ENCYCLOPEDIA
OF THE COLD WAR

ENCYCLOPEDIA
OF THE COLD WAR

Thomas S. Arms

Facts On File®

AN INFOBASE HOLDINGS COMPANY

Encyclopedia of the Cold War

Facts On File, Inc.
460 Park Avenue South
New York NY 10016

Library of Congress Cataloging-in-Publication Data

Arms, Thomas S.
Encyclopedia of the Cold War / Thomas S. Arms.
p.   cm.
Includes bibliographical references and index.
ISBN 0-8160-1975-4
1. Cold War—Encyclopedias.   2. World politics—1945–
—Encyclopedias.   I. Title.
D843.A668   1994
909.82—dc20   90-26899
CIP

Facts On File books are available at special discounts when purchased in bulk
quantities for businesses, associations, institutions or sales promotions. Please call
our Special Sales Department in New York at 212/683-2244 or 800/322-8755.

Text design by Donna Sinisgalli
Jacket design by Heidi Haeuser
Printed in the United States of America

MV KA 10 9 8 7 6 5 4 3 2 1

This book is printed on acid-free paper.

*Dedicated to the memory of my
father and grandfather*

CONTENTS

ACKNOWLEDGMENTS

Where to begin? The problem with writing an acknowledgments section is that you set out to extend the much-deserved thanks to all those who gave their much-appreciated help and you inevitably forget someone whose name should figure prominently. So first of all, an apology for anyone whom I might forget.

High on the list of acknowledgments should appear the name Edward Knappmann, former executive vice president of Facts On File, the original editor of this project and a good friend. His suggestions, advice and patience have been a major help.

For the past four years I have been a regular visitor to the Royal Institute of International Affairs in London and have made extensive use of its staff and libraries for information and ideas. Throughout my research they have provided expert and friendly help at all stages. I have not been as frequent a user of other libraries or foreign policy think tanks, but I have found useful the staff and libraries of the International Institute for Strategic Studies, the Hudson Institute, the Stockholm International Peace Research Institute, the United Nations Information Center in London and the Goethe Institute in London.

Various governments' embassies or foreign ministries have also been a major help. These have included the British Foreign Office, the British Ministry of Defense, the U.S. Department of Defense and the London embassies of West Germany, Poland, the Soviet Union, Japan, China, the Philippines, Indonesia, Turkey, Greece, Norway, Denmark, Canada, France, Italy, Egypt, Hungary, Iceland, the Netherlands, Belgium and Finland. International organizations that have aided this project with material and other information include the United Nations, the European Economic Community, the Organization of American States and the North Atlantic Treaty Organization.

A number of individuals have helped me by sharing their reminiscences and their views of events. These have included three former British foreign secretaries: David Owen, Alec Douglas-Home and Peter Carrington.

I have read a number of books and magazine articles in the preparation of this book. They are all included in the "For Further Information" section at the end of each entry and again in the biliography at the end of the book. I have made particularly extensive use of the memoirs of all the key players in the Cold War period and of the *Facts On File World News Digest* for contemporary reports.

Late in the project I was helped immeasurably by Melanie Knights who played a vital role in providing research assistance for the rewrites. This was not an easy task given the rapid political changes at the end of the Cold War, coupled with the mounting pressure of deadlines.

The last paragraph is devoted to my family, and at the top of the list is my wife, Eileen. She not only had to put up with bad tempers and being followed around the house while I read pearls of wisdom, but she also pitched in at key moments to help with the vital page corrections. My son Simon also deserves a special mention. He spent a week of his school holidays collating the pages of Dad's book when he and his father should have been at the park playing football. My daughter Kimberly, whose birth almost coincided with the start of this project, played a reluctant part by staying out of Daddy's office. And her little brother Christopher, whose arrival almost coincides with completion of the encyclopedia, did his part in letting me sleep.

INTRODUCTION

The Cold War ended not with a bang, but with a whimper. Many had long expected it to end with the ultimate bang of a nuclear holocaust. Instead, it flickered erratically as its flame was turned progressively lower, until finally it winked out, extinguished by the winds of change.

When exactly did it end? In retrospect, it seems to have happened with incredible swiftness, although in fact it was a rather drawn-out process extending over several years. Some date it to late 1989, with the opening of the Berlin Wall and the collapse of most of Eastern Europe's communist regimes, but that was more like the beginning of the end.

Others would cite the signing of the Treaty on the Final Settlement with Respect to Germany in September 1990, and the formal reunification of Germany the following month. This is a logical point, as the Cold War actually grew out of the failure of the World War II allies—the United States, U.S.S.R., Britain and France—to agree on a postwar political structure for Germany.

According to contemporary news accounts, the "formal" conclusion of the Cold War actually came in November 1990, with the Paris summit of the Conference on Security and Cooperation in Europe and the signing of the Conventional Forces in Europe disarmament treaty. That gathering brought together all the nations of Europe (except Albania), including all the member states of NATO and the Warsaw Pact. It was followed in July 1991 by the official disbanding of the Warsaw Pact.

However, some analysts date the real end of the Cold War to the cataclysmic events inside the Soviet Union in 1991: the failed August coup against Mikhail Gorbachev by hard-liners; the eclipse of Gorbachev by Boris Yeltsin; the collapse of the Communist Party; and finally, in December, the dissolution of the U.S.S.R. into the Commonwealth of Independent States (C.I.S.). Although Russia remained dominant within the C.I.S., it was transformed virtually overnight into a "struggling democracy" desperate for Western aid. Some Russian nationalists and "former" communists could be heard grumbling that Moscow's foreign policy was for all intents and purposes now being made in Washington.

Finally, some might argue that, in terms of the United States, the final punctuation mark to an era came with the November 1992 election victory of Bill Clinton over George Bush, "the last Cold War president." Clinton was the first American president who grew up during the Cold War, for whom the definitive public event was Vietnam, not World War II. His election was widely interpreted as signaling a collective shift of the American public's attention away from foreign entanglements and toward the nation's dire domestic problems.

Aside from deciding when the Cold War ended, a more problematic question is deciding why it started. Who was to blame for Europe's division into two armed camps? The conventional explanation, particularly among conservative scholars, has been to put virtually the entire blame upon Stalin and his supposed plans for communist world domination. And indeed there is no question that the Soviet dictator used deceit and naked force to install puppet regimes in Eastern Europe in the late 1940s, earning the permanent enmity of the West in the process.

But since the 1960s, revisionist American historians have argued that the fear of the Red Army's being poised to invade Western Europe—which ultimately served as the reasoning behind NATO and the rearming of West Germany—was misplaced. In this view, the U.S.S.R. was so shattered after the war that it was in no position even to contemplate fighting the West, and that Washington's alarmist fears were in part prompted by skewed intelligence provided by the Gehlen Organization, the former Nazi German spy network in Eastern Europe and the Soviet Union that served as the U.S.'s main source of intelligence on Soviet capabilities and intentions from 1946 until well into the 1950s. (In those years, communist political parties and labor unions constituted a much greater threat than Stalin's armies to the U.S.-backed governments in Western Europe—a threat the CIA successfully combated with its first forays into covert action.)

Gorbachev himself, although no admirer of Stalin, took a similar tack when he toured the United States in May 1992 as a private citizen. Speaking at Westminster College in Fulton, Missouri—seen by many as the symbolic birthplace of the Cold War because of Churchill's famous "iron curtain" speech there in March 1946—he asserted that Stalin "was afraid of war, did not want war, and never would have engaged in a major war." He blamed "the West, and primarily the United States," for having "unleashed a monstrous arms race."

Whatever the murkiness of its origins, after decades of East-West conflict and confrontation the Cold War did not end with a victory in the conventional sense. It was more of a case of one side, the Soviet Union, simply giving up the game and going home. Gorbachev, realizing his country had been bankrupted by its military spending, kept throwing arms-reduction initiatives at the West until finally the United States was forced to start accepting them. Meanwhile, his domestic policies had a transformative effect on Soviet society, but not in the way he intended. With *perestroika* (restructuring), his half-hearted economic reforms succeeded only in making a bad situation worse, increasing popular discontent. And with *glasnost* (openness), his easing of political and social strictures created new forums for that discontent to be expressed, and helped lead to an explosion of civic and nationalist unrest that ultimately doomed the entire Soviet system.

Very few in the West, and virtually none of the establishment "Kremlinologists," ever predicted that the demise of the Soviet Union would occur the way it did. Indeed, it was long an article of faith among American "hawks" that the Soviet communist system was incapable of reforming itself voluntarily. Most Western scenarios for the collapse of the U.S.S.R. involved external war or internal armed revolt as a trigger. Of course, since the Soviet Union has disbanded, things have not exactly gone smoothly: there is ethnic bloodletting within and among the various Central Asian and Caucasian republics, nuclear weapons and fuel (and unemployed scientists) have appeared on the international black market, and near-constant warnings have been heard of a conservative backlash or even a coup against Boris Yeltsin and his fellow Russian reformers. Nevertheless, perhaps the most striking thing about the devolution of the Soviet empire into the C.I.S. was that the process was such a relatively peaceful and orderly one.

Who won the Cold War? That seems simple enough on the surface. "We"—meaning the West, and specifically the United States—did. There has been some debate about credit, however. Conservatives have argued that it was their steadfast anticommunism, and particularly President Reagan's massive arms buildup of the 1980s, that finally pushed the Soviets over the brink. Others have disputed that claim, and they have good cause. The Cold War began with the

interventionism of the Truman administration, while it was President Eisenhower who left office warning about the "military-industrial complex." President Kennedy, in response to a nonexistent "missile gap," ordered a major expansion of the American strategic nuclear arsenal, prompting the Russians to scramble to catch up and thus launching the arms race in earnest. Republicans blamed President Carter for not standing up to Moscow and for allowing America's defenses to weaken; but Carter's early efforts at détente were a direct outgrowth of the Nixon-Kissinger policies, and it was Carter who, after the Soviet invasion of Afghanistan, began the major arms build-up that was continued and accelerated under Reagan. So it can indeed be argued that America's victory in the Cold War was very much a bipartisan affair.

Ironically, some observers have concluded that the real winners of the Cold War have been Germany and Japan, the two defeated Axis powers of World War II. By this argument, the Soviet Union may have lost the Cold War, but the U.S. came in a close second-from-last, its economy similarly disfigured and nearly bankrupted by long-term military spending. Meanwhile, Germany and Japan, protected by their military alliances with Washington, were able to develop into regional and then global economic powerhouses, their industries concentrating on producing high quality consumer trade goods rather than "useless" (outside of war) high-tech military hardware, like the U.S.

Indeed, Japan appears to have won back the "Greater East Asia Co-prosperity Sphere" that it carved out by force before and during World War II, this time peacefully, by trade and investment. And Germany, while preoccupied with the problems and costs of reunification, retains the strongest economy in the European Community and stands ready to achieve economic dominance over the former communist lands to the east, the very territories Germany, like Japan in Asia, had ultimately failed to conquer by force of arms half a century before.

Despite this outcome, it has been argued, primarily by those on the left, that the high levels of U.S. defense spending during the Cold War were in the end dictated not by the nature of the Soviet threat but by domestic economic considerations. That is, American business and government leaders, having realized that it was World War II and not the New Deal that finally ended the Depression, decided to put the postwar U.S. economy on a permanent war footing. This policy of "military Keynesianism," as it has been called, allegedly used defense spending as a system of public investment (of taxpayers' dollars) in private corporations (military contractors) in order to prime the pump of the American economy.

Whether or not there was such a conscious policy, there can be little question that military spending—particularly in the high-tech aerospace field—provided a powerful engine of growth for the U.S. economy over the past five decades, from World War II through all the years of the Cold War. So much so, in fact, that the main opponents of recent specific cutbacks in the U.S. defense budget are often not Pentagon officials but congressmen and senators (including liberal Democrats) whose districts and states stand to lose revenue and jobs from the closure of military bases or the cancellation of weapons systems.

Most Americans have not seen any concrete improvement in their lives as a result of the end of the Cold War. It seems as though the people most directly impacted have been government policymakers, military planners, academic experts and media pundits, some of whom appear almost nostalgic for the certitude of the Cold War years, when everyone knew who the enemy was. For all those decades of superpower blustering, nuclear brinksmanship and proxy wars in the Third World, international relations were for the most part predictable. What lies ahead is not.

About This Book: It is hoped that *Encyclopedia of the Cold War* will serve to show readers where we have been so that they might better understand where we may be going. But with a subject as broad as the Cold War, the choices confronting the author were daunting. The East–West conflict has been the major, and largely overriding, factor in international relations since the end of World War II. At the height of the Cold War there was hardly a political, military or economic development anywhere in the world that was not viewed—correctly or otherwise—through its bipolar prism.

Nevertheless, this book cannot list every event since 1945 and analyze it within the context of the East–West struggle. Instead, the criterion of selection has been that a topic (person, thing or event) must have been directly related to the Cold War or of such importance that it affected the international balance of power. Absent from the pages of this book, for instance, are a vast number of entries that might have been written on the Middle East (although an effort has been made to deal with the overall situation in an entry under that name), because the Palestine-Israel conflict is essentially local, even though the United States and the Soviet Union lined up behind opposing sides. Included, however, is the Suez Crisis because it substantially changed the international equation by effectively removing Britain as a major world power. The original Lebanese Crisis is included as well because the United States dispatched troops to Lebanon to counter a perceived communist threat and developed the Eisenhower Doctrine to justify its actions.

There is also the problem of which personalities to include. Again the choices are daunting, and there are many otherwise worthy people who are omitted. The reader will also notice the preponderance of Americans. This is for two reasons. The Cold War was primarily between the United States and Soviet Union, and the differing nature and structure of the two countries' governments means that there were more frequent changes at the top policymaking levels in Washington than in Moscow. It should also be noted that all of the figures have been placed within the context of the Cold War. In the entry for Richard Nixon, for instance, there is nothing on his economic policies and only a minimal reference to the Watergate scandal.

In addition to people, countries and events, certain diplomatic and military expressions and weapons systems have been included. Technically speaking, the expressions should be part of a dictionary rather than an encyclopedia, but phrases such as "Iron Curtain" and "brinksmanship" are such an integral part of Cold War culture that it would have been impractical to omit them. As for the weapons, not all major systems have been included; only those that have played a major part in Cold War debate are discussed.

Throughout the text, words in small capitals refer the reader to separate entries under that subject. Liberal cross-references have been included. If the reader is unable to find a name or subject in the list of entries, then he or she should consult the index to determine where it appears. Many entries are followed by suggested readings for further research, and a general bibliography is provided at the end of the book.

A

Abel, Rudolf (1902–November 15, 1971) Colonel Rudolf Abel was one of the highest-ranking KGB agents ever arrested in the United States. After a major public trial he was sentenced to a long prison sentence, but he was exchanged in 1962 for American U-2 pilot Lieutenant FRANCIS GARY POWERS.

Abel was the son of Russian émigrés who had fled Czarist Russia to live in Britain when Abel was only a year old. Abel lived in Britain until 1921, when he is believed to have returned to the Soviet Union and joined Soviet intelligence. During World War II he worked in Germany and France as a Soviet agent, and at the end of the war he arranged to be placed in a camp for displaced persons under the name of Goldfus. Using his status as a displaced person, Abel organized immigration to Canada and then, in 1948, surreptitiously crossed the border into the United States and went to New York City, where he established a business as a photographer and artist.

Abel was arrested in New York on June 21, 1957, as an illegal alien. On August 7 he was indicted on espionage charges by a federal grand jury in Brooklyn. At the time, he was the highest-ranking communist spy ever caught in the United States. In his Brooklyn studio federal agents found a shortwave radio, microfilm equipment and other espionage equipment such as hollowed out pencils, nails, coins and earrings. Also found was $6,000 in cash in Abel's pockets and a further $15,000 in various safe deposit boxes.

A 19-count indictment accused Abel of conspiring to provide the Soviet Union with defense data, particularly on arms, equipment, troops disposition and atomic energy. It claimed that he would activate and attempt to activate members of the U.S. armed forces as agents.

The chief witness in the trial against Abel was his former associate, ex-Lieutenant Reino Hayhanen, who had defected to the U.S. embassy in Paris. Abel himself did not testify during his trial but maintained his innocence even after his conviction. Hayhanen, who also had entered the United States illegally, said that Abel had been ordered by KGB headquarters in Moscow to give $10,000 to Mrs. Helen Sobell, wife of MORTON SOBELL, who was serving a 30-year sentence for his conviction in the Rosenberg espionage case. Mrs. Sobell later denied any connection with Abel.

On October 25, 1957, Abel was found guilty on three charges: (1) conspiracy to transmit U.S. defense and atomic secrets to the Soviet Union; (2) conspiracy to gather the secrets; and (3) failure to register as a foreign agent. On November 15 he was sentenced to 30 years in prison.

Abel's lawyers appealed the conviction on legal technicalities, but in March 1960 the Supreme Court upheld the conviction by a 5 to 4 vote. His appeal was based on the claim that he had been convicted on evidence seized from him in violation of the Fourth Amendment, which forbids unreasonable search and seizure. Justice Felix Frankfurter's majority opinion held that "government officers who effect a deportation arrest have a right of incidental search analogous to the search permitted criminal law enforcement officers."

After the shooting down of the United States' U-2 reconnaissance plane in the Soviet Union in May 1960, U.S. president DWIGHT EISENHOWER used the example of Abel to suggest that the Soviet Union "look at their own record" before suggesting that the United States was engaged in provocative espionage. Eisenhower's statement appeared to establish a link between Abel and the captured U-2 pilot, Francis Gary Powers, and this link became the focus of discussions about the two men.

After secret U.S.–Soviet negotiations involving Abel's long-time American lawyer James B. Donovan, Abel was exchanged for Powers on February 10, 1961, at the border crossing at Glienicker Bridge between the American sector of Berlin and the East German town of Potsdam.

Back in the Soviet Union, Abel was showered with honors and became a chief KGB instructor in espionage techniques. He died of lung cancer on November 15, 1971.

For Further Information:
Barron, John. *KGB*. New York, 1974.
Carpozi, George. *Red Spies in the U.S.* New Rochelle, N.Y., 1974.
Newman, J. "Famous Soviet Spies," *U.S. News and World Report*, 1974.

Abgrenzung Abgrenzung (German: demarcation) was a policy developed by the East German government at the height of West Germany's OSTPOLITIK ("Eastern Policy") in an attempt to delimit and emphasize the differences between the two Germanies and thus minimize the chances of reunification. The policy was eliminated following the collapse of the East Germany Communist Party at the end of 1989.

Abgrenzung was developed as a counter to the West German policy of "change through accommodation." Its intention was to make clear to the people of East German that the conclusion of treaties with West Germany and other Western states did not amount to a softening of controversial positions or an accommodation between the two systems.

Through Abgrenzung the East German government also sought to restrict inter-German relations to the governmental level as much as possible. The government justified this position by continuing to identify West Germany as the "class enemy."

For Further Information:
Steele, Jonathan. *Socialism with a German Face: The State that Came in from the Cold.* London, 1977.

Acheson, Dean   **(April 11, 1893–October 12, 1971)**   As U.S. undersecretary of state from 1945 to 1947 and secretary of state from 1949 to 1953, Dean Acheson was a principal architect of America's early Cold War policies. During the 1950s, he was the chief scapegoat for what American conservatives termed the "loss of China," but he returned to prominence as an adviser to presidents Kennedy and Johnson.

A graduate of Yale University and Harvard Law School, Acheson served in the U.S. Navy during World War I. He developed an early interest in government when he served as private secretary to Supreme Court Associate Justice Louis Brandeis for the first two years after the war. For the next 50 years he divided his time between government service and his private law practice in Washington, D.C.

Acheson's first government post was under President Franklin D. Roosevelt as undersecretary of the Treasury in 1933. He resigned that post six months later in protest against Roosevelt's decision to reduce the gold content of the dollar. He rejoined the administration just before the outbreak of World War II and from 1941 to 1944 helped to coordinate the Lend-Lease program, liaised with Congress and contributed to the establishment of such postwar organizations as the United Nations, the INTERNATIONAL MONETARY FUND, the WORLD BANK, the Food and Agricultural Organization and the United Nations Relief and Rehabilitation Agency.

In June 1945 Acheson was appointed undersecretary of state under JAMES BYRNES. During Byrnes' 18 months as secretary of state, he was abroad much of the time and it fell to Acheson to administer the State Department and regularly brief President Truman. Truman came to rely on Acheson's judgment and his ability to mediate between the president and Byrnes, his former political rival.

During the war years, Acheson took the view that an essential component to the maintenance of the postwar peace would be the economic reconstruction of Europe. In the immediate aftermath of the war he took a leading role in pressing for U.S. economic aid to Europe. This eventually took the form of the European Economic Recovery Program, which became known as the MARSHALL PLAN. Acheson pre-

Dean Acheson, who in 1949 became secretary of state under President Truman. He developed the policy of "containing" Soviet influence through economic and military aid, and helped to establish the North Atlantic Treaty Organization (NATO). Oil on canvas by Gardner Cox. National Portrait Gallery, Smithsonian Institution, Washington, D.C.

sented the first outline of general philosophy and tenets of the Marshall Plan at a speech on May 8, 1947, in Mississippi. The following month, Secretary of State GEORGE C. MARSHALL gave Acheson's proposals his full support and formally launched the Marshall Plan in his famous commencement address at Harvard University.

Acheson also helped to formulate U.S. nuclear policy. He opposed Byrnes and Secretary of the Navy JAMES FORRESTAL, who wanted the United States to maintain a nuclear monopoly. Acheson believed that the Soviet Union would soon develop its own nuclear weapons and pressed for an international agency to establish some control over the Soviets. He and HENRY STIMSON, secretary of war from 1940 to 1945, wanted a joint Soviet–American–British commission to coordinate the exchange of information on nuclear weapons and the eventual international control of atomic material. In January 1946, Acheson was appointed chairman of a committee, which included DAVID LILIENTHAL, formed to draw up a report on the subject to be presented to the United Nations. The report included a proposal for an international atomic development agency to assume control of atomic weapons development and offered to end the U.S. atomic weapons program.

The Acheson-Lilienthal report was put to the United Nations by BERNARD BARUCH, a U.S. foreign policy adviser and the delegate to the UN Atomic Energy Commission. He insisted on amending the proposals so that UN Security Council members were prevented from using their veto power when discussing atomic energy. The report became known as the Baruch Plan. Acheson opposed Baruch's amendment on the grounds that the Soviet Union would object. Baruch's amendments prevailed, however, and in June 1946 the Baruch Plan—the first attempt at the control of nuclear weapons—was rejected by the Soviet Union.

At first, Acheson followed the Roosevelt policy of conciliation toward the Soviet Union. But Soviet actions in Eastern Europe, Greece, Turkey and Iran changed his mind, and he quickly became an advocate of the policy of CONTAINMENT, the goal of which was to contain the Soviet Union's sphere of influence. In 1947 he played a major role in persuading Truman to assume Britain's responsibilities in Greece and in the formulation of the subsequent TRUMAN DOCTRINE.

Acheson was one of the most powerful undersecretaries of state ever to hold the post. This was partly because of his undoubted intellectual abilities and partly because of the two secretaries of state with whom he served. Byrnes, who in 1944 was narrowly defeated by Truman in the Democratic nomination for the vice presidency, felt bitter toward his former opponent, and this led to conflicts between the State Department and the White House in which Acheson was regularly called upon to act as a buffer and mediator. Marshall was a traditional military man who saw his role as an administrator, and his primary purpose was to delegate work to his more experienced diplomatic subordinates. Acheson, as one of the most talented men at the State Department, was given the responsibility for much of the policymaking.

In 1947 Acheson returned to his law practice, but two years later he was appointed secretary of state by President Truman. By 1947 the containment policy formulated in the immediate postwar years had begun to bear fruit and had established itself as the cornerstone of U.S. foreign policy. However, it lacked a defense dimension that included Western Europe, and Acheson quickly found himself pressing for a U.S.–European military alliance. This bore fruit in 1949 with the creation of the NORTH ATLANTIC TREATY ORGANIZATION (NATO).

In 1950 Acheson released a report calling on the United States to defend unilaterally the noncommunist world from Soviet expansion. To support this role as the world's policeman, the report proposed an increase in defense spending to 20% of gross national product. Initially, the proposals were opposed by Truman, but the outbreak of the KOREAN WAR led to the report's implementation.

Acheson's foreign policy was Eurocentric. Even his support for U.S. intervention in the Korean War and French intervention in Vietnam was based largely on the premise that these actions were needed to secure European support for American policies around the world. As a Eurocentric secretary of state, Acheson felt uncomfortable in dealing with Asian issues, and it was his handling of events in that part of the world that eventually led to his fall from political grace.

Within European circles, Acheson was regarded as a Cold War warrior who was too intransigent in his dealings with the Soviet Union. Even conservatives such as WINSTON CHURCHILL were frustrated by Acheson's refusal to negotiate with the Soviets over anything other than major issues such as Soviet withdrawal from Eastern Europe.

In the United States, however, Acheson was regarded as too liberal, a reputation based largely on his actions in Asia. Following the collapse of the government of CHIANG KAI-SHEK in China, Acheson produced a white paper in which he defended the Truman administration's China policy on the grounds that the communists gained power because Chiang had lost the support of the Chinese people. He maintained that only direct military intervention by the United States could have prevented such an outcome, but he regarded such intervention as immoral.

American conservatives claimed that the communist victory in the CHINESE CIVIL WAR was a result of communist subversion with the State Department. In 1950 Senator JOSEPH MCCARTHY issued the names of prominent diplomats in the State Department whom he claimed were communists and had been using their positions to influence Acheson's Far East policies. Acheson tried in vain to protect some of the diplomats singled out for attack by McCarthy, such as John Carter Vincent, JOHN PATON DAVIES and JOHN STEWART SERVICE. Acheson's support for these accused diplomats resulted in Acheson himself becoming a target of the witch hunt.

Partly as a result of the conservative backlash, Acheson extended his containment policy to Asia and supported the Korean War. Along with the rest of the Truman administration, Acheson was caught off guard when the Chinese intervened in the war following the UN forces' initial success. American conservatives claimed that the Chinese intervention was further proof that Acheson should replace his containment policy with one of attack and pressed him and Truman to extend the Korean War to the Chinese mainland. Acheson steadfastly rejected this change of policy and suffered further scorn from the increasingly powerful conservative lobby on Capitol Hill.

Branded by conservatives as one of the chief villains of the Truman administration, Acheson left office in 1952 at the height of the McCarthy era. In January 1955, McCarthy accused Acheson and Truman of leading a faction of the Democratic Party that "coddled, covered up and nurtured treason."

In 1953 Acheson resumed his private law practice, although he regularly commented on the Eisenhower administration's foreign policy and became a prolific writer. He was a strong critic of Secretary of State JOHN FOSTER DULLES, America's most conservative postwar secretary of state. In September 1958 he was one of the most vociferous critics of Dulles's defense of Chiang's occupation of QUEMOY AND MATSU ISLANDS, between mainland China and Taiwan. Acheson called it a "horrendous decision."

In 1961 Acheson returned to government as one of the key

advisers to President JOHN F. KENNEDY during the CUBAN MISSILE
CRISIS. He supported immediate action against Cuba, even to
the extent of an air strike to wipe out the Soviet missile bases.
Acheson also directed liaisons with America's European allies
during the crisis.

In March 1968, following the request of the military establishment for an additional 200,000 U.S. troops in Vietnam,
President Lyndon Johnson asked Acheson to assess the request and U.S. war policy. Acheson reversed his earlier support for the war and concluded that the United States could
not win the war and should withdraw as quickly as possible
because of the loss of U.S. domestic support. His report was
given as one of the reasons for Johnson's announcement on
March 31, 1968, that he would de-escalate America's involvement. Acheson died of a heart attack on October 12,
1971.

For Further Information:

Acheson, Dean. *Among Friends: Personal Letters of Dean Acheson*,
    edited by David S. McLellan and David C. Acheson. New York,
    1980.
————. *Grapes from Thorns*. New York, 1972.
————. *The Korean War*. New York, 1971.
————. *Morning and Noon*. New York, 1965.
————. *Power and Diplomacy*. New York, 1958.
————. *Present at the Creation*. New York, 1969.
————. *Private Thoughts on Public Affairs*. New York, 1967.
Barnet, Richard J. *Roots of War: The Men and Institutions Behind
    U.S. Foreign Policy*. New York, 1972.
Davis, Lynn Etheridge. *The Cold War Begins*. Princeton, N.J., 1974.
Isaacson, Walter, and Evan Thomas. *The Wise Men*. New York,
    1986.
May, Ernest, ed. *The Truman Administration and China*. Philadelphia,
    1975.
McLellan, David S. *Dean Acheson: The State Department Years*. New
    York, 1976.
Smith, Gaddis. **Dean Acheson**. New York, 1972.

Adenauer, Konrad   (January 5, 1876–April 19, 1967)

Konrad Adenauer was the first chancellor of the Federal
Republic of Germany. A firm anti-communist, he effected the
political rehabilitation of West Germany and led it firmly into
the Western Alliance. In doing so, he laid the foundations of
West Germany's postwar foreign and domestic policies.

Adenauer, the son of a minor civil servant, was raised in
Cologne and studied law and political science at the universities of Freiburg, Munich and Bonn. He worked for a time in
the Cologne public prosecutor's office before becoming a
Cologne city councillor in 1904. Five years later, his wife's
cousin became mayor and Adenauer was appointed his deputy. He became mayor of Cologne in October 1917. He was
devoted to the city and in 1926 turned down an invitation by
the leaders of the Catholic Center Party to stand as a candidate for reich chancellor of the Weimar Republic.

Adenauer was an early opponent of the Nazi Party, and
when Hitler visited Cologne in February 1933, Adenauer
refused to meet him or allow swastika flags to be flown in his

Konrad Adenauer, first chancellor of the Federal Republic of Germany, effected
the political rehabilitation of his country and brought it firmly into the Western
Alliance. Photo courtesy of the German Ministry of Foreign Affairs.

honor. As a result, Hitler made plans to arrest him, and in
March Adenauer was forced to flee the city. He was lucky to
survive the next 12 years. He was arrested twice but freed each
time. For much of the time he was secluded in a monastery.

When U.S. troops arrived in Cologne in March 1945,
Adenauer was asked to resume his duties as mayor. After
Germany's surrender, however, Cologne fell into the British
sector and Adenauer quickly clashed with the British authorities, who dismissed him from his mayoral post in October
1945. The event is said to have made him anti-British for the
remainder of his political career. Two months later, however,
the British ban on his political activities was lifted, and
Adenauer shifted his attention from Cologne to the national

stage and the newly created Christian Democratic Union (CDU). In February 1946 Adenauer became chairman of the conservative CDU.

National elections throughout West Germany had to wait, however, until the end of the Berlin Blockade. The elections were held in August 1949. The trade union-oriented Social Democratic Party (SPD) under Otto Schumacher was favored to win, but Adenauer's CDU won the most seats, and he was easily able to cobble together a center-right coalition with the centrist Free Democratic Party (FDP) and the conservative, Bavarian-based Christian Social Union (CSU), which gave him a small but workable majority in the new Bundestag (the lower house of parliament).

Adenauer had an advantage over most German politicians of his day in that he had a clear idea of where he wanted to go and how to get there. He was, for a start, instinctively anti-Soviet and anti-communist. This led him away from any move toward reunification with East Germany except on his own terms. Adenauer was convinced, correctly, that the path to reunification lay through the strengthening of the sovereignty of the Federal Republic and that this country would form the basis for a reunited Germany once communist rule eventually collapsed in East Germany. Adenauer also understood that from the war had emerged two superpowers—the United States and the Soviet Union—and that the Soviet Union was a direct threat to West Germany, whose only possible protector was the United States. At the same time, Adenauer gave high priority to winning West Germany a place as an equal partner in the Western Alliance against the Soviet Bloc and reckoned that the best way to achieve this goal was through a general reconstruction and integration of Europe and, in particular, through a close Franco-German relationship.

With the value of hindsight, Adenauer's goals appear obvious and simple. But in 1949 they were considered by many to be radical. Although the Soviet Union had replaced Germany as the main enemy of the West, it was less than five years since German troops had occupied most of Western Europe, and any German leader had to live not only with the legacy of Hitler but also with three-quarters of a century of German aggression.

In 1950 there were still restrictions on Germany's steel production, and the country's defense forces were nonexistent. In March 1950, Adenauer made the premature proposal for a Franco-German union, beginning with a customs union, to combat the threat of communism. The idea was endorsed by a semi-retired CHARLES DE GAULLE but was rejected by the French government as too vague for consideration at that time. Only two months later, however, French foreign minister ROBERT SCHUMAN made the first steps toward rapprochement and European union when he proposed that France and Germany pool their coal and steel resources as the first step toward European integration. The concept was enthusiastically embraced by Adenauer. As a result of the German acceptance of the Schuman Plan, the Allied Powers

announced on May 15 that West Germany was to be accepted into "the community of free European nations" and stated that when the plans for the European Coal and Steel Community had been fully implemented, all forms of economic control would be abolished.

Adenauer was asked to make one further concession, however, for the creation of the ECSC: West Germany was to cede the coal-rich Saarland to France. The French had been slowly annexing the Saar region since the end of the war, and Adenauer had been largely silent for fear of wrecking his long-term plans for Franco-German cooperation. But domestic German public opinion was firmly against French policy toward the Saarland, and complete acquiescence by Adenauer to the French would probably have resulted in the collapse of his government and a hardening of positions on both sides of the Rhine. Adenauer thus played a careful diplomatic game, quietly protesting to the French about their policies in the Saar and seeking support from Britain and the United States for eventual French withdrawal. In 1954 Adenauer won the agreement of French prime minister Pierre Mendes-France for a referendum in the Saarland, and in October 1955 the Saarlanders voted to be reunited with West Germany.

Another major element in Adenauer's strategy was West German participation in a European army. The outbreak of the KOREAN WAR in June 1950 strengthened his hand as many observers feared that the communist offensive in Asia was part of a strategy of diverting American forces away from Europe so that the Red Army could successfully attack West Germany. In August 1950 WINSTON CHURCHILL proposed the formation of a European army with German participation, and in October French defense minister Rene Pleven proposed the creation of the European Defense Community (EDC), which would include Germany. The proposal was enthusiastically embraced by Adenauer, and the West German Bundestag was the first to ratify the subsequent EDC Treaty. But by the time the treaty came before the French National Assembly the Korean War was over, Stalin was dead and the threat of a Soviet attack had receded, but the French public's fear of German militarism had failed to disappear completely. As a result, the French National Assembly rejected the treaty and threw Adenauer's plans into disarray.

Adenauer was furious. He claimed that France had wrecked the "European idea" and warned that without a defense agreement that included West Germany the German people would be driven into an accommodation with the Soviet Union. The crisis was resolved by British foreign secretary SIR ANTHONY EDEN, who proposed that Germany be brought into the WESTERN EUROPEAN UNION and the NORTH ATLANTIC TREATY ORGANIZATION (NATO) and that a check be placed on the possibility of a revived German militarism by formally limiting the size of the German forces and by basing an estimated 50,000 British troops on German soil for the next 50 years. Adenauer, however, always regarded West German membership in NATO as second-best to the EDC.

In an attempt to block formal German membership in the

Western Alliance, the Soviet Union in January 1955 proposed the reunification of Germany on the basis of free elections if the West German government agreed to scrap the EDEN PLAN FOR GERMAN REUNIFICATION. The Soviet approach was rejected by Adenauer, who believed that Moscow had no intention of allowing the creation of a reunified Germany free of Soviet control and that it was only offering the carrot of reunification in order to delay West Germany's integration into the Western Alliance. Throughout his 14 years in office, Adenauer was often criticized by the opposition parties for not doing enough for German reunification.

West Germany's membership in NATO forced the Soviets to deal with Adenauer on a completely different level, and in June 1955, a month after West Germany joined the alliance, the Soviet government invited Adenauer to Moscow to discuss the establishment of diplomatic relations. Adenauer went to Moscow in September and agreed to West German–Soviet diplomatic relations in exchange for the return of German prisoners of war still held in the Soviet Union. The Soviet Union thus became the only country in the world to have diplomatic relations with both East Germany and West Germany up until the late 1960s.

The next step toward German rehabilitation was the creation of the EUROPEAN ECONOMIC COMMUNITY in March 1957. Adenauer, facing general election in the same year, was able to tell the voters that he had not only won West German readmission to the family of nations and secured its defense but that he had also substantially increased the financial well-being of Germany. The result was a landslide victory as the CDU won an absolute majority with 270 seats in the Bundestag. Adenauer was 81 years old, but he steadfastly refused to consider retirement. He believed that he had become indispensable to the postwar development of Germany.

Adenauer now concentrated his efforts on completing his strategy of Franco–German rapprochement. He was aided in this goal by the return to power of de Gaulle in 1958. In September 1958 Adenauer visited de Gaulle at his home in Colombey-les-deux-eglises, and the two men found that they shared a common vision of Europe. In November de Gaulle visited Adenauer at Bad Kreuznach, and from there the friendship blossomed and eventually resulted in the FRANCO-GERMAN FRIENDSHIP TREATY OF 1963.

Adenauer's next major problem was the Berlin Crisis. West Germany had responded weakly to the building of the Berlin Wall. This was partly the result of poor intelligence, which failed to detect the Soviet and East German plan, and partly the result of Adenauer's focus on building up West Germany and avoidance of confrontation with the Soviet Union over the future of East Germany. The policy, however, was unpopular with the German electorate; in September 1961 the CDU lost its absolute majority in the Bundestag and was forced into a coalition with the Free Democratic Party (FDP).

The 85-year-old Adenauer came under increasing pressure to resign in favor of Economics Minister Ludwig Erhard. But the aging German statesman continued to believe in his indispensability, and he did not retire as chancellor until October 1963. Adenauer continued as chairman of the CDU until March 1966, although most of his time was taken up with writing his four-volume memoirs. He died on April 19, 1967.

For Further Information:
Adenauer, Konrad. *Memoirs*, 4 vols. New York, 1966–68.
Augstein, Rudolf. *Konrad Adenauer*. London, 1964.
Crawley, A.M. *The Rise of West Germany, 1945–1972*. New York, 1974.
Fritsch-Bournazel, Renata. *Confronting the German Question*. Oxford, 1988.
Jonas, M. *The U.S. and West Germany*. New York, 1985.
Prittie, Terence. *The Velvet Chancellors*. New York, 1979.

Afghanistan   The Soviet invasion of Afghanistan in December 1979 ended the period of U.S.–Soviet détente. It also severely damaged Soviet relations with the Third World and embroiled Moscow in an unwinnable war.

Afghanistan had long been of strategic importance to Russia and the U.S.S.R. Control of, or at least good relations with, this predominantly tribal Muslim country was vital for Moscow if it was to exert any influence on either the Indian subcontinent or Iran. The importance of Afghanistan increased after an Islamic revolution overthrew the shah of Iran in 1979.

From 1953 the Soviet Union enjoyed a close relationship with the Afghan government in Kabul. Afghanistan was not formally in the Soviet orbit, but it received a considerable amount of aid from the Soviet Union. In April 1978, these relations were strengthened when President Sardar Mohammed Daud was overthrown and replaced by Nur Mohammed Taraki, leader of the Communist People's Democratic Party of Afghanistan. Taraki immediately abolished the constitution and banned all other political parties.

Taraki's government, however, quickly faced an armed insurrection by the deeply religious Islamic tribesmen, who objected to the imposition of an atheistic state. Their supporters fled into neighboring Pakistan and Iran, where they established refugee camps from which the Muslim guerrilla fighters—Mujahideen, as they became known—operated. Taraki himself was overthrown by Deputy Prime Minister Hafizullah Amin, who imposed even stricter communist policies and was in turn overthrown on December 27, 1979, by Babrak Karmal, supported by an estimated 100,000 Soviet troops.

The Soviet invasion of Afghanistan met with immediate and worldwide condemnation. The Carter administration cancelled the 1976 U.S.–Soviet grain agreement and, along with most other Western nations, announced a boycott of the 1980 Moscow Olympics. The United States, Britain and France also increased their naval presence in the Indian Ocean. On January 14, 1980, the United Nations passed a resolution deploring the Soviet invasion of Afghanistan and calling for "the immediate, unconditional and total withdrawal of the foreign troops" in the country. Members of the NONALIGNED MOVEMENT voted 56 to nine in favor of the resolution, with 26 abstaining or absent. Twenty-two other Third World countries not belonging to the Nonaligned Movement also sided with the majority. The anti-Soviet Third World vote was a major blow to Moscow's foreign policy, which at the time was concentrating on developing Third World relations.

Western countries, in particular the United States and Britain, also substantially increased their aid to Pakistan, which became home for an estimated 3 million Afghan refugees and the main conduit for weapons and humanitarian aid to the Mujahideen. China and oil-rich Saudi Arabia were also significant contributors to the Mujahideen cause. Under American pressure, the Mujahideen formed themselves into a loose coalition called the Islamic Unity of Afghan Mujahideen. But this attempt at a unified government-in-exile ran afoul of the traditional tribal rivalries and was hindered by the fact that the political leaders based in Pakistan had little or no control over the military commanders fighting in Afghanistan.

The Afghan government, for its part, was completely dependent on the Soviet Army for its existence. The local army was badly trained and equipped, and from the start of the Afghan War was plagued by defections from its ranks to those of the Mujahideen. It has been estimated that these defections halved the size of the Afghan Army between 1978 and 1985.

A pattern was quickly established with the Soviet forces in control of the major urban centers and the Mujahideen in control of the countryside. The capital of Kabul had to be supplied almost entirely from the Soviet Union by either air or convoy. The Mujahideen concentrated on attacking the Soviet convoys and trying to surround and starve out isolated Afghan Army and Soviet outposts. After 1986, when the United States and Britain supplied the Mujahideen with antiaircraft weapons, they were also able to severely disrupt Soviet transport planes.

The Soviets, for their part, maintained a strong grip on the cities, from which they would launch scorched-earth attacks on valleys known to shelter Mujahideen or their supporters. They also used helicopter gunships for effective attacks on Mujahideen forces. In September 1985, the Soviet and Afghan forces attempted to seal the Pakistani–Afghan border, and there were a number of border violations that for a time threatened to expand the geographic scope of the war.

But following the accession to power of MIKHAIL GORBACHEV in the Soviet Union, Soviet policy in Afghanistan began to shift toward finding a negotiated solution. In May 1986, Najibullah, former chief of the KGB-trained Afghan secret police, succeeded Karmal as general secretary of the People's Democratic Party of Afghanistan, and soon afterward the Kabul government launched a policy of national reconciliation with a special emphasis on Islam. Najibullah also legalized opposition political parties, which won representation in subsequent local and legislative elections (which were boy-

cotted by the Mujahideen). The changes helped to stop the flood of defections from the army and allowed President Najib (as he was called) to consolidate his political position within the country.

Najib's improved position also enabled Gorbachev to start planning to end Soviet involvement in the Afghan War. This was vital to his efforts to reduce defense spending, concentrate on domestic problems, improve East–West relations and end the SINO–SOVIET SPLIT. The constant toll on Soviet soldiers was also making the war increasingly unpopular within the Soviet Union. (By the end of the war, nearly 15,000 Soviet troops and more than one million Afghans had reportedly died.) UN-organized negotiations to find a solution to the Afghan War and to allow the withdrawal of Soviet troops had started as early as 1980. The negotiations were conducted between Afghanistan and Pakistan; but carefully observing and directing the negotiating positions of their client states were the Soviet Union and the United States.

In April 1986, the Soviet Union made a unilateral withdrawal of 8,000 troops as a gesture of goodwill. This led to detailed discussions, and on April 14, 1988, an agreement was signed to allow the withdrawal of Soviet forces. The agreement involved Afghan and Pakistani pledges of noninterference and nonintervention in each other's affairs, American and Soviet guarantees of Afghan neutrality, arrangements for the voluntary and safe return of refugees to Afghanistan, the establishment of a UN monitoring force and, finally, the withdrawal of Soviet forces from Afghanistan.

The withdrawal of the Soviet forces, which then numbered 115,000 troops, started on May 15, 1988, and was completed on February 15, 1989. As the Soviets reached the final stages of their withdrawal, the Mujahideen launched a major offensive on Jalalabad, which straddles the main highway between Kabul and Pakistan. Western embassies in Kabul closed and foreigners fled in the belief that the Najib government would quickly be overrun by the Mujahideen. By March 8 the rebels had seized Jalalabad Airport, but the following day the airport was recaptured by government troops, and on March 12 the advancing Mujahideen forces were halted just a mile and a half from the city line. Despite heavy Mujahideen artillery bombardments, the government forces held onto the city, and by the end of March the Mujahideen offensive had collapsed.

The collapse of the Mujahideen offensive temporarily increased the credibility of the Najibullah government both at home and abroad, and by March 1990 President Najibullah felt secure enough to endorse the possibility of elections and the end of his party's monopoly of power. But he refused to step down before the elections. He was backed by the Soviet government on this issue. The U.S. government and the Mujahideen refused to countenance talks with the Najibullah government or elections unless Najibullah first resigned and allowed an interim government to manage the country until elections were held.

However, both the Soviet Union and the United States modified their positions, and this change among the chief backers led to talks in Geneva on November 19–20 between President Najibullah and some of the Mujahideen leaders. However, key rebel figures refused to attend and responded to the talks by launching an attack on Kabul.

Fighting continued through the rest of 1990 and 1991. At the same time, the economic and political collapse of the Soviet Union negated the need for the United States to continue its support for the Mujahideen, whose divisions and Islamic fundamentalism made them unreliable allies at best. The Soviets, for their part, were keen to sever aid to the Najibullah government in order to conserve funds for home use.

On September 13, 1991, the U.S. and Soviet governments agreed to discontinue their military aid to government and rebel forces in Afghanistan from January 1, 1992. The agreement effectively ended Afghanistan's role as a Cold War pawn.

By early 1992, several key rebel leaders, backed by Pakistan, had agreed to a UN peace plan to form an interim government. The plan was rendered moot in April of that year, when Najibullah resigned and went into hiding, his government collapsed, and a coalition of Islamic rebel armies led by Ahmed Shah Massoud entered Kabul in victory. Their triumph followed several months of huge territorial gains by the rebels that were achieved with little bloodshed, as government army and militia units joined forces with Massoud or reached de facto truces with other rebel factions.

The new government, dominated by moderates, had trouble asserting its control over Kabul, much less the rest of the country. In the months after the rebel victory, sporadic fighting continued between forces allied with the new ruling council and their opponents, who included an Iranian-backed rebel faction and the powerful guerrilla army led by Gulbuddin Hekmatyar. (Hekmatyar's group had received the bulk of CIA arms aid over the years even though he was a fundamentalist who favored an Iranian-style Islamic state and his men had been linked both to killings of more moderate rebels and to a large-scale heroin smuggling racket protected by Pakistani military intelligence.)

Drawn by the rebel victory, hundreds of thousands of Afghan refugees—some of the 3.2 million who had fled to Pakistan and the 3 million who had fled to Iran over the past 14 years—began returning to their homes, despite the continued unrest and a devastated countryside still sown with millions of land mines.

For Further Information:

Griffiths, J.C. *The Conflict in Afghanistan*. Hove, U.K., 1987.

Klass, Rosanne, ed. *Afghanistan, the Great Game Revisited*. New York, 1987.

Maprayil, C. *The Soviets and Afghanistan*. New Delhi, 1986.

Nyrop, Richard F., and Donald M. Seekins, eds. *Afghanistan: A Country Study*. New York, 1986.

Roy, A. *The Soviet Intervention in Afghanistan*. New Delhi, 1987.

Roy, O. *Islam and the Resistance in Afghanistan*. Cambridge, U.K., 1986.

Agee, Philip (July 19, 1935–   ) Philip Agee was a former CIA agent who did much to undermine public confidence in the agency through his exposés of CIA activities.

Agee graduated from Notre Dame University in 1956 and the following year joined the CENTRAL INTELLIGENCE AGENCY. After three years of training, he was assigned to the Latin American Division and until 1968 was a field officer serving in Uruguay, Mexico and Ecuador.

He resigned from the CIA in 1969. At the time he described his reasons as "personal," but he later wrote that he had left "as a reaction against the corruption, ineffectiveness and greed I found among the traditional political forces that we were supporting." He characterized the CIA as "nothing more than the secret police of American capitalism, plugging up leaks in the political dam . . . so that shareholders of U.S. companies operating in poor countries can continue enjoying their ripoff."

In 1969 Agee enrolled at the National Autonomous University of Mexico and soon afterward began to plan a book about his career in the CIA. In 1970 he went to Cuba, where he spent six months on research. The Cuban government provided Agee with two university students to help with his research, but Agee insists that he was under no pressure from the Cuban government and has never worked for them. The CIA believes that he was recruited by the DGI, the Cuban Secret Service.

In 1975 Agee published *Inside The Company: CIA Diary*. In addition to exposing day-to-day CIA activities in Latin America, the book listed the names of nearly 250 CIA officials, informers or collaborators. The book was greeted with stony silence at CIA headquarters in Langley, Virginia, which refused to confirm or deny the book's allegations. But espionage experts confirmed its accurancy and its damage to CIA operations.

As well as writing books, Agee gave a number of public lectures around the world, wrote articles and edited the magazine *Counterspy*, which published the names of CIA agents and exposed their activities. One of those named in *Counterspy* was Richard Welch, then CIA station chief in Athens. His identity was picked up by a Greek newspaper, which republished the details, and on December 23, 1975, Welch was gunned down by leftist guerrillas on the doorstep of his Athens home. The CIA publicly blamed Agee for his death, but it was subsequently revealed that the CIA itself had warned Welch against moving into the Athens house, as it had become well-known locally as the home of previous CIA station chiefs.

Agee continued to expose CIA agents publicly, and in 1978 he edited the book *Dirty Work: The CIA in Western Europe*. His unpopularity with the CIA led him to live abroad, and from 1970 to 1976 he was based in London. He was deported by the British authorities in 1976 on the grounds that he had "maintained regular contacts harmful to the security of the United Kingdom with foreign intelligence agents." Agee left Britain for France, but in 1977 he was expelled and went to the Netherlands, where he was asked to leave at the end of 1977. The United States revoked his passport in 1979. In the 1980s, he lived mostly in Spain and traveled on a passport issued by the Sandinista government in Nicaragua. In 1987, he returned to the United States for the first time in 16 years to promote his new book, *On the Run*.

For Further Information:
Agee, Philip. *Inside the Company: CIA Diary*. New York, 1975.
———. *On the Run*. New Jersey, 1987.

Agency for International Development (AID)   The Agency for International Development was founded in 1961 as a semi-autonomous agency within the U.S. State Department designed to coordinate and rationalize foreign aid programs.

The creation of AID gave new stature to the U.S. foreign aid program by coordinating the work of the International Cooperation Administration, the Development Loan Fund for Peace and various other agencies that dispensed U.S. assistance abroad.

The rationale behind the Foreign Assistance Act that created AID was a mixture of humanitarian instincts and a fear of communism. The bulk of the initial monies went to the Kennedy administration's multi-billion-dollar ALLIANCE FOR PROGRESS in Latin America. The idea was that long-term assistance would allow a country to undertake self-sustaining economic growth and enable it to leave the ranks of the underdeveloped countries. Along with economic growth, democratic political institutions would develop, making the recipient nation an ally of the United States, capable of resisting the appeals of both communist and right-wing dictatorships.

But by 1963, AID was coming under attack from congressional critics, who demanded a discernible link between aid programs and other foreign policy objectives. For fiscal 1963, Congress cut President KENNEDY's $4.9 billion foreign aid request to $3.9 billion. Because military aid was reduced only slightly, economic aid suffered almost all of the $1 billion cut.

To generate support for foreign economic assistance, President Kennedy appointed a bipartisan Citizens Committee to Strengthen the Security of the Free World. Kennedy hoped that the committee's findings would support the need for an ambitious foreign aid program, but the committee's unexpectedly conservative report concluded that the United States attempted to do "too much for too many too soon." In 1964 the AID budget was cut to $3 billion.

During the Johnson administration, the agency concentrated its programs in countries where American foreign policy interests were most directly at stake. With the widening of the VIETNAM WAR, AID took responsibility for handling the economic assistance side of the large U.S. effort in Southeast Asia. There, CIA agents frequently operated under AID cover.

In the 1970s and 1980s, AID shifted the focus of its activities from financing major public works to supporting private-sector activities and the balance-of-payment deficits of developing countries. Congress insisted on tying conditions to most of the aid, mainly related to the implementation of privatization schemes and economic restabilization programs. By the end of the 1980s, there appeared to be a shift of opinion back toward support for major public works projects.

For Further Information:
Aubrey, Henry. *The Dollar in World Affairs*. New York, 1964.
Baldwin, David. *Economic Development and American Foreign Policy, 1943–1962*. Chicago, 1966.
Coffin, Frank. *Witness for Aid*. Boston, 1964.
Morss, E.R. *Foreign Aid, Its Defense and Reform*. Lexington, KY., 1987.
Walton, Richard J. *Cold War and Counterrevolution: The Foreign Policy of John F. Kennedy*. New York, 1972.
———. *The United States and Latin America*. New York, 1972.
Wood, R.E. *From Marshall Plan to Debt Crisis*. Berkeley, Calif., 1986.

Ailleret Doctrine   The Ailleret Doctrine was a French military doctrine developed in 1967 by General Charles Ailleret, the French chief of staff. It was the military expression of the independent foreign policy of President CHARLES DE GAULLE.

The basic tenet of the Ailleret Doctrine was that the French nuclear force must be independent and able to attack in any direction. In this way, France would be free to develop independent relations with both of the superpowers.

Ailleret was killed in an air crash on March 9, 1968. He was succeeded by General Michel Fourquet, who abandoned the Ailleret Doctrine and replaced it with the explicitly anti-Soviet and implicitly pro-United States Fourquet Plan.

For Further Information:
Grosser, Alfred. *The Western Alliance*. New York, 1978.

Air Burst   A term used to describe the detonation of a nuclear warhead in the air.

This technique is usually reserved for attacks on cities or densely inhabited areas. The warhead explodes 2,000–3,000 feet above the ground so that the effect of the radiation, blast and heat covers a larger area. The first atomic bomb used in warfare, at Hiroshima, was exploded in an air burst.

For Further Information:
Mayers, T. *Understanding Nuclear Weapons and Arms Control*. London, 1986.

Air Defense   Air defense comprises those measures used to protect a country or region from air attack.

Defense analysts usually divide air defense into two categories: active and passive. Active air defense consists of defensive weapons such as antiballistic missile systems, fighter aircraft, antiaircraft guns, surface-to-air missiles and electronic countermeasures.

Passive air defense includes such measures as radar or airborne early warning systems, camouflage, hardened missile silos and special civil and military shelters to protect against attack.

For Further Information:
Singh, Jasit. *Air Power in Modern Warfare.* New York, 1985.

Air-launched Cruise Missiles (ALCM)   Air-launched cruise missiles are cruise missiles that are launched from the wings of bomber aircraft. The advantage of this system is that it extends the range of the cruise missile from perhaps 1,200 miles to 1,200 miles plus the range of the bomber.

Another advantage of ALCMs is that the bomber is able to release its weapons before it is picked up by enemy radar and attacked. The missiles themselves are equipped, like ground-based cruise missiles, with computerized guidance systems that enable them to fly low under enemy radar to a predetermined target.

For Further Information:
Singh, Jasit. *Air Power in Modern Warfare.* New York, 1985.

Albania   Albania was the most hard-line and isolated of all the communist states. Throughout most of the Cold War era it isolated itself not only from the Western world, but also from the other Communist Bloc countries.

For most of its history, Albania has been a backward and feudal country dominated by either the Serbians or the Ottoman Turks. Albanian independence was not fully achieved until 1920. A republic was declared in 1925 under President Ahmet Beg Zogu, who became King Zog in 1928. But independence was shortlived; in April 1939, the country was occupied by Fascist Italy as a base of operations against Yugoslavia and Greece.

During World War II, the communists under ENVER HOXHA became the most effective resistance group, fighting first the Italian and then the German occupation. They formally took power on November 29, 1944, when the Germans left the country. Britain and the United States agreed to recognize the communist-dominated provisional government on the condition that it hold free elections. Elections were held in 1945, but they were preceded by a savage purge of anti-communist political leaders, which left Hoxha in control. As a result of these elections, the United States and Britain severed diplomatic relations and blocked Albanian entry into the United Nations until 1955. In 1950, Britain and the U.S. made an unsuccessful attempt to overthrow the Hoxha government.

In the immediate postwar years, Albania and Hoxha were closely tied to Yugoslavia and its leader JOSIP BROZ TITO, and for a time went along with his idea of a Balkan federation. From 1945 to 1948 Albania was almost totally absorbed in the Tito-dominated federation. But Tito's differences with Soviet leader JOSEF STALIN, the historical conflict between Serbia and Albania, and Hoxha's strong commitment to the prewar Comintern led to Hoxha's siding with Stalin. When Tito's nationalism léd Stalin to expel Yugoslavia from the Cominform in 1948, Hoxha took Albania out of the monetary and customs union with Yugoslavia and into a close alliance with the Soviet Union. Titoists within the Albanian communist leadership, such as Koci Xoxe, leader of the secret police, were given show trials and executed.

The determining factor in Albania's foreign policy now became the state of its relationship with Yugoslavia. This relationship was complicated by the fact that a large number of Albanians lived outside of Albania, in the Yugoslav region of Kosovo. The Yugoslavs regularly accused the Albanians of stirring up ethnic unrest in Kosovo, and the Albanians accused the Yugoslav government of suppressing Albanian culture and planning to invade Albania.

The Soviet-Yugoslav split therefore served Hoxha's purpose in that it provided Albania with a superpower protector. The price paid by Albania—total obedience to Moscow foreign policy directives—was a small one for a country used to being under the control of a foreign power for most of its political history.

When Soviet leader NIKITA KHRUSHCHEV ended the dispute with Yugoslavia, relations between Moscow and Tirana began to deteriorate. Hoxha, who felt he had been betrayed by Khrushchev, began to look around for another protector. He found him in Chinese leader Mao Zedong. In the late 1950s, Albania aligned itself more and more with Peking and refused to accept the destalinization campaign launched by Khrushchev.

With the formal SINO-SOVIET SPLIT, Albania allied itself formally with Peking. In 1961, the Soviet Union withdrew economic and technical aid from Albania, evacuated its submarine base at Vlore and broke off diplomatic relations. Soviet advisers and aid were replaced by Chinese. In 1962, Albania withdrew from COMECON and in 1968 left the WARSAW PACT.

Sino-Albanian relations, however, were soured by China's decision in 1972 to seek a rapprochement with the United States. Relations with Peking worsened still further after the death of Mao in 1976. In 1978, it was revealed that the defense minister had been executed for his involvement in an alleged Chinese-supported attempt to overthrow Hoxha. The same year, Albania announced its full support for Vietnam in its dispute with China, and the Peking government retaliated by formally severing all economic and military cooperation with Albania, thus leaving the tiny Balkan state almost completely friendless and isolated, but, according to its leadership, ideologically pure.

Increasing isolation, however, also brought increasing economic hardship on the already impoverished Albanian people. This forced the Albanian leadership to extend tentative feelers toward Western countries, most notably Greece, Italy and West Germany. Ideological and ethnic differences continued to block an improvement in relations with Yugoslavia, although Yugoslavia was Albania's biggest trading partner.

On April 11, 1985, Hoxha died and was succeeded by Ramiz Alia who initially increased contacts with West European countries while at the same time retaining the trappings of a strict Stalinist state. At the Communist Party Congress in November 1986, Alia declared that "Albania is a European nation . . . our Party and people are particularly interested in anything that occurs on our continent."

Throughout the late 1980s, Alia tried to keep Albania aloof from the collapse of communism throughout the rest of Eastern Europe. But he and Prime Minister Carcani were forced into a series of economic liberalization measures and the release of a number of political prisoners. As elsewhere in Eastern Europe, these limited reforms only whetted the public's demand for more democracy.

By January 1, 1991, Alia found himself vowing free democratic elections, but these were postponed until March 31 because of social and ethnic unrest (during which Albanian mobs tore down monuments to Enver Hoxha). In the months before the elections, Albania renewed diplomatic relations with the United States after 52 years, and under strong public pressure, Alia announced a caretaker government to carry the country toward the "free elections."

The elections were won by the existing Communist Party, and international observers declared that the polling procedure had been less than fair. The Democrats, who won over 60 seats, including Alia's in Tirana, boycotted the opening of the new parliament and renewed unrest followed. A general strike was called on May 15 and lasted until the government resigned on June 4. It was followed by a nonpartisan interim parliament led by Ylli Bufi, a communist approved by the Democrats, and a coalition cabinet. (Meanwhile, more than 40,000 Albanian refugees fled to Italy between March and August 1991, but most of them were quickly deported home again.)

The new government collapsed in December 1991 when, following nationwide unrest sparked by food and fuel shortages, the Democrats withdrew from the cabinet. In free national elections held in March 1992, the Democrats routed the Socialists (as the Communists now called themselves) 65% to 25%. Sali Berisha, the Democratic Party leader, announced, "We are saying farewell to Communism once and for all." However, the electoral triumph came at a time of economic and social turmoil: Inflation was running at 150%, unemployment was estimated at 70% and violent crime—long suppressed under Communist rule—had reached epidemic proportions.

For Further Information:
Bethell, Nicholas William. *Betrayed.* New York, 1984.
Pollo, S. *The History of Albania.* New York, 1981.
Schnytzer, A. *Stalinist Economic Strategy in Practice.* New York, 1983.
Winnifrith, Tom, ed. *Perspectives on Albania.* New York, 1991.

Allen, George V.   (November 3, 1903–July 11, 1970)

George Allen was U.S. ambassador to Iran when Soviet troops occupied the northern part of the country in 1946. He was later assistant secretary of state for public affairs; ambassador to Yugoslavia at the height of the Soviet–Yugoslav split;

assistant secretary of state for Near Eastern, South Asian and African affairs and director of the United States Information Agency.

Allen attended Duke and Harvard universities. He received a master of arts degree from Harvard in 1929, after which he joined the U.S. State Department as a career diplomat. He served in a number of posts and at the close of World War II attended the Moscow, Cairo and Potsdam conferences. On April 17, 1946, Allen was appointed ambassador to Iran, which was then the center of a major Cold War crisis.

Under a wartime agreement with Britain and the United States, the Soviet Union had occupied the AZERBAIJAN district in the northern half of Iran to prevent German intervention and secure the supply lines of U.S. LEND-LEASE equipment from the Persian Gulf to the Soviet Caucasus region. British troops secured the southern half.

The Soviets, under the agreement, were supposed to withdraw from Iran within six months of the end of the war against Germany. But in the intervening period they had established a puppet government that demanded autonomy for Azerbaijan. The Soviet troops remained, ostensibly at the request of the new autonomous government, and prevented the Iranian troops from reentering.

Iran complained to the Security Council of the newly formed United Nations on January 3, 1946, and was supported by the United States. Finally, on April 28, 1946, Soviet troops were withdrawn. But the Iranians had to pay a price: a Soviet–Iranian agreement giving the Soviets control of a production company to exploit Iranian oilfields. On top of that, the government still in place in Azerbaijan refused incorporation back into the Iranian state.

Allen was given the task of helping Iranian prime minister Ahmed Qavam to remove the pro-Soviet elements from his government and from Azerbaijan. He also successfully lobbied against the Iranian parliament's ratification of the Soviet-Iranian oil treaty. In the course of his work in Iran, Allen laid the foundations for the strong U.S. postwar presence in Iran that existed up until the overthrow of the shah in 1979. He was responsible for the start of American aid to the Iranian police and army and secured an agreement that American army officers would be the only foreign advisers to the Iranian Army.

In January 1948, Allen was appointed Assistant Secretary of State for Public Affairs and consolidated the work of the Voice of America. President Truman appointed him ambassador to Yugoslavia on October 27, 1949. Once again, the appointment came during a crisis period. On June 28, 1948, there was a formal split between Moscow and Belgrade, and Yugoslavia was expelled from the Cominform (the communist Information Bureau). Within the same week, the Soviets imposed the Berlin Blockade. Both the Soviet Union and the United States were trying to encourage dissension within the other's camp. Allen was given the task of encouraging Yugoslav President Tito to continue his independence from the

Soviet Union. To this end he pressured the U.S. government to increase trade with Yugoslavia and lift travel restrictions.

When President Eisenhower was inaugurated, Allen was first appointed ambassador to India and Nepal, from March 1953 to January 1955, and then assistant secretary of state for Near Eastern, South Asian and African Affairs from January 1955 to January 1958. As assistant secretary, Allen was given the futile task in September 1955 of trying to persuade Egypt's president Gamal Abdel Nasser to cancel his agreement with Moscow to buy Soviet weapons and purchase American arms instead.

On October 16, 1957, Allen was appointed director of the United States Information Agency, the government agency responsible for projecting a positive image of the United States overseas. On January 22, 1960, he testified before the Senate Foreign Relations Committee that the United States had "suffered a tremendous loss of prestige" because it had fallen behind the Soviet Union in the space race.

Allen left the State Department in November 1960 to become president of the Tobacco Institute. He retired in 1969 and died in 1970.

For Further Information:
Brands, H.W. *Cold Warriors.* New York, 1988.
Goode, James. *The United States and Iran, 1946–1951: The Diplomacy of Neglect.* London, 1989.
Spanier, J.W. *American Foreign Policy Since World War Two.* Washington, D.C., 1988.

Allen, Richard   (January 1, 1936–   )   Richard Allen was an influential right-wing foreign policy adviser to presidents Nixon and Reagan and for a short time was President Reagan's national security adviser.

Allen received his B.A. and M.A. degrees from Notre Dame University and during the 1960s was a staff member at Georgetown University's Center for Strategic and International Studies and Stanford University's Hoover Institution on War, Revolution and Peace. He received his doctorate from the University of Munich, where he wrote a dissertation on "The Theory and Practice of the Liberation of Man in Marxism and Leninism."

In 1968 he served as a foreign policy coordinator in Richard Nixon's presidential campaign. He and HENRY KISSINGER, then chief foreign policy adviser to Nelson Rockefeller, met before the 1968 Republican National Convention to draft a compromise Vietnam War plank for the party platform.

After Kissinger's appointment as national security adviser, Allen became his "principal associate." But the two men's personalities and policies clashed. Allen never liked Kissinger's détente policies and later accused him of "opening the bowels of the Adminstration to the New Left." After a short and unhappy stay on the National Security Council, Allen became deputy to Peter Peterson, Nixon's international economic aide. Soon afterward he left that post to found his own consulting firm, Potomac International, advising foreign governments and businesses on relations with Washington.

Allen remained active on the right wing of the Republican National Committee and was chairman of the party's intelligence subcommittee, which was responsible for analyzing details of the Soviet threat. He was also a founding member of the Committee on the Present Danger, a right-wing pressure group opposed to the second STRATEGIC ARMS LIMITATION TREATY (SALT II) and cutbacks in military spending.

Allen also helped to draft the foreign policy plank of the 1980 Republican platform. He took a particularly hard line on intelligence issues, protesting against what he called a "unilateral disarming of our intelligence agencies" and calling for a crash program to reverse the process.

In October 1980 the *Wall Street Journal* published a report claiming that Allen, during the Nixon administration, "apparently used his White House connections to obtain lucrative consulting contracts for himself and his friends." In order to prevent any damage to Reagan's candidacy, Allen immediately resigned his position as chief foreign policy adviser. But immediately after his election victory, Reagan appointed Allen to his foreign relations advisory panel, saying that his staff had found "no evidence of wrongdoing whatsoever" by Allen. Reagan named Allen his national security adviser on December 23, 1980.

Allen's strongly held and forcefully expressed conservative views quickly surfaced and brought him into conflict with Secretary of State ALEXANDER HAIG and high-ranking officials at the State Department. Speaking before the Conservative Political Action Conference on March 21, 1981, Allen warned that Western Europe was threatened internally by "outright pacifist sentiments" and a "grave economic crisis" as serious as that following World War II.

Allen's speech followed an interview given to Reuters News Agency by his close associate Richard Pipes in which Pipes, with the apparent support of Allen, said that war with the Soviet Union was inevitable if it did not abandon communism. Pipes also attacked the policies of West German foreign minister HANS-DIETRICH GENSCHER as too susceptible to Soviet persuasion.

The interview and the Allen speech led Haig to send a personal letter to Genscher expressing "outrage" about the comments. Haig proposed to President Reagan that Allen be told to clear any further foreign policy speeches with the State Department. Relations between Haig and Allen continued to deteriorate, and later in 1981 Haig announced that an unnamed White House aide (which was widely reported to be Allen) was waging "guerrilla warfare" against him.

Later in 1981, doubts about Allen's business dealings again surfaced. It was reported that he had accepted and failed to report a $1,000 gift that Japanese journalists had tried to give Nancy Reagan after a brief interview he had helped to arrange through a former business associate. He also allegedly accepted two wristwatches from Japanese businessmen and continued to work on behalf of and receive payments from his consulting firm.

Shortly before Christmas 1981, Allen went on "administrative leave." A Justice Department and White House investigation cleared Allen of any wrongdoing, but the press controversy had made it difficult for him to continue as national security adviser and he resigned on January 4, 1982, to be replaced by William Clark. Allen, however, was retained as a part-time adviser both to Reagan and the Republican National Committee.

For Further Information:
Brownstein, Ronald, and Nina Easton. *Reagan's Ruling Class.* Washington, D.C., 1982.
Cyr, A.I. *U.S. Foreign Policy and European Security.* New York, 1988.
New American Library. *The Reagan Foreign Policy.* New York, 1987.
Savigear, P. *Cold War or Détente in the 1980s.* New York, 1987.

Allende, Salvador   (July 26, 1908–September 11, 1973)
Salvador Allende was a democratically elected socialist president of Chile who forged close links with Cuba's FIDEL CASTRO and nationalized American business interests. He was subsequently overthrown by a U.S.-supported military coup.

Allende was born into a radical Chilean political family. His grandfather was founder of the Chilean Radical Party, one of the non-Marxist parties that made up Allende's Popular Unity coalition government in 1970.

In 1933, after qualifying as a medical doctor, Allende helped to found the Chilean Socialist Party. His political activities led to a brief jail sentence for "revolutionary activities," and after his release he had difficulty finding a post as a doctor and was forced to accept work as a coroner's assistant. In 1937 he was elected to the Chilean legislature as a socialist deputy and in 1939 became minister of health.

Allende, by his own admission, was an emotional socialist. He had little interest in the mechanics of politics or economics. His main concern was the social welfare of the masses. He did not join the Communist Party because he believed that its emphasis on internationalism ignored Chile's specific problems, although Allende himself accepted basic Marxist beliefs and sought an accommodation with the communists.

Allende's support for the outlawed Communist Party led to his suspension from the Socialist Party in 1952, and he placed last in the four-man presidential campaign that year. It was his first of several attempts to win the presidency. By 1957 the Communist Party had been legalized, and in the 1958 and 1964 elections Allende ran as the joint candidate of the Socialist and Communist parties. The U.S. government, frightened of Allende's links with the communists, provided substantial financial support to the conservative Christian Democratic Party to block Allende's election. The Christian Democrats also received American financial support during Allende's successful 1970 campaign, including $1 million from International Telephone and Telegraph (ITT), which was channeled through CENTRAL INTELLIGENCE AGENCY links.

In February 1970, Allende widened his political base by creating an electoral alliance of left-wing and center-left parties under the banner of the Popular Unity Coalition. The alliance secured Allende 36.3% of the vote in the presidential elections on September 4, 1970. This was enough to put him in first place out of a field of four candidates, but under the Chilean constitution, he had to be confirmed by the legislature because he lacked an absolute majority. Once again, strong pressure was brought to bear by American interests, but the legislature confirmed Allende in office.

Within nine days of his inauguration, Allende established diplomatic relations with Cuba. He also established contact with North Korea and North Vietnam and released from prison hundreds of members of the Chilean terrorist organization Movement of the Revolutionary Left. Allende then moved against American business interests, particularly ITT and Kennecott Copper Corporation.

Allende's socialist economic policies lost him the support of the Chilean business community. A strike by truckers and shopkeepers in 1972 was ended only after he temporarily brought senior army officers into his cabinet.

By this time, Allende had lost control of the economy. Inflation was the highest in the world, and the country was becoming dangerously polarized between the far left and far right. After another strike by Chilean truck owners, the military was brought back into the cabinet. But this time they entered government reluctantly, only too aware that they were sacrificing their historic political neutrality in support of a government in crisis.

On January 10, 1973, Allende announced a new system for the distribution of basic foodstuffs, which in effect, constituted food rationing. This led to a new series of strikes. U.S. government and private American interests provided financial support for the conservative parties in Chilean congressional mid-term elections in March 1973, which resulted in a stalemate. In June 1973 members of the military attempted a coup. This was followed by more strikes and street riots. On September 11, 1973, a second coup, led by General Augusto Pinochet, successfully overthrew Allende, who was killed—or committed suicide—in the course of the coup.

It is not clear what role, if any, the CIA played in the actual coup. However, there is little question that the agency had worked diligently toward such an outcome at the request of the White House, spending $8 million from 1970 to 1973 to destabilize the Chilean economy and foment opposition to Allende. In 1970, before Allende's election, then-national security adviser Henry Kissinger reportedly told a secret White House meeting, "I don't see why we need to stand by and watch a country go communist due to the irresponsibility of its own people." Later that year, after Allende's election, President Richard Nixon was quoted as instructing the CIA to "make the [Chilean] economy scream."

Allende's overthrow was followed by more than 16 years of military dictatorship under Pinochet during which thousands of Chileans were killed, tortured or "disappeared," and the regime gained the reputation of being among the worst abusers of human rights in Latin America. Radical free-market reforms were instituted with the advice of University of Chicago economists. The economy generally performed poorly in the first half of Pinochet's rule and gradually improved in the second half. Pinochet was finally replaced by an elected civilian government in March 1990, although he continued to wield considerable behind-the-scene powers as commander-in-chief of the armed forces.

For Further Information:
De Vylder, S. *Allende's Chile*. New York, 1976.
Forsythe, F.P. *Human Rights and U.S. Foreign Policy*. New York, 1987.
MacEoin, Gary. *No Peaceful Way: Chile's Struggle for Dignity*. New York, 1974.
Petras, James F. *The United States and Chile: Imperialism and the Overthrow of the Allende Government*. New York, 1975.
Uribe Arce, Armando. *The Black Book of American Intervention in Chile*. Boston, 1975.

All-German Council   The All-German Council was proposed in 1950 by the East German government to provide a forum for the negotiation of a new constitution for a reunified Germany.

The council was proposed in a letter sent to West German chancellor KONRAD ADENAUER on November 30, 1950. Adenauer, with the approval of the Western occupying powers, had already proposed his own plan, on March 22, 1950, in which he called for a government based on a free nationwide election, freedom of the press and of all political parties, elimination of interzonal and trade barriers, and a guarantee of political freedom for individuals by the occupying powers. The constitution of a reunified Germany would be drawn up after the election.

The Soviet Union and East Germany countered with their proposal for an All-German Council to establish a provisional all-German government, which would draw up a constitution and then hold elections on the basis of that constitution. East and West Germans would be represented equally on the council and in the provisional government. The West Germans and the Western Powers rejected this suggestion, arguing that, because the East German government had not been freely elected, it should not have equal representation in a provisional government charged with negotiating a constitution. In March 1951 the rejection was emphasized when the West German Bundestag (lower house of parliament) passed a resolution that the restoration of human rights was the foundation of a democratic state and the prerequisite for free elections in East Germany.

For Further Information:
Crawley, A.M. *The Rise of West Germany 1945–1972*. New York, 1974.
Whetsen, Lawrence. *Germany East and West*. New York, 1980.

Alliance for Progress   The Alliance for Progress was established in 1961 as the cornerstone of the KENNEDY administration's Latin American policy to thwart the expansion of Soviet and Cuban influence in the Western Hemisphere. The

Alliance for Progress was first mentioned by John F. Kennedy in a speech in Tampa, Florida during the 1960 presidential campaign. On September 10, he called for a "great common effort to develop the resources of the entire hemisphere, strengthen the forces of democracy and widen the vocational and educational opportunities of every person in all the Americas." Kennedy also called for increased American aid to Latin American countries, land reform, commodity price stabilization programs and an arms agreement for the hemisphere.

Immediately after his election, Kennedy asked ADOLF BERLE, an adviser on Latin America, to form a Latin American Task Force to make immediate and long-range policy recommendations on Latin American problems. Berle advised the president that the best way to combat communist expansion in Latin America was to decrease support for right-wing dictators, to support democratic movements openly and to launch a plan for aid to Latin America similar to the MARSHALL PLAN.

On March 13, Kennedy proposed that the Latin American countries, excluding Cuba, join the United States in a 10-year, 10-point economic and social development program for Latin America that incorporated the ideas first outlined in his Tampa speech and later developed by Berle's task force. Kennedy also asked the U.S. Congress to appropriate $500 million immediately for development in Latin America.

On August 17, 1961, the United States and 19 other American countries meeting in Punta del Este, Uruguay, signed the Alliance for Progress Charter, which implemented an American 10-year, $20-billion economic development plan for Latin America. They also signed the accompanying Declaration of Punta del Este. The main points of the Alliance Charter and accompanying declaration were as follows:

1. To improve and strengthen democratic institutions through self-determination.
2. To accelerate economic and social development throughout Latin America.
3. To carry out extensive housing programs.
4. To wipe out illiteracy.
5. To increase public health programs.
6. To reform tax laws, stimulate private enterprise, eliminate unemployment and encourage monetary policies aimed at price stabilization.
7. To encourage and accelerate the economic integration of Latin America.

The United States was to provide a minimum of $20 billion in aid over the following 10 years. It also pledged to provide development loans running up to 50 years at very low or no interest.

The Alliance for Progress continued to be the cornerstone of the Latin America policy of the Kennedy administration and later the Johnson administration. However, the financial drain of the Vietnam War and continuing NATO commitments, plus eight years of Republican administrations following President Johnson's, moved Latin America down the

United States' list of foreign policy priorities. Successive administrations failed to build on the alliance after the expiration of the initial 10-year period.

For Further Information:
Berle, Adolf A., Jr. *Latin America: Diplomacy and Reality.* New York, 1962.
McClellan, Grant, ed. *U.S. Policy in Latin America.* New York, 1963.
Walton, Richard J. *The United States and Latin America.* New York, 1972.
Wood, R.E. *From Marshall Aid to Debt Crisis.* Berkeley, Calif., 1986.

Allison, John   (April 7, 1905–October 28, 1978)   John Allison was a career American Foreign Service officer who served as President Dwight Eisenhower's ambassador to Japan, Indonesia and Czechoslovakia. His relatively liberal beliefs helped to prevent a major postwar rearmament of Japan.

After graduating from the University of Nebraska, Allison went to Japan as an English teacher. While there he joined the U.S. diplomatic service and between 1932 and 1941 served in a variety of posts in Japan and China. He was interned by the Japanese for the first six months after Pearl Harbor and during the rest of the war years was based in London. In 1947 he was appointed chief of the Far Eastern Division at the State Department.

In April 1953, Allison was sent to Japan as ambassador. He had developed a close relationship with Secretary of State JOHN FOSTER DULLES and at the time shared his staunch anti-communist views. Allison was under instructions from Dulles to persuade the Japanese to rearm as a bulwark against communism in Asia. The Japanese, however, had already written into their constitution a renunciation of war "as a means of settling international disputes." The Japanese also opposed any diversion from the rebuilding of their economy.

Allison became convinced of the rightness of the Japanese position, which was a major boost to the Japanese government in negotiations with the United States. The Japanese–U.S. Mutual Defense Treaty of 1954 did, however, commit Japan to rebuild its armed forces under American guidance in order to make a "full contribution to the strength of the anti-Communist world." (See JAPANESE–U.S. DEFENSE TREATIES.)

In April 1957 Allison was appointed ambassador to Indonesia. By this time he had become convinced that the world was much more complex than Dulles' version of good and evil and that it was wrong and dangerous to base an entire foreign policy on communist versus capitalist. The determining motivation of all countries, Allison maintained, was not political doctrine but national self-interest. Because of this belief, Allison was dismissive of Dulles' fears about the left-wing tendencies of Indonesian president SUKARNO. This led to a clash with Dulles and eventually to Allison's resignation as ambassador to Indonesia in November 1957. Allison served two more years in the foreign service as ambassador to Czechoslovakia. In 1960 he retired to teach at the University of Hawaii.

For Further Information:
Allison, John N. *Ambassador from the Prairie, or Allison Wonderland.* Boston, 1973.

Alsop, Joseph W.   (October 10, 1910–August 28, 1989)   Joseph Alsop was a prominent conservative American journalist throughout most of the Cold War period.

Born into a wealthy and influential New York family, Alsop attended the exclusive Groton School and Harvard College. After graduation in 1932 he joined the *New York Herald-Tribune*, and within five years had his own Washington-based syndicated column.

During World War II Alsop worked in China as public relations aide to U.S. General CLAIRE CHENNAULT, and he emerged from his wartime experiences a staunch supporter of CHIANG KAI-SHEK and an ardent anti-communist.

He continued both his support for Chiang and his opposition to communism when he returned to writing his column for the *Herald-Tribune*, this time in collaboration with his brother Stewart. In 1947 he predicted the communist takeover in Czechoslovakia and in 1948 warned that the withdrawal of American forces from Korea would throw the country into "the expanding Soviet Empire." In 1950 Alsop pressed for increased defense spending as the principal way to combat Soviet expansionism.

Although strongly opposed to the Soviet Union, Joseph Alsop was also adamantly opposed to McCarthyism and regularly defended its victims. He maintained that the communist threat to the United States came from outside rather than from internal subversion.

During the Eisenhower administration the two brothers' column took an increasingly critical view of American foreign policy. This was mainly the influence of Joseph Alsop, whose New Year's message for 1954 was simply "All Is Lost." In 1954 Joseph Alsop also urged the United States to support French action in Vietnam, and through the years he issued warnings about the imminent collapse of Southeast Asia.

In 1953 Stewart and Joseph Alsop coauthored the book *We Accuse!* in which they denounced the ATOMIC ENERGY COMMISSION for refusing to reinstate the security clearance of J. ROBERT OPPENHEIMER, the father of the atomic bomb. Their denunciation of Senator Joseph McCarthy and his accusations against Oppenheimer, which had led to Oppenheimer's dismissal from the commission, played a role in McCarthy's eventual fall from power.

The two brothers ended their writing partnership in March 1958 when Stewart left the column to become a contributing editor for the *Saturday Evening Post.* Joseph Alsop continued writing the column, concentrating mainly on the perceived MISSILE GAP between the Soviet Union and the United States.

By the time JOHN F. KENNEDY was elected president in 1960, Joseph Alsop's nearly 30 years at the top of his profession had established him as an independent political force. He became a friend and confidant of Kennedy and advised him to select LYNDON JOHNSON as his running mate.

It was during the Kennedy years that Alsop began to develop a reputation as a "superhawk." Because of this reputation and his continuing hard line on Vietnam and Communist China, he gradually drifted away from the mainstream of American foreign policy thinking in the late 1960s and early 1970s. He retired in 1973 to concentrate on the study of Greek antiquities.

For Further Information:
Alsop, Joseph, and Stewart Alsop. *We Accuse!* New York, 1953.
———. *The Reporter's Trade.* New York, 1958.
Alsop, Joseph W., with Adam Platt. *I've Seen the Best of It.* New York, 1992.

American Federation of Labor–Congress of Industrial Organizations (AFL–CIO)   The American Federation of Labor–Congress of Industrial Organizations was the giant American trade union federation created by a merger of the two constituent organizations in 1955. Before and after 1955, the American trade union movement played a major role in financing non-communist trade union organizations, sometimes working in conjunction with the CENTRAL INTELLIGENCE AGENCY.

The American Federation of Labor was founded in 1886 to organize workers in craft unions. The Committee for Industrial Organization (the CIO's orginal name) was formed in 1935, at the height of the Roosevelt administration's New Deal, and was aimed at the workers in the growing and unorganized mass-production industries.

The two union blocks competed vigorously for members during the 1930s. Wartime considerations led to cooperation, but this again degenerated into a membership battle in the late 1940s. One of the major causes for friction between the two was the difference in their positions toward communism.

During the early postwar period, the issue of communism in the CIO was continually raised in the U.S. Congress and in the press. John L. Lewis had relied on skilled communist organizers during the founding years of the CIO, and by the end of the war an estimated quarter of the total CIO membership was enrolled in unions whose leaders were either members of, or strongly influenced by, the Communist Party.

By the end of 1945, however, as the Cold War began to develop, anti-communists within the CIO began to mobilize. Philip Murray, then president of the CIO, at first tried to remain neutral, but as Cold War emotions grew, this position became increasingly untenable. During 1947 and 1948, the communist leadership within many CIO affiliates met with resounding defeat. At the Cleveland CIO Convention in 1949, the anti-communist majority voted to end all communist influence. This allowed the CIO leaders to join the AFL–State Department coalition in foreign affairs.

After the sudden death of Murray in November 1952, he was succeeded by Walter Reuther, who had been the leading anti-communist figure within the CIO.

The American Federation of Labor had from the start taken a strong anti-communist position. In this it was strongly influenced by Jay Lovestone, a former leader of the American Communist Party who became virulently anti-communist when he was ordered by the Soviet Union to abdicate in favor of WILLIAM Z. FOSTER. During World War II, Lovestone, working with the AFL-affiliated International Ladies Garment Workers Union, helped rescue hundreds of union officials, politicians and intellectuals from German-occupied Europe. In 1944 he persuaded the AFL to create a fund to assist the organization of "democratic" unions in Europe, Asia and Latin America.

This fund was administered by Lovestone through the Free Trade Union Committee (FTUC), whose anti-communist activities became broadly accepted by the leadership of the AFL. At the end of the war, the FTUC launched an extensive aid program to non-communist unions in France and Italy. The FTUC and the AFL also successfully lobbied the American military government in Germany to permit the organization of centralized unions in the American sector.

In the immediate postwar period, communist and non-communist unions around the world joined forces to form the World Federation of Trade Unions (WFTU). But in the spring of 1948 the WFTU split over the Soviet-initiated attempts to block implementation of the MARSHALL PLAN in Western Europe. The British Trades Union Congress convened a separate meeting of non-communist unions in London to which both the AFL and CIO sent delegates. This conference formed the nucleus of the International Confederation of Free Trade Unions (ICFTU), which was formally inaugurated in December 1949.

By the late 1940s, the AFL's foreign policy had become virtually indistinguishable from that of the U.S. government, and AFL and FTUC representatives were posted in American embassies around the world. The FTUC, through Lovestone, also worked with the CIA in various clandestine operations. These included support for anti-communist trade union activities in Italy, help in the overthrow of Guatemalan president Jacobo Arbenz and the overthrow of Prime Minister Cheddi Jagan of British Guiana.

Walter Reuther of the CIO opposed this rigid anti-communism. He especially objected to the government-supported and often clandestine overseas operations of Lovestone, and at the time of the AFL-CIO merger in 1955, he made an unsuccessful attempt to have Lovestone removed. The disagreements about the approach to the problem of communism continued to bedevil intra-union relations after the merger. In 1959 the disagreements surfaced on the occasion of a visit by top Soviet leaders to the United States when AFL-CIO president George Meany pointedly boycotted two Reuther-led union delegations that met with Soviet premier Nikita Khrushchev.

Lovestone and the anti-communists remained in firm control of the foreign policy of the AFL-CIO and ensured that the American trade union movement took a strong anti-communist position through the 1950s and 1960s. They consistently supported the Vietnam War policies of presidents Johnson and Nixon.

For Further Information:
Draper, Alan. *A Rope of Sand: The AFL-CIO Committee on Political Education, 1955–1967.* New York, 1989.
Godson, Roy. *American Labor and European Politics: The AFL as a Transnational Force.* New York, 1976.
Halpern, Martin. *UAW Politics in the Cold War Era.* Albany, N.Y., 1988.
Lens, Sidney. "Lovestone Diplomacy." *The Nation,* July 5, 1965.
Radosh, Ronald. *American Labor and United States Foreign Policy.* New York, 1969.
Scott, Jack. *Yankee Unions, Go Home: How the AFL Helped the U.S. Build an Empire in Latin America.* Vancouver, 1978.

American University Speech   President John F. Kennedy, delivering the commencement address on June 10, 1963, at American University in Washington, D.C., announced that the U.S., British and Soviet governments had agreed to convene new negotiations on a treaty to ban nuclear weapons tests. Kennedy also announced that the United States had halted atmospheric nuclear tests and would not resume them unless another country did so.

The president's announcements were made in an address devoted to elaborating "a strategy of peace" to prevent a world nuclear holocaust. The speech was regarded as a major statement of U.S. hopes for a relaxation of the Cold War and was given wide press coverage throughout the world, including the Soviet Union.

Kennedy offered the new negotiations and an end to U.S. atmospheric tests as "preliminary but important steps toward a lessening of East-West tensions, disarmament and an eventual world order capable of resolving international conflict without war."

He called on Americans to support this aim by reexamining their own attitudes toward the Soviet Union and the Cold War and contended that peace was possible because "our problems are man-made" and "can be solved by man."

Kennedy asserted that communism was "profoundly repugnant" to Americans but that "we can still hail the Russian people for their many achievements—in science and space, in industrial growth, in culture, in acts of courage." He said that America's Cold War policies must be conducted "in such a way that it becomes in the Communists' interests to agree on a genuine peace" and added that "constructive changes within the Communist Bloc might bring within reach solutions which now seem beyond us."

Soviet leader NIKITA KHRUSHCHEV told veteran American diplomat W. Averell Harriman that Kennedy's American University speech was "the greatest speech by any American President since Roosevelt." The speech cleared the way for renewed negotiations for a NUCLEAR TEST BAN TREATY, which was soon afterward concluded in Moscow.

For Further Information:
Dean, Arthur. *Test Ban and Disarmament: The Path of Negotiations.* New York, 1966.
Lepper, Mary Milling. *Foreign Policy Formulation: A Case Study of the Nuclear Test Ban Treaty of 1963.* Columbus, Ohio, 1973.
Walton, Richard. *Cold War and Counterrevolution: The Foreign Policy of John F. Kennedy.* New York, 1972.

Americans for Democratic Action (ADA)   The Americans for Democratic Action is a liberal anti-communist lobby group founded in January 1947 as an alternative to the Progressive Citizens of America, led by left-wing presidential candidate Henry A. Wallace.

The membership of the ADA has embraced some of the most prominent American liberals of the postwar period, including CHESTER BOWLES, ELEANOR ROOSEVELT, FRANCIS BIDDLE, HUBERT HUMPHREY, Reinhold Niebuhr, Arthur Schlesinger Jr., Wilson Wyatt and Walter Reuther.

The ADA was one of two major liberal coalitions formed in an attempt to aid the Democratic administration of President HARRY TRUMAN. From its inception the ADA rejected the prospect of becoming a political party in its own right, as such a move would be likely to split the liberal vote between itself and the more established Democratic Party.

In its constitution, the ADA specifically forbade members of the Communist Party from joining the ADA, and its first president, Wilson Wyatt, took a tough anti-communist line in foreign policy. He favored Truman's policy of CONTAINMENT toward the Soviet Union and vigorously supported the TRUMAN DOCTRINE.

During the early 1950s, the group backed civil rights legislation, Truman's Fair Deal proposals and the U.S. role in Korea. It opposed American aid to the government of FRANCISCO FRANCO in Spain, fought the INTERNAL SECURITY ACT OF 1950, supported repeal of the Smith Act, attacked the HOUSE UN-AMERICAN ACTIVITIES COMMITTEE, opposed loyalty oaths for teachers and publicly condemned the tactics of Senator JOSEPH MCCARTHY.

Under the chairmanship of economist Robert Nathan from 1957 to 1959, the ADA shifted its emphasis to criticizing the conservative economic policies of President DWIGHT EISENHOWER.

During the 1960 presidential race the ADA supported Hubert Humphrey against John F. Kennedy in the race for the Democratic nomination, and during the Kennedy and Johnson administrations its emphasis shifted toward social and civil rights legislation. But at the height of the Vietnam War, during the Nixon administration, ADA chairman Allard Lowenstein threw the weight of the organization behind the peace movement.

For Further Information:
Diving, Robert A. *Foreign Policy and U.S. Presidential Elections.* New York, 1974.
Gillon, Steven M. *Politics and Vision: The ADA and American Liberalism, 1947–1985.* New York, 1987.
Goulden, Joseph. *The Best Years, 1945–1950.* New York, 1976.
McAuliffe, Mary. *Crisis on the Left: Cold War and Politics and American Liberals, 1947–1954.* Amherst, Mass., 1974.

HMS *Amethyst* Communist attacks on the British warship HMS *Amethyst* during the Chinese Civil War threatened to bring about British intervention on the side of the Nationalist government and undermined the popularity of the British Communist Party.

HMS *Amethyst* was attacked by communist shore batteries on April 20, 1949, when it was traveling up the Yangtze River from Shanghai to Nanking to protect British citizens. It ran aground 15 miles east of Chinkiang while trying to turn around to go back to Shanghai. Eighteen men on the *Amethyst* were killed in the initial attack, including the captain. A series of British ships tried to go to *Amethyst*'s aid but were stopped by communist gunfire.

Indignation over the incident ran high in Britain. Harry Pollitt, the secretary of the British Communist Party, had to be rescued from a stone-throwing crowd when he tried to defend the Chinese communist action in a speech on April 22. He argued that the *Amethyst* had no right to be on the Yangtze.

The Labour government maintained a position of strict neutrality in the CHINESE CIVIL WAR while continuing to recognize the Nationalist government of Chiang Kai-shek. But with the *Amethyst* trapped and under attack, the government came under pressure to react. Prime Minister CLEMENT ATTLEE, however, firmly ruled out "punitive warfare" to rescue the ship. He was saved from a major diplomatic and military disaster when the *Amethyst* finally escaped on July 30.

For Further Information:
Luard, D.E.T. *Britain and China*. Baltimore, 1962.

Andropov, Yuri (June 15, 1914–February 9, 1984) Yuri Andropov was Soviet ambassador to Hungary during the 1956 revolution, later head of the KGB and finally, for only 15 months, leader of the Soviet Union.

Andropov, the son of a railway worker, was born in Nagutskaya in the northern Caucasus. He worked as a telegraph operator and film projectionist before attending Petrozavodsk University, from which he never graduated.

During World War II, he was sent to head the Young Communist League in the Karelo-Finnish Republic after its formation in 1940. After the German occupation of the region, Andropov organized guerrilla activity behind the German lines, and after the war he was rewarded with the post of party chief of Petrozavodsk, capital of the republic.

In 1951 Andropov was transferred to Moscow and the secretariat of the Communist Party's Central Committee. At the same time, he was sent to the Higher Party School, a political–military institution, to complete his university education. In July 1953 he was switched to the Ministry of Foreign Affairs, where he became head of the department that dealt with Poland and Czechoslovakia. At the end of 1953 he transferred to Hungary to become counselor and chargé d'affaires at the Soviet embassy. In 1954 he was promoted to ambassador..

As Soviet ambassador in Hungary, Andropov played a

Yuri Andropov was leader of the Soviet Union for only 15 months (1982–1984) before his death. Photo courtesy of Novosti Press Agency.

major role in the events up to, during and after the 1956 Hungarian Revolution. His handling of his role in these historic events placed the young diplomat on the ladder to the top of the Soviet structure.

In the years before the revolution, Andropov had worked hard to cultivate political contacts among both the pro-Soviet communists and the opposition and reformist wing of the party. He also took an active interest in Hungarian culture and language, and this made him a genuinely popular figure in Hungarian circles.

Andropov initially saw his role in the revolution as trying to mediate a compromise between the Stalinist and reformist wings of the Hungarian Communist Party. It is believed, for instance, that he played an instrumental role in bringing reformist IMRE NAGY back from exile and reinstating him as premier in an attempt to appease the reformists.

But by this time, the reform movement had developed an unstoppable momentum. The Nagy government released the dissident archbishop JOZSEF MINDSZENTY, and crowds burst into the street to tear down the statue of Stalin and demand Hungary's withdrawal from the WARSAW PACT. A party delegation led by Soviet ideologue MIKHAIL SUSLOV arrived in Budapest and set up its headquarters at Andropov's ambassadorial residence.

In the meantime, Andropov continued to talk with the Hungarian government, all the time assuring the Hungarians that Soviet troops would not intervene. But at the same time, he persuaded JANOS KADAR to desert his colleagues in the Hungarian government and agree to replace Nagy after the Soviet invasion. Later, after Nagy was overthrown and took refuge in the Yugoslav embassy, Andropov guaranteed him safe passage to Yugoslavia, only to arrange to have him kidnapped and later secretly tried and executed.

After the Hungarian Revolution, Andropov also encouraged Kadar to introduce some of the basic economic reforms that eventually led to Hungary's becoming the most politically and economically liberal of the East European countries in the 1970s and 1980s. It is believed that Andropov's experiences in rebuilding the Hungarian Communist Party led him to adopt a more reformist position when he became general secretary of the Soviet Communist Party.

In 1957 Andropov left Hungary to return to Moscow as head of the Secretariat's department of liaison with communist parties in other countries. In this capacity he led a delegation to North Vietnam following the CUBAN MISSILE CRISIS to assure the North Vietnamese of Soviet support. In 1962 he became a member of the party's Central Committee.

In 1967 Andropov left the Secretariat and began his 15-year tenure as head of the KGB. At the same time, he became a candidate (non-voting) member of the Politburo. In 1973 he was promoted to full voting member.

Andropov was chosen by Soviet leader LEONID BREZHNEV as head of the KGB because he was regarded as the man most likely to keep the secret police on the straight and narrow and not use it as a personal political weapon. He did not disappoint Brezhnev. Under Andropov, the KGB became less oppressive and shifted its emphasis from political espionage to industrial espionage in order to fill the yawning gaps in Soviet research programs.

Andropov largely did away with the terror tactics of torture, murder and labor camps, but he replaced them with a more subtle way of controlling the population and its dissidents. Some dissidents, such as writer ALEXANDER SOLZHENITSYN, were effectively exiled to the West on the grounds that they could do less harm there and that their release helped to still Western criticism. Others such as dissident scientist ANDREI SAKHAROV were harassed by KGB agents who publicly shadowed their every move, regularly searched their apartments, interrogated them at regular intervals and arranged for them to be robbed or attacked by "hoodlums."

But the most frightening KGB tactic of the Andropov era was the misuse of psychiatric hospitals. On the grounds that anyone who opposed communism must be mentally ill, many dissidents were sent to psychiatric hospitals, where they were locked away and treated with psychoactive or debilitating drugs.

Brezhnev and the other members of the Politburo were obviously pleased with the work done by Andropov at the KGB. In 1979 they honored him by publishing his collected works and speeches. The glowing reviews it attracted in the official Soviet press were a sign that Andropov was being considered for the leadership position.

In May 1982 Andropov left the KGB to take up a post in the party Secretariat. Brezhnev was clearly dying, and the different factions of the party were moving their key people into positions from which to launch a bid for the leadership. Andropov was the candidate of the pragmatic, or reformist, wing of the party. His experiences in Hungary and at the KGB had exposed him to the limits of socialism as well as the corruption and stagnation within the party. His main opponent was Brezhnev's chief lieutenant, KONSTANTIN CHERNENKO.

The reformist position had been strengthened considerably by the death in January 1982 of chief Soviet ideologue Mikhail Suslov, whose insistence on orthodox communism had blocked the reformers for years. Andropov's campaign within the party focused on exposing corruption among the family and friends of Brezhnev. By doing so, he implicitly attacked Brezhnev and, by association, his policies and his hand-picked successor, Chernenko. When Brezhnev died on November 17, 1982, Andropov had already secured the party leadership, and, to provide the impression of a united front, Chernenko was detailed to make the announcement.

Andropov's first priority was the economy, which years of subsidies, lack of investment and poor workmanship had left in a shambles. On November 22, only five days after taking office, Andropov made a major speech in which he confirmed that the economy had fallen short of its production targets for the past two years. To resolve this crisis he proposed decentralization and material incentives to stimulate the economy. He also supported giving greater independence to industrial and agricultural enterprises and linking workers' earnings to productivity. In addition (with the experience of Hungary in mind), he advocated drawing on "the experience of fraternal countries" and encouraging "those who boldly introduce new technology."

In the same speech, Andropov also dealt with East-West relations and nuclear arms issues. He stressed that détente was "by no means a past stage. The future belongs to this policy." He supported a freeze on strategic nuclear arsenals as a first step in a process of mutual arms reduction.

Andropov had already drawn the conclusion that the Soviet Union could not afford to continue sacrificing its domestic economy to the East-West arms race. Throughout 1983 he continued to press for economic reforms and offered reductions in nuclear weapons. But at the same time he had to fight for his policy changes against the well-entrenched Brezhnevites led by Chernenko. On February 9, 1984, Andropov died of acute kidney failure. His policies suffered a temporary setback when he was succeeded by Chernenko, but a year later they were set back on course by MIKHAIL GORBACHEV.

For Further Information:
Barber, Noel. *Seven Days of Freedom: The Hungarian Uprising*. New York, 1974.

Barron, John. KGB: The Secret Work of Secret Agents. New York, 1974.

Ebon, Martin. The Andropov File. New York, 1983.

Angleton, James Jesus   (1917–May 11, 1987)   James Angleton was chief of counterintelligence at the U.S. CENTRAL INTELLIGENCE AGENCY for 20 years, from 1954 to 1974. He was the chief CIA investigator of Soviet penetration into the agency, and ironically was at one time himself suspected of being a top Soviet mole (he was subsequently cleared).

After graduating from Yale in 1943, Angleton joined the Office of Strategic Services, wartime predecessor of the CIA. In 1947 he transferred to the newly created agency and was posted to Italy, where he helped to channel American funds to anti-communist groups.

In 1954 Angleton returned to Washington to establish the CIA's counterintelligence operation, which in 1956 succeeded in obtaining a copy of NIKITA KHRUSHCHEV's secret denunciation of Stalin. Angleton also played a major role in organizing American attempts at infiltrating KGB units, helped to manage the CIA's illegal monitoring of the mail between the United States and Eastern Europe, and developed close relations between the CIA and Israeli Intelligence.

Angleton—with his gray pallor, intellectualism, penchant for growing orchids, and labyrinthine (his critics would say paranoid) mind—became the real-life model for many fictional spymasters. He built the CIA's counterintelligence division into his own private fiefdom. His suspicions of Soviet duplicity ran deep: He saw the Sino-Soviet split as a ruse designed to lull the West, and viewed a number of important Soviet defectors as "false defectors" sent over to spread KGB DISINFORMATION. In retrospect, many analysts consider Angleton's compulsive search for a Soviet deep penetration agent within the CIA as having done far more harm than good. Ironically, one of the few people he did not suspect until it was too late was his friend KIM PHILBY, the notorious Soviet mole within British intelligence.

Angleton's worst fears were fed by the 1962 defection of Anatoli Golitsin, a high-ranking KGB officer, who claimed knowledge of a high-level Soviet mole in the CIA (although Golitsin did not know his name) and of a devious KGB plan for a "strategic disinformation" campaign against the West involving false defectors. He was followed in early 1964 by Yuri Nosenko, another senior KGB officer, who appeared to deflect many of Golitsin's allegations about Soviet penetration of U.S. and British intelligence. Most importantly, Nosenko claimed first-hand knowledge that the KGB had not recruited—indeed, had had nothing to do with—Lee Harvey Oswald, the accused assassin of President John F. Kennedy.

(Oswald "defected" to the U.S.S.R. in 1959 and returned to the United States in 1962. Angleton and others in the CIA apparently found it inconceivable that the KGB would not have tried to recruit Oswald during his stay in Russia, particularly because he claimed to have knowledge of the U-2 spy plane program gained during his Marine service at a secret U-2 base in Japan. Some JFK assassination researchers, on the other hand, point to evidence that Oswald was working for U.S. intelligence all along—perhaps right up until JFK's murder—and argue that the KGB would have had good reason to steer clear of him.)

Nosenko was accepted as a genuine defector by the FBI. He volunteered to tell all he knew to the Warren Commission investigating the assassination. Instead, he was abducted by the CIA and illegally detained for the next five years. He spent three of those years in solitary confinement at a special CIA safe house in Virginia, where he was subjected to physical and psychological torture in an effort to get him to admit that he was in fact a Soviet disinformation agent. Nosenko never broke, but his long ordeal caused a severe split within the CIA between the defector's doubters, led by Angleton, and his supporters. The latter eventually won out, and Nosenko was released and hired as a CIA consultant.

In 1967 President Johnson put Angleton in charge of "Operation Chaos," which was established to discover whether or not the growing U.S. antiwar movement was backed or directed by foreign powers. Operation Chaos was later criticized by the 1975 Rockefeller Commission for breaching the CIA charter by engaging in the collection of domestic intelligence, but most of the blame was attributed to CIA director RICHARD HELMS. The operation continued until 1975 but could find no evidence of foreign influence.

From 1971, Angleton came into conflict with WILLIAM COLBY, who gained considerable influence over CIA policy when he was given control of the agency budget. In February 1973 Colby became head of the Directorate for Operations and recommended to director JAMES SCHLESINGER that Angleton be removed. Angleton was retained, but his staff was reduced and he ceased to act as the counterintelligence liaison with the FBI. Later that year, Schlesinger, against the advice of Angleton, suspended the CIA/FBI mail opening operation on the grounds that the intelligence derived was not worth the risk of CIA involvement. Colby became director of the CIA in August 1973, and in December 1974 he removed Angleton and two of his aides.

After his retirement, Angleton himself was accused of being a Soviet mole—largely on account of the confusion, inefficiency and disorganization caused within the CIA by his mole-hunting operation. In February 1979 he was cleared after an extensive investigation. (Some of Angleton's supporters suggested that Colby was the mole.) At the time, Colby said he never doubted Angleton's loyalty and added that he removed him from the counterintelligence post because of Angleton's failure to produce results in a long search for a possible spy in the CIA. James Angleton died on May 11, 1987.

For Further Information:
Berman, Jerry, and Morton H. Halperin, eds. The Abuses of the Intelligence Agencies. Washington, D.C., 1975.

Epstein, Edward Jay. *Legend: The Secret World of Lee Harvey Oswald.* New York, 1978.

Hersh, Burton. *The Old Boys: The American Elite and the Origins of the CIA.* New York, 1992.

Mangold, Thomas. *Cold Warrior: James Jesus Angleton: The CIA's Master Spy Hunter.* New York, 1991.

Marchetti, Victor, and John D. Marks. *The CIA and the Cult of Intelligence.* New York, 1974.

Oglesby, Carl. *The JFK Assassination: The Facts and the Theories.* New York, 1992.

Wise, David, and Thomas B. Ross. *The Invisible Government.* New York, 1964.

Anglo-American Financial and Trade Agreement (1945)

The Anglo-American Financial and Trade Agreement saved the imperiled British economy in the immediate postwar period, provided a financial base for the Anglo-American "special relationship" and helped to prevent a return to prewar American isolationism.

In 1945, six years of war and the sudden end of the wartime Lend-Lease program had left Britain heavily in debt to the United States. It still had extensive trade in the Far East and Africa, but this was conducted in nonconvertible sterling. Its debt was almost entirely in dollars while its trade in this currency was negligible.

The Labour Government of CLEMENT ATTLEE in August 1945 sent economist John Maynard Keynes to Washington to negotiate a financial deal to help Britain out of its economic problems. Keynes effectively argued for a financial grant of $5 billion to $6 billion on the grounds that Britain contributed more than the United States to the defeat of the Axis Powers in terms of wear and tear on capital equipment. He further argued that, although U.S. Lend-Lease spending was quantitatively greater than British mutual aid to its allies, Britain's aid to the United States had a "negligible" effect on the U.S. economy, while U.S. contributions to the United Kingdom had a "considerable" effect on the total British economy by tying the British debt to the American dollar.

Keynes found some opposition from American negotiators, who seemed more concerned with constructing an international financial structure that shifted the balance of power from Britain to the United States. But the British were also aware that the United States needed Britain as a strong trading partner and a bulwark against the spread of communism in Europe and in its far-flung empire. The result was a financial agreement signed on December 6, 1945. The main points of the agreement were:

1. The United States extended Britain a $3.75 billion line of credit, available until December 31, 1951.
2. Payment on the loan was to be made in 50 annual installments at 2% interest on the amount outstanding and would not begin until December 31, 1951.
3. Interest would be waived when Britain was short of dollars.
4. Britain was not to use the money to pay other creditors and would remove exchange restrictions on current transactions with the United States and all restrictions in imports from the United States.
5. Both governments agreed to lower tariff rates on a reciprocal basis.
6. Britain agreed to reconsider its system of Empire tariff preference.
7. Lend-Lease accounts were settled for $650 million, effectively wiping out a British Lend-Lease debt of $20 billion.

The agreement was approved by the House of Commons on December 13, by 345 votes to 98. WINSTON CHURCHILL urged the Conservative opposition to abstain, arguing that a Conservative government could have negotiated a better deal.

The agreement did not reach the floor of the U.S. Senate for ratification until April 17, 1946. It faced opposition from a number of conservative leaders, who favored a return to prewar isolationism. A sudden change of mind by Republican Senator ARTHUR VANDENBERG helped to shift opinion in favor of the agreement, and it passed the Senate by 46 votes to 30 and the House of Representatives by 219 votes to 155.

For Further Information:
Balogh, Thomas. *The Dollar Crisis.* Oxford, 1949.

Gardner, L.C. *The Foreign Policy of the British Labour Governments, 1945–51.* Leicester, 1984.

———. *Safe for Democracy.* New York, 1984.

Anglo–French Treaty of Alliance and Mutual Assistance (1947)

The 50-year Anglo–French Treaty of Alliance and Mutual Assistance signed at Dunkirk on March 4, 1947, by British foreign secretary ERNEST BEVIN and French foreign minister GEORGES BIDAULT was the first step in a successful three-stage plan by Bevin to tie the United States to the defense of Western Europe.

Bevin believed that before the United States could be persuaded to join an institutional alliance, Europeans must demonstrate their own recognition of the Soviet threat and their determination to defend each other. The Anglo–French Treaty made no mention of the Soviet Union. In fact, it specifically stated that the treaty was designed to thwart German aggression, but its real purpose was to create a climate for the later BRUSSELS TREATY of 1948, which extended the defense pact to Belgium, the Netherlands and Luxembourg, and to pave the way for the creation of the North Atlantic Treaty Organization. The main elements of the treaty were:

1. Joint consultation and action in case of a German threat of aggression.
2. Mutual aid if either country were attacked.
3. Consultation in case of Germany's failure to observe economic penalties.
4. Anglo–French economic cooperation.

For Further Information:
Young, J.W. *Britain, France and the Unity of Europe.* Leicester, 1984.

Angola and Namibia Conflicts   The Southern Africa states of Angola and neighboring Namibia became the focus of East–West tensions after Portuguese colonial rule was replaced by a Marxist government supported by Soviet and Cuban troops. The resolution of the Angola–Namibia conflict was a rare case of U.S.–Soviet cooperation.

Portuguese influence in Angola dated to the 15th century and Prince Henry the Navigator. The country was initially colonized by Portugal in the hope of finding precious minerals, but when they failed to materialize Angola became the center of the Portuguese slave trade.

The battle for Angolan independence started in February 1961 when the Marxist Popular Liberation Movement of Angola (MPLA) launched its first attack on Portuguese installations. The following year, the National Liberation Front for Angola (FNLA) established a government-in-exile in neighboring Zaire. A third opposition party, the National Union for the Total Independence of Angola (UNITA), was established in the southern part of the colony under Jonas Savimbi. Throughout the war against the Portuguese, these three factions spent as much time fighting each other or forming tenuous alliances as they did confronting the Portuguese.

Following the April 1974 military coup in Lisbon, Portugal recognized Angola's right to independence and began to withdraw. The three opposing parties in March 1975 agreed to form a preindependence coalition, but it quickly fell apart and fighting broke out between the MPLA on one hand and a coalition of FNLA and UNITA forces on the other. By the time independence was granted on November 11, 1975, the country was effectively divided among the three parties, with the MPLA in control of the capital at Luanda, the FNLA in the northeastern section of the country and UNITA in control of the south.

The situation was then complicated by the introduction of foreign support for the different factions. The Soviet Union and Cuba supported the MPLA, led by Dr. Agostinho Neto, and airlifted troops and supplies to Luanda. The MPLA proclaimed the People's Republic of Luanda, with Neto as its first president. The FNLA and UNITA forces were supported by Zaire, China, South Africa and the United States. The UNITA–FNLA alliance established an alternative capital at Huambo, and South African forces invaded Angola in support of the Huambo-based government. The South Africans hoped that their military move would draw in the Americans, but the U.S. Congress refused to send American forces overseas so soon after the Vietnam War, and America's European allies, particularly Britain, argued that military support for South Africa could have disastrous long-term effects on the Western position throughout Africa. (However, the U.S. Central Intelligence Agency did give covert military aid to the FNLA and UNITA in 1975, and provided more than $100 million in arms to UNITA between 1986 and 1991.)

Without direct American military support, South Africa was forced to withdraw. By the end of February 1976 the MPLA, aided by Cuban technical and military expertise, had effectively gained control of the whole country. Cuban troops remained to assist the MPLA, which continued to fight remnants of the UNITA army. The MPLA was recognized as the legitimate government of Angola at the meeting of the Organization of African Unity in January 1976.

President Neto died of cancer in September 1979 and was succeeded by Jose Eduardo dos Santos. The MPLA managed to hold parliamentary elections in 1980 (based on the Soviet one-party state model), but shortly afterward the situation began to deteriorate again. The FNLA ceased to be a major problem and surrendered to the MPLA in 1984, but UNITA leader Savimbi forged close links with South Africa, which provided the UNITA forces with extensive supplies through its territory of Namibia (also known as South-West Africa).

The South Africans wanted to maintain the UNITA forces as a buffer between themselves and the 30,000 to 50,000 Cuban troops in Angola and Namibia, where black nationalist forces led by the South-West African People's Organization (SWAPO) were fighting for independence from South Africa. South Africa's links with UNITA also enabled South African troops to engage in hot pursuit across the border into Angola, where SWAPO guerrillas maintained their rear bases.

It quickly became apparent that the problems of Namibia and Angola were inextricably linked. The South Africans refused to countenance independence and free elections in Namibia as long as the Cuban troops were in Angola. They feared that if the left-wing SWAPO came to power it would invite the Cubans into Namibia and then Soviet Bloc troops would be ranged along the Western border of South Africa itself. The Cubans and the Soviet Union refused to withdraw from Angola before the South Africans left Namibia for fear that South African forces in Namibia would invade Angola in support of a UNITA offensive that would overthrow the socialist government in Luanda.

The United States was heavily involved in the diplomatic negotiations because it also feared increased Soviet and Cuban influence in the region. South Africa itself is the Western world's major source of diamonds, gold and other precious minerals, as well as a repository for American and European investment. Namibia is also a large diamond producer and Angola is a major oil producer. In addition to this, the sea lanes around the Cape of Good Hope are the major route for the giant oil tankers between the Middle East oil fields and America and Western Europe.

The American position was difficult. The United States wanted the Cubans out of Angola in order to protect Western interests throughout the region. But it also wanted the internationally reviled South African government out of Namibia in order to defuse a potentially dangerous conflict that could damage Western interests throughout Africa. In 1981, the U.S. assistant secretary of state for African affairs, Chester Crocker, proposed a policy of "constructive engagement" in America's relations with South Africa. The ostensible purpose of this policy was to increase American leverage over

South Africa by maintaining amicable relations with the Pretoria regime.

There was, however, little incentive for the Cubans to withdraw from Angola as long as the Soviet Union continued to provide military equipment and financing for their presence. But after MIKHAIL GORBACHEV became Soviet leader in 1985, the Kremlin began reassessing its activities in the Third World in relation to the Soviet Union's domestic economic problems. The result was a Soviet move to withdraw from Southern Africa, which resulted in unprecedented cooperation between Soviet and American diplomats to pressure the Cubans and Angolans on one hand and the South Africans on the other.

A series of informal talks were held involving the United States, South Africa, Cuba and Angola, which led to formal negotiations in Geneva in early August 1988. On August 8, 1988, Angola, Cuba and South Africa issued a joint statement declaring that a "de facto cessation of hostilities [was] now in effect" in Angola and Namibia. South Africa began withdrawing its troops from Angola on August 10. Soviet deputy foreign minister Victor Adamishin participated behind the scenes as an "unofficial observer."

The formal agreement was not signed until December 22, 1988. It took the form of two treaties, the first providing for free elections in Namibia in November 1989 and full independence in 1990, and the second setting the timetable for the withdrawal of 50,000 Cuban troops from Angola over a 27-month period. The treaties also barred the South Africans from supporting the UNITA forces and the Angolans from supporting the African National Congress (the main black opposition group to the white government in South Africa). At any rate, it was clear that South Africa would find it more difficult to maintain previous levels of supplies to UNITA after 1990 because it would no longer control a common border with Angola.

The withdrawal of troops and the elections took place on schedule. SWAPO won a major share of the seats in the constituent assembly, which was charged with responsibility for writing the independence constitution. But the organization failed to win the two-thirds majority that would have enabled it to write its own constitution for the territory. Sam Nujoma, the leader of SWAPO, was, however, elected Namibia's first president.

Namibia became completely independent on March 21 in a ceremony attended by delegates from 70 countries, including Soviet foreign minister Eduard Shevardnadze, U.S. secretary of state James Baker and South African president F.W. de Klerk. During the two-days of celebrations there were a number of bilateral diplomatic exchanges, including a meeting between Shevardnadze and de Klerk. This was the first meeting between a Soviet minister and a South African head of state.

By the time of Namibian independence, South Africa had started on the road to ending the apartheid racial system and returning to the international community. This process had started with the release of Nelson Mandela, leader of the African National Congress, in February 1990. The internal changes within South Africa led to further changes in Pretoria's foreign policy, including a dropoff in support for the UNITA forces in Angola. This, coupled with the withdrawal of Cuban troops and the collapse of the Soviet Union, pushed the MPLA and UNITA into negotiations under Portuguese auspices. On May 31, 1991, the two sides signed an agreement ending the 16-year-old civil war. The agreement stated that free and fair elections would be held in September 1992.

For Further Information:

Hodges, Tony. *Angola to the 1990s: The Potential for Recovery.* Economist Intelligence Unit, January 1987.

Klinghoffer, Arthur. *The Angolan War.* Boulder, Colo., 1984.

Somerville, Keith. *Angola: Politics, Economics and Society.* Boulder, Colo., 1986.

Stockwell, John, *In Search of Enemies: A CIA Story,* New York, 1978.

Antarctic Treaty   (1959)   The Antarctic Treaty of 1959, at the height of the Cold War, was viewed by many as proof that the United States and the Soviet Union could negotiate agreements and work together. The treaty is regarded as an important forebear of the U.S.–Soviet agreements of the 1960s for scientific cooperation and limits on nuclear testing.

The treaty was a direct result of the activities of the International Geophysical Year (IGY) of 1957–58, the two focal points of which were exploration of space and exploration of Antarctica. During the course of the IGY, a political moratorium in Antarctica was declared, and 12 nations established more than 50 overwintering stations on the continent. Both the United States and the Soviet Union initiated major scientific projects under the auspices of the International Committee of Scientific Unions. The 18 months of scientific cooperation resulted in an unprecedented number of scientific discoveries.

The scientific advantages of continuing the political moratorium in Antarctica quickly became apparent. On May 3, 1958, the Eisenhower administration invited the Soviet Union and the 10 other nations that had participated in the IGY to a conference to negotiate a treaty that would assure the peaceful use of Antarctica, "freedom of scientific investigation" there by "all countries" and a continuation of the successful IGY cooperation.

Eisenhower made it clear that his proposed treaty would not require any nation to renounce its claims or rights in Antarctica. Seven countries—Argentina, Australia, Chile, France, New Zealand, Norway and Britain—have claims of sovereignty to portions of Antarctica, some of which overlap. The invitations went to Belgium, Japan and South Africa, in addition to the Soviet Union and the seven claimant nations.

On June 3, 1958, the Soviet Union agreed to the conference proposals. Secret talks involving representatives from all of the invited governments were held in Washington starting on October 15, 1959. The Antarctic Treaty was signed on

December 1, 1959, setting aside the entire area of Antarctica as a scientific preserve free from military activities.

Among the treaty's provisions was a clause allowing the inspection of other countries' bases to ensure compliance with the provision that there be no military activity. In January 1964 U.S. officials completed the first Western disarmament inspection of Soviet scientific posts—Vostok and Smirny—in Antarctica. The inspection, carried out by a team headed by John C. Guthrie, director of the State Department's Soviet Affairs Office, was said to have found no evidence that the Soviet posts were being used for unauthorized military or nuclear purposes.

In March 1973 the Soviet Union agreed to participate in a U.S. research project that involved drilling holes in the ocean floor off Antarctica.

The treaty was due for review in 1989, and as the review date approached, Third World countries expressed an interest in involving themselves in Antarctic exploration in order to share in the continent's mineral wealth at a later date. In December 1985 the UN General Assembly passed a resolution that called for the expansion of a UN study on Antarctica for "international management and equitable sharing of the benefits" of the continent's rich mineral resources. It was feared that Third World interest could politicize the southern continent and complicate the review conference. Another indication of possible complications was the UN General Assembly resolution, also in December 1985, demanding the expulsion of South Africa from the Antarctica Treaty group.

In June 1987 the United States and the Soviet Union announced a cooperative effort to study ozone and other gases that affect the world's climate, focusing in particular on Antarctica, where a potentially alarming annual depletion in the Earth's ozone layer had first been discovered.

The major points of the 14-article Antarctica Treaty were as follows:

Article I stated that "Antarctica shall be used for peaceful purposes only. There shall be prohibited . . . any (military) measure . . . such as the establishment of military bases and fortifications, the carrying out of military maneuvers, as well as the testing of any type of weapons."

Articles II and III stipulated that "freedom of scientific investigation in Antarctica . . . as applied during the International Geophysical Year, shall continue . . ." Signatories would exchange scientific plans, "scientific personnel . . . between expeditions and stations" and "scientific observations and results from Antarctica."

Article IV froze the signatories' territorial claims in Antarctica "without prejudice to such claims."

Article V prohibited "any nuclear explosions in Antarctica and the disposal . . . of radioactive waste material."

Article VI restricted the geographic scope of the treaty to the area south of 60° South Latitude, including the continent and all the ice shelves, but not the high seas in that area.

Articles VII and VIII committed the treaty's signatories to naming observers who would have complete freedom, including the right of aerial observation, in all of Antarctica to verify compliance with the treaty's obligations. It also committed the treaty's signatories to notifying each other in advance of all expeditions, stations and military personnel to be introduced into the continent.

Article IX called on the signatories to meet in Canberra, Australia, two months after the ratification of the treaty by all the signatory governments, to review progress to date.

Article X pledged the signatories not to violate the United Nations Charter.

Article XI established that any disputes arising from the treaty would be "referred to the International Court of Justice for settlement" if consultation, arbitration, mediation or conciliation failed.

Article XII established that the treaty could be revised at any time by unanimous agreement of the signatories and established that the treaty would remain in force "indefinitely," with a review conference after 30 years and the right of signatories to withdraw after 34 years.

Article XIII established the procedure for other countries to join the treaty.

For Further Information:
Chapman, S. *IGY: Year of Discovery*. Ann Arbor, Mich., 1960.
Special Committee of the International Geophysical Year. *Annals of the International Geophysical Year*, 10 vols. 1959–60.

Antiballistic Missile Treaty of 1972 (ABM Treaty)   The ABM Treaty was signed in May 1972 as part of the STRATEGIC ARMS LIMITATION TREATY (SALT) negotiations between the Soviet Union and the United States. Its purpose was to help maintain the nuclear balance by limiting each side's ability to defend itself from nuclear ballistic missiles with the deployment and use of antiballistic missile systems.

The possibility of a treaty to limit antiballistic missile systems was first raised by President LYNDON JOHNSON in January 1967, when he announced that the Soviet Union had begun building an ABM system around Moscow. He offered to delay America's own ABM system and initiate treaty discussions with the Soviet Union. Johnson, however, made it clear that the postponement of the U.S. ABM system would be reconsidered if discussions were unsuccessful. The Soviets responded with an agreement in principle to discuss "means of limiting the arms race in offensive and defensive missiles."

However, there was no definite Soviet commitment until 1968, when American politics was focused on a presidential election. After the election of Richard Nixon, the Soviets sought a quick start to negotiations, but the Nixon administration demanded time to formulate its position.

Negotiations on ABM systems formally started as part of the SALT I talks on November 17, 1969, in Helsinki, Finland. The American negotiating team was led by GERARD SMITH, and the Soviet negotiators were led by Deputy Foreign Minister Vladimir Semyonov. The talks were held in Helsinki and Vienna.

By the time the talks began, Congress had approved the Safeguard ABM system to protect Minuteman intercontinental ballistic missile (ICBM) sites at Malmstrom Air Force Base in Montana, Grand Forks Air Force Base in North Dakota, Whiteman Air Force Base in Missouri and Warren Air Force Base in Wyoming. The Soviet Union had 64 ABM launchers in place around Moscow and was believed to have the capability to base the system around other industrialized sites in European Russia.

On July 24, 1970, the Nixon administration offered to abandon its ABM sites in the Midwest and limit the number of ABM launchers allowed each country to 100 around the respective capitals. In return, it demanded that the Soviets agree to dismantle their SS-9 offensive missiles.

Almost from the start of the SALT negotiations, the Soviets seemed more interested in the ABM aspect than in the offensive weapons. Nixon, however, made it clear in his "State of the World" address on February 25, 1971, that "to limit only one side of the offense-defense equation could rechannel arms competition rather than curtail it." His position was supported by advisers in the Pentagon and at the White House. However, U.S. diplomats in the ARMS CONTROL AND DISARMAMENT AGENCY at the State Department, and leading senators such as Edmund Muskie and Hubert Humphrey, pressed for a quick ABM Treaty as a first step toward a wider nuclear weapons agreement. The Soviets, aware of the divisions within the American government, delayed progress in the negotiations.

On May 21, 1971, Nixon announced that in order to break the deadlock the two sides had agreed to concentrate on ABM systems and that there would be a separate ABM treaty alongside an agreement to limit offensive weapons.

The treaty was finally signed along with the SALT I agreement at St. Vladimir Hall in the Kremlin on May 26, 1972, at the end of an official visit to the Soviet Union by Nixon. The Senate approved the ABM treaty by a vote of 88–2. The two dissenting senators were James Buckley (R, New York) and James Allan (D, Alabama).

On July 3, 1974, a protocol to the treaty was signed during another visit to Moscow by Nixon. This limited each side to one ABM system each. The Soviet system would protect Moscow and the American system would protect ICBM missile sites in the Midwest.

The treaty played a major role in discussions about the deployment of the STRATEGIC DEFENSE INITIATIVE (SDI, or "Star Wars") proposed by President RONALD REAGAN on March 23, 1981. The Soviet Union and opponents of SDI claimed that it would breach the ABM Treaty. But supporters of SDI claimed that a "broad interpretation" of the 1972 treaty allowed SDI development and deployment.

The ABM treaty was of an unlimited duration but was subject to review every five years and to cancellation by either party upon six months' notice. It was comprised of 15 articles.

Article I committed each signatory "not to deploy ABM systems for a defense of the territory of its country and not to provide a base for such a defense, and not to deploy ABM systems for defense of an individual region except" around areas specified in Article III.

Article II defined an ABM system as a "system to counter strategic ballistic missiles or their elements in flight trajectory."

Article III set out the areas where ABM systems can be deployed. These were the national capital and one ICBM (Intercontinental Ballistic Missile) launcher area. (The 1974 protocol to the 1972 treaty reduced the permitted deployment to the one type of area each side chose to defend.)

Article IV allowed deployment of ABM components, including up to 15 ABM launchers, at "current or additionally agreed" test ranges.

Article V prohibited the development, testing or deployment of ABM systems or components that were sea-based, air- or space-based, or mobile land-based. It also prohibited the development, testing or deployment of rapid-fire and rapid-reload launchers.

Article VI prevented circumvention of the agreement by means of non-ABM technology. It also prevented the deployment of strategic early warning radars except outward-oriented systems along the periphery of national territory.

Article VII allowed the modernization and replacement of permitted ABM systems.

Articles VIII to XI forbade the transfer of ABM systems or components to third parties, or their deployment outside national territory.

Article XII provided for the monitoring of the agreement.

Article XIII outlined the duties and responsibilities of a bilateral Standing Consultative Commission (SCC), which was to be responsible for considering questions of treaty compliance, amendments, reviews and "further measures aimed at limiting strategic arms."

Article XIV established the procedure for amendments and reviews.

Article XV set the duration of the agreement (unlimited) and the conditions for withdrawal ("upon six months' notice should extraordinary events related to the subject matter of this Treaty have jeopardized supreme interests").

For Further Information:
Holst, T.T., and W. Schneider, eds. *Why ABM? Policy Issues in U.S. Defense Policy.* Elmsford, N.Y., 1976.
Newhouse, John. *Cold Dawn: The Story of SALT.* New York, 1973.
Owen, David. *The Politics of Defense.* New York, 1972.

Antisubmarine Warfare   Antisubmarine warfare consists of military operations against enemy submarines.

The most common weapon used against submarines is the depth charge. This was first used by the British Royal Navy during World War I and essentially involves a surface ship's dropping an explosive charge into the water. When the charge reaches a certain depth, it explodes.

During World War II, the Royal Navy developed depth

charge mortars. Two of the more popular versions in use during the 1980s are the British Squid and Limbo depth charges.

Nuclear depth charges have been introduced by the U.S. Navy. They are usually attached to torpedos to ensure that attacking vessels are a safe distance from the explosion. Britain has also developed nuclear depth charges capable of delivery by helicopter for use against deep-diving submarines.

Torpedos, launched from either surface ships or other submarines, are also used in antisubmarine warfare. Commonly used torpedoes are the American Asroc or Sea Lance and the Soviet Union's FRAS-1 or SS-N-14/15/16.

Most surface ships are also equipped with antisubmarine rockets such as the U.S. Alpha rocket or its successor Abe. Many navies also use the Swedish Bofors rocket launcher.

For Further Information:
Compton-Hall, R. *Submarine Warfare*. London, 1985.

ANZUS (Australia, New Zealand, United States) Treaty Organization   Anzus is the South Pacific link in a series of security pacts devised by U.S. foreign policy makers to "contain" the Soviet Union. It is based on a security treaty among Australia, New Zealand and the United States, the aim of which is to provide mutual aid to each of the signatories in case of aggression by an outside force. The organization has been suspended since 1985 because of New Zealand's refusal to allow nuclear ships in its waters.

Policies are determined by the ANZUS Council, which consists of the foreign ministers, or their deputies, of the three signatories, who meet once a year. The organization has never had a permanent staff or secretariat.

The treaty document did not commit any of the signatories to come to the others' defense. It has been criticized by Australian and New Zealand analysts as disproportionately balanced in favor of the United States.

The ANZUS Treaty is regarded by many as a forerunner to the geographically wider-ranging SOUTHEAST ASIA TREATY ORGANIZATION (SEATO); it helped to create the climate that led to the involvement of Australian and New Zealand troops in the VIETNAM WAR.

Australia and New Zealand expressed their desire for a regional defense organization as early as 1944, with the AN-ZAC Agreement. At the time they would have preferred such an organization to have been based on their traditional ties with Britain and other Commonwealth countries, with a peripheral role for the United States. But America's postwar domination of the Pacific region led them to reconsider their position.

By 1946, the Australian and New Zealand governments proposed a defense pact with the United States in return for allowing the United States to retain bases in Japan's former Pacific territories. They proposed that this pact cover the entire Pacific region. At the time, however, America's defense interests in the Pacific were seen to be centered exclusively in the northern area, with any defense arrangements in the South Pacific being centered on U.S. bases in the Philippines.

In 1949 conservative governments came to power in both New Zealand and Australia. They took a distinctly more anti-communist and pro-American stance in foreign policy. In 1950 both New Zealand and Australia made troop commitments to the Korean War. In return, throughout 1950, the United States gave generous but informal assurances that it would come to the aid of New Zealand and Australia in the event of an attack.

In 1950 Australia started to press for a formal defense treaty with the United States. New Zealand external affairs minister F. W. Doidge thought that America's commitment as regional policeman was so strong that a formal treaty was unnecessary. This different emphasis in the foreign policies of Australia and New Zealand was a continuing problem for ANZUS. Australia was more conscious of Asia as her "near north" and the need for a relationship with the United States to contain possible attack from the Asian continent. New Zealanders worried that Pacific security arrangements might bring unwelcome new commitments, weaken traditional ties with Britain and the Commonwealth, and draw New Zealand too closely into a Cold War power bloc in which it would have too small a voice.

In January 1951, U.S. secretary of state JOHN FOSTER DULLES took the first step toward a defense pact with Australia and New Zealand when he hinted that the U.S. government was considering means of reassuring the government and people of New Zealand of U.S. assistance in the event of attack. Difficult negotiations followed, as the United States wanted to merge its defense commitments to Japan and the Philippines with those to Australia and New Zealand. This was acceptable to Australia but not to New Zealand.

New Zealand prime minister Sir Sidney Holland discussed the problem with President HARRY TRUMAN in early 1951, and it was agreed to form a three-party Australia–U.S.–New Zealand pact for the time being. Discussions continued during Dulles's February 1951 tour of the South Pacific, during which he attempted to include the Philippines in the pact. In the end, the problem of the Philippines and Japan was solved by bilateral agreements between those two countries and the United States that did not include Australia and New Zealand. The ANZUS Treaty was signed in San Francisco on September 1, 1951.

Throughout the 1950s and 1960s the governments of Australia and New Zealand were dominated by conservatives who adopted strong pro-American and anti-communist stands. Australia, in particular, launched a series of communist witch hunts that mirrored those taking place during the McCarthy era in the United States. Australia and New Zealand became members of the Southeast Asia Treaty Organization, refused to recognize the People's Republic of China or North Korea and generally supported U.S. policy in the Pacific region. Both New Zealand and Australia committed troops to the Vietnam War.

In 1972 the Australian Labour Party came to power and Australia's foreign policy took a more independent course, while the government retained its firm commitment to ANZUS. The strongest indication of this shift was Australia's withdrawal from Vietnam in 1972. The government of Prime Minister Gough Whitlam also moved quickly to abolish the system of national selective service, released draft resisters from jail, recognized the People's Republic of China, severed diplomatic links with Taiwan and normalized relations with East Germany and North Korea.

Labour Party attacks against America's continued presence in Vietnam increased in 1972, and Australian–U.S. relations were severely strained by the support of prominent Labour politicians for an Australian Seamens' Union ban on American ships visiting Australia. President RICHARD NIXON threatened "retaliatory action" and issued a warning that implied that the Australian action threatened America's defense obligations toward Australia.

The diplomatic crisis was defused by the resumption of the Paris peace talks between North Vietnam and the United States and private assurances from Whitlam that his government treasured the ANZUS pact. But in a speech to the National Press Club in Washington, D.C., in July 1973, Whitlam clarified Australia's changed foreign policy when he said: "My government wants to move away from the narrow view that the ANZUS Treaty is the only significant factor in our relations with the United States, and the equally narrow view that our relations with the United States are the only significant factor in Australia's foreign relations."

This altered perception of Australia's role in the world continued after the Whitlam government, with different emphases according to the political complexion of the party in power. The Australian commitment to ANZUS, however, remained stronger than that of the New Zealand Labour Party (NZLP), which during the 1970s started to develop a strong antinuclear and pacifist wing.

Particularly influential in reshaping New Zealand policies were the actions of the 1972–75 Labour government, which was headed by Prime Minister Norman Kirk from 1972 until his death in 1974. Kirk took the lead in protesting against French nuclear testing, and at the United Nations his government proposed a nuclear-weapons-free zone in the Pacific. His government also took the issue of French tests in the region to the International Court of Justice at The Hague. In 1973 New Zealand's antinuclear policy captured world attention when the government, with Australian support, sent a frigate into the French testing zone. The action helped to drive the testing underground.

In 1973 the NZLP attempted to curtail American use of the New Zealand air and naval base at Harwood, and in 1975 party members passed a resolution stressing New Zealand's independence in foreign affairs and called for legislation to ban foreign warships or aircraft that normally carried, or could be carrying, nuclear weapons. However, the NZLP lost office before the government had a chance to act on the resolution,

On February 4, 1985, the government of Prime Minister David Lange banned visits to New Zealand ports by ships carrying nuclear weapons, thereby removing New Zealand from ANZUS (Australia-New Zealand-United States Treaty Organization). Photo courtesy of the New Zealand Ministry of Foreign Affairs.

and the conservative National Party, which was committed to a pro-American foreign policy, remained in power under Prime Minister Robert Muldoon until the general election of July 14, 1984, returned the NZLP to office.

Labour prime minister David Lange moved quickly to enforce party policy. On February 4, 1985, he banned visits to New Zealand ports by ships carrying nuclear weapons, effectively ending defense cooperation between New Zealand and the United States.

On July 15, 1985, bilateral U.S.–Australian talks were held in Canberra between U.S. secretary of state GEORGE SHULTZ and Australian foreign minister Bill Hayden. These were recognized as a substitute for the annual trilateral ANZUS council. Formal legislation banning nuclear weapons and nuclear-powered warships from New Zealand was introduced by Lange on December 10, 1985. After a meeting in Manila between

Lange and Shultz, the U.S. secretary of state said that the United States would no longer promise to defend New Zealand and that that country was effectively suspended from the ANZUS pact. Shultz stressed that the ANZUS treaty was not terminated and that the United States maintained defensive ties with Australia through the treaty. Australia continued defensive links with both the United States and New Zealand.

The ANZUS Treaty signed in 1951 consisted of a preamble and 11 articles. The preamble recognized the existing commitments of the three signatories, the United States toward the Philippines and Japan, and Australia and New Zealand toward the Commonwealth. It also stated their desire to coordinate collective defense efforts "pending the development of a more comprehensive system of regional security in the Pacific area."

Article One committed each of the signatories to attempt to settle international disputes by peaceful means.

Article Two committed the three countries "separately and jointly by means of continuous and effective self-help and mutual aid" to "maintain and develop their individual and collective capacity to resist armed attack."

Article Three committed the signatories to consult if any of them believed that "the territorial integrity, political independence or security of the parties is threatened in the Pacific."

Article Four stated that an armed attack on any of the signatories would be dangerous to each signatory's own "peace and safety and declare[d] that it would act to meet the common danger in accordance with its constitutional processes." It also stated that "any such armed attack" would be immediately reported to the UN Security Council.

Article Five defined an "armed attack" as an attack on any of the signatories' possessions, ships, armed forces or aircraft in the Pacific.

Article Six said that the treaty did not supersede each signatory's rights and obligations under the UN charter.

Article Seven established a council consisting of each country's foreign minister or his deputy.

Article Eight empowered the foreign ministers to coordinate with other states in the Pacific region until a more comprehensive regional security system was developed.

Article Nine established the ratification process.

Article Ten established the duration of the treaty as indefinite.

Article Eleven set out the distribution pattern of the treaty document.

For Further Information:
Pugh, Michael. *The ANZUS Crisis.* New York, 1989.
Thakur, I.C. *In Defense of New Zealand.* New York, 1986.
U.S. House of Representatives Committee of Foreign Affairs. *Regional Security Developments in the South Pacific.* Washington, D.C., 1989.

Arbatov, Georgi (May 19, 1923–   ) Georgi Arbatov was recognized as the Soviet Union's chief spokesman on East–West relations in the latter years of the Brezhnev era and the early part of Gorbachev's government.

During World War II, Arbatov fought with the Red Army and in 1943, became a member of the Communist Party. After the war he studied at the Moscow Institute for International Relations and stayed on to teach until 1962, when he became chief of the secretariat at the Institute of World Economic and International Relations at the Soviet Academy of Sciences. In 1967 he was appointed director of the U.S. and Canada Institute. In 1981 Arbatov became a member of the Soviet Communist Party's Central Committee.

As director of the U.S. and Canada Institute, a major Soviet think tank, Arbatov became a leading expert on American affairs, and eventually emerged as one of the Soviet Union's chief spokesmen on East–West relations. Ostensibly an academic, he was able to provide an academic gloss to Soviet policy statements.

In December 1981, Arbatov led a delegation of Soviet scholars to a meeting in Philadelphia with the Foreign Policy Research Institute, at which he said that the Soviet Union would be unwilling to talk about a U.S.–Soviet agreement that differed substantially from the SALT II accord (see STRATEGIC ARMS LIMITATION TALKS). Arbatov went on to tour the United States, giving lectures at colleges and foreign policy think tanks across the country. His relaxed manner, excellent English and extensive knowledge of American affairs made him popular with American audiences, to whom he presented a more acceptable face of Soviet foreign policy.

In April 1981 Arbatov found himself at the center of a controversy when he was forced to withdraw from an American television debate on arms control because the U.S. State Department refused to extend his visa. One State Department official was quoted as saying that the U.S. government wanted to get Arbatov out of the country because "his views have been getting too much attention in the press."

In 1981 and 1982, Arbatov was the Soviet representative on an independent international commission on disarmament chaired by Swedish prime minister Olof Palme. The panel issued a list of proposals designed to turn nations back from what it termed "the brink of a new abyss." Recommendations included ratification of the SALT II treaty, a nuclear-weapon-free zone in Central Europe, the removal of battlefield nuclear weapons from Central Europe, drastic reductions in conventional forces in Europe, the establishment of a chemical weapon-free zone in Europe and a ban on the testing of antisatellite weapons.

After MIKHAIL GORBACHEV took over as leader of the Soviet Communist Party he chose Arbatov as one of his key advisers on American affairs. In November 1985, Arbatov was in the Soviet delegation to the Reagan–Gorbachev summit in Geneva. In January 1986 Arbatov chaired a widely publicized television press conference at which he condemned the Reagan administration's STRATEGIC DEFENSE INITIATIVE and attacked Secretary of State GEORGE SHULTZ and Defense Secretary CASPAR WEINBERGER as two senior administration figures "frightened" by the gains made at the Geneva Summit. Arbatov's press conference was timed to coincide with a meeting between Gorbachev and the cochairmen of a Western group called International Physicians for the Prevention of Nuclear War, at which Gorbachev offered to extend the Soviet moratorium on nuclear testing.

During the Brezhnev years, Arbatov had been viewed as a moderating influence within the Soviet establishment. But under Gorbachev his positions were overtaken by more reform-minded figures. At the historic Soviet Communist Party Congress in July 1988, reformers demanded Arbatov's resignation because he was seen as a member of the "old guard." From that time, his influence on Soviet foreign policy steadily waned.

For Further Information:
Arbatov, Georgi. *Cold War or Detente: The Soviet Viewpoint.* New York, 1983.
————. *The Dream World of American Policy.* Moscow, 1982.

Arctic Ocean   The Arctic Ocean is one of the most inhospitable areas of the world and sits astride the shortest route for Soviet and American ballistic missiles, submarines and aircraft to reach each other's territories. The Arctic was thus of major strategic concern to both countries.

The Soviet Union recognized the importance of the Arctic by basing the bulk of its nuclear-powered ballistic submarine fleet and strategic bombers at Murmansk on the Kola Peninsula, inside the Arctic Circle. Its U.S.-targeted, land-based strategic missiles were aimed northward, over the Arctic ice pack.

The U.S. strategic systems were also aimed northward over the Arctic, and the United States still maintains a DISTANT EARLY WARNING LINE extending from Alaska through Canada to Greenland to warn against a missile attack across the Arctic.

The Arctic was also important because, in the event of war, Soviet naval forces would have had to pass through it to reach the GREENLAND-ICELAND-UK GAP and sever the vital North Atlantic sea route between North America and Western Europe. For this reason, a large number of conventional forces were also maintained at Murmansk with the aim of securing the northern coast of NORWAY.

The Arctic is also an important economic region for Russia, with major mining operations in Siberia. There are several major commercial ports on the Arctic Ocean that handle vital exports to Atlantic Rim countries through the Greenland-Iceland-UK Gap and to Pacific Rim countries through the Bering Sea Straits.

For Further Information:
Lindsey, George. *Strategic Stability in the Arctic.* London, 1989.

Arms Control and Disarmament Agency (ACDA)   The United States Arms Control and Disarmament Agency was formed in September 1961 to coordinate government policy on nuclear testing and disarmament.

The bill establishing the agency faced considerable opposition from conservative members of the U.S. Congress, who feared that the establishment of an arms-control agency at a time of rising international tension would send the wrong signal to the Soviets. The leading opponents were Rep. Harold Gross (R, Iowa) and Senator Richard Russell (D, Georgia). One of the most vocal advocates for the agency's creation was Senator Hubert Humphrey (D, Minnesota).

The key figures behind the drafting of the statute setting up ACDA were Arthur Dean, then chairman of the U.S. delegation to the Conference on the Discontinuance of Nuclear Weapons Testing, and John McCloy, special adviser to President Kennedy on disarmament issues. McCloy briefly served as the first director of ACDA but was quickly followed by William Foster, who was in the post from September 1961 to January 1969.

The director of ACDA is the principal adviser to the president and the secretary of state on all issues related to arms control and disarmament and is usually directly involved in any arms control negotiations with the Soviet Union. ACDA offices are housed within the State Department, and the director's primary responsibility is to the secretary of state, but he has direct access to the president, other federal agencies and Congress. This gives him considerable autonomy in arms control and disarmament issues.

Aswan High Dam   Soviet financing of the Aswan High Dam project in Egypt in 1956 was seen by many observers as the Soviets' major breakthrough in their efforts to establish a presence in the Arab world and was a contributory cause of the SUEZ CRISIS.

U.S. secretary of state JOHN FOSTER DULLES offered American aid for the project on December 16, 1955. This was done at the urging of the British government, which wanted to prevent Soviet political penetration into Egypt. Under the initial offer, the United States was to provide a grant of $56 million and Britain $14 million.

The offer, however, was withdrawn on July 19, 1956, because of dissatisfaction with the financial arrangements and Egyptian president GAMAL ABDEL NASSER's increasingly anti-Western statements and policies. Within a week the Soviet Union entered into negotiations with President Nasser to fill the vacuum left by America and Britain.

The first stage of the Aswan project was completed in 1964. NIKITA KHRUSHCHEV himself visited Egypt on May 6–12, 1964, and awarded Nasser the highest Soviet decoration—"Hero of the Soviet Union." He also used the opening of the dam to promise a loan of $280 million on favorable terms. The loan agreement was signed by Khrushchev and Egyptian prime minister Aly Sabry at a ceremony in Moscow on September 22, 1964. The money was allocated for the construction of industrial plants under a second Egyptian five-year plan and for technical assistance in developing new agricultural areas.

At the time of his fall from power, Khrushchev was criticized for being overgenerous toward Egypt. But the loan was soon confirmed, and LEONID BREZHNEV worked hard to build on the political bridgehead established by his predecessor. It was not until after the 1973 Yom Kippur War that Nasser's successor, President ANWAR SADAT, began to move Egypt closer to the United States in the belief that the United States alone had the political muscle to force compromises out of Israel.

The 364-foot-high Aswan High Dam became fully operational in 1970, at a final cost of $1.3 billion. As a result, about 1 million acres of land that formerly could be irrigated only in summer have been converted to year-round irrigation.

The completion of the dam meant that for the first time in Egyptian history, the annual flooding of the Nile River was controlled. In addition to irrigating land, the dam also improves navigation both upriver and downriver and generates electricity.

Many economists and ecologists believe the dam has had a disasterous effect because it has removed silt from irrigation water and has depleted the soil of nutrients.

For Further Information:
Fahim, Hussein M. *Dams, People, and Development: The Aswan High Dam Case.* New York, 1981.
Heikal, Mohammed. *Sphinx and Commissar.* New York, 1978.
Little, Thomas. *Modern Egypt.* London, 1967.

Atlantic Nuclear Force　　A proposal made by Britain to solve the problem of how to structure a NATO-wide Multilateral Nuclear Force (MLF). The proposal, made in December 1964, like the wider discussion surrounding the MLF, never went further than the discussion stage.

During the Kennedy administration the concept of a Multilateral Force of nuclear weapons controlled by all NATO countries became official U.S. policy and was supported by the non-nuclear allies, especially West Germany, which believed that its status as the front-line ally meant that it should have a greater say over the deployment and use of nuclear weapons.

The MLF, however, was opposed by the British Conservative Party and the French government, because it would mean a diminution of the British and French independent nuclear deterrents. But in October 1964 the Labour Party under HAROLD WILSON was voted into office in Britain. A main plank in Labour's election platform was the incorporation of Britain's existing nuclear forces into a broadened MLF.

The British proposals were the main subject of a summit meeting in Washington on December 7–8, 1964, between Prime Minister Wilson and President LYNDON B. JOHNSON. On December 16, Wilson proposed the creation of an "Atlantic Nuclear Force" comprised of the following:

1. All nuclear-armed British Vulcan bombers, except those needed for British commitments outside the NATO area.
2. The British fleet of Polaris missile-firing nuclear submarines to be built under the 1962 NASSAU AGREEMENT.
3. An equal number of U.S. Polaris missile submarines.
4. An internationally manned force similar to the proposed MLF (but not necessarily composed of missile-firing surface vessels), in which NATO's non-nuclear powers could participate and share joint ownership.
5. A French nuclear contingent if France decided to participate in the Atlantic nuclear force.

Instead of helping the discussions aimed at the establishment of the MLF, Wilson's proposals only clouded the issues further and contributed to the eventual collapse of negotiations. Some observers believe that that was the purpose of the Wilson proposal.

However, the main reason for NATO's failure to agree to the MLF centered on the inability of the Alliance members to agree to a political command structure that did not give every Alliance member an effective veto over the use of nuclear weapons and thus destroy the credibility of the deterrent.

For Further Information:
Kissinger, Henry. *The Troubled Partnership: A Reappraisal of the Atlantic Alliance.* New York, 1965.
Neustadt, Richard. *Alliance Politics.* New York, 1970.
Nunnerly, David. *President Kennedy and Britain.* New York, 1972.

Atlantic Policy Advisory Group (APAG)　　The APAG, formed in 1961, is composed of senior planning officials from the foreign ministries of all NATO countries. Its purpose is to take a longer-term and imaginative look at East-West relations in the global context. The group reports to NATO's Permanent Council through its chairman, the assistant secretary general for political affairs.

Atomic Bomb　　The atomic bomb was the first nuclear weapon, and the existence of "the bomb" and its successor, the hydrogen bomb, was a central element in the political and defense strategy of the Cold War.

The explosion of an atom bomb is the result of a sudden release of energy caused by the splitting of the atomic nuclei of heavy elements such as the isotopes of uranium-235. An atom bomb, in addition to producing an enormous shock blast, also releases tremendous heat and lethal radiation.

The theory behind the bomb was developed by ALBERT EINSTEIN, ROBERT OPPENHEIMER, ENRICO FERMI and other nuclear physicists in the years before World War II. After the outbreak of war, they convinced President FRANKLIN D. ROOSEVELT that the United States should build such a weapon before the Germans or Japanese did. The result was the top-secret MANHATTAN PROJECT, staffed by American and British scientists and begun in June 1942.

The first atomic bomb was designed by Oppenheimer, who headed the Project Y Division at Los Alamos, New Mexico. The first experimental bomb was detonated near Alamogordo, New Mexico, on July 16, 1945. The bomb was first used in wartime on August 6, 1945, when the United States

This photo was taken in Nagasaki, Japan on August 9, 1945, just moments after an atomic bomb exploded over the city.

dropped it on Hiroshima. A second bomb was dropped on Nagasaki on August 9, causing the Japanese to surrender. These are the only two occasions that a nuclear weapon has been used in wartime.

For three years, the United States enjoyed a monopoly of atomic power. But in September 1948, President HARRY TRU-MAN announced that the Soviet Union had exploded its first atomic weapon. The Soviet Union was quickly followed by Britain, then France, China and India. In 1949 American scientists under Edward Teller began development of the even more powerful HYDROGEN BOMB, which has largely succeeded the atomic bomb. Large stockpiles of these bombs exist in the former Soviet Union (where at present it is not entirely clear who controls them) and the United States. Hydrogen bombs are also part of the nuclear arsenals of China, Britain and France. A number of other countries are known to have developed nuclear weapons, or the capacity to build them, among them India, Pakistan, Israel, South Africa and North Korea.

For Further Information:
Boyer, Paul S. *By the Bomb's Early Light: American Thought and Culture at the Dawn of the Atomic Age*. New York, 1985.
Herken, Gregg. *The Winning Weapon: The Atomic Bomb in the Cold War*. New York, 1980.
Hersey, John Richard. *Hiroshima*. New York, 1976.
Rhodes, Richard. *The Making of the Atomic Bomb*. New York, 1986.

Sherwin, Martin J. *A World Destroyed: The Atomic Bomb and the Grand Alliance*. New York, 1980.
Mayers, T. *Understanding Nuclear Weapons and Arms Control*. London, 1986.

Atomic Energy Act (1946) The Atomic Energy Act of 1946 was the first law passed by the U.S. Congress for the purpose of controlling atomic energy.

Also known as the McMahon Act after its author, Senator BRIEN MCMAHON, the law created a five-man civilian ATOMIC ENERGY COMMISSION (AEC), which became the sole owner of fissionable material and was given full control over atomic research. It also established a military liaison committee, a technical advisory committee and a joint congressional committee and made illegal the exchange of American atomic secrets until international control was established. This provision caused the British government to embark on its own atomic development program.

The bill was unanimously passed by the Senate on June 1, 1946. It was amended by the House of Representatives to allow the inclusion of two military representatives on the AEC board. The bill passed the House on July 20 by a vote of 265–79.

For Further Information:
United States Senate, Special Committee on Atomic Energy. *Atomic Energy Act of 1946: Hearings Before the Special Committee on Atomic Energy, United States Senate, Seventy-Ninth Congress, Second Session, on S. 1717, A Bill for the Development and Control of Atomic Energy*. Washington, D.C., 1946.

Atomic Energy Commission, United Nations The United Nations Atomic Energy Commission was the forum for the first attempts at nuclear disarmament, including the U.S.-sponsored Baruch Plan (see BERNARD BARUCH).

The first postwar efforts at disarmament were made within the context of the United Nations. The general enthusiasm for the United Nations made it the logical forum for such issues, and in fact, the UN charter gave responsibility to the Security Council for "preparing and submitting plans for the regulation of armaments."

In January 1946, the United Nations established the Atomic Energy Commission (AEC) to prepare plans for the control of atomic energy. The negotiations within the AEC soon revealed the total absence of agreement between the Soviet Union and the United States. It was in the context of these negotiations that the Baruch Plan was unveiled.

The Baruch Plan called for the establishment of an international atomic development agency to survey nuclear raw materials and to assume control of dangerous fissionable materials and production plans. The agency would make its resources available for peaceful use and would control, inspect and license all nuclear activities. It would report any attempt to build atomic weapons to the United Nations, whose members would take appropriate action. The Baruch Plan stipulated that the United States would end the manufacture of nuclear devices at some point in the future and would transfer atomic knowledge to the UN agency in stages. It stressed, however, that there must be no immediate release of atomic knowledge. Baruch also insisted that members of the UN Security Council be denied their right of veto when considering atomic energy and that penalties be fixed for illegal possession or use of atomic bombs and other materials.

The plan was presented to the AEC on June 14, 1946, and was quickly condemned by the Soviet Union as an attempt to undermine the Security Council. The Soviets offered a counterproposal that included a demand for the immediate destruction of all nuclear weapons. The AEC, however, accepted the Baruch Plan and recommended it to the UN General Assembly, which in turn overwhelmingly voted to recommend it to the Security Council, where it was vetoed by the Soviet Union.

The AEC never recovered from the Soviet veto. It recommended two other compromise proposals in 1947 and 1948, but at the end of 1948 its members reported to the Security Council that negotiations had reached a stalemate. In 1952 the Atomic Energy Commission and the Commission for Conventional Armaments were merged to form the United Nations Disarmament Commission. This became the nonnuclear countries' main forum for pressing their case for a reduction in nuclear weapons, but it has had little influence on superpowers.

For Further Information:
Rabimowitch, E., ed. *Minutes to Midnight*. Chicago, 1950.
Coit, Margaret L. *Mr. Baruch*. Boston, 1957.
Becnhoefer, Bernard G. *Postwar Negotiations for Arms Control*. Washington, D.C., 1961.

Atomic Energy Commission (AEC), United States The U.S. Atomic Energy Commission was established by the Atomic Energy Act of 1946, and began operations on January 1, 1947, as the successor to the military-controlled Manhattan Project.

A major purpose behind the creation of the AEC was to place production of atomic materials under civilian control. It was originally planned as a five-man civilian board, but the bill was amended in the House of Representatives to include a two-man military liaison committee.

The AEC was responsible for the development and production of all nuclear weapons and for directing and developing peaceful uses for nuclear technology. This included the development of the first hydrogen bomb and the administration of President Eisenhower's ATOMS FOR PEACE PLAN. In 1975 the AEC was superseded by the newly-formed Energy Research and Development Administration (ERDA) and the Nuclear Regulatory Commission (NRC).

For Further Information:
York, Herbert. *The Advisors: Oppenheimer, Teller and the Superbomb*. San Francisco, 1976.
Huntington, Samuel. *The Soldier and the State: The Theory and Politics of Civil-Military Relations*. Cambridge, Mass., 1957.

Atoms for Peace Plan The Atoms for Peace Plan was a program established in 1953 by President Dwight Eisenhower to extend U.S. aid to other countries to establish nuclear reactors for peaceful research.

The plan was launched by Eisenhower at the United Nations General Assembly on December 8, 1953. In his speech, Eisenhower urged the world's major powers to work together in developing peacetime uses of nuclear power. This, he said, could be a first step toward reversing "the fearful trend of atomic military buildup."

He specifically proposed that all nations with nuclear weapons give part of their nuclear stockpiles to a United Nations–supervised "bank of fissionable materials" in an attempt to strip atomic energy of "its military casing and adapt it to the arts of peace." This UN body later became the International Atomic Energy Agency

Eisenhower later wrote that he had several objectives when he announced his Atoms for Peace program:

1. To involve the Soviet Union in a noncontroversial area of nuclear technology.
2. To spread knowledge of the positive benefits of nuclear power to the Third World.
3. To publicize America's lead in nuclear technology.

U.S.–Soviet talks on Eisenhower's plan were held between Secretary of State JOHN FOSTER DULLES and Foreign Minister V. M. MOLOTOV in February 1954, but the Soviets refused to participate in the program unless it were accompanied by a ban on the production of nuclear weapons. Eisenhower decided to go ahead without the Soviet Union, and on September 6, 1954, he announced that the United States, Britain, Canada, France, Australia and South Africa had agreed to establish an agency to develop "new atomic technology for peaceful use." But he continued to try to attract Soviet participation and in November 1954 dropped his previous insistence that the new UN agency physically hold fissionable material. In 1955, however, the Soviet Union launched its own version of the Eisenhower plan, and the two superpowers developed separate programs and policies.

For Further Information:
Eisenhower, Dwight D. *Mandate for Change*. Garden City, N.Y., 1963.
Steel, Richard. *Pax Americana*. New York, 1967.

Attlee, Clement   (January 3, 1883–October 8, 1967)
As British prime minister from 1945 to 1951, Attlee played a major role in formulating Britain's early Cold War policies. He was a participant at the POTSDAM CONFERENCE, helped organize Britain's withdrawal from India and Egypt, authorized the development of Britain's nuclear weapons, committed British troops to the Korean War and encouraged early British support of American foreign policy.

Attlee was born into a comfortable British middle-class family and studied at Oxford University before practicing law. He soon became interested in social reform, joining the

Fabian Society in 1907 and the Independent Labour Party in 1908.

In 1919 Attlee was elected mayor of the Borough of Stepney in London's East End, and in 1922 was elected to Parliament as the member for Limehouse. He served in Britain's first Labour government in 1924 as undersecretary of state for war. In the second Labour government (1929–31) he was chancellor of the Duchy of Lancaster and postmaster general.

In 1935 Attlee defeated the pacifist George Lansbury in an election for the leadership of the Labour Party. When war broke out, Attlee refused to join a national government headed by Neville Chamberlain. His refusal cleared the way for WINSTON CHURCHILL to succeed to the premiership. Attlee was named Churchill's deputy prime minister and loyally served the wartime leader.

In May 1945, at the end of the war in Europe, Attlee led the Labour Party out of the coalition and forced an election. The extended counting of votes coincided with the Potsdam Conference, and Churchill asked Attlee to attend the conference with him so that both party leaders would be well briefed to finish negotiations regardless of the outcome of the election. Labour won a historic election victory, and Attlee returned to Potsdam as prime minister with the new foreign secretary, ERNEST BEVIN. The close relationship between Bevin and Attlee was a cornerstone of British foreign policy at the start of the Cold War. Most of the negotiations and policies were determined by Bevin, who knew that he could depend on Attlee's full support in the Cabinet, at sometimes hostile Labour Party conferences and at the House of Commons. Attlee said of Bevin, "If you have a good dog why do the barking yourself?"

At Potsdam, Attlee and Bevin continued Churchill's determined stand on Polish independence and negotiated the key issues of the administration of postwar Germany and the Soviet claims for extensive German reparations. It was at Potsdam that Attlee first became convinced of the Soviet Union's postwar expansionist policies.

On his return from Potsdam, Attlee started to implement the British welfare state and the gradual dismantling of the British Empire. He recognized that British withdrawal was an inevitable consequence of its reduced economic position in the world. During his government, Britain withdrew its troops from Egypt and ended its rule of India, Sri Lanka, Burma and Palestine. British economic difficulties made it impossible for the Attlee government to fulfill its commitments in protecting Greece from a communist takeover, and Attlee and Bevin's efforts at persuading President Truman to fill the vacuum led to the Truman Doctrine and the end of America's prewar isolationism.

Attlee also authorized the development of an independent British atomic bomb. In many respects, the decision was a continuation of prewar and wartime British research, which had been moved to the United States to work on the Manhattan Project. But Attlee was motivated too by the realization that if Britain wanted to remain a first-rank power it had to follow the American lead. Attlee believed that possession of nuclear weapons was a useful hedge against an American return to isolationism.

Support for American foreign policy was a key element of Attlee's government. He very quickly came to the conclusion that postwar Britain and Europe were militarily and economically dependent on the United States for the forseeable future. In return, Britain would need to adjust some of its foreign policies accordingly. Attlee's support for the U.S. position on the KOREAN WAR was part of that policy. He quickly committed British troops to the United Nations force, although he was uncomfortable with Truman's tendency to assume that all communist parties and governments were completely controlled by the Soviet Union. He believed, for instance, that a Sino-Soviet split was inevitable due to the historic conflict between China and Russia and that this should be borne in mind in determining policy toward Korea.

Attlee's decision to extend British recognition to the People's Republic of China was one of the few foreign policy conflicts that his government had with the United States. He took the view that recognition should be determined on the basis of political control of territory rather than British agreement with political principles. This remained the basis of British diplomatic recognition throughout the Cold War period.

Close Anglo-American relations were also extended to German issues. Britain and the United States merged their postwar zones in Germany into a single administrative unit under the Bizonal Agreement of 1946, and when the Soviet Union imposed its blockade on Berlin, Attlee ordered every available Royal Air Force transport plane to join American planes in airlifting supplies to West Berlin. During the blockade, Attlee and Truman reached an agreement on air bases in Britain for American nuclear-armed bomber aircraft. A year later, the NORTH ATLANTIC TREATY ORGANIZATION was formed.

Attlee was defeated in the 1951 general election, which returned Winston Churchill and the Conservative Party to power. He resigned from the leadership of the Labour Party in 1955 and was created an earl. Attlee died on October 8, 1967.

For Further Information:
Attlee, Clement. *As It Happened.* New York, 1954.
Burridge, T.D. *Clement Attlee, A Political Biography.* New York, 1985.
McNeill, William H. *America, Britain and Russia: Their Cooperation and Their Conflict.* New York, 1970.
———. *The Foreign Policy of the British Labour Governments, 1945–51.* Leicester, 1984.

August Coup   (1991)   See GORBACHEV, MIKHAIL.

Austin, Warren   (November 12, 1877–December 25, 1963)
Warren Austin was U.S. ambassador to the United Nations during the early and most turbulent years of the Cold War,

from 1946 to January 1953. In the important debates on Korea, the Berlin Airlift and Palestine, it fell to Austin to present the American position to the United Nations.

Austin was educated at the University of Vermont. Upon graduation he practiced law and soon became active in Vermont politics as a Republican. In March 1931 he was elected to fill a U.S. Senate seat vacated by the death of Senator Frank L. Greene.

Austin was a staunch opponent of President FRANKLIN ROOSEVELT's domestic policies, but he was just as staunch a supporter of Roosevelt and Truman's foreign policies. As members of the Senate Foreign Relations Committee, he and Senator Arthur Vandenberg (R, Michigan) worked hard during the war and immediately afterward to promote internationalism and support for a bipartisan foreign policy in the Republican Party.

After World War I, Austin had opposed American membership in the League of Nations, but he was an early and strong supporter of the United Nations and other international organizations aimed at maintaining the peace after World War II. The liberal newspaper PM termed him an "ultra-internationalist."

In June 1946, President Truman appointed Austin ambassador to the United Nations. He was chosen partly because his strong support for the United Nations had earned him national prominence and partly to secure continued bipartisan support for foreign policy.

Austin's Republican credentials, however, kept him out of Truman's inner circle of foreign policy advisers, and he confined himself to being the administration's spokesman at the United Nations. In this role he made a name for himself as an eloquent opponent of the Soviet Union's attempts to use the international organization as a forum for propaganda.

After the initial successes of the UN forces, commanded by General DOUGLAS MACARTHUR, in the KOREAN WAR, Austin leaned heavily toward pressing the advantage to secure the entire Korean Peninsula. This was reflected in a statement he issued on August 17, 1950, in which he said that "the United Nations must see that the people of Korea attain complete individual and political freedom. Shall only a part of this country be assured freedom? I think not. The General Assembly has decided that fair and free elections should be held throughout the whole of the Korean peninsula. The United Nations ought to have free and unhampered access to and full freedom to travel within all parts of Korea."

Austin remained at the United Nations until the start of the Eisenhower administration. In his memoirs, Truman wrote: "He was not one to talk much for the headlines, but behind the scenes he knew how to make his influence felt and to bring factions to agree." A heart ailment curtailed Austin's activities in the last 10 years of his life, but he maintained his interest in foreign affairs and in 1955 became chairman of the pro-Taiwan lobby COMMITTEE FOR ONE MILLION. In September 1958 the committee published a study of Communist China in which it claimed that a "continuing revolt" against communist rule smoldered on Mainland China. Austin died of a heart attack on Christmas Day, 1963.

For Further information:
Finger, Seymour M. *American Ambassadors at the UN.* New York, 1988.
Weiley, Lawrence, and Anne Patricia Simmons. *The United States and the United Nations.* New York, 1967.

Australia   Australia is the dominant Western military power in the Southwest Pacific. Throughout the Cold War it has played a major role in conflicts in Asia, including the Korean and Vietnam wars. Its territory was used for early British atomic bomb tests, and Australia was a key member of both the SEATO and ANZUS alliances.

Australians have traditionally seen themselves as a European country 10,000 miles away from their political, cultural and military base. This has led them to fear the prospect of domination by hostile Asian powers, leaving Australia and New Zealand isolated and vulnerable. In the 1930s, the hostile power they feared was Japan, and Australia forged close political and military links with Britain and its Far Eastern imperial possessions.

The collapse of the British Empire at the hands of the Japanese in 1941 and 1942 led the Australians to turn toward the United States for protection. In December 1941, after the Japanese attack on Pearl Harbor, Australian prime minister John Curtin declared, "I make it quite clear that Australia looks to America, free from any pangs about our traditional links of friendship to Britain." The political and military links between Australia and the United States grew during the war, with General DOUGLAS MACARTHUR establishing his Pacific base in Australia after the fall of the Philippines. The Australians made a major contribution to the battle of the Coral Sea, and American and Australian troops fought side by side on Pacific islands.

In the immediate postwar years, there was a temporary shift back toward Britain and the Commonwealth, but the 1949 communist victory in China meant that the Chinese had replaced Japan as the hostile Asian power. An impoverished Britain was unable to help, and the Australians again looked toward the United States for protection.

In December 1950, the staunchly anti-communist Sir Robert Menzies came to power at the head of a Liberal–Country Party coalition. Menzies stayed in power until 1966. His government was among the first to offer troops to the United Nations force, following the North Korean attack on South Korea. More than 10,000 Australian soldiers fought in Korea, and the Australian Navy played an important role in the INCHON landings. Throughout the conflict, Menzies liaised closely with presidents Truman and Eisenhower and British prime ministers CLEMENT ATTLEE and WINSTON CHURCHILL.

In response to the Australian support in Korea, the United States gave generous but informal assurances that it would come to the aid of Australia in the event of an attack. The

Australians, however, wanted a formal defense treaty with the United States and New Zealand. Negotiations took place through 1951, and the ANZUS Treaty was signed September 1 in San Francisco. The treaty committed the three governments to work together for their common defense, but did not contain an explicit commitment from the U.S. to come to its allies' defense in case of attack.

On September 8, 1954, after the withdrawal of France from Indochina, Australia became a founding member of the SOUTHEAST ASIA TREATY ORGANIZATION (SEATO), along with Britain, the United States, New Zealand, Pakistan, France and Thailand. This treaty committed Australia to do little more than consult with the other signatories in the event of hostilities in Southeast Asia, but it formed the legal basis for Australian troops to be sent to Laos in 1961 and to Indochina during the VIETNAM WAR.

Australia's uranium deposits also became a major source of fuel for American and British nuclear bombs, and Britain's first atomic bomb test was held on the Monte Bello Islands off northwestern Australia. Further tests were held on Australia's Woomera Rocket Range, where British and American rocket systems were also developed and tested. The United States has also built a number of missile bases in Australia, and British and American intelligence organizations maintain electronic listening posts on the continent.

Australia in the 1950s went through an anti-communist hysteria similar to that experienced in the United States. The Australian Communist Party had been active in the major industrial centers since its founding in 1922; after World War I returning servicemen formed themselves into a group known as the Returned Servicemen's League and patrolled the streets in gangs looking for "Bolsheviks." By the late 1940s, the communists were a major force on the Australian docks and an influence in the Labor Party. Allegations of communist infiltration played a major part in the labor party's defeat in the election of December 1949. Sir Robert Menzies, an ardent anti-communist, in April 1950 introduced a bill outlawing the Communist Party, but the controversial measure was blocked by the courts and finally defeated in a referendum on the issue in September 1952.

Menzies tried to revive the anti-communist hysteria in 1954 after the defection from the Soviet embassy in Canberra of Soviet agent Vladimir Petrov. Petrov's defection led to a Royal Commission investigation into Soviet espionage in Australia. The report, published in 1955, claimed that the Soviet Union had used its embassy as a "cloak" for espionage for 11 years. The principal target was the Australian Ministry of Foreign Affairs, where the Soviets were reported to have "met with substantial success between 1943 and 1949." But the commission concluded that there was "no trace of any significant leakage" since then.

The turning point in Australia's foreign policy was the Vietnam War. Menzies, in line with his pro-American and anti-communist foreign policy, was an early and enthusiastic supporter of American intervention in Vietnam. Australian and New Zealand casualties in Vietnam totalled 469. By the end of 1968 the antiwar protest movement in Australia was growing as quickly as that in the United States. In 1969 the protests culminated in a series of violent demonstrations across the country on America's Independence Day, July 4. In September 1969, deputy Labor leader Lance Barnard said that a Labour government would withdraw all Australian troops from Vietnam and end conscription. The Liberal Party, then in the throes of a leadership crisis, preempted Labor by starting a withdrawal from Vietnam in August 1971. It was completed just before the Labor Party's election victory in December 1972.

The Labor prime minister, Gough Whitlam, placed a high priority on improving relations with other Asian countries. The People's Republic of China was recognized immediately, and North Vietnam in February 1973. Whitlam also regularized relations with East Germany and North Korea. In November 1973 Whitlam visited China, and in 1974 he made a tour of Eastern Europe and the Soviet Union. Whitlam also distanced himself from the foreign policies of the United States and Britain and increased ties with the Labor government of New Zealand.

In 1973, the Australian government launched a series of diplomatic attacks on America's continued presence in Vietnam, and Australian–U.S. relations were severely strained. It was later revealed that the CIA had infiltrated agents into Australian labor unions, and may have played a role in the "constitutional coup" that ousted Whitlam in December 1975, replacing him with the more right-wing Liberal Party leader Malcolm Fraser.

In February 1976, after the end of the Vietnam War, the SEATO alliance was dissolved at a ceremony in Manila. The ANZUS alliance thus replaced SEATO as America's major defense pact in the Southeast Asia–Southwest Pacific region. But in 1985, New Zealand effectively withdrew from that alliance when Prime Minister David Lange banned visits to New Zealand ports by ships carrying nuclear weapons. The ban made defense cooperation between America and New Zealand an impossibility.

The United States maintained its defensive links with Australia, and Australia maintained its ties with both New Zealand and the United States, attempting to build a bridge between the two countries. At the same time, Australia continued to try to forge closer political and economic links with other countries in the region.

For Further Information:
Albinski, Henry. *The Australian-American Security Relationship.* New York, 1982.
———. *Politics and Foreign Policy in Australia.* Durham, N.C., 1970.
———. *Australia and China.* Melbourne, 1985.
———. *A History of Australian Foreign Policy.* Melbourne, 1979.
Barclay, Glen St. John. *Friends in High Places: Australian-American Diplomatic Relations Since 1945.* New York, 1985.
Bell, Coral. *Dependent Ally: A Study in Australian Foreign Policy.* New York, 1988.

Bridge, Carl, ed. *Munich to Vietnam: Australia's Relations with Britain and the United States Since the 1930's.* Melbourne, 1991.
Philips, Dennis H. *Cold War Two and Australia.* Boston, 1983.

Austria Austria holds a unique position in Europe as the only country to have been occupied after World War II by Soviet and Western troops, each of whom withdrew after signing a treaty guaranteeing its neutrality. Successive Austrian governments sought to build upon this position, and upon Austria's historical ties in Eastern Europe, by acting as a bridge between East and West.

A common culture, language and political history have meant close relations between Germany and Austria. The two countries were allies during World War I, and their defeat coincided with the collapse of the Austro-Hungarian Empire in 1918.

The merging of Austria and Germany was long a major goal of German foreign policy, and a significant minority of Austrians favored the move. In 1938 Hitler formally absorbed Austria into the Third Reich in the Anschluss. At the outbreak of the war, Austrian troops were integrated into the German Army.

At a meeting of British, American and Soviet foreign ministers in Moscow in October 1943, the three countries declared the Austrian–German union null and void and pledged themselves to restoring Austrian independence as an essential part of the postwar order in Central Europe. At the end of the war, Austria, like Germany, was divided into four sectors: Soviet, American, British and French.

Germany was divided because of fear of a resurgence of German military and economic power. The same fears did not apply to Austria. It was initially divided as a punishment for its acceptance of the Anschluss and as a way of guaranteeing an end to the Austrian–German union, but Austria's relatively small population (7 million in 1989) has never posed a serious threat to any other postwar European country. The fact that it remained divided for 10 years after the war's end was purely a result of Cold War tensions, which made it impossible for East and West to negotiate.

It was not until after the death of JOSEF STALIN in March 1953 that the first serious steps toward Austrian reunification were made. On May 11, 1953, British prime minister Sir WINSTON CHURCHILL set the ball rolling when he proposed a piecemeal approach to improving relations with the new leadership in the Soviet Union. He suggested peace in Korea and an Austrian Peace Treaty as two important steps. Churchill proposed an immediate summit of the four powers to be attended by the heads of the government. His proposal was welcomed by France but treated cautiously by the United States, where DWIGHT EISENHOWER had recently become president, and by the Soviet Union. As a result of this caution and other factors, the summit did take place, but at only foreign-minister level, in Washington, D.C. on July 10, 1953.

The foreign ministers' talks ended on July 14 with agreement that they would meet again to discuss an Austrian Peace Treaty and all-German elections for a unified German state.

No progress was made on the German issues, however, because the Western powers insisted on elections before the formation of an all-German government. Progress on the Austrian Peace Treaty was held up because of Soviet reluctance to conclude negotiations on Austria before reaching an agreement on Germany.

The foreign ministers met again in Berlin on January 25, 1954. They accepted the agenda proposed by V.M. MOLOTOV, the Soviet foreign minister, which consisted of: (1) the Austrian Peace Treaty, (2) German unity and security in Europe and (3) measures for reducing tensions. The meeting, which ended on February 18, 1954, failed to achieve agreement on any of the issues, guaranteeing the continued division of Germany.

For a time it looked as if the same fate would befall Austria, as one of Molotov's demands was that the occupying forces remain in that country until the German issue was resolved. But a combination of internal and external factors brought a change in the Soviet position. The major external factor was the rearming of West Germany and that country's formal links with the Western Alliance, including its acceptance into NATO in 1955. This is believed to have prompted the Soviet leadership to preempt any move into the Western military alliance of any part of Austria by supporting the establishment of a unified but neutral Austrian state. A neutral Austria, with its neighbor Switzerland, would constitute a 600-mile neutral zone between the northern and southern members of NATO.

Within the Soviet Union, 1954 and 1955 saw major internal upheavals as NIKITA KHRUSHCHEV continued his climb to power. In February 1955 a key Politburo member, GEORGI MALENKOV, resigned. At the same meeting of the Supreme Soviet, Molotov agreed that Austria could be considered separately from Germany. The Soviets went on to propose a withdrawal of the occupying forces in return for Austrian neutrality, and Julius Raab, the Austrian chancellor, was invited to Moscow to discuss the issue.

Britain and the United States did not object because they did not consider Austria to be as vital as Germany to Western security interests. In Moscow, Raab agreed that Austria would not join any alliances and that all foreign bases would be withdrawn from Austria. The Austrian chancellor also agreed to pay heavy war reparations to the Soviet Union. The proposed treaty agreed upon in Moscow was acceptable to the British, French and American governments and was signed in Vienna on May 15, 1955.

During the Cold War, Austria enjoyed a close relationship with the Western Alliance but based its foreign policy on being equidistant between East and West. Its historical contacts with Eastern Europe made it the best informed Western country on East European affairs and issues. Vienna was (and remains) a major listening post for Western Alliance diplomats. The Austrian foreign office often acted as a political bridge between East and West, and its banking and commercial system still has extensive ties with Eastern Europe.

Austria has also been one of the main conduits for refugees from Eastern to Western Europe. After the Soviet invasion of HUNGARY in 1956 more than 150,000 Hungarians fled to the West through Austria, many of them remaining there. After the invasion of Czechoslovakia by forces of the Warsaw Pact in 1968, another 104,000 refugees fled westward through Austria. Austria also played host to a number of Polish refugees after the crackdown on the Solidarity movement in 1980, and in 1989 an estimated 40,000 East Germans fled to West Germany across the newly opened border between Austria and Hungary. The United Nations High Commissioner for Refugees has permanently maintained camps in Austria for East European refugees, including Russian Jews immigrating either to Israel or to the United States.

Since 1955 Austria has developed close relations with its neutral neighbor Switzerland, and the two regularly cooperate on military and political issues. They are both founding members of the European Free Trade Agreement (EFTA), and they also provide extensive facilities for the United Nations in Geneva and Vienna.

Like Switzerland, Austria has developed a policy of armed neutrality. The exact details of this policy are determined largely by the restrictions placed on Austria by the 1955 Austrian State Treaty. For instance, under articles 13 and 14, Austria is prohibited from the ownership, manufacture or testing of certain offensive weapons, including nuclear weapons, chemical and biological weapons, guided missles and artillery pieces with a range of more than 20 miles.

To comply with the treaty's terms and at the same time defend Austrian neutrality, the government in 1973 implemented its Territorial Defense Plan. This plan stipulates that in the event of an international emergency, Austria will deploy active formations and mobilize reserves to prevent foreign forces from violating Austrian neutrality. The plan leans heavily on partisan-style defense, and as part of this plan the Austrian Army relies on an active force of 50,000 conscripts. After six months of training, conscripts return to civilian life, where they constitute a reserve force of some 250,000.

In June 1989, Austria applied for membership in the European Community. This further raised questions of the country's neutrality, for although the EC is not a military alliance, it has plans for a political union, which may at some stage involve military cooperation.

For Further Information:
Barker, Elisabeth. *Austria, 1918–72.* New York, 1973.
Bauer, Robert A., ed. *The Austrian Solution—The International Conflict and Cooperation.* Charlottesville, Va., 1982.
Cronin, Audrey Kurth. *Great Power Politics and the Struggle Over Austria, 1945–1955.* Ithaca, N.Y., 1986.
Gann, Lewis, ed. *The Defense of Western Europe.* Dover, Mass., 1987.
Grayson, C.T. *Austria's International Position (1938–1955): The Reestablishment of an Independent Austria.* New York, 1955.
Gruble, K. *Between Liberation and Liberty.* New York, 1955.
Schlesinger, Thomas O. *Austrian Neutrality in Postwar Europe; The Domestic Roots of A Foreign Policy.* Wien-Stuttgart, 1972.
Stadler, Karl. *Austria.* London and Toronto, 1971.

Austrian Peace Treaty   (1955)   See AUSTRIA.

Azerbaijan   Azerbaijan, consisting of two provinces, is the northern region of Iran. (The international border separates it from the independent state of Azerbaijan, formerly a constituent republic of the USSR.) A Soviet-supported communist government was established there immediately after World War II. Establishment of this government led to one of the first disputes of the Cold War, and convinced American foreign policy planners of Soviet designs on Iran, which in turn led to a strong American presence in the country up until 1979.

During World War II Iran was a major conduit for supplies traveling from Britain and America to Soviet troops in the Transcaucasian region. It was also a major supplier of oil to Britain. In 1942 Britain and the Soviet Union concluded an agreement with Iran that permitted the stationing of British and Soviet troops to secure the strategic supply line. American troops were later added to this force. Under this agreement, the troops were permitted to remain until six months after the end of the war. At the LONDON FOREIGN MINISTERS CONFERENCE in September 1945, British foreign secretary ERNEST BEVIN and Soviet foreign minister V.M. MOLOTOV agreed that all foreign troops would be withdrawn from Iran not later than March 2, 1946.

However, American and British intelligence reported that the Soviets were increasing rather than decreasing their forces in northern Iran, especially in the province of Azerbaijan. U.S. president Harry Truman offered to speed up the withdrawal of the small American contingent if the Soviets would do the same. But on December 3, 1945, the Soviets refused the offer and announced that a revolutionary government had been formed in Iranian Azerbaijan, which bordered Soviet Azerbaijan. With approximately 4 million ethnic Azerbaijanis in both provinces, it seemed clear that the Soviets intended to play on nationalist aspirations to unite the Azerbaijanis into one Soviet-controlled province.

On January 19, 1946, Iran formally charged the Soviet Union before the UN Security Council with interference in Iranian internal affairs. But Soviet refusal to discuss the issue blocked effective UN action, and when the March 2 deadline arrived the Soviet Union announced that "some troops" would remain in Iran. Iran attempted to move its troops into Soviet-occupied areas but found the roads blocked by the Soviets.

The British and American governments sent strong notes of protest to the Soviet Union and promised to support Iran. On March 24, 1946, Moscow Radio announced that all Russian troops would be withdrawn from Iran at once. The Iranians were expected to pay a price—a Soviet–Iranian agreement giving the Soviets control of an oil production company to exploit Iranian oilfields. On top of that, the communist government in place in Azerbaijan refused to be incorporated back into the Iranian state. At the same time, Iranian Kurds rebeled and proclaimed the Kurdish Republic of Mahabad.

On June 7, the policy of U.S. military aid to Iran was established when Secretary of State GEORGE MARSHALL announced that Iran would receive $30 million worth of surplus army equipment. On October 6, 1946, the United States and Iran signed an agreement for an American Army mission to visit Iran to assist in "enhancing the efficiency of the Iranian army." In Iran, U.S. ambassador GEORGE ALLEN successfully lobbied against Soviet pressure to ratify the Soviet–Iranian oil agreement.

Soviet pressure on Iran continued, and Iran remained high on the U.S. State Department's list of likely Soviet targets throughout the 1940s and 1950s. American aid helped to suppress the Kurdish and Azerbaijani breakaway governments and secure Iran's independence from the Soviet Union. But the communist influences were well established throughout Iran, and this led to the establishment by the shah of an American-supported internal security operation employing torture and other police-state techniques, which left the United States associated with vested financial interests, extreme rightist groups and the suppression of political and individual liberties.

For Further Information:

Chubin, Shahram, and Sepehr Zabih. *The Foreign Relations of Iran.* Los Angeles, 1974.

Goode, James F. *The United States and Iran: The Diplomacy of Neglect.* London, 1989.

Kuniholm, Bruce. *The Origins of the Cold War in the Middle East.* Princeton, 1980.

B

Baghdad Pact The Baghdad Pact was the Middle Eastern link in a series of defense alliances established to "contain" the Soviet Union. It was formed in 1955 and in 1959 changed its name to the Central Treaty Organization. It was also known as the Middle East Treaty Organization.

The main force behind the formation of the Baghdad Pact was Britain, which wanted to use the alliance both to strengthen its own military and political presence in the Middle East and to contribute to containment of the Soviet Union. (See CONTAINMENT.)

At the core of the initial agreement was a strong political and military link between Britain and Iraq. This was emphasized in the mutual defense pact when it was signed on April 5, 1955, by Britain, Turkey and Iraq. The agreement gave the Royal Air Force bases in Iraq and the right to help train Iraq's Air Force, and it called for close Anglo–Iraqi defense collaboration in peace and war. British foreign secretary Anthony Eden told the House of Commons that the accords could serve as the basis of a general Middle East defense plan.

Iran and Pakistan were the next full members of the Pact. Pakistan joined on September 23, 1955, and Iran on October 12, 1955. The United States, in deference to British wishes, stayed on the periphery of the organization by accepting only observer status. But the United States and Britain both channeled economic and military assistance through the structure of the Baghdad Pact. A Baghdad-based secretariat and permanent council were established.

The Baghdad Pact became one of the major targets of Egyptian leader GAMAL ABDEL NASSER, who regarded it as a threat to his own plans for pan-Arab nationalism. The British humiliation during the 1956 SUEZ CRISIS was a major setback to the pact. With British prestige seriously damaged, the United States joined the Military Committee of the Baghdad Pact on June 5, 1957, in an attempt to strengthen the Western orientation of the alliance and to reinforce the EISENHOWER DOCTRINE and U.S. intervention in Lebanon.

From its inception, Iraq had hoped that the Baghdad Pact would enable it to form a comprehensive regional security system between the signatories of the pact and the signatories of the 1945 Arab League Pact (Egypt, Syria, Iraq, Lebanon, Jordan, Saudi Arabia and Yemen). Egyptian opposition and the formation in 1958 of the United Arab Republic (uniting Egypt and Syria) and the Arab Union (Iraq and Jordan) ended any hope of wider regional defense cooperation. Eden's defense plans for the region were thwarted as well.

The defense alliance was dealt a major blow in July 1958 when the Iraqi military overthrew the Hashemite monarchy and killed King Faisal. The new Iraqi leader, Abdul Karim Kassem, was sympathetic to the ambitions of Nasser, took Iraq out of the Baghdad Pact on March 24, 1959, and ended Iraq's defense agreements with Britain. In the wake of the Iraqi revolution, the United States became an associate member of the pact, the pact's name was changed to the Central Treaty Organization (CENTO), and headquarters was moved to Ankara, Turkey.

Iraq's withdrawal from the alliance increased the importance of both Iran and Pakistan to the United States (Turkey already had a close defense relationship with the United States through its membership in NATO). On March 5, Iran and Pakistan signed bilateral defense agreements with the United States. The agreements, however, fell considerably short of a mutual defense treaty as they committed the United States only to "take such appropriate action . . . as may be mutually agreed upon."

But both Iran and Pakistan increasingly saw the major threat to their security coming from the medium-sized regional powers, Iraq and India, respectively, rather than from the Soviet Union. Both countries tried to invoke the pact to secure American and British military assistance in wars with their neighbors. But the two Western allies refused to be drawn into regional conflicts that did not involve communist aggression.

The alliance was further weakened by Britain's decision in 1968 to withdraw its military forces from the Persian Gulf in 1971. This left the West with its nearest forces at the sovereign British air bases on Cyprus. Further British defense cuts in 1974 forced British defense planners to withdraw specific CENTO troop commitments. In the same year, a U.S. aircraft carrier entered the Persian Gulf for the first time for CENTO naval maneuvers.

By the mid-1970s the alliance was mainly a symbolic organization. It completely collapsed in 1979 after the withdrawal of Iran following the overthrow of the shah. The final blow came on March 12, 1979, when Pakistani foreign minister Afgha Shahi announced that his country was withdrawing because the pact "had lost its meaning" after Iran's withdrawal.

For Further Information:

CENTO Public Relations Division. *The Story of the Central Treaty Organization.* Ankara and Washington, D.C., 1959.

Kuniholm, Bruce. *The Origins of the Cold War in the Near East.* Princeton, N.J., 1980.

Baker, James A., 3rd.   (April 28, 1930–   ) James A. Baker 3rd served as President GEORGE BUSH's secretary of state from January 1989 to August 1992. Traveling widely, he was the chief diplomatic player on the U.S. side during the stunning series of crises and negotiations that ended the Cold War: the collapse of communism in Eastern Europe in 1989, the reunification of Germany in 1990, the dissolution of the Soviet Union in 1991.

Baker, a Texan, got his BA from Princeton University, served in the Marine Corps from 1952 to 1954 and earned his law degree at the University of Texas. He served as an undersecretary of commerce in the Ford administration, was Bush's campaign chairman in his failed 1980 bid for the Republican presidential nomination, and subsequently advised the victorious Reagan-Bush campaign. He served as President Reagan's White House chief of staff from 1981 to 1985 and as secretary of the treasury from 1985 to 1988. In 1988, he rescued Bush's foundering presidential campaign and managed it to victory over Michael Dukakis. Bush rewarded his friend with the plum assignment to the State Department.

Although Baker's foreign affairs experience was limited, he enjoyed a reputation for competence. He was regarded as a skilled negotiator and an adroit handler of the press. While conservative, he was not an ideologue on most issues, and had often been described in Reagan administration circles as the "ultimate pragmatist."

Baker began 1989 by touring North Atlantic Treaty Organization capitals to discuss modernizing the alliance's battlefield nuclear weapons and to try to counter the growing impression in Europe that the Bush administration was responding inadequately to Soviet president MIKHAIL GORBACHEV's ongoing peace initiatives. By the end of the year, Baker had already met several times with Gorbachev and his foreign minister, EDUARD SHEVARDNADZE, and had established a personal rapport with the two men that would serve him in good stead over the next few years.

On December 12, 1989, Baker delivered a major speech in Berlin in which he outlined the U.S. vision of Europe's future in the wake of the ongoing reforms in the Soviet bloc. While the administration had recently been reaffirming U.S. military ties to Europe, Baker now sought to emphasize a heightened American political role on the continent as the European Community (EC) moved toward greater integration and the threat from the East evaporated. He specifically suggested that "institutional and consultative links" between the U.S. and EC be strengthened, that NATO take on a more political role, and that the Conference on Security and Cooperation in Europe (CSCE) be used to promote multi-party elections and free markets in Eastern Europe. Later that day, Baker made a brief trip to Potsdam, East Germany, becoming the first U.S. official of his rank to visit that state.

To some extent out of deference to Gorbachev, the Bush administration generally took a hands-off approach toward Eastern Europe and its transition to democracy. The U.S. limited itself to encouragement and offers of aid, although Baker did visit Czechoslovakia, Bulgaria and Romania in 1990 and Yugoslavia and Albania in 1991.

But because of its treaty obligations, the U.S. was much more directly involved in the issue of German reunification, the centerpiece of the Cold War. Baker and the foreign ministers of the other three allied nations of World War II—the U.S.S.R., Britain and France—met in Ottawa in February 1991 and agreed on the so-called two-plus-four talks, which involved the "Big Four" allies plus the two Germanies. Baker attended ministerial-level meetings in Bonn in May and in East Berlin in June; in Moscow in September, he signed the Treaty on the Final Settlement with Respect to Germany, which paved the way for German reunification the following month.

Throughout 1990 and 1991, it sometimes seemed as if Baker was spending as much time in Moscow as he was in Washington. He and Shevardnadze met frequently in the U.S.S.R., United States and Europe, hammering out the details of arms agreements, pre-summit negotiations and Persian Gulf crisis diplomacy. A major preoccupation of Baker from August 1990 to January 1991 was to organize a consensus in the UN Security Council against Iraq, ultimately leading to the authorization of the use of force to drive Iraq out of Kuwait. The process involved all of Baker's cajoling and arm-twisting skills, and was greatly aided by his increasingly close and cooperative relationship with Shevardnadze. Indeed, when Shevardnadze resigned his post in December 1990, Baker hailed him as a man of "courage, conviction and principle," adding, "I am proud to call this man friend." (The two men had met 25 times over the previous 23 months.)

Baker kept up a similar pace with Shevardnadze's successors, first Alexander Bessmertnykh and then Boris Pankin, in 1991. After the successful July summit in Moscow, followed by the failed coup against Gorbachev in August, Baker found himself back in the U.S.S.R. in September, negotiating a range of issues, including a halt in military aid from both governments to both sides of the Afghan civil war. He also visited and conferred with the leaders of the newly independent Baltic states, becoming the first U.S. secretary of state to visit that region. In mid-December, he returned to the Soviet Union, shortly before its official dissolution. He sought and received assurances that the Soviet nuclear arsenal would remain under some kind of central control and that the key republics would abide by U.S.-Soviet arms-control treaties.

In January 1992, Baker hosted a conference to coordinate aid to the new Commonwealth of Independent States and announced a U.S. military airlift of emergency food and medicine to the former U.S.S.R. The airlift, dubbed Operation Provide Hope and including aid from 14 countries, was carried out in February. The same month, Baker toured six southern, former Soviet republics to initiate diplomatic contacts. He also visited Russia and announced the establishment of a U.S.-Russian-German program to employ former Soviet nuclear weapons scientists in peacetime projects. Meanwhile, throughout the first half of 1992, Baker and Russian foreign minister Andrei Kozyrev carried out a series of negotiations that culminated in the June agreement between President Bush and Russian president Boris Yeltsin to slash deeply both sides' strategic nuclear arms.

Among the other major accomplishments of Baker's tenure was the beginning in October 1991 of the first direct Middle East peace talks between Israel and all of its major Arab adversaries. The invitations to the first round of the talks, which began in Madrid, were issued jointly by the United States and Soviet Union. Capping an intense diplomatic drive, Baker announced the peace conference during his eighth trip to the Mideast region since the end of the Persian Gulf War in February. Baker and the Bush administration had made clear their desire to use the military victory against Iraq to score a diplomatic coup in the long-simmering Arab-Israeli conflict. However, no breakthroughs were achieved at the Madrid conference or at followup talks held in Washington.

President Bush brought Baker back to the White House in August 1992 as chief of staff. It was widely understood that Baker's real assignment was to revive Bush's faltering campaign for reelection.

Balance of Terror   The balance of terror is the term used for the state of mutual apprehension between two major opposing blocs, each of which has enough power to destroy the other. This creates a mutual deterrent, effectively preventing either side from attacking.

The balance, and thus the credibility of the deterrent, depends largely on the credibility of the threat. In the late 1950s, for example, the Soviet Union was still significantly behind the United States in the development of nuclear weaponry, but the dramatic launching of the Sputnik satellite increased the West's fear of the Soviet arsenal.

In more recent years, Western planners resisted pressure from antinuclear groups to announce a "non-first-use" nuclear weapons policy. NATO argued that it would be unlikely to be the first to use nuclear weapons, but to give a categorical assurance to that effect would destroy the delicate balance of terror and invite an attack from the overwhelmingly powerful conventional forces of the Warsaw Pact.

Ball, George   (December 21, 1909–   )   George Ball was U.S. undersecretary of state during the Kennedy and Johnson administrations. He was a key adviser during the Cuban Missile Crisis and strongly opposed the introduction of U.S. combat troops in Vietnam.

After graduating from Northwestern University Law School in 1933, Ball worked first at the U.S. Farm Credit Administration and then at the Treasury Department. In 1935 he went into private law practice in Chicago, and in 1942 joined the Office of Lend-Lease Administration; in 1944 he was appointed director of the U.S. Strategic Bombing Survey.

After World War II, Ball returned to private practice, increasingly specializing in international law. He became closely involved with the European Coal and Steel Community, forerunner to the European Economic Community. Adlai Stevenson was a senior partner in Ball's law firm, and Ball helped him with his campaigns for the U.S. presidency in 1952 and 1956. This put him in touch with JOHN F. KENNEDY, who appointed him undersecretary of state for economic affairs in January 1961.

Ball's main responsibilities in this post involved drafting the Trade Expansion Act of 1962, which cut tariffs on foreign goods and gave the president wide powers to retaliate against foreign import restrictions. Ball was also deeply involved with U.S. policy toward the Congo, supporting the use of force against the rebellion in Katanga province, if necessary, to achieve reunification. This was accomplished in January 1963 through the use of UN troops with American military support.

In November 1961, Ball replaced CHESTER BOWLES as undersecretary of state. During the 1962 CUBAN MISSILE CRISIS he was a member of the inner circle that advised Kennedy and coordinated consultations with European allies following the decision to blockade Cuba. In his early years at the State Department, Ball was mainly responsible for U.S.–European relations, and he supported all moves toward European unity, but he became increasingly interested in events in Southeast Asia.

Ball opposed the Taylor-Rostow report (named after its authors, General Maxwell Taylor and Walt Rostow), which advocated the introduction of U.S. combat troops into South Vietnam, arguing that this would be the start of an ever-increasing American involvement. Ball also opposed the regime of South Vietnam's President NGO DINH DIEM and led American advisers who advocated the withdrawal of U.S. support for Diem in order to force a coup. Diem was eventually overthrown by the South Vietnamese military in November 1963.

Ball continued as undersecretary of state during the administration of President LYNDON JOHNSON, but he was never able to reconcile himself to American military involvement in Vietnam. He regarded the conflict as unwinnable because of the deep commitment of the North Vietnamese and the lack of popular support for the Saigon government. In July 1965, Ball wrote a memorandum entitled "Cutting Our Losses in South Vietnam," in which he proposed a substantial cut in American military forces and a negotiated compromise solution with North Vietnam. He argued that continued U.S. troop increases were not an assurance of victory. Opponents of the Ball memorandum argued that American withdrawal would result in an American loss of face among Asian nations. Ball's counterargument was that such a loss of face would be only short-term and that in the end the United States would emerge with the reputation of a "wiser and more mature nation." He said the alternative was "humiliation."

Ball sent a similar antiwar memorandum to President Johnson in January 1966 in which he opposed the bombing of North Vietnam on the grounds that it would strengthen rather than weaken North Vietnamese morale. Publicly, Ball remained loyal to Johnson and Secretary of State DEAN RUSK both in and out of office. His loyalty was rewarded in May 1966, when Ball was given responsibility for a number of diplomatic tasks performed by former presidential advisor MCGEORGE BUNDY and was named chairman of an interdepartmental group that included the director of the CIA, the chairman of the Joint Chiefs of Staff, the director of the U.S. Information Agency and the assistant to the president for national security affairs.

Ball, however, found himself more and more at odds with the Johnson administration's Vietnam policy and in September 1966 resigned from the State Department, citing "economic reasons" in order to avoid any embarrassing controversy for the president. The importance of Ball's advice was eventually recognized by Johnson, who appointed him in March 1968 to the senior advisory group on Vietnam. In this group, Ball continued to press for de-escalation and was eventually rewarded on March 31 with Johnson's statement that he would gradually pull back U.S. forces.

The following month, Ball was appointed ambassador to the United Nations in succession to ARTHUR GOLDBERG. Johnson told him at the time that no one had disagreed with him more but that there was no one whom he needed more at that moment. Ball was at the United Nations until September 1968, when he left to join HUBERT HUMPHREY's campaign staff as "a principal foreign policy adviser." In December 1968, he published *The Discipline of Power: The Essentials of World Structure*, in which he expounded his ideas on the necessity for a united Europe that would function as a third superpower and a revised American policy in Asia that would include recognition of and trade with communist China.

After the 1968 presidential election, Ball became one of the fiercest Democratic critics of President RICHARD NIXON's Vietnam policy. He was also critical of dtente, the details of Nixon's China policy, and the personal style of diplomacy exercised by HENRY KISSINGER.

Ball played a major role in formulating the foreign policy plank of the 1976 Democratic Party platform. He contributed to JIMMY CARTER's presidential campaign and was one of four front-runners considered for the post of secretary of state. But, in the end, Carter selected the younger CYRUS VANCE. Ball continued to advise the president, however, and on December 4, 1978, Ball was appointed to President Carter's National Security Council to help the administration draft a long-range study on the Persian Gulf in the months before the fall of the shah.

Now. in retirement, George Ball remains a student of American foreign policy and frequently writes for publication.

For Further Information:
Ball, George W. *The Discipline of Power: The Essentials of World Structure.* New York, 1968.
———. *In Diplomacy for a Crowded World.* New York, 1976.
Halberstam, David. *The Best and the Brightest.* New York, 1972.
Hilsman, Roger. *To Move a Nation: The Politics of Foreign Policy in the Administration of John F. Kennedy.* Garden City, N.Y., 1967.
Spanier, J.W. *American Foreign Policy Since World War Two.* Washington, D.C., 1988.
Walton, Richard J. *Cold War and Counterrevolution: The Foreign Policy of John F. Kennedy.* New York, 1972.

Ball, Joseph H.   (November 3, 1905–   )   Joseph Ball was a Republican senator from Minnesota who strongly opposed the Marshall Plan in the late 1940s.

A graduate of Antioch College and the University of Minnesota, Ball was a journalist for many years before being appointed to the Senate in 1940 following the death of Senator Ernest Lundeen. He was elected in his own right in 1942. His election platform stressed postwar international cooperation and the need for an international body to coordinate activities.

Ball's idealistic support for world government led him to oppose the MARSHALL PLAN, not because he opposed aid for postwar Europe, but because he felt that it should be distributed by the United Nations or a similar body. In March 1948 Ball proposed an amendment to the European Recovery Program Bill (the Marshall Plan) that would have established a European peacekeeping force controlled by a Supreme Council composed of 11 United Nations members. Opposition to the amendment was led by Senator ARTHUR VANDENBERG, who said that it would have committed the United States to war on the vote of foreign nations. The Senate voted against the amendment.

Ball lost his Senate seat to Hubert Humphrey in the 1948 election. He returned to journalism until 1953, when he became vice president of States Marine Line, a merchant shipping line.

For Further Information:
Hitchens, Harold L. "Influences on the Congressional Decision to Pass the Marshall Plan." *Western Political Quarterly,* (21) 1968.
Vandenberg, Arthur H., Jr., ed. *The Private Papers of Arthur H. Vandenberg.* Boston, 1952.

Ballistic Missile Early Warning Systems   Ballistic Missile Early Warning Systems (BMEWS) are radar systems based a considerable distance from the likely target of a nuclear attack.

Some BMEWS are located outside the national territory of the country being protected. An example is the early warning station at Flyingdales in Yorkshire, England. The station provides a five-minute warning of a Soviet missile attack on Britain, but it is also an integral part of the U.S. early warning system and provides a 20-minute warning for American targets.

The United States early warning system is also linked into

two Canadian stations for Soviet missile attacks coming over the North Pole. America's western flank is protected by radar stations ranged along the West Coast of the United States.

As satellite technology has progressed, BMEWS have been largely replaced by radar and infrared satellites. Satellites are the preferred early warning system, as they are less likely to be destroyed during a first-strike attack. Satellites also reduce American dependence on foreign bases. The Soviet Union, with its vast territory, never had any need for BMEWS on foreign soil.

Baltic States   The Baltic states of Estonia, Lithuania and Latvia represented a major nationalist challenge to the Soviet Union and eventually played a major part in its internal collapse. During the interwar years the Baltic states were independent republics and bases for White Russian activity. In the 1980s they became leaders in the movement to decentralize political and economic power in the U.S.S.R.

There is a long tradition of conflict between the Baltic states and Russia. During the Middle Ages the Baltic states were powerful members of the Hanseatic Trading League, and the Grand Duchy of Lithuania at one time controlled a territory bordered by the Baltic Sea, Black Sea and Dnieper River. In the 18th century Russia gained control first of Estonia and Latvia and then of Lithuania. Throughout the 19th century there were sporadic attempts to break away from the Russian Empire, most of them allied with parallel attempts in neighboring Poland.

Independence was granted to Estonia by the Soviet-German Treaty of Brest-Litovsk, which took the new Bolshevik government out of World War I. The loss of Estonia was a bitter blow to the new Bolshevik state. As soon as Germany surrendered to the allies, the Bolshevik government declared the Treaty of Brest-Litovsk null and void and started an invasion of Estonia. But the invasion was repulsed by a combination of White Russians and Allied forces and fighting spread to Latvia and Lithuania. By 1919, independent governments were in control of all three states. In February 1920, Lenin signed peace treaties with all three republics in which the U.S.S.R. recognized their independence "in perpetuity."

In the interwar years, early attempts at democratic government quickly foundered and were replaced by authoritarian regimes. The three countries also became a base for White Russian emigrs and Western, mainly British, agents working to subvert the Soviet state. Soviet leader JOSEF STALIN was determined to stamp out what he termed "this nest of spies" and at the same time regain the strategic territory on the Baltic Sea. In 1934, the Baltic states attempted a diplomatic solution by signing non-aggression pacts with both Germany and the Soviet Union. But this was effectively ignored by the great powers in the Molotov-Ribbentrop Pact of August 1939. A secret protocol to this agreement recognized Latvia and Estonia as being in the Soviet sphere of influence. Lithuania was added soon after the start of World War II.

The Baltic states found themselves hopelessly trapped and unable to turn to Germany for help. On October 10, 1939, all three countries signed mutual assistance treaties with the Soviet Union and allowed the Red Army to enter their territory. In July 1940, Stalin ordered elections in which only communist candidates stood, and in August all three states "voted" by a show of hands for incorporation into the Soviet Union.

The immediate result of incorporation was the deportation of over 100,000 nationalists to the Siberian labor camps. This was halted by the German invasion in 1941, but was quickly followed by the German annihilation of 150,000 Jews from the Baltic states. Another 100,000 were sent to German labor camps. A resistance army sprang up, and the fighting resulted in the loss of 450,000 Latvians, 200,000 Estonians and 500,000 Lithuanians. At the end of the war, a further 250,000 people from the Baltic states fled the approaching Red Army for sanctuary in Finland, Sweden, West Germany and the United States.

In 1945, Stalin restored the Soviet governments in Estonia, Latvia and Lithuania, but immediately faced a nationalist guerrilla war that lasted until 1951. He responded with a mass deportation of some 600,000 people, most of whom were replaced by ethnic Russians. Those who survived the Siberian camps and the torture cells (about 250,000) returned to their homes after the death of Stalin in March 1953.

Khrushchev, and later Brezhnev, tried to solve the problem of Baltic nationalism by encouraging Russian immigration to the Baltic states and by dramatically improving the living standard of the region. Major power generating stations were built, the fishing industry was revived and there were investments in factories producing high-technology goods and equipment. The indigenous peoples also declined in relation to the Russian immigrants so that by 1980 of 1.5 million citizens in Estonia, only 900,000 were ethnic Estonians.

The native languages, although not officially suppressed, were discouraged, and Russian became the primary language taught in schools. The Catholic Church in Lithuania was suppressed as was the once powerful Lutheran Church in Estonia and Latvia. Local history was rewritten so that the independent interwar years were explained away as the work of "Western Imperialism" or the "bourgeois period," and the Soviet annexation of the Baltic states was described as "liberation from the yoke of imperialism."

The United States and some other Western governments refused officially to recognize the incorporation of the Baltic states into the Soviet Union, and a few prewar diplomatic missions were extended official courtesies. In de facto terms, however, the West accepted Soviet annexation of the region and, apart from sending in a few agents during the early Cold War years, did nothing to change the status quo.

During the 1970s, much of the nationalist sentiment appeared gradually to evaporate. It remained strongest in Estonia. That country's proximity to Finland and the close relationship between the Finnish and Estonian languages exposed Estonians to Western news broadcasts through Finnish television and radio.

In 1985 Soviet authorities felt secure enough in Latvia to invite 220 American specialists in East-West relations to a forum on U.S.-Soviet relations in the Latvian resort town of Jurmala. But Latvian nationalists used the meeting as a forum to broadcast their continued dissatisfaction with Soviet rule.

As nationalist tensions increased throughout the Soviet Union, the Baltic states took the lead in demanding greater autonomy from Moscow. On the 48th anniversary of the Soviet annexation of the region, in August 1987, thousands marched through the streets of Latvia, Estonia and Lithuania to demand the restoration of independence. An attempt to hold a similar demonstration in Latvia on November 18 (the anniversary of Latvian independence in 1918) was blocked by police.

But Soviet leader MIKHAIL GORBACHEV had by this time decided that a greater degree of autonomy for the Baltic states and other regions would be in keeping with his decentralizing of political and economic power as well as help to defuse nationalist tensions. His tacit approval, however, led only to more demonstrations and more demands.

In June 1988, a group of Latvian writers demanded that Latvia be granted the status of a "sovereign state" within the U.S.S.R., and published their demand in the state-controlled press. That same month, Moscow was forced to grant official recognition to the People's Front of Estonia, a non-communist nationalist political organization that attracted 100,000 followers to its inaugural rally. Similar organizations quickly followed in Lithuania and Latvia.

In October 1988, representatives of Latvian, Lithuanian and Estonian popular fronts met in Talinn, the capital of Estonia, to coordinate policies, attack the Soviet authorities for blocking their activities and, for the first time since 1940, to fly their prewar national flags.

In response to the challenge from the popular fronts, the local communist parties in the three Baltic states also began to demand greater autonomy. On November 16, 1988, the communist-controlled parliament (Soviet) in Estonia demanded the right to veto unilaterally national laws that affected the republic. Latvia and Lithuania quickly followed suit.

Gorbachev tried to slow down the nationalist trend by warning that it "posed the single greatest threat" to his perestroika policies. But by this time, the protest movement had developed an increasing momentum. In February 1989 the Estonian national flag started to fly over all government buildings. In April the government submitted proposals for the return of collective farms to private farmers, the right to form private companies, a system of investment and foreign ownership independent of national laws, and Estonian control over emigration from other parts of the Soviet Union. In response, the ethnic Russians in Estonia held a rally to protest against anti-Russian discrimination.

In February 1989, the Sajudis, the Lithuanian nationalist movement, called for Lithuania to become an independent and neutral state, and a new official holiday was created to celebrate the interwar period of independence. In the Soviet Union's first multicandidate parliamentary elections on March 26, nationalist candidates trampled their non-nationalist opponents.

On May 14, a Baltic assembly of the nationalist movements of the three states adopted a resolution declaring the right of the "sovereign states" of the Baltic region to choose their own economic systems. They also issued a plea to the United Nations to help their republics become independent states. Four days later, the parliaments of Estonia and Lithuania passed radical resolutions on their sovereignty and independence of action from Moscow.

Throughout the rest of 1989, the Baltic states' demands for independence continued. Gorbachev alternately threatened and conceded in the face of Baltic nationalism on one hand and Communist Party pressure to suppress nationalism on the other. In the spring of 1990 Lithuania, followed by Estonia and then Latvia, declared independence, gaining cautious approval in the West, but not formal recognition. Gorbachev initially took a hard-line approach, warning the republics that they were putting the future of perestroika in jeopardy.

Within days of Lithuania's declaration of independence, tanks were rolling through the capital, Vilnius, and military jets were flying over it. Movements of foreign journalists were restricted and foreign diplomats were asked to leave.

In April 1990 Gorbachev incurred the displeasure of President George Bush by cutting off oil and gas supplies to Lithuania and threatening economic sanctions if the republic did not rescind legislation strengthening its demands for independence. Despite threats of U.S. retaliation, the Kremlin stood by its hardline policy.

Lithuania agreed to suspend legislation on independence, and Gorbachev declared Estonia and Latvia's attempts at secession to be illegal. The leaders of the three republics then met for the first time to coordinate strategy. At this meeting they revived the Baltic Council, a trilateral policy group that had existed between 1934 and 1940 before Soviet annexation. On July 2 the Soviet Union lifted its trade embargo to Lithuania, which, in return, froze its March declaration of independence.

The apparent backdown by the Baltic republics was short-lived. The Baltic states' battle for independence had rekindled the spirit of nationalism in the other Soviet republics. When Russia, Georgia and the Ukraine began agitating for control over their own affairs, they in turn encouraged the Baltic states to press harder with their claims.

When Gorbachev declared himself ready to discuss a treaty of union with all the Russian republics, the Baltic republics issued a joint declaration demanding that their secession talks be organized on a "three plus one" basis. They maintained the same stance when Gorbachev published the text of his Treaty of Union in November 1990.

In January 1991 the dispute was exacerbated by a disagreement on the Soviet budget for 1991. Neither the Russian Federation nor Lithuania would pay their contributions. This action lead to what became known as the "Soviet crackdown" in the Baltic states. Soviet Interior Ministry troops seized government buildings, the Latvian police headquarters were attacked and 15 Lithuanians were killed in the unrest. The crackdown attracted international condemnation.

By February all the republics had voted for independence in a series of national referendums. Results in Estonia and Latvia showed that even the sizable Russian minority populations voted in favor of secession. But during the following months the calls for independence were put on hold while negotiations continued with all the republics for a new union treaty.

The situation radically changed with the August 1991 coup in the Soviet Union. With Gorbachev ousted temporarily from power, the Baltic states seized the initiative and declared their total independence from Moscow. The Kremlin coup failed within days, and the three new republics won diplomatic recognition from the European Community and other nations by the end of August. The United States apparently in deference to Gorbachev, delayed granting recognition until September 2. Finally, the Soviet Union formally recognized Baltic independence on September 6. The three republics joined the UN on September 17.

For Further Information:
Hiden, John, and Patrick Salmon. *The Baltic Nations and Europe: Estonia, Latvia, and Lithuania in the Twentieth Century.* New York, 1991.
Kaslas, B.J. *The Baltic Nations: The Quest for Regional Integration and Political Liberty.* New York, 1976.
Manning, C.A. *The Forgotten Republic.* New York, 1952.
Misiunas, Romuald H., and Rein Taagepera. *The Baltic States: Years of Dependence, 1940–1980.* London, 1983.
Nodel, E. *Estonia: Nation on the Anvil.* Boston, 1963.
Remeikis, Thomas. *Opposition to Soviet Rule in Lithuania, 1945–1980.* Chicago, 1980.
Stukas, Arthur. *Awakening of Lithuania.* New York, 1966.
Thomson, Clare. *The Singing Revolution: A Political Journey Through the Baltic States.* London, 1992.
Vardys, V. Stanley. *The Catholic Church: Dissent and Nationality in Lithuania.* Boulder, Colo., 1978.
Ziedonis, Arbids, et al., eds. *Problems of Mininations: Baltic Perspectives.* San Jose, Calif., 1973.

Bandung Conference (1955) The Bandung Conference in 1955 was the first major attempt by Third World non-aligned countries to establish a group identity and policy distinct from both the United States and Soviet Union. It also established communist China as a force in the Third World.

The seven-day conference of African and Asian countries in Bandung, Indonesia, started on April 17, 1955. The conference was sponsored by Indonesia, Burma, Ceylon, India and Pakistan, all of whom were dissatisfied both with the Eisenhower administration's insistence that Third World countries could not remain neutral in the Cold War and with

American reluctance to consult with their governments on Asian issues.

They also wanted to state their collective opposition to colonialism, especially French colonialism in North Africa, and were concerned that the increasing conflict between communist China and the United States could lead to a Third World War. Chinese premier CHOU EN-LAI made a personal appearance at the conference and used it to establish a firm Chinese foothold in the Third World by incorporating in the final communiqu his FIVE PRINCIPLES OF PEACEFUL COEXISTENCE, outlined the previous year during a visit to India. Chou also used the conference to hold out an olive branch to the United States, which led to an end to the first crisis over the QUEMOY AND MATSU ISLANDS.

The major debate, however, centered on the issue of whether Soviet actions in Eastern Europe were as abhorrent to Third World countries as was Western colonialism. The conference, whose attendees represented more than half of the world's population, surmounted the problem by condemning colonialism in "all its manifestations," thus implicitly attacking Soviet actions in Eastern Europe, Western European–controlled colonies, and the alleged economic colonialism of the United States.

The main points in the conference's final communiqu were as follows:

1. The countries at the conference agreed to exchange technical data "on the basis of mutual interest and respect for national sovereignty."
2. They urged the early establishment of a "special United Nations fund for economic development" and collective action for stabilizing international commodity prices.
3. The conference governments promised to "work for closer cultural cooperation," as it was "among the most powerful means of promoting understanding among nations."
4. The conference governments declared "full support" of the principles of "human rights" and "self-determination of peoples and nations" and attacked both Israel and South Africa for their policies.
5. The conference said that "colonialism in all its manifestations is an evil which should speedily be brought to an end."
6. The conference governments supported disarmament negotiations aimed at reducing nuclear weapons.

For Further Information:
Bairoch, Paul. *The Economic Development in the Third World Since 1900.* Los Angeles, 1975.
Brands, H.W. *The Specter of Neutralism: The United States and the Emergence of the Third World, 1947–1960.* New York, 1989.
Coppock, Joseph. *International Economic Instability.* New York, 1962.
Gardner, *In Pursuit of World Order.* New York, 1964.

Barnard, Chester I. (November 7, 1886–June 7, 1961) Chester Barnard was a government consultant on the control of atomic energy and weapons during the administration of President Harry Truman.

Barnard left Harvard after the end of his third year to join the American Telephone and Telegraph Company in 1909. By 1927 he had become president of the New Jersey Bell Telephone Company and had written several books on business organization.

In 1945 he was appointed a consultant to the U.S. representative on the United Nations Atomic Energy Commission and contributed to the Acheson-Lilienthal Report on Atomic Energy. After the report, Barnard worked on a commission concerned with the reorganization of the military. The commission, headed by Congressman Ferdinand Eberstadt of New York, uncovered serious waste and inefficiency in the military establishment.

Barnard became president of the Rockefeller Foundation in 1948 and held that post until 1952. Later he established a health code for the city of New York. He died in 1961.

For Further Information:
Lilienthal, David E. *The Journals of David E. Lilienthal: The Atomic Energy Years, 1945–1960.* New York, 1964.

Baruch, Bernard   (August 19, 1870–June 20, 1965)   Bernard Baruch was an important adviser on economics and foreign policy to successive American presidents and gave his name to the Baruch Plan, the world's first major nuclear disarmament proposal.

Baruch went from the College of the City of New York into the linen business and then to Wall Street, where he amassed a large fortune speculating in stocks. In 1916 he started his involvement in foreign affairs when he was appointed by President Woodrow Wilson to the Advisory Commission of the Council of National Defense. During World War I he was chairman of the War Industries Board and after that served as a member of the Supreme Economic Council at the Versailles Peace Conference.

During World War II President FRANKLIN ROOSEVELT sought Baruch's advice on mobilizing the American economy for the war effort. After the war, President HARRY TRUMAN sent him to the United Nations as the American delegate to the United Nations ATOMIC ENERGY COMMISSION, which was established on January 24, 1946. The U.S. proposals were put forward by Baruch at the commission's first meeting, in June 1946, and were thenceforward known as the Baruch Plan.

In his opening statement, Baruch said, "We are here to make a choice between the quick and the dead. That is our business. Behind the black portent of the new atomic age lies a hope which, seized upon with faith, can work our salvation. If we fail then we have damned every man to be the slave of fear."

The Baruch Plan proposed the creation of an international atomic development authority that would control all military-related atomic work; for a start, the United States would hand control of its atomic weapons over to the authority. The U.S.

government also agreed to stop production of atomic weapons as soon as adequate control machinery was in place. Under the Baruch Plan, an international atomic development authority would work with the UN Atomic Energy Commission, which would have the power to license and inspect all other activities in the atomic energy field.

The Baruch Plan was opposed by the Soviet Union, which demanded unilateral nuclear disarmament by the United States as a precondition for any agreement. The Soviet Union also proposed the establishment of two committees, the first to supervise the exchange of atomic information and the second to prevent the use of atomic energy "to the detriment of mankind."

Negotiations collapsed at the end of 1946 because of the Soviet refusal to accept inspections within its borders. The Soviet government also refused to accept the American proposal that no government be allowed to veto proposals by the international authorities. Some analysts believe that the Soviet Union sabotaged the negotiations because it was already well on the way to testing its first atomic weapon.

Baruch's influence within the Truman administration waned in later years. This was partly because of the failure of his disarmament proposals and partly because the conservative financier clashed with the president over the latter's deficit spending program. Baruch had a minimal role in the second Truman administration and in 1952 publicly backed the Republican presidential candidate, DWIGHT D. EISENHOWER, in protest against the economic policies of the Democratic candidate, Adlai Stevenson. Until his death in 1965, Baruch advised both Republican and Democratic presidents, but he focused his attention on his financial interests.

For Further Information:
Coit, Margaret L. *Mr. Baruch.* Boston, 1957.

Basic Law   The Basic Law, which came into force in the British, French and U.S. zones of occupation in Germany on May 23, 1949, in effect became the constitution of the Federal Republic of Germany. But it differed from most constitutions in that its preamble specifically stated that the law was for a "transitional period" until East and West Germany were reunited, and called on "the entire German people . . . to achieve in free self-determination the unity and freedom of Germany."

The constitution of the Federal Republic of Germany thus determined that the unity of Germany was the ultimate national goal and that the founding of the West German state was intended only as a transitional arrangement. The initial constitution of the German Democratic Republic contained a similar commitment to reunification, but this was dropped when the GDR constitution was amended in 1967.

The Basic Law had to be approved by the British, French and American military governors, and they insisted in a letter to KONRAD ADENAUER on May 12, 1949, that West Berlin be denied voting rights in the newly formed Bundestag (lower house of parliament) or Bundesrat (upper house) because of the complex and tense legal and diplomatic situation in the city. Article 23, however, did allow West Berlin to send 22 deputies to the Bundestag as non-voting members, and it was accepted that the laws of West Germany were applied in West Berlin, but only on the authority of the Western occupying powers.

Basic Treaty   (1972)   The Basic Treaty, signed on December 21, 1972, laid the legal foundations for relations between the Federal Republic of Germany (West Germany) and the German Democratic Republic (East Germany). As such it was one of the main elements of West Germany's OSTPOLITIK (Eastern Policy) and was recognized as making a major contribution to the reduction of East-West tensions.

Formal negotiations for a Basic Treaty started on March 19, 1970, when West German chancellor WILLY BRANDT met with East German premier Willi Stoph in Erfurt, East Germany. It was the first meeting between the leaders of the two Germanies. In Erfurt, Stoph presented a seven-point program demanding that the West German government relinquish its claim to the sole right of representation, cancel the HALLSTEIN DOCTRINE, recognize East Germany and its territorial integrity, renounce the use of force and pay alleged debts amounting to $25 billion.

Two months later, at Kassel, West Germany, the two men met again, and Brandt presented his 20 points, which called for relations between the two Germanies to be regulated on the basis of human rights, peaceful coexistence and nondiscrimination. Further points referred to the renunciation of force, to disarmament, respect of four-power rights, agreements on Berlin, travel and freedom of movement, reunification of families, and cooperation in border matters, transport, postal affairs, telecommunications, academic affairs, education, culture and trade relations.

At the same time, West Germany was already involved in negotiations with the Soviet Union and Poland, while Britain, France, the United States and the Soviet Union were negotiating the QUADRIPARTITE AGREEMENT on Berlin. East Germany had no choice but to join negotiations if it did not want to isolate itself from the general trend of East-West relations. On November 27, 1970, formal negotiations began between West German state secretary Egon Bahr and his East German counterpart Michael Kohl for a treaty on the basis of relations between the two German states.

The Quadripartite Agreement on Berlin went into effect on June 3, 1972. The same day, the West German Bundestag ratified treaties with Poland and the Soviet Union. These agreements acted as a spur to the negotiations between East Germany and West Germany, and on December 21, 1972, the Basic Treaty was signed in East Berlin. The main provisions of the treaty were:

1. The treaty presupposed the existence of two German states, but emphasized their divergent views "on basic questions, including the national question," thus allowing West Germany to remain officially committed to the reunification of Germany as stated in the preamble to the BASIC LAW of the Federal Republic.
2. "Good neighborly relations" were to be pursued on the "basis of equal rights."
3. Relations between the two Germanies were to be based on respect for each other's independence, "autonomy and territorial integrity, the right of self-determination, the protection of human rights and nondiscrimination."
4. The two Germanies agreed to settle any disputes by peaceful means and to "reaffirm the inviolability now and in the future of the frontier existing between them."
5. The two Germanies agreed that "neither of the two States can represent the other" at international organizations or meetings.
6. They agreed to promote peaceful relations between European states and to work for "complete disarmament under effective international control."
7. They accepted that their legal systems were separate and could be applied only within their own territories.
8. The two Germanies agreed to regulate "practical and humanitarian questions" and to "conclude agreements with a view to developing and promoting . . . for their mutual benefit cooperation in the fields of economics, science and technology, transport, judicial relations, posts and telecommunications, health, culture, sport, environment protection and in other fields."
9. The two Germanies agreed to exchange permanent diplomatic missions.

The Basic Treaty provided the foundation for more than 100 treaties, arrangements, protocols and declarations between the governments of the Federal Republic and the German Democratic Republic. They covered, among other things, family reunification, improvements regarding visits in connection with urgent family matters, travel for people living in the border areas, improvements in the transport of noncommercial goods, working conditions for journalists, health and veterinary affairs, noncommercial payments, athletic exchanges, individual transport matters, the handling of damages resulting from auto accidents and the fixing of fees for the use of transit routes, reciprocal exemption from traffic taxes and fees, transport-related construction projects, improvement of the Teltow Canal in Berlin, and construction work on waterways and railways through Each Germany.

For Further Information:
Fritsch-Bournazel, Renata. *Confronting the German Question.* Oxford, 1980.
Griffiths, William. *The Ostpolitik of the Federal Republic of Germany.* Amherst, Mass., 1978.
Pfetsch, Frank. *West German Internal Structures and External Policies: Foreign Policy of the Federal Republic.* New York, 1988.
Viola, T. *Willy Brandt.* London, 1989.
Whetten, Lawrence. *Germany East and West.* New York, 1980.

Batista, Fulgencio **(January 16, 1901–August 6, 1973)**
Fulgencio Batista was a dictator in Cuba during the 1950s.
His corrupt rule created fertile political conditions for the rise
of FIDEL CASTRO.

Batista was born into an impoverished Cuban family. He
enlisted in the Cuban Army in 1921 and rose to the rank of
sergeant. In September 1933, with U.S. support, he headed a
coup that overthrew the dictator Gerardo Machado y Mo-
rales. Between 1933 and 1940 Batista was content to remain
the man behind the throne, but in 1940 he had himself elected
president in a rigged ballot.

Batista's first term of office was marred by corruption,
patronage and some political assassinations, but while he
enriched himself and his friends he also initiated a massive
public works program and expanded the educational system.

In 1944 Batista retired from office to travel and invest his
illicit earnings abroad. While he was out of office corruption
soared out of control in Cuba, and he was widely welcomed
when he returned to power in 1952 after an army coup. But
the welcome quickly soured when it became clear that his
second administration was particularly brutal and corrupt.
Batista forged close links with the American underworld, and
the country became noted for its brothels, drugs and gambling, out of which the dictator took a substantial cut. To stifle
dissent, Batista maintained strict press censorship and imprisoned, exiled or assassinated political opponents.

The conditions created by Batista's dictatorship made the
country ripe for the popular revolution started by Fidel Castro
after his return to Cuba from exile in December 1956. In
interviews with the American press Castro promised free
elections, social reform and an end to corruption. This won
him popular support within the United States and this, plus
the brutality of Batista's regime, made it impossible for the
Eisenhower administration to support Batista, even after the
CIA reported that Castro's July 26 Movement had been
infiltrated by communists.

Throughout 1958, the United States remained aloof from
the civil war in Cuba. American arms shipments to Castro
were seized by U.S. customs officials, and official American
military supplies to Batista were suspended in March 1958. In
December 1958 events swung dramatically in Castro's favor
when a large contingent of Batista's forces deserted to Castro's
ranks during an attack on Santa Clara, the capital of Las Villas
province. On January 1, 1959, Batista fled to the Dominican
Republic. He later went into exile in Portugal.

For Further Information:
Batista, Fulgencio. *Cuba Betrayed.* New York, 1962.
Chester, E.A. *Sergeant Named Batista.* New York, 1954.
Williams, William Appleman. *The United States, Cuba and Castro.*
New York, 1962.

Bay of Pigs The Bay of Pigs was the landing area on the
south coast of Cuba for an abortive American-organized
invasion of the island by Cuban exiles in 1961. The complete

failure of the invasion was a political setback for President
JOHN F. KENNEDY and for American attempts to overthrow
Cuban leader FIDEL CASTRO.

The United States originally welcomed the Cuban revolution that brought Fidel Castro to power on December 31,
1958. But his nationalization of American properties throughout 1959 and 1960 and increasing political, military and
economic links with the Soviet Union led to a breach with
the Eisenhower administration. On March 17, 1960, President DWIGHT EISENHOWER ordered the CIA to "organize the
training of Cuban exiles, mainly in Guatemala, against a
possible future date when they might return to their homeland."

The original plan was that a group of guerrillas would land
at an isolated spot on the Cuban shore and establish a provisional government on Cuban soil. At the same time, dissidents within Cuba would launch a series of acts of sabotage
against power stations and other vulnerable targets. It was
believed that the combination of the landings and the sabotage would lead to a general uprising among the Cuban people
and defections from the armed forces.

All the guerrillas would be drawn from the Cuban exiles
who had fled Castro's regime. It was essential that American
involvement in the plot be kept secret: If it became known,
the United States risked Soviet retaliation in Berlin and would
be correctly accused of violating the OAS charter, which
bound the American states to respect each other's sovereign
territory.

Much of the planning, development and training was conducted between November 1960 and January 1961, when
both President Eisenhower and president-elect Kennedy were
absorbed in the transfer of power. Kennedy was told about the
plan by CIA director ALLEN DULLES on November 29 and gave
his approval to continue the training of the Cuban exiles, but
he paid little attention to the plot until after his inauguration.
The result was that major political decisions about the invasion plan were either delayed or made by CIA officers already
committed to the project.

In February 1961, shortly after his inauguration, President
Kennedy asked the Joint Chiefs of Staff to assess the invasion
plan. The Joint Chiefs, working on the premise that the Castro
government was genuinely unpopular, concluded that it was
impossible for a 1,400-strong invasion force to defeat Castro's
200,000-strong army, but that it could succeed if there was a
general uprising. The Joint Chiefs added that, even if the
invasion failed, it would contribute to the climate of dissatisfaction on the island.

According to Arthur Schlesinger, Kennedy's biographer,
the president remained skeptical about the plan but in March
was forced into a decision when Guatemalan president Miguel
Ydigoras demanded that the Cuban exiles leave his country
by the end of April. At the same time, the CIA reported that
on June 1 the Cubans would receive a large delivery of Soviet
MiG fighter aircraft, which would render the invasion plan
obsolete. Kennedy was also faced with the problem of how to

demobilize the Cuban brigade if he decided against the plan. On March 11, 1961, Kennedy gave the go-ahead to the plan, although he retained the right to cancel it on 24 hours' notice.

On April 10, 1961, American advisers started moving the Cuban brigade out of Guatemala in preparation for an attack on April 17. The men were told that they were to seize and hold for three days three beaches along 40 miles of the Bay of Pigs area. Paratroopers would be dropped inland to gain control of the roads through the swamps, air attacks from Nicaragua on the Cuban Air Force would disable its planes on the ground and a further group of 1,000 dissidents would join the invaders soon after landing.

On April 15 the first air strikes were carried out, but only five planes were destroyed. A second air strike was necessary, but at the last minute it was canceled because the first attack had generated widespread international opposition at the United Nations. This immediately put the attacking Cuban brigades at risk.

When the invasion force arrived on April 17, they found Castro's defense forces waiting for them. Intelligence reports had informed them of the likelihood of the attack, and the air strike confirmed its imminence. The paratroopers landed inland and were quickly isolated and defeated, permitting Castro's tanks to secure control of the roads through the swamps to the beachhead. The bulk of the invasion force at the beachhead immediately encountered heavy resistance. Early on, a Cuban aircraft sank the ship carrying the ammunition and communication equipment, and the ferocity of the Cuban air attack meant that the other ships had to quickly return to sea, leaving the Cuban brigade on the beach without any naval backup. The invaders' air support of four B-26 fighter-bombers was also quickly wiped out by Castro's air force. The possibility of a general uprising was quelled by the immediate mass arrest of 200,000 suspected dissidents.

Within 24 hours it became clear to President Kennedy and other officials in Washington that the mission was in serious jeopardy. On April 19, Kennedy agreed to deploy six unmarked American aircraft to help defend the Cuban brigade's B-26 planes flying from Nicaragua. However, because of a mix-up over timing, the B-26 aircraft arrived at the targets an hour before the American air convoy and encountered heavy fire.

Exiled Cuban leaders in the United States then pressed the Kennedy administration for full-scale American intervention. But by April 20 the invasion force had been completely defeated and its members were either dead or imprisoned.

It was impossible to keep American involvement a secret, and the international opposition increased as the extent of U.S. involvement became more apparent. Within Western Europe there was disappointment in Kennedy, whom many had hoped would retreat from the Cold War interventionist policies of the Eisenhower administration. At the height of the invasion, on April 18, Soviet leader NIKITA KHRUSHCHEV sent a protest note to Kennedy and pledged "all necessary assistance" to Castro. It has been calculated by some that Kennedy's perceived indecisiveness during the Bay of Pigs encouraged Khrushchev to deploy nuclear-armed missiles in Cuba.

The aftermath of the Bay of Pigs invasion saw a series of political and military post mortems to determine the causes of the failure. A report by General Maxwell Taylor that concentrated on the military aspects of the fiasco concluded that one of the main causes had been a gross underestimation of Castro's defense forces and of the Cuban leader's grip on power. A State Department report concluded that the wrong political decisions were made because no expert advice was sought outside a small group of presidential advisers.

Kennedy publicly took full responsibility for the disaster, but privately he seethed against the CIA and forced its top leadership into retirement: Dulles, RICHARD BISSELL and Gen. Charles P. Cabell. For their part, many senior CIA officers and Cuban exiles never forgave Kennedy for his failure to give the invasion full U.S. military support.

For Further Information
Beschloss, Michael R. *The Crisis Years: Kennedy and Khrushchev, 1960–1963.* New York, 1991.
Bonsal, Philip W. *Cuba, Castro and the United States.* Pittsburgh, 1971.
Dulles, Allen W. *The Craft of Intelligence.* New York, 1963.
Higgins, Trumbull. *The Perfect Failure: Kennedy, Eisenhower, and the CIA at the Bay of Pigs.* New York, 1987.
Matthews, Herbert Lionel. *Revolution in Cuba: An Essay in Understanding.* New York, 1975.
Nezerik, A.G. *Cuba and the United States.* New York, 1963.
Williams, William Appleman. *The United States, Cuba and Castro.* New York, 1962.

Belgium   Belgium has been one of the main Western European states behind the formation of the North Atlantic Treaty Organization (NATO) and greater European political and economic integration. It plays host to the headquarters of both the European Community and NATO.

Sandwiched between France and Germany, the flat territory of Belgium lies in the middle of the natural invasion route between the two. As a result, Belgium has been invaded and occupied twice during the 20th century. For this reason, successive postwar Belgian governments have made Western European integration the major pillar of their foreign policy in the belief that a more closely integrated Western Europe would make war between France and Germany less likely.

A corollary to this policy has been the encouragement of closer defense relations with the United States, until Western Europe is in a position to replace the American defense guarantee. This policy found its first expression in 1944 when the Belgian government-in-exile in London joined with its Dutch and Luxembourgian counterparts in a Benelux Customs Union, which took effect in 1948. In 1960 the customs union was succeeded by the Benelux Economic Union, and in 1970 border controls between the three countries were abolished.

A key figure in the formation of the customs union was Belgian foreign minister PAUL-HENRI SPAAK. In 1947 he became prime minister and played a leading role in negotiating the BRUSSELS TREATY of 1948, which established a regional defense alliance among Britain, France and the Benelux countries. The Brussels Treaty demonstrated a Western European commitment to a common defense, a move regarded as essential to draw American support for the defense of Western Europe. This was accomplished with the signing of the North Atlantic Treaty in 1949, which established NATO.

During the negotiations for the Brussels Treaty, Belgium urged the other countries to expand the military nature of the agreement to include economic, social and cultural aspects as well. Spaak argued that the solution to Europe's problems lay in the formation of a "United States of Europe." He went on to play a leading role in several organizations for European union, including the COUNCIL OF EUROPE, the EUROPEAN COAL AND STEEL COMMUNITY and the EUROPEAN ECONOMIC COMMUNITY.

As part of its policy of encouraging European union, Belgium offered Brussels as the home for the European Commission (the administrative arm of the EC) and for NATO (after the French withdrawal).

Belgium also makes a small but significant contribution to NATO forces. In 1989 its armed forces totalled 92,400, including 25,000 personnel deployed at forward bases in West Germany. The small Belgian Navy of four frigates was completely under the command of the NATO naval command for the English Channel. Brussels, along with the Netherlands, also plays a major role in NATO strategy as European receiving point for military supplies and troops from the United States, Canada and Britain.

In 1979, NATO foreign ministers agreed to deploy 572 U.S. cruise and PERSHING II missiles in Western Europe in response to the Soviet deployment of a new generation of intermediate-range nuclear forces. Belgium was earmarked to receive 48 of the Cruise missiles. The decision provoked opposition from the country's antinuclear lobby, and there were major, anti-U.S. and antinuclear demonstrations in Brussels. To forestall a crisis, the Belgian government persuaded NATO to delay installation of the missiles until 1985. The issue was raised again in 1983, and at a two-day debate in November the government of Wilfred Martens won the right to make a final decision on deployment without further consultation of parliament. The missiles were finally deployed in 1984 and 1985 but were withdrawn after the signing of the U.S.-Soviet INTERMEDIATE RANGE NUCLEAR FORCES (INF) TREATY in December 1987.

For Further Information:
Cleveland, Harold Van B. *The Atlantic Idea and Its European Rivals.* New York, 1966.
Florinsky, Michael T. *Integrated Europe.* New York, 1955.
Grosser, Alfred. *The Western Alliance.* New York, 1978.
Meade, J.E. *Negotiations for Benelux.* Princeton, 1957.

Benes, Edvard   See CZECHOSLOVAKIA.

Bentley, Elizabeth   (1908–December 3, 1963)   Elizabeth Bentley was a self-confessed communist whose testimony before congressional committees led to the dismissal or discrediting of a number of government officials, including former assistant treasury secretary HARRY DEXTER WHITE and ALGER HISS.

Bentley was from a moderately well-off family and attended Vassar College and Columbia University. In 1933 she visited Italy to study at the University of Florence, and she was so appalled at the fascist government of Benito Mussolini that she joined the Communist Party upon her return to America in 1935.

Shortly after joining the Communist party, Bentley became romantically involved with Soviet agent Jacob Golos and herself began spying for the Soviet Union in 1940, using the cover of journalism. But after the death of Golos in 1943, she became disenchanted with communism and in May 1945 began working for the Federal Bureau of Investigation as a double agent.

In July 1948, Bentley appeared before the Senate Expenditures Committee and the House Un-American Activities Committee. She testified that she had been a member of two Soviet espionage groups; one was headed by Nathan Gregory Silvermaster, a former government employee, and the other by Victor Perlo, a member of the War Production Board during World War II. Bentley said that the groups had coordinated a number of Soviet espionage agents in Washington, D.C. and that she herself had collected secret military, diplomatic and economic information from top government sources, including Lauchlin Currie, a top wartime aide of President FRANKLIN D. ROOSEVELT; Commerce Department official William Remington; Harry Dexter White; and Alger Hiss. Bentley claimed to have received information directly from about 20 government employees and indirectly from 20 White House, State Department, Treasury, and defense officials.

All those implicated by Bentley's testimony denied the allegations. President HARRY TRUMAN characterized the anticommunist hearing and, by direct implication, Bentley's testimony, a "red herring" designed to distract attention from the failings of the Republican-controlled Congress. However, a number of the officials named by Bentley were dismissed from their posts, and some were proven to have belonged to communist cells.

In 1951 Bentley published her autobiography, *Out of Bondage,* in which she said she was prompted to leave the Communist Party by the activities of "gangster type" Soviet agents. During the 1950s, Bentley worked as a teacher and lectured on communism. She died after surgery for an abdominal tumor in December 1963.

For Further Information:
Barron, John. *KGB: The Secret Work of Soviet Agents.* New York, 1974.
Bentley, Elizabeth. *Out of Bondage.* New York, 1951.

Carpozi, G. *Red Spies in the U.S.* New Rochelle, N.Y., 1974.
Dallin, David J. *Soviet Espionage.* New Haven, Conn., 1953.
Newman, J. "Famous Soviet Spies," *U.S. News and World Report,* 1974.

Beria, Lavrenty Pavlovich   (March 29, 1899–December 23, 1953)

As head of internal security in the Soviet Union, Lavrenty Beria personified the ruthless dictatorship of JOSEF STALIN in the early years of the Cold War. Following the death of Stalin, Beria tried but failed to seize power. His arrest, trial and execution played a major part in the de-Stalinization of the Soviet Union.

Born in Georgia, Beria joined the Communist Party shortly before it came to power in 1917. He was soon drawn into intelligence and counterintelligence work and in 1921 was appointed head of the Georgian security police. He was named party leader in the Transcaucasian provinces in 1931 and played the major role in incorporating those provinces into the Soviet Union. As a reward, in 1938 Beria was sent to Moscow and placed in charge of the Comissariat for Internal Affairs.

This position placed him in charge of the Stalinist purges, which had started earlier in the decade and resulted in the deaths of millions. Beria himself instituted a purge of the police force. During World War II, Beria was promoted to deputy prime minister and played a major role in armaments production while continuing to supervise the security system. After the war, in 1946, Beria was elevated to the Politburo. He had been a member of the Central Committee from 1934.

Beria played a major part in directing subversive activities in Western Europe and in coordinating Communist Party activities in Eastern Europe, especially in countries, such as Romania, Czechoslovakia and Hungary, that did not emerge from the war with communist governments. Once a communist government was installed, Beria saw to it that a Soviet KGB agent was placed in a high-ranking position within the intelligence organization of each country and that the intelligence organizations were closely modeled on those of the Soviet Union.

In the final years of Stalin's life, Beria himself is believed to have become a target of the dictator's paranoia, and a mass purge of the party organization in Georgia is believed to have been directed at Beria. After Stalin's death in March 1953, Beria tried to engineer a coup. He failed, but he emerged as one of the four deputy prime ministers who succeeded to power in the immediate post-Stalin period. Beria was believed to be second only to GEORGI MALENKOV and retained control of security policy.

In July 1953 Beria was arrested, stripped of all his government and party posts, and placed on trial for "criminal anti-party and antistate activities." A statement in the government newspaper *Pravda* said that he tried "to put the Soviet Ministry of the Interior above Party and Government." Beria was sentenced to death and executed in December 1953.

Beria's fall from power coincided with the 1953 anti-communist uprising in East Germany. Some analysts have suggested that Beria clashed with fellow Politburo members, especially the emerging NIKITA KHRUSHCHEV, over Soviet policy in East Germany. He was believed to favor easing political restrictions, and it has been suggested that Beria proposed withdrawal from East Germany. After Beria's arrest, Soviet policy in East Germany hardened considerably.

For Further Information:
Barron, John. *KGB: The Secret Work of Secret Agents.* New York, 1974.
Dallin, David J. *Soviet Espionage.* New Haven, Conn., 1953.
Fairbanks, Charles. *National Cadres as a Force in the Soviet System: The Evidence of Beria's Career.* New York, 1978.
Khrushchev, Nikita. *Khrushchev Remembers.* Boston, 1970.
Lawrence, John. *Beria.* London, 1953.
Wittlin, Thaddeus. *Commissar: The Life and Death of Lavrenti Pavlovitch Beria.* New York, 1973.

Berle, Adolf A.   (January 29, 1895–February 17, 1971)

Adolf Berle was a leading American in the development of policy toward Latin America from the TRUMAN to the KENNEDY administrations.

Berle graduated from Harvard University in 1913 and went on to Harvard Law School. During World War I, he served in Army intelligence and attended the Versailles Peace Conference. After the war he returned to private law practice and lecturing at various universities.

In the early 1930s Berle was an adviser to FRANKLIN D. ROOSEVELT and, after Roosevelt's election to the presidency, helped to draft some of the early New Deal legislation. In 1938 he was appointed assistant secretary of state for Latin American affairs and started a long relationship with that region of the world. Berle remained assistant secretary of state until 1945, when he was sent for a year to Brazil as ambassador.

Berle was a proponent of hemispheric solidarity and neutrality and played an important role in negotiating the 1947 RIO PACT, the first postwar regional defense alliance. The pact stipulated that an attack against any signatory nation would be considered an attack against all, but it added that signatories would not be required to use their armed forces without their consent. The defense pact was reaffirmed the following year when the ORGANIZATION OF AMERICAN STATES was formed to administer it.

Berle returned to his private law practice and teaching in 1947 but maintained his interest in and contacts with Latin America. In March 1953, after meeting with Latin American leaders, Berle produced a secret report for President DWIGHT D. EISENHOWER on the left-wing Guatemalan government of Jacobo Arbenz, focusing on the "precise problem of how to clear out the Communists." Berle rejected direct intervention to overthrow Arbenz but suggested "a good deal of quiet work." His proposals were largely accepted by the Eisenhower administration.

In November 1960, president-elect JOHN F. KENNEDY asked Berle to head a six-man task force to make recommendations on Latin American problems and U.S. foreign policy toward the region. The task force's recommendations led to the administration's ALLIANCE FOR PROGRESS.

Berle was vehemently opposed to FIDEL CASTRO's government in Cuba and in his report stated that communists intended to "convert the Latin American social revolution into a Marxist attack on the United States itself." Berle's answer to this perceived threat was to reduce U.S. support for right-wing dictatorships and increase support for democratic and progressive elements. He also advocated a MARSHALL PLAN for Latin America.

Berle himself took no active part in the planning of the abortive BAY OF PIGS invasion, but he was used by Kennedy in the aftermath as an emissary to try to improve relations with the Cuban exiles and various Latin American countries. Berle left the government in July 1961 but remained active in Latin American affairs as a private citizen until his death.

For Further Information:

Berle, Adolf. *Latin America: Diplomacy and Reality*. New York, 1962.

Berle, Beatrice Bishop, and Travis Beal Jacobs, eds. *Navigating the Rapids, 1919–1971: From the Papers of Adolf A. Berle*. New York, 1973.

Burr, Robert N. *Our Troubled Hemisphere: Perspectives on United States–Latin American Relations*. Washington, D.C., 1967.

Morrison, De Lesseps S. *Latin American Mission: An Adventure in Hemisphere Diplomacy*. New York, 1965.

Berlin   Berlin was at the forefront of Cold War politics from 1945, a divided city that was a Western enclave in the heart of Eastern Europe. As such it was a magnet for disgruntled East Germans, and this led first to the BERLIN BLOCKADE and later to the erection of the BERLIN WALL. In the era of dtente, relations between the two halves of Berlin came to be regarded as a barometer of East–West relations, and the reunification of the city signaled the end of the Cold War.

At a meeting of Allied foreign ministers in London in 1944, it was agreed that both Germany and its capital would be divided into occupation zones. The agreement took effect upon the surrender of the Third Reich. The Soviet Union took the districts of Prenzlauer Berg, Berlin Mitte, Friedrichshain, Kopenick, Treptow, Lichtenberg, Weissensee and Pankow as its occupation zone. The U.S. occupied the districts of Zehlendorf, Steglitz, Tempelhof, Neukolln, Kreuzberg and Schoneberg; and the British sector included the central and western districts of the Tiergarten, Kurfrstendamm, Spandau, Charlottenburg and Wilmersdorf. The French were later allowed to occupy the Reinickendorf and Wedding districts.

Technically, the whole of Berlin was administered by the Allied Control Council on which representatives from each of the four occupying powers sat. But in practice, the Soviets introduced their own communist political and economic system in their sector (as they did in East Germany), and the Western powers introduced a Western political system in their sector. Thus Berlin was divided between two competing political systems, each becoming a showcase for its respective sponsors.

As early as 1945, the Western-occupied zones of Berlin became both a magnet and an escape route for East Europeans fleeing Stalinist persecution. Hundreds of thousands of East Europeans made it first to East Berlin and then crossed the still open border into West Berlin, whence they were able to secure passage to Western Europe, the U.S. or Canada. This exodus was both a major political embarrassment and a drain on the economies of Eastern Europe, as the refugees were usually young and well-educated. The Soviet Union set out to plug this gap, either by forcing the Western powers to withdraw from Berlin or by preventing East Europeans from entering the western half of the city.

The Western powers, for their part, were equally determined to remain in Berlin, for political, military and intelligence reasons. Withdrawal would have been interpreted as defeat and this was politically impossible for the Western governments. Militarily, the 10,000 Western troops in Berlin were vastly outnumbered, but they served a useful purpose as a tripwire, which became invaluable to the NATO forces based in West Germany. Berlin also quickly became an important listening post for Western intelligence services.

However, in negotiating their presence in Berlin, the Western powers made a major tactical error in failing to negotiate a formal agreement for access to West Berlin through Soviet-controlled East Germany. This presented the Soviets with their first opportunity to try to force the withdrawal of Western forces in Berlin—the Berlin Blockade.

The Berlin Blockade was the first major Cold War confrontation in Germany. It was also the first major Cold War defeat for the Soviet Union in East Germany. It involved the Soviet Union closing all land routes from the Western-occupied sectors of Germany to Berlin. Britain and the United States responded with a massive airlift in order to retain their toehold in the middle of the Soviet sector.

Possibly more than any other event of the Cold War, the Berlin Blockade drove governments, parties and individuals into opposing political camps. During the 320-day siege, the political foundations were laid for the governments of East and West Germany and East and West Berlin. The Council of Europe (political forebear of the European Economic Community) and its East European equivalent, the Council for Mutual Economic Assistance (CMEA or COMECON), were established. And, in the last few months of the blockade, the NORTH ATLANTIC TREATY ORGANIZATION was established.

The Berlin Blockade came as the result of years of escalating disagreements between the Soviet Union and the Western powers over the economic and political structure of postwar Germany. The Western powers became convinced in 1948 that the Soviet Union had no intention of reaching an agreement. They went ahead with laying the foundations for what was later to become the Federal Republic of Germany.

An integral part of the Western plans was a common currency for the three Western sectors. The Soviet Union decided to make its stand on the currency issue and let it be known that Western insistence on introducing its currency could lead to a blockade of Berlin.

The four occupying powers failed in a last-ditch effort in Berlin on June 22 to solve the currency crisis. During this meeting the Soviets claimed that Berlin was a Russian-zone city where Americans, British and French were merely guests. After the meeting Marshal Vasily D. Sokolovsky decreed a separate currency reform for the Soviet sector, including all of Berlin. On June 23, the Western Powers announced that their new currency would be introduced in the western sectors of Berlin.

On June 24 the Soviets banned all shipments of any kind from West Germany to Berlin. They also cut off all electric power to the U.S., British and French sectors. Sokolovsky announced that the four-power government of Berlin was "factually dead."

The Western powers were faced with the problem of keeping alive 2,500,000 people in the western sector of Berlin. At the start of the blockade there was sufficient food for 35 days and coal for 45 days. It was estimated that the American and British transports would need to supply 4,500 tons daily in order to maintain the civilian population and occupation forces.

An airlift, codenamed "Operation Vittles," was immediately started by the British and Americans. At the height of the airlift, nearly 13,000 tons of food, fuel and other goods were ferried into Berlin daily. Over 200,000 flights were made by British and American planes over 15 months, carrying a million and a half tons of supplies.

The blockade was finally lifted on May 12, 1949. In return the Western powers agreed to a Four-Power meeting of foreign ministers on May 23 to discuss all questions related to Germany's future. The Soviets dropped their insistence on the adoption of a common Berlin currency and on the suspension of the plan for a West German government.

Many analysts believe that the clear Western victory marked the beginning of the end of the Soviet Cold War offensive in Western Europe. It also confirmed Berlin as the chief pawn in the East-West conflict.

Continued popular dissatisfaction with Soviet rule in East Berlin was underscored by the EAST GERMAN UPRISING of June 1953. The uprising came three months after the death of JOSEF STALIN and shortly after the East German government an-

German children watch the arrival of an American transport plane in West Berlin. In June 1948, after Russian and East German troops blockaded Berlin's Western sector, President Truman ordered the U.S. Air Force to fly in supplies to the beleaguered city.

nounced that real wages would be reduced. This was offset by an easing of political restrictions.

This carrot-and-stick approach resulted in a series of strikes expressing the popular response that the political and economic changes were too little and the drop in real wages unacceptable. On June 16 2,000 demonstrators demanded to see East German Communist Party leader WALTER ULBRICHT. When he failed to appear, what most observers claim was a spontaneous cry was broadcast on West Berlin radio and television for a general strike on June 17.

Tens of thousands of workers went on strike and mass demonstrations took place throughout East Berlin. However, the uprising was quickly put down by Soviet troops. In East Berlin tanks chased the crowd down the main boulevard, the Unter den Linden, and at least one demonstrator was crushed under the treads.

The importance of Berlin as an intelligence outpost for the West was indicated by the BERLIN TUNNEL. The tunnel was a CIA-financed wiretap into the headquarters of the Soviet Army in Berlin and operated from 1954 until it was discovered in April 1956.

The Berlin issue remained relatively dormant from the death of Stalin until 1958, as Soviet politicians concentrated their efforts on jockeying for power. NIKITA KHRUSHCHEV emerged as the undisputed leader in 1957 and proceeded to introduce a series of economic reforms within the Soviet Union. These were opposed by the Stalinist old guard, but he managed to win concessions on domestic issues by taking a harder line on foreign policy, especially in regard to Berlin.

After the 1953 uprising, the importance of West Berlin as an escape route increased as the Soviets and East Germans closed the East-West German border with barbed wire and machine-gun nests. But the Berlin border remained open between 1954 and 1961, under the terms of the 1949 Four-Power agreement, which stipulated that forces of Britain, the United States, the Soviet Union and France could travel anywhere in the city. As a result, an estimated 2,750,000 East Europeans flooded across the Berlin border between 1954 and 1961. The East German authorities tried to stop the flood by introducing stiff passport regulations, threatening imprisonment and confiscating the property of those who attempted to escape or helped others to escape. But none of these measures worked.

Khrushchev, under strong pressure to succeed where Stalin had failed, decided to try again to force Western withdrawal from Berlin. On November 10, 1958, he declared the Soviet Union's intention to sign a separate peace treaty with the East German government and demanded Western withdrawal from Berlin.

The demand for withdrawal was immediately rejected by U.S. secretary of state John Foster Dulles, and a statement from the West German government on November 12 warned that Soviet abrogation of the four-power Berlin statute would "constitute a threat to the freedom" of Berlin and would increase "the already tense situation in the world."

The temperature was heightened on November 14 by a follow-up statement from Khrushchev in which he warned that the Soviet Union was preparing "definite proposals" for the termination of the allied administration in Berlin. But he also added: "we are not saying that we will go to war against the West" over the issue but "if the aggressors attack the Soviet Union [or] the Socialist countries, they will be crushingly repulsed."

On November 27, Khrushchev backed away slightly from his initial demands and amended his plans by proposing that West Berlin become a demilitarized "free city" independent of either East or West Germany. He also warned that the Soviet Union would turn all Soviet occupation functions over to the East German government at the end of six months if the Western powers did not accept the free city proposal.

This proposal was also rejected by Britain and the United States, whose governments argued that a free city in West Berlin, without Western political and military guarantees, would soon be absorbed by East Germany. The Eisenhower administration thus began to strengthen American military forces in Germany in preparation for the deadline on May 27, 1959.

Khrushchev gradually backed away from his hardline position and indefinitely postponed the May deadline. Unable to force Western withdrawal he then set in motion plans to prevent the exodus to the West by blocking the escape route to West Berlin. On August 12, 1961, the East German parliament passed a decree to seal the border. At three minutes past midnight on August 13, 1961, East German troops and police occupied the crossing points on the East Berlin side of the border, tore up the streets and installed roadblocks and barbed wire barricades.

The action caught the West completely by surprise. The Kennedy administration was not certain whether the barricades were designed effectively to imprison the people of East Germany or whether they were meant only to control the embarrassing flood of refugees. In case the latter represented the new Soviet policy, President Kennedy took an initially cautious stand, although Secretary of State DEAN RUSK attacked the barricades as a violation of the 1949 agreement and said that the flight of refugees from east to west was the result not of Western propaganda but of the failure of communism in East Germany. The people, said Rusk, "voted with their feet."

The construction of the actual Berlin Wall did not begin until August 17. At first it was only a six-foot wall topped, in most places, with barbed wire. Even then, the East German and Soviet authorities continued to allow some limited movement between sectors in order to lead the Kennedy administration into the belief that the wall was a temporary aberration. By the time the West realized that the wall was meant to be a permanent barrier, it was too late to pull it down without risking a nuclear war.

In the meantime, the Soviet and East German authorities

A portion of the Berlin Wall in late September 1961, when workers began to reinforce the hastily-built structure.

moved to strengthen the wall. It was rebuilt and reinforced with guard dog patrols, machine-gun nests, flood lights and observation turrets. By 1980 the barrier was more than 850 miles long. East Europeans, however, continued to attempt to cross it. Between 1961 and 1981 there were 37,800 successful escapes through, over or under the wall. These included 466 guards on duty. There have been over a hundred confirmed cases of people killed trying to climb the wall.

Tension in Berlin surfaced again during the CUBAN MISSILE CRISIS. It was generally accepted within the Kennedy administration that the Soviets linked Cuba and Berlin and that tough action against Cuba could result in a Soviet invasion of West Berlin. Conversely, tough NATO action in Berlin could contribute to a Soviet withdrawal from Cuba. In line with this argument, Attorney General Robert Kennedy at one point during the missile crisis proposed bringing countervailing pressure to bear on the Soviets by basing nuclear missiles in Berlin. Khrushchev's failure to place the missiles in Cuba or secure Western withdrawal from Berlin were major factors in his fall from power.

Throughout the 1960s, East-West tensions in Berlin gradually eased and after the election of WILLY BRANDT as West German chancellor in 1969, the situation improved dramatically as Brandt put his OSTPOLITIK policy into effect. On September 3, 1971, the U.S., Britain, France and the Soviet Union signed the QUADRIPARTITE AGREEMENT on Berlin, which regularized West Berlin's postwar status and removed the

constant Soviet threat that had been hanging over the western sector of the city since the end of World War II.

The agreement pledged the signatory powers to strive to promote "elimination of tension and prevention of complications" in the "relevant area." It also obliged the signers to relinquish the "use or threat of force" in solving problems relating to Berlin and to see to it that the document was not "changed unilaterally."

The text also affirmed that although West Berlin would "continue not to be a constituent part of the Federal Republic of Germany" its ties with West Germany would "be maintained and developed." The Soviets also promised to improve "communications" between the two halves of Berlin and to allow visits "for compassionate, family, religious, cultural or commercial reasons, or as tourists."

The four governments agreed to "mutually respect their individual and joint rights and responsibilities, which remain unchanged." The Soviets pledged not to block traffic through East Germany to West Berlin. West Germany was also allowed to perform consular services for West Berlin and represent it at international meetings.

The Quadripartite Agreement paved the way for a number of agreements between the East and West Berlin governments on such issues as sewage, water supply and other municipal matters. The increased contact at official levels contributed to the general improvement in East-West relations.

In 1988 and 1989 presidents RONALD REAGAN and GEORGE BUSH called on Soviet leader MIKHAIL GORBACHEV to end the Cold War symbolically by pulling down the Berlin Wall. During a visit to West Germany in June 1989, Gorbachev said "nothing is eternal" and that the wall had been built for a specific purpose and not out of evil intention. He added: "The wall could disappear once the conditions that generated the need for it disappear. I do not see much of a problem here."

However, the East German government of hardline communist ERICH HONECKER remained totally committed to the maintenance of the Berlin Wall and orthodox communist economic and political policies. Many East Germans, however, continued to reject communism and in 1989, when the Hungarians opened their border with Austria, an estimated 50,000 East Germans took advantage of the standing offer of West German citizenship to flee to West Germany through Hungary and Austria. Thousands of other East Germans sought sanctuary in the West German embassies in Prague and Warsaw, and the East German government was forced reluctantly to allow them to immigrate to the West through East Germany. Honecker tried to apply pressure on other East European governments to close their borders to prevent the exodus of East Germans.

But the other East European governments ignored Honecker, whose hardline policies had left him increasingly isolated within the Warsaw Pact. Hundreds of thousands of East Germans took to the streets to demand Honecker's resignation.

In October 1989, Honecker resigned as president and

In late 1989 and 1990 the Berlin Wall was demolished, symbolically ending the Cold War. Photo courtesy of German Ministry of Foreign Affairs.

leader of the East German Communist Party. He was quickly succeeded by Egon Krenz who, on November 9, 1989, ordered the end of restrictions on emigration or travel to the West. Millions of East Berliners poured into West Berlin and West Berliners poured across the top of the Berlin Wall. The next day, the East German government started knocking holes in the wall to accommodate the human flood. Demolition of the wall continued throughout 1990.

On November 12, 1989, ambassadors from the four occupying powers met for the first time in 18 years to discuss relinquishing their powers in Berlin. This resulted in the "Two Plus Four" talks among the Four Powers and the two German sides, who negotiated the handing over of power to an all-German administration. The most difficult detail to be negotiated was Germany's membership in NATO, crucial to all participants and opposed by the Soviet Union. Once the Soviet Union had yielded on this point, the Four Powers officially handed their administrative powers to Germany with the signing in Moscow of the Two Plus Four Treaty on September 12, 1990.

On June 20, 1991, the German parliament voted by 337 to 320 to make Berlin the new capital of Germany and to transfer the seat of parliament from Bonn to its original home. However, the relocation of government operations was expected to take place gradually over the next decade, and many civil servants were expected to stay in Bonn.

For Further Information:
Beschloss, Michael R. *The Crisis Years: Kennedy and Khrushchev, 1960–1963.* New York, 1991.

Cate, Curtis. *The Ides of August: The Berlin Wall Crisis—1961.* New York, 1978.

Jonas, M. *The U.S. and Germany.* New York, 1985.

Mander, J. *Berlin: The Eagle and The Bear.* New York, 1962.

———. *Berlin: Hostage for the West.* New York, 1962.

Mezerik, A. G., ed. *Berlin and Germany.* New York, 1962.

Schick, Jack M. *The Berlin Crisis, 1958–1962.* Philadelphia, 1971.

Slusser, Robert M. *The Berlin Crisis of 1961; Soviet-American Relations and the Struggle for Power in the Kremlin, June–November 1961.* Baltimore, 1973.

Wyden, Peter. *Wall: The Inside Story of Divided Berlin.* New York, 1989.

Berlin Foreign Ministers' Conference   (1954)   The Berlin Foreign Ministers' Conference of 1954 resulted in a deadlock over the issues of German and Austrian reunification and of Trieste, but set a date for the Geneva Conference on Indochina and Korea. The second conference resulted in the partition of Vietnam.

The conference, which alternated between East Berlin and West Berlin, started on January 25, 1954. It was the seventh meeting of the Big Four foreign ministers since the end of World War II, but the first meeting in five years. The previous meeting, in London in 1949, had ended in bitter disagreement. The Berlin meeting was convened mainly at the request of the Soviet Union and was in response to the West European decision to form a EUROPEAN DEFENSE COMMUNITY (EDC).

The Soviets strongly opposed the formation of the EDC, and Soviet foreign minister V.M. MOLOTOV used the conference as a platform to attack both the EDC and the NORTH ATLANTIC TREATY ORGANIZATION. He also tried to secure some form of Western recognition of communist China.

The Western position, as presented by French foreign minister GEORGES BIDAULT, was that Western defense efforts could not be "the object of negotiation"; that the "pillars of a European settlement" were the Austrian and German peace treaties, and that free German elections were "the essential precondition" to a treaty that must "not leave Germany isolated in the heart of Europe" and must prevent "rebirth of aggressive militarism."

On January 29, Molotov proposed that both the East and West German governments be represented at the conference. But this was opposed by the Western powers and dropped. The Western foreign ministers, through British foreign secretary ANTHONY EDEN, then proposed that an interim all-German government, chosen in free elections throughout all of Germany, would be empowered to negotiate and conclude peace treaties with all former enemy nations. This would end the nine-year occupation of Germany and leave the unified government free to organize its own army for domestic defense, join the EDC and assume any other "international rights and obligations" of the East Zone or West Zone governments consistent with the United Nations Charter.

Molotov countered this proposal, on February 1, with the proposal that the occupying powers and an all-German government draft a peace treaty based on the 1945 POTSDAM CONFERENCE, and that this treaty would "neutralize" Germany by releasing the unified government from "political or military" obligations of the East or West Zone governments. The unified Germany would be barred from "any coalition or military alliance directed against" a former enemy nation. The treaty would also end partition of Germany, specify the withdrawal of all occupation armies and dismantle "all foreign military bases on German territory."

The Molotov proposal was rejected by the British, French and American foreign ministers. It was also opposed by West German chancellor KONRAD ADENAUER, who on February 2 said that the plan was "completely unacceptable" since its ban on political and military alliances would make Germany easy prey for Soviet expansionist policies. He called the Western plan "constructive."

The Soviet and Western positions on Germany were recognized as deadlocked, and Molotov tried to move the conference on from this issue to a proposal for a 50-year all-European security pact that would negate both NATO and the EDC. It would exclude the United States from the defense of Europe but make both America and China "observers" of the application of the treaty. Dulles said it was up to the European delegations whether they wanted to discuss the Molotov proposal. Both the British and French foreign ministers rejected it as unacceptable and accused Molotov of attempting to "wreck" the Atlantic Alliance.

Austrian chancellor Julius Raab had earlier tried to soften the Soviet position on an Austrian State Treaty by offering to abandon claims to oil installations and shipping companies previously owned by Austria and now held by the Soviet Union, to pay $150 million to settle Soviet claims, and to pledge not to join any aggressive military alliance.

Raab's proposals made the chances of progress on Austria more likely, and the foreign ministers agreed to listen to Austrian foreign minister Leopold Figl. On February 12 he told the Big Four foreign ministers that Austria would do everything "likely to facilitate" conclusion of an Austrian State Treaty. The Western foreign ministers, in a dramatic move to secure some kind of agreement in Berlin, offered on February 13 to accept the five remaining disputed articles of the Austrian State Treaty, including Soviet amendments made in 1949.

But Molotov ignored the offer, saying that any agreement would have to be preceded by the neutralization of Austria and agreement on the problems of Germany and Trieste. He blamed the conference's failure on the Western determination to create the EDC. The conference formally ended on February 18. Its only achievement was an agreement to hold an international conference on the Far East, which would include communist China, and to organize an "exchange of views" on the issue of world disarmament.

For Further Information:
Brands, H.W. *The Collapse of the Middle Way.* New York, 1988.
Fontaine, Andre. *History of the Cold War.* New York, 1970.
Guhin, Michael. *John Foster Dulles: A Statesman and His Times.* New York, 1972.

Berlin Tunnel   The Berlin Tunnel was a massive CIA-financed wiretap operation carried out in East Berlin during the 1950s.

The idea for the tunnel was developed by CIA director ALLEN DULLES in conjunction with the freelance German espionage group, the GEHLEN ORGANIZATION. In 1954, CIA and Gehlen operatives tunneled 500 yards under the East Berlin–West Berlin border to tap into the Soviet telephone cables near Schoenfeld Airport.

The operation was run for two years, until April 22, 1956,

when Soviet troops stormed into the tunnel and severed the tap. There have been mixed reports about the value of the Berlin Tunnel. Soviet sources claim that they knew about the wiretap from its earliest days and used it to feed disinformation to American intelligence. But the CIA claims it was an invaluable source of information during a key period in the Cold War.

Berlin Ultimatum (1958) See BERLIN.

Berlin Wall See BERLIN.

Bermuda Summit Conference (1953) The 1953 Bermuda Summit Conference among the British, French and American heads of government was the first such meeting of Western leaders of the Cold War. Its major achievement was an agreement for the storage of U.S. nuclear weapons in Britain.

The summit was first proposed by British prime minister WINSTON CHURCHILL, who felt that Western leaders should coordinate their actions in order to improve relations with the Soviet Union in the wake of the death of JOSEF STALIN.

Churchill's speech on May 11, 1953, was warmly welcomed by the French government but was greeted with suspicion in the United States, where editorial writers and some government officials argued that Churchill was leaning toward "appeasement." U.S. president Dwight Eisenhower only reluctantly agreed to the summit, and it did not take place until December 4–8 because of the illnesses of Churchill and British foreign secretary ANTHONY EDEN and a political crisis in France.

When the meeting finally did take place, Churchill's original proposal had lost much of its impetus, and the summit became largely an exchange of views. The main issues discussed were the EUROPEAN DEFENSE COMMUNITY (EDC), Korea, Indochina, SUEZ, British and American troop levels in Europe, the exchange of atomic information, and relations with the Soviet Union.

French prime minister Joseph Laniel foresaw the difficulties his government would face in securing parliamentary approval for the EDC in the following year. He stressed that France was making a "humiliating sacrifice" of integrating its forces with "those of another nation which had long been its enemy" and that for him to win parliamentary approval his government would have to regain control of the Saarland and receive a promise from Britain and America that they would maintain current troop levels in Europe for at least 20 years.

The French leader gave a glowing report of French actions in Vietnam and suggested that France would eventually defeat the communist forces. Eisenhower promised to increase military assistance. The defeat of France in Vietnam and the issue of the EDC caused the eventual collapse of the Laniel government.

Churchill raised the subject of Suez. Britain and Egypt had recently signed a treaty stipulating the withdrawal of British troops from their Egyptian bases but allowing their return in case of war. He wanted American and French support at the United Nations for his proposal that the UN be given the responsibility of deciding when the peace of the region was threatened so that the troops could return. Eisenhower was reluctant to become involved in the issue.

U.S. secretary of state JOHN FOSTER DULLES gave a report on the recently signed Korean Armistice and caused some concern among the French and British delegations when he threatened that the United States would use nuclear weapons if the North Koreans renewed the attack. Churchill was particularly concerned that the use of nuclear weapons in Korea would lead to a Soviet nuclear attack against Britain.

Churchill proposed to Eisenhower that United States forces in Britain store a certain number of atomic bombs earmarked for use by British bombers in the event of war. Eisenhower's agreement led to increased Anglo-American cooperation on nuclear weapons.

The heads of government also agreed to accept a Soviet proposal for a four-power foreign ministers' meeting to discuss the reunification of Germany and of Austria. The BERLIN FOREIGN MINISTERS' CONFERENCE was subsequently held in February 1954 but failed to make any progress on the issue of German reunification.

Bermuda Summit Conference (1957) The four-day Anglo-American Bermuda Summit Conference in 1957 between U.S. president DWIGHT EISENHOWER and British prime minister HAROLD MACMILLAN reestablished the Anglo-American special relationship after the bitterness of the SUEZ CRISIS and resulted in the United States agreeing to supply Britain with guided missiles and to join the BAGHDAD PACT.

The summit started on March 21 and covered the Suez Canal, the problem of maintaining oil supplies from the Middle East, Cyprus and its relationship to Greece and Turkey and the supply of American intercontinental ballistic missiles to Britain.

Britain requested the American missiles because mounting economic problems had forced it to abandon its own guided missile project, Blue Steel. Under the agreement reached at Bermuda, the United States would supply missiles with a range of 1,500 miles. The U.S. nuclear warheads for the missiles would be stored in Britain but not turned over to British forces unless an emergency arose.

For Further Information:
Grosser, Albert. *The Western Alliance, European–American Relations Since 1945.* New York, 1978.
Macmillan, Harold. *At the End of the Day.* New York, 1973.
Ryan, H.B. *The Vision of Anglo-America.* Cambridge, Eng., 1987.

Bethe, Hans Albrecht (July 2, 1906–) Hans Bethe was a German-born nuclear physicist who helped develop the atomic and hydrogen bombs and later became a prominent antinuclear campaigner.

Bethe received his doctorate in physics from the University

of Munich. He fled Germany during the Nazi era because of his partly Jewish ancestry. Bethe went first to Britain and then, in 1935, to the United States. In 1943 Bethe joined the Manhattan Project and played a leading role in the scientific research that led to the first atomic bomb.

After the explosion of the bomb at Hiroshima, Bethe joined the Emergency Committee of Atomic Scientists, a group led by Albert Einstein that wanted to establish international controls over atomic weapons. Their ideas found fruit in the BARUCH Plan, the U.S. proposals to the UN Atomic Energy Commission, which was rejected by the Soviet Union in 1946.

When the Soviet Union rejected the Baruch Plan, Bethe became a leading advocate of the policy of "finite containment" of Russian expansionism. This policy supported American maintenance of atomic weapons as a deterrent to the Soviet Union but argued that the United States should seek to limit the nuclear arms race through international agreement. The opposing policy of "infinite containment" was propounded by Edward Teller, the "father of the hydrogen bomb." Teller argued that the only way to combat Soviet expansionism was by maintaining the U.S. lead in the arms race. The conflict between Teller and Bethe continued into the 1980s, when the two men clashed over President Reagan's Star Wars policy.

After the Soviet Union exploded its first atomic device in 1949, Teller tried to persuade Bethe to rejoin him to develop an American hydrogen bomb. Bethe at first refused, saying, "No nation has the right to use such a bomb, no matter how righteous its cause."

But the start of the KOREAN WAR changed Bethe's mind, and in 1950 he returned to the government research laboratories at Los Alamos, New Mexico, to help with the research that led to the first hydrogen bomb explosion, on November 1, 1952. Bethe continued to work as a nuclear weapons adviser to presidents Eisenhower and Kennedy while at the same time advocating the policy of finite containment.

In 1956 Bethe was appointed to the president's Science Advisory Committee and in 1958 he became chairman of a panel formed to study the possible effects of a nuclear test ban agreement between the United States and the Soviet Union. The panel was also given the task of developing methods for detecting atomic blasts on foreign soil.

In testimony before the Senate Disarmament Subcommittee Bethe again clashed with Teller, who argued that if the United States agreed to end nuclear tests it could be "sacrificing millions of lives in a dirty nuclear war later" and that a halt on testing would abandon the United States' only advantage over the Soviet Union.

Bethe told the subcommittee on April 17, 1958, that the United States would gain "considerably" from a test ban providing for "a good inspection system with all the trimmings." He added that if tests continued the Soviet Union would "surely attain the same level of capability as we . . . It is more advantageous to stop when . . . you are still ahead."

Bethe won the debate and in 1958 participated in the U.S.-Soviet disarmament talks in Geneva. In March 1960 the two governments agreed to negotiate a ban on nuclear tests except those underground. But it was not until August 5, 1963, that the United States, the Soviet Union and Britain signed the NUCLEAR TEST BAN TREATY. By then Bethe had left the American delegation, although he was still advising President Kennedy.

Bethe returned to Cornell University, where he had been teaching off and on since his arrival in America. In 1967 he was awarded the Nobel Prize for physics for his discoveries about the energy production of stars. From Cornell, Bethe continued as an active advocate of arms control. He was a strong supporter of the second Strategic Arms Limitation Treaty (SALT II) and opposed President Ronald Reagan's STAR WARS proposals. When the U.S. Air Force conducted its first test of an antisatellite missile, in January 1984, Bethe joined other prominent scientists in signing a statement that the new weapon signaled a commitment by the United States to conduct a dangerous arms race in space. Bethe took a leading role in forming the Union of Concerned Scientists to oppose Star Wars as prohibitively expensive, technologically unattainable, easy to defeat and likely to stimulate the arms race.

Bevin, Ernest   (March 9, 1881–April 14, 1951)   As British foreign secretary in the immediate postwar years, Bevin played a key role in the formation of the MARSHALL PLAN, WESTERN EUROPEAN UNION, the TRUMAN DOCTRINE, the NORTH ATLANTIC TREATY ORGANIZATION and the formulation of British and Western policy toward the Soviet Union.

Bevin was appointed foreign secretary in the Labour government of CLEMENT ATTLEE, which took office July 26, 1945. His appointment followed a long career in the British trade union and Labour Party movements following an impoverished childhood. After leaving school at the age of 11, he drifted from job to job before finding regular work as a delivery driver for a mineral water company. He soon became involved in the embryonic Labour Party's trade union affairs and by the end of World War I was the assistant general secretary of the Dockers' Union. In 1922 he amalgamated several unions into the Transport and General Workers' Union (TGWU), which became the largest trade union in the world. He was general secretary of the TGWU until 1940. In 1937 Bevin was elected chairman of the Trades Union Congress (TUC).

When WINSTON CHURCHILL formed his wartime national coalition in May 1940, Bevin was chosen as minister of labor and national service. It was thought that his position within the union movement made him one of the few figures who could introduce the necessarily unpopular measures needed for the war effort, including conscription, a ban on strikes and changes in trade union regulations.

Following the historic Labour victory in the June 1945 general election, Bevin was appointed foreign secretary and immediately accompanied Prime Minister Clement Attlee to the POTSDAM CONFERENCE. Bevin launched a bitter and intense attack on the Soviet Union's handling of Poland and succeeded in securing a promise that Polish elections would be held in the first part of 1946. The failure of the Soviet Union and BOLESLAW BIERUT, the Soviet-supported Polish communist, to fulfill the pledge made to Bevin was a major factor in the deterioration of East-West relations.

Through trade unions, Bevin had earlier established links with the Communist Party of the Soviet Union; in 1920 he organized a group that threatened widespread strikes if the British government intervened on the Polish side in the war between Poland and the Soviet Union. His admiration for the Soviet Union continued throughout the 1930s and during the war, but soon after becoming foreign secretary, Bevin changed his attitudes toward the Soviet Union. In the autumn of 1945 he argued against recognition of the Soviet-sponsored governments in Eastern Europe. From 1946 onward, Bevin became convinced that the Soviet Union was attempting to take over West European governments, including Britain's, by organizing a series of subversive political strikes.

At the Potsdam Conference, the victorious powers had agreed to establish a council of foreign ministers to negotiate the terms of a final peace treaty with Germany. Bevin was Britain's representative at these successive meetings in London and Moscow in 1945 and 1947. Bevin was host for the first meeting, which was held in London in September and October 1945. As a result of continuing difficulties between the Western delegations and the Soviet delegation led by Foreign Minister V.M. MOLOTOV, the meeting broke up on October 2 without having agreed upon a communiqu. The further meetings were also largely fruitless, with the result that a German peace treaty remained unsigned until 1990, when circumstances were very different.

Early on, Bevin recognized that Britain was economically drained by two successive world wars and was in no position to defend Western Europe from Soviet advances. He therefore made it a key element of his policy to transfer a large proportion of Britain's military and political responsibilities to the emerging American superpower.

Bevin's first major effort in this direction involved Greece and Turkey. Britain was heavily involved financially and militarily in supporting the conservative Greek government in the civil war against the communists. At the same time, the Soviet Union was applying heavy pressure on Turkey to give it unfettered access to the Dardanelles. But in early 1947, British chancellor of the exchequer Hugh Dalton informed Bevin that Britain could not contribute any more aid to Greece after March 31.

Bevin immediately sent two diplomatic notes to U.S. secretary of state GEORGE C. MARSHALL explaining that Britain had borne the main burden of military aid but could not contribute any longer. He then suggested that British obligations be carried by the United States. The responsibility was accepted by the administration of President HARRY TRUMAN and was enunciated in the TRUMAN DOCTRINE.

The Truman Doctrine was quickly followed by its economic counterpart, the MARSHALL PLAN, and Bevin played a major role in organizing European support for the plan, working closely with his French counterpart, GEORGES BIDAULT. Under the Marshall Plan, economic aid was offered to all of Europe, including the Soviet Union, and Bevin and Bidault organized a meeting with Molotov in Paris to discuss the proposal. It became clear at this meeting that the Soviet Union would refuse to participate in the plan.

Bevin's initial success in attracting the Americans to the defense of Greece and Turkey, a traditional British sphere of influence, helped to end American isolationism. Bevin, however, believed that an institutionalized American commitment was needed to ensure its defense of European independence. He developed a plan to bring the United States into a treaty organization with Europe in stages. The first two stages were intended to demonstrate that European nations recognized the threat and were determined to defend each other from Soviet aggression.

The first stage was a treaty between the two historic antagonists, Britain and France. On March 4, 1947, a 50-year ANGLO–FRENCH TREATY OF ALLIANCE AND MUTUAL ASSISTANCE was signed. The second stage was the signing of the BRUSSELS TREATY of March 17, 1948, which effectively extended the Anglo-French mutual defense pact to include Belgium, the Netherlands and Luxembourg.

On April 28, 1948, the idea of a single mutual defense system, including and superseding the Brussels Treaty, was publicly put forward in the Canadian House of Commons by External Affairs Minister Louis St. Laurent. It was warmly welcomed a week later by Bevin, who had discussed it at length with Secretary of State Marshall and the chairman of the U.S. Senate Foreign Relations Committee ARTHUR VANDENBERG. Vandenberg drew up a resolution that cleared the way for American membership in the NORTH ATLANTIC TREATY ORGANIZATION, and the North Atlantic Treaty was signed in Washington, D.C., on April 4, 1949.

These fresh postwar alliances were spurred mainly by the Soviet Union's increasingly aggressive policies and repressive measures in Eastern Europe. The most forceful of these was the 1948 BERLIN BLOCKADE. At the start of the blockade, some left-wing Labour Party members suggested that Britain withdraw from Berlin, and these suggestions were broadcast by Soviet radio. But the idea was quickly dismissed by Bevin, who said, "We intend to stay in Berlin . . . The opinion of the whole world will condemn the ruthless attempt by the Soviet Government to create a state of siege in Berlin and so, by starving the helpless civilian population, secure political advantages at the expense of the other Allied Powers." Bevin went on to direct the British position in negotiations with the Soviet Union during the long blockade and completely supported the airlift.

Bevin, however, did not always agree with American foreign policy. On January 6, 1950, Britain offered recognition to the People's Republic of China at a time when the United States was forging close links with the Nationalist Chinese government on Taiwan. Bevin, along with Prime Minister Clement Attlee, believed that the historical differences between China and the Soviet Union would eventually resurface and urged the United States to maintain links with Peking in order to be in a position to exploit a future Sino-Soviet split.

The last year of Bevin's life was taken up with the crisis of the KOREAN WAR. He formulated the British policy of committing troops to the UN forces and basically supporting American foreign policy. But he was firmly against General DOUGLAS MACARTHUR's plans to cross the Yalu River into China or to support Nationalist Chinese troops in an attack on the southern part of mainland China. Bevin believed that such a move would bring the Soviet Union into the war and cause a direct military confrontation between the two superpowers. Because of Bevin's poor health, it fell to Attlee to fly to Washington and present the British views. This position played a major part in Truman's restraints on General MacArthur.

Bevin believed that Western security interests in Asia could be furthered by extending financial aid to the countries in the region. He set up a meeting of Commonwealth foreign ministers in Colombo, Ceylon (now Sri Lanka) in 1950 to funnel development aid to the countries of Southeast Asia. The program allocated $5.25 billion in aid from seven of the wealthier Commonwealth countries to six Asian Commonwealth countries. The Colombo Plan was Bevin's last major effort. The details of the plan were announced a few months before ill health forced his resignation on his 70th birthday. He died five weeks later.

For Further Information:

Barclay, Sir Roderick. *Ernest Bevin and the Foreign Office, 1932–1969.* London, 1975.
Bullock, Alan. *Ernest Bevin, Foreign Secretary, 1945–1951.* New York, 1985.
Saville, John. *Ernest Bevin and the Cold War 1945–50.* London, 1984.
Williams, Francis. *Ernest Bevin: Portrait of a Great Englishman.* London, 1952.
———. *The Foreign Policy of the British Labour Governments, 1945–51.* Leicester, 1984.

Bidault, Georges   (October 5, 1899–January 27, 1983)
Georges Bidault was the dominant voice in French foreign policy from 1944 to 1954. He combined a fierce nationalism with a strong anti-communist position and deep distrust of Germany. Later, his nationalism brought him into conflict with French president CHARLES DE GAULLE over the latter's Algerian policy, and Bidault was forced into exile and political disgrace.

Before the war, Bidault's career centered on an academic life and journalism. He was a distinguished professor of history and wrote articles for the Christian Democratic press warning against the rise of Nazism. Politically, he supported the Catholic Social Movement.

Bidault was taken prisoner in 1940 and the following year was repatriated to France, where he joined the Resistance. In 1943 he succeeded the murdered Jean Moulin as head of the National Council of Resistance, and when General Charles De Gaulle formed his provisional government in 1944, Bidault was named foreign minister. He founded the Popular Republican Movement, a Christian Democratic party that, although small, held a pivotal position in successive coalition governments of the Fourth Republic. This ensured Bidault a place in most French cabinets between 1944 and 1954 either as premier, foreign minister or defense minister.

Bidault's first task was to secure a major place for France at the postwar negotiations for the reconstruction of Europe. Although a committed anti-communist, he also recognized the Soviet Union's dominant position in postwar Europe and its influence over the powerful French Communist Party. One of his first acts therefore was to secure relations with the Soviet Union by signing, in 1944, a Franco-Soviet Defense Treaty. He later endorsed the YALTA and POTSDAM accords.

In May 1945, Bidault flew to Washington, D.C., to meet with U.S. president HARRY TRUMAN to persuade him that France should participate in the postwar occupation of Germany. Truman allocated a portion of the American zone to France. Bidault also tried to persuade Truman to allow French troops to participate in the final occupation of Japan in order to help secure the French position in Indochina. Truman, who opposed French colonialism in Indochina, refused this request unless the French troops were placed under American command. Bidault refused this condition.

Bidault continued to battle for equal status for France in Allied circles. At the LONDON FOREIGN MINISTERS CONFERENCE in 1945 he threatened to walk out after Soviet foreign minister V.M. MOLOTOV tried to exclude Bidault and the Chinese foreign minister from key parts of the negotiations on the grounds that France and China had not really contributed to the defeat of the Axis powers.

Bidault formed a close relationship with British foreign secretary ERNEST BEVIN. By 1947 the two men had agreed that a united Europe was needed to secure American support for the defense of Western Europe and that a key first step was an Anglo-French Treaty. The 50-year Anglo-French TREATY OF ALLIANCE AND MUTUAL ASSISTANCE was duly signed on March 4, 1947. It was the first in a series of postwar European treaties that eventually culminated in the signing of the North Atlantic Treaty and the formation of the NORTH ATLANTIC TREATY ORGANIZATION on April 4, 1949.

Bidault also played a major role in securing European support for the MARSHALL PLAN, which faced opposition from the pro-Moscow French Communist Party. Bidault initially projected himself as intermediary between Marshall and Molotov in an attempt to bring the Soviet Union and the rest of Eastern Europe, most of which had expressed an interest in the plan, into the scheme. He and Bevin invited the Soviet foreign minister to a three-power summit in Paris in June 1947. But Bidault also confided to Jefferson Caffery, U.S.

ambassador to France, "Molotov clearly does not wish this business to succeed, but on the other hand his hungry satellites are smacking their lips in expectation of getting some of your money. He is obviously embarrassed." In Paris, Molotov rejected the Marshall Plan for Eastern Europe and thus helped to tighten Western Europe's economic and political ties to the United States.

Bidault was as concerned about the resurgence of Germany as he was about the threat of the Soviet Union. To most Frenchmen, who had undergone the trauma of occupation, Germany remained far more ominous than Russia. Bidault took a much harder line toward the occupation of Germany than either his British or American counterparts, and in many ways French foreign policy toward Germany in the immediate postwar years was closer to the Soviet Union's than to Britain's or the United States'. France was reluctant to agree to the economic reconstruction of Germany and at first refused to join Britain and the United States in the economic integration of their occupation zones. The French contribution toward the Berlin Airlift was also minimal.

France had particular difficulty in accepting German rearmament and a merger of its armed forces with Germany as envisaged in the EUROPEAN DEFENSE COMMUNITY (EDC). Bidault himself supported the EDC, but at the 1953 BERMUDA SUMMIT CONFERENCE he argued that French support for the plan had to be bought with an agreement for an autonomous Saarland and an Anglo-American commitment to maintain high troop levels in West Germany for a minimum of 12 years. The demands were rejected by the British and American representatives, and the French National Assembly subsequently rejected the proposed EDC.

Simultaneously, Bidault was fighting a rearguard action to maintain French colonial rule in Indochina. After several years of heavy losses, the French were tiring of their costly war against the Vietnamese. Bidault, who strongly supported continued French rule, tried to perform a complex diplomatic juggling act. This involved persuading the Eisenhower administration to continue its economic support for the French forces in Indochina and the possible intervention of American and British troops. At the same time, as the military situation deteriorated in Indochina Bidault struggled to reach an accommodation with the Soviet Union by proposing to include Indochina on the agenda for the 1954 Geneva East-West talks on Korea.

U.S. secretary of state JOHN FOSTER DULLES, who was anxious to keep the Soviets out of negotiations involving Indochina, at first refused to endorse the inclusion of Indochina on the agenda. Bidault told Dulles that if the United States were held responsible for blocking such a conference then the moral obligation to carry on the war in Indochina would shift from French to American shoulders. Dulles, who had failed to secure the British military aid that he deemed essential for successful military intervention, was forced to agree to the talks. By this time the French were within days of losing the watershed battle of DIEN BIEN PHU, and it fell to Bidault, at the Geneva Conference, to propose the division of Vietnam into north and south.

The French defeat at Dien Bien Phu, coupled with the National Assembly's rejection of the EDC, brought about the collapse of the French government and a period of political uncertainty that was compounded by the SUEZ CRISIS and the Algerian War. Bidault was a rabid opponent of Algerian independence and in 1958 played a leading role in the recall of Charles de Gaulle in the mistaken belief that De Gaulle would fight to keep Algeria French and defeat Arab nationalism.

When de Gaulle's true intentions toward Algeria became clear, Bidault, in 1959, broke with him and created the Rally for French Algeria, which campaigned for complete integration of France and Algeria. In 1960 he was banned from entering Algeria, and in 1962 Bidault left France to head the underground political opposition to Algerian independence. The same year his parliamentary immunity was withdrawn, and Bidault was accused of "plotting against the security of the state." Bidault was expelled from Italy, Austria, Spain and West Germany before eventually finding political asylum in Brazil. He did not return to France until the political amnesty of 1968. By this time his political career was destroyed. Bidault died on January 27, 1983.

For Further Information:
Ball, M. Margaret. *NATO and the European Unity Movement*. New York, 1959.

Gouguel-Nyegaard, Franois. *France Under the Fourth Republic*. New York, 1953.

Meisel, James. *The Fall of the Republic*. Ann Arbor, Mich., 1962.

Werth, Alexander. *De Gaulle: A Political Biography*. New York, 1969.

Biddle, Francis **(May 9, 1886–October 4, 1968)**   Francis Biddle was chairman of AMERICANS FOR DEMOCRATIC ACTION, a liberal anti-communist organization active during the early Cold War years.

Biddle was born into a wealthy Philadelphia family and was graduated from Harvard University and Harvard Law School. He started a legal practice in Philadelphia and became involved in national politics in 1934 as chief counsel to a joint congressional committee investigating the Tennessee Valley Authority. In 1941 he was named U.S. attorney general. In September 1945 President HARRY TRUMAN appointed Biddle a member of the international military tribunal established to try Nazi war criminals at Nuremberg.

In January 1947 Truman nominated Biddle as U.S. representative to the United Nations Economic and Social Council. But his liberal views were out of favor with the conservative Republicans on the Senate Foreign Relations Committee, and after his nomination had been held up for five months, Biddle asked Truman to withdraw it.

On April 2, 1950, Biddle was elected national chairman of Americans for Democratic Action. During his three years as chairman the ADA supported civil rights legislation, Truman's Fair Deal economic policies and the U.S. role in Korea.

The ADA opposed American aid to General Franco's regime in Spain, urged reform of the federal loyalty program to prevent civil liberties abuses in the United States and fought the U.S. Internal Security Act of 1950.

Biddle was a staunch opponent of Senator JOSEPH MCCARTHY. In 1951 he published *The Fear of Freedom*, in which he attacked McCarthy, anti-communist hysteria, the HOUSE UN-AMERICAN ACTIVITIES COMMITTEE, the censorship of school textbooks, the introduction of loyalty tests for teachers and the dismissal of teachers for political nonconformity.

During the 1950s and 1960s Biddle wrote and lectured and advised the American Civil Liberties Union. He died on October 4, 1968.

For Further Information:

Biddle, Francis. *In Brief Authority.* Garden City, N.Y., 1962.

Diving, Robert A. *Foreign Policy and U.S. Presidential Elections.* New York, 1974.

Goulden, Joseph. *The Best Years, 1945–1950.* New York, 1976.

McAuliffe, Mary. *Crisis on the Left: Cold War and Politics and American Liberals, 1947–1954.* Amherst, Mass., 1974.

Bikini Island   Bikini Island, an atoll in the western chain of the Marshall Islands in the Pacific Ocean, was the site of U.S. nuclear tests between 1946 and 1958.

Bikini fell under U.S. administration when the Japanese were driven from the Marshall Islands in 1944. In 1947 the United Nations granted trusteeship to the United States. But before that, Bikini became the central point for Operation Crossroads, an experiment to guage the impact of atomic weapons on ships. After this, Bikini, along with nearby Eniwetok Atoll, became known as the Pacific Proving Ground of the United States ATOMIC ENERGY COMMISSION.

On July 1, 1946, the fourth ATOMIC BOMB in history, and the first to be exploded in peacetime, was detonated at Bikini Island. Unlike previous explosions, this one received the maximum advance publicity. The result was that Bikini Island became synonymous with nuclear weapons tests.

The bomb was dropped over a fleet of 73 unmanned U.S. Navy vessels off Bikini Atoll. The bomb, which was detonated in midair, had the explosive equivalent of 20,000 tons, the same size as that dropped on Nagasaki. Five of the ships

A million tons of water are blown into the air by a nuclear explosion on Bikini Atoll in the Marshall Islands archipelago, where the United States performed nuclear tests between 1946 and 1958.

were sunk and 45 were damaged. Ninety percent of the test animals on board the vessels (goats, pigs, sheep, rats and mice) survived the initial blast but died later from radiation sickness.

A second explosion, on July 25, 1946, was the first atomic bomb to be detonated underwater. As a result of this explosion 10 of the 75 unmanned ships moored on the test site were sunk. It was calculated that the explosion was equivalent to the power of 60,000 depth charges of 600 pounds each. A water column half a mile in diameter was sent a mile into the air, topped off by the familiar mushroom-shaped cloud.

A further 19 tests were conducted at Bikini in 1954, 1956 and 1958. On March 1, 1954, America's second hydrogen bomb was exploded at Bikini. The 15-megaton thermonuclear explosion was 759 times more powerful than the 1946 explosions and resulted in an unexpectedly widespread radioactive fallout. Japanese fisherman 70 to 90 miles from the test center were seriously burned by radiation, and residents of Kwajalein Island, 176 miles from Bikini, had hurriedly to be evacuated and remained under U.S. medical supervision for years.

The exposure of the Japanese fishermen created panic in Japan, where it was feared that radiation fallout would contaminate Japanese fishing grounds. The 1954 test revealed the global nature of radioactive contamination and was a factor in the 1958 moratorium on atmospheric nuclear tests. There have been no tests on Bikini since then.

Biological Weapons Treaty (1972) The 70-nation Biological Weapons Treaty of 1972 banned the production, stockpiling or acquisition of biological weapons. The treaty was seen as part of the general process to achieve a Strategic Arms Limitation Treaty (SALT, see STRATEGIC ARMS LIMITATION TALKS); the SALT I and ANTIBALLISTIC MISSILE TREATY were signed six weeks later.

The treaty, which was signed on April 10, 1972, at ceremonies in Washington, D.C., London and Moscow, committed the signatories "not to develop, produce, stockpile or otherwise acquire or retain" biological weapons and "to destroy or divert to peaceful purposes" such weapons "as soon as possible but not later than nine months."

British prime minister Edward Heath called the ban "a true disarmament treaty" because it required the signatory states to destroy their existing stocks of biological weapons.

Bissell, Richard (September 18, 1909–) Richard Bissell was a key figure in the CENTRAL INTELLIGENCE AGENCY when it was at the height of its powers in the late 1950s and 1960s. He was responsible for planning the BAY OF PIGS invasion and a number of assassination attempts. Bissell's activities seriously tarnished the reputation of the agency and damaged United States foreign policy.

Bissell attended Yale University and the London School of Economics before taking up a post teaching economics at Yale in 1935. During World War II, he helped supervise Allied shipping and from 1948 to 1951 was assistant administrator of the MARSHALL PLAN.

In 1954 Bissell joined the CIA as special assistant to director ALLEN DULLES. His initial responsibilities included the development of early high-technology espionage and surveillance techniques, including the U-2 spy planes and surveillance satellites.

In 1959 Bissell assumed responsibility for the CIA's covert operations when he became deputy director for plans. In this capacity he was responsible for attempts to assassinate Cuban leader FIDEL CASTRO, his brother Raul Castro and Congolese leader PATRICE LUMUMBA. He also assumed responsibility for training a group of Cuban exiles to invade Cuba and overthrow the Castro regime.

In 1960 the Belgian Congo became a focal point for East-West tensions when Lumumba turned to the Soviet Union for military assistance in suppressing separatist forces. In September 1960 Bissell, on the authority of Dulles and probably President DWIGHT EISENHOWER, sent CIA scientist Sidney Gottlieb to the Congo with poison for an attempt on Lumumba's life. This attempt failed, as did a second attempt, when CIA officer Michael Mulroney refused to carry out the assassination. Lumumba was eventually murdered by Katanga tribesmen on February 12. There is no evidence to suggest that the CIA was responsible.

CIA plots against Castro started as early as March 1960. They included impregnating his cigars with a disorienting agent before a speech and dusting his boots with a substance that would make his beard fall out. Between 1960 and 1965, the CIA instigated at least eight separate plots against Castro, but none was successful. Several of the plots involved links with organized crime leaders Sam Giancana and John Roselli, who were provided with CIA money, poison and electronic equipment to give to hired assassins.

In testimony before the Senate Select Committee to Study Intelligence Activities in 1975, Bissell said that he had "assumed" that he had the authority from Eisenhower and Dulles to make the assassination attempts. The committee concluded that Bissell exceeded his authority. It never fully established the extent of the involvement by Dulles or the president.

Eisenhower did, however, order the recruitment and training of Cuban exiles as part of a plot to overthrow Castro. The order was given on March 17, 1960, and Bissell was given direct responsibility for the project. On April 17 the CIA-backed army of exiles landed at the Bay of Pigs. It was clear from the outset that the CIA's estimates of Cuban military strength were badly understated and their estimates of the general public's dissatisfaction with the regime badly overstated. The result was an embarrassing debacle for the CIA and the fledgling Kennedy administration.

Before the Bay of Pigs, Bissell had been thought the probable next director of the CIA. Instead he quietly resigned from the agency on February 17, 1962, and moved first to be head of the Institute of Defense Analysis, and then in 1964 to the United Aircraft Corporation.

For Further Information:
U.S. Senate, Select Committee to Study Intelligence Activities. *Alleged Assassination Plots Involving Foreign Leaders*. Washington, D.C., 1975.
Wise, David, and Thomas B. Ross. *The Invisible Government*. New York, 1964.

Bizonal Agreement (1946) The Bizonal Agreement of 1946 combined the British and American occupation zones in Germany in order to combat growing economic chaos and Soviet refusal to integrate all the occupation zones. In August 1948 the area was expanded to include the French zone, and the three zones became the geographic area of the future Federal Republic of Germany.

The creation of "Bizonia" stemmed from basic and irreconcilable differences over the organization and treatment of postwar Germany. The Soviets had consistently demanded $20 billion in war reparations, some of which was to come from their own zone and some from the Western-occupied zones. They also insisted on the right to establish their own political system in their zone.

The United States and Britain, however, rejecting the idea of pastoralizing Germany, decided to reestablish the German economy and reintegrate the country into the international economic and political community. This was made clear in a major policy speech by U.S. secretary of state JAMES BYRNES at Stuttgart on September 6, 1946. Soviet refusal to go along with the Western policy forced Britain and America to seek stability by increasing cooperation between their two zones. This found its expression in the Bizonal Agreement of December 2, 1946.

The agreement was signed in New York by Byrnes and British foreign secretary ERNEST BEVIN. It merged the economies of the two occupation zones effective January 1, 1947, and was designed to make the two zones self-sustaining within three years at a cost to Britain and America of $1 billion.

France remained outside the Anglo-American agreement for a further two and a half years because it believed that Bizonia provided an excuse for the Soviets to continue their control of the Eastern Sector. But the BERLIN BLOCKADE of 1948 forced a change of mind in Paris, and Trizonia was formed with the signing of the Trizonal Agreement of August 5, 1948.

For Further Information:
Gimbel, John. *The American Occupation of Germany: Politics and the Military, 1945–49*. Stanford, Calif., 1968.
Kuklick, Bruce. *American Policy and the Division of Germany: The Clash with Russia over Reparations*. Ithaca, N.Y., 1972.

Blue Streak Blue Streak was the British land-based INTERCONTINENTAL BALLISTIC MISSILE (ICBM) system planned in the 1950s. Its cancellation in 1960 ended Britain's attempts to establish a nuclear deterrent completely independent of the United States.

In the Defense White Paper of February 1955 the British government announced a major shift from conventional to nuclear weapons and announced that one-third of its arms budget for that year would be spent on nuclear arms systems.

The centerpiece of the British nuclear arsenal was to be the land-based Blue Streak, with an estimated range of 2,800 miles. Almost from its inception, the concept of a British land-based nuclear deterrent came under attack. It was argued that such a system was more vulnerable to enemy fire and that, because Britain was a small island, an attack against its land-based ICBMs would have unacceptable repercussions on the rest of the country.

This factor, plus the cost of Blue Streak, led to its cancellation on April 13, 1960. Between 1955 and 1960 a total of $182 million was spent on it. British defense minister Harold Watkinson estimated that a further $1.7 billion would have been needed to complete its development. No Blue Streak missile was ever test-fired.

For Further Information:
Freedman, Lawrence. *Britain and Nuclear Weapons*. London, 1980.
Groom, John Richard. *British Thinking About Nuclear Weapons, 1940–1962*. London, 1974.
Rosecrance, Richard. *Defence of the Realm*. New York, 1968.

Blunting Mission Blunting Mission was the code name given to a Western nuclear attack plan in the 1950s and 1960s. The plan called for British and American airborne nuclear forces based in Britain to launch the first nuclear attack if war with the Soviet Union became imminent. This attack would "blunt" Soviet defenses by destroying anti-ballistic systems and radar. The U.S. American strategic bomber fleet would then arrive from the United States to launch the definitive nuclear attack.

Bohlen, Charles (August 30, 1904–January 1, 1974) Charles Bohlen was one of the leading American diplomatic experts on Soviet affairs. He reached the height of his influence during the KENNEDY administration, when he was regularly consulted by the president on a wide range of foreign policy issues.

Bohlen joined the American diplomatic service two years after graduating from Harvard University in 1927. He quickly established a speciality in Soviet affairs and in 1934 was a member of the first American diplomatic mission to the Soviet Union. In 1939 Bohlen was transferred to Tokyo, and he was in Japan when Pearl Harbor was bombed. He was interned for six months by the Japanese authorities.

Upon his return to Washington in 1942, Bohlen was appointed chief of the State Department's Eastern European Affairs Office. In this capacity he attended the Tehran, YALTA and POTSDAM conferences. After World War II he became personal adviser to Secretary of State GEORGE C. MARSHALL and worked on both the MARSHALL PLAN and the TRUMAN administration's CONTAINMENT policy.

In January 1953 Bohlen was nominated by President DWIGHT EISENHOWER as ambassador to the Soviet Union. Bohlen's close links with the Truman administration and his refusal to denounce the Yalta and Potsdam agreements brought him into conflict with conservative Republican senators. Among his opponents were Senator JOSEPH MCCARTHY, who hinted that he had information showing Bohlen to be a security risk.

Although McCarthy was unable to prove his accusations, they seriously jeopardized Bohlen's chances of confirmation, and it took a personal intervention by Secretary of State JOHN FOSTER DULLES to secure Bohlen's appointment. Bohlen had worked with Dulles at the Japanese peace conference, and although the two men had different views on many issues, they respected each other's intelligence. In his testimony before the Bohlen confirmation hearings Dulles denied that Bohlen was a security risk and stressed that as ambassador Bohlen would have little impact on policy.

Dulles honored his pledge to exclude Bohlen from the policy-making process. During his stay in Moscow Bohlen was used mainly as a messenger and interpreter of State Department telegrams to and from the Soviet leadership. Bohlen later wrote, "I cannot say I accomplished much during my four years." Bohlen, however, was in Moscow during the crucial period just after the death of JOSEF STALIN and during the rise of NIKITA KHRUSHCHEV, and this allowed him to build up contacts and knowledge.

In April 1957 Bohlen was moved from Moscow to be ambassador to the Philippines, and in 1959 Dulles's successor, CHRISTIAN HERTER, appointed Bohlen his special assistant for Soviet affairs. But continued opposition from conservative Republican senators forced Herter to drop plans to nominate Bohlen to a post as assistant secretary.

Bohlen's clashes with the Republican right wing and his Eastern Establishment credentials attracted President John F. Kennedy, and the two men formed a good working relationship. Kennedy called for advice from Bohlen on a wide range of foreign policy issues, especially those related to Soviet affairs. Major issues on which Bohlen advised the president included the LAOS crisis, the Soviet response to the BAY OF PIGS, the erection of the BERLIN WALL in 1961 and the CUBAN MISSILE CRISIS.

The crisis in Laos was sparked off by a civil war between U.S.-supported General Phoumi Nosavan and Prince Souvanna Phouma. The corruption of the Nosavan regime had encouraged the rise of the North Vietnamese-supported communist forces, who took advantage of the power struggle to seize control of the northeastern part of Laos. Bohlen advised Kennedy to shift his support to Prince Souvanna Phouma. When the communists, supported by the North Vietnamese, continued to advance, Bohlen helped in the drafting of the diplomatic notes that resulted in a shaky ceasefire.

Bohlen was not a member of the inner circle advising the president during the Bay of Pigs Crisis, but he was consulted by Kennedy about the possible Soviet response to an invasion.

Bohlen told him that the Soviet Union would not intervene militarily in support of Cuba, but would attempt to extract the maximum propaganda value from the event.

During the Soviet Union's partitioning of Berlin in 1961, Bohlen visited West Berlin in August and advised Kennedy that he should be prepared to use all measures short of war to protect Western rights in Berlin.

During the Cuban Missile Crisis, Bohlen was one of the inner circle daily advising the president. Bohlen proposed sending Khrushchev a carefully worded diplomatic note demanding the withdrawal of the missiles. If that failed he advised that the president ask Congress for a declaration of war. His advice was rejected.

Bohlen left for Paris to be U.S. ambassador to France shortly after the Cuban Missile Crisis. His four years in France coincided with General CHARLES DE GAULLE's pursuit of a more independent foreign policy, French withdrawal from the military structure of NATO in 1966 and the demand that the United States withdraw its military bases from French soil. Bohlen advised first Kennedy and then President LYNDON JOHNSON to avoid an open conflict with de Gaulle no matter how great the provocation.

In December 1967 Bohlen returned to Washington as undersecretary of state for political affairs. He advised Johnson against the bombing of North Vietnam and favored a muted American response to the Soviet invasion of CZECHOSLOVAKIA in 1968 in order to avoid either an embarrassing backing down or a major U.S.-Soviet confrontation. Bohlen retired in January 1969 and died five years later, on January 1, 1974.

For Further Information:
Bohlen, Charles. *Witness to History, 1929–1969.* New York, 1973.
Isaacson, Walter, and Thomas Evan. *The Wise Men.* New York, 1986.
Rostow, Walt W. *The Diffusion of Power: An Essay in Recent History.* New York, 1972.

Bonn Convention   (1952)   The Bonn Convention of May 26, 1952, set down the guidelines for the formal ending of the Allied Occupation of West Germany and the incorporation of West Germany into the Western Alliance.

The main points of the Bonn Convention were:

1. The Occupation statutes would be abolished.
2. Allied forces in West Germany were no longer occupation forces but part of "the defense forces of the free world of which the Federal Republic and West Berlin form a part."
3. West Germany would have full control over its internal and foreign affairs.
4. "Because of the international situation" France, Britain and the United States would continue to claim the right to base their troops in West Germany.
5. France, Britain, the United States and West Germany agreed that a "freely negotiated peace settlement for the

whole of Germany" was their common aim, and the delineation of the final borders of Germany would await such a treaty.

The Bonn Convention was negotiated in tandem with the EUROPEAN DEFENSE COMMUNITY Treaty and was designed as a political and military prelude to the EDC Treaty, which was signed the following day in Paris. The EDC and the Bonn Convention were meant to simultaneously guarantee a German contribution to West European defense and Western control over that contribution. The EDC was also designed to provide a West European defense force to support the United States, which at the time was militarily overstretched by the Korean War and other commitments in the Far East.

The EDC, however, required the ratification of national parliaments and was rejected by the French National Assembly in 1954. The collapse of the EDC after the signing of the Bonn Convention left the West in the politically unacceptable position of being committed to rearming Germany without maintaining any checks on its recent enemy. This problem was solved by incorporating West Germany into the NORTH ATLANTIC TREATY ORGANIZATION and the WESTERN EUROPEAN UNION in 1955.

For Further Information
Jonas, M. *The U.S. and West Germany.* New York, 1985.

Bowles, Chester   **(April 5, 1901–June 25, 1986)**   Chester Bowles was a leading American, liberal foreign affairs expert throughout the height of the Cold War. His main area of expertise was the Third World, and he served twice as ambassador to India.

Bowles made his fortune in advertising during the 1930s and quickly became involved with the liberal wing of the Democratic Party. In 1943 President FRANKLIN ROOSEVELT appointed Bowles director of the Office of Price Administration. Bowles established himself as a leading liberal voice in both the Roosevelt and the TRUMAN administrations. He resigned in 1946 when Congress refused to continue price controls enacted during the war.

Out of office, Bowles became an active supporter of the AMERICANS FOR DEMOCRATIC ACTION, becoming the chairman of the ADA's Committee for Economic Stability. In November 1948 he was elected governor of Connecticut. During his two years in office, Bowles launched a low-income housing program, introduced civil rights legislation and raised welfare payments.

When Bowles was voted out of office in 1950, Truman appointed him ambassador to India. Bowles became a close friend of Prime Minister Jawaharlal Nehru and supported his socialist economic policies and nonaligned foreign policy. He also started a lifelong campaign to shift America's foreign aid program from military to development aid as well as arguing that nonalignment did not, as many American conservatives believed, mean support for communism.

Bowles resigned his ambassadorship when DWIGHT EISEN-HOWER was elected president in 1952 and concentrated on delivering lectures and writing articles and books critical of the Eisenhower administration's foreign policy. In 1958 Bowles was elected to the U.S. House of Representatives after failing to win the Democratic nomination to the Senate. He spent his one term in Congress lobbying for disarmament and an improvement in foreign aid programs, which he regarded as "stingy." He played down the Soviet threat and concentrated on the dangers to global stability poised by poverty and hunger. "Foreign aid," argued Bowles, "is America's best deterrent against the spread of Communism." Bowles also supported political accommodation with the Soviet Union and communist China.

In 1959, Bowles endorsed Senator JOHN F. KENNEDY for the Democratic Party presidential nomination. Bowles' support helped Kennedy to win the backing of the party's liberal wing, and he rewarded Bowles by naming him chief adviser on foreign policy. It was thought that Bowles might be appointed secretary of state, but Kennedy regarded Bowles' liberalism as too controversial for such a senior position, and Bowles was given instead the post of undersecretary of state.

Bowles had the initially important task of persuading leading liberals to take senior State Department positions. But once this job was completed, there was little for the administration's ranking liberal to do but play second fiddle to Secretary of State DEAN RUSK. He increasingly came into conflict with Rusk, Attorney General ROBERT KENNEDY and President Kennedy. He opposed the BAY OF PIGS invasion and American intervention in the Dominican Republic.

By the summer of 1961, Kennedy was thinking of moving Bowles to an ambassadorship. Key liberals came to Bowles' defense, and he managed to stay on as undersecretary of state until November 26, when Rusk urged him to accept a post as roving ambassador. Bowles at first considered quitting the administration and taking his case to the public, but he eventually accepted the job of the president's special representative and adviser on Asian, African and Latin American affairs.

Bowles made extensive tours throughout the Third World, wrote numerous policy documents on foreign aid programs and proposed the neutralization of Southeast Asia as a way of heading off future American involvement. None of the proposals were implemented, and a frustrated Bowles submitted his resignation in December 1962. Kennedy, however, regarded Bowles as more dangerous out of government and persuaded him to return to India as ambassador. Bowles arrived in New Delhi on July 17, 1963.

Bowles' primary concern in India was an improved American aid program. But in this he was blocked by the JOHNSON administration's decision to stop all aid to Pakistan and India during the Indo-Pakistani War of 1965 and President Johnson's anger over the Indian government's opposition to the VIETNAM WAR.

Bowles also tried to shift American foreign policy away from supporting Pakistan and toward support for India. Successive administrations had placed a greater emphasis on Pakistan because of its strategic position close to both China and the Soviet Union. But Bowles argued that India's democratic tradition and large population made it the key to the maintenance of a stable and pro-Western South Asia subcontinent. Bowles left India in April 1969 and returned to lecturing and writing until his death on June 25, 1986.

For Further Information:
Bowles, Chester. *Promises to Keep: My Years in Public Life, 1941–1969.* New York, 1971.
Isaacson, Walter, and Thomas Evan. *The Wise Men.* New York, 1986.
Kepley, *The Collapse of the Middle Way.* New York, 1988.

Boyce, Christopher   (1952–   )   One of the Soviet Union's most valuable spies of the 1970s, Christopher Boyce, with his friend Andrew Daulton Lee, passed highly classified and very damaging data about American spy satellites to the KGB. His exploits were chronicled in the book and film *The Falcon and the Snowman.*

A college dropout with a genius IQ, Boyce was hired in 1974 at the age of 21 by TRW Systems Group, a military-defense contractor in southern California. Although his 1974 security check "was a joke," as he later testified (both his father and his uncle were former FBI agents), Boyce was employed as a clerk monitoring a top-secret global communications network run by TRW under contract to the CIA. Boyce claimed his treason was not motivated by money but by disillusionment when he discovered that the CIA had been meddling in Australia's domestic politics (meddling that climaxed, some believe, with CIA involvement in the "constitutional coup" that ousted Labor Prime Minister Gough Whitlam in 1975).

Boyce used his drug-dealing boyhood friend Lee to pass information—about National Security Agency codes, the Rhyolite surveillance satellites and the "Pyramider" satellite still in development—to KGB agents at the Soviet embassy in Mexico City. Boyce collected about $15,000 and Lee about $60,000 in KGB money before Lee was arrested in January 1977 and Boyce shortly thereafter. Lee was sentenced to life in prison, while Boyce got 40 years. Boyce managed to escape in January 1980 and spent 18 months on the run, supporting himself by robbing banks, before he was recaptured and given another 28 years in prison for his escapades.

Bradley, Omar   (February 12, 1893–April 8, 1981)   General Omar Bradley was a key military figure in the immediate postwar years and was chairman of the Joint Chiefs of Staff during the KOREAN WAR.

Born in Missouri, Bradley graduated from the United States Military Academy in 1915, when he started his career in the Army infantry. Throughout his time in the military, Bradley was a staunch supporter of a strong land army, especially in any possible war against the Soviet Union, and his views ensured that the United States maintained its numbers even while developing its nuclear arsenal and air capabilities.

During World War II Bradley commanded the II Corps in North Africa and Italy and led the American forces during the Normandy invasion. His troops went on to liberate Paris in August 1944 and become the first American forces to make contact with the Red Army.

Bradley's immediate postwar position was as administrator for veterans' affairs. In January 1948 President TRUMAN appointed him army chief of staff and in August 1949, chairman of the Joint Chiefs of Staff. He held that post until his retirement in May 1953.

Bradley was known as a "soldier's soldier," and as chairman of the Joint Chiefs he saw his job as implementing the decisions of the president. He was a keen supporter of the NORTH ATLANTIC TREATY ORGANIZATION and of plans to integrate West Germany into the Western Alliance defense efforts. In 1949 and 1950 he supported Truman's cuts in defense spending and then supported Truman's calls for increased defense spending from 1950 onward.

Bradley's criticism of General DOUGLAS MACARTHUR and support for Truman's recall of MacArthur from Korea was a major aid to the president during the political storm that followed. Bradley maintained that MacArthur's plans for an attack on China would be an unnecessary escalation and would force American troops to leave an endangered Europe undefended in order to fight in the Far East.

As soon as Truman received MacArthur's cabled war plans he sent for Bradley as well as DEAN ACHESON, GEORGE MARSHALL and AVERELL HARRIMAN. Bradley was deeply shocked by MacArthur's insubordination to the president and immediately went to the Joint Chiefs of Staff to organize their unanimous recommendation for the dismissal of the general. Bradley later said that the Joint Chiefs approved the recall of MacArthur because in their opinion his actions "jeopardized the civilian control over the military authorities."

In 1950 Bradley was made a (five-star) General of the Army, only the fourth officer in American history to reach that rank. He retired from the military in May 1953 to become chairman of the board of the Bulova Research and Development Laboratories. He lived quietly in retirement but occasionally testified on defense matters before congressional committees and was a strong supporter of President Lyndon Johnson's VIETNAM WAR policy. Bradley died in New York on April 8, 1981.

For Further Information:
Bradley, Omar Nelson. *A General's Life: An Autobiography.* New York, 1983.
Hewes, James E., Jr. *From Root to McNamara: Army Organization and Administration, 1900–1963.* Washington, D.C., 1963.

Brainwashing   Brainwashing refers to the forcible indoctrination of a person or group of people.

A system of torture and rewards was used by Soviet psychiatrists during the Stalinist era to obtain confessions during the show trials of the 1930s. The term brainwashing, however, came into common usage during the KOREAN WAR when it was thought to have been used successfully by the Chinese against American prisoners of war. Of the 7,000 Americans captured by the communist forces, about a third collaborated with their captors, most of them allegedly as a result of brainwashing. Collaboration included participation in communist broadcasts and signed confessions alleging an American germ warfare program.

Contrary to popular belief, the brainwashing did not always take the form of torture. Often it was a much more subtle technique. American-educated Chinese were assigned to prisoner-of-war camps. Their first task was to destroy the cohesiveness of the military units by separating the men from their leaders and encouraging informers. This increased group insecurity.

At the same time, the prisoners were sent to formal and informal indoctrination courses in communist theory. They were also given selected anti-American newspaper articles and books, culled mainly from American and European publications. Their mail was intercepted, and only letters carrying bad news were delivered. All of this made the prisoners increasingly dependent on their captors, and gradually this dependence led to cooperation with them.

For Further Information:

Gillmor, Don. *I Swear by Apollo: Dr. Ewen Cameron and the CIA-Brainwashing Experiments*. Montreal, 1987.

Hunter, Edward. *Brainwashing in Red China*. New York, 1951.

Lifton, Robert Jay. *Thought Reform and the Psychology of Totalism*. New York, 1967.

Winn, Denise. *The Manipulated Mind: Brainwashing, Conditioning, and Indoctrination*. London, 1983.

Brandt, Willy   (December 13, 1913–October 8, 1992)

Willy Brandt was the chancellor of West Germany from 1969 to 1974. His OSTPOLITIK ("Eastern Policy") established a greater degree of normality in West Germany's relations with Eastern Europe and paved the way for the period of détente of the 1970s.

Brandt was born Herbert Ernst Karl Frahm, the illegitimate son of Martha Frahm, a salesgirl in the town of Lübeck. His grandfather, a truck driver, first introduced him to socialism and encouraged him to take part in the early Social Democratic youth movement. By the age of 14, Brandt was contributing articles to the local Social Democratic newspaper, and before his 17th birthday he was a full member of the Social Democratic Party (SPD).

But the Social Democrats' failure to stand up effectively to the Nazis led Brandt to leave the SPD and join the more extreme Socialist Workers Party in 1932. In that same year he graduated from high school and started writing newspaper articles under the pseudonym "Willy Brandt."

Brandt's activities quickly brought him to the attention of the Gestapo. Fearing arrest, he fled to Norway in April 1933, where he set up an exile office of the German Socialist Workers Party. At the same time he discarded the name Frahm and adopted the name Willy Brandt as his own. In Norway, Brandt continued to write and studied history and philosophy at Oslo University. He also traveled extensively throughout Western Europe, promoting the anti-fascist cause. After the Germans invaded Norway in 1940, Brandt was taken prisoner as a Norwegian soldier. But luckily the German Army failed to recognize his true identity and Brandt was released after a month. He then crossed the border into Sweden, where he continued his journalism and anti-fascist activities. In 1940, Brandt also acquired Norwegian citizenship.

After the war, Brandt returned to Germany first as a journalist for Scandinavian newspapers and then as press attach with the Norwegian Military Mission at the Allied Control Council. At the end of 1947, Brandt relinquished his Norwegian citizenship and rejoined the Social Democratic Party, becoming the director of the BERLIN liaison office of the SPD. The position made him a key link between the Western allies and the Social Democratic mayor of Berlin, Ernst Reuter, during the Berlin Blockade.

In 1949 Brandt was elected to the West German Bundestag, and in 1950 he was elected a member of the Berlin house of representatives. From 1955 to 1957 he was chairman of the latter. In October 1957 he shot to international prominence when he was elected mayor of West Berlin.

Brandt served as mayor of West Berlin during four of the city's most turbulent Cold War years, and his repeatedly tough stand in support of West Berliners' right to be part of the Western Alliance and to make decisions independent of the Western military commanders won him a reputation for toughness and at times bravery. In November 1958 Soviet leader NIKITA KHRUSHCHEV demanded that West Berlin break its ties with West Germany and become "an independent political entity." Realizing that such a move would be a first step to being swallowed up by the Soviet Bloc, Brandt rejected the demand as "unacceptable" and then turned to the Western powers and insisted that they do the same.

Brandt formed a close relationship with President JOHN F. KENNEDY, and both men strongly admired each other. But Brandt also clashed with Kennedy over the American reaction to the building of the Berlin Wall in August 1961. Kennedy, uncertain of the meaning of the wall, waited four days to take any action; then the U.S. response consisted only of a protest note and an acceleration of the military build-up in the United States. A furious Brandt wrote to Kennedy condemning the feeble Western response. As a result, Kennedy sent Vice President LYNDON JOHNSON to West Berlin and dispatched a diplomatic note to the Soviet Union stressing that Berlin was an "ultimate American commitment." He also ordered 1,500 U.S. troops to move from West Germany to West Berlin. Brandt, for his part, embarked on a major diplomatic offensive to increase world political support for West Berlin. Through his efforts in this direction, Brandt became an internationally recognized symbol not only of the divided city but also of a divided Germany.

In the interim, Brandt had also become heavily involved in moving the SPD toward a more politically acceptable position in order to present a national electoral challenge to the dominant Christian Democrats. At a party conference in Bad Godesberg in 1959, he played a major role in drafting the party platform, which renounced doctrinaire Marxism and accepted the principles of a free market economy, private property and freedom of religion.

Brandt's growing importance, both within the party structure and on the national and international stage, made him a logical choice as SPD candidate for chancellor in the September 1961 general elections. The SPD was able to win only 36% of the vote, but Brandt's reputation was further enhanced by his campaign performance and he was the candidate for chancellor in 1965 as well. In 1965 he also became chairman of the Social Democratic Party. In the 1965 election the SPD managed to increase its share of the vote to 39% but still remained out of office. But in October 1966, the Christian Democratic-Federal Democratic coalition government of LUDWIG ERHARD collapsed. The Christian Democrats were forced into forming a grand coalition government under Chancellor KURT KIESINGER. The coalition included Brandt in the post of foreign minister and vice chancellor.

In the previous 10 years, Brandt had been quietly formulating a new West German policy toward the Soviet Bloc. The Christian Democratic governments of KONRAD ADENAUER and Erhard had been firmly against any serious diplomatic relations with Eastern Europe, especially anything that even implicitly recognized the existence of the German Democratic Republic or the ODER-NEISSE LINE as the Polish-German border. The Adenauer government had even gone so far as to issue the HALLSTEIN DOCTRINE, which committed West Germany to breaking diplomatic relations with any government that recognized the East German government.

Brandt was seriously worried about West Germany's position as a front-line state in the Cold War, which could become a hot war. He concluded that the best way to prevent such an outcome was for West Germany to take an active role in improving relations with Eastern Europe. This policy became known as Ostpolitik, or the "Eastern Policy." In practical terms, it meant accepting the division of Europe, which had existed since 1945, and trying to work within the constraints established by that division.

For West Germans, Ostpolitik was a particularly delicate issue. If it was carried to its natural conclusion, the policy meant the acceptance of a divided nation, a politically impossible premise ruled out by the West German constitution. But rejection of Ostpolitik meant a continuing state of high international tension, which was unacceptably dangerous. Brandt had to somehow steer a middle course between these two extremes.

Brandt's Ostpolitik became nominally accepted as a key element of the foreign policy of the grand coalition. And during the coalition's three-year tenure, diplomatic relations were established with ROMANIA and YUGOSLAVIA. But the Christian Democrats in the government acted as a brake on any dramatic West German initiatives in Eastern Europe.

As new elections in September 1969 approached, it became clear that the coalition could not survive, and the constituent parties went into the election on separate platforms. A major issue was Brandt's Ostpolitik. The SPD emerged with 42.7% of the votes and 224 seats in the Bundestag. The liberal Free Democrats (FDP), who were supportive of Brandt's foreign policy, won 30 seats. The result was an SPD-FDP coalition with a majority of 12 seats—just enough to give Brandt the post of chancellor and the freedom he needed to implement his Ostpolitik.

Brandt's first major step toward normalization of relations was a meeting in March 1970 with East German premier Willi Stoph at Erfurt, East Germany. The talks proved initially to be inconclusive. Stoph insisted on international legal recognition for the East German state and indemnification of 100 billion marks (about $25 billion) for losses incurred by East Germany's economy through emigration to West Germany before the building of the Berlin Wall in 1961. At a second meeting at Kassel, West Germany, Brandt presented a list of 20 "principles and elements" designed to lead to a treaty normalizing relations between the two German states. These included the establishment of joint diplomatic missions in each other's capitals. Stoph did not press his earlier demand for indemnification but repeated his demand for legal recognition of the East German government and branded as "absolutely unacceptable" Brandt's use of phrases such as "intra-German" to describe relations between two states with "contradictory social orders" and "utterly different basic interests."

Despite the cool response from East Germany, Brandt pushed forward with his Ostpolitik policy, and it finally bore fruit in August 1970 when, after extended negotiations, he and Soviet premier ALEXEI KOSYGIN signed a West German-Soviet nonaggression pact. The pact included a pledge to renounce territorial claims against each other, to refrain from the use of force in the settlement of disputes between them, and the recognition of all boundaries, including the border between East Germany and West Germany and between Poland and East Germany.

Brandt's recognition of the Oder-Neisse Line as Poland's western border cleared the way for a treaty between West Germany and Poland. This treaty was signed in Warsaw in December 1970 by Brandt and Polish premier Jozef Cyrankiewicz.

The United States, Britain and France, the three Western powers responsible for West Berlin, had mixed and different feelings about Brandt's Ostpolitik policy. France was generally in favor and had formed a close relationship with Brandt, who had reestablished the Franco-German special relationship inaugurated by Adenauer and French president CHARLES DE GAULLE in 1963. The British were won over by Brandt's enthu-

siastic support of their application to join the EUROPEAN ECO-
NOMIC COMMUNITY.

The United States, however, was more suspicious. HENRY
KISSINGER, then national security adviser to the president, was
concerned that Ostpolitik could lead to a resurgence of German nationalism. At the same time, he recognized that West
Germany's Hallstein Doctrine was an increasingly dangerous
political anachronism that had lost support in West Germany.
Kissinger, in order to retain some control of events, offered
his support to Brandt's foreign policy, and in August 1971,
Britain, France, the United States and the Soviet Union made
their own contribution to Ostpolitik when they signed the
QUADRIPARTITE AGREEMENT, which established the right of unhindered traffic between West Germany and West Berlin,
allowed West Berliners to travel to the East and normalized
the city's status in relation to West Germany.

In recognition of his work in defusing East-West relations,
Brandt was awarded the Nobel Prize for peace in October
1971. The East Germans were then forced to take a more
serious view of Brandt's Ostpolitik, and in November 1972
East Germany and West Germany signed a treaty normalizing
relations between them. The treaty also allowed the reunification of families and the release of prisoners. This treaty,
signed only a few days before a West German general election,
helped Brandt's SPD-FDP coalition to increase its majority to
48 seats.

In his second term, Brandt concluded economic agreements with the Soviet Union and Romania. In December
1973 West Germany and Czechoslovakia signed a treaty
recognizing each other's postwar boundaries.

Brandt appeared to be politically impregnable, when in
April 1974 his close aide Gunter Guillaume was arrested and
charged with being a spy for East Germany. The subsequent
scandal forced Brandt to resign the chancellorship the following month. In his letter of resignation to President Gustav
Heinemann, Brandt assumed responsibility for "negligence"
in allowing Guillaume to become a top member of his staff.
Brandt was succeeded in the chancellorship by HELMUT
SCHMIDT.

Brandt, however, continued to play a major role in both
German and international affairs. He maintained his position
as chairman of the SPD, a role that allowed him to wield
considerable influence over party and government policy and
that gave him access to statesmen around the world. In
November 1976 his international stature was further enhanced when he was elected president of the Socialist International.

Brandt was also named chairman of an international commission to study the relationship between the countries of the
Northern and Southern hemispheres, i.e., the developed versus the developing and underdeveloped world. The Brandt
Commission, which made its report in February 1980, concluded that the rich Northern countries should provide $8
billion a year in additional food aid, and that development aid
and loans should be increased to nearly $60 billion annually

over the following five years. The commission also recommended that a form of universal taxation be instituted to raise
the money.

After the election of RONALD REAGAN as U.S. president,
Brandt appeared to move further to the left of the SPD,
especially in regard to nuclear issues. In October 1983 he was
a keynote speaker at a 200,000-strong antinuclear rally in
Bonn at which he publicly opposed the deployment of American Cruise and PERSHING II missiles in Western Europe. In a
debate in the Bundestag in November 1983, Brandt argued
that the missiles might have a "destabilizing effect" by reducing West German popular support for NATO. He added that
his party supported NATO and West Germany's friendly ties
but that "we will be cornered by Reagan." He also rejected
demands for the withdrawal of existing American nuclear
weapons in Germany.

Brandt was highly critical of the Reagan administration's
policies in Central America and was appointed by the Socialist International to mediate between NICARAGUA's Sandinista
government and the opposition Democratic Coalition (CD).
Brandt's assignment was to negotiate an agreement between
the two sides on the conduct of presidential elections scheduled in 1984. But he failed after opposition leader Arturo Cruz
refused to register for the elections, claiming that the election
rules unfairly favored the Sandinistas.

A combination of a poor showing by the SPD in the January
1987 general election coupled with a sex scandal led to the
resignation of 73-year-old Brandt from the chairmanship of
the SPD. In the immediate aftermath of the campaign, Brandt
was accused of not enthusiastically supporting the moderate
SPD candidate for the chancellorship, Johannes Rau. Then
in March, he appointed his close friend Margarita Mathiopoulos, a Greek national, as the party's spokeswoman. The growing band of Brandt critics from within the SPD demanded his
resignation. Mathiopoulos tried to save his career by immediately resigning, but it was too late, and Brandt was forced to
quit the leadership of the SPD after 23 years in the post.

For Further Information:
Binder, David. *The Other German: Willy Brandt's Life & Times.*
Washington, D.C., 1975.
Brandt, Willy. *My Life in Politics.* London, 1992.
———. *People and Politics: The Years 1960–1975.* Boston, 1978.
Homze, Alma, and Edward Homze. *Willy Brandt, A Biography.* Nash-
ville, 1974.
McGhee, George Crews. *At the Creation of a New Germany: From
Adenauer to Brandt: An Ambassador's Account.* New Haven,
Conn., 1989.
Prittie, Terence. *The Velvet Chancellors.* New York, 1979.
———. *Willy Brandt.* New York, 1973.
Whetten, Lawrence. *Germany East and West.* New York, 1980.

Brezhnev, Leonid Ilyich (December 19, 1906–November
10, 1982) Leonid Ilyich Brezhnev was the longest-serving
postwar leader of the Soviet Union. He sought superpower
parity with the United States by sacrificing the Soviet econ-

omy to nuclear weapons development. At the same time, Brezhnev was the architect of dtente, who saw the policy collapse following the Soviet invasion of Afghanistan and the rise of RONALD REAGAN in the United States.

Brezhnev was the son of a Ukrainian steelworker, and his family background provided him with the working-class pedigree essential for a high post in the early days of the Communist Party. Brezhnev himself started working in the steel mills at the age of 15 but at the same time attended night classes at the local metallurgical school. In 1923 he joined the Communist Party.

From his earliest days in the party, Brezhnev was a staunch Stalinist, and in the 1930s helped to carry out the Stalinist purges in the Ukraine that wiped out the Kulaks and imposed collectivization. In 1937 Brezhnev became deputy mayor of his native city of Dneprodzerzhinsk and in 1938 was promoted to the secretaryship of the Ukrainian Communist Party under NIKITA KHRUSHCHEV. This was the start of a long relationship between Brezhnev and Khrushchev, which ensured Brezhnev's continued rise and saved him from political obscurity following the death of JOSEF STALIN.

Brezhnev entered World War II as a political commissar with the military rank of lieutenant colonel. Between 1941 and 1945 he was deputy head of the Political Board of the Southern Front, head of the Political Department of the 18th Army and head of the Political Board of the 4th Ukraine Front. He rose to the rank of major general in 1943. The many military friends and contacts Brezhnev made during this period served as an important base of support in later years.

At the end of the war, Brezhnev was appointed political commissar in the border areas with Romania and Czechoslovakia. Soon afterward he was given the same job in the Ukraine and then Moldavia. These positions involved organizing the imposition of Soviet rule on a largely reluctant people, and Brezhnev's own official biography described his administration as draconian. Brezhnev's tactics, however, won the approval of Stalin, and in 1952 he moved to Moscow as a member of the Central Committee of the Communist Party and a candidate (non-voting) member of the Politburo.

Brezhnev was too closely associated with the Stalinist purges not to be adversely affected by the power struggle following the dictator's death in March 1953. Brezhnev was dropped from the Politburo and did not reappear until 1956, when his old friend Khrushchev had successfully disposed of LAVRENTY BERIA and GEORGI MALENKOV. During his time in the political wilderness, Brezhnev worked to distance himself from Stalin and in 1956 helped Khrushchev to prepare his attack on Stalin, which led to the Polish and Hungarian uprisings. In 1956 Brezhnev again became a candidate member of the Politburo and began his involvement with the development of the Soviet Union's rocket and guided missile program. The following year he was made a full member of the Politburo.

In 1960 Brezhnev became chairman of the Presidium of the Supreme Soviet (parliament), a post equivalent to titular president, and in 1963 he took on the added responsibilities of Central Committee secretary in charge of personnel selection, an appointment that enabled him to increase his political power base by promoting supporters to key positions.

By this time, Brezhnev was regarded as the number-two man in the Soviet hierarchy. He appears to have played little role in the palace coup that ousted Khrushchev in 1964. His strategy appears to have been to observe and at the appropriate moment project himself as the consensus candidate for the leadership. This, at least, is what happened. After Khrushchev was dismissed, a triumvirate emerged with Brezhnev as general secretary of the party, ALEXEI KOSYGIN as premier and Andrei Kirilenko as the designated number-two man in the hierarchy. Brezhnev sought to maintain this consensus structure, but through his contacts with the military he ensured that he retained the deciding vote.

Khrushchev fell from power because men such as ideologue MIKHAIL SUSLOV believed that he had gone too far in is denunciation of Stalin and that this was undermining the socialist structures of the Soviet Union and Eastern Europe. Brezhnev set out to return the Soviet Union to the doctrinaire path of Marxism-Leninism but without the purges and other excesses of the Stalinist years. Dissidents were not summarily executed, but their voices were stilled by a strengthened KGB, and if this did not work, they were sent to labor camps or psychiatric hospitals. He permitted the harassment of Jews and curbed their immigration to Israel.

On the economic front, the Soviet economy returned to a highly centralized structure geared to heavy industry and rapid defense production. The development of the Soviet nuclear arsenal and conventional forces was a key element in Brezhnev's foreign policy. He firmly believed that the only way that the Soviet Union could win a respected place at the world's conference tables was by achieving military parity with the United States and then, from that position, preaching the Khrushchev doctrine of peaceful coexistence, which he renamed DTENTE.

Brezhnev saw dtente as a mutual Soviet-American recognition of each other's interests and "a willingness to resolve differences not by force or saber rattling, but at the conference table." The policy held a certain appeal for U.S. President RICHARD NIXON and his chief foreign policy adviser HENRY KISSINGER, and the working relationship between these men led to the signing of the 1972 SALT I treaty, the first major U.S.-Soviet strategic arms limitation agreement. (See STRATEGIC ARMS LIMITATION TALKS.)

For Brezhnev, however, the highpoint of dtente was the 1975 signing of the Helsinki Accords at the CONFERENCE ON SECURITY AND COOPERATION IN EUROPE. The agreement implicitly recognized Soviet dominance in Eastern Europe but at the same time created future problems for Brezhnev by committing the 35 national signatories to improved human rights.

U.S.-Soviet relations started to deteriorate shortly after the Helsinki Agreement. President JIMMY CARTER's heavy emphasis on human rights issues was interpreted by Brezhnev as interference in the Soviet Union's internal affairs, and this clouded other U.S.-Soviet discussions, including the SALT II treaty. Dtente was dealt its death blow by Brezhnev's decision to invade AFGHANISTAN in December 1979. Its coffin was sealed by the U.S. Senate's rejection of SALT II, the election of President Ronald Reagan and the declaration of martial law in Poland in 1980.

Brezhnev's opposition to Polish reforms was symptomatic of his near-Stalinist line toward Eastern Europe. This was, in Brezhnev's opinion, an area of vital national interest to the Soviet heartland. Poland, in particular, remained the traditional military corridor for an attack from the West on the Russian heartland. In 1968 Brezhnev had ordered Soviet troops into Czechoslovakia to quell the uprising there. To justify the action, the Soviet leader developed the BREZHNEV DOCTRINE, which stated that danger to socialism in one country represented a danger to all socialist states and, as such, could not be tolerated. Practical politics, however, did lead to some relaxation of doctrinaire socialism in Poland, Czechoslovakia and Hungary. But this was kept to a minimum until after Brezhnev's death.

Brezhnev took a similar intolerant view toward the rise of Eurocommunism, which led to a weakening of the Soviet influence among the West European communist parties and contributed to the rise of the French Socialist Party at the expense of the French communists. Brezhnev managed to forge a special relationship with the politically conservative French presidents CHARLES DE GAULLE, Georges Pompidou and VALERY GISCARD-D'ESTAING. But Franco-Soviet relations deteriorated with the election as president of France of Socialist Party leader FRANCOIS MITTERRAND.

Brezhnev's closest relationship with a Western leader was forged with West German chancellor WILLY BRANDT, whose OSTPOLITIK mirrored and supported Brezhnev's dtente. Brandt was a regular visitor to Moscow, and Brezhnev upgraded West German–Soviet relations and visited Bonn more often than any other Western capital. Brezhnev also had a good relationship with Brandt's successor, Chancellor HELMUT SCHMIDT.

Anglo-Soviet relations deteriorated during the Brezhnev years. The Soviet leader was dismissive of Britain's place in world affairs, which he regarded as little more than that of an American lackey. British Labour prime ministers HAROLD WILSON and JAMES CALLAGHAN liked to think that they had a special relationship with Brezhnev, but this was not echoed by the Soviet leader, who downgraded diplomatic relations with Britain. He underestimated the appeal and influence of Conservative leader MARGARET THATCHER, whom he dubbed "The Iron Lady," an epithet that only helped her campaign.

Sino-Soviet relations during the Brezhnev years were marked by a continuation of the deterioration that had started under Khrushchev. Brezhnev's unstinting support for North Vietnam during its war with the United States owed as much to his desire to contain Chinese influence as it did his wish to see the U.S. forces defeated and humiliated. Brezhnev was so frightened of the regime of MAO ZEDONG that at the height of his dtente relationship with Nixon he suggested a preemptive U.S.-Soviet nuclear strike against China. But as U.S.-Soviet relations plummeted following the election of Reagan, Brezhnev sought to improve relations with China. In his last major speech, in March 1982, he called on the Chinese to join in ending Sino-Soviet hostility.

A major foreign policy priority for Brezhnev was the Third World. The emergent countries had been singled out by Khrushchev as an area where communism could make major inroads by projecting itself as the logical alternative to the capitalism of the departing colonial powers. This led to Soviet and Cuban involvement in Ethiopia, Angola and Mozambique. Brezhnev maintained close relations with Cuba, whose troops played a major part in both the Horn of Africa and southern Africa. President Reagan accused Brezhnev of using Cuba as his stalking horse in Central America.

Soviet influence in the strategic Middle East waned significantly during the Brezhnev years. The Soviet Union lost its regional power base in Egypt when its civilian and military personnel were expelled by President Anwar Sadat. It maintained some influence through its relationships with Syria and South Yemen and to a lesser extent Iraq, but these were not significant enough to give them the voice that Soviet foreign policymakers felt necessary. After the fall of the shah of Iran, Brezhnev made tentative attempts to improve relations with Iran, but these fell afoul of the invasion of Afghanistan and the Iran-Iraq Gulf War.

In his later years, Brezhnev succumbed to the temptation of the personality cult. Streets and towns were named after him, and giant Brezhnev posters decorated Moscow walls. In 1976 he promoted himself to field marshal of the army, the highest military rank. The following year he replaced NIKOLAI PODGORNY as president of the Soviet Union and became the first Soviet leader to hold both the top party and government posts. He awarded himself the Order of Victory, the nation's highest military honor, in 1978.

Some observers have interpreted the creation of the personality cult as an essential adjunct to Brezhnev's attempts to protect himself from attacks on his handling of the Soviet economy. Heavy defense expenditure coupled with overcentralization and heavy subsidies led to what MIKHAIL GORBACHEV dubbed the "years of stagnation." Brezhnev's economic failure subsequently led to cutbacks in defense expenditure and a less expansionist foreign policy. After his death, Brezhnev was as reviled within the Soviet Union as he was revered during his life.

For Further Information:
Breslauer, G.W. *Khrushchev and Brezhnev as Leaders.* London, 1982.
Edmonds, R. *Soviet Foreign Policy: The Brezhnev Years.* Oxford and New York, 1983.
Gelman, Harry. *The Brezhnev Politburo and the Decline of Detente.* Ithaca, N.Y., 1984.
Kelley, Donald R., *Soviet Politics in the Brezhnev Era.* New York, 1980.

Brezhnev Doctrine The Brezhnev Doctrine was formulated by Soviet leader LEONID BREZHNEV in the aftermath of the 1968 Warsaw Pact invasion of CZECHOSLOVAKIA. Its purpose was to justify ideologically the invasion of Czechoslovakia and to state publicly how much flexibility Moscow would allow Soviet Bloc countries in their domestic political affairs. The doctrine played a major role in isolating the Soviet Communist Party from communist parties in Western Europe and elsewhere.

The Brezhnev Doctrine was enunciated by Brezhnev at the Polish Communist Party's Fifth Congress in Warsaw on November 12, 1968, three months after the Warsaw Pact invasion of Czechoslovakia. In his speech, Brezhnev mentioned Czechoslovakia only once, but the inference was clear. His choice of Warsaw for delivery of the speech was also important because Poland had the most potent and anti-Soviet nationalist movement.

Brezhnev appealed for unity among the world communist parties and insisted that communist-ruled countries stood for "strict respect" of sovereignty. "But," he added, "when internal and external forces that are hostile to socialism try to turn the development of some socialist country toward the restoration of a capitalist regime . . . [it is] a common problem of all socialist countries." The Warsaw meeting, the first major Socialist Bloc gathering after the invasion of Czechoslovakia, was well attended by communist leaders from around the world. Giancarlo Pajetta, representing the Italian Communist Party, said in response to Brezhnev's speech that international unity depended on "specific national conditions and respect for the autonomy of every party." He added: "In current circumstances we regard it as our duty to trace out and follow our own road to socialism." The Italian Communist Party response to the Brezhnev Doctrine helped lead to the development of EUROCOMMUNISM.

For Further Information:
Gelman, Harry. *The Brezhnev Politburo and the Decline of Detente.* Ithaca, N.Y., 1980.
Luttwak, Edward N. *The Grand Strategy of the Soviet Union.* London, 1983.

Bricker, John W. **(September 6, 1893–March 22, 1986)**
U.S. Senator John Bricker was an old-guard Republican conservative who was severely critical of the YALTA and POTSDAM agreements. During the TRUMAN and EISENHOWER administrations he sponsored the Bricker Amendment, which sought to amend the U.S. Constitution to curb the president's treaty-making powers. The failure of the Congress to adopt the Bricker Amendment marked the end of the isolationist wing of the Republican Party.

After serving in World War I as an army chaplain, Bricker attended Ohio State University Law School, graduating in 1921. An active Republican, he quickly became involved in Ohio politics and was elected governor in 1938. In 1944 he

was THOMAS DEWEY's running mate in the presidential elections, and in 1946 Bricker was elected to the U.S. Senate.

Bricker was a traditional Republican isolationist. He was strongly opposed to the United Nations, condemned secret wartime agreements made by President FRANKLIN ROOSEVELT with the Soviet Union and attacked the Yalta and Potsdam agreements. He opposed American funding for the International Labour Organization and the International Atomic Energy Agency and was severely critical of the United Nations Covenant on Human Rights because it included provision for the suspension of freedom of speech during a national emergency. He also initiated cuts in foreign aid and voted against confirmation of CHARLES BOHLEN as ambassador to the Soviet Union.

During the Truman administration, Bricker first proposed a constitutional amendment to restrict the federal government's treaty-making powers. In 1952 he managed to have his proposal written into the Republican Party platform. But it was not until January 7, 1953, that Bricker formally introduced his amendment. The Bricker Amendment would have voided any treaties that conflicted with the Constitution. It also stipulated that domestic policy could not be overruled by foreign treaties, executive agreements and international organizations unless they were accompanied by supporting federal or state legislation. Finally, the Bricker Amendment would have made it necessary for the president to seek Senate ratification for all understandings reached with foreign governments.

The Bricker Amendment became a major political cause clbre in the early days of the Eisenhower administration, and pro- and anti-Bricker organizations sprung up around the country. It was supported by the American Legion, Daughters of the American Revolution and the American Bar Association. Because its wording also provided a defense of states' rights, the amendment was also actively supported by Southern segregationists.

The major critics were internationalists such as ELEANOR ROOSEVELT and the liberal anti-communist lobby group AMERICANS FOR DEMOCRATIC ACTION. President Eisenhower and Secretary of State JOHN FOSTER DULLES also opposed the amendment because they felt it would shackle American foreign policy. But they initially remained aloof from the debate for fear of splitting the Republican Party. As support for the Bricker Amendment grew, however, Eisenhower had no choice but to express his opposition. In January 1954 he said that the amendment would signal America's intention "to withdraw from its leadership in world affairs."

The Bricker Amendment was put to a vote on the Senate floor on February 25, 1954. It failed 42 votes to 50. The next day, a watered-down version of the amendment sponsored by Senator WALTER GEORGE fell one vote short of the required two-thirds majority. Bricker tried to reintroduce his amendment in 1955, but the proposal and the isolationist lobby were effectively dead.

Bricker lost his Senate seat to Democrat Stephen Young.

He retired from active politics to practice law in Columbus, Ohio, until his death on March 22, 1986.

For Further Information:
Adler, Selig. *The Isolationist Impulse: Its Twentieth Century Reaction.* New York, 1957.
Commager, Henry Steele. "The Perilous Folly of Senator Bricker," *The Reporter* (October 13, 1953).
Spanier, J.W. *American Foreign Policy Since World War Two.* Washington, D.C., 1988.

Bridges, Henry Styles (September 9, 1898–November 26, 1961) U.S. Senator Styles Bridges was a leading conservative Republican of the early Cold War years and was especially critical of President TRUMAN's unenthusiastic support of CHIANG KAI-SHEK. He was also a strong supporter of Senator JOSEPH MCCARTHY and General DOUGLAS MACARTHUR.

Bridges graduated from the University of Maine in 1918 with an agricultural degree. During the 1920s he was an agricultural adviser and in 1934 was elected New Hampshire's youngest-ever governor. In 1936 Bridges was elected to the U.S. Senate, where he opposed the Roosevelt administration's New Deal. In 1940 he was a candidate for the Republican presidential nomination.

By the time Truman became president in 1945, Bridges was regarded as one of the most powerful Republicans in the Senate. On domestic issues he continued to vote conservative. On foreign policy issues he became one of the leading American conservatives.

Bridges subscribed to the belief that the Soviet Union was masterminding a communist plot to control the world. He pressed for a formal break in diplomatic relations with the Soviet Union, successfully lobbied for the end of lend-lease supplies to the Soviets, supported Chiang Kai-shek, opposed aid to Yugoslavia and regarded any Americans with links to communism or the Soviet Union as Soviet-manipulated subversives.

Bridges was deeply involved in trying to push America's policy in China toward a more pronounced anti-communist line. In 1945 he claimed that the Truman administration was planning to "abandon" China to the communists. After the collapse of Chiang Kai-shek's Nationalist government in 1949, Bridges encouraged PATRICK HURLEY, the former U.S. ambassador to China, to pursue his claims that U.S. diplomats had worked for the defeat of Chiang. He also joined the campaign for the dismissal of DEAN ACHESON because of his "loss" of China. He supported Senator Joseph McCarthy's demand for an investigation of "subversives" in the State Department.

In 1950 Bridges became Senate minority leader and continued to attack Truman's foreign policy. During the KOREAN WAR he called for a Nationalist invasion of mainland China and described the dismissal of General MacArthur as a "tragedy."

Bridges continued his strident anti-communist crusade throughout the Eisenhower administration. In 1953 he un-

successfully opposed the appointment of CHARLES BOHLEN as ambassador to the Soviet Union on the grounds that Bohlen had helped to negotiate the YALTA Agreement, which Bridges described as a "traitorous mishandling of American foreign policy."

A consistent supporter of Senator McCarthy, Bridges tried to prevent a Senate censure of McCarthy. When the censure motion went ahead in December 1954, Bridges attacked it as a "blow against patriotic anti-Communism."

In 1955 Bridges opposed U.S. participation in the GENEVA SUMMIT conference on the grounds that all international conferences held the dangers of "appeasement, compromise and weakness." In 1956 he attempted to cut off all aid to Yugoslavia and to reduce aid to India because of its nonaligned status.

In March 1961 Bridges attacked President Kennedy's decision to end the interception of mail sent from communist countries. He also cosponsored a resolution urging Kennedy to resume nuclear testing. Bridges supported Kennedy's tough stand during the 1961 Berlin crisis and at its height tried to prohibit all assistance to nations trading "strategic materials" with communist countries. Bridges was elected five times to the U.S. Senate. He suffered a heart attack on September 21, 1961, and died two months later.

For Further Information:
Bachrack, Stanley D. *The Committee of One Million: "China Lobby" Politics 1953–1971.* New York, 1976.
Griffith, Robert. *The Politics of Fear.* Lexington, Ky., 1970.
Purifoy, Lewis McCarroll. *Harry Truman's China Policy: McCarthyism and the Diplomacy of Hysteria.* New York, 1976.

Brinkmanship Brinkmanship was a term used in the 1950s and 1960s to denote the willingness of an adversary to go to the brink of disaster in protection of perceived national interests.

The term was first used by U.S. secretary of state JOHN FOSTER DULLES in a *Life* Magazine interview published on January 16, 1956. In the article, Dulles defended his "brinkmanship" policies. He said that the United States had gone "to the verge of war" to maintain the peace.

Dulles maintained that "the ability to get to the verge without getting into war is a necessary art." He added: "We walked to the brink and we looked it in the face." Dulles was referring in his interview to the clashes over QUEMOY AND MATSU ISLANDS and BERLIN. But possibly the best example of brinkmanship was the CUBAN MISSILE CRISIS.

For Further Information:
Drummond, Roscoe, and Gaston Coblents. *Duel at the Brink: John Foster Dulles' Command of American Power.* Garden City, N.Y., 1960.

British Army of the Rhine (BAOR) The British Army of the Rhine, through the Cold War, consisted of 55,000 British troops permanently based in West Germany, the second largest foreign military force in the country.

The BAOR was put in place in 1945 as a postwar occupation force but quickly developed into the first British line of defense against a Soviet attack. The BAOR protected a vital section of the NATO Central Front. Its area of responsibility is some 60 miles long in the industrially important section of northern West Germany. Its left flank was protected by the German Army Corps and its right flank by a Belgian Army Corps.

The BAOR, which is still in place in a reduced form, was equipped almost entirely with conventional forces, with a heavy complement of tanks, but it also had some battlefield nuclear weapons under a joint command arrangement with the United States.

Over the years, the British government made repeated efforts to withdraw troops from Germany as an economy measure. In the immediate postwar years this was impossible because the BAOR doubled as an occupation army. It was hoped that the creation of the EUROPEAN DEFENSE COMMUNITY would allow the troops to be withdrawn, but when the French National Assembly rejected the EDC in 1954, Britain had to agree to maintain its forces in Germany as part of a deal to extend the WESTERN EUROPEAN UNION to West Germany.

From the 1960s on there were alternative proposals to reduce the cost to Britain by basing a large number of the soldiers at home, but committing them exclusively to the defense of Germany. This proposal proved unacceptable to Britain's allies.

In July 1991, the British government announced plans for a 20% reduction in the armed forces over three years due to the end of the Cold War. Included in the proposed cuts was a 58% reduction in the BAOR, to 23,000 men.

British Treasury Paper on Post-War Germany (1945)

The British Treasury Paper on Post-War Germany, submitted to the War Cabinet on March 7, 1945, formulated the British economic policy toward occupied Germany. This policy later came to be accepted by the Americans and French.

At the time there was strong pressure for destroying the economic strength of Germany in order to deprive it of capital resources needed for rearmament. The Soviets demanded $20 billion in war reparations, and U.S. treasury secretary HENRY MORGENTHAU presented a plan for the "pastoralization" of Germany.

The British Treasury argued that both policies would place the occupying powers in a position of paying for imports into Germany while the Germans were paying reparations. The Allies would in fact be paying for the German reparations. The paper went on to argue that if Germany were stripped of its capital resources, large sums would be required from other parts of Europe to support the German people, leading to the impoverishment of the rest of Europe.

The best policy, argued the Treasury, was to work for the redevelopment of the German economy and its integration within the general economy of the Western European countries. The paper also suggested that if the Soviet Union

attempted to set up an economic system in its own zone in keeping with its socialist policies and demand for reparations, then the British should carefully reconsider the desirability of the Western sectors reunifying with the Soviet zone.

Brosio, Manlio (July 10, 1897–March 14, 1980) Manlio Brosio was a respected Italian diplomat and secretary general of the NORTH ATLANTIC TREATY ORGANIZATION (NATO) from 1964 to 1971, a time when the alliance was faced with serious internal crises.

Brosio was born in Turin and studied law at that city's university. During World War I he served as an artillery officer and was highly decorated. Brosio entered politics in 1920 as a member of the Liberal Party and quickly became an opponent of the fascist movement. His opposition to Mussolini led eventually to the government's banning him from all political activities.

After the fall of Mussolini in July 1943, Brosio resumed his political career, first as a member of the Italian National Liberation Committee and then as a member of the cabinet in governments between 1944 and 1946. His posts included minister without portfolio, deputy prime minister and minister of defense.

In January 1947 Brosio started his diplomatic career as Italy's ambassador to the Soviet Union. He was in Moscow until 1951 and was deeply involved in the peace negotiations between the Soviet Union and Italy, in reparations and in the exchange of prisoners of war as well as the negotiations leading to the first postwar Soviet–Italian trade agreement.

In January 1952 Brosio was appointed ambassador to Britain and represented Italy in the negotiations over TRIESTE, and eventually signed the final treaty on behalf of the Italian government in 1954. Subsequently Brosio was ambassador to the United States from January 1955 to June 1961 and ambassador to France from 1961 to 1964.

On May 13, 1964, Brosio was appointed secretary general of NATO in succession to DIRK STIKKER. While Brosio was at the top NATO job, the organization faced a number of difficult issues, and his diplomatic skills were credited with keeping NATO on an even keel. Some of the problems included: the debate of the Multinational Nuclear Force and the creation of the NUCLEAR PLANNING GROUP, the withdrawal of France, the HARMEL REPORT on political cooperation, the explosion of the first Chinese nuclear bomb, the VIETNAM WAR, deteriorating relations between Greece and Turkey, the 1968 Soviet invasion of CZECHOSLOVAKIA, DÉTENTE and OSTPOLITIK, the Arab–Israeli Six-Day War in the Middle East and changes in defense planning to incorporate the strategy of FLEXIBLE RESPONSE.

In 1971, shortly before he left NATO, Brosio attacked the MANSFIELD Amendment, which proposed to reduce American forces in Europe. Brosio, in a letter to President Richard NIXON, warned that Senator Mike Mansfield's proposal "could deeply affect the political and moral strength of NATO" and deprive it of the alternative of a nonnuclear response. Brosio's letter was released by the White House and contributed to the proposal's defeat in the Senate by a 61–36 vote.

Brosio retired as NATO secretary general in June 1971, when he was replaced by Dr. Joseph Luns. In September 1971 Brosio was awarded the U.S. Medal of Freedom, the highest U.S. civilian citation. In October 1971 he was asked by the North Atlantic Council to conduct exploratory talks with the Soviet Union on the subject of mutual and balanced force reductions. These talks led to the establishment of the Mutual Balance Force Reduction Talks (MBFR) in Vienna, aimed at reducing conventional forces in Europe. Brosio retired from active politics the following year.

For Further Information:

Calleo, David P. *The Atlantic Fantasy: The U.S., NATO and Europe.* Baltimore, 1970.
Grosser, Alfred. *The Western Alliance, European–American Relations Since 1945.* New York, 1978.
Neustadt, Richard E. *Alliance Politics.* New York, 1970.
Pfaltzgraff, Robert L., Jr. "The United States, Partners in a Multipolar World," *Orbis* (Spring 1973).

Browder, Earl (May 20, 1891–June 27, 1973) Earl Browder was the wartime leader of the American Communist Party (CPUSA). He advocated continued postwar cooperation between communist and capitalist notions. His fall from party leadership as World War II drew to a close indicated a confrontational attitude toward the United States by JOSEF STALIN.

Browder was forced to leave school at age nine to help support his family. In 1912 he joined the Syndicalist League of North America, generally regarded as a forerunner of the American Communist Party.

When the United States entered World War I in 1917, Browder sought a court order to prevent the draft laws from being implemented in Missouri, where he was living. He was imprisoned for conspiracy to block the draft as well as for refusing to register. On his release in 1920 Browder became one of the first members of the CPUSA, and in 1921 he visited Moscow, where he met Lenin.

In 1934 Browder succeeded William Z. Foster as party general secretary when the latter resigned because of ill health. Browder loyally toed the Moscow line. During the Nazi-Soviet nonaggression pact from 1939 to 1941 he attacked World War II as the "second imperialist war." But when the Germans attacked the Soviet Union he urged the United States to enter the war, and after Pearl Harbor he became a keen advocate of increased American military efforts to open a Western front in Europe in order to relieve the pressure on the Eastern Russian Front.

Up until 1944 Browder was the model internationalist and a strict adherent to the Moscow line of the day. But in 1944 he came into direct conflict with Stalin's policies when he proposed that for the sake of America's "national unity," the communists cease to act as a political party and rename themselves the Communist Political Association (CPA).

In May 1945 French Communist Party Leader Jacques Duclos, acting at the behest of Stalin, attacked Browder for engineering the "liquidation of the Communist Party" in the United States and accused him of deviations from "Marxist-Leninist understanding." The following month, the party executive voted Browder out of the leadership and Foster returned to power. In July Foster called Browder a "bourgeois reformist" and accused him of casting away the goal of socialism and "substituting for it a capitalist utopia."

In September 1945 Browder was subpoenaed to appear before the newly formed House Un-American Activities Committee to explain the ideological differences that led to his expulsion from the party leadership. He refused to answer any questions.

In February 1946 Browder was formally expelled from the Communist Party. He traveled to Moscow to appeal to Soviet foreign minister V.M. MOLOTOV for readmission. But the Soviets were set on a policy course and Browder was a pawn who had already been sacrificed. He had become too closely associated with Soviet-American wartime amity and sought to continue the friendship in the postwar years. He was a symbol that did not represent the current state of U.S.–Soviet relations. Browder's removal from the party was a sign of Stalin's hardening attitudes. His reinstatement would have indicated a desire to improve U.S.–Soviet relations at a time when such a desire did not exist.

Molotov tried to soften the blow for Browder by appointing him American distributor of Soviet scientific literature. But Browder wanted to return to party politics. Between 1948 and 1952 he made several vain attempts to gain readmission. In 1950 he was cited for contempt of Congress after he refused to testify before a Senate Foreign Relations subcommittee investigating communist infiltration of the State Department. The contempt ruling put Browder in jail from December 1950 to March 1951, when a federal judge ruled that he was within his rights in refusing to answer irrelevant questions.

The party refused to come to Browder's aid during his contempt trial or his period in prison. This fueled his growing bitterness toward the party structure, and in 1952 he announced that he would no longer seek readmission.

Browder remained a target for Senator Joseph McCarthy, who accused him of aiding the Soviet Union's wartime subversion in China. But Browder himself never again took an active political role, and in 1971, at the age of 80, he said he no longer considered himself a Marxist. Earl Browder died in 1973.

For Further Information:

Spiro, George. *Earl Browder, Communist or Tool of Wall Street: Stalin, Trotsky or Lenin.* New York, 1937.
Starobin, Joseph R. *American Communism in Crisis, 1943–57.* Berkeley and Los Angeles, 1972.

Brown, Winthrop (July 12, 1907–May 25, 1987) Winthrop Brown was American ambassador to Laos from 1960 to

1962, when that country was in a complex civil war. His support for neutralist elements was a major factor in President JOHN F. KENNEDY's decision to shift American foreign policy.

After graduating from Yale Law School in 1929, Brown practiced law in New York. During World War II he helped administer the Lend-Lease program. After the war he joined the diplomatic service and in the 1950s was minister-counselor for economics at the U.S. embassies in London and New Delhi. He was named ambassador to Laos in July 1960.

Laos' strategic position in relation to Vietnam, Cambodia and Thailand made it the key to control of Indochina. When the SOUTHEAST ASIA TREATY ORGANIZATION was formed in September 1954, a special protocol extended the organization's defensive perimeter around Vietnam, Laos and Cambodia, and U.S. secretary of state JOHN FOSTER DULLES drew up a plan that called for Laos to build an army of 25,000 men as a "bulwark against Communism." In pursuit of this policy, the Eisenhower government provided $300 million between 1954 and 1960. More than 90% of the money was military aid.

The military aid was spent in combating the North Vietnamese-supported Pathet Lao who controlled the northeastern corner of the country. But a large proportion was also distributed in graft and patronage, which undermined grass roots support for U.S. policy and strengthened the Pathet Lao. When Prime Minister Prince Souvanna Phouma came to power he struck a neutralist position in the Cold War conflict and tried to negotiate with the Pathet Lao. This alarmed the Eisenhower administration, which in 1958 ordered the CENTRAL INTELLIGENCE AGENCY to install the pro-Western Phoumi Nosavan in power as a replacement for the neutralist Prince Souvanna. The Pathet Lao stopped negotiations and returned to fighting.

Brown arrived in Laos just as Laotian Air Force officer Kong Le staged an anticorruption coup to bring Prince Souvanna back into an anti-Pathet Lao coalition. Brown supported Kong Le's actions, but the Pentagon, CIA and the Far Eastern Desk at the State Department continued to back Phoumi, with the result that civil war broke out between Phoumi and Prince Souvanna. Brown pressed for a reorientation of American policy and risked his career by returning instructions to Washington and asking for further clarification in order to maintain a discussion of policy options.

But the Eisenhower administration, by now convinced that Prince Souvanna and Kong Le were communists, or at least communist sympathizers, continued their support of Phoumi, who in December 1960 marched on Vientiane and drove Prince Souvanna into exile.

Phoumi's victory coincided with the start of the administration of President Kennedy, who supported Brown's calls for a shift in support to Souvanna. In the meantime, Phoumi's campaign against the Pathet Lao was in disarray, and the Soviet Union, seeing a major opportunity in Indochina, started airlifting supplies to the communist forces. President Kennedy, closely following Brown's advice, gradually started shifting American foreign policy from the establishment of an anti-communist bastion in Laos to the establishment of a neutral Laos.

On April 24, 1961, the Soviet Union agreed to a ceasefire in Laos after Kennedy threatened to step up U.S. military action. On May 12 the Geneva Conference on Laos started and the conditions for a neutralized Laos were established. A neutralist Laotian government was finally formed in June 1962.

Brown took little part in either the Geneva negotiations or the talks to form the neutralist government. Responsibility for these discussions was taken over by AVERELL HARRIMAN. Shortly after the new Laotian government was formed, Brown left to become the U.S. ambassador to South Korea. Later he served as special assistant to the secretary of state and from 1968 to 1970 he was deputy assistant secretary of state for East Asian and Pacific affairs. Brown retired from the foreign service in 1970.

For Further Information:
Schlesinger, Arthur. *A Thousand Days.* New York, 1965.
Stevenson, Charles A. *The End of Nowhere, American Policy Towards Laos Since 1954.* Boston, 1972.

Bruce, David   (February 12, 1898–December 4, 1977)
David Bruce was one of America's most respected and skilled postwar diplomats. He was the only U.S. diplomat to hold the three most important ambassadorships in Europe: France, Germany and Britain. In 1968 he signed the Nuclear Non-Proliferation Treaty on behalf of the United States. He also served as negotiator at the Vietnam Peace Talks, liaison officer to communist China and U.S. Ambassador to the NORTH ATLANTIC TREATY ORGANIZATION (NATO).

Bruce was born into a prominent and wealthy Baltimore family. He studied at Princeton University and the University of Maryland, where he received his law degree. His marriage to heiress Ailsa Mellon introduced him to the world of high finance, including a directorship of the Bankers Trust Company and Harriman and Co. During World War II he organized the British base of the Office of Strategic Services, the wartime predecessor of the CIA, and headed OSS operations in Europe between 1943 and 1945.

In 1947 Bruce joined his long-time friend and business associate W. AVERELL HARRIMAN at the Department of Commerce. A year later he was sent to France to head America's Economic Cooperation Administration there. As head of the ECA mission, Bruce was instrumental in distributing American funds, which helped to stabilize the delicate French political situation. He also formed a close relationship with the French politician JEAN MONNET and arranged American support for Monnet's plan to revitalize the French coal and steel industries. Monnet later became one of the founders of the EUROPEAN ECONOMIC COMMUNITY (EEC). Through Monnet, Bruce became an active proponent of European integration and was one of the originators of the concept of a European army.

President HARRY TRUMAN appointed Bruce ambassador to France in April 1949. In this position he played a major role in ensuring that the governments of the Fourth Republic pursued a pro-American foreign policy.

In 1952, Bruce returned to Washington as undersecretary of state. He was also appointed an alternate governor of the International Monetary Fund and a governor of the World Bank. In 1953, President DWIGHT EISENHOWER sent Bruce back to Europe as an observer at the Interim Commission of the EUROPEAN DEFENSE COMMUNITY (EDC) and special representative to the embryonic EUROPEAN COAL AND STEEL COMMUNITY (ECSC). Bruce played an important part in ensuring U.S. support for both projects, an essential element in their success. The ECSC prospered and went on to become, in 1958, the EEC. The EDC, however, collapsed after the treaty was rejected by the French National Assembly in August 1954.

Bruce left full-time diplomatic work between 1955 and 1957 but returned in January 1957 as U.S. ambassador to West Germany. In November 1959 he resigned his diplomatic post to serve as a foreign policy adviser to the campaign of Senator JOHN F. KENNEDY. After his election Kennedy appointed Bruce ambassador to Britain. Bruce's main task was to recreate the special Anglo-American relationship, which had been severely strained by the 1956 SUEZ CRISIS. Bruce succeeded in this task by establishing a personal relationship with Prime Minister HAROLD MACMILLAN that was matched only by the relationship between Kennedy and the British ambassador in Washington, David Ormsby-Gore. At the same time, however, it became clear during Bruce's long tenure in London that the Anglo-American relationship had changed from a partnership to a dependent role for Britain.

Bruce left London for part-time retirement in 1969 after an unprecedented eight years in the post. In July 1970 he was called out of retirement by President RICHARD NIXON to head the American negotiating team at the Paris peace talks on Vietnam. He remained chief negotiator until July 31, 1971, when he resigned because of ill health. Throughout the talks, Bruce accused the North Vietnamese of negotiating in bad faith and attacked their treatment of American prisoners of war.

After Nixon's historic visit to Beijing in 1972, the president asked Bruce to head America's first diplomatic mission to mainland China since 1949. As head of the U.S. liaison office, Bruce dealt mainly with trade and cultural issues, as the U.S. still withheld full diplomatic recognition of the communist government. But Bruce's careful cultivation of Chinese leaders eventually led to a normalization of Sino-American relations.

Bruce remained in China until September 1974, when he was replaced by Republican Party national chairman GEORGE BUSH. Two months later, President GERALD FORD asked Bruce to become ambassador to NATO. He remained in Brussels until his retirement in January 1976. The following month Bruce was awarded the Medal of Freedom for 50 years of distinguished diplomatic service. On December 5, 1977, David Bruce died of a heart attack.

For Further Information
Nunnerley, David. *President Kennedy and Britain.* New York, 1972.
Spanier, J.W. *American Foreign Policy Since World War Two.* Washington, D.C., 1988.

Brussels Treaty   (1948)   The Brussels Treaty of March 17, 1948, was the immediate forerunner of the NORTH ATLANTIC TREATY ORGANIZATION. In 1955 it was extended to include West Germany and became the legal foundation of the WESTERN EUROPEAN UNION.

The Brussels Treaty of 1948 was the second stage in a three-stage, successful attempt by British foreign secretary ERNEST BEVIN to tie the United States to the defense of Western Europe. To do this, Bevin believed he had to show that Europeans were aware of the Soviet threat and recognized the need to cooperate in their joint defense. The first stage was the 50-year ANGLO-FRENCH TREATY OF ALLIANCE AND MUTUAL ASSISTANCE signed on March 4, 1947.

On January 22, 1948, Bevin outlined an agreement among Britain, France, Belgium, the Netherlands and Luxembourg and found the plan quickly endorsed by the TRUMAN administration and the Benelux countries. PAUL-HENRI SPAAK, Belgian prime minister and foreign minister, said, "The hour of choice has arrived. We must choose our friends and allies, not in a spirit of hostility toward anyone, but to preserve peace and liberty."

Bevin then invited the Benelux foreign ministers, and the foreign ministers of the Western occupying powers in Germany, to convene in London to discuss policies toward Germany. At the same time diplomats from Britain, France and the Benelux countries started negotiations aimed at achieving greater political, economic and military cooperation. As the London meeting opened on February 23, Czechoslovakia fell victim to a communist coup. With this background, Bevin had little difficulty in quickly securing a commitment to greater European defense cooperation. The agreement was initialed on March 13 and formally signed within four days. Under the terms of the treaty the five countries agreed to the following:

1.   If any of the five states "should be the object of an armed attack in Europe," the others would "afford the party so attacked all military and other aid and assistance in their power."
2.   In the event of attacks on possessions outside Europe, the five countries would consult.
3.   The treaty was to last for 50 years.
4.   The five states could, by common consent, admit "any other state."
5.   The five states agreed to organize and coordinate their economic programs and increase their mutual trade.

For Further Information:
Albrecht-Carrie, Rene. *The Unity of Europe.* London, 1966.
Mayne, Richard. *The Recovery of Europe.* New York, 1970.

Brzezinski, Zbigniew (March 28, 1928–   ) Zbigniew Brzezinski was national security adviser to President JIMMY CARTER from 1977 to 1981. He was regarded as the Carter administration's leading hard-liner and took a major role in all foreign policy discussions and decisions.

Brzezinski is the son of a Polish aristocrat who served as a diplomat in the anti-communist Polish government before World War II. Following the war and the communist takeover in Poland, the elder Brzezinski took his family to Canada. Zbigniew enrolled in McGill University, where he studied economics and political science. In 1953 he received his Ph.D. in government from Harvard University.

Brzezinski quickly established himself as an expert on communist affairs, writing and teaching extensively on the subject. In 1958 he became an American citizen and in 1961 was appointed director of Columbia University's Institute on Communist Affairs. Brzezinski established his Democratic Party credentials during the 1968 presidential campaign when he was a foreign policy adviser to Hubert Humphrey's presidential campaign.

In 1973 he became director of the Trilateral Commission, an organization that had been established that year to promote U.S., West European and Japanese cooperation in international affairs. It was through the Trilateral Commission that Brzezinski met Jimmy Carter, one of the early members. Brzezinski and Carter became close friends, and, according to Carter, Brzezinski became his "teacher" on foreign policy issues.

In 1976 president-elect Carter chose Brzezinski as his national security adviser, partly to counter Carter's own "liberal" image. Brzezinski's Polish background and generally conservative views were guaranteed to protect him, and by extension the Carter administration, from charges of being "soft on Communism." But the extreme hawkish views ascribed to Brzezinski were often overstated. He was a long-time advocate of U.S.–Soviet dialogue and at the beginning of the Nixon administration called for twice-yearly summit meetings between U.S. and Soviet leaders.

It was unavoidable that comparisons would be drawn between Brzezinski and HENRY KISSINGER, if only because Kissinger had dominated American foreign policy for the previous eight years under presidents Nixon and Ford. There was also the fact that both men came from Central Europe and spoke with pronounced accents. They had both also come from the academic community and had at various times been intellectual sparring partners. Brzezinski, however, never succeeded in creating the public persona projected by Kissinger, and his reputation for brashness alienated him from the media.

On the other hand, Brzezinski was more of a team player than Kissinger. He revived the National Security Council and revived the esprit de corps it had lost in the previous administrations. If anyone dominated foreign policy during the Carter administration it was President Carter, who was determined to control all elements of foreign policy himself.

A large part of Brzezinski's role was to teach and brief the president.

Carter and Brzezinski placed a heavy emphasis on an early conclusion of the Strategic Arms Limitation Treaty (SALT) II with the Soviet Union, but a number of factors delayed an agreement (see STRATEGIC ARMS LIMITATION TALKS). There were substantial disagreements over Backfire bombers and cruise missiles, and the atmosphere was soured by Cuban and Soviet intervention in the Horn of Africa, Zaire and Angola. The Soviets, for their part, were unhappy with the growing Sino–American links negotiated by Brzezinski.

Brzezinzki argued strongly for ratification of the SALT II treaty. Without it, he warned, "the Soviet Union could have one-third more strategic systems" than it already had. In addition, he asserted that the treaty would enable the United States to save an estimated $30 billion in the 1980s while keeping pace with Soviet weapons development. The treaty, however, encountered strong opposition within the U.S. Senate and was eventually shelved by Carter after the Soviet invasion of Afghanistan in December 1979.

One of Brzezinski's special areas of responsibility was relations with China. He regarded it as essential that the United States improve relations with communist China and play the "China Card" often and well in its relations with the Soviet Union. In May 1978 Brzezinski visited Beijing to negotiate the reestablishment of formal U.S.–Chinese relations and to arrange a visit to the United States by Chinese leader Deng Xiao-ping. The final agreement included American acceptance that Taiwan was part of China, but also pledged that the United States would protect Taiwan. Full Sino–American diplomatic relations were announced in December 1978. When Deng visited the United States in February 1979, Brzezinski hosted an "informal reunion of the negotiating team" that had worked out the normalization of relations.

Brzezinski was also one of the key members of the Carter negotiating team in 1979 at the Camp David talks among the United States, Israel and Egypt. In the aftermath of the Camp David accord, Brzezinski was sent on a tour of the Middle East to secure Saudi and Jordanian support for the agreement. Neither country would pledge its support, but both did agree to shun the Arab front, which had vowed strong opposition to the accords and action against Egypt's Anwar Sadat. The result was that for 10 years Egypt was diplomatically isolated within the Arab world, but not to such an extent that it was forced to forsake the Camp David Accords.

The biggest crisis on Brzezinski's watch was the seizure of American diplomatic hostages in Iran. A key factor prompting the embassy takeover in November 1979 was the earlier U.S. decision to admit the exiled shah for medical treatment. A number of senior Carter administration figures had opposed the decision because of the damage it could do to U.S. relations with Iran. But Brzezinski had argued forcefully in favor, maintaining that to refuse the shah entry would be a signal to the world that the United States was a fair-weather friend.

As national security adviser, Brzezinski was part of the team that met daily to discuss the hostage crisis. He was strongly in favor of the decision to send American commandos into Iran to rescue the hostages, a mission that ended in failure in the Iranian desert in April 1980.

The abortive rescue mission also resulted in the resignation of Cyrus Vance, who had been as strongly against the mission as Brzezinski had been in favor of it. The two men did occasionally disagree, but there was often less friction between the State Department and National Security Council than in other administrations. Generally, Brzezinski took the role of behind-the-scenes adviser while Vance acted as administration spokesman on foreign policy.

This system usually worked well. A good example was the two men's presentation of the administration's "new diplomacy." In separate speeches in May 1979, Brzezinski and Vance unveiled details that stressed American recognition that Washington could no longer dictate international events. Speaking before the American Society of Newspaper Editors, Brzezinski said that the purpose of American foreign policy was "to create a framework that is genuinely global, within which the individual needs of nations and peoples can be more fully satisfied." He added that the United States sought "a world community built not on the domination of a single sector, a single culture or a single ideology, but a community which draws on global diversity as the basis for strength in a pluralistic and increasingly just global order."

After the December 1979 Soviet invasion of Afghanistan, Brzezinski was sent to Pakistan to reassure its government that the United States would honor its 1959 defense treaty, which obligated it to take "appropriate action, including the use of armed force," in the event of Pakistan becoming the victim of Soviet or Afghan aggression.

Brzezinski was one of several senior administration figures awarded the U.S. Medal of Freedom a few days before Carter left office in January 1981. After he left office, Brzezinski returned to his former job as international affairs consultant at Dean Witter Reynolds, Inc., and taught at Columbia University. Brzezinski continued to speak out on foreign policy issues. He was critical of President RONALD REAGAN's nuclear policy and attacked Reagan's decision to resume the sale of American grain to the Soviet Union. Brzezinski, however, supported U.S. military aid to the CONTRA REBELS fighting the Sandinista regime in Nicaragua. In January 1987, he was named a member of a Reagan administration defense strategy panel. In September 1988, Vice President GEORGE BUSH, who was campaigning for the presidency, appointed Brzezinski co-chairman of his campaign's national security task force.

For Further Information:
Brzezinski, Zbigniew. *In Quest of National Security.* Boulder, Colo., 1988.
Carter, Jimmy. *Keeping Faith.* New York, 1982.
Forsythe, D.P. *Human Rights and United States Foreign Policy.* Tampa, Fla., 1988.
Jordan, Hamilton. *Crisis: The Last Year of the Carter Presidency.* New York, 1982.
Spanier, J.W. *American Foreign Policy Since World War Two.* Washington, D.C., 1988.
Talbott, Strobe. *Endgame: The Inside Story of SALT Two.* New York, 1979.

Buchan, Alastair   (September 9, 1918–February 3, 1976)
Alastair Buchan was a leading British writer on international relations and founded the London-based International Institute of Strategic Studies in 1958.

Buchan was born into an upper-crust British family and attended Eton and Oxford. His father was governor-general of Canada at the outbreak of World War II, and Buchan was commissioned into the Canadian Army. After the war he joined first the *Economist* and then the *London Observer*, where he worked first as Washington correspondent from 1951 to 1955 and then as the newspaper's diplomatic and defense correspondent.

His period in Washington gave him a deep understanding of, and interest in, the problems of the American political process and the new world role of the United States. This and the contacts he developed were to prove invaluable when he founded and became the first director of the International Institute of Strategic Studies (IISS) in 1958.

The IISS became a world forum for the gathering of strategic information and the encouragement of dispassionate debate on the military and political problems of the Cold War. Some of the figures who worked at the IISS under Buchan included future U.S. secretary of state Henry Kissinger, future West German chancellor Helmut Schmidt and future British defense secretary Denis Healey.

Through the IISS, Buchan created several regular publications that have become accepted primary source material. These included the annual *Military Balance*, which lists the military capabilities of almost every country in the world, and the annual *Strategic Survey*, which reviews the strategic events of the preceding year.

By the time Buchan resigned as director in 1969, the IISS drew members from more than 50 countries, many of them leading defense and political figures. The institute had also established a dialogue with leading figures in the Soviet Bloc.

In 1970 Buchan became commandant of Britain's Imperial Defense College. He is credited with transforming the military college into a serious forum for the study of all the complex issues—sociological as well as economic, technical and political—that affect national defense.

Buchan was appointed Professor of International Relations at Oxford in 1972.

Buckley, William F., Jr.   (November 24, 1925–   ) William F. Buckley Jr. is an American conservative journalist who founded and edited *The National Review*, one of the most prominent publications of the American right. He also writes two syndicated columns, hosts a television discussion program and helped to found the Young Americans for Freedom.

Buckley was born into one of America's wealthiest and most conservative Roman Catholic families. After serving in the army during World War II, he entered Yale University, where he edited the *Yale Daily News*. After graduation in 1950, he wrote the best-selling book *God and Man at Yale*, which attacked the university's liberal and secular orientation and immediately established Buckley as a leading archconservative.

In 1954 Buckley further established his conservative credentials with his book *McCarthy and His Enemies*, which he wrote in collaboration with L. Brent Bozell. Buckley and Bozell accepted that Senator JOSEPH MCCARTHY was guilty of slander and sensationalism but wrote that McCarthyism was a movement "around which men of good will and stern morality can close ranks."

Buckley founded the biweekly *National Review* in 1955 with the aim of producing a conservative platform to compete against two liberal political reviews, *The New Republic* and *The Nation*. In 1962, the *National Review* started publishing Buckley's column "A Conservative Voice," which became widely syndicated. Buckley was a vigorous opponent of the Soviet Union and repeatedly stated, "Better the chance of being dead than the certainty of being Red."

In September 1960 a group of conservative college students gathered at Buckley's home in Sharon, Connecticut, to found the Young Americans for Freedom. Among the policies advocated by YAF were continued nuclear testing and the withdrawal of American aid to communist countries. Buckley later joined the American Conservative Party and was its unsuccessful candidate in the 1965 New York City mayoral election.

In addition to writing his column and editing the *National Review*, Buckley also became a familiar figure on the American college lecture circuit and in 1966 began a syndicated television interview program, "Firing Line."

In 1964, Buckley supported the presidential ambitions of Senator BARRY GOLDWATER and in 1968 supported the campaign of RICHARD NIXON. He was an early and consistent opponent of the anti-Vietnam War movement. From 1969 to 1972, Buckley was a member of the Advisory Committee of the United States Information Agency (USIA). He resigned in 1972 in protest against Nixon's policy of détente with the Soviet Union and rapprochement with communist China. In the 1976 and 1980 presidential elections, Buckley endorsed RONALD REAGAN. In 1982, Reagan rewarded Buckley by naming him a consultant to the National Security Council.

In the 1988 presidential election, Buckley started the campaign by endorsing Republican candidate GEORGE BUSH, but when Bush appeared to water down his support for Reagan's STRATEGIC DEFENSE INITIATIVE, Buckley attacked the candidate in his column under the headline "What's Going On?" But Buckley's main efforts in 1988 were directed toward successfully ousting Connecticut senator Lowell P. Weicker, one of the last liberal Republicans. Weicker was defeated in the U.S. Senate race by the Buckley-backed Democratic candidate Joseph I. Lieberman.

For Further Information:
Buckley, William F. *Up From Liberalism*. New York, 1959.
Burner, David. *Column Right: Conservative Journalists in the Service of Nationalism*. New York, 1988.
Diggins, John P. *Up From Communism, Conservative Odysseys in American Intellectual History*. New York, 1975.
Judis, John B. *William F. Buckley, Jr.: Patron Saint of the Conservatives*. New York, 1988.
Markmann, Charles Lam. *The Buckleys*. New York, 1973.
Winchell, Mark Royden. *William F. Buckley, Jr*. Boston, 1984.

Budenz, Louis F.   (July 17, 1981–April 28, 1972)   Louis Budenz was a former communist whose sensational testimony before Senator JOSEPH MCCARTHY's House Un-American Activities Committee implicated ALGER HISS and China expert OWEN LATTIMORE in communist activities.

Born in Indianapolis, Budenz received his law degree from the Indianapolis Law School in 1912. He practiced as a lawyer for a short time before entering journalism. In 1920 he became editor of the socialist magazine *Labor Age* and in 1935 joined the American Communist Party and edited its newspaper, the *Daily Worker*.

In 1945 Budenz left the party and in April 1946 described it as "the direct arm of the Soviet foreign department." Born into a strict Roman Catholic family, he returned to his Catholic roots by becoming a professor of journalism and economics at Notre Dame University; later in the year he moved to Fordham University. He also made contact with the FBI and between October 1945 and October 1946 helped the bureau to compile a list of Communist Party members and sympathizers.

In October 1946 Budenz went on the radio to declare that "Russia is driving to rule the world and the United States is its principal enemy." On November 22, 1946, Budenz appeared before the HOUSE UN-AMERICAN ACTIVITIES COMMITTEE to claim that every communist in the United States was "part of a Russian fifth column."

Budenz then began a series of appearances before the House Un-American Activities Committee in which he named hundreds of people as communists or communist sympathizers. His first target was Gerhardt Eisler, whom he described as "the number-one Communist spy in the U.S." Eisler was arrested and charged with conspiracy to overthrow the U.S. government, but he left the country illegally after being released on bail.

In 1948 Budenz was a key witness during the Senate Internal Security Subcommittee hearings on communist infiltration in the federal government. He told the senators that "possibly thousands" of Communists had worked their into federal jobs, with "several score" obtaining "fairly important jobs" and "several hundred in relatively important places."

On August 24, 1946, Budenz secretly testified before the

House Un-American Affairs Committee that he regarded Hiss to be "under Communist Party discipline" and "the equivalent to a member of the Communist Party." On April 20, 1950, Budenz accused Professor Owen Lattimore, a key adviser to the government on Chinese affairs, of having been a concealed member of a communist cell. He said that he had never met Lattimore and had no documentary evidence, but that on numerous occasions the party's highest leaders had described Lattimore as a member and subject to party discipline.

Budenz's testimony was regularly attacked as unsubstantiated hearsay, and no one named by Budenz was ever convicted for spying. His charges, however, contributed to the climate of fear in the early Cold War years and ruined the careers of a number of prominent foreign policy figures. In 1956 he left teaching and turned to full-time writing. He died on April 28, 1972.

For Further Imformation:
Griffith, Robert. *The Politics of Fear* Lexington, Ky., 1970.

Bulganin, Nikolai A.   (June 11, 1895–February 24, 1975)
Nikolai Bulganin was Soviet minister of defense in the early Cold War years and the second most powerful man in the Soviet Union following the death of JOSEF STALIN and the liquidation of LAVRENTY BERIA. After a power struggle with NIKITA KHRUSCHEV in 1957 and 1958, Bulganin fell into political disgrace.

Bulganin was born at Nizhny Novgorod, the son of a clerk in a local factory. Little is known about him until 1917, when he joined the Bolshevik Party shortly after the outbreak of the revolution. He was soon appointed to a position in the Cheka, the predecessor of the KGB, and remained there until 1922.

From 1922 to 1927 Bulganin was involved with the Supreme Economic Council, which was charged with the task of rebuilding the economy, and in 1931 he became president of the Moscow Council of Workers Deputies. The same year, he was elected mayor of Moscow, a post he held until 1937, when he became president of the Russian Federation. Bulganin rose rapidly from his Moscow base. In 1934 he was elected to the Communist Party's Central Committee; in 1938 he became a vice president of the Council of People's Commissars and from 1938 to 1941 he was chairman of the State Bank.

After the German invasion in 1941, Bulganin became a member of the Military Council with the rank of lieutenant general. He was given responsibility for organizing the defense of Moscow and the Western Front. He emerged from the war with the rank of marshal. In 1944 he was named deputy defense minister and from 1947 to 1949 served as minister of defense. In 1948, Bulganin was elevated to the ruling Politburo.

As deputy minister and then minister of defense, Bulganin was responsible for the Red Army's occupation of Eastern Europe, North Korea and Iranian Azerbaijan. He also pressed the development of the Soviet Union's atomic weapons program and oversaw its early advances in missile and rocket technology. He faced the problem of ensuring the continued loyalty of war heroes such as Marshal GEORGI K. ZHUKOV, who was initially banished to an obscure provincial post because he lacked a power base within the Communist Party.

In 1949, Bulganin relinquished his defense portfolio in favor of Marshal Alexander Vassilevsky, but he retained effective control over the military from his position on the Politburo. Little is known of his actions between 1949 and the death of Josef Stalin on March 5, 1953. It is generally accepted that in 1949 Stalin started laying the groundwork for another great purge with his accusations of a "Doctors' Plot" against his life. Bulganin protected himself through his links with the secret police and the military, but he may have been on the brink of being purged when Stalin suddenly died.

It is obvious that Bulganin was deeply involved in the political machinations before and after the dictator's death, as he emerged as one of the key figures in the new regime, along with Khrushchev, Beria and GEORGI MALENKOV. In the early days of the post-Stalin power struggle, Bulganin made the far-sighted decision to attach himself to the Khrushchev star. He helped to marshal the military forces that enabled the liquidation of secret police chief Beria in June 1953, and when Khrushchev challenged Malenkov for the party leadership in 1955, Bulganin publicly backed the former.

Khrushchev rewarded Bulganin with the Order of the Red Star for his help in liquidating Beria, and in February 1955 he appointed him premier for his support against Malenkov. This was the start of what became known as the "B and K Era," with Bulganin and Khrushchev touring the world together in an attempt to defuse international tensions and project a more peaceful image of the Soviet Union. During this period the Soviet Union finally agreed to an AUSTRIAN PEACE TREATY and evacuated its troops from that country. A Soviet military base in Finland was voluntarily relinquished and Soviet–Yugoslav relations dramatically improved.

Nikolai Bulganin (at right center), Soviet minister of defense in the early Cold War years, is interviewed by foreign journalists in Moscow, 1955. Photo courtesy of Novosti Press Agency.

The tactics of Soviet diplomacy changed. The barriers of secrecy and reserve were abandoned, and Bulganin and Khrushchev mingled with foreign diplomats in Moscow and made major policy announcements at diplomatic receptions. Leaders of non-communist nations were invited to Moscow and "B and K" traveled widely to Burma, Afghanistan, Britain and Finland selling their policy of PEACEFUL COEXISTENCE.

Bulganin was the titular head of the Soviet delegation to the GENEVA HEADS OF GOVERNMENT SUMMIT of 1955 and used the occasion to make the unrealistic proposal of "a system of collective security," with all of Europe, the Soviet Union and the United States involved. One of the phases of his proposal was the dissolution of the WARSAW PACT and the NORTH ATLANTIC TREATY ORGANIZATION. Bulganin also gave an initial warm welcome to U.S. President DWIGHT EISENHOWER's "OPEN SKIES" proposal, which was unveiled at the Geneva Summit. The idea was later rejected by Khrushchev.

It soon became clear that the Soviet Union's foreign policy was aimed at winning favor among the nonaligned countries and the emerging Third World while maintaining its iron grip on Eastern Europe. Bulganin played a major role in the development and implementation of this policy. During Poland's POZNAN CRISIS of 1956, Bulganin flew to Warsaw to demand that the Polish opposition be silenced and dissidents arrested. He also accompanied Khrushchev to Warsaw later in the year to make certain that WLADYSLAW GOMULKA did not attempt to declare a policy line independent of the Soviet Union. When Hungary erupted shortly afterward, Bulganin took a leading role in ordering Soviet troops into that country. In March 1957, Bulganin signed an agreement with Hungarian premier JANOS KADAR that bound the two countries closer together.

Throughout 1956 and 1957, Bulganin conducted a highly publicized correspondence with Eisenhower, which was clearly aimed at Third World opinion and designed to give the impression that the Soviet Union was taking the initiative in trying to improve East–West relations. On October 17, 1956, just before the U.S. presidential elections, Bulganin wrote to Eisenhower proposing that the United States and the Soviet Union negotiate an agreement to end nuclear weapons tests. Without mentioning the Democratic candidate, ADLAI STEVENSON, by name, Bulganin made it clear that the Soviet Union supported his approach to nuclear issues.

Eisenhower angrily accused Bulganin of interference "in our internal affairs of a kind which, if indulged in by an ambassador, would lead to his being declared persona non grata." The Eisenhower reply was criticized by Stevenson, and the Bulganin letters briefly became an election issue.

The October exchanges were quickly overtaken by the SUEZ CRISIS, and on November 5, 1956, Bulganin wrote to Eisenhower proposing that the Soviet Union and the United States jointly intervene to halt the fighting in Egypt. Eisenhower rejected this as "unthinkable." Later, he wrote to British prime minister ANTHONY EDEN, Israeli prime minister David Ben-Gurion and French premier Guy Mollet and threatened the use of Soviet troops to "crush the aggressors and restore peace in the Middle East."

Bulganin's downfall started in June 1957 when he unsuccessfully challenged Khrushchev for the party leadership. Bulganin managed to win the support of a majority of the Politburo, but Khrushchev outmaneuvered him by appealing to the Central Committee, which endorsed him in power. The other leading members of what became known as the "anti-party group"—Malenkov, V. M. MOLOTOV and Lazar M. Kaganovich—were immediately relieved of their official positions. Bulganin remained an ineffectual premier while Khrushchev completed the process of consolidating power in his own hands. In March 1958, Bulganin was formally dismissed and Khrushchev became both premier and head of the party.

Bulganin "confessed" to having been a prominent member of the "anti-party group" and was dispatched to Stavropol in the northern Caucasus as head of the local economic council. Bulganin's health declined rapidly, and in 1960 he was allowed to return to Moscow on the condition that he remain in retirement. In January 1964 he was seen happily chatting with Khrushchev at a cocktail party and in 1970 he attended the funeral of Molotov's wife.

For Further Information:
Crankshaw, Edward. *Khrushchev's Russia.* Baltimore, 1959.
Duranty, Walter. *Stalin and Co.* New York, 1949.
Leonhard, Wolfgang. *The Kremlin Since Stalin.* New York, 1962.
Schapiro, Leonard. "Bulganin." *London Calling* (July 1955).

Bulgaria   Bulgaria was one of the first East European countries to join the Soviet Bloc and was one of the most loyal of the Soviet Union's allies.

Under the dictatorship of King Boris III, the country sided with the Axis powers during World War II. Boris died in August 1943 after a stormy interview with Adolf Hitler. He was succeeded by his son, King Simeon II, who was faced with a growing antifascist resistance movement organized and led by the Bulgarian Communist Party (BCP). In September 1944, the right-wing Bulgarian government was overthrown and replaced with a government dominated by the BCP.

The Bulgarian communists had enjoyed genuine popularity with the electorate before it was forced underground in 1923, and this, in addition to their resistance activities, gave them a strong political base. They were also helped by the fact that Bulgarians are traditionally pro-Russian.

Under Georgi Dimitrov as prime minister and Vulko Chervenkov as secretary-general of the BCP, the party moved quickly to establish a one-party state. In fact, it moved too quickly for Soviet leader JOSEF STALIN, who was initially concerned that a too hasty purge of opposition parties would provoke a hostile Western reaction before the communists elsewhere in Eastern Europe were in place. Nevertheless, the Bulgarian communists deposed and exiled King Simeon II and secured key government posts, which enabled them to liquidate several thousand opponents in 1945 and placed them in a position to win the elections held in 1946. By 1947, the main opposition party, the Agrarian Union, was effectively dissolved and the smaller parties had either disappeared or had merged with the communist-controlled Fatherland Front.

The Bulgarian Communist Party played an early and major role in helping to establish the foundations of a uniform communist rule throughout the Balkans. Dimitrov, in particular, advocated the establishment of a communist-controlled Balkan confederation. The first step in his plan, which was shared with JOSIP BROZ TITO, was the creation of a federal structure in Yugoslavia under Tito. The second was a communist government in Albania under ENVER HOXHA, then an independent, and a communist Macedonia carved out of Greece and parts of Yugoslavia. Finally, all the Balkan states would be merged into a Balkan superstate. The latter stages of the plan fell apart with the defeat of the communists in the GREEK CIVIL WAR and Tito's split with Moscow. Following that split, in June 1948, Bulgaria sided with the Soviet Union and changed dramatically from being Yugoslavia's closest ally to being one of Tito's sternest critics: The BCP's ranks were purged of "Titoists."

Dimitrov died in 1949 and was succeeded as prime minister by Chervenkov, thus combining the roles of head of government and head of the party. Chervenkov stepped up the purges of suspected Titoists and during a series of show trials attempted to implicate American diplomats in subversion charges. This led to a break in U.S.–Bulgarian relations from 1950 to 1966.

The Bulgarian communists copied the Soviet economic system in the 1940s and early 1950s, nationalizing land and business and organizing farmers into cooperatives. The peasant farmers at first refused to cooperate, and in 1950 the government had to "borrow" 150,000 tons of Soviet wheat because of the refusal of Bulgarian farmers to cultivate the land. The government also instituted a purge of the country's minority Turkish community, and some 250,000 ethnic Turks fled across the border into Turkey.

After the death of Stalin in March 1953, Chervenkov came under strong pressure to relinquish either the premiership or the leadership of the Bulgarian Communist Party. Chervenkov decided to retain the premiership and appointed his young lieutenant, TODOR ZHIVKOV, as general secretary of the BCP. But Chervenkov was too closely associated with Stalin for the new leadership in Moscow. Zhivkov, seeing his opportunity, carefully cultivated NIKITA KHRUSHCHEV and managed to secure his support to have Chervenkov removed from the premiership in 1962. Zhivkov then assumed the leadership of both party and government and became the new strongman of Bulgaria.

In April 1965 there was an attempt by reform-minded members of the Bulgarian Communist Party to overthrow Zhivkov and develop a policy more independent of the Soviet Union. The plot was discovered at the last minute and crushed. Zhivkov said in a speech a week afterward, "In the West . . . the reactionaries are screaming about a plot that aimed to separate us from the Soviet Union . . . There is no force that can separate Bulgaria from the Soviet Union. We are linked for life and death."

Zhivkov went on to earn a reputation as the leader of the Soviet Union's most loyal satellite. He took a leading role in denouncing the Chinese Communist Party; Bulgarian troops participated in the 1968 Warsaw Pact invasion of Czechoslovakia, which crushed the PRAGUE SPRING movement; and Bulgaria was the first East European country to join the Soviet Union in the boycott of the 1984 Los Angeles Olympics. In return for this loyalty, Zhivkov was in 1977 awarded the title of "Hero of the Soviet Union."

In the 1970s Zhivkov oversaw a general improvement in relations between Bulgaria and the West alongside the improvement in U.S.-Soviet relations. But relations between Bulgaria and the West, and in particular between Bulgaria and Italy, became strained in November 1982 after Mehmet Ali Agca, a Turkish citizen, claimed Bulgarian involvement in his attempt to assassinate Pope John Paul II in 1981. Another cause of conflict between Bulgaria and the West was Zhivkov's policy of forced "Bulgarization" of the ethnic Turkish minority. The policy led thousands of ethnic Turks to flee across the border into Turkey, and in 1989 Soviet leader MIKHAIL GORBACHEV pointed out to Zhivkov that the policy was damaging Bulgaria's international reputation. There were also disputes with Greece over Bulgaria's diversion of the Nestos River and with Yugoslavia over Macedonia.

Zhivkov ruled Bulgaria like an old-style Stalinist leader. Signs of a Stalinist-type personality cult were evident throughout Bulgaria. Zhivkov's portrait was omnipresent as were his words of wisdom. He regularly broadcast long and didactic speeches on television. In the 1970s Zhivkov also displayed dynastic ambitions by promoting his daughter, Lyudmila Zhivkova, to the Politburo. She was made chairman of the State Committee on Culture as well. Her sudden death in 1981 was a major setback for Zhivkov's plans, but Zhivkov retained his iron grip over the country's political structure. Other political figures were denied any opportunity to present a challenge to Zhivkov by his policy of regularly rotating party and government posts in order to prevent anyone from developing a political base.

But Zhivkov's rule could not survive the dramatic changes in the Soviet Bloc in 1989. On November 10 he was forced to resign by reformist foreign minister Peter Mladenov, who succeeded him as leader of the BCP. Shortly afterward, Mladenov purged the Politburo of hard-line communists and announced that free elections would be held in the next year.

The elections were held in June 1990 and resulted in the only communist electoral victory in Eastern Europe at that time. The Bulgarian Socialist Party—the successor to the communists—won a total of 211 seats in the 400-seat Grand National Assembly. But the elections were marred by reports of voter intimidation and irregularities in several election districts.

Andrei Lukanov was elected premier and immediately called for a coalition government with the non-socialist parties, but his proposal was rejected by the opposition coalition, the Union of Democratic Forces (UDF).

Continuing pressure from the UDF led to anti-government riots and the resignation of Mladenov as president on July 6. On August 1, the UDF managed to force the socialists to accept its leader, Zhelyu Zhelev, as the new president.

The government then set out to dismantle some of the trappings of the old communist state. The body of Georgi Dimitrov was removed on July 18 from its ornate mausoleum in Sofia and cremated, and former communist leader Zhivkov was summoned to appear before the parliament to answer charges of abuse of power and embezzlement. His formal trial started in February 1991.

New elections were held in October 1991, and this time the UDF eked out a victory over the socialists. The new UDF leader, Filip Dimitrov, 36, became the country's youngest-ever premier in November. His cabinet included no socialists. President Zhelev won a new five-year term in January 1992 in Bulgaria's first direct presidential election.

For Further Information:

Boll, Michael M. *Cold War in the Balkans: American Foreign Policy and the Emergence of Communist Bulgaria, 1943–1947*. Lexington, Ky., 1984.

Brzezinski, Zbigniew. *The Soviet Bloc: Unity and Conflict*. Cambridge, Mass., 1960.

Crampton, R.J. *A Short History of Modern Bulgaria*. New York, 1987.

Devedjiev, Hristo H. *Stalinization of the Bulgarian Society, 1949–1953*. Philadelphia, 1975.

Fejto, F. *A History of the People's Democracies: Eastern Europe Since Stalin*. New York, 1974.

Rakowska-Harmstone, T. *Communism in Eastern Europe*. Bloomington, Ind., 1984.

Bullitt, William   (January 15, 1891–February 15, 1967)
William Bullitt was the first American ambassador to the Soviet Union in 1933 and in the postwar years claimed that presidents Roosevelt and Truman had "sold out" Eastern Europe and China.

Bullitt was born into one of Philadelphia's most patrician families and attended Yale University and Harvard Law School. He dropped out of law school to enter journalism and became first a war correspondent and then the Washington bureau chief of Philadelphia's *Public Ledger*.

At the outbreak of World War I, Bullitt moved into the State Department as head of the Bureau of Central European Affairs. He traveled with President Wilson to the Versailles Peace Conference, but in the middle of the conference he was sent on a secret mission to negotiate a truce between the White Russians and the Bolsheviks.

Bullitt was long-time friend of President FRANKLIN ROOSEVELT, and shortly after Roosevelt assumed office, he asked Bullitt to arrange American recognition of the Soviet government. In November 1933 Bullitt became the first U.S. ambassador to the Soviet Union.

Bullitt had originally been sympathetic to the Soviets. In the immediate postwar years he had broken with the Wilson administration over its refusal to extend recognition to the new government in Russia. But within a short time in the Soviet Union Bullitt became disillusioned with JOSEF STALIN's Soviet state and was publicly denouncing Soviet suppression of civil liberties. In 1936 he cabled Washington that "we should not cherish for a monent the illusion that it is possible to establish really friendly relations with the Soviet government or with any Communist Party or Communist individual."

In the climate of the times, Bullitt's increasingly anti-Soviet views failed to find an audience in Washington and Roosevelt transferred him to Paris as ambassador, where he stayed until 1940. From 1940 to 1944 he was Roosevelt's special adviser on Soviet affairs and was one of the few who expressed doubts about the feasibility and desirability of U.S.-Soviet wartime cooperation. This led him into conflict with a number of adminstration figures, and he was forced to resign in 1944.

Bullitt returned to journalism to denounce the foreign policies of Roosevelt and Truman in articles for *Time* and *Life* magazines. He was also critical of Secretary of State GEORGE C. MARSHALL, whom he accused of giving "faulty advice" to Roosevelt at the Teheran and Yalta conferences and of being the central figure in the fall of China.

During the Korean War Bullitt continued to expound his conservative views in *The Reader's Digest*. He pressed for a policy of "total victory" by supporting CHIANG KAI-SHEK in an invasion of Mainland China.

In April 1952, Bullitt became involved in the ALGER HISS case when he testified before the Senate Internal Security Subcommittee that he had been told by Edouard Daladier, the former prime minister of France, that Alger Hiss and his brother Donald were Soviet agents. Daladier said he did not recall the conversation. Bullitt continued to write until his death from leukemia on Februry 15, 1967.

For Further Information:

Brands, H.W. *Cold Warriors*. New York, 1988.

Lafeber, Walter. *America, Russia and the Cold War, 1945–1971*. New York, 1972.

Taubman, William S. *Stalin's American Policy*. New York, 1982.

Bundy, McGeorge   (March 30, 1919–   )   McGeorge Bundy was a foreign policy adviser during the KENNEDY and JOHNSON administrations. He was a member of the inner circle that advised the president during the CUBAN MISSILE CRISIS and played an important role in developing policy in the early stages of America's involvement in Vietnam.

Bundy was born into a prominent New England family. His father, Harvey H. Bundy, served as assistant secretary of state during the administration of President Herbert Hoover.

Bundy graduated from Yale in 1940 and during World War II served as an intelligence officer.

After the war he helped Henry Stimson complete his memoirs, helped to implement the MARSHALL PLAN, worked as a foreign policy adviser on Thomas Dewey's presidential campaign and in 1949 started teaching at Harvard University.

Bundy's establishment background led him toward the Republican Party, and he nominally supported General DWIGHT D. EISENHOWER in the 1952 and 1956 presidential campaigns. But he was a long-time opponent of RICHARD NIXON, and when the party nominated Nixon for the presidency in 1960, Bundy switched his allegiance to the Democrats and organized a committee of scientists and professionals to support John F. Kennedy.

The two men developed a close rapport during the election campaign, and after Kennedy's victory Bundy was offered a choice of senior positions in the defense and state departments. Bundy declined these, however, and instead asked to be made Kennedy's special assistant for national security affairs.

It was his job to collate information from the defense and state departments and present it in a concise and easily understandable form to the president. He also organized National Security Council meetings, assembled Kennedy's numerous foreign policy task forces and controlled access to the president for anyone wanting to discuss defense and foreign policy.

Bundy's influence grew after the BAY OF PIGS invasion in 1961 because Kennedy blamed the debacle on bad advice from the State Department and the CIA. Kennedy turned increasingly to Bundy and Bundy's sources for advice and information. Bundy had learned of the presence of Soviet missiles on Cuba before the president, and it fell to him to organize a special bipartisan group to advise Kennedy during the crisis. Bundy at first argued against an air strike to destroy the missile bases. But at a later meeting, on October 23, he came out in favor of an air attack because Kennedy's proposed compromise—to impose a blockade—would constitute an act of war under international law. Bundy argued that if an act of war was to be committed, then it should be a swift and decisive act.

Bundy was heavily involved in the development of the Vietnam policy of the Kennedy and Johnson administrations. He gave ambivalent support to the 1963 coup that overthrew the regime of NGO DINH DIEM, arguing that the administration should not prevent any coup that appeared potentially successful but at the same time should maintain the "option of judging and warning on any plan with poor prospects of success."

Bundy remained at the White House after Kennedy's assassination and became one of President Lyndon B. Johnson's closest foreign policy advisers. In May 1965, Johnson sent Bundy to the Dominican Republic to negotiate a settlement to a civil war there. At the last minute, his plan collapsed, but U.S. diplomat ELLSWORTH BUNKER (q.v.) was able to revive it and reach a settlement in August.

There has been some dispute over the position Bundy took on the VIETNAM WAR. This is largely caused by the way in which Bundy performed his job as adviser. He saw his role as largely offering alternatives and counseling the president to maintain his options until a major decision was unavoidable.

During the Kennedy administration and the early part of the Johnson administration, Bundy's advice reflected this open-option approach. But by the early part of 1965, he became convinced that a decision should be made in favor of escalation in Vietnam because the alternative would undermine international trust in America's determination to stop the spread of communism. His advice was reported to be a crucial factor in Johnson's decision to resume bombing of North Vietnam.

Although Bundy was one of Johnson's closest advisers, the two men had, at times, a stormy personal relationship. In December 1965, Bundy resigned from the administration to accept the presidency of the Ford Foundation. In 1967 he started to reverse his earlier support for the Vietnam War, and he wrote to Johnson opposing a further escalation. In October 1968 he called for a reduction in the number of U.S. troops.

In March 1973 Bundy was a prominent witness for the defense in the case of Daniel Ellsberg, who was accused of leaking the "Pentagon Papers." Bundy testified that the publication of the papers had not damaged American security interests.

Bundy remained at the Ford Foundation until 1979, when he left for a teaching post at New York University. Twenty-four professors at the university protested Bundy's appointment on the grounds of his complicity in a "genocidal war."

For Further Information:
Anderson, Patrick. *The Presidents' Men.* New York, 1968.
Halberstam, David. *The Best and the Brightest.* New York, 1972.
Stavins, Ralph. *Washington Plans an Aggressive War.* New York, 1971.

Bundy, William P. (September 24, 1917–) William Bundy served as deputy assistant secretary of defense for international security affairs during the KENNEDY administration and as assistant secretary of state for Far Eastern affairs during the JOHNSON administration. Along with his brother McGeorge Bundy, William Bundy was one of the key architects of the Johnson administration's VIETNAM WAR policy.

After serving in the U.S. army during World War II, Bundy graduated from Harvard Law School in 1947 and joined the prominent law firm of Covington and Burling in Washington, D.C. Three years later he joined the CENTRAL INTELLIGENCE AGENCY, where he was in charge of evaluating international intelligence. In 1960 he joined President Dwight Eisenhower's Commission on National Goals, and in January 1961 President John F. Kennedy named him deputy assistant secretary of defense for international security affairs.

Bundy's primary responsibility was the coordination of military aid programs, and in that capacity he became deeply involved in American policy in Southeast Asia. In October 1961 he strongly supported the request from South Vietnamese president NGO DINH DIEM for a U.S.-Vietnamese defense treaty and increased across-the-board American military assistance. Bundy advised Kennedy and Defense Secretary ROBERT MCNAMARA to launch an "early hard-hitting operation" against North Vietnam. "It is now or never," he wrote, "if we are to arrest the gains of the Vietcong." Kennedy decided against committing U.S. ground forces but did substantially increase American support forces and equipment aid.

Bundy's influence grew during the Johnson administration when, in February 1964, he was named assistant secretary of state for Far Eastern affairs. In October 1964 he was cochairman, with Assistant Secretary of Defense JOHN MCNAUGHTON, of a National Security Council working group formed to review American policy toward U.S. air attacks on North Vietnam and the size of American ground forces. The group, which reported in November, recommended "a policy of sustained reprisal against North Vietnam—a policy in which air and naval action against the North is justified by and related to the whole Vietcong campaign of violence . . . in the South."

Bundy opposed a negotiated settlement at the time on the grounds that it would not lead to a stable peace and that the negotiations would probably undermine South Vietnamese morale. He was, however, initially reluctant to support the introduction of large-scale U.S. ground forces, but eventually accepted this as well. The committee's report was officially adopted by Johnson in February 1965 and determined the course of the war until 1968. Its acceptance also meant that Bundy played a major part in selecting North Vietnamese targets for American air attacks.

Later, when Johnson shifted American policy toward finding a negotiated settlement, Bundy continued to press for the bombing of North Vietnam as a means of driving the North Vietnamese to the negotiating table and pressuring them into concessions. But by 1967–68 he opposed negotiations as "useless," although he also opposed a further escalation of the war on the grounds that it would strengthen North Vietnamese morale, persuade the South Vietnamese that U.S. support was limitless, and damage relations with U.S. allies. Bundy left government at the end of the Johnson administration. In 1972 he was appointed editor of *Foreign Affairs*.

Bunker, Ellsworth　(May 11, 1894–September 27, 1984)
Ellsworth Bunker was a leading American diplomat during the 1960s and 1970s. Major assignments included ambassador to the Organization of American States, ambassador to South Vietnam and ambassador-at-large.

Bunker joined his family's sugar-refining business after graduating from Yale University in 1916. He was appointed chairman of the board in 1948 and in 1951 started a second career as a senior U.S. diplomat. His first posting was as ambassador to Argentina. Other postings included ambassador to Italy and to India. In 1962 Bunker became a State

Department troubleshooter, acting as mediator in disputes between Holland and Indonesia, Saudi Arabia and Egypt, the United States and Panama, and warring factions in the Dominican Republic.

Bunker's efforts in ending the civil war in the Dominican Republic in 1965 prompted the influential columnist WALTER LIPPMANN to describe him as "America's most accomplished diplomat." In April 1967, President JOHNSON appointed Bunker ambassador to South Vietnam, where he earned a reputation as one of the administration's leading hawks. He supported the repressive South Vietnamese government of President Nguyen Van Thieu, opposed the decision to halt the U.S. bombing of North Vietnam and consistently exaggerated the progress of South Vietnamese and American forces.

President RICHARD NIXON kept Bunker at his Saigon post, and Bunker maintained his hawkish position. He supported the U.S. invasion of Cambodia in 1970 as necessary to give "more time to develop the South Vietnamese forces." In 1971 Bunker tried to liberalize the South Vietnamese electoral process by offering to finance the campaign of Thieu's opponent, General Duong Van Minh. But the offer backfired after Minh and Vice President Nguyen Cao Ky withdrew from the campaign, charging the United States with interference in the domestic political process. As a result, Thieu was reelected unopposed.

Bunker returned to Washington, D.C., in March 1973 and was named ambassador-at-large. In November 1973 he took over Panama Canal Treaty negotiations and, except for a short break during Middle East peace negotiations in late 1973 and early 1974, handled the delicate talks until their conclusion in 1977. Bunker retired from public life after the treaty was signed in June 1978. He died on September 27, 1984.

For Further Information:
Smith, R.B. *An International History of the Vietnam War*. New York, 1986.
Spanier J.W. *American Foreign Policy Since World War Two*. Washington, D.C., 1988.

Burgess, Guy Francis de Moncy　(July 14, 1911–August 30, 1963)　Guy Burgess was one of three British diplomats who spied for the Soviet Union during the early Cold War years.

Burgess was educated at the exclusive Eton College and then at Cambridge University, where he developed a reputation as an outrageous homosexual and a drunkard. While at Cambridge, he became friends with DONALD MACLEAN and KIM PHILBY, and the three of them were recruited by Soviet intelligence while still students.

During World War II, Burgess found a job with British intelligence and in 1944 he was offered a temporary post at the Foreign Office, which soon became permanent. His reputation was mixed. Minister of State Hector McNeil was full of praise for Burgess, but a department head dismissed him from one post because he was "dirty, drunk and idle."

In 1950 Burgess was sent to Washington, D.C., as the Far Eastern affairs attach at the British Embassy. In this job, he was responsible for helping to coordinate British and American policies during the early stages of the KOREAN WAR and had access to vital American and British documents, which he passed on to Soviet intelligence. While in Washington, Burgess stayed in the home of Philby, a visit that later led British and American intelligence to suspect the loyalties of the more highly-placed Philby.

Toward the end of 1950, British counterintelligence (M15) was closing in on Burgess' coconspirator MacLean, who was then in London. Philby instructed Burgess to engineer his return to London in order to warn MacLean and help him organize his escape. This Burgess did by affecting increasingly abusive and outrageous behavior, and in May 1951 he was dismissed from the British Embassy in Washington and returned to London.

Soon afterward, with the help of Anthony Blunt, another British offical working secretly for the Soviets, Burgess passed a warning to MacLean. He then hired a car and drove with MacLean to Southampton. Burgess was meant to return to London after delivering MacLean to the boat at Southampton, but he became afraid that British counterintelligence was closing in on him as well, and the two men caught the ferry to France and then in Paris boarded a plane for Moscow. In the Soviet Union, Burgess was given a minor post in the KGB and continued his reputation for heavy drinking and outrageous homosexual behavior. He died on August 30, 1963.

For Further Information:
Boyle, Andrew. *The Climate of Treason.* New York, 1980.
Connolly, Cyril. *The Missing Diplomats.* London, 1952.
Knightley, Phillip. *Philby.* London, 1988.
Philby, Kim. *My Silent War.* New York, 1968.

Bush, George Herbert Walker (June 12, 1924–   )
George Bush has had a major impact on American foreign policy since he was appointed ambassador to the United Nations in 1971. In 1974 he was given the task of overseeing the normalization of Sino-American relations. In 1976 Bush was appointed director of the CENTRAL INTELLIGENCE AGENCY and in 1980 was elected vice president of the United States. He was elected president in November 1988 and was in office during the final stages of the Cold War.

Bush was born into a prominent and wealthy American political family. His father was Senator Prescott Bush of Connecticut; Bush was educated at the exclusive Philips Andover Academy and, after a period of wartime service as a naval pilot, Yale University. After graduating from Yale in 1948, Bush moved to Texas and, using capital supplied by his family, became a millionaire in his own right by developing an oil supply business.

In 1966 Bush was elected to the U.S. House of Representatives from Texas. He served two terms as a congressman before unsuccessfully challenging Democrat Lloyd Bentsen for a U.S. Senate seat. Out of Congress, Bush was soon appointed ambassador to the United Nations in 1970. He became heavily involved in trying to stem the international drug trade and in October 1971 unsuccessfully coordinated President RICHARD NIXON's attempted "Two Chinas" policy of admitting communist China to the United Nations while allowing Taiwan to retain its seat as Nationalist China.

Following the 1972 elections, Bush was appointed chairman of the Republican National Committee, where he had the difficult task of minimizing the damage to the party of the Watergate scandal. In September 1974, President GERALD FORD appointed Bush to the high-profile diplomatic post of head of the U.S. Liaison Office in Beijing. Bush was essentially the American ambassador, but since the U.S. still recognized Nationalist China as the official government of China, the Beijing post was called a liaison office. Bush established a close rapport with the Chinese leadership and developed an Asian perspective at a vital point in his career.

In December 1975, President Ford brought Bush back to Washington to be director of the CIA. The agency was going through a crisis of confidence following a series of damaging revelations in the wake of the Watergate scandal. Bush is credited with rebuilding morale within the agency and regaining a degree of public confidence in it by implementing limited reforms. The reforms included the upgrading of the interagency committee on covert operations to cabinet level, a presidential order prohibiting agency abuses, measures to tighten security and an enlargement of the responsibilities of the director to allow him greater supervision and control of agency activities.

Bush had been considered as a vice presidential candidate as early as 1972 and was a serious contender for the nomination in 1976, but Ford instead chose Senator Robert Dole as his running mate. Bush announced his candidacy for the Republican presidential nomination in 1979 and was one of the frontrunners with RONALD REAGAN. His campaign against Reagan was one of the most bitter primary campaigns in the postwar period and is perhaps best remembered for Bush's description of Reagan's financial policies as "voodoo economics."

Because of Bush's apparent antipathy for Reagan and his policies, he was a surprise choice as Reagan's running mate in the 1980 election. But the move united the right and left wings of the Republican Party and made Reagan more acceptable to the political middle ground.

Bush had no trouble sensing the lurch to the right that Reagan represented, and he adjusted his views accordingly. He became an active and loyal vice president. His chameleon-like change led to charges from moderate Republicans and Democrats that Bush lacked a firm ideological base and was too willing to compromise principle to expediency. Conservative Republicans remained suspicious and accused him of riding Reagan's coattails as a means to get elected president, after which they felt he would abandon them.

Bush quickly carved out a White House role for himself as a foreign affairs expert and became one of Reagan's chief foreign policy advisers. In 1981 he was named chairman of the White House foreign crisis management team over Secretary of State ALEXANDER HAIG and national security adviser RICHARD ALLEN. His appointment is believed to have contributed to the resignation of both men.

After the December 1981 crackdown on SOLIDARITY in Poland, Bush was named chairman of a special situation group to monitor events in Poland and report to the president. Bush also played a major role in the planning of the U.S. invasion of Grenada and is reported to have been the leading voice urging Reagan to withdraw American marines from Lebanon. He represented Reagan at the funerals of LEONID BREZHNEV, YURI ANDROPOV and KONSTANTIN CHERNENKO and on each occasion met the succeeding Soviet leader.

Bush, who knew many foreign leaders from his days at the UN and CIA, was used repeatedly as the president's special envoy. One of his main tasks was to win West European support for the Reagan administration's nuclear strategies. Bush regularly toured Europe arguing for the Reagan position on Intermediate Range Nuclear Force negotiations, Strategic Arms Reduction Talks (see STRATEGIC ARMS REDUCTION TREATIES) and the *Strategic Defense Initiative*.

Bush was also a regular visitor to other parts of the world. In November 1982 he toured Africa to defend the Reagan administration's policy of "constructive engagement" with South Africa and U.S. support for South African insistence on linking a settlement of the Namibia problem to the withdrawal of Cuban troops from Angola. He encountered strong opposition throughout the tour but stoutly maintained the Reagan position.

Bush was also a regular visitor to Latin America where he defended the Reagan administration's hardline policy toward the Sandinista regime in Nicaragua and support for the CONTRA REBELS. During the 1984 presidential election campaign, Bush said that the Sandinista government had "aborted" democracy in Nicaragua and that "most of the rebels fighting there felt that the revolution that put the Sandinistas into power had been betrayed."

Bush became increasingly involved in Latin American issues after the 1984 election, both as head of the administration's campaign to staunch the flow of illegal drugs into the U.S. from Latin America, and in planning U.S. policy toward Nicaragua. From the start of the Iran-Contra scandal, Bush was linked to some of the key developments in the case. Some observers felt that he was the logical person to have coordinated the operation because of his CIA background, but Bush consistently denied any illegal involvement, and the subsequent investigations into the scandal generally did not criticize him. Critics claimed that Bush's involvement was covered up to avoid any damage to his chances in the 1988 presidential election.

Bush won the November 1988 presidential election by a clear margin over Democratic Party candidate Michael Dukakis, with 54% of the popular vote compared to 46% for Dukakis and 426 electoral college votes compared to 112 for Dukakis. However, Bush's judgment was repeatedly called into question in the final months of the campaign by critics who faulted his surprise decision to choose the obscure and undistinguished conservative Senator Dan Quayle as his running mate.

In office, Bush gained further criticism for his failure to respond quickly to the diplomatic initiatives of Soviet leader Mikhail Gorbachev. Critics in America and abroad claimed that Bush was letting Gorbachev win the public relations battle in Europe. The debate over the apparent "rudderlessness" of the Bush foreign policy reached its zenith in the weeks before the NATO heads of government summit meeting in May 1989. NATO leaders were split over the issue of modernization of tactical nuclear weapons. Bush and British prime minister MARGARET THATCHER maintained that the weapons had to be modernized to offset the withdrawal of intermediate range nuclear weapons. But West German chancellor HELMUT KOHL opposed the modernization program and called for negotiations with the Soviet Union to reduce short-range systems.

The issue appeared to be on the verge of seriously damaging the alliance, on the eve of NATO's 40th anniversary celebrations. Bush managed to defuse the crisis with a compromise that linked negotiations on short-range systems to progress at East-West talks on conventional weapons. He then announced his own unilateral defense initiative by reducing American troop levels in Europe by 20%. Both actions were hailed as statesmanlike and a public relations coup and vindicated the administration's first few months of inaction.

The real breakthrough in disarmament talks followed a Bush initiative in January 1990, when he proposed a drastic reduction of both Soviet and American forces in Europe. At the CONFERENCE ON SECURITY AND COOPERATION (CSCE) summit in November, the Conventional Forces in Europe (CFE) treaty was signed, reducing forces on both sides to 195,000 in Central Europe. Also signed at the CSCE summit was the Charter of Paris, which expressed the "steadfast commitment" of all members to democracy. The summit marked the formal end of the Cold War.

Bush supported moves in Eastern Europe to pursue democracy and break with communism, but his initial responses to events in the area had been cautious. He visited Hungary and Poland in July 1989, and in November he gave Polish president LECH WALESA the Freedom Medal during his visit to the U.S. But the initial aid packages Bush offered to Poland and other emerging Eastern European democracies were faulted by some foreign policy analysts as inadequate.

Bush supported German unification, while his administration demanded and got guarantees that Germany would remain a full member of NATO and renounce all links with the WARSAW PACT. However, he turned down an invitation to attend the Unity Day celebrations on October 3, 1990.

Bush and Gorbachev held the first post-Cold War superpower summit July 30–31, 1991, in Moscow. It was the fourth official summit between the two men and the 16th meeting between the leaders of the U.S. and U.S.S.R. since the first Cold War summit in 1959. The highlights of this summit were the signing of a Strategic Arms Reduction Treaty (START) that would cut both sides' nuclear arsenals by about 30% and the announcement that the two countries were ready to cosponsor a Middle East peace conference in October.

But events moved with incredible swiftness after that, and Bush was hard-pressed to keep up with them. Less than a month after the successful summit, Soviet hard-liners failed in an attempt to oust Gorbachev, Russian president BORIS YELTSIN emerged as a major force by leading the opposition to the coup, and the Soviet Communist Party fell from power. Bush was faulted by critics for his tentativeness: his initial failure to condemn the coup outright, his delay in recognizing the independence of the Baltic states (the U.S. became the last major Western nation to do so, in September 1991) and his administration's seeming diplomatic preference in the months that followed for the sinking star that was Gorbachev rather than the rising one that was Yeltsin.

Regaining the initiative, Bush on September 27 announced the unilateral reduction of about 2,400 U.S. nuclear weapons. The cuts included the removal from Europe and the destruction of U.S. tactical missiles and atomic artillery shells, the removal from U.S. Navy ships of nuclear cruise missiles and depth charges, a halt to the effort to develop a rail-basing system for the MX intercontinental ballistic missile (ICBM) and an end to the 24-hour alert status of American long-range strategic bombers. Bush called on Moscow to respond in kind.

On December 25, 1991, the Soviet Union officially transmuted into the COMMONWEALTH OF INDEPENDENT STATES, and Gorbachev resigned. Bush hailed Gorbachev's role in the "historic and revolutionary transformation of a totalitarian dictatorship." He also announced that the United States would recognize the independence of all 12 of the former Soviet republics, but for the time being would establish formal diplomatic relations with only six of them: Russia, Ukraine, Kazakhstan, Belorussia (now Belarus), Armenia and Kirghizia. Bush said that Washington would delay formal ties with Azerbaijan, Georgia, Moldavia (now Moldova), Tadzhikistan, Turkmenistan and Uzbekistan pending commitments to "responsible security policies and democratic principles" by those states.

In November, the U.S. Congress authorized Bush to divert $500 million from the defense budget to Soviet aid: $400 million to help the Soviet republics dismantle nuclear weapons, and $100 million to transport emergency food and medicine to the soon-to-be defunct U.S.S.R. Bush followed up in January 1992 by promising $645 million in new aid, pending approval by Congress. But as the year went on, the whole issue of American foreign aid for its former enemy—at a time when the U.S. was mired in economic recession—became more and more of a political football, with neither the president nor

lawmakers eager to get out in front on an issue that threatened to antagonize many voters.

Bush, in his January 28 State of the Union address, declared, "By the grace of God, America won the Cold War." He praised "those who won it" by fighting "in places like Korea and Vietnam." He also paid tribute to the American taxpayer, who he said had "shouldered the burden" of the Cold War era.

In the speech, Bush called for a total of $50 billion in U.S. defense cuts between 1993 and 1997, for a total military reduction of about 30%. (He was actually proposing an additional 5% reduction on top of the 25% in cutbacks that the Defense Department was already undertaking.) Bush also announced a new initiative for further deep cuts in strategic nuclear arsenals.

Yeltsin meanwhile announced his own arms proposals. After several months of hard bargaining, Yeltsin traveled to Washington June 16–17 for the first official U.S.-Russian summit, where he and Bush reached a surprise agreement to deeply slash both sides' strategic weapons. If the accord were implemented, by the year 2003 the United States would have cut its 9,986 nuclear warheads to 3,500, while Russia would have trimmed its 10,237 warheads to 3,000. (Under the 1991 START pact, the U.S. would have been left with 8,556 warheads to Russia's 6,449.) The main concessions came from Yeltsin: He agreed to abandon the concept of strategic parity, or roughly equal balance of arms; and he agreed to both sides' eliminating all of their land-based multiple-warhead ICBMs, which was Russia's main strength. In return, the U.S. agreed to cut its submarine-launched ICBMs—where America had its main advantage—by 50%.

For the American public, however, the dramatic collapse of the arms race over the past year had lost its novelty, and Bush reaped little apparent political advantage from his stunning agreement with Yeltsin. Indeed, as the year wore on, Bush could increasingly be heard complaining that his administration was getting insufficient credit for its handling of the end of the Cold War.

A similar process had occurred in the wake of Bush's greatest single triumph—the U.S. victory in the 1991 Persian Gulf war against Iraq. After Iraq invaded Kuwait in August 1990, Bush had carefully stage-managed the U.S. military buildup in Saudi Arabia and the forging of an anti-Iraq coalition through the United Nations Security Council. The latter was made easier by the tacit and sometimes active support of Gorbachev's U.S.S.R. against its former ally, Iraq. Bush's defense of what he called the "New World Order" became the first major post-Cold War crisis, the first international armed conflict in which the Soviet Union lined up squarely behind the U.S. rather than across from it.

The smashing success of Operation Desert Storm, the air and ground war against Iraq in January and February 1991, initially gave Bush a huge surge in public opinion polls. But a year later that support had largely evaporated, and the president found himself going into an election year with sinking popularity. The Cold War was over, the arms race was running in reverse, and the average American voter by all accounts was more concerned with the stagnating U.S. economy than with receding military triumphs or happy summits with former enemies who arrived with begging bowl in hand. George Bush was defeated for reelection by the Democratic candidate, Governor Bill Clinton of Arkansas.

For Further Information:
Beschloss, Michael, and Strobe Talbott. *At the Highest Levels; The Inside Story of the End of the Cold War.* New York, 1993.
Brzezinski, Zbigniew. *In Quest of National Security.* Boulder, Colo., 1988.
Bush, George, with Victor Gold. *Looking Forward.* Garden City, N.Y., 1987.
Duffy, Michael. *Marching in Place: The Status Quo Presidency of George Bush.* New York, 1992.
Green, Fitzhugh. *George Bush: An Intimate Portrait.* New York, 1989.
King, Nicholas. *George Bush: A Biography.* New York, 1980.
Smith, Jean Edward. *George Bush's War.* New York, 1992.
Sufrin, M. *George Bush.* New York, 1989.

Bush, Vannevar   (March 11, 1890–June 28, 1974)   Vannevar Bush was a member of the committee that recommended dropping the ATOMIC BOMB on Hiroshima and later became an early advocate of U.S.-Soviet arms control negotiations.

Bush was educated at Tufts College, Harvard and the Massachusetts Institute of Technology, receiving his doctorate in engineering in 1916. Three years later he joined the faculty of MIT, and he rose to become dean of the engineering school in 1931. He patented a number of inventions, including a forerunner of the computer.

During World War II Bush was chairman of the Office of Scientific Research and Development, where he was responsible for coordinating collaboration between the military and civilian scientists. The most dramatic result of this collaboration was the atomic bomb.

President TRUMAN appointed Bush to the committee created to help formulate atomic policy in the closing days of the war. Bush supported the committee's recommendation that the bomb be dropped on a civilian-military Japanese target without warning. But soon after the end of the war, he advocated the international control of atomic energy. In 1952 he tried to persuade Truman to negotiate with the Soviets before exploding the first hydrogen bomb.

During the 1950s Bush attacked the abuses of Senator JOSEPH MCCARTHY's anti-communist hearings, especially those involving prominent scientists. He came to the defense of J. ROBERT OPPENHEIMER, the former chairman of the Atomic Energy Commission, who was suspended in 1953 because of his prewar involvement with leftist groups.

Following Oppenheimer's suspension, Bush told a House government operations subcommittee that the security phobia of the times retarded weapons research by destroying morale and making scientists feel they were "regarded with suspicion." In December 1954 he was awarded the Procter Prize by the Scientific Research Society of America. In his acceptance speech, Bush said that "our enemy" had been "so successful" in spreading "suspicion and distrust" in the United States that "we are carrying on the process now without his prompting. Useful men are denied the opportunity to contribute to our scientific efforts because of their youthful indiscretions."

Bush became chairman of the MIT Corporation, the school's governing body, in 1957 and its honorary chairman in 1959. He continued to write on national defense issues until his death on June 28, 1974.

For Further Information:
Levine, Robert A. *The Arms Debate.* Cambridge, Mass., 1963.
Roberts, Chalmers M. *The Nuclear Years: The Arms Race and Arms Control.* New York, 1970.

Byrnes, James F.   (May 2, 1879–April 9, 1972)   James F. Byrnes was President TRUMAN's first appointment as secretary of state and played an important role at the POTSDAM CONFERENCE and in the first 18 months of the postwar period.

Byrnes was admitted to the South Carolina bar in 1903 after working as a law clerk and court stenographer. He was elected to the U.S. House of Representatives in 1910 and to the U.S. Senate in 1930. During the early years of the New Deal, Byrnes was one of President Franklin Roosevelt's keenest supporters on Capitol Hill, but as the president's policies swung further to the left, Byrnes returned to his conservative Southern roots and joined the Democratic opposition to the New Deal.

Byrnes continued to support Roosevelt's foreign policy, however, and in 1941 he was rewarded with an appointment to the Supreme Court. After only 16 months he resigned from the Court at Roosevelt's request to supervise the production of war and consumer goods, as director of economic stabilization, and established a formidable reputation as an administrator. As one of Roosevelt's principal advisers, he accompanied the president to the YALTA CONFERENCE and later helped to steer the agreement through Congress. His main task was to explain the "Declaration of Liberated Europe," which accepted the principle of Soviet-dominated provisional governments in Eastern Europe to be followed by free elections.

Byrnes was the front-runner for the Democratic Party's vice presidential nomination in 1944, but the party bosses felt that he was too closely associated with the South and opted for HARRY TRUMAN as the compromise choice. In July 1945 Truman appointed Byrnes secretary of state.

Byrnes felt that he could work with the Soviet Union and that JOSEF STALIN was basically a politician who would eventually compromise on the principle of a revived Germany, free elections in Eastern Europe and the withdrawal of Soviet troops. He went into the Potsdam Conference prepared to exercise his considerable talent for negotiating political compromises and succeeded in achieving one of the few postwar agreements with the Soviet Union.

One of the major issues bedeviling East–West relations in the closing days of World War II, and its immediate aftermath, was the issue of German war reparations. The Soviets demanded that Germany pay $20 billion, half of which would go to the Soviet Union. The British and Americans wanted to ease the German burden because they feared that a destitute Germany would severely damage the prospect of European economic recovery.

Byrnes negotiated a settlement that permitted the collection of reparations only after the imports essential to the maintenance of the German economy had been paid for by German exports. Also, the occupying powers were allowed to collect their reparations only from the sectors they controlled, except for the Soviet Union, which was allowed to take from the British and American zones "10% of such industrial capital equipment as is unnecessary for the German peace economy." The Soviet Union was also given an additional 15% in return for food and other commodities from its zone.

The agreement on reparations was part of what became known as the "Byrnes Package Deal," which also included agreements on Italy and the German–Polish border. The British and Americans received concessions on reparations and a Soviet agreement to grant Italy admission to the United Nations. The Soviets won concessions on the German–Polish border that resulted in German territories east of the Neisse River being placed under Polish administration.

At the follow-up LONDON CONFERENCE OF FOREIGN MINISTERS in September 1945, Byrnes encountered his first difficulties with the Soviet Union. East and West clashed on a number of issues, including Soviet demands for a say in the administration of Japan and for British and American recognition of the Soviet-imposed governments in Romania and Bulgaria. The ministers failed to reach any agreement on these and other issues and the meeting broke up on October 2 without issuing a communiqu.

Following the failure of the London Conference, Byrnes initiated a series of minor conciliatory gestures. First the United States recognized the provisional governments in Austria and Hungary in return for a Soviet promise that free elections be held. Byrnes then sent a special representative with known liberal views—Mark Etheridge, publisher of the *Louisville Courier-Journal*—to Bulgaria and Romania. Finally, Byrnes drafted a cordial letter to Stalin from Truman, which stressed America's genuine desire for an agreement on European peace treaties.

Another conference of foreign ministers was arranged for Moscow and started on December 16, 1945. At this meeting Soviet foreign minister V.M. MOLOTOV agreed to Byrnes's demand that a conference be held to discuss treaty terms. Byrnes, for his part, agreed to Molotov's demand that the Soviets be allowed a role in the occupation of Japan, although it was made clear that the Soviet role would not jeopardize American dominance.

Byrnes's second major foreign policy compromise was strongly criticized by the growing band of anti-Soviet congressional leaders. Truman was also angry and summoned Byrnes to the White House to accuse him of "losing his nerve at Moscow." The president was especially angry about Byrnes's inability to negotiate the withdrawal of Soviet troops from the Azerbaijan province of Iran.

In response to growing public, congressional and presidential pressure, Byrnes started to shift his foreign policy into a more anti-Soviet position. This became apparent in early 1946 with Byrnes's handling of the Iranian crisis. When the deadline for Soviet withdrawal of troops from Iran passed, Byrnes demanded an immediate withdrawal and rebuffed various Soviet attempts for compromise. The issue was resolved only after the Soviets and Iranians announced a formal agreement.

Byrnes also started to move toward the unification of the Western-occupied sectors of Germany. On September 6 he visited Stuttgart, where he told a German audience, "It is the view of the American government that the German people throughout Germany, under proper safeguards, should now be given the primary responsibility for the running of their own affairs . . . The United States favors the early establishment of a provisional Government for Germany." He added, "If complete unification cannot be secured, we shall do everything in our power to secure maximum possible unification." Byrnes ended this major speech by implicitly warning the Soviet Union: "We do not want Germany to become a satellite of any power. Therefore, as long as there is an occupation army in Germany, American armed forces will be part of that occupation."

By the time of Byrnes's Stuttgart speech, he and Truman had more or less agreed that Byrnes would resign as secretary of state. The two men never worked well together. Byrnes never forgave Truman for being in the job he felt rightfully belonged to him, and he often failed to inform the president of his actions. His relations with State Department officers were also poor, and, although he hardened his position on the Soviet Union, he was unable to shake his public image as an appeaser.

Byrnes formally resigned as secretary of state in January 1947. In 1950 he was elected governor of South Carolina, and he fought several battles to maintain racial segregation in the state. Byrnes retired from politics in 1955.

For Further Information:

Acheson, Dean. *Present at the Creation: My Years in the State Department*. New York, 1969.

Byrnes, James F. *All in a Lifetime*. New York, 1958.

———. *Speaking Freely*. New York, 1947.

Curry, George. *James F. Byrnes*. New York, 1965.

Horowitz, David. *From Yalta to Vietnam: American Foreign Policy in the Cold War*. New York, 1967.

Callaghan, James (March 17, 1912–) James Callaghan was the British foreign secretary from 1974 to 1976 and then prime minister from 1976 to May 1979. In the 1980s he took a leading role in opposing his Labour Party's policy of unilateral nuclear disarmament.

Callaghan was educated in the British state school system through secondary school, after which he joined the civil service. He quickly became active in trade union affairs, and at 19 he joined the Labour Party. By 1936, Callaghan was a full-time trade union official and began to rise through the ranks of Britain's Trades Union Congress.

During World War II, Callaghan served as a lieutenant in British Naval Intelligence. He was elected to Parliament in the Labour landslide of 1945. His first involvement in foreign affairs was 1956, when he was the Labour Party spokesman on colonial affairs.

When Labour returned to power in 1964 Callaghan became chancellor of the Exchequer. He resigned that post in 1967 after Prime Minister HAROLD WILSON forced him to devalue the pound. But shortly afterward, Callaghan was brought back into the government as home secretary. After the Conservative victory of 1971 he became the shadow spokesman on foreign affairs, and then in 1974, when the Labour Party was returned to office under Wilson, he was appointed secretary of state for foreign and Commonwealth affairs.

Callaghan was a conservative Labourite who placed a strong emphasis on Britain's special relationship with the United States. This was reflected in his first major speech as foreign secretary in March 1974, when he stressed the need for the "fullest and most intimate" cooperation between Europe and the United States. He added that a close European defense alliance with the United States could not be maintained "without parallel cooperation on trade, money and energy."

One of Callaghan's first foreign policy problems was the Cyprus crisis following Turkey's invasion of the northern third of the island in July 1974, ostensibly to protect the Turkish minority community in Cyprus. Cyprus was one of Britain's residual imperial responsibilities. It maintained two sovereign military bases on the former colonial possession and, along with Greece and Turkey, was joint guarantor of the island's independence.

The Turkish invasion of the island led to calls from Greeks and Cypriots for Britain, as a guarantor, to intervene to expel the Turks. But both Britain and the United States feared the repercussions of a British attack on a fellow NATO ally and backed away from this. The conflict brought Greece and Turkey to the brink of war and seriously threatened cohesion of the NATO alliance's southern flank. Callaghan, along with U.S. secretary of state HENRY KISSINGER, helped to mediate a ceasefire that prevented a further deterioration of the security situation, although it failed to achieve the aim of Turkish withdrawal from the island. The British and American failure to force Turkey to withdraw led to the temporary withdrawal of Greece from the military structure of NATO and to calls for the closure of American bases in Greece.

Britain's chronic economic problems seriously undermined its ability to maintain a global military presence. This was confirmed in December 1974 when the Labour government reduced the budget for defense spending over the following 10 years by $11 billion. This cut involved a reduction in British forces in Hong Kong and Cyprus and a pullout from Singapore and Mauritius. The strategic island of Diego Garcia was effectively handed over to the United States, and it became a major air base in the Indian Ocean, although it remained under British sovereignty.

Callaghan was always lukewarm toward the policy of détente of the 1970s, although he helped to negotiate an Anglo-Soviet agreement for $2.4 billion in low-interest credits for the Soviet Union. The agreement was announced during a visit to Moscow by Prime Minister Wilson in February 1975 during which he announced a "new phase in Anglo-Soviet relations." The Soviet Union, however, took up only a small percentage of the credit available.

Most of Callaghan's efforts as foreign secretary were absorbed by the ongoing Rhodesia crisis and the wider issue of Southern Africa. The white supremacist government of Ian Smith in Rhodesia had declared itself independent of Britain in 1965, and the following year civil war had broken out between black nationalists and the Smith government. Britain refused to recognize the independence of Rhodesia and organized an international economic embargo of the rebel colony.

The Smith government managed to circumvent the embargo by cultivating close relations with the racist government in South Africa and the right-wing dictatorship in Portugal, which allowed goods to be imported through its colonies of Mozambique and Angola.

But the collapse of Portuguese rule in Angola and Mozambique in 1975 was followed by the establishment of left-wing governments in both those countries. This not only increased the pressure on Rhodesia but also created diplomatic and military opportunities for the Soviet Union in Southern Africa. Thus the pressure increased on Callaghan to find a solution to the problems of southern Africa, including Rhodesia, South Africa and South African-administered Namibia.

Callaghan believed that the best hope the West had of preventing the spread of communism in Africa and winning the long-term support of Africa's black nationalists was to prove that Western diplomacy could achieve black majority rule in Rhodesia, Namibia and eventually South Africa. He further argued that the Western powers must at all costs steer away from military alliances with South Africa.

In December 1974, Callaghan signaled the Labour government's intention to abrogate Britain's 1955 Simonstown Agreement with South Africa, under which Britain maintained a naval task force at Simonstown, South Africa. Callaghan said: "Wider British interests dictate that we should not appear to give aid and comfort to apartheid." The agreement was formally ended in June 1975.

Following the collapse of Angola and Mozambique, Callaghan also played a major role in dissuading President GERALD FORD and Secretary of State HENRY KISSINGER from sending American troops into Angola or giving full support to the South African invasion of that country. He argued that any country that became identified with South African support for the anti-Soviet forces would "find itself pilloried all over Africa."

But at the same time, Callaghan was highly critical of Soviet and Cuban support for Marxist movements in Angola and Mozambique and nationalist movements throughout Southern Africa. Between March 15 and 19, 1976, he had three meetings with Soviet ambassador Nikolai Lunkov to express British concern over foreign intervention in Southern Africa. He expressed the same concerns to Soviet foreign minister ANDREI GROMYKO when he visited London on March 25. Gromyko denied any interest in Southern Africa.

Callaghan also encouraged American involvement in trying to negotiate a solution to the Rhodesian problem, and Kissinger made several trips to Southern Africa on behalf of the British government. This led to the Rhodesia Geneva Conference, opened in October 1976, which was the first major roundtable conference of all the parties since Smith's unilateral declaration of independence. The conference, however, soon break down.

In April 1976, Wilson resigned as prime minister, and Callaghan was elected by the Labour members of Parliament to succeed him. Shortly afterward JIMMY CARTER was elected U.S. president, and the two men formed a close relationship.

James Callaghan, British prime minister from 1976 to May 1979, with U.S. President Jimmy Carter. Photo courtesy of the Labour Party.

Callaghan appointed Dr. David Owen, another conservative Labourite and Atlanticist, as foreign secretary, and Owen named Callaghan's son-in-law, journalist Peter Jay, as ambassador to Washington.

Under Callaghan and Owen, American involvement in Southern Africa and the coordination of British and American policy in that region increased considerably. America's ambassador to the United Nations, Andrew Young, and Assistant Secretary of State Richard Moose regularly visited Southern Africa. The increased pressure eventually forced Smith to form an alliance with "moderate" black leader Bishop Abel Muzorewa in the hope that this would satisfy American and British public opinion. But this ploy failed. It was not until six months after Callaghan left office that a final solution to the Rhodesia problem was reached.

One of the major problems faced by Callaghan as prime minister was the decision on the replacement of the British Polaris fleet. Britain operated four American Polaris submarines, which represented the country's entire nuclear deterrent. By the mid-1970s pressure was growing on the British government to make a decision on the successor to Polaris, which would become obsolete by 1995. The United States offered its Trident submarine and missile systems, but the Labour Party's growing antinuclear lobby wanted Callaghan either to opt for a formal policy of unilateral nuclear disarmament or to defer a decision indefinitely so that Britain would become a nonnuclear power by default. Callaghan, however, opted for the Trident system, a decision confirmed by the successor Conservative government.

Callaghan's Labour government did not have a majority of seats in the House of Commons and remained in office through an informal arrangement with the centrist Liberal Party. The Lib-Lab Pact, as it was called, came under pressure in 1978 because of Callaghan's decision to impose government sanctions against companies that breached the government's 5% wage guidelines. In July 1978, Liberal leader David Steel announced that the Lib-Lab Pact would end with the parliamentary session, and in December 1978 the wage guidelines policy collapsed when the House of Commons passed a Conservative amendment criticizing the sanctions used by the government to enforce the guidelines. This effectively destroyed the government's "Social Contract" with the trade unions, and a series of damaging strikes led in March 1979 to a second vote of no confidence in the Callaghan government. The prime minister was forced to call an election for May, which the Conservatives under Margaret Thatcher won with a comfortable 43-seat majority.

Immediately after the election, Callaghan was reelected leader of the Labour Party, but he faced increasing opposition from the party's growing left wing. Callaghan resigned the leadership after the party adopted a number of left-wing positions at its October 1980 party conference. Among the proposals adopted was a commitment to unilateral nuclear disarmament. A number of conservative Labourites left the party at this time to form the Social Democratic Party. But Callaghan remained in the party and became one of the fiercest critics of Labour's unilateralist nuclear policy and other left-wing proposals.

For Further Information:
Callaghan, James. *Time and Chance*. New York, 1984.
Kellner, Peter, and Christopher Hitchens. *Callaghan: The Road to Number Ten*. London, 1976.

Cambodia   Cambodia was a tragic victim of the Cold War, a small country in the path of two conflicting countries and ideologies. The result of this conflict was to plunge the country into a self-destructive civil war that has resulted in the deaths of millions.

Cambodia became a French colony in 1863 under the Franco-Cambodian Treaty, which gave France control of foreign affairs and defense. In 1887, Cambodia became a part of the Indochina Union. The French left the traditional political and social structures largely intact, which made it much easier for the royal family, under Norodom Sihanouk, to regain political power when the French reluctantly granted Cambodia its independence in 1953. In 1955, Sihanouk abdicated his throne to run for president in a national election and won decisively.

Sihanouk at first sought economic and military aid from the United States. But he soon realized that this made him a target for communist forces inside and outside his country, and he switched to a neutral and nonaligned foreign policy in order to avoid being dragged into the conflict between communist and non-communist forces being waged in neighboring Laos and Vietnam. At the same time, he forged close relations with communist China because of the traditional rivalry between Vietnam and Cambodia. This led to the suspension of American aid and the imposition of an economic blockade by Thailand and South Vietnam.

In 1956, South Vietnamese Army units invaded Cambodia, and with covert U.S. support, Thailand and South Vietnam organized the right-wing Khmer Serei movement in an attempt to topple Sihanouk. But Sihanouk had established a wide enough popular base to defeat the initial challenge.

By 1964, the United States was deeply embroiled in the VIETNAM WAR and Sihanouk had become convinced that America was prepared to sacrifice Cambodia in the interests of wider Cold War strategy. In 1965, he severed U.S.–Cambodian diplomatic relations and allied Cambodia even more closely with China and North Vietnam. He also agreed to allow the Vietnamese communists to use Cambodian territory for attacks on South Vietnam. But simultaneously, Sihanouk feared the eventual success of the Vietnamese communists.

By this time, both the far-left and far-right elements within Cambodia had become distrustful of Sihanouk's political balancing act and began to move against him. The left-wing forces established the Khmer Rouge guerrilla group and the far-right coalesced behind General Lon Nol who, in 1966, was elected prime minister. Sihanouk, as president, retained power. In 1967, leftist demonstrations toppled Lon Nol and a communist-inspired revolt erupted in Battambang Province. This combination of events convinced Sihanouk that the greatest threat to Cambodia came from the left, and he bowed to pressure from the army and cracked down on left-wing elements in Cambodian society.

In 1968, Sihanouk agreed to allow the United States and South Vietnamese armies to conduct hot-pursuit raids into Cambodian territory in search of Viet Minh and Viet Cong forces. But the agreement was made half-heartedly. Sihanouk refused to reestablish diplomatic relations with the United States or sever official ties with North Vietnam and China. The American CENTRAL INTELLIGENCE AGENCY (CIA), along with Lon Nol (who returned to the premiership in 1969) and the Khmer Serei, began to plot the overthrow of Sihanouk.

In March 1970, while Sihanouk was visiting France, Lon Nol demanded the withdrawal of all Vietnamese communist forces from Cambodian territory. The following week, Lon Nol officially deposed Sihanouk, who formed a government-in-exile in Beijing. Lon Nol reestablished diplomatic relations with the United States and brought Cambodia formally into the Vietnam War. On May 1, 1970, U.S. and South Vietnamese forces invaded Cambodia in an attempt to wipe out Vietnamese communist bases. The move resulted in an outcry against U.S. policy in Southeast Asia, both domestically and around the world.

At first the major opposition faced by American-led forces was from the Vietnamese communists. But soon they were also fighting the Khmer Rouge, who replaced the exiled

Sihanouk as the only alternative to Lon Nol. In 1971, the United States escalated its air attacks in Cambodia. As a result, millions of refugees from Khmer Rouge areas flooded into the capital Phnom Penh, widening the conflict and increasing the internal security threat to Lon Nol.

In August 1973, the United States stopped its bombing of Cambodia and started to withdraw from Southeast Asia. American Air Force planes had dropped more than 539,000 tons of bombs on Cambodia. The Khmer Rouge had by this time firmly established itself throughout the Cambodian countryside and rejected all of Lon Nol's peace overtures.

On April 17, 1975, the revolutionary forces entered Phnom Penh. Lon Nol was forced to flee to sanctuary in Indonesia, and the U.S. embassy was quickly evacuated. Sihanouk returned to Cambodia in September as titular chief of state. The reverence with which he was held by the peasantry made him a useful ally for the Khmer Rouge, and they had maintained contact with him while he had been in Peking. But it quickly became apparent that Sihanouk was not in power, and a doctrinaire communist state was established.

In May 1975, U.S.-Cambodian relations plummeted even further when Cambodian forces seized the U.S. Navy warship *Mayaguez* off the Cambodian coast. President Ford denounced the seizure as an act of piracy, and American Marines were sent in to rescue the ship and its crew, with the loss of three U.S. helicopters and 15 Marines.

By April 1976, Sihanouk had served his purpose and was forced out of office by Khieu Samphan, who changed the country's name to Kampuchea. Samphan was replaced in 1977 by Pol Pot, who officially declared the Communist Party the governing body of Cambodia. Samphan started, and Pol Pot continued, one of the bloodiest terror campaigns in history. Pol Pot was determined to establish a perfect communist state. To this end private property was abolished; educational, legal and monetary systems were dismantled, and all newspapers were suspended. Phnom Penh was virtually evacuated as millions were sent to "reeducation camps" or agricultural cooperatives. The economy collapsed overnight, and anyone who resisted or was suspected of "bourgeois tendencies" was summarily executed. Bodies were piled up on street corners of Phnom Penh, where they were allowed to rot. In 1978, the ambassadors of Sweden, Denmark and Finland described Phnom Penh as a "ghost city," and the United States accused the Khmer Rouge government of massacring its population "in order to destroy every vestige of existing society." As many as 3 million people may have been killed by the Pol Pot regime.

In the late 1970s tensions between Cambodia and Vietnam also grew, for several reasons. One reason was the traditional rivalry between the two countries. Another was the SINO-SOVIET SPLIT, as Cambodia had allied itself with China and Vietnam with the Soviet Union. And, finally, the self-destructive doctrinaire communism of Pol Pot threatened to destabilize Vietnam. In 1979, in a 15-day blitzkrieg, Vietnam overran Cambodia, occupied the capital and ousted the Pol Pot regime. A new Vietnamese-backed regime under Heng Samrin, leader of the Kampuchean National United Front for National Salvation, was installed.

China vowed retaliation against Vietnam and attempted an invasion of that country, which was repulsed. The Pol Pot regime formed a government-in-exile in Thailand and, with Chinese support, managed to hold onto its seat in the United Nations; from the refugee camps in Thailand it launched a guerrilla war against the Vietnam-backed regime.

The Western countries faced an acute moral dilemma. Strategic considerations dictated that they oppose the new government in Phnom Penh, but the only effective opposition remained the morally repugnant Khmer Rouge. Sihanouk was brought out of retirement and encouraged to form an alternative to the Khmer Rouge. This he did and in June 1982 he became head of a loose coalition of anti-Vietnamese forces including the Khmer Rouge. This enabled the United States and other Western countries to channel military and other aid to the new Kampuchean National Liberation Front, which in turn increased its guerrilla activities in Cambodia.

In 1988, the Vietnamese were forced to maintain 150,000 troops in Cambodia, which was now governed by Hun Sen. The cost of maintaining this force was borne either directly or indirectly by the Soviet Union. But the end of the Sino-Soviet split, improving East–West relations and the Soviet Union's own economic problems meant that the Soviet Union was forced to reduce its aid substantially; Vietnam in turn was forced to seek a negotiated solution to the Cambodian civil war.

Several attempts to find a negotiated solution were initiated in the 1980s by Indonesia, the Association of Southeast Asian Nations and the French government. These initially foundered either on the anti-Vietnamese coalition's inability to agree to a common program or on a shift in the military situation. But in September 1989, events took a dramatic turn when the Vietnamese started the unilateral withdrawal of their forces from Cambodia. The guerrilla forces launched a major offensive against the Hun Sen regime, but when this offensive failed to produce immediate results it became clear to both sides that a negotiated solution was the only alternative.

On June 5, 1990, a conditional ceasefire agreement was signed in Tokyo between the Hun Sen government and Prince Sihanouk, but the Khmer Rouge refused to attend the negotiations or be party to the agreement. In July 1990, U.S. secretary of state JAMES BAKER announced that the U.S. government was withdrawing its recognition of the rebel forces in an attempt to encourage a negotiated solution to the civil war.

Throughout 1991 negotiations continued in Paris, Bangkok and Jakarta under United Nations auspices. Gradually the Khmer Rouge were brought into the process and on June 24 a formal ceasefire was declared, along with plans for the establishment of a Supreme National Council to administer the country with the aid of UN peacekeeping forces during an interim period before elections. The Supreme National

Council was comprised of all four members of the rebel alliance and the Hun Sen government. At the end of November Prince Sihanouk returned to his country after a long exile. But when members of the Khmer Rouge attempted to return they were stoned by angry mobs. Khmer Rouge intransigence continued to threaten the UN-brokered peace process through 1992.

For Further Information

Barnett, Anthony. *The Cambodian Revolutions.* New York, 1981.

Barron, John, and Paul Anthony. *Murder of a Gentle Land.* Pleasantville, N.Y., 1977.

Becker, Elizabeth. *When the War Was Over: The Voices of Cambodia's Revolution and Its People.* New York, 1986.

Burchett, Wilfred G. *The China-Cambodia-Vietnam Triangle.* Chicago, 1981.

Carney, Timothy M. *Communist Party Power in Kampuchea.* Ithaca, N.Y., 1977.

Chandler, David P. *A History of Cambodia.* Boulder, Colo., 1992.

Haggart, M.T. *The United States and Cambodia.* Washington, D.C., 1971.

Haley, P. Edward. *Congress and the Fall of South Vietnam and Cambodia.* New Jersey, 1982.

Issacs, Arnold R., Gordon Hardy, MacAllister Brown, and Editors of Boston Publishing Co. *Pawns of War: Cambodia and Laos.* Boston, 1987.

Osborne, M.E. *Politics and Power in Cambodia: The Sihanouk Years.* New York, 1973.

Penfold, Helen. *Remember Cambodia.* Robinsonia, Pa., 1979.

Shaplen, Robert. *Bitter Victory.* New York, 1986.

Shawcross, William. *Sideshow: Kissinger, Nixon, and the Destruction of Cambodia.* New York, 1979.

Sihanouk, Norodom. *My War with the CIA.* New York, 1973.

Zasloff, Joseph J., and Alan E. Goodman. *Indochina in Conflict: A Political Assessment.* Lexington, Mass., 1972.

Campaign for Nuclear Disarmament (CND)   The British-based Campaign for Nuclear Disarmament (CND) was one of the most influential of the anti-nuclear weapons pressure groups, particularly during the early 1960s and mid-1980s.

CND was formally founded in London on January 6, 1958, but it had its origins in the 1954 H-bomb National Campaign, the 1957 National Council for the Abolition of Nuclear Weapons Tests and the Direct Action Committee Against Nuclear Weapons (DAC).

In 1958 CND and DAC organized the first protest march from London to the British atomic weapons factory at Aldermaston in Berkshire. By the 1960s, CND's annual Easter marches (from Aldermaston to London after 1958) had become international events. In 1962, more than 150,000 people, including a number of prominent British Labour members of Parliament, participated in the Easter march.

As a result of CND pressure, the British Labour Party in 1964 campaigned on a platform that included the cancellation of plans to buy the U.S. Polaris nuclear missile submarines. But after his party's election victory, Labour prime minister HAROLD WILSON decided to go ahead with Polaris. This

was a major blow to CND, which went into decline for the next 15 years.

The pressure group was given a new lease on life by the decision of the NORTH ATLANTIC TREATY ORGANIZATION (NATO) to deploy intermediate-range Pershing II and cruise missiles in Western Europe in response to the Soviet deployment of SS-20s. The debate was further fueled by the decision of British Labour and Conservative governments to replace the aging Polaris submarines with American Trident submarines. CND's national demonstration in London in October 1980 attracted 100,000 supporters, and in 1983 400,000 CND supporters gathered in London's Hyde Park.

CND also supported the women's "peace camp" outside the American cruise missile base at Greenham Common in Berkshire. The women established a permanent vigil outside the camp gates, and in December 1982 a total of 30,000 women drew international attention to the peace camp by linking arms around the base. Other "peace camps" were established at the second proposed cruise missile base at Molesworth in Cambridgeshire, at the Faslane Polaris base, the Upper Heyford U.S. air base in Oxfordshire and several other nuclear bases and installations in Britain. The success of these campaigns was a major factor in the Labour Party's decision to adopt a policy of unilateral nuclear disarmament in the 1980s (a policy it later abandoned).

Various right-wing British conservatives attempted to smear CND with the label of "Communist front organization." It was true that members of the British Communist Party and other far-left political groups supported CND, and generally speaking it did draw the bulk of its support from the left of the political spectrum. But there was no evidence that it was controlled by the Soviet Union. In any event, the issue became moot with the waning of the Cold War in the late 1980s.

For Further Information:

Minnion, John, and Philip Bolsover, eds. *The CND Story.* London, 1983.

Ruddock, Joan. *The CND Scrapbook.* London, 1987.

Canada   Canada played an important part within the Cold War Western Alliance as the second North American country committed to the defense of Europe and as the state over which passed the arctic flight paths of U.S. and Soviet strategic missiles. It has had a contradictory relationship with the United States, on the one hand joining with it in a continental defense system and making Canadian bases available to it, and on the other criticizing U.S. foreign and defense policies.

Unlike the United States, Canada had a history of involvement, albeit at times reluctant, in European affairs through its links with the British Commonwealth and the language and cultural links between French-speaking Quebec and France. Tens of thousands of young Canadians enlisted to fight with the British at the start of both world wars, and Canada played an active role in supporting British foreign policy.

Canada entered World War II as a primarily agricultural country very much in Britain's shadow. The war, however, spurred industrial and financial development and the country, emerged from the conflict as a middle-ranking industrial power and, like the United States, a major creditor nation. The war also resulted in the first formal U.S.-Canadian agreement for the defense of North America.

But the government of Prime Minister William Lyon MacKenzie King was determined that Canada maintain an identifiably separate foreign policy despite the new relationship with the United States. This has continued as a hallmark of Canadian postwar foreign policy, which has been similar to and generally supportive of the United States and the policy of collective security, but at the same time has been independent of and generally more liberal than specific policies of U.S. administrations.

In the initial Cold War years, the government of MacKenzie King was at first suspicious of the anti-Soviet rhetoric coming from Washington and tried to encourage a continuation of the wartime alliance with Moscow. This made the Canadians more susceptible to the activities of the Soviet KGB, which used Canada either as a source for shared U.S.-Canadian secrets or as a back door through which to smuggle illegal agents into the United States.

The main elements of Canadian foreign policy are support for international organizations such as the Commonwealth and the United Nations, close relations with the Third World, an extensive foreign aid program and a willingness to criticize U.S. policy. The support for the United Nations has led successive Canadian governments to make strong contributions to UN peacekeeping forces throughout the world; this support for the peacekeeping forces has been described as a "national passion."

Early and enthusiastic Canadian support for the United Nations made the Canadians initially cautious of the proposed NORTH ATLANTIC TREATY ORGANIZATION. Many felt that peace should be maintained by the forces of the United Nations and that regional alliances undermined the authority of the global body. But despite the initial caution, Canada, once it made up its mind, was an enthusiastic supporter of NATO. In the treaty negotiations, however, the Canadians tried to widen the scope of the alliance to encompass political and economic affairs. This goal was incorporated as Article 2 of the North Atlantic Treaty but has never been actively pursued.

The anti-communist hysteria that swept the United States in the late 1940s and 1950s never really hit Canada, and this was reflected in Canadian attitudes toward East-West relations. Canada sent forces to fight alongside U.S. troops in the KOREAN WAR, but the government made it clear that it regarded the war not as an attempt to contain or roll back communism but as a UN action to uphold the peace settlement that had divided Korea at the 38th Parallel.

The Canadians were also critical of the U.S. refusal to recognize the communist government of China, although the Canadians also withheld recognition until 1970. But it was during the Vietnam War that Canadian criticism was most keenly felt. Not only did Canada refuse to support U.S. action, but it also provided a refuge to thousands of young Americans fleeing conscription.

Nevertheless, the defense relationship between Canada and the United States has been strengthened. In 1958 the two countries established the North American Defense Command (NORAD) for defense against air attacks. The United States also built a string of radar stations across Canada as part of the DISTANT EARLY WARNING LINE (DEW) to warn of any Soviet missile or air attack across the Arctic Ocean, the most direct and likely route. Canada also contributed an infantry brigade, 12 air squadrons and ships to NATO forces.

Canada's policy toward nuclear weapons has been at times contradictory. During World War II, Canadian scientists worked with their British colleagues on the development of atomic weapons. Canada also supplied the uranium for the MANHATTAN PROJECT and many of the U.S. and Britain's subsequent nuclear weapons.

Canada, however, decided against the development of its nuclear weapons. But in 1957 the military developed plans for the deployment of nuclear-armed warheads in its bomber contribution to NORAD and to Starfighter planes and Honest John missiles based in West Germany. The plan provoked an outcry in Canada, and to still the criticism Conservative prime minister John Diefenbaker agreed to the deployment of the missiles but withheld the nuclear warheads. This compromise solution was opposed by the Liberal Party, which was divided on the issue: Party leader LESTER PEARSON argued in favor of deployment and the party's left wing, led by Pierre Trudeau, argued against. Following Pearson's election as prime minister in 1963, Canadian forces in Germany were armed with nuclear warheads, but after Trudeau assumed office in 1968, they were denuclearized.

During the 1968 election campaign, Pierre Trudeau argued that Canada's foreign policy was in danger of being determined by its defense relationship with the United States and that Canada should attempt to relax its defense ties to Washington and NATO and develop a more independent, Canada-first foreign policy. This was pursued after the Liberals' election victory in June 1968. In April 1969, Trudeau said that Canada would give priority to "surveillance of our own territory and coastlines" ahead of continental defense, NATO obligations and peacekeeping duties. As a result, Canada's contributions to NATO were substantially reduced, although it continued to maintain a token force of 7,000 troops in West Germany. The Defense White Paper of 1970 also decided to reduce Canadian involvement in NORAD. At the same time, Trudeau set out to increase links with the Far East, Africa and Latin America.

Trudeau did, however, support the development of the U.S. Cruise missile, and Canada made available a testing ground on the MacKenzie River. The first air-launched cruise missiles were deployed on U.S. bombers based in Canada, and

Canada was an early and keen supporter of the deployment of Cruise and PERSHING II missiles in Western Europe.

During the 1980s, Trudeau was particularly critical of the REAGAN administration's policies toward Central America and East-West relations. At the UN disarmament conference in June 1982, Trudeau called for a freeze on new nuclear weapons and a reduction in stocks. In October 1983, Trudeau announced that he was launching a personal crusade to improve East-West relations and facilitate a U.S.-Soviet agreement on reducing nuclear arms. To this end, he embarked on a series of foreign trips and proposed a conference of the five major nuclear weapons states (the United States, the Soviet Union, Britain, France, China) to discuss nuclear arms reductions. The initiative foundered on the British and French refusal to reduce their nuclear arsenals before the superpowers did and on President Reagan's basic distrust of the proposal.

Canada's Liberal government was also highly critical of President Reagan's enthusiastic support for oppressive right-wing governments in Central America, opposed his attempts to overthrow the Sandinista regime in Nicaragua and "regretted" the U.S. invasion of Grenada in 1983.

Trudeau's distinctive foreign policy turned the issue of foreign affairs into an election issue, with the Conservatives adopting a more pro-American and anti-Soviet position. In September 1984 the Conservatives under Brian Mulroney were returned to office, and Canadian foreign policy took a marked turn toward the United States. Mulroney supported President Reagan's STRATEGIC DEFENSE INITIATIVE, and at the start of 1989 Reagan and Mulroney signed a U.S.-Canada Free Trade Agreement. The close relationship continued under President Bush, who met with Mulroney frequently.

Meanwhile, Mulroney became the first Canadian prime minister in nearly two decades to visit the Soviet Union when he traveled to Moscow in November 1989 for talks with President MIKHAIL GORBACHEV. Gorbachev returned the favor by visiting Canada in May 1990.

For Further Information:

Balawyder, Aloysius. *Canada-Soviet Relations, 1936–1980.* Winnipeg, 1982.

Bowen, R.W. *Innocence Is Not Enough.* New York, 1988.

Clarkson, Stephen. *Canada and the Reagan Challenge.* Toronto, 1985.

English, Harry, ed. *Canada-United States Relations.* New York, Washington, 1976.

Hurs, Donald, and John Miller. *The Challenge of Power: Canada and the World.* New York, 1979.

Stacey, C.P. *Canada and the Age of Conflict: A History of Canadian External Policies.* Toronto, 1981.

Vans, G.S. *Canada.* New York, 1988.

Canada–United States Regional Planning Group   The Canada–United States Regional Planning Group is a NATO organization that helps to coordinate U.S. and Canadian defense policies. It meets alternately in the United States and Canada, usually at ministerial level, and develops plans for the defense of North America, which it recommends to the military committee of the NATO Alliance. Among the responsibilities of the planning group are the North American radar stations in the DISTANT EARLY WARNING LINE (DEW).

Captive Nations Resolution   The Captive Nations Resolution was a U.S. congressional resolution requiring the president to issue a statement attacking Soviet control of Eastern Europe.

The resolution first passed Congress in 1950 and was passed every year thereafter throughout most of the Cold War period. The resolution urged Americans to "study the plight of Soviet-dominated nations and to recommit themselves to the support of the just aspirations of those captive nations."

The resolution was regarded as little more than a minor political concession to right-wing Americans determined to replace the containment policy with their plan to "roll back" communism. But the Soviets and the communist governments in Eastern Europe attacked it as interference in the internal affairs of East European countries and as a thinly disguised call for rebellion.

When Vice President RICHARD NIXON visited Moscow in 1959, he was subjected to a tirade by NIKITA KHRUSHCHEV against the Captive Nations Resolution. According to Nixon's memoirs, Khrushchev called the resolution stupid and frightening and asked whether war would be the next step. "Heretofore," Khrushchev told Nixon, "the Soviet government thought Congress could never adopt a decision to start a war. But now it appears that, although Senator McCarthy is dead, his spirit still lives. For this reason the Soviet Union has to keep its powder dry."

Carlucci, Frank   (October 18, 1930–   )   As U.S. ambassador to Portugal, Frank Carlucci played a vital role in preventing a communist coup. He was also deputy director of the CENTRAL INTELLIGENCE AGENCY deputy secretary of defense, national security adviser and finally secretary of defense at the end of the REAGAN administration.

After graduating from Princeton University, Carlucci joined the navy and saw active service in Korea as a gunnery officer. After a short spell in business, he became a U.S. Foreign Service officer specializing in African affairs. In 1960 he was the victim of a stabbing in the Congo when he rescued a carload of Americans from a rioting mob. Carlucci also served in Zanzibar and Brazil.

In 1971, Carlucci resigned from the diplomatic service to become director of the Office of Economic Opportunity. The following year he became deputy director of the White House Office of Management and Budget and formed a close relationship with the director, Caspar Weinberger.

In 1974, President GERALD FORD appointed Carlucci ambassador to Portugal. At the time, the country was threatened with a communist takeover following the military coup that deposed the right-wing dictator Marcelo Caetano. As the country moved further and further to the left, Carlucci was attacked by the ruling Portuguese officers as the embodiment of American and imperialist policies. In reality, he was pressing a reluctant Secretary of State HENRY KISSINGER not to cut off aid to Portugal and working with West German chancellor HELMUT SCHMIDT to finance the Portuguese Socialist Party, which finally prevailed against the communists.

Carlucci has always managed to maintain good relations with both major American political parties, and after the election of JIMMY CARTER he was asked to take over as deputy director of the Central Intelligence Agency (CIA). Morale at the agency was at an all-time low following post-Watergate revelations about illegal CIA activities. Carlucci was given the task of helping to restore morale by repairing CIA relations with a suspicious Congress.

After RONALD REAGAN was elected president in 1980, he appointed Casper Weinberger secretary of defense. Weinberger made it a condition of the job that Carlucci become his deputy. The appointment encountered heavy opposition from Republican conservatives, who saw Carlucci as too much of a pragmatist and too closely associated with the foreign policies of Henry Kissinger and Jimmy Carter. As the conservatives came to the fore in the early Reagan days, Carlucci's influence waned, and in 1982 he left the government for a job in business.

Then in 1986, the Reagan administration was hit by the Iran-Contra scandal. National security adviser John Poindexter, who helped organize the illegal sale of weapons to Iran and funds to the CONTRA REBELS in Nicaragua, was forced to resign. Weinberger, who had established himself as a chief adviser to Reagan, successfully urged the president to turn to Carlucci as the man best qualified to reorganize the National Security Council and restore morale.

Carlucci's appointment as national security adviser came at a critical moment in the development of Reagan's foreign policy. Carlucci, through careful cultivation of Congress, managed to rescue Reagan's Central American policy and helped to direct the administration's negotiations for the U.S.-Soviet INTERMEDIATE RANGE NUCLEAR FORCES (INF) Treaty of December 1987. He also traveled widely in Europe and Latin America.

Reagan came to rely heavily on Carlucci's advice, and when Weinberger resigned in November 1987, Carlucci was appointed in his place as defense secretary. With the prospect of only a year in office, many observers believed that Carlucci was only a stopgap appointment with little real power. This was not the case. Carlucci's excellent relations with Congress helped to ensure the smooth passage of the INF Treaty. At the same time, he advocated U.S. withdrawal from the 1972 ANTIBALLISTIC MISSILE TREATY while instituting a Pentagon study to cut back Reagan's prized STRATEGIC DEFENSE INITIATIVE.

In March 1988 Carlucci became the first American defense secretary since the end of World War II to hold a bilateral discussion with his Soviet counterpart when he met Dmitri Yazov in Berne, Switzerland. The discussions were devoted primarily to a debate of military concepts, with Yazov virgor-

ously defending the notion that Soviet military strategy was purely defensive in nature. Carlucci used the meeting to attack Soviet military aid for Nicaragua. After the meeting, Carlucci told reporters that the talks had built "a bridge of communications" between the United States and the Soviet Union. But he added, "It doesn't mean that the problems have been solved, that the millennium is here." Five months later, in August, Carlucci continued his talks with Yazov when he became the first American defense secretary to visit Moscow on his own.

Carlucci also oversaw the end of negotiations for the withdrawal of American air bases in Spain and found them a new home in Italy. In January 1988 he visited American naval vessels providing escort services to merchant ships operating under the U.S. flag in the war-torn Persian Gulf. In April he announced that the navy's rules of engagement in the Gulf were being expanded to permit U.S. warships to protect merchant ships not flying the U.S. flag from armed attack in certain "unspecified circumstances." Carlucci again returned to private industry at the start of the Bush administration.

For Further Information:
Brzezinski, Z. *In Quest of National Security*. Boulder Colo., 1988.
Spanier, J.W. *The American Foreign Policy Since World War Two*. Washington, D.C., 1988.

Carrington, Lord (Peter) (June 6, 1919–   ) Peter Carington, sixth Baron (the family name has one "r") Carrington, served as Britain's defense secretary and foreign secretary and finally as secretary-general of the NORTH ATLANTIC TREATY ORGANIZATION from 1984 to 1988.

Carrington was born into the British aristocracy. He was educated at Eton and the Royal Military College at Sandhurst and succeeded to the peerage on his father's death when Peter was 19 years old. During World War II, he served with the Grenadier Guards in northwestern Europe and was awarded the Military Cross.

In 1946, Carrington took an active interest in politics in the House of Lords as a Conservative Party peer. When the Conservatives returned to office in 1951, Carrington became a junior minister in the Ministry of Agriculture. In 1954 he became parliamentary secretary to the minister of defense and two years later was appointed British High Commissioner in Australia. He returned to Britain in 1959 to take up the post of First Lord of the Admiralty. From 1964 to 1970, Carrington was leader of the opposition in the House of Lords.

After the Conservative election victory in 1970, Carrington returned to government as secretary of state for defense. In this post, he implemented the previous Labour Government's decision to withdraw British forces from the Persian Gulf. In 1972, Carrington left the Ministry of Defense to become chairman of the Conservative Party, and from 1974 to 1979 he was again leader of the opposition in the House of Lords.

In 1979, the Conservative Party and Lord Carrington re-

Peter Carrington, British defense secretary, foreign secretary and secretary-general of NATO (North Atlantic Treaty Organization) from 1984 to 1988. Photo courtesy of NATO.

turned to government. This time, Carrington was appointed secretary of state for foreign and Commonwealth affairs. His first major task was to resolve the long-running Rhodesian problem. His skillful handling of constitutional talks led to elections and the emergence of the independent republic of Zimbabwe. After the Soviet invasion of AFGHANISTAN in December 1979, Carrington turned his attention to the Middle East and East-West affairs. He was the first Western statesman to visit the Persian Gulf, Pakistan and the border areas with Afghanistan after the Soviet invasion, and in July 1981 went to Moscow to present the EEC proposals on Afghanistan. Lord Carrington's increasing involvement in the Middle East and East-West affairs distracted him from other parts of the world, and in April 1982 he handed in his resignation after Argentina invaded the British South Atlantic colony of the Falkland Islands.

From 1982 to 1984, Carrington was involved in various businesses. In June 1984 he took over from JOSEPH LUNS as secretary-general of NATO. During his four years as secretary-general, the issues Carrington had to deal with included the long-running dispute between Greece and Turkey over the Aegean and Cyprus, the withdrawal of American air bases from Spain and Spanish entry into NATO, negotiations on U.S.-Soviet INTERMEDIATE RANGE NUCLEAR FORCES (INF) in Europe and U.S.-Soviet Strategic Arms Reduction Talks (START), the deployment of U.S. CRUISE and PERSHING missiles and the subsequent revival of the European antinuclear and anti-NATO lobby, and Afghanistan.

Possibly the greatest long-term problem that arose during Carrington's tenure at NATO was the impact of MIKHAIL GORBACHEV. Carrington believed that the Soviet leader's unilateral diplomatic initiatives were clearly aimed at driving a wedge between a Europe looking for détente and the more conservative United States under President RONALD REAGAN. Carrington worked hard to steer a middle course between the two Western positions, urging Reagan to maintain the 1972 ANTIBALLISTIC MISSILE TREATY and to reconsider his refusal to link U.S.-Soviet strategic weapons negotiations to the STRATEGIC DEFENSE INITIATIVE. At the same time he warned the Europeans on May 5, 1987, that the Soviets seemed to be aiming at a "denuclearization" of Europe through the removal of shorter-range weapons. This, he contended, would be "absolutely fatal" to the West. Carrington left NATO on July 1, 1988, to become chairman of Christies, the international art auction house.

Most recently he has served as the EC's chief mediator in the Yugoslavian civil war.

For Further Information:
Carrington, Lord Peter. *Reflect on Things Past.* New York, 1988.

Carter, Jimmy (October 1, 1924–   )   Jimmy Carter was president of the United States from 1977 to 1981. He placed a heavy emphasis on human rights issues. Major events of his administration included the signing of the SALT II Treaty and the Camp David accords; the overthrow of the shah of Iran and the seizure of American diplomats in Iran; and the Soviet invasion of AFGHANISTAN.

Carter was the son of a Georgia peanut farmer and a nurse. In his autobiography, Carter described his father as "quite conservative" and an unbending foe of racial integration while his mother Lillian "was and is a liberal." When she was 68, Lillian Carter joined the Peace Corps and served two years in India.

Carter attended Georgia Southwestern College from 1941 to 1942, Georgia Institute of Technology from 1942 to 1943 and graduated from the U.S. Naval Academy at Annapolis in 1946. He spent seven years in the navy, rising to the rank of lieutenant before resigning his commission in October 1953. Most of his time in the navy was spent on submarines. From 1952 to 1953 he established a naval training program for prospective personnel on America's nuclear submarines.

Carter left the navy to take over the family peanut business following his father's death. He built it into a thriving concern. Carter also became active in local politics and in 1962 was elected to the Georgia State Senate. In 1966, although still a

Jimmy Carter, president of the United States from 1977 to 1981.

political unknown, Carter managed to place third in the Democratic primaries for governor of Georgia. His second challenge, in 1970, resulted in a victory as he secured 59.3% of the vote. As governor, Carter established his liberal credentials by appointing a number of blacks to prominent positions and battling against racial discrimination. He also increased spending on education, welfare, hospitals and pollution control.

During the 1972 U.S. presidential campaign, Carter was prominent in the movement to stop candidate George McGovern and nominated Senator HENRY JACKSON at the Democratic National Convention. It was in 1972 that Carter decided to run for president in 1976. In 1973, Robert Strauss, chairman of the Democratic National Committee, selected Carter as the party's national campaign coordinator for the 1974 midterm elections. In this capacity, Carter traveled to 30 states and laid the groundwork for his presidential bid.

By 1975, Carter was well known within Democratic Party circles but still virtually unknown to the wider voting public. This "outsider" position proved to be a major asset in the presidential election, however. The 1975–76 campaign came at the end of the Watergate scandal and other scandals involving the CENTRAL INTELLIGENCE AGENCY and several other government departments. The scandals badly shook the Washington political establishment that had controlled national politics since the end of World War II. Carter represented an untainted "breath of fresh air" that captured the public imagination. The result was a narrow but decisive

victory for Jimmy Carter over incumbent President GERALD FORD in the election on November 2, 1976.

During his campaign, Carter had said he wanted to construct a foreign policy based on "morality." He also promised a major reduction in the defense budget. On December 2, Carter named CYRUS VANCE as secretary of state. Vance, a well-known liberal, had established a reputation as an envoy of President LYNDON JOHNSON in Cyprus and Korea and as deputy secretary of defense. Vance, after receiving the nomination, said the issue of strategic arms negotiation was "paramount" and added that early attention would be given to the Middle East.

Carter's appointment of Vance was not popular among conservatives. Partly to forestall criticism from the right, he appointed a well-known anti-communist, Polish-born ZBIGNIEW BRZEZINSKI, as his national security adviser. At the United Nations, Carter placed another well-known liberal, black activist Andrew Young, and as secretary of defense he appointed Harold Brown. Carter, however, was determined from the start that he would remain in firm control of America's foreign and defense policies.

On his inauguration day, Carter broke with tradition to issue a separate statement to the world as well as his inaugural address to his country delivered from the steps of the Capitol. In it Carter promised that American foreign policy would "be guided . . . by our desire to shape a world order that is more responsive to human operations."

Carter's emphasis on human rights was one of the hallmarks of his administration. He established a bureau of human rights at the State Department headed by an assistant secretary of state. The first person named to the post was Patricia Derian. Under Carter and Derian, human rights considerations played an increasing part in allocations of American aid and political support, and the basic criteria were applied to both left-wing and right-wing governments. This meant that some of the right-wing governments that had enjoyed varying degrees of support under previous administrations—such as Guatemala, El Salvador, Nicaragua and South Africa—now suffered major cutbacks. The new emphasis increased the credibility of American criticism of Soviet Bloc countries' violations of human rights but also undermined some traditional anti-communist allies such as Nicaraguan president Anastasio Somoza, who in 1979 was overthrown by a popular revolt led by the left-wing Sandinistas.

Carter's relations with the Soviet Union were uneasy. The Soviets had formed a working relationship with the Kissinger-dominated administrations of RICHARD NIXON and GERALD FORD and could relate to HENRY KISSINGER's balance-of-power diplomacy. Carter was badly received by the Kremlin for the same reason he had been well received by the American voting public—he was an unknown quantity from outside the political establishment. The Soviet government, although it claimed to be revolutionary, was under LEONID BREZHNEV one of the most conservative bureaucracies in the world. Its leaders hated change and resisted being forced to adapt its foreign policies to changed personalities and circumstances. The Soviets were also uneasy with a foreign policy that placed morality and human rights before balance-of-power diplomacy.

The Soviets were particularly worried about the appointment of Zbigniew Brzezinski and the effect this would have on the VLADIVOSTOK ACCORDS and the SALT II negotiations. During the campaign, Carter sent veteran diplomat AVERELL HARRIMAN to Moscow to meet with Soviet President Brezhnev and reassure him that Carter wanted to quickly sign a SALT II Treaty based on the Vladivostok Accords. But within a few weeks of Carter's inauguration, Brezhnev and Carter faced a substantive disagreement over strategic weapons reductions.

Carter took a leading role throughout the negotiations during the following two and a half years. He was responsible for the major policy decisions, at key times personally intervened in negotiations with Soviet diplomats and read every document and briefing paper related to the subject. He also several times proposed a personal summit between himself and Brezhnev in the belief that much of the deadlock was the result of a mutual personal suspicion, which could be sorted out in a face-to-face meeting.

By the beginning of 1979, Carter's chances for reelection had become increasingly doubtful as inflation soared out of control and the Democratic Congress clashed more and more with the White House. Carter needed a foreign policy success and therefore decided to compromise on SALT II and accept the principle of parity in strategic weapons with the goal of substantial reductions tabled for a later date. The agreement was signed on June 18, 1979, in Vienna by Brezhnev and Carter.

Even before Carter left for the signing ceremony, the SALT II Treaty was being savagely attacked. General Edward Rowney, the U.S. military representative at the negotiations, refused to go to Vienna in protest against what he thought were dangerous concessions. And Senator Henry Jackson, the most prominent critic of SALT II, accused Carter of following in the appeasing footsteps of Britain's Neville Chamberlain. On the eve of Carter's departure, he said, "To enter into a treaty which favors the Soviets, as this one does, on the grounds that we will be in a worse position without it, is appeasement in its purest form." Jackson's attack presaged a tough battle between the White House and the U.S. Senate over ratification of the treaty. Unable to guarantee its passage, Carter never submitted it to the Senate, and after the Soviet invasion of Afghanistan in December 1979 managed to save some political face by shelving it in protest against the Soviet action.

The invasion of Afghanistan and the revolution in Iran were the major foreign policy crises of Carter's administration. The United States had become increasingly dependent on the shah of IRAN, MOHAMMED RIZA PAHLEVI, as its chief military ally in the increasingly important Persian Gulf. But the shah's relationship with the United States and the political repres-

sion enforced by his feared secret police, Savak, were opposed by his subjects. In January 1979, the shah was forced to flee Iran after massive demonstrations organized by the Islamic clergy. Shortly afterward, the exiled Islamic clerical leader Ayatollah Ruhollah Khomeini returned to Teheran and established an Islamic state. The United States tried to establish a relationship with the new regime but was denounced by Khomeini as the "Great Satan."

The depth of anti-American feeling in Iran was underscored when Iranian protesters seized control of the American Embassy on November 4, 1979, and took hostage the American diplomats there. The Khomeini regime tacitly supported the hostage-taking, and Carter eventually decided to attempt to rescue the hostages with American commandos. This rescue mission, in April 1980, ended in failure after three of the eight helicopters involved developed mechanical trouble and crashed at a rendezvous site in the Iranian desert. This humiliating failure further undermined public confidence in Carter, as Carter was further hurt by Iran's refusal to release the hostages until he had left office.

Throughout the first year of the Iranian revolution, there were repeated reports that the Iranian Tudeh (Communist Party) would take advantage of the political turmoil to seize control in Teheran. American policy planners worried that a communist foothold would give the Soviet Union access to a warm-water port and put it within a few miles of the Arab oilfields in Iraq, Kuwait, Bahrain, Saudi Arabia and elsewhere in the Persian Gulf.

The American fears appeared to be justified in December 1979 when an estimated 150,000 Soviet troops invaded Afghanistan. Carter responded by increasing the U.S. naval presence in the Indian Ocean and Persian Gulf, organizing a Western boycott of the 1980 Moscow Olympics, shelving the SALT II Treaty and suspending the U.S.-Soviet grain trade agreement.

A further note of instability was injected into the region in the autumn of 1980 when Iraq's president Saddam Hussein decided to take advantage of the political turmoil in Iran to invade the country and assert Iraq's long-standing claim to full control of the vital Shatt al-Arab waterway. The subsequent Iran-Iraq War became a dominant feature of international relations for most of the 1980s.

The conflict in the Persian Gulf could easily have spilled over into the explosive Arab–Israeli conflict if it had not been for Carter's greatest foreign policy achievement: the Camp David Accords between Israel and Egypt. Carter had initially abandoned Kissinger's step-by-step approach to MIDDLE EAST negotiations in favor of a comprehensive Middle East peace settlement to be hammered out at an international conference involving the Soviet Union. This was opposed by the Israelis, who feared that Soviet involvement would lead to participation by the Palestine Liberation Organization (PLO).

This stalemate posed a major political threat to Egyptian president Anwar Sadat, who had staked his political career on closer ties with the United States and Israel. In November

1977 Sadat broke the deadlock by flying to Israel and personally addressing the Israeli parliament, the Knesset. Carter took advantage of the momentum created by Sadat's initiative to return to the step-by-step approach favored by the Egyptian leader. Over the next year, the United States acted as mediator at numerous negotiating sessions. These finally culminated in face-to-face negotiations at the presidential retreat at Camp David, Maryland, among Carter, Sadat and Israeli prime minister Menahem Begin. The Camp David Accords resulted in the staged return to Egypt of the Sinai Desert, the establishment of Israeli–Egyptian diplomatic relations, clearance for Israel to use the Suez Canal and the start of negotiations on a separate Israeli–Egyptian peace treaty. The accords removed a major threat to Israel, and introduced an element of stability to the unstable eastern Mediterranean, but Egypt's participation split the Arab world.

In Africa, the Carter administration enjoyed a peripheral success in helping to resolve the long-running civil war in Rhodesia against the white supremacist regime of Prime Minister Ian Smith, who in November 1965 declared independence from Britain. The Carter administration, through Cyrus Vance, Andrew Young and Assistant Secretary of State Richard Moose, joined with Britain to increase the pressure on both South Africa and Rhodesia to attend a constitutional conference chaired by British foreign secretary LORD CARRINGTON. The London conference ended in December 1979 with an agreed constitution, which led to the end of the civil war, black majority rule under Robert Mugabe and independence. The resolution of the Rhodesia crisis also supported the Western assertion that it was better placed to secure basic human rights in the Third World than was the Soviet Union.

Carter's relations with America's European allies were mixed. In principle they supported his strong stand on human rights, but in practice they regarded his foreign policy as politically naive. Their concern appeared to be underscored by Carter's handling of the controversy over the NEUTRON BOMB soon after taking office. The neutron bomb, or enhanced radiation weapon, is a small hydrogen bomb with only one-tenth of the blast, heat and fallout produced by a normal hydrogen bomb. The bomb is designed to be detonated in the air. The radiation or neutrons emitted by the blast kill the occupants in a limited area but leave physical infrastructure such as roads and buildings intact.

When knowledge of the bomb became public, the Soviet Union and European antinuclear campaigners dubbed the enhanced radiation weapon the "capitalist's bomb" because it left property intact while killing people. Carter was unable to deliver an effective rebuttal and was forced to shelve deployment and development of the weapon.

The neutron bomb's primary purpose was to counter the Soviet Union's overwhelming superiority in conventional weapons, but by the end of the 1970s an additional Soviet threat appeared in the form of highly mobile intermediate-range nuclear missiles. Carter responded by agreeing to deploy American cruise and PERSHING II MISSILES as a counter to the Soviet INF forces. Despite objections from European antinuclear campaigns, Carter this time stuck by the NATO-wide decision to deploy. The policy was also supported by President RONALD REAGAN until the INF Treaty of December 1987 agreed on the mutual withdrawal of Soviet and American INF weapons.

America's Western allies also generally supported the SALT II Treaty on the grounds that the absence of an agreement was worse than a bad interim agreement. There was also support for Carter's tough stand on Afghanistan and the boycott of the 1980 Moscow Olympics. The Europeans welcomed the Camp David Accords but also pressed for greater consideration of the Palestinian cause.

The end of the Carter administration saw the initial rise of the SOLIDARITY movement in Poland. Carter praised the striking workers for setting "an example for all those who cherish freedom and human dignity." In November 1980 Carter issued a statement warning the Soviet Union that any military intervention in Poland "would be most serious and adverse for East-West relationships in general and particularly relations between the United States and the Soviet Union."

Following his failure to win reelection in the November 1980 election, Carter established an international affairs institute, the Carter Center, in Atlanta, Georgia, and through this remained active in foreign affairs. He spoke out on defense and East-West relations, acted as an observer at elections in Nicaragua in 1984 and Angola in 1992 and acted as an unofficial presidential emissary to the Middle East and China. He mediated negotiations between the Ethiopian government and rebel forces in 1989 and has won renewed public respect for his charitable activities.

For Further Information:

Brzezinski, Zbigniew. *In Quest of National Security*. Boulder, Colo., 1988.

Carter, Jimmy. *Keeping Faith*. New York, 1982.

Forsythe, D.P. *Human Rights and United States Foreign Policy*. Tampa, Fla., 1988.

Jordan, Hamilton. *Crisis: The Last Year of the Carter Presidency*. New York, 1982.

Spanier, J.W. *American Foreign Policy Since World War Two*. Washington, D.C., 1988.

Talbott, Strobe. *Endgame: The Inside Story of SALT Two*. New York, 1979.

Casey, William J. (March 13, 1913–May 6, 1987) William Casey was director of the CENTRAL INTELLIGENCE AGENCY during the REAGAN administration. He was credited with restoring morale in the service, but he came under heavy criticism for the extralegal aspects of his covert operations.

Casey attended Fordham University and St. John's Law School in New York, after which he went into private law practice. During World War II, Casey distinguished himself as the station chief in London for the Office of Strategic Services, the wartime forerunner of the Central Intelligence Agency.

Casey won the Bronze Star for his work in organizing French Resistance actions in support of the Normandy invasion.

Casey was appointed general counsel to the MARSHALL PLAN in 1947, and he was one of those consulted about the creation of the CIA. But the main thrust of his postwar activities was toward building up his private practice in the New York law firm of Hall, Casey, Dickler and Howler. Later he branched out into venture capital and became a millionaire several times over.

Casey, however, maintained close contact with his wartime comrades, many of whom went on to senior positions within the Republican Party. In 1969 he started to take more direct involvement in government affairs when President RICHARD NIXON appointed him a member of the General Advisory Committee on Arms Control and Disarmament and a member of the Presidential Task Force on International Development.

Casey was appointed chairman of the Securities Exchange Commission in 1971 and the following year was named undersecretary of state for economic affairs, a post he held for a year. In that position, Casey played an important role in developing the economic aspects of President Nixon's détente policies. In April 1972 he said, "We are seeking to build and expand East-West trade as a pivotal element in a structure of peace. We see economic interdependence as a great force for peace."

In 1973, Casey was named president of the Export-Import Bank, where he continued to have a major impact on the questions of East-West trade. He remained in that post until after the 1976 presidential election, when he briefly returned to private law practice, this time as a member of the law firm of Rogers and Wells.

Casey was a long-time friend of Ronald Reagan and was chosen by Reagan to manage his 1980 presidential campaign. Following Reagan's landslide victory, Casey was rewarded with the post of director of the CIA. He quickly established himself as one of Reagan's closest foreign policy advisers and was the first CIA director to hold Cabinet rank.

Casey's nomination, however, was not plain sailing. A number of members of the Senate Intelligence Committee preferred Admiral Bobby Inman, then director of the NATIONAL SECURITY AGENCY, as CIA director, but Reagan's strong support secured the post for Casey.

The previous decade had seen serious scandals at the CIA involving assassination attempts and illegal wiretapping. These had led to increasing skepticism in Congress and among the public about the CIA's role and had badly damaged the agency's morale. Casey was well aware of the problem and said during his nomination hearing that "the CIA suffers from institutional self-doubt . . . the morale of much of the agency is said to be low. Too often the agency has been publicly discussed as an institution which must be tightly restrained, stringently monitored or totally reorganized."

Casey made the restoration of morale and the CIA's covert operations his major priority. He launched a major recruit-ment drive and increased pay and benefits for agents. At the same time, he successfully lobbied for a reduction in the number of congressional oversight committees, a freer hand in the management of covert operations and official approval for conducting covert operations within the borders of the United States. He also succeeded in pushing through the Intelligence Identities Protection Act, which stopped journalists such as ex-CIA agent PHILIP AGEE from publicly identifying CIA agents or collaborators.

Casey, as it was later claimed by a congressional investigating committee, had a "passion for covert operations." According to *Washington Post* reporter Bob Woodward in his 1987 book *Veil*, these operations included a bungled Lebanese assassination plot, aid to Chad in its conflict with Libya and an effort to frustrate a campaign by the Italian Communist Party in the local Italian elections in May 1985.

But the focus of Casey's covert operations was Central America, in particular El Salvador and NICARAGUA. In Nicaragua the CIA organized and armed the CONTRA REBELS opposed to the Sandinista government of Daniel Ortega and also coordinated other activities aimed at destabilizing the Sandinista regime.

In March 1982, Casey secured President Reagan's approval for a $19 million covert program for the CIA to train a paramilitary force of Latin Americans to operate against Nicaragua. The figure was increased to $22 million the following year despite congressional opposition.

In April 1984, it was revealed that the CIA, under Casey's direction, had directed the mining of Nicaraguan ports. The operations had been directed from a U.S. ship outside the 12-mile territorial limits of Nicaragua. Speedboats had been launched from the ship to lay the mines in shipping lanes around the ports of Corinto and Puerto Sandino. The mines had been laid by commandos trained and directed by the CIA.

Exposure of the mine-laying operation resulted in an outcry, both abroad and within Congress. A sense-of-the-Congress resolution condemning the operation was quickly passed by both houses, and the CIA was forced to abandon the operation. The project was a clear breach of the law requiring the CIA to keep the Senate Intelligence Committee informed of major covert operations, and committee chairman Daniel Patrick Moynihan threatened to resign in protest against the lack of consultation. Casey had to appear before the committee on April 26 to apologize, and Moynihan withdrew his resignation threat.

The problems of obtaining congressional support for funding covert operations in Central America led the Reagan administration to seek funding for the Contra rebels from outside sources, arranged by the CIA and by the NATIONAL SECURITY COUNCIL. Casey, if not always directly involved, was usually apprised of the situation.

The most famous of these extralegal operations was the Iran-Contra affair, in which the National Security Council, with the knowledge of Casey, organized the sale of American weapons to Iran and then diverted the proceeds to the Nicaraguan Contra rebels. After his death, Casey was blamed by the Tower Commission investigating the scandal for allowing the CIA to lose control of the operation to the NSC and for failing to tell President Reagan or Congress about it. (It later proved, however, that both President Reagan and Vice President George Bush had been fully informed, and had approved the plan at the start.)

A subsequent report by the House and Senate committees investigating the arms scandal was more critical of Casey's activities. It said that Casey wanted to construct an "off-the-shelf, self-sustaining" nongovernmental organization for covert enterprises and charged that Casey had "subverted" the democratic process by manipulating intelligence data to influence decisions.

Casey died before either the Tower Commission report or the congressional investigation into the Iran-Contra arms scandal was published. He developed a cancerous tumor in his brain and suffered a cerebral seizure in December 1986, shortly before he was due to testify before the Senate Intelligence Committee on the Iran-Contra scandal. He resigned in January 1987 and died on May 6, 1987, without having left the hospital.

For Further Information:
Brzezinski, Zbigniew. *In Quest of National Security.* Boulder, Colo., 1988.
Burns, E.B. *At War in Nicaragua.* New York, 1987.
Woodward, Robert. *Veil: The Secret Wars of the CIA, 1981–87.* New York, 1987.

Castro, Fidel   (August 13, 1926–   )   Fidel Castro led the Cuban Revolution that established a pro-Soviet socialist government in Cuba, 90 miles off the coast of the United States. His agreement to allow Soviet missiles on Cuban soil led to the CUBAN MISSILE CRISIS and his strong anti-Americanism and support for revolutionaries in Africa and Latin America led the U.S. government to attempt to overthrow or kill him on several occasions. (For details, see CUBA.)

Catalytic War   A war in which a minor nuclear power launches a unilateral nuclear attack on one of the two major nuclear powers and the attacked country mistakenly believes that the attack is coming from the other major power and counterattacks that country.

Defense planners in the early years of the Cold War were seriously worried about such an eventuality, but the introduction of sophisticated fail-safe mechanisms, hotlines and radar systems made it possible to identify quickly the source of an attack.

Ceausescu, Nicolae   (January 26, 1918–December 25, 1989)   Nicolae Ceausescu became leader of Romania in 1965. He was one of Eastern Europe's most authoritarian rulers, but his determination to pursue a foreign policy independent of Moscow led to cordial relations with the West until this position was undermined by MIKHAIL GORBACHEV'S perestroika policies. Ceausescu was overthrown and executed in December 1989.

Ceausescu was born into a peasant family in the village of Scornicesti in southwestern Romania. He never completed his secondary education and by 1931 had joined the Romanian Communist Youth Movement. His political activities led to his arrest in 1933 and again in 1940. He escaped from prison shortly before King MICHAEL led the antifascist coup of August 1944.

The coup brought Romania from the German to the Allied side at the end of World War II and led to the country's occupation by the Red Army. The Soviets forced the monarch to give key posts to Communist Party leaders, and Ceausescu was named secretary of the Union of Communist Youth. He attached himself to the Stalinist GHEORGHE GHEORGHIU-DEJ, who assumed dictatorial powers in 1952.

Ceausescu's position as the protégé of Gheorghiu-Dej led to his rapid advancement through government and party ranks. From 1948 to 1950 he was minister of agriculture and from 1950 to 1954 he was deputy minister of the armed forces with the rank of major general. In 1955 he was made the Politburo member in charge of political and ideological activities in the army, a position that enabled him to build a decisive political base in the military.

Between 1947 and 1956 the Romanian Communist Party, which renamed itself the Romanian Workers' Party, carried out one of the most vicious purges in Eastern Europe as it sought to consolidate its power and impose Stalinist policies through the physical extermination of its opponents. Ceausescu, as minister of agriculture, was responsible for the campaigns against landowners and wealthy peasants. Under the government's reform program, land had at first been given to the small- and middle-size farmers, but when forced collectivization was started in 1949, it was taken away again. All peasants owning more than 37 acres were declared "class enemies," and an estimated 150,000 were sent to concentration camps along the Danube–Black Sea canal.

Gheorghiu-Dej, Ceausescu's mentor, was a committed Stalinist, and Romania was one of the few East European countries that did not fully de-Stalinize after 1956. This partly explains Ceausescu's commitment to the personality cult, largely out-of-date Stalinist economic policies, and authoritarian measures to enforce them. Gheorghiu-Dej died in 1965, and Ceausescu succeeded him after a brief power struggle. He remained dictator of Romania until his ouster and execution in the revolution of December 1989. (For further details, see ROMANIA.)

For Further Information:
Almond, Mark. *The Rise and Fall of Nicolae and Elena Ceausescu.* London, 1992.
Behr, Edward. *Kiss the Hand You Cannot Bite: The Rise and Fall of the Ceausescus.* New York, 1991.
Fischer, Mary Ellen. *Nicolae Ceausescu: A Study in Political Leadership.* Boulder, Colo., 1989.
Sweeney, John. *The Life and Evil Times of Nicolae Ceausescu.* London, 1991.

Central Command (CENTCOM)   The official name for the U.S. rapid deployment force (RDF) established by President JIMMY CARTER in 1979.

The establishment of a rapid deployment force was first proposed by Defense Secretary Harold Brown in 1978. The main purpose of the force was to protect Western interests in the Persian Gulf. It was decided that such a force would need to be highly mobile in order to overcome the military advantage the Soviet Union gained from its proximity to the region.

Throughout 1978 and 1979, allies and pro-Western countries were sounded out on the possibility of basing all or part of the RDF on their soil. The Arab and African countries responded coolly because they felt that playing host to such a force would damage their nonaligned status and make them a target for a Soviet attack. The Arab countries also had mixed feelings about improving American capability to intervene in their region while America remained wholly committed to the defense of Israel.

Therefore, when the details for the Central Command were announced in the December 1979 defense budget, they called for an RDF based in the United States at a cost of $9 billion. The 1979 plan called for the army to earmark 110,000 troops for the force and the Marines an estimated 45,000. These troops would be ferried to trouble spots by a long-range, wide-body transport plane whose cost would be $6 billion. Another $3 billion would be spent on specialized cargo vessels, which would be stocked with artillery, vehicles, ammunition, tanks and supplies and deployed at sea, over the horizon from potential trouble spots.

In the event of a crisis, U.S. Marines would be flow in and fitted out with the sea-based equipment. Their mission would be to fight a holding action until army reinforcements arrived.

Headquarters for the RDF was later established at McDill Air Force Base, Florida. The force was renamed Central Command and its intervention capabilities were expanded outside of the Middle East. The troops for CENTCOM are not based in Florida but attached to other bases elsewhere in the United States. Some of the cost of seaborne supplies has been reduced by agreements with Kenya, Egypt and Oman for refueling facilities and forward supply bases. These countries, however, have refused to have American combat troops based on their territory.

CENTCOM formed the U.S. command structure during the victorious war against Iraq in January and February 1991, as well as during the five-month U.S. military build-up in Saudi Arabia that preceded the conflict.

Central Front   The border between East and West Germany. This area was the only place where American and Soviet troops faced each other and contained the highest concentration of weapons and troops in the world. The Central Front had been regarded as the most likely place for World War III to begin.

Defense analysts believed that a Soviet attack on the Central Front would have been directed at one of two points: the north German plains, which were protected by British, German and Belgian forces, or the Fulda Gap, which was protected by American forces. Among the Western forces based on the Central Front were 300,000 American troops, 55,000 British troops and 450,000 West German troops, as well as Belgian, Canadian, Dutch and French forces.

Central Intelligence Agency   The Central Intelligence Agency is the United States' organization responsible for overseas intelligence and counterintelligence operations. It is the West's largest intelligence organization.

The CIA had its roots in the wartime Office of Strategic Services (OSS), which was established with British help to gather intelligence during World War II. In the immediate aftermath of the war, President Harry Truman disbanded the OSS because he feared that it could lead to government excesses. But as the Cold War intensified, he came to the conclusion that an intelligence agency was necessary to protect American interests.

In 1946, Truman signed a directive establishing the National Intelligence Authority (NIA) and its operative arm, the Central Intelligence Group (CIG), as well as the top post of director of Central Intelligence (DCI). The National Security Act of 1947 melded the NIA and CIG together, and on September 18, 1947, the Central Intelligence Agency formally came into existence.

Serving as DCI have been Rear Adm. Sidney Souers (1946), Lt. Gen. HOYT VANDENBERG (1946–47), Rear Adm. ROSCOE HILLENKOETTER (1947–50), Gen. WALTER BEDELL SMITH (1950–53), ALLEN DULLES (1953–61), JOHN A. MCCONE (1961–65), William F. Raborn Jr. (1965–66), RICHARD M. HELMS (1966–72), JAMES R. SCHLESINGER (1972–73), WILLIAM E. COLBY (1973–76), GEORGE BUSH (1976–77), Adm. Stansfield A. Turner (1977–81), WILLIAM J. CASEY (1981–87), William J. Webster (1987–91), Robert M. Gates (1991–1993) and R. James Woolsey, Jr. (1993–   ).

The CIA's main original function was to collect and analyze intelligence. Its collection methods grew increasingly sophisticated over the years, employing such high technology approaches as the U-2 and SR-71 spy planes and ever more advanced models of satellites. However, it was the agency's covert activities that garnered it the most publicity—some good, most bad—throughout the Cold War.

In addition to its regular intelligence duties, the CIA was also enjoined "to perform such other functions and duties related to intelligence affecting the national security as the National Security Council may from time to time direct." This directive became the mandate for the CIA's clandestine service to intervene actively around the world, usually at the direction of the president. The success of the CIA campaign that kept the Italian communists from winning Italy's general elections in 1948 led senior U.S. officials to become convinced that such covert operations were an invaluable tool of statecraft. That belief led to the CIA's paramilitary "rollback" campaigns of subversion against Eastern Europe and the

Soviet Union in the late 1940s and 1950s, which failed ignominiously, as well as the more successful operations that overthrew elected leftist governments in Iran in 1953 and Guatemala in 1954. The CIA met what was perhaps its worst covert action failure on the beaches of the Bay of Pigs in Cuba in 1961.

From the 1960s through the early 1970s the CIA became preoccupied with its vast paramilitary campaigns in Vietnam and Laos. Despite its charter prohibiting it from domestic operations, it also became involved—at the behest of President LYNDON JOHNSON—in spying on the American anti-war movement. Following the Watergate scandal in the mid-1970s, the CIA had its dirty linen aired in public by the investigations of the Senate's Church Committee and the House's Pike Committee, which disclosed bungled attempts to use the Mafia to murder Fidel Castro and a host of other misdeeds.

In reaction against those revelations, President JIMMY CARTER's DCI, Stansfield Turner, conducted a wholesale housecleaning of the clandestine service, forcibly retiring many of the CIA's most experienced covert operators. Agency morale sank under Turner but rose again with the increased funding and more swashbuckling attitude of William Casey during the Reagan administration. The 1980s again saw the CIA involved in major paramilitary campaigns around the globe, particularly in Afghanistan, Angola and Nicaragua. But the Iran-Contra scandal led to a new outcry, and with the death of Casey and his replacement by William Webster, the agency again receded for the most part from the public limelight. Webster's successor, Robert Gates, was confirmed by the Senate in November 1991 despite contentious Senate Intelligence Committee hearings at which Gates—a career CIA man who had most recently been serving as President Bush's deputy national security adviser—was accused by fellow CIA officers of having slanted intelligence reports to fit the foreign policy objectives of the Reagan administration in the 1980s. Gates denied the charges and was approved by the committee 11–4 and by the full Senate in a 64–31 vote. Gates was a Soviet specialist who had long expressed skepticism about the genuineness of President Mikhail Gorbachev's efforts to reform the Soviet Union.

For Further Information:

Agee, Philip. *On the Run.* New Jersey, 1987.
Ameringer, Charles D. *U.S. Foreign Intelligence: The Secret Side of American History.* Lexington, Mass., 1990.
Buncher, Judith F. *The CIA and the Security Debate, 1971–1975.* New York, 1976.
Dulles, Allen. *The Craft of Intelligence.* New York, 1963.
Hersh, Burton. *The Old Boys: The American Elite and the Origins of the CIA.* New York, 1992.
Jeffreys-Jones, Rhodri. *American Espionage: From Secret Service to CIA.* New York, 1977.
Mangold, Thomas. *Cold Warrior: James Jesus Angleton, The CIA's Master Spy Hunter.* New York, 1991.
Marchetti, Victor, and John D. Marks. *The CIA and the Cult of Intelligence.* New York, 1974.
O'Toole, G.J.A. *The Encyclopedia of American Intelligence and Espionage: From the Revolutionary War to the Present.* New York, 1988.
Ranelagh, John. *CIA, A History.* London, 1992.
U.S. Commission on CIA Activities within the United States. *Report to the President by the Commission on CIA Activities within the United States.* Washington, D.C., 1975.
U.S. Senate Select Committee on Intelligence Activities. *Alleged Assassination Plots Involving Foreign Leaders.* Washington, D.C., 1975.
U.S. Senate Select Committee on Intelligence Activities. *Intelligence Activities and the Rights of Americans.* Washington, D.C., 1976.
Wise, David, and Thomas B. Ross. *The Invisible Government.* New York, 1964.

Central Treaty Organization (CENTO) See BAGHDAD PACT.

Chambers, Whittaker **(April 1, 1901–July 9, 1961)** Whittaker Chambers was a key figure in the communist "witch hunt" in the United States in the late 1940s and early 1950s. A self-confessed communist agent, Chambers was the key witness in the perjury trial of former senior U.S. State Department official ALGER HISS.

Chambers joined the Communist Party in 1925, when he started writing for the *Daily Worker*. In 1932 he became a Soviet agent, passing documents obtained from U.S. government officials to the Soviet Union. But within five years he was disillusioned with communism and by 1938 he had renounced the party and converted to Quakerism. He became a fervent anti-communist and worked as an editor of the conservative *Time* magazine.

Between 1938 and 1948 Chambers briefed FBI agents on the activities of the Communist Party and his contacts with U.S. government officials. He implicated a number of senior liberal Democrats. The most prominent was Alger Hiss, who had attended the YALTA and POTSDAM conferences, had helped in the formation of the United Nations and by 1948 was president of the Carnegie Endowment for International Peace.

On August 3, 1948, Chambers appeared before the House Un-American Activities Committee to accuse Hiss of being a communist. Hiss denied the accusations. He also denied knowing Whittaker Chambers but did recognize Chambers as a journalist named George Crosley who had sublet his apartment and still owed him money. Chambers said that he had introduced himself to Hiss as Carl Crosley. Thus started a series of accusations and counteraccusations that eventually led to Hiss' imprisonment for perjury and a still unresolved debate as to the guilt of Hiss and the honesty of Chambers.

During the course of the investigations by the HOUSE UN-AMERICAN ACTIVITIES COMMITTEE, Chambers described Hiss as "a dedicated and rather romantic Communist" who had been introduced to him by the head of the communist underground in Washington, D.C. Hiss attacked Chambers as "a self-confessed liar, spy and traitor" and challenged Chambers to repeat his accusations outside the confines of the committee hearings, where Chambers was protected by congressional immunity. On August 27, 1948, Chambers appeared on the television show "Meet the Press" and declared, "Alger Hiss was a Communist and may be one now." In September Hiss sued Chambers for slander. Chambers repeated the accusations to the Associated Press, and Hiss filed a second suit.

In November 1948, at a pretrial discovery hearing, Chambers produced more than 60 documents as proof that he and Hiss had spied for the Soviet Union. The documents were part of the "Pumpkin Papers," which Chambers said he had kept in a hollowed-out pumpkin as protection against assassination by communist agents. In December these microfilmed papers were dramatically subpoenaed by the House Un-American Activities Committee. They included a number of classified State Department documents, which had been initialled by Hiss. Two weeks later, Hiss was indicted on perjury charges.

During the 1949 trial, Chambers was the key witness. He was attacked as "a thief, a liar, a blasphemer and a moral leper." Psychologists testified that Chambers had "a psychopathic personality." The defense lawyers also attacked various inconsistencies in Chambers' story, including his testimony before a New York grand jury in October 1948 that he had no direct knowledge of Soviet espionage activities in the U.S. But Chambers' basic accusations seemed to be corroborated by the fact that each of the Pumpkin Papers documents had either been initialled by Hiss, written in his handwriting or been typed on Hiss's typewriter.

The first trial ended in a hung jury. But a second trial found Hiss guilty of perjury on January 21, 1950, and he served 44 months in prison. Hiss maintained his innocence and made vain attempts to clear his name. Chambers was equally emphatic in his assertions that he had told the truth during the Hiss trial.

After the Hiss trial, Chambers left *Time* to work on his Maryland farm and become a general commentator on behalf of the American right wing. His main contribution to the conservative cause was his best-selling 1952 autobiography *Witness*, in which he warned that the greatest threat to the American system was secular liberalism.

Although Chambers supported the basic anti-communist thrust of Senator JOSEPH MCCARTHY's "witch hunt," he deplored the senator's style and tactics and refused to back him. In August 1957 Chambers joined the right-wing *National Review*, where he continued to attack liberals and advocate a return to religion-inspired political doctrine. Chambers left the *National Review* in December 1958. He died of a heart attack on July 9, 1961.

On March 26, 1984, President RONALD REAGAN posthumously awarded Chambers the Medal of Freedom and, in May 1988 Chambers' farm outside Westminster, Maryland, was granted national historic landmark status as the hiding place for the Pumpkin Papers.

For Further Information:
Buckley, William F., Jr. *Odyssey of a Friend: Whittaker Chambers. Letters to William F. Buckley, Jr., 1954–61.* New York, 1969.

Chambers, Whittaker. *Witness.* New York, 1952.
Smith, John Chabot. *Alger Hiss: The True Story.* New York, 1976.
Weinstein, Allen. *Perjury: The Hiss-Chambers Case.* New York, 1978.

Charles River Doctrine   The Charles River Doctrine was the first major theory of "stable nuclear deterrence." It is named after the Charles River in Massachusetts because it was developed primarily by academics based at universities and think tanks along the river.

The leading proponents of the Charles River Doctrine were HENRY KISSINGER, Jerome Wiesner and Thomas C. Schelling. During the 1950s and early 1960s they held a number of seminars and wrote papers that argued that the essence of arms control should be stable nuclear deterrence rather than complete disarmament. The Charles River Doctrine was first fully embraced by the Kennedy administration and later became the guiding principle of successive arms-limitation negotiations.

Charter 77   Throughout the latter part of the 1970s and most of the 1980s, Charter 77 was the main dissident organization in Czechoslovakia. It started on January 6, 1977, when a manifesto signed by 230 prominent Czech intellectuals was published in various Western newspapers. The manifesto announced the formation of Charter 77, an association of dissidents "bound together by the will to devote themselves, individually and collectively, to the respecting of civil and human rights in our country and the world." Among the signatories were the playwright Vaclav Havel; his wife Jelena; Jiri Hajek, who had been foreign minister under ALEXANDER DUBCEK; and playwright Pavel Kohout.

The day after the publication of the manifesto, several of the signatories were arrested. The dissidents responded by publishing a second manifesto on January 8, condemning the official reaction to the first. This was signed by 300 individuals.

The Czech authorities denounced the signatories as "piqued ineffectual wrecks and self-appointees" and launched a series of widespread arrests and crackdowns on dissident activities. The United States responded by charging Czechoslovakia with violating the 1975 HELSINKI ACCORDS on human rights, the first time that the United States publicly accused another country of violating the Helsinki Final Act.

Western pressure made it difficult for the Czech authorities either to expel or detain Charter 77 members for long periods of time, but regular harassment continued throughout the 1970s and 1980s. Charter 77 continued to attract followers, and in 1979 the Communist Party was forced to conduct a purge of its own membership.

Charter 77 was never meant to be a political party, and when the Czech Communist Party began to crumble at the end of 1989, its activities were largely taken over by the Civic Forum.

For Further Information:
Kusin, Vladimir. *From Dubcek to Charter 77: A Study of Normalization in Czechoslovakia, 1968–1978.* New York, 1978.
Skilling, H. Gordon. *Charter 77 and Human Rights in Czechoslovakia.* Winchester, Mass., 1981.
Volgyes, Ivan. *Politics in Eastern Europe.* Chicago, 1986.

Chemical and Biological Weapons Control Treaty (1972)
The Chemical and Biological Weapons Control Treaty of 1972 prohibited the stockpiling of biological weapons. The treaty was signed on April 10, 1972, at ceremonies in Washington, London and Moscow. Negotiations had been conducted in 1971 within the United Nations Conference of the Committee on Disarmament.

The 22 signatory countries (which included the United States, Britain and the Soviet Union) agreed "not to develop, produce, stockpile or otherwise acquire or retain" biological weapons and "to destroy or divert to peaceful purposes" such weapons "as soon as possible but not later than nine months [from the effective date of the treaty]."

The signing ceremony was used by President RICHARD NIXON as a platform for an implied condemnation of Soviet military aid to North Vietnam. But the treaty also helped to create the final climate of U.S.-Soviet goodwill prior to the signing of the more important STRATEGIC ARMS LIMITATION and ANTIBALLISTIC MISSILE treaties in Moscow the following month.

Chemical Weapons   Chemical weapons are those weapons designed to kill or incapacitate the enemy by the release of chemical agents.

Most chemical weapons are delivered in either artillery shells or bombs. There are two types: binary and unitary. Binary weapons consist of two chemicals housed in separate compartments. Individually, they are harmless, but upon impact they mix and become poisonous. Unitary chemical weapons contain a single poisonous chemical. Most current chemical weapons are binary.

Chemical weapons, such as nerve gas and chlorine gas, have existed since World War I, when they were responsible for thousands of deaths. Their inhumane nature led in 1925 to the GENEVA PROTOCOL ON GAS WARFARE, which banned the use of asphyxiating, poisonous or other gas or bacteriological weapons. The agreement prevented the use of chemical weapons by any of the great powers during World War II, but the Soviet Union and the United States have continued to stockpile such weapons and have issued protective clothing to troops in case of a breach of the agreement. The United States has claimed that the Soviet Union used chemical weapons in Laos and AFGHANISTAN, and it is known that chemical weapons were used by Iraq during its war with Iran (1980–1988).

For Further Information:
Adams, Valerie. *Chemical Warfare, Chemical Disarmament, Beyond Gethsamane.* New York, 1989.
Hersh, Seymour. *Chemical and Biological Warfare.* Garden City, N.Y., 1969.
Spiers, Edward. *Chemical Warfare.* New York, 1986.

Cheney, Richard Bruce (Dick)   (January 30, 1941–   )
Richard (Dick) Cheney served as President GEORGE BUSH's defense secretary beginning in 1989. He had to contend with a continuous stream of Soviet disarmament proposals, a rapidly shrinking U.S. military budget and an American armed forces establishment in search of new missions in the wake of the end of the Cold War. He was also one of the primary architects of the victorious Persian Gulf War against Iraq.

Cheney was born in Nebraska, received his bachelors and masters degrees from the University of Wyoming and did post-graduate work at the University of Wisconsin from 1966 to 1968. He avoided the draft during the VIETNAM WAR through deferments, first as a student, then as a married man with a child. He held various White House jobs from 1970 to 1975, culminating with his stint as President GERALD FORD's chief of staff. He was elected to the House of Representatives from Wyoming in 1979. He became House Republican whip in 1987, and was in his sixth term in Congress when he was tapped by Bush to be defense secretary in March 1989, after the Senate rejected the president's first choice, former Senator John Tower (R-Texas). Cheney, a popular Washington insider who was considered a conservative but not an ideologue, won swift Senate approval.

In May 1989, Cheney sparked a diplomatic flap and was forced to apologize after he voiced pessimism about the chances of Soviet president MIKHAIL GORBACHEV and his reform program. But he sounded several more warnings in 1990, arguing that the United States had to keep its military guard up because Gorbachev could be overthrown by hard-liners who would reverse his policies and restart the Cold War. Cheney went on to make his visit to the U.S.S.R. in October 1990, where he met Gorbachev and afterward said he was convinced that "we have entered a new era of U.S.-Soviet relations." But in August 1991, after the failure of the attempted coup against Gorbachev, Cheney was the first senior American official to suggest that he favored Russian president BORIS YELTSIN over Gorbachev.

A major preoccupation of Cheney's tenure was determining how and where to cut the defense budget in view of the declining threat from the Soviet bloc. In early 1990, he ordered freezes in civilian hiring and military construction by the Pentagon, and put forward a list of more than 80 U.S. bases and military facilities at home and overseas that could be closed or have their operations reduced. In June, he submitted to Congress a plan to reduce U.S. military forces by 25% over a five-year period.

However, Cheney's continued skepticism about Soviet reforms and his refusal to contemplate deep cuts in U.S. strategic weapons systems rankled liberals in Congress, who accused the administration of outdated Cold War thinking that would preclude a major "peace dividend" for the U.S.

civilian economy. Cheney, for his part, frequently sparred with members of Congress in 1990–91 over the fate of particular weapons systems that Cheney wanted cut back or eliminated (like the Seawolf attack submarine or Osprey tilt-rotor aircraft), but which certain lawmakers fought to save because the programs provided jobs in their districts. (This controversy did not end with the Bush administration.)

Chennault, Claire L.   (September 6, 1890–July 27, 1958)

General Claire Chennault was a U.S. Army aviation officer who created CHIANG KAI-SHEK'S wartime air force and in the postwar years was a leading spokesman for the conservative "China lobby."

After graduating from Louisiana State Normal College, Chennault became first a high school teacher and then, during World War I, a pilot with the U.S. Army. Chennault was a brilliant aviator and developed several innovative tactics such as formation flying and the use of paratroopers.

In July 1937 he left the U.S. Army and moved to China to help Chiang Kai-shek's government build an air force to fight the invading Japanese. Before American entry into World War II he created the Flying Tigers, a group of American volunteer pilots serving the Chinese government. During the war, in uniform again, he was chief of the United States Army Air Force in China as well as Chief of Staff of the Chinese Air Force. At all times Chennault worked closely with Chiang Kai-shek and the two men became close friends.

In 1945 Chennault retired from the army and returned to the United States. But within a year he had secured $2 million in American aid and formed a 12-plane airline to fly emergency relief to famine-stricken areas in China. As Chiang Kai-shek's military position vis-à-vis the Chinese communist forces worsened, Chennault became a key lobbyist in his efforts to win increased U.S. support. Before the House Foreign Affairs Committee in March 1948, Chennault urged Congress to send at least $1.5 billion in military aid to China over the following three years, as well as U.S. personnel down "to the company level." To justify this Chennault said that a communist victory in China would allow the Soviet Union to direct its full force against Europe. The next year he proposed a $700-million U.S. military airlift to Chiang's forces.

In 1949, as the communist forces took firm hold of mainland China, Chennault's airline, Civil Air Transport Company (CAT), helped to transport Chiang's forces to safety in Taiwan. In March 1954 CAT planes also helped to supply the trapped French forces at DIEN BIEN PHU in Vietnam. During the KOREAN WAR, Chennault favored General DOUGLAS MACARTHUR's plans to support a Nationalist Chinese invasion of mainland China. In articles published in *Reader's Digest*, he regularly warned that the Chinese communists were the "Asian arm" of the Soviet Union and unless stopped would spread their influence into Southeast Asia.

Chennault was a supporter of Senator JOSEPH MCCARTHY and in 1954 signed a pro-McCarthy petition just before the anti-

communist crusader's censure by the Senate. But Chennault was too involved with his Asian airline to become deeply involved in American politics. CAT became a financial success and just before Chennault's death on July 27, 1958, Congress passed a bill promoting him to lieutenant general.

For Further Information:
Chennault, Maj. Gen. Claire Lee. *Way of a Fighter*. New York, 1949.
Koen, R.Y. *China Lobby in American Politics*. New York, 1960.

Chernenko, Konstantin   (September 24, 1911–March 10, 1985)

Konstantin Chernenko was leader of the Soviet Union from February 1984 until his death in March 1985. During his short tenure in the post, Chernenko attempted to restore the policies of his mentor LEONID BREZHNEV.

Chernenko was born into a Siberian peasant family and spent most of his youth working as a farm laborer. In the 1920s he became active in the Communist Youth Movement, Komsomol, and gradually rose through the local Communist Party structure to become regional party secretary of Krasnoyarsk in 1941.

In 1948 Chernenko was transferred to the newly formed Moldavian Republic, where he was placed in charge of the regional propaganda department. The move to Moldavia was the major breakthrough in Chernenko's career, because two years later Leonid Brezhnev was appointed Moldavian party leader. The two men formed a close political and personal relationship, which continued until the death of Brezhnev and eventually brought Chernenko to the leadership of the Soviet Union.

In 1956 Brezhnev moved to Moscow to become a candidate (non-voting) member of the Politburo, and Chernenko moved with him to join the Central Committee staff as head of a mass propaganda section. In 1960, when Brezhnev became chairman of the Presidium of the Supreme Soviet (parliament), a post equivalent to president, he appointed Chernenko office manager and chief of staff. Chernenko retained this post until Brezhnev's death.

When Brezhnev was elected first secretary of the Central Committee in 1965, Chernenko became head of the Central Committee General Department, which had responsibility for overseeing the workings of the party. Chernenko headed the General Department until 1983.

In 1971 Chernenko was elected to the Communist Party's Central Committee, and in 1976 he became the Central Committee secretary in charge of administration and security. He was made a candidate member of the Politburo in 1977 and a full member in 1978.

Toward the end of Brezhnev's life, Chernenko emerged into second place in the party hierarchy, accompanying Brezhnev in his travels and serving as the Soviet leader's principal spokesman. In 1979 Chernenko was a member of the Soviet delegation at the Brezhnev–Carter summit meeting in Vienna, which culminated in the signing of the second Strategic Aims Limitation Treaty (SALT II). As Brezhnev became increasingly ill in the 1980s, Chernenko took responsibility for deciding who should see the Soviet leader and often took his place in meetings with foreign leaders.

Chernenko was clearly Brezhnev's choice to succeed him. But Chernenko never was able to establish his own political power base separate from that of Brezhnev, and in the last years of Brezhnev's life party reformers led by former KGB chief YURI ANDROPOV began a series of attacks on the Soviet leader and his ruling circle. This Kremlin power struggle culminated in Andropov's, rather than Chernenko's, succeeding Brezhnev following the latter's death in 1982.

In a show of party unity, Chernenko nominated Andropov at the Central Committee plenary session that approved Andropov's succession as general secretary of the Soviet Communist Party. Chernenko's nomination speech appears to have spared him the fate of many Brezhnev loyalists, who were purged in a widespread crackdown on corruption in the party and government. In 1983 Chernenko assumed the powerful posts of party ideology leader and propaganda leader formerly held by MIKHAIL SUSLOV.

In April and May 1983 there was speculation that Chernenko had also been purged when he dropped out of the public eye. But his disappearance was due to illness, and he reemerged in June and assumed a major party role, substituting for the ailing Andropov in the annual Red Square parade in November. Chernenko at this stage became the main hope of the party's old guard who faced the loss of their jobs and positions in Andropov's purges. When Andropov died on

February 9, 1984, this old guard attempted to turn the clock back by electing Chernenko to replace Andropov.

Chernenko moved quickly to silence dissidents who had shown signs of beginning to find a voice under Andropov. On February 16, dissident Yuri Orlov started a five-year term of internal exile and Crimean Tatar nationalist Mustafa Dzhemilev was sentenced to a sixth term of detention for anti-Soviet agitation. On April 20, Nenn Targo, a member of an Estonian human rights organization, was sentenced to 10 years of hard labor and five years of internal exile for "anti-Soviet agitation and propaganda."

The new Soviet leader also set out to strengthen ties between Moscow and Eastern Europe. In May 1984, Chernenko and Polish leader WOJCIECH JARUZELSKI signed a 15-year economic cooperation agreement designed to reduce Polish economic dependence on the West and restore Poland's position as one of the Soviet Union's leading trading partners. The agreement called for "new forms and methods" in planning long-term economic and technical cooperation between the two countries. Close coordination of five-year plans was specified, as was direct contact between Soviet and Polish factories.

Chernenko took a hard line in nuclear weapons negotiations with the United States and Western Europe, demanding the withdrawal of American cruise and Pershing II missiles from Western Europe before continuing talks on intermediate-range nuclear forces. He also tied a ban on the Reagan administration's proposed STRATEGIC DEFENSE INITIATIVE to arms-control negotiations. His defense budget of November 1984 increased military spending by 12%.

Chernenko never met with President RONALD REAGAN or Secretary of State GEORGE SHULTZ, although he did have a brief meeting with then Vice President GEORGE BUSH after Andropov's funeral. Chernenko did, however, meet with other world leaders, including Canadian prime minister Pierre Trudeau, Spain's King Juan Carlos, West German foreign minister HANS-DIETRICH GENSCHER and British foreign secretary Sir Geoffrey Howe. Howe reported that Chernenko was backtracking on the arms-control proposals made by Andropov.

Chernenko does not appear to have made any effort to come to terms with the Soviet Union's crumbling economic structure. This failure ensured that the reformers placed in positions of power by Andropov would have to wait for Chernenko either to fail or die. In April 1984 their position was strengthened when MIKHAIL GORBACHEV was named a full member of the Soviet Politburo and leapfrogged several more conservative party members to take the number-two position behind Chernenko.

Just before Christmas 1984, Chernenko was reported to be ill and missed the funeral of Soviet defense minister DIMITRI USTINOV. Chernenko was suffering from lung and liver infection brought on by pulmonary emphysema, hepatitis, cirrhosis of the liver and hypoxia. His illness forced the Warsaw Pact to postpone a regular summit meeting. As it dragged on, Chernenko offered to resign from the Politburo. His resigna-

Konstantin Chernenko, leader of the Soviet Union from February 1984 to March 1985, in Red Square on November 7, 1984. Photo courtesy of Novosti Press Agency.

tion was rejected and he died on March 10, 1985. Chernenko was succeeded by Gorbachev, who hailed his predecessor as "a true Leninist."

For Further Information:
Zemtsov, Ilya. *Chernenko: The Last Bolshevik. The Soviet Union on the Eve of Perestroika.* New Brunswick, N.J., 1989.

Chernobyl The 1986 Chernobyl nuclear disaster in the Soviet Union severely damaged the reputation of Soviet industry around the world. It resulted in one of MIKHAIL GORBACHEV's first efforts to loosen restrictions on the reporting of accidents in the Soviet Union, and it led to increased East-West cooperation on nuclear safety issues.

In the early hours of April 26 there was a surge of power during maintenance on Chernobyl's number four reactor. The surge produced steam and hydrogen that led to an explosion in the reactor building. The resultant fire nearly caused a meltdown of the reactor core, but that was averted. The explosion, however, did spew out radiation that spread as far as Scandinavia and Britain. A total of 50,000 people had to be immediately evacuated from the surrounding area. Two people died in the explosion or fighting the fire, and at least 50 others died from radiation burns. Hundreds were hospitalized.

The Soviet Union at first tried to impose a news blackout on the disaster. But evidence from radiation monitors in Scandinavia and elsewhere and from American spy satellites confirmed the explosion and fire and their location. Soviet authorities starting on April 28 issued a series of statements admitting that an accident had occurred but minimizing its effects, and criticizing the Western media for exaggeration and "anti-Soviet" lies.

Then on May 14, Gorbachev appeared on national Soviet television, speaking for 25 minutes to give details of the explosion and to reassure viewers that "the most serious consequences have been averted." During his broadcast, Gorbachev also proposed a "serious deepening of cooperation in the framework of the International Atomic Energy Agency," including the creation of an international regime on the safe development of nuclear power, which would include a system for the issue of prompt warnings at nuclear reactors; an IAEA conference on nuclear energy; steps to enhance the role of the agency and the active involvement of the World Health Organization and UN Environmental Program in agency activities.

The crippled number four reactor was entombed in concrete, but the numbers one, two and three reactors were allowed to stay on line and continue to generate electricity.

In April 1992, the Ukrainian official in charge of Chernobyl's clean-up claimed that the 1986 accident had ultimately caused between 6,000 and 8,000 deaths.

For Further Information:
Marples, David R. *Chernobyl and Nuclear Power in the USSR.* London, 1987.

Chiang Ching-kuo (March 18, 1910–January 13, 1988)
See CHINA REPUBLIC OF.

Chiang Kai-shek (October 31, 1887–April 5, 1975)
Chiang Kai-shek was the leader of Nationalist China. He ruled mainland China from 1927 to 1949, when the communist victory in the CHINESE CIVIL WAR forced him to flee to the island of Taiwan. There he established the Nationalist government, which, with American support, presented itself as the government of all China and the alternative to the communists in power in Peking (now Beijing).

Chiang was born in Chekiang Province, 100 miles south of Shanghai, the son of a salt merchant. His father died when he was nine years old, and Chiang spent the rest of his childhood in abject poverty. Somehow he managed to gain admission to the Paoting Military Academy in 1906 and did well enough there to be sent to Japan in 1907 for two years of advanced instruction. In Japan he met his mentor Sun Yat-sen, the founder of the Kuomintang and of modern China.

When revolts broke out in China in 1911, Chiang joined Sun as one of his military commanders. In 1921 Chiang became chief of staff of Sun's Canton-based Nationalist government. At this stage, the Kuomintang was allied with the Chinese communists and actively solicited help from the Bolsheviks in the newly created Soviet Union. In 1923 Chiang was sent to the Soviet Union to study Soviet institutions and military structure and on his return was made commandant of the Soviet-inspired Whampoa Military Academy.

Chiang later said that it was during his visit to Moscow that he became a convinced anti-communist. Others maintain that he did not turn against communism until it became obvious that the Chinese Communist Party threatened his own control of the Kuomintang after the death of Sun in 1925. In 1927 he moved against the Chinese communists in a bloody coup that left thousands dead. Chiang was left in control of the Kuomintang and the remnants of the Chinese Communist Party, under MAO ZEDONG, fled to southern Kiangsi.

The expulsion of the communists, however, did not leave Chiang in complete control of China. The Kuomintang was based almost entirely in the southern half of the country. The northern part was controlled by groups of competing feudal warlords, and many regarded Chiang as little more than another warload, although clearly the most powerful one. In 1927, however, he moved against the warloads in his Northern Expedition, and the following year entered Peking. Chiang at this stage laid titular claim to all of China, although the country still remained badly fragmented, with warloads continuing to operate in many areas and the Chinese communists expanding their base of operations in Kiangsi.

In 1931 Chiang's problems were compounded by the Japanese invasion of Manchuria and the creation of the puppet state of Manchukuo. But Chiang continued to regard the communists as the major threat to his government and decided to ignore the Japanese until Mao's forces were eliminated. He encircled their Kiangsi base and in 1934 appeared to be on the verge of victory, but in October the communists broke out of the siege and marched 6,000 miles to a more secure sanctuary in the northwestern province of Shenshi.

By this time, the threat of Japan to the whole of China had become clear. The communists, with the support of the Soviet Union, called for a Kuomintang–communist alliance against the Japanese, but Chiang rejected this and continued to direct his troops against the communist positions. Public opinion, however, was increasingly swinging toward war against Japan. In December 1936, in the Sian Incident, Chiang was kidnapped by warlords from the north who refused to release him until he agreed to a military alliance with the communists against the Japanese.

The uneasy alliance, known as the United Front, lasted until 1941. Shortly after its collapse the United States entered the war against Japan and threw its entire financial and military support behind Chiang's Nationalist government. Chiang and his wife, who came from the financially powerful Soong family, carefully cultivated influential American contacts such as HENRY LUCE, editor and publisher of *Time* and *Life* magazines. These were later to play a vital role in ensuring continued American recognition after Chiang's flight to Taiwan.

The U.S. government had long maintained that it had a special interest in fostering a strong and democratic China, and President FRANKLIN D. ROOSEVELT continued the policy during the war years. He insisted on treating Chiang as one of the Big Four Allied leaders, much to the annoyance of both JOSEF STALIN and WINSTON CHURCHILL. Roosevelt went so far as to plan a postwar world order in which China was to be responsible for maintaining stability in Asia. It was at Roosevelt and Chiang's insistence that China was included as a permanent member of the United Nations Security Council, a position that was held for many years by the Nationalist government on Taiwan.

There were, however, some voices of dissent within senior American circles, the most prominent of which was General Joseph Stilwell, the American-appointed chief of staff to the Chinese defense forces during most of the war. Stilwell had little time for internal Chinese politics and became increasingly annoyed at Chiang's diversion of his best troops and American supplies away from the fighting with Japan to the internal struggle with the communists. Stilwell was supported by American diplomats in China such as JOHN PATON DAVIES and JOHN STEWART SERVICE. They also became increasingly disillusioned with the corruption within Chiang's government. Chiang, through his powerful American contacts, managed to have Stilwell dismissed and replaced by the more malleable General PATRICK J. HURLEY.

Stilwell, however, had succeeded in raising some doubts about Chiang's government, and the Roosevelt administration shifted from unqualified support for Chiang to support for a Kuomintang–communist coalition to fight Japan and provide a stable postwar government for China. General Hurley and then General GEORGE C. MARSHALL were instructed to try to negotiate a rapprochement between the two Chinese factions, but both failed and postwar China collapsed into civil war. Chiang, who had based his government on a loose coalition with the military, the merchant classes and the landed classes, faced a guerrilla army with a solid popular base among China's large peasant class.

With three million troops to Mao's one million, Chiang, with some help from American military transport, managed to gain the upper hand in the first few months of the civil war. But by 1947 the initiative had clearly swung to the Chinese communists. Peking fell to the communist forces in October 1949, and almost simultaneously Chiang and the remnants of his army, along with the gold and silver bullion reserves of the Nationalist government, crossed the Taiwan Straits to the island of Taiwan.

Chiang remained in power until his death on April 5, 1975. He was ultimately succeeded by his son, Chiang Ching-Kuo. (For further developments, see CHINA, REPUBLIC OF.)

For Further Information:
Boorman, Howard L., and Richard Howard, eds. "Chiang Kai-shek." *Biographical Dictionary of Republican China.* New York, 1967.
Bueler, William M. *U.S. China Policy and the Problem of Taiwan.* Boulder, Colo., 1971.
Chiang Kai-shek. *Soviet Russia in China: A Summing Up at Seventy.* New York, 1965.
Crozier, Brian. *The Man Who Lost China: The First Full Biography of Chiang Kai-shek.* New York, 1976.
Furuya, Keiji. *Chiang Kai-shek, His Life and Times.* New York, 1981.
Lattimore, Owen. *China Memoirs: Chiang Kai-shek and the War Against Japan.* Tokyo, 1990.
Tuchman, Barbara. *Stilwell and the American Experience in China, 1911–1945.* New York, 1971.

Chile See **Allende, Salvador.**

China, People's Republic of The People's Republic of China (Communist China) was for many years considered to be as great a threat to Western interests as the Soviet Union. It fought against UN forces in Korea and supported the North Vietnamese and the Khmer Rouge, as well as communist guerrilla forces throughout Asia and elsewhere. America's relations with the People's Republic were further bedeviled by America's traditional and at times idealized involvement with China and its close relations with Nationalist Chinese leader CHIANG KAI-SHEK. However, the SINO–SOVIET SPLIT eventually led to closer relations between the United States and communist China.

The rise of communism in China was inextricably tied to the anticolonial and nationalist movement at the start of the 20th century. This movement at first crystallized around the Kuomintang, led by Dr. Sun Yat-sen, who became president of the Republic of China in 1911.

While Sun was consolidating his power base, MAO ZEDONG was developing the ideas that were to become the philosophical foundations of the Chinese Communist Party (CCP). By 1920 Mao was a convinced Marxist, and in 1922 he helped to found the CCP. The anti-imperialist policies of the communists led them into a coalition with the Kuomintang in 1923.

By 1925 Mao had formed the basis of his theory of the revolutionary potential of the peasantry (rather than the industrial workers of Marx and Lenin's "revolutionary vanguard"), and he gathered around him the figures who were to become the nucleus of the Chinese communist government. In April 1927, however Chiang Kai-shek, who succeeded Sun, carried out a bloody and extensive purge of the Chinese communists that left only a handful of leaders alive. Mao managed to escape the purge, and with a group of Hunan peasants he established a base in the southern province of Kiangsi. There he began to put into practice his theory of a peasant-based revolution, which Mao believed would "rise like a tornado or tempest—a force so extraordinarily swift and violent that no power, however great, [would] be able to suppress it."

Mao's closest associate in these early years in Kiangsi was CHU TEH, a military genius who worked with Mao to apply his basic political philosophies to military doctrine. The result was the successful development of guerrilla warfare operating from bases in the countryside. But Chiang gradually encircled the communist forces and was on the verge of defeating them when they broke out in October 1934 and started the historic 6,000-mile Long March to the more secure northwestern province of Shenshi.

In 1936 Mao, in association with a group of sympathetic northern warloads, kidnapped Chiang and forced him to form a Kuomintang–communist "United Front" against the invading Japanese. The war against Japan enabled Mao's communists to expand both their base of operations and their army. Using Chu Teh's guerrilla tactics and Mao's peasant politics, the Chinese communists grew to an army of about 700,000 men controlling a population of nearly 85 million by the end of World War II. The communists were also clearly popular. Mao instituted widespread agrarian reforms in the areas he controlled, and American observers who visited the communist areas during the war favorably contrasted his administration with the corrupt and inefficient government in the areas controlled by Chiang Kai-shek.

From their solid northern base, the communists were in a good strategic position when the CHINESE CIVIL WAR broke out at the end of WORLD WAR II. In the first year they suffered setbacks against Chiang's numerically stronger Nationalist forces, but they were able to regroup in the countryside while the Nationalist Army stayed in the cities. By 1947 the communists were on the offensive, and the northern cities were beginning to fall under their control. The People's Republic of China was proclaimed by Mao on October 1, 1949.

The "lose of China" to communism, as it was dubbed by American conservatives, was a major blow to U.S. foreign policy. The United States had long claimed a special interest in and felt a special responsibility toward China. A number of prominent Americans also had close relations with Chiang Kai-shek, who, along with Madame Chiang, had carefully cultivated American contacts. These prominent figures, such as former ambassador PATRICK JAY HURLEY, demanded American support for the overthrow of Mao and the reinstatement of Chiang. They also demanded the dismissal of State Department officials such as JOHN STEWART SERVICE and JOHN PATON DAVIES, who had been critical of Chiang's wartime government. The result was that the United States withheld diplomatic recognition of Communist China and continued to recognize Chiang's Nationalist government—which had fled to the island of Taiwan—as the legitimate government of all of China. Through American pressure, Chiang's government also continued to hold China's seat in the United Nations General Assembly and on the UN Security Council.

Mao's first priority thus became the adoption of tactics to protect his government from an American-supported counterattack by Chiang. The United States was regarded as the primary enemy of communist China until the Sino-Soviet Split. In December 1949 Mao had gone to Moscow and negotiated the SINO-SOVIET TREATY OF FRIENDSHIP, ALLIANCE AND MUTUAL ASSISTANCE, which only fueled American claims that the Chinese communists were puppets of Moscow and part of a grand strategy orchestrated from the Soviet Union.

Further confirmation of the Chinese communist role in the world was supplied by the KOREAN WAR. On November 25, 1950, the Chinese communists entered the war on the side of the North Koreans, and in the subsequent months they almost defeated the American-led UN forces. Reports of Chinese brutality and BRAINWASHING coupled with the difficult and interminable armistice negotiations did nothing to improve the American view of communist China.

It has been argued, however, that communist China's involvement in Korea was a logical extension of its concern about an American-supported attack by Chiang's forces. Shortly after the outbreak of the Korean War Chiang offered his forces to the UN, and General DOUGLAS MACARTHUR flew to Taiwan to discuss the possibility of a Nationalist Chinese attack on the southern mainland of China to relieve the pressure on UN forces in Korea. MacArthur also pressed Truman to let him cross the YALU RIVER, which divides China and Korea, to attack North Korean bases in Manchuria. All of these plans were thwarted by President HARRY TRUMAN, who stated, "We have never at any time entertained any intention to carry hostilities into China."

American support for Chiang's government threatened to bring the United States and China to war in 1954 and in 1958 over the Nationalist-held islands of QUEMOY AND MATSU just off the coast of mainland China. The heavily fortified islands provided a potential stepping stone for a Nationalist invasion of China and were already being used as a base for guerrilla attacks. In August 1954 the Chinese communists attacked in an attempt to force Chiang's troops off the islands. The Eisenhower administration responded by signing a mutual defense treaty with Taiwan. This treaty, however, also bound Chiang not to attack communist China without the permission of the U.S. government.

By the following April, tensions over Quemoy and Matsu had wound down. But they quickly surfaced again in 1958 after another buildup of Nationalist forces on the islands. In August 1958 the Chinese communists launched another major artillery bombardment of the islands, and the United States responded by ordering the Seventh Fleet into the Taiwan Straits to protect Nationalist China. But the following month, the Chinese communists and the United States began negotiations through their respective embassies in Warsaw. This was the established channel of communication between the two countries until HENRY KISSINGER's visit to Beijing in 1971.

Throughout the 1950s and 1960s, communist China was viewed by the West as the major destabilizing force throughout Asia. It invaded and annexed Tibet and forced the Dalai Lama into exile. It also supported communist guerrilla movements in Thailand, Malaysia, Indonesia, Laos, Vietnam, the Philippines and elsewhere. The only Western-supported Asian country with which it enjoyed close relations was Pakistan; China and Pakistan shared a dispute with India. But despite their attempts to destabilize pro-Western governments and American attempts to isolate communist China, the Beijing government quickly became a major force within the emerging Third World, which looked to the Chinese experience as a model of anticolonialism. The Chinese communists also established diplomatic relations with Western European governments who believed that the United States was wrong to attempt to isolate the world's most populous country.

The international position of communist China was further complicated by the Sino-Soviet Split, which started in the 1950s and erupted into a final break in the mid-1960s.

At the height of the Sino–Soviet Split, in 1964, communist China became the fifth country to explode a nuclear bomb. The weapon, which was developed largely by the Chinese themselves with some help from Soviet scientists in the early 1950s, was built mainly in response to American threats to use atomic weapons against communist China. But by the time the Chinese successfully tested their first device, the major threat to Peking had shifted to Moscow, and China's first missiles were intermediate-range weapons aimed at the Soviet Union.

Changes within China had by this time also had a major impact on Chinese communist policies. The biggest changes were wrought by the CULTURAL REVOLUTION, a major upheaval beginning in 1966 orchestrated by Mao and LIN BIAO to wrest power back from LIU SHAOQI and DENG XIAOPING. Mao and Lin succeeded in their aim, but at the price of near-civil war, which badly damaged the Chinese economy and for several years effectively removed communist China as a major player on the world stage.

By the time the first phase of the Cultural Revolution ended in 1969, Mao was chronically ill. The running of the country was left largely to CHOU EN-LAI and later to Mao's wife, Chiang Ch'ing (Jiang Qing), whose radical domestic policies ensured that the Cultural Revolution continued.

In the years before Mao's death, Deng reappeared on the Chinese political scene after having been denounced by the Cultural Revolution. It appears that Mao, at the urging of Chou, had rehabilitated Deng because the excesses of the Cultural Revolution had alienated many of the technocrats who looked toward Deng for leadership and who were needed to restore the Chinese economy. But within the Chinese leadership, Deng and his emphasis on economic pragmatism still had a number of enemies, most notably the "Gang of Four" led by Chiang Ch'ing. While Chou was alive, he was able to maintain Deng's faction over the Gang of Four. But after Chou's death in January 1976, the Gang of Four moved against Deng in a power struggle that preceded and followed the death of Mao on September 9, 1976.

Deng was removed from his government posts and vilified in the state press as "the foremost capitalist roader" who "had never been a Marxist." With Deng in disgrace and Mao and Chou dead, there was no obvious candidate to assume the leadership of the party and state. The compromise choice of the moderates and hard-liners was Hua Guo-feng, who removed the Gang of Four from power in October 1976 and restored Deng to the government in July 1977. Deng's powerful and long-standing political base within the party now made him the de facto leader of communist China, although Hua still retained the more significant titles.

Deng then began a major economic shift away from the traditional socialist structures to a more incentive-oriented system. The changes started at the party congress in August 1977 at which Deng and his supporters were officially rehabilitated. The more pragmatic economic line was further consolidated at a plenary meeting of the Central Committee in December 1978, when the party called for "readjustment, restructuring, consolidation and improvement." At the same meeting, the slogan "See truth from facts" was adopted as official party policy.

This new economic line was followed by increased criticism of the policies of MAO ZEDONG and improved relations with the West as Deng sought private foreign capital to fund ambitious industrialization schemes and markets for Chinese goods. In January 1979 Deng became the first Chinese communist leader to visit the United States, where he met President JIMMY CARTER. This was soon followed by the establishment of formal Sino-American diplomatic relations and the exchange of ambassadors. Deng said, "This is not the end but just a beginning."

From September 1980, the aging Deng started to distance himself from the day-to-day running of the country by resigning a number of his government and party posts. But it was clear that he continued to make the key administrative appointments and determine the basic principles that shaped Chinese policy. The country, which had been virtually closed to the West during Mao's rule, continued to open as American and European businesses invested in Chinese enterprises and China imported Western technology. The private Western investment was encouraged by Western governments because Deng continued his hard-line policy against the Soviet Union. This meant that the Soviet Union was forced to maintain an expensive army on both its Eastern and Western borders, while China became more economically integrated and thus more dependent on the West.

While Deng encouraged a more and more liberal economic structure, he refused to introduce a parallel political structure. He believed that the communist and capitalist structures could and should work side by side, with the capitalist economic system feeding and supporting the communist political system. The result was widespread corruption as Chinese entrepreneurs took advantage of the centralized political control and economic freedom to bribe party officials to approve their industrial schemes. At the same time, the economic liberalization raised the hopes of dissident groups that the reforms would be mirrored in the political sector. When these failed to materialize, student-led pro-democracy and anticorruption riots broke out in December 1986. They were suppressed but flared up again in May 1989, when it seemed as if the demonstrators were on the verge of overthrowing Deng and possibly the entire communist system. But, on Deng's orders, the demonstrators were brutally crushed by Chinese troops, who shot hundreds of demonstrators in Beijing's Tiananmen Square on June 3–4.

Deng did not reappear in public until June 9, when he praised the military and denounced the pro-democracy demonstrators. "A very small number of people started to cause chaos which later developed into a counterrevolutionary rebellion," he said. "Our basic direction, our basic strategy and policy will not change." Communist Party general secretary Zhao Ziyang, blamed for being too liberal in his approach to the civil unrest, was ousted two weeks later and replaced by Deng protégé Jiang Zemin. A major concern of Deng was how to relinquish power in such a way as to ensure the continuation of his policies. On November 9, 1989, he stepped down from his last official post—chairman of the Central Military Commission—and was replaced by party leader Jiang. But Deng remained the de factor paramount ruler of China, and Western analysts expected him to wield substantial political power for the foreseeable future.

The bloody massacre in Tianamen Square was denounced throughout the world. The U.S. and European nations imposed sanctions—mostly involving a temporary halt to high-level official contacts and military cooperation—that were allowed to lapse over the next year or so. The West essentially decided that China was too big and too important a country and market to isolate and antagonize permanently. Relations with China became a political issue in the United States, where the Democratic Congress tried to stiffen the mild sanctions imposed on China by President BUSH and to link China's "most favored nation" trading status with the United States to improvements in Beijing's human rights record. Bush managed to beat off such efforts, but he left himself open to Democratic charges of moral weakness and double standards in his foreign policy. Some noted that China, which had opened its economy to foreign investment but maintained a totalitarian communist political system, had won greater rewards from the United States than had the Soviet Union, whose economy was still mostly closed but whose political system was now much freer than China's.

Meanwhile, Beijing was reported to have viewed the collapse of communism in Eastern Europe in 1989–90 and in the U.S.S.R. in 1991 with great trepidation. Hard-line Chinese officials had no sympathy for MIKHAIL GORBACHEV. When the Soviet president resigned in December 1991, China's official news agency assailed his record, saying that he had left a legacy of "political chaos, ethnic strife and economic strife" in the U.S.S.R.

For Further Information:

Brandt, Conrad. *A Documentary History of Chinese Communism.* New York, 1966.

Ch'en Jerome. *Mao and the Chinese Revolution.* New York, 1965.

Eckstein, Alexander. *China's Economic Revolution.* Cambridge, England, 1977.

Fairbank, John King. *Chinabound: A Fifty Year Memoir.* New York, 1982.

———. *China: A New History.* Cambridge, Mass., 1992.

———. *China Watch.* Cambridge, Mass., 1987.

———. *The Great Chinese Revolution, 1800–1985.* New York, 1986.

———. *The United States and China.* Cambridge, Mass., 1983.

Fitzgerald, C.P. *Mao Tse-tung and China.* New York, 1977.

Hsu, C.Y. *The Rise of Modern China.* New York, 1983.

Kahn, E.J. *The China Hands: America's Foreign Service Officers and What Befell Them.* New York, 1975.

Kubek, Anthony. *Modernizing China: A Comparative Analysis of the Two Chinas.* New York, 1987.

Meisner, Maurice. *Mao's China and After: A History of the People's Republic.* New York, 1986.

Myers, Ramon H., ed. *Two Societies in Opposition: The Republic of China and the People's Republic of China After Forty Years.* Stanford, Calif. 1991.

Snow, Edgar. *Red Star Over China.* New York, 1937.

Spence, Jonathan D. *The Search for Modern China.* New York, 1990.

Tuchman, Barbara. *Stilwell and the American Experience in China, 1911–1945.* New York, 1971.

Wakeman, Frederic. *History and Will: Philosophical Perspectives of Mao Tse-tung's Thought.* New York, 1973.

Zagorian, Donald. *The Sino–Soviet Conflict, 1956–61.* Princeton, 1962.

China, Republic of   Since October 1949, the government of the Republic of China (Nationalist China), on the island of Taiwan, has claimed to be the legitimate government of all China. American support for the government on Taiwan throughout the 1950s and 1960s posed a major threat to the communist government of the People's Republic of China (mainland China) and soured relations between Beijing and Washington. The Nixon administration's reestablishment of relations with Beijing eliminated the threat to Beijing of Nationalist China, which quickly became a Cold War anachronism.

Nationalist China claimed to be the political heir of the Nationalist government established by Dr. Sun Yat-sen in 1911. It was dominated by Sun's successor, CHIANG KAI-SHEK, who remained on the mainland of China fighting both the Japanese and the Chinese communists until the communist victory in the CHINESE CIVIL WAR forced him to flee to Taiwan in October 1949. There he established a Nationalist government that, with American support, presented itself as the government of all China and the alternative to the communists in power in Beijing.

America's perceived special interest in China led first the Roosevelt administration and then the TRUMAN administration to try to negotiate a settlement to the conflict between Chiang's Kuomintang and the Chinese Communist Party led by MAO ZEDONG. But the United States could never claim strict neutrality because while attempting to mediate it also made it clear that it recognized Chiang's Nationalist state as the legitimate government of China. The Truman administration, although discouraged by reports of corruption within the Kuomintang, maintained this position throughout the subsequent Chinese Civil War. By the time Chiang was forced to Taiwan, the anti-communist hysteria in the United States had reached such heights that it was politically unthinkable to recognize a communist government. Therefore the United States continued to support Chiang's government-in-exile as the legitimate Chinese government. Chiang's powerful American contacts helped to continue this policy for nearly a quarter of a century through a pressure group called COMMITTEE FOR ONE MILLION.

On Taiwan, Chiang helped to perpetuate the political myth that he headed the true Chinese government by maintaining in office all the members of the Chinese legislature (the Yuan) who had been elected in the last Kuomintang-organized general election on mainland China, in 1947–48. These officials were instructed to continue to represent the mainland constituencies over which they no longer had any control or right to visit. They were to remain in office until they died or until the Nationalist government could reestablish itself on mainland China and organize fresh elections. By 1989, approximately one-third of these aging officials remained in office.

Chiang also immediately declared a state of emergency and martial law, which was maintained after his death by his son, Chiang Ching-kuo, until the late 1980s. This state of emergency was ostensibly for the dual purpose of protecting the island from attack by the Chinese communists and preparing for the imminent reconquest of the mainland. But martial law also served to impose the will of the two million exiled Chinese on the 15 million native citizens of Taiwan.

Chiang probably would have faded into obscurity if it had not been for the KOREAN WAR, which started in June 1950. Reinforcing American fears of Chinese communism, the war enabled Chiang to project himself as a loyal regional ally. Chiang also tried to use the war as a means to win American support for his projected reconquest of the mainland. He argued that a Kuomintang attack from the south would divert Chinese communist troops massing on the border with Korea and eventually lead to the collapse of Mao's government. General DOUGLAS MACARTHUR, commander of the American and UN forces in Korea, flew to Taiwan to discuss the plan with Chiang, and these discussions are believed to have played a major part in the Chinese decision to intervene in the war.

Truman, however, ruled out American support for Chiang's plan. He believed that this would only cause the Soviet Union to come to China's aid and lead to a clash between Soviet and American troops. But at the same time, the Truman administration was not prepared to see the Chinese communists invade Taiwan. He stationed America's Seventh Fleet in the Taiwan straits and gave it the dual task of preventing a communist attack on Chiang and preventing Chiang from attacking mainland China.

In 1954 Chiang enjoyed another resurgence when the Chinese communists appeared to be on the verge of capturing QUEMOY AND MATSU, two small islands a few miles off the coast of the mainland that had been occupied by more than 100,000 Nationalist troops. The islands were clearly being used by Chiang as a potential springboard for an attack on the mainland. As if to reinforce this view, Chiang sent commandos from the islands to attack communist positions on the mainland. In September 1954 the communists started shelling the two islands. This led to the signing in December 1954 of the U.S.–Taiwan Mutual Defense Treaty, which committed the two countries to come to the other's aid if either was attacked. But at the same time, Chiang was forced to sign a secret agreement in which he pledged not to invade the mainland without the permission of the U.S. government.

The Quemoy and Matsu crisis quieted down in 1955 but flared up again in 1958 after Chiang again built up his forces on the islands. The result was another communist attack on the islands. American forces were put on a war alert and President DWIGHT EISENHOWER warned that he would use nuclear weapons. This led to a communist ceasefire, and during the lull U.S. secretary of state JOHN FOSTER DULLES flew to Taiwan to tell Chiang Kai-shek that he must renounce the use of force to achieve his return to the mainland. Dulles made it clear that the United States would not provide military or logistic support for a Nationalist invasion but would continued to defend Taiwan. Faced with the implied threat of a withdrawal of American support, Chiang had no choice but to renounce the use of force and reduce the Nationalist presence on Quemoy and Matsu.

From 1960, Chiang continued to pay lip service to the policy of a return to the mainland, as it remained the binding element in the Kuomintang. But in reality, he was tightening his political hold on Taiwan and building up the Taiwanese economy. The former policy involved the establishment of a repressive political structure supported by a pervasive secret police force under the command of Chiang's son, Chiang Ching-kuo. His father left the running of the country more and more to his son, who gained a reputation for ruthlessness and authoritarianism. Chiang Ching-kuo himself boasted of breaking up more than 500 separate communist conspiracies over a four-year period. As a result of this action an estimated 2,500 suspected communists were executed.

The death knell for Chiang's dreams of a glorious reconquest of China was sounded by President RICHARD NIXON on his historic visit to communist China in 1972. This was quickly followed by Nationalist China's replacement at the United Nations by the People's Republic of China. Chiang, however, continued to lay claim to the title of president of China until his death on April 5, 1975, when he was succeeded by C.K. Jen. It was recognized that Jen was an interim president and that the younger Chiang would take control. He did so in 1978 when he was elected to a six-year term as head of the party and president.

Despite his desire to engineer the end of communist rule on the mainland, Chiang Ching-kuo made some attempts to ease tensions with Beijing, moving Taiwan's ruling Kuomintang Party away from the idea—advocated by his father—of retaking the mainland by force. Chiang Ching-kuo also worked to expand the base of the Nationalist Party to include more native Taiwanese, who made up 84% of the island nation's total population. He also engineered the economic miracle of Taiwan with its sustained average growth of almost nine percent each year in the 1970s and 1980s.

In the year before his death, Chiang introduced a number of domestic political reforms, including an end to martial law and an easing of limitations on the press and restrictions on travel to the mainland. But Chiang Chin-kuo, like his father, remained a firm symbol of intractable anti-communism, and it was not until after his death on January 13, 1988, that serious political reforms were introduced and the first tentative moves toward a rapprochement with Beijing were made.

Lee Teng-hui, a native Taiwanese, was sworn in as president immediately after the death of Chiang Ching-kuo. In February 1988 Lee pushed through a plan to reform the Yuan (national assembly) by increasing the number of seats filled by native Taiwanese, and soon afterward he allowed citizens of Nationalist China to visit family on the mainland and to invest and trade with communist China.

National elections were held in December 1989, and while the ruling KMT won the majority of the contests, the opposition Democratic Progressive Party (DPP) won more than 30% of the vote. Lee was reelected to a six-year term in 1990, and in April 1991 he formally lifted the country's 43-year-old state of emergency. In December 1991 elections, the KMT won 254 seats to the DPP's 66.

For Further Information:

Bachipack, Stanley D. *The Committee of One Million: "China Lobby" Politics, 1953–1971.* New York, 1976.

Chi, Hsi-sheng. *Nationalist China at War: Military Defeats and Political Collapse, 1937–45.* Ann Arbor, Mich., 1982.

Clubb, Oliver E. "Formosa and the Offshore Islands in American Policy, 1950–55," *Political Science Quarterly* (December 1959).

Fairbank, John King. *Chinabound: A Fifty Year Memoir.* New York, 1982.

———. *China: A New History.* Cambridge, Mass., 1992.

———. *The Great Chinese Revolution, 1800–1985.* New York, 1986.

———. *The United States and China.* Cambridge, Mass., 1983.

Gold, Thomas B. *State and Society in the Taiwan Miracle.* Armonk, N.Y., 1986.

Hinton, Harold C. *An Introduction to Chinese Politics.* New York, 1978.

Kahn, E.J. *The China Hands: America's Foreign Service Officers and What Befell Them.* New York, 1975.

Kubek, Anthony. *Modernizing China: A Comparative Analysis of the Two Chinas.* New York, 1987.

Lasater, Martin L. *The Taiwan Issue in Sino-American Relations.* Boulder, Colo., 1984.

Long, Simon. *Taiwan: China's Last Frontier.* New York, 1991.

Myers, Ramon H., ed. *Two Societies in Opposition: The Republic of China and the People's Republic of China After Forty Years.* Stanford, Calif., 1991.

Spence, Jonathan D. *To Change China: Western Advisers in China, 1620–1960.* New York, 1980.

China, White Paper on　The White Paper on China issued by the U.S. State Department in August 1949 blamed the communist takeover of China on corruption and inefficiency in the Nationalist Chinese government. The paper was roundly condemned by American anti-communists and played a major part in subsequent attacks on President HARRY S. TRUMAN, Secretary of State DEAN ACHESON and State Department officers who helped develop America's policy toward China.

Throughout 1949 the Truman administration came under strong pressure from American conservatives to intervene in the CHINESE CIVIL WAR on the side of the Nationalist Chinese under CHIANG KAI-SHEK. Truman, however, was reluctant to do this because American foreign service officers were virtually unanimous in the opinion that Chiang's corrupt and inefficient government was incapable of holding onto power in the face of the genuinely popular rebellion led by the communists under MAO ZEDONG.

To justify his hands-off policy, Truman authorized the release of the State Department White Paper on China, which was published on August 5, 1949, two months before the final communist victory. The 1,054-page White Paper charted the decay of the Kuomintang from before WORLD WAR II to 1949 and chronicled American efforts to mediate in the war between the Kuomintang and the Chinese Communist Party.

In the paper's conclusion, Secretary of State Acheson wrote that it would be futile for the United States to resort to "full-scale intervention on behalf of a Government which had lost the confidence of its own troops and its own people." Such intervention, probably requiring "participation of American armed forces," would have "been resented by the mass of Chinese people . . . diametrically reversed our historic policy" and been "condemned by the American people."

He predicted that the Chinese would wake up to the fact that the communists served only the Soviet Union's interests and would "throw off the foreign yoke."

The Chinese Nationalists tried to stop publication of the White Paper, which they said would destroy their last chance of resisting the communist drive into southern China. Many members of the U.S. Congress called it a "whitewash" intended to cover up blunders in U.S. policy toward China. President Truman, in announcing publication of the White Paper, said it would dispel the "misapprehension, distortion and misunderstanding" that had surrounded U.S.–Chinese relations in the preceding years.

For Further Information:

Fairbank, John K. *The United States and China*. Cambridge, Mass., 1971.

Feis, Herbert. *The China Tangle*. Princeton, 1953.

Purifoy, Lewis McCarroll. *Harry Truman's China Policy: McCarthyism and the Diplomacy of Hysteria, 1947–1951*. New York, 1976.

U.S. State Department. *U.S. Relations With China*. Washington, D.C., 1949.

Valeo, Frances, ed. *The China White Paper*. Washington, D.C., 1949.

Chinese Civil War   The Chinese Civil War between the Nationalist government of Chiang Kai-shek and the communist forces of Mao Zedong led to the establishment of a communist government in China. The civil war had its roots in the confusion that surrounded the collapse of Imperial authority and the rise of Republican China. Russia had always had an interest in neighboring China, and this interest was carried over to the new Soviet government, which formed close links with the Nationalist government of Dr. Sun Yat-sen in China. This encouraged the growth of the Chinese Communist Party, which was incorporated into Sun's ruling Kuomintang.

By the time Sun died in 1925, the Chinese communists were in a powerful position within the Kuomintang. Sun was succeeded by Chiang Kai-shek, who distrusted both the communists and the Soviet Union. In 1927 Chiang expelled the Chinese communists from the Kuomintang. The communists, under Mao Zedong, established their own army and administration based in the southern province of Kiangsi and soon found themselves fighting the government troops of Chiang Kai-shek.

Throughout the 1930s, Chiang concentrated on establishing a blockade around the communist-held region. By October 1934 the blockade had the communists on the verge of defeat, but they were able to break through and began their historic Long March to a new base in northwest China. At the same time as he was fighting the communists, Chiang was also in conflict with northern warlords and the Japanese, who invaded Manchuria in 1931 and established the puppet state of Manchukuo. After being kidnapped by the communists and

pressured by warlord allies, Chiang reluctantly agreed in 1936 to an anti-Japanese alliance with the communists. But by 1941 the alliance was crumbling and Chiang again moved to surround the communist forces.

By the time the United States entered the war against Japan, the Chinese communists and Nationalist government were spending as much time fighting each other as they were the Japanese. One of the major elements of President FRANKLIN ROOSEVELT's wartime China policy was to stop this civil war so that all of China's forces could be used against Japan to open a second front in the Asian war and relieve the American forces island-hopping across the Pacific. General Joseph Stilwell became Roosevelt's chief envoy in his efforts to effect a communist–Kuomintang reconciliation. But Stilwell's dislike of Chiang and respect for the communists' military prowess led to a clash with the Nationalist leader, and Roosevelt was forced to recall him. He later sent General PATRICK J. HURLEY to try to negotiate a settlement of the communist–Kuomintang conflict.

As World War II drew to a close, Roosevelt had another reason for wanting an end to the Chinese Civil War. He had envisaged a postwar world structure based on four major regional powers: Britain, the United States, China and the Soviet Union. Each country would have a veto in the Security Council of the United Nations and would hold effective responsibility for maintaining peace and stability in its region of the world. A China wracked by civil war was obviously incapable of serving as the regional overseer, and its absence would create a dangerous political vacuum.

Hurley succeeded in establishing negotiations between Chiang and Mao, but the two men maneuvered their military forces to be in the best position to occupy the areas that had been held by the Japanese. At the same time, Roosevelt and Soviet leader JOSEF STALIN agreed at the YALTA CONFERENCE that the Soviet Union would enter the war against Japan and occupy Manchuria. The Red Army moved on August 8, 1945. At the end of the war, therefore, the Soviet Union controlled Manchuria; the Chinese communists controlled northwest China and were rapidly moving eastward; the Japanese still occupied south and east China, and Chiang Kai-shek's government controlled the southwestern corner.

Chiang was in a poor military position, but in a much better political position than Mao's forces. His Kuomintang Party was recognized as the government of China by the United States, Britain and the Soviet Union. The United States was committed in establishing political unity in China, but this commitment was somewhat negated by its policy of recognizing and supporting the Kuomintang as the legitimate government of all China.

To this end, the United States moved quickly to help Chiang establish his authority in the areas being vacated by the Japanese. The surrendering Japanese force—some three million troops—was ordered by Supreme Allied Commander DOUGLAS MACARTHUR to remain in south and east China for an additional three months to maintain order while the United

States organized a sea lift of Nationalist troops to those areas so that Chiang could accept the Japanese surrender and establish his authority.

The Soviet position at this stage in the conflict was unclear. Stalin had told a procession of American envoys that the Soviet Union was not interested in China; it was too heavily committed to Eastern Europe and too busy rebuilding European Russia to become involved with supporting the Chinese communists. Furthermore, Stalin repeatedly stated that Chiang was the only man strong enough to unite China. Nevertheless, when the Red Army invaded Manchuria in August 1945, only 10,000 Chinese communist guerrillas were operating there; by November 1945 there were an estimated 215,000. By the time the Red Army evacuated Manchuria in May 1946, the Chinese communists had a well-equipped force in northeast China under the command of LIN BIAO, whose army played a key role in the remainder of the conflict. Mao candidly admitted that this could not have been achieved without the help of "big brother" in the Soviet Union. But Stalin appears to have turned a deaf ear to other urgent requests for aid from Mao, arguing that he could not at that stage risk a direct conflict with the United States.

By the start of 1946, therefore, the country was effectively divided in half. The northern half was controlled by the Chinese communists and the southern half by the Kuomintang. While this division was taking place, the United States was continuing its efforts to negotiate a settlement between the two protagonists. General Hurley had resigned in November 1945 after a disagreement with President HARRY TRUMAN, and the president had sent General GEORGE C. MARSHALL in his place.

Throughout 1946 Marshall worked to assemble a coalition government for China. Chiang Kai-shek refused to accept the communists into government until Mao's forces laid down their arms and accepted his authority. Mao in return refused to disarm without guarantees about the communists' status in the government. Despite these apparently intractable positions, Marshall negotiated a truce and established the ground rules for an integrated army and a national assembly to draft a new constitution. Marshall felt confident enough to return to Washington in March 1946 to organize a comprehensive aid program for China. While he was away, however, Kuomintang and Chinese communist forces clashed when Chiang attempted to move into Manchuria, and the truce evaporated.

CHOU EN-LAI, the chief communist negotiator, walked out of the negotiations in November 1946 and the fighting resumed in earnest. On January 3, 1947, Truman recalled Marshall to Washington to become secretary of state. The United States then threw all of its political support and some military support behind Chiang Kai-shek. Truman was reluctant to make a full commitment to Chiang for two main reasons: He felt that American public opinion would not support the massive manpower commitment that would be required to defeat the Chinese communists; and persistent reports of human rights abuses by Chiang's government and Chiang's own obstinacy in dealing with American officials undermined Truman's confidence in the Nationalist Chinese leader.

Chiang's first and perhaps most important military blunder, after the breakdown of negotiations, was to attempt to move into Manchuria. The Soviet Union, in accordance with its policy of recognition for Chiang, had agreed to hand over formal authority to Chiang's forces as they withdrew. Lin Biao's army, however, was already in place. Marshall had advised Chiang against the move on the grounds that the Nationalist government would be overextending its supply lines. But the advice was rejected, and the Nationalist and Communist Party forces clashed as soon as Chiang's troops landed. The result was a major defeat for Chiang, who lost almost his entire Manchurian force and a large supply of American weapons.

The Nationalist forces never recovered from this setback. For a time Chiang's fortunes appeared to improve when in 1947 he launched another northern attack and captured the communist capital at Yenan on March 19. But Mao's forces recaptured Yenan the following year. Part of Chiang's problem was that his generals suffered from what historians have since termed a "walled-city" mentality. That is, they based their forces in cities. The communists responded by occupying the countryside and enacting a new Land Law at the end of 1947. The new law confiscated and redistributed the land among the peasants and had the effect of securing peasant support for the communists and cutting the Kuomintang forces off from their food supplies. With the success of this tactic, the Kuomintang forces rapidly disintegrated.

The final, decisive battle came at the strategic rail junction at Suchow in October and November 1948. The Chinese communists successfully encircled the 250,000-man Nationalist garrison, and nearly all of the troops and American equipment again fell into the hands of Mao's forces. Mao took the next few months to consolidate his position in North China, eliminating the Nationalist garrisons at Peking and Nanking.

Then on February 5, 1949, the Chinese communist forces crossed the Yangtze River and started their drive south. Nanking, Chiang's own capital, fell in April. Shanghai and Hankow were occupied in May. On October 1, 1949, Mao proclaimed the new government in Peking, and on December 8 Chiang quit the mainland for the island of Taiwan.

The success of the Chinese communists established a communist government as a regional superpower in Asia. This was to have a major impact on the Far East and other parts of the world. In the Far East, it meant that left-wing anticolonialist forces fighting in Indochina, Burma, Indonesia, Korea and elsewhere could count on political and military support from the government in China. In the wider, international communist movement, Mao's successful revolution established a second inspirational focal point for the world's communists. China's long and proudly ethnocentric history ruled out the possibility of its becoming another Soviet satellite. Its refusal to do so later created the first major split in the international communist movement.

In the early Cold War years, however, most American politicians viewed Mao as a key pawn in an international chess game carefully planned and played in Moscow. Conservative Republicans went a step further and accused President Truman, Secretary of State Marshall and Undersecretary of State DEAN ACHESON, as well as various key diplomats, of being responsible for the "loss of China," because of their refusal to extend unlimited financial, political and military aid to Chiang Kai-shek. The conservatives' position was improved by the enormous affection the American public held for Chiang and his wife, both of whom had forged strong links with the American political and business communities.

Chiang was able to build on these connections to secure continued American military support and diplomatic recognition of his Kuomintang as the legitimate government of China even though his forces were confined to Taiwan. During the Hurley and Marshall missions the Chinese communists regularly accused the United States of being prejudiced in favor of Chiang Kai-shek. U.S. support for Chiang's forces during the fighting and diplomatic recognition after he fled to Taiwan appeared to confirm this belief and increase their suspicion of American motives. This distrust is believed to have played a major role in the Chinese communists' decision to intervene in the KOREAN WAR and later to aid the North Vietnamese in the VIETNAM WAR.

For Further Information:
Beal, John Robinson. *Marshall in China.* Garden City, N.Y., 1970.

Curtis, Richard. *Chiang Kai-shek.* New York, 1969.

Dulles, Foster Rhea. *American Policy Toward China 1949–1969.* New York, 1972.

Fairbank, John King. *The United States and China.* Cambridge, Mass., 1971.

Kahn, E. J. *The China Hands: America's Foreign Service Officers and What Befell Them.* New York, 1975.

Morwood, William. *Duel for the Middle Kingdom: The Struggle Between Chiang Kai-shek and Mao Tse-tung for Control of China.* New York, 1980.

Rose, Lisle A. *Roots of Tragedy: The United States and the Struggle for Asia 1945–1953.* Westport, Conn., 1976.

Spence, Jonathan D. *The Search for Modern China.* New York, 1990.

———. *To Change China: Western Advisers in China, 1620–1960.* New York, 1980.

Tuchman, Barbara. *Stilwell and the American Experience in China.* New York, 1970.

Chinese Cultural Revolution   See CULTURAL REVOLUTION, CHINESE.

Chou En-lai   (1898–January 8, 1976)   Chou En-lai (Jou Enlai) was premier of the PEOPLE'S REPUBLIC OF CHINA (Communist China) from 1949 until his death in 1976 and was also foreign minister for most of that time. Regarded by many as the epitome of the diplomat, Chou was responsible for virtually all of China's foreign policy during these crucial

years, and he played a major role in determining domestic policies as well.

Chou was not a communist ideologue. He was a pragmatist and master of diplomatic negotiation whose main contribution to the Chinese revolution was to restrain the extremists and keep open the door to the outside world.

Chou was born in 1898 into a prosperous middle-class Chinese family. From the start, his father intended that Chou should have a career in the civil service. His family's efforts to provide the young Chou with the best possible education took him to Chinese, Western and Japanese schools, where he was exposed to a variety of cultures and philosophies, including Marxism.

In May 1919 Chou took a leading role in the student demonstrations that started China on the revolutionary path. He was arrested and jailed for a short time before leaving to study in Paris. In France, Chou met a number of the individuals who later became leading figures in the Chinese Communist Party. Chou himself became a communist at this time and in 1924 returned to China and joined the south China-based alliance of the communists and Kuomintang. Chou was placed in charge of the Canton branch of the Communist Party and was named deputy head of Whampoa Military Academy.

In 1927 Kuomintang leader CHIANG KAI-SHEK turned against the communists in a bloody purge. Chou narrowly escaped with his life and joined MAO ZEDONG at Nankow, where, in April 1927, he was elected to the Chinese Communist Party's Politburo. Chou was given political responsibility for the army but was forced to hand control back to Mao in 1934 after a series of military reverses forced the Chinese communists to make the Long March from Nankow to Yenan in the northwest.

Chou's remarkable skill as a negotiator was first displayed after the Long March, when in December 1936 he helped to save Chiang Kai-shek's life after Chiang was kidnapped in Sian by the communists and forced to agree to a "United Front" against the invading Japanese. From 1937 to 1945 Chou was the communist representative at Chiang's headquarters in Chungking. Later he represented the communists in negotiations to establish a communist-Kuomintang coalition government and met regularly with American mediators General PATRICK J. HURLEY, General ALBERT WEDEMEYER and General GEORGE C. MARSHALL.

When the People's Republic of China was founded in October 1949, Chou's ability to mix with all levels of society and his extensive foreign contacts made him the obvious choice for the premiership and the post of foreign minister. As premier he was responsible for the entire administrative structure of government. And every year he would issue an annual report on the government's work. These continued for nearly three decades and were regarded as communist China's definitive state-of-the-nation report.

He held the post of foreign minister until 1958, when he relinquished the title, but little of the duties and responsibilities, to Chen Yi. Chou was recognized as the voice of the People's Republic. He traveled extensively and worked hard to establish communist China's credentials in the emerging Third World and in the Western world as the alternative to American-supported Taiwan.

His biggest problem was American antagonism. In Chou's view, the United States was China's chief enemy because it continued to recognize the Kuomintang government on Taiwan as the legitimate government of China and this government made regular threats to invade the mainland. The United States also blocked the admission of communist China to the United Nations and maintained troops in Korea and Japan. But Chou had an instinctive preference to diplomatic rather than military battle. There are strong indications that Chou was initially opposed to the North Korean invasion of South Korea in June 1950 and held off sending in Chinese troops until he was convinced that China was under threat from General DOUGLAS MACARTHUR's forces in Korea and Chiang's in Taiwan. Once committed, however, Chou was a tireless advocate of the military solution in Korea and proved a tough negotiator during the long armistice talks.

Another major Sino-American flashpoint of the Cold War years was the Kuomintang-held islands of QUEMOY AND MATSU off the coast of mainland China. The islands were heavily fortified by Chiang's forces, and Chou regarded them as a threat; on two occasions his government tried to drive the Kuomintang forces off with heavy artillery bombardments. Each time, the Eisenhower administration intervened to protect Taiwan while at the same time preventing a Kuomintang counterattack.

Chou's negotiating talents flourished best when he was faced with antagonists whom he hoped to neutralize or neutrals whom he hoped to win over. At the GENEVA CONFERENCE ON INDOCHINA AND KOREA in 1954 he deftly employed these skills to destroy a popular perception of communist China as an anarchic country out to destroy the world order through total noncooperation. During the conference Chou persuaded the Viet Minh leader HO CHI MINH to first negotiate and then to accept a division of Vietnam, which brought temporary peace to Southeast Asia. His diplomacy won plaudits from all the delegations; in India on his way back to China after the conference, Chou used his new-found prestige to launch a regional diplomatic initiative known as the FIVE PRINCIPLES OF PEACEFUL COEXISTENCE. These efforts to establish friendly relations with other Asian nations were expanded the following year at the BANDUNG CONFERENCE, but they collapsed in the face of the SOUTHEAST ASIA TREATY ORGANIZATION.

Sino-Soviet relations were primarily the responsibility of party leader Mao. He was the philosophical and spiritual leader of the party and thus responsible for relations with the communist government in Moscow. Chou, however, was responsible for the day-to-day administration of Sino-Soviet relations. He attended the final stage of Mao's long negotiations in Moscow to seal the Sino-Soviet alliance in February 1950 and coordinated relations between the two countries during the Korean War. He also represented China at the funeral of JOSEF STALIN.

Chou placed a high priority on establishing bilateral relations with Eastern Europe that would be independent of relations with the Soviet Union. In January 1957, after the upheavals in Poland and Hungary, he toured Eastern Europe. His message was basically supportive of the Soviet Union as he urged the Eastern Europeans to show deference to Moscow and remain united against the West. But at the same time, he quietly urged the Soviets to abandon "great power chauvinism." This infuriated Soviet leader NIKITA KHRUSHCHEV and led to the slide in Sino-Soviet relations that resulted in the formal split in 1960.

In 1961 Chou tried to repair the damage at the 21st Soviet Party Congress, but he left early after being rebuffed by Khrushchev. Throughout the rest of his life Chou followed Mao's anti-Soviet line while privately urging the Chinese leader to compromise and steer a more pragmatic course. In 1966, for instance, Chou is believed to have advocated a form of limited cooperation with the Soviets in Vietnam, and low-level negotiations were started, but the plan was vetoed by Mao. After Sino-Soviet border clashes in 1969, however, Chou did manage to stage successful negotiations with Soviet premier ALEXEI KOSYGIN to avoid future military flare-ups.

Chou was also responsible for keeping the door open to the United States. From 1958 onward, an informal channel of communication was established through the American and Chinese embassies in Poland. This was eventually rewarded by a trip to China in July 1971 by U.S. national security adviser HENRY KISSINGER and in February 1972 by President RICHARD NIXON. During the trip, Nixon acknowledged that Taiwan was part of China. Although Nixon met with Mao, all negotiations were conducted with Chou. Three years after Chou's death, the United States recognized the People's Republic and severed diplomatic relations with Taiwan. In his memoirs, Nixon wrote that one of his most outstanding memories of his trip to China was the "brilliance and dynamism" of Chou En-lai.

Chou's pragmatic approach was especially evident in his handling of domestic affairs. He also stood out as a restraining influence whenever the Maoist revolution entered one of its more extreme stages, such as during the Great Leap Forward in 1955–56 and the CULTURAL REVOLUTION of 1966–76. He never took an anti-Maoist position, though, for doing so would have resulted in his own downfall from power.

During the Cultural Revolution, however, he did risk his position by using his prestige to protect several threatened ministers. This could have been the end of his political career if Chou had not also employed his diplomatic skills to make himself indispensable as an intermediary between the various communist factions. After the Cultural Revolution, Chou moved quietly to protect Mao from a right-wing backlash while at the same time moving to curb the power of the People's Liberation Army and the Red Guards.

For the last three years of his life, Chou was seriously ill with high blood pressure and cancer. He still maintained an interest in policies, but he shed many of his day-to-day responsibilities. Chou En-lai died of cancer on January 8, 1976.

For Further Information:

Clubb, Oliver Edmund. *China and Russia: The "Great Game."* New York, 1971.

Levi, Werner. *Modern China's Foreign Policy.* London, 1955.

Li Tien-min. *Chou En-lai.* New York, 1970.

Meisner, Maurice. *Mao's China and After: A History of the People's Republic.* New York, 1986.

Churchill, Winston   (November 30, 1874–January 24, 1965)

Sir Winston Churchill was one of the greatest political figures of the 20th century. He led Britain from the brink of defeat to ultimate victory in World War II and, along with JOSEF STALIN and FRANKLIN ROOSEVELT, negotiated the YALTA Agreement. He later became the first of the major Western leaders to warn of the communist threat and coined the term "IRON CURTAIN." Churchill's insistence on the threat led to the development of the British nuclear deterrent, and he played a leading role in early moves toward European unity. After the death of Stalin, Churchill initiated the early actions to improve East–West relations.

Churchill was born into one of Britain's most prestigious families. His uncle was the Duke of Marlborough and his father, Lord Randolph Churchill, was a controversial Conservative member of Parliament. But perhaps the greatest influence on Churchill's life was his American mother, Jennie Jerome Churchill, the daughter of wealthy New York financier Leonard Jerome.

Churchill was educated at the exclusive English public school Harrow and then the Royal Military Academy at Sandhurst. In the army he saw service in India and the Sudan, but he made his mark as a journalist and writer, not as a soldier. In 1899 he went to South Africa to report the Boer War for the London *Morning Post*. He returned a national hero after a daring escape and in 1900 capitalized on his popularity by being elected Conservative member of Parliament for Oldham.

In 1904 Churchill left the Conservatives for the Liberal Party over the issue of free trade, and in 1908 joined the Liberal government of Herbert Asquith as president of the Board of Trade. In 1911 Churchill was promoted to home secretary, in which capacity he developed a lifelong antipathy for communism and for the British trade union movement. Before World War I, Churchill was transferred to the Admiralty. He played a vital role in strengthening British naval forces before the war and remained at the Admiralty until November 1915, when, discredited by the disastrous Gallipoli campaign, he resigned from the government to join the fighting in France as a lieutenant colonel. In 1916 Churchill returned to Parliament and the following year was named minister of munitions, in which post he helped to develop the world's first tanks.

In the immediate aftermath of the war, Churchill was named secretary of war. He was instrumental in sending British troops to fight against the new Bolshevik government in the Russian Civil War and in dispatching arms to the Poles, who were fighting Soviet troops in the Ukraine. Churchill's early support for the White Russians earned him the lasting enmity of Stalin. Churchill moved to the Colonial Office in 1921, where he helped establish British policies in the Middle East and produced the White Paper that confirmed Palestine as a Jewish "national home" while recognizing continued Arab rights.

Churchill lost his seat in the general election of 1922 but was back in the House of Commons in November 1924. In the intervening two years he had abandoned the Liberals and rejoined the Conservative Party, which promptly rewarded him with the post of chancellor of the exchequer under Prime Minister Stanley Baldwin. His first move was the disastrous decision of 1926 to bring Britain back on the gold standard. This created deflation and widespread unemployment, and led to the general strike of 1926. In 1929, the Conservatives were voted out of office. Churchill was excluded from the Conservative shadow cabinet and immediately launched an attack on Baldwin's India policy.

Former prime minister Winston Churchill (center), escorted by President Truman (left), arrives at Westminster College in Fulton, Missouri in 1946. Speaking on this occasion, Churchill warned the world against Soviet aggression, coining the term "Iron Curtain."

When the national (all-party coalition) government was formed in 1931, Churchill found himself excluded by every major party. The Liberals distrusted him after his departure in 1924. The Labour Party distrusted him because of his antiunion and anti-communist stands, and the Conservatives because of his opposition to the party's colonial policies. All party leaders regarded Churchill as too flamboyant and mercurial to hold senior political office.

During his time in the political wilderness, which lasted until 1939, Churchill became obsessed with the danger of German rearmament and repeatedly urged first Baldwin and then Neville Chamberlain to awaken to the dangers posed by Nazi Germany. By 1939, Churchill had become the national spokesman for all those urging the government to prepare for war and was a symbol for action and national resolve. When war finally broke out, Chamberlain had no choice but to return Churchill to the cabinet in charge of the Admiralty. Repeated German successes led to Chamberlain's resignation in May 1940. Parliament turned to Churchill as the man who had at every turn opposed the Germans.

Churchill responded by forming a new national government and mobilizing the country for what he knew would be a total war. His strategy was simple: victory was essential, and any and every sacrifice necessary would be made to achieve that goal. Nazi Germany was the enemy. Anyone who opposed Germany was an ally, despite any previous political differences with Britain. From the earliest days of the war, it was clear that Churchill urgently sought an alliance with both the United States and the Soviet Union—with the United States because he saw a common history, culture and political philosophy endangered by Nazism; with the Soviet Union because communism was the natural enemy of fascism. Both countries, of course, had natural and industrial resources greater than Britain's.

When Adolf Hitler launched his surprise attack on the Soviet Union in June 1941, Churchill immediately pledged Britain's aid to the Russian people. On December 7, 1941, the United States entered the war after the Japanese bombing of Pearl Harbor, and in May 1942 the grand alliance among the United States, Britain and the Soviet Union was formalized.

With Germany fighting a war on two fronts, and America supporting Britain, it was only a matter of time before the Allies defeated the Axis Powers. By December 1943, when the Allied leaders met in Teheran, the beginnings of victory were visible, and the leaders discussed the final stages of the war and plans for the postwar world. The differences between the plans of Churchill and Stalin became apparent at Teheran, as did Roosevelt's policy of attempting to undermine the continuation of the British Empire, an entity central to Churchill's ideas of world order.

After the successful invasion of France, discussions on postwar Europe increased, and in October 1944 Churchill and Foreign Secretary ANTHONY EDEN flew to Moscow for what was to become a controversial meeting with Josef Stalin. The controversy centered on a discussion between Stalin and Churchill on spheres of interest in the Balkans. Churchill told Stalin, "Let us settle our affairs in the Balkans. Your armies are in Romania and Bulgaria. We have interests, missions and agents there. Don't let us get at cross-purposes in small ways. So far as Britain and Russia are concerned, how would it do for you to have 90% predominance in Romania, for us to have 90% of the say in Greece and go fifty-fifty in Yugoslavia." Churchill then wrote the proposals on a scrap of paper and passed them to Stalin, who marked them with a large tick and passed them back in agreement.

Churchill later said that his proposals were meant to refer only to the immediate postwar period and Stalin knew that this was so. But Soviet officials later chose to interpret the discussion as a typical great power division of permanent spheres of influence and used it to help justify their continued political and military presence in Eastern Europe.

At the Moscow Conference the two European leaders also had their first major disagreement over the future of Poland. In the following weeks the disagreements grew to include the future of Germany and the structure of the proposed United Nations.

The next major Anglo–Soviet clash came in Greece. The German garrison evacuated Athens on October 2, 1944, and was quickly replaced by British troops. Churchill had had his eye on Greece since the early days of the war. He regarded it as the key to the Balkans and part of the "soft underbelly of Europe." Stalin also had a keen interest in Greece because of its proximity to the Dardanelles and position on the edge of the Balkans. As British troops landed in Athens, Stalin threw his support behind the Greek communists. The result was a civil war between the British-supported Greek government and the Soviet-supported Greek communists. The situation was further complicated by the personal intervention of Churchill, who had himself declared regent by Greece's King George.

Churchill's actions in Greece are believed to have convinced President Roosevelt that Britain was determined to continue its imperialist traditions in Europe and to have inclined him more toward the Soviet position in the weeks preceding the historic Yalta Conference. At Yalta, the future of Poland dominated the discussions, and Churchill took the lead in demanding that the Soviet Union allow the Polish people to determine their own future. Stalin maintained that Poland, as the corridor through which Russia's enemies had historically passed, could not be relinquished. The presence of the Red Army in Poland left Churchill and Roosevelt with only the powers of persuasion. In this position they agreed to major changes in Polish borders in return for Soviet pledges for free Polish elections. The elections failed to materialize, and Poland became a key Soviet satellite and a major East–West point of conflict.

The discussions on Poland continued at the POTSDAM CONFERENCE, which took place in the middle of the British general election in July 1945. Both Churchill and Labour leader CLEMENT ATTLEE (wartime deputy prime minister) attended the start of the conference, so that the prime minister would be well informed regardless of the way the election went. Halfway through the conference, both returned to Britain for the announcement of the election result. It was a landslide victory for the Labour Party and Attlee, and the new British foreign secretary, ERNEST BEVIN, returned to complete the negotiations.

Churchill never accepted his 1945 election defeat. During the campaign he was cheered at every election meeting he addressed. But the war had induced a national mood for change, which was represented by the Labour Party and its proposed welfare state. Churchill was cheered because he was a war hero. But he was also leader of the Conservative Party, which represented a return to discarded prewar values.

After the election, Churchill threw himself into the role of leader of the opposition and chief antagonist of the foreign policy of Stalin. On March 5, 1946, he helped lay one of the ideological foundation stones of the Cold War in his "IRON CURTAIN" speech at Westminster College in Fulton, Missouri. The central purpose of the speech was to propose an Anglo–American postwar partnership, but the section that is most remembered was Churchill's references to Soviet domination of Eastern Europe. He said, "Nobody knows what Soviet Russia and its Communist international organization intends to do in the immediate future, or what are the limits, if any, to their expansive and proselytizing tendencies . . . From Stettin in the Baltic to Trieste in the Adriatic an iron curtain has descended across the continent of Europe. The Communist parties, which were very small in all these eastern states of Europe, have been raised to preeminence and power far beyond their numbers and are seeking everywhere to obtain totalitarian control . . . Whatever conclusions may be drawn from these facts—and facts they are—this is certainly not the liberated Europe we fought to build up. Nor is it one that contains the essentials of permanent peace . . ."

In the House of Commons, Churchill supported the foreign policy of Attlee and Bevin, including the Berlin Airlift (see BERLIN BLOCKADE), the merging of the British and American zones in Germany, the Labour government's position on negotiations with the Soviet Union for a German Peace Treaty, moves toward European union and the formation of the NORTH ATLANTIC TREATY ORGANIZATION as a means of protecting Western Europe from Soviet encroachments. At Zurich, in September 1946, he proposed the formation of "a council of Europe" and attended the first assembly of the council at Strasbourg in 1949.

Many hoped that Churchill's early advocacy of European union would lead to British involvement in the unified structures after Churchill returned to government. But Churchill, with his strong sense of history, opposed active British involvement, seeing his country's role as an independent link between America, Europe and the British Empire. In 1954, however, when the EUROPEAN DEFENSE COMMUNITY collapsed in the face of French opposition, Churchill and Eden saved the concept of European unity and enabled German rearmament by agreeing to the permanent basing of 50,000 British troops in West Germany.

Churchill returned to government as prime minister after the Conservative victory in the general election of October 1951. Shortly afterward, in January 1952, he flew to Washington to meet with President HARRY TRUMAN in order to buoy up the Anglo-American special relationship that was at the center of his foreign policy. This involved reassuring Truman of Britain's commitment to the KOREAN WAR, acceptance of a U.S. naval commander for NATO forces in the Eastern Atlantic and the coordination of policies on the issue of German rearmament. Churchill hoped, in return, to renew the wartime Anglo–American cooperation in nuclear weapons research. But Truman was by this time bound by the McMahon Act, which prohibited the transfer of American nuclear secrets abroad.

Churchill was convinced that Britain needed its own atomic bomb in order to maintain its prewar status as a great power, and he expanded and accelerated the nuclear research begun by the previous Labour government. On October 3, 1952, Britain became the world's third nuclear power when it exploded an atomic weapon in the Monte Bello Islands 50 miles off the northwestern coast of Australia. In a report to the House of Commons on October 23, Churchill gave details of the explosion and said that the test would result in a much closer interchange of atomic secrets between Britain and America. In 1955, shortly before his retirement as prime minister, Churchill authorized the production of a British hydrogen bomb.

Churchill also encouraged the development of an independent British land-based missile delivery system for Britain's nuclear weapons. This missile eventually became the BLUE STREAK program, which was canceled in 1960 because of the prohibitive cost.

Britain's postwar economic problems remained the largest challenge in Churchill's efforts to return his country to its prewar status in international relations. He was reluctantly forced to withdraw British defense, political and military commitments around the world. Rather than completely abrogate those commitments, Churchill managed to persuade the United States to take direct responsibility. Churchill's larger-than-life personality and his reputation as wartime leader and preeminent international statesman ensured that the British government retained a major say in most regions of the world. Many American leaders continued to turn to Churchill and his associates for guidance and advice.

Although Churchill is often cast as the archetypal Cold War warrior, this was not the case. Churchill did not see the East-West conflict in purely ideological terms, as many American statesmen did, but more in the terms of traditional 19th-century power politics. He regarded Josef Stalin as the major obstacle to peace in Europe, and after the Soviet leader's death in March 1953 he proposed a concerted Western effort to improve relations with the new Soviet leadership.

In May 1953 Churchill proposed a summit of Western

leaders to coordinate policies for a major East-West summit. The idea would be to explore areas of mutual East-West interest that could lead to the resolution of some problems and create a climate of improved relations. Churchill's proposal received a mixed reaction from the Soviet Union and was well received by the French government, but it was treated with suspicion by the staunchly anti-communist Eisenhower administration. Eventually, however, President Eisenhower agreed to a summit. But a political crisis in France, followed first by the illness of Sir Anthony Eden and then Churchill's stroke, led to the postponement of the Bermuda Summit to December. The successive delays robbed the meeting of its urgency, and it failed to achieve the commitments that Churchill sought, but it did implant the seed of East-West negotiations, which bore fruit in the second half of the decade.

The year 1954 was dominated by the problems of the FRENCH INDOCHINA WAR. The Eisenhower administration tried in vain to persuade Churchill and Eden to join the United States in supporting the French troops in Vietnam. But Churchill was convinced that Vietnam was a lost cause and a political quagmire to be avoided. He instead tried to persuade Eisenhower and U.S. secretary of state JOHN FOSTER DULLES to accept the Geneva Accords negotiated by Eden. Churchill failed in this task, but during his trip to Washington in June he won Eisenhower's endorsement for Britain's policy toward Egypt in the wake of Churchill's acceptance of the phased withdrawal of British troops from the Suez Canal Zone. The false British belief in American support contributed to Eden's later decision to collaborate with France and Israel to recapture the canal (see SUEZ CRISIS).

Churchill retired as leader of the Conservative Party and prime minister on April 5, 1955. Shortly afterward, his successor, Sir Anthony Eden, announced that Churchill's hoped-for summit of British, French, American and Soviet leaders would take place in Geneva. Churchill had celebrated his 80th birthday only 6 months before, and age made it increasingly difficult for him to play an active part in politics. He continued to sit in the House of Commons and was reelected again in 1959, but he ceased to be a major influence on world affairs.

Churchill received a number of honors in his lifetime. He was offered a hereditary dukedom and declined it, but in 1953 he was created a Knight of the Order of the Garter. In the same year he won the Nobel Prize for literature. On April 9, 1963, he was accorded the unique distinction of being made an honorary citizen of the United States by Act of Congress.

For Further Information:

Bonham-Carter, Lady Violet. *Winston Churchill As I Knew Him.* London, 1965.

Churchill, R.S., ed. *The Sinews of Peace: Postwar Speeches by Winston S. Churchill.* London, 1948.

Churchill, Sir Winston. *The Second World War.* New York, 1948–1954.

Feis, Herbert. *Churchill, Roosevelt and Stalin: The War They Waged and the Peace They Sought.* Princeton, 1957.

Gilbert, Martin. *Churchill: A Life.* New York, 1991.

Lord Moran. *Churchill: The Struggle for Survival, 1940–1965.* New York, 1966.

Manchester, William Raymond. *The Last Lion, Winston Spencer Churchill.* Boston, 1983.

Chu Teh   (December 18, 1886–July 6, 1976)   Chu Teh was the Chinese communist military leader who led the Chinese Red Army to victory over the Nationalist forces of CHIANG KAI-SHEK and developed theories of guerrilla strategy that have been employed by revolutionary groups around the world.

Chu was born into a peasant family in China's Szechwan Province and attended Yunnan Military Academy. He graduated in 1911, the same year as the overthrow of the Chinese Imperial government, and joined the anti-Imperial forces. In 1923 Chu traveled to Europe to continue his studies at Göttingen and Berlin. While in Berlin, Chu joined the Communist Party, and in 1926 was expelled by the German government for his revolutionary activities.

He returned to China and became an officer in the Kuomintang Army of Chiang Kai-shek. When Chiang purged the Kuomintang of communists in 1927, Chu managed to escape and joined MAO ZEDONG at his new base in Kiangsi province. The two quickly formed a close relationship. Chu became commander of the Chinese Red Army and Mao became the army's political commissar and chairman of the Communist Party.

Mao had by this time already developed his theories of a peasant-based revolution, but he lacked the expertise to develop a military strategy to put his political theories into action. This task was left to Chu, who was responsible for the development of the Chinese communists' guerrilla tactics, which eventually brought them to power. These tactics relied heavily on the support of the peasant community and based the communist troops in the countryside, where they could live off the land but not at the expense of the peasants and their families.

The Kuomintang forces were allowed control of the cities and large towns. Whenever Chiang's forces ventured out to attack, Chu's army retreated. When Chiang's forces moved back to the city, Chu's forces attacked. The communists' main priority remained the countryside, and their control of it meant that the Kuomintang forces were eventually forced to retreat from the cities for lack of food and other supplies. Chu's tactics were so successful in the 1920s and early 1930s that the Chinese communist influence extended to several thousand square miles and Mao was able in 1931 to declare the founding of the Chinese Soviet Republic.

But Chiang developed an effective counter to Chu's tactics that involved a huge encirclement of the communist-controlled areas. He gradually tightened this circle and by October 1934 was on the verge of victory when Chu, in a brilliant flanking movement, broke out of the encirclement and led the communist forces, some 200,000 strong, 6,000 miles on the Long March to Shenshi Province in northwest China.

After Chiang was kidnapped in 1936 and forced into an anti-Japanese alliance with the Chinese communists, Chu's Red Army was renamed the Eighth Route Army. This force waged a successful guerrilla war against the Japanese in northern China, while in southern China a group of communists left in Kiangsi formed the New Fourth Army and employed successful guerrilla tactics in the Shanghai area. The success of Chu's tactics increased the political power of the Chinese communists; in 1941 the New Fourth Army was attacked by Nationalist forces and the uneasy alliance ended.

Neither the Chinese communists nor the Kuomintang were prepared at this stage to enter into a full-scale civil war. The country was effectively divided between the communist areas in the northwest, the Kuomintang-held areas in the southwest and the Japanese-held areas in the eastern half of the country. Chu continued to employ his guerrilla tactics in the north, and by the end of World War II the Chinese Communist Army had grown to about 700,000 men in control of a population of nearly 85 million people. Chu was thus in an excellent strategic position at the start of the CHINESE CIVIL WAR.

During the first two years, Chiang managed to move his forces into the northern cities and towns, but Chu repeated the peasant-based tactics he had successfully employed in Kiangsi. By the summer of 1946, Chiang's forces were effectively isolated in the urban areas and by 1947 they started to retreat from the north. The Chinese Red Army, under the field command of LIN BIAO, went on the offensive. In 1948 Chu proved that his army could successfully fight conventional battles as well as employ guerrilla tactics. In 1949 the Chinese Red Army crossed the Yangtze River virtually unopposed. It then moved swiftly through the rest of China, and on October 1, 1949, the People's Republic of China was proclaimed. Chu Teh became the first commander in chief of the People's Liberation Army (PLA).

Chu's first task was to protect the new government from a Kuomintang counterattack. He encouraged the signing of the SINO–SOVIET TREATY in 1950. But Chu became increasingly worried that Chiang would be successful in using the KOREAN WAR to gain American support for a counterattack in southern China, while the Americans under General DOUGLAS MAC-ARTHUR crossed the Yalu into northern China. On November 25, 1950, Chu ordered his forces across the Yalu to support the North Koreans.

The Chinese achieved an immediate success and drove the UN forces back to the southern corner of Korea. On December 26, 1950, Chu Teh announced in a radio broadcast that if the United States did not abandon Korea the Chinese would drive them back by their might. Two days earlier he had told a Peking rally that the PLA successes in Korea would "bring about a new upsurge" of communism through Asia. Mac-Arthur, however, eventually succeeded in pushing the Chinese back to the 38th parallel. Chu Teh remained com-mander-in-chief throughout the Korean War and the long armistice negotiations.

After the Korean War, Chu gradually slipped into the background. He was first and foremost a military commander and contributed little to communist doctrine or to peacetime government. But Chu's key role in the communist victory and the early years of the People's Republic assured that he would continue to be held in high regard throughout the party and the country. In 1959 he was appointed to the largely ceremonial position of chairman of the Standing Committee of the National People's Congress, the Chinese parliament. During the CULTURAL REVOLUTION he supported Mao Zedong and Lin Biao. When Mao became too ill to greet foreign dignitaries, Chu took over this responsibility.

For Further Information:
Clubb, Oliver Edmund. *Twentieth Century China.* New York, 1964.
Hsu, C.Y. *The Rise of Modern China.* New York, 1983.
Meisner, Maurice. *Mao's China and After: A History of the People's Republic of China.* New York, 1986.
Solomon, R.H. *Mao's Revolution and the Chinese Political Culture.* New York, 1971.

Civil Defense Administration   See FEDERAL CIVIL DEFENSE ADMINISTRATION.

Civil Defense Systems   In general military jargon, civil defense systems include all measures taken to protect the civilian population during a war. This includes protection from conventional weapons, such as the air raid shelters used in London during World War II. But during the Cold War, civil defense became synonymous with the construction of fallout shelters to protect civilians during a nuclear attack.

In the late 1950s and 1960s, following the Soviet Union's launching of the SPUTNIK satellite and fears of a "MISSILE GAP" in favor of the Soviet Union, a campaign was organized in the United States to build nuclear fallout shelters and devise mass evacuation plans in the event of a Soviet nuclear attack on the United States. Later, as it became clear that the reported missile gap was nonexistent, the emphasis on civil defense lessened as America's defense policy shifted back toward nuclear deterrence as the best way to protect the homeland.

The effectiveness of fallout shelters during a nuclear war has long been debated. Certainly, the effects of a nuclear blast would kill most civilians within a 10-mile radius of most blast sites. The subsequent firestorm would claim additional lives, and the fallout, which could be carried by the wind for hundreds of miles, would remain fatal for weeks afterward. Most major countries, however, have civil defense systems for the maintenance of essential services in the event of a nuclear war.

Some antinuclear organizations have actively campaigned against civil defense systems on the grounds that these programs foster the belief that a nuclear war is survivable and winnable.

For Further Information:
Zuckerman, Edward. *The Day After World War III: The United States Government's Plan for Surviving a Nuclear War.* New York, 1984.

Clark, Mark   (May 1, 1896–April 17, 1984)

General Mark Clark served as American high commissioner in Austria in 1945–47 and as United Nations supreme commander in Korea during the latter part of the KOREAN WAR.

Clark graduated from West Point in 1917 and was wounded in action during the World War I. In World War II he helped plan the Allied invasion of North Africa and was second in command after the troops landed. He took command of the Fifth Army in Italy.

In 1945 Clark was appointed high commissioner in the U.S. occupation zone in Austria (which, like Germany, had been divided into American, British, Soviet and French sectors). One of the first problems he had to face was the question of German assets in Austria. The Soviets were demanding that Germany pay the Soviet Union $10 billion in war reparations, and in September 1946 Clark complained that the Soviets were taking "almost everything on the ground that [was] a German asset." This left the Austrians without enough food to feed themselves and the strong possibility that the economy would soon collapse completely.

Clark took a tough stand in negotiations with the Soviet Union and eventually came to a working arrangement with it. With Soviet cooperation he arranged for American food supplies to be distributed to Austrians in the Soviet sector; he reduced Soviet stripping of assets and curbed inflation by stopping Soviet access to Austrian currency reserves.

When Clark returned to the United States in May 1947 he declared that he saw no reason for optimism in American-Soviet relations because of the Soviet Union's noncooperative attitude. He also accused the Soviets of reducing the Austrians to a starvation diet by seizing their food industry and other resources in violation of the POTSDAM agreement of 1945. He also claimed that the Russians encouraged Austrians to join the Communist Party by offering them higher wages if they did so.

In April 1952 U.S. President HARRY TRUMAN appointed Clark commander-in-chief of the U.S. Army Forces in the Far East and United Nations supreme commander in Korea. He took over at a time when peace negotiations with the Chinese communists and North Koreans were deadlocked, and in December 1952 he advised president-elect Eisenhower to return to the offensive and launch an attack against Chinese bases in Manchuria.

Eisenhower rejected the advice and instructed Clark to reach a diplomatic solution. He did this by alternating between concessions and threats of a nuclear attack. On July 27, 1953, the truce was signed. A month later Clark retired from the army after 40 years of service. Announcing his retirement, Clark said that the United States should use any and every weapon, including the atom bomb, if the communists broke the Korean truce.

In 1954 former President Herbert Hoover was asked to prepare a series of reports on executive departments in the U.S. government. He asked Clark to investigate the CENTRAL INTELLIGENCE AGENCY, with special attention to claims that poor intelligence had led to the Korean War and that the CIA had been infiltrated by communist agents. In his report, issued on June 18, 1955, Clark found no valid ground for charges of communist infiltration. He did express concern about the "lack of adequate intelligence data from behind the Iron Curtain," but he blamed the State Department rather than the CIA.

However, Clark did draw attention to "administrative flaws" and proposed a reorganization that included the appointment of an "executive officer" and a nonpartisan "watchdog commission" to ensure that the CIA acted within democratic limits. The watchdog proposal was rejected by Eisenhower.

From 1954 to 1966 Clark was president of Citadel Military College.

For Further Information:
Berger, Carl. *The Korea Knot: A Military Political History.* Philadelphia, 1964.
Donnelly, Desmond. *Struggle for the World.* New York, 1965.
Moseley, Philip E. "Hopes and Failures: American Policy Towards East and Central Europe, 1941–1947," *Review of Politics* (1975): 461–85.

Clay, General Lucius D.   (April 23, 1897–April 16, 1978)

General Lucius Clay was a key figure in the postwar reconstruction of Germany. He opposed pastoralization of the former enemy, favored the incorporation of West Germany into the Allied camp and was military governor of the U.S. zone in Germany during the BERLIN BLOCKADE and airlift.

Educated at West Point, Clay entered the U.S. Army Corps of Engineers upon graduation in 1918. He quickly developed a reputation as a strong administrator, and throughout his military career he concentrated on the administrative rather than the combat side of the army.

During World War II he was first the army's director of matériel, a post that involved coordinating production and procurement of supplies. In 1944 he was appointed deputy director for war programs and general administrator in the Office of War Mobilization and Reconversion. However, Clay had his eye on the senior administrative post in the American occupation forces in Europe.

In March 1945, as a preliminary to this post, he was appointed deputy to General DWIGHT EISENHOWER, then supreme commander of Allied forces. In March 1946 Clay's staff was separated from Eisenhower's and he was appointed deputy military governor of the U.S. zone in Germany. He held that post until March 1947, when he was appointed the military governor.

From the moment he joined Eisenhower's staff, Clay played an important role in the negotiations involving the occupation of Germany by the four Allied powers (Britain, France, the United States and the Soviet Union). These early relations with the Soviet Union convinced him that Stalin was determined to pursue an expansionist policy in Europe, and Clay became an early advocate of a revived Germany as a bulwark against Soviet expansionism.

In this position, he opposed the "pastoralization" of Germany as proposed by U.S. treasury secretary HENRY MORGENTHAU and supported by the Soviet Union. At first, Clay encountered strong opposition within Washington's governing circles. But as Cold War positions hardened, he found that his early anti-Soviet and pro-German stands increased his standing.

In 1946 he won approval to stop the dismemberment of German factories and suspend German reparations payments from the American zone. He justified this move by arguing that the punitive measures agreed upon at the Allies' postwar conferences at Teheran, YALTA and POTSDAM were meant to be imposed on an economically productive, integrated Germany. As the Soviets showed no inclination to integrate their sector with the American, British and French sectors, the Americans were left with the choice of either attempting to create a self-sufficient Germany in the U.S. zone or saddling the U.S. Treasury with an obligation to subsidize the German economy, including reparations to the Soviet Union, for the foreseeable future.

Clay's policies made him extremely unpopular with the Soviet government, and they were the cause of the first official Soviet postwar attack on American policies when the Allied foreign ministers met in Paris in July 1946. At the meeting Clay was personally denounced by Soviet foreign minister V.M. MOLOTOV.

Molotov's attack, however, did not deter Clay. He continued his policy of strengthening Germany, slowing down decartelization and de-Nazification plans. He believed that a total purge of Nazis would have severe economic repercussions, as would decartelization, the breakup of the large corporate alliances that had controlled the German economy under the Nazis. Clay also quickly introduced new political structures in the American zone. When the zone was merged with the British and French zones, Clay's structures became the political basis of the Federal Republic of Germany.

By the spring of 1948 Clay was becoming increasingly worried about Soviet intentions toward the West. On March 5, 1948, he cabled the U.S. Army director of intelligence that "for many months I have felt and held that war was unlikely for at least ten years. Within the last few weeks, I have felt a subtle change in the Soviet attitude which I cannot define but which now gives me a feeling that it may come with dramatic suddenness."

Despite this feeling of unease, Clay was a strong supporter of the MARSHALL PLAN and the extension of its aid program to the Western-occupied sectors of Germany. On June 7, 1948, it was announced that Germany would participate in the Marshall Plan, a constitution for the Federal Republic was to be drawn up and the economic policies in the three Western-occupied zones were to be coordinated as of June 20. The Soviets had made it clear for some time that they would cut off Berlin if the Western Allies tried to introduce the new federal currency there, and on June 24 they imposed the Berlin Blockade (q.v.).

Clay immediately organized the Berlin Airlift in conjunction with the British military governor, Sir Brian Robertson. At the same time he pushed U.S. President HARRY TRUMAN to reopen the land routes with armed convoys. Truman, backed by Secretary of State GEORGE MARSHALL, rejected Clay's advice for fear that it would unnecessarily escalate the situation.

The Berlin Airlift was an administrative triumph for Clay. From June 24, 1948, to May 12, 1949, nearly 200,000 flights were made by British and American planes. They carried more than a million and a half tons of supplies to Berlin. At the height of the airlift, nearly 13,000 tons a day were being ferried into Berlin. Clay's hard line, however, had alienated him from senior figures in the Truman administration, and he was excluded from the United Nations negotiations that ended the blockade.

In his memoirs, Clay blamed himself for the Berlin Blockade. He believed that he should have had the foresight in 1945 to secure in writing a basic access agreement to Berlin. Most historians, however, believe that this lapse was understandable given the generally pro-Soviet climate of American thinking immediately before the Potsdam Conference.

On the day the blockade was lifted the French, British and American military governors agreed to a constitution for the Federal Republic of Germany. Three days later Clay left Germany to be replaced by a civilian high commissioner for the U.S. zone, JOHN MCCLOY. He retired from the army to become chairman and chief executive officer of the Continental Can Company and became active in politics. Clay played a crucial role in persuading Eisenhower to run for president and helped him to select his cabinet. During the Eisenhower administration he headed a presidential commission that planned the interstate highway network. He also continued to advise on German affairs.

In August 1961 the Soviet and East German governments again threatened to cut off Western access to Berlin. President JOHN F. KENNEDY immediately sent Clay to West Berlin to reassure the West Berliners of American support. Under the Four Power Treaty on Berlin, officials of all the occupying powers had the right to visit each other's sectors. To underscore America's determination to retain that right, Clay ordered armed convoys to accompany American diplomats into East Berlin, and Soviet and American tanks faced each other across the Berlin border for the first time. American forces were withdrawn after the Soviet Union pulled back its tanks.

In December 1962 Kennedy appointed Clay chairman of the Permanent Advisory Committee on Foreign Aid with the assignment to set new guidelines for the distribution of U.S. aid. In March 1963, much to Kennedy's chagrin, the committee recommended that aid levels be reduced by at least $500 million a year and not be extended in situations "inconsistent with our beliefs, democratic tradition and knowledge of economic organization and consequences."

In August 1963 the U.S. Congress used the committee's report to slash foreign aid by a third. In the political battle that followed, Clay claimed that his committee's report had been misinterpreted by Congress and he supported Kennedy's pleas for a reversal of the congressional vote. He particularly deplored the $225 million cut in military aid and the $150 million cut in the Alliance for Progress Program.

In November 1965 Clay was among 104 well-known Americans who signed a statement supporting the Johnson administration's Vietnam policy. This was his last active involvement in political affairs. In 1970 Clay retired from Continental Can.

For Further Information:
Clay, Lucius. *Decision in Germany*. New York, 1950.
Davis, Franklin M., Jr. *Come as a Conqueror; The United States Army's Occupation of Germany, 1945–1949*. New York, 1967.
Davison, Walter Phillips. *The Berlin Blockade: A Study in Cold War Politics*. Princeton, 1958.
Smith, Jean Edward, ed. *The Papers of General Lucius D. Clay: Germany 1945–1949*. Bloomington, Ind., 1974.
Tusa, Ann, and John Tusa. *The Berlin Blockade*. New York, 1989.

Clayton, William   (February 7, 1880–February 8, 1967)
William Clayton was one of President HARRY TRUMAN's key foreign economic advisers. As such he helped to develop the MARSHALL PLAN. Some historians have called him "the stepfather" of that scheme.

Clayton left school at age 16 to work as a stenographer for a cotton broker in St. Louis. By the time he was 24 he had established his own brokerage agency, which eventually became the world's largest cotton brokerage firm.

He joined the ROOSEVELT administration in 1940 as assistant secretary of commerce responsible for the foreign activities of the Reconstruction Finance Corporation. In December 1944 he was appointed assistant secretary of state for economic affairs, and in 1946 Truman appointed him undersecretary of state for economic affairs.

Clayton was an early advocate of U.S. economic aid to its allies in order to prevent a postwar economic slump and the expansion of the Soviet Union. To this end he successfully lobbied in 1946 for a U.S. loan to Britain of $3.75 billion.

In March 1947 Clayton presented a memorandum to Truman in which he asserted that the war had left Britain unable to meet its peacetime military and political commitments and that if the United States did not act quickly to fill the vacuum it would be filled by the Soviet Union. Clayton went on to urge the president to launch a $5 billion program of U.S.-controlled economic aid for Western Europe.

Clayton's proposals prompted Secretary of State GEORGE MARSHALL to order a State Department-sponsored aid program that called for minimal U.S. control. Clayton, although pleased that the principle had been accepted, opposed the structure of the State Department plan because he wanted a

larger injection of immediate aid and he wanted greater American control of the allocation of funds. The State Department proposals, however, became the basis for the Marshall Plan.

In 1948 Clayton retired from government and returned to his cotton brokerage business. He remained a director of the company until his death in 1967.

For Further Information:
Gimbell, John. *The Origins of the Marshall Plan*. Stanford, Calif., 1976.
Hartmann, Susan. *The Marshall Plan*. Columbus, Ohio, 1968.

Clifford, Clark   (December 26, 1906–   )   Clark Clifford was a trusted and influential adviser to four Democratic American presidents and in 1968 succeeded ROBERT MCNAMARA as secretary of defense. In this position he played a major role in persuading President Lyndon B. Johnson to de-escalate the VIETNAM WAR.

After graduating from Washington University Law School in 1928, Clifford entered practice as a trial attorney, later switching to corporate and labor law. During World War II he met Vice President HARRY TRUMAN when he became assistant to Truman's naval aide. Clifford and Truman formed a close friendship that became the basis of the former's political career.

Truman succeeded to the presidency in 1945, and in 1946 Clifford became his special counsel and helped with the writing of his speeches. Initially the president relied on Clifford mainly for advice on labor issues, but soon was turning to him for advice on relations with the Soviet Union. Clifford was an early supporter of GEORGE F. KENNAN's containment policy, and in 1946 composed a memorandum on U.S.–Soviet relations in which argued in favor of an anti-Soviet Western alliance and the willingness to wage nuclear and biological warfare against Moscow until it sought accommodation with the West.

Clifford was also responsible for writing the 1947 speech in which Truman asked Congress for military and economic aid for Greece and Turkey. The speech laid the foundations for the TRUMAN DOCTRINE.

Clifford left the Truman administration in 1950 to return to his private law practice, although throughout the 1950s he remained a major behind-the-scenes political figure in Washington circles. Among his personal clients was Senator JOHN F. KENNEDY. In 1960 he joined the staff of Kennedy's presidential campaign, and acted as liaison officer with the Eisenhower administration after Kennedy's election victory.

In May 1961 Clifford was appointed to the newly formed Foreign Intelligence Advisory Board to oversee intelligence activities following the debacle of the BAY OF PIGS invasion. Clifford became the panel's chairman in April 1963. After Kennedy's assassination, Clifford reorganized the White House staff for President JOHNSON and was offered the post of attorney general, which he refused. However, he continued to advise the president regularly, especially on the war in South Vietnam, about which he at first took a hawkish line.

In January 1968 Clifford agreed to take on the post of secretary of defense in succession to Robert McNamara. It was widely assumed by observers that he would continue his hawkish stand on the war, but he soon adopted a more dovish position. He was greatly influenced by the lack of enthusiasm for the war among American allies and by the destabilizing effect of the Viet Cong/North Vietnamese TET OFFENSIVE, which took place in January–February 1968. Two days before he was sworn in as secretary of defense, Clifford was also named chairman of the president's Ad Hoc Task Force on Vietnam. The panel was created to study the best way to raise an additional 200,000 troops requested by the military for the war effort, but Clifford reassessed the brief to include an examination of the American role in Vietnam. As a result, the military's request for 200,000 troops was refused.

Instead, the task force recommended the immediate deployment of 23,000 additional troops in Vietnam, and Clifford expressed serious reservations about the administration's Vietnam policy. From this point on, Clifford worked incessantly to reverse the pro-war positions of Johnson, Secretary of State DEAN RUSK and national security adviser WALT ROSTOW. He was rewarded on March 31, 1968, with Johnson's televised statement that he was deescalating the war. Later, at Clifford's insistence, he stopped all bombing of North Vietnam. Clifford left office in January 1969 and returned to his private law practice, and from 1969 onward he was an advocate of unilateral American withdrawal from Vietnam.

Clifford returned to government service in 1977 under President Jimmy Carter, who used the veteran adviser on sensitive diplomatic missions to Greece, Turkey, Cyprus, India and Pakistan. Clifford also advised Carter on ways to curb the excesses of the American intelligence community.

Clifford's sterling reputation in Washington was severely tarnished in 1991 when he became linked to a burgeoning scandal surrounding the criminal activities of the Bank of Commerce and Credit International (BCCI). Clifford was indicted in the case in July 1992. He did not go trial, however, because of ill health.

For Further Information:
Dougan, C.A. *A Nation Divided*. Boston, 1984.
Hoopes, Townsend. *The Limits of Intervention*. New York, 1969.
Karnow, Stanley. *Vietnam: A History*. New York, 1984.
Smith, R.B. *An International History of the Vietnam War*. New York, 1986.

Cline, Ray (June 4, 1918–   )   Ray Cline directed American intelligence operations in the Far East during the 1950s and was deputy director for intelligence at the CENTRAL INTELLIGENCE AGENCY from 1962 to 1966.

Cline was teaching history at Harvard when he was recruited into the OFFICE OF STRATEGIC SERVICES (OSS), the wartime forerunner of the CIA, at the start of World War II. His wartime experiences gave him a taste for intelligence work,

but he never completely divorced himself from academia and drifted back and forth between the two.

Immediately after the war he worked in the office of the chief of military history at the Department of the Army, helping to compile a history of World War II. In 1949 he was posted to the American Embassy in London and in 1951 officially joined the Central Intelligence Agency. In 1954 Cline was appointed director of U.S. Naval Auxiliary Communications at Taipei in Taiwan.

Relations between communist China and the United States were then at their nadir. American soldiers returning from Korea were full of stories of Chinese atrocities, and the Chinese lived in fear of an American-supported invasion by the Nationalist Chinese on Taiwan. Cline was responsible for intelligence-gathering flights over communist China and for parachuting agents into the country.

Cline's importance within the CIA grew, and he played a major role in persuading the EISENHOWER administration to publish its copy, procured by the CIA, of Soviet leader NIKITA KHRUSHCHEV's secret speech before the 20th Party Congress in 1956, in which Khrushchev denounced the excesses of JOSEF STALIN.

In 1962 Cline was appointed deputy director of intelligence at the CIA and was regarded as a possible contender for the directorship. But he was not a political animal and clashed with CIA director Admiral William Raborn. Rather than stay and argue, Cline asked to be transferred to West Germany in 1966, where he became the CIA station chief, based at the U.S. Embassy in Bonn. In 1969 he transferred to the State Department to become director of the State Department's Bureau of Intelligence and Research.

In 1973 Cline left official government work to become director of Georgetown University's Center for Strategic and International Studies. He also retained his interest in Asian affairs as a member of the Committee for Free China. In 1986 he became chairman of the U.S. Global Strategy Council. Since leaving government service, Cline has written and lectured extensively on espionage.

For Further Information:
Cline, Ray. *Secrets, Spies and Scholars*. New York, 1976.
Cline, Ray, and Herbert Block. *The CIA: Reality vs. Myth*. New York, 1982.

Coalition Defense   Coalition defense is an American policy for the development of a global defense.

The main thrust of a global defense is that the United States forms a military alliance with a country or group of countries in strategic regions of the world. These countries provide the forward bases and all or most of the troops, and the United States provides strategic military aid in the form of weapons, technical advice and possibly logistic support. The best and most successful example of coalition defense is the NORTH ATLANTIC TREATY ORGANIZATION (NATO).

Coalition defense reached its zenith during the EISENHOWER

administration, when Secretary of State JOHN FOSTER DULLES was its leading advocate. The results of Dulles' efforts included the BAGHDAD PACT (Central Treaty Organization) and the SOUTHEAST ASIA TREATY ORGANIZATION (SEATO).

For a coalition defense policy to be successful, all the members of the alliance must have a high degree of political cohesion. This has always been the case in NATO, most members of which shared a common belief in a pluralistic political system and had strong historic and cultural links with each other as well as a clearly defined and visible common enemy. The absence of these factors was a major reason for the failure of SEATO and the Baghdad Pact.

Cohn, Roy   (February 20, 1927–August 2, 1986)   Roy

Cohn was a hard-line politically connected, anti-communist lawyer who served as chief counsel to U.S. Senator JOSEPH MCCARTHY's Permanent Investigations Subcommittee. In this capacity he contributed to the anti-communist hysteria of the 1950s.

Cohn was the son of a New York state judge and received his law degree from Columbia University when he was only 20. He entered politics as an assistant U.S. attorney for the southern district of New York, where he specialized in uncovering "subversive" activities. His work included the espionage trial of JULIUS AND ETHEL ROSENBERG in 1951.

His work in New York brought him to the attention of right-wing congressmen, and in September 1951 he transferred to Washington, where he started as a special assistant to the U.S. attorney general. In this capacity he conducted a grand jury investigation of charges of subversion among United Nations employees. This brought him to the attention of Senator Joseph McCarthy, who hired him as his subcommittee's chief counsel in January 1953.

The two men were both dedicated right-wingers, and Cohn became McCarthy's chief lieutenant in his anti-communist crusade. He took part in many of the interrogations and was regarded as being as rude and aggressive as McCarthy himself. McCarthy once remarked, "[Cohn] is as indispensable as I am."

In April 1953 Cohn and the subcommittee's chief consultant, David Schine, conducted a tour of Western Europe in search of pro-communist literature in embassy libraries. Their report resulted in a number of books being withdrawn from American embassies but prompted President DWIGHT EISENHOWER to issue a warning against "book burners."

The friendship between Cohn and Schine eventually caused the collapse of Cohn's political career. In November 1953 Schine was drafted into the army, and Cohn used his political influence to obtain soft assignments for his friend. This coincided with McCarthy's own investigation into subversion in the army, and Cohn went so far as to threaten to discredit the army unless Schine was given special treatment. The army, however, kept a special file on Cohn's threats and countered by threatening to expose him.

McCarthy's hearings on the army went ahead anyway in April 1954, and McCarthy's performance during these hearings was a major factor in the Senate's decision to censure him. Cohn, because he was listed as a principal in the investigation, temporarily withdrew from the subcommittee while the hearings were in progress. But other members of the subcommittee were by this time disgusted with his bullying tactics, and he was forced to resign on July 19, 1954. Shortly afterward, the Republican majority on the subcommittee issued a report stating that Cohn had been "unduly aggressive and insistent" in the Schine affair. The minority Democrats insisted that he had "misused and abused the powers of his office and brought disrepute to the committee."

Cohn returned to New York, where he entered a law firm. In 1957 he became a professor of law at New York Law School, and in the 1960s he promoted boxing matches. As a lawyer his clients included J. Edgar Hoover, Terence Cardinal Cooke, Aristotle Onassis and alleged Mafia "boss of bosses" Carmine Galante. He counted RONALD REAGAN among his close personal friends.

During the late 1950s, Cohn was a prime target of the Internal Revenue Service, which eventually collected more than $300,000 in back taxes from him but claimed he owed as much as $7 million. He was three times tried and acquitted on federal charges, including bribery, extortion, obstruction of justice and blackmail. In June 1986 he was disbarred from practicing law in New York state. Roy Cohn died of AIDS on August 2, 1986.

For Further Information:

Hoffman, Nicholas von. *Citizen Cohn: The Life and Times of Roy Cohn.* New York, 1988.
Rovere, Richard H. "The Adventures of Cohn and Schine," *The Reporter* (July 21, 1953): 9–16.

Colby, William   (January 4, 1920–   )   William Col-

by was director of the CENTRAL INTELLIGENCE AGENCY during the NIXON and FORD administrations. Prior that he was CIA station chief in Vietnam during the early 1960s. He was director of the CIA at the height of public and congressional attacks on the agency.

Colby was a career espionage agent. After graduating from Princeton University in 1940 he joined the wartime predecessor of the CIA, the OFFICE OF STRATEGIC SERVICES. After the war the OSS was disbanded, and Colby returned to his studies to obtain his law degree from Cornell University. He practiced law in New York for three years before joining the newly created CIA in 1950.

His first postings were to Europe, where he served in Sweden and Italy. In the latter post, Colby worked closely with U.S. ambassador to Italy CLARE BOOTH LUCE in trying to discredit the Italian Communist Party and channeling American funds to the pro-American Christian Democrats.

In 1959 Colby was appointed CIA station chief for Vietnam. It was a vital role because the United States was directing the main thrust of its support for South Vietnam through covert operations of the CIA. In 1962 Colby's influence over American policy in Vietnam was increased when he was appointed head of the Far East division of clandestine services. One of his first actions was the organization of a 30,000-strong private army of Laotian tribesmen, who launched commando-type raids against communist forces in Laos, China and North Korea.

In 1964 Colby established the Vietnam Counterterror Program, which employed kidnapping, intimidation and assassination against leading Vietnamese communists. In 1967, he also started Operation Phoenix, which coordinated American and Vietnamese attacks on communist bases. In April 1968 Colby was appointed assistant director in Saigon of Civil Operations and Rural Development Support (CORDS), an American program designed to "win the hearts and minds of the people" through the development of health and social service programs. After becoming director of the program in November 1968, Colby linked it to CIA operations, and CORDS fell into disrepute and eventually failed.

In 1970 and 1971 Colby's actions in Vietnam came under the scrutiny of the U.S. Congress, and he was called before congressional committees to justify his programs. When asked point-blank if the CIA had performed assassinations, Colby refused to answer.

In June 1971 Colby returned to Washington as budget director for the CIA. This ensured that he was aware of all major CIA covert operations, including the attempt to block the election of Chilean Marxist SALVADOR ALLENDE and Operation Chaos, which investigated possible foreign links with domestic dissidents, especially antiwar activists. In violation of the CIA charter, the agency compiled files on 10,000 U.S. citizens and groups and indexed 300,000 names on computer records. Colby, when he realized the legal implications of Operation Chaos, shifted the focus of the operation from the antiwar movement to anti-terrorist activities. However, he blocked efforts to destroy the illegal information that had already been gathered.

In January 1973 Colby became deputy director of plans under CIA director James SCHLESINGER. At Schlesinger's request, Colby compiled a list of questionable CIA activities. These activities were termed "family jewels" and included attempted assassinations of foreign statesmen, intercepting domestic mail and experiments with mind-control drugs.

In August 1973 Colby was named director of the CIA and shortly afterward became entangled in publicly defending the questionable CIA activities that he had documented for Schlesinger. In 1974 and 1975 the CIA was investigated by one Senate and one House committee, a presidential commission and scores of investigative reporters. In September 1975 Colby was threatened with contempt of Congress for refusing to give the House of Representatives' Pike Committee uncensored classified documents. The clash was resolved only after intervention by President GERALD FORD.

Ford, however, was generally unimpressed with Colby's handling of the various investigations. Colby tried to give the appearance of cooperating with the investigations while at the same time denying any major wrongdoing and refusing to disclose selected information on the grounds of national security. After a damaging report in the *New York Times*, Ford sought assurances that the CIA would act within the law. Colby replied with a "full assurance" that the agency was "not conducting activities comparable to those alleged" in the *Times*. He continued, "Even in the past, I believe the agency essentially conformed to its mission of foreign intelligence. There were occasions over the years in which improper actions were taken . . . but I believe these were few, were quite exceptional to the thrust of the agency's activities, and have been fully eliminated."

On September 9, 1975, Senator Frank Church, chairman of the Senate Select Intelligence Committee, announced that the CIA continued to maintain a secret cache of deadly poisons "in direct contravention" of a 1969 order by President NIXON to destroy biological and chemical weapons. The revelations concerning the chemical weapons were the last straw for Ford, and in a major reshuffle of advisers and cabinet officers on November 3, 1975, Colby was dismissed as director of the CIA. Ford simply said that Colby did not fit on his new team. The President offered Colby the post of ambassador to NATO, but Colby declined, set up his own law practice in Washington, D.C. and wrote his memoirs.

For Further Information:
Berman, Jerry, and Morton H. Halperin, eds. *The Abuses of the Intelligence Agencies.* Washington, D.C., 1975.

Colby William Egan, and Peter Forbath. *Honorable Men: My Life in the CIA.* New York, 1978.

Colby, William Egan, with James McCargar. *Lost Victory: A Firsthand Account of America's Sixteen-Year Involvement in Vietnam.* Chicago, 1989.

Marchetti, Victor, and John D. Marks. *The CIA and the Cult of Intelligence.* New York, 1974.

Wise, David, and Thomas B. Ross. *The Invisible Government.* New York, 1964.

Collins, General Lawton J.   (May 1, 1896–September 11, 1987)   General Lawton Collins was a World War II hero who won prominence during the Cold War as U.S. Army chief of staff during the KOREAN WAR and then as President EISENHOWER's special representative to Vietnam. His experiences there left Collins skeptical of the wisdom of American involvement in Southeast Asia, and he was one of the first "dove" generals.

Collins graduated from the United States Military Academy at West Point in 1917. By the start of World War II he had reached the rank of brigadier general. He saw active duty in the Pacific, where he won the nickname "Lightning Joe" when in command of a division on Guadalcanal. Later he helped direct operations in Europe.

Collins was named army chief of staff in August 1949 and become a strong advocate of the development of nuclear weapons in the belief that this would help to free U.S. divisions tied down in Europe.

Collins was deeply involved in army planning operations during the Korean War and supported President HARRY TRUMAN's dismissal of General DOUGLAS MACARTHUR. In 1953 President DWIGHT EISENHOWER appointed Collins U.S. representative to the NORTH ATLANTIC TREATY ORGANIZATION. After the partition of Vietnam, Collins became involved in American policy there.

In November 1954 Eisenhower sent Collins to Saigon as his special representative with the rank of Ambassador. Collins' task was to strengthen the government of Premier NGO DINH DIEM so that it could successfully withstand an attack from communist North Vietnam. Collins started a military training program, improved internal security, suggested the inclusion of Buddhist elements in the government and laid the foundations for an agrarian reform program. But Diem and Collins clashed, and the South Vietnamese leader refused to implement the American's proposals or programs.

After fighting broke out in Saigon between Buddhist fundamentalists and Diem's supporters in March 1955, Collins was recalled to Washington to brief the president personally. He strongly recommended that the United States withdraw its support from the Diem regime. The State Department offered a compromise proposal that allowed Diem to remain titular head of the government while real power was transferred to Phan Huy Quat. This was accepted by Collins and was about to be implemented when Diem crushed the Buddhist resistance and Eisenhower shifted his full support back to Diem.

By this time Collins had become the focal point for American opposition to the Diem regime. In that position it was impossible for him to return to Saigon, so in May 1955 he was assigned again to NATO, where he remained until he retired and went into business in 1957. Collins' experiences in Vietnam left him convinced that the United States' ability to prevent communist expansion by positively influencing events in South Vietnam was severely limited. This led him to be one of the early military critics of the Vietnam War. Collins died of a heart attack on September 11, 1987.

For Further Information:
Barnet, Richard J. *Roots of War.* New York, 1972.
Bartor, Victor. *Vietnam: A Diplomatic Tragedy: The Origins of the United States Involvement.* Dobbs Ferry, N.Y., 1965.
Lansdale, Edward G. *In the Midst of Wars: An American's Mission to Southeast Asia.* New York, 1972.

Colombo Plan for Cooperative Economic and Social Development in Asia and the Pacific   The Colombo Plan was a British-inspired scheme to provide financial assistance to Asian and Pacific countries. It played a major role in creating a pro-Western outlook among most of the countries.

The Colombo Plan was one of the last foreign policy initiatives of British foreign secretary ERNEST BEVIN. It was outlined by Bevin at a meeting of Commonwealth foreign ministers in Colombo, Ceylon (now Sri Lanka), on January 9–13, 1950. Its initial aim was to help Burma achieve the political stability necessary to defeat communist insurgents, but it was soon extended to the rest of Asia and the Pacific.

The United States did not participate in the initial formation of the Colombo Plan but quickly became involved as a donor country. The plan provided aid to 20 member countries from seven donor countries—Britain, India, the United States, Japan, New Zealand, Australia and Canada. The aid extended included capital projects in agriculture, communications, education and energy; technical cooperation in industry, fishing, education, health and other areas; and educational fellowships. Between 1950 and 1983 the total aid allocated through the Colombo Plan amounted to $72 billion. More than half of the money, $41.2 billion, was provided by the United States.

For Further Information:
Barclay, Sir Roderick. *Ernest Bevin and the Foreign Office.* London, 1975.
Saville, John. *Ernest Bevin and the Cold War, 1945–50.* London, 1984.
Stavrianos, L.S. *Global Rift: The Third World Comes of Age.* New York, 1981.
Williams, Francis. *Ernest Bevin: Portrait of a Great Englishman.* London, 1952.
———. *The Foreign Policy of the British Labour Governments, 1945–51.* Leicester, 1984.

Cominform (Communist Information Bureau)   The Cominform was an international communist propaganda bureau begun in 1947. Its stated aim was to disseminate propaganda designed to encourage international communist solidarity. Some analysts suggest, however, that its main purpose was to act as a Soviet-sponsored coordinator in directing communist parties elsewhere in the world to subvert democratic governments.

The Cominform was established by the Soviet Union partly in response to the MARSHALL PLAN. It was launched at a meeting of East European leaders at Wiliza Gora in Silesia on September 22–23, 1947, and it involved the communist parties of the Soviet Union, Poland, Yugoslavia, Hungary, Romania, Czechoslovakia, Bulgaria, Italy and France.

Most observers agree that the founding of the Cominform was tantamount to a declaration of ideological war on the part of JOSEF STALIN and that it was a political precursor to the WARSAW PACT, which was formed in 1955.

The Cominform was the first international communist organization to be announced since the Comintern had been formally dissolved in 1943 in deference to the Soviet Union's Western allies. A manifesto issued after its meeting called for communist parties to "place themselves in the guard of Opposition" against U.S. "expansion and aggression . . . whether in the sphere of state administration, politics, economics or ideology."

Cracks appeared within the international communist

structure almost as soon as the Cominform was formed. These mainly concerned relations between the Soviet Union and Yugoslavia. JOSIP BROZ TITO, the communist leader of Yugoslavia, refused to allow his country to be dominated by the Soviet Union. Josef Stalin, who was determined that the communist revolution be directed from Moscow, expelled Yugoslavia from the Cominform on June 28, 1948, after Tito refused the Soviet Union access to Yugoslav state secrets.

Yugoslavia had started out as one of the most enthusiastic supporters of the Cominform, and because of this the organization was headquartered in Belgrade. After the break in 1948, however, the bureau was moved to Bucharest.

Two of the most active members were the French and Italian communist parties, which were given the specific task of obstructing the implementation of the Marshall Plan and the TRUMAN DOCTRINE. The combination of their failure and the parties' slavish support of Soviet foreign policy played a major role in keeping the French and Italian communist parties out of office in the postwar years.

The Cominform was disbanded on April 17, 1956, as part of NIKITA KHRUSHCHEV's attempt to improve Soviet relations with Yugoslavia.

For Further Information:
Borkenau, Franz. *European Communism.* London, 1953.
Shulman, Marshall D. *Stalin's Foreign Policy Reappraised.* Cambridge, Mass., 1963.
Triska, Jan F., and David D. Finley. *Soviet Foreign Policy.* New York, 1968.
Ulam, Adam B. *Titoism and the Cominform.* Cambridge, Mass., 1952.

Command, Control, Communications and Intelligence (C3I)

Command, Control, Communications and Intelligence—better known as C3I—is the phrase used to describe a military force's capacity to monitor intelligence and convey information and orders reliably, quickly and secretly.

In the latter years of the Cold War C3I capacity of both superpower blocs came under criticism for being too vulnerable. Defense analysis maintained that heavy reliance on computer systems makes it possible for communications to be easily intercepted or jammed by electronic countermeasures.

Committee for One Million Against the Admission of Communist China to the United Nations

The Committee for One Million Against the Admission of Communist China to the United Nations, later known as the Committee of One Million, was a right-wing American pressure group formed in October 1953 to block communist Chinese membership in the United Nations and to reject any attempts to improve Sino-American relations. The committee had a powerful impact on America's China policy up to the early 1970s.

The committee was formed in the period after the KOREAN WAR when a number of Western countries were urging the EISENHOWER administration to normalize relations with communist China by dropping its bar to Peking's membership in the UNITED NATIONS.

This was anathema to many American conservatives, who regarded support for the Nationalist Chinese government of CHIANG KAI-SHEK and opposition to the communist Chinese as a major pillar of American foreign policy. On October 23, 1953, a total of 210 prominent Americans signed a petition calling on the United States to block communist China's admission to the UN and handed the petition over to the White House at a special meeting with President Dwight Eisenhower.

The event was the first step in a drive to obtain one million American signatures on the petition, hence the organizers called themselves "The Committee for One Million . . ." The one millionth signature was obtained on July 6, 1954, and shortly afterward the committee changed its name to the "Committee of One Million . . ." and reorganized itself into a permanent lobby organization chaired by former ambassador to the UN WARREN AUSTIN and administered by ex-communist MARVIN LIEBMAN.

The committee widened its scope of activities to encompass the whole range of Sino-American activities and general opposition to communism. Liebman produced a regular newsletter that kept members informed of communist aggression in Southeast Asia and "appeasement" of communism in the West. The newsletter also campaigned against the relaxation of the American economic boycott of communist China, supported military and economic ties with Taiwan and kept members informed of other nations' attempts to secure communist Chinese entry into the United Nations.

The Committee of One Million remained a potent force in U.S. foreign policy until President Richard NIXON's rapprochement with Beijing in 1971 and 1972. It disbanded shortly afterward.

For Further Information:
Bachrack, Stanley D. *The Committee of One Million: "China Lobby" Politics, 1953–1971.* New York, 1976.
Koen, R.Y. *China Lobby in American Politics.* New York, 1960.

Commonwealth of Independent States (CIS)

The Commonwealth of Independent States officially came into being on December 25, 1991, with the dissolution of the former U.S.S.R. The CIS was an alliance of fully independent states made up of 11 of the 15 former Soviet constituent republics.

The developments that led to the formation of the commonwealth came with stunning rapidity in the four months following the failure of the August 19–21 coup attempt by Communist Party hardliners to oust President MIKHAIL GORBACHEV. Gorbachev resigned as CP leader August 24, and the Supreme Soviet August 29 voted to suspend all activities of the ruling Communist Party, effectively ending its 74-year reign. Over the next few months, Gorbachev's powers steadily waned, and Russian President BORIS YELTSIN—who had led the opposition to the coup—became the country's preeminent political figure. Gorbachev's final failure came on November

25, when representatives of seven republics balked at signing a treaty for a new, loosely confederated Union of Sovereign States that had been proposed by Gorbachev.

On December 8, the leaders of the three Slavic republics—Russia, Ukraine and Byelorussia (which shortly thereafter formally changed its name to Belarus)—signed an inital agreement forming a Commonwealth of Independent States. Gorbachev vehemently rejected the move as illegal but no longer had the power to oppose it. On December 17, after a two-hour discussion between Yeltsin and Gorbachev, the Russian president said that Gorbechev now accepted that the demise of the Soviet Union was imminent. Yeltsin on December 19 issued decrees ordering the Russian government to seize the Kremlin and to take over or replace the functions of the entire Soviet central government, with the exceptions of the defense and atomic energy ministries.

The unofficial end of the U.S.S.R. came on December 21 when 11 of the 12 republics signed agreements to create a commonwealth. (Georgia, which had declared transitional independence earlier in the year and was embroiled in a civil war, did not join. The three Baltic republics of Estonia, Latvia and Lithuania had been recognized as independent states by the Soviet Union on September 6.) The 11 participating states were: Armenia, Azerbaijan, Belarus, Kazakhstan, Kyrgyzstan (formerly Kirghizia), Moldova (formerly Moldavia), the Russian Federation, Tajikistan, Turkmenistan, Ukraine and Uzbekistan. (Azerbaijan has since withdrawn.)

The pact was signed at a meeting of the republic's presidents in Alma-Ata, the capital of Kazakhstan. Among the key points of the agreement:

- The CIS was not a state but an alliance of fully independent states. CIS policy would be arrived at through coordinating bodies such as a council of heads of state (made up of state presidents) and a council of heads of government (made up of states premiers).
- The individual states would assume ownership of the former Soviet government civilian facilities on their soil.
- The CIS would honor the former Soviet Union's arms control treaties and commitments. Marshal Yevgeny Shaposhnikov, the Soviet defense minister, would retain temporary command of all Soviet military forces pending agreement on a new CIS military structure. (According to further agreements reached on December 30, strategic weapons would be under the effective control of Russia's Yeltsin, who on December 25 took possession of the Soviet nuclear-war codes from Gorbachev. In the case of war, however, the leaders of all four CIS nuclear states—Russia, Ukraine, Belarus and Kazakhstan—had to agree on the use of the weapons, while the rest of CIS states would have to be consulted on the matter.)
- Russia, Ukraine and Belarus would keep their memberships in the United Nations General Assembly, while Russia would take over the Soviet seat on the Security Council. The other eight CIS states would seek their own

UN memberships. (The eight states were admitted to the UN in March 1992.)

The official end of the U.S.S.R. came on December 25, when Gorbachev announced his resignation in a nationally televised speech. A half-hour later, the red hammer-and-sickle Soviet flag atop the Kremlin was replaced with the white, red and blue flag of prerevolutionary Russia.

The long-term prospects for the commonwealth were uncertain. On the positive side was the obvious need for the various states to retain cordial economic and trade relations. On the negative side was the ethnically based bloodshed in the southern republics that had began under Gorbachev and showed no signs of abating (the worst cases at the end of 1991 were a secessionist movement in Moldova and the ongoing war between Armenia and Azerbaijan), and the mounting rivalry between Russia and Ukraine over such issues as the disposal of tactical nuclear arms and ownership of the Black Sea naval fleet. The disposition of the former Soviet Union's conventional armed forces remained a thorny issue at the several CIS summits held in the first half of 1992.

Communist Control Act   (1954)   The Communist Control Act of 1954 outlawed the Communist Party in the United States and made its members subject to the provisions and penalties of the INTERNAL SECURITY ACT of 1950. It was followed by the Espionage and Sabotage Act, which authorized the death penalty for peacetime espionae and sabotage.

Original supporters of the bill, including Senator HUBERT HUMPHREY, wanted to make membership in the Communist Party a punishable felony. But President Dwight EISENHOWER and FBI director J. EDGAR HOOVER argued that this would hinder rather than help the federal government's fight against communism by driving the party completely underground.

Faced with this opposition, the House of Representatives passed a watered-down version of the bill that outlawed the Communist Party but provided no penalties for membership. The Senate, however, rejected the House substitute and passed a bill that made membership punishable by a $10,000 fine and five years' imprisonment (virtually identical with the previous version). The bill was then sent to a joint committee, where the House members persuaded the committee members from the Senate to drop the penalties.

They argued that if Communist Party membership were made a felony then the Fifth Amendment would bar the government from compelling communists to register under the Internal Security Act, would drive the party underground, and would thus make it more difficult to keep members under surveillance and would turn communists into martyrs. The watered-down version of the bill was finally signed into law by Eisenhower on August 24. He signed the Espionage and Sabotage Act on September 3, 1954.

For Further Information:
Brown, Ralph S., Jr. *Loyalty and Security: Employment Tests in the U.S.* New Haven, Conn., 1958.

Caughey, John W. *In Clear and Present Danger: The Crucial State of Our Freedoms.* Chicago, 1958.

Conference on Security and Cooperation in Europe (CSCE)

The Conference on Security and Cooperation in Europe (CSCE) was one of the pillars of the détente process. The final agreement, signed in Helsinki in August 1975, does not have the force of a treaty, but it implicitly recognized the boundaries of postwar Europe while at the same time establishing a mechanism for reducing political and military tensions and improving human rights. It eventually led to a second CSCE summit in Paris in November 1990 that formally marked the end of the Cold War.

The initiative for the CSCE conference came from the Soviet Union in 1971, and President RICHARD NIXON formally agreed to a security conference during his trip to Moscow in May 1972. Preparatory talks started in Helsinki on November 22, 1972, and full negotiations started the following year in Geneva.

The final document was signed in Helsinki on August 1, 1975, at a summit conference attended by the leaders of 33 European nations, the United States and Canada. The meeting was the largest summit conference in European history. The document became known as the HELSINKI ACCORDS. Its main points were as follows.

1. The participating states pledged to "broaden, deepen and make continuing and lasting the process of détente."
2. The signatories agreed that they had "sovereign equality" and the right to "freedom and political independence" and "freely to choose and develop" their systems.
3. Although "frontiers [could] be changed by peaceful means and by agreement," all of the signatories' frontiers were "inviolable."
4. "The threat or use of force" was renounced as a means of settling disputes and the participants pledged to "refrain from direct or indirect assistance to terrorist or to subversive activities" aimed at overthrowing a signatory state.
5. The signatories pledged to respect "fundamental freedoms, including the freedom of thought, conscience, religion or belief."
6. The signatories pledged to resolve disputes through peaceful mediation.
7. The European states promised to give 21 days' notice of military maneuvers involving more than 25,000 troops with the purpose of building confidence and avoiding the possibility of accidental attack.
8. The signatories promised to work toward facilitating the increase of trade among them.
9. The signatories pledged to make it easier for families separated by the division of Europe to be reunited and for citizens of different countries to marry one another and travel to other countries.
10. The participating states agreed to reduce tension in the Mediterranean and to improve relations with non-European Mediterranean states.
11. The signatories agreed to encourage the freer flow of information, including newspapers, magazines and educational and cultural exchanges.
12. The participating states promised to reduce visa and travel restrictions for foreign journalists and not to expel foreign journalists without providing a reason and an opportunity for appeal.

British prime minister HAROLD WILSON praised the Helsinki Accords, saying that while they could not "in themselves, diminish the tension and insecurity" of postwar Europe, they did represent "a moral commitment, to be ignored at our mutual peril, and the start of a new chapter in the history of Europe."

Soviet leader LEONID BREZHNEV said the accords represented "a victory for reason." He went on to stress that the major principle of the agreement was that "No one should try to dictate to other peoples, on the basis of foreign policy considerations of one kind or another, the manner in which they ought to manage their internal affairs."

Brezhnev's insistence that he had won a major victory on this point led American conservatives to attack the Helsinki Accords savagely. RONALD REAGAN, then a potential presidential candidate, said, "All Americans should be against it." Senator HENRY JACKSON said that the accords represented "a sign of the West's retreat" from "a crucial point of principle," by implicitly recognizing Soviet dominance of Eastern Europe and the absorption of the Baltic States of Estonia, Latvia and Lithuania. President GERALD FORD sought to defuse this criticism by stressing that "our official policy of non-recognition is not affected by this conference. We are not committing ourselves to anything beyond what we are already committed to by our own legal and moral standards." He also stressed that the Helsinki Accords did not comprise any legal commitments.

Three follow-up CSCE conferences were held in Belgrade, Madrid and Vienna. At each conference, all of which were attended by all 35 signatory nations, the West accused the Eastern Bloc countries of breaking the accords' pledges on human rights, while those countries in turn rejected the criticism on the grounds that it constituted interference in their domestic affairs. The conference did, however, increase the flow of information and trade and helped to reduce military tensions.

The CSCE remained a valuable forum for discussion in the years leading up to the end of the Cold War. That event officially arrived on November 10–21, 1990, in Paris, when the CSCE held its second full summit. The number of CSCE full members—which included all European nations except Albania (which had observer status), plus the U.S. and Canada—had been reduced to 34 from 35 with the reunification of Germany the previous month. The summit brought together 11 presidents (including GEORGE BUSH of the U.S. and MIKHAIL GORBACHEV of the U.S.S.R.), 22 prime ministers and many foreign ministers and other senior officials.

The highlights of the summit were the signing of a sweeping arms reduction treaty that had grown out of the Conventional Forces in Europe (CFE) negotiations, and a document called the Charter of Paris for a new Europe. The charter proclaimed an end to "the era of confrontation and division in Europe," and vowed "a new era of democracy, peace and unity." It pledged a "steadfast commitment to democracy based on human rights and fundamental freedoms; prosperity through economic liberty and social justice; and equal security for all our countries." To implement those goals, the document called for the creation of a secretariat in Prague, a conflict-resolution center in Vienna and an elections-resource center in Warsaw. CSCE foreign ministers were to meet at least once a year.

The CSCE foreign ministers met twice in 1991. In June, meeting in Berlin, they discussed crisis-intervention procedures and admitted Albania as a full member. In September, gathering in Moscow, the ministers discussed human rights issues and voted to admit three new members—the newly independent Baltic states of Estonia, Latvia and Lithuania—bringing the CSCE's total to 38.

For Further Information:
Bell, Coral. *The Diplomacy of Détente: The Kissinger Era.* New York, 1977.

Congolese Civil War   The Congolese Civil War (1960–63) was the first East–West clash in Africa and helped to set the pattern for other such African conflicts.

The mineral-rich Congo had been administered by the Belgian government since 1905. Among the European colonial powers in Africa, the Belgians had the worst record for preparing the indigenous Africans for eventual self-rule. This, in addition to the Belgian policy of exploiting tribal differences in order to divide and rule, resulted in a higly unstable situation when the Congo eventually achieved independence.

The Belgian government at first resisted moves toward independence, but after a series of violent attacks, the Belgians decided to withdraw quickly, leaving an unprepared and divided African community to run the country. Belgian rule officially ended on June 30, 1960. The following day PATRICE LUMUMBA, whose Congolese National Movement had won an overwhelming majority in hastily arranged elections, took office as prime minister.

During the previous 12 months, Lumumba had emerged as the only Congolese leader with widespread national appeal. But his political leanings were toward the left of the political spectrum, leaving him isolated from Belgian business interests and from the United States. The situation was further exacerbated by the election of a pro-Western president of the Congo, Joseph Kasavubu, and by the Belgian mining industry's support for a secessionist movement in the province of Katanga, whose mineral resources provided half of the Congo's tax revenues.

Almost as soon as Lumumba took power as prime minister, the army mutinied, and Katanga Province, led by Moise Tshombe, formally seceded from the rest of the country. The result was another outbreak of violence, and the Belgian government ordered paratroopers into the country to protect the 90,000 whites still there. Lumumba interpreted this move as a reassertion of colonial rule; he turned to the United Nations to stop Katangan secession and to the Soviet Union for aid against the Belgians. Soviet Premier NIKITA KHRUSHCHEV saw the request as an opportunity to establish a political toehold among the emergent countries of Africa. On July 15, he cabled Lumumba: "If the Western powers continue their criminal actions against the Congo the USSR will not shrink from resolute measures to curb the aggression." Soon afterward he sent Soviet military equipment and several hundred "technicians" to the Congo.

The UN Security Council created a peacekeeping force and authorized it in July 1960. But the UN forces were limited to maintenance of the status quo. This was not enough for Lumumba, who demanded the reunification of the country under his authority and turned toward the Soviet Union for help.

Lumumba's links with the Soviet Union attracted American interest. The CENTRAL INTELLIGENCE AGENCY (CIA) hatched several plots to assassinate him, none of which was successful. Because of its concerns over the Soviet Union and Lumumba, the United States initially supported Katangan leader Tshombe as the major source of opposition to Lumumba. But in September 1960 President Kasavubu dismissed Lumumba from the premiership, closed the Soviet and Czech embassies and placed a greater reliance on the UN peacekeeping force, which had been dispatched to the country in July.

At this stage, Khrushchev, who had initially supported the UN force, turned against it. In a speech before the UN General Assembly on September 24, 1960, Khrushchev accused Secretary General DAG HAMMARSKJOLD of "disorganizing the life of the state and paralyzing the legitimate government." He called on the General Assembly to "give a rebuff to the colonialists and their stooges and call Mr. Hammarskjold to order so that he should not abuse his position." In October, the Soviet Union announced that it would not contribute to the cost of the UN peacekeeping operations in the Congo.

These initial events coincided with a change of government in the United States. The new administration of President JOHN F. KENNEDY, inaugurated in January 1961, felt that Western interests would best be served by a united Congo, and that if the UN were unable to do the job, then the United States should be prepared to intervene directly in order to prevent the Soviet Union from establishing a political base in the center of Africa.

Soviet influence in the Congo was dealt a serious blow by the murder of Lumumba. Ousted from office and imprisoned in November 1960, he had remained a popular and powerful figure, and the government had decided to hand him over to Katangan rebels, who killed him in January 1961.

In the summer of that year, a coalition government took office under Prime Minister Cyrille Adoula. This coalition was able to unite most of the Congolese factions behind the UN forces, which took over key installations in Elisabethville and extended their operations against Tshombe's forces. But Tshombe still had substantial support in Western conservative circles, which worked to undermine American support for the United Nations and the central government in the Congo. Tshombe's conservative connections also lost him the support of the rest of Africa and the support of Kennedy, who placed a strong emphasis on forging close relations with the first generation of African leaders.

In January 1962, after American political intervention, Tshombe signed the Kitona Agreement, which accepted the authority of the central government. But it soon became clear that the Katangan leader was only playing for time in the hope that Britain and Belgium, which supported him, would be able to effect a change in Kennedy's policy. On December 24, 1962, Tshombe launched a fresh attack against the UN forces. Both the United States and the Soviet Union prepared for military intervention, but without warning Tshombe's attack collapsed after only a week. In June 1963 Tshombe fled the country, but the following year returned, renounced the cause of secessionism and became prime minister. He was overthrown in a CIA-backed coup a year later by army chief of staff Joseph-Désiré Mobutu.

Mobutu, who later changed his name to Mobutu Sese Seko and changed the Congo's name to Zaire, remained in power for the next two decades. He amassed a huge personal fortune through his notorious corruption, and remained a willing tool of CIA covert operations in Africa, particularly against neighboring Angola.

For Further Information:
Abi-Saab, Georges. *The United Nations Operation in the Congo, 1860–1964.* New York, 1978.
Davidson, Basil. *Africa in Modern History: The Search for a New Society.* New York, 1978.
Dayal, Rajeshwar. *Mission for Hammarskjold: The Congo Crisis.* Princeton, 1976.
Kalb, Madeleine G. *The Congo Cables: The Cold War in Africa—From Eisenhower to Kennedy.* New York, 1982.
Kanza, Thomas R. *The Rise and Fall of Patrice Lumumba: Conflict in the Congo.* Boston, 1979.
Weissman, Stephen. *American Policy in the Congo, 1960–1964.* Ithaca, N.Y., 1974.

Containment Containment was the official United States policy toward the Soviet Union from 1947 to the end of the Cold War. In essence, it meant that the United States worked to contain the Soviet Union's sphere of influence to what it had been at the end of World War II.

The intellectual basis for containment was developed by GEORGE F. KENNAN. He first set out the policy in a special State Department report that has since become known as the "Long Telegram." He publicly elaborated on his report in an anony-mous article in the July 1947 issue of *Foreign Affairs*, in which he foresaw that the Soviet Union would probe for weak links in the Western Alliance. To meet this threat Kennan recommended "a long-term patient but firm and vigilant containment of Russian expansive tendencies through . . . the adroit and vigilant application of counterforce at a series of constantly shifting geographical and political points, corresponding to the shifts and maneuvers of Soviet policies."

Kennan hoped that when the Soviet Union realized that the West was determined to repel aggression, tensions would eventually ease. When this happened the Soviet leaders would lose their justification for a police state and would liberalize their regime.

For many conservative Republicans, the containment policy was too moderate. They advocated a "roll-back" policy to push the Soviets out of Eastern Europe, North Korea and elsewhere and eventually topple the communist government in Russia. However, when the Republicans came to power in 1952, they continued the containment policy with the construction of an elaborate series of alliances.

For Further Information
Horowitz, David, ed. *Containment and Revolution.* Boston, 1967.
Kennan, George F. *On Dealing with the Communist World.* New York, 1963.
Mr. X [George F. Kennan]. "The Sources of Soviet Conduct." *Foreign Affairs* (July 1947).

Conventional War A conventional war is a war that does not involve nuclear weapons.

Most defense analysts believed that any East–West conflict would start off as a conventional war, probably launched by the Soviet Union because of its overwhelming advantage in conventional weapons. It was believed highly likely that any such conventional war would quickly escalate into a nuclear conflict.

Cooper, Senator John Sherman (August 23, 1901–February 21, 1991) John Cooper was a liberal Republican who served as ambassador to Nepal and India before being elected to a full term in the U.S. Senate, where he took a leading role in opposing the VIETNAM WAR and the deployment of the U.S. antiballistic missile system.

Cooper graduated from Yale Law School in 1926 and soon afterward entered politics in his native state of Kentucky. He was elected to the state legislature in 1928, where he served one term before becoming a county judge. During World War II, Cooper served with the U.S. Army, and immediately afterward he helped to reorganize the Bavarian judicial system.

In 1946 Cooper won a special election to fill a Senate vacancy. He also won special Senate elections in 1952 and 1956, but on each occasion he failed to win reelection at the general elections. In 1950 he became a consultant to Secretary of State DEAN ACHESON and in 1955 was appointed ambassador to India and Nepal.

Throughout the 1950s, Cooper was a prominent spokesman on international affairs and a vehement opponent of the anti-communist hysteria that was sweeping the country. He was among the first Republicans to endorse the censure of Senator JOSEPH MCCARTHY and opposed a proposal that the United States blockade the Chinese coast and press for a UN resolution condemning the Soviet Union as "a supporter of aggression in the Far East." He also opposed President DWIGHT EISENHOWER's decision to send American troops into Lebanon.

In 1960 Cooper won his first full term to the Senate by a wide margin. Firmly established in the Senate, he continued his role as a liberal Republican by voting against his party on more than a third of the roll call votes. His record made him unpopular with conservative Republicans, but President JOHN F. KENNEDY—a Democrat—praised him as an "outstanding Republican."

Cooper was an early opponent of the Vietnam War. In January 1966 he criticized the renewed bombing of North Vietnam. In August 1967 he called on the United States to make the first move toward negotiations by unconditionally ending the bombing of North Vietnam and supported a proposal to bring the issue before the United Nations. In 1969 Cooper successfully introduced an amendment to a procurement bill barring the president from using funds for U.S. combat support in Laos and Thailand. In May 1970, Cooper and Senator Frank Church joined forces to introduce another amendment to an appropriations bill barring the president from spending any funds without congressional approval after July 1 for American troops fighting in CAMBODIA, for support of advisers or troops from other countries aiding Cambodia or for air combat operations. The measure also barred the introduction of U.S. ground troops into Thailand and Laos and forbade the spending of funds for "free world forces" used to provide military support for the Laotian or Cambodian governments.

The Senate deleted the Cooper–Church Amendment from its bill, but a modified version of the amendment, restricting the powers of the president in the Vietnam War, was passed in December 1970. In 1971 Cooper charged that President RICHARD NIXON violated this amendment by ferrying South Vietnamese troops into battle in Cambodia and providing air cover for them.

Cooper's opposition to the Safeguard antiballistic missile system was based on a fear that it would provoke an East–West arms race. He supported Senator MIKE MANSFIELD's call for a moratorium on both sides on weapons development projects.

Cooper retired from the Senate in 1973 and was appointed U.S. ambassador to East Germany. He remained in Berlin until 1976, when he retired to Kentucky.

For Further Information:
Berman, W.C. *William Fulbright and The Vietnam War*. Ohio, 1988.
Dougan, C.A. *A Nation Divided*. Boston, 1984.

U.S. Senate Committee on Foreign Relations. *The Vietnam Hearings, 1966*. New York, 1966.

Coordinating Committee for Multilateral Strategic Export Controls (COCOM)   COCOM, founded in 1953, is a group of representatives from 16 nations that meets in Paris to coordinate controls on the export of goods and technology of military potential to what were the Eastern Bloc countries. The committee members include Australia, Japan, and all of the NATO countries except Iceland.

COCOM is a nontreaty organization, but has close links with NATO. The COCOM secretariat is based in Paris, and meetings take place throughout the year to review the list of controlled items and COCOM's procedures. Less frequent meetings take place at ministerial or senior officials level.

The restricted goods and technology are in three basic areas: the industrial or "dual use" category, which includes equipment that can be used for civilian and military purposes, such as computers; the munitions category, which covers explicit conventional weapons equipment; and the atomic energy category, which covers nuclear-related items.

In the 1980s differences arose between COCOM members over what should be included on the "dual use" list. A number of countries, West Germany and Japan in particular, wanted to export more computer equipment to the Eastern bloc countries. These differences became more pronounced with the introduction of reforms in the Soviet Union. With the fading of the Cold War, however, COCOM agreed in 1991 to loosen restrictions on the sale of militarily useful high technology items to the Soviet Union and Eastern Europe.

Council for Mutual Economic Assistance (CMEA or COMECON)   The Council for Mutual and Economic Cooperation was formed in 1949 to increase economic cooperation among the Soviet Bloc countries. It was meant as a Soviet version of the MARSHALL PLAN, but it was unable to compete with the American program because of the Soviet Union's inability to deliver large amounts of financial aid. It disbanded in 1991.

In the immediate aftermath of the West Europeans' acceptance of the Marshall Plan, the Soviet Union called a meeting of Eastern Bloc foreign ministers in 1947 and formed the Communist Information Bureau (COMINFORM), which acted as a political counter to the Marshall Plan. But the Soviet Bloc remained without an economic framework for another 18 months, when COMECON was formed.

The formation of COMECON was announced on January 25, 1949. Initially it was comprised of seven countries: the Soviet Union, East Germany, Poland, Czechoslovakia, Hungary, Romania and Bulgaria. Membership was later extended to include Cuba, Mongolia and Vietnam.

The initial Soviet statement said that the council would promote "exchange of experience in the economic field, the rendering of technical assistance to each other and the rendering of mutual assistance in regard to raw materials, foodstuffs, machinery, equipment, etc." There was no indication that the Soviet Union would finance the economic recovery of Eastern Europe in the way that the Marshall Plan was aiding Western Europe.

The statement also said that the council would admit "other countries of Europe that share the principles of the Council and wish to participate in broad economic cooperation with" the original members. The statement implied that members of the Marshall Plan would have to reject the U.S. plan to join COMECON. The French Communist Party immediately demanded that France do so.

A later charter said that the council "aims to unite and coordinate the efforts of the member countries in order to improve the development of socialist economic integration; to achieve more rapid economic and technical progress in these countries, and particularly a higher level of industrialization in countries where this is lacking; to achieve a steady growth of labor productivity; to work gradually towards a balanced level of development in the different regions, and a steady increase in standards of living in the member states."

The creation of COMECON encountered substantial opposition from the governments of Soviet-occupied countries, which regarded the organization as an agency for developing the Soviet Union at the expense of the satellite countries. But the Soviet Union's iron grip on Eastern Europe ensured that Moscow's will prevailed.

Between 1949 and 1951, trade between COMECON members was planned by yearly agreements. After 1951, the agreements were extended on longer terms. In 1956 the council established the Standing Commission for Foreign Trade, which ensured that most of the members' foreign trade was with each other and conducted through state monopolies.

In 1971 a major step was taken toward further economic integration when COMECON adopted the "Comprehensive Program for Further Extension and Improvement of Cooperation and the Development of Socialist Economic Integration among Comecon Countries." Over a 10-year period this led to a 300% increase in trade among COMECON members.

In the 1980s the original emphasis on mutual trade shifted toward joint production and standardization of equipment. To facilitate this, some 25 standing commissions were created, ranging from the Standing Commission on Iron and Steel to standing committees on statistics and monetary and financial relations. The national five-year economic plans of member states were coordinated by the COMECON secretariat.

The Soviet Union's grip on COMECON started to loosen as the East European economies strengthened in the 1970s. In 1983 and 1984 there were interstate disagreements over the pricing of food and petroleum, with the satellite countries complaining that they were paying too much for Soviet oil exports and receiving too little for their food exports. The Soviet Union agreed to a large increase in food imports from its COMECON partners (the first in 10 years) but offset this by a further increase in oil prices.

A number of countries were not official members of COMECON but sent observers to council meetings and established strong trading links. These countries included Afghanistan, Angola, Ethiopia, Laos, Mozambique, South Yemen and Yugoslavia.

With the end of the Cold War, COMECON members officially agreed to disband after a June 28, 1991, meeting in Budapest.

For Further Information:
Grzybowski, Kazimierz. *The Socialist Commonwealth of Nations.* New Haven, Conn., 1964.
Reshetar, *The Soviet Polity.* New York, 1971.
Sobel, Vladimir. "COMECON," in *The Soviet Union and Eastern Europe,* ed. George Schopflin. New York, 1986.

Council of Europe   The Council of Europe was the first postwar West European attempt to create a "United States of Europe." Because of early nationalist aspirations, the council failed to achieve its promise, but it became one of the organizational building blocks that led to the creation of the EUROPEAN ECONOMIC COMMUNITY.

The Council of Europe grew out of the desire for European unity following the BRUSSELS TREATY of 1948 among Britain, France, Belgium, Holland and Luxembourg. The Low Countries, which had the most to gain from European unity, began to press for an expansion of European cooperation beyond the military terms of the Brussels Treaty to the wider political and economic arena and proposed a consultative assembly.

Although British foreign secretary ERNEST BEVIN was the main architect of the Brussels Treaty, he had doubts about the concept of a United States of Europe. As the center of an empire, Britain still had to consider its commitments and ties outside of Europe. He at first proposed the creation of a council of ministers but eventually agreed to a consultative assembly, which was established on May 5, 1949.

The stated aim of the council, whose assembly members are either elected or appointed by their national parliaments, is to achieve "greater unity between its members, facilitate their economic and social progress and to uphold the principles of parliamentary democracy." The 170 members of the assembly meet once a year for a month. They do not represent their national governments, but rather represent their nations' public opinion as a whole. Some of the offshoot organizations include the European Commission on Human Rights and the European Court of Human Rights.

The original members of the Council of Europe were Britain, Belgium, Denmark, Ireland, France, Italy, Luxembourg, Holland and Norway. They were later joined by Austria, Cyprus, West Germany, Greece, Iceland, Liechtenstein, Malta, Portugal, Spain, Sweden, Switzerland and Turkey.

Hungary joined the council in 1990, followed by Czechoslovakia and Poland in 1991.

Council of Foreign Ministers   The Council of Foreign Ministers was established on July 17, 1945, at the POTSDAM CONFERENCE at the end of World War II. The council was comprised of the foreign ministers of the United States, Britain, France and China, and its purpose was to prepare the way for a full peace conference at which a formal peace treaty would be signed with Germany.

Repeated meetings of the council ended in failure as relations between the Soviet Union and the other Allied powers deteriorated. A formal peace treaty was not signed until 1990, under very different circumstances.

Counting Rules   The counting rules were designed to allow the United States to verify Soviet compliance with the SALT I and SALT II agreements without on-site inspections.

Under these rules any Soviet missile that had been tested with MULTIPLE INDEPENDENTLY TARGETED REENTRY VEHICLES (MIRVs) would be counted as a MIRVed missile. Also, any launching system that had launched a MIRVed missile would be counted as a MIRV launcher.

Cuba   Cuba's proximity to the United States—only 90 miles from the Florida Keys—and its hard-line pro-Moscow communist government led successive American administrations to fear the island both as a base for subversive activities throughout the Western Hemisphere and as a platform for a Soviet attack on the United States. These fears led to the BAY OF PIGS INVASION, the CUBAN MISSILE CRISIS and American efforts to isolate the government and assassinate its leader, FIDEL CASTRO.

America's close involvement with Cuba extends back to the mid-19th century, when several attempts were hatched by Southern American adventurers to seize the island. After the U.S. Civil War, the federal government offered to buy Cuba from Spain. By the end of the 19th century, a total U.S. investment of $50 million and an annual trade of $100 million meant that the Cuban economy was virtually controlled by the United States.

This investment was threatened by the Cuban War of Independence, which broke out in 1895. In 1898, the U.S. intervened on the side of the rebel forces. When the war ended and independence was declared in 1899, American troops remained on the island, and, in the imperialist atmosphere of the times, there were numerous calls to annex Cuba. Over the next half-century, the United States remained the dominant power in Cuba, at times controlling the island's defense and foreign affairs and also intervening to ensure friendly governments.

In September 1933 the United States supported a coup led by FULGENCIO BATISTA. Between 1933 and 1959 Batista controlled Cuba, either through puppets or by having himself elected to the presidency in rigged ballots. Batista's regime became increasingly corrupt and oppressive. He forged close links with the American Mafia, and the country became noted for its brothels, drugs and gambling, out of which the dictator took a substantial cut. To stifle dissent, Batista maintained strict press censorship and imprisoned, exiled or assassinated his political opponents.

Fidel Castro was born into a middle class family and graduated with a law degree from the University of Havana. He became involved in politics while still at the university and joined the left-wing, but not Marxist, Cuban People's Party. In 1952, Castro was selected as a People's Party candidate for a seat in the house of representatives, but before elections could be held, Batista overthrew the government and cancelled the poll.

A year later, Castro started organizing a revolution. In July 1953, he was arrested after leading a raid on a military barracks in Santiago. Castro conducted his own defense at the subsequent trial and used the event to stage a political attack on the Batista regime. His calls for free elections, land reform, profit-sharing and industrialization won a wide hearing and became the main pillars of his movement.

Castro was released from prison in 1955 and, along with his brother Raul, went to Mexico to form the 26th of July Movement (after the date of his attack on the military barracks). On December 26, 1956, Fidel and Raul returned by boat to Cuba with a small group of guerrillas. They suffered heavy losses on their arrival, but Castro, Raul and a few other men escaped and managed to establish a base in the Sierra Maestra jungles from which they conducted a series of intermittent forays against government forces. Castro's populist politics struck a chord with many Cubans, and his guerrilla band grew in numbers and support.

Many people in the United States supported Castro's revolutionaries. His policies were favorably compared in the American press to the corrupt right-wing dictatorship of Batista. Most American officials subscribed to the view that Castro was a revolutionary but not a communist. Castro himself did not announce his formal conversion to Marxism-Leninism until 1961. But there were a few who believed that, even in his earliest days, Castro was heavily dependent on the Soviet Union. The EISENHOWER administration was inclined, therefore, toward Batista but was forced into an official policy of nonintervention by the popular support for Castro.

In December 1958, Castro launched a major attack on Santa Clara, the capital of Las Villas Province. Shortly after the attack, the demoralized Batista forces defending the city surrendered and then defected to Castro's army. With this major moral and military victory behind him, Castro quickly moved against Havana, and on December 31 he marched into the city while Batista fled into exile in the Dominican Republic.

In the immediate aftermath of the collapse of the Batista government, Castro appeared to be inclined toward a pluralistic democratic government. He visited the United States in April 1959, where he was greeted by enthusiastic crowds. But during this visit, Castro also met with Vice President RICHARD NIXON, who reported that the new Cuban leader was "either incredibly naive about Communism or under Communist discipline."

In May 1959, against the objections of the United States, Castro nationalized the sugar cane industry, which had been dominated by an American corporation, the United Fruit Company. He also started the mass trials and executions of political opponents. In August he accused the United States of participating in a plot to overthrow him. In September 1959, Castro signed trade agreements with the Soviet Union, followed by agreements with the rest of Eastern Europe and China. In 1960 he closed down opposition newspapers, seized the American-owned sugar refinery, a meat-packing plant, cement and glass factories and other American assets. The Eisenhower administration retaliated by ending military aid in February 1960 and, in July 1960, suspending a law requiring that the United States buy about half of Cuba's annual sugar crop at premium prices. In December 1960, Castro announced his support for Soviet foreign policy and communist philosophies and his implacable opposition to the United States. One of the last official diplomatic acts of the Eisenhower administration was the severing of U.S.–Cuban diplomatic relations.

As early as March 17, 1960, President Dwight Eisenhower ordered the CENTRAL INTELLIGENCE AGENCY to start training Cuban exiles "against a possible future date when they might return to their homeland." The original plan was that a group of guerrillas would land at an isolated spot on the Cuban shore and establish a provisional government on Cuban soil. At the same time, dissidents within Cuba would launch a campaign of sabotage against power stations and other vulnerable targets. It was believed that the combination of landings and sabotage attacks would lead to a general uprising and the collapse of Castro.

The plan was inherited by President JOHN F. KENNEDY, whose initial indecisiveness allowed the scheme to develop its own uncontrolled momentum. By April 1961, the BAY OF PIGS invasion went ahead, but without either the planning or American support required for success. The invaders encountered stronger than expected opposition from the Cuban military and the whole operation collapsed within days. The Bay of Pigs was a major boost for Castro. He was able to point to a tangible threat from the United States, which had the effect of rallying the Cuban people behind him and against the "Yanqui Imperialists." The Bay of Pigs also encouraged Castro to seek military ties with the Soviet Union to protect his government against another attack.

In July 1962, Foreign Minister Raul Castro and Finance Minister CHE GUEVARA traveled to Moscow to negotiate a defense treaty with the Soviet Union. In October 1962, American U-2 aerial reconnaissance flights over Cuba revealed that the Soviet Union was building launching pads for medium-range and intermediate-range ballistic missiles. The intelligence led to the CUBAN MISSILE CRISIS. Kennedy called up American reserves for a possible invasion of the island and imposed a naval blockade. The world teetered at the brink of World War III until Soviet leader Nikita KHRUSHCHEV agreed to withdraw the missiles and dismantle the launching pads in return for an America pledge not to invade Cuba.

American attempts to overthrow Castro thereafter shifted from invasion to CIA-directed covert attempts to assassinate or overthrow the Cuban leader. At least eight attempts before and after the Cuban Missile Crisis were later revealed by the Senate's Church Committee in 1975; they involved links with the Mafia and the use of poisoned cigars, poisoned pills, a poison pen and a poison-impregnated skin diving suit. Castro himself claimed that at least 24 CIA-organized attempts had been made on his life.

U.S. administrations also sought to isolate Castro's government within the Western Hemisphere. Cuba was expelled from the ORGANIZATION OF AMERICAN STATES, and most Latin American states severed diplomatic relations with Havana. Washington let it be known that having friendly relations with Castro was considered an unfriendly act toward the United States. It was not until 1975 that the OAS allowed its members to normalize relations with Cuba. Castro, for his part, continued to strengthen ties with the Soviet Union and in the 1960s and early 1970s provided assistance to revolutionary movements in South America, in particular Bolivia, Venezuela and Guatemala.

At home, Castro introduced a Soviet-style political structure. The Cuban Communist Party is the only legal political party, press and television are heavily censored and most businesses are owned by the state. But extensive Soviet aid

Cuban revolutionary leader Fidel Castro (right) with ally Leonid Brezhnev of the Soviet Union. Photo courtesy of Novosti Press Agency.

also enabled Castro to redistribute wealth, introduce a free public health system, expand educational opportunities and provide full employment. These improvements in the everyday life of Cubans, and Castro's undoubted charismatic quality, have ensured his continued leadership of Cuba.

A major American irritant to Cuba is the American military base at GUANTANAMO BAY. The strategically placed base was captured by U.S. Marines during the Spanish–American War, and the American presence was legalized by a treaty in 1903 that gave the United States "complete jurisdiction and control over the area." The base, with approximately 3,000 men, provides the United States with a unique foothold on the communist-governed island. The U.S. Navy's lease on the base expires at the end of the century.

In September 1960, Castro threatened to seize the base but was deterred by a counterthreat from Eisenhower to take "whatever steps are necessary" to protect it. Successive administrations, however, have been careful not to jeopardize the base by using it for either a conventional or subversive attack on Cuba. It was not, for instance, included in the plans for the Bay of Pigs operation. Neither have the base facilities been involved in any of the various CIA plots to assassinate Castro. Guantanamo was, however, included in advanced contingency plans for a U.S. attack on Cuba during the Cuban Missile Crisis and it also serves as a listening post for radio communications to and from Cuba.

In the late 1970s, Castro became militarily involved in supporting revolutionary movements in Africa. He sent 40,000 Cuban troops to Angola to support the pro-Soviet MPLA government in its struggle against the South African-backed UNITA forces. He also sent troops in as advisers to aid the pro-Soviet Ethiopian government when that country was invaded by Somalia. In the 1980s Castro helped to supply the Sandinista government in Nicaragua.

A large proportion of these costs was borne either directly or indirectly by the Soviet Union, which used Castro's revolutionary zeal to further the cause of international communism. But following the accession to power of Soviet leader MIKHAIL GORBACHEV, Soviet support began to drop off as Gorbachev diverted funds to the Soviet Union's chronic domestic economic problems. This also forced Castro to reduce his defense expenditures. In 1988 he agreed to the withdrawal of Cuban troops from Angola and reduced the Cuban presence in the Horn of Africa.

But the domestic cost of Castro's revolutionary activities was adversely affecting the Cuban people, and in 1989 there were signs of discontent with his government. In April 1989, a group of human rights activists were arrested for planning to hold a demonstration outside the Soviet Embassy in Havana during a visit by Gorbachev. In July 1989 there was a widespread purge of the military, after several high-ranking officers were found guilty of drug smuggling and either executed or sentenced to long prison terms. Some analysts believe that the drug issue was a facade covering up a power struggle inside Cuba.

As the economy worsened in 1990–91, the government was forced to institute increased food and gasoline rationing. Cubans were encouraged to ride bicycles; more bicycles were imported, and plans were made to increase Cuba's own production. Castro continued publicly to fault the retreat from socialism in Eastern Europe and the Soviet Union, and vowed that the Cuban people would endure any sacrifices before they would surrender to U.S.-led capitalist forces.

In September 1991, Gorbachev, after talks with visiting U.S. secretary of state JAMES BAKER, announced that Moscow would soon begin negotiations with Cuba over a withdrawal of Soviet military forces from the island. He also said that Soviet-Cuban economic relations in the future would be based on "mutually beneficial trade," rather than the barter system currently in effect. (Under the chief arrangement of that system, the U.S.S.R. received overvalued Cuban sugar in exchange for Soviet oil, which amounted to a $2 billion annual Soviet subsidy to Castro.)

Cuba, complaining that it had not been consulted, said that Gorbachev's announcements "constituted inappropriate behavior both from the point of view of international norms and of the agreements which exist between the two countries."

For Further Information:

Benjamin, Jules R. *The United States and the Origins of the Cuban Revolution: An Empire of Liberty in an Age of National Liberation.* Princeton, N.J., 1990.

Brenner, P. *From Confrontation to Negotiation.* Boulder, Colo., 1988.

Cannon, Terence. *Revolutionary Cuba.* New York, 1981.

Chayes, Abram. *The Cuban Missile Crisis: International Crises and the Rule of Law.* New York, 1973.

Fall, Bernard. *Anatomy of a Crisis.* Garden City, N.Y., 1969.

Gonzalez, Edward. *Cuba Under Castro, the Limits of Charisma.* New York, 1974.

Harnecka, M. *Fidel Castro's Political Strategy.* New York, 1987.

Mezerik, A.G. *Cuba and the United States.* New York, 1963.

Schlesinger, Arthur. *A Thousand Days.* New York, 1965.

Sherman, P. *The Soviet Union and Cuba.* London, 1987.

Smith, W.S. *The Closest of Enemies.* New York, 1987.

Szulc, Tad. *Fidel: A Critical Portrait.* New York, 1986.

Welch, Richard E. *Response to Revolution: The United States and the Cuban Revolution, 1951–1961.* Chapel Hill, N.C., 1985.

Cuban Missile Crisis   The 1962 Cuban Missile Crisis brought the world to the brink of a U.S.–Soviet nuclear confrontation. It also marked a major turning point in U.S.–Soviet relations and led to an American pledge not to invade Cuba.

Following the 1961 American-led attempt to invade Cuba at the BAY OF PIGS, the government of FIDEL CASTRO sought closer military ties with the Soviet Union. In 1962, Finance Minister CHE GUEVARA and Foreign Minister Raul Castro went to Moscow to negotiate Soviet military aid.

The Soviets refused to sign a formal military alliance with Cuba, but they decided to install nuclear missiles in Cuba. Such missiles, argued Soviet planners, would have the dual effect of protecting Cuba from American attack and providing the Soviet Union with a strategic military base in the Western Hemisphere to counter similar such American bases in Turkey. In July 1962, American U-2 reconnaissance planes detected an increase in Soviet shipments to Cuba. On August 29 a U-2 flight spotted a Soviet defensive missile system. President JOHN F. KENNEDY regarded this as acceptable, but to be on the safe side he ordered 150,000 U.S. reserve troops to active duty and increased the number of U-2 flights over Cuba. Soviet leader NIKITA KHRUSHCHEV responded by promising that "armaments and military equipment sent to Cuba are designed exclusively for defensive purposes."

On September 6, Kennedy confirmed that the new Soviet arms shipments did not constitute a serious threat, but, in a clear message to the Soviet Union, he added that if at any time Cuba were to "become an offensive military base of significant capacity for the Soviet Union, then [the United States would] do whatever must be done to protect its own security and that of its allies."

The hurricane season delayed U-2 flights until October 11 to 14. These flights revealed that the Soviet Union had started building launching pads for offensive ballistic missiles at San Cristobal. The CIA at once informed national security adviser MCGEORGE BUNDY, who informed President Kennedy the following morning. Kennedy immediately formed an inner cabinet of advisers, which became known as the Executive Committee, or ExCom.

Intelligence reports revealed that Soviet ships carrying a cargo of ballistic missiles had recently left ports on the Black Sea bound for Cuba. They were expected to reach the Caribbean within 10 days. This left Kennedy just over a week to decide his course of action. The advice from ExCom ranged from invasion, to surgical air strikes against the missile bases, to acquiescence. In the interim, American forces were placed on full alert and 100,000 troops were moved to Florida.

For a time, Kennedy appeared to incline toward a "surgical" strike against the missile bases. But a Pentagon analysis revealed that this would leave the airports, where the Soviets had based nuclear-armed Ilyushin bombers, untouched. A limited strike thus appeared to leave the U.S. mainland open to the possibility of a nuclear retaliatory strike. The only certain military solution, argued defense planners, would be a full-scale assault on Cuba. But the State Department opposed this course because they believed Khrushchev would use an American attack on Cuba to justify a similar movement against West Berlin, which would in turn lead either to American humiliation or to World War III.

It was ROBERT MCNAMARA who proposed the course of action that was eventually taken—a naval blockade. As Arthur Schlesinger later wrote, "It avoided war, preserved flexibility and offered Khrushchev time to reconsider his actions."

Kennedy signed the quarantine order on October 23. The day before he gave a nationwide radio and television address in which he publicly revealed the existence of the Soviet bases in Cuba. "This urgent transformation of Cuba into an impor-

tant strategic base . . . constitutes an explicit threat to the peace and security of all the Americas," he declared.

Kennedy went on to claim that the Soviet action had upset the nuclear balance. "[This decision] is a deliberately provocative and unjustified change in the status quo which cannot be accepted by this country."

Kennedy made it clear that the American objective was the "withdrawal or elimination" of the missiles from Cuba and in pursuit of that objective ordered the following steps:

1. "A strict quarantine on all offensive military equipment under shipment to Cuba."
2. Increased surveillance of Cuba.
3. It became the declared policy of the nation "to regard any nuclear missile launched from Cuba against any nation in the Western Hemisphere as an attack by the Soviet Union on the United States, requiring a full retaliatory response upon the Soviet Union."
4. Reinforcement of the American base at GUANTANAMO and the placing of other forces on a "stand-by alert basis."
5. A call for an emergency meeting of the Organization of American States to invoke the RIO PACT.
6. A call for an emergency meeting of the United Nations Security Council.
7. A personal appeal to Khrushchev "to halt and eliminate this clandestine, reckless and provocative threat to world peace."

The Soviet Union quickly issued a statement in which it reaffirmed its claim that the missiles were of a defensive nature and warned that the naval blockade "is taking a step along the road of unleashing a thermonuclear world war." Castro, in a 90-minute television address, assailed the American blockade as "a violation against the sovereign rights of our country and all the peoples," and he placed Cuban defense forces on a war footing.

The United States quickly won the support of the OAS to invoke the Rio Treaty, which in 1948 had established a joint security pact for the defense of the Western Hemisphere against attack from outside. The UN Security Council was faced with the American draft resolution calling for "the immediate dismantling and withdrawal from Cuba of all missiles and other offensive weapons" and the sending to Cuba of a UN observer corps to ensure compliance. There was also a counter-resolution from Cuba that demanded that the U.S. withdraw its "illegal blockade" and a similar Soviet draft resolution.

Secretary General U THANT of the UN intervened at this stage to propose a cooling-off period during which the Soviet Union would suspend its arms shipments and the United States would lift its blockade. The proposal was welcomed by Khrushchev but rejected by Kennedy because it left the missiles already in Cuba untouched. Khrushchev's response to U Thant's proposal was the first sign of a Soviet retreat. It soon became known that the Soviet leader had ordered the cargo ships to slow down in order to give himself more time to consider the options. At the suggestion of the British ambassador, David Ormsby-Gore, Kennedy overrode the U.S. Navy's objections to moving the blockade closer to Cuba and thus gave the Soviet leader even more thinking time.

On October 24, Pentagon spokesmen reported that 12 of the 25 Soviet ships bound for Cuba had changed course to avoid contact with the blockade. By the following day all but one of the ships had turned back. That ship, the tanker *Bucharest*, was carrying only oil. It was stopped on October 25 and allowed to continue on to Havana. The same day, Adlai Stevenson displayed the American photographs of Soviet missile emplacements before the UN Security Council.

U Thant in the meantime stepped up his diplomatic activity. He appealed to both Kennedy and Khrushchev to avoid a direct naval confrontation. On October 26, the Soviet and American leaders cabled U Thant accepting his appeal for caution but strongly denouncing each other's actions. Kennedy realized that the Soviet decision not to immediately challenge the blockade meant that he had won the first round, but work continued on the missiles and missile bases already in Cuba, and he warned that if that did not stop "further action" would be taken and he strongly implied that the action would be an American invasion of Cuba.

Khrushchev by this time recognized that he was faced with an impossible situation. If he moved against Berlin he faced nuclear retaliation. If he completed and used the missile bases already in Cuba he faced nuclear retaliation. If he simply left in Cuba the missiles already in place, then the United States would invade Cuba and the Soviet Union would lose its communist foothold in the Western Hemisphere. If he tried to break the blockade, then the result would be a direct Soviet–American military confrontation, which could quickly escalate out of control.

On October 26, Soviet diplomat Alexander Fomin approached John Scali, the diplomatic correspondent for the American Broadcasting Corporation, and asked him to convey to Secretary of State DEAN RUSK a Soviet offer to the effect that the Soviet Union would pledge never again to introduce offensive nuclear weapons into Cuba and to withdraw the weapons already in place in return for a public American pledge not to invade Cuba. The message was passed on and was received positively by Rusk and Kennedy. The response from Khrushchev was a pair of apparently conflicting cables. The first, more conciliatory, cable implied a willingness to dismantle the bases in return for an American guarantee not to invade Cuba. The second, more truculent, cable demanded that American missiles in Turkey be withdrawn in return for the Soviet withdrawal from Cuba.

Kennedy decided to ignore the second message. On October 27 he sent Khrushchev a message accepting his first cable and offering to negotiate a settlement along the lines of Khrushchev's proposal as soon as work was stopped on the missile bases and the offensive weapons were rendered inoperable. The message was delivered by Robert Kennedy to Soviet ambassador ANATOLY DOBRYNIN. When he handed over

the letter, Robert Kennedy added the oral message that unless assurances were received within 24 hours the United States would take military action by October 30.

The following day Khrushchev cabled Kennedy to give in to the American demands.

Khrushchev's cable was welcomed by Kennedy as a "statesmanlike decision" and an "important and constructive contribution to peace."

The two leaders, however, faced one other major obstacle in the form of Castro, who refused to allow a UN inspection team on Cuban soil to verify the withdrawal of the missiles. Politburo member ANASTAS MIKOYAN was sent to Havana to try to persuade Castro to accept the UN inspection team. The two men argued for four weeks, but Castro was implacable. In the end, Kennedy dropped his insistence on UN verification teams and relied on American intelligence.

Khrushchev's withdrawal of the missiles was hailed as an American victory because it prevented the Soviet Union from gaining a strategic military position in the Western Hemisphere. But in another way it was a defeat for Kennedy because he was forced to accept publicly the presence of a communist government in the Western Hemisphere. Kennedy himself refused to use the word victory or defeat to describe the end of the crisis.

At the same time, the Cuban Missile Crisis clearly frightened the leaders of both the Soviet Union and the United States and led both countries to move toward easing international tensions in order to avoid a repetition of the event. In the months immediately following the Cuban Missile Crisis, the two countries established the Washington–Moscow HOT LINE, and in August 1963 they signed the first NUCLEAR TEST BAN TREATY.

For Further Information:
Blight, James G. *The Shattered Crystal Ball: Fear and Learning in the Cuban Missile Crisis.* Savage, Md., 1990.

Blight, James G., and David A. Welch. *On the Brink: Americans and Soviets Reexamine the Cuban Missile Crisis.* New York, 1989.

Brugioni, Dino A. *Eyeball to Eyeball: The Inside Story of the Cuban Missile Crisis.* New York, 1991.

Chayes, Abram. *The Cuban Missile Crisis: International Crises and the Rule of Law.* New York, 1973.

Detzer, David. *The Brink: Cuban Missile Crisis, 1962.* New York, 1979.

Fall, Bernard. *Anatomy of a Crisis.* Garden City, N.Y., 1969.

Medland, William J. *The Cuban Missile Crisis of 1962: Needless or Necessary?* New York, 1988.

Mezerik, A.G. *Cuba and the United States.* New York, 1963.

Schlesinger, Arthur. *A Thousand Days.* New York, 1965.

Thompson, Robert Smith. *The Missiles of October: The Declassified Story of John F. Kennedy and the Cuban Missile Crisis.* New York, 1992.

Cultural Revolution, Chinese   China's Cultural Revolution from 1966 to 1976 turned the country in on itself as MAO ZEDONG turned to the nation's youth to help seize control of the Chinese Communist Party from his deputies DENG XIAO-

PING and LIU SHAOQI. Mao's actions nearly resulted in a civil war, and the conflict removed China from the international stage during a crucial time in Southeast Asia and delayed needed political and economic reform.

By 1965, Mao had lost effective control of the party apparatus to Liu and Deng, who had attempted to modify some of the more Stalinist economic policies imposed by Mao in the 1950s and to reintroduce market forces. Without the support of the party apparatus, Mao needed to seek support outside the party if he was to combat Liu and Deng.

He turned first to LIN BIAO, minister of defense, who agreed to increase Maoist political training in the ranks. Defense expenditures and basic military training were also substantially increased, with the result that the People's Liberation Army became a major pro-Mao force. By 1964 Lin and Mao felt strong enough to start purging the army of Deng and Liu's supporters, and the following year they turned their attention to cultural figures. In February 1966 the supporters of Deng and Liu fought back within party circles. Mao, however, turned to the students for additional support and struck a responsive chord among the Chinese youth.

The army was given responsibility for education and cultural affairs, and the schools were effectively shut. Students were organized into battalions called "Red Guards." The Red Guards were encouraged to hold mass meetings with Mao and were presented with the *Quotations from Chairman Mao Tsetung,* which became known as "Mao's little red book." They were then encouraged to go out through the country and create local rebellions and overthrow the "capitalist roaders" who supported Deng and Liu. The party was purged to such an extent that the only effective power left in the country was the army, which took over administration of the government.

By the summer of 1967, the country teetered on the brink of civil war. After a series of particularly disturbing armed clashes in the industrial city of Wuhan, Mao started to move against the excesses of the Cultural Revolution. By 1968 the country had returned to near normality and the schools were reopened. By 1969, the first, crucial phase of the Cultural Revolution was at an end. The party had been extensively purged, and Mao and the military were left in control. Mao took complete control after the death of Lin Biao in September 1971.

Although the major violence and upheavals had ended in 1969, the current Chinese government under Deng considers that the Cultural Revolution did not officially end until the death of Mao and the arrest of the Gang of Four in 1976.

For Further Information:

Dittmer, Lowell. *Liu Shao-chi and the Chinese Cultural Revolution.* Berkeley, Calif., 1974.

Hsu, C.Y. *The Rise of Modern China.* New York, 1983.

MacFarquhar, Roderick. *The Origins of the Cultural Revolution.* London, 1974.

Wilson, Dick. *Mao: The People's Emperor.* New York, 1979.

Curzon Line   The Curzon Line was agreed upon at the YALTA CONFERENCE in 1945 as the postwar eastern boundary of Poland. It resulted in Poland's loss of 52,000 square miles of territory, which became part of the Soviet Union. For many Poles the Curzon Line represents Soviet imperialism and the West's inability to stop it.

The Curzon Line was drawn during the Soviet–Polish War of 1919–20 by British foreign secretary Lord Curzon, who was asked to mediate in the war. At the time the line was drawn, the Polish armies were being pushed westward, and Lord Curzon's armistice line reflected the Soviet advances. The northern point of the line divided the former Suvalki Province between Lithuania and Poland. It then ran south with a bulge eastward toward Grodno, then back westward to the Bug River. It followed the river past Brest-Litovsk to Sokoly, where it went almost due west, bending around Przemysl and then heading south to the Carpathian Mountains and the border with Czechoslovakia.

The Curzon Line was rejected by the Poles, who had managed to push the Soviets back and occupy a large slice of Russian territory. When the final treaty was signed in March 1921, the new Soviet–Polish border was drawn farther to the east. The recovery of this territory became a major goal of Stalin's foreign policy, and the German-Soviet Pact of 1939 divided Poland along a line roughly similar to the Curzon Line.

In wartime negotiations with Britain, the United States and the exiled Polish government in London, JOSEF STALIN insisted that Poland's new eastern border follow the Curzon Line with a few alterations. This was rejected by the Poles, who were at first supported by British prime minister WINSTON CHURCHILL and U.S. president FRANKLIN ROOSEVELT. But at the Yalta Conference in February 1945 the two Western leaders acceded to Stalin's demands on the Curzon Line in return for a redrawing of Poland's borders with Germany.

Czechoslovakia   Czechoslovakia was one of the pivotal states in the Eastern Bloc. Bordering West Germany, East Germany, Poland, Hungary and Austria, it was strategically located. Politically, its strong democratic traditions led to the PRAGUE SPRING reform movement of 1968 and the country's subsequent invasion by the WARSAW PACT countries. Between 1967 and 1989 the Czech Communist Party took a lead within the Eastern Bloc in suppressing moves toward democracy, but it was forced to give way to forces for change in December 1989.

Czechoslovakia is a creation of 20th-century nationalism. Before 1918 it was part of the vast Central European empire of Austria-Hungary. When that empire was dissolved at the end of World War I, the areas occupied by the Czechs and the Slovaks became Czechoslovakia. It quickly established itself as one of the most advanced countries in Eastern Europe, with a strong industrial and political base.

But from its inception, the country suffered from problems with neighboring Germany. The new country included the Sudetenland, an area in northern Bohemia inhabited by 3 million ethnic Germans. The rise of Adolf Hitler led to increasing demands within both Germany and the Sudetenland for the area to be ceded to Germany. In 1938, to appease German demands, the British and French governments, nominally the allies and protectors of Czechoslovakia, agreed to cede the Sudetenland to Germany. The remainder of Czechoslovakia was occupied by Nazi Germany in March 1939.

A provisional Czechoslovak government was established by the exiled president, EDVARD BENES, first in Paris and then in London. In December 1943 Benes signed an alliance with the Soviet Union, which was used as the legal basis for the Soviet presence in the country in the immediate postwar period. The treaty also enabled Benes to become the only East European leader allowed by the Soviets to return to his country in the postwar period. It is generally accepted that Soviet leader JOSEF STALIN allowed Benes to return because he realized that the Czech leader's international stature was needed to give legitimacy to the new Czech government.

Benes, for his part, accepted the political reality of working closely with the Soviet Union, and his first 25-member cabinet contained seven communists. For three years, Benes kept his country out of the Soviet orbit. Free multiparty elections were held in 1946, and the communists polled 40% of the vote, a figure that was attributed to the electorate's gratitude toward the Soviet Union for liberating their country from German occupation.

Following the 1946 election, the key government positions were taken by members of the Communist Party, including the premiership, held by KLEMENT GOTTWALD. But Benes maintained the Western multiparty system. Soon after the election, however, the popularity of the communists seriously declined because of events elsewhere in Eastern Europe, and the party moved to grab power by replacing non-communist police officers with party members.

In protest against this policy, the non-communist cabinet members tendered their resignations in February 1948 in the hope of forcing an early general election. But the Social Democratic Party refused to join the rest of the non-communist bloc, and in the ensuing political confusion the communist-controlled police moved to arrest its opponents. They suppressed nonparty newspapers, placed party members in key positions, surrounded the capital with armed activists supported by the Soviet Red Army and introduced a Soviet-style constitution. Benes, who was seriously ill, resigned in June 1948 and died shortly afterward. He was immediately succeeded by Gottwald.

Gottwald continued his Stalinist-type purges of all noncommunists and party deviationists. Thousands were arrested, subjected to show trials and imprisoned or executed. The most famous of these show trials was that of Communist Party general secretary Rudolf Slansky.

Gottwald was one of the most slavish disciples of Josef Stalin and Soviet policy. Industry was completely nationalized and the farms collectivized. In the autumn of 1948 Gottwald went on holiday to the Crimea, where he met with Stalin and

was told exactly how to run the country. It became increasingly difficult, however, for Gottwald to impose the Soviet strictures on the Czechoslovak people, so in 1949 Soviet advisers were placed in key positions to ensure that orthodox policies were introduced.

In June 1949 Gottwald started a purge against the Roman Catholic Church, interning archbishops and bishops and confiscating church lands. A state office for church affairs was set up to bring the church under party control, dissident clergymen were brought to trial, and an effort was made to appoint clergy who were prepared to collaborate with Gottwald.

Gottwald, however, began to face increasing opposition from Communist Party members who resented the Soviet stranglehold on national political life. In 1950, with the help of the Soviet-controlled security police, he began a purge of party members. Vladimir Clementis, the foreign minister, was dismissed from office, as was GUSTAV HUSAK, the Slovak regional premier. Both were accused of bourgeois nationalism. In February 1951 Husak was arrested and imprisoned, and in December 1952 Clementis was executed. Also executed was Rudolf Slansky, the party general secretary, who along with 10 other party members was accused of leading an antistate conspiracy. An estimated 200 leading communists were executed during the purge, and thousands more were sent to concentration camps.

At the behest of Moscow, Gottwald introduced an expensive industrialization campaign at the expense of consumer items. (This helped lead to the workers' riots at PILSEN, which were ruthlessly suppressed.) Gottwald died in March 1953, only nine days after Stalin. He was succeeded from 1953 to 1957 by ANTONIN ZAPOTOCKY, and then in 1957 by ANTONIN NOVOTNY. The latter in particular maintained the Stalinist style and policies of Gottwald despite the de-Stalinization campaign elsewhere in the Socialist Bloc.

But by 1963, it became clear that the country needed a large degree of economic reform. The reforms proposed involved decentralized decision making and improved incentives in what became known as "market socialism." As the economic reforms began to take effect, they were joined by demands for matching political reforms. In Czechoslovakia the demands took on a greater meaning because of the ethnic rivalry between the Czech-speaking and Slovak-speaking populations.

Novotny was prepared to accept limited economic reforms as a financial necessity, and he allowed the political rehabilitation of some of those purged during the Stalinist years. But he refused to introduce any significant parallel political reforms, especially any that would increase the political influence of the Slovak minority.

This refusal led to a powerful alliance between the Slovaks and the political reformers. The battle between reformers and conservative hard-liners came to a head at a meeting of the Central Committee of the Czechoslovak Communist Party in October 1967. The hard-liners were led by Novotny and the reformers by Slovak leader ALEXANDER DUBCEK, who managed to win the support of a majority of the Central Committee members, and on January 5, 1968, Dubcek succeeded Novotny as general secretary of the Communist Party. Novotny, however, did manage to retain the largely ceremonial position of president.

Within a few short weeks Dubcek started to loosen the repressive political ropes of the Novotny regime, and a heady political perfume known as the Prague Spring swept through the country, carrying the party leadership toward more and more liberal reforms. Speaking at a conference in Brno on March 16, Dubcek promised the "widest possible democratization" for the country and greater autonomy for the government, the courts, the trade unions and economic enterprises. Shortly afterward, on March 22, Novotny was forced to resign as president.

In April the Communist Party published its reformist "action program" with the stated aim of purifying communism of its "former aberrations" and "to build socialism in this country in a way corresponding to our conditions and traditions." The document's pledges included:

1. Guarantees of freedom of speech, press, assembly and religious observance.
2. Electoral laws to provide a broader choice of candidates and greater freedom for the non-communist parties within the National Front.
3. Upgrading of the power of parliament and the government at the expense of that of the Communist Party apparatus.
4. Broad economic reforms to give enterprises greater independence, to achieve a convertible currency, revive a limited amount of private enterprise and increase trade with Western countries.
5. An independent judiciary.
6. Federal status for Slovakia on an independent basis and a new constitution by the end of 1969.
7. Full and fair rehabilitation of all persons who had been unjustly persecuted between 1949 and 1954 and "moral, personal and financial compensation" to persons affected by the rehabilitation.
8. Exclusion from important posts in the country's social and political life for those people who had taken part in past persecutions.

The document caused consternation among all the other East European communist parties, and a summit meeting of Eastern Bloc leaders was hastily called in Dresden on March 23 in an attempt to urge Dubcek to restrain his reforms. East Germany took the lead in criticizing Dubcek, and on March 27 the Czech government formally accused East Germany of interfering in Czech internal affairs.

Dubcek refused to back away from any of his reforms. On April 24 he told the Central Committee of the Czechoslovak Communist Party, "We cannot go back and we cannot go halfway." He added the warning that "moving along unexplored paths requires caution and courage."

On July 16 a second summit meeting of Eastern Bloc countries, this time excluding Czechoslovakia, warned Dubcek that his liberalization drive was "completely unacceptable." On July 22 it was announced that the entire Soviet Politburo would go to Prague and move its troops into Czechoslovakia in an attempt to halt the growing threat of a "counterrevolution" in Czechoslovakia. Dubcek replied that the party leadership was determined to continue its liberalization program. He declared, "We paid too dearly and are still paying for the methods of the past." But he also renewed the pledge that Prague would remain loyal to communism, to the socialist camp and in particular to the Soviet Union.

The Soviet–Czech meeting started on July 29 in the Czech village of Cierna near the Soviet border. It was accompanied by the biggest peacetime military maneuvers in Soviet history along the border, a clear attempt to intimidate the Czech leadership. The meeting continued until August 1. LEONID BREZHNEV opened the meeting with a demand that Dubcek restore censorship, abolish all "anti-Communist political clubs, remove liberals from key government positions and allow the stationing of Soviet troops along the Czech–West German border." MIKHAIL SUSLOV, who was in charge of ideological matters, then attacked Dubcek's reform program as heresy.

On the second day, Czech president LUDVIG SVOBODA made an impassioned defense of his country's right to carry out its program of liberalization. On the third day, the Soviets tried to split the Czechoslovaks between the conservatives and progressives. When this failed, they effectively accepted defeat by departing Czechoslovakia without an agreement.

When the talks ended, thousands of demonstrators gathered in Prague and were told by National Assembly president Josef Smrkovsky, "We explained our position and succeeded." On August 3 Dubcek went on national television to assert, "We promised you that we would stand fast. We kept our promise."

Also on August 3, Czech leaders met with Soviet and other East European leaders in Bratislava and were rewarded with a communiqué promising that other East European leaders would cooperate with the Dubcek government on the basis of "equality, sovereignty and national independence."

The Czechs at this point believed that they had won the right to develop their own political system. Dubcek was hailed as a national hero and there were spontaneous pro-Dubcek demonstrations throughout the country. But the Soviets had already decided that the changes in Czechoslovakia represented too much of a threat to their own communist government and to the pro-Soviet communist governments elsewhere in Eastern Europe. On August 10, during a visit to Czechoslovakia by Yugoslav leader JOSIP BROZ TITO, the Soviet press agency Tass announced that new joint military exercises, involving Soviet, East German and Polish troops, had begun in southern East Germany, Poland and the western Ukraine in areas bordering on Czechoslovakia. At the same time, the Soviet Union resumed its criticism of the Czech press.

Then, on the night of August 20–21, an estimated 200,000 troops from five Warsaw Pact countries crossed the borders from East Germany, Poland, the western Ukraine and Hungary. More troops were flown directly to the capital, which was quickly occupied. By the end of August 21, the troops had successfully occupied the entire country. Over the course of the week a total of 650,000 foreign troops entered Czechoslovakia.

Before dawn on August 21, the Czechoslovak Communist Party's Central Committee broadcast a statement that the invasion was taking place "without the knowledge" of the country's leaders. An estimated 1,000 members of the Central Committee held an emergency meeting in a factory outside Prague, but the meeting was largely ineffectual because the party leaders, including Dubcek, were arrested shortly after the invasion.

The Soviet Union issued a statement on August 21 claiming that the Warsaw Pact countries had acted after the Czechoslovak party and government leaders had requested "urgent assistance" to repulse the threat "emanating from the counterrevolutionary forces" within Czechoslovakia. The statement added, "The further aggravation of the situation in Czechoslovakia affects the vital interest of the Soviet Union and other Socialist states, the interests of the security of the states of the Socialist community. The threat to the Socialist system in Czechoslovakia constitutes at the same time a threat to the mainstays of European peace."

There was no organized resistance to the invasion and occupation, but Czech citizens, led by students, resorted to a wide variety of means to hamper the invaders. Crowds roamed the streets of the major towns and cities shouting support for Dubcek and insults at the Soviets. Swastikas were painted on tanks and armored cars and barricades were raised to slow the progress of the troops. An estimated 35,000 Czechoslovaks fled across the border to Hungary.

The most stubborn resistance was established around the national radio station in Prague, where students erected barricades using paving stones, buses and trolleys and then threw Molotov cocktails, stones and refuse at the soldiers to prevent them from entering the building. Their defense enabled the radio to report details of the invasion until 11 A.M. on August 21. After the closure of the state radio station, about a dozen pirate radio stations sprung up to continue uncensored broadcasts.

On August 22, a crowd of 20,000 peaceful demonstrators marched on St. Wenceslas Square in the center of Prague to

Czechs defy Soviet tanks in the streets of Prague in August 1968. Photo courtesy of Popperfoto.

demand the withdrawal of the occupying forces. By August 23, rumors spread of arrests by the secret police. The same day, lists appeared in doorways and on shop windows giving the license plate numbers of the cars used by the secret police. At noon there was a one-hour general strike. The following day three young men were shot and killed by Soviet soldiers after they had been caught distributing anti-Soviet leaflets in Prague.

The United Nations Security Council, by a vote of 10 to 2, supported a seven-nation resolution condemning the invasion and calling for the withdrawal of the occupying forces. The Soviet Union vetoed the resolution. During the debate on August 22 the Czechoslovak delegation called the invasion illegal and unjustifiable.

The invasion also sparked widespread condemnation from communist parties outside the Eastern Bloc, including the communist parties of France, Italy, Romania, Yugoslavia and China. The invasion set in motion a chain of events that led to the estrangement of the Western European communist parties from the Soviet Union.

In the United States, the invasion ended secret talks between the JOHNSON administration and the Soviet Union for the start of STRATEGIC ARMS LIMITATION TALKS, which had been scheduled to begin in October 1968. President Lyndon Johnson said, "The Soviet Union and its allies have invaded a defenseless country to stamp out a resurgence of ordinary human freedom. It is a sad commentary on the Communist mind that a sign of liberty is deemed a fundamental threat to the security of the Soviet system."

In the meantime, the Czech party leadership, including Dubcek, were taken under guard to Moscow and forced to accept a reversal of their reform program. Dubcek, after his return, appealed to his countrymen "not to permit provocations" that would precipitate punitive measures by the occupation forces "and to try to prevent panic from entering our ranks."

In April 1969 the hard-liners' control of the party apparatus was completed when Dubcek was ousted as party leader by Gustav Husak. In his speech before the party's Central Committee, Husak warned that the party would not tolerate any "counterrevolutionary" threats to its existence. Husak went on to purge some 400,000 Communist Party members, impose a rigid and wide-ranging censorship and enact a harsh penal code. Soviet forces took up permanent positions on the frontier with West Germany, and Soviet party leader Leonid Brezhnev justified the invasion with his BREZHNEV DOCTRINE.

In January 1970, Dubcek was appointed ambassador to Turkey, but after being expelled from the Communist Party he was recalled to Prague six months later. He was given the post of inspector of forestry administration in Bratislava. Dubcek officially became a non-person, and his name was dropped from news reports, but he remained a focal point for dissidents.

In May 1975, Husak was named president of the republic while still retaining the positions of chairman of the National Front and general secretary of the Communist Party. The thrust of Husak's economic, foreign and domestic policies was strict adherence to orthodox communism and a close relationship with the Soviet Union. He realized that the underlying tensions within Czechoslovakia and the experience of the Prague Spring and the Benes years made Czechoslovakia a country where even limited reform was impossible and that the only alternative to the orthodox communist system was a Western form of government.

For this reason, Husak largely turned his back on the political and economic reforms advocated by Soviet leader MIKHAIL GORBACHEV. But the Czech leader's repressive measures also led to the formation of Eastern Europe's most successful dissident group—CHARTER 77—which was formed in 1977 to monitor compliance with the human rights provisions of the 1975 HELSINKI ACCORDS. Hundreds of members, many of them prominent politicians and intellectuals, were arrested and imprisoned for their association with the group.

In December 1987 Husak resigned as general secretary of the party to be replaced by Milos Jakes, although Husak retained the presidency. The personnel shift was the Czechoslovak Communist Party's response to Gorbachev's calls for reform. But it quickly became apparent that the changes were only cosmetic. Jakes was at best only moderately interested in reform, and Husak still retained considerable power as state president.

However, the Czechoslovak Communist Party was unable to withstand the pressures for change that built up in Eastern Europe in 1989. The fall of hard-line East German leader ERICH HONECKER, Husak's main ally in the Warsaw Pact, and the opening of the BERLIN WALL sparked a series of demonstrations in Prague. Night after night hundreds of thousands of Czechs gathered in Wenceslas Square to demand the resignation of Communist Party leaders, the end of the party's monopoly on power, and multiparty government. On December 9, 1989, Husak was forced to resign as president, and a multiparty coalition government, with Communists a minority, was quickly established.

Dissident playwright Vaclav Havel, 53, was elected president December 29 by the federal assembly (parliament), replacing Husak. Havel, one of the founders of leading, umbrella opposition group Civic Forum (which in turn had grown out of the Charter 77 group), was the first noncommunist to get the post in more than 40 years. The day before his election, the assembly had effectively rehabilitated Dubcek by unanimously electing him parliamentary chairman (speaker). "The autumn of 1989 developed the ideals of the Prague Spring of 1968 and inspires our nation today toward new creative actions," Dubcek said. The previous week, the Communist Party had issued a formal apology "to all citizens who suffered from repression . . . and those who were ousted from the party in 1968."

The sudden success of the 1989 "Velvet Revolution" seemed to surprise Czechoslovakia's democratic activists as much as it did the Communist Party and its allies in the

U.S.S.R. Soviet President Mikhail Gorbachev managed to adapt to the situation, however, even though he had reportedly hoped for the formation of a new, reformist communist government in Prague rather than a noncommunist one. Havel traveled to Moscow in February 1990, where he met Gorbachev, and the two men agreed on a phased withdrawal of all Soviet troops from Czechoslovakia. (The pullout began February 26, 1990, and was completed June 21, 1991.) Havel traveled widely abroad, where he was hailed as a hero of democracy. Just before his visit to Moscow, he had made a triumphant visit to the United States, where he met with President BUSH and addressed a joint session of Congress.

Czechoslovakia held parliamentary and regional elections on June 8–9, 1990, the country's first free voting in over four decades. Civic Forum and its Slovak sister party, Public Against Violence (PAV), captured 46% of the national vote and 170 seats in the 300-seat assembly. The communists came in a distant second with 13% of the vote and 47 seats.

Throughout 1990 and 1991, Czechoslovakia's new democracy was beset by growing pains. Civic Forum and PAV divided into left- and right-wing factions. The government set up special commissions to begin screening employees of the civil service and state-owned companies for communists and their collaborators, who would then be fired (elected officials were excepted). Havel and others opposed the process as a "witch hunt," relying as it did on the files of the now-disbanded secret police. (The government went further in December 1991, passing a law providing prison terms of up to five years for anyone convicted of promoting communism or fascism.) But the greatest threat arose out of the revival of Slovak nationalism, which had been suppressed since World War II.

The country was made up of the Czech Republic in the west and the smaller Slovak Republic in the east. About two-thirds of Czechoslovakia's 15 million people were ethnic Czechs, while most of the remainder were Slovaks, who had long complained of economic and political domination by the Czechs. Reflecting the gradual drifting apart of the two groups, the country was renamed the Czech and Slovak Federative Republic in 1990. The process picked up steam over the next two years, as Slovak politicians agitated for greater autonomy or even full independence. Havel, a Czech who was often jeered during his appearances in Slovakia, opposed a national breakup and repeatedly called for a public referendum in which Slovaks could vote on the issue of sovereignty. (Polls indicated that a majority of both Czechs and Slovaks opposed a complete split.)

New elections were held in June 1992 in which more than 70 parties competed. The result was a victory for right-wing parties led by Finance Minister Vaclav Klaus in the Czech Republic, and for resurgent leftist (including reformed communists) and nationalist parties led by Vladimir Meciar in Slovakia. After two weeks of negotiations, Klaus and Meciar agreed both to the formation of a national caretaker government and on preparations for the division of the Czech and Slovak republics into separate, sovereign countries.

For Further Information:
Bradley, John Francis Nejez. Czechoslovakia: A Short History. Edinburgh, 1971.
Czerwinski, Edward J. The Soviet Invasion of Czechoslovakia: Its Effects on Eastern Europe. New York, 1972.
Fischer-Galati, G.S., ed. Eastern Europe in the 1980s. London, 1980.
Havel, Vaclav. Open Letters: Selected Writings, 1965–1990. New York, 1991.
Kusin, Vladimir V. The Intellectual Origins of the Prague Spring: The Development of Reformist Ideas in Czechoslovakia, 1956–1967. Cambridge, England, 1971.
Mlnar, Z. Nightfrost in Prague. New York, 1980.
Renner, Hans. A History of Czechoslovakia Since 1945. New York, 1989.
Salomon, Michel. Prague Notebook; The Strangled Revolution. Boston, 1971.
Shawcross, William. Dubcek. New York, 1990.
Silnitsky, Frantisek, et al., eds. Communism and Eastern Europe. New York, 1979.
Svitak, Ivan. The Czechoslovakia Experiment, 1968–1969. New York, 1971.
Szulc, Tad. Czechoslovakia Since World War II. New York, 1971.
Tokes, Rudolf, ed. Opposition in Eastern Europe. Baltimore, 1979.
Valenta, J. Soviet Intervention in Czechoslovakia 1968: Anatomy of a Decision. Baltimore, 1979.
Wheaton, Bernard, and Zdenek Kavan. The Velvet Revolution: Czechoslovakia, 1988–1991. Boulder, Colo., 1992.
Wheeler, George Shaw. The Human Face of Socialism: The Political Economy of Change in Czechoslovakia. New York, 1973.

D

Dardanelles   The Dardanelles are the straits that separate the Aegean Sea (and the Mediterranean) from the Sea of Marmara and the Bosporus Strait to the Black Sea. In the post–World War II period the Soviet Union tried to establish control over the Dardanelles. Its efforts to do so played a major role in spurring the TRUMAN DOCTRINE, the admission of Greece and Turkey to the NORTH ATLANTIC TREATY ORGANIZATION and the placement of U.S. military bases in those two countries.

Davies, John Paton   (April 6, 1908–   )   John Paton Davies was an American career diplomat whose views on China made him a prominent victim of McCarthyism.

The son of American missionary parents in China, Davies joined the American diplomatic service after graduating from Columbia University in 1931. During World War II he served in China, first as an adviser to General JOSEPH STILWELL and then on the political staff of Ambassador PATRICK HURLEY.

In his reports back to Washington Davies repeatedly expressed the opinion that the Nationalist government of CHIANG KAI-SHEK was riddled with corruption and that the Chinese communists were likely to oust Chiang from power. At Davies' suggestion, U.S. president FRANKLIN ROOSEVELT sent a wartime military mission to the communist-controlled areas of China. Davies also urged the administration to create a working relationship with the Chinese communists in order to prevent a Sino–Soviet alliance should the communists come to power as he expected.

His opinions clashed with those of Hurley, who was an unqualified supporter of Chiang Kai-shek. Hurley maintained that Davies was pro-communist and, after Hurley resigned as ambassador, he publicly accused Davies of sabotaging American policy in China and lobbied for his removal from the State Department.

At first Davies' career appeared to be unaffected by the accusations of Hurley and the right-wing China Lobby. From 1947 to 1951 he served on the prestigious State Department Policy Planning Staff, and was director of political affairs at the U.S. mission in Bonn from 1951 to 1953. Between 1948 and 1953 he was subjected to eight security investigations. Each one cleared him.

But in 1951 Senator JOSEPH MCCARTHY took up the case against Davies and in 1954, after a ninth investigation by the State Department Loyalty Board, Davies was ruled disloyal and dismissed on the basis of Hurley's earlier testimony. Davies moved to Peru but returned to Washington in 1964 to clear his name. He was finally successful in 1968.

For Further Information:
Kahn, E.J. *The China Hands.* New York, 1973.
Purifoy, Lewis McCarroll. *Harry Truman's China Policy: McCarthyism and the Diplomacy of Hysteria, 1947–1951.* New York, 1976.

Dean, Arthur   (October 16, 1898–November 30, 1987)   Arthur Dean was a prominent New York lawyer who served presidents FRANKLIN ROOSEVELT, DWIGHT EISENHOWER, JOHN KENNEDY and LYNDON JOHNSON. His duties included the Korean armistice negotiations and disarmament talks. He also played a key role in President Johnson's decision to stop the bombing of North Vietnam and not seek reelection.

Dean graduated from Cornell Law School in 1923 and joined the law firm of Sullivan and Cromwell, in which JOHN FOSTER DULLES was a senior partner. The two men formed a close relationship, and when Dulles became secretary of state, he used Dean on several diplomatic missions, including heading the American delegation to the Korean armistice negotiations. The talks were difficult, and in December 1953 Dean suspended them. But he had become convinced that the negotiations and future relations with China could be made easier if the United States recognized the Chinese communist government, and he made the mistake of telling a journalist from the *Providence Journal* (January 3, 1954) that the Eisenhower administration should take "a new look" at the possibility of recognizing communist China.

Dean's interview resulted in a chorus of protests from the powerful China lobby. Senator Herman Welker accused Dean of supporting "appeasement" and of collaborating with communist China. In March, Dulles asked Dean to resign from the negotiations. Dean did so but continued to call publicly for recognition of the People's Republic. He specifically recommended Britain's two-China policy, which recognized communist rule on the mainland and Nationalist rule on Taiwan.

In 1958 Dean represented the United States at the Law of the Sea Conference in Geneva. He upheld the traditional American position of a three-mile territorial limit against opposition from the Soviet Union and Iceland, which wanted the limit extended to 12 miles—the Soviets because of their fear of Western espionage and the Icelanders because of their economic dependence on home fishing waters. Dean eventually offered a compromise territorial limit of six miles. When this was rejected, Dean served formal notice that the United States would continue to observe the three-mile limit.

In February 1961 President Kennedy appointed Dean the American representative at the Geneva talks on ending nuclear weapons tests and also at the United Nations General Assembly. Dean reassessed America's entire arms control policy and subsequently proposed a number of concessions to the Soviets on the issue of on-site inspections. But a draft treaty presented in April 1961 was rejected by the Soviets because it would have hampered a series of forthcoming nuclear tests.

Dean, who also drafted the legislation that created the ARMS CONTROL AND DISARMAMENT AGENCY in September 1961, then proposed in conjunction with LLEWELLYN THOMPSON, that Kennedy shift his emphasis from a blanket test ban treaty to a more limited treaty. Dean and Thompson hoped that a step-by-step approach would help to build an atmosphere of trust that would eventually result in a total test ban treaty and further disarmament measures. President Kennedy accepted the plan, but when Dean presented his two proposed agreements in Geneva the Soviets rejected them also. At the suggestion of the Soviets, test ban negotiations were then taken over by special higher-level emissaries, and Kennedy chose W. AVERELL HARRIMAN as his representative. Harriman successfully negotiated a U.S.–British–Soviet partial test ban treaty, which was signed in Moscow on August 5, 1963.

Dean returned to his New York law practice in February 1963, but remained active in foreign affairs and joined a nonpartisan citizens' panel formed to advise the president on foreign affairs and another created to study ways of preventing the spread of nuclear weapons. In 1967 Dean was asked to join President Lyndon Johnson's senior advisory group on the Vietnam War. Dean was among those who forcefully advised Johnson to halt the bombing of North Vietnam and de-escalate the war. He also told Johnson that if he sought reelection in 1968 it would have a major divisive effect on the country. Johnson announced the de-escalation and his decision not to seek reelection on March 31, 1968.

Dean continued to act as an informal foreign policy adviser to succeeding presidents, but the emphasis of his work shifted to writing and his law practice.

For Further Information:

Dean, Arthur. *Test Ban and Disarmament: The Path of Negotiation.* New York, 1966.

Jacobson, Harold K. *Diplomats, Scientists and Politicians.* Ann Arbor, Mich., 1966.

Lepper, Mary Milling. *Foreign Policy Formulation: A Case Study of the Nuclear Test Ban Treaty of 1963.* Columbus, Ohio, 1971.

Sobel, Lester. *Disarmament and Nuclear Tests, 1960–1963.* New York, 1964.

Defense Intelligence Agency (DIA)   The U.S. Defense Intelligence Agency (DIA) was created in October 1961 as part of a major reorganization of the Department of Defense by Secretary of Defense ROBERT S. MCNAMARA. A major figure in the creation of the DIA was CYRUS VANCE, who later became secretary of state under President JIMMY CARTER. In 1961 he was general counsel at the Pentagon.

The DIA became responsible for coordinating and evaluating the separate intelligence operations of the armed forces. One of its main tasks was to assess regularly Soviet military strengths. The DIA report on the Soviet Union was often cited in defense debates both in the United States and abroad.

de Gasperi, Alcide   **(April 3, 1881–August 19, 1954)**
Alcide de Gasperi, Italy's most prominent political leader in the early Cold War years, established the Christian Democratic Party as the dominant force in Italian postwar politics. His strong anti-communist position also blocked the powerful Italian Communist Party from power and resulted in strong links with the United States.

De Gasperi was born in the Trentino region; now part of Italy, until 1918 it was part of the Austro-Hungarian Empire. De Gasperi began his professional career as a journalist, and at the age of 24 he was editor of the regional newspaper *Il Nuovo Trentino*. In 1911 de Gasperi formally started his political career when he was elected to the Austrian parliament, where he campaigned for the Trentino region to be transferred to Italy.

At the end of WORLD WAR I, the Austro-Hungarian Empire was dissolved, and the Trentino region was ceded to Italy. De Gasperi was elected to the Italian parliament in 1921 as a member of the newly formed Christian Democratic organization called the the Italian Popular Party (PPI).

De Gasperi's strong belief in Christian Democratic principles brought him into conflict with Benito Mussolini's Fascist Party government and he was arrested and imprisoned in 1927. After intervention by the pope, de Gasperi was released after 16 months and moved to the sanctuary of the Vatican.

During WORLD WAR II, de Gasperi took a leading role in organizing the resistance to Mussolini's rule and reorganized the PPI into the Christian Democratic Party. When the fascist government fell in 1943, de Gasperi was appointed minister without porfolio. In December 1945 he became prime minister and formed his first government, remaining in office until 1953.

Wartime resistance activities had enabled the pro-Soviet Italian Communist Party (PCI) to become a major force in Italian politics, and the PCI's cooperation had been an essential element in the successive post-fascist wartime coalition governments. Between 1943 and 1945, membership in the PCI grew from 5,000 to 1.7 million. De Gasperi's Christian Democratic Party represented the only credible non-fascist challenge to the communists at this time, and the United States threw its resources behind it in order to prevent a communist government from being elected.

De Gasperi's first government continued the policy of cooperation with the communists, and members of the PCI sat in his cabinet. In the Cold War atmosphere of the time, they tried to swing Italian foreign policy toward either a neutral or a pro-Soviet position and pressed for widespread nationalization programs and land reform. But de Gasperi leaned toward the United States and in January 1947 confirmed this tilt in a visit to Washington, which resulted in the U.S. Export–Import Bank's extending Italy a $100 million credit. He also persuaded the TRUMAN administration to divert six wheat-laden ships bound for the U.S. Army in Germany to Italian ports to stave off famine. De Gasperi described his mission as a "great success both from the concrete and moral standpoint."

On his return to Italy, de Gasperi also introduced conservative law-and-order measures to protect the state and prevent a communist coup. This, plus his trip to Washington, led to protests from the communists. De Gasperi responded by resigning and forming a government without the PCI. The Italian communists have remained out of the national government.

Out of office, the PCI, with encouragement from the Soviet-controlled COMINFORM, organized a series of damaging anti-government strikes, and in September 1947, PCI leader Palmiro Togliatti warned that he could call on "30,000 well-armed partisans." Togliatti also denounced the U.S. "world dictatorship" for trying to "spread another war." De Gasperi, however, weathered the disturbances and emerged the chief bulwark against communism in Italy.

To protect that bulwark, the United States expanded its already generous aid to Italy. In 1947 alone, the Truman administration released Italian assets frozen during the war and increased emergency food aid, and in December Congress voted Italy a further $200 million in financial aid. The United States also supported the Christian Democratic Party secretly, channeling millions of dollars through the CIA offices for the party's campaign funds.

De Gasperi became an enthusiastic supporter of the Western Alliance and increased European integration. Italy became a founding member of the NORTH ATLANTIC TREATY ORGANIZATION and the EUROPEAN COAL AND STEEL COMMUNITY. De Gasperi was an enthusiastic supporter of the MARSHALL PLAN and staked his political career on the EUROPEAN DEFENSE COMMUNITY.

The problem of the EDC was closely linked to the additional problem of Trieste, and in the 1950s these two issues posed a major threat to both de Gasperi and his policy of close Western ties. Trieste is an Adriatic port city then claimed by both Italy and Yugoslavia and, in the postwar period, occupied by American, Yugoslav and British troops. Italian public opinion demanded ownership of Trieste. The British and Americans, however, were reluctant to do anything that might drive Yugoslavia back into the Soviet camp.

The Italian communists were able to make substantial political gains as a result of the British and American posi-tions, and the U.S. ambassador to Italy, CLARE BOOTHE LUCE, warned that a failure to solve the Trieste problem to Italy's satisfaction could result in a communist victory in the elections of 1953. De Gasperi, for his part, warned that anything less than full Anglo–American support could jeopardize Italian membership in NATO, American bases in Italy and Italian ratification of the European Defense Community Treaty.

Luce's fears appeared to be at least partially justified by the results of the June 7–8 election, in which de Gasperi's four-part centrist coalition emerged with the slimmest majority in Italian political history. De Gasperi formed a single-party government, but within the month the government fell and de Gasperi was forced to hand the premiership over to Giuseppe Pella, although he retained considerable political power as the leader of the Christian Democratic Party.

The fall of de Gasperi was a blow to the American and British governments and encouraged negotiators to press for a settlement favorable to Italy. The Trieste Treaty was eventually signed on October 5, 1954. Shortly afterward, the Italian government confirmed its membership in the EDC. The French National Assembly, however, rejected the defense community, and after hearing the news de Gasperi suffered a heart attack and died on August 19, 1954.

For Further Information:
De Gasperi, Maria. *De Gasperi: Man Alone.* New York, 1965.
Grindrod, Muriel. *The Rebuilding of Italy.* London, 1955.
Hughes, Stuart. *The United States and Italy.* Cambridge, Mass., 1953.
Kogan, Norman. *A Political History of Postwar Italy.* New York, 1966.

de Gaulle, Charles   (November 22, 1890–November 10, 1970)   For 30 years, from 1940 to his death in 1970, Charles de Gaulle towered over the political landscape of France. His vehement France-first foreign policy created major divisions within the Western Alliance, led to French withdrawal from NATO and created an independent pro-Western force on the world stage.

De Gaulle was born into the lesser French nobility. His family had supplied officers for the French Army since the 13th century. De Gaulle attended the French military academy at Saint-Cyr and graduated in 1912.

During WORLD WAR I de Gaulle was wounded three times, captured at Verdun and awarded the Legion of Honor. He became a close friend of Marshal Henri-Philippe Petain, who secured several key posts for him in the inter-war years. In 1934 de Gaulle created a stir in political and military circles when, with remarkable foresight, he published a book, called *Toward a Modern Army*, that criticized the supposedly impregnable Maginot Line and proposed a modernized army with an elite mobile tank force at its head.

The book and its proposals were attacked by the French defense experts of the time. But when the German tanks rolled past the Maginot Line, Prime Minister Paul Reynaud invited de Gaulle into his cabinet as under secretary of defense and sent him to London for talks with Prime Minister WINSTON

CHURCHILL. In London de Gaulle came to the conclusion that France would fall and Britain would remain firm. When the fall of France came a few weeks later, de Gaulle fled to London and on June 28 the British recognized him "as the leader of all the Free French wherever they may be, who will rally to him in defense of the Allied cause." It was at this point that de Gaulle began to see himself as the incarnation of France.

This belief brought him into early conflict with the British and Americans. Churchill once described the Cross of Lorraine (the symbol of de Gaulle's Free French Army) as "the heaviest cross I have ever had to bear." U.S. President FRANKLIN ROOSEVELT's relationship with de Gaulle was even worse. During the war Roosevelt saw de Gaulle as "more and more unbearable" and suffering from a "messianic complex" that made him a "potential dictator." The relationship between Roosevelt and de Gaulle deteriorated to the point that Roosevelt tried to maneuver de Gaulle into handing over the French leadership to General Henri-Honoré Giraud in 1943.

De Gaulle was heavily influenced by his wartime experiences with Roosevelt and became convinced that the United States was trying "to settle Europe's future in France's absence." Later he became more certain that the United States was an aggressive power that posed a threat to European and world stability. He considered Britain to be an American satellite, at best, and Washington's Trojan horse at worst.

In contrast to his relations with the Western Powers, de Gaulle enjoyed a good wartime relationship with Soviet leader JOSEF STALIN. As soon as the Soviet Union entered the war on the Allied side, Stalin recognized de Gaulle as the Free French leader and instructed the French communists, who provided the core of the French Resistance, to follow his orders. This relationship was crucial to de Gaulle at a time when he was starting to build a political base.

By the time Paris was liberated in August 1944 de Gaulle had become accepted as the leader of the French nation, and his triumphant march from the Arc de Triomphe to the Cathedral of Notre Dame on August 26, 1944, confirmed his own belief in himself and in his power.

De Gaulle, however, found it difficult to settle into postwar party politics. In January 1946 he resigned, only to return to politics again in April 1947, when he formed the Rally of the French People (Rassemblement du Peuple Français). The RPR, which became known simply as the Gaullist Party, was the political extension of de Gaulle's belief that he was the embodiment of France and was somehow above the free-for-all of party politics. The Gaullist Party, declared de Gaulle, was "a party against parties."

After years of cooperating with the communists, de Gaulle now turned against them because of their unswerving support for the Soviet Union. In July 1947 he accused the Soviet Union of endangering "the same rights and liberties" as Nazi Germany had and predicted an "immense and unpardonable war" unless, with the help of American financial aid, traditional European governments again became strong enough to attract people flirting with communism. De Gaulle was at-

tacked by Soviet foreign minister Andrei Vishinsky as an "admirer and imitator" of Hitler.

But the Gaullists failed to obtain the support of big business, or, more importantly in the days of the MARSHALL PLAN, the support of successive American administrations, who placed their confidence and money in governments headed by less mercurial French politicians such as JULES MOCH and ROBERT SCHUMAN. In July 1955 de Gaulle retired a second time, telling journalists, "We shall not meet again until the tempest again looses itself on France."

In 1958 the political tempest again loosed itself on France in the form of the Algerian War, and on June 1, 1958, the national assembly elected de Gaulle premier and invested him with almost dictatorial powers. At the end of that year, under the new Fifth Republic whose constitution he had designed himself, he was elected to a seven-year term as president. He went on to shock his military and right-wing supporters by agreeing to Algerian independence in 1962.

On February 13, 1960, France successfully tested an atomic bomb in the Sahara Desert, thus becoming the world's fourth nuclear power. De Gaulle announced, "Hurrah for France! Since this morning she is stronger and prouder." The comments made it clear that he considered the test's success to be a major step toward fulfilling his policy of returning France to a dominant position in Europe. The development of the French nuclear deterrent was also tied to de Gaulle's refusal to believe that the United States would use its nuclear weapons to defend European soil.

As the decade wore on, de Gaulle oversaw the cooling of France's ties with the United States and Britain and the warming of ties with the U.S.S.R. The process climaxed with France's withdrawal from the military structure of NATO in 1966. (For further details, see under FRANCE.)

De Gaulle won a second term in 1966 but was badly shaken by the massive student-worker uprising of 1968. He resigned after losing a nationwide referendum in 1969, and died on November 10, 1970.

Charles de Gaulle, the most powerful figure in France for three decades, at a press conference in November 1959. Photo courtesy of Popperfoto.

For Further Information:

Cook, Don. *Charles de Gaulle: A Biography.* New York, 1983.

Crozier, Brian. *De Gaulle.* New York, 1973.

Kulski, Wladislaw. *De Gaulle and the World.* Syracuse, N.Y., 1966.

Lacouture, Jean. *De Gaulle.* New York, 1970.

Mairidis, Roy C., and Bernard Brow. *The De Gaulle Republic: Quest for Unity.* Homewood, Ill., 1960.

Mauriac, François. *De Gaulle.* New York, 1966.

Monticone, Ronald C. *Charles de Gaulle.* New York, 1975.

Newhouse, John. *De Gaulle and the Anglo-Saxons.* New York, 1970.

Pinder, John. *Europe Against De Gaulle.* London, 1963.

Deng Xiaoping (1904–)

Deng Xiaoping became the leader of the PEOPLE'S REPUBLIC OF CHINA in 1977. He encouraged closer relations with the West and introduced economic reforms. These changes were carried out without a parallel political liberalization, however, and this led to a bloody repression of pro-democracy demonstrations in 1989.

Deng was born in Szechwan Province, the son of a wealthy landowner. In 1920 he left China to study in France, where he met CHOU EN-LAI and joined a branch of the Chinese Communist Party that Chou had founded in Europe. After completing his work-study program in France, Deng returned to China via Moscow, where he undertook further studies at the Oriental University.

Between 1926 and 1927, while the Chinese communists and CHIANG KAI-SHEK's Kuomintang Party were nominally cooperating, Deng taught at the Chungshan Military Academy. After Chiang's attack on the communists, Deng went underground in Shanghai; he eventually joined MAO ZEDONG in Kiangsi, where he became head of the Propaganda Bureau of the Red Army. During the communists' "Long March" into northwest China in 1934–35, Deng was deputy commander of the army's 12th Division.

Deng was named political commissar of a division of the Eighth Route Army in 1937 and in 1943 was promoted to director of the General Political Department of the People's Revolution Military Commission. He joined the Central Committee in 1945 and during the CHINESE CIVIL WAR was the chief political commissar of the Second Field Army, which spearheaded the successful campaign against the Kuomintang forces.

After the founding of the People's Republic of China on October 1, 1949, Deng was named the party leader for southwest China. In 1952 he was summoned to Beijing, and over the next few years held a number of senior posts in the party and government, including Secretary General of the Central Committee, Vice Chairman of the National Defense Council, Minister of Finance and Vice Premier.

The early 1950s saw the laying of the basic political and economic foundation stones of communist China. Deng during this period adopted the relatively moderate economic policies that were to mark the remainder of his political career. He also allied himself with LIU SHAOQI, in opposition to the pro-Soviet Kao Kang and the radically-minded Mao. In April 1955 the moderates and anti-Soviet figures were significantly strengthened when Deng was promoted to the Politburo, Liu was promoted to the number-two position behind Mao and Kao was purged.

The main thrust of Deng's influence at this stage was felt in the economic sphere as he moved to reduce Soviet control of Chinese factories and the railway system. But the Soviet Union continued to exert a strong influence over China's military and foreign policy, and agriculture and intellectual activity were controlled by Mao.

In 1956 Mao launched his "Hundred Flowers" campaign, designed to ease restrictions on the Chinese intelligentsia and stimulate political debate. The encouraging of debate was intended to demonstrate the intellectual supremacy of communist philosophy, but, coinciding as it did with the Soviet invasion of Hungary, the Hundred Flowers campaign only led to an attack on the Chinese Communist Party. This undermined Mao's position within the party and improved that of Deng and Liu. In 1958 Mao tried to recover lost ground with his economic program called the "Great Leap Forward." This quickly failed, and Mao was eclipsed by Liu and Deng.

To correct the errors of the Great Leap Forward, Deng proposed radical changes for Chinese farmers, including an increase in the size of their private plots and material rewards for individual enterprise. Justifying the changes, he said, "For the purpose of increasing agricultural production, any by-hook-or-by-crook method can be applied. It doesn't matter whether a cat is black or white so long as it catches mice."

Deng played a leading role in the formalization of the SINO–SOVIET SPLIT. He was part of a delegation to Moscow in 1957 that criticized NIKITA KHRUSHCHEV's anti-Stalinist line and the Soviets' rapprochement with Yugoslavia. In September 1960, Deng represented China at an international meeting of communist parties in Moscow. Deng repeated the 1957 attack on Khrushchev and widened the ideological assault to encompass a condemnation of Khrushchev's policy of PEACEFUL COEXISTENCE. He accused the Soviet Union of leading the communist parties of the world along the road of capitulation

Chinese leader Deng Xiaoping (right) with U.S. vice president Walter Mondale in Beijing on August 26, 1979. Photo courtesy of Popperfoto.

to imperialism. In 1963 a last attempt was made to heal the Sino–Soviet rift; Deng again led the Chinese delegation. His continued intransigence did nothing to bring the two countries together.

During this period, Mao continued to be eclipsed by Deng and Liu. But he was planning his comeback with the aid of Defense Minister LIN BIAO. In 1966 Mao launched the CULTURAL REVOLUTION, with the aim of toppling Liu and Deng and restoring Mao and his doctrines to power. In this respect, the movement was a success. Deng was branded a "capitalist roader" and was removed from all his party and governmental posts in 1967. His movements over the next six years are largely a mystery, but in April 1973 he reappeared on the Chinese political scene at a state dinner for Cambodia's Prince Norodom Sihanouk.

In August 1973, Deng was reappointed to the Central Committee, and in January 1974 he was back on the Politburo. In 1974 and 1975 Deng took over many duties from the ailing Chou En-lai, although he never formally assumed the title of Premier. Deng attended almost all of Chairman Mao's meetings with foreign visitors and met privately with U.S. secretary of State HENRY KISSINGER in 1974. In May 1975 he became the highest-ranking Chinese official to visit Western Europe when he went to France for talks with French president VALERY GISCARD-D'ESTAING. In December 1975, Deng gave the keynote speech at a state dinner for U.S. president GERALD FORD. He used the occasion to accuse the Soviet Union of being "the most dangerous source of war" in the world.

Following further power struggles and the death of Mao, Deng became China's paramount leader in 1977, a position he continued to hold into the 1990s. (For detailed developments, see CHINA, PEOPLE'S REPUBLIC OF.)

For Further Information:

Hsu, C.Y. *The Rise of Modern China*. New York, 1983.

Camilleri, J. *Chinese Foreign Policy: The Maoist Era and its Aftermath.* Seattle, 1980.

Meisner, Maurice. *Mao's China and After: A History of the People's Republic.* New York, 1986.

Denmark   Denmark is one of the most pacific of the NATO allies and at the same time one of the most strategic, as its land mass blocks the entrance to the Baltic Sea.

Denmark managed to remain largely aloof from Great-Power politics until the middle of the 19th century, when the emergence of global navies and continental railways increased its strategic importance. Lacking the resources to defend itself, Denmark has ever since been faced with three foreign policy options: neutrality, alliance with a great power, or a foreign policy that bends to the will of the most threatening great power.

Neutrality has been the preferred alternative of most Danes and was the cornerstone of Danish foreign policy from 1864 to 1949. Strict neutrality kept Denmark out of World War I but led to its humiliating occupation by Nazi Germany during World War II.

This experience produced a strong anti-appeasement and pro-alliance lobby, as evidenced by the postwar slogan "Never again a 9th of April" (the date of the German invasion in 1940). There were, however, differences over the structure and type of alliance that Danes would join. In line with their pacifist traditions, they initially steered away from the Western powers and looked to the United Nations to provide a protective structure.

But these hopes were quickly dashed, and the Danish government began to toy with a Swedish-promoted idea of a Nordic Defense Group to include Norway, Denmark and Sweden, bolstered with United States military supplies. The Nordic Defense Group failed to materialize when Norway decided in March 1949 that because it shared a northern border with the Soviet Union, it needed the direct protection of the United States, Canada and Britain. At the same time, the United States indicated that it would be unwilling to supply a separate Scandinavian grouping. Denmark, unable to provide for its own defense, reluctantly agreed to join the NORTH ATLANTIC TREATY ORGANIZATION (NATO) as the only alternative.

But from its earliest days, Denmark was one of the least enthusiastic members concerning both NATO and American foreign policies. In January 1950 it recognized communist China, and its contribution to the United Nations' effort in the KOREAN WAR was limited to a hospital ship, 10 ambulances and several cargo ships. At a meeting of Scandinavian foreign ministers in March 1951, Denmark agreed to continue to support the UN intervention in Korea but pressed for a negotiated solution to the conflict rather than a military one. In 1952 Denmark was one of the leading countries behind the formation of the Nordic Council.

Denmark, however, made a valuable contribution to the defense of the continental United States and the North Atlantic when in April 1951 it signed a 20-year U.S.–Danish treaty (renewed for a further 20 years in 1971) on the defense of Danish-owned Greenland. Under the agreement, Denmark retained control of Greenland's naval and air bases, but the United States and other NATO countries were allowed the use of them. The United States was also given the right to base troops in Greenland and to administer some districts jointly with Denmark. Greenland's proximity to the Arctic regions of the Soviet Union meant that it quickly became a vital link in the U.S. Strategic Air Command and in the DISTANT EARLY WARNING (DEW) LINE. Until 1991, two important U.S. air bases were maintained at Thule and Soendrestroenfjord. In 1991, the agreement was extended for the Thule base only, for the duration of the existence of NATO (it can be cancelled on six months' notice by either party).

The Danish government took a leading role in reestablishing links with Eastern Europe in the 1970s. It also opposed American policy in Vietnam and in 1973 recognized North Korea. A strong pacifist tendency forced reductions in the Danish defense budget between 1968 and 1973. These seriously undermined the Danish defense capability, and to avoid further damage and to take defense out of the arena of partisan politics, the government in 1973 introduced a four-year defense budget.

This did not stop the other NATO countries from criticizing the Danish defense policy, particularly at time when the Soviet Union had dramatically increased the size of its Baltic fleet. In October 1980, U.S. defense secretary Harold Brown wrote to his Danish counterpart Poul Soegaard complaining about the level of Danish defense spending and warning that he would find it difficult to justify a U.S. commitment to reinforce Denmark unless that country was "able, and seen to be able, to carry out its assigned role in NATO."

In December 1979 Denmark supported a six-month delay in the implementation of NATO's decision to deploy U.S. cruise and PERSHING II missiles in response to the deployment of Soviet intermediate-range nuclear forces. The delay was meant to give the Soviet Union an opportunity to negotiate a reduction in its forces before American deployment started to go into effect. In December 1983 the Danish parliament voted by 87 to 75 to oppose the NATO deployment of cruise and Pershing II missiles. NATO foreign ministers meeting a few days later tried to satisfy the Danish reservations by stressing that deployment could be "halted or reversed" in the event of a U.S.–Soviet agreement. But in May 1984, Denmark became the first NATO country to withdraw from the program to deploy the missiles when the parliament voted to stop payments to the plan (under the NATO agreement countries that did not deploy the weapons would financially contribute to the program).

The Soviet Union several times attempted to exploit Danish pacifist sentiments either with threats or with political inducements. In March 1957, Denmark was warned by Premier NIKOLAI BULGANIN not to allow its territory to be used for NATO nuclear bases. In a letter to Premier Hans Hansen, Bulganin warned that any country that allowed its territory to be used as a base for nuclear weapons would be subject to a retaliatory strike. In case of war, he wrote, this would "be tantamount to suicide for countries the size of Denmark." This was followed in June 1957 by NIKITA KHRUSHCHEV's proposal for a Baltic "zone of neutrality and . . . peace forever." The zone would include Denmark, Finland, Norway and Sweden. The proposal was repeated in 1983 by Soviet leader YURI ANDROPOV, who offered the added inducement of discussions on de-nuclearizing the Soviet Baltic region and the Baltic Sea.

Soviet foreign policy did have some success in that it led in 1957 to the Danes banning nuclear weapons from their soil. But British and American ships carrying nuclear weapons were allowed to continue to visit Danish ports, and this policy was not questioned until April 1988, when the Folketing (parliament) voted to ban NATO ships carrying nuclear weapons. The resolution threatened Danish membership in NATO because Britain and the United States had a policy of refusing to disclose whether or not their ships carried nuclear weapons. The ban also threatened British reinforcement of Denmark with its 14,000-strong mobile force, because the troops would have to be deployed across the North Sea by the British Navy. U.S. secretary of state GEORGE SHULTZ warned that the resolution would have "extremely serious" consequences for Danish–American relations. He said that the resolution went "to the very heart of the meaning and interlocking nature of our mutual commitments with the NATO Alliance."

The resolution was unacceptable to the minority conservative-led coalition of Premier Poul Schluter, and he called an election on the issue. The election in May 1988 quickly turned into a referendum on Danish membership in NATO. The election failed to produce a clear mandate on the issue, and in June 1988 Schluter formed another government after reaching a compromise on the nuclear question. Under the terms of this compromise, Denmark would inform the ships of other nations of its antinuclear policy but would not insist on specific guarantees that the ships did not carry nuclear weapons.

For Further Information:
Fitzmaurice, John. *Politics in Denmark.* New York, 1981.
Gann, Lewis H., ed. *The Defense of Western Europe.* Dover, Mass., 1987.

Dewey, Thomas   (March 24, 1902–March 16, 1971)
Thomas Dewey was governor of New York and twice unsuccessful Republican nominee for the U.S. presidency. His support for President HARRY TRUMAN's liberal anti-communism is believed to have driven a number of prominent Republicans to the far right following his second presidential defeat.

Dewey grew up in Michigan and was educated at the University of Michigan and Columbia University Law School before starting to practice law. In 1942 he was elected governor of New York, a post he held until 1955, and in 1944 was the Republican Party's candidate for the presidency, opposing Franklin D. Roosevelt. He was nominated again in 1948 to run against Harry Truman.

Dewey consistently supported President Truman's calls for a bipartisan foreign policy. He supported the TRUMAN DOCTRINE and the MARSHALL PLAN. Dewey also opposed conservative elements in his own party who wanted to ban the American Communist Party. His only major foreign policy difference with the president was over support for Nationalist China, which Dewey wanted to be strengthened. But in the 1948 presidential campaign he refrained from making any strong attacks on Truman's policy in China on the grounds that any foreign policy divisions between the two major candidates would only encourage Soviet aggressiveness and exacerbate Cold War tensions.

The Republican Party was confident that Dewey would defeat Truman in the 1948 election. Dewey had been a national figure since before the war (he had first become famous as a racket-busting prosecutor in New York City), while Truman had leapt from virtual anonymity to the White

House. They were also encouraged by the presidential candidacy of former Democrat and former Vice-President Henry A. Wallace, who had established the left-liberal Progressive Citizens of America Party, which was expected to draw votes away from Truman. But Truman won strong support from the trade unions, black voters and the Jewish community. This plus Truman's whirlwind campaign, compared to Dewey's sedate and statesmanlike effort, secured Truman 49.5% of the popular vote compared to Dewey's 45.1%.

A number of prominent Republicans blamed Dewey's defeat on his refusal to attack Truman as being "soft on Communism." Prominent Republicans such as Senate Republican leader Robert Taft reluctantly supported Senator JOSEPH MCCARTHY's witch-hunting activities because they believed that attacking communism would win votes. This left the Republicans with a strong faction supporting a right-wing foreign policy.

After his defeat in 1948, Dewey remained prominent within Republican Party circles, although he never again ran for national office. He played a major role in recruiting DWIGHT EISENHOWER for the 1952 Republican presidential nomination and helped to secure the vice-presidential nomination for RICHARD NIXON on the grounds that he was "a responsible McCarthy." After his election victory in 1968, Nixon offered Dewey the post of his choice, either chief justice or secretary of state. He declined both jobs. Dewey died of a heart attack on March 16, 1971.

For Further Information:

Divine, Robert. *Foreign Policy and U.S. Presidential Elections*, 2 vols. New York, 1974.

Schlesinger, Arthur, and Fred Israel, eds. *History of American Presidential Elections*, 4 vols. New York, 1971.

Dien Bien Phu Dien Bien Phu was the site of the final victory of the Vietnamese independence forces over the French in Indochina in 1954. The battle nearly resulted in American military intervention in Vietnam that same year; it did lead to the withdrawal of all French forces from Vietnam and the division of the country along the 17th parallel.

After World War II, the newly-reinstalled French colonial administration found itself fighting a communist-led independence movement, the Viet Minh, headed by HO CHI MINH. From early in the conflict the United States provided the French with military and financial aid to fight the Viet Minh. Despite American aid, the French found it difficult to defeat the guerrilla army and in November 1953 selected the village of Dien Bien Phu as the site at which to concentrate their forces for a major pitched battle.

Dien Bien Phu, which had changed hands several times during the war, is located near the Laotian border in northwestern Vietnam and about 80 miles from China. Military experts have criticized French commander, General Henri Navarre's choice of Dien Bien Phu as a battleground. The village was accessible only by air and was situated in a large bowl-shaped valley about 10 miles across. The French occupied the bottom of this bowl and the Viet Minh controlled the mountains that surrounded it. Any aircraft trying to supply the French troops had to fly past a deadly antiaircraft barrage from entrenched mountain positions, and the French garrison was soon surrounded and subjected to daily artillery bombardments.

Navarre's fatal strategic errors sapped both the morale of the remaining French forces in Indochina and the will of the politicians in Paris. The French government concluded that American military intervention was essential to keep the war effort alive. On March 20, 1954, General Paul Ely, French chief of staff, flew to Washington for talks with Secretary of State JOHN FOSTER DULLES. On April 3 Dulles and Admiral Arthur Radford, chairman of the Joint Chiefs of Staff, met congressional leaders to discuss the possibility of American intervention. The consensus was that the United States could not act alone, and it was therefore decided to seek joint action with Britain, France, Australia, New Zealand, Thailand and the Phillippines. It was felt that the key to an allied intervention was British support.

Britain, however, was reluctant to intervene only a few weeks before a scheduled Geneva Conference on Korea and Indochina and was concerned that Anglo-American intervention would result in a counter-intervention by Chinese and possibly Soviet forces. Even in France there was little enthusiasm for Dulles' plan, as French popular support for continuing the war was fast dwindling.

The EISENHOWER administration prepared for unilateral intervention in the hope that this would be sufficient to stop the Viet Minh and that it would persuade Britain to join the war. On April 23, two American aircraft carriers were ordered to the area, and a group of 60 B-29 bombers based in the Philippines were prepared for action on April 28. Britain, however, continued to refuse to commit its forces, and the Geneva Conference on Korea and Indochina opened on April 26 with the French garrison at Dien Bien Phu on its last legs.

At the conference, Dulles made one last, vain attempt to persuade British foreign secretary Sir ANTHONY EDEN to join the conflict. When he failed, a bitter Dulles announced that he was personally withdrawing from the conference and left Undersecretary of State WALTER BEDELL SMITH in charge of the U.S. delegation.

On May 7, 1954, Dien Bien Phu fell. The French suffered 5,000 casualties, and 10,000 French troops were taken prisoner. What little support there had been for the war within France quickly evaporated, and the emphasis shifted to the Geneva negotiations, which resulted in what was intended to be the temporary division of the country along the 17th parallel.

For Further Reading

Billings-Yun, Melanie. *Decision Against War: Eisenhower and Dien Bien Phu, 1954.* New York, 1988.

Cameron, Allan W. *Vietnam Crisis: A Documentary History.* Ithaca, N.Y., 1971.

Fall, Bernard B. *Hell in a Very Small Place.* Philadelphia, 1966.

Grauwin, Paul. *Doctor at Dienbienphu.* New York, 1955.
Karnow, Stanley. *Vietnam: A History.* New York, 1984.
Keegan, John. *Dien Bien Phu.* New York, 1974.
Kimche, Jon. *Spying for Peace; General Guisan and Swiss Neutrality.* London, 1961.
Randle, Robert E. *Geneva, 1954: The Settlement of the Indochinese War.* Princeton, 1969.
Roy, Jules. *The Battle of Dienbienphu.* New York, 1965.

Dillon, C. Douglas   (August 21, 1909–   ) C. Douglas Dillon played a major role in the 1950s and 1960s in the development of American foreign aid policies. During the KENNEDY administration he was secretary of the treasury.

Dillon was born into a leading New York financial family and attended the exclusive private school of Groton before going on to Harvard University. When Dillon was 21 his father bought him a seat on the New York Stock Exchange, and seven years later he was a vice president of Dillon, Read and Co., the investment banking firm founded by the elder Dillon.

During World War II Dillon saw action in the Pacific with the U.S. Navy, and in 1946 he was appointed chairman of the board of Dillon, Read. He was a major contributor to DWIGHT EISENHOWER's presidential campaign in 1951–52 and helped to organize the campaign in New Jersey.

Dillon's reward was the ambassadorship to France. In this position he frequently stood in for Secretary of State JOHN FOSTER DULLES at the GENEVA CONFERENCE ON INDOCHINA AND KOREA in 1954 and assisted Special Ambassador DAVID BRUCE in attempting (unsuccessfully) to persuade the French to accept the EUROPEAN DEFENSE COMMUNITY.

In January 1957 Dillon returned to Washington as deputy undersecretary of state for economic affairs, in which capacity he supervised the entire U.S. foreign aid program. He was also appointed an alternate governor of the INTERNATIONAL MONETARY FUND and a member of the Development Loan Fund. In July 1959 Dulles promoted Dillon to undersecretary of state for economic affairs.

Dillon set out to reorganize America's foreign aid policy, arguing that communist technical advances demanded more rapid development of the West's economic strength. The United States, he asserted, could no longer grant foreign aid on an emergency basis. His specific proposals included a five-year extension of the Reciprocal Trade Agreements Act and more money for the Development Loan Fund, especially for African and Asian countries. He also urged Congress to approve U.S. membership in the Organization of Trade Cooperation, an agency designed to administer the General Agreement on Tariffs and Trade. Finally, he recommended more private investment and greater use of the Export-Import Bank to help underdeveloped nations. Dillon's proposals met with considerable success.

In April 1959 Dillon was promoted again, this time to undersecretary of state, the number two position in the State Department. He continued to concentrate on economic issues, especially in Latin America, and laid some of the groundwork for what later became President John F. Kennedy's

ALLIANCE FOR PROGRESS. In December 1960, Dillon's persistent efforts to convince the West Europeans to develop more ambitious foreign aid programs led to the establishment of the ORGANIZATION FOR ECONOMIC COOPERATION AND DEVELOPMENT (OECD), which marked the beginning of a coordinated foreign aid policy by the Western developed nations.

Dillon was a major contributor to Vice President RICHARD NIXON's presidential campaign and was surprised when Kennedy asked him to join his cabinet as treasury secretary. The appointment of a man with his financial expertise was meant to reassure the financial community, which was apprehensive about the "easy money" proclivities of the Democrats. Despite his position as a leading Republican, Dillon formed a close personal and working relationship with Kennedy, which enabled him to push through most of his policies.

Kennedy also gave Dillon a number of foreign policy assignments. Probably the major assignment was to head the American delegation sent to Punta del Este, Uruguay to inaugurate the Alliance for Progress in August 1961. At that meeting Dillon pledged $20 billion in low-interest loans over the following 10 years to improve Latin America's living standards. Dillon also sat on the National Security Council and took part in the discussions during the CUBAN MISSILE CRISIS of October 1963.

Dillon was never able to achieve the rapport with President LYNDON JOHNSON that he enjoyed with Kennedy, and he resigned in March 1965 to return to Wall Street. He was, however, retained as a financial and foreign policy adviser. He was one of the members of the senior advisory group who advised Johnson to de-escalate the VIETNAM WAR in March 1968 and was chairman of the advisory committee to the U.S. Treasury on international monetary affairs.

Over the following 20 years Dillon continued to act as a part-time adviser on financial and foreign issues. In 1971 he was appointed chairman of the privately-controlled Rockefeller Foundation, and in 1975 he served on the Ford administration's special commission investigating CIA activities, and another official committee reviewing U.S. Middle East policy. After the election of President RONALD REAGAN he expressed strong criticism of the administration's proposed increase in defense spending. On July 6, 1989, Dillon was awarded the Presidential Medal of Freedom, America's highest civilian award.

For Further Information:
Aubrey, Henry. *The Dollar in World Affairs.* New York, 1964.
Baldwin, David. *Economic Development and American Foreign Policy, 1943–1962.* Chicago, 1966.
Canterbery, E. Ray. *Economics on a New Frontier.* Belmont, Mass., 1968.
Coffin, Frank. *Witness for Aid.* Boston, 1964.
Wood, R. F. *From Marshall Plan to Debt Crisis.* Berkeley, Calif., 1986.

Disarmament and Arms Control Negotiations   Disarmament and arms control negotiations have been a major factor in East–West relations since the earliest days of the Cold War and have encompassed conventional forces as well as strategic and intermediate-range nuclear weapons.

In fact, disarmament negotiations have been a major part of international relations for centuries, and are based on the premise that countries cannot fight if they are not armed. For such negotiations to succeed there must be a climate of trust between the negotiating parties, because arms control negotiations can be broken, giving the offending country a quick and easy advantage. The absence of such trust consistently bedeviled East–West attempts to stop the spiraling arms race that characterized the Cold War.

The first postwar efforts at disarmament were made within the context of the United Nations. (See ATOMIC ENERGY COMMISSION, UN)

By the early 1950s the KOREAN WAR, the BERLIN BLOCKADE, the formation of opposing military blocs in Europe and conflicts in Southeast Asia and elsewhere had pushed all talk of arms reduction into the background. What movement there was in this field concentrated on the creation of confidence-building measures such as the establishment of verification procedures; measures to prevent surprise attacks and minimize the possibility of a catastrophic error; and agreements on the testing of nuclear weapons as first steps toward arms reductions.

President DWIGHT EISENHOWER's 1955 "OPEN SKIES" Plan was the leading effort at confidence-building through verification measures. Eisenhower offered to exchange military blueprints and charts, giving descriptions and locations of all military and naval installations of any kind. He also proposed that Britain, France, the United States and the Soviet Union have a fixed number of airfields and aircraft equipped for photographic reconnaissance to inspect each other's territory. This proposal foundered on the Soviet fear that Western aerial reconnaissance would be used for general espionage purposes.

The first major step toward disarmament was the NUCLEAR TEST BAN TREATY signed in August 1963 by the United States, Britain and the Soviet Union. The treaty banned all testing of nuclear weapons in the atmosphere, outer space or underwater. The Nuclear Test Ban Treaty made no overt effort to reduce or in any way limit nuclear weapons arsenals, but it proved that East–West agreements on nuclear issues were possible and thus helped to slow the arms race and make future negotiations possible.

Disarmament efforts suffered a major setback with the CUBAN MISSILE CRISIS. This destroyed some of the climate of goodwill created by the Test Ban Treaty, but it did lead to the establishment of the HOT LINE between the American and Soviet leaders—a direct telex link that enabled the two superpowers to communicate in times of crisis in order to avoid a misunderstanding that could lead to a nuclear catastrophe.

The next round of U.S.–Soviet talks was SALT I (STRATEGIC ARMS LIMITATION TALKS), which began in Helsinki in 1969. These talks resulted in the May 1972 ANTIBALLISTIC MISSILE TREATY and the SALT I agreement. The first treaty limited the antiballistic missile systems allowed by the Soviet Union and the United States, and the second was an interim agreement limiting the construction of INTERCONTINENTAL BALLISTIC MISSILES and ballistic missile submarines until agreement was reached in a SALT II Treaty.

Negotiations on SALT II started in late 1972 and were eventually concluded in June 1979, when the SALT II Treaty was signed in Vienna by U.S. president JIMMY CARTER and Soviet president LEONID BREZHNEV. Although the treaty called for the destruction of some Soviet weapons, it also implicitly recognized U.S.–Soviet parity in their nuclear arsenals. This was anathema to American conservatives, who set out to block ratification of the treaty in Congress. The SALT II treaty was finally killed by the Soviet invasion of AFGHANISTAN in December 1979 and the election of President RONALD REAGAN in the fall of 1980.

While the U.S.–Soviet SALT I and SALT II negotiations were in progress, two other important sets of wider East–West talks were being conducted that involved all the European states and Canada as well as the two superpowers. The first was the CONFERENCE ON SECURITY AND COOPERATION IN EUROPE (CSCE), which started in Helsinki in November 1972, and the second was the Mutual Balance Force Reduction Talks (MBFR), which started in Vienna in January 1973. The MBFR talks, concentrating on the reduction of conventional weapons in Europe, foundered on the Soviet Union's refusal to accept NATO estimates of the size and quality of their tank forces and other conventional forces, and eventually came to an end in 1988. The CSCE negotiations did not specifically deal with arms negotiations but resulted in the signing in August 1975 of a pact that included an agreement to give 21 days' notice of military maneuvers involving more than 25,000 men, with the purpose of building confidence and avoiding the possibility of accidental attack.

The 1980s were dominated by two sets of U.S.–Soviet arms control negotiations. The first was the intermediate-range nuclear forces (INF) negotiations designed to reduce the number of Soviet and American intermediate-range nuclear weapons in Europe, and the other was the Strategic Arms Reduction Talks (START, see STRATEGIC ARMS REDUCTION TREATIES) aimed at reducing the intercontinental or strategic ballistic missiles in the nuclear arsenals of the two superpowers. The INF negotiations resulted in the signing in December 1987 of the INF treaty, which stipulated the scrapping of American and Soviet INF weapons in Europe (see INTERMEDIATE-RANGE NUCLEAR FORCES TREATY).

The START negotiations were hampered by the Soviets' insistence on including President Reagan's proposed STRATEGIC DEFENSE INITIATIVE in the talks. SDI, or "Star Wars," was a proposed defensive "shield" based in outer space. The Soviets claimed that such a system would be a breach of the 1972 ABM Treaty and would render irrelevant the terms of any treaty reducing strategic weapons. Reagan, and later President George Bush, refused to include SDI in the negotiations, and at the end of 1989 this issue continued to block a proposed 50% reduction in the U.S. and Soviet nuclear weapons arsenals.

Through 1988, 1989 and 1990, however, East and West agreed to major reductions in conventional forces in Europe at the Conventional Weapons in Europe (CFE) talks, which replaced the unsuccessful MBFR negotiations. The CFE treaty was signed November 19, 1990, in Paris by the leaders of all NATO and Warsaw Pact countries.

For Further Information:
Dean, Arthur. *Test Ban and Disarmament: The Path of Negotiation.* New York, 1966.
Newhouse, John. *Cold Dawn: The Story of SALT.* New York, 1973.
Smith, Gerard. *Doubletalk: The Story of the First Strategic Arms Limitation Talks.* Garden City, N. Y., 1980.
UN Department for Disarmament Affairs. *The United Nations Disarmament Yearbook,* Vol. 13. New York, 1989.

Disinformation   Disinformation is false intelligence information or propaganda planted by a government either to mislead opposing intelligence services or to shape public opinion. Both the CIA and the KGB operated disinformation departments, and the tactic has been used effectively by all the major intelligence services.

Disinformation usually involves the use of double agents, who channel the false information to the opposition, usually mixed with enough legitimate intelligence to make the false information believable. Well-disguised disinformation can have a disastrous long-term effect on policy decisions and intelligence activities.

Disinformation can also take the form of false propaganda aimed at influencing public opinion, even to the extent of sabotage. For instance, in the 1960s the Soviet Union considered leaking radioactive waste into waters around the Polaris submarine base at Faslane, Scotland. Once the radioactivity was discovered, environmental pressure groups would have been encouraged to campaign against the base on the grounds that it was a menace to the environment.

For Further Information:
Barron, John. *KGB: The Secret Work of Secret Agents.* New York, 1974.
Blackstock, Paul. *The Strategy of Subversion.* Chicago, 1964.
Dulles, Allen. *The Craft of Intelligence.* New York, 1963.
U.S. Senate. *Select Committee on Intelligence Activities Alleged Assassination Plots Involving Foreign Leaders.* Washington, D.C., 1975.

Distant Early Warning (DEW) Line   The Distant Early Warning Line is a string of radar stations stretching from Alaska to Britain, through Canada, Greenland and Iceland, the aim of which is to detect a ballistic missile or bomber attack while the attacking force is still over the ARCTIC OCEAN.

At the end of 1989, plans were under way to modernize and enhance the North American early warning system to protect against low-flying aircraft capable of flying under the DEW Line. The current DEW Line is along the 70th parallel, about 1,800 to 2,400 miles north of important North American targets.

For Further Information:
Fox, Annette B., et al. *Canada and the United States: Transnational and Transgovernmental Relations.* New York, 1976.

Djilas, Milovan   (June 12, 1911–   )   Milovan Djilas was Yugoslavia's leading dissident. Formerly the right-hand man to JOSIP BROZ TITO, he was imprisoned in 1956. Released in 1966, he continued to criticize the Yugoslav regime in books and articles published in the West.

Djilas was born in Montenegro and studied law at Belgrade University, where he first became active in radical politics. Almost as soon as he left the university, he was arrested for antiroyalist activities and sentenced to three years in prison.

Soon after his release in 1936, Djilas met Josip Broz Tito, secretary general of the Yugoslav Communist Party, and the two men immediately struck up a close friendship and working relationship. In 1938 Djilas was elected to the party's Central Committee, and in 1940 he was elevated to the Politburo, where he quickly established himself as the number-two man to Tito.

Djilas's standing within the party and the country was further enhanced by the major role he played in organizing partisan resistance to the German occupation of Yugoslavia during World War II.

Unlike other East European communist parties, Yugoslavia's communists came to power without any help from the Soviet Union, and Tito, with Djilas at his side, was in control of the country before the Red Army was in a position to occupy the Balkans. This provided Tito with a popular base within Yugoslavia, which in turn allowed him to operate independently of Moscow.

Serious differences emerged between Yugoslavia and the Soviet Union in 1947 when JOSEF STALIN tried to dictate senior appointments within the Yugoslav Communist Party. In March 1948 the Soviet Communist Party wrote to the Central Committee of the Yugoslav party making serious charges against Tito's policies and demanding that he mend his ways. Tito responded by liquidating a number of Stalinist Yugoslavs and purging the army. Then on June 28, 1948 the Soviet-controlled Cominform (Communist Information Bureau) denounced Tito and called on the Yugoslav Communist Party to overthrow him or face expulsion from the Cominform. Yugoslavia was duly expelled, and the following year Stalin broke the Yugoslav–Soviet defense treaty.

Djilas was a key supporter of the break with Moscow. The Soviet Union listed him among the Yugoslav political figures who should be overthrown by the Communist Party for having retreated from Marxism-Leninism and inspiring a "hateful policy" against the Soviet Union. Djilas' complete disillusionment with the philosophy of communism was yet to set in, but Stalin's heavy-handed efforts to control Yugoslavia had turned him against the Soviet Union and made him suspicious of internationalist aspects of communism. The following year, Djilas represented Yugoslavia at a United Nations peace debate at which the Soviet Union proposed a nonaggression pact among China, France, Britain, the United States and the Soviet Union. Djilas accused Moscow of "monstrous hypocrisy" in proposing a nonaggression pact while applying "aggressive pressure" against his country.

In January 1953 Djilas became one of Yugoslavia's four vice presidents and in December was chosen president of the Yugoslav federal parliament. His promotions coincided with the death of Stalin and the first attempts at a Yugoslav–Soviet rapprochement. Djilas' continuing vehement opposition to the Soviet Union brought him into increasing conflict with Tito, who wanted to heal the rift. In January 1954 he was removed from all political posts, and in April 1954 resigned from the Yugoslav Communist Party.

In December 1954 Djilas, in an interview to foreign journalists, claimed that Tito had halted the move toward genuine democracy in Yugoslavia, and he called for the establishment of an opposition democratic socialist party. As a result of this interview, Djilas was arrested for criticizing the government in the foreign press and was given an 18-month suspended prison sentence. But he continued to give interviews and write articles. The Yugoslav press was closed to him, so all of his work was published abroad where he became recognized as Yugoslavia's leading dissident intellectual. In December 1956 he had an article published in the American magazine *New Leader* in which he praised the Hungarian Revolution (see HUNGARY). Tito, who had just finalized his rapprochement with the Soviet Union, was reported to be furious and Djilas was arrested and imprisoned.

But even in prison Djilas continued to write and managed to smuggle his manuscripts to Western publishers. One of his best known works was *The New Class*, published in 1957, in which he charged that the rulers of communist societies were a "new class of owners and exploiters" who ran their countries "on behalf of their own narrow caste's interests." In October 1957, as a result of his book, Djilas was sentenced to a further seven years of "strict imprisonment" for creating hostile propaganda. At his trial, Djilas told the court that he stood by his book "in the way it was written from the first to the last letter."

Djilas was released on parole in 1961 but was imprisoned again the following year for his book *Conversations with Stalin,* based on talks Djilas held with Stalin prior to the 1948 rift. But the continued detention of Djilas was souring U.S.-Yugoslav relations, which Tito was trying to nurture, and in December 1966 Djilas was granted amnesty. He moved to Belgrade, where he continued to write articles and books critical of the regime. In December 1968 the Yugoslav authorities allowed him to attend a conference at Princeton University that was billed as a meeting of the world's most respected intellectuals. The conference was called by the International Association for Cultural Freedom to debate

"The United States, Its Problems, Its Image and Its Impact on the World."

But in 1969 the Yugoslav government reimposed its travel ban on Djilas, although he was allowed to remain at large. During the 1970s he shifted the emphasis of his activities toward human rights. Encouraged by the rise of Eurocommunism in Western Europe, he called upon Western European communist parties, in February 1977, to persuade the Yugoslav government to show greater respect for human rights. According to Djilas, there were 600 political prisoners in Yugoslavia, which represented the same percentage of the population as in the Soviet Union. Djilas publicly welcomed President JIMMY CARTER's emphasis on human rights, saying that it had "a great positive echo in the countries of Eastern Europe."

Djilas was by this time too prominent a dissident and too closely tied to East–West relations to be returned to prison, so the authorities arrested his cousin, Vitomir Djilas, who was jailed for disseminating hostile propaganda.

In April 1984 Djilas was among a group of dissidents arrested at a meeting in a Belgrade apartment on suspicion of "hostile activity." They were released after 24 hours. But by 1984 the major internal threat to Yugoslavia had shifted from anti-communist dissidents such as Djilas to the nationalist forces within the country. The authorities gradually relaxed their pressure on Djilas, and in January 1987 lifted their ban on his travels.

For Further Information:
Djilas, Milovan. *Conversations With Stalin.* New York, 1962.
———. *Land Without Justice.* New York, 1958.
———. *Memoir of a Revolutionary.* New York, 1973.
———. *The New Class.* New York, 1957.

Dobrynin, Anatoly (November 16, 1919–) Anatoly Dobrynin was Soviet ambassador to the United States from 1962 to 1986, when he returned to Moscow to join the Secretariat of the Soviet Communist Party. As ambassador in Washington, Dobrynin formed good personal relations with successive American administrations and played an important role in U.S.–Soviet relations.

Dobrynin served as an engineer in an aircraft plant from the start of World War II until 1944, when he joined the Soviet diplomatic service. His first major foreign posting was in 1952 to Washington as a counselor in the Soviet Embassy. This enabled him to establish his credentials as an expert on American affairs fairly early in his career. By 1954 he had impressed his superiors sufficiently to be promoted to the number two position in the embassy.

In 1955, Dobrynin returned to Moscow, where he assumed the role of roving ambassador and assistant to Foreign Minister Dmitri Shepilov. In July 1957 he joined the Secretariat of the United Nations as undersecretary without portfolio and the following year became the undersecretary in charge of the Department of Political and Security Council Affairs. This made Dobrynin the highest-ranking Soviet official in the UN

Secretariat. He formed a good working relationship with Secretary General DAG HAMMARSKJOLD, further encouraging the cordial relations between Hammarskjold and the Soviet leadership that existed from the late 1950s up until the CONGOLESE CIVIL WAR.

In February 1960 Dobrynin returned to Moscow to take charge of the American Department at the Soviet Ministry of Foreign Affairs. In 1961 he was named the new ambassador to the United States, and he presented his credentials to President JOHN F. KENNEDY on March 30, 1962. Dobrynin stayed in Washington for 24 years, during which time he became a member of the Communist Party Central Committee and was involved in every major East–West issue. He attended virtually all meetings between the American and Soviet foreign ministers and heads of state and initiated several key diplomatic efforts.

Dobrynin moved to Washington at a time when BERLIN was still at the top of the East–West agenda. Only two weeks after presenting his credentials, Dobrynin started exploratory talks with Secretary of State DEAN RUSK on the Berlin issue. Dobrynin proposed that the Western forces in Berlin be replaced by UN forces for a fixed period, with West Berlin eventually becoming a demilitarized zone. This was rejected by Rusk, who stuck to the position that the presence of Western forces in Berlin was not negotiable.

It was not until the QUADRIPARTITE AGREEMENT of 1971 that a working solution was found to the Berlin problem, but Dobrynin's dogged determination to negotiate rather than to conduct affairs through threats and counterthreats marked a major shift in Soviet policy toward Berlin and the West in general.

Dobrynin, however, did not have a close relationship with Soviet leader NIKITA KHRUSHCHEV, as was demonstrated most dramatically during the 1962 CUBAN MISSILE CRISIS. Throughout the crisis, Dobrynin sent anxious cables back to Moscow requesting fresh instructions and clarifications every time the Kennedy administration produced new evidence about the missile buildup. The Politburo simply instructed him to deny the existence of offensive missiles in Cuba. Knowing that this was an untenable position, Dobrynin was forced into increasingly weak diplomatic improvisations. Presidential advisor Arthur Schlesinger's account of the crisis said that Dobrynin "gave every indication of ignorance and confusion." In April 1989 Dobrynin admitted that the presence of the missiles had been such a closely guarded secret within the Kremlin that he himself had not learned about them until the crisis broke.

Dobrynin was able to form a better relationship with Khrushchev's successor, LEONID BREZHNEV. Following the overthrow of Khrushchev in October 1964, Dobrynin was assigned to inform President LYNDON JOHNSON that the new Soviet leadership planned "no change in basic foreign policy." Johnson replied that "we intend to bury no one and we do not intend to be buried." Dobrynin enjoyed good but not close relations with the Johnson administration. This was largely due to friction over Southeast Asia and the 1968 WARSAW PACT invasion of CZECHOSLOVAKIA.

However, at the end of the Johnson administration, Dobrynin played an important role in preparing the ground for the STRATEGIC ARMS LIMITATION TALKS (SALT I), which were held during the subsequent NIXON administration.

Dobrynin probably reached the peak of his influence during Nixon's years as U.S. president. He and HENRY KISSINGER, then the national security adviser, managed to strike up a rapport, as both enjoyed secret diplomacy and negotiating carefully constructed balances of power. Dobrynin quickly became the major channel of communication between Kissinger and Nixon and the Soviet Politburo. The American ambassador in Moscow became virtually superfluous to superpower relations. In his book *White House Years*, Kissinger wrote that "Dobrynin moved through the upper echelons of Washington with consummate skill. His personal role . . . was almost certainly beneficial to U.S.–Soviet relations." He added: "If someday there should come about the genuine relaxation of tensions and dangers, Anatoly Dobrynin will have made a central contribution to it."

At the suggestion of Kissinger, President Nixon arranged for the Soviet ambassador to arrive unseen through a seldom-used door in the East Wing of the White House. The rationale behind the arrangement was that Dobrynin would be more forthcoming and helpful in private and unpublicized meetings. Within a short time, Nixon, Kissinger and Dobrynin were meeting weekly, usually over lunch. Secretary of State WILLIAM ROGERS was rarely at these meetings, as Nixon and Kissinger wanted to establish direct control over the conduct of U.S.–Soviet relations. This served only to increase Dobrynin's importance.

Because of his close relationship with Kissinger and Nixon, Dobrynin was often used by the two men as an intermediary with the North Vietnamese. He was used to send messages to Hanoi, which set up the PARIS PEACE TALKS, and after the talks were established he often acted as a conduit for additional pressure when they became deadlocked.

But Dobrynin's major efforts were directed toward the SALT I talks. The formal negotiations began in Helsinki on November 17, 1969. The American negotiating team was led by GERARD SMITH, and the Soviet negotiators were led by Deputy Foreign Minister Vladimir Semyonov. But most of the policy for the American team was established and directed by Kissinger, working with a small group in Washington known as the Verification Panel. Soviet policy was directed by Foreign Minister ANDREI GROMYKO, and Dobrynin acted as the link between the two.

By the end of 1970, the formal negotiations in Helsinki were effectively deadlocked. To break the deadlock Kissinger turned to secret negotiations with Dobrynin. These negotiations established the principle of two separate treaties—the first to deal with antiballistic missile systems only, and the second to deal with offensive weapons. The two treaties were eventually signed in Moscow in May 1972.

The departure of first Nixon and then Kissinger from the U.S. government could have resulted in Dobrynin being transferred to another post. But by this time, he was so well informed and well connected within Washington circles that he was more useful to both countries remaining at the U.S. post. This was especially true after the election of JIMMY CARTER as president. The Soviet leaders had found it easier to deal with Nixon and Kissinger because they spoke in geopolitical terms the Soviets could understand. Carter, however, was more interested in morality and human rights, subjects that the Soviets neither understood nor felt comfortable with.

During the Carter administration, Dobrynin found a great deal of his time taken up with human rights issues. But he also helped with the SALT II negotiations. He did not have as close a relationship with Carter as he had enjoyed with Nixon, but he was assured easy access to Secretary of State CYRUS VANCE.

Dobrynin was perhaps most uncomfortable with President RONALD REAGAN, whom he regarded as threatening the delicate balance of détente with his military build-up and strong anti-Soviet line. But by this time, both the United States and the Soviet Union had become dependent on Dobrynin's unrivaled experience in dealing with the leaders in both countries. It was not until March 1986 that Dobrynin was finally called back to Moscow to become the Communist Party secretary responsible for supervising foreign relations.

In Moscow, Dobrynin became the chief adviser on East–West and disarmament issues to Foreign Minister EDUARD SHEVARDNADZE and Soviet leader MIKHAIL GORBACHEV. On May 23, 1986, he was a key figure at a conference of top Soviet diplomats called back to Moscow for a realignment of Soviet foreign policy. Later in 1986 he attended the Reykjavik Summit between Gorbachev and Reagan. In December 1987 he was back in Washington for the signing of the U.S.–Soviet INF TREATY.

On September 30, 1988, Dobrynin fell victim to a purge of former Brezhnevites and was ousted from his post in the party Secretariat. But Gorbachev decided that Dobrynin's experience outweighed his previous political connections and on October 28 appointed him his special adviser on foreign policy.

For Further Information:
Bialer, Seweryn. *Stalin's Successors.* New York, 1980.
Kissinger, Henry. *The White House Years.* New York, 1979.
———. *Years of Upheaval.* New York, 1982.
La Feber, Walter. *America, Russia and the Cold War: 1945–1984.* New York, 1985.

Dominican Republic, U.S. Invasion of (1965)   The American invasion of the Dominican Republic in April 1965 was launched ostensibly to protect American lives and prevent a communist takeover of the island. The move was generally regarded as an overreaction, and damaged U.S. relations with Latin America. However, it underscored American determination to prevent a "second Cuba."

From 1930 to 1961, the Dominican Republic was ruled by Rafael Trujillo, one of the cruelest and most absolute dictators in Latin American history. Trujillo was assassinated in 1961. For just over a year, his political heirs attempted to hang onto the reins of power, but eventually they agreed to free elections, which were held in 1962 and won by the reformist Juan Bosch and his Dominican Revolutionary Party.

The conservative forces remained a power within the army, however, and they overthrew Bosch in September 1963. Pressure from the U.S. government forced them to hand over power to a temporary civilian government until elections could be held in 1965. The civilian government was headed by former foreign minister, Donald Reid y Cabral.

Reid set out to reform the military in advance of the elections. The officers countered by plotting another coup. On April 24, 1965, Reid moved first by sending an army unit to arrest the conspiratorial officers. But the officers turned the tables on Reid by seizing the arresting officers and mobilizing against the government.

In the resultant confusion, several different factions moved to seize power. These included former President Bosch, the army, three different communist groups, and supporters of the exiled Joaquin Balaguer, a former associate of Trujillo. There were widespread looting and rioting and reports that an estimated 1,000 Americans in the Dominican Republic were in danger.

President LYNDON JOHNSON quickly decided to send a detachment of U.S. Marines to organize the evacuation of American citizens and other foreign nationals. They landed on April 28. Fighting among the various factions continued in the capital, Santo Domingo, and President Johnson was sent reports that there was a strong possibility that one of three communist factions—pro-Soviet, pro-Chinese, Cuban-supported—would seize power through Juan Bosch. He was advised that the Dominican Army was not in a position to stop the rebel forces.

Johnson decided to send a major force of U.S. Marines and paratroopers to the Dominican Republic to prevent what he believed to be an imminent communist coup. By May 5, some 19,000 American troops were in Santo Domingo, and before the crisis was resolved the number rose to 30,000.

A special meeting of the ORGANIZATION OF AMERICAN STATES was called to deal with the crisis, and the United States was generally condemned for what most members regarded as a breach of the noninterference clause of the OAS charter. The United States, however, won support from the right-wing Latin American dictatorships. U.S. ambassador Ellsworth Bunker maintained that the sending of U.S. forces to the Dominican Republic was "not intervention in any sense." He said the action was taken "purely and solely for humanitarian purposes."

In a television broadcast on May 2, Johnson said that the U.S. goal in the Dominican Republic was "to save the lives of our citizens and the lives of all people" and was "in keeping with the principles of the American system . . . to help prevent another Communist state in this hemisphere."

With the American forces in place, a cease-fire was signed on May 5 by the rebel military forces and a rival military junta backing Brigadier General Elias Wessin y Wessin. The truce was negotiated by a commission from the OAS and the U.S. ambassador to the Dominican Republic, W. Tapley Bennett. On May 29, the U.S. forces were partially replaced by an OAS peacekeeping force with members supplied by right-wing governments in Paraguay, Honduras, Nicaragua and Brazil.

The situation on the island, however, remained tense. Johnson sent three separate peace missions to Santo Domingo to negotiate an agreement for an interim government to lead the country until elections could be held. Success was finally achieved in June 1965 by Ellsworth Bunker, who persuaded all sides to accept an interim government under Garcia Godoy and to hold elections in June 1966.

The two main candidates were the left-wing Bosch and the American-supported Joaquin Balaguer. The elections were won by Balaguer, who projected himself as a symbol of moderation and orderly change. The validity of the elections has often been challenged, but the instances of fraud were not widespread enough to influence the result, although it could be argued that the presence of American and Brazilian troops intimidated many voters.

For Further Information:
Bosch, Juan. *The Unfinished Experiment: Democracy in the Dominican Republic.* New York, 1965.
Lowenthal, Abraham F. *The Dominican Intervention.* Cambridge, Mass., 1972.
Martin, John Bartlow. *Overtaken by Events, The Dominican Crisis from the Fall of Trujillo to the Civil War.* New York, 1966.
Slater, Jerome. *Intervention and Negotiation: The United States and the Dominican Republic.* New York, 1970.

Dowling, Walter   (August 4, 1905–July 1, 1977)   Walter Dowling was an American career diplomat who served in a number of important posts, including that of U.S. ambassador to South Korea from 1956 to 1959 and U.S. ambassador to West Germany from 1960 to 1963.

Dowling graduated from Mercer University in 1925 and joined the American diplomatic service in 1932. He served in a variety of European posts before World War II and during the war served in Rio de Janeiro. After the war he returned to Europe, where he served in Austria and West Germany. His tasks included standing in for Secretary of State JOHN FOSTER DULLES during the negotiations for the Austrian Peace Treaty.

In May 1955 President DWIGHT EISENHOWER appointed Dowling ambassador to South Korea. His first job was to complete negotiations for a treaty of friendship, commerce and navigation. The treaty was signed in December 1955 and was considered to be a good start to Dowling's ambassadorship. But between 1955 and 1959 U.S.–Korean relations

deteriorated as American public opinion swung against the dictatorial government of President SYNGMAN RHEE. In January 1959, Dowling was recalled after Rhee hired armed guards to remove opposition parliamentarians forcibly so that a law could be passed abolishing local elections and suppressing opposition newspapers.

Dowling returned to South Korea to mediate a dispute between America's two closest regional allies, South Korea and Japan. Relations between the two countries were traditionally poor because of the historic exploitation of Korea by Japan and the Japanese prejudice against Koreans living in Japan. On February 13, 1959, the Japanese Diet (parliament) approved plans to repatriate some 5,000 of the 600,000 Koreans in Japan to North Korea.

The South Korean government protested and warned that it would use "every power at its disposal" to prevent the repatriation. There was little that Rhee could do to stop the scheme, however, as the Koreans involved had voluntarily accepted homes and jobs in North Korea. Dowling managed to prevent Rhee from using military force to prevent the repatriation and persuaded the Japanese to mollify the South Korean leader by improving conditions for Koreans remaining in Japan.

In January 1960, Dowling moved to Bonn as U.S. ambassador to the Federal Republic of Germany. His main task was to reaffirm the American commitment to the defense of West Berlin, which was again under pressure from the Soviet Union. On September 22, 1960, Dowling made a major symbolic gesture of that commitment when he forced an East German border guard to back down after he tried to stop the ambassador from entering the Soviet sector because he was not accredited to the East German government.

Dowling left Germany and the diplomatic service in April 1963 and became a visiting professor at Mercer University in Macon, Georgia.

For Further Information:
Schick, Jack M. *The Berlin Crisis: 1958–1962.* Philadelphia, 1971.
Smith, Jean. *The Defense of Berlin.* Baltimore, 1963.
Yung-hwan, Jo, ed. *U.S. Foreign Policy in Asia: An Appraisal.* Santa Barbara, Calif., 1978.

Downey, John T.   (1930–   )   John T. Downey was an American CIA agent held captive by the communist Chinese for 20 years, beginning in 1952.

Downey was recruited from Harvard University into the CENTRAL INTELLIGENCE AGENCY and was sent almost immediately to Taiwan, where he was assigned the task of flying over mainland China to drop American and Chinese CIA agents into communist China at the height of the KOREAN WAR.

In 1952 Downey's plane was shot down and he and his copilot, George Fecteau, were captured. They were placed on trial in 1954 and confessed to espionage. On November 22, 1954, the two men were sentenced to life imprisonment.

The EISENHOWER administration denied that the men had been engaged in espionage, claiming that the charges against them were "utterly false." President Dwight EISENHOWER said that the United States would do everything "humanly possible within peaceful means" to obtain the release of the Americans.

In the late 1950s, a Sino–American diplomatic channel was opened between the United States and Chinese embassies in Warsaw, and the case of Downey was regularly raised by American diplomats, who stressed that his release would contribute to improved relations. But the Chinese refused to move on his case until the Americans agreed to communist Chinese membership in the United Nations and the establishment of Sino–American diplomatic relations.

The tie between the fate of Downey and Fecteau and Sino–American relations became clear to the public after the start of the thaw in relations between Beijing and Washington in 1971. In December 1971, Fecteau was released. At the same time, Downey's sentence was reduced to a further five years because of his good behavior.

Finally, in 1973, the U.S. admitted that Downey had been a CIA agent. Later that year, on the date that the United States and China agreed to establish diplomatic liaison offices in each other's capitals, the Chinese announced that they would conduct a further review of Downey's case. It is believed that Downey would have remained in prison until the exchange of ambassadors, but in March 1973 his mother suffered a stroke, and the Chinese, anxious to encourage the continuing positive trend in Sino–American relations, released Downey early on compassionate grounds. He returned to his home in New Britain, Connecticut, on March 12.

At a press conference the following day, Downey said he looked on his 20-year imprisonment as "to a large extent wasted," adding, "I don't see that it benefited anybody."

Downey said that during his first eight or nine months in jail he was questioned closely by his Chinese captors and that he "revealed about every bit of information [he] had." Asked about the Chinese people, he said he felt "sympathy with them in some respects" and found they were "more behind their government than I dreamed would be possible."

The CIA operation that had led to Downey's capture had been a major flop. The Chinese communists claimed that of the 230 Nationalist and U.S.-trained agents sent into China between 1951 and 1954, 106 had been killed and the other 124 captured. American intelligence sources have never confirmed or denied these figures.

In May 1975, Downey married Audrey Lee, a Chinese student at Yale University.

Dropshot   Dropshot was the code name for the earliest American plan for waging a nuclear war.

The plan, drawn up in 1949, called for the dropping of 300 atomic bombs on 100 urban and industrial areas in the Soviet Union. It was estimated that Dropshot would knock out 40% of the Soviet industrial capacity and result in 7 million fatalities.

Dropshot was not a plan for all-out nuclear war. At the time, most war planners could not envisage such a scenario. The nuclear bombing was meant to be carried out in conjunction with conventional bombing, which would soften up the Soviet Union for a tank and infantry attack. Atomic bomb production was at such a low level at the time that it was estimated that the 300 warheads necessary for Dropshot would not be available until 1957. In 1988, however, it was estimated that the United States had nuclear weapons for 10,000 Soviet targets.

Dual-Capable Systems   Dual-capable systems are systems capable of delivering either conventional or nuclear weapons.

These systems can be aircraft, missiles or artillery pieces. The North Atlantic Treaty Organization, for example, is equipped with the dual-capable Tornado fighter-bomber, 155mm howitzer and Honest John missile. Members of the WARSAW PACT were equipped with the dual-capable SU-7 fighter-bomber and Scud missile.

Dual-Key Systems   A dual-key system is a nuclear defense system that is under the authority of two national governments.

In many cases this means literally that the keys are held by ranking officers from two governments and that in order for a system to be activated the keys have to be turned simultaneously by both, under the direct command of their respective governments.

The system was devised in the 1950s to allay West European nations' arguments that they had no say over the protection of their own territories and that a trigger-happy American president could start a nuclear war in Europe, or alternatively, could sacrifice Western Europe to a conventional or nuclear Soviet attack in order to preserve its nuclear weapons to protect American territory.

The dual-key system is also used in some nuclear weapons systems owned and operated entirely by the United States. In this circumstance it is intended as an additional safeguard against the accidental launching of a nuclear weapon.

Dubcek, Alexander   (November 27, 1921–November 7, 1992)   See under CZECHOSLOVAKIA.

Duclos, Jacques   (October 2, 1896–April 25, 1975) Jacques Duclos was secretary of the French Communist Party from 1931 to 1964. He worked to ensure that the French communists maintained a policy of strict support for Soviet policies.

Duclos was born and raised in a small village in the Pyrenees Mountains, the son of a carpenter and innkeeper. His formal education ended at the age of 11 when he was apprenticed to a pastry chef. At the age of 16 he ran away to Paris, where he started an informal study of the French classics.

During World War I, Duclos served in the French Army and was wounded severely at the battle of Verdun. He was taken prisoner in 1917. His wartime experiences led Duclos toward left-wing politics, and following the Armistice he joined the French Socialist Party. The party soon split into two factions: the majority, liberal-left group under Léon Blum, which followed a political tradition closer to that of modern-day Social Democrats, and the radical left-wing group, which was inspired by the Bolshevik Revolution in Russia and wanted to repeat the event in France.

Duclos allied himself with the pro-Soviet faction, and at a party conference at Tours in 1920 he joined other left-wingers in breaking away from the Socialist Party and helping to form the French Communist Party. Lenin, and later JOSEF STALIN, regarded the French Communist Party as one of the most important in Europe and from its earliest days sought to direct its policies and tie it closely to Moscow. Duclos was one of the internationalists who supported direction from Moscow.

In 1926 Duclos was elected to the French parliament as one of the Parisian deputies. At the time, the party was involved in a major internal battle over how much direction to accept from the Soviet Union. This involved a number of purges, which finally resulted in the pro-Soviet Duclos being elected to the Politburo and becoming first secretary of the party in 1931.

In 1935, after riots forced the resignation of Premier Edouard Daladier, the communists joined with the socialists in the formation of a "Popular Front" government under Blum. Duclos, in 1936, became a vice president of the Chamber of Deputies, a post he held until 1939.

The German–Soviet Non-Aggression Pact at the start of World War II dealt a major blow to the French Communist Party, and many members tore up their party cards in protest. Duclos remained loyal to Moscow and, after the German attack on Russia, emerged as an even more powerful figure within the party. During the war, Duclos led a semi-clandestine existence organizing the communist resistance in Paris, and he played a leading role in the Paris uprising in August 1944.

His activities dramatically increased the popularity of the Communist Party, which won 28.4% of the seats in the National Assembly elections in 1945. In the elections in November 1946, its share of the seats rose to, and peaked at, 30.5%. The party at the time represented the largest block of votes, but its unswerving loyalty to Moscow made it an unacceptable political partner for the other French parties, except for a brief period after the war. After the Cold War began in earnest, the party's fortunes began to decline. In 1951 its share of the National Assembly seats was cut to 17.8%.

Duclos, for his part, continued his policy of strict support for Moscow. In 1945, he was used by Stalin to launch an attack on American Communist Party leader EARL BROWDER, who had called for a postwar continuation of the wartime alliance between the communists, the noncommunist left, and the liberals. Duclos, in an article in the party newspaper L'Humanité, attacked Browder for "opportunist errors" and insisted that the class war would continue long after World War II ended. Duclos' attack led to Browder's dismissal as leader of the American Communist Party.

Under Duclos, the French Communist Party became an active member of COMINFORM and a severe critic of the MARSHALL PLAN, the BRUSSELS TREATY, the NORTH ATLANTIC TREATY ORGANIZATION, United Nations intervention in Korea, French intervention in Indochina, American policy toward communist China, the formation of the EUROPEAN COAL AND STEEL COMMUNITY and Western policy in Germany and Berlin. At the same time, the French communists supported the communist takeovers throughout Eastern Europe.

Duclos was arrested in May 1952 after communist-organized riots to protest the arrival of General MATTHEW RIDGWAY as NATO supreme commander. During the riots French police fought off 5,000 demonstrators. One demonstrator was shot to death, 37 policemen and many rioters were injured and 700 were arrested. Duclos was charged with plotting against the security of the state, but he was released in July after the court ruled that his parliamentary immunity had been violated.

However, Duclos' private diary had been confiscated at his arrest and had fallen into the hands of the right-wing newspapers France-Soir and Le Figaro, which published extracts indicating that the French Communist Party was working for the French Army's "certain defeat" in Indochina, Korea and Tunisia.

Despite the growing backlash against communists, Duclos remained true to his convictions, and in March 1953 he attended the funeral of Stalin. In 1956 he supported the Soviet invasion of Hungary and the crackdown in Poland. In 1964, at the age of 68, Duclos relinquished the secretaryship of the party, but his charismatic personality ensured that he remained the major force in French communism.

The highpoint of Duclos' political career came in the French presidential elections of June 1969. Less than a year after the Warsaw Pact invasion of CZECHOSLOVAKIA, which Duclos had supported, he managed to poll a surprising 21% of the vote as the official Communist Party candidate. The election marked the beginning of a revival in Communist Party fortunes, which peaked in 1981 when four communists were given ministerial posts following the election of socialist president FRANCOIS MITTERRAND. Duclos died on April 25, 1975.

For Further Information:

Albright, D.E. Communism and Political Systems in Western Europe. Boulder, Colo., 1979.
Hoffman, Stanley, et al. In Search of France. New York, 1963.
Machin, H., ed. National Communism in Western Europe. New York, 1983.

Dulles, Allen (April 7, 1893–January 30, 1969) As deputy director of the CENTRAL INTELLIGENCE AGENCY from 1951 to 1953 and as director from 1953 to 1961, Allen Dulles was one of the dominant figures of the Cold War. His influence on American policy was further enhanced by the position of his brother, JOHN FOSTER DULLES, who was President DWIGHT EISENHOWER's secretary of state.

After graduating from Princeton University in 1916, Dulles entered the diplomatic service. In 1917 he was posted to Switzerland, where he started his lifetime affair with espionage as the intelligence officer for the American legation. Between the world wars, Dulles moved between the diplomatic service and work as an international lawyer and developed close links with the German upper classes. His experience made him a logical choice for the wartime post of Berne station chief for the OFFICE OF STRATEGIC SERVICES (OSS), the wartime forerunner of the CIA.

In the immediate aftermath of the World War II, Dulles was appointed Berlin station chief. Difficulties in dealing with his Soviet counterpart and the activities in Germany of Soviet intelligence helped to convince him that the West should shift its attention from the humbling of postwar Germany to a closer watch of Soviet activities.

When the OSS was disbanded in 1945, Dulles returned to the United States and joined the campaign to establish an American peacetime intelligence service to deal with the Soviet threat. President HARRY TRUMAN soon realized the need for such a service and in January 1946 established the Central Intelligence Group (CIG) to coordinate and evaluate defense intelligence reports. Dulles was among those who argued that the CIG could not operate effectively as long as it remained under military control, and he testified before Congress about restructuring the system. In 1947 the NATIONAL SECURITY ACT was passed, creating the Central Intelligence Agency.

During the 1948 elections, Dulles was foreign policy adviser to presidential candidate THOMAS E. DEWEY. But he remained in close contact with the embryonic CIA and advised the government on the establishment of a covert operations agency that eventually became the Office of Policy Coordination (OPC) under the direction of his wartime OSS colleague FRANK WISNER. Dulles also helped to raise funds to influence the Italian elections and wrote a National Security Council report on improving clandestine and covert operations.

On August 23, 1951, Dulles was named deputy director of the CIA, and after the election of Dwight Eisenhower he was appointed director of the agency. From the start, Dulles placed a heavy emphasis on covert operations, especially in Eastern Europe, and in that respect worked closely with Wisner, who had become the CIA's deputy director for plans. Later, as American technology improved, he shifted his emphasis to high-technology espionage such as the U-2 and SR-71 spy planes.

Dulles's activities often skirted the law and sometimes flagrantly violated it. He justified his actions on grounds of necessity in the Cold War power struggle. Among the abuses was the decision in 1953 to intercept all mail between Eastern Europe and American citizens. This practice continued for 20 years. He also helped to engineer the overthrow of several governments. These included the elected governments of Iranian premier MOHAMMED MOSSADEQ and left-wing Guatema-

lan president Jacobo Arbenz, whose land reforms threatened American commercial interests. During Dulles's tenure at the CIA, the agency also authorized the assassination of Congolese leader PATRICE LUMUMBA (although it is believed that Lumumba was actually murdered by local Congolese) and provided aid to the unpopular government of South Vietnamese president NGO DINH DIEM and to other anti-communist regimes.

Dulles was also heavily involved in early CIA activities in Cuba and the BAY OF PIGS invasion. In March 1960 Eisenhower ordered the CIA to start unifying the Cuban opposition with the purpose of training a Cuban guerrilla army that would overthrow FIDEL CASTRO. Dulles placed RICHARD BISSEL, deputy director of plans, in charge of the operation, and Bissel planned the Bay of Pigs invasion as well as several plots for the assassination of Fidel Castro and his brother Raul. Bissel reported directly to Allen Dulles.

Two days after his election, on November 10, 1960, president-elect JOHN F. KENNEDY announced that he would retain Allen Dulles as director of the CIA. Although he disagreed with many of Dulles's methods and far-right policies, Allen Dulles had, in the public view, become a leading figure in America's fight against world communism, and Kennedy retained him as proof that he was not "soft on Communism."

On November 18, Dulles and Bissel briefed Kennedy on the CIA's Cuban plans, and Kennedy approved the continuation of the training program for Cuban guerrillas. He finally gave his approval for the Bay of Pigs invasion in April 1961. To distract attention from CIA involvement in the Bay of Pigs, Dulles delivered a speech in Puerto Rico on invasion day, leaving Bissel in charge of the operation. It has since been argued that Kennedy might have sent in more reinforcements if Dulles had been present to argue in favor of such an action.

In the aftermath of the failed invasion, Dulles served on a committee that conducted a postmortem into CIA involvement in the affair. The committee failed to agree whether or not the agency should be blamed and whether or not the invasion could have succeeded. Dulles argued that the invasion would have had a reasonable chance if the original plans for air strikes had been carried through. The committee recommended that the CIA continue to conduct covert operations but not paramilitary activities, unless these stipulations could be plausibly denied.

The Bay of Pigs irreparably tarnished Allen Dulles and allowed Kennedy to start to curb his power and that of the CIA. Attorney General ROBERT KENNEDY took a special interest in the agency's covert operations, and the president cut back the agency's budget. On July 31, 1961, it was announced that Dulles would soon retire, and on September 27, 1961, Kennedy accepted his resignation.

Dulles returned to his New York law practice and, after the assassination of Kennedy in 1963, was appointed a member of the Warren Commission. He died in Washington on January 30, 1969.

For Further Information:
Dulles, Allen W. *The Craft of Intelligence.* New York, 1963.
Mosley, Leonard. *Dulles: A Biography of Eleanor, Allen and John Foster Dulles and Their Family Network.* New York, 1978.
U.S. Senate Select Committee to Study Intelligence Activities. *Alleged Assassination Plots Involving Foreign Leaders.* Washington, D.C., 1975.
Wise, David, and Thomas B. Ross. *The Invisible Government.* New York, 1964.

Dulles, John Foster   (February 25, 1888–May 24, 1959)

The policies and personality of John Foster Dulles, for many people, typified American foreign policy during the Cold War. He was an unbending opponent of the Soviet Union and a firm believer in the existence of a monolithic communist conspiracy to overthrow the Western political system. Through Dulles's role as President DWIGHT EISENHOWER's secretary of state, these beliefs became an integral part of U.S. policy.

After studying at Princeton University and the Sorbonne in Paris, Dulles attended law school at George Washington University. He graduated in 1911 and joined the New York law firm of Sullivan and Cromwell. Dulles distinguished himself during World War I as an intelligence officer and after the war served on President Woodrow Wilson's staff at the Versailles Peace Conference.

Dulles's experiences at Versailles gave him a taste of international relations, so that when he returned to New York he concentrated on international law and by the 1930s was recognized as one of the leading American authorities. He was a strong supporter of the League of Nations and during World War II advocated the formation of the United Nations. He later acted as an adviser to the Roosevelt administration on America's UN policy and, finally, in 1945 was one of the delegates to the SAN FRANCISCO CONFERENCE.

When a Democrat, HARRY TRUMAN, succeeded Roosevelt as president, in an effort to maintain a bipartisan foreign policy he persuaded the Republican Dulles to remain as an adviser to his administration. Dulles quickly became disillusioned with the Soviet Union and from 1945 to 1948 concentrated on a study of JOSEF STALIN, communism and how communist ideology fitted into Soviet foreign policy. He became utterly convinced that the Soviet Union was determined to overthrow the West by any means at its disposal and that this would be Moscow's ultimate aim regardless of who was in power. He interpreted the basic differences between the United States and the Soviet Union as a conflict between good and evil with the United States, of course, as the leading force for good.

Having established these basic precepts, it was a natural progression for Dulles to regard a tough anti-communist policy as the essential ingredient of a "moral crusade." It also justified his refusal to negotiate with the Soviet Union, his support for the "liberation" of Eastern Europe as opposed to Truman's "containment" policies, his support for a strong military establishment, his support for anti-communist military dictatorships, and his belief that, in the predominantly bipolar world political system, it was anti-American for third-party countries to profess neutrality in the superpower conflict. At home, Dulles placed a heavy emphasis on morality, arguing that the United States had to be seen to be good if it was to stand any chance of winning the moral crusade against the Soviet Union.

During the 1948 presidential campaign, Dulles worked as foreign policy adviser to the Republican candidate, New York governor THOMAS E. DEWEY. His efforts were rewarded in 1949 when Dewey, who had lost the election but remained governor, appointed him to the U.S. Senate seat vacated by the resignation of Robert Wagner. In the Senate, he became a strong supporter of Nationalist China, the NORTH ATLANTIC TREATY ORGANIZATION and the MARSHALL PLAN. Dulles lost his seat to Herbert Lehman in the election of 1950.

Out of office, Dulles wrote *War or Peace,* in which he criticized Truman's containment policies. He elaborated on his policies further in a 1952 article for *Life* in which he argued that "containment" only offered the "status quo," and what was needed was an active policy of liberation.

Despite Dulles's criticisms, Truman continued to use Dulles' expertise on specific projects during his second term. The most important such project was the negotiations for the final U.S. peace treaty with Japan. Dulles firmly believed that Japan should be allowed to develop both economically and

John Foster Dulles, secretary of state from 1953 to 1959, formulated the Eisenhower administration's policy of "massive retaliation" against the Soviet Union.

militarily and ally itself with the United States to provide a bulwark against the spread of communism in Asia. Dulles was unable to win support for a build-up of Japanese forces, but he did succeed in negotiating a U.S.–Japan security pact that allowed America to continue basing troops on Japanese soil.

Dulles was an ambitious man who sincerely believed that he was the best foreign affairs specialist in the West and the best man for the job of secretary of state. He was Dewey's choice for the post had he been elected in 1948, and when opinion polls predicted a Republican landslide, Dulles actually contacted Secretary of State GEORGE C. MARSHALL to discuss the technical details of the transition. By 1950, Dulles had built up a powerful political base within the Republican Party, and it was generally thought that if the party won the 1952 presidential election, Dulles would be secretary of state regardless of the president's opinion. Dulles was asked to draft the party's foreign policy plank and in November 1952, after the election of Dwight Eisenhower as president, was duly designated as the next secretary of state.

Initial relations between Eisenhower and Dulles were cool. Eisenhower dislike Dulles's arrogance and was suspicious of his liberation rhetoric. But gradually the two men formed a close friendship, and Dulles was given more freedom in shaping foreign policy than any other postwar secretary of state. Dulles, however, always regarded the president as the chief foreign policy maker and saw his role as chief foreign policy adviser. He was always careful to clear major speeches or policy pronouncements with Eisenhower, and on most evenings he would visit the Oval Office for a review of the world situation. The close relationship between the two men was based on a shared perception of the Soviet threat to the West, although Eisenhower disagreed with Dulles on the tactics to be deployed in combating that threat and tended to act as a brake on the policies of his secretary of state.

One of Dulles's first problems in office was the "witch hunt" conducted by Republican Senator JOSEPH MCCARTHY. By the time Dulles took office, McCarthy's attacks on American diplomats had reached their peak. Dulles did little to defend his staff against these attacks, and this, plus his rather independent conduct of foreign policy and neglect of departmental management, damaged morale among the diplomatic corps for the next 10 years. It was Dulles, after McCarthy's innuendoes, who removed men such as John Carter Vincent, JOHN PATON DAVIES and JOHN STEWART SERVICE, as well as several hundred other State Department employees who were accused of homosexuality, drunkenness or [political] "incompatibility."

The other major problem Dulles initially faced was how to end the KOREAN WAR without appearing to give in to the communist menace. He and Eisenhower accomplished this by a series of carrot-and-stick diplomatic maneuvers. Communist China was warned of American determination by the enlargement of the South Korean Army, the basing of nuclear weapons in Okinawa and the withdrawal of the U.S. Seventh Fleet, which had served as a buffer between mainland China

and Nationalist China, from the Taiwan Straits. At the same time, Dulles pushed South Korean president SYNGMAN RHEE into an armistice.

Dulles regarded Western Europe as "the world's fire hazard," and he lavished a great deal of attention on it. He was a strong supporter of European unification as a bulwark against the further spread of communism, and he personally campaigned for the proposed EUROPEAN DEFENSE COMMUNITY (EDC) and European army. When it became apparent that the initialed agreement would have difficulty winning approval in the French National Assembly, Dulles threatened France with an "agonizing reappraisal of American policy." The threat failed. The National Assembly voted against the EDC, but a crisis was avoided by a strengthening of NATO and by West Germany's entry into the military alliance.

In the Middle East, Dulles attempted to contain Soviet expansion with a NATO-type structure. Concerned with the left-wing policies of Iranian premier MOHAMMED MOSADDEQ, he helped to engineer the CIA-led coup that overthrew Mosaddeq in August 1953 and established the United States as the preeminent Western power in Iran. The Middle East, however, also produced several moral dilemmas for Dulles. In the 1950s the region continued to be dominated by the colonial policies of Britain, and Dulles was almost as opposed to British colonialism as he was to communism.

Dulles's opposition to British colonialism brought him into personal conflict with British foreign secretary Sir ANTHONY EDEN, who in November 1952 had taken the unusual step of asking Eisenhower not to appoint Dulles secretary of state. Each man regarded his country as the natural leader of the Western world and himself as the West's major foreign affairs specialist. The Dulles-Eden conflict came to a head during the SUEZ CRISIS (Eden was by then prime minister), which resulted in a major Anglo-American schism. This was repaired only after Eden had resigned and Prime Minister HAROLD MACMILLAN accepted American leadership.

The Suez Crisis was a complex diplomatic potpourri of colonialism versus nationalism and communism versus the West. Egyptian leader GAMAL ABDEL NASSER was an Arab nationalist who himself as the leader of the Arab world against British colonialism. Dulles initially admired Nasser and believed that it was in America's interest to establish good relations with him. In conjunction with Britain, he offered American aid to build the ASWAN HIGH DAM. But Nasser also wanted American military aid, which was blocked in the United States by the pro-Israel lobby. Nasser turned to the Soviet Union for the military supplies he wanted, and as a result Dulles withdrew American aid for the dam. Nasser retaliated by nationalizing the Suez Canal on the grounds that the revenue from tolls would be needed to pay for the dam. He also received further financial aid from the Soviet Union. The resultant Suez crisis not only strained French- and Anglo-American relations but also increased Soviet influence in Egypt and the wider Arab world.

Dulles's strident anti-communism was another cause of his

unpopularity among many European leaders. They wanted and needed American military, political and economic support to protect them against communism. But at the same time, they believed that their long-term security could be guaranteed only through negotiation with the Soviet Union. Many of them, including British prime minister WINSTON CHURCHILL, wanted to explore the possibility of coexistence following the death of JOSEF STALIN. Dulles was opposed to negotiation, and the few East–West summit meetings that took place during the Eisenhower administration were at the insistence of Eisenhower and over the objections of Dulles.

As secretary of state, Dulles also helped to formulate the "NEW LOOK" DEFENSE POLICY, which shifted the emphasis of defense from conventional to nuclear forces. "New Look" provided Dulles with a new diplomatic weapon: nuclear deterrence, that is, the threat to use nuclear weapons in order to deter a conventional or nuclear attack. Dulles wanted to use the nuclear threat to defeat communist-led national movements in the crumbling French empire in Southeast Asia. Congress refused to support the necessary resolution allowing American military intervention, but deterrence remained U.S. policy.

At the GENEVA CONFERENCE ON INDOCHINA AND KOREA in 1954, Dulles and, later, Undersecretary of State WALTER BEDELL SMITH remained aloof from the negotiations. They refused to sign the agreement of July 21, which divided Vietnam into North and South and promised reunification following free elections in 1956. Dulles was skeptical of communist intentions, and to counter them he formed the SOUTHEAST ASIA TREATY ORGANIZATION (SEATO) in September 1954.

Dulles was allowed to use the threat of nuclear reprisals against China during the QUEMOY AND MATSU ISLANDS crises in 1954 and 1955. The crises, which involved the Chinese communist shelling of the Nationalist-held islands of Quemoy and Matsu, also led to the negotiation of a mutual security treaty between Taiwan and the United States. The Quemoy and Matsu crises were a good example of what Dulles coined

"BRINKMANSHIP," a tactic of going to the brink of war as a kind of diplomatic dare. In an interview in 1956 with *Life* magazine he attributed his diplomatic successes to his willingness to employ this tactic.

The secretary of state attempted to use the nuclear threat when the problem of Quemoy and Matsu flared up again in 1958. This time, Soviet leader NIKITA KHRUSHCHEV responded by pointing out that the Soviet Union also had nuclear weapons. The Soviet threat undercut congressional support for strong action, and Dulles was forced into a major policy shift in which he initiated contacts with Beijing and publicly pointed out that Quemoy and Matsu were excluded from the U.S.–Taiwan security agreement.

In 1958 Dulles was found to have terminal cancer. The medical diagnosis roughly coincided with the start of a gradual shift in American foreign policy away from the moral crusade advocated by Dulles. Disarmament, improved relations with the Third World and negotiation with the Soviet Union became major goals of American policy. Dulles devoted his energies to opposing this shift despite his considerable physical pain. His illness finally forced his resignation on April 15, 1959, and he died on May 24.

For Further Information:
Beal, John Robinson. *John Foster Dulles: A Biography.* New York, 1957; rev. ed. in 1959: *John Foster Dulles: 1888–1959.*

Drummond, Roscoe, and Gaston Coblentz. *Duel at the Brink: John Foster Dulles' Command of American Power.* Garden City, N.Y., 1960.

Dulles, Eleanor Lansing. *John Foster Dulles: The Last Year.* New York, 1963.

Gerson, Louis L. *John Foster Dulles.* New York, 1967.

Goold-Adams, Richard. *The Time of Power: A Reappraisal of John Foster Dulles.* Boston, 1962.

Guhin, Michael. *John Foster Dulles: A Statesman and His Times.* New York, 1972.

Hoopes, Townsend. *The Devil and John Foster Dulles.* Boston, 1973.

Immerman, Richard H. ed. *John Foster Dulles and the Diplomacy of the Cold War: A Reappraisal.* Princeton, 1990.

_E_

East German Uprising (1953)   The East German uprising of June 1953 dramatically underscored the East German people's dissatisfaction with the Communist Party leadership and the Soviet occupying forces. It also helped to maintain Western public pressure for political freedom in Eastern Europe and is believed to have contributed to the downfall of the Soviet security chief LAVRENTY BERIA, who was made the scapegoat for the affair.

The uprising came three months after the death of JOSEF STALIN and shortly after the abolition of the Russian Control Commission in East Germany on May 28, 1953, and its replacement by a Soviet High Commission. At the same time the East German government announced that real wages would be reduced. This was offset by an easing of political restrictions, including a promise that "requests for permission to resume business from persons who [had] closed or handed over their concerns [to the state would] be granted immediately."

This carrot-and-stick approach resulted in a series of strikes that condemned the political and economic easing as too little and the drop in real wages as unacceptable. On June 16 some 2,000 demonstrators, led by striking construction workers, marched to the House of the Ministries in East Berlin. The crowd demanded to see East German Communist Party leader WALTER ULBRICHT. When he failed to appear, there was a cry—which most observers claim was spontaneous—for a general strike on June 17. Three demonstrators also crossed into West Berlin to an American radio station to demand free elections, a reduction in the cost of living and an amnesty for striking workers.

These demands, and the call for a general strike, were broadcast into East Berlin by American radio and West Berlin radio and television. On June 17, tens of thousands of workers went on strike and mass demonstrations took place throughout East Berlin, centering on Marx-Engels Platz. The red flag was torn down from the Brandenburg Gate, fires were started in several public buildings and demonstrations were sparked in other East German cities.

The uprising was quickly put down by Soviet troops. In East Berlin tanks chased the crowd down the main boulevard, the Unter den Linden, and at least one demonstrator was crushed under the treads. On June 18 one of the demonstrators, Willi Gottling, was charged with acting as a Western agent and summarily executed. His death and the prompt and repressive intervention of the Soviet troops led to a quick end to the uprising.

For Further Information:
Black, Cyril, ed. _The East German Rising._ London, 1954.
McCauley, Martin. _The German Democratic Republic Since 1945._ New York, 1983.
Stefan, Brant. _The East German Rising._ London, 1954.

East-West Trade   Trade between the Western and Soviet Bloc countries was a major weapon and issue of the Cold War, as well as a useful barometer of the state of East–West relations. When tensions increased, trade plummeted, and when relations improved, trade increased.

Throughout the Cold War, diplomats on both sides of the East–West divide argued over the political, military and economic desirability of increased East–West trade. Those in the West in favor of such links claimed that increasing trade would increase the Soviet Bloc's dependence on the Western economies, deplete those countries' hard currency reserves, and increase the West's political leverage over the Soviet Bloc. Those opposed to trade said that a trade partnership would give the Soviet Union access to Western military secrets and would financially underwrite communism.

Within the Soviet Union, those in favor of trade said that it would give access to much-needed consumer goods, agricultural products and high technology (areas in which the Soviet Union consistently lagged behind the West). It also would provide a market for Soviet oil, gas and gold (of which the Soviet Union was the world's largest producer). Those opposed to East–West trade were concerned that such a relationship would lead the Soviet Bloc to become economically dependent on the West and that this would circumscribe its political activities. Each argument was dominant at various times throughout the Cold War, according to the state of political relations, the personalities in power, economic concerns and the countries involved.

The economic division of the world, in particular Europe, was ensured by the MARSHALL PLAN, by the Soviet Bloc's refusal to participate in the plan and by the creation of the alternative COUNCIL FOR MUTUAL ECONOMIC ASSISTANCE (CMEA or COMECON) to coordinate and encourage trade among the Soviet Bloc countries. Western economic cohesion was further enhanced by the formation of other bodies such as the General Agreements on Tariffs and Trade (GATT), which slightly predated the Marshall Plan; the ORGANIZATION FOR EUROPEAN ECONOMIC COOPERATION (OEEC), which was established to coordinate the distribution of the Marshall Plan and later developed into the Organization for Economic Cooperation and Development (OECD); the EUROPEAN COAL AND STEEL COMMUNITY; and the EUROPEAN ECONOMIC COMMUNITY. The INTERNATIONAL MONETARY FUND and the WORLD BANK were also major elements in the Western trading structure. The Soviet Union, for its part, eventually extended the geographic scope of COMECON beyond Eastern Europe to include Vietnam, Cuba and Mongolia. Associated members included Afghanistan, Angola, Ethiopia, Laos, Mozambique and South Yemen.

Trade between East and West, particularly between the Soviet Union and the United States, did not start to decline seriously until 1948. In the first six months of 1947, American imports from the Soviet Union totalled $36.5 million. In the same period in 1948 they had dropped to $7.4 million. The U.S. government in 1948 started curbing its sales of military and military-related equipment to the Soviet Union, as did other Western countries. In 1953 the NATO countries formed the COORDINATING COMMITTEE FOR MULTILATERAL STRATEGIC EXPORT CONTROLS (COCOM), which coordinated national restrictions on the export of goods and technology of military potential to the Soviet Bloc countries. The committee originally comprised only NATO members but was later expanded to include Japan and Australia.

The Cold War in trade continued throughout the 1950s and 1960s, and it was not until the OSTPOLITIK policy of West German chancellor WILLY BRANDT, followed by a more general détente, that trade between the two blocs began to increase substantially. Part of Brandt's Ostpolitik was a trade agreement with East Germany. This encouraged other Western governments to increase their trade with Soviet Bloc countries. Soviet imports from Western industrialized countries increased from $13.5 billion in 1975 to $26.4 billion in 1983, and exports to the West increased from $8.6 billion to $26.6 billion.

The major East–West trade issues of this period were the U.S.–Soviet grain trade agreement of 1972 and the NIXON administration's proposal to grant the Soviet Union Most Favored Nation (MFN) trading status. The grain trade agreement had a multiple purpose: to highlight the weakness of the Soviet agricultural system, to dispose of a surplus of American grain and to increase the dependence of the Soviet Union on the U.S. economy. But the agreement was constantly under attack, and the proposal to grant the Soviet Union Most Favored Nation status failed after the U.S. Congress attached an amendment linking MFN status to Jewish emigration from the Soviet Union.

The West Europeans, taking their lead from U.S. secretary of state HENRY KISSINGER and Brandt, also increased their exports to and imports from the Soviet Union. Their exports consisted mainly of consumer goods and non-military high-technology equipment. The main import was natural gas, and the Soviet Union built a multi-billion-dollar pipeline to deliver it. The pipeline heavily increased the West Europeans' dependence on the Soviet Union for their energy needs, and the United States became increasingly concerned about the security dimension of this dependence.

President RONALD REAGAN tried to prevent the building of the pipeline by applying sanctions to any U.S. or foreign companies supplying equipment for the pipeline. After complaints about the sanctions, Reagan quietly dropped them and the pipeline went ahead. Conversely, the Reagan administration also restored the U.S.–Soviet grain trade agreement, which had been suspended by the CARTER administration in 1979 in retaliation for the Soviet invasion of Afghanistan. The reason for the restoration was that the American farmers had become more dependent on the Soviet market than the Soviets had on American supplies.

Trade relations between the West and Eastern Europe were never as strained as those between the West and the Soviet Union. The West at various times used trade as a weapon to drive a wedge between Moscow and its satellites in Eastern Europe. The first such case was YUGOSLAVIA after its break in 1948 with the Soviet Union. Later, the independent foreign policy of ROMANIA's president, NICOLAE CEAUSESCU, led to that country's being awarded Most Favored Nation status by the United States despite its repressive internal politics.

The East Europeans were more dependent on Western markets than the Soviet Union was. Unlike the Soviet Union, they had little in the way of valuable natural resources to earn them hard currency; therefore, they had to compete in the world market for sales of consumer, military and heavy industrial goods. This competition required extensive capital investment. The Soviet Union was unable to provide it, and the East Europeans turned increasingly toward Western banks for loans.

This relationship worked reasonably well in the 1960s and 1970s, when the growth of the world economy caused a boom in exports, which enabled the East European countries to service existing loans and take out new loans for further investment in industrialization. But the recession that followed the quadrupling of oil prices in 1973–74 cut exports and left countries such as Poland, Yugoslavia, Romania and Bulgaria with heavy foreign debts, idle factories and expensive state subsidies. Attempts to pay off the debts by reducing or eliminating subsidies led to shortages and higher prices, increased public dissatisfaction and aided the rise of dissident organizations such as Poland's independent trade union SOLIDARITY. The issue played a major role in the collapse of the communist governments throughout Eastern Europe. After new governments came to power in Eastern Europe in 1989, the Western countries rushed to bolster the new political structures with economic aid and trading benefits.

Although the Soviet Union did not itself become dependent on Western banks, it indirectly, albeit reluctantly, underwrote the borrowings of its East European satellites by continuing to subsidize its trade with those countries and by providing massive subsidies to countries such as Cuba and Vietnam. This, plus heavy defense expenditures, left the Soviet Union with little money for new investment in its own industries, which suffered a relative decline in the late 1970s and early 1980s. This in turn led to the accession of reformist Soviet leader MIKHAIL GORBACHEV and his *perestroika* (restructuring) policies, which introduced a large element of Western-style free market economics into the Soviet economy. Gorbachev also introduced parallel political reforms, known as *glasnost* (openness). The combined economic and political reforms led to a substantial increase in trade between the Soviet Union and the West as the Western countries sought to support Gorbachev economically. This process continued through the final days of Gorbachev and the U.S.S.R. in 1991, as Western foreign aid became more important than trade to the increasingly desperate Soviet economy.

Trade between the West and China was even more politically motivated than that between the Soviet Union and the West. During the 1950s and 1960s there was virtually no trade because of the United States' refusal to recognize communist China. What little trade existed was conducted indirectly, mainly through the British colony of Hong Kong.

After President Richard Nixon's visit to China in 1971, however, the United States began to encourage trade with China as a means of increasing the political pressures on the Soviet Union. This trade increased considerably after the accession to power of DENG XIAOPING, who introduced a number of economic reforms similar to Gorbachev's later *perestroika* policies. But Deng's economic reforms were not accompanied by political reforms, and this led to frustration among a younger generation demanding democratic institutions. The frustrations led to several weeks of mass demonstrations in several cities in the spring of 1989, culminating in a crackdown by the government, including a bloody massacre in Tiananmen Square in Beijing in June, and the temporary reversal of many of Deng's economic policies. In response to the massacre, Western countries imposed a series of economic sanctions on China, but the refusal of President GEORGE BUSH to take a hard line led to their early abandonment. Trade relations and Western investment in China, though slowed down, have continued.

For Further Information:

Baldwin, David A., and Helen V. Milner, eds. *East–West Trade and the Atlantic Alliance.* New York, 1990.

Funigiello, Philip J. *American-Soviet Trade in the Cold War.* Chapel Hill, N.C., 1988.

Hanson, Philip. *Trade and Technology in Soviet-Western Relations.* New York, 1981.

Haus, Leah A. *Globalizing the GATT: The Soviet Union's Successor States, Eastern Europe, and the International Trading System.* Washington, D.C., 1992.

NATO Economics Directorate. *External Economic Relations of CMEA Countries: Their Significance and Impact in a Global Perspective.* Brussels, 1984.

U.S. Congress Joint Economic Committee. *Soviet Economy in the 1980s: Problems and Prospects.* Washington, D.C., 1983.

Wallace, William V., and Roger A. Clarke. *Comecon, Trade and the West.* New York, 1986.

Eaton, Cyrus   (December 27, 1883–May 9, 1979)   Cyrus Eaton was a wealthy American industrialist who formed close links with the Soviet leadership, established the PUGWASH CONFERENCES for the exchange of views by scientists and intellectuals from East and West, and worked for a U.S.–Soviet rapprochement.

Eaton, the son of a Canadian storekeeper, started his career working for the industrialist John D. Rockefeller. By 1929 Eaton had established a personal fortune of $100 million through control of hundreds of public utility companies and the Goodyear Tire and Rubber Company. He lost most of his fortune in the Wall Street crash of 1929 but rebuilt it by shrewd investments in railways and steel. In 1954 he became chairman of the Chesapeake and Ohio Railway.

In the late 1940s, Eaton became increasingly concerned about the dangers of the Cold War and started working to promote better East–West relations. In April 1954 he organized a conference of scientists and intellectuals from East and West at his summer home in Pugwash, Nova Scotia. The meeting was the first of a series of "Pugwash conferences," which helped to maintain a dialogue at a time when official contacts were minimal. At the conference in April 1958 nuclear scientists called for a ban on atmospheric nuclear tests, and the conference in Moscow in December 1960 was used by the Soviets to signal their willingness to reopen arms negotiations with the KENNEDY administration.

Eaton's stand on East–West relations made him a favorite target of American conservatives, who denounced him as the Soviets' "favorite capitalist." After a meeting between Eaton and NIKITA KHRUSHCHEV in Paris in May 1960, Senator Thomas Dodd called for the prosecution of Eaton under the 1799 Logan Act, which prohibited private citizens from dealing with foreign governments.

For his part, Eaton became increasingly critical of American foreign policy. During the Eisenhower administration he regularly attacked Secretary of State JOHN FOSTER DULLES and called for American recognition of communist China. In the 1960s and 1970s he opposed American involvement in VIETNAM.

Eaton's relations with the Soviet leadership, on the other hand, were cordial and warm. When he visited the Soviet Union in September 1958 he was given a 90-minute meeting with Khrushchev, and in July 1960 the Soviet leader awarded him the Lenin Peace Prize.

Eberstadt Survey Committee   The Eberstadt Survey of 1948 laid the foundations for a major reorganization of the U.S. military. The survey was the military section of the

Hoover Commission report on the reorganization of the government's executive branch.

The 14-member bipartisan survey committee, headed by Congressman Ferdinand Eberstadt, reported on December 16, 1948, that the United States was "not getting its money's worth of military strength."

The committee uncovered serious waste and inefficiency in the military establishment and listed six major areas "in which improvement . . . [was] both possible and necessary." Its recommendations were as follows:

1. Control. The central military authority should be strengthened but without lessening civilian control. This included the appointment of a chairman of the Joint Chiefs of Staff.
2. Budget. The committee recommended the overhaul and improvement of military budget structures and procedures. They found that defense costs were too much of a drain on the economy, despite "a growing belief" that communist strategy was "to force the United States" into ruinous expenditures and so win a "victory by bankruptcy."
3. Teamwork. The committee called for closer coordination between departments responsible for military and foreign policies. This included the Defense Department, the Central Intelligence Agency and the State Department.
4. Science. Scientific research and planning should be more closely related to strategic planning.
5. Mobilization. Plans should be quickly drawn up for complete civilian (including economic, industrial and manpower) mobilization in case of war.
6. "Unconventional" warfare. The committee called for adequate provision for "new and unconventional" means of warfare. These included nuclear, chemical and biological warfare.

The report was well received by the TRUMAN administration, and most of its proposals were accepted and implemented either by President Truman or by President Eisenhower.

Eden, Anthony   (June 12, 1897–January 14, 1977)   Anthony Eden was the most influential British foreign secretary of the 20th century. He held the post before and during World War II and attended the Teheran, YALTA and POTSDAM conferences. He was again foreign secretary from 1951 to 1955, when he succeeded WINSTON CHURCHILL as prime minister. In 1956 he made the disastrous decision to involve Britain in a French and Israeli attack on Egypt.

Eden was born into the British upper classes, the third son of a British baronet. He attended the exclusive British public school Eton and while still at school volunteered for service in World War I. By the time the war ended, he was the youngest brigade major in the British Army. After the war he attended Oxford University and after graduating in 1922 went into politics, securing election to the House of Commons in 1923.

In August 1931, Eden began his long diplomatic career when he was asked by Prime Minister Stanley Baldwin to join the Foreign Office as a junior minister. From the start he specialized in defense, colonial and Middle East issues.

In February 1933 Eden became the first British minister to meet Adolf Hitler and in 1935 was the first British minister to meet JOSEF STALIN, who used the occasion to propose a collective security pact against Hitler. In June 1935 Eden was elevated to cabinet rank and made minister of League of Nations affairs, in which position he became involved in shaping British policy on the Italian invasion of Ethiopia. In December 1935 he became the youngest British foreign secretary in almost 100 years.

After his first meeting with Hitler, Eden cabled Baldwin, "I find it very hard to believe that the man himself wants war." But as foreign secretary his opinions changed, and he pressed first Baldwin and then Neville Chamberlain to take a strong stand against the German dictator. He finally resigned in February 1938 to protest against Chamberlain's appeasement of Germany and Italy. When war broke out he returned to Chamberlain's government as Dominions secretary. When Winston Churchill formed his wartime national government, Eden was named secretary of war, and in December 1940 he moved back to the Foreign Office.

During the war, Eden worked closely with Churchill on every major policy issue and played a leading role in all wartime negotiations, including the Atlantic Charter with the United States, the lend-lease agreements, the alliance with the United States, the alliance with the Soviet Union, and the Teheran, Cairo, Yalta and Potsdam conferences. Churchill and Eden developed a close relationship, and Churchill advised King George VI that should anything happen to him, Eden was best qualified to succeed him as prime minister. The two men, however, did not always agree, and there was often a strong element of rivalry in the relationship.

One of Eden's most difficult assignments was negotiating the wartime alliance with the Soviet Union, and the protracted talks revealed many of Stalin's postwar ambitions. Eden left for Moscow in December 1941 while the battle of Moscow was raging just outside the city. Stalin proposed a secret Anglo-Soviet protocol that would give East Prussia to Poland, confirm the Baltic states' status as part of the Soviet Union, divide Germany and set the Russian–Polish frontier along the CURZON LINE. In return, he offered Britain military bases in France, Belgium, Holland, Norway and Sweden. Stalin's demands were passed on to American secretary of state Cordell Hull, who completely rejected them; President FRANKLIN D. ROOSEVELT cabled Stalin that he could not agree on any frontiers until after the war. Eden and Churchill, however, felt the need to mollify Stalin and accepted Soviet sovereignty over the Baltic states. The Polish question was left open.

During the war, Eden became heavily involved in trying to repair relations between Stalin and the London-based Polish government-in-exile. In the closing days, he also played a major role in securing the commitment of British troops in fighting communist forces in Greece. He represented Britain at the SAN FRANCISCO CONFERENCE of 1945, which founded the United Nations.

Although Churchill and Eden agreed on most points, Eden felt that his superior was alarmingly anti-communist and during the first three years of the Grand Alliance, he tried to soften Churchill's views. He even went so far as to tell Roosevelt and Hull of his views about Churchill's attitudes toward the Soviet Union, and there is evidence to suggest that this influenced Roosevelt to at times overcompensate for Churchill's antipathy in his own dealings with Stalin.

But by the spring of 1944, Eden was beginning to have serious doubts about the Soviet Union. He wrote in a Foreign Office paper, "I confess to a growing apprehension that Russia has vast aims and that these may include the domination of Eastern Europe and even the Mediterranean and the communizing of much that remains."

Both Churchill and Eden, however, were political pragmatists in the traditional mold of European statesmen. The concessions they eventually made to Stalin at Yalta were mainly a recognition of the European balance of power as it existed at the end of World War II.

In July 1945, Eden lost office with the Labour Party's landslide victory in the general election. As opposition foreign affairs spokesman, he at first expressed his "deep desire for friendship with Russia, as close and cordial a friendship as we have with the United States . . ." In February 1946 he told the House of Commons that he was convinced that the dominant factor in Soviet foreign policy was not expansionism but the fear of another invasion by Germany and that "the determination not to allow Germany to be in a position to do this again . . . resulted in a Soviet determination to have as friendly neighbors as they can."

Eden's immediate postwar views of the Soviet Union brought him into direct conflict with Churchill, who delivered his "IRON CURTAIN" speech at Fulton, Missouri in March 1946. Eden publicly responded to the speech with a studied silence and privately tried to organize a Conservative Party revolt against Churchill's position. It was not until the communist coup in Hungary in the spring of 1947 that Eden started to move toward Churchill's position on the Soviet Union. After that he worked with his close Labour friend, Foreign Secretary ERNEST BEVIN, to develop a bipartisan British foreign policy that gave added strength to the Labour government's support for the TRUMAN DOCTRINE, the MARSHALL PLAN, the Berlin Airlift, the KOREAN WAR and the NORTH ATLANTIC TREATY ORGANIZATION.

After the general election of October 1951 Eden returned to power as foreign secretary and deputy prime minister. He was the recognized heir apparent to Churchill. But during the Conservatives' six years in opposition, Britain's wartime debts had forced it out of the superpower league. Eden was never able to accept this. He continued to regard his country as the world's preeminent power and the natural leader of a vast empire. This brought him into increasing conflict with the foreign policy makers of the United States, in particular JOHN FOSTER DULLES, who by then correctly viewed America as the dominant world power.

When Eden returned to the Foreign Office the main issues facing Britain were German rearmament, European unity, the Korean War and Indochina, Iran, Egypt, and the Suez Canal. In Iran, Prime Minister MOHAMMED MOSSADEQ sparked a crisis with his nationalization of the Anglo-Iranian Oil Company, and Eden worked with the United States to arrange Mossadeq's overthrow.

The British Labour government had supported the United Nations forces in Korea and sent British forces to fight the North Koreans and Chinese. But both Prime Minister CLEMENT ATTLEE and Eden differed from the Americans on the nature of communism and the Chinese communists. The United States took the view that the Chinese communists were operating within the grand design of a Soviet-controlled strategy. The British, on the other hand, viewed China's action as the result of a misinterpretation of what the Chinese regarded as a threat to their national interests. Eden feared that the United States was irrational in its policies toward China. He would have liked to commit more troops to the Korean War in order to increase British influence, but he was prevented from doing so by the dire state of the British economy.

Eden agreed with Churchill in supporting European unity but without formal British participation. They both saw Britain in its traditional role as a world power on the geographic periphery of Europe. This meant opposition to British membership in both the EUROPEAN DEFENSE COMMUNITY (EDC) and the EUROPEAN COAL AND STEEL COMMUNITY, forerunner to the EUROPEAN ECONOMIC COMMUNITY.

But at the same time, it was central to Eden's foreign policy that the continental European states unite both economically and militarily to provide an adequate buffer between Britain and Soviet-controlled Eastern Europe. Therefore, when the French National Assembly rejected the proposed EDC in 1954, Eden intervened to preserve military unity. One of the main reasons for the French rejection was fear of German rearmament without British participation. Eden therefore successfully countered French fears by proposing to extend the BRUSSELS TREATY of 1948 to West Germany and Italy and pledge to maintain 50,000 British troops on garrison duty in Germany.

Eden was also responsible for the last of the attempts made to reunify Germany in the 1950s. The EDEN PLAN FOR GERMAN REUNIFICATION was formally unveiled at the February 1954 meeting of Soviet, British, French and American foreign ministers. At the core of the plan was a proposal for free and secret-ballot elections to be held as soon as possible throughout all of Germany. The government of a unified Germany would be formed after the elections.

Soviet foreign minister V. M. MOLOTOV rejected the Eden Plan and restated the Soviet demands for a unified provisional government before elections, the banning of political parties "hostile to democracy and peace" and a pledge that a reunified Germany would refrain from any military alliances. The failure of the Eden Plan set the final seal on the postwar division of Germany.

Eden also became a pivotal figure in the debate over the future of Indochina and Western involvement in the region. As the French faced defeat at DIEN BIEN PHU in 1954, the EISENHOWER administration, fearful of communist expansion in Southeast Asia, called on Britain to join it in rushing to the aid of the French troops. Eden, however, regarded the Indochinese War as unwinnable and refused. The issue threatened to split the Western Alliance. To prevent this split Eden, attending the GENEVA CONFERENCE ON INDOCHINA AND KOREA in 1954, proposed two treaties. The first was among the Western powers, China and the Soviet Union and guaranteed the neutrality of Laos, Cambodia and Vietnam. The second was a military alliance among the non-communist countries of Southeast Asia. The proposal was reluctantly accepted by Dulles and resulted in the 1954 Treaty on Indochina and the formation of the SOUTHEAST ASIA TREATY ORGANIZATION.

From the start of the 1951 Conservative government, Eden had been waiting for the aging Churchill to retire so that he could assume the role of prime minister. The moment finally arrived in April 1955. As an appointed leader, Eden felt the need for a mandate from the British electorate and called a general election the following month, which resulted in a substantially increased majority for the Conservative Party.

Eden was never particularly interested in domestic British political issues and continued to focus on foreign policy as prime minister. He and Churchill hoped that after Stalin's death in 1953 the Soviet Union would develop a more moderate leadership in the Kremlin and foster improved East–West relations. As prime minister, Eden's main contribution to relaxed East–West tensions was to act as host during a visit to Britain by Soviet leaders NIKOLAI BULGANIN and NIKITA KHRUSHCHEV in April 1956.

But by 1956 Eden's attention was increasingly directed toward Egypt, the Suez Canal and Egyptian leader GAMAL ABDEL NASSER. Eden was an imperialist determined to maintain Britain's global role. The Suez Canal was the vital link between Britain and its possessions in the East and the oil fields of the Persian Gulf. Nasser's seizure of the canal threatened that link and Britain's role in the world.

Nasser's moves came at a time when Eden's health was seriously declining, and there has been speculation that if the British statesman had been in better health he would have realized that Britain could not win a military struggle against the potent force of rising nationalism. Eden, however, became determined to overthrow Nasser and regain control of the canal. This led to Britain's involvement in a French and Israeli plot of dubious legality that became the November 1956 SUEZ CRISIS.

Militarily, Britain had the power to crush the Egyptians. But the British economy was totally dependent on American support. The United States opposed the outdated colonial character of the operation and threatened to withdraw its support of the British economy unless British and French troops withdrew from the canal zone. Eden was forced to capitulate to the American demands. The affair severely strained Anglo-American relations, underscored British dependence on America in the eyes of the rest of the world and marked the end of Britain's role as a superpower.

Throughout the crisis Eden's health continued to decline, and on November 21, 1956, with the crisis still not fully resolved, he was ordered by his doctors to take a vacation. Eden left Deputy Prime Minister R. A. Butler to complete the British withdrawal from the Suez, and on January 9, 1957, he resigned both the prime ministership and his parliamentary seat, citing ill health as the reason. In retirement, Eden concentrated on writing his three volumes of memoirs. He was made Earl of Avon in 1961 and died on January 14, 1977.

For Further Information:

Aster, Sidney. *Anthony Eden.* New York, 1976.
Campbell-Johnson, Alan. *Eden: The Making of a Statesman.* New York, 1955.
Carlton, David. *Anthony Eden: A Biography.* New York, 1981.
Eden, Anthony. *Facing the Dictators.* New York, 1962.
———. *Full Circle.* New York, 1960.
———. *The Reckoning.* New York, 1965.
Rhodes James, Robert. *Anthony Eden.* New York, 1987.
Rothwell, Victor. *Anthony Eden: A Political Biography, 1931–1957.* New York, 1992.

Eden Plan for German Reunification The Eden Plan for German Reunification was put forward by Sir ANTHONY EDEN, then British foreign secretary, at the BERLIN CONFERENCE of Soviet, British, American and French foreign ministers held on January 25–February 18, 1954. The details of the proposal were presented by Eden on January 29. At their core was the demand for free elections to be held as soon as possible throughout all of Germany.

Details of the election would be worked out by the high commissioners of the four occupying powers, who would begin to draft an electoral law within two weeks of the end of the Berlin conference and report not more than a month later. The electoral law would guarantee full freedom for political meetings and other activities associated with democratic voting.

An international commission comprised of the occupation powers and possibly some neutral nations would supervise the voting and the post-election activities of the interim German government. Its decisions would depend on majority vote.

In the elections, Germans of both zones would choose a national assembly to prepare a constitution for the unified government. The occupying powers would exercise only those powers related to the stationing of armed forces in Germany, the special status of Berlin as an occupied city, the reunification of Germany and the conclusion of a German peace treaty.

The German government formed after the elections would

be free to make its own international commitments, organize its own army for domestic defense and join the proposed EUROPEAN DEFENSE COMMUNITY.

The Soviet foreign minister, V. M. MOLOTOV, rejected the Eden Plan. He restated the Soviet Bloc's demand for the formation of a provisional government before elections, insisted on the banning of political parties "hostile to democracy and peace," and proposed that the reunified Germany be effectively neutralized.

Einstein, Albert   (March 14, 1879–April 18, 1955)

Albert Einstein was one of the most brilliant scientific minds in history. His theory of relativity was the scientific basis for the development of atomic energy. During World War II he played an important role in urging the development of the atomic bomb and afterward played an equally important role in urging the control of nuclear weapons.

Einstein was born in Ulm, Germany, the son of nonreligious German Jews. Early conflicts with the German school system led Einstein to teach himself physics and mathematics, and in 1905, while working in Switzerland, he published his theory of relativity. The theory maintained that if the speed of light is constant and that natural laws are uniform throughout the universe, then both time and motion are relative to the observer. Previous to the publication of Einstein's *On the Electrodynamics of Moving Bodies*, it was thought that space and time were fixed absolutes.

Einstein progressed from the Theory of Relativity to the conclusion that matter is concentrated energy. This theory is best explained in the famous equation $E = MC^2$ (energy-mass × speed of light, squared). It was this theory, published in his paper entitled "Does the Inertia of a Body Depend Upon Its Energy Content?" that became the theoretical basis for atomic research.

The Theory of Relativity established Einstein as the world's leading scientist, and he traveled extensively, lecturing and delivering papers. In 1921 he was awarded the Nobel Prize for physics.

After World War I Einstein became an active Zionist and several times visited Palestine and toured the United States to raise money for the Jewish settlements there. Einstein was also a committed pacifist. During World War I he was an outspoken critic of German militarism. His Jewishness and pacifist activities brought him into conflict with Nazism, and in 1933, when Hitler came to power, Einstein renounced his German citizenship and fled Europe for the United States, where he took up a teaching post at Princeton University.

After the outbreak of war in Europe, Einstein was concerned that Nazi Germany was close to developing an atomic bomb, and in 1939 he urged President FRANKLIN ROOSEVELT in a letter to start development of an American atomic bomb. Einstein's letter eventually led to the start of the MANHATTAN PROJECT.

Einstein himself did little work at the Los Alamos laboratories where the first atomic bomb was built. His pacifism made him unsuitable. When, after the defeat of Germany, he learned that the bomb had been successfully tested, he immediately wrote to President Truman urging him not to use it. After the war, Einstein campaigned for a supranational government to control nuclear power. The constitution for such a government would be written by Britain, the United States and the Soviet Union. In August 1946 Einstein helped to form the Emergency Committee of Atomic Scientists to advance the peacetime uses of atomic energy, and in April 1948 he warned that U.S. rearmament would not avert but actually "threaten us with war."

Einstein strongly opposed development of the hydrogen bomb. In February 1950 he warned that if man succeeded in making the hydrogen bomb, "radioactive poisoning of the atmosphere and hence annihilation of any life on earth" would be "brought within the range of technical possibilities."

Einstein's pacifism and repeated calls for international control of nuclear weapons led him into conflict with the HOUSE UN-AMERICAN ACTIVITIES COMMITTEE, which in April 1951 accused him of belonging to a communist-front organization. In June 1953 Einstein accused Senator JOSEPH MCCARTHY's committee of having "managed to instill suspicion of all intellectual efforts into the public by dangling before their eyes a danger from without." He urged American intellectuals to fight against McCarthy's reactionary nationalism by refusing to testify before the House Un-American Activities Committee. Einstein also supported fellow scientist J. ROBERT OPPENHEIMER and urged clemency for convicted spies JULIUS AND ETHEL ROSENBERG. Einstein died on April 18, 1955.

For Further Information:
Clark, Ronald. *Einstein: The Life and Times.* New York, 1971.
Michelmore, Peter. *Einstein: Profile of the Man.* New York, 1962.

Eisenhower, Dwight D.   (October 14, 1890–March 28, 1969)

Dwight D. Eisenhower was president of the United States from 1953 to 1961. The former military leader was a staunch anti-communist, but he balanced this with a realistic sense of the possible. He started his presidency at the height of the Cold War with American troops fighting in Korea. The last few years of the Eisenhower administration saw some of the first efforts to reduce East–West tensions.

Eisenhower was raised in Abilene, Kansas, where his father worked in a creamery. Ike, as he was known from his childhood, won appointment to the United States Military Academy at West Point. He graduated in 1915, 61st out of a class of 164. Eisenhower's poor scholastic record did not hold him back. During World War I he served as a tank instructor and received the Distinguished Service Medal. During the 1920s he attended the Command and General Staff School and the Army War College.

Eisenhower caught the attention of General DOUGLAS MACARTHUR, who brought him onto his staff as an aide, and in 1933 he went with MacArthur to the Philippines to reorganize the Filipino army. When war broke out in Europe in 1939, Eisen-

Dwight D. Eisenhower, president of the United States from 1953 to 1961.

hower had attained the rank only of lieutenant colonel. By the time of the bombing of Pearl Harbor, Eisenhower was a brigadier general and chief of staff of the Third Army. In that position he won the attention of the army chief of staff, General GEORGE C. MARSHALL, who promoted Eisenhower over 366 senior officers to command American troops in Europe.

The qualities that attracted Marshall were the same that resulted in Eisenhower's becoming supreme commander in Europe and eventually being courted by both major political parties as their presidential candidate. From a military point of view, Eisenhower was a good strategist. But that was not the determinant factor, for there were greater military thinkers within the American army. Eisenhower, however, combined his military gifts with extraordinary diplomatic and political talents that enabled him to win acceptance of his policies while at the same time retaining the respect and friendship of those with whom he worked. These traits, combined with a sincere humility and a strong moral purpose, made him one of the best-liked public figures of his time. However, Eisenhower was never regarded as an impressive or dynamic political figure because his tendency to seek compromise steered him away from taking major initiatives.

During World War II, Eisenhower directed the invasion of North Africa in 1942, Sicily and Italy in 1943 and finally Normandy in 1944. At the end of the war, President HARRY TRUMAN appointed Eisenhower army chief of staff. Early in the postwar period Eisenhower supported continuing close relations with the Soviet Union, but he quickly shifted to an anti-communist position and accepted Truman's containment policies and efforts to provide financial and military

support to Western Europe. Eisenhower resigned from the military in 1948 to become president of Columbia University. But he became disillusioned with the academic world and in 1951 was back in the army as commander of the Armed Forces of the NORTH ATLANTIC TREATY ORGANIZATION (NATO).

As early as 1948 Eisenhower was mentioned as a presidential candidate, and a "Draft Eisenhower League" was formed to enter his name in presidential primaries. Eisenhower, however, was opposed to military men in politics and refused to let his name be associated with any political movement or party. But between 1948 and 1952, he reconsidered his position. He let it be known that he was a Republican and became concerned that the isolationist position of the main Republican contender, Senator Robert Taft, would damage American interests in Europe if they became government policy. In June 1952, Eisenhower resigned from the army and returned to the United States to campaign for the Republican nomination, which he won after a spirited battle on the convention floor. In the subsequent presidential election, he took 41 out of the 48 states.

Eisenhower appointed JOHN FOSTER DULLES as his secretary of state, and Dulles was given a great deal of freedom in developing and implementing American foreign policy. Eisenhower, however, always took a keen interest in foreign affairs, and most evenings he and Dulles would hold a foreign policy review in the Oval Office. Dulles was one of the most strident anti-communist figures of the Cold War. Eisenhower acted as a brake on his more extreme views while accepting his basic belief that the United States was the leading force for good in the battle against the evil of Soviet communism.

The president's first major foreign policy task was the resolution of the KOREAN WAR. He had promised to end the unpopular war, but he had to do so in such a way that he did not compromise his anti-communist position. He started by fulfilling a campaign promise to visit Korea as soon as possible after his election. The trip was made in November 1952 and served no useful purpose other than to reassure the American electorate that the war was receiving the attention of a wartime hero.

After his inauguration, Eisenhower employed a diplomatic carrot-and-stick approach to pressure both communist China and the reluctant South Korean president, SYNGMAN RHEE, into accepting an armistice. To increase the pressure on the Chinese, he removed the Seventh Fleet from the Taiwan Straits. The fleet had been blocking an invasion attempt by Nationalist Chinese leader CHIANG KAI-SHEK. He also announced the basing of nuclear weapons in Okinawa and increased American airpower in Korea. At the same time, he rejected Rhee's demands that U.S. forces resume fighting if the Korean Peninsula was not unified within 90 days of the signing of an armistice agreement. The agreement was eventually signed on July 27, 1953.

After the Korean War, the administration continued to face problems in the Far East. Two of the major difficulties were Vietnam and the battle between communist China and

Nationalist China for the islands of QUEMOY AND MATSU. By the end of 1953, it became clear that the French in Vietnam faced the possibility of defeat at the hands of the Viet Minh. Throughout the early months of 1954 Eisenhower and Dulles worked to construct a regional grouping of the United States, France, Britain and Southeast Asian nations to support the French position in Vietnam. But neither the French nor the British were enthusiastic about the project, and DIEN BIEN PHU fell before Eisenhower could muster the congressional support needed for American intervention. At the subsequent GENEVA CONFERENCE ON INDOCHINA AND KOREA, Vietnam was temporarily divided along the 17th parallel. The American delegation, led by WALTER BEDELL SMITH, remained aloof from the negotiations and refused to sign the treaty; the foundations of future American intervention were laid by Smith's announcement that the United States "would view any renewal of the aggression . . . with grave concern and as seriously threatening international peace and security."

Despite the problems of the Far East, Eisenhower, in common with most Americans, believed that the most dangerous communist threat was to Western Europe, and he believed strongly in increased European unity as the best means of combating Soviet expansionism in that part of the world. He and Dulles were strong supporters of the EUROPEAN DEFENSE COMMUNITY, and the president was disappointed when the French National Assembly refused to endorse the defense agreement because of a fear of German rearmament. The problem, however, was solved by West Germany's admission to NATO and the strengthening of the alliance.

Eisenhower's military background made it inevitable that he would become heavily involved in defense issues. During his tenure as army chief of staff and at NATO, Eisenhower had supported nuclear weapons and high-technology defense equipment, but not at the expense of ground forces. By 1954 it had become clear that the U.S. economy could not afford both nuclear weapons and a large standing army. He therefore initiated his "NEW LOOK" DEFENSE POLICY, which shifted the emphasis from conventional to nuclear forces in order to achieve "more bang for the buck." The policy also accepted the theory of nuclear deterrence, which became the mainstay of American strategic thinking.

Eisenhower's first term coincided with the height of the career of the far-right demagogue, Senator JOSEPH MCCARTHY, and his eventual fall. Unlike Truman, Eisenhower refused to attack personally McCarthy for his communist "witch hunt." This was partly because he sympathized with the professed aim of rooting out communist subversion, partly because he did not want to lose the support of right-wing Republicans and partly because he refused to "get down into the gutter with that guy." The result was that Eisenhower managed to remain largely aloof from the debate over McCarthy and had little to do with his eventual fall from grace.

On September 24, 1955, Eisenhower suffered a "moderately severe heart attack." He made a rapid recovery, but the experience made him carefully consider running for a second term. He was persuaded to run by favorable opinion polls and the Republican Party leadership. He defeated Adlai Stevenson by 457 electoral votes to 74, once again carrying 41 of the 48 states.

The closing stages of the 1956 presidential campaign were marked by two major foreign policy crises. The first was the SUEZ CRISIS, which resulted in a major, but temporary, split between Britain and the United States. The Suez Crisis also played a part in General CHARLES DEGAULLE's later decision to seek a more independent French foreign policy. The other crisis was the Hungarian Revolution of 1956, which dramatically underscored the West's inability to intervene in support of anti-communist movements in Eastern Europe (see HUNGARY).

The Anglo-French defeat and the resultant divisions within the Western Alliance greatly improved the Soviet Union's position within Egypt and the wider Arab world. Eisenhower became increasingly concerned about communist expansion in the Middle East and on March 7, 1957, he received congressional support for a resolution on the Middle East, which became known as the EISENHOWER DOCTRINE. This resolution gave the president authority to use American forces to support nations facing "overt armed aggression from any country controlled by international Communism."

Tensions continued to mount in the Middle East in 1957 and 1958, and anti-British and anti-American forces took power in Iraq and threatened Jordan and Lebanon (see LEBANON CRISIS). Camille Chamoun, president of Lebanon, requested American support, and the U.S. Marines were ordered in on July 15, 1958, to prevent a coup by Pan-Arab forces suspected of links with the Soviet Union.

In November 1958 the focus shifted back to Western Europe and a fresh BERLIN Crisis. The Soviet leader NIKITA KHRUSHCHEV, continuing to take advantage of the post-Suez disarray in the Western Alliance, demanded that the West agree that Berlin become an autonomous free city within six months. If it refused, the Soviets would hand control of the major highways between Berlin and West Germany to the East Germans, who would most likely close them. Khrushchev hoped that his proposal would fill a vacuum created by the divisions within the West. But Eisenhower, with great difficulty, managed to persuade the French and Germans to join him in an agreed counterproposal, which was submitted at a four-power summit on Berlin held in May 1958. The summit resulted in the traditional East–West deadlock with the West reunited and the crisis eased.

Throughout his administration, Eisenhower demonstrated a willingness to negotiate with the Soviet Union. In this he differed markedly from John Foster Dulles, who was opposed to any and all negotiations with the Soviet Union. In 1953, following the death of JOSEF STALIN, Eisenhower replied positively to peace feelers from the new Soviet leader. But the continuing power struggle in the Kremlin delayed any real progress. In July 1955 he overrode Dulles' objections and attended a four-power summit in Geneva on German unification and disarmament. But the high point in Soviet–American relations during the Eisenhower administration was Khrushchev's visit to the United States, from September 15 to September 27, 1959. It was the first Soviet–American postwar summit and resulted in the initial tentative steps toward the limitation of nuclear weapons when the Soviet Union and the United States became signatories to the ANTARCTIC TREATY, which established a nuclear-free zone on that continent. A second Eisenhower–Khrushchev summit, which was scheduled for 1960 in Moscow, was canceled after the Soviets shot down a U.S. U-2 spy plane over Soviet territory.

In April 1959 ill health forced Dulles to resign as secretary of state. He died just over a month later. Eisenhower appointed CHRISTIAN HERTER as Dulles's replacement, but in his last 18 months as president he took a greater personal interest in foreign policy and embarked on a series of foreign trips to Third World countries. In September 1960 Eisenhower instituted a financial aid program in Latin America to encourage "social evolution" rather than communist revolution.

His support for social evolution in Latin America was one of the reasons that Eisenhower remained neutral in the struggle in CUBA between FIDEL CASTRO and FULGENCIO BATISTA, whom Eisenhower called a "self-enriching and corrupt dictator." In the final days of the Batista regime the CIA reported that communists had "penetrated the Castro movement," and CIA director ALLEN DULLES recommended that the United States should rescue Batista. Eisenhower rejected the advice in the hope that "some kind of non-dictatorial third force, neither Castroite nor Batistiano," would emerge from the Cuban struggle.

Batista fled the country on New Year's Day 1959, and Castro marched into Havana. The Eisenhower administration awarded the new Cuban government almost immediate diplomatic recognition, but the honeymoon was short-lived. Within a few months Eisenhower became convinced that Castro was a communist or was controlled by communists. The Cuban leader helped to confirm Eisenhower's beliefs by nationalizing American assets, canceling elections, arresting and executing political opponents and declaring himself a socialist. In July 1960, Eisenhower suspended imports of Cuban sugar, and on July 31, 1961, severed diplomatic relations. But Eisenhower's major decision related to Cuba was his approval in March 1960 of a CIA plan to train a group of Cuban exiles who would invade the island and overthrow Castro. This plot culminated in the unsuccessful BAY OF PIGS invasion.

After his second term, Eisenhower retired to his farm near Gettysburg, Pennsylvania. In retirement he remained aloof from party politics, but during the KENNEDY administration he issued statements opposing increased defense expenditures and supporting reduced American troop commitments in Western Europe. Eisenhower supported American involvement in Vietnam, but in private discussions with President LYNDON JOHNSON he expressed doubt about the effectiveness of American conventional forces winning a guerrilla war. Eisenhower died of a heart attack on March 28, 1969.

For Further Information:
Adams, Sherman. *Firsthand Report: The Story of the Eisenhower Administration.* New York, 1961.
Alexander, Charles. *Holding the Line: The Eisenhower Era, 1952–1961.* Bloomington, Ind., 1975.
Ambrose, Stephen E. *Eisenhower.* 2 vols. New York, 1984.
Brands, H.W. *Cold Warriors: Eisenhower's Generation and American Foreign Policy.* New York, 1988.
Burk, Robert Fredrick. *Dwight D. Eisenhower, Hero & Politician.* Boston, 1986.
Cook, Blanche Wiesen. *The Declassified Eisenhower: A Divided Legacy.* Garden City, N.Y., 1981.
Divine, Robert A. *Eisenhower and the Cold War.* New York, 1981.
Eisenhower, Dwight D. *The White House Years, Mandate for Change, 1953–56.* Garden City, N.Y., 1963.
———. *The White House Years, Waging Peace, 1956–61.* Garden City, N.Y., 1965.
Hughes, Emmet John. *The Ordeal of Power: A Political Memoir of the Eisenhower Years.* New York, 1963.
Parmet, Herbert S. *Eisenhower and the American Crusade.* New York, 1972.
Steel, Richard. *Pax Americana.* New York, 1967.

Eisenhower Doctrine   The Eisenhower Doctrine was formulated by President DWIGHT EISENHOWER in 1957 to deal with a perceived Soviet threat in the Middle East following the SUEZ CRISIS. Its ultimate result was the landing of United States marines in Lebanon.

The Suez Crisis had several unwelcome repercussions in the Middle East. It seriously damaged British influence, which in turn created a political vacuum in this volatile part of the world. It also greatly enhanced Soviet prestige because the Soviets had supported Arab nationalist GAMAL ABDEL NASSER in his fight against the British, French and Israelis. Nasser's pan-Arabism, and, by association, the Soviet Union, moved to fill the political vacuum.

On January 1, 1957, Eisenhower and Secretary of State JOHN FOSTER DULLES met with congressional leaders, who were told by Eisenhower, "The existing vacuum in the Middle East must be filled by the United States before it is filled by Russia." He went on to request authorization for a special economic fund and the use of military force if necessary in the Middle East. On January 5, 1957, House Joint Resolution 117 was introduced into the Congress. It received final approval on March 7.

The Eisenhower Doctrine was generally favored by Britain and France and attacked by the Soviet Union. The Arab world was divided on the issue, with Egypt and Syria vehemently opposed to it; Iraq, Saudi Arabia and Jordan cautiously critical and Lebanon looking upon it as its guarantee of peace.

The first test of the Eisenhower Doctrine came in Jordan. In March 1957 the Anglo-Jordanian treaty, which had established British control of the Jordanian Army, was terminated by Jordan. King Hussein, under strong pressure, had appointed a left-wing, pro-Nasser prime minister. When Hussein later dismissed the prime minister, he immediately found himself the victim of a pro-Nasser propaganda barrage. Hussein responded by imposing martial law, but his position was perceived as precarious. Eisenhower sent units of the Sixth Fleet to the Eastern Mediterranean in April, and the State Department issued a statement saying that the United States regarded the "independence and integrity of Jordan as vital." On April 29, an emergency economic grant of $10 million was extended to Jordan. The situation stabilized, and on May 1, 1957, the Sixth Fleet was recalled from the Eastern Mediterranean.

In April 1957 the Syrian government began issuing anti-American and pro-Nasser propaganda, accusing the U.S. of fomenting the crisis in Jordan. Eisenhower, fearful that the Syrians had fallen under Soviet control and were likely to become a source of attacks on neighboring Arab countries, let it be known that the United States would support an Arab attack against Syria and stepped up military supplies to friendly Arab states. The attack never came, but it had the effect of containing Syrian influence for a time.

But the most forceful use of the Eisenhower Doctrine was in Lebanon (see LEBANON CRISIS). That country's unstable political division between Christians and Muslims made it inevitable that outside forces would attempt to exploit the split to their own advantage. In April 1958 President Chamoun, a Christian and pro-American, pushed through a constitutional amendment that allowed him to run for an unprecedented second term. The result was a Muslim uprising in Beirut. Chamoun claimed that Egypt and Syria, which had formed a political union in January, were fomenting the uprising, and requested American help.

The American landings were strongly opposed by the Soviet Union, Egypt, Syria and the new gov- ernment in Iraq, and anti-American and anti-British demonstrations took place outside American embassies throughout the Arab world. But the troops had the desired effect of stabilizing the Middle East situation. The last of the American troops sent to enforce the Eisenhower Doctrine withdrew from Lebanon on October 25, 1958.

For Further Information:
Campbell, John C. *Defense of the Middle East.* New York, 1960.
Polk, William. *The United States and the Arab World.* Cambridge, Mass., 1969.

Electromagnetic Pulse (EMP) An electromagnetic pulse is a shock wave from a weapon blast, usually from a nuclear device, that is designed to destroy or seriously damage electronic equipment.

EMP weapons are usually aimed at computer systems, wiping out memory banks by creating electrical and magnetic fields. ·The vulnerability of computers to EMP weapons and the heavy reliance of modern armies on computers is a major concern for military planners.

ELINT (Electronic Intelligence) Program The ELINT (Electronic Intelligence) Program was an American espionage plan that involved sending American spy planes parallel to or over Soviet borders to be detected so that American electronics specialists could investigate the activated Soviet radar signals.

The program was launched in the late 1950s and involved the use of American EC-130s. The planes were packed with electronic surveillance equipment that would pick up the faint emissions of Soviet air-defense radar, microwave signals and ground communications. These would be captured and sent to the NATIONAL SECURITY AGENCY's headquarters outside Washington, D.C., for analysis.

Best results were achieved when the planes deliberately flew across the Soviet border. On September 2, 1958, one such plane was shot down by a MiG 218 over Soviet Armenia, causing the death of its 17-man crew. To maintain the secrecy of the ELINT program, the plane was initially listed as missing, although the Air Force made a tape recording of the MiG pilots' tracking and shooting down of the plane.

On September 12 the Soviet Union revealed that an American plane had crashed in Soviet Armenia but said nothing about its having been shot down. The EISENHOWER administration demanded further information about how the plane had crashed and the fate of its crew. The Soviets replied with a charge that the plane had violated Soviet airspace, but gave no further details. On September 24 the bodies of six of the crew were returned by the Soviet authorities.

President Dwight Eisenhower and Secretary of State JOHN FOSTER DULLES were convinced that the rest of the crew had bailed out before the plane crashed and were alive. In February 1959, in an effort to secure their release, the Eisenhower administration released the transcript of the tape recording of the MiG pilots and accused the Soviets of shooting down an unarmed plane.

The Soviet Union denounced the tape as a "fake" and a "gross forgery." Soviet broadcasters charged that "the fake [recording] is so transparent that a child could see through it. The script sounds as if it were written in Hollywood by someone who knew nothing of contemporary Russian language." Independent experts, however, accepted the tape's authenticity.

At a press conference called for the release of the tapes, Eisenhower refused to reveal the source of the recording. He also specifically denied that the American plane had deliberately crossed the Soviet border "to cause scrambling" by Soviet fighters in order to monitor Soviet air defenses.

Eisenhower's denial and the provocative nature of the ELINT program angered two employees at the National Security Agency (NSA), Bernon Mitchell and William Martin, and led to their defection to the Soviet Union in 1960. At a press conference in Moscow on September 6, 1960, the two men revealed details of the ELINT Program and said that their decision to defect was not due to the "fact that the United States . . . is delving into the secrets of other nations" but to the fact that the United States "knowingly makes false and deceptive statements both in defending its own activities and in condemning the activities of other nations."

The Eisenhower administration, and later the Kennedy administration, continued to press the Soviet Union for information about the unaccounted crewmen. This included a personal appeal from Vice President RICHARD NIXON and a meeting between Soviet leader NIKITA KHRUSHCHEV and American Ambassador LLEWELLYN THOMPSON. In January 1961 the Soviet magazine *Ogonek* published an article that claimed that 11 of the crew had parachuted out of the plane and had been captured on the outskirts of the Armenian city of Yerevan. The article was denounced by the Soviet authorities as an error, and in November 1962 the Kennedy administration officially listed the crewmen as "missing, presumed dead."

For Further Information:
Bamford, James. *The Puzzle Palace*. New York, 1982.

Ellsberg, Daniel (April 7, 1931–) Daniel Ellsberg was a defense analyst for the Rand Corporation who leaked the top secret "Pentagon Papers" to the press. The documents proved to be a considerable embarrassment to the U.S. government and hastened American withdrawal from Vietnam.

After two years in the Marines, Ellsberg attended Harvard University, where he wrote an analysis of strategic military planning for his graduate dissertation. He graduated in 1959 and joined an Air Force-sponsored think tank, the RAND CORPORATION. In 1964 he left to join the staff of JOHN T. MCNAUGHTON, an assistant secretary of defense.

Ellsberg started off a hawk on the VIETNAM WAR. In 1967, after he had returned to the Rand Corporation, he was employed as a researcher on a project for the Pentagon, a history of the U.S. involvement in Southeast Asia. His research convinced him that the war was unjust and that the United States was guilty of "foreign aggression." Ellsberg became a speaker at antiwar rallies, wrote numerous antiwar articles for magazines and newspapers and dispatched hundreds of letters to prominent political figures urging an immediate withdrawal from Vietnam.

In October 1969 Ellsberg used his top secret clearance to obtain a copy of the history on which he had worked for the Pentagon. He photocopied it and offered it first to the prominent "dove," Senator J. WILLIAM FULBRIGHT, who refused to use it. He then offered it to the *New York Times*, which began publishing excerpts in June 1971. The NIXON administration obtained an injunction against the *New York Times*, and Ellsberg leaked copies of his "Pentagon Papers" to the *Washington Post* and *Boston Globe*. Each time the government was forced to seek an injunction against the publisher, and each time Ellsberg found another platform. Finally, on June 30, the Supreme Court ruled in favor of the *Time*'s right to publish the leaked documents.

In the interim, Ellsberg had gone into hiding. He surrendered to the authorities on August 28 and was indicted on charges of theft of government property and violation of the Espionage Act. Ellsberg admitted that he was the source of the leaks but denied breaking any laws. During the course of the trial, it was revealed that G. Gordon Liddy and E. Howard Hunt, two convicted Watergate conspirators, had, under the orders of White House adviser John Ehrlichman, burgled the office of Ellsberg's psychiatrist in an effort to uncover embarrassing information about Ellsberg. It was also revealed that the FBI had tapped the telephones of Ellsberg's friends and that the judge trying his case, Matthew Byrne, had been offered the directorship of the FBI. When Byrne ordered the prosecution to turn over transcripts, the government announced that it had lost all the relevant records. On May 11, 1973, Byrne accused the government of "gross misconduct" and declared a mistrial. The case cost an estimated $5 million. The U.S. government dropped its charges against Ellsberg on June 6, 1973.

Ellsberg continued as a prominent figure in the antiwar movement. After the American withdrawal from Vietnam in 1975, he joined the nuclear disarmament campaign.

For Further Information:
Bannon, John F., and Rosemary Sy. *Law, Morality and Vietnam: The Peace Militants and the Courts*. Bloomington, Ind., 1974.
Dougan, C.A. *A Nation Divided*. Boston, 1984.
Ellsberg, Daniel. *Papers on the War*. New York, 1972.

El Salvador Beginning in 1980, the Central American country of El Salvador was embroiled in a bitter civil war involving the U.S.-financed, right-wing military and left-wing guerrillas, supported by Nicaragua and Cuba. With the waning of the Cold War, the two sides signed a peace treaty in January 1992.

Since its independence from Spain in 1821, El Salvador has suffered from chronic political instability and the dominance of an arch-conservative and highly politicized military. Throughout the 1970s, the country was ruled by the military-dominated National Conciliation Party (PCN), whose draconian methods led to the growth of guerrilla activities. The military responded to the start of guerrilla activity with roaming right-wing death squads, widespread imprisonment of political dissidents and other abuses of human rights.

In October 1979 President General Carlos Humberto Romero was overthrown in a civilian-military coup that installed a junta committed to elections. The junta offered a political amnesty to guerrillas, but this was rejected. In March 1980, the government's credibility was seriously damaged by the assassination of the Roman Catholic archbishop of San Salvador, Oscar Romero y Galdames, the country's leading and most outspoken critic of the military's human rights record. Shortly afterward the formerly disparate guerrilla groups formed a coalition called the Farabundo Marti National Liberation Front (FMLN), named after the leader of a peasant revolt in the 1930s. In December 1980 Jose Napoleon Duarte, El Salvador's leading moderate conservative politician, was sworn in as president.

But the FMLN continued to ignore peace feelers it felt were

not made in good faith and launched its first major offensive in January 1981. This was accompanied by a general strike called by the FMLN's political wing, the Revolutionary Democratic Front (FDR). The strike failed to attract popular support, but the initial success of the guerrilla offensive led to the declaration of martial law nine days later.

Government forces met with initial success, but fighting continued in the area north of the capital, San Salvador. The FMLN offensive also strengthened the political position of the conservative military officers, which in turn led to an increase in the activities of the death squads and a postponement of elections. These activities increased popular support for the FMLN, and by May 1981 the guerrillas claimed to control four provinces. In August the FMLN launched a series of bomb attacks on economic targets in San Salvador. The army retaliated with indiscriminate attacks on the civilian population in guerrilla-held areas. By the end of 1981 there were an estimated 300,000 refugees from the civil war.

The FMLN, which had established diplomatic offices in Mexico, gained full political support from Cuba, Panama, Yugoslavia and Nicaragua and some degree of support from France, Mexico and the Netherlands. The Cuban and Nicaraguan support included military supplies, and this alienated the United States, which increased its support to the El Salvador government, claiming that Nicaragua and Cuba were trying to extend their revolutionary activities in Central America. During 1983, El Salvador received an estimated $80 million in U.S. military aid. In 1982 some 1,600 Salvadoran troops received training in the United States, and American military advisers were reported to be actively involved in the fighting. In that same year, an estimated 20,000 civilians were killed. Between 1980 and 1989, the United States provided an estimated $3.3 billion in economic and military aid to the El Salvador government.

The United States found itself in a difficult position in El Salvador. It had evidence that the FMLN was receiving military supplies from Cuba (and probably the Soviet Union) through Nicaragua. The FMLN leadership openly subscribed to Marxist policies and had stated that its aim was to form a "people's state" following a "prolonged popular war." The Reagan administration believed that this combination of factors meant that the Soviet Union planned to establish a bloc of communist states in Central America, which would pose a threat to the Panama Canal and Mexico and would stand as a political barrier between the United States and South America.

On the other hand, the United States could not afford to be seen to be supporting one of the world's most politically repressive regimes. The United States thus adopted a two-pronged policy of supplying extensive military aid while at the same time demanding political reform as a price for this aid. The installation of Duarte as president in 1980 was one of the results of American pressure. In March 1982, the United States supported Duarte's Christian Democratic Party (PDC) in legislative elections. But the right-wing parties emerged with 60% of the vote and Major Roberto D'Aubuisson, who had been linked with the death squads and was leader of the extreme right-wing National Republican Alliance (ARENA), emerged as the most powerful political figure and was elected president of the Constituent Assembly.

The United States, however, managed to moderate D'Aubuisson's powers by privately threatening to cut off aid. This threat led to the admission of five members of the PDC to the cabinet. The moderate conservatives regained control of the Constituent Assembly in December 1982 after a split within the right-wing coalition. The death squads, however, continued their activities. In October 1983 the weekly number of deaths attributed to these roaming assassins reached 200. As a result, the United States demanded that several high-level political figures linked to the squads be dismissed. In presidential elections in March 1984, Duarte was backed by the United States and was elected with 53.6% of the vote, compared to 46.4% for D'Aubuisson.

Following his election, Duarte ordered a purge of the military, reorganization of the police force, and the end of the death squads. The election of Duarte encouraged the FMLN to seek negotiations with the new government, and the first set of talks was held between the FMLN and the government of President Duarte in October and November 1984. These resulted in a series of oft-broken ceasefires. Duarte's political base was further strengthened by legislative and local elections in March 1985, which gave his PDC a clear majority in the Constituent Assembly. This majority enabled Duarte to embark on a series of extensive social reforms that weakened the FMLN's political base and led to further negotiations.

Economic problems, exacerbated by a severe earthquake in October 1986, led to public discontent with Duarte, although this was blunted by increased American aid. But the Central American peace plan signed in Guatemala City in August 1987 encouraged hopes for a negotiated solution to the civil war. The agreement was signed by the leaders of Costa Rica, Honduras, Nicaragua and El Salvador. Its provisions included:

1. An amnesty for the region's guerrilla forces.
2. Negotiations between the region's governments and "unarmed internal political opposition groups."
3. Promotion of "an authentic, democratic, pluralist and participatory process" in each country with respect for human rights and social justice.
4. A ban on aid to guerrilla forces in the region.

Discussions between the government and the FMLN formally opened in October 1987. But the murder of Herbert Anaya Sanabria, president of El Salvador's Human Rights Commission, led to an early breakdown, and in December 1987 a new guerrilla offensive resulted in the deaths of 1,500 more people.

In municipal and legislative elections, Duarte's PDC suffered a major setback at the hands of ARENA, which won more than 80% of the municipal elections. The PDC also had its share of seats in the 60-seat National Assembly reduced from 33 to 30, while ARENA jumped from 13 to 23. After a split within the Christian Democrats, ARENA secured control of the assembly. ARENA continued to be dominated by D'Aubuisson, but its candidate for the March 1989 presidential elections was Alfredo Cristiani, who won with 53.8% of the vote despite continued American backing for the Christian Democrats.

Cristiani tried to present a moderate image in order to retain American support and offered further talks with the FMLN. His pledges to respect human rights won him the early support of U.S. president GEORGE BUSH. At his inauguration in June 1989, Cristiani offered a five-point peace plan, and at an August meeting in Tela, Honduras he persuaded the leaders of the Central American countries to call on the FMLN to start a dialogue with the government to achieve "a just and lasting peace."

Negotiations between the FMLN and the government were held in October 1989 in Costa Rica, but these talks broke down on a number of points. The FMLN first claimed that the government proposals basically constituted a surrender. In addition, they wanted the army to be more fully represented at negotiations, and they demanded a reduction in the size of the army, the trial of D'Aubuisson, the separation of the various security police forces from the army, and a stop to Cristiani's economic privatization program.

Fresh talks were set for November 14 in Venezuela, but on November 11 the FMLN launched a major offensive that took them into the center of San Salvador and nearly toppled the government. By Christmas 1989, the guerrilla offensive had subsided and the government was proposing fresh talks.

New peace talks under the auspices of the United Nations got under way in May 1990. In September 1991 in New York, the Salvadoran government and representatives of the five main rebel groups signed a broad agreement on the country's political and economic future. That accord led to the signing on January 16, 1992, in Mexico City of a formal peace treaty ending the 12-year-old civil war. Under the treaty, a formal cease-fire would run from February 1 through October 31, by which date the FMLN was to be fully disarmed and become a legal political party. That process was to be monitored by up to 1,000 UN military and civilian observers. Meanwhile, the government agreed to cut its armed forces in half by 1994 and purge the worst human rights violators. The national guard and treasury police would be absorbed into the regular army, and a new national civilian police force that would include both former rebels and government troops was to be created.

For Further Information:
Dunkerley, James. *The Long War: Dictatorship and Revolution in El Salvador*. London, 1982.
———. *Power in the Isthmus*. London, 1988.
Feinberg, Richard E., ed. *Central America: International Dimensions of the Crisis*. New York, 1982.
Gettleman, Marvin, et al., eds. *El Salvador: Central America in the New Cold War*. New York, 1986.

Miller, Nicola. *Soviet Relations with Latin America, 1959–1987*. New York, 1989.

Erhard, Ludwig   (February 4, 1897–May 5, 1977)   Professor Ludwig Erhard was the second chancellor of the Federal Republic of Germany. As the first economics minister, he was the man most responsible for the postwar German economic miracle, which reinforced the country's political and military status in the Western Alliance. As chancellor, he fended off advances from French president CHARLES DE GAULLE and strengthened ties with the United States.

Erhard was born in Bavaria and served in the German Army during World War I; he was badly wounded at the battle of Ypres in 1918. After the war he studied economics at Frankfurt University. In 1928 he joined the Industrial Research Institute of Nuremberg. He lost this post after refusing to join the Nazi Party. During the war he was a freelance economics consultant and developed a postwar reconstruction plan for Germany. This kept him relatively untainted from association with the Nazis. In 1945 the American occupying forces, after reading his plan, employed Erhard as an economics adviser.

Erhard joined the Bavarian state government in 1946 as minister of economics. When the British and American zones were merged, he went to Frankfurt to become director of economics, where he was responsible for the currency reform

Ludwig Erhard was the second chancellor of the Federal Republic of Germany, from 1963 to 1966. Photo courtesy of the German Ministry of Foreign Affairs.

that laid the economic foundations of the Federal Republic of Germany. In 1949 he was named the economics minister in the first government of Chancellor KONRAD ADENAUER.

It was as economics minister that Erhard had his greatest impact on Germany and the whole of Western Europe. He laid the foundations for the economic revival of Germany that within 10 years turned it from an postwar economic disaster zone to the most powerful economy in Western Europe. West Germany at the time was an ideal candidate for an eminent economic theorist such as Erhard. Having had its political and economic structures completely destroyed by the war, it provided a real-life laboratory in which he could build a new economic structure from scratch.

Western Europe at the time was busy implementing the welfare state policies being pioneered by the postwar Labour government in Britain. But at the heart of Erhard's policies was the belief that the solution to Germany's economic problems lay "not in the leveling of scarcities but in the just sharing of a growing prosperity." The logical consequence of this policy was a firm belief in free trade and a free market. Thus, while Britain was still enduring food rationing, Erhard in 1948 abolished rationing. Prices rose alarmingly, but within a short time production increased to cope with the public's demand for consumer goods, and the economy began to blossom.

Erhard was elected federal chancellor by the Bundestag on October 16, 1963. It was a popular decision, for the aged, right-wing Adenauer was regarded by many as having outlived his usefulness. Adenauer, however, strongly opposed the selection of Erhard, whom he publicly reviled as a political lightweight. Erhard consistently refused to retaliate against Adenauer.

In his final days as chancellor, Adenauer became increasingly concerned about what he regarded as American appeasement toward the Soviet Union and sought to forge a Franco-German reconciliation that would become the basis of a politically and militarily united Europe and eventually replace German dependence on American military guarantees. The result was the FRANCO-GERMAN FRIENDSHIP TREATY signed in January 1963.

Erhard did not share the pro-French views of Adenauer or the European concepts of Charles de Gaulle. He was committed to the ideal of European unity but rejected completely the view that Europe should become a third force independent of the United States; he believed that the American presence in Europe was essential to West German security. This strained Franco-German relations and led De Gaulle to strengthen his relations with the Soviet Union.

Erhard's "Atlanticist" attitude encountered heavy opposition from the strong Gaullist wing within his own Christian Democratic Union and even more so among coalition partners in the Christian Social Union. The Gaullists attempted a revolt in 1964, and Erhard was forced to bring them into line by publicly quoting from the section of the federal constitution that gave the chancellor the sole responsibility for determining the course of West German foreign policy. Er-

hard's position within the party was considerably strengthened by his success at the polls in the 1965 general election.

While Franco-German relations deteriorated, U.S.-German relations improved considerably during Erhard's government. Erhard managed to forge a close friendship with President LYNDON JOHNSON and, despite growing public opposition, supported American policy toward both China and the VIET-NAM WAR. There were problems, however, over the Multinational Nuclear Force proposed for NATO and the negotiation of German offset payments for American troops in Germany. Erhard's major foreign policy achievement was the establishment of full diplomatic relations with Israel.

The final two years of Erhard's government were plagued by economic problems. Faced with the prospect of a budget deficit in 1967, Erhard called for substantial tax increases. This was opposed by his other coalition partners, the Free Democratic Party, who walked out of the government. Erhard resigned in December 1966 and retired to relative political obscurity. He died on May 5, 1977, of heart failure.

For Further Information:
Prittie, Terence. *The Velvet Chancellors: A History of Postwar Germany.* London, 1979.
Rosolowsky, D. *West Germany's Foreign Policy.* Westport, Conn., 1988.

Espionage Espionage, or spying, is the collection of information about another state's secrets. Because of the constant threat of nuclear war, the Cold War period saw a steep increase in the growth and types of espionage activities, to include covert operations and disinformation aimed at destabilizing the main protagonists in the East-West conflict.

Most intelligence can be gathered from public sources such as radio, television, newspapers, books and public speeches. Great effort is expended by the world's intelligence services in scouring public sources, storing the information, developing retrieval systems and analyzing it for signs of political, economic and military trends.

A great deal more secret information is gathered by electronic means, using satellites, listening devices, radio and radar intercepts and other equipment. These systems have made almost obsolete the old-fashioned information-gathering agent in the field, whose primary purpose now is to administer, interact with other intelligence services and at times direct covert paramilitary operations.

Espionage, or the gathering of intelligence, has been an integral part of political affairs since ancient times. It is often called the world's second oldest profession. It has always been important to learn as much as possible about the enemy's political and military affairs and equally important to keep one's own affairs secret.

The first known book on espionage was written in 400 B.C. by the Chinese defense and intelligence expert Sun Tzu. He wrote about the use of penetration agents, double agents, agents in place and deception agents as well as counterintelligence operations. The first major national intelligence operation was developed by England during the reign of Queen Elizabeth I. By the 19th century, intelligence and counterintelligence organizations were an integral part of every major European country's defense establishment.

After World War I, Britain emerged with the world's dominant intelligence service. During the interwar years, Britain took the lead in espionage activities against the young Bolshevik government in the Soviet Union. The Soviets' decision in the 1920s and 1930s to recruit graduates of Cambridge University stems from its early fears of British intelligence activities.

In the Soviet Union itself, the intelligence services played a dual role, spying on foreign governments and services and at the same time monitoring the domestic civilian population. This gave the Cheka, and later the NKVD and KGB, a sinister and inordinately powerful role within the Communist Party and the government.

The United States had virtually no espionage network before World War II. The FEDERAL BUREAU OF INVESTIGATION was responsible for counterintelligence operations within the United States but had no authority to gather intelligence overseas. At the start of the war, the United States formed the OFFICE OF STRATEGIC SERVICES (OSS) to gather and assess foreign intelligence and conduct secret operations. The United States relied heavily on British expertise in establishing the OSS and its Cold War successor, the CENTRAL INTELLIGENCE AGENCY.

In the immediate aftermath of the war, President HARRY TRUMAN disbanded the OSS because he feared that it could lead to government excesses. But as relations with the Soviet Union deteriorated, he came to the conclusion that an intelligence agency was necessary, and the CIA was created under the NATIONAL SECURITY ACT OF 1947. The CIA, however, was not the only American intelligence operation. The Defense Department maintained its own intelligence branch (the Defense Intelligence Agency), the FBI continued its counterintelligence operations, the ATOMIC ENERGY COMMISSION established its own intelligence unit and the NATIONAL SECURITY AGENCY (NSA) was formed to deal with the growing field of electronic espionage.

The CIA, however, became the dominant intelligence agency in the United States and the Western world. During the Cold War, its influence and power were further increased by the overhanging threat of nuclear war. This deterrent threat prevented the superpowers from launching a conventional war against each other for fear that it would quickly escalate into a nuclear conflict. Instead, the United States and the Soviet Union resorted to covert operations to secure political gains that in pre-nuclear days would have been achieved with conventional military forces. Some of these covert operations have included the overthrow of Jacobo Arbenz in Guatemala (see GUATEMALA INTERVENTION), the overthrow of SALVADOR ALLENDE in Chile, the attempted assassinations of Congolese leader PATRICE LUMUMBA and Cuban leader FIDEL CASTRO, the abortive BAY OF PIGS operation in Cuba,

the overthrow of Iranian Premier MOHAMMED MOSADDEQ and the attempted overthrow of the Albanian government.

The CIA also involved itself in illegal activities such as intercepting mail to and from the Soviet Bloc and maintaining extensive files on anti-Vietnam War protesters and other dissident Americans. The agency's domestic operations were a breach of its charter, and this, plus disclosure of some of the more unsavory covert operations, led to severe criticism of the CIA in the 1970s. Its budget and staff were cut, morale sank and agency operations came under close scrutiny of the Senate Intelligence Committee. By the mid-1980s, however, the administration of President RONALD REAGAN had restored the CIA to its former position.

Another reason the CIA turned more toward covert operations was technological advances that made the business of gathering intelligence increasingly electronic. This aspect was handled by the National Security Agency, which was formed in November 1952 and is based at Fort Meade, Maryland, outside Washington, D.C. By the start of the 1980s, the NSA had the capability to intercept every form of communication. In the 1950s and 1960s it operated spy planes such as the U-2, which flew over the Soviet Union and reported the presence of Soviet missiles in Cuba. In the late 1970s and 1980s the surveillance emphasis shifted to space-based satellites capable of detecting the smallest details. The NSA is also responsible for breaking foreign codes, developing new American codes and developing electronic surveillance equipment for use in the field by CIA and other agents.

Throughout the Cold War period, American intelligence worked closely with the British intelligence establishment. These are primarily the SIS, or MI6, which is responsible for gathering foreign intelligence and conducting foreign covert operations; MI5, which is responsible for counterintelligence; and GOVERNMENT COMMUNICATIONS HEADQUARTERS (GCHQ) at Cheltenham. The relationship with GCHQ was formalized by the 1947 UKUSA AGREEMENT, which effectively established a partnership between GCHQ and the NSA covering electronic intelligence. The British, working in conjunction with the governments of Australia and New Zealand, were responsible for monitoring radio, telegraph, telex and telephone traffic to and from Britain, China, the Middle East, Australia and New Zealand, while NSA was responsible for the rest of the world.

The working relationship between the CIA and MI5 and MI6 is less formal but nevertheless close. Both intelligence establishments have agreed not to operate agents in the other's territories, and they have liaison officers based in Washington and London. The two countries' intelligence networks have also worked jointly in several covert operations, including the overthrow of Mohammed Mosaddeq in Iran and attempts to subvert the government of Albania and support dissidents in Soviet Georgia, the Baltic states, the Ukraine and Moldavia.

British intelligence, however, was plagued with Soviet double agents recruited from the British upper classes. Three of these recruits, KIM PHILBY, DONALD MACLEAN and GUY BURGESS, passed on valuable nuclear secrets, exposed Western agents and disrupted covert operations before fleeing to the Soviet Union. Their activities in the early years of the Cold War created within some circles of the CIA a climate of suspicion toward MI5 and MI6. British intelligence did, however, have a major success in the recruitment of KGB agent OLEG PENKOVSKY, who passed on valuable secrets before being executed by the Soviet Union in 1963.

One of the best-informed Western intelligence officers in the early Cold War years was General Reinhard Gehlen, former head of German Army Intelligence on the Eastern Front and a close friend of Adolf Hitler. Germany's status as a defeated and occupied enemy meant that it was impossible to develop a formal German intelligence service. But, at the same time, Gehlen's wartime experience had left him with extensive and invaluable files on Soviet operations in Eastern Europe as well as a network of in-place agents. In July 1946 the CIA hired this fiercely anti-communist Nazi as a freelance agent, and he founded the private GEHLEN ORGANIZATION, which became one of the most important Western intelligence agencies operating in Eastern Europe. Gehlen agents were particularly active in East Germany, where they infiltrated East German intelligence at almost every level. In 1956, a year after formal Allied control of West Germany ended, the Gehlen Organization was brought under German government control and became the Federal Intelligence Service (BND). Gehlen became its first president.

The BND, however, also suffered from infiltration by East German agents. This was because the West German constitution automatically extended its citizenship to East Germans. West Germans also had family contacts in East Germany. This made it possible for East German intelligence to send its agents into West Germany under the guise of refugees and to use family connections to blackmail or threaten West Germans into providing information to the East German government. The most famous East German infiltrator was GUNTER GUILLAUME, who managed to become a key aide to West German chancellor WILLY BRANDT. His exposure in 1974 forced Brandt's resignation.

Another important element in the Western intelligence network is the French Service de Documentation Exterieure et de Contre-Espionage (SDCE). The SDCE worked closely with the CIA and British Intelligence durng the 1940s and 1950s and played a vital role in exposing the presence of Soviet missiles in Cuba. But close Franco-American cooperation stopped after President CHARLES DE GAULLE took France out of NATO in 1966. In 1968, Philippe Thyraud de Vosjoli, a retired high-ranking officer in the SDCE, published his memoirs, in which he claimed that, like the British and Germans, the SDCE had been infiltrated by the communists.

Soviet intelligence, which was dominated by the KGB, or Committee of State Security, developed an expertise for infiltrating foreign agencies. It relied on the dedication of private individuals to the political ideology of communism to betray their own countries for the sake of the greater cause. The Soviets' successful infiltrations and the employment of double agents helped them with their early development of nuclear weapons through spies such as KLAUS FUCHS. Agents such as Philby also enabled the Soviets to thwart British and American covert operations in the Balkans and the Soviet republics.

The KGB, which still operates on a partially reformed basis as an agency of the Russian government, traces its lineage back to the Cheka, which was formed under Felix Dzerzhinsky, shortly after the Bolshevik Revolution in 1917. The Cheka organized the first Red Terror, in which thousands died. It was dissolved in 1922 and replaced by the State Political Directorate (GPU) and the People's Commissariat of Internal Affairs (NKVD). In 1934, the GPU was made a division of the NKVD, which gained control of border guards, internal troops, labor camps, the police, intelligence gathering and general internal security. It was the NKVD that orchestrated the great Stalinist purges of the 1930s.

The eight years between the end of World War II and the death of JOSEF STALIN saw a series of power struggles for control of the Soviet security service, and the organization was variously split and regrouped into several different bureaucracies. The NKVD was controlled by LAVRENTY BERIA, who used the organization to spy on other leading communists and to build his own political power base. In June 1953, however, he was arrested and shot. The security services again reorganized, and on March 13, 1954, the KGB officially came into being. The new organization took over from the NKVD the responsibilities for intelligence, counterintelligence and internal control. The KGB also developed a new directorate for electronic intelligence, similar to the American National Security Agency.

The new KGB, however, was more carefully controlled by the ruling Politburo, and for the next 13 years the Politburo was careful to appoint easily controlled technocrats to the post of KGB director. This damaged morale within the Soviet intelligence service, which did not improve again until the appointment in 1967 of YURI ANDROPOV as head of the KGB.

The KGB was the most powerful Soviet intelligence agency, but not the only one. The military also controlled a vast intelligence network known as the GRU, or Chief Intelligence Directorate.

Both the GRU and KGB had large numbers of agents posted overseas at Soviet embassies and trade missions or working under cover as journalists. They also maintained close liaison with the East European and Cuban intelligence services, all of which were closely modeled on the KGB.

The Chinese intelligence service, known as the Social Affairs Department, is also closely modeled on the KGB. It is closely tied to the Chinese Communist Party and, like every other branch of the party, was heavily purged during the CULTURAL REVOLUTION of the 1960s. Chinese agents have been active throughout the Far East and conducted a successful counterintelligence compaign against CIA and Taiwan operations in the 1950s and 1960s.

Another important country in the world intelligence community is Israel. The activities of its Mossad and Shin Bet agents have played a major role in ensuring that country's military successes against its larger Arab neighbors. The Israelis cooperate closely with the CIA and passed on useful intelligence about Soviet activities in the Middle East.

For Further Information:
Andrew, C. *Secret Service.* London, 1985.

Bamford, James. *The Puzzle Palace.* New York, 1982.

Barron, John. *KGB: The Secret Work of Soviet Secret Agents.* New York, 1974.

Blackstock, Paul. *The Strategy of Subversion.* New York, 1964.

Boyle, Andrew. *The Climate of Treason.* London, 1979.

Buncher, Judith F. *The CIA and the Security Debate, 1971–1975.* New York, 1976.

Dulles, Allen. *The Craft of Intelligence.* New York, 1963.

Knightley, Phillip. *Philby.* London, 1988.

———. *The Second Oldest Profession.* London, 1986.

Marchetti, Victor, and John D. Marks. *The CIA and the Cult of Intelligence.* New York, 1974.

Philby, Kim. *My Silent War.* New York, 1968.

Wise, David, and Thomas B. Ross. *The Invisible Government.* New York, 1964.

Yakovlev, Nikolai. *CIA Target: The USSR.* Moscow, 1982.

Ethiopia   See HORN OF AFRICA.

Ethridge, Mark   (April 22, 1896–April 5, 1981)   Mark Ethridge was a Kentucky newspaper publisher who was sent by Secretary of State JAMES F. BYRNES to ROMANIA and BULGARIA to observe elections. He reported that Soviet interference made free elections impossible there.

Ethridge entered journalism even before graduating from high school and left the University of Mississippi after his first year to become a full-time reporter. After World War I, he worked on a number of major newspapers, including the *Washington Post* and the *New York Sun,* and in 1936 was appointed vice president and general manager of the *Courier-Journal* and *Times* in Louisville, Kentucky. He became publisher in 1944.

Under Ethridge, the two newspapers became the most liberal print voices in the South, supporting Roosevelt's New Deal policies and racial justice. Ethridge's policies won him an admirer in Secretary of State James F. Byrnes, and in 1945 he asked Ethridge to be his special representative to elections in Romania and Bulgaria. He hoped that Ethridge's liberal credentials would prejudice him in favor of postwar cooperation with the Soviet Union, Byrnes' own view at the time.

But in his subsequent report to Byrnes, Ethridge stated that the Soviet Union's "constant and vigorous intrusion . . . into the internal affairs of these countries is so obvious to the impartial observer, that Soviet denial of its existence can only be regarded as a reflection of party line." Ethridge went on to warn that the Soviet Union planned further aggression in Greece and Turkey. He added that neither Romania nor Bulgaria had a broadly representative government "in the Yalta sense" of the term.

Byrnes took a copy of Ethridge's report to the MOSCOW FOREIGN MINISTERS' CONFERENCE in December 1945, and as a result of the report he insisted that the Bulgarian and Romanian governments broaden their political bases. Byrnes' demands, however, had little effect on the structure of the governments in those countries.

In December 1946 the United Nations created a commission to investigate Greek charges that Yugoslavia, Albania and Bulgaria were aiding the communists in the GREEK CIVIL WAR. Ethridge was appointed the American representative to the commission. His work on the commission convinced him that unless major Western aid was extended to the Greek and Turkish governments, they would fall under authoritarian communist rule. His cables to U.S. president HARRY TRUMAN to that effect played a major part in the president's enunciation of the TRUMAN DOCTRINE, which extended military and economic aid to Greece and Turkey.

Ethridge returned to his newspaper duties in June 1947. In 1962 he was named vice president and editor of Long Island's *Newsday.* He retired in 1963 and died on April 5, 1981.

For Further Information:
Ethridge, Mark, and C.E. Black. "Negotiating on the Balkans, 1945–1947." In Raymond Dennett and Joseph E. Johnson, eds. *Negotiating with the Russians.* Boston, 1951.

Kertesz, Stephen D. ed. *The Fate of East Central Europe.* South Bend, 1956.

Eurocommunism   Eurocommunism was the term given to the independent course taken by the West European communist parties in the 1970s and 1980s. It was the result of a decline in electoral support, a reaction to the WARSAW PACT invasion of Czechoslovakia, and popular support for West European political and economic integration.

Before World War II, the European communist parties were closely linked to the Soviet party through the Comintern and followed policies tailored to Soviet interests. During the war, the communists played a leading role in the resistance to Nazi rule. When the fascists collapsed, the communists emerged a powerful political force, and in the immediate postwar years communists served in the cabinets of Belgium, France, Italy, Denmark and Norway. The two biggest communist parties were in France and Italy.

Soviet leader JOSEF STALIN and the local communist leaders counted on political and economic turmoil in the aftermath of the war to create favorable conditions for the rise of communist governments in Western and Eastern Europe. But American aid in the form of the MARSHALL PLAN, and later the formation of the EUROPEAN COAL AND STEEL COMMUNITY and the EUROPEAN ECONOMIC COMMUNITY, laid stable economic foundations that thwarted these expectations.

Stalin reacted to American aid and moves toward West European integration with the creation in 1947 of COMINFORM (the Communist Information Bureau) to disseminate communist political propaganda and to work toward the subversion of West European capitalist society. The French and

Italian communist parties were two of the staunchest supporters of Cominform and its policies.

But the climate of suspicion against the Soviet Union engendered by the Cold War was soon extended to local communists and began to have a detrimental impact on the West European communist parties' electoral performances. The drop was especially dramatic in the smaller West European countries. In 1946, the Dutch Communist Party polled 503,000 votes, and in 1956 it polled 270,000. In Norway, the communists in 1945 won 11.9% of the total vote to emerge as the fourth largest party, but by 1957 its support had dropped to just 3.4% of the vote.

The Italian and French communist parties managed to retain their large shares of their national electorates, but they failed to grow. American opposition ensured that the Italian communists stayed out of office, and in France, President CHARLES DE GAULLE's introduction of new electoral rules after 1958 reduced the communist representation in the National Assembly from 147 to 10.

Parallel with the communists' failure to break through on the electoral front was a growing popular movement toward political and economic integration among the West European states. This resulted in the formation of the European Coal and Steel Community in 1952 and the European Economic Community in 1957. These were steadfastly opposed by the Soviet Union and the local communist parties, which feared that West European integration would lead to a capitalist European power bloc able to thwart Soviet and communist interests.

Thus, by the mid-1960s, the West European communist parties had failed to achieve the political breakthrough that had seemed so close at the end of the war, and were beginning to reassess their policies and their relationship with the Soviet Union. This reassessment was given a dramatic impetus by the Warsaw Pact invasion of CZECHOSLOVAKIA and the subsequent BREZHNEV DOCTRINE, which confirmed the right of the Soviet Union to intervene in the domestic affairs of other communist states. The Italian Communist Party responded by declaring that "in current circumstances we regard it as our duty to trace out and follow our own road to socialism."

The Italians were soon followed by most of the other West European communist parties, including the Spanish and Portuguese after those countries shed their fascist governments. To mark this change in direction, the West European communists introduced the term "Eurocommunism." This action involved not only criticism of the Soviet Union but also support for membership of the EEC and even limited involvement with NATO.

In June 1976 the political shift resulted in major electoral gains for the Italian Communist Party (PCI), which forced the ruling Christian Democrats into an unofficial "historic compromise" with the communists. PCI leader Enrico Berlinguer went straight from his success at the polls to a meeting in Berlin of East and West European Communist Party leaders, at which he said that Soviet socialism was marked by "errors" and repeated his support for communist pluralism and open debate within the movement. He was supported by Yugoslav leader JOSIP BROZ TITO and others, but his strongest support came from the leader of the Spanish Communist Party, Santiago Carillo, who said, "For years Moscow was our Rome. Today we have grown up. More and more we lose the character of being a church."

At a March 1977 summit of the French, Spanish and Italian Communist Party leaders, Carillo again took the lead in attacking the Soviet Union: "In the Soviet Union and Eastern Europe what is missing is democracy." He added that Eurocommunists demanded a strict respect for "the richness of individual and collective liberties." Berlinguer tried to strike a balance in his criticism of the Soviet Union by praising Moscow's "great conquests in the social domain," while at the same time noting its "authoritarian traits and limitations of liberty." The most reluctant Eurocommunist was French communist Georges Marchais, and the French Communist Party remained the most loyal of Moscow's allies in Western Europe through the 1980s.

The adoption of a more independent political course, however, appears to have worked against the communist parties in the long term because it robbed them of their separate identity vis-à-vis the European social democratic parties, which have been the Communists' main competitors for the role of standard-bearer for the European Left. The result has been that a number of communist voters abandoned the communists in France, Italy and Spain in favor of the socialists in those countries. This led to the election of a socialist, President FRANCOIS MITTERRAND, in France and a socialist government under Prime Minister Felipe Gonzalez in Spain. It also resulted in an increase in the votes cast for the Italian Socialist Party, and its leader Bettino Craxi became the longest-serving postwar prime minister.

For Further Information:
Albright, D.E. *Communism and Political Systems in Western Europe.* Boulder, Colo., 1979.
Antonian, Armen. *Toward a Theory of Eurocommunism: The Relationship of Eurocommunism to Eurosocialism.* New York, 1987.
Aspaturian, Vernon V., Jiri Valenta, and David P. Burke, eds. *Eurocommunism Between East and West.* Bloomington, Ind., 1980.
Kriegel, Annie. *Eurocommunism: A New Kind of Communism?* Stanford, Calif., 1978.
Leonhard, Wolfgang. *Eurocommunism: Challenge for East and West.* New York, 1979.
Machin, H., ed. *National Communism in Western Europe.* New York, 1983.
Middlemas, K. *Power and the Party: Changing Faces of Communism in Western Europe.* New York, 1980.
Stern, Geoffrey. *Rise and Decline of International Communism.* New York, 1990.
Tokes, Rudolf L., ed. *Eurocommunism and Detente.* New York, 1978.

European Coal and Steel Community (ECSC)   The European Coal and Steel Community (ECSC) was the first Western European attempt at economic integration and led to the formation of the European Economic Community in 1957.

The formation of the ECSC was the result of an initiative by French foreign minister ROBERT SCHUMAN. In May 1950 Schuman proposed that the coal and steel resources of France and Germany be pooled under a common authority as a major step toward the unification of Europe. The common pool would be open to all European countries, and Schuman expressed the hope that it would lead to eventual "European federation."

The treaty establishing the ECSC took effect after Italian ratification in June 1952. The other members were France, West Germany, Belgium, Holland and Luxembourg. The main elements of the treaty were:

1. The elimination of national restrictions in trade in coal and steel within the six-nation area.
2. Restrictions on monopolistic private cartels.
3. The establishment of international bodies to govern the common pool.
4. A 50-year life for the treaty.

Under the presidency of Monnet, the ECSC was an early political and economic success and encouraged the negotiations toward European union. These received a temporary setback when the next step, the EUROPEAN DEFENSE COMMUNITY, was rejected by the French National Assembly in 1954, but efforts were revived with the creation in 1955 of the European Atomic Energy Authority (EURATOM) and by the 1957 Treaty of Rome, which established the European Economic Community. The ECSC and EURATOM were incorporated into the umbrella structure of the European Economic Community upon its formalization in 1957.

For Further Information:
Lodge, J. *Institutions and Policies of the European Community*. London, 1982.
Mason, Henry. *The European Coal and Steel Community*. The Hague, 1955.
Mayne, Richard. *The Recovery of Europe*. New York, 1970.
Mayne, Richard, ed. *Handbooks to the Modern World: Western Europe*. New York, 1986.
Schuman, Robert. *Pour L'Europe*. Paris, 1963.

European Defense Community (EDC) The European Defense Community was an abortive attempt in the early 1950s by the West Europeans, with help from the United States, to establish a European defense structure to counter the Soviet Union's overwhelming conventional superiority and to bolster the overstretched American forces and provide an acceptable vehicle for German rearmament. As a result of the failure of the EDC, West Germany joined NATO and the WESTERN EUROPEAN UNION, and Britain made a formal defense commitment to mainland Europe.

The initial impetus for the EDC was the need for German rearmament within politically acceptable bounds. In the immediate aftermath of the war, the Allied powers, and especially the Soviet Union, were determined that Germany's warmaking ability should be destroyed and permanently restrained. But it soon became apparent to the United States that West Germany's cooperation was essential to the defense of Western Europe as a whole.

In May 1950, U.S. secretary of state DEAN ACHESON, who was convinced of the need for German rearmament, visited Paris and London to see how the United States could assuage European fears of a revival of German militarism. Both British foreign secretary ERNEST BEVIN and French foreign minister ROBERT SCHUMAN agreed that the issue should be discussed further, but both wanted to keep the discussions private because of the strong anti-German feeling running throughout European public opinion.

The start of the KOREAN WAR six weeks later dramatically changed the situation. Europeans were convinced that the communist offensive in Korea was a diversion to draw U.S. troops away from the defense of Western Europe and that the Red Army would soon come sweeping across the German plain. At a meeting of the Council of Europe on August 7, 1950, an Anglo–French resolution calling for the appointment of a European minister of defense and a unified European army was passed by 89 votes to five.

The British support was organized by WINSTON CHURCHILL, who made it clear that the European army should include German units. This immediately encountered strong opposition in France and from sections of the British Labour Party. The deadlock was broken by the PLEVEN PLAN, proposed by French prime minister René Pleven on October 24, 1950, which suggested the following:

1. That a European defense minister be appointed and that he be responsible to a European assembly, which would be either elected or appointed by the governments of its members.
2. That a European defense council comprised of West European defense ministers be created.
3. That the European defense council adopt a single defense budget.
4. That each member of the European defense council contribute forces from its own national forces.
5. That West Germany contribute to the European army and be represented on the council, but not have its own national army.

By legally committing all of the German forces to a common European army, the Pleven Plan overcame European fears of a revival of German militarism. A modified version of the plan formed the basis for further discussion of the EDC.

Plans for the EDC, however, were dealt a blow when it became clear that neither the British Labour nor Conservative party was prepared to commit British troops to the common European army. This left France alone to deal with Germany. This situation was partially resolved by Britain's reassurance that it would come to the aid of any signatory of the BRUSSELS TREATY attacked by Germany.

The EDC then needed the approval of the members of the NORTH ATLANTIC TREATY ORGANIZATION. This was obtained at a meeting of NATO foreign and defense ministers at Lisbon in February 1952. The LISBON AGREEMENT also substantially reorganized the alliance structure to strengthen American ties and committed the European members to major expenditure on conventional weapons.

The way was clear for the signing of the European Defense Community Treaty by the foreign ministers of France, West Germany, Belgium, Italy, the Netherlands and Luxembourg. The main points of the treaty signed in Paris on May 27, 1952, were as follows:

1. A European army would be set up under supranational control and made available to NATO.
2. There would three kinds of EDC national army "groupments": infantry (13,000 men), armored (12,000 men) and mechanized (12,600 men). Three or four groups each of different nationality would form a European army corps.
3. EDC units would wear a common uniform and be internationalized at corps level. EDC air units would consist of national half-brigades integrated at tactical command level.
4. A bureau of nine members chosen for competence (not nationality) would administer EDC forces.
5. The European Coal-Steel Assembly would control the EDC budget, approve the work of the bureau and consider the creation of an elected European assembly.
6. An EDC council of national representatives would harmonize bureau and national policies.

The day before the signing of the EDC Treaty, a "Convention on Relations" among the United States, Britain, France and the Federal Republic of Germany was signed in Bonn. This established the guidelines of the post-EDC relationship between West Germany and the main Western powers. Under this convention, West Germany was freed from Allied controls except for certain Allied privileges in matters of defense. The purpose of the convention was to reassure France and other European countries of American and British determination to control Germany while at the same time admitting West Germany to the Western Alliance. The main points of the convention were as follows:

1. The Allied Occupation statute was repealed.
2. The occupation status of the Allied armed forces in Germany was ended.
3. The Allied forces retained the right to maintain military forces in West Germany and do whatever was necessary to repel external or internal threats to the security of West Germany and West Berlin or declare a state of emergency in a security crisis.
4. The Allies would consult with the West Germans insofar as possible on such steps, but the Germans would have no veto over Allied defensive actions.

5. Foreign troops other than U.S., French and British could be brought into West Germany without German consent only in military emergencies.
6. West Germany would have full control of all its internal and foreign affairs except those affected by the Allied prerogatives on security.
7. The peace contract could be altered or discarded "in event of the unification of Germany or the creation of a European federation" or "upon the occurrence of any other event which all of the signatory states recognize to be of a similarly fundamental character."

For the EDC Treaty to take effect it had to be ratified by the national parliaments. The Benelux countries and West Germany quickly ratified the treaty, but it soon became apparent that French public opinion remained opposed to an alliance with the country that had attacked France three times in less than 100 years. The collapse of the pro-EDC government of Joseph Laniel in June 1954 threw the debate into confusion, and the new French prime minister, Pierre Mendes-France, tried to renegotiate the treaty to include clauses openly discriminatory toward West Germany. He failed and consequently refused to recommend the treaty to the French National Assembly, which defeated it on August 30, 1954, by 314 votes to 264.

The French vote, which effectively killed the EDC, threw the Western Alliance into panic. It was now committed to German rearmament and could not retreat from that position without pushing the Germans toward the neutrality being offered by the Soviet Union. In an attempt to resolve the crisis, British foreign secretary ANTHONY EDEN called a nine-power conference in London consisting of the six EDC countries, the United States, Canada and Britain. At the conference he proposed a solution:

1. West Germany would enter NATO and regain its sovereignty.
2. The Brussels Treaty of 1948 would be amended to include West Germany and Italy in the Western European Union.
3. The powers of the SUPREME ALLIED COMMANDER FOR EUROPE (SACEUR) over the use and supply of national army units under his command would be expanded.
4. Britain would maintain a force of four divisions and a tactical air force on the mainland of Europe.
5. West Germany would not manufacture nuclear, biological or chemical weapons.
6. The German defense forces would not exceed 500,000 and would be under the command of SACEUR.
7. The region of the Saarland, jurisdiction over which was disputed between Germany and France, would be "Europeanized," but France would retain economic control.

For Further Information:
Ball, Margaret. *NATO and the European Unity Movement.* New York, 1959.

Grosser, Albert. *The Western Alliance*. New York, 1978.

Laqueur, Walter. *Europe Since Hitler*. New York, 1970.

Manderson-Jones, R.B. *The Special Relationship: Anglo–American Relations and Western European Unity, 1947–1956*. London, 1972.

European Economic Community   The European Economic Community is a multinational organization designed to create political and economic unity in Western Europe in order to reduce the possibility of another European war, to establish political and economic structures capable of defending against Soviet attack and to be capable of competing economically with the United States.

The first formal moves toward European integration started with the May 1950 proposal by French foreign minister ROBERT SCHUMAN that France and Germany pool their steel and coal resources and that this action lead to eventual "European federation." Schuman's proposal resulted two years later in the formation of the EUROPEAN COAL AND STEEL COMMUNITY.

The next step in Schuman's integration plans, the EUROPEAN DEFENSE COMMUNITY, was rejected by the French National Assembly in 1954 but was quickly followed by the creation of the European Atomic Energy Authority (EURATOM) in 1955.

The concept of a European federation had been the postwar dream of European statesmen such as Schuman and JEAN MONNET. The concept was enthusiastically welcomed by the smaller European countries such as Belgium, Holland and Luxembourg, which had already agreed to form the Benelux Customs Union. West Germany and Italy were eager to be politically and economically rehabilitated, and France saw itself as able to dominate the new structure. The only unenthusiastic country was Britain, which adopted its traditional island policy of interest in, but detachment from, European affairs.

The subsequent treaty establishing the EEC was signed in Rome in February 1957 and included the following provisions:

1. The gradual abolition of customs duties between the signatory countries.
2. A common tariff on goods imported from outside the community.
3. The establishment of a European parliament.
4. The establishment of a council of ministers to coordinate national policies.
5. The establishment of a European court of justice.
6. Free movement of labor throughout the community.
7. The establishment of a European investment bank to finance development in the member countries.

The EEC was steadfastly opposed by the Soviet Union, which feared it as a European-based capitalist trading bloc with the potential to develop into a political and military alternative to the Soviet Bloc. The EEC started its life with six members: France, West Germany, Italy, Belgium, Holland and Luxembourg. By 1990 the original members had been joined by Britain, Ireland, Denmark, Greece, Spain and Portugal.

The issue of British membership was to be a major problem for the EEC until Britain, along with Ireland and Denmark, was finally admitted in 1973. European enthusiasts had mixed feelings about British membership. They felt that a truly united Europe had to include Britain, but feared that Britain's attachment to the United States and to its former empire would cause it to act as a brake on moves toward political integration.

In Britain there were equally mixed feelings toward the EEC. Britain in general favored and encouraged moves toward European integration, but leaders such as WINSTON CHURCHILL and ANTHONY EDEN believed that Britain still retained a great-power role beyond the borders of Europe and that it would be detrimental to British interests to become part of a Eurocentric organization. Ireland was not a charter member because of its economic and political ties with Britain, and Denmark had stayed out because of trade agreements with Britain and a historical aversion to alliances. Greece, Spain and Portugal had been denied admission because of their fascist/military governments.

By 1961, Britain had reconciled itself to the loss of its great-power status and in October of that year application was made for membership in the EEC. But in 1963 French president CHARLES DE GAULLE vetoed British membership. He made it clear that he regarded Britain as an American pawn and that he wanted to create a European community free of dependence on U.S. military and economic power and able to act independently in its own interests.

Britain reapplied after de Gaulle's resignation and was finally admitted on January 1, 1973. In the interim, the EEC had developed a number of institutions that worked to the financial disadvantage of Britain once it had joined. These included the Common Agricultural Policy (a system of common guaranteed prices for agricultural products) and a social and development fund that channeled contributions from member states to needy areas. British concern about the unfairness of these policies to British interests led to additional negotiations, which further delayed political integration.

By the mid-1980s, however, most of these issues had been dealt with. Spain, Portugal and Greece had been admitted after the establishment of democratic institutions in those countries, and the EEC was able to move faster toward political and monetary union. The Single European Act was passed in February 1986, revising the 1957 Treaty of Rome so that the remaining barriers to internal trade and commerce would completely disappear by 1992. By 1990 most of the members, with continuing reservations from Britain, had also agreed on monetary union and the need for a central European Bank.

Formal bureaucratic and legislative mechanisms had also developed or were in the latter stages of development. These included a commission that acted as a European civil service, a directly elected parliament with increasing legislative powers, ministerial councils for various political responsibilities (including finance, agriculture, fisheries, foreign affairs, transport, social affairs, sport and environment) and an ultimate political authority of national heads of government known as the European Council. There was also an active European Court of Justice which mediated disputes between members.

In the field of foreign affairs the members of the community spoke increasingly as one voice. Policy was hammered out at regular meetings of national foreign ministers known as the General Affairs Council. The presidency of the council (which rotated every six months among the member states) would speak for the EEC as a whole at international forums such as the United Nations and in dealings with other states.

The EEC, however, did not have any political mechanism for dealing with defense or security issues. This was recognized as a shortcoming by most of the member countries and there were attempts to introduce a defense element into the EEC. These were thwarted, however, by Ireland, which found it politically impossible to join in any defensive arrangement with Britain while the two countries remained divided over the issue of Northern Ireland.

The political importance of the EEC grew considerably with the collapse of communist governments in Eastern Europe in 1989 and 1990. The governments of East Germany, Poland, Czechoslovakia, Hungary, Romania and Bulgaria looked increasingly toward the EEC for financial aid and investment to support their emerging governments. Approaches were also made about eventual membership in the community.

The 12 EEC nations, in a December 1991 summit in Maastricht, the Netherlands, agreed to a political treaty pledging "ever closer union" among their nations and a monetary pact that would set the introduction of a single currency for the EEC by 1999. The treaties were the culmination of the community's moves toward political and economic integration in recent years. However, the treaties were still subject to ratification by the member states, and potential roadblocks to passage were expected in a number of countries, such as Britain.

The Maastricht treaty called for a common defense role to be taken up by the WESTERN EUROPEAN UNION, a long established but largely dormant organization. The WEU would "elaborate and implement" EEC decisions on defense and serve as a "bridge" between the EEC and the NORTH ATLANTIC TREATY ORGANIZATION. However, the EEC failed its first major collective security test, which was presented by the series of civil wars that followed the break-up of YUGOSLAVIA in 1991. Particularly in the fighting in Bosnia-Herzegovina, the EEC's mediation efforts bore little fruit, and military intervention seemed to be an option that no European nation would seriously consider.

For Further Information:
Archer, Clive, and Fiona Butler. *The European Community: Structure and Process.* New York, 1992.
European Commission. *Steps to European Unity.* Brussels, 1988.
Hackett, Clifford P. *Cautious Revolution: The European Community Arrives.* New York, 1990.
Lodge, J. *Institutions and Policies of the European Community.* London, 1982.
Mayne, Richard. *The Recovery of Europe.* New York, 1970.
Mayne, Richard, ed. *Handbooks to the Modern World: Western Europe.* New York, 1986.
Pinder, John. *European Community: The Building of a Union.* New York, 1991.
Sbragia, Alberta M., ed. *Euro-Politics: Institutions and Policymaking in the New European Community.* Washington, D.C., 1991.

European Recovery Program   See MARSHALL PLAN.

Executive Committee of the National Security Council (ExCom)   The Executive Committee of the National Security Council (ExCom) was a special bipartisan committee created by President JOHN F. KENNEDY at the start of the CUBAN MISSILE CRISIS in 1962. Its purpose was to advise the president on the policy to pursue during the crisis. The members were Vice President LYNDON JOHNSON, Secretary of State DEAN RUSK, Defense Secretary ROBERT MCNAMARA, Attorney General ROBERT KENNEDY, Chairman of the Joint Chiefs of Staff General MAXWELL TAYLOR, CIA director JOHN MCCONE, Treasury Secretary DOUGLAS DILLON, Ambassador to the United Nations ADLAI STEVENSON, national security adviser MCGEORGE BUNDY, Undersecretary of State GEORGE BALL, Deputy Secretary of Defense ROSWELL GILPATRIC, special adviser on Soviet affairs LLEWELYN THOMPSON, Deputy Undersecretary of State for Political Affairs U. ALEXIS JOHNSON, Assistant Secretary of State for Inter-American Affairs Edwin Martin, former Secretary of State DEAN ACHESON and former Undersecretary of State ROBERT LOVETT. All of ExCom's meetings were held in the strictest secrecy, to avoid unnecessary panic and to prevent the Soviet Union from becoming aware of the fact that the United States knew of the missile installations.

President Kennedy encouraged the widest possible discussion of alternative courses of action. In the first few days two alternatives dominated the discussion: acceptance of the missiles' emplacement as a Soviet fait d'accompli or a surgical air strike to remove the missiles. Both courses were unpalatable to the president, and committee members were urged by Robert Kennedy to come up with more alternatives. The ultimately successful course of action was suggested by Defense Secretary Robert McNamara, who proposed a naval quarantine. This was imposed on October 22, and six days later Soviet Premier NIKITA KHRUSHCHEV agreed to dismantle and remove the missiles under United Nations supervision.

Executive Order 10450   Executive Order 10450 was issued by U.S. president DWIGHT EISENHOWER on April 27, 1953. It instituted a strict program to assure loyalty and security among all employees of the government's executive branch; it contributed to the dismissal of many federal employees suspected of communist links.

The order superseded President HARRY TRUMAN's loyalty checks and provided for rechecks of all employees who had undergone full field investigations under the Truman LOYALTY

REVIEW BOARD. Senator JOSEPH MCCARTHY, embroiled in his investigation of suspected communist subversion, called Eisenhower's order "pretty darn good" and "a tremendous improvement over the old method."

Under Executive Order 10450, federal employment became contingent upon whether retention was "clearly consistent with the interests of national security." This led to dismissals for personal habits or associations with left-wing organizations. Among those to suffer from the order were Dr. ROBERT OPPENHEIMER, who had led the manufacture of the atomic bomb, and senior State Department officials such as JOHN PATON DAVIES.

F

Failsafe Failsafe is a system to prevent the start of an accidental nuclear war. This system employs a number of double checks at various stages and with various people to confirm that the order to launch a nuclear attack has been given and should be executed.

At the lowest level, two American officers are required to launch a U.S. INTERCONTINENTAL BALLISTIC MISSILE (ICBM). Once launched, on-board computers also regularly check with ground-based headquarters to make certain that the missile should continue its mission. Bombers equipped with nuclear weapons also make regular checks with headquarters. At the top level, the HOT LINE between the president of the United States and the leader of the Soviet Union and now of its successor, the Russian Federation, allows instant communication. Since the dissolution of the Soviet Union, however, there is some uncertainty over the control of Soviet nuclear weapons, not all of which are located in the territory of the Russian Federation.

Fairbank, John King (May 24, 1907–September 14, 1991) John Fairbank was one of the American "China Hands" falsely accused in the 1950s of having supported the Chinese communists in wartime. He managed to weather the storm of McCarthyism and in the 1960s and 1970s played a role in reopening Sino-American diplomatic links.

Fairbank's career as a Sinologist started within three years of his graduation from Harvard University in 1929. In 1936, after three years at Tsinghua University in Beijing, he joined the faculty at Harvard University. During the war he became a prominent adviser to the government on Chinese affairs, serving on the China desk of the OFFICE OF STRATEGIC SERVICES (the wartime forerunner of the CENTRAL INTELLIGENCE AGENCY), as special assistant to the U.S. ambassador to China and then as deputy director of Far Eastern operations for the Office of War Information.

In 1946 Fairbank returned to Harvard and wrote *The United States and China,* in which he attacked CHIANG KAI-SHEK's government as a "corrupt regime of carpetbagging generals and politicians." The following year Fairbank urged the American government to accept that the Chinese communists had defeated the Nationalist forces of Chiang and to forge links with the new government.

Fairbank's position made him a natural target for the China Lobby and for Senator JOSEPH MCCARTHY. On August 14, 1951, Elizabeth Bentley, a former communist spy, testified before the House Un-American Activities Committee that Fairbank had connections with Chinese communists. A week later her testimony was supported by LOUIS BUDENZ, a former communist, who accused Fairbank of being a communist. As a result of these accusations, Fairbank's passport was revoked and he was refused admission to Japan, where he had been offered a teaching post.

Fairbank repeatedly petitioned the Senate for the right to defend himself publicly before the appropriate Senate committee, and was given the opportunity on March 11, 1952. Fairbank appeared before the Senate Internal Security Subcommittee and claimed that it used tactics similar to those employed by the Soviet Union. He denied as "absurd and false" Budenz's claim that he was a communist. He also denied that the Institute of Pacific Relations, of which he was a trustee, was controlled by communists. The State Department reissued Fairbank's passport on August 15, 1952.

Throughout the rest of the 1950s and early 1960s Fairbank concentrated on his academic career. He again rose to prominence when the JOHNSON administration began to reassess American relations with China. On March 8, 1966, Fairbank appeared before the Senate Foreign Relations Committee to support a policy of changing the American posture of isolation and containment of communist China to one of containment without isolation. He also supported the American military presence in Korea and Vietnam.

On March 20, 1966, Fairbank joined other prominent Sinologists in signing a statement that called for a U.S. rapprochement with communist China. The statement called for an end to American opposition to a UN seat for communist China; bilateral negotiations aimed at establishing diplomatic representation; a Sino-American exchange of scholars and journalists; and an end to the American embargo on trade with China.

On December 10, 1966, Fairbank was named an adviser to the State Department on Chinese affairs. In this position he played a prominent role in the events that led to the reestablishment of Sino-American relations.

For Further Information:
Fairbank, John K. *The United States and China.* Cambridge, Mass., 1958.

Harper, Alan D. *The Politics of Loyalty: The White House and the Communist Issue, 1946–1952.* Westport, Conn., 1969.

Kahn, E.J. *The China Hands.* New York, 1973.

Purifoy, Lewis McCarroll. *Harry Truman's China Policy: McCarthyism and the Diplomacy of Hysteria, 1947–1951.* New York, 1976.

Fallout   Fallout is the term for radioactive materials that fall to earth following a nuclear explosion. Fallout can follow both ground bursts and air bursts. In an AIR BURST, the fallout consists of radioactivated air particles. In a GROUND BURST, it consists of air particles and dust.

A nuclear explosion produces three main kinds of fallout: local, tropospheric and stratospheric. The local fallout is the radioactive fallout in the immediate area of the explosion. Its extent is determined entirely by the explosive yield of the nuclear device.

Tropospheric fallout occurs when radioactive air and dust particles are blown into the earth's troposphere and remain trapped there. From there, they are blown over a larger area of the earth's surface in the course of the following weeks.

Stratospheric fallout can take years to fall to earth in the form of dust and radioactivated rain. It occurs when radiated particles are blown into the earth's stratosphere. Stratospheric fallout is worldwide.

Far Eastern Commission and Allied Council for Japan   The Far Eastern Commission and Allied Council for Japan were established at the end of World War II to oversee the Allied occupation of Japan and former Japanese-occupied territories. They were meant to provide a platform for the views of Britain, the Soviet Union and Nationalist China, but American dominance quickly made the commission and council redundant.

The establishment of the commission and council was agreed upon at the MOSCOW FOREIGN MINISTERS CONFERENCE in December 1945. The commission was comprised of 11 members: the Soviet Union, Britain, the United States, China, France, the Netherlands, Canada, Australia, New Zealand, India and the Philippines. Its main functions were "to formulate the policies, principles and standards" that Japan had to carry out to fulfill the terms of surrender and to review "any directive" issued by the supreme commander of the Allied occupation forces. The commission was not allowed any say in military operations or postwar territorial adjustments, and the United States, Britain, China and the Soviet Union retained the right of veto over any decisions.

The Allied Council for Japan was comprised of representatives from the Soviet Union, China, Britain and the United States and was chaired by the supreme commander. Its purpose was to advise the supreme commander on the surrender, occupation and control of Japan. But the council's power was negated by the granting of "sole executive authority" to the supreme commander. President HARRY TRUMAN was given the authority to appoint the supreme commander, and he gave the job to General DOUGLAS MACARTHUR, whose ad-

ministrative style effectively excluded the other Allied representatives.

Federal Bureau of Investigation (FBI)   The Federal Bureau of Investigation (FBI) is the American law enforcement agency responsible for counterintelligence operations inside the United States. It is an agency of the Department of Justice.

The FBI was founded in 1908 as the Bureau of Investigations. Its initial purpose was to apprehend criminals who crossed state lines in an attempt to avoid arrest. In 1921, a young lawyer in the Justice Department, J. EDGAR HOOVER, was appointed assistant director of the bureau. He was promoted to director in 1924 and remained in the post until his death in 1972; during which time he completely dominated the organization.

Throughout the 1920s and most of the 1930s Hoover's energies were concentrated on improving the caliber of individual FBI agents and fighting Prohibition-related gangsterism. The name of the bureau was changed to the Federal Bureau of Investigation in 1935.

Hoover had established his name during the "Red Scare" of 1919–21, when he had directed the arrest of thousands of suspected communists and anarchists for the Justice Department. When he moved to the FBI, the extremely conservative Hoover repeatedly asked that the bureau be given responsibility for rooting out "subversive" activity. But it was not until 1936 that President FRANKLIN D. ROOSEVELT gave the FBI the authority to investigate espionage and sabotage. In the prelude to war, Roosevelt also gave the FBI the authority to expand its surveillance to far-right political groups, the American Communist Party, trade union organizations and civil rights groups. The FBI also had responsibility for checking the loyalty of federal employees.

Hoover used this wide-ranging authority to build a massive file on American communists and anyone suspected of liberal tendencies with which he disagreed. He also compiled damaging files on leading politicians that he used to extend his own influence and to maintain his stay at the head of the FBI well past the official retirement age.

During the war, Roosevelt made it clear that he wanted the FBI to cease its antisubversive and counterintelligence activities when the fighting stopped. But Hoover was convinced that the Soviet Union had placed communist agents into the highest echelons of American government, and in the early years of the Cold War he and the FBI played a prominent role in the investigations surrounding such figures as ALGER HISS, WHITTAKER CHAMBERS, JOHN PATON DAVIES, JOHN STEWART SERVICE, JULIUS AND ETHEL ROSENBERG and HARRY DEXTER WHITE. The FBI's counterintelligence operations also played an important part in exposing the operations of British spies KLAUS FUCHS, KIM PHILBY, GUY BURGESS and DONALD MACLEAN.

FBI investigations convinced President HARRY S TRUMAN of the need for an expanded loyalty program for federal employees. Hoover demanded and got an even tougher program, winning for the FBI the right to conduct the loyalty investigations. Hoover also won permission to wiretap the telephones and open the mail of suspected subversives.

Hoover had an ambivalent relationship with the anti-communist, Senator JOSEPH MCCARTHY. The FBI director supported many of McCarthy's statements and the FBI provided McCarthy with information. But at the same time, Hoover feared that McCarthy's investigators were becoming too powerful and in some ways challenging the supremacy of the FBI.

After McCarthy's fall from power in 1954, Hoover lost the Eisenhower administration's support for some of his anti-communist activities. As a result he turned to extralegal activities, including illegal wiretaps and burglaries. In 1956 Hoover started his Counter Intelligence Program (COINTELPRO), which involved harassment of Communist Party members, including writing anonymous letters to employers demanding that they be dismissed. COINTELPRO's activities were later extended to the Socialist Workers' Party, Black Power groups, the civil rights movement and its most prominent leaders, and the anti-VIETNAM WAR movement.

By the time RICHARD NIXON was elected president in 1968, Hoover's political power base and his scope for extralegal activities had seriously declined. When Nixon wanted his political opponents or antiwar activists watched, he turned to the CIA instead of the FBI. In January 1971 antiwar activists raided the FBI offices in Media, Pennsylvania, and stole a number of embarrassing confidential documents, which were leaked to the *New York Times* and *Washington Post*. The revelations led to a series of calls for the retirement of Hoover and a reform of the bureau's activities. Hoover was forced to end COINTELPRO and curtail other schemes.

In the midst of this controversy, Hoover suddenly died on May 2, 1972. In 1975 the Senate Select Committee on Intelligence Activities started investigating Hoover's activities while head of the FBI. It was this investigation that uncovered many of Hoover's extralegal and unconstitutional activities.

Hoover was succeeded first by Patrick Gray, who was forced to resign as acting director after being implicated in some of the bureau's illegal activities. The charges were later dropped. Gray was followed in the directorship in quick succession first by William Ruckelshaus and then by former FBI agent and Kansas City police chief, Clarence M. Kelley. It was Kelley who had to deal with the Senate committee investigating illegal FBI activities and who revealed the existence of COINTELPRO and illegal wiretaps. He was faced with a difficult task of restoring bureau morale and public faith in the FBI. Kelley resigned in 1977 after the election of JIMMY CARTER as president. He was succeeded in 1979 by William Webster, who in April 1983 claimed that there were 1,000 Soviet spies operating in the United States. In March 1987 he moved to the directorship of the CENTRAL INTELLIGENCE AGENCY and was replaced at the FBI by Federal District Judge William S. Sessions.

For Further Information:
Hoover, J. Edgar. *The Masters of Deceit: The Story of Communism in America and How to Fight It.* New York, 1958.

Ungar, Sanford. *FBI.* Boston, 1975.
U.S. Senate Select Committee on Intelligence Activities. *Report.* Washington, D.C., 1976.

Federal Civil Defense Administration   The American civil defense program was launched by the TRUMAN administration in January 1951, but from its inception there was doubt about its effectiveness, and by the 1970s civil defense planning was almost moribund.

Following the explosion of the first Soviet atomic bomb and the start of the KOREAN WAR, there was a great fear of a Soviet attack on the United States. In response to this fear, President Harry Truman established the Federal Civil Defense Administration on January 12, 1951.

Even before the start of the Civil Defense Administration, experts had expressed doubts about the effectiveness of any physical protection from nuclear attack. In February 1950, Dr. VANNEVAR BUSH, wartime director of weapons research, had told the Senate Armed Services Committee that "it is almost impossible to design an atom bomb-proof building."

Political pressure was such, however, that Truman went ahead and created the Civil Defense Administration and asked Congress for a $500 million budget. A skeptical Congress slashed the budget request to $75 million. Truman called the cut a "reckless evasion of responsibility."

The Civil Defense Administration continued to be poorly funded, and during the first six years most of its activities involved the construction of a limited number of fallout shelters and the printing of publicity material. It was not until the 1958 GAITHER REPORT warned that the Soviet Union was closing the gap in nuclear weaponry that civil defense became a priority.

Civil Defense administrator Leo Hoegh argued for the spending of $22.5 billion on fallout shelters "in order to save an estimated 50 million American lives." Hoegh, however, ran into opposition from Secretary of State JOHN FOSTER DULLES, who argued, "It's hard to sustain simultaneously an offensive and defensive mood in a population. For our security, we have been relying above all on our capacity for retaliation. From this policy we should not deviate now."

President Eisenhower decided against an all-out program to build shelters, but on August 8, 1958, he signed legislation that increased civil defense funding by giving the federal government and the states a joint responsibility for civil defense and authorized federal financial help for state civil defense projects.

During the KENNEDY administration the Federal Civil Defense Administration became the Office of Civil and Defense Mobilization; civil defense became the responsibility of the secretary of defense, and the budget was trebled. President John F. Kennedy, who placed a high priority on civil defense, in February 1962 asked Congress to authorize $450 million for an incentive program to provide fallout shelters for 20 million people by mid-1963. The proposal was rejected by Congress. But one of the results of the CUBAN MISSILE CRISIS was a three-month emergency program to speed up civil defense efforts, and on October 25, 1962, the Defense Department reported that "potential fallout shelter spaces" for 60 million people had been identified in more than 112,000 structures throughout the United States. But in succeeding administrations, the skeptics of civil defense predominated, and civil defense planning eventually became moribund.

Current thinking echoes that of Dr. Bush in 1951 in that most experts believe it is impossible to predict the extent of direct explosive or fallout damage from a nuclear attack and that it would be inordinately expensive and probably useless to try to protect the civilian population with fallout shelters.

For Further Information:
Tuckerman, Edward. *The Day After World War III: The United States Government's Plan for Surviving a Nuclear War.* New York, 1984.

Fermi, Enrico (September 29, 1901–November 30, 1954) Enrico Fermi played a prominent role in the wartime development of the atomic bomb and in the postwar years advised the ATOMIC ENERGY COMMISSION on nuclear policy.

Born and raised in Rome, Fermi started his academic career at the University of Rome, where he developed a model of the atom and succeeded in splitting the uranium nucleus. In 1938 Fermi won the Nobel Prize for physics, and he and his Jewish wife were given permission by the fascist government to travel to Stockholm to receive the prize. Fermi had secret plans, however, to go from Sweden to the United States.

He was soon joined in America by the Danish physicist Niels Bohr. The two men successfully repeated a German experiment that led them to conclude that a nuclear chain reaction could be created by splitting the uranium-235 isotope. It is this chain reaction that causes the explosion of an atomic bomb.

The two scientists were seriously concerned that Nazi Germany had a significant lead in the race for an atomic bomb and drafted a letter to President FRANKLIN ROOSEVELT urging him to start development of an American atomic bomb. They asked ALBERT EINSTEIN, as the most respected scientist of the day, to sign it.

As an eventual result of this letter, the MANHATTAN PROJECT was started to develop the atomic bomb. Much of the initial work was done at the University of Chicago, where Fermi was teaching. In December 1942 Fermi succeeded in producing the first self-sustaining, controlled nuclear reaction. In 1944 he became associate director of the Los Alamos laboratories where the atomic bomb was constructed.

In 1945 Fermi was appointed to the scientific panel charged with advising the president on nuclear policy. In this capacity he recommended dropping the atomic bomb on Japan, on the grounds that it would end the war and save lives.

After the war Fermi returned to the University of Chicago and in 1946 was appointed to the General Advisory Committee, a scientific panel created to advise the newly formed Atomic Energy Commission. In 1949 he joined the other scientists on the committee in opposing development of the hydrogen bomb, but a year later he helped to develop it, although he retained his doubts about the morality of the weapon. Fermi died of cancer on November 30, 1954.

For Further Information:
Feis, Herbert. *The Atomic Bomb and the End of World War Two.* Princeton, 1966.
Hewlett, Richard G., and Francis Duncan. *A History of the United States Atomic Energy Commission: Atomic Shield, 1947–1952.* University Park, Pa., 1969.
De Latil, Pierre. *Enrico Fermi, the Man and His Theories.* New York, 1964.
Lilienthal, David E. *The Journals of David E. Lilienthal: The Atomic Energy Years, 1945–1960.* New York, 1964.
Segre, Emilio. *Enrico Fermi, Physicist.* Chicago, 1970.

Finland During the Cold War, Finland developed a special relationship with the Soviet Union in which its policies accommodated Soviet interests, and the Soviet Union did not seek political control over Finland's affairs. This form of indirect subordination came to be referred to as "Finlandization."

Postwar Finland was in a difficult position in its relations with the Soviet Union. For 100 years before the Bolshevik Revolution in 1917 it had been a part of the Russian Empire, and even before that it had been heavily influenced by the Czarist court. In 1918, it declared itself independent, then fought a two-year war with Bolshevik forces to affirm that independence.

The Soviet Union, however, continued to pose the greatest threat to Finnish sovereignty, and at the outset of WORLD WAR II invaded and defeated Finland in the "Winter War" of 1939-40. Finland allied itself with Germany against the Soviets, and joined in Hitler's invasion of the U.S.S.R. in 1941. As early as 1943, the Finnish government realized that the Soviet Union would emerge from the war as the superpower in Europe. It began to plan a postwar foreign policy that would ensure Finland's independence from the Soviet Union by placating any fears that the Soviet Union might have about Finnish hostility. This policy was largely the work of URHO KEKKONEN and President Juho Passikivi, and it became known as "the Passikivi-Kekkonen Line."

In February 1943 the Finnish government, without any prompting from the Soviets, pledged not to join any postwar alliance opposed to the Soviet Union. The second step toward fending off the Soviets was the decision to cede to the Soviet Union a large area of southeastern Finland, including the important city of Viipuri. The territory was formally transferred when the Soviet-Finnish Treaty was signed in Paris on February 10, 1947.

The final step in the Passikivi-Kekkonen Line was the FINNISH–SOVIET AGREEMENT OF FRIENDSHIP AND MUTUAL ASSISTANCE (q.v.), signed in Moscow on April 6, 1948. The treaty committed Finland to neutral status, confirmed close economic and cultural relations with the Soviet Union and allowed

Soviet troops to enter Finland if Finland was attacked or if foreign troops attacked the Soviet Union through Finland. Finnish defense forces were also limited to 41,900 troops, and they were forbidden the possession of nuclear weapons, bombers and submarines.

The Passikivi-Kekkonen Line was strengthened on February 15, 1956, when Kekkonen was elected president in succession to Passikivi. He went on to be confirmed in office in five successive elections. As president, Kekkonen strove to increase economic ties with the Soviet Union, especially in the traditionally Finnish area of Karelia, where Finland developed a number of major construction contracts that enabled it to maintain commercial, political and family ties across the border.

In 1961 Finland joined the European Free Trade Agreement (EFTA) as an associate member, but to allay Soviet fears it balanced that with similar tariff-free arrangements with the Soviet Union. In the 1970s Finland continued its economic balancing act by negotiating trade agreements with both the EUROPEAN ECONOMIC COMMUNITY and COMECON. Until the latter part of the 1980s, trade with both European economic blocs was balanced at about 20 percent each. The balance shifted toward the EC toward the end of the 1980s because of economic difficulties in Eastern Europe, but Finland's largest trading partner continued to be the Soviet Union. Since then, however, Finnish trade with the former Soviet republics has plummeted, and the Finnish economy has been severely damaged. Finland has applied for membership in the European Economic Community, but cannot be admitted before 1995.

For Further Information:
Alapuro, Risto. *State and Revolution in Finland.* Berkeley, Calif., 1988.
Allison, Roy. *Finland's Relations with the Soviet Union, 1944–84.* London, 1985.
Kirby, D.G. *Finland in the Twentieth Century.* Minneapolis, 1980.
Maude, George. *The Finnish Dilemma: Neutrality in the Shadow of Power.* New York, 1976.
Penttila, Risto E.J. *Finland's Search for Security Through Defense, 1944–89.* Basingstoke, England, 1991.

Finletter, Thomas   (November 11, 1893–April 24, 1980)   In the immediate postwar years Thomas Finletter played a major role in increasing the power of the American Air Force, and in the 1950s he became a foreign policy adviser to ADLAI STEVENSON.

Finletter was educated at the University of Pennsylvania; after graduating from the university's law school in 1920, he moved to New York to practice law. In 1941 he was appointed special assistant to Secretary of State Cordell Hull and in 1943 assumed responsibility for economic planning in Allied-controlled areas.

In July 1947 President HARRY TRUMAN appointed Finletter to chair the Temporary Air Policy Commission, which had been formed to survey air defense policies. In his report,

Finletter urged that the United States spend $18 billion immediately to increase its air force by 95 planes. He argued that air superiority was an essential defense requirement in the nuclear age. The Finletter report was universally praised and played a major role in the buildup of the American Air Force.

In May 1948 Finletter was appointed chief of the Economic Administration Mission to Britain with the task of overseeing $1.2 billion in American aid to the United Kingdom. He returned to his law practice in 1949 but in 1950 rejoined the government as secretary of the air force and continued his drive for increased air power as a vital element in the maintenance of the nuclear deterrent.

Finletter became a keen admirer of Adlai Stevenson when the two men worked together during the formation of the United Nations. He supported him in the 1952 presidential election, and in the following years he formed an informal advisory panel known as the Finletter Group, which was regarded as Stevenson's private think tank. During the 1956 presidential election, Finletter organized the Stevenson campaign in New York state, and in 1960 he helped to organize a draft-Stevenson movement.

Throughout the 1950s Finletter spoke and wrote on foreign and defense policy issues. In 1954 he wrote *Power and Policy* in which he attacked the Eisenhower administration for losing nuclear supremacy to the Soviets; toward the end of the decade he was writing about the widening "missile gap" between the United States and the Soviet Union. In 1955 Finletter countered Eisenhower's disarmament proposals with a disarmament plan to be enforced by UN troops.

In 1961 President JOHN F. KENNEDY appointed Finletter U.S. ambassador to NATO. He was America's representative at alliance headquarters during the Berlin Crisis in 1961 and the CUBAN MISSILE CRISIS in 1962. As ambassador, Finletter was charged with the task of helping to secure allied support for the Anglo-American plan for a Western nuclear strike force. Finletter resigned in July 1965 and returned to his New York law practice.

For Further Information:
Finletter, Thomas. *Power and Policy.* New York, 1954.
Hammond, Paul. *Organizing for Defense: The American Military Establishment in the Twentieth Century.* Princeton, 1961.

Finnish-Soviet Agreement of Friendship and Mutual Assistance (1948)   The 1948 Finnish-Soviet Agreement of Friendship and Mutual Assistance established the main pillars of Finnish-Soviet relations during the Cold War period. The main elements of the agreement were Finnish neutrality, qualified by a special emphasis on the preservation of good relations with the Soviet Union. The treaty embodied the concept of "Finlandization," which some observers believed was the ultimate Soviet foreign policy aim for Western Europe. (See FINLAND.)

From 1946 onward, successive Finnish governments under

Juho Kusti Passikivi and URHO KEKKONEN sought to structure a foreign policy that accommodated the Soviet Union while preserving Finnish independence. This "Passikivi-Kekkonen Line" was legally embodied in the treaty signed in Moscow on April 6, 1948. The main points of the treaty were:

1. A Soviet-Finish defense alliance would take effect if Germany or a state "allied with" Germany attacked Finland or struck at the Soviet Union through Finland.
2. The Soviet Union promised not to send troops into Finland except by "mutual agreement."
3. The Soviet Union promised not to meddle in Finland's internal affairs.
4. Finland was not obligated to join in the defense of the Soviet Union unless its own territory was violated.
5. Both nations would consult each other in case of "a threat of military attack" by Germany or a German ally.
6. Both Finland and the Soviet Union promised not to join any alliance aimed at the other country.
7. Both countries pledged themselves to closer economic and cultural relations.

For Further Information:
Mazour, Anatole. *Finland between East and West.* Princeton, 1956.

First Strike Capability   First strike capability is the ability to launch a successful nuclear attack without the fear of massive retaliation.

If a nation pursues a policy of developing and maintaining this capability then it has a "first-strike strategy." The United States had a first-strike capability in the late 1940s and early 1950s when it enjoyed first a monopoly of nuclear weapons and then a massive lead in the production of such weapons and their delivery systems.

But by the late 1950s the gap between the nuclear arsenals of the Soviet Union and the United States had narrowed considerably. By the 1960s there existed a rough parity, which created a BALANCE OF TERROR that prevented either country from attacking the other for fear of risking a massive counter-attack, or SECOND STRIKE.

Five Principles of Peaceful Coexistence   The Five Principles of Peaceful Coexistence were developed in the mid-1950s by Chinese premier CHOU EN-LAI to persuade other Asian nations that China had no revolutionary intentions toward other Asian nations.

The principles were outlined in a communique signed by Chou and Indian prime minister Jawaharlal Nehru after Chou stopped off in New Delhi on his way home following the 1954 GENEVA CONFERENCE ON INDOCHINA AND KOREA. The principles were discussed at the BANDUNG CONFERENCE in 1955 and were generally welcomed by other Asian countries, but they fell afoul of the anti-communist and anti-Chinese rhetoric of the Eisenhower administration. The principles did, however, keep Nehru from taking India into the SOUTHEAST ASIA TREATY ORGANIZATION. The five principles were:

1. Mutual respect for each other's territorial integrity and sovereignty.
2. Nonaggression.
3. Noninterference in each other's internal affairs.
4. Equality and mutual benefit.
5. Peaceful coexistence.

Flexible Response   The policy of flexible response is one of the mainstays of Western defense policy. It stipulates that the Western Alliance maintain credible forces at all defense levels (conventional, tactical nuclear, intermediate nuclear and strategic nuclear forces) in order to have the flexibility to deter an attack at each level and to decide which form of warfare to use in deterring attack.

The policy was developed during the KENNEDY administration as a reaction to the preceding EISENHOWER administration's heavy reliance on massive nuclear retaliation to any attack. Kennedy and his advisers feared that this policy had the dual effect of making nuclear war more likely and at the same time weakening America's ability to respond to lower-level conflicts.

The major drawback of the flexible response policy is the cost of maintaining sufficient numbers of forces at all levels to deter an attack. The cost has meant that in some areas of the world, such as Western Europe, the Western Alliance had to pay lip service to the concept of flexible response while in reality continuing to rely on massive nuclear retaliation to deter the Soviet Union's overwhelming superiority in conventional weapons.

Force d'Action Rapide (FAR)   The Force d'Action Rapid is a French rapid-deployment force of 40,000 troops created in 1982 by President FRANCOIS MITTERRAND.

The creation of the FAR was part of a general defense reorganization and is partly a way of cutting defense spending by basing more troops in metropolitan France. It was also a symbol in part of Mitterrand's greater commitment to the Western Alliance, as he made it clear that these troops would spearhead a French commitment if the West were attacked. The FAR was strengthened by the decision in 1988 to base a joint French and German brigade in West Germany.

Ford, Gerald   (July 14, 1913–   )   Gerald Ford was president of the United States at the height of détente. His administration, however, was hamstrung by congressional suspicion of the presidency in the post-Watergate and post-VIETNAM WAR era and by the fact that Ford had not been elected to the White House.

Ford attended the University of Michigan, where he won fame as an All-American football player. He went on to Yale Law School and graduated in 1941. Ford served in the navy during World War II and in 1945 returned to Grand Rapids, Michigan, to practice law.

In the immediate postwar years the Republican Party was

Gerald Ford, president of the United States from 1974 to 1977.

split between the prewar isolationists and a growing internationalist wing led by Senator ARTHUR VANDENBERG. One of the leading isolationists was Michigan congressman Bartel Jonkman. Vandenberg persuaded Ford to challenge Jonkman for the Republican nomination in the 1948 congressional elections. Ford's challenge was successful, and he went on to defeat the Democratic candidate with 61% of the vote.

In the House of Representatives, Ford adopted a conservative but internationalist Republican position. He supported President HARRY TRUMAN's foreign policies but opposed his social welfare programs. After the election of DWIGHT EISENHOWER, Ford developed a reputation as a party loyalist, backing the White House on every major issue.

In 1953, Ford joined the Defense Subcommittee of the House Appropriations Committee and quickly developed an expertise in military spending. He supported high defense spending and military assistance to pro-American countries. In 1960 he was considered by RICHARD NIXON as his running mate in presidential elections that year. "I don't know of anyone," Nixon said in July 1960, "whose views on domestic and foreign policy are more consonant with mine than Jerry [Ford]."

Ford had no problem transferring his loyalty on foreign affairs issues to the Democratic administration of JOHN F. KENNEDY. In January 1964, Ford was elected House minority leader. Until then, he had enjoyed a reputation as an advocate of bipartisan foreign policy, but his staunch support for the Vietnam War led him into conflict with liberal Democrats, and he regularly criticized President LYNDON JOHNSON for not being aggressive enough in his conduct of the war.

Ford was a loyal supporter of President Nixon's Vietnam War policies. In September 1969 he voted against all efforts to curb military spending or place a time limit on U.S. troop involvement in Vietnam. Ford voted in favor of extending the draft in 1971 and against the 1973 War Powers Act, which curbed the president's powers to send troops abroad. Ford also supported Nixon's decision to intensify the bombing of North Vietnam in 1972 and the mining of North Vietnamese harbors.

On October 12, 1973, Nixon nominated Ford to replace the disgraced Spiro Agnew as vice president. Ford had little trouble in securing congressional approval. He had been a well-liked figure in the House, and his reputation for personal honesty was a welcome contrast to Nixon's Watergate scandal and Agnew's financial corruption.

As vice president, Ford was a loyal supporter of the president right up to the time of Nixon's resignation on August 9, 1974. A month after succeeding Nixon, Ford granted Nixon a legally questionable, full pardon for all federal crimes he may have committed while in office.

The major issue during Ford's presidency was the state of the American economy. During his first year in office inflation rose by 18 percent. Ford responded by increasing taxes and cutting federal spending. But by the end of 1974 it was clear that the country was in a recession, and Ford shifted back to tax cuts and deficit spending.

Ford's economic policies strained relations with Congress and left the president with little time to devote to foreign policy issues. His control of foreign policy was limited by the fact that he was an appointed president, and therefore without an electoral mandate, and also by the congressional restrictions placed on the president in the post-Watergate and post-Vietnam era.

The residual American presence in Vietnam remained a major foreign policy preoccupation. Nixon's policy had been to withdraw American troops, but in such a manner that South Vietnamese forces were left with a marked military advantage and continued to have access to U.S. financial help and military equipment. But by the end of 1974, it was clear that the cease-fire negotiated by Secretary of State HENRY KISSINGER and Le Duc Tho was not holding, and in January 1975 Ford asked Congress for an additional $522 million in military aid for South Vietnam and Cambodia. "With adequate United States material assistance," said Ford, "they can hold their own. We cannot turn our backs on these embattled countries."

Congress refused the president's request. On April 23 Ford announced that the war was over for the United States, and five days later he ordered the emergency evacuation of all U.S. personnel as Viet Cong troops closed in on Saigon. On May 7, 1975, Ford proclaimed: "America is no longer at war."

Five days later, on May 12, tensions in Southeast Asia again rose when Cambodian forces seized the American merchant vessel the *Mayaguez* in the Gulf of Thailand. The Cambodians claimed that the *Mayaguez* was on a spy mission. Ford attacked the seizure of the ship as "an act of piracy" and demanded the release of the vessel and its 39-member crew. The Cambodians did not reply, and on May 14 American forces launched a ground, air and sea attack on Tang Island, where the vessel and crew were held. The *Mayaguez* and all of its crew were safely retrieved and Ford was praised by congressional leaders from both parties.

In addition to Vietnam, Ford inherited the policy of détente with the Soviet Union and the STRATEGIC ARMS LIMITATION TALKS (SALT) process. For many people, the high point of the détente era was reached in July and August 1975 when the leaders of 33 European nations, Canada and the United States met in Helsinki to sign the Helsinki Accords of the CONFERENCE ON SECURITY AND COOPERATION IN EUROPE. The agreement was criticized by many conservatives for apparently accepting the postwar division of Europe, but the accords also pledged the signatories (including the Soviet Union) to the freer exchange of information and travel, respect for "fundamental freedoms, including the freedom of thought, conscience, religion or belief" and the reunification of families split by the division of Europe.

Despite détente, the SALT process became bogged down during the Ford administration. It started in 1972 with the signing of the Strategic Arms Limitation Talks One and ANTIBALLISTIC MISSILE TREATIES in Moscow. SALT I was meant only to be an interim agreement that would lead to a SALT II treaty designed to reduce rather than simply limit the strategic nuclear systems of the two superpowers. In October 1974 Ford sent Henry Kissinger to Moscow in pursuit of a SALT II agreement, and in November 1974 Ford met Soviet leader LEONID BREZHNEV in Vladivostok.

After the Vladivostok meeting the two leaders reached a preliminary SALT II accord, which included an agreement to limit the numbers of all strategic offensive nuclear weapons and delivery vehicles, including multiple independently targeted reentry vehicles (MIRVs). Kissinger described the accord as a "breakthrough" that would "mean that a cap has been put on the arms race for a period of ten years."

Formal U.S.–Soviet negotiations resumed in Geneva in January 1975. In February 1975 Ford described the differences between the two delegations as "minor," but by the spring of 1975 the talks were running into difficulty over the continued Soviet arms buildup, which American officials regarded as a violation of the spirit if not the letter of the 1972 SALT I agreement. A planned summertime summit meeting between Brezhnev and Ford was postponed and in November 1975 Ford was forced to concede that "the timetable doesn't look encouraging" for a new SALT pact in the near future.

The immediate post-Vietnam period created opportunities for the Soviet Union to expand its influence in the Third World. A major area of interest was Southern Africa (see ANGOLA AND NAMIBIA CONFLICTS). The region's position along the major oil tanker route from Europe and North America to the Persian Gulf made it of major strategic interest. Southern Africa's potential vulnerability to Soviet influence was underscored by the collapse of the Portuguese Empire, the international isolation of South Africa and the illegal, white-dominated government in Rhodesia (Zimbabwe).

In 1975 Cuban and Soviet forces intervened in Angola in support of the Marxist MPLA (Movimiento Popular de Libertacao de Angola). Ford initially authorized the provision of covert aid to the rival FNLA (Frente Nacional de Libertacao de Angola) and UNITA (Uniao Nacional para a Independencia Total de Angola), in conjunction with South Africa and some West European countries. South African president P.W. Botha ordered his own troops into Angola and on December 31 issued an appeal for American involvement in Angola to be increased "not only in the diplomatic but all other fields" to keep the former Portuguese colony from being "hounded into the Communist fold." The U.S. Congress, however, had blocked aid to Angola, thus limiting Ford to diplomatic and economic measures.

As part of its efforts to limit Soviet influence in the region, the Ford administration also became diplomatically involved in the long-running Rhodesia Crisis. The white-dominated government of the British colony, led by Ian Smith, had in 1965 declared itself unilaterally independent from Britain to avoid sharing power with the black majority. The civil war that resulted, coupled with the withdrawal of the Portuguese, threatened to create additional opportunities for the Soviets. Ford sent Secretary of State Henry Kissinger to mediate a solution to the Rhodesia Crisis. Working closely with British foreign secretary Anthony Crosland, Kissinger persuaded Smith to agree to preparations for a coalition government that would include moderate black leaders. The so-called internal settlement did not end the crisis, but it was a major step in the ultimate resolution.

Another African problem during the Ford administration was the conflict between Somalia and Ethiopia in the strategic HORN OF AFRICA at the mouth of the Red Sea. Ethiopia had been an American ally in the region, and the Soviet Union had backed Somalia, where it maintained an important missile base at Berbera. But in September 1974 Ethiopia's Emperor Haile Selassie was overthrown by Marxist military officers. Somalia immediately sought to take advantage of the internal turmoil in Ethiopia by invading the country and pressing its claim to the Ethiopia-occupied Ogaden Desert. The new Marxist government in Addis Ababa appealed to the Soviet Union for help, and Brezhnev turned on Somalia to support the strategically more important Ethiopia with Soviet weapons and advisers and Cuban troops. Ford provided aid to Somalia, but was again blocked by Congress from providing the level of support he wanted.

There were several problems in Western Europe during the Ford administration. The collapse of Portugal's African empire led to a left-wing revolution at home, and for a time it appeared that a pro-Soviet government would come to power in Lisbon. As the government moved further to the left, Ford became increasingly inclined to reduce American support but was dissuaded by FRANK CARLUCCI, the American ambassador in Lisbon. The communist threat eventually receded and Portugal returned to a more moderate form of government.

The Ford administration also saw the rise of EUROCOMMUNISM. The process had started after the Soviet invasion of Czechoslovakia in 1968 as West European communist parties found their pro-Soviet positions an increasing electoral disadvantage. By 1975 almost all of the West European communist parties, with the exception of those of France and Portugal, were publicly dissociating themselves from Moscow. This led to a sharp increase in the size of the communist vote, especially in Italy, where it looked as if the communists would join the government. The move worried Ford and Kissinger, and in November 1975, the secretary of state warned that Italy "could be lost to NATO" because of communist political victories. But Ford refused to authorize support for anti-communist covert operations similar to the ones employed by the Eisenhower administration in the 1950s.

Ford announced his candidacy for the 1976 Republican presidential nomination in July 1975. His support for détente had by this time alienated Ford from the conservative wing of the party, and he faced strong opposition from right-wing challenger RONALD REAGAN. Going into the convention, however, Ford was slightly ahead in delegate votes, and this and his incumbency gave him the edge. However, he lost the presidency to Georgia governor JIMMY CARTER, who capitalized on the voters' post-Watergate disenchantment with the Washington establishment by promising to bring a new morality to government.

Out of office, Ford continued to speak out on major subjects. He supported the MX MISSILE program and the NEUTRON BOMB and opposed the final SALT II agreement negotiated by Carter. For the first three years of the Carter administration, Ford considered running against Carter in the 1980 election, and there were various draft-Ford movements in the early primaries. But in May 1980 he ruled himself out of the race by endorsing Ronald Reagan.

For Further Information:

Ford, Gerald, *Public Papers of the President: Gerald R. Ford*. 3 vols. Washington, D.C., 1975–1977.

———. *A Time to Heal: The Autobiography of Gerald R. Ford*. New York, 1979.

Mollenhoff, Clark R. *The Man Who Pardoned Nixon*. New York, 1976.

Osborne, John. *White House Watch: The Ford Years*. Washington, D.C., 1977.

Reeves, Richard. *A Ford, Not a Lincoln*. New York, 1975.

Schapsmeier, Edward L., and Frederick H. Schapsmeier. *Gerald R. Ford's Date with Destiny: A Political Biography*. New York, 1989.

Foreign Aid Foreign aid was one of the chief economic weapons of the Cold War, as both power blocs sought to buy influence in Third World countries through extensive aid programs.

The first Cold War example of American foreign aid was the TRUMAN DOCTRINE announced by President HARRY TRUMAN on March 12, 1947. Faced with the growing prospect of a communist takeover in Greece and Turkey, Truman announced that the United States was extending $400 million worth of military and economic assistance to those two countries.

The Truman Doctrine was quickly followed by the MARSHALL PLAN, which was unveiled on June 4, 1947, by Secretary of State GEORGE C. MARSHALL. He and his deputy DEAN ACHESON argued that the problems of Greece and Turkey were only a small part of a wider threat facing the whole of Western Europe and that a massive aid program was necessary to save war-ravaged Western Europe from an economic and political collapse, which would create a vacuum into which the Soviet Union could easily step.

The Marshall Plan (also known as the European Recovery Program) was spread over a four-year period and resulted in $12.5 billion being funneled into the reconstruction of Western Europe. It played the most important role in boosting European industrial output to 35% above prewar levels and agricultural output to 18% above prewar levels by 1952.

The Marshall Plan also demonstrated the benefits of aid for the American economy. The United States ended the war as the world's largest creditor nation. In order to prevent inflation it needed to recycle its surplus capital and create markets for its goods. One of the stipulations of the Marshall Plan was that most of the $12.5 billion be spent on American products. This provided a major boost to the American postwar economy and strengthened trading patterns, which continued to work to the advantage of the United States.

The Marshall Plan also had a political purpose, declaring clearly that the aid was designed to "prevent the growth or advance of national or international power which constitutes a substantial threat to U.S. security and well-being . . . [and] orients foreign nations towards the U.S." The committee that laid down the ground rules for the aid program also made it clear that the United States must have full knowledge "of the manner in which the means provided are distributed and used" and that the recipient countries must use the money for "the development and support of free and democratic institutions." These conditions conflicted with the Soviet Union's political ambitions in Eastern Europe, and the Soviets refused to participate in the plan or to allow their East European satellites to participate.

One of the offshoots of the Marshall Plan was the ORGANIZATION FOR EUROPEAN ECONOMIC COOPERATION (OEEC), which was created initially to coordinate Marshall Plan aid and then, after the aid ceased, continued to work for economic cooperation among European countries. In 1961 the OEEC changed its name to the Organization for Economic Cooperation and Development, expanded its membership to include Canada and the United States and took on the additional role of channeling funds from Europe and North America to developing countries.

Other international foreign aid institutions are the INTERNATIONAL MONETARY FUND (IMF) and the associated WORLD BANK. Both were heavily capitalized by the United States in their early years and have a strong bias toward private-sector investment and free-market economic policies. This led the Soviet Bloc countries to boycott the organizations until the end of the 1980s, when a number of East European countries applied for membership as the power of their communist parties waned.

In the first two years of the Cold War, the main thrust of America's foreign aid program was directed toward Western Europe. But as tensions increased elsewhere in the world, so did the amount of American aid. President Truman became especially concerned about the political allegiance of the Third World and the emerging new nations. He and his advising economists believed that an extension of American aid to this region would diminish the appeal of communism as the aid helped these countries make the transition to a modern economy.

In his inaugural address of January 20, 1949, Truman announced his extended foreign aid policy in what became known as the POINT FOUR PROGRAM (also referred to as the International Development Act). The first three points were continued support for the United Nations and its related agencies, continuation of the program for world economic recovery, and strengthening of "freedom-loving nations" against the dangers of aggression. Truman's fourth point was to make American investment capital and scientific and technical expertise available to underdeveloped countries in order to raise the world standard of living. Truman requested that the program be started with a budget of $45 million. By March 1951, a total of 350 technicians were at work on more than 100 technical cooperation projects in 27 countries. By 1953 Congress had increased the budget to $155,600,000.

There were also a number of regionally based foreign aid programs. One of the first such programs was the COLOMBO PLAN, organized by British foreign secretary ERNEST BEVIN but largely financed by the United States. The Colombo Plan coordinated economic aid to Asian and Pacific countries. The United States did not participate in the initial formation of the Colombo Plan but quickly became involved as a donor country. The plan provided aid to 20 member countries from six donor countries. Between 1950 and 1983, the aid allocated through the Colombo Plan amounted to $72 billion. More than half of the money—$41.2 billion—was provided by the United States.

The main thrust of the initial U.S. policy toward Latin America was to extend the 19th-century Monroe Doctrine to create a hemispheric defense treaty. This was formalized in the RIO PACT of 1947. Formal American aid was channeled through Truman's Point Four Program. This was considered inadequate by a number of Latin American specialists such as ADOLF BERLE and NELSON ROCKEFELLER, and Rockefeller used his family money to found the American International Association for Economic and Social Development (AIA) to channel private funds into Latin American development projects. He also encouraged the Rockefeller Foundation to become more heavily involved in Latin America.

A U.S. federal government aid program specifically for Latin America did not get under way until August 1961, when President JOHN F. KENNEDY's ALLIANCE FOR PROGRESS took effect. At the core of this program was a proposed 10-year, $20 billion economic development plan for Latin America. The Alliance for Progress continued to be the cornerstone of the Latin America policy of the Kennedy and later the Johnson administrations. However, the financial drain of the VIETNAM WAR, continuing NATO commitments, and eight years of Republican administrations following Johnson moved Latin America down America's list of foreign policy priorities, and successive administrations failed to build on the alliance after the expiration of the initial 10-year period.

Shortly after the unveiling of the Alliance for Progress, the Kennedy administration launched the AGENCY FOR INTERNATIONAL DEVELOPMENT (AID) to coordinate and rationalize foreign aid programs. Within two years of its formation, AID was coming under attack from congressional critics who demanded a discernible link between the aid programs and foreign policy objectives. The result was a series of congressional cuts in the AID budget as money was shifted from economic and development aid to military assistance. In the 1970s and 1980s, AID shifted the focus of its activities from financing major public works to supporting private sector activities and the balance of payments deficits of developing countries.

Although most Western aid came from the United States, as the world economy recovered from the war, considerable sums also came from the West European countries and Japan. Oil-rich Arab countries also generously extended aid in support of general Western interests following the quadrupling of oil prices in 1973–74. The European countries generally extended their aid to former colonial possessions. Britain, for instance, established an extensive aid program to Commonwealth countries. In 1975, the EUROPEAN ECONOMIC COMMUNITY signed a trade and aid agreement (the Lome Convention) with the EEC members' 46 former colonial possessions in Africa, Asia and the Caribbean. The pact committed the EEC to some $4 billion in development aid, guaranteed duty-free access to all the industrial and most of the agricultural exports of the developing countries, established a committee to promote commercial and industrial cooperation, and pledged $450 million in aid for those nations whose export earnings depended heavily on any of 12 basic commodities if the price of those commodities fell below a determined level.

Japan provided little aid during the initial Cold War years, and in fact was a major recipient of American aid. After the Japanese economy recovered from the war, the Japanese were at first reluctant to extend foreign aid because of their sensitivity to charges of revived Japanese imperialism. But Japan's growing trade surplus with the rest of the world led to increasing calls for the Japanese to recycle that surplus in the form of development aid. In 1989 the Japanese government pledged $10 billion in foreign aid for that year, making it the world's largest national supplier of development aid.

From the earliest years of the Cold War, military assistance played an important role in American aid packages. The purpose of the Truman Doctrine, for instance, was to extend military as well as economic assistance to Greece and Turkey. In 1951, at the height of the Korean War, the U.S. Senate approved $500 million in military and approximately $100 million in economic aid to the South Korean government. Other major recipients of American military aid have been Egypt, Israel, Turkey and Pakistan.

At times it was difficult to separate military and economic assistance. For instance, "the hearts and minds" campaign during the Vietnam War was designed to achieve military objectives by winning the support of the Vietnamese peasantry with development aid projects.

The first stages of American Cold War foreign aid were designed to protect European democratic institutions and governments. But as the Cold War spread beyond the borders of Europe, the premises on which the United States based its assistance underwent a change. The basic requirement for American aid became opposition to communism, and the establishment of a democratic government was a secondary consideration at best. This led to support for a number of dictatorial and military governments which, at best, paid only lip service to democratic principles. As a result, the foreign aid program came under increasing scrutiny by liberal elements of the U.S. Congress and the American public.

Occasionally the Soviet Union and the United States used foreign aid to compete directly and overtly for influence in a third country. An early and dramatic example of this was the competition to fund and build the ASWAN HIGH DAM in Egypt. In 1955, Secretary of State JOHN FOSTER DULLES offered American aid to build the dam, which was designed to provide electrical power and irrigation water. The American offer was extended at the urging of the British government, which wanted to prevent Soviet political penetration in Egypt. Under the original offer, the United States was to provide $56 million for building the dam and Britain $14 million. But Egyptian leader GAMAL ABDEL NASSER's increasingly anti-Western statements led to the withdrawal of the American offer, and the Soviet Union stepped in to fill both the financial and the political void.

The Soviet financing of the Aswan Dam was an example of the type of project the Soviet Union generally sought to aid: a grand-scale, high-profile scheme closely linked to the political ambitions of leading individuals and capable of winning the Soviets maximum political influence for minimum expenditure. This policy was largely forced on the Soviet Union by its economic circumstances. Unlike the United States, the Soviet Union had finished the war a debtor country, and its initial postwar economic foreign policy was aimed at using its military gains to rebuild the Soviet economy as quickly as possible.

For a start, Soviet leader JOSEF STALIN demanded and received the right to collect $10 billion in war reparations from Germany. This he did by virtually stripping the Soviet sector of its economic base. With reparations and political control were Soviet-created, jointly-owned state corporations, or joint stock companies, in the satellite countries. These were started in Mongolia during the 1920s and involved the creation of companies in key areas (such as transporation, mining, energy and communications) in which the Soviet Union would provide half the required capital. In return, it would receive half of all income. At the time of the dissolution of the joint venture, it usually demanded and received a sum equivalent to half the value of the assets. If the host country did not have the money for the initial capitalization, the Soviet Union offered loans to cover costs, thus increasing Soviet revenues and the satellite countries' dependence.

At the end of the war, the Soviet government confiscated all German assets in Hungary, Romania and Bulgaria. In Hungary this represented 201 companies, many of them large and in key sectors. In Romania there were 400 former German companies. These assets provided the Soviet contribution to a number of joint stock companies in those nations. Other such companies were formed with the Chinese, Albanian, Yugoslav, Polish and Czech governments. In addition, the satellite countries also agreed to supply the Soviet Union with goods at preferential prices. Poland, for instance, sold coal to the Soviet Union at cut-rate prices for nearly 10 years after the war.

The announcement of the Marshall Plan in 1947 forced the Soviet Union into a more generous attitude toward Eastern Europe, especially as two countries, Poland and Czechoslovakia, initially tried to join the plan. In January 1948, the Soviets extended a $450 million loan to cover construction of a new Polish steel mill. A further Soviet loan of $100 million was extended to Poland in 1950. Romania and Bulgaria were allowed to reduce their war reparations and Czechoslovakia was provided with 600,000 tons of grain and an industrial loan of $32 million.

The creation of the COUNCIL FOR MUTUAL ECONOMIC ASSISTANCE (CMEA or COMECON) in response to the Marshall Plan was not meant to create a conduit for Soviet aid but to establish a Soviet-controlled mechanism to encourage trade between Eastern Bloc countries, so that their economies would become increasingly interdependent and less likely to be tempted by trade with the West.

The unrest that followed the death of Stalin in March 1953 persuaded the new Soviet government to extend aid to Eastern Europe in order to ensure Soviet control. A soft loan of $125 million was extended to East Germany after the uprising there in 1953, and remaining reparations were annulled. After the riots in Poland in 1956, the Soviet Union extended a complex aid package of $320 million to the Poles. The Hungarian Revolution was followed by a Soviet aid package to that country of $250 million and $100 million from other Soviet Bloc countries. In the aftermath of the Warsaw Pact's invasion of Czechoslovakia in 1968, the Czechs signed a favorable $1 billion trade agreement with the Soviet Union. And after the initial crushing of Poland's free trade union SOLIDARITY in 1981, the Soviet Union was forced to sell billions of dollars of its gold reserves to help ease the Polish foreign debt problem that had led to the creation of Solidarity.

As stated above, Soviet cash aid to Third World countries usually took the form of grants for high-profile projects such as the Aswan Dam. Other examples of this type of aid were a Soviet-built flour mill at Bhilai in India, a sports coliseum built by the Soviet Union for Indonesia's President Sukarno and a Soviet-built palace for Ghanaian leader Kwame Nkrumah.

Soviet aid for less glamorous projects normally consisted of goods and equipment supplied on a credit basis with repayment in the form of cash or goods. In some cases, however, exports were supplied by the Soviet Union for immediate repayment in a hard (Western) currency. When the trading partner was unable to pay, the resultant trade deficit was often converted into a foreign aid credit for the purchase of additional Soviet goods. Some of the main recipients of this type of Soviet aid were Cuba, Vietnam, North Korea, Nicaragua, Angola, Ethiopia and, at times, Egypt.

Even more so than U.S. foreign aid, Soviet aid was directed toward political objectives. Between 1961 and 1965 $500 million in aid was promised to Mongolia to prevent that country from falling into the Chinese orbit. At the start of the Korean War, the Soviets extended an outright gift of $250 million in aid to North Korea as well as a loan of $75 million. By 1964, the Soviet aid to North Korea had totaled $560 million. Before the start of the Vietnam War, the Soviets extended some $500 million in aid to North Vietnam. A further $500 million was provided by other communist countries. It is difficult to estimate the amount of aid extended to North Vietnam between 1965 and 1975. Between 1980 and 1985. Between 1980 and 1985, Vietnam received an estimated $1 billion a year in Soviet aid, and in 1986 it was announced that the figure would be doubled to $2 billion a year for the following five years.

The first Soviet loan to Cuba—$100 million—was made in February 1960 for a number of industrial development projects. But the most important Soviet–Cuban aid agreement concerned sugar. Banned from the American market, Cuba persuaded the Soviet Union to purchase virtually all of its sugar crop at prevailing world prices, even though the Soviet Union had little need of it and either destroyed or redistributed it to other countries. In 1988 it was estimated that the Soviet Union was paying up to $5 billion a year to maintain a communist government in Cuba. Some of that money, however, went toward the financing of Cuban troops and aid in support of pro-Soviet governments in Nicaragua, Angola and Ethiopia.

By the start of the 1980s, nearly 40 years of competition for world influence (along with the arms race) had left both the Soviet Union and the United States with billions of dollars in unpaid Third World debts and expensive trade deficits. In 1988 the U.S. trade deficit was $137.3 billion. The Soviet economy, however, was unable to support the burden, and Soviet leader MIKHAIL GORBACHEV was forced into a basic restructuring of the Soviet economy, which involved major cuts in foreign and military aid to Moscow's allies.

For Further Information:
Berliner, Joseph. *Soviet Economic Aid.* New York, 1958.
Clark, Paul G. *American Aid for Development.* New York, 1972.
Eberstadt, Nicholas. *Foreign Aid and American Purpose.* Washington, D.C., 1988.
Gimbel, John. *The Origins of the Marshall Plan.* Stanford, Calif., 1976.
Goldman, Marshall. *Soviet Foreign Aid.* New York, 1967.
Hogan, M. J. *The Marshall Plan.* New York, 1987.
Pollard, Robert. *Economic Security and the Origins of the Cold War, 1945–50.* New York, 1985.

Formosa Doctrine The Formosa Doctrine was formulated by the EISENHOWER administration and passed by the U.S. Congress in order to authorize President Dwight Eisenhower to extend military aid to the Nationalist Chinese government on Taiwan after the communist Chinese shelling of Nationalist forces on the islands of QUEMOY AND MATSU in 1954. (Formosa is the name given the island by the Portuguese in the 16th century. It was known by this name in the West until recently.)

Eisenhower asked for the authority to extend American military support to Taiwan and the Pescadores Islands on January 24, 1955, five months after the mainland Chinese had started an artillery barrage of Quemoy and Matsu. In response to the president's request, the U.S. Senate, by a vote of 83 to 3, passed a resolution authorizing Eisenhower "to employ the armed forces of the United States as he deems necessary for the specific purpose of securing and protecting Formosa and the Pescadores against armed attack, this authority to include the securing and protecting of such related positions and territories of that area now in friendly hands and the taking of such other measures as he judges to be required or appropriate in assuring the defense of Formosa and the Pescadores."

The Senate resolution cleared the way for Secretary of State JOHN FOSTER DULLES to fly to Taiwan to negotiate a mutual defense treaty with Nationalist Chinese leader CHIANG KAI-SHEK. Eisenhower, however, was fearful that such an agreement might be interpreted by Chiang as American support for an invasion of mainland China. Therefore, as a price for the mutual defense treaty, Dulles also negotiated a secret treaty with Chiang that prevented him from launching an attack against the mainland without American permission.

For Further Information:
Clubb, Oliver Edmund. "Formosa and the Offshore Islands in American Policy, 1950–1955," *Political Science Quarterly* (December 1959).

Forrestal, James V.   (February 15, 1892–May 22, 1949)
James Forrestal served first as secretary of the navy and then as secretary of defense under President HARRY TRUMAN. He was the most rabidly anti-communist member of the Truman administration, and his extreme right-wing views eventually led to his resignation.

After attending Dartmouth College and Princeton University, Forrestal became a Wall Street bond salesman before World War I. During the war he served as a pilot, and he returned to join the prestigious Wall Street brokerage firm of Dillon, Read, where he became president in 1938.

In 1940 President ROOSEVELT appointed Forrestal undersecretary, and in May 1944 secretary of the navy. Forrestal was among the first to warn Roosevelt and then Truman of Soviet expansion, and he opposed postwar demobilization.

In 1946 Forrestal was behind the decision to send an American warship to Greece and Turkey, which were under threat from communists. At the same time he pressed for increased pay for the armed forces. Forrestal also opposed General GEORGE MARSHALL's efforts to negotiate an agreement between the Chinese communists and the Nationalist Chinese government and supported economic aid to Germany and Japan to turn those countries into effective bulwarks against Soviet expansion.

Forrestal was a keen advocate of the TRUMAN DOCTRINE, the MARSHALL PLAN and, although he did not live to see it, the NORTH ATLANTIC TREATY ORGANIZATION. He opposed the creation of the state of Israel on the grounds that it would alienate the Arab world and lead to a Soviet foothold in the Middle East.

On July 26, 1947, Truman named Forrestal the first secretary of defense in the newly-created Defense Department. It was a difficult job, as Forrestal had to balance and coordinate three services that had thitherto worked separately. The strains of the task began to take their toll, and Forrestal began to exhibit signs of paranoia. He became increasingly concerned about the activities of the Communist Party and began to support extreme-right political causes.

In 1948 he lost a budget battle with Truman when the president cut back his 1949 defense budget request from $18 billion to $15 billion. Forrestal began to fear that the United States was on the brink of a war with the Soviet Union, which it would lose. He also reported to aides that he was being followed by Zionists and communists.

After Truman's reelection victory in 1948 he asked Forrestal to resign, which he did in March 1949. Shortly afterward Forrestal suffered a nervous breakdown and was admitted to Bethesda Naval Hospital in Maryland. On May 22, 1949, he committed suicide by jumping from his 13th-floor window.

For Further Information:
Davis, Vincent. *Postwar Defense Policy and the U.S. Navy, 1943–1946.* Chapel Hill, N.C., 1966.
Rogow, Arnold A. *James Forrestal: A Study of Personality, Politics and Policy.* New York, 1963.

Forward-Based Systems (FBS)   Forward-based systems are nuclear weapon systems controlled by one country and based in another country or on aircraft carriers, aircraft or submarines, in order to place the weapons at the ready and closer to the target country.

The term is usually used to refer to U.S. nuclear weapons in Western Europe. It was introduced by the Soviet Union during the Strategic Arms Limitation Treaty (SALT) I negotiations. In both the SALT I and the SALT II negotiations, the Soviet Union at first insisted that the U.S. forward-based systems be included in calculations involving the U.S. strategic force. (See STRATEGIC ARMS LIMITATION TALKS.)

A combination of U.S. refusal and the difficulties of categorizing strategic, intermediate-range and tactical weapons led the Soviets to drop their demand. At Vladivistok in 1974 the two countries agreed that forward-based systems would not be treated as strategic weapons. Later, the Soviets on occasion revived the problem to justify their maintenance of a slightly larger strategic nuclear deterrent.

Foster, William   (April 27, 1897–October 14, 1984)   William Foster was the first director of the ARMS CONTROL AND DISARMAMENT AGENCY during the KENNEDY and JOHNSON administrations and played an important role in negotiating the "HOT-LINE" accord and the partial NUCLEAR TEST BAN TREATY of 1963 and the Nuclear Nonproliferation Treaty of 1968. During the TRUMAN administration he was undersecretary of defense and in 1958 was chief delegate to the Geneva Conference on the Prevention of Surprise Attacks.

Foster dropped out of college to fight in World War I. After the war he graduated from M.I.T. and went into business, eventually becoming president of Welded Steel Products Inc. Foster was recruited in 1946 by AVERELL HARRIMAN to be undersecretary of commerce. When Harriman in 1948 went to Paris to oversee the MARSHALL PLAN, Foster accompanied him as his deputy. In June 1949 he was named deputy administrator of the Economic Cooperation Administration.

In September 1951 Foster was appointed deputy secretary of defense. He was mainly concerned with problems in Asia. After a visit to South Korea, Taiwan and Vietnam in October 1952 he said that there was no possibility that the South Koreans could carry on the war alone within the foreseeable future. He thought the Nationalist Chinese troops were "able and well-led" and that Vietnam should have "priority next to Korea." He also advocated greater cooperation among Southeast Asian governments to fight communists in the region.

Although Foster was a Republican, he left the Pentagon in January 1953 when DWIGHT EISENHOWER took office as president. He worked for a number of companies in the chemical industry until November 1958, when he was asked to head the U.S. delegation to the Geneva Conference on the Prevention of Surprise Attacks. Foster started his negotiations from the premise that the major threat to world security was nuclear-capable delivery systems. He therefore proposed a comprehensive inspection system to control the development of these systems.

This was rejected by the Soviet delegation, which emphasized disarmament rather than control. Their demands included the withdrawal of bases from foreign soil, the reduction of conventional forces, abolition of nuclear weapons, and the creation of a nuclear-free zone in Central Europe. The conference failed to reach an agreement, but it marked a turning point in American disarmament policy, as it was the first time that the U.S. government had offered concrete proposals for arms control. The talks also helped to establish Foster as a leading American nuclear weapons negotiator.

In September 1961, President John F. Kennedy appointed Foster as the first director of the Arms Control and Disarmament Agency (ACDA). During the Kennedy administration Foster helped to develop the American positions for negotiations on the partial Nuclear Test Ban Treaty, which was signed in Moscow on August 6, 1963, and helped in the drafting of President Kennedy's September 1961 proposal for "General and Complete Disarmament in a Peaceful World," which proposed nuclear disarmament and a drastic reduction in conventional weapons.

In the aftermath of the CUBAN MISSILE CRISIS in 1962 the American and Soviet governments agreed that a "hot line" linking Washington and Moscow should be established to ensure a secure communications link that could be used to defuse international crises. The American position on negotiations for the hot line was developed by Foster, and a U.S.–Soviet agreement establishing the link was signed on June 20, 1963.

Foster stayed at ACDA throughout the Johnson administration and negotiated the 1968 Nuclear Non-Proliferation Treaty. Foster left ACDA in January 1969 and became president of Porter International Company.

For Further Information:
Burns, Eedson L.M. *A Seat at the Table.* Toronto, 1972.
Dean, Arthur. *Test Ban and Disarmament: The Path of Negotiation.* New York, 1966.
Jacobson, Harold D. *Diplomats, Scientists and Politicians.* Ann Arbor, Mich., 1966.
Lepper, Milling. *Foreign Policy Formulations: A Case Study of the Nuclear Test Ban Treaty.* Columbus, Ohio, 1971.
Sobel, Lester. *Disarmament and Nuclear Tests: 1960–1963.* New York, 1964.

Fourquet Plan   The Fourquet Plan was the successor to the AILLERET DOCTRINE, which had emphasized an "omnidirectional" or "all-points" nuclear deterrence to ensure an independent French foreign policy.

The Fourquet Plan was developed in 1969 in response to the Soviet invasion of Czechoslovakia following the PRAGUE SPRING of 1968. Developed by General Michel Fourquet, French chief of staff, it identified the Soviet Union as the target of France's nuclear force. The new doctrine also rejected the main premise of the Ailleret Doctrine that an omnidirectional nuclear force would ensure French neutrality and security in the event of a U.S.–Soviet war.

Other main elements of the Fourquet Plan were a graduated FLEXIBLE RESPONSE strategy, a heavier reliance on tactical nuclear weapons and an implied link with the U.S. strategic force as the ultimate deterrent. The Fourquet Plan was superseded in March 1976 by the MERY PLAN developed by General Guy Mery, French chief of staff.

France   France played an important and changing role throughout the Cold War. In the early years, it was a catalyst for European unity and close U.S.–European relations. But the rise of CHARLES DE GAULLE saw the unabashed pursuit of French national interests at the expense of the United States and Britain and the development of a special Franco-Soviet relationship that encouraged early moves toward détente. Subsequent French presidents moved France back toward greater cooperation with the United States, while maintaining a national independence that served to inspire other governments to do the same.

The key to French foreign policy through the Cold War period must be sought in French history, its wartime experience and the towering personality of General Charles de Gaulle.

Between 1870 and 1940, France was invaded by Germany on three occasions. Twice it was defeated, while World War I left it victorious but drained. During World War II, humiliating defeat was followed by occupation and even more humiliating collaboration between leading French figures and the German forces. This experience left France with a deep-seated fear of Germany and a desperate need to recover its national self-respect.

De Gaulle set out to win back France's national self-respect shortly after he fled to London in June 1940 and was recognized by the British as the leader of the "Free French." From this point, de Gaulle saw himself as the living embodiment of the French nation who somehow stood above all political factions. This unshakable belief was a driving force behind the later creation of the Fifth Republic, the development of an independent French nuclear capability and an independent foreign policy.

Installed as head of the provisional government after Paris was liberated in August 1944, de Gaulle announced that the French people would be allowed to decide their own form of government through an elected constituent assembly.

In the political infighting that followed, de Gaulle continued to project the image of being above party politics but let it be known that he preferred a strong elected executive at the head of the government. Other French political figures preferred a more parliamentary system. In January 1946 de Gaulle suddenly resigned as provisional president in the hope that popular demand would sweep him back into office and give him the mandate he required to impose the system of government he preferred. But the French public failed to appreciate the subtleties of de Gaulle's political machinations.

When he resigned they accepted the resignation and turned to the socialist leader Felix Gouin to form the first government under the constitution of the Fourth Republic.

De Gaulle tried to stage a comeback in April 1947 when he formed the Rally of the French People (RPR), which became known simply as the Gaullist Party. But the French voters were by this time more interested in less mercurial figures. In July 1955 de Gaulle retired a second time, telling journalists "We shall not meet again until the tempest again looses itself on France."

The leaders of the Fourth Republic were less concerned with French national pride than with trying to rescue the economy and protect France from Soviet expansionism. Their concern about these issues led them to support European unity, defense ties with the United States and the MARSHALL PLAN.

In March 1947 French foreign minister GEORGES BIDAULT met with his British counterpart, ERNEST BEVIN, at Dunkirk to sign the 50-year ANGLO–FRENCH TREATY OF ALLIANCE AND MUTUAL ASSISTANCE, which is regarded as the first step in a successful three-stage plan to tie the United States to the defense of Western Europe. Bidault also played a major role in securing European support for the Marshall Plan, which faced strong opposition from the powerful French Communist Party.

An important element in France's postwar foreign policy strategy was to secure equal status with the other great powers. Bidault and others argued that although France had not played a major role in the defeat of Germany, French participation was essential to the rebuilding of Europe. The argument carried some weight. France was made a member of the Allied Council and given a zone of occupation in Germany and Berlin. But the British, Americans and Soviets tended to treat France as a junior partner.

Another reason for France's reduced status among the Allies was its slightly softer line toward the Soviet Union. French policy makers tended to attribute Soviet aggression to a fear of Western aggression. Bidault made a major effort to bring the Soviet Union and Eastern Europe into the Marshall Plan, and France contributed little to the breaking of the BERLIN BLOCKADE for fear that it would antagonize the Soviets. The French also refused to participate in the initial merging of the Western sectors in Germany.

In a further effort to regain prestige, France played a leading role in the first steps toward European unity. The formation of the EUROPEAN COAL AND STEEL COMMUNITY (ECSC)—immediate precursor to the EUROPEAN ECONOMIC COMMUNITY—was the result of an initiative by French foreign minister ROBERT SCHUMAN in May 1950. Schuman believed that a federated Europe and increased economic interdependence would reduce the risk of war between European states. It was also the best way in which Western Europe could stand economically and militarily free of the United States and offered the best long-term prospect of thwarting Soviet expansionism. Schuman's close colleague JEAN MONNET was the first president of the European Coal and Steel Community after its formation in 1952.

The ECSC pooled the coal and steel resources of France and Germany and was the first major step toward a Franco–German rapprochement. Statesmen such as Monnet, Bidault and Schuman saw the logic of this policy, but many Frenchmen understandably continued to harbor strong feelings against Germany. The French public had particular difficulty in accepting German rearmament and a merger of France's armed forces with Germany, as envisaged in the EUROPEAN DEFENSE COMMUNITY (EDC). The French government supported the EDC, but at the Bermuda Conference of 1954 Bidault argued that French support for the plan had to be bought with an agreement for an autonomous Saarland and an Anglo-American commitment to maintain current high troop levels in West Germany. The demands were rejected by the British and the Americans, and the French National Assembly narrowly rejected the proposed EDC.

The collapse of the EDC coincided with the collapse of French rule in Indochina. Under the terms of the POTSDAM Treaty in 1945 the French had been reinstated as the political power in Vietnam. Their efforts to reestablish that authority led to the FRENCH INDOCHINA WAR between the French colonial army and the Vietnamese nationalist forces led by the communists under HO CHI MINH. The United States, concerned about the spread of communist influence in Asia, became a strong supporter of the French forces. In 1954, the French gathered a large army at DIEN BIEN PHU for what they hoped would be an offensive that would turn the course of the war in favor of France. Instead the French were quickly surrounded and defeated after an extended siege. The fall of Dien Bien Phu resulted in 5,000 French casualties and 10,000 French troops taken prisoner.

Dien Bien Phu destroyed the will of the French to continue the war in Indochina. At the 1954 GENEVA CONFERENCE ON INDOCHINA AND KOREA France agreed to withdraw and to accept the temporary partition of Vietnam into North, controlled by the communist Viet Minh, and South, controlled by Vietnamese forces that had collaborated with the French, pending a national election that would have reunified the country under a single government. This was against the wishes of U.S. president DWIGHT EISENHOWER and Secretary of State JOHN FOSTER DULLES, who, assuming that the Viet Minh would win any such election, tried to persuade the French to remain in Vietnam with increased American support. French withdrawal led the Americans to commit themselves to support directly the government of South Vietnam, in an attempt to establish it permanently. This resulted in the subsequent VIETNAM WAR.

France's other major colonial problem was Algeria. The French had been in Algeria since conquering it in 1830. By the start of World War II, there were an estimated 400,000 Frenchmen living in Algeria. In 1944 de Gaulle had extended French citizenship to Algerians and in 1947 Algeria had become an autonomous French department. Many Frenchmen regarded Algeria as an integral part of France, and the European settlers saw themselves as Frenchmen rather than Algerians. The politically oppressed Arab majority, however, never accepted French rule. In the early 1950s they became increasingly influenced by the Arab nationalism preached by Egypt's GAMAL ABDEL NASSER.

In 1954 a group of Algerian nationalists led by Ahmed Ben Bella formed the National Liberation Front (FLN) and started an armed resistance against French rule. As the resistance gained strength a French army of 500,000 men was sent to Algeria to quell it. The French also involved themselves with the British and Israelis in the 1956 Suez War (see SUEZ CRISIS), which attempted to topple Nasser. The French, however, were unable to quell the Algerian revolt, and the long and brutal struggle destroyed the Fourth Republic. Right-wing activists, angry at what they regarded as a sellout of the European settlers in Algeria, plotted to overthrow the government and replace it with either the military or de Gaulle, whom they believed favored their position.

In May 1958 pro-Gaullist riots organized by the right wing broke out in Paris. The tempest he had spoken of in 1955 was breaking. De Gaulle let it be known that he would return to government if the National Assembly agreed to vote him the powers necessary to deal with the crisis. On June 1, 1958, the National Assembly invested de Gaulle with almost dictatorial powers and elected him premier. De Gaulle then set about to design a constitution that was tailor-made for his beliefs and personal talents. The constitution for the Fifth Republic placed effective power in a president who stood above and directed the political parties in the National Assembly. In December 1958 de Gaulle was elected president for a seven-year term that began on January 8, 1959.

The new French president set about resolving the Algerian crisis. He had been brought to power by military elements who believed that he supported the maintenance of French authority in North Africa. In fact, de Gaulle regarded Algeria as an albatross that was preventing France from taking its rightful place on the world stage. In November 1960 he proposed an independent Algeria, and the proposal was endorsed in a referendum in January 1961. French Algerians revolted, de Gaulle stood firm in the face of repeated assassination attempts, the revolt collapsed, and Algeria became an independent state in September 1962.

De Gaulle's distrust of the Americans and British began to have its effect on French foreign and defense policy shortly after his accession to power. The French leader sincerely believed that it would not be in America's interest to launch a retaliatory nuclear attack on the Soviet Union should the Soviets launch either a conventional or nuclear attack on Europe. Therefore, the only certain way of protecting French national interests was for France to have its own nuclear deterrent. On February 13, 1960, France successfully tested an atomic bomb in the Sahara Desert, thus becoming the world's fourth nuclear power.

De Gaulle now set about his policy of distancing France from Britain and the United States and, at the same time, improving relations with the Soviet Union. He blocked British entry into the European Economic Community, barred American nuclear warheads from French territory and denied French rocket sites to the United States. He also established diplomatic relations with communist China and condemned American involvement in the Vietnam War, which he thought should be resolved by a strict policy of neutrality by all the great powers.

The French leader believed that the differences between the great power blocs, East and West, would gradually blur and disappear and that if France maintained good relations with both the United States and the Soviet Union, it would emerge in a powerful role. His policy of détente with the Soviet Union and cool relations with the Anglo-American West reached its peak in 1966 when he took France out of the military structure of NATO and made a triumphant tour of the Soviet Union and Eastern Europe. He later wrote, "My design consists . . . in disengaging France, not from the Atlantic Alliance, which I intend to maintain as an ultimate precaution, but from the integration realized by NATO under American command; in forging with each of the states of the Eastern Bloc, and first with Russia, relations aimed at an easing of tensions, then at understanding and cooperation; in doing the same, when the moment comes, with China; finally in providing ourselves with a nuclear power of such force that nobody could attack us without risking terrible wounds."

Another major element of de Gaulle's foreign policy was rapprochement with Germany in order to create the core of a Europe-oriented political and defense structure that would be more independent of the United States. In this aim, he found common cause with West German chancellor KONRAD ADENAUER, and on January 22, 1963, the two men signed the FRANCO-GERMAN FRIENDSHIP TREATY to end the "centuries-old rivalry" between the two countries.

De Gaulle's relationship with U.S. president DWIGHT EISENHOWER had been formed during the war when Eisenhower had been supreme commander of Allied troops in Europe. In September 1959 Eisenhower visited Paris for talks with de Gaulle, who proposed that the supranational command structure of NATO be dissolved and replaced with an organization composed of France, Britain and the United States, which would coordinate the political policies of the three nations in every area of the world. This was rejected by Eisenhower, who feared it would lead to the complete dissolution of NATO and a backlash from the developing world.

President JOHN F. KENNEDY and de Gaulle met during Kennedy's European tour in June 1961. The West was in the middle of another Berlin Crisis, and de Gaulle advised Kennedy to take a strong stand and make it clear to NIKITA KHRUSHCHEV that the West was prepared to fight for Berlin and that such a fight would quickly lead to an all-out East–West war.

Franco–American relations reached their nadir during the administration of President LYNDON JOHNSON. In March 1966, de Gaulle took France completely out of the military structure of NATO. The move caused a major crisis within the Western Alliance, and NATO's headquarters had to be moved quickly from outside Paris to Brussels; American bases in France had to be rapidly dismantled. Johnson's immediate reaction was uncharacteristically diplomatic, but he later described the action as "ill-considered and dangerous." De Gaulle's stand on Vietnam also damaged relations with Johnson. On August 30, 1968, he visited Cambodia and called for an American pledge to withdraw its forces within a "fixed and suitable period."

De Gaulle was elected to a second term in January 1966, but in March 1968 students at the University of Nanterre rioted over the issue of education reform. The riots spread to Paris, and in May 1968 there was a near-revolution as police and students fought a month-long battle. The issues had changed from educational reform to complete political, social and economic reform. De Gaulle went on national radio to warn that he would restore law and order "with all the means at his disposal." Hundreds of thousands of Gaullist supporters swept into the streets to support their leader, and the left-wing students backed down.

But de Gaulle's faith in his belief that he was France was shaken. If a large proportion of students and workers rioted against his government then he could not, in all honesty, claim to represent all of France. In April 1969 de Gaulle called a referendum on the issue of the future regional structure of France. He made it clear that if he lost the referendum he would resign. The issue was relatively minor, but its timing and de Gaulle's stand turned it into a vote on the wider issue of an endorsement of de Gaulle's political beliefs. He lost and retired to his modest home in Colombey to write his memoirs. He died the following year.

The major issue that now faced France was whether Gaullism could survive without de Gaulle. Initially, a limited form of Gaullism survived under Georges Pompidou, who succeeded de Gaulle as president and leader of the RPR. Pompidou, however, substantially altered the Gaullist foreign policy. He encouraged British entry into the EEC and formed a particularly close relationship with Prime Minister EDWARD HEATH. Pompidou also eased tensions with the United States. He was responsible too for altering France's nuclear policy. Under de Gaulle France had adopted the AILLERET DOCTRINE, which declared that the French nuclear deterrent must be completely independent and able to strike in any direction at any time. But in 1969 Pompidou's FOURQUET PLAN specifically identified the Soviet Union as the target of the French nuclear forces and implied a link with the United States strategic force as the ultimate deterrent.

Pompidou's sudden death in April 1974 caught the Gaullists unawares, and they were divided over the choice of a successor. A sizable proportion of the party broke ranks with the mainstream and supported VALERY GISCARD-D'ESTAING, leader of the small Independent Republican Party. Giscard went on to narrowly defeat the Socialist candidate FRANCOIS

MITTERRAND in the May 1974 presidential elections. A special concern of Giscard's was the strengthening of the Franco-German Alliance, and in 1976 he declared that French and German security interests were inextricably bound together and that French defense of Germany was a vital element in the defense of the French national territory. Giscard also strove to involve France more in African affairs. He maintained a large French military presence on the continent through a number of bilateral treaties and in 1978 sent French troops to rescue Europeans and support the Zairean government of President Mobutu Sese Seko, who was being threatened by Soviet- and Cuban-backed guerrillas of the Congolese National Liberation Front.

Giscard lost the May 1981 presidential elections to Mitterrand. The Socialist Party leader had earlier formed a "Common Program" with the communists and some left-wing members of the Radical Party. Following legislative elections in June 1981, Mitterrand appointed four communists to his Cabinet. It was the first time since 1946 that the pro-Moscow French Communist Party had been represented in the French government, and the situation caused concern in Washington. But Mitterrand, if anything, was more of an Atlanticist than any of his predecessors and soon broke with the Communist Party. He supported the deployment of American cruise and PERSHING II MISSILES in Europe, sent French troops to protect Chad from an invasion by Libya, joined America and Britain in a military intervention in Lebanon, and supported President RONALD REAGAN's "STAR WARS" plan. During a visit to the United States in March 1984, Mitterrand said that the United States could depend upon France to be "a constant ally that can be counted upon to bring an original contribution" to the search for world peace. Mitterrand was reelected president in 1988.

The French government was supportive of Soviet president MIKHAIL GORBACHEV and his reform policies. Mitterrand visited the Soviet Union in 1989, and Gorbachev traveled to France in 1989, 1990 and 1991, where he signed friendship and economic aid treaties. France also played a key role in the two-plus-four talks that led to the reunification of Germany in October 1990.

Mitterrand and U.S. president BUSH enjoyed a warm working relationship, but the French continued to let their independent streak show on occasion. At a September 2, 1991, meeting of the ruling Socialist Party, Foreign Minister Roland Dumas said that the deterioration of the Soviet Union meant that "American might reigns without balancing weight." He added, "Our American friends . . . must realize that being the world's top power creates not only possibilities and rights but also duties." He suggested that the European Community and the United Nations should seek to balance U.S. power.

For Further Information:
Aldrich, Robert, and John Connell, eds. *France in World Politics.* New York, 1989.
Hartley, Anthony. *Gaullism: The Rise and Fall of a Political Movement.* New York, 1972.

Kissinger, Henry. *The Troubled Partnership*. New York, 1966.

Kulski, Wladislaw. *De Gaulle and the World*. Syracuse, N.Y., 1966.

MacKay, D. *The United States and France*. Westport, Conn., 1983.

Newhouse, John. *De Gaulle and the Anglo-Saxons*. New York, 1970.

Williams, Philip. *Crisis and Compromise: Politics in the Fourth Republic*. London, 1964.

Franco, General Francisco   (December 4, 1892–November 20, 1975)

General Francisco Franco was one of the few fascist dictators to survive World War II. His tough anti-communist position secured him a generous amount of American aid, but his ruthless suppression of political opposition and past associations with Hitler and Mussolini were a considerable embarrassment to the West.

Franco was the second son of a naval paymaster. After attending the Spanish Infantry Academy at Toledo he fought in Morocco, where he earned a reputation for bravery. In 1923, he was given command of the Spanish Foreign Legion. His successful campaign against the Rif rebellion in Morocco made him a national hero.

After the fall of the Spanish monarchy in 1931, the new Republican government adopted an antimilitary policy, and Franco was placed on the inactive list. When the conservatives regained power in 1933, he resumed his active command and the following year was promoted to major general. In May 1935, he was appointed chief of the Spanish Army's general staff. After the February 1936 general election, the country divided into two opposing power blocs, the left-wing Popular Front and the right-wing National Bloc. Franco, who at this stage was not a member of any political party, appealed to the government to declare a state of emergency. The appeal was rejected, and Franco was sent into virtual exile in Tenerife.

In July 1936, Franco declared a military rebellion. That same day fighting broke out on the mainland, and Franco flew to Morocco, where he took command of the right-wing rebel forces. The Italian Fascist leader Benito Mussolini provided him with air transport for an invasion of the Spanish mainland, and the German Third Reich provided him with air cover and military equipment in Spain. The resultant war became a testing ground for many of Germany and Italy's tactics and equipment used in World War II. The war finally ended on April 1, 1939, with a victory for Franco.

Franco was essentially a military dictator, and throughout his long rule his power base was entirely in the military. However, he formed a working relationship with the Spanish fascist Party, the Falange, which became the official ruling party of Spain. But Franco always controlled the party through the military. During World War II he was a pro-German neutral, and his keeping Spain out of the war was one of his greatest diplomatic achievements.

His most difficult period came immediately after the war. Franco was the only major fascist leader left in Europe and an object of censure for every European country that had either fought against or been occupied by Germany. Spain was barred from membership in the United Nations, which, in December 1946, recommended the withdrawal of diplomatic representatives from Spain. Franco might well have been toppled in the 1950s if it had not been for the Cold War.

The EISENHOWER administration, in particular, was more impressed with Franco's anti-communism than put off by his fascism. The need for strategic bases on the Iberian Peninsula outweighed any reluctance to be associated publicly with the Franco dictatorship. Negotiations for American air bases started early in the TRUMAN administration, prompted by the outbreak of fighting in Korea; an agreement was signed on September 26, 1953. It provided for American aid to Spain in return for the use of the bases, which gave the United States a strategic air presence in the Mediterranean and North Africa. It was agreed that the Spanish flag would fly over all U.S. bases and that U.S. personnel would not wear their uniforms outside the bases.

In December 1959, President Dwight Eisenhower visited Spain and personally embraced Franco. He later wrote in his memoirs, "I found him personable and agreeable—indeed, sufficiently so that I wonder what the consequence would be if he became willing to hold free elections?" The strong relationship with the United States protected Franco both within and without Spain, but it was not strong enough to guarantee him membership in the two primary Western "clubs"—the NORTH ATLANTIC TREATY ORGANIZATION and the EUROPEAN ECONOMIC COMMUNITY. These remained closed to dictatorships, and Spain was not granted admission until several years after the death of Franco.

The main thrust of Spain's foreign policy, other than the establishment of a special relationship with the United States, was directed toward the recovery of Gibraltar from Britain, the maintenance of good relations with the emerging Arab world and colonial problems. In 1966 Franco closed the border with Gibralter in an unsuccessful effort to force the British to cede sovereignty. The increasingly bitter dispute between Spain and Britain only isolated Franco further from NATO's second-most-important member.

In the 1960s and 1970s, as Spain's domestic economy improved, Franco started to relieve some of the more repressive elements of his regime. Censorship was relaxed and some opposition groups were allowed to operate unofficially. Workers were allowed to strike, and after 1972 the special tribunals were abolished and military courts had their powers curbed.

In 1968–69 disorders began in the Basque province. The rebellion led by the separatist movement ETA proved to be the greatest challenge to Franco's authority. The continuing disturbances in this traditional stronghold of Republicanism led to some of the worst excesses of Franco's last years and lost him some support from army officers who disliked the military's repressive role in the region.

The final years of Franco's rule were absorbed by the problems in the Basque country and the restoration of the monarchy under Prince Juan Carlos. In June 1973, Franco separated the duties of head of state and head of government, shedding a substantial part of his own authority and ensuring that Juan Carlos would be a constitutional monarch. He appointed his long-time friend and committed Falangist, Admiral Luis Carrero Blanco, as prime minister, with the intention that he continue the Francoist regime. But Carrero Blanco was assassinated shortly afterward by Basque separatists. When Franco died on November 20, 1975, the way was clear for King Juan Carlos to reintroduce democracy to Spain.

For Further Information:
Beaulac, Willard Leon. *Franco: Silent Ally in World War II.* Carbondale, Ill., 1986.
Coles, Sydney. *Franco of Spain.* New York, 1955.
Crozier, Brian. *Franco, A Biographical History.* London, 1967.
Fusi Aizpurua, Juan Pablo. *Franco: A Biography.* New York, 1987.
Manuel, F. E. *The Politics of Modern Spain.* Westport, Conn., 1974: reprint of 1938 edition.
Preston, Paul. *The Politics of Revenge: Fascism and the Military in Twentieth-Century Spain.* Boston, 1990.
Trythall, John W. *Franco.* New York, 1970.

Franco–German Friendship Treaty (1963) The Franco–German Friendship Treaty of 1963 ended centuries of rivalry between the two countries and established a close partnership that became a foundation stone of West European unity.

The traditional enmity between the two countries over the Alsace and Saar regions was a primary cause of the Franco–Prussian War, World War I and World War II. French suspicion of Germany was the main reason for the collapse of the EUROPEAN DEFENSE COMMUNITY. It became clear by the early 1960s that moves toward European unity could not be achieved unless the two traditional rivals were brought closer together.

The result was the Franco–German Friendship Treaty, signed by President CHARLES DE GAULLE and Chancellor KONRAD ADENAUER in Paris on January 22, 1963. A joint statement issued after the signing ceremony proclaimed the belief of the two leaders that the treaty sealed "the reconciliation of the German people and the French people, ending a centuries-old rivalry," and was a "historic event that profoundly [transformed] the relations between the two peoples." The "reinforcement of cooperation between the two countries," they declared, "constitutes an indispensable stage on the way to a united Europe which is the aim of the two peoples."

The main points of the treaty were:

1. The French and West German heads of government were to meet at least twice a year to coordinate policies; foreign ministers four times a year; defense ministers four times a year and officials from key ministries were to meet monthly.
2. The two governments agreed to "consult before any decision on all important questions of foreign policy . . . with a view to reaching as far as possible an analogous position."
3. The two governments agreed to bring their two countries closer together on defense issues, to exchange personnel and to "endeavor to organize work in common from the

stage of drawing up appropriate armament plans and of the preparation of plans for financing them."
4. The two countries agreed to stimulate the teaching of each other's languages, coordinate educational programs, organize student and cultural exchanges and increase the exchange of information between French and German scientific institutes.

The Franco–German relationship continued to be developed by successive governments in both countries, with possibly the closest relationship being that between President VALERY GISCARD-D'ESTAING and Chancellor HELMUT SCHMIDT. On January 22, 1988, President FRANCOIS MITTERRAND and Chancellor HELMUT KOHL marked the 25th anniversary of the treaty with a new treaty that formally established joint councils on defense and economic issues. The treaty included a provision for the establishment of a 4,000-man Franco–German brigade to be based in West Germany.

For West Germany, closer cooperation with France was a step toward bringing France back to the NATO unified military command. In France, its pledge to defend West Germany was seen as an inducement for West Germany not to become a neutral nation as part of a possible future reunification with East Germany. The pact, however, was criticized by other West European leaders, who feared that it would undermine NATO and the WESTERN EUROPEAN UNION.

For Further Information:
Bretano, Heinrich von. *Germany and Europe.* New York, 1964.
Mayne, Richard. *The Recovery of Europe.* New York, 1970.

Frank–Falin Clause The Frank–Falin clause recognizing that West Berlin was a de facto part of West Germany and West Berlin was inserted in most treaties between the Federal Republic of Germany (West Germany) and Soviet Bloc countries, including East Germany.

The clause stated: "In accordance with the Quadripartite Agreement of September 3, 1971, this agreement (or this treaty) shall be extended to Berlin in accordance with established procedures." The clause clearly indicated that a treaty concluded by the government of West Germany also applied to West Berlin as long as the Western powers responsible for Berlin had no objections, thus acknowledging West Germany's de facto responsibility for West Berlin's foreign policy matters.

Freedom House Freedom House is a New York-based political think tank and advocacy group that places a strong emphasis on human rights issues.

Freedom House was founded in 1941, and its charter specifically states that it should be neither anti-fascist nor anti-communist. Its early supporters included ELEANOR ROOSEVELT and U.S. presidential candidate Wendell Wilkie. Other members have been ZBIGNIEW BRZEZINSKI and U.S. arms negotiator MAX KAMPELMAN. Freedom House's main focus is on foreign affairs, although it also became involved in domestic issues such as the U.S. civil rights movement in the 1960s.

The organization publishes several books each year, mainly on human rights issues, and a bimonthly magazine, *Freedom at Issue*. The magazine prints a register of political rights and civil liberties in every country, ranked on a scale of one to seven. The register is often quoted by commentators and political figures. Freedom House also sends observers to foreign elections.

Free Rocket   A free rocket is a missile that is neither guided nor controlled after its launch.

All of the early nuclear-armed missiles, such as Thor, Jupiter and Atlas, were free rockets. Such systems were relatively cheap and easy to produce and relied heavily on the explosive yield of their nuclear warheads for their military value.

But the introduction of hardened silos and sophisticated antiballistic missile (ABM) systems meant that the superpowers had to develop equally sophisticated guidance systems to zero in on hardened targets and avoid the radar detection of ABM systems.

Freikauf   Freikauf was the system of using West German money to buy freedom for East Germans wishing to move to the West. Sometimes the money was paid by the West German government, sometimes by private charitable organizations and sometimes by East German professionals through West German lawyers.

The East German authorities regarded Freikauf (literally translated as "buying out") as recompense for the money expended by the state for free education, health care and subsidies for food, housing and other essentials. In 1988 an estimated 20,000 East Germans emigrated to West Germany as a result of Freikauf payments.

French Indochina War   The French Indochina War from 1945 to 1954 was the result of the French desire to reestablish its colonial authority over postwar Vietnam. The French defeat resulted in the partition of Vietnam into communist North Vietnam and American-supported South Vietnam.

France had been the colonial power in Vietnam since 1880. However, from the 1920s onward the French faced an increasingly powerful nationalist movement known as the Viet Minh and led by communists under HO CHI MINH.

During World War II, Vietnam was administered by the Vichy government in France on behalf of the Japanese, who operated freely in the country. It was not until the fall of Vichy in 1945 that the French were expelled or imprisoned by the Japanese. During the World War II, Ho's Viet Minh had become the only effective nationalist guerrilla organization fighting both the Japanese and French collaborators. The sudden surrender of Japan following their expulsion of the French left Ho's Viet Minh the only cohesive political unit in

Vietnam at the end of the war. On September 2, 1945, Ho proclaimed the Democratic Republic of Vietnam.

The French, however, were determined to reassert their authority. Under the terms of the POTSDAM TREATY they were reinstated as the political power in Vietnam. The British were given immediate authority to secure the southern half of Vietnam and the Nationalist Chinese under CHIANG KAI-SHEK were given authority in the North. The treaty did not recognize Ho's government. The British secured the south of the country, drove the Viet Minh out of Saigon and freed imprisoned French officials. But Chiang, who was increasingly preoccupied with his own civil war, did little in North Vietnam, and Ho was able to consolidate his position around Hanoi. French forces arrived in Vietnam on September 23, 1945, and effectively drove the Viet Minh out of the southern half of the country.

Neither side, however, wanted a long-drawn-out conflict, and they reached a negotiated settlement in March 1946 that extended French recognition to the Viet Minh government and gave Vietnam the status of a "free state" within the French Union. French troops were to be progressively withdrawn from Vietnam over a period of five years.

The agreement lasted only nine months as it became clear that the two sides remained basically irreconcilable, with the Viet Minh committed to complete independence and the French committed to the reassertion of their authority. On November 23, 1946, tensions erupted with the French naval bombardment of Haiphong Harbor. Three weeks later, the Viet Minh attacked French forces in Hanoi.

From 1946 to 1949 the French appeared to have the upper hand in the subsequent war, but after 1949, the new communist government in China started to provide aid to the Viet Minh. This alarmed the United States, which, after 1950, became increasingly supportive of the French forces. American military aid to French operations in Vietnam totaled $2.9 billion. The aid included covert operations directed by the CENTRAL INTELLIGENCE AGENCY, American aircraft, American personnel to service the aircraft and, toward the end of the French involvement, American transport planes and naval detachments.

In 1949 the French organized a new and formally independent government known as the State of Vietnam. Although this government had formal responsibility for all of Vietnam, its effective authority was concentrated in the southern part of the country, and it became the nucleus of the later Republic of South Vietnam. The French hoped that the State of Vietnam would attract anti-communist nationalists, but as the communists symbolized nationalism, the new government attracted few genuinely nationalist figures. The formation of the government, therefore, had the effect of increasing the popularity of the Viet Minh.

Between 1950 and 1954 the balance of power swung dramatically in favor of the Viet Minh, who fought an increasingly effective guerrilla war. The French tried to counter the guerrilla attacks with conventional forces. In 1954 they gathered a large conventional army at DIEN BIEN PHU for what they hoped would be a decisive battle; it was, but not in their favor.

The position was badly chosen. The French Army was in a large natural bowl ringed by hills and mountains, which were quickly occupied by a tightening circle of Viet Minh guerrillas. The siege of Dien Bien Phu reinforced growing public disenchantment with the war in metropolitan France. The EISENHOWER administration tried to organize a British, French and American force to rescue the French army. The British, however, felt that the cause was lost, and in the middle of the American diplomatic maneuverings the pro-war government of Premier Joseph Laniel fell, and the new French premier, Pierre Mendes-France, announced that he was prepared to negotiate with the Viet Minh.

The result was the 1954 GENEVA CONFERENCE ON INDOCHINA AND KOREA, which formally divided Vietnam into North and South with the Viet Minh in control of the northern half and the American-supported regime in the south. The French agreed to withdraw all their forces, and elections were scheduled for 1956 to unify the country under one government. The United States refused to sign the Geneva Accords and quickly replaced the French as the major Western power in Vietnam (see VIETNAM WAR). The war had resulted in the loss of 92,000 French lives. Another 114,000 French soldiers had been wounded, and 20,000 were listed as missing in action.

For Further Information:
Hammer, Ellen. *The Struggle for Indochina*. New York, 1954.
Kahin, George McTurnan. *Intervention: How America Became Involved in Vietnam*. New York, 1986.
Karnow, Stanley. *Vietnam: A History*. New York, 1984, 1991.
Lancaster, Donald. *The Emancipation of French Indo-China*. New York, 1961.
Sutherland, Ian. *Conflict in Indo-China*. South Melbourne, Australia, 1990.

Fuchs, Klaus   (December 29, 1911–January 28, 1988)
Klaus Fuchs was a naturalized British atomic scientist who passed valuable atomic secrets to the Soviet Union.

The son of a German Lutheran pastor, Fuchs was a student at the University of Kiel when Hitler came to power. He reacted against Nazism by joining the German Communist Party. His parents, concerned about their son's safety, sent Fuchs to Britain shortly before the outbreak of World War II to study at Bristol and Edinburgh universities.

Fuchs was interned as an enemy alien at the start of the war and was shipped to Canada, where he is believed to have made his first contact with Soviet intelligence. In 1942 he was allowed to return to Britain, became a naturalized British subject and obtained a job as a statistician for the British atomic research project. Soon afterward, in 1943, he started passing information to the Soviet Embassy in London.

In 1944 Fuchs was chosen as part of the British team to go to New York to work on the MANHATTAN PROJECT, the top-secret program to develop the first atomic bomb. In New York, Fuchs made contact with Harry Gold and passed American

atomic secrets to Gold and, allegedly, to JULIUS AND ETHEL ROSENBERG.

In 1945, after the successful test firing of the atomic bomb, Fuchs returned to Britain with the other British members of the research team. In Britain, he was appointed head of the theoretical physics division of the Atomic Energy Establishment at Harwell.

In 1949 investigators from the U.S. FEDERAL BUREAU OF INVESTIGATION discovered a British link while investigating the case against the Rosenbergs and Gold. Fuchs was pinpointed as the chief suspect and eventually was made to confess. He was sentenced to 14 years' imprisonment.

Fuchs was a model prisoner and was released after nine years. He immediately went to East Germany, where he was granted citizenship and appointed deputy director of the Central Institute for Nuclear Research. It was later reported that he was working in the Soviet Union.

For Further Information:
Nizer, Louis. *The Implosion Conspiracy*. New York, 1973.

Fulbright, J. William   (April 9, 1905–   )   Senator J. William Fulbright was a leading foreign affairs specialist in the U.S. Congress from his election to the House of Representatives in 1942 to his departure from the Senate in 1975. He was chairman of the Senate Foreign Relations Committee from 1959 to 1975.

After graduating from the University of Arkansas in 1925, Fulbright attended Oxford University in England as a Rhodes scholar. Upon his return to the United States, Fulbright took a law degree at George Washington University and then returned to the University of Arkansas as a law instructor. In 1939 he was appointed president of the university.

In 1942 Fulbright, a Democrat, was elected to the U.S. House of Representatives. He immediately secured a place on the House Foreign Affairs Committee and began his long involvement with U.S. foreign policy. He supported President FRANKLIN D. ROOSEVELT's wartime and postwar policies. This support included introducing a resolution in the House supporting American participation in postwar international organizations dedicated to peace. Passage of the resolution was an important precondition of American membership in the United Nations.

In 1944 Fulbright won election to the Senate and almost immediately introduced a bill to establish a federally financed exchange scholarship fund. Enacted into law in 1945, the program became known as the Fulbright Scholarships and is considered one of the greatest accomplishments of Fulbright's career.

Fulbright was an early internationalist and fought to give greater power to the United Nations, including the power to limit conventional and atomic weapons, and for a World Court with the authority to make binding decisions. He also wanted to abolish the veto in the Security Council, which he saw as a barrier to effective international government. His internationalism also led him to adopt a more dovish position on early Cold War relations with the Soviet Union, but his position changed after the Soviets rejected the BARUCH Plan. Fulbright supported the TRUMAN DOCTRINE, the MARSHALL PLAN and the NORTH ATLANTIC TREATY ORGANIZATION, but early foreign policy disagreements with President HARRY TRUMAN never healed, and the two men rarely spoke after Fulbright called for Truman's resignation in 1947 following the Democrats' mid-term defeat in the congressional elections.

During the 1950s Fulbright had several public clashes with the right-wing Senator JOSEPH MCCARTHY. These involved a quarrel over the nomination of Philip Jessup as a delegate to the United Nations and McCarthy's allegations in 1954 that the Fulbright scholarship program had been infiltrated by communists. In early 1954 Fulbright was the only senator to vote against further appropriations for McCarthy's Permanent Investigations Subcommittee, and he took a leading role in the move to censure the Wisconsin senator.

Fulbright was even more critical of President DWIGHT EISENHOWER's foreign policy than he had been of Truman's, declaring it too ideologically oriented. He stressed the need to supply economic and technical aid to allies rather than military aid and opposed the administration's dependence on nuclear weapons. He opposed the establishment of the SOUTHEAST ASIA TREATY ORGANIZATION, the EISENHOWER DOCTRINE and the FORMOSA DOCTRINE.

In 1959 Fulbright became chairman of the Senate Foreign Relations Committee and was considered as a possible secretary of state by President JOHN F. KENNEDY, with whom he had a good relationship. Fulbright was rejected because of his conservative record on civil rights issues.

During the Kennedy administration, Fulbright worked to achieve a major shift in American policy toward the Soviet Union. He wanted it moved from ideological grounds to a traditional great-power rivalry wherein policies were determined by national rather than uncompromising ideological interests. Fulbright played down the influence of communism in the Third World, where, he said, the West could make great gains through the judicious use of economic aid. Fulbright's thinking had a major impact on the Kennedy administration, especially in the president's efforts to develop closer relations with the emerging nations of Africa.

Although Fulbright fought for quiet diplomacy in the conduct of U.S.–Soviet relations, he took a hard line during the CUBAN MISSILE CRISIS. During the meeting on October 22, 1962, between Kennedy and congressional leaders, Fulbright argued for an immediate invasion of Cuba. He argued that this was less likely to result in a direct clash between American and Soviet forces than a U.S. naval blockade of the island, which involved American ships' stopping Soviet ships in international waters.

Fulbright was a close friend of LYNDON JOHNSON, and when the latter became president following the assassination of Kennedy, he gave his unreserved support to Johnson's foreign policy. This included the GULF OF TONKIN RESOLUTION of 1964, which gave Johnson almost blanket authority to conduct the VIETNAM WAR as he wished. Fulbright later bitterly regretted his support and in 1968 held hearings that raised serious questions about the actual occurrence of the incident in the gulf. Fulbright charged that the resolution was passed "on information which was not true." Two years later the Gulf of Tonkin Resolution was repealed.

His last 10 years in the Senate were dominated by the Vietnam War, with Fulbright maintaining that America's conflict was not primarily with an ideologically dominated communist monolith, as claimed by administration officials, but with a nationalist movement. In February 1966 he held televised hearings into the administration's Vietnam policy. Both critics of the administration's policy, including GEORGE F. KENNAN and JAMES GAVIN, and supporters, such as Secretary of State DEAN RUSK and General MAXWELL TAYLOR, gave evidence. Fulbright used the hearings to question the ethics of using the South Vietnamese people to fight America's ideological war. Fulbright continued his attacks on the morality of the war in a series of lectures at Johns Hopkins University in April 1966.

The lectures were published in the 1967 bestseller *The Arrogance of Power*, along with Fulbright's proposals for ending the war. These included de-escalation of American involvement, an end to the bombing of North Vietnam, truce negotiations and a referendum on the issue of reunification. If this course failed, then, Fulbright said, the United States should commit itself to an indefinite defense of specific areas of South Vietnam.

Fulbright's lectures, articles and books established him as the leading congressional "dove." He continued in this role during the NIXON and FORD administrations and tried to shift control of the war from the White House to the Senate. In February 1969 he introduced a "national commitments" resolution, which stipulated that the legislative and executive branches must both agree before U.S. troops could be sent abroad. In 1972 he supported legislation requiring the secretary of state to submit to Congress the text of any international agreement made by the executive. In 1971, after the Nixon administration invaded Cambodia and provided support for a South Vietnamese invasion of Laos, Fulbright held "end-the-war" hearings aimed at the introduction of further legislation to curb the president's power to wage war without legislative approval. The hearings resulted in the 1973 War Powers Act.

Fulbright was also a stern critic of the Safeguard antiballistic missile (ABM) system. He claimed that the system had little defensive value and was "purely a political gimmick." In June 1969 he signed a Senate petition calling for a moratorium on the Safeguard system, and in August of that year voted in favor of an unsuccessful amendment to the defense procurement bill to bar funds for the ABM. Fulbright blamed the military bureaucracy of the Pentagon for the decision to go ahead with the ABM. In his 1970 book *The Pentagon Propaganda Machine* he claimed that militarism was "slowly undermining democratic procedure and values."

Fulbright continued to write books critical of American foreign relations. In 1972 he published *The Crippled Giant*, which examined postwar American foreign policy. In this book he claimed that American foreign policy makers were "driven by a sense of imperial destiny." He claimed that this encouraged the use of unbridled force, which would eventually destroy American democracy and leave it a "moral wasteland."

It was not until HENRY KISSINGER became secretary of state that Fulbright softened his attacks on American foreign policy. He supported Kissinger's policy of détente and his attempts to achieve progress through quiet diplomacy rather than through the threat or use of force. In 1974 Fulbright lost his Senate seat in the Democratic primaries to Arkansas governor Dale Bumpers. His defeat was attributed to his preoccupation with foreign affairs at the expense of his constituency's interests. Fulbright opened a law office in Washington, D.C. and in 1976 registered as a lobbyist for the Saudi Arabian government.

For Further Information:

Berman, W.C. *William Fulbright and the Vietnam War*. Kent, Ohio, 1988.

Fulbright, J. William. *The Arrogance of Power*. New York, 1967.

———. *The Crippled Giant*. Cambridge, Mass., 1972.

———. *Prospects for the West*. Cambridge, Mass., 1963.

Fulbright, J. William, with Seth P. Tillman. *The Price of Empire*. London, 1989.

Johnson, Haynes, and Bernard M. Gwertzman. *Fulbright: The Dissenter*. New York, 1968.

G

Gaither Report The Gaither Report was commissioned by President DWIGHT EISENHOWER to study Soviet offensive capabilities. The report, which was leaked to the press a month after the launching of the Soviet satellite SPUTNIK, warned that the Soviet Union was likely to achieve superiority in missiles by 1959 and called for a massive increase in defense spending and civil defense. The subsequent debate over the "missile gap" became a major issue in the 1960 presidential election campaign.

The Gaither Report was prepared by a blue-ribbon committee chaired by H. Rowan Gaither, former president of the Ford Foundation. Officially the committee was called "The Security Resources Panel of the Office of Defense Mobilization Science Advisory Committee." Its purpose was to examine America's civil defense capabilities, the deterrent value of the American defense forces and the economic and political consequences of any significant change in the defense program.

The report was secretly presented to President Eisenhower in November 1957, and a week later a roughly accurate synopsis appeared in the press. The report's key observations included:

1. The Soviet gross national product was one-third that of the United States but was increasing at a much faster rate than that of America.
2. Soviet spending on heavy industry and defense was equal to that of America.
3. The Soviet Union had sufficient fissionable material for at least 1,500 nuclear weapons in 4,500 long- and short-range jet bombers, 250–300 long-range submarines and an extensive air defense system.
4. The Soviet Union had been producing ballistic missiles with a 700-mile range for more than a year.
5. The Soviet Union could, by late 1959, possibly launch an attack against the United States with 100 intercontinental ballistic missiles carrying megaton nuclear warheads; if such an attack came, the American civilian population would be unprotected and the aircraft in the U.S. Strategic Air Command would be vulnerable.

To address these problems, the committee recommended the following:

1. That the U.S. government start building fallout shelters on a massive scale.
2. That the U.S. government improve the country's air defense capability.
3. That the U.S. government pool technological resources with its allies to increase the Strategic Air Command's offensive power and the alliance's ability to fight a limited war.
4. That the U.S. government step up its antisubmarine activities.
5. That the Pentagon be reorganized and interservice rivalries ended.

President Eisenhower disagreed with many of the basic assumptions and conclusions of the report. For a start, he thought that the committee had failed to take into account the advantage America gained over the Soviet Union from the dispersion of its forces over a number of overseas bases. He also agreed with Secretary of State JOHN FOSTER DULLES' opposition to a major program of building fallout shelters.

The Gaither Report fueled criticism of the Eisenhower administration's defense policies. As early as January 1956 Senator HENRY JACKSON had maintained that a "missile gap" existed between the Soviet Union and the United States and that the United States should invest in a crash program to develop its force of intercontinental ballistic missiles. Following the Gaither Report, Senator JOHN F. KENNEDY in January 1958 joined Jackson in accusing the Eisenhower administration of allowing a missile gap to develop. Kennedy pursued the issue throughout his presidential campaign, and it helped to counter arguments that he would be "soft" on defense. Later, his secretary of defense, ROBERT MCNAMARA, disowned the missile gap.

For Further Information:
Bottome, Edgar M., *The Missile Gap*. Rutherford, N.J., 1971.
Halperin, Morton. "The Gaither Committee and the Policy Process," *World Politics* (April 1961).
Huntington, Samuel P. *The Common Defense: Strategic Programs in National Politics*. New York, 1961.
Witkin, Richard, ed. *The Challenge of Sputnik*. Garden City, N.Y., 1958.

Galbraith, John Kenneth (October 15, 1908–   ) John Kenneth Galbraith was a leading liberal economist and diplomat who served as the influential U.S. ambassador to India during the KENNEDY administration. He later became president of the Americans for Democratic Action and a leading critic of American involvement in Vietnam.

Galbraith was born and raised in Ontario, Canada and studied at the University of Toronto before attending the University of California, Berkeley, where he was awarded his doctorate in economics in 1934. After receiving his Ph.D., Galbraith attended Cambridge University in England and then took a teaching post at Harvard and adopted American citizenship. He joined the faculty of Princeton University in 1939 but two years later moved to Washington and joined the wartime Office of Price Administration. His rigorous application of price controls made him unpopular with businessmen, and he was forced to resign in 1943.

Galbraith then moved from government service to journalism as a member of the editorial board of *Fortune* magazine. In 1945 he took a leave of absence to serve as joint director of the U.S. Strategic Bombing Survey, followed by a period as an economics adviser to the State Department. Galbraith returned to *Fortune* until 1949, when he resumed teaching economics at Harvard.

At Harvard, Galbraith developed a reputation as the leading liberal American economist; he wrote several popular books on economics and produced a television series on the subject. Perhaps the best known of his publications is *The Affluent Society*, published in 1958. Others included *American Capitalism* (1952) and *The New Industrial State* (1967).

Galbraith also became increasingly active in liberal Democratic Party politics. He worked as a speechwriter for ADLAI STEVENSON during the 1952 presidential campaign and afterward became a vocal critic of the Eisenhower administration's economic policies. Galbraith was an early supporter of JOHN F. KENNEDY's bid for the presidency and played a major role in winning support for Kennedy within liberal and academic circles. During the Kennedy campaign he served as an adviser on agricultural economics.

Kennedy initially offered Galbraith the post of chairman of the Council of Economic Advisers. Galbraith, however, had long been interested in India and asked to be sent there as ambassador. Good relations with India were considered a vital element in the Kennedy administration's foreign policy. The president had decided to give a high priority to developing closer links with the Third World and its leaders, and India, the world's largest democracy, was the most important of the Third World countries.

Galbraith formed a close relationship with Indian leader Jawaharlal Nehru and won some early laurels by immediately putting a halt to CIA covert operations in India. Nehru, a founder of the NONALIGNED MOVEMENT, based his foreign policy on maintaining a neutral position on the Cold War while at the same time developing close relations with both the United States and the Soviet Union. This unique position gave Nehru an opportunity to arbitrate regularly in disputes between the superpowers. Galbraith played a major role in

persuading Nehru to arbitrate the 1961 negotiations that established the neutral status of Laos.

While India enjoyed good relations with both the superpowers, its relations with China were tense, and in October 1962 they erupted into a border war in the Himalayas. The Sino-Indian Border War coincided with the CUBAN MISSILE CRISIS and thus found Washington preoccupied. This meant that Galbraith was left to deal with the situation in the Himalayas largely on his own. As the Chinese offensive progressed, the Indians turned increasingly toward the United States for military supplies and guidance, which Galbraith quickly secured. Faced with the possibility of American intervention in support of India, the Chinese withdrew in November 1962.

Galbraith also built up American economic aid to India, which during his tenure totaled $670 million. Among his contributions was the formulation of what Galbraith called the "mass consumption standard." This meant that American investment should be "strongly guided to those industries that directly or ultimately served the needs of the masses of the people.

While in India, Galbraith also visited Vietnam on a personal mission for Kennedy in November 1961. Kennedy wanted Galbraith to make a personal assessment of the security situation and the regime of President NGO DINH DIEM. Galbraith was critical of the inefficiency and corruption of both the Diem regime and the South Vietnamese military, and he reported that the South Vietnamese were losing the war. He went on to urge the president not to oppose any coup attempt and to "measurably reduce" the American commitment to Vietnam until the Diem regime was replaced. He also stressed that the United States should strive to find a political rather than military solution to the problem of Vietnam.

Galbraith left India in 1963 to return to his teaching post at Harvard. He retained his interest in foreign affairs and became an increasingly vocal critic of the VIETNAM WAR. In 1966 he told the Senate Foreign Relations Committee that he rejected the view that "Vietnam is a testing place of American democracy . . . or that it is strategically or otherwise important to U.S. interests." The following year, in April 1967, Galbraith was elected president of the liberal-minded AMERICANS FOR DEMOCRATIC ACTION and used that position to call for a bombing halt in North Vietnam. During the 1968 presidential primaries, Galbraith was foreign policy spokesman for antiwar candidate Senator EUGENE MCCARTHY, and in 1972 supported Senator George McGovern's presidential bid.

During the 1970s, Galbraith returned to his academic career. He taught at Harvard, took up a fellowship at England's Cambridge University and hosted a BBC television program on the history of economics. He retired from his Harvard teaching post in 1975 but continued to write and broadcast on political, economic and foreign policy issues.

For Further Information:
Galbraith, John K. *The Affluent Society.* Boston, 1958.
———. *Ambassador's Journal.* Boston, 1969.

———. *A Life in Our Times.* Boston, 1981.
———. *The New Industrial State.* New York, 1967.
Hession, Charles H. *John Kenneth Galbraith and his Critics.* New York, 1972.

Galosh (ABM-1B)   Galosh is the NATO codename for the Soviet Union's antiballistic missile (ABM) system deployed around Moscow.

The Soviet development of an ABM system led the United States to develop its own similar system. To avoid an escalating arms race in ABM systems, the two countries signed the ANTIBALLISTIC MISSILE TREATY in 1972 limiting their respective antiballistic missile systems.

The Galosh system, still in place, involves 100 operational launchers that fire surface-to-air missiles with a range of about 210 miles and armed with 1-megaton nuclear warheads. The above-ground launchers are located in four complexes to the north and west of the city. The radar used to locate attacking systems and aid in guiding the Galosh missiles is operated from a complex to the south of Moscow. Under the terms of the 1972 ABM Treaty, both the Soviet Union and the United States were allowed only one ABM system. This system could protect either a military installation or the capital city.

Gates, Robert M.   See CENTRAL INTELLIGENCE AGENCY.

Gates, Thomas   (April 10, 1906–March 25, 1983)   Thomas Gates served variously as undersecretary of the navy, deputy secretary of defense and secretary of defense during the EISENHOWER administration. From 1976 to 1977 he led the U.S. Liaison Mission to China.

After graduating from the University of Pennsylvania in 1928, Gates joined the family banking firm of Drexel and Co. During World War II he became involved in naval intelligence in Europe. After the war he returned to Drexel until October 1953, when he was named undersecretary of the navy. Gates was generally a supporter of Eisenhower's "NEW LOOK" DEFENSE POLICY and secured a nuclear delivery role for the navy by stressing that service's ability to provide mobile launching platforms.

In March 1957 President Dwight Eisenhower appointed Gates secretary of the navy. Gates initiated research into the development of nuclear-armed submarines, which eventually became the POLARIS MISSILE program. He also diverted funds from the development of diesel-powered ships to build the first nuclear-powered aircraft carrier.

In 1958 the Pentagon was reorganized to give more power to the defense secretary. Gates was unhappy with the new arrangement and resigned in protest on February 3, 1959. But by June 1959 he was back in government as the deputy secretary of defense. He was appointed secretary of defense on December 1, 1959, after the resignation of Neil McElroy.

Defense issues during the final year of the Eisenhower administration were dominated by the MISSILE GAP debate, and a great deal of Gates' time was devoted to dismissing charges that the United States was under threat as a result of cuts in defense spending. Gates also became involved in the debate surrounding the shooting down of the U-2 spy plane in May 1960. Called to testify before the Senate Foreign Relations Committee, Gates defended the flights on the grounds that they provided the United States with "vital information" on the Soviet Union's war potential.

During his testimony, Gates revealed that he and other top defense and foreign policy advisers had decided at a meeting on May 9 that President Eisenhower should publicly assume responsibility for the U-2 flight over the Soviet Union. Gates said, "The prestige of the presidency should not be involved in an international lie, particularly when it would not stand up to the facts."

After JOHN F. KENNEDY's election to the presidency in November 1960, Gates suspended navy and air force projects for new supersonic aircraft and canceled the proposed Skybolt missile system on the grounds that he did not want to commit the new Democratic administration to projects developed at the last minute by the Eisenhower administration. The cancellation of Skybolt caused panic in British defense circles, as Britain was dependent on the American system for delivery of its nuclear weapons. Kennedy mollified the British by offering them Polaris as a replacement.

Gates returned to business in 1961 as president of the Morgan Guaranty Trust Company. In March 1976 President GERALD FORD named Gates to head the United States Liaison Mission to communist China. Gates remained at the post for a year and had little impact on policy, as most of the contacts were at a more senior level. Gates retired from government service in 1977.

For Further Information:
Borklund, C.W. *Men of the Pentagon: From Forrestal to McNamara.* New York, 1966.
Huntington, Samuel. *The Common Defense: Strategic Programs in National Politics.* New York, 1961.
Schilling, Warner, et al. *Strategy, Politics and Defense Budget.* New York, 1962.

Gavin, General James   (March 22, 1907–   )   General James Gavin was a World War II hero who in the 1950s took charge of the U.S. Army's missile development program. In this position he became a fierce critic of President DWIGHT EISENHOWER's defense policies and supported the MISSILE GAP theory. President JOHN F. KENNEDY appointed Gavin ambassador to France, and he later advocated limiting American ground forces in Vietnam to defense operations only.

Gavin first joined the army as a private in 1924, but the following year secured an appointment to the U.S. Military Academy at West Point, and he graduated in 1929. He quickly carved out a niche for himself in air operations and in April 1942 was appointed chief of military operations of the Airborne Command.

Gavin saw active service during World War II commanding

paratroop regiments at the invasions of both Sicily and Normandy and then at the battle of the Bulge. After the war, Gavin, by then a brigadier general, served briefly in an administrative post in Berlin before resuming his post at the Airborne Command. In 1952 he returned to Germany as commander of the Seventh Corps and in 1954 was given the rank of lieutenant general and appointed the army's assistant chief of staff for plans and operations.

Gavin's post at plans and operations put him in charge of the army's missile development program. He soon became a strong and prominent advocate for the increased development of army missiles and urged that they be armed with nuclear warheads. This brought him into conflict with President Eisenhower's "NEW LOOK" DEFENSE POLICY, which stressed the development of air force-controlled strategic bombers armed with nuclear weapons. Eisenhower downgraded the use of tactical nuclear weapons, strategic missiles and conventional weapons.

Gavin argued that missiles were a greater deterrent to the Soviet Union than manned bombers, and in March 1958 he resigned from the army in order to state his case publicly. Shortly afterward he published *War and Peace in the Space Age*, in which he warned that America's heavy reliance on nuclear-armed strategic bombers had left it incapable of fighting limited wars. The book was read by Senator John F. Kennedy, who invited Gavin to become one of his advisers on defense issues. In 1959 Gavin was one of those who claimed that a dangerous "missile gap" existed between the United States and the Soviet Union. The phrase was picked up by Kennedy, and the missile gap (and thus military preparedness) became a major issue in the 1960 presidential campaign. The so-called gap was later found to be nonexistent.

After Kennedy's election, Gavin was appointed ambassador to France. During his stay in Paris, Anglo-French relations plummeted as President CHARLES DE GAULLE exploded the French nuclear bomb, expelled American nuclear weapons from French soil and vetoed British membership in the EUROPEAN ECONOMIC COMMUNITY (EEC). Gavin tried to improve relations by proposing that the United States provide France with nuclear equipment and information in exchange for increased access for American goods to the EEC. Gavin resigned after the proposal was rejected. He claimed that the reason for his resignation was that his lack of a large private income made it impossible for him to maintain the embassy.

While in Paris, Gavin also became involved in negotiations over Laos, and in April and May 1961 he held discussions with neutralist Laotian leader Prince Souvanna Phouma. He urged Kennedy not to commit any American troops in the Laotian civil war and supported the proposed neutrality of that country. He also helped to persuade the president to shift his support away from the right-wing government of General Phoumi Nosavan.

Upon his return to the United States, Gavin rejoined the Boston research and management firm Arthur D. Little and became the chairman of the board in June 1964. He had first joined the company immediately after his retirement from the army.

During the Johnson administration, Gavin was one of the few military figures who favored de-escalation of America's involvement in the VIETNAM WAR. In January 1966 he developed the "Enclave Theory," in which he proposed that American military forces refrain from all offensive operations and instead concentrate their efforts on maintaining fortified support bases and cities. These enclaves would later become bargaining instruments in diplomatic negotiations. To bring about the negotiations, Gavin proposed a halt to bombing raids on North Vietnam. Parts of this theory were later incorporated into President RICHARD NIXON's "Vietnamization" program.

In 1967 Gavin seriously considered running as the Republican Party's "peace candidate" but was dissuaded from doing so by New York governor NELSON ROCKEFELLER. He continued, however, to speak out on the war. He told the Senate Foreign Relations Committee that American bombing missions over North Vietnam were "militarily as well as morally wrong" and in 1968 further developed his enclave theory in his book *Crisis Now*. In May 1970 Gavin called for the withdrawal of all American forces from Vietnam in order to avoid a "catastrophic" confrontation with China. Gavin retired as chairman of Arthur D. Little in 1974.

For Further Information:
Gavin, James. *Crisis Now*. New York, 1968.
———. *War and Peace in the Space Age*. New York, 1958.
Halberstam, David. *The Best and the Brightest*. New York, 1972.
Krepinovich, A.F. *The Army and Vietnam*. Baltimore, 1986.
Smith, R.G. *An International History of the Vietnam War*. New York, 1986.

Gdansk Riots (1970) The Gdansk Riots of 1970 led to the resignation of Polish communist leader WLADYSLAW GOMULKA and underscored the difficulties that the Soviet Bloc countries faced in reforming their heavily subsidized and centralized economies.

The riots were partly the result of years of pent-up political frustration and partly the result of massive price increases introduced as part of an economic reform program.

The long-standing historical enmity between Poland and Russia made Poland the most difficult to manage of the Soviet Union's East European satellite states. These difficulties led to the POZNAN CRISIS of 1956, which established, after several tense weeks, the Polish Communist Party's right to choose its own leadership and domestic policies independent of the Soviet Union.

The Polish communists chose as their leader Wladyslaw Gomulka, a former party secretary general who had been imprisoned for his opposition to Stalinist policies. Upon his accession to power, Gomulka was greeted as a hero by the Polish people, who believed that he would introduce major political and economic reforms.

But Gomulka remained wedded to his communist principles and maintained strict censorship of the press and central control of the economy. By the mid-1960s the Poles, including many inside the party, had become disillusioned with Gomulka. In March 1968 there were widespread student riots, and at the Polish party conference of November 11–16, 1968, some party members attacked the Soviet invasion of Czechoslovakia and tried to identify themselves more closely with the EUROCOMMUNISM emerging in Western Europe.

Gomulka's political problems were exacerbated by the stagnation of the Polish economy, which was a direct result of heavy state subsidies for essential food and fuel products and a centrally directed economic system. To try to mollify his political critics, Gomulka decided to reform the economic system, and on May 19, 1970, he introduced an incentive program for individual workers.

But this measure was inadequate unless it could be successfully coupled to a reduction in state subsidies so that funds could be redirected toward industrial development. This created the further problem of coordinating the inevitable food price rises so that they could be paid for with increased wages. The need for food price rises was increased by poor grain harvests in 1969 and 1970, which raised the subsidy level. The government also wanted to decrease domestic meat consumption in order to increase meat exports to finance imports of Western technology.

On December 13, 1970, the government announced a round of price increases, including 11%–33% in prices of meat and meat products; 8%–25% for cheese, flour, fish and milk; and 10%–20% for coal. The same day, Deputy Premier Stanislaw Kociolek went to Gdansk to meet with workers at the Lenin Shipyard. The meeting was arranged to discuss workers' objections to the wage incentive program, but it quickly turned into an attack on the price increases.

On December 15, 1970, the workers walked out of their jobs at the Lenin Shipyard and marched on the local Communist Party headquarters to demand that someone hear their grievances. Police tried to stop the crowd from reaching the building, and violence erupted. Riot police were bused in from all over northern Poland, and an estimated 300 people were killed.

Riots soon spread to other parts of Poland. In the cities of Sopot and Gdynia riots were accompanied by the looting and burning of shops. Telephone wires were cut in the Silesian mining town of Katowice, and tanks were ordered into the Baltic port of Szczecin to stop the spread of riots by that town's shipyard workers.

On December 20 Gomulka's resignation was announced in a radio broadcast. EDWARD GIEREK was named the party's new first secretary, and he went on Polish television the same day to announce that the recent disturbances had resulted from "hasty concepts of economic policy," which would be removed. On January 1, 1971, the minimum salary was raised 17.6% and allowances for children went up 25%. Then on January 25 the wage incentive scheme was dropped, and on February 15, 1970, the food price rises were revoked.

Gehlen Organization The Gehlen Organization was a freelance West German espionage network that worked closely with the CIA in the late 1940s and early 1950s and later became the West German Federal Intelligence Service (BND).

The Gehlen Organization was founded by General Reinhard Gehlen, head of German Army Intelligence on the Eastern Front during World War II. Because of this position, at the end of the war Gehlen had in place an extensive network of anti-communist agents throughout Eastern Europe. He also had extensive files on Soviet activities in the region.

Gehlen used this information to protect himself from prosecution as a war criminal and to secure American financial backing for the establishment of the Gehlen Organization in July 1946. The organization quickly won a reputation for employing ex-Nazis as its operatives and for adopting a hardline anti-communist stance. (Aside from the moral question of employing Nazis and possible war criminals, some critics have since argued that the United States did itself major practical damage by relying on such a biased intelligence source. The paranoia and distrust of the crucial early Cold War years was fed by Gehlen and his cohorts, who succeeded in convincing key U.S. policymakers that the Soviet Army was poised to invade Western Europe. That overheated view turned out to be erroneous, as some U.S. officials had argued at the time.)

The Gehlen Organization, naturally enough, specialized in espionage and counterespionage activities in East Germany. Gehlen agents infiltrated East German Intelligence at every level and played a major role in building the CIA-backed BERLIN TUNNEL, which gave the CIA access to telephone lines at the Soviet Army headquarters in East Berlin. The Gehlen Organization's infiltration of East Germany was so successful that East German Intelligence offered a reward of one million marks for the murder of General Gehlen. On the other hand, Gehlen's group was also deeply penetrated by Soviet double-agents.

The organization was successful in digging up information on the Soviet Union. It provided the first detailed dossier on the operations of SMERSH, the KGB assassination squad. It also secured the first full text of Soviet leader NIKITA KHRUSHCHEV's secret speech denouncing Stalin before the 20th Soviet Communist Party Congress in 1956.

Gehlen was able to act as a freelance spymaster because the occupying powers in West Germany—Britain, France and the United States—refused to allow the establishment of an autonomous West German Intelligence service. But after the formal end of direct Allied control in 1955, the government of Chancellor KONRAD ADENAUER moved to bring the Gehlen Organization under its political direction. In April 1956 responsibility for the organization's finances and operations was formally transferred to the West German government, and the Gehlen Organization was transformed into the BND. General Gehlen was its first president. He died in 1979.

For Further Information:
Cookridge, E.H. *Gehlen: Spy of the Century*. London, 1971.
Gehlen, Reinhard. *The Gehlen Memoirs*. New York, 1972.

Geneva Conference on Indochina and Korea (1954)

Geneva Conference on Indochina and Korea (1954)   The Geneva Conference on Indochina and Korea resulted in the end of the FRENCH INDOCHINA WAR, the partition of Vietnam and the formation of the SOUTHEAST ASIA TREATY ORGANIZATION.

The conference was originally called to discuss Korea, but the French asked that Indochina be included on the agenda as a result of the worsening French position in the Indochina War. Failure to make any progress on the Korean issue, plus a further deterioration in the French military position, led to Indochina's dominating the conference.

The conference opened on April 26 with foreign ministers from 19 nations, including communist China, present. At the time, the French were fighting a major battle at DIEN BIEN PHU, and the U.S. government was pressing Britain and France for a strong military and political stand both in Indochina and at Geneva. But the British did not want to be drawn into a war in Indochina, and the French government by this time was encountering strong domestic opposition.

The first week of the conference was completely occupied with the issue of Korea. The South Koreans started by demanding free Western-style elections in a united Korea. The North Korean delegation responded by demanding the withdrawal of all foreign troops and the appointment of an all-Korean commission to arrange elections.

The first week of the conference also saw the appearance of CHOU EN-LAI, China's prime minister and foreign minister, on the international stage. Speaking after U.S. secretary of state JOHN FOSTER DULLES, Chou denied that China had been the aggressor in Korea and accused the United States of trying to impose "the Kuomintang remnant clique" on the Chinese people. He went on to call on the Asian nations to "consult among themselves . . . seeking common measures to safeguard peace and security in Asia." The speech was well received in a number of non-communist Asian nations and helped to strengthen China's international position.

Events in Indochina, however, quickly dominated the fringe discussions and soon took center stage at the conference. Dulles believed that he could persuade the French to carry on fighting if they had British and American support and that U.S. congressional support could be assured if Britain agreed to a military commitment. Dulles was also concerned that French collapse in Indochina would result in the collapse of the government of French prime minister Joseph Laniel, which would endanger the proposed EUROPEAN DEFENSE COMMUNITY. British foreign secretary ANTHONY EDEN, however, was afraid that British and American intervention in Indochina would result in a countervailing intervention by China and the Soviet Union, and that this must be avoided at all costs.

At a meeting on April 30, Dulles tried to persuade Eden to accept his plan of action for Indochina. When he failed, a bitter Dulles refused to stay in Geneva to be associated with any political agreement on Indochina. Therefore, on May 1, he announced that he was personally withdrawing from the Geneva Conference and leaving the U.S. delegation under the chairmanship of Undersecretary of State WALTER BEDELL SMITH.

With the American plan in disarray and Dulles back in Washington, Eden took over as de facto leader of the West at the conference. He immediately shifted the focus of the conference from a coordinated Western intervention to a political solution. He started talks with Soviet foreign minister V.M. MOLOTOV, who was keen to reach a political agreement and made it clear to Eden that he feared that failure would strengthen a radical China's position in the region. This was one of the first signs of the coming SINO-SOVIET SPLIT. Eden's position was strengthened on May 7 with the surrender of the French forces at Dien Bien Phu, resulting in the death, wounding or capture of 15,000 French troops. The defeat left France completely demoralized.

Back in Washington, Dulles continued to try to organize Western intervention. He instructed Smith to oppose Eden's attempts to negotiate a political solution and pressed Laniel to request American military intervention. But this effort was thwarted when the Laniel government fell on June 12 over the issue of the war in Indochina. The new prime minister, Pierre Mendes-France, announced that he would negotiate a peace settlement with the Viet Minh by July 20 or resign.

At the same time, British prime minister WINSTON CHURCHILL had become worried that the differences between Dulles and Eden were seriously affecting the Anglo-American Alliance. He and Eden flew to Washington on June 25 to try to repair the damage. They offered to join with the United States in the formation of a Southeast Asia Treaty Organization, which promised British support against future communist aggression in the region, but at the same time the two men made it clear that they did not believe that the current situation was the right time or place for a stand against the Chinese and Soviets.

Dulles and President Dwight Eisenhower welcomed the formation of SEATO but remained opposed to the political solution of the immediate problem, and Dulles steadfastly refused the entreaties of Mendes-France to return to the Geneva Conference. By this time, the French prime minister had decided upon the temporary partition of Vietnam. Mendes-France wanted the dividing line along the 18th parallel, while the Viet Minh insisted that their claim extend from the 13th to the 16th. On July 20, the two sides agreed on the 17th parallel and the agreement was signed on July 21, 1954.

To the very end, the U.S. delegation refused to take part in any negotiations that led to the handing over of territory to communists. Smith refused to sign the agreement and announced that the United States "took note" of the Geneva settlement that temporarily partitioned Vietnam only until free elections could be held.

The main points of the agreement were as follows:

1. The French would evacuate the North Vietnamese Red River delta stronghold of Hanoi within 80 days and Haiphong within 10 months.
2. Communist forces in South Vietnam were to be withdrawn to "concentration areas" from which they were to be evacuated to the north within 10 months.
3. Elections for a unified government were to be held throughout all of Vietnam within two years.
4. Communist forces in Laos were to be concentrated in the two Laotian provinces of Samneua and Phongsaly on the North Vietnamese border.
5. The communists would respect the territorial and political integrity of Cambodia and the rest of Laos.
6. Cambodia and Laos were to be demilitarized and were to retain only forces needed for self-defense. But the French would maintain military units at Seno and at a second Laotian base. They were also to continue training Laotian troops.
7. Prisoners of war and captured civilians were to be exchanged within 30 days.
8. Civilians were to be allowed to move voluntarily from North Vietnam to South Vietnam and vice versa.
9. The agreements were to be supervised by a commission composed of India, Poland and Canada. (For subsequent developments see VIETNAM WAR.)

On September 8, 1954, Australia, Britain, France, New Zealand, Pakistan, the Philippines, Thailand and the United States signed the treaty forming SEATO.

For Further Information:
Cable, James. *The Geneva Conference of 1954 on Indochina.* Hampshire, England, 1986.
Randle, Robert E. *Geneva, 1954: The Settlement of the Indochinese War.* Princeton, 1969.

Geneva Heads of Government Summit (1955) The Geneva Heads of Government Summit Conference of 1955 was the first postwar summit meeting between the heads of government of Britain, France, the Soviet Union and the United States. U.S. president DWIGHT EISENHOWER unveiled his "OPEN SKIES" proposal at the five-day summit, and the four leaders agreed on a set of discussion points for German reunification, a European security treaty and disarmament negotiations. But the "Spirit of Geneva" collapsed at a follow-up conference of foreign ministers.

The summit conference was first proposed on May 11, 1953, by Prime Minister WINSTON CHURCHILL, who believed that efforts should be made to improve relations with the new Soviet leadership following the death of JOSEF STALIN. Because of illnesses, political crises in France and failure of a Big Four foreign ministers' meeting, no progress on the summit was made until 1955, when the signing of the Austrian State Treaty, which provided for the end of the occupation and the neutralization of Austria, helped to melt the Cold War ice and paved the way for a meeting.

The major items on the agenda were the issues of German reunification and disarmament. The purpose of the summit was to define the crucial world problems and then issue a directive to the foreign ministers to work out the details and conduct negotiations. The major participants were President Eisenhower; British prime minister ANTHONY EDEN, who had recently succeeded Churchill; Edgar Faure, who headed the French delegation as prime minister; and NIKOLAI BULGANIN, the head of the Soviet delegation as chairman of the Council of Ministers. NIKITA KHRUSHCHEV as head of the Communist Party also played a major role.

President Eisenhower, as the only head of both state and government, was chosen chairman of the meeting. In his opening remarks he gave precedence to "the problem of unifying Germany and forming an all-German Government based on free elections." He also raised the issue of political freedom in Eastern Europe and stressed that "the American people feel strongly that certain peoples of Eastern Europe . . . have not yet been given the benefit of . . . our wartime declaration."

At the opening session, Faure described the continuance of a divided and unarmed Germany as "brutal" and dismissed the thought that its problems could be solved by reducing Germany further as a political power. Eden then went on to present a Western proposal for a security pact that would include Germany and the Big Four. Under this agreement each member (including the Soviet Union) would declare itself ready to aid any victim of aggression "whoever it might be." Eden also proposed a system of reciprocal control to restrict German armaments and "to examine the possibility of a demilitarized area between East and West."

Bulganin refused to discuss Eastern Europe as "moves toward interference in the affairs of these states." He felt that an all-European security system should precede the unification of Germany, since the "remilitarization of Western Germany and her integration into military groupings of the Western powers [was] the main obstacle" to German unification. Bulganin went on to reiterate a proposal made by Soviet foreign minister V. M. MOLOTOV at the BERLIN FOREIGN MINISTERS' CONFERENCE of 1954. This called for the establishment of a European security system that would bring about the simultaneous termination of the NORTH ATLANTIC TREATY ORGANIZATION and the WARSAW PACT. In an attempt to meet Bulganin's points, the West agreed to consider together the question of German reunification and Bulganin's proposal for a European security system.

On July 21, Eisenhower seized the initiative by launching his Open Skies plan, which called for the exchange of military blueprints and charts and the maintenance by each nation of a fixed number of airfields and aircraft equipped for photographic reconnaissance to inspect each other's territory. Bulganin promised to study the proposals, but Khrushchev, in a private discussion with Eisenhower later that day, said, "I don't agree with the Chairman [Bulganin]."

The final communiqué agreed that foreign ministers should discuss the following:

1. A security pact for Europe, "including provisions for inclusion of member states of an obligation not to resort to force and to deny assistance to an aggressor."
2. "Limitation, control and inspection" of armed forces.
3. The "establishment between East and West of a zone in which the disposition of armed forces would be subject to mutual agreement."
4. The settlement of the German question "and the reunification of Germany by free elections" to be carried out "in conformity with the national interests of the German people and the interests of European security."
5. The establishment of "a system for the control and reduction of all armaments and armed forces under effective safeguards."
6. "Freer contacts and exchanges as are of mutual advantage of the countries and people concerned."
7. The "elimination of barriers which interfere with free communication and peaceful trade between people."

The summit conference was hailed as a diplomatic triumph and a major breakthrough in the Cold War. The speeches and discussions showed a marked departure from the vitriolic recriminations that had characterized most earlier meetings. The same spirit carried over to the follow-up meeting of foreign ministers, which started on October 27, 1955, in Geneva.

Moscow, however, was in the midst of a major internal power struggle, and the Soviet leadership was divided on the direction of its policy toward the West. On November 4 Foreign Minister Molotov returned to Moscow for the November 7 anniversary of the Bolshevik Revolution. When he returned to Geneva on November 8, Molotov had substantially hardened the Soviet position on the whole range of issues, and the Western powers suspended the talks.

For Further Information:
Eisenhower, Dwight D. *The White House Years, Mandate for Change, 1953–56.* Garden City, N.Y., 1963.
———. *The White House Years, Waging Peace, 1956–61.* Garden City, N.Y., 1965.
La Feber, Walter. *America, Russia and the Cold War, 1945–1971.* New York, 1967.
Mackintosh, J.M. *Strategy and Tactics of Soviet Foreign Policy.* New York, 1963.

Geneva Protocol on Gas Warfare (1925) The Geneva Protocol on Gas Warfare, adopted in 1925, was a reaction to the use of gas warfare in World War I. It banned the use of asphyxiating, poisonous or other gas or bacteriological weapons.

The international agreement effectively prevented the use of gas, chemical or germ warfare during World War II, although both sides held stockpiles of such weapons and Germany, in particular, developed an extremely potent nerve gas.

The agreement remains in effect and has generally prevented the widespread use of chemicals, germ or gas warfare, although these weapons were used in the Iran–Iraq War of 1980–88, and the United States claimed that the Soviet Union used chemical weapons in Laos and Afghanistan.

Genscher, Hans-Dietrich   (March 21, 1927–   ) Hans-Dietrich Genscher served as West Germany's foreign minister from May 1974 to May 1992, making him the longest-serving foreign minister in the Western world. He played an important role in the implementation of OSTPOLITIK, in moves toward European integration, in German reunification and in discussions on the deployment of American nuclear missiles in Europe.

Genscher was born in the Prussian province of Saxony and in 1943, before he finished his high school education, was drafted into the German air force (Luftwaffe). He went from the air force to the wartime national labor service and then to the German Army before being taken prisoner by American forces in 1945.

After his release, Genscher returned to his home, which was by then part of the Soviet-occupied sector of Germany. He studied law and economics, first at the Martin Luther University in Halle and then at the University of Leipzig, where he passed his bar exams in 1949.

Genscher quickly became involved in anti-communist politics and by 1952 had made himself so unpopular with the authorities that he was forced to flee to West Germany. Genscher settled in Bremen, joined the local branch of the centrist Free Democratic Party (FDP) and in 1954 passed the Hamburg bar exam and went into practice, specializing in tax law.

Genscher quickly became identified with the rightwing of the FDP and steadily rose through the party ranks. In 1959 he was named general secretary to the party's parliamentary

Hans-Dietrich Genscher, West German and German foreign minister from 1974 to 1992, in December 1984. Photo courtesy of the German Ministry for Foreign Affairs.

faction. In September 1965 Genscher started his formal parliamentary career when he was elected to the Bundestag as deputy for North Rhine-Westphalia. Genscher became a member of the Bundestag Finance Committee and quickly developed a reputation as an expert in constitutional law and foreign policy.

In January 1968 Genscher was chosen as the FDP deputy chairman, and in 1969 played a leading role in the negotiations that led to the coalition Social Democratic (SPD)–FDP government. Genscher was given the key post of minister of the interior, where he was responsible for the crackdown on terrorism perpetrated by the Red Army Faction (also known as the Baader-Meinhof Gang). Genscher also personally negotiated with the Palestinian terrorists who kidnapped—and subsequently killed—11 members of the Israeli team competing at the 1972 Munich Olympics. At one point during the negotiations, Genscher offered himself as a substitute hostage.

As the minister responsible for internal security, Genscher was also involved in the events surrounding the arrest of East German spy Gunter Guillaume, a close aide of Chancellor WILLY BRANDT. Genscher had warned Brandt that Guillaume was under suspicion, but he was later criticized for not having acted quickly enough. Genscher was almost forced to resign, and his political career was saved by Brandt's decision to accept full responsibility.

In May 1974 Genscher became chairman of the FDP, and on May 17 he was sworn in as foreign minister. His appointment was opposed by many SPD members, who were embittered by his role in the Guillaume affair and who pointed out that Genscher had limited foreign affairs experience and that his only foreign language was a fractured English. He maintained his position, however, and until 1985 he combined the foreign minister's job with the vice chancellorship and leadership of the FDP.

For his first eight years as foreign minister, Genscher served in an SPD-FDP coalition. Then in 1982 he led his party into a coalition government with the Christian Democratic Union and Christian Social Union. His retention of the foreign affairs portfolio ensured the contination of the Ostpolitik policy under the more conservative Chancellor HELMUT KOHL.

Genscher became foreign minister at a time when West Germany and Berlin were no longer the major source of conflict between East and West. The HALLSTEIN DOCTRINE had been abandoned in 1967, Ostpolitik was launched in 1970, the QUADRIPARTITE AGREEMENT on Berlin had been signed in 1971, and in 1973 East and West Germany both became members of the United Nations. The basic issue that caused the East–West friction—the division of Germany—was not resolved until 1990. But the policies and events of the early 1970s resulted in a de facto recognition of that division and a willingness by both sides to work within the limits of that recognition. This freed West Germany to take a more active part in discussions on other areas of the world, such as South Africa, the EUROPEAN ECONOMIC COMMUNITY and the Middle East, as well as to develop its relations with the United States

on a more equal partnership basis. It also allowed the Bonn government more room to develop relations with East Germany, the Soviet Union and the rest of the Eastern Bloc countries.

Genscher himself did not share Brandt's enthusiasm for Ostpolitik. Genscher's foreign policy was consistent with the centrist politics of the party he led. He supported Ostpolitik and improved relations with Eastern Europe, but the purpose behind his support was the desire to secure a better quality of life for Germans in the East and to reduce East–West tensions in order to improve the security for Germans on both sides of the border. Genscher has been described as the ultimate tactician whose primary goal is to steer a middle course between any two extremes. German commentators have coined the expression "Genscherism" to describe his tactics and policies.

One of Genscher's first tasks as foreign minister was to tie up some of the loose ends of Ostpolitik. In June 1974 East Germany and West Germany exchanged diplomatic representatives who had the status but not the title of ambassador.

A high priority was attached to pressing the Eastern Bloc countries to fulfill their promise to allow ethnic Germans in their countries to immigrate to West Germany. Some 40,000 ethnic Germans in the Soviet Union had applied for permission to immigrate to West Germany. During a visit to Moscow in November 1974, Chancellor Helmut Schmidt and Genscher secured a Soviet promise that these ethnic Germans would be allowed to leave for West Germany at a rate of about 4,000 a year. In 1976 Genscher negotiated a further agreement allowing for 125,000 ethnic Germans living in Poland to emigrate to West Germany in return for a long-term, low-interest trade credit of $400 million and an indemnification of $500 million to settle Polish pension claims against Germany dating from World War II.

Ostpolitik was the first major step toward the creation of general East–West détente, which reached its height with the 35-nation CONFERENCE ON SECURITY AND COOPERATION IN EUROPE held in Helsinki in July and August of 1975. As a sign of West Germany's continuing commitment to détente, Genscher arranged a meeting between Schmidt and East German leader ERICH HONECKER. It was the first such meeting in five years and was described by the West German spokesman as "useful, relaxed and factual."

Eastern Europe had been a traditional market for German industrial goods and a traditional source of its raw materials. Ostpolitik reopened that market, with dramatic consequences for trade. For instance, between 1973 and 1974 trade between West Germany and the Soviet Union alone doubled from $1.5 billion a year to $3 billion a year.

Genscher believed that East–West trade reduced the possibility of war. In this he conflicted with many American political figures, who were concerned that the increasing trade between West Germany and the Soviet Bloc would make the Germans susceptible to Soviet political pressure. The most dramatic example of this conflict arose over the

Soviet gas pipeline deal. In November 1981 the Soviet Union signed a $15 billion agreement with a West German-led construction consortium to build a pipeline from Siberian gas fields to Western Europe. At the Ottawa Summit of Western heads of government in November 1981, President RONALD REAGAN tried to persuade Schmidt to shelve the pipeline deal, arguing that it would turn the West European economies into hostages of the Soviet Union. In December 1981, Reagan used the crackdown in Poland to ban the sale of oil and natural gas equipment to the Soviet Union by American companies, and in June 1982, in an attempt to scuttle the deal, the ban was widened to include foreign subsidiaries and licensees of American companies. Genscher played a leading role in organizing the resistance to Reagan's ban, and the U.S. president was forced to lift the ban quietly in 1983.

An increasingly difficult problem between West Germany and the United States during Genscher's tenure as foreign minister was the presence of British and American forces—conventional and nuclear—in West Germany. Both sides had ambivalent and at times contradictory feelings on the issue. The United States maintained 300,000 troops and several thousand tactical nuclear weapons in West Germany, and Britain maintained a force of 50,000 men and tactical nuclear weapons. As West Germany's economic strength, trade surpluses and criticism of American actions grew, so did American resentment over the cost of maintaining its presence in West Germany. American resentment found its expression in the attempts of Senator MIKE MANSFIELD to reduce American troop levels in Europe.

The Mansfield Amendment set alarm bells ringing in West Germany. Genscher was insistent that West Germany could be secure only if its defense were linked to that of the United States at every level—conventional, theater nuclear and strategic nuclear. It was this belief that led Genscher and Schmidt in December 1979 to press NATO allies to deploy U.S. cruise and PERSHING II MISSILES in Western Europe. They argued that the missiles were needed to force the Soviets to negotiate the reduction or withdrawal of their new generation of intermediate-range nuclear missiles.

But while West Germans wanted American protection, they also wanted peace. Being in the front line of a divided Europe, they knew that if war broke out Germany would be destroyed. The hard-line rhetoric of President Reagan worried a number of Germans, and Schmidt's SPD turned against the deployment of U.S. intermediate nuclear force (INF) weapons. Genscher, true to his policy of compromise, never completely condemned the INF weapons, but he became increasingly anxious that an INF agreement be signed as soon as possible and at times appeared over-eager in his support of Soviet diplomatic initiatives. An INF TREATY withdrawing both American and Soviet INF weapons from Europe was finally signed in Washington in December 1987.

Genscher was one of the early supporters of Soviet leader MIKHAIL GORBACHEV. He believed that it was essential that the West respond positively to Gorbachev's various foreign policy and arms control initiatives in order to shore up the Soviet leader's domestic power base. This was another reason for Genscher's support for an early INF Treaty. He also opposed President Reagan's hard-line interpretation of the 1972 ANTI-BALLISTIC MISSILE TREATY and the threat to breach the SALT II accords. But Genscher's biggest point of disagreement concerned American and British proposals to modernize NATO tactical nuclear weapons in West Germany in the wake of the signing of the INF Treaty.

Genscher argued that to authorize the modernization program at a time when the Soviet Bloc appeared to be radically restructuring its foreign policy would send the wrong signal to Moscow and strengthen the position of Soviet hard-liners. He called on NATO to start negotiations immediately with the Warsaw Pact on tactical nuclear weapons. U.S. president GEORGE BUSH and British prime minister MARGARET THATCHER argued that the withdrawal of the intermediate-range weapons made it imperative that the tactical nuclear weapons be modernized so that they remained a credible deterrent in the face of the overwhelming Soviet conventional forces.

The issue appeared to be on the verge of seriously damaging the Western Alliance on the eve of NATO's 40th birthday celebrations. Bush managed to defuse the crisis with a compromise solution that linked negotiations on short-range systems to progress at East–West talks on conventional weapons.

Genscher was a strong proponent of both the FRANCO-GERMAN FRIENDSHIP TREATY of 1963 and greater political integration through the European Economic Community. When Genscher became West German foreign minister the EEC was preoccupied with budgetary issues and the political and economic absorption of Britain. Genscher, working with Italian foreign minister Emilio Colombo, moved the EEC back toward its goal of political integration when the two launched the Colombo Plan, which led to the Single European Act of 1985. The act committed the member states to the complete lifting of trade barriers and economic integration by 1992. In 1990, Genscher also took a leading role in trying to bring about monetary union within the EEC.

Genscher saw the alliance with France in 1963 as one of the main diplomatic ropes trying France to the Western Alliance. He also viewed the relationship with France as the core of a possible future European defense force. In January 1988 France and Germany formally established joint councils on defense and economic issues. The new treaty also included a provision for the establishment of a 4,000-man Franco-German brigade to be based in West Germany. Genscher encouraged French moves to revive the WESTERN EUROPEAN UNION as a vehicle for increased European defense and security cooperation.

While the Germans used the Franco-German Treaty to tie France to the wider Western Alliance, the French saw it as a device for ensuring that West Germany would not be tempted into reuniting with East Germany in a neutral German state, which would then become a threatening power in its own right or be dominated by the Soviet Bloc. As the communist parties in Eastern Europe, especially in East Germany, collapsed in 1989, the possibility of German reunification became likely. Genscher held several meetings with his East German counterpart Oskar Fischer, and West German chancellor Kohl met with East German prime minister Hans Modrow.

Genscher's greatest triumph was his key role in the negotiations that led to the reunification of Germany in 1990. He attended the February summit in Ottawa that paved the way for the "two-plus-four" talks (the two Germanies plus the four World War II Allied powers), which took place over the following months. Genscher worked particularly closely with Soviet foreign minister EDUARD SHEVARDNADZE, meeting with him several times. The talks culminated with the September 12 signing in Moscow of the Treaty on the Final Settlement with Respect to Germany, which was followed the next month by Germany's formal reunification.

In 1991, Genscher came under increasing criticism both at home and abroad on a number of policy issues. Among the complaints: Germany's seemingly reluctant aid for the U.S.-led Persian Gulf war against Iraq; its slowness in responding to the collapse of the Soviet Union; and its push for early recognition of Croatia, which critics viewed as having accelerated the bloody disintegration of Yugoslavia. His strong support for greater European unity also faced mounting opposition within Germany.

Nevertheless, Genscher's overall popularity and status as a political icon remained relatively strong. Thus it came as something of a surprise when he announced his resignation on April 27, 1992. He did not specify a reason, although he was said to be concerned about his health, after having had two heart attacks. He formally retired on May 18 and was replaced by a protegé, Justice Minister Klaus Kinkel.

For Further Information:
Pfetsch, Frank. *Internal Structures and External Relations: Foreign Policy of the Federal Republic of Germany.* New York, 1988.
Whetten, Lawrence. *Germany East and West.* New York, 1980.

George, Walter   (January 29, 1878–August 4, 1957)   U.S. senator Walter George was a conservative Georgia Democrat whose support was vital for President HARRY TRUMAN's foreign policy initiatives. During the EISENHOWER administration he was chairman of the Senate Foreign Relations Committee and supported most of the administration's foreign policy but also played an important role in stimulating East–West negotiations.

After graduating from Mercer University Law School in 1901, George started a successful 20-year career as a lawyer, culminating in his appointment to the Georgia Supreme Court. In 1922 he was elected to the U.S. Senate, where he became known for his conservatism, especially on financial issues. On foreign affairs issues, however, George was more outward-looking than other conservatives of the day, who tended to adopt an isolationist stance.

In 1940 George assumed the chairmanship of the Senate Foreign Relations Committee and helped to push through President FRANKLIN ROOSEVELT's lend-lease program. However, George's main interest lay in fiscal matters, and in August 1941 he resigned the chairmanship of the Foreign Relations Committee to head the Senate Finance Committee. He held this post until 1947 and again from 1949–1953. George remained a member of the Foreign Relations Committee and supported the Truman administration's proposals for the Marshall Plan, the Truman Doctrine and the North Atlantic Treaty Organization. His conservative credentials gave him credibility with Senate conservatives who opposed these pillars of the Truman foreign policy and thus helped to secure their passage through Congress.

In January 1955 George returned to the chairmanship of the Senate Foreign Relations Committee and became a supporter of President Dwight Eisenhower's foreign policy. In the same month that he assumed the chairmanship, George sponsored a resolution giving Eisenhower unlimited authority to use American military power to protect Taiwan, following the communist Chinese shelling of QUEMOY AND MATSU ISLANDS.

George also supported Eisenhower in his differences with Secretary of State JOHN FOSTER DULLES, who opposed any negotiations with the Soviet Union. In 1954 British prime minister WINSTON CHURCHILL proposed an East–West summit meeting with the new Soviet leadership. Under pressure from Dulles, Eisenhower gave a cool response to Churchill's proposal, saying that such a summit should be preceded by peaceful Soviet gestures in "deeds, not words." George, however, went on the television program "Meet the Press" on March 20, 1955, to add his voice to the chorus supporting Churchill's proposed conference. Dulles was forced to back down, and the summit took place in July 1955.

The emphasis in George's positions began to shift from the containment of the late 1940s to the encouragement of international discussion. On April 23, 1955, he said that the United States "ought to be willing to talk with" the communist Chinese government "because we certainly owe a high obligation to all mankind everywhere."

In 1955, almost any other senator would have been castigated by Dulles and Republican conservatives for suggesting that the American government conduct discussions with the communist Chinese. But George's established conservative credentials and his 33 years in the Senate ensured that he was listened to with respect.

In Georgia, however, George faced a stiff challenge from white supremacist Herman Talmadge in the 1956 election. George had been easily reelected to the Senate in six successive elections. He was suffering from heart disease and did not feel well enough to mount what was expected to be a tough campaign. In May 1956 he announced that he would not seek reelection, and in January 1957 Eisenhower appointed him U.S. ambassador to the North Atlantic Treaty Organization. George died only seven months later, on August 4, 1957.

For Further Information:
Farnsworth, David N. *The Senate Committee on Foreign Relations (1947–1957).* Urbana, Ill., 1961.

German-German Border Commission   The German–German Border Commission was established in 1972 in the wake of the signing of the Basic Treaty as an attempt to define the border between East and West Germany.

Because the wartime Allied Powers had never meant to divide Germany permanently, they had never delineated the boundary between the Soviet- and Western-occupied sectors. The issue was further complicated by the exchange of bits of border territory among the Allies in the immediate postwar period. This led to conflicting West German and East German claims as to the exact position of the boundary and resulted in divided villages.

By 1988 most of the border had been agreed upon. The only outstanding area of difference was the Elbe River, which marks the boundary between East and West Germany from Lauenburg southeast almost to Wittenberge. The West Germans claimed that the boundary ran along the eastern bank of the river, and the East Germans claimed that it ran down the middle. The river was carefully guarded by East German patrols. Elsewhere in the disputed area, where the border was not set by the river the East Germans sealed it with a five-kilometer-wide no-go zone that could be entered only with special passes. The zone was guarded with barbed wire, dogs, and armed guards with orders to shoot to kill anyone trying to escape to the West. The precautions all became moot with the collapse of the communist regime in 1989 and German reunification in 1990.

German-Polish Treaty (1970)   The German–Polish Treaty was signed on December 7, 1970, to normalize relations between the Federal Republic of Germany (West Germany) and Poland. The treaty was one of the high points of West German chancellor WILLY BRANDT's OSTPOLITIK policy and helped to establish the climate for the détente era.

Relations between the two countries had been strained since the end of World War II because of West Germany's refusal to recognize the ODER-NEISSE LINE as the German-Polish border. The United States, Britain and the Soviet Union had agreed on the border pending the signing of a final German Peace Treaty. The Soviet Union and Poland interpreted this to mean that the border had been set, and the West Germans, with the support of the other Western Powers, interpreted it to mean that the boundary was temporary.

In 1950 the East German government accepted the Oder-Neisse line in the GORLITZ AGREEMENT. The agreement was denounced by the West German government of Konrad Adenauer as "traitorous." The issue of the former German territories was an emotional one in West Germany because millions of Germans had fled the area to West Germany and left behind land, homes, possessions and families.

Social Democratic leader Willy Brandt, however, was determined to normalize relations with Eastern Europe in order to move West Germany and Europe out of the deadlock created by unresolved post-World War II problems. At the core of any normalization agreement was an implied recognition of Polish border claims. Brandt started negotiations with Poland shortly after becoming chancellor on October 21, 1969. A little more than a year later the treaty was signed.

Because of the emotions raised by the Polish issue, the West German government refused to allow the use of the word "recognition" in the German–Polish Treaty. But the intention was clear, and it was seen as a major sacrifice for the West Germans.

In a national television address following the signing ceremony in Warsaw, Brandt said, "We did not take this decision lightheartedly. We are haunted by memories, by frustrated hopes. But . . . we are convinced that, in order to achieve a European peace order, tensions must be eliminated, treaties on the renunciation of force observed, relations improved and suitable forms of cooperation found. In the pursuit of these aims we have to start from what actually exists and from what has developed."

The main points of the treaty were as follows:

1. Both countries stated their desire to "establish durable foundations for peaceful coexistence" and accepted that "the inviolability of frontiers and respect for the territorial integrity and sovereignty of all States in Europe within their present frontiers are a basic condition for peace."
2. West Germany and Poland were "in mutual agreement" that the Oder-Neisse Line "shall constitute the western state frontier" of Poland.
3. Both countries declared that they "have no territorial claims whatsoever against each other and they will not assert such claims in the future."
4. Poland and West Germany pledged themselves to settle "all their disputes exclusively by peaceful means."
5. Both countries agreed to "take further steps toward full normalization and a comprehensive development of their mutual relations."

For Further Information:
Press and Information Office of the Government of the Federal Republic of Germany. *The Treaty Between the Federal Republic of Germany and the People's Republic of Poland.* Wiesbaden, 1971.

Germany   The division of postwar Germany into a communist eastern half and a capitalist western half, and the subsequent developments within and between the two Germanies, lay at the very heart of the Cold War. Situated in East and West Germany were the largest concentration of opposing armed forces in the world. The reunification of Germany in October 1990 was thus a major event in the end of the Cold War.

Between 1870 and 1945, Europe suffered three wars as the result of German aggression. Two of them developed into world wars. World War I resulted in about 10 million soldiers being killed in actual fighting. Another 7 million were permanently disabled and 15 million seriously wounded. Approximately 10 million civilians died as a result of disease and famine. During World War II, as many as 50,000,000 deaths from all causes occurred; the Soviet Union alone suffered an estimated 20,000,000. France suffered a humiliating defeat in the Franco-Prussian War of 1870, lost 1,300,000 men in World War I and suffered a political collapse, then a second humiliating defeat and occupation in 1940.

As a result of this experience, the Allied powers agreed at the Moscow Foreign Ministers Conference in 1943 to work together to construct a new order in Germany. Their discussions were based on a paper prepared by British foreign secretary ANTHONY EDEN, who proposed that Germany should be "totally occupied" and, for this purpose, divided into three zones of American, Soviet and British troops under a joint Allied Command.

The issue was first discussed in detail by the Allied heads of government—Prime Minister WINSTON CHURCHILL, JOSEF STALIN and President FRANKLIN D. ROOSEVELT—at the November 1943 Teheran Conference. Stalin was in rough agreement with the Eden proposal. Roosevelt suggested breaking Germany into five parts with key economic zones under UN control. All three leaders, however, agreed that Germany should be divided, and the issue was referred to a special committee under the European Advisory Commission.

The commission was slow to react, and the three allied governments began to develop separate proposals. The Americans, under Treasury Secretary HENRY J. MORGENTHAU, proposed one of the most severe plans for postwar Germany. The Morgenthau Plan called for the destruction of German industry and the "pastoralization" of the country. The proposal was supported by the Soviets, but the British leaned toward a variation of Eden's original proposal and some sort of plan to reintegrate a democratized Germany back into Europe. The Morgenthau Plan was eventually abandoned by President HARRY TRUMAN.

The dismemberment of Germany was the first issue raised at the YALTA CONFERENCE in February 1945. Roosevelt again proposed his five-part division. Churchill resubmitted Eden's proposal with the addition of a zone of occupation for France. Churchill's proposal was broadly accepted, but it was agreed to leave the exact boundaries of the occupation zones for later discussion. It was also agreed at Yalta that BERLIN, which was in the middle of the Soviet Zone, would be divided into four occupation zones. But, significantly, there was no discussion on British, American and French access to their Berlin zones.

Another key item on the Yalta agenda was the issue of German war reparations. The Soviet Union wanted Germany to pay the Allies $20 billion in reparations, with half of that money going to the Soviet Union. Churchill opposed any reparations and stressed that the crippling reparations levied on Germany at the end of World War I had largely created the political climate that led to the rise of Hitler and the start of World War II. Differences over this issue were to play an

important role in the postwar development of East and West Germany.

It was significant that no final or detailed decision on the division of Germany or reparations was reached before the German surrender in May 1945. There was a rough agreement that British forces would occupy the northwestern sector of Germany and Americans the southern and that the American forces would not cross the Elbe River. The Soviets would be responsible for the eastern sector, and the Polish–German border would be temporarily moved westward. In the absence of detailed international agreements, the determining factor became the positions of the various military forces at the time of the German surrender.

At the POTSDAM CONFERENCE in July–August 1945 (attended by Churchill, Truman, Stalin and CLEMENT ATTLEE), the British and Americans agreed that although Germany was divided, it should be treated as a single economic unit. They believed that they had secured Stalin's agreement on this point, but it subsequently became clear that Stalin had intended from the start to treat his zone as a separate political and economic unit. The Potsdam Conference also approved further German reparations payments to the Soviet Union and established the Allied Control Council to administer jointly the country. A Council of Foreign Ministers was established to negotiate a German peace treaty and deal with other issues.

Neither the Foreign Ministers' Council nor the Allied Control Council succeeded in developing a joint administration for Germany. In the absence of any agreed political structure, the occupying powers imposed their own political and economic systems in their respective zones. But there were further basic differences. The British, French and American forces saw their main task as rooting out leading Nazis and creating and rebuilding German political and economic structures so that the country could stand on its own. Stalin's main purpose was to take German capital equipment to rebuild Soviet industry and to install a communist government that, he hoped, would eventually dominate a reunited Germany.

The first major Allied difference over postwar Germany erupted in May 1946 over the issue of reparations payments to the Soviet Union. The Americans and British were becoming increasingly concerned that the Soviets were depriving Germany of the economic means to feed itself, let alone conduct trade. At the same time, the Western Allies were finding it increasingly difficult to house and feed the millions of German refugees who were fleeing the Eastern zone to avoid harsh Soviet treatment. On May 3, 1946, the United States stopped the delivery of reparations materials to the Soviet Union from the U.S. zone until Soviet policy changed.

The next step toward long-term division came in December 1946 when the British and the Americans decided to merge the economies of their two sectors in order to combat growing economic chaos in the Soviet sector. The merger, known as the BIZONAL AGREEMENT, took effect on January 1, 1947. The French joined the Bizonal Agreement in August

1948, and the cooperation among the three zones created the foundation for the Federal Republic of Germany (West Germany).

Even before the Bizonal Agreement, a great deal of administrative work had been handed over to the Germans, and Lander (state) governments had been set up following elections in the American zone in June 1946, the British zone in April 1947 and the French zone in May 1947. Four parties emerged from these elections: the conservative Christian Democratic Union (CDU), the trade union-oriented Social Democratic Party (SPD), the centrist Free Democratic Party (FDP) and the conservative Bavarian-based Christian Social Union (CSU). It was clear from these early elections that the dominant party in the Western zone was the CDU led by KONRAD ADENAUER, who became increasingly convinced that an agreement with the Soviet Union was impossible.

In January 1948 the terms of the Bizonal Agreement were altered to create the elected two-chamber German Economic Council, which became the nucleus of the future West German government. In June, after the French joined Bizonia, it was agreed to summon a constituent assembly to create a federal German government that would incorporate all three zones. An Allied military security board would enforce the Allied plans for the continued demilitarization of Germany, the German coal and steel industries of the Ruhr Valley would be placed under international control, and relations between the German assembly and the Allies would be regulated by an occupation statute.

The Western Allies' plans brought an immediate and strong protest from Stalin, who hoped to bring all of Germany under the communist government he was establishing in East Germany. The Soviets had moved quickly to establish a communist economy. In July 1945 all private banks had been closed, farms larger than 250 acres had been nationalized without compensation and all individuals and businesses had been ordered to surrender all their currency, title deeds and other valuables. Four main antifascist parties were legalized: the Communist Party of Germany (KPD), the Christian Democratic Union (CDU), the Social Democratic Party (SPD) and the Liberal Democratic Party (LDPD). It was clear from the start, however, that the Communist Party under WALTER ULBRICHT, Wilhelm Pieck and OTTO GROTEWOHL dominated the scene, and communists were moved into key administrative positions by the Soviet authorities. In April 1946 the Communist Party and the SPD merged to form the communist-dominated Socialist Unity Party (SED), which won an overwhelming victory in local elections that year.

In response to the creation of the German Economic Council in the West, the Soviets established an Economic Council in East Germany, and in March 1948 a congress of the Socialist Unity Party started work on a constitution for a separate East German state.

Thus by the spring of 1948, the foundation had been laid for the formal division of Germany into two states. The final catalyst that confirmed this division was the BERLIN BLOCKADE, which started in June 1948. At the Yalta Conference it had been agreed that Berlin—the spiritual heart of Prussian militarism—would be divided into four sectors and occupied by all four of the Allied Powers in the same way as the rest of Germany. The four-power occupation of Berlin would have been of only symbolic significance if the Allies had stuck by their original intention to treat all of Germany as one economic unit. But as the divisions grew, the Western presence in the heart of the Soviet sector became an increasing irritant to the Soviet Union. The success of their communist experiment in Germany depended heavily on isolating East Germany from the temptations of the capitalist West. The Western Allies, for their part, had decided that the security of Western Europe depended on their determination not to retreat from any position coveted by the Soviet Union. Furthermore, the maintenance of an American presence in West Berlin became a major symbol of America's commitment to the defense of Western Europe.

On March 30, 1948, the Soviets started the first of their attempts to force Western troops out of Berlin when they began stopping and searching Western military trains between West Germany and the Western sectors of Berlin. The British and Americans responded with a small airlift. On April 22 the Soviets canceled the Nord Express to Berlin and pressed for the cancellation of night and bad-weather flights to Berlin. On June 11 all rail traffic between Berlin and West Germany was halted for two days.

On June 18 the Western powers decided to go ahead with a planned currency reform in their sectors of Germany (excluding Berlin). The reform wrought a dramatic and almost overnight improvement in the West German economy and was followed by the Soviet introduction of its own currency reform for East Germany. Berliners were forced to change their money into one of the two rival currencies. To help them make up their minds, communists stormed and occupied Berlin city hall and tried to force the city assembly to pass a resolution agreeing that the Soviet currency would operate throughout the city. But the assembly instead voted that the Soviet currency would operate in the Soviet sector and the Western currency in the other three zones.

The vote confirmed the Soviets' course, and on June 24 Soviet forces stopped all road and rail traffic between West Berlin and West Germany. The Western powers were faced with the problem of keeping alive 2,500,000 people in the Western sector of Berlin. At the start of the blockade there was sufficient food for 35 days and coal for 45 days. It was estimated that the American and British transports would need to supply 4,500 tons of material daily in order to maintain the civilian population and occupation forces.

An airlift was immediately started by General LUCIUS CLAY, military governor of the American Sector, and General Sir Brian Robertson, military governor of the British Sector.

The blockade was not lifted until May 12, 1949. Possibly more than any other event in the Cold War, it polarized East and West and set down the clear political and geographic boundaries that divided Europe. During the 320-day blockade city governments for West and East Berlin and national governments for West Germany (the Federal Republic of Germany) and East Germany (the German Democratic Republic) were established. The NORTH ATLANTIC TREATY ORGANIZATION was established, American nuclear-armed bombers were based in Britain, the COUNCIL OF EUROPE was founded in Western Europe, and the COUNCIL FOR MUTUAL ECONOMIC ASSISTANCE (CMEA or COMECON) was founded in Eastern Europe.

The BASIC LAW, the constitution for the Federal Republic of Germany, was passed by the West German Parliamentary Council only four days before the end of the Berlin Blockade, on May 8, 1949. At the insistence of the Western Allies, Berlin was specifically excluded from the provisions of the West German constitution, although the Western Allies agreed that West German laws would be applied in West Berlin but only on the authority of the Western Occupying Powers.

The preamble of West Germany's Basic Law specifically stated that it was to cover a "transitional period" until East and West Germany could be reunited. It also called on "the entire German people . . . to achieve in free self-determination the unity and freedom of Germany."

The Basic Law also stipulated that all Germans were entitled to the right of citizenship in the Federal Republic of Germany. It divided West Germany into 11 Lander (states) and established a bicameral federal legislature comprised of the Bundestag (lower house) and Bundesrat (upper house). The members of the Bundestag would be directly and universally elected by proportional representation. The members of the Bundesrat would be elected from the parliaments of each Lander, which were directly elected. The government would be headed by a chancellor, who required an absolute majority of the votes in the Bundestag. Provision was made for a federal head of state, a president with mainly symbolic political powers. Elections were held in August 1949, and Konrad Adenauer was elected West Germany's first federal chancellor.

The constitution of the German Democratic Republic was adopted on May 30, 1949. The new East German state was formally proclaimed in October 1949. The first constitution provided for a parliamentary government of all "democratic" (i.e., communist-led) organizations of more than 40 members to be represented in a unicameral parliament, which ensured communist control. Private ownership of property was recognized with the proviso that it must not jeopardize "public welfare." The constitution outlawed "incitement to boycott against democratic institutions." Wilhelm Pieck became president, Otto Grotewohl chancellor and Walter Ulbricht, the secretary-general of the SED, became deputy chancellor.

As the SED was the only recognized "democratic" organization, East Germany became a one-party state. The East German constitution underwent several changes after 1949. A new constitution was promulgated in April 1968 that described the German Democratic Republic as a socialist state under the "leadership of its Marxist-Leninist Party." The 1968 constitution also declared that East Germany was "linked irrevocably and permanently with the U.S.S.R. and other Socialist states."

Thus at the end of 1949 there were two opposing German states, each militarily occupied and politically and economically supported by an opposing superpower. The states had rival political and economic systems and each claimed the right to represent the entire German nation (the East German government formally dropped this claim in 1968). Each German state became a showcase for the political and economic ideology of its respective sponsor, and the success or failure of each state became closely tied to the success or failure of each superpower.

In the contest between the two Germanies, West Germany got off to an early and good start. The combined factors of political stability, currency reform and the Marshall Plan created an overnight economic boom in the Federal Republic. In the second half of 1949, steel and coal production doubled and overall industrial production rose by nearly 50%. In East Germany, the economy was hamstrung by the continuing payment of war reparations to the Soviet Union. The result was a flood of both political and economic refugees from East to West. Tens of thousands of East Germans also continued to live in East Germany and work in either West Berlin or West Germany.

The westward flow of East Germans was obviously having a detrimental effect on the East German economy, as many of those moving to the West were university graduates or skilled workers. In 1954 the Soviet Union closed the inter-German border with machine gun nests and barbed wire. But the border between East and West Berlin remained open, and between 1954 and 1961 more than 27 million East Europeans fled to the West through Berlin. On August 12, 1961, the East German parliament passed a decree to seal the border. At three minutes past midnight on August 13, 1961, East German troops and police occupied the crossing points on the East Berlin side of the border, tore up the streets and installed road blocks and barbed wire barricades. Four days later, the East German authorities started construction of the Berlin Wall. The wall plugged what the East Germans termed the "Berlin Gap" and marked the beginning of a revival in the East German economy. East Germany was able to become the most thriving nation in Eastern Europe, but it still lagged far behind its rival in the West. The Berlin Wall also became one of the most potent symbols of the Cold War.

Throughout the 1950s there were continuing attempts to reunite the two German states. In March 1950 Adenauer proposed the formation of a government based on a free nationwide election, freedom of the press and for all political parties, elimination of interzonal and trade barriers and the guarantee of political freedom for individuals by all four of the Occupying Powers. The constitution of a reunified Germany would be drawn up after elections. The Soviet Union and East Germany countered with a proposal for an ALL-GERMAN COUN-

CIL that would establish a provisional all-German government to draw up a constitution and then hold elections on the basis of that constitution. East and West German governments would be represented equally on the council and in the provisional governments. The West Germans and the Western Allies rejected this proposal on the grounds that the East German government had not been freely elected and therefore should not have equal representation in a provisional government charged with negotiating a constitution.

In 1952 Stalin became increasingly worried about Western attempts to incorporate West Germany into the Western defense structure and offered to agree to a reunification of the German nation in return for a promise of perpetual neutrality. This was rejected by the Western Occupying Powers and by the pro-Western Adenauer, although it was considered by the opposition SPD. From that point onward the possibility of West Germany leaving the Western Alliance in return for reunification remained a factor in Western attitudes toward the Federal Republic, and it was the major consideration behind the FRANCO–GERMAN FRIENDSHIP TREATY of 1963.

From about 1950 onward, the Soviet Union began gradually to shift its policy from trying to reunite Germany under its terms to consolidating its position and the position of the German Communist Party. This policy was intensified after the EAST GERMAN UPRISING of June 1953 when workers rioted following an attempt to raise prices. To help the East German economy, the Soviets annulled the remaining $3.2 billion in reparations payments, and a soft loan of $125 million was extended to the East German government. On March 25, 1954, it was announced that the German Democratic Republic had become a sovereign state. In the same year East Germany became a full member of COMECON, and was a founder member of the WARSAW PACT when it was created in May 1955.

As time passed, power changed hands from the Soviet Union to the East German Communist Party. The Soviet Union, however, continued to maintain a massive military presence in East Germany, which in 1989 was comprised of about 380,000 troops and an entire Tactical Air Force. The Western Group of Soviet Forces, as they were called, served as a forward base threatening NATO forces in West Germany and by their presence enforced the continued loyalty of the East German population. The East German Armed Forces in 1989 consisted of 173,100 active troops.

At the same time, West Germany was being politically, militarily and economically integrated into the Western Bloc. Along with France it was a founding member of the EUROPEAN COAL AND STEEL COMMUNITY in 1952, and in 1957 it was among the founding members of the EUROPEAN ECONOMIC COMMUNITY. Other West European countries, however, had as much suspicion of West Germany as the Soviets did of East Germany. This suspicion led to the initial exclusion of West Germany from NATO and to the failure of the proposed EUROPEAN DEFENSE COUNCIL because it involved West German rearmament. After the failure of the EDC, West Germany was

admitted to NATO and Britain agreed to maintain a force of 50,000 men in West Germany as the BRITISH ARMY OF THE RHINE. In 1989 there were also 240,000 American troops, 52,000 French troops and 25,000 Belgian troops. West German active troops totaled 494,000 in 1989.

At the height of the Cold War, in the 1950s and 1960s, a country's political position in regard to the East–West conflict was largely determined by which German state it recognized. The Soviet Bloc countries and their allies recognized East Germany, and the Western Bloc countries and any neutral countries that desired good relations with the United States recognized West Germany as the legitimate government of all Germany. This policy was encouraged by Adenauer's HALLSTEIN DOCTRINE of 1955, which declared that the recognition of the German Democratic Republic by another state constituted an "unfriendly act" toward West Germany. The only exception to the Hallstein Doctrine was the Soviet Union, as it was regarded to be occupying a sector of the German nation. West German–Soviet diplomatic relations were established in 1955.

The Hallstein Doctrine was quietly dropped in 1967 and was gradually replaced by the OSTPOLITIK ("Eastern Policy") of Chancellor WILLY BRANDT. In practical terms, Ostpolitik meant accepting the division of Europe that had existed since 1945 and trying to work within those constraints in order to prevent the Cold War from breaking out into a hot war that would destroy both German states. Another factor in the thinking behind Ostpolitik was Brandt's belief that the best way to improve conditions for Germans living in East Germany was to establish relations with the Eastern Bloc.

In 1970 Brandt met with East German Premier Willi Stoph to discuss normalizing relations between the two Germanies. In December 1972 the two men signed the Basic Treaty, which laid the legal foundations for relations between the two German states. The treaty renounced the use of force; called for the respect of Four-Power rights and existing agreements on Berlin; established cooperation in border matters, transport, postal affairs, telecommunications, academic affairs, education, culture, trade relations; assured the right of West Germans to visit and travel in East Germany; and relaxed the travel restrictions on East Germans.

The Basic Treaty also established a form of joint diplomatic recognition. But it was politically impossible for any West German government to abandon totally the principle of a single German nation and the stated desire for eventual reunification. Therefore the two Germanies, at the insistence of Brandt, recognized each other as two states within a single German nation. The East Germans were reluctant to accept this concept because they feared it undermined their own legitimacy. But the Soviets saw this joint recognition as a vital element in their own plan to win Western recognition of postwar borders and forced the resignation of the reluctant Ulbricht, who was replaced with the more amenable ERICH HONECKER.

Ostpolitik went on to become one of the foundation stones

of the détente period of the 1970s and substantially eased East–West tensions over Berlin. It also led to the signing of the Berlin QUADRIPARTITE AGREEMENT OF 1971, which regularized West Berlin's postwar status and removed the constant Soviet threat that had been hanging over the western sector of the city since the end of World War II.

Brandt resigned as chancellor in 1974 after it was discovered that his close aide GUNTER GUILLAUME was an East German spy. However, he remained a major influence on West German foreign policy as chairman of the SPD until 1987. Brandt was succeeded in the chancellorship by the SPD's HELMUT SCHMIDT. He and Foreign Minister HANS-DIETRICH GENSCHER, leader of the centrist Federal Democratic Party, continued Brandt's Ostpolitik. In 1975, during the CONFERENCE ON SECURITY AND COOPERATION IN EUROPE, Schmidt and Honecker held a fringe meeting that was described as "frank and friendly."

Implicit in the policy of Ostpolitik was mutual recognition and maintenance of the division of Europe as the status quo. Both German states therefore sought not only to establish relations in each other's power blocs, but also to extend and strengthen relations with its allies. East Germany, in particular, knew that its continued existence depended entirely on the domination of the communist system throughout Eastern Europe. By the 1970s, East Germany had become the most prosperous and consumer-oriented country within the Soviet Bloc, although it still lagged far behind West Germany. The East German government had been one of the major opponents of CZECHOSLOVAKIA's PRAGUE SPRING and had enthusiastically participated in the August 1968 Warsaw Pact invasion of Czechoslovakia. Later, Honecker took a hard line in urging Czech leaders to crack down on dissident organizations such as CHARTER 77. He also urged the Polish authorities to crack down on the SOLIDARITY trade union and was reported to have recommended a Soviet–East German invasion of Poland in 1980. East Germany actively supported Soviet foreign policy in the Third World by sending military and technical advisers to pro-Soviet countries and by becoming a major source of foreign aid. Domestically, East Germany became one of the most repressive regimes in the Soviet Bloc.

West Germany, on the other hand, became a strong proponent of West European political integration through the European Economic Community. As its economic power grew, so did its political weight. It played an increasing role in Third World development through bilateral aid and such international agencies as the INTERNATIONAL MONETARY FUND and the WORLD BANK. West Germany was a member of the Western contact group on Namibia and one of the group of seven largest industrialized countries (G7), whose leaders met once a year to coordinate economic and political policies. Relations between West Germany and the United States grew even closer, and many American observers believed that West Germany replaced Britain as America's closest ally in Europe.

The height of détente, however, coincided with a world recession, which put increasing pressure on an American economy overburdened by extensive military commitments. This, plus some differences over policy issues, led to repeated calls in the U.S. Congress for reductions in American forces in Europe. At the same time, the Soviet Union deployed a new generation of intermediate-range nuclear missiles (the SS-20s) that were aimed specifically at West European targets. Genscher and Schmidt responded by seeking to strengthen the U.S. defense commitment to Western Europe at every level—conventional, theater nuclear and strategic nuclear. As part of this policy, they persuaded NATO allies, in December 1979, to deploy cruise and PERSHING II missiles in Western Europe. They argued that the missiles were needed to force the Soviets to negotiate the reduction or withdrawal of their SS-20s.

The deployment of the American missiles, however, also sparked off a divisive debate in Germany and the rest of Western Europe. The Germans wanted protection, but they also wanted peace, and many Germans feared that deployment of the missiles was another twist in the arms spiral that brought the world closer to a nuclear disaster that would leave both East and West Germany a pile of irradiated ashes. Their fears were reinforced by the hard-line rhetoric of U.S. president RONALD REAGAN, and the SPD gradually turned against the deployment of the missiles. By then, however, conservative CDU leader HELMUT KOHL had replaced Schmidt as chancellor, and he and Genscher continued the pro-deployment policy.

But the U.S.–German disagreement on INF weapons had exposed a serious difference of emphasis between West Germany and the United States toward relations with the Soviet Bloc. The United States in the 1980s had abandoned détente and returned to the hard-line policy of CONTAINMENT and tough negotiating from a strong military posture. West Germany believed that the way ahead lay in expanding political and economic ties with the Soviet Bloc by continuing détente. The situation was complicated further by the accession of MIKHAIL GORBACHEV to the Soviet leadership.

Gorbachev quickly launched a series of diplomatic and arms control initiatives designed to drive a wedge between West Germany and the United States. At the same time, he introduced a series of domestic economic and political reforms (perestroika) and adopted a more Western political style oriented to public relations. The result was that the Soviet Union appeared far less threatening to West German security. In fact, Reagan's continuing hard line was regarded by many Germans as more threatening to world peace than Gorbachev's foreign policy, and the Soviet leader grew in popularity in West Germany.

In East Germany, however, the Soviet leader and his policies became increasingly unpopular with the country's leaders. Erich Honecker steadfastly refused to introduce any of the political or economic reforms advocated by Gorbachev. He had established an elaborate communist bureaucracy supported by economic corruption, heavy subsidies and political repression. Any political or economic reforms would undermine this system and therefore the reason for the existence of the German Democratic Republic.

Other East European countries, however, eagerly embraced *glasnost* and *perestroika*, especially HUNGARY, which had been gradually pursuing similar policies ever since the Hungarian Revolution of 1956. In 1989 Hungary took the dramatic step of opening its border with Austria. For many East Germans, it was as if the Hungarians had punched a back door through the Berlin Wall. They could travel freely to Hungary, as it was a Warsaw Pact country, and from there they could go to West Germany, where the Basic Law guaranteed them West German citizenship and a standard of living roughly double that of the East.

An estimated 50,000 East Germans quickly fled West through Hungary. Thousands more sought sanctuary in the West German embassies in Prague and Warsaw. Honecker attempted to persuade the other East European leaders to reverse their *glasnost* policies and stop the flood of East Germans, but they refused. Gorbachev, in keeping with his new policy of nonintervention in the affairs of other East European states, refused to step in. Honecker was reluctantly forced to allow trainloads of East Germans to travel from Poland and Czechoslovakia through East Germany to the West.

The combination of Gorbachev's refusal to intervene, plus the establishment of an escape corridor and the collapse of communist influence in Poland and Hungary, led to demonstrations in the streets of East Germany. Hundreds of thousands demanded the immediate resignation of Honecker and an end to communist rule. In October 1989 Honecker resigned as president and leader of the East German Communist Party. He was quickly succeeded by Egon Krenz who, on November 9, 1989, ordered the end of restrictions on emigration. This effectively ended the need for the Berlin Wall. Millions of East Berliners poured into West Berlin, and the following day the East German government started dismantling the wall to accommodate the human flood.

With an estimated 2,000 East Germans per day flooding into West Germany, the East German state at the start of 1990 faced political and economic collapse. Effectively abandoned by the Soviet Union and the other Warsaw Pact countries, it was forced to turn toward West Germany for political and economic aid. The price demanded by Chancellor Kohl for this aid was reunification of the German nation.

At a February 1990 summit in Ottawa, a surprise agreement was reached to hold "two-plus-four" talks on reunification, consisting of the four victorious World War II Allied powers—the U.S., U.S.S.R., U.K. and France—plus the two Germanies. The talks began in March, and subsequent rounds were held in May, June and July. Meanwhile, in March, East Germany held free elections, which were led by the Christian Democratic Union. In April, CDU leader Lothar de Maiziere became premier in a broad coalition government that favored rapid reunification. The following month, plans for a monetary union treaty between East and West were agreed upon, and the treaty took effect July 1.

The last major obstacles to reunification fell shortly thereafter. On July 16, after two days of talks in the Soviet Union between Kohl and Gorbachev, Moscow agreed that a unified, sovereign Germany could belong to NATO. In return, Kohl agreed on the following key points: Germany would help finance the Soviet Union's 380,000 troops in East Germany during their three- to four-year withdrawal period; as long as Soviet troops remained, no integrated NATO troops would be stationed in East German territory; a unified German Army would ultimately be cut to a strength of 370,000 (as of 1990, West Germany had about 480,000 troops and East Germany about 170,000); and Germany would refrain from producing or possessing atomic, biological or chemical weapons and would sign the nuclear nonproliferation treaty.

A second key matter was resolved July 17 at the two-plus-four talks, when all sides agreed on a plan to guarantee that Poland's current western border, known as the ODER-NEISSE LINE, would remain the official demarcation with a united Germany. (Poland and Germany signed a treaty finalizing the agreement on November 14.)

On August 23, the East German parliament agreed to an October 3 reunification date, voting to join the Federal Republic under Article 23 of West Germany's constitution. On August 31, East and West Germany signed a treaty on political, social and legal matters relating to reunification.

On September 12 in Moscow, the foreign ministers of the two-plus-four countries signed the Treaty on the Final Settlement with Respect to Germany. The treaty formally ended the Allied powers' responsibilities over Germany. The next day, West Germany and the U.S.S.R. signed a 20-year friendship pact.

Finally, on October 3—"Unity Day"—Germany became a united nation for the first time since the end of World War II, 45 years earlier. The landmark Cold War development came less than one year after the opening of the Berlin Wall on November 9, 1989, which had heralded the downfall of East Germany's communist regime. Buoyed by his successful leadership of the unity drive, Kohl's CDU December 2 won an easy victory in the first general election in a reunified Germany.

In 1991 and 1992, Germany was preoccupied with dealing with the economic, social and political costs of reunification, as well as with relations with Eastern Europe and the Soviet Union. As the government began soberly reckoning with the huge cost of integrating the devastated East German economy with the far more prosperous West, eastern citizens protested their high unemployment. Some complained that Western capitalists and entrepreneurs were more concerned with reaping profits from the privatization of the east's state-run industries than they were with creating new jobs.

Among the social problems were those posed by the release of Stasi (the former East German security service) files—which revealed the names of prominent citizens who had served as informers for the communist regime—and the huge influx of economic refugees and asylum-seekers from the former Eastern Bloc countries. The government's generous policy toward refugees angered many Germans, particularly in the east, and provided a rallying cry for violent neo-Nazi protests, which broke out in late 1991 and then erupted with even greater fury in August and September 1992.

Germany signed friendship pacts with Poland, Czechoslovakia and Romania in 1991 and 1992. However, Germany came in for some criticism when it led an aggressive drive to grant European diplomatic recognition to the republics of Croatia and Slovenia in late 1991, speeding the breakup of YUGOSLAVIA. The German move alarmed Serbian nationalists, who saw it as an expression of a German desire to dominate the region as it had during World War II, when hundreds of thousands of Serbs died under fascist rule. Some observers viewed Germany's Balkan diplomacy as ill-conceived and reckless, suggesting that it had the effect of fueling Serbian aggression in the region's ethnic civil wars, which spread to Bosnia in 1992.

Meanwhile, Kohl's government remained committed to Gorbachev, and it failed to realize that the Soviet leader's stock was so low with his countrymen that he would not last out 1991. (In the United States, the Bush administration similarly miscalculated.) Kohl visited the U.S.S.R. in July 1991 for cordial talks with Gorbachev. Germany reacted sluggishly to the short-lived coup against Gorbachev the following month, initially signaling that it could live with the hard-line communist usurpers. Russian president BORIS YELTSIN, who had led the opposition to the coup, received a distinctly lukewarm reception when he visited Germany in November. Confronted with the inevitable—the formal dissolution of the Soviet Union on December 25, 1991—Germany moved the next day to grant diplomatic recognition to Russia.

According to European Community figures released in January 1992, $80 billion in aid had been pledged to the Soviet Union and its successor, the COMMONWEALTH OF INDEPENDENT STATES, by foreign countries and international organizations. More than 57% of that total was from Germany, but most of that aid was related to the 1990 reunification process.

For Further Information:

Brant, Stefan. *The East German Rising*. London, 1954.
Carr, J. *Helmut Schmidt*. New York, 1985.
Crawley, A.M. *The Rise of West Germany, 1945–1972*. New York, 1974.
Fritsch-Bournazel, Renata. *Confronting the German Question*. Oxford and New York, 1988.
Griffiths, William. *The Ostpolitik of the Federal Republic of Germany*. Cambridge, Mass., 1978.
Jonas, M. *The U.S. and West Germany*. New York, 1985.
Mander, J. *Berlin: The Eagle and the Bear*. New York, 1962.
Mezerik, A.F., ed. *Berlin and Germany: Berlin Crisis, Wall, Free State, Separate Treaty, Cold War, Chronology*. New York, 1962.
Pfetsch, Frank. *West Germany, Internal Structures and External Relations: The Foreign Policy of the Federal Republic*. New York, 1988.
Prittie, Terence. *The Velvet Chancellors*. New York, 1979.
Strauss, Franz Joseph. *The Grand Design*. New York, 1965.
Viola, T. *Willy Brandt*. London, 1989.
Whetten, Lawrence. *Germany East and West*. New York, 1980.

Gero, Erno (July 8, 1898–March 12, 1980)

Erno Gero had a brief but important role in the Cold War when he served as first secretary of the Hungarian Communist Party in the three months before the uprising of 1956.

Gero was one of the early members of the Hungarian Communist Party, joining in 1918 as the Bolsheviks came to power in Russia. Like so many prewar European communists, Gero looked toward the newly formed Soviet Union as an inspiration and in the interwar years lived for a time in Moscow. He also fought with the International Brigades during the Spanish Civil War.

When Stalin was looking for pro-Soviet Hungarians to install in the postwar Hungarian government, Gero was a logical choice for a cabinet post. He was successively minister of transport, minister of finance and, after 1950, minister of state and foreign trade. From 1955 to 1956 he was deputy prime minister.

Gero's period in power coincided with NIKITA KHRUSHCHEV's efforts to publicize the abuses of Josef Stalin and heal the breach with Yugoslavia. But the Soviet leader's policies undermined the rationale for the dominant role of the Hungarian Communist Party and its links with the Soviet Union. In July 1956, at the behest of Khrushchev, the Stalinist Hungarian leader MATYAS RAKOSI was removed from power and replaced by Erno Gero.

Gero, again at Khrushchev's insistence, concentrated his efforts on rapprochement with Yugoslavia. He joined talks between Khrushchev and JOSIP BROZ TITO at Yalta in September. The following month Gero traveled to Belgrade to start talks on reestablishing ties between the Yugoslav and Hungarian communist parties. While he was in Yugoslavia students rioted and demanded Gero's removal from power as well as the withdrawal of Soviet troops and the trial of Rakosi.

Gero returned on the following day, October 23, 1956, and went on the radio to pledge to defend socialism and to charge that the mob leaders sought to "restore capitalism." On October 25 Gero was replaced as first secretary by Janos Kadar, and a few days later he fled the country for Moscow as the anti-Soviet prime minister, IMRE NAGY, took over the government and declared that "the revolution had triumphed."

After Soviet tanks quelled the uprising, Kadar assumed the reins of government. Gero was seen as an embarrassing symbol of the pre-uprising government and was ordered to remain in Moscow. He was eventually allowed to return but was expelled from the party in 1962. He lived quietly in retirement until his death on March 12, 1980.

For Further Information:

Kovrig, Bennet. *Communism in Hungary from Kun to Kadar*. Stanford, Calif., 1979.
Vali, Ferenc. *A Rift and Revolt in Hungary: Nationalism vs. Communism*. Cambridge, Mass., 1961.
Zinner, Paul. *Revolution in Hungary*. New York, 1962.

Ghana   Ghana was the first West African country to achieve independence and under Kwame Nkrumah developed a form of socialism and nationalism that inspired many other African independence movements. Nkrumah was eventually overthrown by the military, who claimed that his policies had ruined the country.

Most of Ghana was under direct British rule from 1901 to 1957, when it was known as the Gold Coast and British Togoland Trust Territory (the Togo portion being a part of a former German colony). British influence in Ghana dated back to the 17th century, when the region had been an important source of slave labor for sugar and tobacco plantations in the American colonies and the Caribbean.

Ghana's early political development was forged almost entirely by the American-educated Kwame Nkrumah, who became interested in Marxism-Leninism and its relationship with Third World causes while studying at the University of Pennsylvania in the 1930s. Nkrumah returned to Ghana in 1945, where he immediately threw himself into liberation politics. In September 1948 he founded the *Accra Evening News* as a vehicle for his political views. In June 1949 he founded the Convention People's Party, and the following year he started a campaign of civil disobedience, which eventually led to his arrest by the British authorities.

Nkrumah's overwhelming popularity with the people led the British quickly to release him, and in 1950 he was elected to Ghana's parliament. By 1952 he was prime minister. When Ghana became independent in March 1957, Nkrumah moved quickly to establish a one-party state and authoritarian rule, which enabled him to implement his political ideas. In 1958 the Constitution Act and Preventive Detention Act were passed, giving Nkrumah wide extralegal powers to suppress opposition. In 1960 he was named president. The following year "Nkrumahism" became the official ideology of the nation, and Ghana officially became a one-party state led by Nkrumah's Convention People's Party.

Through Nkrumah, Ghana became the most influential black African member of the NON-ALIGNED MOVEMENT, the driving force behind the formation of the Organization of African Unity, a primary opponent of the apartheid government in South Africa and a champion of anticolonial liberation struggles in Africa and beyond. Nkrumah's rise coincided with the Soviet Union's attempts to gain influence in the Third World by supporting national liberation movements. His attraction to Marxism made him an early and obvious target for Soviet FOREIGN AID.

Conversely, U.S. president JOHN F. KENNEDY also saw major benefits in cultivating the increasingly influential international figure of Nkrumah and offered massive American aid. In fact, the most impressive aid project in Ghana was the $200-million U.S.-built Volta Dam sponsored by the U.S. AGENCY FOR INTERNATIONAL DEVELOPMENT and Kaiser Industries and completed in 1965. The dam created a lake of 3,500 square miles and powered an electricity generating station capable of producing 768 megawatts of power.

The Soviet aid was not on such a grand scale, but Soviet loans totaled nearly $100 million by 1961, and a series of state farms, technical schools, a fish processing plant, a hospital, planes for the Ghanaian state airline, and a military airfield had been provided.

But Nkrumah's penchant for grandiose and expensive public projects and industrialization schemes, as well as the massive corruption of his government, placed an increasing burden on the Ghanaian economy. At independence, Ghana had foreign reserves of $500 million. By 1964 they had dropped to $100 million. In the same period, foreign debt increased tenfold. Unable to finance Western imports, the Ghanaians turned increasingly to barter arrangements with the Soviet Union, supplying a larger and larger proportion of their cocoa crop in return for Soviet trade credits. But Ghanaians were unable to find enough Soviet products they wanted to import, with the result that by 1963 they accumulated Soviet trade credits worth $700 million, which they could not convert into the hard currency needed to pay off the Western debt.

Nkrumah's growing dependence on the Soviet Bloc led many Western conservatives, and leading figures in the Ghanaian military, to regard Ghana as a Soviet client state. In 1966 Nkrumah, while on a peace mission to Vietnam, was overthrown in a military coup led by General Joseph Ankrah.

Nkrumah was succeeded by a series of short-lived military and civilian governments. In April 1969 Ankrah was replaced by brigadier General Akwasi Arifa, who led the country to civilian rule under President Edward Akufo-Addo. He in turn was overthrown in January 1972 by General Ignatius Acheampong. In July 1978 General Frederick Akuffo seized power in a bloodless coup and set about organizing a return to civilian rule, only to be overthrown by Flight Lieutenant Jerry Rawlings on the eve of election day. The civilians did regain control in September 1979 under President Hilla Limann, but in December 1981 Rawlings seized power in another military coup. Despite radical rhetoric, Rawlings generally has enjoyed good relations with Western governments and financial institutions.

For Further Information:
Agbodeka, Francis. *Ghana in the Twentieth Century.* New York, 1972.
Armah, Kwesi. *Nkrumah's Legacy.* London, 1974.
Davidson, Basil. *Black Star: A View of the Life of Kwame Nkrumah.* London, 1973.
Dei-Anang, Michael. *The Administration of Ghana's Foreign Relations, 1957–1965.* New York, 1975.
Krassowski, A. *Development and the Dept Trap: Economic Planning and External Borrowing in Ghana.* Mystic, Conn., 1974.

Gheorghiu-Dej, Gheorghe   (November 8, 1901–March 19, 1965)   Gheorghe Gheorghiu-Dej was the Stalinist dictator of Romania from 1952 until his death in 1965. During the 1950s he slavishly followed the Soviet lead, but during the last few years of his rule he laid down the foundations for

Romania's increasingly independent economic and foreign policies.

Gheorghiu-Dej began his revolutionary career during World War I and after the war joined the banned Romanian Communist Party. In 1933 he helped to organize a major railway strike. For his part in the strike, he was sentenced to 12 years' imprisonment. He was released from prison in August 1944 following the overthrow of the fascist government of General Ion Antonescu.

Out of prison, Gheorghiu-Dej was named secretary general of the Communist Party, and at the insistence of the Soviet Union was appointed to the cabinet of pro-Western prime minister Nicolae Radescu. He was minister of communications from 1944 to 1946 and after 1946 was responsible for many of the basic economic planning decisions.

Although Gheorghiu-Dej held relatively minor positions in the cabinet, his power in the immediate postwar years was disproportionately large because of his position as general secretary of the Communist Party at the time of the Soviet occupation of Romania. He played a major role in forcing King MICHAEL to dismiss Radescu; subsequent police-state tactics led to the communist victory in the November 1946 elections. In 1952 Gheorghiu-Dej assumed dictatorial powers when he succeeded Petro Groza as prime minister.

Between 1947 and 1956 the Romanian Communist Party, which renamed itself the Romanian Workers' Party, imposed one of the most vicious purges in Eastern Europe as Gheorghiu-Dej sought to consolidate his power and impose Stalinist policies through the physical extermination of his opponents. One of the most vicious campaigns was against landowners and wealthy peasants. Under the government's original reform program, land had been given to the small- and middle-size farmers, but when forced collectivization was started in 1949, the land was taken away again. All peasants owning more than 37 acres were declared "class enemies," and an estimated 150,000 were sent to infamous concentration camps along the Danube–Black Sea canal.

Gheorghiu-Dej was a committed Stalinist, and Romania was one of the few East European countries that did not fully de-Stalinize after 1956. Gheorghiu-Dej used a Stalinist personality cult and centralized economic policies to achieve rapid industrialization and to suppress the ethnic Hungarian minority in Transylvania.

But it was not until 1962 that the Romanian chief came into conflict with the new leadership in Moscow. The cause was his ambitious industrialization plans, which clashed with the plans of Soviet leader NIKITA KHRUSHCHEV, who wanted the Soviet-controlled COMECON secretariat to allocate specific economic duties to specific Soviet Bloc countries in order to avoid duplication of effort. The proposal was vehemently opposed by Gheorghiu-Dej, who feared that Khrushchev's plan would lock Romania into the position of primary producer.

Because of Gheorghiu-Dej's opposition to Khrushchev's plan, COMECON was forced to accept Romania's right to reject economic proposals that were incompatible with its national interest. Within a short time, Gheorghiu-Dej's independent economic line was extended into the foreign affairs field when he supported Peking in the SINO–SOVIET SPLIT. These policies were continued by NICOLAE CEAUSESCU after the death of Gheorghe Gheorghiu-Dej on March 19, 1965.

For Further Information:
Jelavich, Barbara. *History of the Balkans—Twentieth Century.* New York, 1983.
Jowitt, Kenneth. *Revolutionary Breakthrough and National Development: The Case of Romania, 1944–1965.* Los Angeles, 1971.
Polonsky, A. *The Little Dictators: The History of Eastern Europe Since 1918.* London, 1975.
Rakowska-Harmstone, T. *Communism in Eastern Europe.* Indianapolis, 1984.

Gierek, Edward   *See* POLAND

Gilpatric, Roswell (November 1906–   )   Roswell Gilpatric was U.S. deputy secretary of defense during the KENNEDY administration and at the start of the JOHNSON administration. In this capacity he was responsible for several strategic decisions involving American foreign policy in Vietnam. He was also responsible for the sale of American weapons abroad. He had previously served as assistant secretary of the air force and later undersecretary of the air force in the closing years of the TRUMAN administration.

After graduating from Yale Law School in 1931, Gilpatric joined the New York law firm of Cravath, Swaine & Moore and became involved in Democratic Party politics. During World War II he advised corporations involved in defense production. This placed him in regular contact with senior Democrats in Washington.

In May 1951 President Harry Truman appointed Gilpatric assistant secretary of the air force with special responsibility for production and procurement. His skill in this post led to his promotion to undersecretary, in which capacity he was instrumental in introducing a lighter and more maneuverable jet fighter. Gilpatric resigned from the Pentagon after the election of DWIGHT EISENHOWER.

During the Eisenhower administration, Gilpatric concentrated on his law practice, but he also became involved in various defense study groups. In 1960 he was named chairman of the board of trustees of the Aerospace Corporation, a nonprofit organization sponsored by the Air Force to encourage ballistic missile development. After John F. Kennedy secured the Democratic presidential nomination, Gilpatric was named by Kennedy to two defense study groups. Kennedy was at first undecided whether to appoint Gilpatric or ROBERT MCNAMARA as defense secretary. After a postelection meeting among the three men, Gilpatric agreed to serve as McNamara's deputy, and the two developed a close relationship.

In April 1961 Gilpatric was named head of a task force to investigate ways of preventing communists from gaining power in Vietnam and Laos. Gilpatric urged the president to increase U.S. military aid to South Vietnam, dispatch U.S. ground troops to the country and send air force general Edward Lansdale to Vietnam to prepare further proposals. Kennedy increased aid, but he did not send Lansdale to Vietnam, and he indefinitely postponed a decision on the introduction of ground troops. Gilpatric's views were supported in a slightly later report by General MAXWELL TAYLOR and WALT ROSTOW.

On August 24, 1963, Gilpatric gave Pentagon approval to the State Department cable to HENRY CABOT LODGE, then ambassador to South Vietnam, which effectively gave U.S. government backing for a military coup against South Vietnamese president NGO DINH DIEM. Gilpatric's approval of the cable led to one of his few disagreements with McNamara, who was away on vacation at the time. This in turn damaged Gilpatric's relations with Kennedy, who was more concerned about the breakdown in policy consensus than with the actual wording of the cable.

As Vietnam took on an increasingly important role in American strategic thinking, McNamara played a more direct part in the policy decisions. As partial compensation, Gilpatric was given a larger role in determining America's defense relations with Europe. He acted as the Pentagon spokesman during the 1961 BERLIN Crisis, telling the press on June 6 that U.S. forces in Europe would use nuclear weapons in response to a major Soviet conventional attack. In October 1961 Gilpatric held a series of meetings with European defense ministers that resulted in the Europeans' agreeing to an arms buildup based on purchases of American weapons. In the same month, he officially laid to rest the allegations of a MISSILE GAP between the Soviet Union and the United States.

Gilpatric was a member of the inner circle that advised Kennedy during the CUBAN MISSILE CRISIS. He opposed direct intervention and supported the naval blockade of the island.

Gilpatric had mixed feelings about Kennedy's desire for disarmament negotiations with the Soviet Union and the 1963 NUCLEAR TEST BAN TREATY. He opposed the test ban, not because he thought it a significant military risk, but because he feared "that any easing of tensions would soon find the western democracies inviting disaster by letting down their guard." He preferred that the two negotiating teams discuss only reciprocal or unilateral arms reductions.

During 1963 Gilpatric toured Europe to canvass U.S. allies' opinions on the American plan for a multinational nuclear force. The force failed to advance beyond the planning stages as a result of British apathy and French opposition. Later Gilpatric also turned against the concept.

Gilpatric's last year in office was marred by a scandal involving the allocation of defense contracts for the TFX fighter aircraft. It was discovered that Gilpatric's law firm, Cravath, Swaine & Moore, had done a great deal of defense-related work for General Dynamics, which was awarded the TFX contract over a bid by Boeing that was actually lower. The affair was investigated by the Senate Permanent Investi-

gations Subcommittee, which narrowly voted its confidence in Gilpatric, and by the Justice Department, which cleared him of conflict-of-interest charges.

Gilpatric resigned on January 9, 1964, and returned to his law practice. In September 1964 President Lyndon Johnson appointed Gilpatric to a nonpartisan advisory panel on foreign policy, and later made him chairman of a secret panel to study ways to prevent the spread of nuclear weapons. Among the panel's proposals was the scrapping of the multinational nuclear force.

From 1965 onward, Gilpatric was instrumental in the opposition to the development and deployment of the U.S. antiballistic missile (ABM) system. In November 1965 he was appointed joint head of a White House citizens' committee that urged a three-year U.S.–Soviet moratorium on such systems. His opposition was stepped up after President RICHARD NIXON committed the government to the ABM system. Gilpatric continued to lecture and write on defense and disarmament issues throughout the 1970s.

For Further Information:
Borklund, C.W. *The Department of Defense.* New York, 1968.
———. *Men of the Pentagon: From Forrestal to McNamara.* New York, 1966.

Giscard d'Estaing, Valéry   (February 2, 1926–   )

Valéry Giscard d'Estaing was the first non-Gaullist president of France's Fifth Republic. He continued France's independent foreign policy while quietly shifting its emphasis toward better relations with the United States. He also played a major role in preventing Africa from becoming a superpower battlefield.

Giscard was born in Coblenz in Germany, the son of a wealthy financier and member of the minor French nobility. He attended the prestigious École Nationale d'Administration in Paris, the source of France's top civil servants, and joined the Ministry of Finance after World War II. French finance minister Edgar Faure was impressed by Giscard's ability and, in 1952, appointed him his chief of staff. Giscard's interests, however, were in politics rather in the civil service, and in 1956 he was elected to the National Assembly as a member of the conservative National Center of Independents and Peasants.

Giscard quickly won a reputation as one of the most intellectual members of the National Assembly. After CHARLES DE GAULLE came to power in 1959 he was named secretary of state for finance with responsibility for formulating and implementing the national budget. In January 1962 Giscard became France's minister of finance and shortly afterward founded the small pro-Gaullist Independent Republican Party.

Giscard quickly became France's chief symbol of conservative, austerity economics. Government spending was cut, wage and price controls were introduced and taxes were increased. As a result of these measures, France achieved its first balanced budget in 36 years, and inflation was lowered from 5% to 2.5%. But Giscard's measures became increasingly unpopular with industry and workers, and in 1966 he was dismissed by de Gaulle.

Out of the cabinet, Giscard concentrated on building his power base within the Independent Republican Party and took an increasingly anti-Gaullist line on foreign policy issues such as autonomy for Quebec and British membership in the EUROPEAN ECONOMIC COMMUNITY. Following de Gaulle's resignation in 1969, Giscard rejoined the cabinet as minister of finance for President GEORGES POMPIDOU, and during the following three years he oversaw an annual growth rate in the French economy of 6%. The French "economic miracle," however, came to a sudden end with the 1973 oil crisis and the ensuing world inflation.

Following the death of Pompidou in April 1974, Giscard announced that he was a candidate for the presidency. His two main rivals were the official Gaullist candidate Jacques Chaban-Delmas and Socialist leader FRANCOIS MITTERRAND. Giscard recognized that the voters wanted a change from Gaullism, but not the extreme change offered by Mitterrand. His campaign slogan was "Change without risk." None of three candidates received the absolute majority required and so the top two candidates—Giscard and Mitterrand—went into a run-off vote on May 5, 1974. Giscard won by the narrowest margin in French history—50.7% of the vote compared to 49.3% for Mitterrand.

Giscard's first meeting with a foreign leader was with West German chancellor HELMUT SCHMIDT at the end of May 1974. The close relationship between the two men became one of the main pillars of the Franco-German Alliance and helped the movement toward greater economic and political integration within the EEC. Schmidt also helped to move France's foreign policy closer to the United States and NATO.

France's relations with Britain improved under Giscard but remained slightly distant. Giscard did make a state visit to Britain in July 1976, and he and Prime Minister JAMES CALLAGHAN agreed to meet once a year. The frequency of the Anglo-French summits was later increased to twice a year.

Giscard tried to continue the Gaullist concept of France as an independent third force in international relations. To this end, he continued the special Franco–Soviet relationship started by de Gaulle, but as East–West tensions increased Giscard moved France closer to the United States. His first meeting with Soviet leader LEONID BREZHNEV, in December 1974, showed no sign of any future problems, and Brezhnev spoke of the "perfect convergence of our points of view down to the last details." In October 1975 Giscard visited Moscow, where the first perceptible signs of a cooling in Franco–Soviet relations were recognized over the application of détente. Giscard called for "détente in armaments . . . and détente in ideological rivalry so that competition between economic and social systems should [not] result in excessive tensions." Brezhnev declared, however, "It goes without saying that in the development of cooperation between states with different socio-economic and ideological systems, specific differences

cannot be eliminated . . . International détente in no way puts an end to the struggle of ideas."

Giscard and U.S. president GERALD FORD held their first meeting in December 1974 when they met on the French Caribbean island of Martinique. The French had been angered over unilateral measures to protect the dollar in the wake of the 1973 oil crisis. Giscard persuaded Ford to agree to greater coordination of Western countries on energy and economic issues. At this same meeting, Giscard agreed to pay the United States $100 million to compensate for financial losses incurred when de Gaulle had expelled U.S. forces and bases from French territory in the 1960s. The agreement for greater international cooperation on economic issues led Giscard to convene the November 1975 economic summit of heads of government of the United States, Britain, Japan, France, Canada and West Germany. This group was later expanded to include the president of the EEC and the Italian prime minister and became the Group of Seven (G7) industrialized countries, which met regularly once a year.

Giscard had a good working relationship with both Ford and Secretary of State HENRY KISSINGER, whom he respected for his "realpolitik" view of the world. His relationship with the CARTER administration, however, was at times strained because Giscard regarded Carter's emphasis on human rights as naive and damaging to détente. But the two presidents put on a strong show of unity when Carter visited France in January 1978, and the two men strolled together down the Champs-Elysees waving to the Parisian crowds.

In January 1979 Giscard hosted the Guadeloupe summit meeting attended by Carter, Callaghan and Schmidt. The meeting endorsed the projected second Strategic Arms Limitation Talks (SALT II) and discussed problems in Iran and the Middle East, economic aid for Africa, the conflict between Vietnam and Cambodia, and ways to reduce Soviet fears that improved Western relations with China would lead to a reduced Western commitment to détente.

Giscard placed a heavy emphasis on France's role in Africa. In his view, the economic and political problems of emerging African nations provided tempting opportunities for the Soviet Union, which threatened to attract American intervention and turn Africa into another battleground for the superpowers. He therefore worked to prevent conflict by increasing French military, political and financial aid, mainly to French-speaking African countries, regardless of their political policies. During his presidency, France maintained a force of 12,000 troops in Africa; helped to put down rebellions in Mauritania, Zaire and Chad; and extended billions of dollars in French aid.

Giscard also worked hard to develop close relations with communist China in order to emphasize France's independence from the Soviet Union. DENG XIAOPING visited France in May 1975 and applauded France's foreign policy of "defending" its "national independence and reinforcing the union of Europe." Prime Minister Hua Guofeng visited in October 1979 and was extended the courtesies due to a head of state.

Giscard visited China in October 1980 and said that the Chinese leaders shared his views on the need for a multipolar world in which the United States and the Soviet Union did not monopolize decision-making.

Regular meetings between Giscard and Brezhnev continued, and at a summit meeting in May 1979 the two leaders signed a 10-year economic agreement and set the frequency of the summit meetings at once a year instead of once every two years. But at the same meeting, Brezhnev failed to persuade France to join the third round of strategic arms limitation talks, and Giscard failed to win Soviet approval for a general European conference on the reduction of conventional arms on the continent.

In June 1975 Giscard visited POLAND and signed documents strengthening economic, political and cultural relations. Among the agreements was one granting Poland credits worth $1.75 billion for the purchase of French products over the following three years and another increasing French purchases of Polish coal. Giscard reportedly wanted to take a hard line on Poland following the crackdown on the SOLIDARITY trade union in December 1980 but was dissuaded by Schmidt.

Giscard's initial reaction to the Soviet invasion of AFGHANI-STAN was muted criticism. But after a meeting with Schmidt, Giscard agreed to a joint statement saying that the Soviet intervention was "unacceptable and create[d] grave dangers for the stability of the region and for peace." The two leaders also said that the détente had become "more difficult and more uncertain." It could not, they said, survive another blow of the same magnitude as the Afghan crisis.

This French commitment to Western solidarity did not last long. Giscard became increasingly concerned at the rapid increase in East–West tensions and in May 1979 flew to Warsaw for a hurried meeting with Brezhnev. The meeting angered Schmidt, Prime Minister MARGARET THATCHER and Carter, all of whom were given only a day or two's notice of the summit. Giscard's gesture also failed to extract any concessions from Brezhnev on Afghanistan. Government representatives said afterward that the talks "revealed positions that were far apart and remain far apart." Giscard also raised the problem of the Soviet Union's deployment of intermediate-range nuclear weapons (SS-20s) in Europe and warned that NATO would be likely to match them with American missiles unless the deployment was halted. Brezhnev also failed to respond to Giscard's warning, and at the meeting of NATO foreign ministers in December 1979 it was agreed to deploy American cruise and PERSHING II missiles.

Giscard's attempts to save the relationship with the Soviet Union proved embarrassing during the 1981 presidential elections, which he contested with Mitterrand. French public opinion had swung clearly away from the Soviet Union, and in March 1981 *Pravda*, the Soviet Communist Party's newspaper, praised Giscard as a "prudent and careful politician" and criticized Mitterrand for lacking a "clear and consistent political program" and for trying "to suit the interests of a very broad range of voters."

Mitterrand grabbed the opportunity presented by *Pravda's* virtual endorsement of Giscard and said that it was natural that Giscard "should receive a wage for his journey to Warsaw." He added, "Why is Pravda displeased with me? Because I did not wait 11 days to protest against the invasion of Afghanistan, like the outgoing candidate." Giscard lost the presidential election in May 1981, taking 48% of the vote compared to 52% for Mitterrand.

Giscard continued to speak out on foreign policy and economic issues and in September 1984 was reelected to the French National Assembly in what some observers interpreted as the start of a political comeback. In April 1986 he failed in his bid to be elected president of the Assembly, but he did well in the June 1988 National Assembly elections. In January 1989 he was included in a group of members of the Trilateral Commission who visited Moscow for talks with Soviet leader MIKHAIL GORBACHEV. During the 1989 European Parliament elections, he led a Gaullist–UDF coalition that won the most French seats, with 28.9% of the vote compared to 23.6% for the French Socialists.

For Further Information:
Aldrich, Robert, and John Connell, eds. *France in World Politics.* New York, 1989.
Kennan, George F. *The Fateful Alliance.* New York, 1984.
MacKay, D. *The United States and France.* Westport, Conn., 1983.
Meisel, James. *The Fall of the Republic.* Ann Arbor, Mich., 1962.

Glassboro Summit   (1967)   The Glassboro Summit was the fifth postwar summit between U.S. and Soviet leaders and the only one between President LYNDON JOHNSON and Premier ALEXEI KOSYGIN. Although it did not produce any startling breakthroughs, the meeting is believed to have played a major part in paving the way for subsequent Strategic Arms Limitation talks.

In June 1967 the Johnson administration learned that Premier Alexei Kosygin would be leading a Soviet delegation to the United Nations and would welcome a summit meeting with the American president. Johnson welcomed the initiative and proposed that they meet at an Air Force base in New Jersey, roughly halfway between UN headquarters in New York and the U.S. capital in Washington. Kosygin accepted New Jersey but refused to meet at an American military establishment. Thus they agreed on the unlikely venue of the home of Dr. Thomas Robinson, the president of Glassboro State College in Glassboro, New Jersey, on June 23 and June 25.

Because of the short preparation time, the two leaders started the talks at cross-purposes. Johnson wanted to use the talks to try to start formal STRATEGIC ARMS LIMITATION TALKS (SALT). Kosygin, whose position in the Kremlin was weakening, had no authority over strategic arms negotiations and had asked for the meeting to try to secure American concessions in the Middle East. Each time Johnson raised the issue of strategic arms talks, Kosygin switched the subject to the Middle East and implied that the strategic negotiations would be fruitless because the United States wanted to talk only about limiting ANTIBALLISTIC MISSILE (ABM) systems while the Soviets felt ABM and offensive nuclear weapons should be linked (these positions were reversed in 1969).

Although no issues were resolved at Glassboro, the meeting underscored the American commitment to SALT. A year later, the United States and the Soviet Union agreed to negotiate limitations of strategic nuclear weapons systems as well as anti-ballistic missile systems.

Goldberg, Arthur   (August 8, 1908–January 19, 1990)

Arthur Goldberg, a former Supreme Court associate justice, was U.S. ambassador to the United Nations during the JOHNSON administration. He was a staunch opponent of U.S. involvement in Vietnam during both the Johnson and Nixon administrations. He also supported other liberal foreign and domestic policies.

Goldberg was the son of Russian Jewish immigrants. Raised in Chicago, he worked his way through college and law school. After law school he developed an expertise in trade union law and eventually became special counsel to the AFL-CIO. President JOHN F. KENNEDY appointed Goldberg secretary of labor in 1961 and in 1962 raised him to the Supreme Court, where he took a solid liberal position.

In 1965 President Johnson asked Goldberg to step down from the Supreme Court to become U.S. ambassador to the United Nations after the death of ADLAI STEVENSON. Goldberg was told by the president that he would have a direct influence on American foreign policy and on ending the VIETNAM WAR, which was of special concern to Goldberg. In fact, he was unable to influence the administration's Vietnam policies, which became increasingly hard-line and in direct conflict with Goldberg's beliefs. Goldberg's refusal to fall into line with administration thinking soured his relationship with Johnson.

Goldberg made several attempts to start peace negotiations through the United Nations, but these were blocked either by the North Vietnamese or the Johnson administration. The major stumbling blocks he faced were President Johnson's refusal to stop bombing North Vietnam and the North Vietnamese refusal to countenance negotiations until the bombing was halted. It was not until after the TET OFFENSIVE in early 1968 that Goldberg can be said to have influenced American policy in Southeast Asia. Following the offensive, Johnson ordered a review of American policy. Goldberg wrote an eight-page memorandum urging a complete halt to the bombing. His carefully reasoned argument added to the weight of other similar advice and contributed to Johnson's announcement on March 31 that he was halting the bombing raids and de-escalating U.S. involvement.

On issues other than Vietnam, Goldberg was able to play a greater role. He helped to draft the cease-fire resolution that stopped the fighting during the 1965 Indo-Pakistani War and in 1966 introduced a resolution declaring that South Africa had forfeited all right to administer Southwest Africa (Namibia). In the aftermath of the 1967 Arab–Israeli war, Gold-

berg worked to prevent a universal condemnation of Israel and garnered support for the British-sponsored U.N. Resolution 242, which became the basis for future Middle East negotiations. The resolution asserted Israel's right to exist while at the same time calling for its withdrawal from the West Bank and the Gaza Strip.

Goldberg resigned as ambassador in April 1968. During the NIXON administration he became a prominent critic of the Republican president's foreign and domestic policies. He supported recognition of communist China, urged the ratification of the Nuclear Non-Proliferation Treaty, demanded that the president accept the principle of a "prompt withdrawal of all American forces" from Vietnam, organized lawyers to lobby against the war and formed a national citizen's committee to oppose Nixon's proposal to continue funding development and deployment of an antiballistic missile system.

In March 1970, Goldberg announced that he was a candidate for governor of New York. He narrowly won the Democratic Party nomination but was defeated by incumbent Nelson Rockefeller. It was later revealed that during the campaign, Rockefeller had commissioned a derogatory biography of Goldberg. After his defeat, Goldberg returned to his law practice but continued to speak out on public issues.

For Further Information:
Bohlen, Charles. *The Transformation of American Foreign Policy.* New York, 1969.
Finger, Seymour M. *American Ambassadors at the UN.* New York, 1988.
Johnson, Richard. *The Administration of United States Foreign Policy.* Austin, Tex., 1971.

Goldwater, Barry   (January 1, 1909–   )

U.S. senator Barry Goldwater was an ultraconservative Republican and was the Republican candidate for president in 1964. After his humiliating defeat in that election, the right-wing conservatives lost control of the Republican Party and did not fully regain it until the election of Ronald Reagan in 1980.

Goldwater left the University of Arizona after his first year to join the family retailing business. By 1937 he was the president of Goldwater, Inc. During World War II he served as a pilot in the Far East, and after the war he became involved in Arizona politics. He was elected to the U.S. Senate in 1952.

Goldwater quickly established himself as an ultraconservative on domestic and foreign issues. On the domestic scene, he opposed farm price supports, federal aid for education, tax reductions for low-income families and minimum wage laws. On foreign issues, he pressed for a reduction of foreign aid and retaliation against nations trading with communist China.

Goldwater supported Senator JOSEPH MCCARTHY's anti-communist crusade and was one of the 22 senators who voted against his censure in December 1954. He told a Wisconsin Republican convention that "because Joe McCarthy lived, we are a safer, freer, more vigilant nation today."

Throughout most of the 1950s Goldwater concentrated his activities on domestic issues. He was particularly interested in trying to curb the activities of organized labor. Walter Reuther, president of the United Automobile Workers, labeled Goldwater "this country's number one political fanatic."

By the 1960 Republican National Convention, Goldwater was recognized as the leader of the party's right wing. He became increasingly identified with extreme far-right groups. He defended the John Birch Society from its critics and hailed as "the wave of the future" the Young Americans for Freedom founded by journalist WILLIAM F. BUCKLEY.

Goldwater was a fervent opponent of President JOHN F. KENNEDY's foreign policy. He voted against the confirmation of CHESTER BOWLES as undersecretary of state because of Bowles' positions on disarmament and recognition for communist China. He also led the conservative attack against Kennedy's pledge not to invade Cuba. During the debate on the NUCLEAR TEST BAN TREATY in September 1963 Goldwater proposed an amendment that would have made ratification contingent upon the removal of all Soviet troops and weapons from Cuba. When his amendment was rejected, he joined 18 other senators in voting against the treaty.

By the autumn of 1963, Goldwater appeared to be the leading contender for the Republican Party's 1964 presidential nomination, and in January 1964 he announced his candidacy. The primary campaign was a closely fought contest that polarized the Republican Party. At the party convention, Goldwater won the nomination on the first ballot with 883 votes to 214, but the divisions persisted throughout the campaign.

Johnson's campaign advertisements focused heavily on Goldwater's ultraconservatism. Goldwater was portrayed as the enemy of Social Security and world peace. Goldwater added fuel to Johnson's campaign by proposing to use nuclear weapons in the VIETNAM WAR and attacking Medicare and the War on Poverty. The result was a landslide victory for Johnson, with Goldwater winning only 38.4% of the vote and carrying only five states.

After the election Goldwater went into a temporary retirement, but was reelected to the Senate in November 1968. He supported RICHARD NIXON's 1968 presidential campaign. Goldwater became one of the chief supporters of the Vietnam War during the Nixon administration, and even after the withdrawal of American forces and the 1973 peace treaty he called for increased American support for the South Vietnamese government. He also strongly opposed efforts to normalize relations with China. In 1982 he visited Taiwan and pressed for the sale of American weapons to the Nationalist Chinese.

Goldwater supported Reagan in both the 1976 and the 1980 elections. He was a harsh critic of President JIMMY CARTER's foreign policy, which he described as marked by "an unseemly haste, an almost feverish eagerness to reach agreements." In 1978 Goldwater led a group of conservative senators in filing suit in U.S. District Court in Washington against the Carter administration's decision to abrogate the U.S. defense agreement with Taiwan. They argued that the treaty could not be abrogated without the backing of the Senate.

The court ruled against them, and the U.S. Supreme Court declined to hear their appeal.

In January 1981, Goldwater was named chairman of the Senate Intelligence Committee. He was also chairman of the Armed Services Committee. During the Reagan administration, Goldwater appeared to shift away from his hard-line conservative views of the past. He opposed Reagan's decision to send U.S. Marines into Lebanon in 1983, saying, "we have no business playing policeman over there. . . ." In January 1985 he came out in favor of defense cuts, although he proposed that they be tied to cuts in domestic spending. Goldwater retired in 1986.

For Further Information:
Goldwater, Barry. *The Conscience of a Conservative.* New York, 1960.
Novak, Robert. *The Agony of the GOP, 1964.* New York, 1965.
White, F. Clifton. *Suite 3505; The Story of the Draft Goldwater Movement.* New Rochelle, N.Y., 1967.

Golitsin, Anatoli   See ANGLETON, JAMES JESUS.

Gomulka, Wladyslaw   (February 6, 1905–September 1, 1982)   Wladyslaw Gomulka was the dominant political figure in postwar Poland, and his career illustrated the limitations of East European political independence from the Soviet Union and the problems that East European leaders faced in balancing Soviet demands against the pressure of national aspirations.

Gomulka came from a working-class background, and his father was an active socialist. Gomulka joined the Socialist Party at age 15 and then, in 1926, switched his allegiance to the Polish Communist Party. Shortly afterward he was arrested for his political activities. Throughout the 1930s Gomulka organized strikes and was in and out of prison; after the division of Poland in 1939 he moved to the Soviet-occupied sector of the country.

He returned to his political activities when Germany invaded the Soviet Union in 1941. In July 1942 he moved to Warsaw to organize the communist resistance to German occupation. At the same time he became the party's district secretary in Warsaw and a member of the Central Committee. In November 1943 Gomulka was named secretary general of the Workers' Party.

When the Red Army entered Poland in July 1944, Gomulka moved to Lublin to join the Moscow-supported provisional government headquartered there and quickly established himself as number two in the party hierarchy behind Stalin's close associate BOLESLAW BIERUT. Gomulka was named deputy premier in January 1945 and in June 1945 was given responsibility for the administration of all Polish lands recovered from Germany. At the party conference in December 1945, he was formally elected secretary general and joined the Politburo.

But in the early war years differences began to arise between Gomulka and the Soviet Union. Gomulka was utterly ruthless in crushing political opposition and establishing the supremacy of the Polish communists. He was also a committed ideologue and during the war helped to write the party's ideological manifesto. But, at the same time, he argued that communism had to be tailored to suit different nations, and in the case of Poland, he believed that this meant the party could not carry through the forced collectivization of agriculture that had become a hallmark of the Soviet economy. He also opposed the formation of COMINFORM, the Communist Information Bureau.

This brought Gomulka into direct conflict with JOSEF STALIN, who had him accused of "political deviation" and "Titoism." Gomulka was forced to admit defeat in September 1948 and on September 5 was replaced as secretary general by Bierut. He was stripped of all his government posts on January 21, 1949, and ousted from the party on November 14, 1949. He was finally arrested on July 10, 1951, and imprisoned after being found guilty of "Titoism."

The persecution, arrest and imprisonment of Gomulka played a major role in establishing his political credentials. Throughout this period he refused to admit his guilt; his considerable bravery won him widespread respect and established him as the leader of the reformist wing of the party and the natural alternative to the Stalinists.

Stalin's death in 1953 led to the release of a number of East European communists accused of deviation during the Soviet leader's last years, but because of Poland's special place in Russian history Gomulka was considered a greater threat than most other East Europeans, and he remained in prison until April 6, 1956.

Before Gomulka could be rehabilitated several events were necessary to clear the way for him. The first of these was the Soviet–Yugoslav rapprochement, which indicated to East European communists that the Soviet leadership had accepted that nationalism and communism could exist in the same political structure. The next was NIKITA KHRUSHCHEV's de-Stalinization campaign, which reached its peak with Khrushchev's now-famous speech on February 26, 1956, at the 20th Party Congress in Moscow. This was quickly followed by the sudden death of Boleslaw Bierut on March 12.

But the event that ensured Gomulka's political return was the outbreak of riots among workers in POZNAN. The de-Stalinization campaign had unleashed Polish nationalist aspirations, which found expression in demands for better pay and working conditions. On June 29 a crowd of 50,000 gathered in the main square of the industrial city of Poznan to demand better working conditions, free elections, the withdrawal of Soviet troops and the return to power of Gomulka. Troops opened fire. There was a riot. The police headquarters and prison were stormed and 70 people were killed.

Polish communists turned to Gomulka as the man most likely to win the confidence of the masses. On August 4, 1956, he was readmitted to the party. In September and October the leading Stalinists within the party were forced to resign from their posts, and Gomulka was asked to resume the post of first secretary at the party plenum in October.

This caused political eruptions in Moscow. The new leadership was prepared to accept a nationalist leader in Yugoslavia for the sake of international communist solidarity and because Yugoslavia was of minimal strategic importance to the Russian heartland. But Poland was the traditional invasion route for armies attacking Russia, and throughout history Polish nationalism had led to wars with Russia. The result was a surprise visit to Warsaw by the Soviet leadership just as Gomulka was preparing to deliver his acceptance speech at the party congress.

The purpose of the delegation, which was led by Khrushchev, was designed to prevent the election of Gomulka. The party congress was interrupted while the Polish Politburo drove out to the airport to meet with the Soviets, who told the Poles that Gomulka could not lead the Polish party and that the reform programs planned by Gomulka and the other members of the Politburo could not be allowed to continue. Khrushchev went on to warn the Poles that Soviet tanks had crossed the Soviet–Polish border and were moving toward Warsaw.

At this stage Secretary General Edward Ochab told Khrushchev that the Polish Communist Party was determined to press ahead with the election of Gomulka and that Polish workers were ready to fight the Soviet tanks. The Polish Politburo returned to the conference to complete the election of Gomulka while the Soviet leadership went to their embassy. That night there was a second meeting between Gomulka and Khrushchev, at which Gomulka repeated the Polish insistence that Poles must be allowed to choose their own leaders, but he mollified Khrushchev by promising him that Poland would not withdraw from the WARSAW PACT.

It was a delicate balancing act on the part of Gomulka. In order to maintain order within Poland he had to be seen to be leading a Polish government whose primary loyalties were to Poland rather than the Soviet Union. But, at the same time, he knew that the Soviet tanks could easily crush Poland. Khrushchev did not want to invade Poland, and his main concern was that Poland remain firmly in the Soviet camp. Gomulka's pledge that Poland would remain in the Warsaw Pact answered that concern and made it possible for the Soviet leader to accept the new Politburo gracefully. It was a major political victory for Gomulka, and an estimated 250,000 Poles swept into the Warsaw city center to cheer him.

From that high point in 1956, Gomulka's popularity gradually declined over the next 14 years. He presided over a stagnating economy and instituted only limited reforms, in effect allowing the country to develop into a somewhat less repressive version of a Stalinist state. [For further details, see POLAND.]

Gomulka's political fortunes dipped further after he strongly supported the 1968 Soviet invasion of Czechoslovakia. But the main issue remained the poor economy, and the final straw came with the explosion of the GDANSK RIOTS in December 1970. Faced with the uprising, Gomulka resigned December 20 and was replaced by Edward Gierek. Gomulka disappeared into a quiet retirement, and died on September 1, 1982.

For Further Information:
Bethell, Nicolas. *Gomulka: His Poland, His Communism.* New York, 1969.

Goodwin, Richard   (December 7, 1931–   )   Richard Goodwin was a liberal foreign policy adviser and speechwriter to presidents KENNEDY and JOHNSON. During the Kennedy administration he was heavily involved in Latin American affairs. He resigned from the Johnson administration over the VIETNAM WAR and became a leading critic of U.S. involvement in Southeast Asia.

Goodwin graduated first in his class from Tufts University and Harvard Law School. After working on various congressional committees, he joined the staff of then-Senator John F. Kennedy in 1959 as a speechwriter. Following Kennedy's election to the presidency in November 1960, Goodwin helped to draw up the program for the ALLIANCE FOR PROGRESS, and in January 1961 was named White House Assistant Special Counsel specializing in Latin American affairs.

Goodwin worked directly under ADOLF BERLE and quickly earned a reputation as one of the most liberal thinkers in the Kennedy administration. Goodwin's often abrasive manner made him unpopular with U.S. career diplomats, but his intelligence won him the respect and the ear of the president. Kennedy came to rely increasingly on Goodwin and other White House officials after the failed April 1961 BAY OF PIGS invasion, which had been recommended by the CIA and the Pentagon.

In June 1961 Goodwin came under attack for allegedly holding an unauthorized meeting with Cuban guerrilla leader CHE GUEVARA. Questioned by the Senate Foreign Relations Subcommittee on Latin America, Goodwin explained that he had spoken with Guevara for less than half an hour at a diplomatic cocktail party in Uruguay. Goodwin's evidence was corroborated by American diplomats, and Goodwin himself followed up the attacks by taking a hard line against Cuba, recommending economic and political isolation of the island.

In November 1961 Goodwin left the White House to become deputy assistant secretary of state for Inter-American Affairs. In the State Department Goodwin found many of his policies blocked by the career diplomats whom he had alienated while working in the White House. In July 1962 he temporarily moved over to help Sargent Shriver at the Peace Corps and was considered for the post of presidential adviser on the arts.

During the Johnson administration, Goodwin rejoined the White House staff first as a speechwriter and then, in December 1964, as a special assistant to the president, concentrating on developing the "Great Society" Program.

Goodwin left the Johnson administration in September 1965 in protest against the growing U.S. involvement in Vietnam. He supported the campaigns of antiwar candidate

EUGENE MCCARTHY and then ROBERT F. KENNEDY in 1968. After Kennedy's death, he offered his services to NELSON ROCKEFELLER. After the 1968 election, Goodwin worked as a journalist and author. In 1974 he published *The American Condition*, in which he expressed a deep pessimism about the future of freedom in the United States. In this book, Goodwin asserted that he "had come to the rejection of politics as a vehicle for social change in America."

For Further Information:
Goodwin Richard. *The American Condition.* New York, 1974.
———. *Triumph or Tragedy: Reflections on Vietnam.* New York, 1966.
Levinson, Jerome, and Juan de Onis. *The Alliance that Lost Its Way: A Critical Report on the Alliance for Progress.* Chicago, 1970.
Lumar, Shiv. *U.S. Intervention in Latin America.* Chicago, 1987.
Walton, Richard. *The United States and Latin America.* New York, 1972.

Gorbachev, Mikhail Sergeyevich   (March 2, 1931–   )   As president of the Soviet Union and general secretary of the Communist Party of the Soviet Union, Mikhail Gorbachev was credited with launching a series of initiatives to improve East–West relations dramatically and to reform the Soviet Union politically and economically. Despite serving as a catalyst to end the Cold War, he ended up presiding—against his will—over the formal dissolution of the U.S.S.R. in December 1991.

Gorbachev was born into a peasant family and studied law at Moscow State University. He became an active member of the Communist Party while still at university and was soon an official of Komsomol, the communist youth league, in his home territory of Stavropol. In 1962 he moved into agricultural organization and by 1963 was head of the agricultural department for the entire Stavropol region. He continued to rise through the local party hierarchy to become, in April 1970, first secretary of the Stavropol Territory Party Committee, making him effective governor of the province at the relatively young age of 39.

Gorbachev made a name for himself boosting local agricultural production and came to the attention of MIKHAIL SUSLOV, the head of party ideology under LEONID BREZHNEV, and KGB chief YURI ANDROPOV. Acting as Gorbachev's mentors, they arranged for him to be elected to the Supreme Soviet in 1970 and the Central Committee in 1971 and placed him on overseas delegations to Belgium, West Germany and France. In 1978 Gorbachev was taken to Moscow to join the secretariat of the Central Committee and oversee national agricultural production.

He was not successful as the party secretary responsible for agriculture. The Politburo's strict adherence to collective farming plus the uncertain weather meant continued crop failures. It has been argued that Gorbachev became convinced of the need for drastic economic reform during this period. He did, in fact, try to introduce some limited reforms in agriculture such as devolving authority for agricultural production to regional groups and assigning some farmers to specific plots and rewarding them according to results.

The poor harvests, however, had little impact on Gorbachev's continuing rise through the party hierarchy. He became a candidate (nonvoting) member of the Politburo in November 1979 and a full member in October 1980. When Andropov succeeded Brezhnev in 1982, Gorbachev became his right-hand man responsible for political and economic reform and a purge of corrupt officials and practices. Gorbachev's profile rose increasingly, and in May 1983 he led a Soviet delegation to Canada. It seemed that after the death of Andropov in 1984, Gorbachev would succeed his mentor. But the party's old guard, who had been frightened by the Andropov–Gorbachev purge of their ranks, elected one of their own, KONSTANTIN CHERNENKO, as general secretary.

In recompense, Gorbachev was given the powerful role of party ideologue. He consolidated his power base and waited for the ailing Chernenko to eventually die. Now universally recognized as the heir apparent, Gorbachev led a Soviet delegation to Britain. Conservative prime minister MARGARET THATCHER made a point of meeting the Soviet politician and declared afterward, "I like Mr. Gorbachev. We can do business together." The ensuing close relationship between Gorbachev and the staunchly anti-communist Thatcher helped to establish Gorbachev's reformist credentials elsewhere in the world.

Following the death of Chernenko, Gorbachev was elected general secretary of the party on March 11, 1985. In his acceptance speech he vowed to follow the "strategic line" of policies set by the party and his predecessors. He emphasized the need for rapid economic development as the most important goal and called for "further perfection and development of democracy" and "socialist self-government." On nuclear weapons negotiations with the United States, which were scheduled to resume the following day, Gorbachev said he wanted a "termination" of the arms race and offered "a freeze of nuclear arsenals and an end to further deployment of missiles."

Gorbachev's foreign and domestic policies, summed up by the terms *perestroika* (economic restructuring) and *glasnost* (political and social openness), were directed by his absolute priority to improve the Soviet economy and place more consumer goods on the shelves of Soviet shops. Failure to do so, he argued, undermined the socialist revolution at home and abroad. The need to improve the Soviet economy was given added impetus by projections that showed Soviet oil reserves declining. For decades, oil exports had financed investment in prestige industrial projects and successive large defense budgets.

The drop in oil revenues, plus economic mismanagement and corruption during the later years of the Brezhnev administration, made it imperative that the industrial and service sectors of the economy be restructured before it was further undermined. This, in Gorbachev's view, meant decentralization and incentive schemes for workers and managers. It also meant a relaxation of subsidized price structures, which would result in sacrifices by consumers. To win support for the necessary sacrifices, Gorbachev opened up the Soviet political system to give the people a greater say in government.

Many of the economic and political problems faced by the Soviet Union were mirrored among its allies. Their economic shortcomings had been subsidized by loans and aid from the Soviet Union, but Gorbachev moved to reduce that aid and the Soviet Bloc countries were encouraged to imitate the Gorbachev-type reforms, which appeared to move their economic systems toward capitalism. Countries such as Hungary had started several years earlier, but others such as Mongolia and Vietnam became avid reformers, as did Poland. East Germany, Czechoslovakia and Cuba fought against the reforming spirit for their own special reasons.

Defense was the biggest nonproductive sector of the economy, and Gorbachev moved to reduced expenditures significantly. He withdrew large contingents of Soviet troops from East Germany, Hungary, Mongolia and the Sino-Soviet border. He also withdrew all Soviet troops from Afghanistan. Each withdrawal was offered as a unilateral concession to the West or to China in order to win concessions from the West over nuclear weapons negotiations and to heal the SINO-SOVIET SPLIT.

The long-running dispute between China and the Soviet Union was patched up when Gorbachev visited Beijing in May 1989. His visit was marred, however, by Chinese students demonstrating for the resignation of the Chinese Communist Party leadership.

Gorbachev's rapid-fire diplomatic initiatives, unilateral concessions and personal charm made him a major success with a Western public hoping for an end to the Cold War. This produced problems for Western governments that wanted to maintain their defensive strategy. It also produced splits within the Western Alliance, with different governments taking different views on what concessions to offer Gorbachev in return for his initiatives. The British and Americans took the hardest line, and West Germany took the lead in pressing for greater Western concessions on nuclear weapons issues.

Gorbachev himself took a fairly hard line on the maintenance of the Soviet nuclear arsenal, which grew in importance as the more expensive conventional forces were reduced. He agreed to the scrapping of the SS-20 and SS-23 missile systems as enshrined in the INTERMEDIATE-RANGE NUCLEAR FORCES (INF) TREATY of 1987. But he was totally opposed to President RONALD REAGAN's space-based STRATEGIC DEFENSE INITIATIVE (SDI) and proved a tough negotiator in the Strategic Arms Reduction Talks (START).

Gorbachev and Reagan met on five occasions. No two Soviet and American leaders had met more often. The first meeting was in November 1985 in Geneva. In the joint communiqué, both men agreed to the "principle" of a "50% reduction in nuclear arms," as well as "the idea of an interim INF agreement." The two, however, clashed over Reagan's

SDI plan. After the three-day summit, Reagan told reporters that he viewed the meeting as a "fresh start" in U.S.–Soviet relations and added, "We've packed a lot into the last two days and we are headed in the right direction."

The two men met again in Reykjavik, Iceland in October 1986, when Gorbachev demonstrated his diplomatic skill by getting Reagan to agree to eliminate within 10 years all ballistic missiles and nuclear bombs. Reagan's advisers were appalled at the proposal, and the president was forced to make an embarrassing reversal, claiming that there had been a misunderstanding. The talks, which were intended to lay the groundwork for a later, more detailed summit in the United States, broke down over the SDI issue.

Gorbachev did not meet Reagan again until he went to Washington, D.C., in December 1987 to sign the INF Treaty. The visit was a diplomatic triumph for Gorbachev, who was warmly welcomed by American crowds. He especially won high praise for stopping the Soviet motorcade, ignoring security agents and plunging into the crowd to shake hands and proclaim in English, "Hello, I'm glad to be in America."

Gorbachev and Reagan met in Moscow in June 1988 for the signing of the ratified INF Treaty. Gorbachev had by this time won over Reagan to such an extent that the American president withdrew his famous description of the Soviet Union as an "evil empire."

Gorbachev visited New York City in December 1988 to address the United Nations. He vowed in his speech to cut Soviet armed forces by 20%, or 500,000 men, by 1991. He also met with Reagan for the final time of Reagan's presidency and conferred with president-elect GEORGE BUSH. The Soviet leader held his first formal summit with Bush aboard a ship at Malta in December 1989. No agreements were reached, but both men vowed to step up the pace of arms reduction talks. Their second summit was held May 31-June 3, 1990, in Washington D.C., where they signed protocols on strategic arms, chemical weapons, trade and other bilateral issues. Gorbachev went on to visit Minnesota and California, where he had a fond reunion with Reagan.

At Bush's request, the two leaders met in September 1990 for a brief summit in Helsinki, Finland, where they displayed unity on the Persian Gulf crisis. Bush wanted to show Iraq and the world that the superpowers were in accord on opposing Iraq's invasion of Kuwait and on supporting the forceful U.S.-led response to it.

The two men met next at the CONFERENCE ON SECURITY AND COOPERATION IN EUROPE summit in November 1990 in Paris. There they and the other heads of the NORTH ATLANTIC TREATY ORGANIZATION and WARSAW PACT nations signed the Conventional Forces in Europe treaty limiting the deployment of nonnuclear arms on the continent. The CSCE summit was hailed as the formal end of the Cold War.

That ending was further punctuated by the disbanding of the Warsaw Pact in July 1991. That same month, the first post-Cold War superpower summit was held in Moscow, at which Gorbachev and Bush signed the long-awaited START treaty calling for the reduction of long-range strategic weapons. They also announced the joint U.S.-Soviet sponsorship of a Middle East peace conference.

In his final, major arms-control proposal, in October 1991, Gorbachev topped an initiative presented by Bush the previous week by taking Soviet strategic bombers off alert, ordering the destruction of all ground-based tactical nuclear weapons and setting the removal of all short-range nuclear arms from the Soviet Navy, among other sweeping steps.

Gorbachev's so-called "new thinking" was also demonstrated in his policies toward Moscow's increasingly wayward satellite states. In March 1989, meeting with Hungarian communist leader Karoly Grosz, Gorbachev pledged not to interfere with the political reforms under way in Eastern Europe. The vow amounted to a rejection of the BREZHNEV DOCTRINE, which justified Soviet foreign intervention to preserve communist regimes. The withdrawal of Soviet forces from Eastern Europe began in April 1989 with initial tank and troop pullouts from Hungary and East Germany, and by the end of that year the collapse of the region's communist governments, essentially unopposed by Moscow, was in full swing.

The Soviet president was instrumental in the reunification of GERMANY in 1990. He met with German chancellor HELMUT KOHL in July and agreed, in return for a range of concessions, that a united, sovereign Germany could belong to NATO, thus removing a key stumbling block. The two-plus-four treaty was signed in Moscow in September, paving the way for Germany's "unity day" the next month.

Meanwhile, glasnost and perestroika were proceeding apace inside the Soviet Union. In the field of human rights alone, Gorbachev freed dissident Anatoly Shcharansky from jail and pardoned physicist ANDREI SAKHAROV in 1986. Moscow began permitting a sharp increase in the number of Soviet Jews allowed to emigrate in March 1987 and eased emigration restrictions on all Soviet citizens in May 1991; new laws were enacted curbing the use of mental hospitals to detain political dissidents in January 1988; a law guaranteeing religious freedom for all citizens was passed in October 1990.

The Supreme Soviet (the standing national legislature) also passed Gorbachev's most comprehensive package of economic reforms in October 1990. They called for a phasing-out of state controls on the prices of nonessential goods and services, a sell-off of state properties and the establishment of a convertible currency. In a follow-up action in July 1991, the legislature approved the sale, or "denationalization," of state-owned enterprises.

In the political realm, in March 1989 the Soviet Union held its first nationwide elections since 1917 to select members to nonreserved seats in the new Congress of People's Deputies. Independents routed communist candidates in many districts, and BORIS YELTSIN, ousted from the Politburo by Gorbachev in 1988, won Moscow's at-large seat. (He was elected Russian president in 1990.) Then in February 1990, the Communist Party, pressured by Gorbachev, renounced its monopoly on political power, paving the way for a multiparty system.

Gorbachev's dizzying and unending series of international initiatives and domestic reforms clearly made him the most respected and well-liked statesman on the world stage from the mid-1980s through the early 1990s. In December 1989, *Time* magazine named him "Man of the Decade," and in October 1990 he was awarded the Nobel Prize for peace for his crucial role in ending the Cold War. However, the frequently voiced joke that he was more popular abroad than at home proved in the end to be all too true.

In essence, he seemed to have been undone by two key trends. One was that the half-way policies of perestroika failed, and in fact seemed to deepen the country's economic misery. (Reformers argued that the "restructuring" did not go far enough toward a true market system, while many ordinary citizens found themselves nostalgic for the relative plenty they had enjoyed during the Brezhnev era of "stagnation.") The other was that the policies of glasnost succeeded, although probably in ways undreamed of by their architect. The civic and social spheres were indeed "opened," releasing nationalist, ethnic and political currents that swept away the old system. For all his transformative policies, Gorbachev—a self-described dedicated Marxist committed to a unitary Soviet state—was part of that system, and he was swept away with it.

The beginning of the end came in November and December 1990. Gorbachev, responding to economic and nationalist ferment, consolidated his presidential powers, elevated Communist Party (CP) loyalists to prominent posts and boosted the authority of state security forces. The moves were viewed as a victory for CP hardliners and alarmed Gorbachev's liberal allies. Foreign Minister EDUARD SHEVARDNADZE, his long-time adviser, resigned and warned of an impending dictatorship. Then, in March 1991, a referendum on national unity revealed the growing strength of separatist sentiment, as six republics boycotted the vote and Ukraine voters backed independence.

The turning point was the bungled coup by CP conservatives against Gorbachev on August 19–21, 1991. Gorbachev was put under house arrest while vacationing on the Black Sea in the Crimea. Back in Moscow, it was announced that he had been incapacitated with an unspecified illness and was being replaced by an eight-man state emergency committee. The committee's key members were Vice President Gennadi Yanayev, KGB chairman Vladimir Kryuchkov, Premier Valentin Pavlov, Defense Minister Dmitri Yazov and Interior Minister Boris Pugo. All had been appointed to their positions by Gorbachev.

The coup leaders pledged to continue Gorbachev's reforms while at the same time restoring law and order, economic stability, territorial integrity and national honor. "Whereas only yesterday a Soviet person finding himself abroad felt himself a worthy citizen of an influential and respected state, now he is often a second-rate foreigner, the attitude to whom is marked by either contempt or sympathy," the committee said in a statement.

The coup appeared to have been poorly planned, and it quickly fizzled in the face of uncertainty over the support of the military and overwhelming opposition both within the country and abroad. Hundreds of thousands of pro-democracy protesters rallied against the coup in cities around the nation. The most visible, organized and influential defiance took place in Moscow and was led by Russian president Yeltsin and his followers, who faced down tanks while decrying the coup leaders as "traitors" and "putschists."

Gorbachev was released unharmed and returned to Moscow August 22. By then, most of the conspirators were in custody, while Pugo shot himself to death. In the wake of the coup, Yeltsin emerged as the country's most popular politician, and Gorbachev's fortunes went into a steep decline, although it seemed to take the international community (the U.S. in particular) months to come to grips with that fact.

Gorbachev quit as CP leader August 24, although he remained a party member. He also issued a series of decrees curbing the party, disbanding the Central Committee, placing all the party's property under the control of the Soviet parliament and banning its political activity in public institutions. The Supreme Soviet followed up August 29 by voting to suspend all party activities. The series of moves effectively ended the 74-year reign of Soviet communism.

The Congress of People's Deputies September 5 approved a Gorbachev plan to transfer sweeping powers to the republics, creating an interim political structure to run the country while the Kremlin and the republics redefined their relationship. The new provisional executive body, the State Council, September 6 formally recognized the independence of the three BALTIC STATES. Meanwhile, most of the other republics had already declared their own nominal independence. In October and November, 10 of the remaining 12 republics signed a Soviet economic union treaty, but the political power of Gorbachev's central government continued to erode as Russia under Yeltsin decreed for itself increasingly sweeping powers.

The three Slavic republics of Russia, Ukraine and Belarus (Byelorussia) December 8 signed an agreement forming a COMMONWEALTH OF INDEPENDENT STATES (CIS) to replace the Soviet Union. Gorbachev said the move was illegal but could do nothing to stop it. The five Central Asian republics December 13 agreed to join the CIS. Yeltsin met with Gorbachev December 17 and afterward said that the Soviet president accepted as imminent the demise of the U.S.S.R.

Yeltsin December 19 decreed the Russian takeover of the Kremlin and most of the remaining Soviet government functions and ministries. On December 21, 11 of the 15 former Soviet republics (excepting Georgia, which was embroiled in civil war, and the Baltics) joined together in the CIS. Accepting the inevitable, Gorbachev resigned in a brief, bitter speech to the nation December 25. The Soviet flag over the Kremlin was replaced by the Russian flag, and the U.S.S.R. officially passed into oblivion.

After the demise of the Soviet Union, private citizen Gorbachev continued to occupy himself as an author, foundation head and world traveler, visiting the U.S. and other countries, garnering acclaim and awards, gratefully accepting the honors abroad that always seemed to have eluded him at home.

For Further Information:

Beschloss, Michael, and Strobe Talbott. *At the Highest Levels; The Inside Story of the End of the Cold War.* New York, 1993.

Doder, Dusko. *Gorbachev: Heretic in the Kremlin.* New York, 1990.

Gorbachev, Mikhail. *Perestroika: New Thinking for Our Country and the World.* London, 1987.

———. *Reykjavik.* New York, 1987.

Hough, Jerry F. *Russia and the West: Gorbachev and the Politics of Reform.* New York, 1988.

Kaiser, Robert G. *Why Gorbachev Happened: His Triumphs and His Failure.* New York, 1991.

Sheehy, Gail. *Gorbachev: The Making of the Man Who Shook the World.* London, 1991.

———. *The Man Who Changed the World: The Lives of Mikhail S. Gorbachev.* New York, 1990.

Gorlitz Agreement (1950)

In the Gorlitz Agreement, between the government of East Germany (German Democratic Republic) and the Polish government, the East German government recognized the ODER-NEISSE LINE as the eastern border of Germany and effectively ceded large portions of prewar Germany to Poland. The formal agreement was signed on June 7, 1950, and included five economic agreements providing for a 60% increase in German-Polish trade, exchange on production methods, currency exchange and a cultural treaty.

The West German government denounced the agreement as "traitorous." The United States maintained that the agreement was illegal because the POTSDAM CONFERENCE made it clear that the eastern border of Germany could not be formally decided until a German peace treaty was signed. No such treaty was signed until 1990.

Gorshkov, Admiral Sergei (February 26, 1910–May 13, 1988)

Admiral Sergei Gorshkov transformed the Soviet Navy from a small coastal defense force in the 1950s to a global force capable of projecting Soviet political and military might around the world.

Gorshkov was born into a teaching family in the Ukrainian town of Kamenets-Podolsk. He joined the Soviet Navy at the age of 17. At the time, the navy was suffering from political disgrace following the anti-Bolshevik Kronstadt Mutiny of 1921. It also suffered from the lack of both a political purpose and funds.

Gorshkov's first command was a patrol boat in the Black Sea. This was followed by seven years with the Pacific Fleet, where he commanded destroyers. At the outbreak of the war with Germany, Gorshkov was a rear admiral in command of the Azov Flotilla in the Black Sea. He cooperated closely with the Red Army in the battle for the Caucasus and for a time even commanded the 47th Army.

In December 1943, Gorshkov planned and executed the landings of the Red Army in the Crimea, and in April 1944 he helped to seize the Danube estuary, which led to the Soviet victories in Belgrade and Budapest. After the war, Gorshkov was placed in command of the Black Sea Fleet and in December 1955 was named commander-in-chief of the Soviet Navy.

Throughout its long history Russia has been first and foremost a European land power. This is mainly because it has lacked warm-water ports accessible to the historical and cultural heartland centered on Moscow and Leningrad. Because of these historic and geographic circumstances the navy was starved of funds and talent and was largely restricted to the role of coastal defense.

This was the naval philosophy inherited by Gorshkov, but from the start, he saw the navy as the major instrument for projecting Soviet influence and power far beyond its land-locked European base. He initially faced opposition from Soviet leader NIKITA KHRUSHCHEV, who placed a high priority on the development of intercontinental ballistic missiles. The CUBAN MISSILE CRISIS, however, taught Soviet planners that strategic missiles were not enough. Missiles alone meant that every time the Soviet Union faced American opposition it was faced with the choice of either a nuclear holocaust or a humiliating concession.

To overcome this problem, the Soviet military required conventional forces capable of being moved and maintained anywhere in the world. This demanded a global navy. Following the fall of Khrushchev in 1964, Gorshkov's calls for such a navy were welcomed. Between 1964 and 1976 the navy expanded almost 14-fold. Soviet combat surface ships equipped with surface-to-air missiles appeared in the Mediterranean in 1964. These were reinforced with cruise-missile submarines between 1966 and 1967, and their stationing was declared permanent. In 1968, Soviet warships moved into the Indian Ocean; in 1969 the practice of periodic sorties was introduced; and in 1980 the nucleus was established in the eastern Atlantic for what was to prove a permanent West Africa patrol. In the 1970s and 1980s Soviet naval bases were established at Aden in South Yemen and at Cam Ranh Bay in Vietnam.

Gorshkov regarded the navy as a diplomatic as well as military tool and set out his views in *The Sea Power of the State*, published in 1976. The book has since been accepted as a major military treatise and has won him wide respect in political and naval circles around the world. Gorshkov argued that the navy was a flexible instrument that could be used in limited conflicts and in support of state interests far from the Soviet frontiers. Above all, he maintained, a strong navy was the indisputable mark of a great power.

The Sea Power of the State not only won Gorshkov international respect, but by association it also increased Western respect for the Soviet Navy. This strengthened Gorshkov's claim that a strong navy brought political benefits and doubtless contributed to his being awarded five Orders of Lenin and the title Hero of the Soviet Union.

Gorshkov placed a heavy emphasis on submarine development, so much so that Khrushchev, in his memoirs, mistakenly referred to the Soviet naval chief as a submariner. It was appropriate that when Gorshkov retired on December 11, 1985, his successor, Admiral Vladimir N. Chernavin, was a specialist in submarine warfare.

For Further Information:
Gorshkov, Sergei. *The Sea Power of the State.* New York, 1976.
Watson, Bruce, and Susan Watson, eds. *The Soviet Navy.* Boulder, Colo., 1987.

Government Communications Headquarters (GCHQ) Cheltenham

Government Communications Headquarters (GCHQ) is the British electronics intelligence agency. It works closely with its counterpart in the United States, the NATIONAL SECURITY AGENCY (NSA).

British electronics intelligence started as an arm of naval intelligence during World War I. It came to prominence during World War II, when its scientists working at Bletchley Park broke the Germans' Enigma code. This enabled the British to read all of Germany's top-secret military cables throughout most of the war.

The British offered the Enigma intelligence to the United States in return for a long-term agreement on the exchange of electronic intelligence. This was formalized in the UKUSA Agreement in 1947. The agreement effectively established a partnership between GCHQ and the NSA covering electronic intelligence. The British operation was directly responsible for monitoring radio and telegraph, telex and telephone traffic to and from Britain, China, the Middle East, Australia and New Zealand.

The electronics intelligence organization moved to the outskirts of the country town of Cheltenham, about 70 miles west of London, in 1952. In addition to monitoring electronic traffic, the staff also develops and breaks codes and works on new methods of electronic surveillance.

For Further Information:
Bamford, James. *The Puzzle Palace.* New York, 1982.

Graduated Deterrence

Graduated deterrence is a term used to describe the maintenance of a defensive posture capable of deterring attack at the conventional, tactical nuclear, intermediate-range nuclear and strategic nuclear levels. This term has also, at times, been extended to include deterrence at a political level and is closely tied to the policy of FLEXIBLE RESPONSE.

Greek Civil War

The Greek Civil War of 1944–49, fought between the British- and American-supported government and Greek communists, was the major factor in the formulation of the TRUMAN DOCTRINE and caused the United States to adopt a practice of stepping in to political vacuums created by British withdrawals. It also led to the establishment of American military bases in Greece.

The Greek Civil War had its roots in the Greek resistance during World War II. A large proportion of the resistance was led by the communist National Liberation Front (EAM) and its military wing, the People's National Army of Liberation (ELAS). In September 1944 the Germans withdrew, and the British landed and returned the London-based government-in-exile to power. The Greek government had been broadened to include the EAM. But left-wing elements in the ELAS refused to work with the British-supported government and publicly threatened to take over the country.

The British believed that the only chance of averting civil war was to disarm the ELAS guerrillas. This was opposed by the communist members of the government, and on December 1, 1944, six EAM ministers in the Greek government resigned. The next day the communists declared a general strike in Athens, and on December 3 fighting broke out between police and the ELAS.

The British commander in Athens was ordered by Prime Minister WINSTON CHURCHILL to open fire on "any male in Athens who assails the British authority or Greek authority with which we are working." Churchill added, "We have to hold and dominate Athens. It would be a great thing for you to succeed in this without bloodshed if possible, but also with bloodshed if necessary."

Churchill decided that the situation was serious enough to require a personal visit. He and Foreign Secretary ANTHONY EDEN arrived in Athens on Christmas Day 1944 and called a conference with ministers and representatives of the ELAS, which resulted in a New Year's truce and the withdrawal of ELAS guerrillas from the Athens area.

On February 12, 1945, a pact was signed between the government and the EAM-ELAS faction that provided the latter would turn in its arms within 14 days. On February 14 martial law was ended and a political amnesty declared for all those who handed in their arms by March 15. It appeared as if British intervention had succeeded in averting civil war. But a combination of factors intervened to prevent a peaceful conclusion.

The first problem was chronic political instability among the non-communist parties. Between April 1944 and the end of the civil war in 1949 there were 17 governments and 12 prime ministers. The resultant political vacuum encouraged the creation of extremist political factions on both the far left and far right. The left wing was dominated by the communists and the right wing was dominated by the fanatical X Organization, whose activities encouraged a communist backlash.

The other factors were the Greek government's territorial claims against neighboring Balkan states and the establishment of communist governments in those states, in particular Yugoslavia and Albania. The Yugoslav leader, JOSIP BROZ TITO, was especially anxious to establish his authority in the Balkans by helping to establish a friendly communist government in Greece. Greek claims on Yugoslav and Albanian territory provided him with an added incentive to support the EAM-ELAS guerrillas.

This support encouraged the Greek communists to continue fighting the British-supported government. They retreated to bases in the mountainous north from which they could be easily supplied by Yugoslavia and Albania and regroup for attacks on the southern half of the country. The Soviet Union was unable to provide more than political support at the United Nations, although it claimed a directing role as the world's major communist power. The Soviet Union's demands on this issue eventually played a major role in the communists' defeat.

The Athens-based government was supported by 40,000 British troops and financial aid from Britain. On January 24, 1946, the British government extended a $40 million loan to stabilize the Greek drachma and $2 million for direct assistance.

The British scheduled elections in Greece for January 25, 1946, but fighting led to their postponement until March 31, 1947. When they were finally held Organization X was barred from participating because it failed to register in time; the communists boycotted the ballot and set out to prevent voting with violence and political intimidation. Only half of the electorate succeeded in voting, and the results were questionable, as many of the "voters" had actually died during the war.

On July 8, Tito claimed that "Greek provocateurs, reactionaries and troops are without reason firing mortars across our frontier, trying to provoke us." He said that Yugoslavia would undergo only partial demobilization so long as other countries remained armed. The Yugoslav ambassador was recalled on August 21, 1947, and the Soviet ambassador returned to Moscow six days later. On September 21, 20 British warships arrived at Nauflion. Greek premier Constantin Tsaldari said that fighting in Salonika had reached "war" status.

The Greek government was being kept in power entirely by British military and financial aid. British and American intelligence reported that the Greek government would fall in 1947 unless British aid was substantially increased, but the British were having their own severe financial problems. Foreign Secretary ERNEST BEVIN tried to maintain aid but came up against strong opposition from chancellor of the exchequer Hugh Dalton, who told him that British aid to Greece would stop after March 31, 1947.

On February 21, 1947, Bevin cabled U.S. secretary of state GEORGE C. MARSHALL informing him that Britain could no longer meet its commitments to protect Greece, and requested American aid for Greece and Turkey (which was being pressed by the Soviet Union to hand over military control of the Dardanelles). It was clear from the cable that if the United States accepted the British request then it was effectively shouldering the burden of protecting the non-communist world. On March 12 President Truman went before Congress to ask for $400 million in aid for Greece and Turkey. He set the request within the context of a deteriorating world situation that required American action to prevent the political vacuum from being filled by communist governments. The policies established in this speech became known as the Truman Doctrine.

The communist powers responded to the Truman Doctrine by creating a communist government in Greece that they could recognize. ELAS leader General Markos Vafthiades broadcast his intention to create the government in August 1947, but it was not until December 24, 1947, that the "Free Greek Government" was proclaimed. At this time the ELAS had between 20,000 and 30,000 guerrillas based mainly in the mountainous north and at camps in Albania and Yugoslavia. They were pushing southward, and by February 1948 they were reported to be within 20 miles of Athens.

But along with financial aid, Truman had also sent military advisers led by General James Van Fleet. The American financial aid helped to stabilize the Greek government, and the U.S. and British military assistance started to drive the ELAS guerrillas back toward the mountains.

The final blow to the Greek communists came from the Soviet Union and Yugoslavia. As American assistance started to take effect, Yugoslavia and the Soviet Union fell out over the issue of Soviet domination of the world's communist parties. The Greek Communist Party, like those around the world, was split between supporters of Tito and Stalin. The Stalinist faction won. On July 10, 1948, Tito announced that he was closing Yugoslavia's borders to the Greek communist guerrillas, and on July 23 Yugoslav foreign minister Edvard Kardelj announced that Yugoslavia was withdrawing "moral and political" support.

The Greek government forces started their spring offensive on April 16, 1948. On August 8 they announced that they had reached the Albanian frontier. On January 27, 1949, Greek guerrillas broadcast an offer for peace negotiations if the government would stop taking U.S. aid, agree to a ceasefire, grant an amnesty to all political prisoners and negotiate for a "government acceptable to both sides." Two days later the government replied that the only terms for peace were that the "bandits" lay down their arms. On May 6 Miltiades Porphyrogenis, justice minister of the Free Greek Government, said the rebels would be satisfied with an "honest free election" and the reinstatement of the Communist Party to legitimate Greek politics.

On August 28 the Greek Army captured the last major rebel stronghold in the Grammos Mountains after a three-day drive up 8,000-foot Grammos Peak. On October 16 the Greek rebel radio said that they had halted military operations "to avoid the total destruction of Greece."

For Further Information:
Bullock, Alan. *The Life and Times of Ernest Bevin.* London, 1960.
Gage, Nicholas. *A Place for Us.* Boston, 1989.
Grivas, George. *On Guerrilla Warfare.* New York, 1964.
Nachmani, Amikam. *International Intervention in the Greek Civil War: The United Nations Special Committee on the Balkans, 1947–1952.* New York, 1990.
O'Ballance, Edgar. *The Greek Civil War, 1944–1949.* New York, 1966.
Stavrakis, Peter J. *Moscow and Greek Communism, 1944–1949.* Ithaca, N.Y., 1989.

Vlavianos, Haris. *Greece 1941–49: From Resistance to Civil War: The Strategy of the Greek Communist Party.* London, 1992.

Greenland–Iceland–UK Gap   The Greenland–Iceland–UK (GIUK) Gap refers to the relatively narrow area of the North Atlantic through which the Soviet Navy would have had to pass in order to threaten the vital North Atlantic sea lanes.

The Soviet Union's western fleet, especially its hunter-killer submarines, was based at Murmansk on the Barents Sea. This meant that for the Soviet Navy to seriously threaten the North Atlantic it would have had to round the northern tip of Norway and come down through the North Atlantic either to the east of Iceland between Britain and Iceland or to the west of Iceland between Greenland and Iceland.

NATO forces took advantage of this geographic situation by concentrating a large proportion of their naval power and air surveillance in the GUIK Gap. Air surveillance was shared by British and American forces based at Reykjavik Air Force Base in Iceland. The British had the major responsibility for naval patrols. The British, Dutch, Canadians and Americans also had responsibility for the defense of Norway should the Soviet Union have attacked the NORTHERN FLANK across the Kola Peninsula in an attempt to establish air bases in Norway.

Grenada   The Caribbean island of Grenada was the target of an American invasion in 1983 following a left-wing coup. Although it was America's first successful military action after the VIETNAM WAR, its strategic significance was questionable.

Grenada was a British colony until it gained independence in February 1974. After independence, Grenada remained in the Commonwealth and recognized the British queen as its sovereign. She was represented by a governor general. At independence, the island's politics were dominated by Sir Eric Gairy, the right-wing leader of the Grenada United Labour Party (GULP).

In March 1979 Gairy was overthrown in a bloodless coup led by Maurice Bishop, leader of the left-wing New Jewel Movement (NJM). Gairy fled to exile in the United States. Bishop's left-wing policies alienated him from Britain, the United States and the island's historic allies in the English-speaking Caribbean, who formed the Organization of Eastern Caribbean States (OECS). Bishop turned increasingly toward the Soviet Bloc countries for financial and military aid, which was provided by Cuba, the Soviet Union and East Germany.

The Cubans built and operated an airport at Port Salines, which American officials feared would become a Caribbean staging post for the ferrying of supplies from the Soviet Union or Cuba to Central and South America. U.S. objections to the Port Salines project further strained U.S.–Grenadan relations, and in 1983 the Bishop government warned that it was expecting an American invasion.

In an effort to improve relations with the United States, Bishop released a number of political prisoners and announced that he would rewrite the constitution. This was unpopular with a left-wing faction of the NJM led by Party Deputy Bernard Coard, who on October 13, 1983, had Bishop placed under house arrest. Six days later, thousands of Bishops's supporters rioted and freed him from imprisonment. But the same day, the Coard-controlled People's Revolutionary Army rearrested Bishop, executed him, staged a successful coup and imprisoned the other key members of the New Jewel Movement.

Sir Paul Scoon, the governor-general of the island, asked the Organization of Eastern Caribbean States to intervene and restore order. The OECS in turn asked for American assistance. The result was that on October 25, 1983, some 7,355 American troops invaded the island, along with about 300 troops from Jamaica. The official State Department justification for the invasion was the danger posed to the 1,000 American residents on the island and the threat to American national interests posed by the Port Salines airport.

The fighting was over in a few days. The United States put the final death toll at 18 American troops, 45 Grenadians (including 18 patients at a mental hospital mistakenly bombed by a U.S. jet) and 24 Cubans. The U.S. invaders encountered over 700 Cubans on the island, most of them airport construction workers armed with small arms who put up unexpectedly fierce resistance.

On November 9 a nonpolitical interim council was appointed to run the government until elections could be held. The United States started withdrawing its troops in mid-November and by December 1983 had reduced its presence to 300 men. Elections held in December 1984 were won by the centrist New National Party led by Herbert Blaize.

For Further Information:
Ashby, T. *The Bear in the Backyard.* Lexington, Mass., 1987.

Burrowes, R.A. *Revolution and Rescue in Grenada.* Westport, Conn., 1988.

Davidson, Scott. *Grenada: A Study in Politics and the Limits of International Law.* Brookfield, Vt. 1987.

Lumar, Shiv. *U.S. Intervention in Latin America.* Chicago, 1987.

Miller Nicola. *Soviet Relations with Latin America, 1959–1987.* New York, 1989.

O'Shaughnessy, Hugh. *Grenada: An Eyewitness Account of the U.S. Invasion and the Caribbean History That Provoked It.* New York, 1984.

Payne, Anthony. *Grenada: Revolution and Invasion.* New York, 1984.

Gromyko, Andrei   **(July 6, 1909–July 2, 1989)**   As the longest-serving foreign minister of the postwar years, Andrei Gromyko played a leading part in the conduct of Soviet foreign policy from the 1950s to the 1980s.

Gromyko started his career as an academic, lecturing in agricultural economics at the Moscow Institute of Economics of the Academy of Sciences from 1936 to 1939. The post was a relatively obscure one and saved Gromyko from Stalin's "Great Purge" of the 1930s, which left the ranks of the Soviet diplomatic service sadly depleted.

The purge provided opportunities for bright young men to

move quickly through the ranks. Gromyko joined in 1939 and was immediately appointed chief of the U.S. division of the Soviet Foreign Office. Before he could complete his English-language course, Gromyko was posted to Washington, D.C., as counselor at the Soviet Embassy. In 1943 he was named ambassador to the United States and in 1946 permanent representative to the United Nations and deputy foreign minister. He was appointed ambassador to Britain in 1952 and a year later returned to Moscow as deputy foreign minister, and finally he became foreign minister in 1957, a post he held until becoming president in July 1985.

Gromyko owed his success and political longevity in large part to his good fortune in being at the right place at the right time and his ability to act as a faithful executor of policies developed by others. In the early years his influence was limited. It was not until the Brezhnev period, especially during Leonid Brezhnev's final years in power, that Gromyko became the major shaper as well as executor of Soviet foreign policy. He did not join the Politburo until 1973.

When Gromyko joined the diplomatic service, Britain was the world's major superpower and the United States was still encased in its traditional isolationism. With the Soviet diplomatic service purged of its American experts, Gromyko emerged from World War II as one of the few Soviet experts on the United States, and at roughly the same time America emerged from its prewar isolation to take the role of leader of the Western world. JOSEF STALIN and his Foreign Minister V.M. MOLOTOV were forced to turn increasingly to the young Gromyko (only 36 at the end of the war) for advice. As a result, Gromyko was included in the Soviet delegations to the YALTA and POTSDAM conferences, where he advised Molotov and Stalin on likely American responses. He also headed the Soviet delegation to the 1944 Dumbarton Oaks conference that led to the founding of the United Nations.

During the early part of his career, Gromyko formed a close relationship with Molotov, and he became known as the latter's protégé. When Molotov fell out of favor with Stalin in 1949, Gromyko's career started to falter, although he soon displayed his ability to project himself as the faithful servant of whoever was in power in the Kremlin. He kept his post and continued to rise gradually while Molotov's more distant associates disappeared. After Stalin's death in March 1953, Molotov was restored to his former post, and Gromyko's career returned to the fast track with his appointment as Molotov's deputy in 1954, candidate membership in the Central Committee in 1956 and full membership in 1957.

Gromyko demonstrated his chameleon-like adaptability again in 1957 when Molotov was dismissed after losing in a power struggle to NIKITA KHRUSHCHEV. Instead of dismissing the protégé with the mentor, Khrushchev promoted Gromyko to foreign minister. Khrushchev liked to draw attention to Gromyko's "civil servant" status and in his memoirs described him as "a good civil servant who always went by the book." The Soviet leader was clearly in charge of policy, but he also relied heavily on Gromyko's knowledge of the mechanics of foreign policy.

The start of Gromyko's tenure as Soviet foreign minister coincided with the first tentative moves toward arms limitation negotiations, and Gromyko, proving himself an expert negotiator, oversaw or was directly involved in the talks surrounding the ABM TREATY, the NUCLEAR TEST BAN TREATY, the QUADRIPARTITE AGREEMENT, the Nuclear Nonproliferation Treaty, SALT I, SALT II and the INF and START negotiations and the CONFERENCE ON SECURITY AND COOPERATION IN EUROPE.

Gromyko played an embarrassing role during the CUBAN MISSILE CRISIS. On October 18, 1962, he visited Washington, D.C. for routine talks with President JOHN F. KENNEDY. The purpose of the visit was to prepare the ground for a new Soviet initiative on Berlin. But Kennedy was more concerned about Cuba. He knew about the presence of Soviet missiles there, but Gromyko did not realize this and was taken aback when Kennedy brought the conversation around to Cuba. He told Kennedy that Soviet aid had "solely the purpose of contributing to the defense capabilities of Cuba . . . ," and he stated, "If it were otherwise the Soviet Government would never become involved in rendering such assistance." Kennedy was later able to accuse Gromyko of lying, which contributed to the humiliation of Khrushchev and the withdrawal of the Soviet missiles.

Gromyko is understood to have taken a hard line during the various crises in BERLIN. He also helped to construct Soviet foreign policies designed to win over the emerging Third World, which led to Soviet and Cuban intervention in Angola and Ethiopia as well as support for the North Vietnamese. In Eastern Europe he consistently followed the party line. The bulk of his efforts were directed toward developing and executing Soviet policy toward Western Europe and the United States. This may have resulted in less attention being given to Asia and may have contributed to the SINO–SOVIET SPLIT of the 1960s and 1970s.

During the Brezhnev years, Gromyko became heavily involved in constructing the diplomatic apparatus of détente. The policy suited the archetypal diplomat, who saw his role as publicly eschewing ideology and furthering his country's national interest while avoiding armed conflict with the West. In 1973 Gromyko's contribution to Soviet foreign policy was recognized when he was made a full member of the Politburo without going through the normal stage of candidate membership.

Gromyko now became the chief architect of Soviet foreign policy. ZBIGNIEW BRZEZINSKI, President JIMMY CARTER's national security adviser, later wrote that during U.S.–Soviet summit meetings Gromyko would whisper instructions in Brezhnev's ear and would sometimes disagree with his superior.

When Brezhnev died in November 1982, Gromyko gave his unqualified support to former KGB chief YURI ANDROPOV in the brief power struggle with Brezhnev's protégé KONSTANTIN CHERNENKO. Andropov rewarded Gromyko by naming him first

Luttwak, Edward. *The Grand Strategy of the Soviet Union*. London, 1983.

Ulam, Adam. *Expansion and Coexistence: The History of Soviet Foreign Policy, 1917–1967*. New York, 1968.

Soviet foreign minister Andrei Gromyko (left) in March 1976 with James Callaghan, Britain's foreign minister. Photo courtesy of the Labour Party.

deputy chairman of the Council of Ministers. Gromyko's opposition to Chernenko might have spelled the end of the career of Moscow's "Great Survivor" had Chernenko, who succeeded Andropov in 1984, lived long enough or been in better health during his brief 11 months as general secretary.

The poor health of both Andropov and Chernenko placed heavy burdens on Gromyko, who took complete control of Soviet foreign policy as well as playing a larger role in the development of domestic economic policy. His detailed exposure to the Soviet Union's economic problems convinced him that drastic reform was essential, and he proposed MIKHAIL GORBACHEV as general secretary in a speech that was unusually eulogistic and almost totally devoid of party phraseology.

Gorbachev had been facing tough opposition from the old guard, who were planning a last-ditch attempt to prevent his nomination. Gromyko's unstinting support was a key factor in Gorbachev's accession to power.

On July 2, 1985, Gromyko was replaced as foreign minister by EDUARD SHEVARDNADZE. The same day, Gromyko was named to the ceremonial post of president of the Soviet Union. The move was interpreted not as a demotion but rather as an honorable retirement post. Gromyko himself is understood to have accepted the impossibility of a survivor of the Stalinist years being able to sell to the Soviet public the policies of *glasnost* and *perestroika*. He retained his seat on the Politburo and conducted a tour of the country gathering information on economic problems. He finally retired from public office on September 30, 1988.

For Further Information:

Bialer, Seweryn. *Stalin's Successors*. New York, 1980.

Gilman, Harry. *The Brezhnev Politburo and the Decline of Détente*. New York, 1984.

Gromyko, Andrei Andreevich. *Memoirs*, Foreward by Henry A. Kissinger. New York, 1989.

Grotewohl, Otto   (March 11, 1894–September 21, 1964)

Otto Grotewohl was the leader of the Social Democratic Party (SPD) in East Germany immediately after World War II. In return for the joint chairmanship of the communist-controlled Socialist Unity Party (SED) he took the SPD into the SED, a move that led to his denunciation by the West German branch of the party. In 1949 he was named prime minister of the German Democratic Republic.

Grotewohl was the son of a tailor and after school was apprenticed to a printer. He quickly became involved in politics and joined the SPD at the age of 18. He briefly flirted with the left wing of the party, which later broke away to become the German Communist Party, but decided that better opportunities lay with remaining in the SPD mainstream. The communists never fully trusted him because of what they regarded as an early betrayal.

Grotewohl quickly made a name for himself as an orator and intellectual. At the age of 26 he was elected to the Brunswick Landtag (state parliament), and two years later was appointed the Brunswick minister of education. In 1929 he was elected to the federal Reichstag. He also left the print trade and through political and business contacts rose to become president of the Brunswick Insurance Company.

After Hitler came to power, Grotewohl was forced to resign as president of the insurance company and earned his living as a salesman. He was arrested by the Gestapo in 1938 but released after being held for a year without trial. He was arrested again in July 1944 following the attempted assassination of Hitler.

The watershed in Grotewohl's career came in the immediate aftermath of the war. He was faced with the opportunity of fleeing to the Western zone or of remaining in the Soviet zone. He decided that there were more opportunities for him in the Soviet zone, and he was quickly chosen as chairman of the Central Committee of the SPD in the Soviet zone.

The SPD was the most popular party in the Soviet zone, and Grotewohl was a respected politician. The Soviets and the East German Communist Party needed his support to lend credibility to their rule. In return for bringing the SPD into the communist-controlled Socialist Unity Party, they offered Grotewohl joint chairmanship of the SED along with communist Wilhelm Pieck. With the Soviet troops backing Pieck and Communist Party secretary WALTER ULBRICHT, the title of joint chairman was never more than symbolic, but Grotewohl decided he had no other choice, and the SPD joined the SED in April 1946.

Grotewohl's move brought a chorus of protest from Social Democrats in both East and West Germany. The West German SPD broke relations with Grotewohl's party, and thousands of protesting SPD members in East Germany were arrested and either imprisoned or executed for treason.

By the end of 1949, Grotewohl was faithfully following the Communist Party line. In January 1949 he publicly warned that the West was "preparing for war," and in March 1949 he supported the entry of the Socialist Unity Party into the Soviet-controlled COMINFORM and promised to support the Soviet Union in any future war with the United States. In October 1949, Grotewohl was named prime minister of the newly formed German Democratic Republic. In June 1950 he was the East German signatory to the GORLITZ AGREEMENT, which recognized the ODER-NEISSE LINE as the eastern border of German. The West German government denounced the agreement as "traitorous," and the United States maintained that the agreement was illegal.

Grotewohl attempted to act as a brake on Ulbricht's extreme nationalization programs, but his inability to influence policies was revealed by his repeated failures. His influence, however, did increase slightly after the EAST GERMAN UPRISING in 1953, and there were a number of relaxations on private property. But this influence was short-lived, and Grotewohl was again quickly eclipsed by Ulbricht. The political eclipse was completed in 1960 when, following the death of Pieck, Ulbricht created the post of chairman of the Council of State, took that office and combined it with his own position as first party secretary, thus making the prime minister's job redundant, even though Grotewohl continued to hold the title.

By this time Grotewohl was not physically capable of offering a challenge to Ulbricht. He was weakened by leukemia and in November 1960 suffered a severe heart attack while visiting the Soviet Union. Grotewohl repeatedly requested permission to retire but was refused because the SED continued to require his symbolic value. Grotewohl finally died on September 21, 1964. The East German government acclaimed him as a "true son of the German people." The SPD in West Germany said that his memory "would remain stained with the blot of having sacrificed the Social Democratic Party in the Russian occupation zone and of having shared in the guilt over the death and imprisonment of SPD members" in East Germany.

For Further Information:

Brant, Stefan. *The East German Rising.* London, 1954.
Fritsch-Bournazel, Renata. *Confronting the German Question.* Oxford and New York, 1988.
McCauley, Martin. *The German Democratic Republic Since 1945.* New York, 1983.
Whetten, Lawrence. *Germany East and West.* New York, 1980.

Ground Burst A ground burst is the detonation of a nuclear device at ground level or below ground level.

This type of detonation would be used against a hardened target such as a missile silo. Against such a target the effects of radiation, which follow an air burst, would be useless. In order for the target to be destroyed it must be subjected to the maximum possible effect of blast and heat. This can be done only when the nuclear warhead is detonated at ground level.

Ground-launched Cruise Missile (GLCM) The Ground-launched Cruise Missile (GLCM) is a cruise missile launched from a ground base. Like its air and sea-launched counterparts, the GLCM has an estimated range of 1,250 miles. It is a slow missile, but its computer guidance system allows it to fly under enemy radar by following the contours of the land.

American GLCMs were the cause of a major revival of the European antinuclear lobby in the 1980s after NATO foreign ministers agreed in December 1979 to deploy American GLCMs and PERSHING II missiles in Western Europe in response to the Soviet deployment of intermediate-range SS-20s.

Despite a number of demonstrations, the missiles were deployed in Britain, West Germany, Italy, Belgium and the Netherlands. The European-based GLCMs and the SS-20s were the main subject of the U.S.–Soviet Intermediate-range Nuclear Force (INF) negotiations in the 1980s. In December 1987 President RONALD REAGAN and Soviet leader MIKHAIL GORBACHEV signed the INF Treaty, which agreed to the withdrawal of both systems. Withdrawal of the U.S. GLCMS started the following year, before the full complement of 464 missiles had been sent across the Atlantic.

GRU (Glavnoye Razvedyvatelnoye Upravleniye) The GRU, or Chief Intelligence Directorate, was responsible for Soviet military intelligence activities. It was also involved in industrial espionage and provided advisers to left-wing guerrilla groups.

The GRU was founded in 1920 as a consequence of an unsuccessful Soviet invasion of Poland. The GRU suffered badly during the Stalinist purges of the 1930s but still managed to perform credibly during World War II. Richard Sorge, one of the most successful Soviet spies, was a GRU agent.

In the early 1950s many of the GRU's responsibilities were taken over by the rival KGB. In 1958 the GRU suffered a major setback when it was discovered that one of its senior officers, Lieutenant Colonel Yuri Popov, was a CIA agent. KGB chairman Ivan Serov was ordered to take charge of the GRU and purge it of potential double agents. In 1962, however, it was discovered that another GRU agent, OLEG PENKOVSKY, was working for both British and American intelligence. Serov was dismissed and replaced by Lieutenant General Petr Ivanovich Ivashutin, the first deputy chairman of the KGB. After that the KGB dominated the upper echelons of the GRU, although the GRU remained a separate entity responsible to the Soviet General Staff.

Guantanamo Bay Guantanamo Bay, on the southeastern end of Cuba, is the site of a U.S. naval base. The base, with approximately 3,000 men, provides the United States with a unique foothold on the communist-governed island. The U.S. Navy's lease on the base expires at the end of the century.

The bay is one of the largest and best sheltered in the world and commands a strategic position that gives the United States control of the Windward Passage, the shipping route linking the Atlantic Ocean to the Caribbean and the Panama Canal. It was this strategic position that led the U.S. Marines to capture the site during the Spanish–American War. The American presence was legalized by a treaty in 1903 that gave the United States "complete jurisdiction and control over the area."

By 1959, when FIDEL CASTRO seized power from FULGENCIO BATISTA, the United States had a major naval installation, an air strip and 5,000 troops based at Guantanamo. In September 1960, after the United States announced trade restrictions against Cuba in retaliation for the seizure of American assets, Castro warned that he would attack Guantanamo.

On November 1, 1960, President DWIGHT EISENHOWER warned that the United States would take whatever steps were necessary to protect the Guantanamo base. He said that the treaties governing the base could be changed only by agreement between the United States and Cuba and that the United States had "no intention of agreeing to modification or abrogation of these agreements." When the United States severed diplomatic relations with Cuba on January 2, 1961, a White House statement reaffirmed the status of the Guantanamo base.

Successive administrations, however, have been careful not to jeopardize the base by using it for either a conventional or subversive attack on Cuba. It was not, for instance, included in the plans for the BAY OF PIGS operation. Neither have the base facilities been involved in any of the various CIA plots to assassinate Castro. Guantanamo was, however, included in advanced contingency plans for a U.S. attack on Cuba during the CUBAN MISSILE CRISIS, and it serves as a listening post for radio communications to and from Cuba.

Castro has consistently condemned the presence of the base as a dangerous anachronism from the days when the United States routinely intervened in Cuba's internal affairs. He knows, however, that a military move against the base would only provide the United States government with an excuse to attack Cuba. The Cuban leader has tried to force the removal of the base by denying it essential supplies from the Cuban hinterland such as water, electricity and food. But each time the United States has demonstrated its commitment to stay by bringing supplies in from outside the island or establishing them on the base.

In May 1966, Castro ordered an island-wide "state of alert" following a series of U.S.–Cuban shooting incidents along Guantanamo's perimeter fence, but two days later the Cuban Communist Party newspaper Granma made it clear that Cuba had no intention of seizing the base.

Guatemalan Intervention   The United States' intervention in Guatemala in 1954 led to the overthrow of a constitutional, elected government. It was the first such postwar U.S. intervention in the Western Hemisphere and graphically demonstrated American determination to prevent the establishment, even by democratic means, of left-wing governments in what it considered its own "backyard."

In 1944 the right-wing dictator Jorge Ubico was overthrown. In the following 10 years, the political center of the country moved gradually to the left under the elected government of the reformist president Juan Jose Arevalo. In the free political atmosphere, the Communist Party was able to form a strong political base within the trade union movement.

Presidential elections in 1950 resulted in a victory for another reformer, Jacobo Arbenz. He quickly set out to introduce a serious land reform program, largely at the expense of the American-owned United Fruit Company, which was Guatemala's largest employer and principal landowner. Because of the company's dominance of Guatemalan agriculture, the country was unable to use the land for vital crops and was forced to import food.

The Agrarian Reform Law, promulgated on June 17, 1952, provided for the expropriation of land not under cultivation, with compensation to be paid in the form of government bonds. The value of the land, however, was fixed on the basis of current tax assessments, which, due to the company's influence, were severely underestimated. This meant that the United Fruit Company received compensation of less than $630,000; the U.S. government, acting on the company's behalf, claimed that the company was owed $15.9 million.

To secure passage of the Agrarian Reform Law, Arbenz had turned to the Communist Party for support. This led to inevitable claims from American anti-communists that Arbenz was either a communist or a puppet of the communists.

In the summer of 1953, the EISENHOWER administration began to act. ALLEN DULLES, director of the Central Intelligence Agency, was directed to organize the overthrow of Arbenz and his replacement with the pro-American Colonel Carlos Castillo Armas. A group of about 200 Guatemalan troops was trained in neighboring Honduras to provide the core of an invasion force. At the same time, U.S. secretary of state JOHN FOSTER DULLES prepared the diplomatic ground for a coup by securing the passage of the "Declaration of Solidarity for the Preservation of the Political Integrity of the American States Against the Intervention of International Communism" at a meeting of the ORGANIZATION OF AMERICAN STATES at Caracas in March 1954.

On May 17, Dulles reported that Guatemala was importing weapons from Czechoslovakia. Two days later the government of Nicaraguan dictator Anastasio Somoza broke diplomatic ties with Guatemala, and on May 24 President Eisenhower announced that the United States was airlifting arms to Nicaragua and Honduras and imposed a naval quarantine on Guatemala. Britain, however, was reluctant to cooperate with a quarantine, and Eisenhower was forced to turn to Armas's troops in Honduras.

The invasion force entered Guatemala on June 18, 1954. At the same time the CIA launched a series of radio broadcasts exaggerating the size of the invasion army in the hope that it would lead to a popular uprising inside Guatemala. Arbenz, however, retained popular support and had a firm grip on the situation inside Guatemala, and the small army of Castillo Armas was soon under threat. On June 22, two of Armas's three bombers, which had been attacking the capital city, were shot down. President Eisenhower was faced with the choice of replacing the planes with U.S. aircraft or withdrawing CIA support. Henry Holland, assistant secretary of state for inter-American affairs, advised against further U.S. intervention, while both Allen Dulles and John Foster Dulles pressed for it. The planes were supplied.

After the United States publicly committed itself to Armas, the Guatemalan Army turned against Arbenz, who had no choice but to resign on June 27. He fled first to Mexico and then to Czechoslovakia. After a series of coups, Armas came to power, reversed the land reform program and restored the property of the United Fruit Company and other large landowners.

For almost four decades, Guatemala has suffered under a series of army dictatorships and military-dominated civilian regimes. It has been conservatively estimated that more than 100,000 civilians have been killed by government troops and death squads fighting both leftist guerrillas and nonviolent social reformers. Guatemala has earned a reputation as Latin America's worst violator of human rights.

For Further Information:

Carmack, Robert M., ed. *Harvest of Violence: The Maya Indians and the Guatemalan Crisis.* Norman, Okla., 1988.

Cook, Blanche Wiesen. *The Declassified Eisenhower: A Divided Legacy.* Garden City, N.Y., 1981.

Fried, Jonathan L., ed. *Guatemala in Rebellion: Unfinished History.* New York, 1983.

Galeano, Eduardo H. *Guatemala: Occupied Country.* New York, 1969.

Gillin, John, and K.H. Silvert. "Ambiguities in Guatemala." *Foreign Affairs* (April 1956).

Pike, Frederick B. "Guatemala, the United States and Communism in the Americas," *Review of Politics* (April 1955).

Taylor, Philip B. "The Guatemala Affair: A Critique of United States Foreign Policy," *American Political Science Review* (September 1956).

Guerrilla Warfare   Guerrilla warfare involves usually non-uniformed combatants employing hit-and-run tactics and unorthodox military measures against a larger conventional force. This type of warfare usually depends on grassroots support.

Guerrilla warfare is not, as is often believed, a 20th-century phenomenon. It has been an accepted military strategy for centuries and was used extensively during the American Revolution. The Russians used it against Napoleon during his retreat from Moscow in 1812, and the term *guerrilla* was first used in Spain to describe Spanish and Portuguese partisans fighting Napoleon's troops during the Duke of Wellington's Peninsular Campaign from 1809 to 1813. Other guerrilla campaigns included the Boer War in South Africa and the successful Arab Revolt directed by T.E. Lawrence during World War I.

Guerrilla warfare holds a strong appeal for communists, as such a war requires a great deal of popular support and can thus be characterized as a "people's war." During the interwar years, Chinese Communist Party leader MAO ZEDONG expressed the political relationship between communism and guerrilla warfare thus: "Guerrilla warfare must fail . . . if its political objectives do not coincide with the aspirations of the people and their sympathy, cooperation and assistance cannot be gained."

The identification of communist movements with guerrilla warfare was strengthened during World War II, since key guerrilla leaders, such as JOSIP BROZ TITO in Yugoslavia, came from the ranks of the Communist Party. The wartime guerrilla organizations formed in Eastern Europe during the war had strong links with the Soviet Union and in the postwar period went on to form the core of the Soviet-supported governments.

Since World War II, a number of communist (and non-communist) popular leftist movements have employed guerrilla operations, and many have received aid from the Soviet Union. Among these have been rebellions in Greece, China, Vietnam, Malaysia, Cuba, El Salvador and Nicaragua. In the later stages of the Cold War, the West's dissatisfaction with leftist and Soviet-supported governments led it to support right-wing guerrilla groups. The most notable recent examples are the Nicaraguan Contras, the Mujahideen in AFGHANISTAN, the UNITA forces in ANGOLA, the Renamo guerrillas in Mozambique and the forces opposed to the Vietnamese- and Soviet-supported government in Cambodia.

A number of guerrilla operations have been employed by political movements inspired more by the fight against colonialism or neo-colonial foreign domination, than by any close identification with communism (or capitalism), although the Soviet Union usually tried to identify with nationalist elements, with varying degrees of success. These include the national liberation movements in the Algerian civil war, the Cypriot Rebellion, the Rhodesia/Zimbabwe civil war, the Eritrean and Tigrean struggle against Ethiopia, the war in Namibia, the Sudanese civil war and the Mozambican and Angolan struggles against Portugal.

Some guerrilla operations are more akin to terrorist activities than to the more sophisticated guerrilla warfare. It is difficult, at times, to draw a distinction between the two. Some of the groups that sometimes have employed such tactics include the PLO (Palestine Liberation Organization), the Mau Mau in Kenya, the ANC (African National Congress) in South Africa and the Irish Republican Army (IRA).

Guevara, Ernesto ("Che")   (June 14, 1928–October 8, 1967)   Che Guevara played an active role in the Cuban Revolution and helped forge the initial ties between FIDEL CASTRO and the Soviet Union. He became a cult figure in the West in the 1960s as a socialist revolutionary strongly opposed to U.S. foreign policy and favoring world revolution. His life, ideas and death inspired millions of people, especially the youth movement of the 1960s and 1970s.

Guevara was born into a comfortable middle-class Argentine family and qualified as a doctor. He became involved in revolutionary politics at an early age. In 1953 he went to Guatemala, where Jacobo Arbenz was attempting a social revolution. The overthrow of Arbenz in 1954, in a coup supported by the CENTRAL INTELLIGENCE AGENCY, is believed to have been a major factor in Guevara's anti-Americanism.

Guevara left Guatemala for Mexico where he met Fidel Castro as he and his brother, Raul Castro, were planning their return to Cuba to overthrow the dictator FULGENCIO BATISTA. He returned to Cuba with Castro and distinguished himself in the guerrilla war that brought Castro to power.

After the Marxist government was established, Guevara adopted Cuban citizenship and joined the government. He served in a number of positions, including president of the National Bank, minister for industry and head of the National Institute for Agrarian Reform. He also headed a number of diplomatic missions, during which he became well known for his virulent attacks on American foreign policy.

In April 1965 Guevara dropped out of Cuba's political life and returned to his previous role of roving revolutionary. Most of his activities during this period were clouded in secrecy, but he is believed to have visited North Vietnam and the Congo. In September 1966 he joined a guerrilla group in Bolivia and was killed by CIA-led Bolivian security forces on October 8, 1967.

For Further Information:
Grivas, George. *On Guerrilla Warfare.* New York, 1964.
Guevara, [Ernesto] Che. *Guerrilla Warfare.* New York, 1961.
———. *Reminiscences of the Cuban Revolutionary War.* New York, 1963.
Mao Tse-tung. *On Guerrilla Warfare.* New York, 1961.
Rojo, Richard. *Che Guevara.* New York, 1970.

Guillaume, Gunter   (1927–   )   Gunter Guillaume was the most celebrated East German spy of the Cold War period. He rose to the position of personal assistant to West German chancellor WILLY BRANDT, and his exposure, at the height of détente and OSTPOLITIK, led to Brandt's resignation and to widespread doubts about the Ostpolitik policy.

Guillaume joined the East German Army as an officer in 1949 and was quickly recruited into intelligence activities. In the early 1950s he was transferred to the HAUPTVERWALTUNG AUFTLARUG (HVA), the main East German intelligence agency, and started training as a "sleeper," that is, an undercover agent who enters a target country and sets out to establish himself in a position of trust. The problems of a divided country made West Germany particularly susceptible to sleeper agents, especially as the West German constitution recognized East Germans as citizens of West Germany.

In 1956 Guillaume entered West Germany as a refugee from the East. He described himself as a moderate social democrat and joined the Social Democratic Party (SPD), which was then in opposition. At his subsequent trial, a number of SPD officials and politicians described him as a hard-working and conscientious party member who displayed no sign of communist sympathies. By 1962 he had risen to a high enough level within the party apparatus that he was investigated by West German security services and cleared.

Guillaume's big breakthrough came when he was recruited to work in the office of Chancellor Willy Brandt in 1970. He was checked again by the security services and again he was cleared. On February 1, 1973, Brandt asked Guillaume to become his personal assistant. That summer HANS-DIETRICH GENSCHER, then minister for the interior, warned Brandt that Guillaume was suspected of being an East German spy. He asked Brandt to keep him on his staff to aid the investigation but to restrict his access to top secret information. Brandt thought it "rather unlikely" that Guillaume was an agent and allowed him continued access to all papers.

Guillaume was picked up for questioning by West German officials on April 25, 1974, at Cologne Airport when he stepped off a plane bringing him home from a vacation in France. He immediately made a statement admitting that he was an officer in the East German Army and had been working for East German intelligence. The arrest occurred only a few hours before East and West Germany signed two new agreements related to the Ostpolitik policy.

Within hours of the arrest, Brandt came under heavy attack from the opposition Christian Democratic Union (CDU), which criticized government security as a "scandal" and described Guillaume as "the most important and best-placed" East German agent ever uncovered in West Germany. On May 6, 1974, Brandt resigned after admitting "negligence" in allowing Guillaume to become a top member of his staff. It was never revealed specifically what secrets Guillaume had had access to, but Brandt admitted that it was information that could be "extremely damaging" if passed on to East Germany.

A subsequent inquiry by the West German Bundestag (parliament) blamed structural weaknesses and a breakdown in communication among West Germany's three security forces for the employment of Guillaume. Several high-level West German trade union officials who were in close contact with Guillaume were subsequently arrested but were cleared.

Guillaume was formally charged with high treason and breach of official secrets on March 10, 1975. His wife, Christel, was also charged with treason and aiding the breach of official secrets. The trial, which started on July 24, 1975, was held behind closed doors in the State Supreme Court of North Rhine-Westphalia in Düsseldorf. Guillaume was sentenced to 13 years' imprisonment and his wife to eight years. In prison, Guillaume developed high blood pressure and a kidney ailment. He and his wife were exchanged on October 1, 1981, for nine West German agents held in East German prisons. Four other East German agents were released at the same time. According to a West German government spokesman, as part of the exchange East Germany also promised to free an undisclosed number of political prisoners and allow about 3,000 East Germans to join relatives in the West.

Gulf of Tonkin Resolution   The Gulf of Tonkin Resolution provided U.S. president LYNDON JOHNSON with the wide-ranging executive powers he required to involve the United States in the VIETNAM WAR. The resolution followed an incident involving the U.S. Navy destroyers *Maddox* and *C. Turner Joy* in the Gulf of Tonkin off the coast of North Vietnam.

In 1964 President Johnson and his chief foreign policy advisers were becoming increasingly convinced that South Vietnam would fall under a communist government unless American ground troops were committed to its defense. Plans were drawn up for congressional approval of such action, but the White House knew that such approval would not be forthcoming unless it could be shown that the North Vietnamese had attacked U.S. forces.

The United States at this stage had 17,000 personnel in South Vietnam, in the main supplying air support for South Vietnamese ground forces and aid for covert operations. One of these covert operations involved testing North Vietnamese radar operations and providing support for the landing of South Vietnamese forces on the coast of North Vietnam. American ships were despatched to the coast of North Vietnam and ordered to remain at least three miles off the coast—the territorial limit recognized by the United States.

North Vietnam, however, claimed a 12-mile territorial limit, and on August 2, 1964, three North Vietnamese patrol boats attacked the USS *Maddox*, which was operating 10 miles off the North Vietnamese coast in the Gulf of Tonkin, near the strategic port of Haiphong. The American aircraft carrier USS *Ticonderoga*, which was farther out to sea, sent fighter planes to assist the Maddox and one North Vietnamese patrol boat was sunk and two were disabled.

Johnson did not immediately retaliate. He simply instructed the *Maddox* to continue its patrols, sent a second destroyer, the USS *C. Turner Joy*, to join the *Maddox* and warned the North Vietnamese of "grave consequences which would inevitably result from any further unprovoked offensive military action against United States forces."

On the night of August 4 it was reported that the *Maddox* and *C. Turner Joy* had again been attacked. This second attack, however, may have been a false alarm triggered by a radar malfunction, as none of the U.S. crew later reported having seen the two North Vietnamese patrol boats at which the *Maddox* and *C. Turner Joy* had returned fire. The Pentagon, however, announced that an "undetermined number of North Vietnamese PT-boats" had made a "deliberate attack" on the American ships about 65 miles offshore. Johnson retaliated by ordering U.S. aircraft to bomb an oil depot and North Vietnamese patrol boat bases. He also submitted to Congress his resolution requesting wide-ranging executive powers to commit troops to Vietnam.

The Gulf of Tonkin Resolution, which was submitted to Congress on August 5, 1964, expressly authorized "all necessary measures" the president might take "to repel any armed attack" against U.S. forces and "to prevent further aggression." The resolution also approved in advance "all necessary steps, including the use of armed force," that the president might take to help any nation that requested aid "in defense of its freedom" under the Southeast Asia Collective Defense Treaty.

The resolution was unanimously passed by the House of Representatives and, in the Senate, only two members dissented: Wayne Morse of Oregon and Ernest Gruening of Alaska. Morse accused the United States of acting as a provocateur.

The North Vietnamese government claimed that the United States had fabricated the story of the second attack and said that the American retaliation "exposes even more clearly the design to invade North Vietnam and extend the war here as declared many times by the United States." Soviet premier NIKITA KHRUSHCHEV promised that the Soviet Union would "stand up for . . . other Socialist countries if the imperialists impose war on them." The communist Chinese government said that it fully supported the "just stand" of North Vietnam.

For Further Information:
Halberstam, David. *The Best and the Brightest.* New York, 1972.
Herring, George C. *America's Longest War: The United States and Vietnam, 1950–1975.* Philadelphia, 1986.
Kahin, George McTurnan. *Intervention: How America Became Involved in Vietnam.* New York, 1986.
Karnow, Stanley. *Vietnam, A History.* New York, 1991.
Windchy, Eugene. *Tonkin Gulf.* Garden City, N.Y., 1971.

H

Haig, Alexander (December 2, 1924–) After distinguishing himself as a U.S. Army officer in the VIETNAM WAR, Alexander Haig carved out a political career as military adviser to HENRY KISSINGER, White House chief of staff for President RICHARD NIXON, supreme commander of NATO forces and then secretary of state for President RONALD REAGAN.

Haig attended Notre Dame University and the U.S. Military Academy at West Point before entering the army in 1947. His graduating class yearbook noted Haig's "strong convictions and even stronger ambitions." During the Korean War, Haig saw combat in five campaigns, including the INCHON landings, and emerged from the fighting heavily decorated. After the war, he taught at West Point and at the U.S. Naval Academy, took courses at the Naval War College, and studied international relations at Georgetown University.

In 1964, Haig's career took a decidedly political turn when he was appointed military assistant to Secretary of the Army CYRUS VANCE. He moved up with Vance when the latter was appointed deputy secretary of defense in 1965. Haig was assigned to Vietnam in 1966, where he won the Distinguished Service Cross while commanding a battalion in the battle of Ap Gu. When he returned to the United States the following year, Haig was assigned to West Point, and in 1968 became deputy commander of the Academy. He moved back into the political stream the following year when Henry Kissinger, then national security adviser to President Nixon, asked Haig to become his chief military aide. In this position, Haig acted as liaison between the White House and the Pentagon on security issues. He screened all intelligence reports and presented daily security summaries. President Nixon also sent Haig to Vietnam on several fact-finding missions, and he played a leading role in the PARIS PEACE TALKS ON VIETNAM, visiting South Vietnam to persuade President Nguyen Van Thieu to accept the cease-fire terms negotiated by Kissinger in October 1972. Haig also visited China as part of the Kissinger advance party for Nixon's historic trip.

Haig was promoted to brigadier general in 1969 and major general in 1972. In September 1972 he was promoted two grades to four-star general, and he returned to the Pentagon as vice chief of staff in January 1973. But Haig had been at the Defense Department for only six months when Nixon asked him to retire from the military and take over as White House chief of staff from Watergate conspirator H. R. Haldeman. Haig is credited with effectively running the White House in the last confused days of the Nixon administration. He was one of the key Nixon aides not implicated in the Watergate conspiracy.

After GERALD FORD succeeded to the presidency, Haig moved back to the military as SUPREME ALLIED COMMANDER, EUROPE (SACEUR). He was generally regarded as an excellent SACEUR during his four and a half years in Brussels. During his tenure, he was a forceful spokesman for a strong alliance and for increased NATO preparedness. He is also credited with having introduced a number of improvements in NATO strategy and training. But after the election of JIMMY CARTER he came into increasing conflict with what he regarded as the too-liberal foreign policy of the new U.S. administration. He retired from the military on July 1, 1979, because of "strong differences of opinion" with the Carter administration.

Upon his return to the United States, Haig considered a political career and was talked about as a possible candidate for the Republican presidential nomination. In the short interim, he became a popular speaker on the college lecture circuit, a professor of political science at the University of Pennsylvania and president of United Technologies Corporation. He met RONALD REAGAN at the Republican nominating convention and acted as a foreign policy adviser in the final months of the Reagan campaign. Reagan nominated Haig as secretary of state on December 16, 1980.

In March 1981 Haig outlined the Reagan administration's foreign policy as focused on the threat posed by the Soviet Union. Addressing congressional committees, he said that the United States was confronted with three major trends: the spread of power among many nations, some of which were not reluctant to employ violence; increased Western vulnerability to international turbulence and violent change; and increasing Soviet military power, which enabled the Soviets to practice "an imperial foreign policy." Haig described the last threat as the most alarming.

Haig placed a high priority on combating international terrorism and said, "When you get to the bottom line, it is the Soviet Union which bears a major responsibility today for the proliferation and hemorrhaging, if you will, of international terrorism."

He accused the Soviet Union of aiming to dominate Cen-

Retired General Alexander Haig was President Reagan's first secretary of state. Photo courtesy of the North Atlantic Treaty Organization.

tral America and of having a "hit list" prepared as part of that effort. Unrest in Central America, Haig maintained, was part of a "four-phased operation" aimed at putting the communists in control. The first phase had already been accomplished with the "seizure of Nicaragua." Haig claimed that El Salvador was next, to be followed by Honduras and Guatemala. Haig also kept open the possibility of military action against Cuba in order to stop the flow of arms to communist rebels in Central America. Haig's overheated rhetoric alarmed many moderates.

During Haig's tenure at the State Department, riots broke out in Poland, and the independent trade union SOLIDARITY was formed. In January 1981, Haig wrote a strong letter to Soviet foreign minister ANDREI GROMYKO warning him against intervening in Poland. The letter was released by the Soviets, who replied that the internal affairs of Poland "cannot be a subject of discussion between third countries, including the U.S.S.R. and the U.S." In June 1981 Haig repeated his warnings about Poland when he expressed concern over the "increase of Soviet threats" and said that "any external or internal repression from the Soviet Union will have profound and lasting effects."

Among the many problems inherited by Haig was the Soviet occupation of AFGHANISTAN. Support for the Mujahideen fighting against the Soviet forces became a key part of

Haig's foreign policy, and he also extended substantial military and financial aid to Pakistan, which provided sanctuary for the Afghan rebels. Haig employed the Kissinger policy of linkage to tie the Soviet withdrawal from Afghanistan to progress in U.S.–Soviet relations in other fields. In January 1981 he specifically ruled out any arms-control negotiations in the immediate future unless Soviet behavior in other parts of the world improved. However, he lifted the Carter administration's embargo on U.S. grain shipments to the Soviet Union, arguing that it was damaging American farmers more than the Soviet Union.

Haig's last few months as secretary of state were absorbed by the Anglo–Argentine war over the Falkland Islands in the South Atlantic. In the period between the Argentine invasion of the British colony and the arrival of the British task force, Haig shuttled between the two American allies, trying to negotiate a solution to the crisis. In the end, the United States was forced to come out in support of Britain and supplied substantial logistical aid during the successful recapture of the islands. This support caused some damage to American interests in Latin America.

Haig's reputation with the American public was seriously damaged by his actions in the immediate aftermath of the attempted assassination of President Reagan on March 30, 1981. In the resultant confusion he declared before television cameras, "As of now, I am in control here, in the White House, pending the return of the Vice President and in close touch with him." The statement was meant to reassure the public that events were under control, but it was widely interpreted as a sign of overambition and a possible breach of the presidential succession as laid down in the constitution.

Haig described himself as "the vicar" of American foreign policy. But he never had the power that had been enjoyed by some of his predecessors, and he was often locked in internal debates with Vice President GEORGE BUSH, national security adviser William Clark and Defense Secretary Caspar Weinberger. This eventually led to Haig's resignation on June 25, 1982. Shortly afterward he established Worldwide Associates, a foreign affairs consultancy based in Washington. He also renewed his relationship with United Technologies and joined the boards of several other companies. In March 1987 Haig announced that he was a candidate for the Republican presidential nomination. But he failed to produce a strong challenge in the early primaries and dropped out of the race.

For Further Information:
Brzezinski, Zbigniew. *In Quest of National Security.* Boulder, Colo., 1988.
Haig, Alexander. *Caveat: Realism, Reagan and Foreign Policy.* New York, 1984.

Hallstein Doctrine   West Germany's Hallstein Doctrine of 1955 stated that the Federal Republic of Germany would consider recognition of East Germany by another state as an "unfriendly act" toward West Germany.

The doctrine grew out of the assertion of Chancellor KON-

RAD ADENAUER that the West German government, having been freely elected, was the "only legitimate government of the German people" and alone had "authority to speak for the German people."

The doctrine, named after West German foreign minister Walter Hallstein, meant that the West German government and its allies would refuse to maintain diplomatic relations with any country that maintained diplomatic relations with East Germany. The only exception was the Soviet Union. The document was effective: By 1960 East Germany was recognized only by Communist Bloc countries and a few socialist countries in the Third World.

The policy was maintained for 15 years and made it impossible for the two Germanies to conduct a dialogue at governmental level, although there were growing trade links, and in the late 1960s the West German government moved toward trying to establish a working relationship with East Germany without abandoning its aim of a reunified Germany. By 1970 the Hallstein Doctrine had been officially supplanted by Chancellor WILLY BRANDT's OSTPOLITIK.

For Further Information:
Planek, Charles R. *The Changing Status of German Reunification in Western Diplomacy, 1955–1966.* Baltimore, 1967.

Hammarskjold, Dag   (July 29, 1905–September 18, 1961)
Dag Hammarskjold is generally regarded as the most effective secretary general of the United Nations, having held the office for eight-and-a-half years at the height of the Cold War. He died in a suspicious plane crash while on a peace mission to the Congo.

Hammarskjold was born into a distinguished Swedish political family. His father, Knut Hjalmar Hammarskjold, was prime minister during World War I. Dag Hammarskjold studied law and economics at Uppsala and Stockholm universities. Between 1930 and 1941 he held a number of high-ranking positions in the Swedish civil service, eventually becoming chairman of the board of directors of the Bank of Sweden from 1941 to 1948.

In 1946 Hammarskjold entered the Swedish diplomatic service as a financial specialist. He was the Swedish delegate to the 1947–48 Paris Conference to organize the MARSHALL PLAN and Sweden's delegate to the Organization for European Economic Cooperation from 1948 to 1953. In 1951 Hammarskjold was appointed Swedish deputy foreign minister and delegate to the United Nations.

Hammarskjold was elected secretary general on April 7, 1953, by a vote of 57 to one. The one negative vote was from Taiwan because of Sweden's recognition of communist China. He was reelected unanimously to his second five-year term on September 26, 1957.

Hammarskjold was the only truly charismatic secretary general of the United Nations. He looked upon the United Nations as an international government, had a presidential conception of the role of the secretary general and often took the initiative in international affairs rather than acting merely as a mediator. But he realized the United Nation's limitations in dealing with the superpower relationship and concentrated on peacekeeping operations in the Middle East, Southeast Asia and Africa.

Hammarskjold did not, however, shun East–West relations. His first diplomatic triumph was in 1955 when he flew to communist China to secure the release of 15 captured U.S. airmen. In November and December 1956 he took a strong stand against the Soviet invasion of Hungary and tried to organize a visit to Budapest, but was stopped by the Hungarian and Soviet governments. Hammarskjold also condemned the Franco-British-Israeli attack on Egypt in November 1956, and his moral influence and swift organization of the UN Emergency Force for the Middle East were vital to restoring peace in the Sinai and Suez.

In a rare public expression of agreement, U.S. ambassador to the United Nations HENRY CABOT LODGE and Soviet ambassador to the United Nations Vasily V. Kuznetsov lauded Hammarskjold's service to the United Nations at his reelection on September 26, 1957. Lodge credited Hammarskjold with many of the United Nation's accomplishments in the previous five years, and Kuznetsov pledged continued Soviet cooperation with Hammarskjold's peace efforts.

But from the start of 1958, Hammarskjold came under increasing Soviet attack for his "independent action." The anti-Hammarskjold campaign became most bitter in 1960, when the United Nations became involved in the Congo Crisis. Soviet premier NIKITA KHRUSHCHEV denounced Hammarskjold as a "tool of the colonialists" for not using force to support PATRICE LUMUMBA, the Soviet-backed premier of the Congo whose government was attempting to deal with a Western-sponsored rebellion.

In 1960, Soviet-Bloc delegates to the General Assembly called for the abolition of the secretary general's office and its replacement by a three-man committee (popularly known as the "troika"), with one member each from the West, the Soviet Bloc and a neutral nation. Hammarskjold replied that his office protected the small powers and that he would remain in office as long as they wished. He was supported in his opposition to the troika by the Eisenhower and later the Kennedy administrations.

On September 12, 1961, Hammarskjold left New York for the Congo to try to arrange a cease-fire between UN forces and the Katangan rebel forces. He landed in Leopoldville on September 13, after UN troops had launched an attack on Katangan forces and proclaimed the abolition of the government of Moise Tshombe. In Leopoldville he was supposed to meet with Tshombe and Premier Cyrille Adoula and President Joseph Kasavubu to discuss the future structure of the Congolese government. But Tshombe's military reverses kept him away from the meeting.

Lord Lansdowne, British minister of state at the Foreign Office, then arranged a meeting between Tshombe and Hammarskjold in Ndola, Northern Rhodesia (Zambia). The plane left for Ndola on September 17. The plane was about to land when it suddenly diverted and then crashed. A number of observers believe the plane was shot down either by Katangan or Soviet forces. The coroner, however, ruled that the crash was accidental. Hammarskjold was posthumously awarded the 1961 Nobel Prize for peace. The Soviet Union refused to join in the laudatory eulogies of Hammarskjold and used his death to push for their proposed troika, but it was blocked and U THANT was elected secretary general.

For Further Information:
Peskow, Bo. *Dag Hammarskjold; Strictly Personal: A Portrait.* New York, 1969.
Weiley, Lawrence, and Patricia Anne Simmons. *The United States and the United Nations.* New York, 1967.

Hammer, Armand   (May 21, 1898–Dec. 10, 1990)   Armand Hammer was a millionaire American businessman, philosopher and art collector who on several occasions acted as an unofficial mediator between the Soviet Union and the United States.

Hammer, whose father was a doctor, trained for a medical career and during World War I was an army medic in France. But before he even finished medical school, Hammer had made his first million dollars through business deals with the new communist leadership in the Soviet Union.

Hammer became a friend and confidant of many of the early Soviet leaders, including Lenin, Trotsky and Stalin. Hammer cared little about political ideology, and he respected the Soviet leaders as men trying to improve the social conditions of their country. The Soviet leaders in turn respected Hammer for his business acumen. This mutual respect not only helped Hammer to negotiate his own business deals, but also led many major foreign companies to engage him as an agent. His biggest deal in these early years was an exchange of a million tons of American grain in return for Russian furs, precious stones and caviar. The grain helped to relieve widespread famine. This deal established Hammer as a popular hero in the Soviet Union.

While in the Soviet Union, Hammer was exposed to Russian art treasures and became a collector and promoter of Russian art. This further strengthened his links with the Soviet Union and became profitable as well, as the prices of Russian art treasures soared.

Hammer's contacts were used extensively during World War II, but as U.S.–Soviet relations cooled in the early Cold War years, the American businessman kept a low profile for fear of attack by McCarthyite right-wingers. Hammer announced his retirement in 1956, but a year later he was back in the business world after buying the near-bankrupt Occidental Oil Company. Within 10 years he transformed Occidental into the 11th largest oil company in the United States.

Hammer started to come into his own with the era of détente that began in the early 1970s. Throughout the Cold War period Hammer had maintained his contacts with the Soviet leadership, and once the NIXON administration had decided to pursue détente, he was in a position to play a leading role in negotiating new trade agreements, both for himself and for the United States and the Soviet Union.

In July 1972 Hammer announced that Occidental Oil had agreed to provide scientific and technical information in the areas of agricultural fertilizers; hotel construction; oil and gas exploration and production; chemicals; metal treating and plating; and conversion of garbage into fuel—in return for Soviet oil, natural gas and metals. In April 1974 he signed contracts with the Soviet government that involved a $20 billion fertilizer deal.

Hammer's role as an art connoisseur also helped to foster better U.S.–Soviet relations. In 1973 he arranged for a loan of 48 post-Impressionist paintings from the Soviet Union to be shown in the United States. He organized another exchange of Soviet art treasures for the U.S. bicentennial celebrations and a third in 1986.

On October 20, 1976, Hammer met with Soviet leader LEONID BREZHNEV in the Kremlin to discuss the "diminishing volume" of U.S.–Soviet trade following the JACKSON AMENDMENT, which linked most-favored-nation status for the Soviet Union to the easing of Soviet emigration restrictions. When the two men met again, in August 1977, Brezhnev used Hammer as a conduit to President Jimmy Carter, telling Hammer that he would like to meet Carter as soon as a SALT (Strategic Arms Limitation) II agreement was concluded. Hammer used the meeting to raise the issue of American businessman Francis Jay Crawford, who had been arrested in June of that year on charges of illegal currency dealings. Brezhnev promised him that Crawford's trial would not be a severe one.

The Soviet invasion of Afghanistan in December 1979 ended East–West détente, and the official communications channels, although still open, became chilly and correct. Hammer, however, retained his close links with Brezhnev, and the two men met in February 1980, when the Soviet president told Hammer that he was interested in talks with the United States on the Afghan situation. The proposal never went any further because of State Department skepticism about Brezhnev's sincerity.

After the Chernobyl nuclear disaster in 1986, Hammer financed the dispatch to the Soviet Union of an international medical team of radiation specialists. He was thanked personally by Soviet leader MIKHAIL GORBACHEV. After the Armenian earthquake disaster, Hammer sent a check for $1 million to the disaster relief fund. In February 1987 he was one of the participants in a Soviet-sponsored peace forum held in Moscow.

Hammer was implicated in the Watergate scandal of the Nixon administration. He pleaded guilty to concealing $54,000 in illegal contributions to Richard Nixon's 1972 campaign fund. He was fined $3,000 and placed on probation for one year. He was pardoned by President Bush in 1989.

For Further Information:
Hammer, Armand, with Neil Lyndon. *Hammer: A Witness to History.* New York, 1987.

Hardened Site A hardened site is one constructed to withstand a nuclear attack. Such sites are also likely to be protected against chemical, biological or radiological attack.

Most hardened sites are of silo-based nuclear missiles. But some civil defense installations can also be called hardened sites. These are usually protected by concrete and earth and are buried deep underground. Missile silos are usually constructed out of concrete topped by steel doors. The command and control facilities for the missiles are similarly protected.

Hardened sites are usually attacked by a GROUND BURST nuclear weapon, which buries itself in the ground as it detonates. It is also possible to attack hardened sites with conventional "smart weapons" equipped with sophisticated computer guidance systems, which can direct a conventionally armed missile to the entrance of a hardened site, burrow through the protective covering, and detonate a conventional bomb inside the silo or control area.

Harmel Report The 1967 Harmel Report, named after Belgian foreign minister Pierre Harmel, was the first NATO-wide expression of support in favor of the policy of détente. The report also established guidelines for greater political cooperation among NATO members.

At a meeting of NATO foreign ministers in December 1966, Harmel proposed a study to delineate the alliance's political tasks in the changed conditions brought about by an easing of Cold War tensions. The study quickly became known as the Harmel Report or "Harmel Exercises" and was approved at a meeting of NATO defense, foreign and finance ministers in Brussels on December 13–14, 1967.

The Harmel Report initially called for coordination of allies' national policies on such matters as détente and other foreign policy issues, economic and military aid, arms control and disarmament, and scientific and technological development. However, to meet French objections to such broadsweeping reforms and commitments, the final report was modified by calling only for closer political consultation among the allies concerning: European security and the problem of German reunification; arms control and disarmament, including "parallel disarmament" between NATO and the Warsaw Pact; and developments on NATO's southeastern flank, such as the Cyprus dispute, the Arab–Israeli conflict and the build-up of Soviet naval forces in the Mediterranean.

"The ultimate political purpose of the alliance is to achieve a just and lasting peaceful order in Europe, accompanied by appropriate security guarantees," the report said. "Military security and a policy of détente are not contradictory but complementary. Collective defense is a stabilizing factor in world policy. It is the necessary condition for effective policies directed towards a greater relaxation of tensions."

For Further Information:
Grosser, Alfred. *The Western Alliance.* New York, 1978.

Harriman, W. Averell (November 15, 1891–July 26, 1986) W. Averell Harriman's political career extended from before World War II to well into the 1970s. Much of this time he was at the center of the American government's foreign policy decision-making process, especially on decisions concerning relations with the Soviet Union.

Harriman was born into one of the wealthiest families in American history. His father was E.H. Harriman, owner of the Union Pacific Railroad. After graduating from Yale in 1913 Averell Harriman joined the family business, and within two years he was a vice president. After founding a shipping company and merchant bank, he was elected chairman of the board of Union Pacific in 1932 and successfully steered that company through the worst of the Depression.

In 1937 President Franklin Roosevelt appointed him chairman of the Business Advisory Council of the Department of Commerce. Just before America's entry into the war, he moved into the foreign affairs field as coordinator of LEND-LEASE aid to Britain and the Soviet Union. In 1943 he was appointed ambassador to the Soviet Union and in that capacity attended both conferences, at Teheran and YALTA, where most of the postwar political boundaries were drawn.

Harriman's experiences as ambassador in Moscow made him skeptical of promises made by JOSEF STALIN during negotiations. In 1945, shortly before Roosevelt's death, Harriman sent a cable warning the president that Stalin was determined to establish a buffer zone of satellite nations in Eastern Europe and that he planned to control both the domestic and foreign policies of these countries. He also claimed that the Soviet Union aimed to subvert countries in Western Europe through the local communist parties.

Harriman urged Roosevelt to take an early stand against the Soviet Union and to use America's economic muscle to prevent Soviet domination of Eastern Europe. Harriman's anti-Soviet views were radical in 1945 and provided him with a sound ideological base in the early Cold War years when other prewar and wartime Democrats fell by the political wayside because they were regarded as "soft on Communism."

Harriman's warning was never read by Roosevelt, who died before it reached him. But the cable was one of the first documents read by President HARRY TRUMAN, and he later said that it had had a profound impact on his thinking.

Ten days after assuming the presidency, Truman met in Washington with Soviet foreign minister V.M. MOLOTOV. At the president's request, Harriman preceded Molotov to give Truman a full briefing and expand further on his cabled warning. The result was a stormy first meeting between the new American president and the Soviet foreign minister. Using "words of one syllable" Truman attacked the Soviet Union for failing to live up to the Yalta agreements, especially those relating to Poland. Molotov, for his part, objected to being "lectured" by the novice president. He left Washington convinced that Truman was likely to take a harder line than Roosevelt would have at the forthcoming POTSDAM CONFERENCE.

Harriman's next foreign policy coup was persuading Truman to end lend-lease shipments to the Soviet Union. He saw this as part of his plan to use American economic muscle to force political concessions out of Moscow. Most historians now believe that Harriman was wrong to suggest the withdrawal of American aid. By withdrawing U.S. financial support, the Truman administration threw away a potential political lever and forced the Soviet Union into tightening its political stranglehold on Eastern Europe in order to extract reparations and other financial benefits.

Harriman left Moscow to become ambassador to Britain in March 1946, but he was there for only a few months before Truman brought him back to Washington as secretary of commerce. In June 1947 he was appointed chairman of the president's Committee on Foreign Aid, a job that involved securing congressional approval of the MARSHALL PLAN and then implementing it. In November 1947 Harriman's committee warned that if Congress blocked the plan, all of Europe, the Middle East and North Africa would fall to the Soviet Union.

In 1950 Harriman became special assistant to Truman. He played a major policy role prior to the KOREAN WAR and acted as liaison between the president and General DOUGLAS MAC-ARTHUR. From 1951 to 1953 he returned to the foreign aid field as director of the Mutual Security Agency, which was responsible for the distribution of foreign aid.

During the Eisenhower administration, Harriman concentrated on establishing a domestic political base. In 1952 he declared himself a candidate for the Democratic presidential nomination, but his patrician manner alienated many party delegates, and Harriman finished fourth on the first two convention ballots. Three years later, however, he was elected governor of New York. He used the position as a forum from which to attack Eisenhower's foreign policies in the hope of winning enough national attention to secure him the 1960 Democratic presidential nomination. But his failure in 1958 to win reelection as governor of New York ended his ambitions for higher elected office.

In 1959 Harriman threw his substantial political weight behind the presidential campaign of JOHN F. KENNEDY. He visited the Soviet Union for talks with NIKITA KHRUSHCHEV and toured West Africa on fact-finding missions for the candidate. Kennedy decided against appointing Harriman secretary of state because of his age, then 69. Instead, the elder statesman was appointed first ambassador at large, then assistant secretary of state for Far Eastern affairs and finally Kennedy's undersecretary of state for political affairs.

As ambassador at large, Harriman's first task was trying to defuse the crisis in LAOS, where the American-supported sections of the military were in conflict with communist insurgents and the Soviet-supported government. Harriman successfully advised Kennedy to support the creation of a neutralist government in Laos, backed up with American troops based in Thailand. Harriman went on to become the U.S. representative to the conference called in Geneva to negotiate the formation of a neutral coalition government. In the middle of the conference the communist Pathet Lao won a decisive battle against the American-supported military

forces of General Phoumi Nosavan. Harriman recommended another show of American force, and 1,800 troops were airlifted to Thailand and the Seventh Fleet was despatched to the Gulf of Thailand.

On July 23, 1962, the Geneva accords guaranteeing the freedom and neutrality of Laos were signed by 14 Western, communist and Asian nations, including the United States, the Soviet Union, North Vietnam, South Vietnam, Britain and France. Although the accords were later violated by China, North Vietnam and the United States, they kept Laos from becoming the venue for a superpower clash.

In March 1963, Harriman was promoted to undersecretary of state for political affairs and was made responsible for negotiating the NUCLEAR TEST BAN TREATY with the Soviet Union. The treaty faced two main problems: the Soviet demand for a simultaneous NATO–Warsaw Pact nonaggression treaty and the absence of the French and the Chinese. Harriman persuaded the Soviet negotiators that both were unnecessary, and on July 25, 1963, he initialed the treaty on behalf of the United States.

From the outset, Harriman was unhappy about U.S. involvement in Vietnam, and his reports to Kennedy expressed skepticism about the Pentagon's optimistic military analyses. Harriman, however, dropped out of the mainstream of foreign policy decision-making following Kennedy's assassination. He had had a close rapport with Kennedy, which did not transfer easily to President LYNDON JOHNSON.

In 1965 and 1966 he was an ambassador at large charged with the task of persuading American allies and neutrals to support U.S. policy in Vietnam. After Johnson announced his de-escalation policy in March 1968, Harriman was dispatched to Paris as U.S. negotiator for talks with the North Vietnamese. Harriman failed to get the talks off the ground. He was impeded first by North Vietnam's insistence on a total cessation of American bombing as a precondition for talks, then by South Vietnam's refusal to enter into conversations with the National Liberation Front and finally by disagreement over seating arrangements. In January 1969 HENRY CABOT LODGE replaced Harriman as chief American negotiator.

After the election of RICHARD NIXON, Harriman became one of the most prominent elder statesman opposing the VIETNAM WAR. On May 25, 1971, in testimony before the Senate Foreign Relations Committee, he urged Congress to use its "power over the purse" to compel a pullout, preferably by the end of the year.

During JIMMY CARTER's 1976 election campaign Harriman was a foreign policy adviser to the Democratic candidate, and he flew to Moscow to explain Carter's foreign policy to Soviet leader Leonid Brezhnev. Brezhnev expressed concern over what he regarded as anti-détente statements by the candidates. Harriman told him that election "campaigns are meant to attract the American voter and less thought is given to reaction abroad."

At 84, Harriman was obviously too old for an active role in the CARTER administration. He was, however, often called upon to advise the president and express his opinion on East–West relations, and he represented the president at the funerals of Lord Mountbatten in 1979 and JOSIP BROZ TITO in 1980. On May 9, 1985, the Soviet government awarded Harriman the Soviet Order of the Patriotic War (first class) for his contribution to the wartime alliance. He died on July 26, 1986, of kidney failure.

For Further Information:

Harriman, W. Averell. *America and Russia in a Changing World.* New York, 1971.

———. *Special Envoy to Churchill and Stalin, 1941–1946.* New York, 1975.

Isaacson, Walter, and Evan Thomas. *Wise Men.* New York, 1986.

Spanier, J.W. *American Foreign Policy Since World War Two.* Washington, D.C., 1988.

Hauptverwaltung Auftlarug (HVA)   The Hauptverwaltung Auftlarug (Chief Intelligence Administration) was the primary East German intelligence organization, and its main responsibility was to direct Eastern Bloc intelligence activities in West Germany. Within West Germany, the HVA had three main targets: NATO bases and the West German government and industry.

The HVA was started in the immediate aftermath of World War II under the cover name Institute of Economic Relations. The division of Germany gave the intelligence organization almost unlimited opportunity to send in spies disguised as refugees. These agents either worked themselves into positions of trust or recruited West Germans who had family in the Eastern Bloc. A favorite tactic among HVA agents was to seduce secretaries, who fed their lovers top secret information from NATO and West German government offices.

East German intelligence was also active in the Scandinavian countries and helped to train the intelligence organizations of Ethiopia and South Yemen.

The HVA's most famous coup was its spy GUNTHER GUILLAUME, who arrived in West Germany from the East in 1957 and rose to be personal assistant to Chancellor WILLY BRANDT. The exposure of Guillaume led to the resignation of Brandt in 1974.

Healey, Denis   (August 30, 1917–   )   Denis Healey was regarded as the leading defense and foreign affairs expert in the British Labour Party from the 1950s until his retirement in 1989. He was defense secretary from 1964 to 1970 and chancellor of the exechequer from 1974 to 1979. Healey has often been referred to as "the best Prime Minister Labour never had."

Healey came from a working-class Yorkshire family. His father placed a heavy emphasis on education, and Healey managed to secure a scholarship to Balliol College, Oxford, from which he graduated in 1938 with a double first, the equivalent of a magna cum laude degree.

Healey volunteered for the army at the outbreak of World War II in September 1939 and was quickly promoted to major.

Former British defense secretary Denis Healey in October 1983. Photo courtesy of the Labour Party.

He participated in the landings in North Africa and at Anzio and was cited for bravery during the latter.

While at Oxford, Healey had joined the Communist Party. He never denied this early fascination with communism and described it as a reaction to fascism and the class-oriented politics of the day. By the end of the war, he had turned firmly against the Communist Party and had become an active member of Labour. In 1946 he helped to draft Labour constitutional amendments proscribing his former comrades, describing communist philosophy as "claptrap" and Stalin as a totalitarian menace as great as Hitler.

Immediately after the war, in 1945, Healey joined Labour Party headquarters as secretary of the international department. In this position he became a close associate and admirer of Labour foreign secretary ERNEST BEVIN, who laid the foundations of Britain's strong pro-American foreign policy in the early Cold War years. Healey himself played an important role in urging Bevin and CLEMENT ATTLEE to acquire the atomic bomb to maintain Britain's international muscle.

Healey failed in his first attempt to be elected to Parliament in 1945 but in 1952 was elected to the House of Commons as the member for South East Leeds. He continued to develop his expertise in defense and foreign affairs and in 1958 was one of those behind the founding of the London-based International Institute for Strategic Studies. He was named to Labour's shadow cabinet in 1959 and after the Labour victory in 1964 became secretary of state for defense.

Healey was known as a man who refused to accept conventional wisdom and was prepared to argue obscure and technical details with the formidable British civil servants. He was known as abrasive and often referred to as a bully, but despite this his six-year tenure at the Ministry of Defense is regarded as the most successful ministry in the history of postwar British defense.

Healey inherited a British defense force that was still largely committed to a global imperial role, but Britain did not have the economic means to maintain the role. Healey's first priority was to fulfill a Labour campaign pledge to reduce defense spending substantially. This found expression in the 1966 Defense White Paper, which set out Britain's withdrawal from east of Suez and allowed the defense establishment to concentrate its overstretched forces on the European theater.

The Defense White Paper reduced defense spending by £72 million and promised that Britain would not "accept commitments overseas which might require her to undertake major operations without the cooperation of allies" and would not "attempt to maintain defense facilities in any independent country against its wishes." In August 1966 Healey further added that the 80,000-strong British force in Malaysia and Singapore would be reduced by half by 1970–1971 and withdrawn completely by 1975.

The White Paper also transferred full responsibility for the British contribution to NATO's nuclear forces from the Royal Air Force to the Royal Navy, whose Polaris submarines would be based entirely in the Atlantic. The paper also committed the government to phasing out the Royal Navy's aircraft carrier force, which had been the cornerstone of its global strike force.

The 1966 White Paper led to the resignation of the naval chief of staff, Admiral Sir David Luce, and Minister of the Navy Christopher Mayhew. There was strong opposition from the British press and from the Conservative opposition, but after the Conservatives came to power in 1970 the new defense secretary, Lord CARRINGTON, continued Healey's policies.

With the reduction in the Far Eastern commitment, Healey was able to increase substantially Britain's contribution to the defense of Europe. In May 1968 he announced a 40% increase in British contributions to NATO troop strength and the addition of naval vessels to the allied Mediterranean command. British troops also helped to fill the gap left by the withdrawal of Canadian forces from West Germany in 1969.

After the Conservative election victory in 1970, Healey became the Labour Party's spokesman on economic affairs and in February 1974, following Labour's return to government, was named chancellor of the exchequer in the government of HAROLD WILSON. Healey's tenure at the treasury was not as successful as his previous ministry. The British economy was caught in the trap of world inflation sparked by the quadrupling of oil prices in 1973–74 plus the continuing expense of the British "welfare state." The result was inflation, which soared above 20%; the introduction of an unpopular prices and incomes policy; high taxes; and the embarrassment of being forced to borrow $3.9 billion from the International Monetary Fund in 1976.

Until 1975–76 Healey had been regarded as the leading contender to succeed Wilson as prime minister. But when Wilson suddenly resigned in March 1976, the country's poor economic performance led to Healey's defeat in the second round of balloting for the premiership, and Wilson was succeeded by Foreign Secretary JAMES CALLAGHAN. Healey, whose main interest remained foreign affairs, hoped to take over the Foreign Office following the election of Callaghan and was disappointed when the post was given to the up-and-coming Dr. David Owen. Healey remained at the treasury until Labour was voted out of office in May 1979.

In opposition, Healey was named the Labour spokesman on foreign affairs at a time when the party was moving rapidly to the left. Healey himself had always been on the right wing of the party, especially on defense and nuclear issues. Labour's swing to the left led the party to adopt a position favoring unilateral nuclear disarmament. The issue caused a major split within the party, and a number of prominent members of the Labour right broke away to form the Social Democratic Party. They tried to recruit Healey to their ranks, but he decided to remain within Labour in an attempt to swing the party back toward a more centrist defense and foreign policy position. In 1980 he again stood for the leadership of the party but was defeated by Michael Foot. He served as deputy leader from 1980 until 1983, when he resigned from the post and was succeeded by Roy Hattersley.

Labour's advocacy of unilateral nuclear disarmament played a major part in the party's defeat in the 1983 and 1987 general elections. This strengthened Healey's argument against the position, which was eventually dropped by Labour Leader Neil Kinnock in 1989. In November 1989, Healey announced that he would retire from the House of Commons at the next general election.

For Further Information:

Healey, Denis. *Labour, Britain and the World*. London, 1963.
———. *Labour and a World Society*. London, 1985.
———. *The Time of My Life*. London, 1989.

Heath, Edward   (July 9, 1916–   )   Edward Heath was Conservative British prime minister from 1970 to 1974. His major contribution was taking Britain into the European Economic Community in 1972.

Heath first became actively involved in Conservative Party politics while attending Oxford University, where he was elected president of the University Conservative Association in 1937. In 1938, as chairman of the Federation of University Conservative Associations and president of the Oxford Union, he actively opposed Neville Chamberlain's policy of appeasement toward Germany.

Heath served in the army during World War II, earning the rank of major, and was cited for bravery. After the war he worked first in the Ministry of Civil Aviation from 1946 to 1947 and then briefly as editor of the *Church Times* before joining a London merchant bank. He was elected to Parliament in the general election of February 1950.

Heath's first major post was as minister of labor under Harold Macmillan from October 1959 to July 1960, when he was appointed Lord Privy Seal with responsibility for handling the negotiations for British entry into the EUROPEAN ECONOMIC COMMUNITY. The negotiations were a success, but British entry

Edward Heath, British prime minister from 1970 to 1974. Photo courtesy of British Conservative Central Office.

was blocked by the veto of French president CHARLES DE GAULLE.

In October 1963 Heath was appointed trade and industry secretary and president of the Board of Trade. After the Conservative defeat in the October 1964 general election Heath became a major opposition figure, and after the resignation of SIR ALEC DOUGLAS-HOME he was elected leader of the Conservative Party in July 1965. He became prime minister when the Conservatives were returned to office in June 1970.

Heath's foreign policy priority was to gain French approval for British entry into the EEC. One of de Gaulle's major reasons for blocking British membership was Britain's special relationship with the United States, which de Gaulle believed would give the United States a backdoor influence on EEC policy. Heath set out to assuage French fears by attempting to distance himself from President RICHARD NIXON, even though Nixon made it perfectly clear that he sought a close and special relationship with the Conservative prime minister. At the same time, Heath carefully cultivated a close relationship with de Gaulle's successor, President Georges Pompidou. The result was that Anglo-American relations temporarily cooled during the Heath government, and in January 1972 Britain joined the Common Market. Heath was awarded the first Europe Prize for Statesmanship in December 1971.

Heath's emphasis on relations with the EEC also led him to distance himself from the British Commonwealth countries. He and Defense Secretary Lord CARRINGTON continued the previous Labour government's policy of withdrawing British defense forces from east of Suez and concentrating them in Europe, and at the Commonwealth Heads of Government Summit in Singapore in January 1977 Heath adopted an aggressive stance when the meeting attempted to impose an embargo on British arms sales to South Africa.

Heath's relations with the Soviet Union were poor, and they reached their nadir in September 1971, when Foreign Secretary Sir Alec Douglas-Home ordered the expulsion from Britain of 105 Soviet citizens suspected of espionage. Heath also opposed American withdrawal from Vietnam on the grounds that it would encourage the Soviet Union to take the offensive in Europe. He took the lead in encouraging better relations between communist China and the West.

In the early part of the Heath government Britain enjoyed an economic boom, but by 1973 this had begun to slow as a result of high inflation, further excerbated by the Arab oil embargo and the quadrupling of world oil prices following the 1973 Yom Kippur War. In November 1973 British coal miners and electrical workers refused overtime work in support of their demands for sharp pay increases. This led to an acute energy shortage, and the government was forced to ration fuel supplies and put the nation on a three-day work week.

In February 1974 Heath called a general election on the issue of who governs the country—the unions or the government. Neither Labour nor Heath's Conservatives won a majority in the elections, and Heath tried but failed to negotiate the formation of a coalition government with the centrist Liberal Party. He was forced to resign, and Harold Wilson formed a minority Labour government.

Although he was leader and prime minister, Heath had never been a popular figure within the Conservative Party. He was keenly admired for his intelligence, grasp of detail and negotiating skills, but his abrasive and offhand manner made him a number of enemies within the party. His middle-of-the-road policies, which attempted to produce a conservative government with a human face, also found opposition from a growing right wing, which wanted to adopt a more doctrinaire conservative approach. In 1975 the Conservatives' right wing ousted Heath from the leadership and replaced him with their candidate, MARGARET THATCHER.

Thatcher, who had served as education secretary under Heath, took a much harder line toward the EEC and revived the special relationship with the United States. Heath, who resented being ousted from the leadership, was excluded from successive Thatcher cabinets and eventually became Thatcher's leading critic within the Conservative Party.

For Further Information:
Heath, Edward. *Europe.* London, 1990.
Laing, Margaret. *Prime Minister.* London, 1974.

Heavy Intercontinental Ballistic Missile (Heavy ICBM)

This is a term devised during the second STRATEGIC ARMS LIMITATION (SALT II) negotiations to describe an ICBM significantly larger than a light ICBM. An example of American heavy ICBMs is the Titan II. Examples of Soviet heavy ICBMs are the Satan and Stiletto.

Helms, Richard   (March 30, 1913–   )   Richard

Helms was an important and controversial figure in the U.S. CENTRAL INTELLIGENCE AGENCY (CIA). His positions included deputy director for plans and, from 1966 to 1973, director of the CIA. In 1973, he was appointed U.S. ambassador to Iran.

After graduating from Williams College in 1935, Helms worked on newspapers until 1942, when he was commissioned a lieutenant in the U.S. Navy. The following year he transferred to the OFFICE OF STRATEGIC SERVICES (OSS), wartime predecessor of the CIA. He remained in U.S. intelligence after the war and helped to lay the foundations of the CIA. His main tasks in the early years were covert operations and training and recruitment.

In 1952 Helms was deputy to the chief of the plans division, with responsibility for supervising U.S. espionage inside the Soviet Union. He also took responsibility for the agency's illegal domestic surveillance, which included opening mail between the United States and Eastern Europe.

During the KENNEDY administration and the early years of the JOHNSON administration, Helms was involved in CIA attempts to assassinate Cuban leader FIDEL CASTRO and Congolese leader PATRICE LUMUMBA. For the attempt on Castro's life, Helms recruited American underworld figures. Subsequent investigations revealed that he had withheld information about the plots from President Lyndon Johnson and Attorney General ROBERT KENNEDY.

Helms was appointed deputy director for plans in February 1962 after RICHARD BISSELL resigned in the wake of the disastrous BAY OF PIGS invasion. In April 1965, Helms was appointed deputy director of the agency under Admiral William Raborn. Because of Raborn's inexperience in intelligence matters, Helms performed many of the director's tasks, and in June 1966 was appointed CIA director.

During Helm's tenure, the CIA was involved in a number of illegal activities. These included investigation of Americans traveling abroad, interception of mail and surveillance of VIETNAM WAR dissidents and black activists. The agency developed a data base of 300,000 names of American domestic dissidents with possible foreign links, and it also infiltrated political activist organizations and secretly provided funding to universities and student groups in an attempt to influence their policies and positions. The CIA's covert funding to educational organizations was exposed in 1967 and led to a presidential investigation and a reduction in, but not a total end to, these activities.

In the 1960s and early 1970s, Helms also directed CIA attempts to prevent the election to the presidency of Chile of the socialist SALVADOR ALLENDE. These attempts included paying half of the campaign costs of the conservative Christian Democratic Party in the 1964 presidential campaign. The agency also created other left-wing Chilean parties in an attempt to splinter Allende's Socialist Party and worked closely with right-wing groups in the Chilean military and intelligence community. In 1970, President RICHARD NIXON instructed Helms to prevent Allende from taking power. This resulted in an unsuccessful coup attempt that year. In 1977 Helms pleaded guilty to two misdemeanor counts for failing to cooperate fully with a Senate inquiry into the CIA role in the overthrow of Allende. He was fined $2,000 and given a two-year suspended sentence.

Helms's rise to power in the agency coincided with the height of postwar liberalism in the United States. Although Helms himself was far from liberal, most of his close political contacts were within the liberal establishment. This made President Richard Nixon suspicious of him. The relationship between the two men was also soured by Helms's refusal to cooperate with the White House's attempt to cover up the Watergate scandal. In January 1973 Nixon nominated Helms as ambassador to Iran. After a stormy Senate hearing, the former CIA director was confirmed in February.

Helms's ambassadorship was hamstrung by a series of investigations into the CIA. He frequently had to travel back to Washington to testify before congressional investigating committees. During these investigations, Helms publicly denied the existence of covert domestic projects. His testimony, especially in regard to Chile, conflicted with the evidence, and in 1977 the Justice Department prepared a perjury indictment against him. But Helms's lawyers negotiated a deal whereby the former CIA director pleaded guilty to two misdemeanors. Shortly afterward, Helms retired as ambassador and opened a consulting firm in Washington, D.C.

After the election of RONALD REAGAN, Helms was partially rehabilitated. In March 1982 he helped to plan and direct tests of U.S. readiness for nuclear war. In December 1982 he was appointed to the Scowcroft Commission's inquiry into the MX MISSILE system. On October 20, 1983, Reagan awarded Helms the National Security Medal for "exceptional meritorious service." Helms said that he felt the award "exonerated" him from the 1976–77 perjury charges. Other observers felt that the award was a sign of Reagan's commitment to restore the morale of the American intelligence community.

For Further Information:
Marchetti, Victor, and John D. Marks. *The CIA and the Cult of Intelligence.* New York, 1974.
Powers, Thomas. *The Man Who Kept the Secrets: Richard Helms & the CIA.* New York, 1979.
U.S. Senate Select Committee on Intelligence Activities. *Foreign and Military Intelligence.* Washington, D.C., 1975.

U.S. Senate Select Committee on Intelligence Activities. *Foreign and Military Intelligence*. Washington, D.C., 1976.

Helmstadt–Berlin Autobahn

The Helmstadt–Berlin Autobahn was, during the immediate postwar period, the only road link between West Berlin and the Western-occupied sectors of Germany. The absence of others made it easier for the Soviets to impose the 1948 Berlin Blockade.

In June 1945 it was discovered that none of the Western powers had made formal arrangements for the transport of men and supplies across the Soviet zone to their sectors of occupied Berlin. A conference of the Allied military representatives met at the Berlin headquarters of the Soviet military commander, Marshal GEORGI ZHUKOV.

The Western commanders thought that the meeting was little more than a formality and that Zhukov would agree to effective unlimited access along two autobahns and three railway lines and to free use of the air. Zhukov, however, maintained that access was a "privilege," not a right, and rejected the Western demand. After several hours of arguments, the Western commanders agreed to a single road access, the Helmstadt–Berlin Autobahn, a single railway line via Magdeburg and one main air route from Magdeburg and two branch air routes. Even then, Zhukov refused to give the Western commanders a written agreement. The West was not given formal rights to use the Helmstadt–Berlin Autobahn until the QUADRIPARTITE AGREEMENT of 1971, when two other road links were also formalized.

Helsinki Accords

See CONFERENCE ON SECURITY AND COOPERATION IN EUROPE.

Herter, Christian   (March 28, 1895–December 30, 1966)

Christian Herter was the successor to JOHN FOSTER DULLES as secretary of state under President DWIGHT EISENHOWER. He never wielded the power or influence enjoyed by Dulles and often stayed in the shadows as Eisenhower took control of foreign policy for the last 18 months of his administration.

Herter was initially educated in France, where his parents were expatriate American artists. He returned to the United States for his secondary education and graduated from Harvard University in 1915. At first he went on to study architecture, but in 1916 he joined the American diplomatic service.

Herter left the diplomatic service in 1921 to become assistant to Herbert Hoover at the Department of Commerce. After working as a journalist, he successfully ran for a seat in the Massachusetts House of Representatives in 1930. He held that seat until 1942, when he successfully contested a seat in the U.S. House of Representatives. He remained in Congress until 1952, when he successfully ran for governor of Massachusetts.

In 1957 Herter was named undersecretary of state. The post was generally recognized as his reward for not challenging RICHARD NIXON for the Republican vice presidential nomina-

tion. Dulles at first opposed Herter's appointment, but the two gradually formed a close relationship, and the dying Dulles ended by designating Herter as his successor.

Herter assumed the post of secretary of state in April 1959. Eisenhower had already decided that no one could really replace Dulles and that he himself would spend his last 18 months in office concentrating on foreign policy. He set off on a series of foreign travels to Asia, Africa and Latin America. Herter accompanied him on all these travels but remained very much in the shadows.

Herter did have three major problems to contend with during his short period as secretary of state. The first was the Berlin Crisis of 1958, in which Herter mediated a common Western position on a Soviet threat to turn Berlin into a free city. His success on this score led to an effective Soviet capitulation at East–West summit meetings in May and August of 1959.

Herter also helped to arrange the KRUSHCHEV visit to the United States in September 1959 and some of the first tentative steps toward limiting nuclear weapons. Progress on the latter issue suffered a major setback after the Soviet Union downed the U-2 spy plane piloted by Lieutenant Francis GARY POWERS. It fell to Herter to admit to the flights and defend them.

The last few months of Herter's tenure at the State Department were dominated by Cuba. He had at first successfully advised Eisenhower to exercise restraint in dealing with FIDEL CASTRO, but after Castro nationalized American corporate interests Herter shifted his position in favor of economic reprisals and obtained a resolution from the ORGANIZATION OF AMERICAN STATES censuring Castro.

During the Kennedy administration, Herter acted as the president's special representative in talks with the European Economic Community. He continued to act as a foreign trade negotiator under President Lyndon Johnson and died at his post on December 30, 1966.

For Further Information:
Noble, Bernard. *Christian A. Herter*. New York, 1970.
Spanier, J.W. *American Foreign Policy Since World War Two*. Washington, 1988.

Hillenkoetter, Roscoe   (May 8, 1897–June 18, 1982)

Rear Admiral Roscoe Hillenkoetter was the first director of the CENTRAL INTELLIGENCE AGENCY (CIA).

Hillenkoetter graduated from the U.S. Naval Academy at Annapolis in 1920. After serving on both submarines and surface ships, he became involved in naval intelligence, serving either as assistant naval attaché or full naval attaché in Spain, Portugal and France. In 1942 and 1943 Hillenkoetter served with the U.S. Pacific Fleet as officer in charge of intelligence. He was made a rear admiral in 1946.

In May 1947 President HARRY TRUMAN appointed Hillenkoetter director of the Central Intelligence Group. In July 1947 Congress passed the National Security Act, the Central

Intelligence Group became the Central Intelligence Agency, and Hillenkoetter became its first director.

Throughout 1947 and 1948, Hillenkoetter worked to establish the CIA's network of agents and helped to draft the Central Intelligence Act (1949), which exempted the director of the CIA from all federal laws requiring public disclosure of agency activities. Hillenkoetter, however, failed to master the intricacies of the Washington bureaucracy and found himself at odds with rival agencies and Congress.

He often clashed with FRANK WISNER, director of the Office of Policy Coordination (OPC), which had been established in 1948 to direct covert anti-communist operations. The OPC was nominally under the CIA, but Hillenkoetter had no authority in the direction of OPC policy or activities. These were determined by Wisner in discussion with the departments of State and Defense and the White House.

Hillenkoetter's relations with Congress were also tense. He and the CIA were regularly blamed for failing to predict major international upheavals. He was most heavily criticized after the North Korean invasion of South Korea, and Truman summoned him to the White House to explain the lack of advance intelligence on North Korean intentions. Hillenkoetter said that the agency had been warning about the possibility of an attack for a year, but that it was impossible to predict the exact date of an attack. Truman was not satisfied and replaced Hillenkoetter with General WALTER BEDELL SMITH in September 1950.

Hillenkoetter returned to sea as commander of the U.S. Navy's Seventh Task Force in the Formosa Straits. He reached the rank of vice admiral before retiring from the navy in 1957, when he became a director of the defense contractors Electronic and Missile Facilities Inc.

For Further Information:
Marchetti, Victor, and John D. Marks. *The CIA and the Cult of Intelligence.* New York, 1974.

Hilsman, Roger (November 23, 1919–   )   Roger Hilsman helped to develop the KENNEDY administration's early Vietnam policies as director of the State Department's Bureau of Intelligence and Research and later as undersecretary of state for political affairs. He resigned from the State Department in protest against President Lyndon Johnson's escalation of the war.

During World War II, Hilsman fought in Burma and later joined the OFFICE OF STRATEGIC SERVICES, wartime forerunner to the CENTRAL INTELLIGENCE AGENCY. In 1951, he earned a doctorate in international relations. Hilsman first taught at Princeton University and then became chief of the foreign affairs division of the Library of Congress's legislative reference service.

In 1961 President John F. Kennedy appointed him director of the State Department's Bureau of Intelligence and Research. The bureau compiled analyses of immediate foreign policy problems and conducted research for long-term plan-

ning. In January 1962 Hilsman wrote the policy memorandum "A Strategic Concept for South Vietnam." In this document he recommended the following:

1. That the U.S. administration view the war as primarily a political rather than military conflict.
2. That the U.S. and South Vietnamese governments develop programs and policies designed to win the allegiance of the rural population.
3. That strategic hamlets be established to give villagers greater security and to provide the South Vietnamese with a string of political bases.
4. That the South Vietnamese government switch the emphasis of its military tactics from conventional to guerrilla warfare.

In November–December 1962, Hilsman made a fact-finding mission to South Vietnam along with Michael Forrestal. The two men produced a report that questioned the optimistic accounts of the war by senior American military figures and the usefulness of continued American support for South Vietnamese president NGO DINH DIEM. In July 1963 Hilsman discussed with Kennedy the possibility of overthrowing Diem, and in August he helped to draft the cable to HENRY CABOT LODGE, U.S. ambassador to South Vietnam, that instructed Lodge to inform South Vietnamese military leaders that the United States would support a military coup. The coup was carried out in November 1963.

Hilsman was appointed undersecretary of state for political affairs in May 1963. In this capacity he attended a Vietnam strategy meeting in Hawaii in November 1963, and from this point onward took an aggressive antiwar stand. In December 1963 Hilsman also held out an olive branch to communist China when, in a speech before the Commonwealth Club of San Francisco, he said that the United States was in favor of keeping the "door open" to negotiations with China.

Hilsman's dovish views conflicted with those of President JOHNSON and Secretary of State DEAN RUSK, who were preparing for an escalation of the VIETNAM WAR. In February 1964 Hilsman resigned his post at the State Department and joined the teaching staff of Columbia University. Out of office, Hilsman became an outspoken critic of the war. In June 1967 he published *To Move a Nation,* which described Kennedy's Vietnam policy and attacked the escalation of the war under Johnson. He appeared on television to assert that the bombing offensive against North Vietnam in February 1965 had not been "in retaliation for a massive introduction of North Vietnamese" into South Vietnam but "to try to force Hanoi to its knees." He also confirmed that there was "no hard evidence" of a large-scale presence of North Vietnamese troops in the South prior to 1965.

For Further Information:
Hilsman, Roger. *To Move a Nation: The Politics of Foreign Policy in the Administration of John F. Kennedy.* New York, 1967.
Johnson, Richard. *The Administration of United States Foreign Policy.* Austin, Tex., 1971.

Spanier, J.W. *American Foreign Policy Since World War Two.* Washington, D.C., 1988.

Hiss, Alger (November 11, 1904–   )   Alger Hiss was a prominent American diplomat who in 1948 was accused of being a communist and a spy for the Soviet Union. The allegations sparked a series of investigations and trials as well as a major political furor that involved even President HARRY TRUMAN. It helped to establish the career of RICHARD NIXON and the power of the HOUSE UN-AMERICAN ACTIVITIES COMMITTEE. The issue of Hiss's guilt or innocence of subsequent perjury charges became a political marker on which the American left and right divided for decades after.

Hiss attended Johns Hopkins University and Harvard Law School, graduating from the latter in 1929. He went from Harvard to the prestigious position of law secretary to Associate Justice Oliver Wendell Holmes of the Supreme Court. After a year in Washington he moved to New York to a private law practice.

In 1933 Hiss returned to Washington, where he joined the Roosevelt New Deal, working initially for the Agricultural Adjustment Administration. In 1936 Hiss joined the State Department as assistant to the assistant secretary of state for economic affairs and in 1939 moved to the State Department's Far Eastern department. He moved to the newly created Office of Special Political Affairs in March 1944 and by 1945 was the office director, playing a major role in the negotiations that led to the establishment of the United Nations.

In February 1945 Hiss was a member of the American delegation to the YALTA CONFERENCE and for a time was temporary secretary general of the SAN FRANCISCO CONFERENCE, which established the United Nations. In 1946 he went to London as principal adviser to the U.S. delegation to the first session of the General Assembly.

At the end of 1946, Hiss left government services to become president of the Carnegie Endowment for International Peace. He had been recruited for the post by the board chairman, the conservative JOHN FOSTER DULLES, and appeared set to continue his rise through the upper echelons of the foreign policy establishment. Then on August 3, 1948, the journalist and former communist WHITTAKER CHAMBERS testified before the House Un-American Activities Committee (HUAC) that during the 1930s he and Hiss had both belonged to a Washington-based underground communist organization.

The allegation was vehemently denied by Hiss, who appeared before the HUAC two days after Chambers. Under oath, Hiss denied that he had ever known Chambers, ever belonged to or sympathized with the Communist Party or any of its "fronts," or ever knowingly maintained a personal friendship with a communist. Hiss, however, did say that Chambers resembled a freelance journalist whom he knew as George Crosley who had sublet his apartment and borrowed money from him. Chambers testified that Hiss had known him as Carl Crosley.

On August 25, 1948, Hiss and Chambers confronted each other at a televised HUAC hearing. The day before Hiss had written to HUAC accusing it of using "verdict-first" and "testimony-later tactics" against him and challenged the committee to find any blemish on his government record. At the hearing Chambers and Hiss gave radically differing accounts of their relationship and Hiss' political beliefs.

Hiss said he had never been a communist. Chambers insisted that Hiss was "a dedicated and rather romantic Communist . . . my closest friend in the Communist Party." Hiss said they had met in 1934 or 1935 when he was chief counsel to the Senate Munitions Investigating Committee when Chambers came to his office, introduced himself as freelance journalist George Crosley and asked for information for a series of articles on munitions. Chambers said he was introduced to Hiss as Carl Crosley in 1934 by the chief of the communist underground in the United States.

Hiss said that Chambers had sublet his Washington apartment for the summer of 1935 but had never paid the rent. Chambers said that as a communist underground courier, he was given free use of the apartment "because Mr. Hiss and I were communists and that was the communist way."

Chambers maintained that Hiss gave him his spare car as "a contribution to the underground work." Hiss had no recollection of how he disposed of the car as "it happened too long ago and never seemed important" until Chambers' accusations.

Hiss said the two men had last seen each other when Hiss had thrown him out of his apartment in 1935. Chambers said they had last met in 1938, after Hiss had refused to join Chambers in quitting the Communist Party. Hiss dared Chambers to repeat his allegations outside the protected precincts of Congress, saying that he would sue if he did so. The journalist took him up on the challenge and on August 27 went on the television program "Meet the Press" to declare, "Alger Hiss was a communist and may still be one." A month later Hiss filed a suit for slander against Chambers, claiming damages of $75,000.

During the pretrial investigations for the slander trial Chambers further raised the temperature by accusing Hiss of espionage, claiming that Hiss had given him classified State Department documents for delivery to the Soviet Union. He went on to produce the documents, which included four memoranda in Hiss's handwriting. In December Chambers handed over five rolls of microfilmed classified documents, which Chambers said had been hidden in a hollowed-out pumpkin on his farm outside Westminster, Maryland. The documents became known as the "Pumpkin Papers" and were dramatically produced by HUAC member RICHARD NIXON, who called them "definite proof of one of the most extensive espionage rings in the history of the United States."

President Harry Truman at this stage intervened in the case to claim that the allegations against Hiss were a "red herring" designed to detract attention from the Republican-controlled Congress' failure to control inflation.

In December Hiss and Chambers presented their evidence before a New York grand jury, and on December 15 Hiss was indicted on two counts of perjury. The grand jury charged that he had lied when he told them that he had never given any State Department documents to Whittaker Chambers in the 1937–1938 period and that he had not seen Chambers after entering the State Department in 1936. Hiss pleaded not guilty to both charges.

The start of the trial was postponed six times before it finally got underway in the New York Federal Court on May 31, 1949. The crux of the trial was whom the jury believed, the patrician diplomat Alger Hiss or the portly self-confessed communist Whittaker Chambers. Hiss's attorney, Lloyd Paul Stryker, got off to a good start by forcing Chambers to admit that he himself had committed perjury when giving testimony about his communist activities. Stryker used this admission to brand Chambers as "a thief, a liar, a blasphemer and a moral leper." In his summation, he called Chambers a "psychopathic . . . sadist" whose charges against Hiss were "preposterous."

Stryker was also able to call a formidable string of character witnesses in defense of Hiss. These included Supreme Court associate justices Felix Frankfurter and Stanley Reed, both of whom praised the character and record of Hiss. Hiss himself made an excellent impression in the witness box, where he once again denied being a communist or a communist sympathizer or having given any secret documents to Chambers in 1937 and 1938.

Set against this testimony, however, was Chambers's encyclopedic knowledge of Hiss's career during the 1930s. But this would have been insufficient without the corroborative evidence of the Pumpkin Papers. It was established at the trial that the handwritten documents were in Hiss's handwriting and that the typed documents had been typed on a Woodstock typewriter owned by Hiss in the 1930s. Hiss claimed that the typewriter had been given away by his wife in December 1937 and had not been in their posession when the 1938 documents produced by Chambers had been typed on it.

The first Hiss trial ended in July with a hung jury, with the jurors split eight to four for conviction. During the second trial, which started on November 17, 1949, the prosecution produced Mrs. Hede Massing, former wife of communist Gerhart Eisler, who testified that she and Hiss had both been members of the communist underground in Washington.

Hiss changed lawyers for his second trial. The new lawyer, Claude Cross, concentrated on trying to discredit the prosecution's documentary evidence by attempting to prove that Chambers could have procured the documents from other sources in the State Department. Cross then claimed that Chambers set out to frame Hiss by typing the papers on the Woodstock typewriter after acquiring the typewriter from the people to whom Mrs. Hiss had given it. The jury, however, found Hiss guilty of perjury on January 21, 1950. He was sentenced to five years' imprisonment.

Hiss started his prison sentence in March 1951 and was released in November 1954. He was barred from practicing law until 1975, when he was readmitted to the Massachusetts Bar. During the interval Hiss worked as a salesmen for various companies. He continued to argue his innocence forcefully. In 1957 he published *In the Court of Public Opinion*, in which he claimed that he had been denied a fair trial and convicted on the basis of manufactured evidence. Hiss said that Nixon and other Republicans had attacked him in an effort to discredit the New Deal and influence the 1948 and 1952 presidential elections.

In July 1978 Hiss filed a petition asking the Federal District Court in New York to overturn his 1950 perjury conviction on the grounds that he had not received a fair trial. The petition was refused. Not satisfied, Hiss applied for leave to appeal to the Supreme Court but was refused in 1983.

The most extensive published investigation of the Hiss case was probably Allen Weinstein's book, *Perjury: The Hiss-Chamber Case*, published in 1978. After interviewing members of the 1930s communist underground and examining previously classified FBI documents, Weinstein concluded that Hiss had been a Communist and that he had passed classified documents to Chambers. However, his conclusion has been challenged by some historians, who have criticized him for refusing to allow anyone to examine his evidence although he had publicly offered to do so.

For Further Information:
Chabot-Smith, John. *Alger Hiss: The True Story*. New York, 1976.
Chambers, Whittaker. *Witness*. New York, 1952.
Hiss, Alger. *In the Court of Public Opinion*. New York, 1957.
Weinstein, Allen. *Perjury: The Hiss-Chambers Case*. New York, 1978.

Ho Chi Minh (Nguyen That Thanh)   (May 19, 1890–September 3, 1969)   Ho Chi Minh was the leader of the Vietnamese Communist Party who drove the French out of Vietnam and laid the foundations for the ultimate victory over the United States in Vietnam. He was also, along with Chinese Communist Party leader MAO ZEDONG, a leading figure in the promotion of nationalist communism and peasant-originated communism.

Ho was born Nguyen That Thanh. He did not adopt the name Ho Chi Minh, meaning "He Who Enlightens," until 1940. In the intervening years he used several aliases during revolutionary activities that spanned several decades and continents. Ho's first job was as a cook on a French steamer, which took him around Africa and the United States. He spent World War I in Britain and France working at a series of manual jobs.

In 1917, while in France, Ho became a member of the Socialist Party and organized the Vietnamese living there. During the 1919 Versailles Peace Conference, Ho petitioned the Great Powers to pressure France into granting greater political independence to Vietnam. The petition was ignored by the world leaders attending the conference, but it helped to establish Ho as a leader of the Vietnamese community both in France and back home.

After the Bolshevik Revolution, Ho became interested in communism and in 1920 joined the French Communist Party. He spent 1923 and 1924 in Moscow and then organized a group of Vietnamese exiles in Canton. When China's Kuomintang leader CHIANG KAI-SHEK moved against the communists, Ho sought refuge in Moscow. During the next two years he traveled to Paris, Bangkok, Brussels and Hong Kong, and he formed the Indochinese Communist Party (PCI) at a meeting in Bangkok in 1930. The French authorities sentenced Ho to death in absentia.

When France was defeated by Nazi Germany in 1940, Ho crossed from China into Vietnam and founded the Viet Minh, the League for the Independence of Vietnam. But it was not until the end of the war that Ho's opportunity to seize power came, as a result of two events. The first was the Japanese decision in 1945 to attack and defeat Vichy French forces in Vietnam and the second was the atomic bomb attack on Hiroshima and the sudden Japanese surrender. These two events in quick succession left a political vacuum in Vietnam, and Ho rushed to fill it by declaring Vietnamese independence on September 2, 1945.

France, however, refused to accept the declaration. In October 1945, French troops landed in Saigon to reassert French authority. Within three months the French had complete control over the southern half of the country. Ho was forced into negotiations that resulted in Vietnam being recognized as a "free state with its own government, army and finances," but it was integrated into the Paris-controlled French Union. The agreement was unsatisfactory to Communist Party nationalists, and the uneasy truce was broken by an incident at Haiphong in November 1946 when a French cruiser opened fired on the town and killed 6,000 Vietnamese. The result was the eight-year-long FRENCH INDOCHINA WAR.

The Viet Minh maintained its power base in the north of the country and in the countryside. They waged a guerrilla war against the French forces, which sought to engage Ho's forces in a conventional battle. In an attempt to force a decisive battle, they eventually concentrated a large force on a poorly chosen site at DIEN BIEN PHU. It was surrounded by the Viet Minh and decisively defeated on May 7, 1954. Dien Bien Phu was a major blow to French morale, already weakened by the long drawn-out war. The government of Pierre Mendes-France committed itself to a negotiated solution, and the 1954 GENEVA CONFERENCE ON INDOCHINA resulted in the temporary division of Vietnam, with complete control of the northern part of the country going to Ho. The Geneva Conference called for country-wide elections to unify Vietnam under a single government after two years, but the United States was assisting the provisional South Vietnamese government to resist this. Although Ho could conceivably have gained complete control—the Viet Minh would certainly have won the scheduled elections—the Soviet and Chinese communists pressured him into compromise for the sake of wider East–West issues.

Ho spent the next five years consolidating his power base at home and abroad, with the ultimate aim of achieving the reunification of Vietnam. He visited the Soviet Union, China, Indonesia, India and Eastern European countries. He also attempted to act as a mediator in the Sino-Soviet dispute. In 1959, the PCI declared at its Third Congress that it sought the reunification of Vietnam by whatever means. At the time, this meant extending aid to the South Vietnam-based Viet Cong, who were conducting a guerrilla war against the U.S.-supported government of NGO DINH DIEM.

At the same conference, Ho relinquished the title of general secretary of the party and took on the largely ceremonial position of head of state. He remained, however, the most important political figure in North Vietnam during the Vietnamese war with the United States. Ho projected himself as the father of a divided nation and encouraged the Vietnamese to call him "Uncle Ho" ("uncle" being an even more respected title in Vietnam than "father").

As the symbol of Vietnamese nationalism, Ho Chi Minh helped to hold the North Vietnamese together after the United States started bombing raids. He also took the lead in refusing to negotiate with the United States until the bombing stopped. In February 1967, President LYNDON JOHNSON attempted to start peace talks with Vietnam by writing directly to Ho, offering to stop the bombing of North Vietnam "as soon as I am assured that infiltration into South Vietnam by land and by sea has stopped."

Ho, in a famous reply, wrote back to President Johnson accusing the United States of aggression and of "transforming South Vietnam into an American colony" and committing "war crimes and crimes against humanity." He went on to say that if the United States wanted peace talks "it must first unconditionally halt the bombing as well as all other acts of war against the Democratic Republic of Vietnam."

Johnson did not halt the bombing until March 31, 1968, after the North Vietnamese TET OFFENSIVE. Shortly afterward began the U.S.–Vietnam peace talks. Ho Chi Minh died on September 3, 1969.

For Further Information:
Halberstam, David. *Ho.* New York, 1971.
Karnow, Stanley. *Vietnam: A History.* New York, 1984.
Lacouture, Jean. *Ho Chi Minh.* New York, 1968.

Home, Lord (Sir Alec Douglas-Home)   (July 2, 1903–   )

Lord Home (pronounced "Hume") was twice British foreign secretary and once prime minister during the 1960s and early 1970s. He was a staunch anti-communist, and his wide experience of foreign affairs made him one of the more respected spokesmen on international affairs.

Home was born into the British aristocracy, the heir to a Scottish earldom. He attended the prestigious British public school Eton and then went on to Oxford, where he became involved in Conservative Party politics. At the age of 28, before he succeeded to his title and hereditary seat in the House of Lords, Home was elected to the House of Commons.

He became a close friend of Neville Chamberlain, and in 1937, when Chamberlain became prime minister, Home was appointed Chamberlain's parliamentary private secretary, a post he held until 1939. In this position he was privy to Chamberlain's negotiations with Adolf Hitler at Munich in 1938, and in the face of later criticism of the negotiations, Home remained a consistent supporter of Chamberlain's policy. Home's close association with Chamberlain and the "appeasement" policy kept him out of office during World War II, but after the Allied victory in Europe he served as undersecretary of state for foreign affairs in WINSTON CHURCHILL's short-lived caretaker government of 1945.

Home lost his Commons seat in the 1945 Labour landslide victory but was reelected to Parliament in 1950. The following year he had to relinquish his seat when he succeeded to his peerage and moved to the House of Lords. In 1951, Churchill appointed Home secretary of state for Scotland, and in 1955 Prime Minister ANTHONY EDEN appointed him secretary of state for Commonwealth relations. Home held this post until 1960, during which time he served also as deputy leader of the House of Lords, leader of the House of Lords and Lord President of the Council.

In July 1960, Home was appointed foreign secretary by Prime Minister HAROLD MACMILLAN. Home and Macmillan were united in their strong anti-communist stance, but they were also united in their opposition to the foreign policy of U.S. President DWIGHT EISENHOWER, which they saw as too blinkered in its approach to Moscow. Home and Macmillan projected Britain as a mediator between the Soviets and the Americans.

This approach was welcomed by President JOHN F. KENNEDY, who formed a close relationship with Macmillan that was mirrored in the relationship between Home and U.S. secretary of state DEAN RUSK. The more important relationship, however, was between the two heads of government, and Home was content to take a back seat to the prime minister, although he was carefully consulted on every foreign policy issue.

Despite the close Anglo-American relationship during the early 1960s, there were some differences. The first came over the CUBAN MISSILE CRISIS. Kennedy, for security reasons, did not tell the British government of his decision to impose a blockade on Cuba until 24 hours beforehand. This caused considerable embarrassment for Home and Macmillan, who had argued that the special relationship with Kennedy gave Britain added power in world councils.

America's unilateral decision to abandon the SKYBOLT missile project in 1963 was even more damaging. The move was a considerable embarrassment to the British, who had been counting on the system to replace their own failed Blue Steel program. The problem was resolved at a meeting between Macmillan and Kennedy in Nassau in December 1962, which was also attended by Home and Rusk. The two countries reached the NASSAU AGREEMENT, under which the United States agreed to sell Polaris submarines to Britain. This re-

sulted in greater British dependence on American nuclear weapons technology.

Home played a major role in the negotiations for the NUCLEAR TEST BAN TREATY and signed the treaty on behalf of the British government at the ceremony in the Kremlin on August 5, 1963. The treaty was the first serious step toward nuclear disarmament. Home said after the signing ceremony, "Although this treaty is not in itself an act of disarmament, it does put a brake on the arms race in the nuclear field."

Britain was still a colonial power during the 1950s and 1960s, and one of Home's major achievements was to direct the process of decolonization, first as Commonwealth secretary and then as foreign secretary, prime minister and once again foreign secretary. Many of the colonial liberation movements struggling for national independence at this time were attracted to the political example of the Soviet Union, which, as much for geopolitical as for ideological reasons, supported such groups. Home took the view that Britain should clearly side with the forces of nationalism in order to prevent increasing Soviet influence in the Third World.

One of Home's greatest successes as Commonwealth secretary was the defeat of the communist insurgency in Malaysia. He continued the British policy of a strong defense posture coupled with an extensive aid program to win the support of the peasantry. By 1957 the communists were effectively defeated as a political force, and Malaysia became an independent nation within the Commonwealth. Under an Anglo-Malaysian defense treaty, British troops remained on the Malay Peninsula and the emergency was not formally ended until 1960. British troops were not withdrawn until 1971.

By the summer of 1963, the Conservative government of Macmillan was under serious threat from the sex–spy scandal known as the Profumo Affair. In October 1963, Macmillan announced that he was retiring for reasons of health. He asked Home to read his resignation as leader to the Conservative Party Conference at Blackpool, thus signaling his support for Home as a successor who had escaped unblemished from the Profumo Affair and was thus best able to unite the party and restore its political fortunes.

Home, however, faced a problem with his peerage. Although he was not legally banned from holding the premiership while in the House of Lords, convention and parliamentary practice made it a virtual impossibility. Home took advantage of recent legislation that enabled him to renounce his peerage and stand for election as Sir Alec Douglas-Home to the House of Commons. He was formally elected Macmillan's successor in October 18 and won reelection to the Commons the following month.

As prime minister, Home faced growing opposition from the Labour Party to the Nassau Agreement and the government's nuclear policy. Labour deputy leader George Brown argued that Britain eventually would have to face the fact that it did not have the resources to be a nuclear power and contended, "We can get a greater sharing of common control of other weapons, not our own alone." Home, however, resolutely defended the maintenance of a British deterrent, and it remained British policy.

In November 1963, Home attended the funeral of President Kennedy and was one of the first foreign leaders to meet with President LYNDON JOHNSON. After his return to London, Home set the tone for the continued special relationship (and indirectly conceded Brown's point) when he said that the United States was clearly "where the power resides," and that Britain would continue to regard the Anglo-American alliance as the cornerstone of British foreign policy.

Home flew to Washington again in February 1964 for two days of talks with Johnson. Johnson agreed to support the continued presence of British troops in Malaysia, and Home agreed to support America's policy in Vietnam. Home continued to support American policy after the GULF OF TONKIN incident and the start of the U.S. bombing of North Vietnam, although he was wary of committing British forces to the conflict.

The last few months of Home's premiership were dominated by negotiations with Rhodesian prime minister Ian Smith over the independence of that British colony in southern Africa. Home refused to agree to a constitution for an independent state that was not approved of by both Rhodesia's blacks and whites. The constitution was rejected by the colony's blacks, and in November 1965, after Home left office, Smith announced Rhodesia's unilateral declaration of independence from Britain. This led to a long-running guerrilla war with its inevitable opening for Soviet influence because of its seemingly unequivocal support of African independence from colonial power.

Home's strength lay in foreign affairs, and he himself recognized that he was a poor manager of the British economy. This showed in his inability to improve the deteriorating British balance of payments. The economic problems and the after-effects of the Profumo Scandal led to a Labour victory in the general election of October 1964.

Home never considered himself more than a caretaker prime minister and party leader, and in January 1965 he resigned as Conservative leader and was replaced by EDWARD HEATH, who promptly named Home as his spokesman on foreign affairs. After the Conservative election victory in June 1970, Home returned to office as foreign secretary.

Under Heath, the emphasis of Britain's foreign policy shifted from the special relationship with the United States and the Commonwealth to membership in the EUROPEAN ECONOMIC COMMUNITY. One of Home's responsibilities during this period was to prevent too much of a deterioration in Anglo-American relations at a time when Heath was concentrating on bringing Britain into the EEC. Home was helped in this respect by the high regard in which he was held by both President RICHARD NIXON and HENRY KISSINGER.

During Home's second tenure as foreign secretary, relations with the Soviet Union were poor, and they reached their nadir in September 1971 when Home ordered the expulsion from Britain of 105 Soviet citizens suspected of espionage.

Home also opposed American withdrawal from Vietnam on the grounds that it would encourage the Soviet Union to take the offensive in Europe. He continued to oppose the introduction of British troops into the VIETNAM WAR, although he was generally supportive of the U.S. position. In March 1973, he was the British signatory to the Paris Peace Treaty ending the Vietnam War.

Home also signed the September 1971 QUADRIPARTITE AGREEMENT on Berlin, which regularized Berlin's postwar status, and the April 1972 treaty prohibiting the stockpiling, acquisition or retention of biological weapons.

The rift in Anglo-Soviet relations caused by the expulsion of Soviet spies was not healed until Home visited the Soviet Union in December 1973. After two days of talks with ANDREI GROMYKO, the two foreign ministers issued a communiqué that "noted with satisfaction" the improvement in relations between the two countries. Only a few days later, however, Home warned a meeting of NATO foreign ministers that his visit to Moscow had convinced him that the Soviets hoped to weaken the West's resolve to defend itself.

Home made a second attempt to resolve the Rhodesia crisis and negotiated a new agreement with Ian Smith in 1971. This agreement was approved by the British Parliament in December 1971 but was once again rejected by Rhodesia's black majority the following year.

Home remained foreign secretary until the Conservatives' election defeat in February 1974. In March 1974, at the age of 70, he announced his retirement from the House of Commons. Later that year he was created a Life Peer in the queen's birthday honors list and returned to the House of Lords, where he became one of the most active members.

For Further Information:
Home, Lord. *Letters to a Grandson.* London, 1986.
———. *The Way the Wind Blows.* London, 1976.

Honecker, Erich   (August 25, 1912–   )   Erich Honecker was the leader of East Germany from 1971 until 1989. He developed a close relationship with Soviet leader LEONID BREZHNEV, but his failure to match the political and economic reforms of MIKHAIL GORBACHEV in the Soviet Union contributed to the collapse of East German communism at the end of 1989.

Honecker was born in what later became West Germany, the son of a German coal miner who was an early and active member of the German Communist Party. By the time he was 10 years old, Honecker was a member of the German Communist Youth League, and he became a full-fledged member of the party at the age of 17. In 1930 he was sent to Moscow to attend the school of the Communist Youth International and in 1931 returned to Germany and was appointed secretary of the Communist Youth League for the Saarland.

In December 1935, Honecker was arrested by the Gestapo and soon afterward was convicted of conspiracy to commit high treason. He was placed in solitary confinement in Brandenburg Prison, where he remained until he was freed by Soviet troops in 1945.

After his release, Honecker remained in the Soviet sector and allied himself with the Moscow-oriented "[Walter] Ulbricht Group," which gave him the task of forming a communist paramilitary youth organization, the Free German Youth. This group led the attack on the BERLIN City Council at the start of the Berlin Blockade and in 1953 helped to suppress the EAST GERMAN UPRISING.

Honecker joined the Central Committee of the Communist-controlled Socialist Unity Party (SED) in 1946. In 1949 he was elected to the East German parliament, and in 1950 he became a candidate (non-voting) member of the SED Politburo. He developed a reputation as an unswerving ally of hard-line German communist WALTER ULBRICHT and helped his mentor to retain power after the death of Soviet leader JOSEF STALIN in 1953.

In 1956, Honecker returned to Moscow to attend the prestigious Communist Party Institute of Higher Political Studies. After completing the two-year course he was named a full member of the SED Politburo and secretary of the SED Central Committee with special responsibility for the armed forces and security affairs. As the head of security and the military, Honecker supervised the building of the Berlin Wall.

Honecker developed steadily closer relations with the Soviet Union and took a hard line in demanding a separate national identity for East Germany, opposing moves toward reunification and proposing total integration of the East German state in the Soviet Bloc. In 1968 he took a leading role in urging the WARSAW PACT invasion of CZECHOSLOVAKIA, which suppressed the PRAGUE SPRING movement, and organized the roundup of East German dissidents sympathetic to the cause of Czech leader ALEXANDER DUBCEK.

Honecker at first opposed the OSTPOLITIK policy of West German chancellor WILLY BRANDT. But when the Soviet Union decreed that the policy was advantageous to the Eastern Bloc he changed his course and finally came into conflict with SED leader Ulbricht, who remained opposed to Brandt and Ostpolitik. The Soviets are believed to have then engineered the resignation of Ulbricht in May 1971 and replaced him with the more amenable Honecker.

Honecker certainly toed the Moscow line during the era of détente. He, for instance, offered no serious objections to the 1971 QUADRIPARTITE AGREEMENT on Berlin, after Soviet leader LEONID BREZHNEV told him that it was a vital element of the Soviet Union's foreign policy.

Honecker's motivations were complex. He was first and foremost a communist committed to the cause of internationalism. He regarded the Soviet Union as the leader of the International Communist Movement and saw as his primary role the maintaining of Soviet-style communism in Germany. He believed that the greatest threat to German communism was German nationalism and that the best means of combating it was through a close relationship with the Soviet Union,

isolation from West Germany and a heavily centralized economic and political structure.

Until 1985, this generally coincided with Soviet foreign and domestic policies. Honecker supported détente, but only in order to win diplomatic recognition for the German Democratic Republic. But he was adamantly opposed to German reunification, as he made clear in a speech in January 1972, when he said, "Between the German Democratic Republic and the imperialistic Federal Republic of Germany there is no unity and there can be no unity. This is as obvious as the fact that rain falls down to earth and does not flow upward to the clouds."

Honecker also used détente to try to win greater recognition of East Germany's separate political identity by West Germany, and in 1974 he was rewarded by the exchange of permanent representatives, which implicitly recognized the existence of two German states. Honecker also used the issue of reunification of German families to win political and economic concessions from the Bonn government.

At the 30-nation CONFERENCE ON SECURITY AND COOPERATION IN EUROPE (CSCE) held in Helsinki in the summer of 1975, Honecker appeared to bring the détente between the two German states to a new high when he met with West German chancellor HELMUT SCHMIDT. Honecker, however, refused to discuss the Berlin Wall. He said, "The frontier and the wall remain as existing realities. It is a fact that stabilized borders constitute an aid to peace."

The late 1970s saw Honecker moving toward improved relations with West Germany. In March 1976 the two Germanies reached an agreement on postal service and telecommunications, and in October 1979 they agreed to waive motor vehicle tax and road-user fees for trucks and buses in order to facilitate intra-German trade and family visits.

The relationship between the two Germanies continued to be heavily affected by the general state of East–West relations. Following the Soviet invasion of AFGHANISTAN in December 1979 and the banning of the SOLIDARITY trade union in Poland, relations between Bonn and East Berlin plummeted. In October 1980 Honecker called upon the Federal Republic to recognize East German nationality and argued that the permanent representative missions in the two Germanies should be converted into embassies.

By the early 1980s, however, the overall improvement in relations between the two Germanies had developed its own momentum, which temporary setbacks were unable to check. Honecker therefore decided to try to use the improvement to gain much-needed hard currency for the East German state. In June 1982 the West German government provided $835 million in interest-free credit to the East Germans, and Honecker made the relatively minor concession of agreeing to allow West Berliners to make day visits to East Berlin. He also proclaimed that former East German citizens who had "left the GDR illegally" before January 1981 would be allowed back to visit friends and relatives. In October 1983, Honecker announced that the self-triggering antipersonnel devices along the east–west German border would be removed.

Official contacts between Honecker and the West German leadership were kept to a minimum. Honecker and Chancellor HELMUT KOHL met briefly at the funeral of Soviet leader YURI ANDROPOV in February 1984, and in September 1985 Honecker met the conservative leader of the Bavarian-based Christian Social Union, FRANZ JOSEF STRAUSS. In September 1987 Honecker became the first East German head of state to visit West Germany and used the visit to stress "the realities" of the "existence of two independent, sovereign German states." He added, "Socialism and capitalism cannot be united any more than fire and water."

Honecker at this stage appeared to have won international recognition of the existence of two Germanies, and many West German officials publicly doubted the wisdom of reunification. But the success of Honecker's communist Germany continued to rely heavily on the existence of communism elsewhere in Eastern Europe, in particular in the Soviet Union. The admission by Soviet leader MIKHAIL GORBACHEV that the Soviet Bloc countries were in need of a major reform of their political and economic systems was a fatal blow to the political career of Honecker.

In 1989, Honecker's health deteriorated, while at the same time his regime was shaken by huge pro-democracy protests and a mass immigration of refugees to West Germany. On October 18, the Communist Party's Central Committee replaced Honecker with Egon Krenz. The committee said that Honecker retired for health reasons, but Western analysts believed he was forced out because of his uncompromising resistance to political reform.

Events moved swiftly after that. East Germany opened its borders and the Berlin Wall fell in November. In December, Honecker was expelled from the Communist Party, placed under house arrest, and charged with corruption and abuse of power. He was released from detention in January 1990 because of his poor health. Hounded by an angry public, he took refuge at a Soviet Army base near Berlin in April. In November, following the reunification of Germany, a warrant was issued for his arrest on charges of manslaughter in connection with his alleged responsibility for shooting deaths at the Berlin Wall. Soviet authorities refused to turn him over and flew him to Moscow in March 1991. However, his welcome there ran out with the demise of the U.S.S.R., and in late 1991 he took refuge in the Chilean Embassy in Moscow. After months of negotiations, he was flown to Germany in July 1992 to face 49 counts of manslaughter.

For Further Information:
Childs, David, ed. *Honecker's Germany.* Boston, 1985.
Fritsch-Bournazel, Renata. *Confronting the German Question.* Oxford, 1988.
Honecker, Erich. *The German Democratic Republic, Pillar of Peace and Socialism.* New York, 1979.
Lippmann, Heinz. *Honecker and the New Politics of Europe.* New York, 1972.
Whetten, Lawrence. *Germany East and West.* New York, 1980.

Hoover, J. Edgar   (January 1, 1895–May 2, 1972)   J. Edgar Hoover was the director of the FEDERAL BUREAU OF INVESTIGATION (FBI) of the U.S. Justice Department for 48 years. He built the FBI into an effective crime-fighting and counterespionage organization. He was one of the most powerful American anti-communist political figures.

After working his way through George Washington Law School, Hoover took a job as clerk with the Justice Department. After three years he was appointed an assistant to Attorney General A. Mitchell Palmer and was charged with the task of rounding up thousands of alleged communist and anarchist immigrants for deportation (the infamous "Palmer Raids").

Hoover was appointed deputy director of what was then the Bureau of Investigation in 1921 and in 1924 was promoted to director. He transformed the almost unknown investigative unit into a nationally respected police force. His breakthrough came in the 1930s when the FBI was given the power to carry firearms and to make certain intrastate arrests. Hoover used these powers to focus on the high-publicity "public enemies" of the period such as John Dillinger, Pretty Boy Floyd, Baby Face Nelson, Ma Barker and Bonnie Parker and Clyde Barrow.

His success in dealing with these gangsters, coupled with a highly effective public relations operation, brought Hoover public approbation, which he used to secure his position as director. His public admiration was such that no president was ever able to remove him from office. The public regarded him as ethically superior to any politician, giving his strong anti-communist views added weight and substance.

In 1936, President FRANKLIN D. ROOSEVELT gave the FBI the responsibility for the investigation of espionage and sabotage. During the war years, Hoover concentrated his efforts on far-right organizations, but he also kept close watch on communists and quickly shifted the focus of FBI activities to the Communist Party and other left-wing groups when the war ended.

Hoover convinced himself that Moscow had infiltrated communist agents into the highest levels of the U.S. government, and in the early Cold War years the FBI played a prominent role in the investigations of such figures as ALGER HISS, WHITTAKER CHAMBERS, JOHN PATON DAVIES, JOHN STEWART SERVICE, JULIUS AND ETHEL ROSENBERG and HARRY DEXTER WHITE.

Beginning in the TRUMAN administration, Hoover wrote and spoke extensively on the "communist menace." His major work on the subject, *Masters of Deceit: The Story of Communism in America and How to Fight It,* was written largely by his staff and published in 1958, when it reached the bestseller list. It was a right-wing conservative view of the history of the Communist Party in the United States and urged all Americans to be on their guard against communists or liberals whose actions were supportive of the Soviet Union.

Hoover's influence started to wane with the election of

JOHN F. KENNEDY as president in 1960. Since Roosevelt's day, Hoover had had direct access to the White House. Under Kennedy his access was limited to the attorney general, ROBERT KENNEDY, who wanted Hoover to increase FBI investigations of organized crime and hire more ethnic minorities. His clashes with Kennedy led Hoover to concentrate on building a stronger political base in Congress. He did this by using FBI agents to conduct political investigations for key senators and congressmen. He had performed similar tasks for presidents Truman and Eisenhower and repeated the work for Johnson and Nixon.

Robert Kennedy left the Justice Department in 1964 and was replaced by Nicholas Katzenbach, who left two years later, feeling that he could no longer effectively serve as attorney general because of Hoover's obvious resentment toward him. Katzenbach was replaced by Ramsey Clark, who also had a difficult relationship with Hoover. Each successive attorney general clashed with Hoover over the FBI's wiretapping and mail-opening activities and its positions against civil rights. Hoover was slowly forced to modify some of his activities. The number of wiretaps authorized by the attorney general declined from 107 to 43 between 1966 and 1968, and in July 1966 Hoover ended the mail-opening and illegal entry operations. He also extended the COINTELPRO program to the Klu Klux Klan and the American Nazi Party.

In the early 1970s, Hoover's ability to order unconstitutional and illegal activities against his perceived opponents was circumscribed by press reports detailing some of the FBI's more questionable actions. In the midst of the controversy over the disclosures, Hoover died suddenly on May 2, 1972. It was widely noted that no president had had the nerve to fire him.

For Further Information:

Gentry, Curt. *J. Edgar Hoover: The Man and His Secrets*. New York, 1991.

Hoover, J. Edgar. *The Masters of Deceit: The Story of Communism in America and How to Fight It*. New York, 1958.

Lamphere, Robert J., and Tom Shachtman. *The FBI–KGB War: A Special Agent's Story*. New York, 1986.

Mitgang, Herbert. *Dangerous Dossiers: Exposing the Secret War Against America's Greatest Authors*. New York, 1988.

Powers, Richard Gid. *Secrecy and Power, the Life of J. Edgar Hoover*. New York, 1987.

Robins, Natalie S. *Alien Ink: The FBI's War on Freedom of Expression*. New York, 1992.

Theoharis, Athan G., ed. *Beyond the Hiss Case: The FBI, Congress, and the Cold War*. Philadelphia, 1982.

———. *From the Secret Files of J. Edgar Hoover*. Chicago, 1991.

Theoharis, Athan G., and John Stuart Cox. *The Boss: J. Edgar Hoover and the Great American Inquisition*. Philadelphia, 1988.

Ungar, Sanford. *FBI*. Boston, 1975.

U.S. Senate Select Committee on Intelligence Activities. *Report*. Washington, D.C., 1976.

Hopkins, Harry L.   August 17, 1890–January 29, 1946)

As special adviser to presidents Roosevelt and Truman, Harry Hopkins played a major role in determining American foreign policy in the closing days of World War II and the first days of the Cold War.

Hopkins started his working life as a social worker after graduating from Grinnell College in 1922. In 1931 FRANKLIN ROOSEVELT, then governor of New York, appointed him head of the state's Temporary Relief Administration. The appointment was the start of a lifelong friendship and close working relationship rarely equalled in political history.

During World War II Hopkins was Roosevelt's special adviser. At times he actually lived in the White House. He accompanied Roosevelt to all the major wartime conferences and undertook a number of wartime missions as a special emissary to either London or Moscow. In May 1945 Truman sent Hopkins to Moscow to try to salvage the U.S.–Soviet wartime alliance, which was being put under heavy pressure by Stalin's refusal to allow free elections in Poland and the Red Army's occupation of Eastern Europe.

Hopkins, who had formed a close relationship with Stalin at previous wartime meetings, took a hard line with the Soviet leader, demanding that he honor his Yalta promise to hold elections in Poland. At the same time, he assured the Soviet leader that the United States was sympathetic to his concern that the Soviet Union have friendly governments on its Western border. As a result of the Hopkins mission, Stalin reluctantly agreed to include some pro-Western ministers in the provisional Polish government.

The two men also set the agenda for the forthcoming POTSDAM CONFERENCE and finalized the terms for the Soviet Union's entry into the war against Japan. Hopkins also persuaded Stalin to accept the principle that the United Nations Security Council be allowed to discuss any issue brought to its attention; the Soviet leader had previously wanted the permanent members to be allowed to veto consideration of an issue.

Hopkins would have doubtless continued to play an important role in the development of postwar American foreign policy, but poor health forced his resignation soon after his return from Moscow. He died six months later, on January 29, 1946.

For Further Information:

Sherwood, Robert. *Roosevelt and Hopkins*. New York, 1948.

Horn of Africa   The Horn of Africa's national and tribal conflicts and its strategic position on the oil route through the Red Sea led to its becoming a proxy battleground for the United States and Soviet Union.

The Horn of Africa is occupied by Ethiopia, Somalia and Djibouti. The conflicting territorial claims of these three countries made the region one of the more politically unstable in Africa. In the early years of the Cold War, the opportunities for conflict were lessened by the continuing imposition of British and French colonial administration on most of the region. The British were responsible for British Somaliland and the administration of the United Nations Trust Territories of Eritrea and Italian Somaliland. The French were the colonial authorities in Djibouti (French Somaliland). Ethiopia was ruled by the absolute monarch Haile Selassie.

In 1952, Eritrea became an autonomous unit within the Ethiopean Empire. Eritrea was indispensable to the economy of Ethiopia, as it contained the empire's only major seaport (Massawa) and oil refinery. In 1962, against the wishes of the Eritrean parliament, the province was fully absorbed into Ethiopia, and the same year the Marxist Eritrean People's Liberation Front (EPLF) was founded to fight for Eritrean independence. British Somaliland gained its independence from Britain in 1960 and was merged with Italian Somaliland to form Somalia. But the Somali government also claimed the northern province of Kenya, the Ogaden region of Ethiopia, and Djibouti. The French maintained their colonial rule in Djibouti until 1977, and after that retained a military presence in the former colony to protect it from attack by Somalia.

Between 1963 and 1964 there were sporadic clashes between Somali and Kenyan forces and Ethiopian and Somali forces. But the Somali government was unable to secure international support for its attempt to create a "Greater Somalia" and after four years of fighting was forced to seek a diplomatic accommodation with its neighbors. This was opposed by the Somali military, which in 1969 seized power. The new ruler, Major General Muhammad Siad Barre, proclaimed a socialist state and moved the country's foreign policy toward the Soviet Union in the hope that Moscow would help Somalia gain control of the disputed territories.

The Soviet Union responded by supplying extensive military aid to Somalia, and in return it was allowed to establish a missile base at Berbera on the Red Sea. The Soviet influence in the region was further increased by its close relations with Egypt and, after 1968, with South Yemen, where it built a submarine base. The United States reacted by increasing its military and economic aid to Ethiopia, which led to an arms race between the two regional powers and an uneasy stalemate.

In 1973 drought and famine struck Ethiopia, causing the deaths of an estimated 100,000 people. This was accompanied by increased guerrilla activity in Eritrea and also in the neighboring province of Tigre, where another Marxist guerrilla organization, the Tigrean People's Liberation Front, launched an offensive. Dissatisfaction at the government's inability to deal with either the separatists or the drought led to antigovernment demonstrations in February 1974. The civilians were joined by military units, and on September 12, 1974, Haile Selassie was deposed by the military and was imprisoned.

The government was taken over by the Armed Forces Coordinating Committee, commonly referred to as the Dergue. The military quickly abolished the monarchy and ordered the execution of the emperor and the political leaders from the imperial regime. In December 1974, the Dergue declared Ethiopia a socialist state and started a widespread nationalization of industries, banks and agricultural land. Farmers were forced onto cooperative farms, with the result that agricul-

tural production dropped, aggravating the already severe famine. Thousands who opposed the socialization of the economy were either imprisoned or shot. At the same time, the Soviet Union replaced the United States as the major foreign influence in Ethiopia.

The turmoil within Ethiopia was reflected in the Dergue, and in February 1977 the hard-line socialist Lieutenant Colonel Mengistu Haile Mariam killed Brigadier General Teferi Benti and his supporters and replaced him as chairman of the Dergue and head of state.

Somalia and the various separatist guerrilla armies saw the internal turmoil within Ethiopia as a golden opportunity to realize their own territorial and political ambitions. In December 1974 the Eritrean People's Liberation Front launched a major offensive, which was soon followed by a similar offensive in Tigre. In 1977, Somalia invaded the Ethiopian-held Ogaden region.

The Somali invasion of Ethiopia placed the Soviet Union in a difficult position, as it now had two client states fighting each other for a disputed territory. The Soviets initially tried to mediate in the dispute, but when it became apparent that neither side would compromise, the Soviets ended their military aid to Somalia and increased their support to the traditional power in the region, Ethiopia. An estimated 15,000 Cuban troops were sent to Ethiopia. Also sent were Soviet-piloted aircraft and Soviet officers to command Ethiopian forces. In 1978 the Soviet Union and Ethiopia signed a treaty of friendship and cooperation.

Somalia reacted by cutting its ties with the Soviet Union and turning first to the Arab countries and then to the United States and Britain for aid. The Western powers, however, were reluctant to extend aid until Somalia dropped its claims to the Ogaden. By the beginning of 1978 the Soviet–Cuban–Ethiopian counteroffensive had driven the Eritrean and Tigrean separatists into their mountain strongholds and the Somalis out of the Ogaden. Somali president Siad Barre barely escaped being overthrown.

In March 1978, to prevent the collapse of Barre, the United States signed an aid agreement with the Somali government. In August 1980, the two countries signed an agreement giving U.S. naval and air forces access to military facilities at Berbera and Mogadishu in return for a minimum of $25 million a year in military aid. The U.S.–Somali bases agreement completed a superpower realignment in the Horn of Africa, with the Soviet Union replacing the United States as the major influence in Ethiopia and the United States replacing the Soviet Union in Somalia. This reversal demonstrated that the driving force behind Cold War conflict was not so much ideology but power, and that behind Third World countries' policies was not ideology but nationalism.

The Soviet and Cuban presence in Ethiopia, plus the restraining influence of the United States, prevented a second full-scale Somali attack on the Ogaden. But the Ethiopian and Cuban forces were unable to inflict a complete defeat on the separatist movements in Eritrea and Tigre. The Eritrean guerrillas gradually grew in strength and numbers and won increasing support from the Arab world. In early 1984, the EPLF launched a major counteroffensive that inflicted severe losses on the government forces. The effect of the guerrilla offensives was aggravated by a worsening drought and famine, which was claiming millions of Ethiopian lives.

In May 1989 military commanders attempted to overthrow Mengistu while he was visiting East Germany. Mengistu rushed home and crushed the coup, but it severely weakened his political base and forced him to seek negotiations to end the war with the Eritrean and Tigrean guerrillas. By the end of 1989, the guerrillas had driven the government forces out of their provinces and were advancing on the capital at Addis Ababa. Negotiations between the separatist movements and the Ethiopian government were started in Rome in December 1989.

With the waning of the Cold War, both the U.S. and U.S.S.R. seemed to lose interest in what happened to their former clients in the Horn of Africa. Mengistu was overthrown by a rebel coalition in May 1991, and the Eritreans began planning for independence. Meanwhile, Somalia's Siad Barre was ousted in January 1991, and the country descended into anarchy, culminating in a devastating famine in 1992.

For Further Information:

Bailey, Glen. *An Analysis of the Ethiopian Revolution.* Athens, Ohio, 1980.
Harris, M.F. *Breakfast in Hell.* New York, 1987.
Legum, Colin. *Horn of Africa in Continuing Crisis.* New York, 1979.
Potholm, Christian P. *Liberation and Exploitation: The Struggle for Ethiopia.* Washington, D.C., 1977.
Spencer, J.H. *Ethiopia at Bay.* Algonac, Mich., 1987.
Vivo, Raul. *Ethiopia's Revolution.* New York, 1978.
Wubneth, M. *Ethiopia.* Boulder, Colo., 1988.

Hot Line   The hot line was the direct communications link between the president of the United States and the secretary general of the Communist Party of the Soviet Union.

The installation of the hot line was one of the byproducts of the CUBAN MISSILE CRISIS. Both governments had previously proposed such an arrangement to ensure a secure communications link that could be used to defuse international crises. The need for such a link was demonstrated when both President JOHN F. KENNEDY and NIKITA KHRUSHCHEV were forced to resort to public broadcasts during the Cuban Missile Crisis in order to communicate with each other.

Revised proposals for a Washington–Moscow hot line were turned over to the U.S. and Soviet delegations to the 17-nation Geneva disarmament conference, and a "memorandum of understanding" on the creation of a teletype link was signed in Geneva on June 20, 1963. The hot line has been modernized several times since its initial installation. It is still open today.

House Un-American Activities Committee (HUAC)   The House Un-American Activities Committee was one of the U.S. Congress's vehicles for investigating alleged communist subversion in the United States, from 1945 to 1975. Its activities, methods and aims were often criticized as unconstitutional, but they reflected the political mood of the country in the early Cold War years. As the national political mood changed, however, the committee became something of a national joke. In its last five years the committee changed its name to the Internal Security Committee.

HUAC began its first investigations of alleged communist subversion shortly after the end of World War II, but its efforts did not attract much attention until the end of 1947. Under the chairmanship of Representative Karl Mundt (R-South Dakota) the committee in 1948 launched an investigation into alleged communist infiltration of government agencies. The HUAC inquiry was attacked by President HARRY TRUMAN as a "red herring" designed to distract attention from the Republican-controlled Congress's failure to combat inflation. The information gathered in this investigation helped in the grand jury indictment of former senior State Department official ALGER HISS.

In 1951 and 1952, HUAC investigated alleged communist infiltration in the American motion picture industry. Celebrated movie stars, writers and producers were brought before the committee to testify about their former connections with the American Communist Party. Following the hearings, 24 people in the film industry claimed that they had been blacklisted by movie studios and had been denied jobs because of the stigma attached to an appearance before the HUAC. Twenty-three of these people unsuccessfully sued the HUAC and its then-chairman Representative John Wood (D-Georgia).

The committee investigated reports of communism in trade unions in February and March 1952 and that same year published a report about Soviet espionage entitled *The Shameful Years.* Also in 1952, the committee recommended the death penalty for espionage and attacked Harvard University and the Massachusetts Institute of Technology (MIT) for failing to suspend alleged communists on their faculties.

Committee chairman Representative Harold Velde (R-Illinois) opened an investigation of communist "infiltration" into American education in February 1953. The committee investigated "subversion" at Harvard and in the public school systems of Philadelphia and New York City. In Philadelphia the hearings resulted in the suspension of 26 teachers, and in New York the HUAC cited for contempt of Congress nine witnesses who refused to testify.

Velde hit the headlines in November 1953, when he issued HUAC subpoenas to former president Truman, former secretary of state JAMES BYRNES and former attorney general Tom Clark. Velde wanted the three men to answer allegations that Truman had appointed HARRY DEXTER WHITE after he knew that the FBI suspected him of being a communist spy. All three men rejected the subpoenas, and President DWIGHT EISENHOWER made a nationally televised address in support of them. No further actions were taken on the subpoenas.

Liberals and moderates hoped after the censure of Senator JOSEPH MCCARTHY in July 1954 that HUAC would also suffer. Instead it replaced McCarthy as Capitol Hill's main standardbearer of the anti-communist cause.

In March 1954, chairman Velde announced that a probe of America's clergy was "entirely possible." This ignited a series of protests from church groups and fellow congressmen, which effectively blocked the investigation. Velde accused the church leaders who attacked his allegations of being guilty of the "sin of subversion."

In 1956, HUAC turned its attention to the alleged unauthorized use of U.S. passports, and its members argued that American citizens who disseminated anti-American opinions overseas should be denied passports. But in 1958 the U.S. Supreme Court ruled that the State Department had not been authorized to withhold passports on the basis of "beliefs and associations."

In 1957, under the chairmanship of Representative Francis Walter (D-Pennsylvania), HUAC investigated suspected communists in the California education system. The committee released the names to local school boards with the result that many teachers lost their jobs. Demonstrations broke out during HUAC hearings in San Francisco in 1959; the committee countered with a movie, *Operation Abolition*, which depicted the demonstrations as communist-inspired and directed.

By the end of the Eisenhower administration, HUAC's activities were starting to be called into question, and liberal congressmen were proposing the committee's abolition. Public opponents, however, were few in number, and the HUAC continued. In December 1962, the committee launched an investigation of alleged communist infiltration of the antiwar organization Women's Strike for Peace. WSP chairman Dagmar Wilson testified before the committee that the organization was not communist-controlled but added that communists and fascists were nevertheless welcomed.

During the VIETNAM WAR HUAC conducted an investigation into alleged communist infiltration of the antiwar movement. The purpose of the hearings was to win support for a bill imposing fines of up to $20,000 and prison terms of up to 20 years for giving material aid to a hostile foreign power or impeding the movement of armed forces personnel or matériel.

In August 1966, just as the hearings were about to begin, a federal district court judge enjoined the panel from starting its investigation on the grounds that HUAC procedures violated the rights of witnesses. The committee chairman, Representative Joe Pool (D-Texas), regarded the court order as an unconstitutional interference by the judiciary in the legislative branch and prepared to start the hearings in defiance of the injunction. A constitutional crisis was averted when the order was overturned by the appeals court. During the subsequent four-day inquiry, antiwar activists showed their contempt for the HUAC by either refusing to testify or disrupting the proceedings from the audience. The bill was

dropped after witnesses from the Johnson administration opposed it as unnecessary and possibly unconstitutional.

In 1969 the committee, now seen as a relic of the McCarthy era, changed its name to the Internal Security Committee. The new committee, however, continued to investigate communist "infiltration," and in 1970 published a list of 57 campus speakers said to be "members, officers or supporters" of "radical" organizations. Federal judge Gerhard Gesell attempted to block publication of the report on the grounds that it violated the constitutional right of free speech, but he was overruled by a resolution passed in the House of Representatives.

Opposition to the committee continued to grow through the 1970s, and it was finally abolished in January 1975. Its responsibilities and files were transferred to the House Judiciary Committee.

For Further Information:
Bentley, Eric, ed. *Thirty Years of Treason*. New York, 1971.
Diggins, John P. *The Rise and Fall of the American Left*. New York, 1992.
Goodman, Walter. *The Committee: The Extraordinary Career of the House Committee on Un-American Activities*. New York, 1968.

Hoxha, Enver   **(October 16, 1908–April 11, 1985)**   Enver Hoxha was the leader of communist Albania from 1944 until his death in April 1985. He ensured that his tiny country remained the most Stalinist and most isolated state within the Communist Bloc.

Hoxha was educated in Albania and Montpelier, France, where he was exposed to radical politics. In 1936, he returned to Albania to take up a teaching post in the capital, Tirana.

Following the Italian occupation of Albania in 1939, Hoxha founded the Albanian Communist Party and became its first leader. During the war years he formed a close military relationship with Yugoslav partisan leader JOSIP BROZ TITO and with the Soviet Union. Within a short time, the Communist Party and Hoxha were at the center of the most effective resistance group in Albania. The communists formally took power on November 29, 1944, when the Germans left the country.

Britain and the United States agreed to recognize Hoxha's provisional government on the condition that it hold free elections. Elections were held in 1945, but they were preceded by a savage purge of anti-communist political leaders, which left Hoxha in control. As a result of these elections, the United States and Britain severed diplomatic relations and blocked Albanian entry into the United Nations until 1955. In 1950, Britain and America made an unsuccessful clandestine attempt to overthrow the Hoxha government.

In the immediate postwar years, Albania and Hoxha remained closely tied to Yugoslavia and Tito, and for a time Hoxha went along with Tito's idea of a Balkan federation. From 1945 to 1948 Albania was almost totally absorbed in the Tito-dominated federation. But Tito's differences with the Soviet leader JOSEF STALIN, the historical conflict between

Serbia and Albania, and Hoxha's strong commitment to the prewar Comintern led Hoxha to side with Stalin. When Tito's nationalism led Stalin to expel Yugoslavia from the COMIN-FORM in 1948, Hoxha took Albania out of the monetary and customs union with Yugoslavia and into a close alliance with the Soviet Union.

The determining factor in Hoxha's foreign policy now became his relationship with Yugoslavia, which was complicated by the fact that a large number of Albanians lived outside of Albania in the Yugoslav region of Kosovo. The Yugoslavs regularly accused the Albanians of stirring up ethnic unrest in Kosovo, and the Albanians accused the Yugoslav government of suppressing Albanian culture and planning to invade Albania.

The Soviet–Yugoslav split therefore served Hoxha's purpose in that it provided Albania with a superpower protector. When Soviet leader NIKITA KHRUSHCHEV ended the dispute with Yugoslavia, relations between Moscow and Tirana began to deteriorate. Hoxha, who felt he had been betrayed by Khrushchev, began to look around for another protector. He found it in Chinese leader MAO ZEDONG.

With the formal SINO–SOVIET SPLIT, Albania allied itself formally with Peking. In 1961 the Soviet Union withdrew economic and technical aid from Albania, evacuated its submarine base at Vlore and broke off diplomatic relations. Soviet advisers and aid were replaced by Chinese assistance. Albania withdrew from COMECON in 1962 and in 1968 left the WARSAW PACT.

Sino–Albanian relations were soured by China's decision in 1972 to seek a rapprochement with the United States. Relations with Beijing worsened still further after the death of Mao in 1976. In 1978, Hoxha announced his full support for Vietnam in its dispute with China, and the Beijing government retaliated by formally severing all economic and military cooperation with Albania, thus leaving the tiny Balkan state almost completely friendless—but ideologically pure, according to Hoxha.

Internally, Hoxha stood at the head of the most Stalinist and repressive state within the Communist Bloc. Contacts between Albanian citizens and foreigners were forbidden. The secret police and the Communist Party controlled virtually ever aspect of Albanian life, and the economy was completely centralized.

In his later years, Hoxha became the target of a power struggle as former colleagues maneuvered to succeed him. The most noteworthy of these struggles was with long-serving prime minister Mehmet Shehu, who is believed to have been shot by Hoxha in 1981 in a pistol fight after the two men argued.

Increasing isolation also brought additional economic hardship on the already impoverished Albanian people. This forced the Albanian leaders to extend tentative feelers toward Western countries, most notably Greece, Italy and West Germany. But Hoxha blocked any major improvement in diplomatic relations.

For Further Information:

Fischer-Galati, G.S., ed. *Eastern Europe in the 1980s*. London, 1980.
Mlnar, Z. *Nightfrost in Prague*. New York, 1980.
Silnitsky, Frantisek, et al., eds. *Communism and Eastern Europe*. New York, 1979.
Tokes, Rudolf, ed. *Opposition in Eastern Europe*. Baltimore, 1979.
Valenta, J. *Soviet Intervention in Czechoslovakia 1968: Anatomy of a Decision*. Baltimore, 1979.

Hudson Institute   The Hudson Institute is a conservative think tank founded by nuclear strategist Herman Kahn (1922–83) in 1962. Kahn argued, in his books *On Thermonuclear War* and *Thinking About the Unthinkable*, that nuclear war could be conducted as rationally as conventional warfare, and he dismissed those who asserted that the use of nuclear weapons was tantamount to the end of civilization.

In September 1961, Kahn left the RAND CORPORATION to start raising money for the Hudson Institute, which was formally launched the following year. The institute won a number of major government contracts to develop nuclear strategies, including scenarios for the possible outbreak of nuclear war. As part of these scenarios, the institute became a keen supporter of the CIVIL DEFENSE programs of the early 1960s.

Kahn himself conceived a $200 billion shelter plan with caverns 1,000 feet underground and capable of withstanding direct hits by nuclear bombs of up to five megatons. Such a shelter, he argued, would contain an economic and industrial complex "to provide a base for rebuilding the country" after a nuclear war.

After Kahn's death in 1983, the institute moved its headquarters from Croton-on-Hudson, New York to Indianapolis. The institute also broadened the scope of its research to embrace the role of a more traditional think tank. Issues covered by its irregular reports include domestic, political and economic affairs as well as strategic problems. The institute publishes a quarterly newsletter, a compilation of articles entitled *Hudson Opinion*, and awards the annual Doolittle Prize for National Security for distinguished service in that field.

Hukbalahap Rebellion   The Hukbalahap Rebellion was a communist-led rebellion in the Philippine province of central Luzon from 1946 to 1954. It failed after a massive injection of American aid.

The rich agricultural area of the Luzon plain was excellent recruiting ground for the Philippine Communist Party. The territory was controlled by a few wealthy landowning families who exploited the local poverty-stricken peasants. During the 1930s, the communists built a solid base of support among the peasant sharecroppers and during World War II organized a coalition to operate an anti-Japanese guerrilla army known as the Hukbalahap, or Anti-Japanese People's Liberation Army.

By the end of the war the Hukbalahap had not only helped to drive out the Japanese but had also seized a number of the large estates and had established their own regional government to enforce Hukbalahap laws and collect taxes. They were determined to retain their power base, and at the end of the war they refused to surrender their arms to either the Americans or the Philippine government that was installed after independence on July 4, 1946.

The Hukbalahap participated in elections before independence, and the Huk leader, Luis Taruc, won a seat in the Philippine Congress, but the government forced him out of office. Denied political representation, the Hukbalahap army retreated to the jungle, resolved to take power through military means.

In March 1948, President Manuel Roxas declared the Hukbalahap to be an illegal organization and launched a campaign of indiscriminate terror against the peasant population in an attempt to wipe out the rebels' power base. This policy only drove the peasants further into the arms of the rebels, and had the effect of destroying morale within the government forces as well.

As a result of the atrocities committed at the orders of President Roxas and his successor, Elpidio Quirino, the United States at first remained aloof from the conflict. From 1947 to 1950 the United States supplied only minimal military aid to the Philippines, and a request by Quirino for additional aid was firmly rejected on the grounds that it was not needed.

But the success of communists elsewhere in Asia caused President HARRY TRUMAN to reverse his policy. By the start of 1950, the Hukbalahap were on the offensive and marching toward the capital, Manila. In the spring of 1950 the U.S. military aid already agreed upon for the Philippines was speeded up, and Truman received from Congress a supplementary appropriation. In 1951, the annual U.S. military aid allocation was increased threefold, and the U.S. military presence on the islands was increased.

At the same time, a joint U.S. Military Advisory Group was assigned to the Philippines to help direct operations against the Hukbalahap. The American advisers recommended that responsibility for suppressing the rebellion be transferred from the police to the armed forces. Intelligence operations were also reorganized and placed under the direction of CIA station chief EDWARD LANSDALE, a U.S. Air Force officer. The United States also supplied $250 million in grants and low-interest loans to help the Filipino economy while the government was diverting its cash resources to fighting the rebellion.

The combination of American aid, weapons and organization tipped the scales in favor of the Philippine government. In October 1950, the Huks suffered a major setback when an intelligence coup resulted in the capture of the entire Politburo of the Philippine Communist Party.

The Hukbalahap, however, maintained a strong base among the Luzon peasantry, buoyed by the corruption and continued unpopularity of the Quirino government. In 1953 Quirino was defeated in the presidential elections by the defense minister, Ramon Magsaysay, who was strongly supported by the United States and received CIA money for his election campaign. Magsaysay promised a land reform program, and in 1954 Hukbalahap leader Luis Taruc surrendered to government forces and the rebellion effectively came to an end.

Successive governments failed to fulfill their promise of land reform, and in the 1960s a renewed communist-led guerrilla war was started. This has never reached the threatening levels of the Hukbalahap rebellion, but it has remained a major problem for successive governments.

For Further Information:
Kerkvliet, Benedict J. *The Huk Rebellion: A Study of Peasant Revolt in the Philippines.* Berkley, Calif., 1977.
Kim, Sung Yong. *United States Philippine Relations, 1946–1956.* Washington, D.C., 1968.
Lahica, Eduardo. *The Huks: Philippine Agrarian Society in Revolt.* New York, 1971.
Lansdale, Edward G. "Lessons Learned: The Philippines, 1946–1956," *Alert* 6 (December 11, 1962).
Shalom, Stephen R. *The United States and the Philippines: A Study of Neocolonialism.* Philadelphia, 1981.

Humphrey, Hubert H.   (May 27, 1911–January 13, 1978) Senator Hubert H. Humphrey was a prominent liberal Democrat who combined his domestic liberalism with a tough Cold War anti-communist stand. He served as vice president under LYNDON JOHNSON from 1965 to 1969 over which period he adopted first a dovish and then hawkish stand on the VIETNAM WAR. In 1968 Humphrey was the Democratic Party's candidate for the presidency.

Humphrey came from an active Democratic family in South Dakota, where his father worked as a pharmacist. He attended the University of Minnesota but was forced to drop out to help with the family business during the Depression. He returned to the University of Minnesota in 1937 and graduated in 1939. In 1940, he earned his master's degree in political science from Louisiana State University.

Humphrey was deferred from army service because of a double hernia and color blindness. He taught briefly and then threw himself into Minnesota Democratic Party politics as a liberal committed to Franklin Roosevelt's New Deal policies. He made his first bid for elected office in 1943, when he unsuccessfully ran for mayor of Minneapolis. His second attempt, two years later, was successful.

In office, Humphrey quickly established a reputation as a liberal on social and economic issues and a staunch Cold Warrior on security and foreign policy matters. At the national level, he was one of the founders of the AMERICANS FOR DEMOCRATIC ACTION in January 1947. At the state level he successfully campaigned to expel a group of communists from the newly merged Democratic-Farmer-Labor Party and at the same time gained control of the party himself.

Humphrey shot into national prominence at the 1948 Democratic Party Convention, at which he gave a stirring pro-civil-rights oration that electrified the convention. Arguing that the United States "must be in a morally sound position" to act as "the leader of the free world," he proclaimed, "The time has arrived for the Democratic Party to get out of the shadow of states' rights and walk forthrightly into the bright sunshine of human rights." In November 1948, Humphrey was elected to the U.S. Senate with the support of 60% of the Minnesota voters.

In the Senate, Humphrey continued in his role as a crusading liberal, supporting civil rights, improved educational facilities, labor rights, social welfare and tax reform. The first bill he introduced eventually became Medicare. He also continued his tough anti-communist stand, supporting a 1950 amendment to the McCarran (INTERNAL SECURITY) ACT that empowered the president to order the internment of suspected subversives during periods of emergency. In 1954 he introduced the Communist Control Bill, which, in its original form, would have outlawed the Communist Party and provided criminal penalties for membership. He later admitted that the act was "not one of the things I'm proudest of."

In 1953 Humphrey joined the Senate Foreign Relations Committee and became chairman of the committee's disarmament subcommittee. In this position he played a major role in keeping the issue of disarmament alive through the 1950s. Humphrey was also a proponent of increased U.S. foreign aid, especially food aid. In 1954 he helped to pass Public Law 480, which authorized the sale and distribution of U.S. agricultural surpluses abroad. In 1961 he helped to expand the law into the more ambitious Food for Peace program. These moves further increased Humphrey's popularity with his agricultural constituents.

Humphrey made an unsuccessful bid for the Democratic Party's vice presidential nomination in 1956 and was the first to declare himself a candidate for the 1960 presidential elections. The Democratic race turned into a bitter two-man struggle between Humphrey and JOHN F. KENNEDY, which Kennedy won with 60.8% of the primary vote. During the Kennedy administration, Humphrey was a loyal Senate majority whip, and after the assassination of Kennedy he helped to smooth the transition to the Johnson administration. He was rewarded when LYNDON JOHNSON named him as his vice presidential running mate for the election of 1964.

As vice president, Humphrey started off opposed to Johnson's Vietnam War policies. In February 1965, he wrote a memorandum to Johnson in which he argued that escalation and a military solution were the "Goldwater position" and that the public would not understand why grave risks were justified to support the "chronic instability in Saigon." He urged the president to cut his losses and apply his negotiating skills to attaining a peaceful settlement.

Johnson was infuriated by Humphrey's memorandum and for the next year excluded the vice president from the foreign policy-making machinery. It was not until February 1966 that Humphrey reentered the foreign affairs field, when he was sent on a nine-nation tour of Asia, including South Vietnam. At the end of this trip, he declared, "The tide of battle in Vietnam has turned in our favor," and from then on he became an active supporter of the war effort.

Humphrey's support for the Vietnam War alienated him from his liberal supporters and moved him firmly into the center of Democratic Party politics. In 1968 he won the Democratic nomination for the presidency, but the bitter primary battle with the anti-war candidates Senator Eugene McCarthy and Senator Robert F. Kennedy and the demonstrations and riots outside the Democratic convention in Chicago left the party badly divided and led to Humphrey's defeat by Republican Richard Nixon in November.

After his defeat, Humphrey briefly taught at the University of Minnesota and Macalester College before returning to the Senate in 1971. The following year he made an unsuccessful third bid for the Democratic Party presidential nomination. Back in the Senate, Humphrey reversed his previous support for the Vietnam War and endorsed a resolution of the Democratic Policy Council condemning Nixon's Vietnam policy and calling for a withdrawal of all American forces by the end of 1971. Shortly after that, he criticized the administration's slow movement on arms control negotiations with the Soviet Union and urged the United States to accept a Soviet offer to limit deployment of the antiballistic missile.

Humphrey's last years in the Senate were devoted mainly to domestic issues. In 1974, he was briefly touched by scandal when it was revealed that he had received illegal contributions from dairy producers. He acknowledged the contributions, but denied that he had known that they were from corporate funds and thus illegal. In August 1977 Humphrey was diagnosed with terminal cancer. He continued to work in the Senate until his death on January 13, 1978.

For Further Information:
Cohen, Dan. *Undefeated: The Life of Hubert H. Humphrey.* Minneapolis, 1978.
Eisele, Albert. *Almost to the Presidency: A Biography of Two American Politicians.* Blue Earth, Minn., 1972.
Griffith, Winthrop. *Humphrey: A Candid Biography.* New York, 1965.
Humphrey, Hubert. *The Education of a Public Man: My Life and Politics.* New York, 1976.
Solberg, Carl. *Hubert Humphrey: A Biography.* New York, 1984.

Hungary Hungary was consistently one of the leaders for reform among the Socialist Bloc countries. In 1956 it was the scene of the first major revolution against Soviet domination and in the 1970s and early 1980s instituted reforms similar to Mikhail Gorbachev's later *perestroika* and *glasnost* policies. At the end of the 1980s it led the way in the reintroduction of a multiparty political system and in seeking closer political and economic relations with Western Europe.

During World War II, the Hungarians reluctantly sided with the Germans and Italians. Hungary had no sympathy with the Axis powers or fascist philosophy. It did, however, have a deep fear of communism as a result of a short-lived, repressive communist government in 1919–20. The Soviet Union was well aware of its unpopularity within Hungary when it invaded and occupied the country in 1944–45, and in part for this reason the Soviets took their time in establishing a Soviet-style state in Hungary.

The first postwar government established by the Soviet Union was a left-of-center coalition government that included only two communist members. Elections on November 5, 1945, resulted in a majority for the centrist Smallholders Party. But the Soviet Union, which maintained its military presence in the country, insisted that the coalition government continue and that communists be given control of the police. The Smallholders were allowed to name the prime minister. Communist control of the police, however, led to intimidation and the first purges of anti-communist politicians. Fresh elections were held on August 21, 1947. Before the balloting, however, an estimated one million people were disenfranchised and major anti-communist figures were arrested. The Soviet-controlled Communist Party emerged as the dominant force.

The Hungarian Communist Party then established a political system closely modeled on the Soviet state. Its leader MATYAS RAKOSI, a close friend and admirer of Soviet leader JOSEF STALIN, used many of the same political tactics employed by Stalin to impose his personal authority on the party and government. Farms were forcibly collectivized, an industrialization program was introduced and thousands were imprisoned or executed. The property of the powerful Roman Catholic Church was expropriated, and the Hungarian primate, JOZSEF Cardinal MINDSZENTY, was imprisoned, becoming a symbol of Hungarian resistance.

Within the party, however, there were two major ideological camps. One, known as the "Muscovite wing," was led by Rakosi and demanded unswerving loyalty to the Soviet Union, Stalin and Rakosi. The other, the "Nationalist wing," was more populist and nationalist in its policies, while still supporting socialism. In 1949 Rakosi turned on the Nationalist wing, arrested its members and executed its leader, Laszlo Rajk.

Rakosi now held absolute power until the death of his Soviet mentor, Stalin, on March 5, 1953. Uncertainty in the Soviet Union following Stalin's death undermined the position of Stalinists throughout Eastern Europe. On July 4, 1953, Rakosi was replaced by IMRE NAGY, a member of the Muscovite wing, but with discernible leanings toward the Nationalist wing. Nagy immediately set about to de-Stalinize Hungary and announced the restoration of land to private farmers, remission of fines for nonfulfillment of crop quotas, a de-emphasis of the industrialization program, price reductions, wage increases, a more liberal attitude toward private enterprises and the release of some political prisoners.

Nagy's policies were an immediate success with the Hungarian people. But the Soviet Union, which still occupied the country, was uncertain about what its attitude should be. The new collective Soviet leadership had yet to develop a position on Stalinist policies. For a time the economic reformer GEORGI MALENKOV held sway in Moscow, and while he and his policies were in the ascendant Nagy remained in power. But on February 8, 1955, Malenkov was forced to resign, and the Soviet Union made an uncertain lurch back toward Stalinism. The moves were mirrored in Eastern Europe, and on April 14, 1955, Nagy was expelled from the party and government.

Rakosi was reinstated and returned Hungary to its pre-1953 Stalinist course. Then came the Soviet Union's rapprochement with Yugoslavia's nationalist communist leader JOSIP BROZ TITO and NIKITA KHRUSHCHEV's "secret speech" of February 24, 1956, in which he denounced the cult of Stalin and, by implication, Stalinism itself. The two events combined to shake the very foundations of communist parties throughout Eastern Europe. Local communists interpreted Moscow's actions as a green light for widespread de-Stalinization. In Poland, for instance, WLADYSLAW GOMULKA, the former first secretary of the Polish Communist Party, who had been under arrest since 1950, was rehabilitated on April 6 and 30,000 political prisoners were released.

The initial changes in Hungary were not so dramatic. Rakosi was dismissed on July 18, 1956. But his replacement, ERNO GERO, was seen as an old-guard Stalinist who would implement only cosmetic changes. Dissatisfaction in Hungary was running high, but the spark that lit the Hungarian Revolution came from Poland. On June 28, 1956, workers in POZNAN rioted in front of a group of foreign businessmen attending the Poznan International Trade Fair. Polish security police opened fire and 53 people were killed and 300 wounded. The Soviet Union demanded a crackdown on dissent. Instead, the Polish Communist Party sided with the rioters and reelected Gomulka as first secretary in the face of strong Soviet opposition.

While these dramatic changes were occurring in Poland, Hungarians were also starting to demonstrate against Stalinism. On June 27 a crowd of several thousand gathered in Budapest to listen to a series of speakers denounce the crimes of Stalin and his Hungarian supporters. Then on October 20, Hungarian students demonstrated outside the Budapest radio station and demanded that it broadcast their 16-point program, which included demands for free elections and the withdrawal of Russian troops. The demands were refused and the students published their program in the form of a manifesto. Demonstrations and marches broke out throughout Budapest. Gero was in Yugoslavia on a diplomatic mission for the Soviets, and before he could return the crowds were demanding the dismissal of Gero, the reinstatement of Imre Nagy and the trial of Rakosi.

Gero, in a speech broadcast on October 23, warned against attempts to harm Soviet relations. He pledged to defend socialism and charged that some of the demonstrators sought to "restore capitalism." On the same day, a Russian armored division moved 80 tanks and artillery into Budapest. But Gero had lost his base of support within the party, and on October 24, 1956, Nagy was readmitted to the Central Committee and Politburo and named premier. He went on Budapest Radio to pledge his government to extend democratization, raise living standards and develop an independent Hungarian communism.

For five days the Hungarians fought street battles with Soviet tanks in the center of Budapest. Then on October 29, the Red Army forces began to withdraw to their bases and by November 1, Budapest was free of Soviet troops. On October 31, 1956, Nagy announced: "The revolution has triumphed. We will tolerate no interference in our internal affairs." The Soviet press agency, Tass, issued a statement that the Soviet government "was ready to enter into negotiations . . . for the withdrawal of Soviet troops from Hungary." Nagy sent a delegation led by Defense Minister Colonel Pal Maleter to negotiate Soviet withdrawal and announced that Hungary had left the Warsaw Pact and freed Cardinal Mindszenty from prison.

Then on November 1, JANOS KADAR, who had succeeded Gero as first secretary of the Hungarian Communist Party, disappeared, and on November 2 there were reports of Soviet tanks on the northeast border. But despite these disquieting events, talks for an orderly withdrawal of Soviet troops began between the Hungarian delegation and Soviet ambassador YURI ANDROPOV on the evening of November 3, 1956. At about midnight, KGB men stormed the conference and arrested the entire Hungrian delegation. At the same time, 200,000 troops and 4,000 Soviet tanks invaded Budapest "to help the Hungarian people crush the black forces of reaction and counterrevolution." An estimated 50,000 Hungarians died on November 4.

Nagy went on Budapest Radio to appeal for help, but the Soviet force was overwhelming. He fled to the Yugoslav Embassy for sanctuary while Cardinal Mindszenty sought protection in the U.S. legation. Janos Kadar reappeared as the Soviet-supported leader of the government. He had abandoned Nagy to help the Soviets plan the invasion.

While the revolution was rising and falling in Hungary, the Western alliance was seriously split over the British, French and Israeli attack on the Egyptian forces at the Suez Canal. This hindered an effective Western response to the revolution, although most analysts believe that there was little that could have been done to help landlocked Hungary without risking a world war. In the aftermath of the revolution more than 150,000 Hungarians fled to the West. After Nagy had spent three weeks in the Yugoslav Embassy, Kadar offered him safe conduct out of the country. But he was arrested as soon as he boarded the bus and was imprisoned in Romania. On June 16, 1958, the Hungarian government announced that Nagy and four other codefendants had been tried, found guilty of treason and executed.

The suppression of the Hungarian revolution continued throughout the rest of the 1950s. Between 1956 and 1961 an estimated 2,500 people were executed and nearly 30,000 imprisoned for political crimes. But the popular revolution had also had a positive effect on Hungarian life. The Communist Party took it as a warning that its power would have to be exercised within limitations politically acceptable to the population. The result was that from 1962, the country was the most politically and economically liberal country in Eastern Europe.

The rule of terror was discontinued. Hungarian citizens were no longer required to attend compulsory political meetings, and nonparty members ceased to be discriminated against in the competition for jobs. A major breakthrough came in 1968 with the introduction of the New Economic Mechanism (NEM), when the party shifted the economy from a Stalinist-style central planning system to one that gave greater freedom to factory managers and placed the emphasis on the profitability of business enterprises. The NEM also freed collective farms from central control and allowed the development of more private farms.

A parallel political reform was planned for 1969 but was temporarily shelved because of the Warsaw Pact invasion of CZECHOSLOVAKIA in August 1968. Kadar feared that any substantial changes in the political structure so soon after the decision to suppress the PRAGUE SPRING would be misinterpreted in Moscow. But the measures were gradually introduced in the late 1960s and early 1970s and involved encouraging the trade unions to work more in the interests of their members rather than as a vehicle for the party. The parliament was encouraged to hold more active debates, and there were elections with multiple candidates, although all the candidates came from the Hungarian Socialist Workers' Party. The judiciary was also given more freedom, and Kadar encouraged the press to take a more independent investigative role in exposing abuses of power at the mid-level.

These reforms backfired on the party; instead of satisfying the people's need for political freedom, they merely whetted their appetite for more. As a result, there was a tactical retreat from reform in 1974 and 1975, and several noted reformers were removed from their party positions. A number of key reformers, however, retained their jobs and in 1979 a second reform debate was launched.

Between 1979 and 1985 the Hungarian economy was again decentralized, state monopolies were broken up and a number of key subsidies were either substantially reduced or removed altogether. In 1981 the Hungarian government took the dramatic step of announcing that it would apply for membership in the INTERNATIONAL MONETARY FUND and the WORLD BANK, two organizations that had long been boycotted by the Socialist Bloc because of their emphasis on free-market economic structures.

Membership in the IMF was approved in May 1982, and in December 1982 the IMF approved a $580 million loan to Hungary. Earlier in the year a consortium of Western banks, led by the Manufacturers Hanover Trust Co. of New York, had extended Hungary a $260 million three-year loan. In return for the IMF loan, Hungary agreed to control imports and domestic spending and encourage exports in order to build up its currency reserves.

Hungary was now leading the Eastern Bloc in economic reforms and drew the attention of British prime minister

MARGARET THATCHER, who flew to Budapest to encourage the "Hungarian experiment" in the belief that the economic changes would lead to an improved standard of living and political reform not only in Hungary, but also elsewhere in Eastern Europe. Thatcher's interest was soon mirrored by other Western leaders. In October 1984 Kadar became the first East European leader to visit French president FRANCOIS MITTERRAND and in the same year was visited by the Australian foreign minister Bill Hayden and a trade delegation from China.

Political reform also moved ahead. In 1983 the Hungarian parliament passed a law requiring that at least two candidates run for each parliamentary seat and in June 1985 independents were allowed to run for office in the general election and won 25 of the 352 parliamentary seats. In December 1985, U.S. secretary of state GEORGE SHULTZ met in Budapest with Kadar and expressed optimism for the future of U.S.–Hungarian relations and indicated his support for an extension of Hungary's most-favored-nation trading status.

The introduction of MIKHAIL GORBACHEV's *glasnost* and *perestroika* policies in the Soviet Union increased the focus of attention on Hungary. Hungary was seen both inside and outside the Soviet Union as a role model for Gorbachev's reforms, and, at the same time, Gorbachev's decision to refrain from interfering in the domestic affairs of the East European countries freed the Hungarian government to speed up its reform program.

In June 1986, Gorbachev visited Budapest for talks with Kadar and told a group of Hungarian factory workers that the Soviet Union "follows with respect the efforts made in Hungary . . . to find solutions to the by-no-means-simple economic and social problems."

But by this time, the reform movement had passed Kadar by. Although he had started many of the political and economic reforms, his guiding principle had always been a devout commitment to Marxism-Leninism. Kadar had turned against Nagy because he believed that the Hungarian premier had abandoned communism. He introduced political and economic reforms because he believed that these were needed to win popular support for the basic communist policies that he pursued. In November 1986, the Hungarian government for the first time commemorated the 1956 revolution, indicating the start of a major reassessment of the uprising and Hungary's relationship with the Soviet Union and the West.

Kadar had, until this time, successfully blocked any attempt to reassess the official party history of the Hungarian Revolution, as any such reassessment would undermine his own position. But the demands for increased reforms grew. Kadar was by this time physically and mentally impaired by age and without a clear successor in the party. In May 1988 he was ousted as general secretary and leader of the Hungarian Socialist Workers' Party, but was retained in the ceremonial position of party president. Karoly Grosz replaced Kadar as general secretary. In May 1989, Kadar lost both the party presidency and his seat on the Central Committee.

(Kadar died on July 6, 1989. He was given a state funeral, and in his eulogy Grosz said that with Kadar's passing a significant era of national history had closed. On the same day that Kadar died, Nagy was posthumously rehabilitated.)

Grosz further accelerated the reform process. In June, the Hungarian government criticized the 1968 Warsaw Pact invasion of Czechoslovakia and in July started negotiations with the Soviet Union for the withdrawal of Soviet troops from Hungary. The same month relations with Romania started to deteriorate because of NICOLAE CEAUSESCU's decision to persecute the ethnic Hungarians in Transylvania. Grosz also established diplomatic relations with Israel and South Korea, and during a visit to the United States he told President RONALD REAGAN, "I will reorganize [Hungary's] economy. This can only be done . . . if the people enjoy more rights, more freedoms. Therefore, we are modernizing our political system and our political practice."

In September 1988, Hungary became the first Eastern Bloc country to officially tolerate independent political parties other than the Communist Party when the government officially recognized the Hungarian Democratic Union. The HSWP, however, was at this stage divided over the pace of the reform process. Grosz, who headed the "pragmatic wing" of the party, wanted to maintain a slow but steady pace, while the "radical wing" headed by Imre Pozsgay advocated immediate and radical reforms.

By the start of 1989, the radical reformers were in control of both the party and the government, and the reform process moved quickly forward on all fronts, helped by the process of reform in the Soviet Union and POLAND. In January the Hungarian parliament approved bills legalizing freedom of assembly and the right to form independent and opposition groups outside the Communist Party. A draft constitution submitted in March 1989 called for a multiparty political system, a separation of powers between the HSWP and the government and a special court to resolve constitutional issues. In August 1989, opposition parties won three parliamentary by-elections. Multiparty elections in two stages, were held March 25 and April 8, 1990. A total of 54 parties ran more than 1,600 candidates; the final results left the center-right Democratic Forum and its coalition partners in control with over 60% of the seats.

The Hungarian government also completely revised its assessment of the 1956 uprising. The 1958 trial of Imre Nagy was ruled "judicially unlawful," his 1956 speeches were broadcast on Hungarian radio, and Nagy's body, which had been buried in an unmarked grave, was exhumed and reinterred at a solemn nine-hour memorial service in Budapest attended by a crowd of 250,000. The funeral was organized by the opposition political parties, but the service had the full support of the government, and the honorary pallbearers were Premier Miklos Nemeth, Imre Poszsgay, Deputy Premier Peter Megyessy and Parliamentary Speaker Matyas Szuros.

Throughout these changes the Soviet Union remained aloof. In March 1989 Grosz had visited Moscow for talks with

Gorbachev at which the Hungarian received Gorbachev's promise not to interfere in the changes in Hungary. Grosz was by this time so confident of the reform process that he discussed the possibility of Hungary withdrawing from the Warsaw Pact and becoming a neutral country. By the start of 1990 some Hungarian politicians were stressing that Hungary's natural political roots were in Western Europe and suggested that Hungary should join the EUROPEAN ECONOMIC COMMUNITY and the political structure of NATO.

In May 1989 the government had begun dismantling the 150-mile-long barbed wire fence along the border with Austria. This action quickly led to a series of events that brought about the collapse of the Socialist Unity [Communist] Party in East Germany as tens of thousands of East Germans taking advantage of their right to travel to Hungary, entered Hungary and then crossed the border into Austria on their way to West Germany.

For Further Information:

Balogh, Sandor. *The History of Hungary After the Second World War, 1944–1980.* Budapest, 1986.

Brzezinski, Z.K. *The Soviet Bloc: Unity and Conflict.* Cambridge, Mass., 1960.

Felkay, Andrew. *Hungary and the USSR, 1956–1988: Kadar's Political Leadership.* New York, 1989.

Gati, Charles. *Hungary and the Soviet Bloc.* Durham, N.C., 1986.

Kertesz, Stephen Denis. *Between Russia and the West: Hungary and the Illusions of Peacemaking, 1945–1947.* Notre Dame, Ind., 1984.

Kovrig, Bennet. *Communism in Hungary from Kun to Kadar.* Stanford, Calif., 1979.

Shawcross, William. *Crime and Compromise: Janos Kadar and the Politics of Hungary Since Revolution.* London, 1974.

Vali, Ferenc. *A Rift and Revolt in Hungary; Nationalism vs. Communism.* Cambridge, Mass., 1961.

Zinner, Paul. *Revolution in Hungary.* New York, 1962.

Hurley, Patrick Jay **(January 8, 1882–July 30, 1963)** Patrick Hurley was a major influence on American policy toward China in the early years of the Cold War. He developed a close friendship with CHIANG KAI-SHEK while ambassador to China and accused American foreign service officers of aiding the Chinese communists.

Hurley was born in Choctaw Indian Territory in Oklahoma into an Irish immigrant family. He worked in coal mines and as a cowboy before attending Baptist Indian University. After obtaining a law degree from National University he opened a law practice in Tulsa, Oklahoma. Hurley invested wisely in oil and banking and by the 1920s was one of the richest men in the state.

He financed Herbert Hoover's 1928 campaign in Oklahoma and was rewarded with the post of assistant secretary of war and then secretary of war. After Hoover's defeat in 1932, Hurley returned to his business interests in Oklahoma, but he maintained a law practice in Washington and became increasingly prominent in Republican circles.

He was obvious choice for a post when President Franklin Roosevelt broadened his wartime political base by bringing Republicans into the administration. Hurley was first given the job of coordinating the running of the blockade of Bataan. This was followed by his appointment as minister to New Zealand. In August 1944 he was named Roosevelt's personal representative to China and three months later ambassador.

China represented a major foreign policy problem at the time. The long-running conflict between the Kuomintang Nationalist government and the Chinese communists was seriously damaging the war effort and souring relations with the American-appointed commander-in-chief, General Joseph Stilwell. Hurley was directed to persuade Nationalist government leader Chiang Kai-shek to set aside his long-standing differences with the Chinese communists and join forces under the command of Stilwell to fight the Japanese. Hurley, however, fell under the spell of Chiang and his wife and became an ardent supporter of the Nationalist cause. He clashed with foreign service officers such as JOHN PATON DAVIES and JOHN STEWART SERVICE, who maintained that Chiang's corrupt government would fall to the communists because it lacked popular support. Hurley came to believe that only communists could take such a position.

In September 1945 Hurley returned to the United States and delivered a speech in which he claimed that American diplomats in China were refusing to carry out American policy. He faced criticism from liberal Democrats who were pressing for his dismissal. Hurley tried to outmaneuver his critics by offering his resignation to President Harry Truman but was himself outmaneuvered when the president accepted it. In his resignation letter Hurley charged the foreign service officers with aiding the Chinese communists and hindering his attempts to save the Nationalist government.

Hurley became a leading figure in the right-wing China Lobby. On June 19, 1950, he accused Service and Davies of supplying the Chinese communists with secret information and advising them on how to defeat the American policy of helping Chiang Kai-shek. Successive State Department investigations cleared Davies and Service, but Hurley continued to agitate for their removal; his demands were picked up by Senator JOSEPH MCCARTHY, and the two diplomats were forced out of the State Department in 1953.

Hurley remained prominent in national Republican politics and ran three times, unsuccessfully, for a Senate seat from New Mexico.

For Further Information:

Buhite, Russell D. *Patrick J. Hurley and American Foreign Policy.* Ithaca, N.Y., 1973.

Fairbank, John K. *The United States and China.* Cambridge, Mass., 1971.

Purifoy, Lewis McCarroll. *Harry Truman's China Policy: McCarthyism and the Diplomacy of Hysteria, 1947–1951.* New York, 1976.

Husak, Gustav **(January 10, 1913–November 18, 1991)** Gustav Husak succeeded Alexander Dubcek as communist leader of Czechoslovakia. He played a leading role in quashing the PRAGUE SPRING of 1968 and went on to lead one of the more repressive governments in Eastern Europe before being forced to resign in December 1987.

After studying law at Comenius University in his home town of Bratislava, Husak became involved in Communist Party politics. During World War II, he remained in Czechoslovakia and led the Slovak resistance against German occupation.

His wartime activities made him a hero among the Slovak community, and after the war he became the Slovak premier. In 1948 he played the major role in coordinating the communist takeover in the Slovakian section of Czechoslovakia.

But Husak was too closely identified with Slovakian national interests for the liking of Communist Party leader KLEMENT GOTTWALD, who aimed to suppress all nationalist tendencies and impose a Stalinist internationalism. In 1950, Husak was purged from the party along with several other major figures. He was accused of "bourgeois nationalism." In an attempt to regain his position within the party, Husak publicly recanted, but despite his self-criticism, he was arrested in 1951 and in 1954 was sentenced to life imprisonment.

It was not until 1960 that Husak was released, and it took him another three years to be politically rehabilitated and gain readmission to the party. Husak's prominent position during the purges of the Gottwald years and his wartime experiences and many years in prison led a number of people to regard him as a reformist figure, and when the Prague Spring erupted in 1968, he was catapulted back into the senior position of deputy prime minister. In reality, however, Husak was as much of a hard-line Stalinist as the ousted ANTONIN NOVOTNY, and his differences with the previous regime were of a personal rather than an ideological nature.

After the Warsaw Pact invasion of Czechoslovakia in August 1968, Husak was one of the few members of the Dubcek government with whom Soviet leader LEONID BREZHNEV was prepared to talk. He quickly reestablished himself in his old role as leader of the Slovaks and on August 23 went to Moscow to negotiate a solution to the crisis. The terms he agreed to included the basing of Soviet troops in Czechoslovakia, tighter party control over cultural and political activities and reduced economic cooperation with the West.

While in Moscow, Husak also convinced Brezhnev of his loyalty to Soviet policies and his acceptability to the Kremlin, the Czechoslovak people and the Czechoslovak Communist Party. With the Red Army occupying the country and with the support of the Soviet Union, Husak was able to reveal his Stalinist positions and he quickly became the alternative to Dubcek. In April 1969, his faction gained control of the party when Husak replaced Dubcek as party leader. He remained in power for the next two decades. (For further developments see under CZECHOSLOVAKIA.)

Hydrogen Bomb   The hydrogen bomb was the successor to the atomic bomb and the mainstay of the strategic nuclear arsenals of the United States, the Soviet Union, Britain, France and China. Hydrogen bombs have an explosive yield of up to 60 megatons, the equivalent of 60 million tons of TNT. The 20-kiloton atomic bomb dropped on Hiroshima had an explosive yield of only 20,000 tons of TNT.

The development of the hydrogen bomb began as early as 1942 when Edward Teller and Enrico Fermi started investigating the possibility of achieving a controlled nuclear explosion through fusion rather than fission (as with the atomic bomb). The name "hydrogen" bomb is derived from the fact that the fusion is created by the burning of the deuterium isotope of hydrogen.

Development of the hydrogen bomb was delayed until the atomic bomb project was completed. In the immediate aftermath of the war there was not the same pressing need for the "super bomb".

Then in August 1949 the Soviet Union exploded its first atomic bomb, and the American political and military establishment was jolted into reviving the development of the hydrogen bomb under the direction of Teller. However, a number of members of the General Advisory Committee of the ATOMIC ENERGY COMMISSION opposed development of the hydrogen bomb on moral grounds and the fear that it would provoke a nuclear arms race with the Soviet Union. Despite these objections, President HARRY TRUMAN gave the final approval for development of the hydrogen bomb—code-named "Super Project"—on January 31, 1950.

Work progressed rapidly at the laboratories at Los Alamos, and the first hydrogen bomb was tested on November 1, 1952, at America's Eniwetok testing grounds in the Marshall Islands in the South Pacific. The explosion completely obliterated an island, and left a crater more than a mile in diameter.

The Soviet Union was not far behind in its development of the hydrogen bomb, which was engineered largely by ANDREI SAKHAROV, who later regretted the development of the weapon and became a leading Soviet dissident. The first successful Soviet testing of a hydrogen bomb was on August 12, 1953. The British were the next to test a hydrogen bomb successfully, on May 15, 1957 (although it has recently been alleged that this test was faked, for political reasons), and were followed by the Chinese on June 17, 1967, and France on August 24, 1968. By the end of the 1960s, the hydrogen bomb had replaced the atomic bomb as the main nuclear weapon in the superpowers' strategic arsenals.

For Further Information:
Gilpin, Robert. *American Scientists and Nuclear Weapons Policy.* Princeton, 1962.
Schilling, Warner R. "The H-Bomb Decision," *Political Science Quarterly*, 81 (1961): 24–46.
York, Herbert F. *The Advisers: Oppenheimer, Teller and the Superbomb.* San Francisco, 1976.

Iceland Iceland is the only NATO country without any armed forces. It is a sparsely populated island whose strategic position at the center of the GREENLAND-ICELAND-UK GAP made it an invaluable asset to the Western Alliance.

For most of its history, Iceland was a Danish colony. Home rule was granted in 1874, and in 1918 Iceland became autonomous within the Kingdom of Denmark and declared itself a neutral European power. But the strategic position of the sparsely populated island made it impossible for Iceland to remain aloof from any European conflict.

During World War II, it was considered a prime target for the Germans wishing to gain access to the North Sea from their Baltic ports and captured Norwegian sites, and for the British who needed to secure the supply routes from North America to Britain and from Britain to the Arctic ports of the Soviet Union. The Icelandic population of 100,000 was in no position to affect events, and the race to occupy the islands was won by the British in May 1940.

The British, however, were militarily overextended and persuaded U.S. president FRANKLIN D. ROOSEVELT to replace them on July 5, 1941—five months before the attack on Pearl Harbor. The U.S. Marines' wartime occupation was a friendly one, and it continued for two years after Iceland declared its full independence from Denmark in 1944. In 1946, the Icelandic and American governments negotiated the withdrawal of American forces within six months, although the United States was allowed the continued use of the airbase at Keflavik for a further five years to help ferry American forces to and from Germany.

The onset of the Cold War quickly convinced the Icelanders that they could not return to their 1918 neutrality. The island was now even more strategic, as it lay at the center of the Greenland-Iceland-UK (GIUK) Gap, which represented the primary route for Soviet warships from European bases to the North Atlantic. In 1949, Iceland became a charter member of the NORTH ATLANTIC TREATY ORGANIZATION, and in 1951 the Icelandic government asked the United States to return to the base at Keflavik. A new defense agreement was signed in 1951 authorizing the stationing of U.S. troops there under NATO command. Iceland is also a member of the COUNCIL OF EUROPE, the WESTERN EUROPEAN UNION and the Nordic Council.

Iceland itself has no armed forces other than a Coast Guard, which is used mainly for fishery protection duties. In 1990 the United States had 3,000 military personnel based at Keflavik. Their main purpose was to monitor shipping through the GIUK Gap, and they performed this task with a combination of radar and air surveillance. The aircraft based at Keflavik include a squadron of F-15 fighter aircraft, antisubmarine warfare helicopters and P-3 Orion antisubmarine warfare aircraft. The United States also maintained four radar stations at each corner of the island, these forming an important part of the DISTANT EARLY WARNING (DEW) LINE against Soviet missile attack.

There has always been a vociferous neutralist lobby in Iceland, which usually finds expression through the left-wing People's Alliance. Normally, however, general support for NATO and the continued presence of American forces runs at between 60% and 70% of the island's population. Support, however, tends to drop when the islanders feel that their economy is threatened by another NATO country. The most striking example was during the fishing disputes between Britain and Iceland during the 1960s and early 1970s. The Icelandic economy depends heavily on exports of fish, and the island was one of the first to extend its territorial limits first to 12, then to 50 and finally to 200 miles to protect its fishingstocks. The British refused to accept their exclusion and sent Royal Navy frigates to protect British fishing vessels being harassed by Icelandic Coast Guard vessels. Diplomatic relations were severed, and Iceland was on the verge of withdrawing from NATO and expelling American forces when the dispute was resolved at a NATO foreign ministers' meeting at Oslo in June 1975.

More recently, the Icelanders have come into dispute with the United States over the Icelandic decision to continue the killing of whales. The Icelanders claim that the whales disrupt the feeding patterns of Icelandic cod and need to be culled. But the Reagan administration, under strong pressure from American environmentalists, supported calls for a ban on whaling. At the height of this dispute, Icelandic support for NATO dropped to 55%.

Inchon Inchon was the site of a bold amphibious landing by UN troops behind communist lines during the KOREAN WAR and marked the beginning of the UN forces' first major counteroffensive. The landing was a major success, and its conception and execution is regarded by military strategists as a brilliant maneuver by the commander of the UN forces, General DOUGLAS MACARTHUR.

MacArthur's strategy was boldly simple. The North Koreans had attacked on June 25, 1950, and successfully surprised South Korean forces, who were in full retreat when the first detachment of 500 American troops arrived on July 5. MacArthur conducted a skillful retreat toward the southeastern port city of Pusan, where he established a secure defensive perimeter supplied by sea from Japan.

The North Koreans' rapid push south had left their supply lines dangerously overextended and exposed. The UN forces had established dominance in the air and at sea, and this, coupled with the North Koreans' exposed supply line, offered an opportunity for MacArthur to land a UN force behind the main North Korean attack force, sever their supply lines and trap them in a north–south pincer movement.

Inchon was chosen as the site for the landing because it was the port city for Seoul, which had political significance as the capital of South Korea and military significance as a vital staging post for North Korean troops. There were serious dangers implicit in the plan. There was the possibility that the North Koreans would repulse the landing. It also required a diversion of resources from the defense of Pusan. MacArthur was confident that the plan would succeed and drew a historical parallel with Wolfe's victory over Montcalm at Quebec. He said, "The enemy commander will reason that no one could be so brash as to make such an attempt." He added, "I realize that Inchon is a five-thousand-to-one gamble, but I'll accept it. I am used to taking those odds."

On September 15, 1950, an invasion fleet of 261 American and British vessels landed 40,000 U.S. Marines and South Korean troops at Inchon. The UN losses were light. One U.S. destroyer, USS *Collette*, was severely damaged, and 15 U.S. Marine assault troops injured. None were killed. It had been almost common knowledge in Japan that MacArthur was planning a major amphibious attack, but the North Koreans had only 4,000 troops ready to repulse the landing.

The landings were preceded by a naval attack on September 11 by American and British destroyers, which were sent in to draw point-blank fire from Inchon's fortifications on Wolmi Island. The North Koreans gave away their defense positions by trying to sink the "sitting duck" destroyers, and Wolmi and Inchon were then bombarded for two days by guns and planes from the fleet. Inchon was two-thirds destroyed in this bombardment.

U.S. Marines equipped with scaling ladders seized Wolmi and a causeway connecting it with Inchon on September 15. The remainder of the U.S. Marines' First Division and South Korean Marines landed at Inchon. The U.S. Army 7th Division followed on September 16.

Simultaneous with the landing at Inchon, the UN forces launched a successful counteroffensive in the south that enabled them to break out of the Pusan Perimeter. Within five days Seoul had been liberated and the North Korean troops were in full retreat.

For Further Information:
Leckie, Robert. *The Korean War*. New York, 1963.
MacArthur, Douglas. *Reminiscences*. New York, 1964.
Rees, David. *Korea: The Limited War*. New York, 1964.

Independent European Program Group (IEPG)   The IEPG was established in November 1975 by the "Eurogroup" of NATO countries to increase European cooperation in defense procurement and to increase arms sales to the United States.

The IEPG, which is not formally linked to NATO, was also established to give France an opportunity to increase its defense cooperation without rejoining the military structure of the NATO Alliance. The members of the group are Denmark, West Germany, Britain, Belgium, France, Italy, Greece, Luxembourg, Norway, the Netherlands, Portugal and Turkey.

Indonesia   The Southeast Asian archipelago nation of Indonesia, with a population of 175 million, is the world's largest Muslim country, and the fifth biggest overall. It occupies a strategic position between the Indian and Pacific oceans. The strongly nationalist government has swung from pro-communist to rabidly anti-communist while always maintaining a leading role in the NON-ALIGNED MOVEMENT.

From the 17th century until World War II, Indonesia was a Dutch colony. Marxism was brought to Indonesia by the Dutch communists, and the Communist Party of the Indies was founded in 1920. The membership was soon dominated by Indonesian nationalists, who were attracted to the party's anticolonial message. During the early 1920s, the Indonesian Communist Party (PKI) was the only significant political organization fighting Dutch colonial rule, although by 1926, the PKI had been ruthlessly suppressed by the colonial authorities.

The PKI was replaced by the charismatic figure of Sukarno. By the time he had acquired his degree in civil engineering in 1926, Sukarno had mastered nine languages and already established a reputation as a leader and great orator. In 1927, at the age of 26, he gave up engineering to concentrate full time on politics.

Sukarno argued that Islam and Marxism had an ideological common ground against Dutch colonial rule. Sukarno's premise provided the philosophical foundation for the anticolonial movement and united its diverse strands behind his leadership and his party, the Indonesian National Association (PNI). He was quickly recognized by the Dutch as a major threat; he was imprisoned from 1929 to 1931, and in August 1933 was arrested again and exiled to the outer islands, where he remained until soon after the Japanese landed in January 1942.

Sukarno welcomed the Japanese as liberators. During the war, he acted as their chief Indonesian supporter and adviser and helped to recruit over 250,000 Indonesians to work in Japanese factories. But at the same time, Sukarno used the Japanese to establish his own political base. In 1944, as the war turned against the Japanese, they attempted to secure Sukarno's continued support by promising Indonesian independence.

But before the Japanese could grant independence they had lost the war, and Sukarno, pressed by more radical nationalists, unilaterally declared independence on August 17, 1945. The victorious Allied powers refused to recognize Indonesian independence and demanded a return to Dutch colonial rule. The result was a "police action" as the Dutch government, with British help, unsuccessfully attempted to reassert its authority. This finally ended in December 1949, when Sukarno returned in triumph to Jakarta and was soon afterward elected the first president of the United States of Indonesia.

Sukarno initially set himself up as titular and philosophical leader of Indonesia. As such he developed the "five principles" on which he based his political beliefs. These were nationalism, internationalism, democracy, social prosperity and belief in God. They remain the stated principles of the Indonesian government even though Sukarno himself has long since been officially discredited. Sukarno preferred to remain aloof from the daily grind of politics.

Sukarno became increasingly attracted to communism and visited both Moscow and Peking. His attraction to the PKI increased after the elections of 1955, when the communists emerged as the country's single largest political party. In 1956, Sukarno dismantled parliament and turned toward a planned economy under his direct leadership. He called the new political-economic structure "Guided Democracy and Guided Economy."

His decision to assume dictatorial powers led to a number of resignations from Sukarno's cabinet, including that of the vice president. The powerful regional governments also protested loudly. The Eisenhower administration became increasingly worried about Sukarno's links with the communists. In 1957 Lieutenant Colonel Achmad Hussain, the Indonesian Army commander in central Sumatra, sounded out the CIA representative in Jakarta about the possibility of American aid for an attempt to overthrow Sukarno.

Hussain had the support of a number of other regional army commanders as well as a number of the disenchanted regional political leaders. President DWIGHT EISENHOWER, Secretary of State JOHN FOSTER DULLES and CIA director ALLEN DULLES all favored some sort of covert action to help the rebels, although Desmond Fitzgerald, who was then head of CIA political and paramilitary warfare, advised against CIA involvement because he doubted the abilities of the rebel forces.

The CIA, however, went on to furnish arms, paramilitary advisers and air support in the form of B-26 bombers. The U.S. Army also drew up plans for a possible invasion of Indonesia. American support and the rebel cause suffered a major setback in May 1958 when one of the CIA B-26 pilots, Allen Pope, was shot down after mistakenly bombing a church. Pope was captured, tried and sentenced to death. His capture exposed American support for the rebels and forced President Eisenhower to terminate CIA aid for the rebellion. Pope was not executed but was imprisoned until 1962, when Attorney General Robert Kennedy finally negotiated his release.

The CIA intervention turned out to be a greater aid than a danger to Sukarno. He used it to rally national support behind his cause and to eliminate his political enemies, and by 1960 he had emerged as the undisputed dictator of Indonesia. Three years later he was named President for Life.

Sukarno adopted an increasingly anti-American policy, partly because of the U.S. support for the rebels and partly because of the American insistence on viewing the world in East–West terms. Sukarno maintained that the major issue was no longer the Cold War, because a balance of power existed between the superpowers. The main threat to world peace, he said, was the increasing conflict between the Third World and the developed world.

Indonesia became a charter member of the Non-Aligned Movement and in 1963 virtually broke relations with the United States. Then, after receiving $1 billion in Soviet military aid, it turned on Moscow as well. Sukarno also set out to crush the emerging state of Malaysia because he regarded it as part of a British imperialist plot to encircle Indonesia. In January 1965, Sukarno took the extreme step of withdrawing from the United Nations over its support for Malaysia. Sukarno, however, maintained close relations with Peking, and most of the Indonesia Communist Party's links were to China. Sukarno had a close friendship with CHOU EN-LAI.

Sukarno's policies virtually destroyed Indonesia's economy, and this plus his foreign policy left him isolated from the intelligentsia and the military. In 1962 two assassination attempts were reported, and another three took place in 1963. However, Sukarno retained his charismatic hold over the masses, who chanted his slogans and gathered in crowds of millions to demonstrate their support.

Sukarno's power came to an end when the Communist Party he had nurtured was linked to a failed coup attempt in September 1965. Troops under Lieutenant Colonel Untung kidnapped and then murdered six top army generals and seized several key areas of Jakarta, including the government radio station, from which they announced the formation of a Revolutionary Council. Untung claimed that he had acted to prevent a coup scheduled to take place October 5 against Sukarno.

General Suharto, the leader of the Jakarta garrison, retaliated with an anti-communist and anti-Sukarno coup and by October 1 had seized power back from the PKI, arrested and imprisoned some 50,000 members of the Communist Party, and put himself forward as the challenger to Sukarno. At least 500,000 alleged communists, landless peasants and ethnic Chinese were slaughtered in army-organized communal massacres over the next two years. By March 1966, Suharto had emerged as undisputed leader. He stripped Sukarno of his remaining powers and the following year was named president. Sukarno died in June 1970.

Suharto began to reverse Sukarno's maverick pro-Peking

foreign policy. In 1966 the Communist Party was banned; Indonesia rejoined the United Nations and ended its conflict with Malaysia. In 1967 Indonesia became a founding member of the Association of Southeast Asian Nations and broke relations with communist China.

Suharto established what he called a "New Order" under a military junta that favored Western economic methods. To combat criticism of a military dictatorship, a political party—Golkar—was formed, but this was no more than a political vehicle for the military leadership and the security police, known as Kopkamtib.

According to the Indonesian constitution, power is shared by an elected parliament and an indirectly elected president. But in real terms, the country is an authoritarian state led by a president who is backed by the military and a rubber-stamp legislature.

Legislative election campaigns are carefully controlled by the government to prevent the eruption of political divisions. Each party must agree to submit speeches in advance to the national election committee and not to discuss personalities, religion, foreign policy or any other contentious issue other than economic development.

For Further Information:
Cline, Ray. *The CIA: Reality vs. Myth.* Washington, D.C., 1982.
Crouch, Harold. *The Army and Politics in Indonesia.* Ithaca, N.Y., 1978.
Dahm, Bernhard. *Sukarno.* Ithaca, N.Y., 1969.
Fryer, D.W., and James C. Jackson. *Indonesia.* Boulder, Colo., 1976.
Griswold, Deirdre. *Indonesia, the Second Greatest Crime of the Century.* New York, 1979.
Kosut, Hal, ed. *Indonesia; The Sukarno Years.* New York, 1967.
Leifer, Michael. *Indonesia's Foreign Policy.* Boston, 1983.
May, Brian. *The Indonesian Tragedy.* Boston, 1978.
McMahon, Robert J. *Colonialism and Cold War: The United States and the Struggle for Indonesian Independence, 1945–1949.* Ithaca, N.Y., 1981.
Neill, Wilfred T. *Twentieth-Century Indonesia.* New York, 1973.
Special Operations Research Office. *U.S. Army Area Handbook for Indonesia.* Washington, D.C., 1964.
Weinstein, Franklin B. *Indonesian Foreign Policy and the Dilemma of Dependence: From Sukarno to Soeharto.* Ithaca, N.Y., 1976.

Intercontinental Ballistic Missile (ICBM) An intercontinental ballistic missile is a land-based rocket-propelled missile capable of delivering a nuclear warhead more than 3,000 nautical miles.

The 1972 US–Soviet STRATEGIC ARMS LIMITATION Treaty (SALT I) further defined an ICBM as a strategic ballistic missile capable of ranges in excess of the shortest distance between the northeastern border of the continental United States and the northwestern border of the continental Soviet Union.

The Soviet Union had, and its successor states still possess, a larger arsenal of land-based ICBMs than the United States, but the United States has a greater number of submarine-launched ballistic missiles, which are less vulnerable to attack.

Intermediate-Range Ballistic Missile (IRBM) An intermediate-range ballistic missile is a missile with a range of between 1,500 to 3,000 nautical miles.

The Soviet Union maintained, and the Russian Republic and China maintain, a number of IRBMs on their mutual border. It was the stationing of Soviet IRBMs in Cuba that sparked off the 1962 CUBAN MISSILE CRISIS. Several of the early American nuclear-armed missiles, Thor and Atlas types, were IRBMs based in Turkey.

Intermediate-range Nuclear Forces (INF) Treaty (1987)
The Intermediate-range Nuclear Forces (INF) Treaty, signed in Washington, D.C., in December 1987, eliminated Soviet SS-20 missiles and American Cruise and Pershing II missiles. It was the first U.S.–Soviet agreement to eliminate an entire class of nuclear-armed missiles.

The negotiations for the INF Treaty had their genesis in a West European concern about the deployment of Soviet SS-20 missiles in European Russia from 1978. The missile was almost invulnerable to attack, as it was mounted on wheeled transport vehicles. The missiles' payloads varied from a single warhead of 1 megaton to three Mirved reentry vehicles of 150 kilotons each.

The SS-20's maximum range was 5,000 miles, which meant that it could hit targets only in Western Europe, the Middle East, South Asia and China. It was the first major Soviet missile to be targeted exclusively on these areas. The West Europeans feared that they would be used to force the Europeans to make political concessions unless the United States countered with the deployment of its own intermediate-range nuclear missiles in Western Europe.

President JIMMY CARTER and U.S. secretary of state CYRUS VANCE agreed with this assessment, and at a meeting of NATO foreign ministers in December 1979 it was agreed to deploy American cruise and PERSHING II missiles in Britain, Italy, West Germany, Belgium and Holland to counter the SS-20s. Accompanying the deployment decision was a NATO commitment to seek U.S.–Soviet negotiations for the reduction or withdrawal of intermediate-range nuclear forces on both sides.

Ironically, the NATO decision to protect Western Europe with American missiles sparked a series of vociferous protests from many Europeans. Groups such as the British-based CAMPAIGN FOR NUCLEAR DISARMAMENT were revived and organized antinuclear demonstrations across Europe. The protesters were worried that the increase in intermediate-range systems was adding another twist to the nuclear arms spiral, lowering the nuclear threshold and making it more, rather than less, likely that a war between the superpowers would result in a nuclear exchange confined to the European theater.

As the protests grew, so did the pressure on the governments of the European members of NATO to force the United States either to reach a quick agreement with the Soviet Union or to retreat from the December 1979 decision. This pressure was increased by a series of "peace initiatives" by the

Soviet leadership, which until 1985 were generally short on substance and long on rhetoric and were clearly designed to drive a wedge between the American and European members of NATO.

The situation was further complicated by the American negotiators' initial plans to link the INF weapons negotiations to talks aimed at reducing the strategic nuclear arsenals of the superpowers. These Strategic Arms Reduction Talks (START) became increasingly bogged down by President RONALD REAGAN's STRATEGIC DEFENSE INITIATIVE ("Star Wars"), which the Soviets regarded as a breach of the 1972 ANTIBALLISTIC MISSILE TREATY.

Slow progress on the strategic front led the U.S. and Soviet negotiators to sever the absolute link between intermediate-range and strategic systems and to run separate but parallel sets of negotiations. The INF negotiations started in Geneva on November 30, 1981. The American delegation was led by veteran U.S. arms negotiator PAUL NITZE, and the Soviet delegation was led by Yuli Kvitsinsky. The American negotiating position was based on President Reagan's 1981 "Zero Option" of the complete withdrawal of both Soviet and American intermediate-range systems.

In February 1982, the Soviet Union publicly revealed its proposal to reduce the number of intermediate-range systems from 1,000 to 600 each by the end of 1985 and then to 300 units on each side toward the close of 1990. The proposal included the French and British nuclear deterrents. The United States rejected this proposal at the insistence of Britain and France, who maintained that their systems were strategic rather than intermediate-range and that the cuts would have a disproportionate effect on their relatively tiny nuclear arsenals. The Soviet negotiators, however, continued to insist that the French and British systems should be included in the negotiations, as they were based in Europe and the Soviet intermediate-range systems were deployed as a counter to them.

To try and break the diplomatic log-jam, Nitze and Kvitsinsky took a personal initiative in the summer of 1982, exceeded their authority and between them came up with a basis for further negotiations. The "Walk in the Woods Agreement" proposed equal limits on missiles deployed by the two sides, entailing radical reductions in the Soviet intermediate-range arsenal in both Europe and Asia. In return, the United States would deploy fewer of its Pershing II and cruise missiles than originally planned. The proposal was quickly disowned by the two governments, and Kvitsinsky was officially reprimanded. The Kremlin opposed the agreement because it failed to take the British and French forces into account, and the United States was against it because it departed from President Reagan's "Zero Option" proposal.

In December 1982, the new Soviet leader YURI ANDROPOV again stressed the Soviet intention to link the negotiations to the British and French forces when he proposed to reduce the number of Soviet INF weapons to 162 to match those of Britain and France. In return, NATO would forego the deployment of the 572 cruise and Pershing II missiles scheduled for deployment in Western Europe. The U.S. State Department replied: "We cannot accept that the U.S. should agree to allow the Soviets superiority over us because the British and French maintain their own national deterrent forces."

The stand-off between the two negotiating positions strengthened the hand of the peace campaigners in Western Europe and threatened the deployment of the American intermediate-range missiles. This led President Reagan, in April 1983, to propose an "interim" agreement on medium-range systems along the lines of the Nitze-Kvitsinsky discussions. At the same time, however, he reiterated his long-term commitment to the Zero Option. Soviet foreign minister ANDREI GROMYKO rejected Reagan's proposal because it again ignored Britain and France.

The next American initiative came from President Reagan in an address to the UN General Assembly in September 1983. He called for the reduction of Soviet INF systems on a "global basis" in return for an American agreement not to "offset the entire Soviet global missile deployment through U.S. deployments in Europe."

The first American INF forces started to arrive in Britain in November 1983 and were accompanied by a U.S. offer of global limits for each side of 420 warheads. Throughout the negotiations the Soviet side had threatened to withdraw from the negotiations if the United States went ahead with deployment. The Soviets fulfilled the threat on November 23, 1983, a week after the arrival of the cruise missiles in Britain and the day after the West German Bundestag reaffirmed its commitment to deployment.

The Soviet Union stayed away from formal negotiations until March 12, 1985. This was partly a means of applying additional pressure on the West Europeans and partly the result of uncertainties within the Kremlin following the death of Andropov, the succession of the ailing KONSTANTIN CHERNENKO and finally his death and succession by MIKHAIL GORBACHEV. The new negotiations combined strategic, space and medium-range negotiations under one umbrella. The U.S. delegation was headed by MAX KAMPELMAN. The Soviet delegation was led by Viktor Karpov.

In April 1985, Gorbachev played a major card in the public relations war for West European public opinion when he declared a six-month moratorium on the deployment of Soviet INF forces and called on the United States to do the same. The White House rejected the Soviet call and said "the proposal for a moratorium seems to revive prior Soviet efforts designed to freeze in place a considerable advantage."

In October 1985, Gorbachev took a different tack and proposed a 50% reduction in Soviet and American strategic weapons and asked Britain and France to join him in separate talks on the reduction of INF forces in Europe. The Western powers were not as dismissive of this suggestion as in the past. The United States countered with a proposal to reduce INF Soviet and American forces in Europe to 120 each, and British prime minister MARGARET THATCHER, under growing pressure from the antinuclear lobby and some pressure from the United States, avoided an immediate rejection. The French, however, rejected the Soviet proposal.

In January 1986, Gorbachev proposed a worldwide ban on nuclear weapons by the year 2000. Part of this proposal included the "complete liquidation" of all U.S. and Soviet intermediate-range nuclear missiles in Europe. He also indicated that the nuclear forces of Britain did not have to be immediately included in the reductions as long as the two nations pledged not to increase their nuclear weapons arsenal.

In February 1986, Reagan formally replied with a proposal to again separate the INF and START talks and concentrate on reaching an agreement to eliminate U.S. and Soviet INF forces over a three-year period. The Reagan plan was dubbed the modified Zero Option.

Reagan and Gorbachev met in Reykjavik, Iceland in October 1986 and agreed to an interim proposal of a limit of 100 warheads each on INF missiles with the elimination of such weapons in Europe. It was implicitly accepted that the 100 Soviet INF weapons would be based in Asia as a deterrent to China. The two men also agreed in principle to a 50% reduction in strategic weapons with mutual ceilings of 6,000 warheads and 1,600 bombers and missiles. But the talks collapsed when Gorbachev attempted to tie these reductions to an agreement that would restrict SDI research to the laboratory.

The major breakthrough came on February 28, 1987, when Gorbachev agreed to a separate INF treaty "without delay" based on the agreement in principle that he and Reagan had reached in Reykjavik. The initial response of the Reagan administration was positive.

On April 15, U.S. secretary of state GEORGE SHULTZ flew to Moscow, where Gorbachev expanded his initial February offer to include shorter-range missiles (those with a strike range of 300 to 600 miles) "within a relatively short and clearly defined time period." Gorbachev also offered to eliminate battlefield tactical nuclear weapons (those with a range of under 300 miles). Gorbachev's initiative was dubbed the "double zero option" and caught Shultz by surprise. He left Moscow without giving a firm response because of the need to consult NATO allies about the proposed expanded scope of the cuts. The NATO allies, while welcoming the proposal, were wary of it, as the Western shorter-range and tactical nuclear weapons were meant to counter the Soviet Union's conventional superiority.

In June U.S. negotiators in Geneva formally proposed the global elimination of American and Soviet intermediate nuclear forces. With regard to shorter-range systems, the United States proposed "global and equal" constraints during negotiations to eventually eliminate the weapons. The United States at that time had no shorter-range weapons but was considering the option of converting some of its Pershing II missiles into such weapons.

The next breakthrough came in July when Gorbachev said in an interview that he was willing to accept a worldwide elimination of Soviet and American INF weapons that would include the 100 missiles that would have been based in Soviet Asia. This concession was apparently wrung from the Soviets by the American threat to counter the INF weapons in Soviet Asia with 100 American INF weapons in Alaska within striking distance of Soviet territory.

The issue of tactical nuclear weapons was quietly shelved, and on September 18, after three days of talks between Shultz and Soviet foreign minister EDUARD SHEVARDNADZE, the two superpowers announced that a treaty had been agreed to in principle, and after a few final details had been ironed it would be signed in Washington that year at a Gorbachev–Reagan Summit. The final summit agenda and the treaty were agreed upon at a meeting between Shultz and Shevardnadze in Geneva on November 23 and 24. This meeting also solved the final problems related to verification of the treaty terms.

The treaty basically called for the destruction of all U.S. and Soviet missiles with approximate ranges of 300 to 3,400 miles. These weapons included the American INF weapons, the 120 Pershing IIs and 309 Cruise missiles and the Soviets' 65 SS-4s and 405 SS-20s. It also included the Soviets' 220 shorter-range SS-12s and the 33 SS-23s. West Germany's 72 shorter-range Pershing 1A missiles, with their U.S.-controlled nuclear warheads, were not part of the treaty.

The signing ceremony was the highlight of a three-day visit to Washington, D.C., by Gorbachev on December 8–10, 1987. It was the first trip to Washington by a Soviet leader since LEONID BREZHNEV visited President RICHARD NIXON in 1972. Gorbachev made use of his considerable charm and grasp of Western-style public relations, and an ABC News–*Washington Post* opinion poll gave the Soviet leader a 59% "favorable" rating.

The INF Treaty itself was signed in the East Room of the White House on December 8. The main points of the treaty were:

1. The Soviet Union and United States "shall eliminate all [their] intermediate-range missiles and launchers of such missiles, and all support structures and support equipment . . . no later than three years" from the ratification of the treaty "and thereafter no such missiles, launchers, support structures or support equipment shall be possessed by either Party."
2. The Soviet Union and United States "shall eliminate all [their] shorter-range missiles and launchers and support launchers . . . no later than 18 months" after ratification of the treaty.
3. Neither government "shall produce or flight-test any intermediate-range missiles . . . or produce, flight-test or launch any shorter-range missiles."
4. The United States will not replace its withdrawn nuclear missiles in Western Europe with new systems, and the Soviet Union will not replace withdrawn intermediate-range or shorter-range systems with new weapons.
5. Each country will be allowed to send on-site inspectors to elimination plants to verify the destruction of the

weapons specified in the treaty. They will also be allowed to visit bases in the Soviet Union and the United States and in third countries.

6. Each country has the right to continuous monitoring of the other country's development and deployment of intermediate-range and shorter-range nuclear missiles for 13 years after ratification of the treaty.
7. Intermediate-range and shorter-range missiles "which have been tested prior to" the ratification of the treaty "but never deployed . . . shall be eliminated within six months" of ratification.
8. The two countries established a "Special Verification Commission" to "resolve questions relating to compliance with the obligations assumed; and agree upon such measures as may be necessary to improve the viability and effectiveness of this Treaty."
9. The treaty "shall be of unlimited duration," but each country has the right to withdraw at six months' notice "if it decides that extraordinary events . . . have jeopardized its supreme interests."

Internal Security Act   (1950)

The Internal Security Act, also known informally as the McCarran Act, was one of the main legislative embodiments of the wave of anti-communism that swept the United States in the late 1940s and early 1950s. Introduced by conservative Democratic Senator Patrick McCarran of Nevada, its main purpose was to expose alleged "subversives" through the registration of communist and communist-front groups.

President HARRY TRUMAN called the legislation "unnecessary, ineffective and dangerous" and sided with liberal opponents who argued that the act would endanger the liberties guaranteed by the U.S. Constitution (specifically, that it would violate Bill of Rights prohibitions of congressional abridgement of freedom of speech [First Amendment] and of compelled self-incrimination [Fifth Amendment]). These, in the 1960s and 1970s, were the grounds on which most provisions of the law were eventually repealed or allowed to lapse by Congress or invalidated by successive decisions of the Supreme Court.

The bill passed both houses of Congress on September 17, 1950, by large majorities. Many senators and representatives voted for its final passage because it was too politically risky to vote against anti-communist legislation. Truman vetoed the act on September 22, but Congress overrode his veto.

The main points of the Internal Security Act were:

1. All communists were to register with the U.S. Justice Department.
2. The officers of all organizations, but not their members, listed by the Justice Department as communist-front organizations, were to register with the Justice Department.
3. In time of war, insurrection or invasion, potential saboteurs and spies could be interned, their cases to be handled by a nine-man detention review board named by the president.
4. All communist organizations were to report their financial activities and label their propaganda as coming from a communist organization.
5. Members of the Communist Party were to be denied federal jobs and U.S. passports.
6. Members of the Communist Party were to be prohibited from working in defense plants.
7. Those regarded by the Justice Department as subversive aliens were to be deported.
8. The statute of limitations on espionage was extended from three to 10 years.
9. A Subversive Activities Control Board with members designated by the president was established to administer and carry out the provisions of the bill.

For Further Information:
Feuerlich, Roberta. *Joe McCarthy and McCarthyism: The Hate That Haunts America.* New York, 1972.
Goldston, Robert. *The American Nightmare: Senator Joseph R. McCarthy and the Politics of Hate.* Indianapolis, 1973.

International Atomic Energy Agency (IAEA)

The International Atomic Energy Agency is an autonomous agency of the United Nations formed in 1957 to encourage the peaceful use of nuclear energy and help prevent the spread of nuclear weapons.

The IAEA was formed as a result of President DWIGHT D. EISENHOWER's ATOMS FOR PEACE proposal in 1954 and 1955. Eisenhower initially wanted a UN-controlled atomic energy agency to act as a bank for nuclear materials, including those of the Soviet Union and United States. But the Soviets rejected this proposal, and the IAEA was created to encourage the peaceful use of nuclear energy.

After the signing of the Nuclear Non-Proliferation Treaty (1972) the IAEA was given the added task of helping to prevent the spread of nuclear weapons. The treaty requires all signatories to be bound by IAEA safeguards. Under these provisions IAEA inspectors visit nuclear facilities in the states that have signed the Non-Proliferation Treaty to ensure that nuclear materials are not being diverted from peaceful to military purposes.

International Development Act   See POINT FOUR PROGRAM.

International Monetary Fund (IMF)

The International Monetary Fund was signed into existence on December 27, 1945, following the Bretton Woods Conference of July 1944. It works closely with the World Bank. Because of their close ties to American economic policies, the two organizations were accused by the Soviet Union and others of being economic vehicles for American imperialism.

Initially, the IMF had 44 member countries and a "quota" (capital) of $8.8 billion. In 1993 it has 175 members and is capitalized at $185 billion. The Soviet Union attended various planning sessions for both the IMF and World Bank but never applied for membership. Poland and Czechoslovakia did join both institutions, but the IMF's heavy emphasis on private-sector investment led to Poland's resignation in 1950, followed by that of Czechoslovakia in 1954. The main purposes of the IMF, as set in the Articles of Agreement, are as follows:

1. To promote international monetary cooperation.
2. To facilitate the expansion and balanced growth of international trade.
3. To promote exchange stability.
4. To assist in the establishment of a multilateral system of payments.
5. To give confidence to members by making the general resources of the fund temporarily available under adequate safeguards, thus providing to correct maladjustments in their balance of payments.

Iron Curtain   A term coined by British prime minister WINSTON CHURCHILL to describe the dividing line between the democratic countries of Western Europe and the Soviet-occupied countries of Eastern Europe.

Churchill first used the phrase in a memorandum to President HARRY TRUMAN on May 12, 1945, a few days after the German surrender. He expressed "deep anxiety" about the Soviet Army's occupation of Eastern Europe and fear that the Soviet armed forces would remain in place as the Western armies demobilized. He then added, "An iron curtain is drawn upon their front. We do not know what is going on behind. There seems little doubt that the whole of the regions east of the line Lübeck-Trieste-Corfu will soon be completely in their hands."

It was not, however, the right time for Churchill's memorandum. Truman was at this stage intent on pursuing President Franklin D. Roosevelt's policy of postwar cooperation with the Soviet Union. The day before Churchill's "Iron Curtain" memorandum, he cabled the prime minister to beware of giving Stalin the impression that Britain and America were "ganging up" on the Soviet Union. And he replied to Churchill's memo: "From the present point of view it is impossible to make a conjecture as to what the Soviet may do when Germany is under the small forces of occupation and great part of such armies as we can maintain are fighting in the Orient against Japan."

Relations between the United States and the Soviet Union, however, were already starting to deteriorate, and within the year Truman was coming around to Churchill's view of the situation. But the Western public was still unwilling to accept that their wartime ally was acting against their interests and wanted to believe that the Soviet Union would continue to cooperate with America and Western Europe. Churchill, then out of office, set out to burst this balloon in his speech at Westminster College at Fulton, Missouri, on March 5, 1946.

Before a distinguished audience which included President Truman, he warned, "Nobody knows what Soviet Russia and its Communist international organization intends to do in the immediate future, or what are the limits, if any, to their expansive and proselytizing tendencies . . . From Stettin in the Baltic to Trieste in the Adriatic an iron curtain has descended across the continent of Europe. The Communist parties, which were very small in all these eastern states of Europe, have been raised to preeminence and power far beyond their numbers and are seeking everywhere to obtain totalitarian control . . . this is certainly not the liberated Europe we fought to build up. Nor is it one that contains the essentials of permanent peace."

The real purpose of Churchill's speech was to call for an Anglo-American alliance to counter the threat from behind the Iron Curtain. He went on, therefore, to dismiss the idea that the Soviet Union desired war. "What they desire," he said, "is the fruits of war and the indefinite expansion of their power and doctrines. From what I have seen of our Russian friends and allies during the war, I am convinced that there is nothing they admire so much as strength, and there is nothing for which they have less respect than for weakness, especially military weakness . . . If the Western democracies stand together in strict adherence to the principles of the United Nations Charter, their influence for furthering these principles will be immense and none is likely to molest them. If, however, they become divided or falter . . . then indeed catastrophe may overwhelm us all."

Although Churchill's speech was later hailed as far-sighted and statesmanlike, at the time it was attacked by many as warmongering. A group of 105 British Labour members of Parliament made a motion condemning it as "inimical to the cause of world peace." President Truman, although he had come to accept many of Churchill's beliefs about Soviet foreign policy, said little publicly but let it be known privately that he was embarrassed by the speech.

Soviet leader JOSEF STALIN replied to the Iron Curtain speech in an interview in *Pravda* in which he said, "To all intents and purposes, Mr. Churchill now takes his stand among the warmongers. A point to be noted is that in this respect Mr. Churchill and his friends bear a striking resemblance to Hitler and his friends . . . Mr. Churchill begins to set war loose also by a racial theory, maintaining that only nations speaking the English language are fully fledged and called upon to decide the destinies of the entire world . . ."

For Further Information:
Mickelson, Sig. *America's Other Voice: The Story of Radio Free Europe and Radio Liberty.* New York, 1983.
Tyson, James L. *U.S. International Broadcasting and National Security.* New York, 1983.

Ismay, General Lord Hastings Lionel   (June 21, 1887– December 17, 1965)   General Lord Ismay was the first secretary-general of the NORTH ATLANTIC TREATY ORGANI-

General Lord Hastings Ismay was the first secretary-general of the North Atlantic Treaty Organization (NATO). Photo courtesy of NATO.

ZATION (NATO) and played a major role in establishing the structure of the alliance and the early policy decisions.

Hastings Lionel Ismay was born into a prominent British family in India. His father, Sir Stanley Ismay, became chief judge of the Mysore Chief Court. Ismay was educated at Charterhouse and the Royal Military College, Sandhurst. After his graduation, he started a long involvement in British colonial and commonwealth affairs.

He twice engaged in fighting on the Northwest Frontier of India, in 1908 and 1920, and during World War I saw action in British Somaliland. In 1926 Ismay was appointed assistant secretary to the Committee of Imperial Defense and in 1931 returned to India as military secretary to the viceroy. Other posts included chief of military intelligence for the Middle East and deputy secretary of the Committee of Imperial Defense.

Ismay rose to international prominence during World War II when he was chosen by Prime Minister WINSTON CHURCHILL as chief of staff. No one was nearer to Churchill among those planning the war, and Ismay accompanied the prime minister to important overseas conferences, including those at Casablanca, Cairo, Moscow, Teheran and YALTA. After Churchill's election defeat in 1945, Ismay remained chief of staff and accompanied Prime Minister CLEMENT ATTLEE and Foreign Secretary ERNEST BEVIN to the POTSDAM CONFERENCE.

At the end of 1946, Ismay was made a life peer and retired from the British Army. Shortly afterward he went to India with the new viceroy, Lord Mountbatten. He was Mountbatten's principal adviser during the negotiations that culminated in the independence of India and Pakistan. After Churchill's return to power in 1951, Ismay was named secretary of state for commonwealth relations.

In the meantime, the onset of the KOREAN WAR had convinced western Europe that it needed to strengthen and reorganize the military and political structure of the North Atlantic Treaty Organization. One of the results of this decision was the creation of the post of NATO secretary-general, who, as a prominent political figure, would be responsible for coordinating NATO policies. It was decided that the military commander of NATO forces, SUPREME ALLIED COMMANDER FOR EUROPE (SACEUR), should be from the United States because of American military dominance within the alliance, but that the political post should be held by a European. The selection of a Briton as the first secretary-general underscored Britain's importance at the time as the second most powerful member of the Western alliance.

Ismay's tasks as secretary-general of NATO included the establishment of NATO headquarters outside Paris; the implementation of the LISBON AGREEMENT; the expansion of the WESTERN EUROPEAN UNION and the implementation of the EDEN PLAN FOR GERMAN REUNIFICATION in the wake of the collapse of the EUROPEAN DEFENSE COMMUNITY; West German membership in the alliance; the establishment of basic alliance structures; and dealing with the negotiations for and later failure of the EDC, the SUEZ CRISIS and the Hungarian Uprising.

At the start of Ismay's tenure at NATO, the defense of the alliance was based almost entirely on conventional weapons. This was reflected in NATO's overambitious conventional weapons force goals set at Lisbon in 1952. Economic necessity, coupled with advances in technology and the Eisenhower administration's emphasis on nuclear weapons and air power, forced Ismay to make the initial feasibility studies into the use of nuclear weapons and the possibility of a Multinational Nuclear Force. In his farewell speech, Ismay reported that during his five years NATO munitions production had increased by 500% and that in the same period defenses had shifted from conventional to "new weapons." He warned, however, that NATO could not impose or forbid the acquisition of nuclear weapons by its member states.

After leaving NATO in May 1957, Ismay retired to his farm in Gloucestershire.

For Further Information:
Ismay, Lord. *The Memoirs of General Lord Ismay.* New York, 1960.

Italy   Italy has played an important role in the Cold War as the Western European country with the largest and most powerful Communist Party and as the headquarters of NATO's naval operations in the Mediterranean.

The Italian Communist Party (PCI) grew alongside and in extreme opposition to Benito Mussolini's Fascist Party. The

PCI was founded in 1921 and very quickly grew to be one of the largest communist parties in Europe outside the Soviet Union. Mussolini seized power in 1922, and from 1926 the PCI went underground and through strong links with trade unions managed to maintain a powerful political base.

Wartime resistance activities further strengthened the position of the PCI. But the war also saw the rise of other anti-fascist groups, such as the Christian Democrats (CD), led by ALCIDE DE GASPERI, and the Socialist Party of Proletarian Unity (PSIUP). Although politically disparate, these three parties were united in their opposition to Mussolini and Nazi Germany and established a Committee of National Liberation (CLN) that organized the armed resistance in Northern Italy between March 1944 and May 1945.

Between 1943 and 1945, the membership of the PCI grew from 5,000 to 1.7 million, dwarfing the Socialists and making it impossible for any Italian government to exclude communists from a postwar coalition. By 1945, de Gasperi's Christian Democrats represented the only credible non-fascist challenge to the PCI. The occupying U.S. forces threw their support behind the Christian Democrats in order to prevent a communist victory in Italy, and de Gasperi formed his first government in 1945.

De Gasperi, however, was forced to include communists in his government in order to secure the broad-based political support required for postwar reconstruction. The communists tried to swing Italian foreign policy toward either a neutral or a pro-Soviet position and pressed for widespread nationalization programs and land reform. But de Gasperi leaned toward the United States, and in January 1947 confirmed this tilt in a visit to Washington that resulted in the U.S. Export–Import Bank extending Italy a $100 million credit. He also persuaded the Truman administration to divert six wheat-laden ships bound for the U.S. Army in Germany to Italian ports to stave off famine.

On his return to Rome, de Gasperi also introduced conservative law-and-order measures to protect the state and prevent a communist coup. This, plus the prime minister's trip to Washington, led to protests from the communists. De Gasperi responded by resigning and forming a government without the PCI. The Italian communists remained out of the government for the rest of postwar Italian political history.

Out of office, the PCI, with encouragement from the Soviet-controlled Communist Information Bureau (COMINFORM), organized a series of damaging anti-government strikes, and in September 1947, PCI leader Palmiro Togliatti warned that he could call on "30,000 well-armed partisans." Togliatti also denounced the United States as a world dictatorship trying to "spread another war." De Gasperi, however, weathered the disturbances and emerged as Italy's chief bulwark against communism.

To protect this bulwark, the United States increased its already generous aid to Italy. In 1947 alone, the Truman administration released Italian assets frozen during the war,

increased emergency food shipments and increased emergency financial aid by $200 million.

The newly created CENTRAL INTELLIGENCE AGENCY (CIA) also launched its first covert operations in support of the Christian Democrats. These operations consisted of a "black propaganda" campaign against the PCI coupled with the channeling of an estimated $10 million into the election campaign funds of the Christian Democrats. The result was a major election victory for the Christian Democrats at the crucial vote on April 18, 1948. The CIA's success also increased the American political establishment's confidence in the efficacy of covert operations.

With the communists safely out of government, de Gasperi was able to increase Italy's ties with the West. Italy became a charter member of the NORTH ATLANTIC TREATY ORGANIZATION and the EUROPEAN COAL AND STEEL COMMUNITY. De Gasperi was an enthusiastic supporter of the MARSHALL PLAN and staked his political career on the EUROPEAN DEFENSE COMMUNITY. (He died of a heart attack after hearing that the French National Assembly had rejected the EDC in 1954.)

Italian approval of the EDC was closely linked to the problem of TRIESTE, and in the 1950s these issues posed a major threat to the Christian Democrats and their policy of close Western ties. Trieste, an Adriatic port city, was claimed by both Italy and Yugoslavia, and in the postwar period it was occupied by American, Yugoslav and British troops. Italian public opinion demanded the ownership of Trieste. The British and Americans, however, were reluctant to do anything that might drive Yugoslavia back into the Soviet camp.

The PCI was able to make substantial political gains as a result of the British and American positions, and the U.S. ambassador to Italy, CLARE BOOTHE LUCE, warned that a failure to solve the Trieste problem to Italy's satisfaction could result in a communist victory in the elections in 1953. De Gasperi, for his part, warned that anything less than full Anglo-American support could jeopardize Italian membership in NATO, American bases in Italy and Italian ratification of the EDC Treaty.

Luce's fears appeared to be at least partially justified by the results of the June 1953 elections, in which de Gasperi's four-party coalition emerged with the slimmest majority in Italian political history. De Gasperi formed a government, but within the month the government fell and de Gasperi was forced to hand the premiership over to Giuseppe Pella. The fall of de Gasperi was a blow to the American and British governments and encouraged negotiators to press for a settlement favorable to Italy; the Trieste Treaty was eventually signed on October 5, 1954. Shortly afterward, the Italian government confirmed its membership in the EDC.

Italy was now firmly entrenched in the Western pro-European integration camp; in 1955 it became a member of the WESTERN EUROPEAN UNION and in 1957 was a charter member of the EUROPEAN ECONOMIC COMMUNITY. Naples became the headquarters for NATO's Southern Command and for the U.S. Mediterranean fleet and a number of American air bases. A U.S. Senate report defined Italy as "essential to military control of the Mediterranean," which in turn provides access to three continents. The major military installations provided by Italy to the United States and NATO include the naval complex at Naples and naval facilities at Sgonella, Sicily and La Maddalena, Sardinia. Air force facilities are located at Aviana Air Base and at San Vito Air Station. The U.S. Army utilize facilities at Camp Darby near Livorno and installations at Camp Ederle at Vicenza. Ten NATO Air Defense early-warning sites are located throughout the country, and nuclear weapons are stored in Italy.

Although Italy maintained a firm pro-American and pro-EEC policy, its foreign policy in the 1970s and 1980s took a more independent course from Washington, especially in regard to relations with the Arab world. Historically, Italy has had a major influence on and close relations with all the countries bordering the Mediterranean. This made Italy more sympathetic to the Arab and Palestinian cause in the Arab–Israeli conflict. In 1977 Italy was host to the EEC heads of government summit, which called for recognition of a Palestinian homeland. The Italian position on the Middle East conflict was also affected by Italy's strong dependence on Arab oil for its energy needs. A large proportion of that oil was imported from Libya, which made it difficult for the Italian government to give full support to the American government's hard-line stance against Libyan leader Colonel Muammar El-Qaddafi.

The Italian economy grew significantly during the postwar period, and by the late 1980s Italy was almost on a par with Britain. The country, however, still suffered from structural imbalances that divided Italy between the wealthy, industrialized north and the poor, peasant-based economy of the south. The Italian government's ability to tackle this problem was hindered by political instability, which led to the creation of 46 governments between 1945 and the end of 1989. All of these governments were dominated by the Christian Democrats, and they moved from center-right to center-left, depending on the political complexion of the Christian Democrats' coalition partners. Generally speaking the governments were center-right from 1947 to the mid-1960s and thereafter were either solidly in the center or center-left.

The Italian communists remained the second largest political party and controlled a number of key city and provincial governments although they were kept out of national government. The communists' failure to achieve a political breakthrough by the mid-1960s led them to reassess their policies and their relationship with the Soviet Union. This led to the rise of EUROCOMMUNISM, and the PCI took a leading role in its development.

After the Warsaw Pact's invasion of CZECHOSLOVAKIA in 1968 and the enunciation of the BREZHNEV DOCTRINE, the Italian communists declared that "in current circumstances we regard it as our duty to trace out and follow our own road to socialism." This separate road led to a condemnation of the invasion of Czechoslovakia, criticism of Soviet internal and foreign policies, support for Italian membership in the EEC and even limited involvement with NATO.

In June 1976, the political shift resulted in major electoral gains for the PCI, forcing the Christian Democrats into an unofficial "historic compromise" with the communists under which the communists agreed not to topple the Christian Democratic government in return for a limited say in government without actual membership in the coalition. The rise of Eurocommunism and the PCI caused considerable concern in the United States, where figures such as HENRY KISSINGER refused to accept that the Italian communists had completely abandoned their allegiance to Moscow in favor of a nationally oriented communism.

Within the United States there were calls among some officials to reassess America's relationship with Italy in light of the increased influence of the PCI and the possibility of communists being included in a coalition government. But such demands never went beyond the discussion stage because the historic compromise represented the post-1947 peak of the PCI. Without its strong links to Moscow and anti-Western stance, the Italian communists lost a great deal of what made them politically different from the democratically oriented Italian socialists. Since the war, the Socialist Party had been overshadowed by the giant PCI, but in the late 1970s it started to grow as former communist voters switched their allegiance.

In 1972, the PCI polled 28.4% of the vote. This jumped to 36% in 1976 and then fell back to 28.3% in June 1987. The Socialists, in the same period, went from 9% to 11%, which enabled them to control the balance of power, and in 1983 Socialist leader Bettino Craxi became the first non-Christian Democratic prime minister of the postwar period.

The rise of the Socialist Party was quickly followed by the political and economic collapse of the communist systems in Eastern Europe. The Italian Communist Party, in an attempt to distance itself from failure, abandoned the hammer and sickle emblem, and in 1990 the party's name was changed to the Democratic Party of the Left.

For Further Information:

Albright, D.C. *Communism and Political Systems in Western Europe.* Boulder, Colo., 1979.

Grindrod, Muriel. *The Rebuilding of Italy.* London, 1955.

Hughes, H. Stuart. *The United States and Italy.* Cambridge, Mass., 1965.

Kogan, Norman. *A Political History of Postwar Italy: From the Old to the New Center-Left.* New York, 1981.

Machin H., ed. National Communism in Western Europe. New York, 1983.

Miller, James Edward. *The United States and Italy, 1940–1950: The Politics and Diplomacy of Stabilization.* Chapel Hill, N.C., 1986.

Nichols, Peter. *Italia, Italia.* New York, 1974.

Novak, Bodgan. *Trieste, 1941–1954.* Princeton, 1976.

Sassoon, Donald. *The Strategy of the Italian Communist Party: From the Resistance to the Historic Compromise.* London, 1981.

Smith, E. Timothy. *The United States, Italy and NATO, 1947–52.* Hampshire, England, 1991.

Urban, Joan. *Moscow and the Italian Communist Party: From Togliatti to Berlinguer.* Ithaca, N.Y., 1986.

Wollemborg, Leo J. *Stars, Stripes, and Italian Tricolor: The United States and Italy, 1946–1989.* New York, 1990.

J

Jackson, Charles (March 16, 1902–September 19, 1964)
Charles Jackson was a propaganda specialist recruited by President DWIGHT EISENHOWER as an adviser on international public opinion. One of the few relatively liberal voices in the Eisenhower administration, he was subjected to a series of conservative attacks, which eventually led to his resignation after only a year.

After graduating from Princeton University in 1924, Jackson took over the family business, but he was forced to sell the company during the Depression. In 1931 he joined *Time* magazine, becoming a vice president of the parent company, Time, Inc., in 1940. During World War II, Jackson helped General Eisenhower organize a psychological warfare squad to generate support in occupied Europe for the Normandy Invasion; after the war he helped to establish Radio Free Europe.

In 1952 Jackson joined the Eisenhower campaign team and played an important role in developing campaign strategy and writing speeches. In November 1952 Eisenhower named Jackson a special assistant for Cold War planning. His task was to formulate diplomatic initiatives so that Eisenhower was seen to always be on the psychological offensive in his dealings with Moscow. Jackson's first major contribution was writing Eisenhower's response on April 15, 1953, to peace feelers from the new Soviet leadership.

Speaking before the American Society of Newspaper Editors, Eisenhower listed a series of "deeds, not words," which he said were a necessary prelude to negotiations. These deeds included an "honorable armistice" in Korea leading to "free elections in a united Korea"; "an end to the direct and indirect attacks upon the security of Indochina and Malaya"; "a treaty with Austria which [would] free that country from economic exploitation and from occupation by foreign troops"; a broader European community "conducive to the free movement of persons, of trade and of ideas" and including "a free and united Germany with a government based upon free and secret ballot"; and "full independence for the East European nations."

Jackson, however, was already starting to clash with conservatives in the administration. In February 1953 he advised the president to consider clemency for convicted spies JULIUS AND ETHEL ROSENBERG on the grounds that their execution would damage relations with America's European allies, who were advocating mercy. For the same reason, Jackson also urged the president to use his position to check the communist witch-hunt of Senator JOSEPH MCCARTHY. Eisenhower refused to "be drawn into the gutter."

But news of Jackson's position was leaked to McCarthy, who attacked the presidential adviser as a man "unsympathetic to strong patriotism." McCarthy's assistant, Roy Cohn, described Jackson as one of a group of "dangerous liberals" who were threatening to subvert the White House. On March 3, 1954, Jackson resigned from the White House to return to Time, Inc. He died of cancer on September 19, 1964.

For Further Information:
Meyerhoff, Arthur E. *The Strategy of Persuasion; The Use of Advertising Skills in Fighting the Cold War.* New York, 1965.

Jackson, Henry M. (May 31, 1912–September 1, 1983)
Senator Henry M. Jackson's career in the U.S. Congress stretched across 43 years, and he became one of America's leading experts on defense and foreign policy. A New Deal liberal, Jackson opposed the McCarthyism of the late 1940s and 1950s but took a tough anti-communist stand on foreign policy. In the Senate, he led the attacks on both Strategic Arms Limitation treaties and the détente policy.

Jackson graduated from the University of Washington Law School in 1935 and went into private practice for three years before being elected district attorney for Snohomish County. In 1940 Jackson was elected to the House of Representatives as a liberal Democrat.

After the war, Jackson opposed the activities of the HOUSE UN-AMERICAN ACTIVITIES COMMITTEE and voted against the 1950 INTERNAL SECURITY ACT. But at the same time, he supported the MARSHALL PLAN and the creation of the NORTH ATLANTIC TREATY ORGANIZATION.

Jackson was elected to the U.S. Senate in 1952 and became a member of Senator JOSEPH MCCARTHY's Permanent Investigations Subcommittee. Jackson became a leading anti-McCarthyite on the subcommittee, at one time resigning over an article written by the committee staff director. During the nationally televised Army–McCarthy hearings in 1954, Jackson accused McCarthy and his aide ROY COHN of personally attempting to "wreck the Army" unless special privileges were given to their former associate, G. David Schine, who had recently been drafted.

In 1955 Jackson was made a member of the Armed Forces Committee and the Joint Committee on Atomic Energy. He became a strong critic of Eisenhower's defense policies and a leading exponent of the "MISSILE GAP," which theory held that the United States had fewer missiles than the Soviet Union. Jackson also championed the development of the nuclear submarine and supported its major proponent, Admiral HY-MAN G. RICKOVER. By 1960 Jackson had emerged as the foremost Democratic spokesman in the Senate on defense issues. His strong pro-defense policy was heavily influenced by the fact that Boeing Aircraft Company, a leading supplier of the Pentagon, was based in Seattle. Jackson was sometimes referred to as the senator from Boeing.

Jackson was considered as the Democrats' vice presidential candidate in the 1960 elections but at the last minute was passed over in favor of Senator LYNDON JOHNSON. Jackson's relations with the Kennedy administration were cool and distant. He was in principle opposed to President JOHN F. KENNEDY's attempts to improve relations with the Soviet Union and curb the arms race, and this led him to try and block the creation of the ARMS CONTROL AND DISARMAMENT AGENCY and oppose the NUCLEAR TEST BAN TREATY.

Jackson was a strong supporter of President Johnson's policies in Vietnam although he criticized officials who overoptimistically predicted an easy and imminent victory in the VIETNAM WAR. He blamed the defeat on America's peace campaigners.

Jackson's increasingly conservative stand on foreign policy issues left him isolated from his liberal roots in the Democratic Party, and he emerged as the leading party conservative when the Democrats split in 1968 over the issue of the Vietnam War. Jackson, however, remained a liberal on domestic issues.

In 1968, president-elect RICHARD M. NIXON offered Jackson the post of secretary of defense, but Jackson refused the position. He was, however, a strong supporter of Nixon's Vietnam policies, and Republicans provided funds to help Jackson defeat a peace candidate in the 1970 Democratic primaries in Washington state. The Republican leadership also pressured the Washington State Republicans to choose a weak opponent for Jackson to help ensure his reelection. In November 1971, Jackson announced his candidacy for the Democratic presidential nomination, but he withdrew in February 1972 after coming in third behind HUBERT HUMPHREY and Alabama Governor George Wallace in the Florida primary.

Although Jackson supported Nixon's Vietnam policies, he was a strong opponent of détente and of HENRY KISSINGER. He opposed the Strategic Arms Limitation Treaty (SALT I) and agreed to ratification only after an amendment was inserted instructing future negotiators that any permanent treaty on offensive nuclear weapons should "not limit the United States to levels of intercontinental strategic forces inferior to" those of the Soviet Union.

Jackson was also responsible for the JACKSON AMENDMENT to the East–West Trade Relations Act, which denied the Soviet Union most-favored-nation trade status as long as it barred emigration of its citizens. The bill was passed in December 1974.

Jackson used his chairmanship of the Permanent Investigations Subcommittee to launch an attack on the U.S.–Soviet Grain Trade Agreement. Jackson described the deal as a "great grain robbery" that would result in depleted U.S. grain reserves, higher food prices and a crisis in the livestock industry. His pressure led to a temporary halt of grain shipments to the Soviet Union in October 1974.

Jackson was even more critical of the SALT II accords than of SALT I. He accused President JIMMY CARTER of following in the appeasing footsteps of Britain's Neville Chamberlain. On the eve of Carter's departure to sign the treaty in Vienna, he said, "To enter into a treaty which favors the Soviets, as this one does, on the grounds that we will be in a worse position without it, is appeasement in its purest form." Jackson's attack presaged a tough battle between the White House and Congress over ratification of the SALT II Treaty which, because of congressional opposition, was never put to the vote.

In November 1980, Jackson was named a member of president-elect RONALD REAGAN's foreign relations advisory panel and was reportedly considered for a cabinet post in the Reagan administration. In April 1982, Jackson cosponsored a proposal with Senator John Warner calling for a long-term freeze on the nuclear arsenals of the United States and the Soviet Union at "equal and sharply reduced levels." The resolution was backed by 58 other senators and President Reagan but was attacked by liberals because it did not block the Reagan administration's plans to deploy new nuclear-armed systems pending a U.S.–Soviet arms agreement.

Jackson remained active until his sudden death from a burst blood vessel on September 1, 1983.

For Further Information:
Brands, H.W. *Cold Warriors.* New York, 1988.
Ognibene, Peter J. *Scoop: The Life and Politics of Henry M. Jackson.* New York, 1975.
Spanier, J.W. *American Foreign Policy Since World War Two.* Washington D.C., 1988.

Jackson Amendment   The Jackson Amendment of 1972 tied American government efforts to liberalize U.S.–Soviet trade to Soviet emigration. The amendment was considered by many to be a major obstacle to détente.

The measure was introduced by Senator HENRY JACKSON of Washington as an amendment to the Nixon administration's East–West Trade Relations Act, which sought to grant the Soviet Union most-favored-nation trade status. Both the Soviet and American leaderships saw the act as one of the cornerstones of détente.

Jackson, however, felt that détente was too one-sided and that the United States was giving away too much without seeing any corresponding improvement of human rights within the Soviet Union, especially the rights of Soviet Jews, many of whom wished to emigrate to Israel or the United States. In response to Jackson, the Soviet Union eased its emigration restrictions slightly but imposed a punitive emigration tax. This was justified on the grounds that those leaving the Soviet Union should compensate the country for their education and other benefits.

But Jackson regarded the emigration tax as a form of "ransom," and in October 1972, along with 75 Senate cosponsors, he introduced his amendment, which denied the Soviet Union most-favored-nation status as long as it barred emigration or imposed "more than a nominal tax . . . on any citizen as a consequence of emigration."

The Soviet leadership responded vehemently to the amendment, which it regarded as an unjustified interference in domestic affairs. In June 1974 Secretary of State HENRY KISSINGER received a pledge from the Soviets to allow the emigration of 45,000 Jews a year. However, Jackson found the figure inadequate, and the trade bill was passed with the Jackson Amendment.

Japanese–U.S. Defense Treaties   The postwar period has seen the United States and Japan sign three major defense treaties, in 1951, 1954 and 1960. These have all tied Japan closer to the Western camp, committed the United States to the defense of Japan and allowed the Japanese to keep down defense spending.

At the end of the war, the Japanese military was completely disarmed and disbanded. The Allies, at this juncture, wanted the complete destruction of Japanese militarism, and General DOUGLAS MACARTHUR persuaded the Japanese that there were economic advantages to be gained from becoming "the Switzerland of Asia." The Japanese leadership accepted this argument, and the 1947 constitution renounced the use of military force except in self-defense.

But as U.S.–Soviet relations deteriorated and tensions increased in Korea and Indochina, American foreign policy shifted from an insistence on the demilitarization of Japan to a willingness for it to become an Asian bulwark against Soviet and Chinese communism. The Japanese, who by now had enthusiastically embraced the cause of national disarmament, opposed the shift in American policy because they needed all of their funds to rebuild the national economy and had been badly scarred by the experiences of Nagasaki and Hiroshima as well as disillusioned in general with the country's military class.

The first treaty, in 1951, avoided Japanese rearmament. Its main purpose was to formalize the basing of American forces in Japan. These forces would help to maintain order within Japan, protect Japan from attack and be used for military operations elsewhere in the Far East. At the same time, it served to strengthen the postwar political and economic links between the United States and Japan and ended Japan's official status as an occupied country.

The Japanese–U.S. Defense Treaty was signed on September 8, 1951, in San Francisco, five hours after the signing of the final Japanese Peace Treaty. The treaty allowed for the basing of American troops on Japanese soil and for rent to be paid to the Japanese government. The pact determined that American land, sea and air forces could be stationed "in and about Japan" to safeguard "international peace and security in the Far East," help protect Japan "against armed attack from without" and help, "at the express request of the Japanese Government," to put down "large-scale internal riots and disturbances in Japan, caused through instigation or intervention by an outside power or powers."

Japan was prohibited from granting bases or "the right of garrison or maneuver" to any third power without American consent. The treaty was to run indefinitely or until the American and Japanese governments agreed there were adequate UN or other "individual or collective security dispositions" to safeguard "international peace and security in the Japan area."

The American negotiating team for the 1951 treaty was headed by JOHN FOSTER DULLES. An integral factor in Dulles' negotiating position was the belief that as Japan regained its economic feet it would take over greater responsibility for defense, while remaining tied to his tough anti-communist policies. When Dulles became secretary of state in 1953 he set out to negotiate a new treaty that would commit Japan to rearmament. But the Japanese were by now fully committed in their opposition to rearmament. The Japanese negotiators were encouraged by the position of American ambassador JOHN ALLISON, who believed Dulles was wrong to want to reduce the Japanese nation to the status of forward bastion of American strategic strength in the Far East. Nevertheless, the Japanese–U.S. Mutual Defense Treaty, signed on March 8, 1954, did commit Japan to a significant degree of rearmament, but with American financial aid and under American direction.

Under the terms of the treaty, the United States provided $100 million in "equipment, materials and services or other assistance." Japan guaranteed that these goods would not be sold to other parties and promised to take "all reasonable measures" toward assuming its own military burden and to accept the guidance of an American military advisory mission. The United States was also given the right to intervene in the Japanese budgetary process to guarantee a Japanese payment of $155 million a year for the support of American troops in Japan.

By the late 1950s it was clear that a new treaty was needed to reflect Japan's increasing economic strength and recognition of its position as a "partner" with the United States rather than a subjugated former enemy. The new treaty superseded the previous treaty and removed the restrictions on Japanese sovereignty as well as the political condescension of previous agreements.

The treaty returned full sovereignty to Japan in defense matters and made the United States and Japan equal partners in a defensive alliance designed to maintain "internal peace and security in the Far East." The United States and Japan would consult on common action "at the request of either party whenever the security of Japan or international peace and security in the Far East [was] threatened." The treaty added that the United States and Japan would "maintain and develop their capacities to resist armed attack" and allowed the continuance of American land, air and naval bases in Japan "for the purpose of contributing to the security of Japan and the . . . Far East."

The clause allowing American bases to remain in Japan was strongly opposed by the Japanese Socialist Party, and the treaty encountered difficulty in getting through the Japanese Diet (parliament). Prime Minister Nobusuke Kishi ordered the police to remove left-wing members from the Diet bodily, and in their absence his Liberal Democratic Party passed the treaty. The action sparked a series of anti-American and anti-Kishi riots aimed at preventing ratification of the treaty and a visit by President Dwight Eisenhower, who was due to arrive in Tokyo on the day the treaty took effect.

On June 10, 1959, White House press secretary James Hagerty arrived in Tokyo on an advance trip for the president. His car was stopped and stoned for an hour and a half before a U.S. Marine helicopter managed to rescue him. Eisenhower's aides urged him to call off the visit. But Kishi, whose political future was now tied to both the treaty and the Eisenhower trip, refused to withdraw his invitation to the president. However, on June 12, a few days before Eisenhower's scheduled arrival, a girl was crushed to death during a riot. Kishi was forced to announce the "postponement" of the president's trip and a week later resigned as prime minister. The treaty, however, went ahead and was signed on January 19, 1960.

From the signing of the 1960 treaty American pressure increased for the Japanese to spend more on defense. But the constitutional restrictions had been joined by a commitment to restrict defense spending to 1% of the gross national product (GNP). This limitation was not formally lifted until January 24, 1987, although the size of the Japanese GNP meant that the Japanese defense budget had grown to the fifth largest in the world.

Japan's seemingly reluctant financial aid to the U.S.-led military coalition that defeated Iraq in the 1991 Persian Gulf War became a sore point between Washington and Tokyo. There was also a continuing political uproar in Japan over the government's efforts to modify the "peace constitution" so that Japanese troops could participate in United Nations peacekeeping operations overseas.

For Further Information:

Dunn, Frederick S. *Peacemaking and the Settlement with Japan*. Princeton, 1963.

Scalapino, Robert A. *American-Japanese Relations in a Changing Era*. New York, 1972.

Jaruzelski, General Wojciech (July 6, 1923–) General Wojciech Jaruzelski took over the leadership of POLAND and the Polish United Workers' (Communist) Party in the early 1980s when the SOLIDARITY trade union was first threatening communist rule. He first negotiated with the union,

General Wojciech Jaruzelski was named prime minister of Poland in February 1981. Photo courtesy of the Polish Ministry of Foreign Affairs.

then suppressed it, then legalized it in a bid to end Poland's political and economic crisis. After being narrowly elected president in 1989, Jaruzelski appointed postwar Poland's first non-communist prime minister. Jaruzelski resigned in December 1990 after the election of Solidarity leader LECH WALESA as president.

Jaruzelski was born into a traditional Polish military family and was educated at an exclusive Jesuit school. Shortly after the start of World War II, he was deported to the Soviet Union to work as forced labor in the Soviet coal mines in Kazakhstan.

Despite his hard experiences, Jaruzelski was won over to communism and in 1943 was singled out by the Soviet authorities for training in the Soviet officer candidate school. In 1944 he was commissioned a lieutenant in the Soviet-sponsored Polish Army and participated in the liberation of Warsaw and Berlin. Between 1945 and 1947 he further consolidated his communist credentials by fighting against Poland's anti-communist guerrillas. He joined the Communist Party in 1947.

In 1951 Jaruzelski graduated with distinction from the general staff academy in Warsaw and was moved onto the promotion fast track. At the age of 33 he became Poland's youngest brigadier general, and was made a two-star general in 1960. In 1962 he was named deputy minister of defense and from 1965 to 1968 was also chief of the General Staff. He joined the party's Central Committee in 1964 and in 1968 was awarded his third star and named minister of defense. He became a full member of the Politburo in 1971.

One of Jaruzelski's first actions as minister of defense was to organize the Polish contingent of the Warsaw Pact force that suppressed the PRAGUE SPRING in Czechoslovakia in August 1968. Jaruzelski worked hard to improve the fighting efficiency of the Polish Army and to forge close links with the Soviet Army while at the same time increasing his political influence within the Politburo. But despite his strong party links and military background, he at times seemed to take a line on domestic issues at odds with that of Moscow and the hard-liners within the Polish Communist Party. For instance, after a series of riots among workers in 1976 he emphatically declared, "Polish troops will not fire on Polish workers." Jaruzelski repeated this assertion at the height of the Solidarity strikes and riots in 1980 and refused pressure from Politburo hard-liners to force workers out of occupied factories.

At the end of 1980, the Soviet Union began to show signs of considering intervention in Poland in order to prevent the spread of the Solidarity-inspired political and economic reforms. Twenty-six Soviet divisions were massed on the Polish border, ostensibly for regularly scheduled maneuvers but with the real purpose of at least intimidating the Poles into controlling the independent trade union movement. The Communist Party turned to Jaruzelski. His liberal credentials made him acceptable to Solidarity while at the same time he wielded considerable strength as leader of the armed forces; this, plus his personal links to Moscow, satisfied the Kremlin.

In February 1981, Jaruzelski was named prime minister while at the same time retaining the defense portfolio. The combination of these two posts meant that Jaruzelski became Poland's strongest political figure while not actually being leader of the Communist Party. In his first address to the Polish Sejm (parliament) on February 12, Jaruzelski appealed for a 90-day strike-free period to enable his government to deal with the economic crisis. At the same time, he promised to continue the policy of "democratic renewal" and reaffirmed Poland's commitment to the Warsaw Pact.

Jaruzelski faced the same problem as every postwar Polish leader had faced: the need to balance fervent Polish nationalism against the constant threat that the Soviet Union would intervene to suppress that nationalism in order to maintain its control of Eastern Europe. Jaruzelski's first month as prime minister was a political success as he opened dialogues with Solidarity, Rural Solidarity, striking students and the powerful Roman Catholic Church. But in early March textile workers in Lodz broke the 90-day moratorium on strikes. Jaruzelski demanded and received legislation suspending the right to strike for two months. "Our backs are against the wall," he told the parliament. "We need social discipline and work. The government believes that a suspension of strikes will bring social peace and douse the flames of new conflicts." Then in

September, Jaruzelski ignored his own previous dictum and ordered the army and police to crack down on "deepening anarchist tendencies" and "unbridled hooliganism."

On October 18, 1981, Jaruzelski's hold on power in Poland was completed when he replaced Stanislaw Kania as first secretary of the Polish United Workers' (Communist) Party. Again Jaruzelski retained his posts of prime minister and minister for defense. His election by the Central Committee was welcomed by both Solidarity and the Kremlin. Soviet leader LEONID BREZHNEV sent him a message of congratulations and pledged his "understanding and approval." Walesa described Jaruzelski as "an improvement" over Kania.

However, the increasing social and economic unrest, and the threat of Soviet intervention to suppress it, led Jaruzelski to declare martial law on December 12, 1981. In the face of widespread Western condemnation, he succeeded in cracking down on Solidarity and forcing it underground. The general considered himself a Polish patriot and believed he had saved his country by averting a Soviet invasion.

Martial law was not lifted until July 1983, although Solidarity remained banned. But Jaruzelski found he could not solve the country's continuing economic crisis without the cooperation of the workers' movement. Finally, in 1989, he began "round-table" talks with the opposition and met with Walesa, a process that resulted in the legalization of Solidarity and major political reforms. These led to new elections to the Sejm (parliament)—now empowered to elect the country's president—in which Solidarity candidates won a crucial share of power.

Jaruzelski at first ruled himself out as a candidate for the presidency, saying that his imposition of martial law had irreparably damaged his image among the general populace. "I know well that public opinion associates me more often with martial law and less often with the policy of reform," he said. "A tired society has the right to ask when the sun will shine again over Poland." Instead, Jaruzelski endorsed General Czeslaw Ksczak, the interior minister.

The Communist Party Central Committee, however, pressed Jaruzelski to run for office, stressing the need for continuity. When the Sejm met in joint session on July 19 for the presidential vote, Jaruzelski's name was the only one before the legislators. He, however, still needed a simple majority to be elected. Several Solidarity representatives boycotted the session in protest at Jaruzelski's candidacy, and the Solidarity members voted in bloc against him, as did a number of former Communist Party supporters. The result was that Jaruzelski won by only one vote.

Jaruzelski tried to persuade Solidarity to join the communists in a grand coalition, but Walesa refused to be a "mere decoration" in a communist-controlled government.

On July 29, Jaruzelski resigned as general secretary of the United Workers' Party. The move honored a preelection promise and was designed to enable Jaruzelski to distance himself from the party in order to effectively deal with Solidarity. His move, however, did not particularly impress Walesa, who still refused to accept Jaruzelski's formula for a coalition government. The result was that Jaruzelski was forced to accept Walesa's proposal for a coalition government dominated and led by Solidarity. On August 24, the Sejm confirmed Solidarity activist Tadeusz Mazowiecki as Poland's first postwar non-communist premier.

According to the Polish constitution, Jaruzelski was the pre-eminent leader, with wide-ranging executive powers. But his inability to form a communist-dominated government and events elsewhere in Eastern Europe highlighted the erosion of his political base, and effective political power was transferred to Solidarity.

Jaruzelski resigned after Walesa was elected president in a national vote in December 1990. In his farewell speech, the general said he was "sorry" for "each harm, pain and injustice" suffered by the Polish people during his nine years in power.

For Further Information:

Ascherson, Neal. *The Struggles for Poland.* New York, 1988.
Brumberg, Abraham, ed. *Poland: Genesis of a Revolution.* New York, 1983.
Sharman, T. *The Rise of Solidarity.* Vero Beach, Fla., 1987.

John Paul II, Pope   (May 18, 1920–   )   Pope John Paul II became the first Polish pope upon his election in 1978. His accession to the papal throne inspired a surge of anti-Soviet nationalism in his homeland and in other predominantly Catholic countries in Eastern Europe.

Pope John Paul II was born Karol Wojtyla to a lower-middle-class family in a village outside Krakow, Poland. He was the first member of his family to attend university. Wojtyla was studying at Krakow when World War II broke out in 1939. During the war he worked as a forced laborer.

Wojtyla became a parish priest in 1946, at a time when Poland was subjected to Soviet occupation and Stalinist terror. Priests were condemned by the regime of Boleslaw Bierut as saboteurs and spies. Communism, of course, opposed all religion as a main institutional rival for the loyalties of the working class. But the historical position of the Roman Catholic Church as the traditional repository of Polish nationalism presented an additional threat to the Communist Party. Throughout its long history, Polish language and culture had been periodically suppressed by the occupying empires of Russia, Sweden, Germany and Austria-Hungary. The church had kept those traditions and the belief in the Polish state alive, and it viewed the Soviet Union as merely another one of the long line of repressive European empires.

STEFAN Cardinal WYSZYNSKI, the primate of the Polish Church, became the country's leading human rights campaigner and in 1952 was imprisoned by the authorities. His imprisonment became one of the symbols of Stalinist repression in Poland, and it was natural that his release was demanded by Polish anti-Stalinists such as WLAYDSLAW GOMULKA,

who became first secretary of the Polish Communist Party after the POZNAN CRISIS of 1956.

Wyszynski was released almost at the same time that Gomulka was elevated to the party leadership. The cardinal was returned to his position as primate and regained control of church appointments. One of his first appointments was Wojtyla's elevation to the office of auxiliary bishop in 1958. In 1968 Wojtyla was named archbishop of Krakow, and he became a cardinal in 1971.

When Pope John XXIII assumed the papacy in 1958, he argued in favor of a dialogue with the communist authorities in order to preserve the institutional and hierarchical structures of the Catholic Church within the Soviet Bloc. This ultimately found its expression in his encyclical *Pacem in Terris*, in which the Pope said peaceful coexistence between East and West was not only desirable, but also necessary if mankind was to survive.

Pope Paul VI, who succeeded to the papacy in 1963, continued John XXIII's policy of détente with the Soviet Bloc, and gradually the Vatican moved toward an acceptance of communist rule over Eastern Europe. In 1978, Paul VI was succeeded by John Paul I, an immensely popular man dubbed the "smiling Pope." John Paul I served for only 34 days before he suddenly died. On October 16 he was succeeded by Wojtyla, who took the name John Paul II as a tribute to his immediate predecessor. He was the first non-Italian to be elected pope since Adrian VI in 1522, and he was the first Polish pope. John Paul II made it clear that he did not intend to forget his homeland and that he intended to reassess his two predecessors' policy of détente in light of his own experiences.

The election of Cardinal Wojtyla to the papacy sent shock waves throughout Eastern Europe, especially in Poland, Czechoslovakia, Hungary, Lithuania, the Ukraine and Belorussia, where there were large and devout Roman Catholic communities. Polish Catholics regarded John Paul II as "their Pope," and for them he combined the roles of priest and world statesman while at the same time fulfilling the Poles' intense need for national pride.

The authorities were uncertain about how to react to the Polish pope and at first gave in to the overwhelming national pride; for the first time since the end of World War II, a mass was broadcast on the radio, during the installation of John Paul II. Then, at Christmas, they allowed a message from the pope to his countrymen to be published in the Catholic press. But the authorities destroyed any goodwill that might have been created by censoring the pastoral message and deleting extensive references to St. Stanislaus, an 11th-century Polish martyr and national hero.

A bigger test for the Polish authorities came in 1979 with the events connected to John Paul II's triumphant homecoming. The pope made it clear that he wanted to time his visit to coincide with the celebration on May 13 of the one-thousandth anniversary of the murder of St. Stanislaus. The Communist Party refused to allow this.

John Paul II's nine-day visit started instead on June 2. Crowds poured into Warsaw for several days before the pope's arrival. It was estimated that a million people entered the city, which has a population of 1.2 million. The capital was sealed off to private traffic at midnight on June 2, and roadblocks were reported as far away as 70 miles outside the city. The pope's official event was a meeting with EDWARD GIEREK, leader of the Polish United Workers' (Communist) Party. In their talk, John Paul II said, "Peace and the drawing together of people can be achieved only on the respect for the objective rights of the nation, such as the right to existence, the right to freedom . . ."

John Paul II's visit united Poles and inspired Polish national pride as had no other event since the end of World War II. It substantially increased the influence of the Roman Catholic Church in Poland and helped to create the conditions that gave rise to the independent trade union SOLIDARITY in August 1980. On August 20, 1980, shortly after the strikes started in the Lenin Shipyard at Gdansk, he said, "We in Rome are united with our countrymen in Poland." On January 15, 1981, the pope granted an audience at the Vatican with Solidarity leader LECH WALESA. But at this meeting, he tempered his obvious support by expressing the hope that Solidarity would continue its work with "prudence and moderation" as well as with "courage."

The pope's appeals for moderation continued throughout most of 1981. In March he broadcast an appeal that an agreement "for the strengthening of international peace" be reached by Solidarity and Polish government negotiators, and on December 13 he issued a prayer for Poles "to peacefully build a peaceful future." But following the declaration of martial law, John Paul II issued a statement that "the church is on the side of the workers." The statement refrained from any direct criticism of the communist government, but it recalled "with emotion" the papal audience with Walesa.

John Paul II's next visit to Poland came in June 1983, after the declaration of martial law. It was preceded by an appeal for a general amnesty of political prisoners, which was rejected by the government of General WOJCIECH JARUZELSKI. The visit itself was in a low key because of the delicate political situation, but the pope continued to stress respect for Polish nationalism and urge the restoration of basic human rights. He also repeatedly called for a return to the principles set forth in the agreements the government had reached with Solidarity in August 1980. During this trip, the pope met twice with Jaruzelski and once with Walesa. John Paul II visited Poland again in 1987, when he went to Gdansk and praised the "eternal significance" of the Solidarity movement and again met with Walesa. The third visit was marred by violence when Gdansk police broke up a demonstration of Solidarity supporters marching from the pope's mass to the Lenin Shipyard.

Walesa and the pope met again at the height of the 1989 roundtable negotiations between Solidarity and the Polish government. When Solidarity eventually triumphed, a close friend of John Paul II, Tadeusz Mazowiecki, was chosen as premier.

John Paul II's influence on Eastern Europe was not confined to his homeland. In Czechoslovakia, Frantisek Cardinal Tomasek, faced with severe persecution, was prepared to compromise with the communist authorities in order to preserve the church hierarchy. The pope was critical and urged him to take a harder line in dealings with the government. John Paul II also took a keen interest in Lithuania and in March 1984 called on all Catholics in Europe to remember their "brothers and sisters in Lithuania."

In December 1989 John Paul II and Soviet president MIKHAIL GORBACHEV met at the Vatican. It was the first meeting between a pope and a Soviet leader and had the effect of bestowing a papal seal of approval on Gorbachev and his policies of *perestroika* and *glasnost*. The two men agreed in principle to establish diplomatic relations, and Gorbachev invited John Paul II to visit the Soviet Union. He also announced the reestablishment of the Catholic Church in the Ukraine, where it had been officially abolished by JOSEF STALIN in 1946.

Gorbachev sought papal approval to gain additional support from a universally popular figure for his economic and political reforms. The government of LEONID BREZHNEV had been extremely critical of John Paul II because he represented a threat to Soviet control of Eastern Europe. In May 1981, John Paul II was shot and seriously wounded by a Turkish gunman, Mehmet Ali Agca. The subsequent investigation produced some suspicion that Agca, who had right-wing political connections in Turkey, had been employed by the Bulgarian Secret Police under orders from the KGB, but this was later dismissed by the Italian authorities.

John Paul II had a significant influence on the events that led to the collapse of communist governments in Eastern Europe. But he was not merely anti-Soviet. John Paul II has traveled more widely than any pope in history. He has visited right-wing military dictatorships where he has been as outspoken about human rights, as he had been during his visits to Poland. John Paul II has maintained that respect for human rights is "the very basis of social and international peace."

John Paul II has been as critical of materialism in the United States as he has been of the human rights record of the Soviet Bloc, and the politics of the Cold War were anathema to him. In February 1988 the pope issued a major encyclical—the 20,000-word *Social Concerns of the Church*—condemning the rivalry between the East and West. He said the Cold War subjected poor nations to imperialistic "structures of sin" that denied them freedom and development. He added that both capitalism and Marxism are "imperfect" systems urgently "in need of radical correction."

While the pope has opposed the suppression of human rights by right-wing governments, he has also banned the preaching of liberation theology. Observers believe that John Paul II took this stand for several reasons. One is that liberation theology is closely tied to Marxist social ideas, implying support for or at least compromise with left-wing groups. The pope could not reconcile this with his experiences in Poland.

John Paul II and other conservatives within the Vatican also fear that liberation theology debases the universality of the gospel by tying the church's activities to a specific political interpretation of history. Finally, liberation theology also implies a decentralization or devolution of power away from the Vatican, which the pope has opposed across a broad spectrum of church affairs.

For Further Information:
Frossard, Andre. *Be Not Afraid.* New York, 1984.
Johnson, Paul. *John Paul II and the Catholic Restoration.* London, 1982.

Johnson, Lyndon Baines　(August 27, 1908–January 22, 1973)　Lyndon Baines Johnson was a leading U.S. senator before becoming vice president in 1961 and then president in 1963 after the assassination of JOHN F. KENNEDY. At his urging, the largest body of progressive social legislation, including landmark civil rights and medical care laws, since the New Deal was passed by Congress. However, he was also responsible for committing the United States to a full-scale war in Vietnam which overshadowed his entire presidency. He also laid the groundwork for the SALT I negotiations.

Johnson was the son of a small farmer in Texas. He started his career as a schoolteacher after graduating from Southwest Texas State Teachers College in 1930. But after only two years he went to Washington, D.C., as a secretary to Texas Representative Richard Kleberg. He used his time to establish political contacts, which bore fruit in 1933 when he was

Lyndon B. Johnson assumed the U.S. presidency after John F. Kennedy's assassination in 1963. Although he initiated a vast program of social reform, Johnson's term in office was dominated by the Vietnam conflict.

appointed Texas director of the National Youth Administration. Four years later he was elected to Congress.

Johnson made his first bid for a Senate seat in 1941 and, by 87 votes, finally won election to the upper house in 1948. In the House of Representatives Johnson had made a reputation as a New Deal supporter. But in the Senate he shifted to the right to reflect the political complexion of his enlarged constituency. In 1953 he became Democratic leader in the Senate, and he used the position to increase his political power base through the distribution of favors to Senate colleagues. By the mid-1950s, Johnson was regarded as the most expert political manipulator in the Senate. Throughout his career his political interests were firmly rooted in domestic affairs; he was, at least while he was in the Senate, considered to be weak in his grasp of foreign policy issues.

During the EISENHOWER administration, Johnson took a conservative stand on foreign policy and was cautious in his criticism of the anti-communist hysteria created by Senator JOSEPH MCCARTHY and others. (However, when it was clear that public opinion had turned against McCarthy, Johnson was instrumental in securing unanimous Democratic support for the Senate's 1954 censure of the Wisconsin Senator.)

In 1956 Johnson was Texas' "favorite son" candidate for president at the Democratic National Convention. In July 1960 he announced his candidacy for the nomination, but was hampered by the geographic narrowness of his power base, (confined almost exclusively to Texas) and by the fact that he did not announce until shortly before the convention. John F. Kennedy won the nomination on the first ballot with 806 votes, but Johnson did surprisingly well, polling 409. Kennedy chose him as running mate, partly as a result of Johnson's performance at the convention and partly in order to balance his liberal eastern establishment image with the more conservative southern Democrat image of Johnson.

Johnson hated being vice president, which he saw as a ceremonial office with no power attached to it. Kennedy seemed to have little confidence in him and excluded him from most decision-making. He was used extensively for goodwill missions and during the Kennedy administration visited 34 countries. Johnson's most important trip was his May 1961 mission to Southeast Asia to help formulate U.S. aid policy for South Vietnam. The visit convinced him of the need to provide full American backing, and during the tour Johnson told the South Vietnamese General Assembly that the United States was ready "immediately" to help expand South Vietnam's armed forces and to "meet the needs of your people on education, rural development, new industry and long-range economic development."

Johnson became president on November 22, 1963, when Kennedy was assassinated. The new president won high praise for maintaining political stability and continuity in the aftermath of the Kennedy assassination, and this helped him to defeat Republican candidate BARRY GOLDWATER decisively in the 1964 presidential elections.

Johnson's first major foreign policy tests came in Latin

America. In January 1964 anti-American riots broke out in Panama and the Panamanian government suspended diplomatic relations with the United States, demanding a revision of the Panama Canal Zone Treaty. Johnson took a hard line and insisted that order be restored before any negotiations could begin. In April 1965 he again took a hard line, sending 30,000 troops into the Dominican Republic when the interim post-Trujillo government was threatened by a right-wing military coup and several groups of left-wing rebels.

Johnson's foreign policy, and indeed his entire presidency, quickly came to be dominated by his decision to commit large American air and ground forces in the VIETNAM WAR. He was convinced before he became president that Vietnam was on the verge of falling to a communist conspiracy; that the "loss" of Vietnam would lead to the "loss" of Southeast Asia; and that American military support could save the region. In February 1964 Johnson authorized secret plans to provide American air support for South Vietnamese air strikes, and in June he signaled his intention for a large-scale military commitment when he appointed a military officer, General MAX-WELL TAYLOR, as ambassador to South Vietnam. Taylor was a committed hawk, as was General William Westmoreland, whom Johnson had appointed commander of the 17,000-strong American force in South Vietnam.

Johnson realized that execution of his plan for a major military commitment would require congressional support and that this would not be forthcoming unless Congress was shown a specific military action or threat against American interests. This was ostensibly provided in August 1964 when it was reported that two U.S. Navy destroyers patrolling the Gulf of Tonkin off the coast of North Vietnam were attacked by North Vietnamese vessels. Whether the attack actually took place has been a matter of debate ever since. But Johnson withheld evidence to the contrary, exaggerated the event and used it to secure passage of the GULF OF TONKIN RESOLUTION, which authorized the president to use "all necessary measures" to "repel any armed attack" against U.S. forces and "to prevent further aggression." The resolution also approved in advance "all necessary steps, including the use of armed force," that the president might take to help any nation that requested aid "in defense of its freedom" under the Southeast Asia Collective Defense Treaty.

The 1964 presidential campaign, in which Johnson capitalized on public fear that Goldwater would irresponsibly lead the country into war, prevented him from authorizing any large-scale troop commitments or bombing raids until 1965. In February 1965, Viet Cong guerrillas provided Johnson with the excuse he needed when they attacked American forces at Pleiku and Qui Nhon. Johnson immediately ordered retaliatory air raids on North Vietnamese military and industrial sites, and on April 1 authorized the use of American troops in offensive actions anywhere in South Vietnam. At the end of 1964, there were 23,300 American military personnel in Vietnam; a year later there were 184,300. Troop levels reached their peak in 1968, at over 536,000.

Johnson, however, always realized that a purely military solution was impossible and that he would have to negotiate with the North Vietnamese government, which by this time had sent troops to fight with the Viet Cong in the south. His plan, worked out in conjunction with national security adviser MCGEORGE BUNDY and Defense Secretary ROBERT MCNAMARA, was to step up the American troop commitments and bombing raids gradually in the hope that the increasing pressure would force the North Vietnamese to the negotiating table. Another reason for the Johnson administration's gradual step-by-step escalation was the fear that a major escalation would precipitate Soviet or Chinese intervention or both.

The North Vietnamese ignored the peace feelers extended through various diplomatic channels. They believed that they were winning the war and refused to start any negotiations until Johnson halted his bombing raids of North Vietnamese targets.

From the start of the war there was a left-liberal, student-dominated war protest movement in the United States. By 1967 this movement had grown to encompass the liberal wing of the Democratic Party, and many of the hawks in the Johnson administration began to doubt the wisdom of continuing the war effort. Johnson remained fully committed to it until the TET OFFENSIVE of February 1968 forced him to make a major reassessment. In October 1967, the North Vietnamese had started operations in the Central Highlands along the borders of CAMBODIA and LAOS. The Americans and the South Vietnamese responded with a massive show of strength that resulted in the deaths of an estimated 10,000 Vietnamese, compared to the loss of 500 American lives.

The Central Highlands operation, however, was a communist feint designed to draw the American forces away from the cities. As the U.S. troops consolidated their position in the highlands, the communist forces struck at the unprotected urban areas. They chose the start of the Vietnamese lunar New Year, Tet, as the date for launching their offensive. A total of 36 of South Vietnam's provincial capitals were attacked, and in Saigon a Viet Cong suicide squad stormed the U.S. Embassy compound.

The Tet offensive reinforced an increasingly popular view that the United States was fighting an unwinnable war and sparked a fresh round of antiwar protests. General Westmoreland maintained that the Viet Cong and North Vietnamese forces had "suffered a military defeat" despite "some temporary psychological advantage" and asked Johnson for an additional 200,000 troops, which would have brought the total American forces in Vietnam to over 700,000.

Meeting such a request would have involved a politically unpopular decision to call up Army Reserve forces. Johnson was reluctant to do this without further advice. He therefore formed a senior advisory group to study the request. They counseled him against Westmoreland's plan and urged him to stop the bombing of North Vietnam and de-escalate American involvement in the war.

Johnson accepted their advice and on March 31, 1968,

appeared on national television to announce a unilateral halt to air and naval bombardment of North Vietnam except in the area immediately north of the so-called "demilitarized" zone along the border between North and South. At the close of his 40-minute speech he spoke of the national divisions over the war and acknowledged that his own presence in office only served to continue and exacerbate those divisions. Therefore, he announced that he would neither seek nor accept nomination for another term as president.

Johnson's statement had the desired effect on the North Vietnamese, who three days later agreed to open peace negotiations in Paris. The PARIS PEACE TALKS started in May.

The Vietnam War dominated the Johnson presidency, but it was not the only significant foreign policy or Cold War event of the period. In June 1967 the Arab–Israeli Conflict erupted into the Six-Day War when Israeli forces launched a surprise attack on Egypt, Syria and Jordan. At the height of the conflict, the Soviet Union accused Israel of ignoring Security Council resolutions for a cease-fire and threatened to take "necessary actions, including military," unless Israel agreed to halt operations. Johnson responded by moving the U.S. Sixth Fleet closer to the Syrian coast and made it clear through diplomatic channels that the United States was prepared to resist Soviet intrusion into the Middle East. The Soviet Union backed off, but the incident had decisively drawn the Arab–Israeli conflict into the wider Cold War.

President Johnson also had to deal with a major crisis in the NORTH ATLANTIC TREATY ORGANIZATION when French president CHARLES DE GAULLE announced in February 1966 that he was pulling France out of the military structure of NATO and ordered American bases in France to be closed. Johnson refrained from a political attack on de Gaulle in the belief that such a move would only further inflame French nationalism and offend French pride.

U.S.–Soviet relations during the Johnson administration were overshadowed by the Vietnam War, but despite the fighting in Southeast Asia, Johnson succeeded in laying the groundwork for the first STRATEGIC ARMS LIMITATION TALKS (SALT I).

Formal U.S.-Soviet negotiations were set to start on September 30 with a meeting in Leningrad between Johnson and Premier ALEXEI KOSYGIN. But on August 20, 1968, WARSAW PACT forces invaded CZECHOSLOVAKIA and the talks were indefinitely postponed. On the issue of Czechoslovakia itself, Johnson and the other NATO leaders had decided there was little that the West could do for the leaders of the PRAGUE SPRING reform movement but to offer moral support and express moral condemnation if the Soviet Union suppressed it.

After leaving the White House in January 1969, Johnson retired to his Texas ranch, where he concentrated on writing his memoirs and completing work on the Lyndon Baines Johnson Library complex on the Austin campus of the University of Texas. Johnson died of a heart attack at his ranch on January 22, 1973.

For Further Information:

Bornet, Vaughn Davis. *The Presidency of Lyndon B. Johnson.* Lawrence, Kan., 1983.

Divine, Robert A., ed. *The Johnson Years.* Lawrence, Kan., 1987.

Evans, Rowland, and Robert Novak. *Lyndon B. Johnson: The Exercise of Power.* New York, 1966.

Goldman, Eric F. *The Tragedy of Lyndon Johnson.* New York, 1969.

Goodwin, Doris Kearns. *Lyndon Johnson and the American Dream.* New York, 1976.

Johnson, Lyndon B. *The Vantage Point: Perspectives on the Presidency, 1963–1969.* New York, 1971.

Kearns, Doris. *Lyndon Johnson and the American Dream.* New York, 1976.

VanDeMark, Brian. *Into the Quagmire: Lyndon Johnson and the Escalation of the Vietnam War.* New York, 1991.

Johnson, Ural Alexis   (October 17, 1908–   )   Alexis Johnson was a career American diplomat who was an early hawk on the VIETNAM WAR while deputy undersecretary of state for political affairs. He later served as ambassador to Japan and chief of the U.S. delegation to the first STRATEGIC ARMS LIMITATION TALKS.

Johnson joined the State Department in 1935 and developed an expertise in Asian affairs after serving in Korea, China and Japan. From 1953 to 1958 he was U.S. ambassador to Czechoslovakia. In 1961, President JOHN F. KENNEDY appointed Johnson deputy undersecretary of state for political affairs.

Johnson continued his involvement with Asian affairs by concentrating his attentions on the growing problem of Southeast Asia. In October 1961 he was asked by Kennedy to draw up a reply to the request from South Vietnamese president NGO DINH DIEM for a defense treaty and increased military aid. Johnson advised that the United States introduce ground troops to achieve the ultimate objective of "defeating the Vietcong and rendering Vietnam secure under a non-Communist government." His recommendations were backed up by others, including General MAXWELL TAYLOR and WALT ROSTOW, but Kennedy decided to defer a decision on the introduction of American combat troops.

At the suggestion of General Taylor, Johnson in January 1962 became a member of the Special Group Counterinsurgency, which was formed to coordinate U.S. efforts to support counterinsurgency operations throughout Southeast Asia. Johnson was also a member of the special bipartisan group that advised Kennedy during the CUBAN MISSILE CRISIS.

President LYNDON B. JOHNSON appointed Johnson deputy ambassador to Vietnam in July 1964. He continued to advocate an escalation of the U.S. commitment and in January 1965 submitted a plan for bringing the war to a conclusion. The plan was never put into effect.

In July 1966 Johnson was appointed U.S. ambassador to Japan and in January 1969 became undersecretary of state for political affairs. In this position he stressed the growing economic importance of the Pacific Rim Asian countries. He supported the Nixon Doctrine and vehicles for regional economic cooperation such as the Southeast Asian Agricultural

Development Conference and the Asian Development Bank. Johnson also proposed a reduction of U.S. troop levels in South Korea.

In January 1973 Johnson was appointed chief of the U.S. delegation to the Strategic Arms Limitation Talks in Geneva. He had little control over the actual policy-making, which was dominated by Secretary of State HENRY KISSINGER and President RICHARD NIXON. Johnson retired after the election of President Jimmy Carter.

Joint Intelligence Organization (JIO)   Britain's Joint Intelligence Organization is the body responsible for coordinating the work of Britain's different intelligence agencies. It is responsible to the cabinet.

The JIO's main responsibility is to prepare intelligence assessments drawn from the reports and cables of military intelligence, counterintelligence (MI5), the Secret Intelligence Service (MI6), the British Foreign Office, GOVERNMENT COMMUNICATIONS HEADQUARTERS (GCHQ) at Cheltenham, and intelligence operations of other nations, particularly the U.S. CENTRAL INTELLIGENCE AGENCY and the intelligence agencies of Canada, Australia and New Zealand.

At the head of the JIO is the Joint Intelligence Commitee (JIC), which is comprised of the director of MI6, the director general of MI5, the director of GCHQ Cheltenham, the director of intelligence at the Ministry of Defense, the deputy chief of staff at the Ministry of Defense, the coordinator of intelligence and security, Foreign Office officials and intelligence representatives from the United States, Canada, Australia and New Zealand.

K

Kadar, Janos **(May 26, 1912–July 6, 1989)** Janos Kadar was leader of the Hungarian Socialist Workers' (Communist) Party from after the Hungarian Revolution of 1956 until 1988. He was at first reviled for his role in bringing Soviet troops into Hungary and engineering the trial and execution of the revolution's leaders. But later he introduced political and economic changes that turned Hungary into the leader of the East European reform movement.

Kadar was born in the Adriatic seaport of Fiume, the illegitimate son of a soldier and a Yugoslav peasant woman. He spent the first six years of his life in foster homes before being reunited with his mother and moving to Budapest just as the Austro-Hungarian Empire was breaking up at the end of World War I.

Kadar's formal education was rudimentary, and from his early teens he started work at low-paid manual jobs. His deprived childhood and financial hardship led Kadar to embrace Marxism. In 1931 he secretly joined the banned Communist Party.

Hungary was occupied by German and Austrian troops during World War II. Kadar went underground and became a leading member of the Hungarian Resistance. He was arrested by the Gestapo but escaped in time to greet the Red Army when it marched into Budapest in December 1944.

The occupying Soviet Union appointed Kadar to the key post of head of the Budapest police. He also became a member of the Hungarian Communist Party's Politburo and the Central Committee. In 1946 he was a deputy secretary general of the party and three years later became minister of the interior.

In 1949, Communist Party leader MATYAS RAKOSI, head of the party's "Muscovite wing," moved against the party's "national wing," arrested its members and executed its leader, Laszlo Rajk, who was Kadar's mentor. Kadar managed to avoid the first round of arrests by persuading Rajk to confess to "Titoism," but in 1951 he was also taken into custody, tried and found guilty of treason, Titoism and spying.

Kadar was sentenced to four years' imprisonment in Hungarian labor camps. Because he repeatedly attempted to escape, Kadar was moved from camp to camp, tortured and beaten. His fingernails were torn out and never regrew. It was rumored that he was also castrated. After two and a half years, Kadar was released following the death of Stalin and resumed his career within the party, but at a much lower level.

He eventually worked his way back to a high party position, and emerged as the Soviet-sponsored leader of the government after the crushing of the Hungarian revolution by Soviet troops in 1956. He retained power for more than three decades, and presided over major political and especially economic reforms.

(For further details, see under HUNGARY.)

For Further Information:

Brzezinski, Z.K. *The Soviet Bloc: Unity and Conflict.* Cambridge, Mass., 1960.
Kovrig, Bennet. *Communism in Hungary from Kun to Kadar.* Stanford, Calif., 1979.
Vali, Ferenc. *A Rift and Revolt in Hungary; Nationalism vs. Communism.* Cambridge, Mass., 1961.
Zinner, Paul. *Revolution in Hungary.* New York, 1962.

Kahn, Herman See HUDSON INSTITUTE.

Kampelman, Max **(November 7, 1920–   )** Max Kampelman is a U.S. diplomat who has been heavily involved in East–West relations and disarmament negotiations since the end of the Carter administration.

Kampelman worked his way through New York University and was a conscientious objector during World War II. He received his M.A. and Ph.D. degrees in political studies from the University of Minnesota, where he met future senator and vice president HUBERT HUMPHREY and future ambassador to the United Nations JEANE KIRKPATRICK.

When Humphrey was elected to the Senate in 1948, he asked Kampelman to join his staff as a legislative counsel. Kampelman had by this time established a reputation as a liberal Democrat but with a strong anti-communist flavor. In 1954, he alienated many of his liberal friends by helping to secure passage of the Communist Control Act, which deprived the American Communist Party of "rights, privileges and immunities attendant upon legal bodies" but stopped short of making party membership a crime.

In 1955 Kampelman left Humphrey's staff to become a partner in the Washington office of the New York-based law firm of Fried, Frank, Harris, Shriver and Kampelman. But he remained active in national Democratic Party politics and helped Humphrey to secure the 1968 Democratic Party presidential nomination. He again supported Humphrey's campaign for the Democratic nomination in 1972.

In 1976 Kampelman joined a bipartisan but right-wing anti-Soviet group called the Committee on the Present Danger. The group, whose membership included RONALD REAGAN and Jeane Kirkpatrick, demanded increased defense spending and a harder line in relations with the Soviet Union. Kampelman, however, remained more liberal on domestic issues and was thus acceptable to both Democrats and Republicans when President JIMMY CARTER appointed him U.S. ambassador and chairman of the American delegation to the CONFERENCE ON SECURITY AND COOPERATION IN EUROPE (CSCE) in 1980. He was quickly reconfirmed in office in 1981 by the incoming President Reagan.

The CSCE process was in the midst of its first review conference, which was being held in Madrid. When Kampelman arrived in December there were signs of an imminent Soviet invasion of Poland. Kampelman set the tone for the Reagan administration's tough negotiating stance throughout the conference when in his first speech he warned that if Soviet forces moved in violation of the HELSINKI ACCORDS, "East–West relations as we know them could not continue." Kampelman was a key figure at the review conference for the next two and a half years and helped to draft the final statement, which recognized the right of workers to form free trade unions and set future meetings to discuss human rights and arms limitations.

After the Madrid conference, Kampelman was retained as a State Department consultant and in June 1984 headed an American delegation to observe presidential elections in El Salvador. In January 1985, Kampelman was appointed head of the U.S. negotiating team to the Strategic Arms Reduction Talks (START) in Geneva. The Soviets refused to negotiate strategic systems until the U.S. agreed to include President Reagan's proposed STRATEGIC DEFENSE INITIATIVE ("Star Wars") program in the negotiations. Kampelman urged Reagan to press deployment of the MX MISSILE system in order to increase his negotiating leverage.

The negotiations continued to be deadlocked until the Reykjavik Summit between Soviet leader Mikhail Gorbachev and Reagan helped to improve the atmosphere. In October 1986 Kampelman announced that the United States was prepared to eliminate intermediate-range nuclear forces in Europe and reduce them in Asia and would consider the elimination of all ballistic missiles.

The negotiations then moved quickly toward a treaty on intermediate-range systems, with a great deal of the negotiations being handled by Secretary of State GEORGE SHULTZ and his Soviet counterpart EDUARD SHEVARDNADZE. Kampelman, however, remained an active participant. The INTERMEDIATE-RANGE NUCLEAR FORCES (INF) TREATY eliminating intermediate-range nuclear missiles from Europe was signed by Reagan and Gorbachev in Washington, D.C., on December 8, 1987.

After the signing of the treaty, Kampelman remained in Washington to help the Reagan administration secure congressional ratification, and in June 1988 he was sent to Central America to assess the situation after the collapse of Nicaraguan peace talks.

Katyn Massacre   The massacres at Katyn Forest near Smolensk and at several other sites in the Soviet Union of more than 14,000 Polish officers and over 7,000 landowners, border police and municipal officials in the early days of World War II severely strained wartime relations between the Soviet Union and the Polish government-in-exile in London. In the postwar years, the memory of the Polish officers was invoked by Polish dissidents to engender mistrust and hatred of the Soviet Union.

On April 7, 1943, General Wladyslaw Sikorski, leader of the London Poles, told WINSTON CHURCHILL that he had proof that the Soviet Red Army had murdered 15,000 Polish officers. Six days later, on April 13, the Germans, who had invaded the Soviet Union in June 1941, broadcast that they had found a mass grave of 14,500 Polish officers in the Katyn Forest. It appeared from the officers' notebooks that they had been killed in April 1940, some months after the Soviet Union, then acting in concert with Germany, had occupied eastern Poland.

The Germans immediately accused the Soviets and proposed an international inquiry. Sikorski asked the International Red Cross to send a delegation to Poland to investigate. He also asked the Soviet government for its "observations." The Soviets claimed that the bodies were those of Polish prisoners of war who had been engaged in construction work and executed by the Germans. The Soviets went on to claim that the timing of the Polish and German announcements indicated Polish collusion with the Nazis, and Stalin broke off diplomatic relations with the London Poles on April 26, 1943. The break in diplomatic relations later gave Stalin an excuse to recognize a communist Polish government in exile led by BOLESLAW BIERUT.

In 1988 Soviet leader MIKHAIL GORBACHEV admitted that his government had "made mistakes" in its past relations with Poland and shortly afterward announced that a joint Polish–Soviet commission of historians would investigate the circumstances surrounding the Katyn Massacre. The investigation came to be regarded in Poland as a test of Gorbachev's stated policy of *glasnost* (openness) and his professed desire to rebuild Soviet–Polish relations on a new basis. In May 1990, while Polish president WOJCIECH JARUZELSKI was visiting the Soviet Union, it was announced by the Soviet authorities that new evidence had come to light that proved that the Soviet Union had been responsible for the Katyn Massacre. Gorbachev officially apologized to Jaruzelski. Later, President Boris Yeltsin of Russia turned over to President Lech Walesa of Poland a document, which he said that Gorbachev had concealed, that appeared to be a copy of the actual execution order signed by Stalin.

For Further Information

Davies, Norman. *Heart of Europe: A Short History of Poland.* Oxford, 1984.

Donnelly, Desmond. *Struggle for the World.* New York, 1965.

Stehle, Hansjakov. *The Independent Satellite: Society and Politics in Poland since 1945.* London, 1965.

Keegan, George (July 4, 1921–   )   George Keegan was head of U.S. Air Force Intelligence during the 1970s. His criticism of the NATIONAL INTELLIGENCE ESTIMATE of Soviet military capabilities led to a major reappraisal, which claimed that the CIA had underestimated Soviet military expenditures.

Keegan joined the U.S. Army Air Force as a second lieutenant after graduating from Harvard University in 1944. He quickly rose through the ranks to major general. It was apparent that his skill lay in intelligence assessment, and during the VIETNAM WAR he was chief of intelligence for the Seventh Air Force in Vietnam from 1967 to 1969 and then chief of intelligence for the U.S. Pacific Command in Hawaii from 1969 to 1970. He became chief of Air Force Intelligence in Washington, D.C. in 1971.

Keegan was highly critical of the CENTRAL INTELLIGENCE AGENCY and its assessments of Soviet military capability, which he maintained were greater than reported by the CIA. Keegan's criticism reached its peak in 1974 when the CIA-prepared National Intelligence Estimate for that year argued that détente was working and that the Soviet Union was not trying to use improved relations to gain a military advantage or make inroads in the Third World.

Keegan ordered his staff to write a rebuttal of the CIA report. They cited Soviet officials to justify their claim that the Soviet Union was using détente to lull the United States into a false sense of security that would enable them to acquire American high technology and shift the strategic balance in favor of the Soviet Union. Keegan's report led to an independent assessment reporting that the CIA had greatly underestimated Soviet military expenditures. The new report helped to justify the increased defense expenditures of the Reagan administration.

Keegan retired from the air force in January 1977. The day before he retired, the usually reticent Keegan explained his views in an interview with the *New York Times*. He cited a massive Soviet military and civil defense shelter program, the stockpiling of emergency stores of food and the development of a wide range of ICBMs as evidence of Soviet strategic intentions. "American strategy," Keegan said, "is premised on the principle of war avoidance while that of the Soviet Union is premised on war winning."

Keegan said that the Soviets' efforts had given them a definite edge in military strength and that by every criterion used to measure strategic balance the Soviets had taken a significant lead over the United States. Keegan attached special importance to the Soviet civil defense program, which he said implied that the Soviets believed they could survive a nuclear war.

After retiring from the air force, Keegan founded the Institute for Strategic Affairs and became cochairman of the Coalition for Peace through Strength. He was a stern critic of President JIMMY CARTER's Salt II treaty and a supporter of President Reagan's hard-line stand on defense issues.

Kekkonen, Urho   (September 3, 1900–August 31, 1986)   Urho Kekkonen, the dominant Finnish politician of the postwar period, was the man responsible for FINLAND's neutrality and close relations with the Soviet Union—in return for the Soviets' respect for Finnish independence.

Kekkonen did not become actively involved in Finnish politics until 1936, after he received his law doctorate. In that same year he joined the Agrarian Party and was quickly named minister of justice. He went on to become speaker of the parliament, prime minister five times, foreign minister twice and finally president from 1956 to 1981.

Over the years Kekkonen emerged as the political and intellectual embodiment of Finland and a genuinely respected statesman on both sides of the Iron Curtain. His foreign policy not only ensured Finnish independence but also created the

On February 15, 1956, Urho Kekkonen was elected president of Finland. Due to his efforts Finland maintained its independence and close relationship with the Soviet Union. Photo courtesy of the Finnish Ministry of Foreign Affairs.

political foundations for rapid economic growth. In the 1978 presidential elections, all six of Finland's largest parties paid tribute to Kekkonen's achievements by jointly endorsing his reelection for his fifth and final term. Ill health forced Kekkonen's resignation on October 27, 1981. He was replaced by Mauno Koivisto and died five years later, on August 31, 1986.

For Further Information:

Alison, Roy. *Finland's Relations with the Soviet Union, 1944–1984.* New York, 1985.

Korhonen, Keijo. *Urho Kekkonen: A Statesman for Peace.* Helsinki, 1975.

Maude, George. *The Finnish Dilemma: Neutrality in the Shadow of Power.* New York, 1976.

Puntila, L.A. *The Political History of Finland.* Helsinki, 1975.

Kennan, George F.   (February 16, 1904–   )   George F. Kennan was one of the designers of America's early Cold War policies and the chief architect of the policy of CONTAINMENT. He continued to have an impact on American foreign policy through the 1980s. His posts included ambassador to the Soviet Union and ambassador to YUGOSLAVIA, but his real influence lay in the advice he offered outside the formal machinery of government as a writer, historian and academic.

After graduating from Princeton University in 1925, Kennan joined the American diplomatic service and was posted to Eastern Europe. In 1931 he attended Berlin University to study Russian language and culture and was posted to Moscow in 1933. Kennan's first Moscow posting, lasting three years and coming at the height of JOSEF STALIN's Great Purges, left him with a strong dislike of communism. But he also developed a love of Russian culture, history and language, which enabled him to communicate easily with and understand the Soviet leadership.

During the opening years of World War II, Kennan was based in Prague and Berlin, and was briefly interned by the Germans from December 1941 to May 1942. In 1943 he joined the European Advisory Commission, where he worked on plans for postwar Germany, and the following year was appointed counselor to the U.S. Embassy in Moscow.

Throughout the war, Kennan argued against a close alliance with the Soviet Union, and after the Soviets' 1944 counteroffensive against the Germans he argued for a "realistic political showdown" with the Kremlin. In opposition to President FRANKLIN D. ROOSEVELT and other key figures in the administration, Kennan advised against a postwar Soviet–American collaboration, and when the Soviets occupied Eastern Europe in the closing stages of the war he proposed that the United States cut off economic aid to the Soviet Union in an attempt to force Soviet withdrawal.

Kennan was initially a voice in the wilderness, but when American foreign policy makers became increasingly concerned about Soviet intentions they turned to Kennan for his advice. This initially found its expression in Kennan's "Long Telegram" of 1946, in which he maintained that Soviet foreign policy was based on the inevitability of conflict between capitalism and communism and that Stalin intended to protect the communist heartland of the Soviet Union by surrounding it with friendly client states and then attempt to topple the European capitalist states through subversion, thus leaving the United States isolated and vulnerable. This assessment became one of the foundation stones of the Truman administration's foreign policy.

In April 1947 Kennan was appointed head of the State Department's newly created policy planning staff and was charged with responsibility for long-range foreign policy planning. One of Kennan's first projects was the initial planning for what became the MARSHALL PLAN.

But possibly Kennan's major contribution to American foreign policy was an article in the July 1947 issue of *Foreign Affairs* in which he proposed the policy of containment and the rationale behind it. Kennan wrote the article under the pseudonym of Mr. X because he did not want a State Department official to become officially associated with an anti-Soviet position at a time when the United States was still publicly committed to postwar cooperation. His identity, however, was quickly established, and the article itself became regarded as one of the opening shots of the Cold War.

In the article Kennan publicly repeated many of his assertions in the "Long Telegram," such as the belief that the Soviet Union would use political subversion to probe at the weak spots in the capitalist West. To meet this threat, Kennan proposed "a long-term patient but firm and vigilant containment of Russian expansive tendencies through . . . the adroit and vigilant application of counterforce at a series of constantly shifting geographical and political points, corresponding to the shifts and maneuvers of Soviet policies."

Kennan argued that this containment policy did not offer a quick victory over the Soviet Union but rather a maintenance of the status quo. Kennan hoped that when the Kremlin saw the determination of the West to repel aggression, tensions would be gradually reduced. This would lead the Soviet leaders to lose their justification for the maintenance of a police state and they would be forced to liberalize their regime. Many observers believe that Kennan's 1947 assessment was unusually prescient and that it very closely corresponds with the subsequent course of the Cold War.

Kennan, however, stressed that the main threat from the Soviet Union was from political subversion rather than conventional or nuclear weapons and that a major Western military buildup would serve only to arouse Soviet suspicions, aggravate the situation, fuel a dangerous arms race and extend the period required for the success of his containment policy. For these reasons, Kennan opposed the formation of the NORTH ATLANTIC TREATY ORGANIZATION in 1949 and the decision to integrate West Germany into the Western defense structure. He was also against the decision to send UN peacekeeping forces across the 38th parallel, which separated North and South Korea, on the grounds that this would lead to communist China's entry into the war (see KOREAN WAR). Kennan's stand on these issues led him into increasing conflict with Secretary of State DEAN ACHESON, and in 1951 he resigned from the State Department and took up a teaching post at Princeton.

In 1952 Kennan returned to the diplomatic service as U.S. ambassador to Moscow. But he became increasingly critical of the internal policies of Stalin and expressed his criticism publicly. When Kennan left Moscow briefly to attend a London conference the Soviet government declared him persona non grata and barred him from reentering the country.

Kennan hoped to be reassigned to another ambassadorship by the new secretary of state, JOHN FOSTER DULLES, but the Republicans had condemned containment as "negative, futile and immoral" and promised "liberation" for Eastern Europe. In those circumstances it was almost impossible for Dulles to appoint the author of containment to an official position, and Kennan returned to Princeton.

Kennan became one of the fiercest critics of Dulles and Eisenhower's Cold War policies. In 1957 he delivered a series of lectures for the British Broadcasting Corporation (BBC) in which he called for a reassessment of U.S. policy toward the Soviet Union. He argued that Stalin's death had been followed by a liberalizing trend within the Soviet Union and that the United States was failing to notice or exploit the change. He specifically recommended that the United States and the Soviet Union negotiate the neutralization of Eastern and Central Europe and "disengage" their forces in the area. In 1959 Kennan went one step further in suggesting that America and the Soviet Union abolish nuclear weapons.

Presidential hopeful JOHN F. KENNEDY wrote to Kennan expressing admiration for the general tenor of his BBC broadcasts and other writings, although he made it clear that he had serious reservations about Kennan's specific recommendations. Three days after his election, Kennedy offered Kennan the post of ambassador to Yugoslavia. Kennan arrived in Belgrade in February 1961 at a time when U.S.–Yugoslav relations were deteriorating and Yugoslav–Soviet relations were improving. Kennan's efforts to reverse the trend were hampered by congressional opposition, and he resigned in protest in May 1963.

Kennan became a prominent critic of American involvement in the VIETNAM WAR. He argued that Vietnam was not vital to American strategic interests and that escalation of the war effort would destroy the possibility of a negotiated settlement and lead to a rapprochement between the Soviet Union and communist China. In February 1966 he appeared before a televised session of the Senate Foreign Relations Committee and said that the Johnson administration's "preoccupation with Vietnam" meant that Europe and the Soviet Union were not receiving proper diplomatic attention. He emphatically denied the applicability of his containment policy in Southeast Asia and advised a minimal military effort to maintain a U.S. presence in Vietnam until a peaceful settlement could be reached.

Kennan took a different attitude toward Europe, and after the WARSAW PACT invasion of CZECHOSLOVAKIA in 1968 he called for the stationing of an additional 100,000 American troops in West Germany until the Warsaw Pact forces left Czechoslovakia. Critics claim that Kennan's apparently conflicting stands on Czechoslovakia and Vietnam exposed an irrational Eurocentrism in Kennan's analyses.

Through the 1970s and 1980s, Kennan continued to write and lecture on foreign policy and the Soviet Union. In June 1981 he was awarded the $50,000 Albert Einstein Peace Prize in recognition of his efforts to improve U.S.–Soviet relations. In November 1981 he attacked the Reagan administration's perception of the Soviet Union as "so extreme, so subjective, so far removed from what any sober scrutiny of external reality would reveal, that it is not only ineffective but dangerous." He said that Americans must recognize the Soviets as "another great people," embrace "the good with the bad" and understand that the positions of both the United States and the Soviet Union were the product "not of any inherent iniquity but of the relentless discipline of history, tradition and national experience."

For Further Information:
Fleming, D.F. The Cold War and Its Origins, 1917–1960. Garden City, N.Y., 1961.

Gellman, Barton D. Contending with Kennan: Toward a Philosophy of American Power. New York, 1984.

Hixson, Walter L. George F. Kennan: Cold War Iconoclast. New York, 1989.

Kennan, George F. Memoirs, 1925–1950. Boston, 1967.

———. Memoirs, 1950–1963. Boston, 1972.

———. On Dealing with the Communist World. New York, 1964.

———. Russia and the West Under Lenin and Stalin. New York, 1951.

Miscamble, Wilson D. George F. Kennan and the Making of American Foreign Policy, 1947–1950. Princeton, 1992.

Spanier, J.W. American Foreign Policy Since World War Two. Washington, D.C., 1988.

Stephanson, Anders. Kennan and the Art of Foreign Policy. Cambridge, Mass., 1989.

Mr. X. "Sources of Soviet Conduct," Foreign Affairs (July 1947): 566–82.

Kennedy, John F.   **(May 29, 1917–November 22, 1963)**
John F. Kennedy was considered by many to be one of America's most charismatic and inspiring presidents. He was elected at the height of the Cold War, and during his nearly three years in office he tried to defuse East–West tensions while maintaining a strong defensive posture.

Kennedy was born into a leading Irish Catholic political family in Boston. He attended the prestigious Choate Preparatory School and Harvard University. His father, Joseph P. Kennedy, was one of the richest men in America and from 1938 to 1940 was U.S. ambassador to Britain. Joseph Kennedy was politically ambitious for all his sons and played a major role in their careers by providing advice, contacts and virtually unlimited financial resources.

John Kennedy started on the road to fame as early as 1940, when his book Why England Slept, about prewar British foreign

John F. Kennedy, seen here in May 1961, was president of the United States at the height of the Cold War. One of his greatest challenges was the Cuban Missile Crisis of 1962, which followed the discovery of Soviet long-range missile installations in Cuba. Photo courtesy of the United States Army.

policy, became a best-seller. During World War II in the Pacific he commanded a U.S. Navy PT boat, which was sunk in 1943. His wartime exploits became the subject of another best-seller and a film. Kennedy published, with the assistance of his aide Theodore C. Sorensen, another best-seller, *Profiles in Courage*, while convalescing from a back operation in 1956. This book won a Pulitzer Prize in 1956.

In 1946 Kennedy was elected to the House of Representatives from Massachusetts as an anti-communist, conservative Democrat. In 1949 he attacked President HARRY TRUMAN for the "loss of China," and in 1950 he contributed to the senatorial election campaign of the California Republican, Representative RICHARD NIXON. In November 1950 he made a speech in praise of the anti-communist crusader Senator Joseph McCarthy. These early positions, which appear to have been taken at least partly for the sake of political expediency, later damaged his attempts to establish a more liberal reputation in the late 1950s.

In November 1952, Kennedy dislodged the patrician Massachusetts Republican Henry Cabot Lodge from his U.S. Senate seat. During his first few years in the Senate, Kennedy concentrated on establishing his power base in Massachu-

setts. In 1954 he made his first major foray into foreign policy when he opposed aid to the French fighting at DIEN BIEN PHU in Vietnam. He told the Senate that "no amount of military assistance" could prevent a Vietnamese victory and that the only way to stop communist expansion in Southeast Asia was through the support of independence movements.

In 1956, Kennedy made an unsuccessful bid at the Democratic Party convention for the party's nomination for vice president. Despite the lateness of the attempt, the voting went to three ballots. This encouraged Kennedy to start laying the groundwork for a bid to win his party's presidential nomination for the 1960 elections. From 1957, he took an increasing interest in foreign affairs and joined the Senate Foreign Relations Committee. Kennedy started off as a committed Cold Warrior. He supported the EISENHOWER DOCTRINE and increased defense spending, and he introduced legislation for the provision of federal funds for "educational materials" to inform the public of the nature and extent of the communist threat. In 1958, after the launching of the Soviet satellite *Sputnik*, he attacked the Eisenhower administration for the alleged "MISSILE GAP" between the Soviet and American strategic forces. The Missile Gap became an issue in the 1960 campaign, but it was later shown to be nonexistent.

Kennedy won the presidential election of 1960 in the closest race of the 20th century. In the electoral college, Kennedy won 303 to 219, and in the popular vote he beat Republican opponent Richard Nixon by only 118,574 votes. In office, Kennedy maintained a tough position on defense issues and relations with the Soviet Union. His policy toward Third World countries differed markedly from that of the Eisenhower administration. President DWIGHT EISENHOWER and Secretary of State JOHN FOSTER DULLES had divided the world into pro- and anti-American camps; Kennedy looked for and found variations of the political spectrum. He supplied economic aid to dissident communist governments such as Yugoslavia and Poland in order to weaken the Soviet grip there. He also sought to expand economic and political links with Third World countries through the Peace Corps, ALLIANCE FOR PROGRESS and the Food for Peace programs, as well as strengthening bilateral links with the emerging African states and key nonaligned countries such as India.

At the same time, Kennedy substantially expanded the American defense establishment. He felt that the Eisenhower administration's heavy reliance on strategic nuclear weapons made it more likely that a local conflict would quickly escalate to a superpower nuclear exchange. He therefore expanded counterinsurgency, conventional and tactical nuclear forces so that the United States could counter force at all levels without having immediately to threaten nuclear retaliation.

Kennedy placed a heavy emphasis on foreign affairs right from the start of his administration. His inaugural address was devoted almost exclusively to the subject. He pledged his government "to pay any price, bear any burden, meet any hardship, support any friend, oppose any foe, to assure the survival and success of liberty." He went on to promise America's allies the "loyalty of faithful friends." Emerging countries were promised that "one form of colonial control shall not have passed away merely to be replaced by a far more iron tyranny."

Other countries in the Western Hemisphere were promised an "alliance for progress" to cast "off the chains of poverty." And the Soviet Union was asked "that both sides begin anew the quest for peace, before the dark powers of destruction unleashed by science engulf all humanity in planned or accidental self-destruction." After stressing the need for increased defense spending he added, "Let us never negotiate out of fear. But let us never fear to negotiate." The stirring inaugural address concluded with the famous words, "And so, my fellow Americans: Ask not what your country can do for you—ask what you can do for your country. My fellow citizens of the world: Ask not what America will do for you, but what together we can do for the freedom of man."

Despite the stirring words, Kennedy's first year in office brought a series of foreign policy setbacks. The first involved Cuba and the BAY OF PIGS. Plans for a CIA-organized invasion of Cuba had been started by the Eisenhower administration. Kennedy, according to his aide Arthur Schlesinger, was skeptical of the plan, which involved the CIA in training 1,500 exiles in Guatemala for an invasion of Cuba. During the changeover of administrations, however, the president-elect did not give the project the attention it demanded, and it developed a momentum of its own. In April 1961 Guatemalan president Miguel Ydigoras demanded that the Cubans leave his country. Since there was no place for them to go but to Cuba, the invasion was launched. The result of the poorly conceived, planned and executed operation was a foreign policy disaster that badly damaged the credibility of the president.

The president also suffered a setback in Southeast Asia. The American government had been trying to establish a stable pro-Western government in Laos as a buffer between China and the rest of the region. Communist guerrillas, however, had established a foothold and were threatening the politically corrupt, Western-supported government. After a series of political and military reversals, Kennedy was forced to accept the neutralization of Laos.

In June 1961 Kennedy met with Soviet premier NIKITA KHRUSHCHEV in Vienna. The meeting, in retrospect, appears to have been a mistake. Kennedy had, within the first six months of his administration, suffered two major foreign policy setbacks. Khrushchev interpreted these, plus the young president's relative inexperience in foreign affairs, as a sign of weakness, which many believe encouraged Khrushchev to provoke the July 1961 BERLIN Crisis.

At the Vienna conference, Khrushchev threatened to sign a separate peace treaty with the East German government, end the occupation, cancel administrative and access rights of Western troops in West Berlin and declare Berlin a "free city." Kennedy decided that if he did not take a tough stand on Berlin, he risked losing all of Western Europe. In July he reaffirmed the American will to defend West Berlin by ordering 250,000 reservists to active duty and asking Congress for another increase in the defense budget. At the same time, he outlined a sweeping civil defense program designed to demonstrate his willingness to risk nuclear war over the issue of Berlin. The Soviets responded by increasing their own military presence in East Germany, building the Berlin Wall in August and letting the issue of a German peace treaty die.

From this point, Kennedy's handling of relations with the Soviet Union began to improve as he adopted a tougher but more realistic approach. Southeast Asia remained a major area of conflict for both superpowers, with the major emphasis, following the neutralization agreement, shifting from Laos to Vietnam. Kennedy was seriously disturbed that the United States was being locked into support for the corrupt and unpopular government of President NGO DINH DIEM. He tried to force reform and later tacitly accepted the need for Diem's overthrow.

Kennedy also sent two of his top foreign policy advisers, General MAXWELL TAYLOR and WALT ROSTOW, on a fact-finding mission to Vietnam. The two men proposed a massive injection of American military and economic aid and the introduction of American ground combat forces. Kennedy authorized the aid, which tied the United States more closely to the survival of South Vietnam, but steered clear of the major commitment of combat troops proposed by the Taylor-Rostow report. The number of U.S. military "advisers," however, increased from 700 to 15,000 during the Kennedy administration, and this was one of the major stepping stones toward America's full involvement in the disastrous VIETNAM WAR.

Kennedy's biggest Cold War challenge and success was the CUBAN MISSILE CRISIS. In August 1962, American spy planes discovered that the Soviet Union had started to install missiles in Cuba. Kennedy issued a statement warning that if Cuba became "an offensive military base of significant capacity for the Soviet Union, then this country will do whatever must be done to protect its own security and that of its allies." On October 10, photographs taken by a U-2 SPY PLANE determined that the Soviet missiles were of an offensive nature and that the United States faced a major new nuclear threat.

The president responded by forming a special bipartisan committee to advise him on the crisis. The group became known as the EXECUTIVE COMMITTEE OF THE NATIONAL SECURITY COUNCIL, or ExCom. The members of the committee offered advice ranging from a surgical air strike to an invasion to a naval quarantine. Kennedy assembled 100,000 American troops in Florida and announced a naval quarantine, which took effect on October 22. Six days later, Khrushchev agreed to dismantle and remove the missiles under United Nations supervision.

A major priority for Kennedy was a U.S.–Soviet NUCLEAR TEST BAN TREATY. Talks for a comprehensive ban on nuclear testing had been dragging on for years, bogged down on the issue of verification and on-site inspections of underground nuclear tests. Kennedy decided that the fact of an agreement was essential if East–West tensions were to be reduced. He therefore announced in June 1963 that the United States was prepared to settle for a limited ban that would exclude the controversial underground tests. He added that he was sending the respected American diplomat AVERELL HARRIMAN to Moscow to negotiate the treaty. Kennedy's speech had the desired effect of convincing Khrushchev of his sincerity, and the treaty was soon initialed, on July 25, 1963.

With the exception of France, Kennedy managed to form a good working relationship with almost all of America's allies. He had an especially close relationship with British prime minister, HAROLD MACMILLAN. The relationship went through a bad patch after the United States unilaterally canceled the Skybolt missile project it had promised to Britain, but the problem was resolved at a meeting between Kennedy and Macmillan in December 1962, at which Kennedy promised to sell U.S. POLARIS submarines to Britain.

Kennedy, under pressure from West German chancellor KONRAD ADENAUER, also tried to create a Multilateral Nuclear Force (MLF) under a multinational NATO command. The purpose of the force was to reassure the Germans of the continuance of the nuclear umbrella. The plan encountered French opposition, British apathy and skepticism from American defense planners.

The Multilateral Nuclear Force and the Anglo-American deal on Polaris angered French president CHARLES DE GAULLE, who saw them as an attempt to establish Anglo-Saxon preeminence in Western Europe at the expense of France. The French president, who had been planning to distance France from the United States, barred American nuclear warheads from French territory and denied the United States rocket sites on French soil. He also established diplomatic relations with communist China and closer relations with the Soviet Union. In 1966, he took France out of NATO's military structure.

In November 1963, Kennedy accepted an invitation to visit Texas to help reunite the liberal and conservative wings of the state's Democratic Party. On November 22, 1963, while being driven in a motorcade through Dallas, he was assassinated by rifle fire.

Lee Harvey Oswald was arrested and charged with the killing, but was himself slain while in police custody days later by Jack Ruby. A presidential commission of inquiry appointed by President Johnson (known as the Warren Commission after its chairman, Chief Justice Earl Warren) subsequently concluded that Oswald was Kennedy's lone assassin, but suspicions of a wide conspiracy have refused to die.

For Further Information:
Beschloss, Michael R. *The Crisis Years: Kennedy and Khrushchev, 1960–1963.* New York, 1991.
Fireston, Bernard J. *The Quest for Nuclear Stability: John F. Kennedy and the Soviet Union.* Westport, Conn., 1982.
Giglio, James N. *The Presidency of John F. Kennedy.* Lawrence, Kan., 1991.
Higgins, Trumbull. *The Perfect Failure: Kennedy, Eisenhower, and the CIA at the Bay of Pigs.* New York, 1987.
Hilsman, Roger. *To Move a Nation: The Politics of Foreign Policy in the Administration of John F. Kennedy.* Garden City, N.Y., 1967.
Newman, John M. *JFK and Vietnam: Deception, Intrigue, and the Struggle for Power.* New York, 1992.
Parmet, Herbert S. *Jack: The Struggles of John F. Kennedy.* New York, 1980.
———. *JFK, The Presidency of John F. Kennedy.* New York, 1983.
Paterson, Thomas J., ed. *Kennedy's Quest for Victory: American Foreign Policy, 1961–1963.* New York, 1989.
Rust, William J. *Kennedy in Vietnam.* New York, 1985.
Schlesinger, Arthur M., Jr. *A Thousand Days.* New York, 1965.
Sorensen, Theodore C. *Kennedy.* New York, 1965.
Thompson, Robert Smith. *The Missiles of October: The Declassified Story of John F. Kennedy and the Cuban Missile Crisis.* New York, 1992.

Kennedy, Robert F.   (November 20, 1925–June 6, 1968)
Robert Kennedy was attorney general in the administration of his elder brother, JOHN F. KENNEDY, and a close adviser to the president during the CUBAN MISSILE CRISIS. In 1968, as an anti-VIETNAM WAR candidate, he was on the verge of winning Democratic Party presidential nomination when he was assassinated.

Kennedy was born into a wealthy Boston Irish Catholic family. His father, Joseph P. Kennedy, was ambassador to Britian, and carefully groomed his sons for political careers. Kennedy attended first Harvard and then the University of Virginia Law School, from which he graduated in 1951.

He helped to manage John Kennedy's successful campaign for the U.S. Senate in 1952 and the following year was named an assistant counsel for the Senate Permanent Subcommittee on Investigations chaired by Senator JOSEPH MCCARTHY. Six months later he resigned his post in protest against McCarthy's tactics, but he rejoined in December 1954 as chief counsel for the subcommittee's Democratic minority. In 1957 Robert Kennedy became chief counsel for Senator John McClellan's Senate Rackets Committee, which investigated crime and corruption in the union movement. He resigned this post in 1959 to manage his brother's presidential campaign.

After the campaign, Kennedy was appointed attorney general. The appointment was widely attacked as nepotistic, but many analysts have since asserted that Robert Kennedy was one of the country's best attorneys general. As head of the Department of Justice, he instituted investigations of the Ku Klux Klan, organized crime and the Teamsters' Union.

As the president's brother, Robert Kennedy had an influence far beyond the confines of the Justice Department. This became more pronounced after the disastrous BAY OF PIGS invasion weakened the president's trust in professional advisers. Robert Kennedy became a member of the "Inner Cabinet" and John F. Kennedy's closest adviser on a wide range of foreign as well as domestic policies. He was used for a number of diplomatic missions to Europe and the Far East and became involved in monitoring CIA activities on behalf of the president. Robert Kennedy was one of the most liberal of the president's advisers and among other things strongly recommended the removal of restrictions on American travel to China, Albania, North Korea and Cuba.

During the Cuban Missile Crisis of October 1962, Robert Kennedy was a member of ExCom, the group of advisers that met to consider the U.S. response to the discovery of Soviet offensive missiles in Cuba. Kennedy strongly opposed proposals for a general air strike and invasion of Cuba and supported the idea of a naval quarantine. He acted as chairman at a crucial meeting of the committee that established a consensus in favor of a naval blockade of Cuba.

At the height of the crisis, Soviet leader NIKITA KHRUSHCHEV sent two conflicting cables suggesting ways to defuse the situation. The first proposed the withdrawal of the missiles in return for an American pledge not to invade Cuba. The second cable, which came the following day, demanded the withdrawal of U.S. missiles in Turkey in exchange for the removal of Soviet missiles in Cuba. Faced with these conflicting demands, Robert Kennedy proposed that the administration simply act as if the second cable had never been received and respond favorably to the first. Robert Kennedy helped to draft the reply and then personally delivered a copy of it to the Soviet ambassador. The next day, the Soviets agreed to the U.S. proposal that Soviet missiles be withdrawn in return for an end to the American blockade and a promise not to invade Cuba.

Robert Kennedy was devastated by the assassination of his brother in November 1963 and for several months afterward delegated most of his Justice Department responsibilities to subordinates. He had never liked or worked well with LYNDON JOHNSON, and the antipathy between the two men grew after Johnson succeeded John Kennedy as president. In August 1964, Kennedy resigned as attorney general and successfully ran for election as U.S. senate from New York.

In the Senate, Kennedy at first basically supported the Johnson administration's policy in Vietnam. But he quickly moved into the dove camp and became one of the leading opponents of American involvement in the Vietnam War. In November 1967 he argued that the American "moral position" in Vietnam had been undermined by the Johnson administration, claiming that "we're killing innocent people because we don't want to have the war fought on American soil."

By 1967, as they prepared for the presidential primary elections, Kennedy and Senator EUGENE MCCARTHY were vying for the leadership of the antiwar movement and the liberal wing of the Democratic Party. Kennedy's family name and larger political base appeared to put him in the stronger position to win the party's presidential nomination if he decided to run. On March 16, 1968, after some weeks of public indecision, Kennedy announced his candidacy. McCarthy, who had announced earlier and had already made a surprisingly strong showing against President Lyndon

Johnson in the New Hampshire primary, became his main opponent after Johnson withdrew from the race on March 31. Kennedy won the Nebraska and Indiana primaries but was soundly defeated by McCarthy in Oregon. The California primary with its huge bloc of convention votes was generally regarded as decisive. Kennedy won with 46% of the vote, compared to McCarthy's 42%, seemingly assuring himself of the nomination.

Shortly after leaving a victory rally the night of June 5, Kennedy was shot at close range in the crowded kitchen of a Los Angeles hotel. He died the next day. Sirhan Sirhan, a Palestinian, was captured at the scene and later convicted of the assassination.

For Further Information:
Chester, Lewis, Godfrey Hodgson, and Bruce Page. *An American Melodrama.* New York, 1969.
Halberstam, David. *The Unfinished Odyssey of Robert Kennedy.* New York, 1969.
Kennedy, Robert. *Thirteen Days: A Memoir of the Cuban Missile Crisis.* New York, 1969.
White, Theodore H. *The Making of the President.* New York, 1968.

KGB The Committee for State Security, or KGB, was the main Soviet security organization. Its duties included overseas intelligence gathering, counterintelligence, the extensive secret police operations and guarding the borders. It was generally accepted that a large number of Soviets overseas were members of the KGB, whether they were representatives of international organizations, journalists, diplomats or Soviet trade delegates.

The Russian state has a long history of secret police activity, extending back to czarist days. This was continued after the Bolshevik Revolution, when the Council of People's Commissars established the Cheka (an acronym, in Russian, for Extraordinary Commission to Combat Counterrevolution and Sabotage) under Felix Dzerzhinsky.

The Cheka, which organized the first "Red Terror," was abolished in 1922 and replaced by the State Political Directorate (GPU) and the People's Commissariat of Internal Affairs (NKVD). In 1934 the GPU was made a division of the NKVD, which gained control of border guards, internal troops, labor camps, the police, intelligence gathering and general internal security. It was the NKVD that orchestrated the great Stalinist purges of the 1930s.

In 1941 the People's Commissariat for State Security, or NKGB, was formed to relieve the NKVD of responsibility for the secret police. In 1946 both the NKGB and NKVD were elevated to the status of state ministries under the effective control of LAVRENTY BERIA, who became a member of the Politburo.

The eight years between the end of World War II and the death of JOSEF STALIN saw a series of power struggles for control of the Soviet security service, and the organization was variously split and regrouped into several different bureaucracies. Beria managed to gain complete control just before Stalin's death, but in June 1953 he was arrested and shot. The security services again reorganized, and on March 13, 1954, the KGB officially came into being.

The KGB was organized into five main directorates, whose responsibilities were overseas operations, counterintelligence and the secret police, the Border Guards and the KGB military corps, suppression of dissidents, and electronic espionage.

Under Soviet leader MIKHAIL GORBACHEV the KGB adopted more liberal policies. For the first time, the KGB offices were opened to foreign and Soviet newsmen and interviews were given to the media. The activities of the second and fourth directorates (responsible for the secret police and control of dissidents, respectively) were also reduced and greater emphasis placed on industrial espionage.

But as Gorbachev's reform policies sparked greater social unrest, he was forced in late 1990 and early 1991 to grant the KGB increased powers to combat nationalist ferment and "economic sabotage." Hardline KGB chief Vladimir Kryuchkov issued dire warnings about alleged CIA plots to use Western aid and anticommunist elements to infiltrate and destabilize the Soviet government and economy.

Despite Gorbachev's efforts to use the KGB to help save *perestroika* and *glasnost*, Kryuchkov led other hardliners in the attempted coup against the Soviet president in August 1991. Although the coup failed, it ultimately led to the fall of the Communist Party and Gorbachev and the dissolution of the U.S.S.R.—and the KGB along with it. Kryuchkov was arrested and replaced by Vadim Bakatin, and the KGB was purged of those who supported the coup. With the end of the Soviet Union in December 1991, the KGB, like most Soviet institutions, became part of the Russian government. It was promptly split into two, along the lines of most Western spy agencies, with its internal security functions going to a domestic ministry and the KGB retaining responsibility only for foreign espionage. In 1992, mindful of the unhappy memories associated with the KGB, Moscow renamed it the Russian Foreign Intelligence Service. The new agency was headed by Yevgeny Primakov, a Gorbachev protégé and former diplomatic troubleshooter who advocated openness and even cooperation with the CIA.

For Further Information:

Andrew, Christopher, and Oleg Gordievsky, eds. *Instructions from the Centre: Top Secret Files on KGB Foreign Operations, 1975–1985.* London, 1991.

Barron, John. *KGB: The Secret Work of Soviet Secret Agents.* New York, 1974.

Bialoguski, Michael. *The Case of Colonel Petrov.* New York, 1955.

Buranelli, Vincent, and Nan Buranelli. *Spy/Counterspy: An Encyclopedia of Espionage.* New York, 1982.

Dallin, David J. *Soviet Espionage.* New Haven, Conn., 1963.

Knightley, Phillip. *Philby: KGB Masterspy.* London, 1988.

Parrish, Michael. *Soviet Security and Intelligence Organizations, 1917–1990: A Biographical Dictionary and Review of Literature in English.* New York, 1992.

Penkovsky, Oleg. *The Penkovsky Papers.* New York, 1965.

Wise, David. *Molehunt: The Secret Search for Traitors That Shattered the CIA.* New York, 1992.

Khmer Rouge   See CAMBODIA.

Khrushchev, Nikita   **(April 17, 1894–September 11, 1971)**
As Soviet leader from the 1950s until 1964, Nikita Khrushchev reversed the Stalinist trend of Soviet communism. He also built up the Soviet nuclear arsenal, increased Soviet influence in the Third World and introduced an element of reform into the Soviet economy. Khrushchev presided over the Soviet Union at the time of the building of the Berlin Wall, the CUBAN MISSILE CRISIS, the SINO–SOVIET SPLIT and the launching of SPUTNIK.

Khrushchev was born into a working-class Russian family and after a basic village education started work at the age of 15 as a pipefitter. His factory work exempted Khrushchev from military service during World War I, and on the factory floor he became involved in workers' organizations, but not, initially, the Communist Party.

It was not until 1918 that Khrushchev joined the Communist Party. In January 1919 he was made a political commissar in the Red Army and was attached to units fighting against invading Polish troops and White Army units attacking from newly independent Lithuania. In 1922 he returned to school to complete his education and in 1925 entered full-time party work as secretary of the Petrovosko-Mariinsk District. In 1925, Khrushchev attended the 14th Party Congress in Moscow as a nonvoting delegate and witnessed JOSEF STALIN's triumph over Leon Trotsky.

Nikita Khrushchev at a press conference on August 5, 1959. Photo courtesy of Novosti Press Agency.

Khrushchev early recognized the importance of a close relationship with Stalin and his supporters, and he cultivated a friendship with Stalin's close associate Lazar Kaganovich, secretary general of the Communist Party in the Ukraine. In 1931, Kaganovich secured Khrushchev a full-time party post in the Moscow city machinery. In 1934 he was elected a member of the Central Committee, and by 1935 he was secretary general of the Moscow Communist Party, effectively mayor of the capital city. He became a candidate (nonvoting) member of the Politburo in 1938 and the following year a full member.

Khrushchev survived Stalin's Great Purges by supporting the dictator and all his policies. He was one of only three provincial party secretaries who survived the mass executions of the 1930s. After the joint German-Soviet invasion of Poland in 1939, Khrushchev was given responsibility for organizing the integration of the Soviet sector into the U.S.S.R. After the German invasion of the Soviet Union in 1941, he was given the rank of lieutenant general and placed in charge of organizing the resistance movement in the Ukraine and moving vital industrial machinery eastward.

After the liberation of the Ukraine in 1944 Khrushchev was placed in charge of reestablishing political and economic life in the region. This led to his first major clash with Stalin. The Ukraine in 1946 suffered one of the worst famines in its history, and Khrushchev concentrated his efforts on restoring food supplies and an efficient distribution network. Stalin, on the other hand, demanded that the emphasis be placed on postwar industrial production. This led to Khruschev's demotion in 1947. But in 1949, he was back in favor and in his previous job as head of the Moscow party machinery.

At the 19th Party Congress in 1952, Khrushchev was given the task of drawing up new party statutes. His changes included the abolition of the old Politburo and its replacement by the Presidium of the Central Committee. This left more power in the hands of the committee secretaries, of whom Khrushchev was one.

The party was thrown into turmoil and a classic power struggle by the sudden death of Stalin on March 5, 1953. The new 10-member presidium, announced within 24 hours of Stalin's death, included GEORGI MALENKOV, LAVRENTY BERIA, V.M. MOLOTOV, NIKOLAI BULGANIN, Kaganovich and Khrushchev. No one completely dominated the party, but Malenkov appeared to be designated as first among equals, with a strong challenge from Beria, the long-time head of the NKVD (forerunner of the KGB). Khrushchev appeared to be very much in the background.

But he suddenly shot to prominence on March 14 when it was announced that Malenkov had resigned his position as secretary of the Central Committee and had been succeeded by Khrushchev. Malenkov retained his post as party chairman. Shortly afterward, Beria was removed from power, tried and executed. This left Khrushchev as the main challenger to Malenkov, and Soviet domestic politics were dominated by the power struggle between the two men for the next four years.

The two could not have been more different. Malenkov was a suave and sophisticated Russian with a strong feel for international affairs and a firm intellectual background. Khrushchev was proud of his peasant and working-class background and displayed a ready and earthy sense of humor. He was a political tactician without a rigid ideological doctrine. His decisions were usually determined by the needs of the moment, rather than the requirements of Marxism-Leninism.

Khrushchev had always taken a special interest in agriculture and within the Presidium was given special responsibility for this important and troublesome sector of the economy. In September 1953 he won high praise for his admission of the critical problems facing Soviet agriculture and the innovative methods he proposed to resolve the crisis. In 1954 he launched his Virgin Lands program, which opened new arable lands in Kazakhstan and western Siberia. The program was a success in its first few years, and this played a major role in Khrushchev's continuing rise. But the Virgin Lands region was particularly susceptible to dramatic and unpredictable climatic change, which undermined the program after Khrushchev came to power.

Malenkov, for his part, pressed for increased production of consumer goods in order to fulfill some of the long-suppressed material aspirations of the Soviet people. However, he faced opposition from party hard-liners and the military, which was pressing for increased defense spending. Khrushchev made the tactical decision to side with the hard-liners and the military, and in February 1955, at a party plenum called to discuss the budget, Malenkov lost the economic debate and resigned as party chairman.

At Khrushchev's suggestion, Defense Minister Nikolai Bulganin succeeded Malenkov. The Soviet Union then entered into a period when the government appeared to be largely controlled by both Bulganin and Khrushchev. This suited Khrushchev, who was strongly opposed to the reintroduction of a Stalinist personality cult and was quite prepared to share the public limelight while privately wielding superior power through his control of the party machinery. Malenkov remained a member of the Presidium and the focal point for the anti-Khrushchev lobby. It was not until June 1957 that Khrushchev gained complete control after an attempt to oust Khrushchev by Malenkov, Molotov and Kaganovich badly backfired and they themselves were catapulted into disgrace.

Having disposed of Malenkov, Khrushchev adopted many of his economic and foreign policies. He strongly pursued the policy of increased production of consumer goods and tempered his previously bellicose statements on East–West relations and nuclear issues. Khrushchev was also responsible for the Soviet space program, which threw the West into a panic when the Sputnik satellite was launched in October 1957. The space program was a major component of Khrushchev's plan to increase the building of nuclear missiles, which many analysts now believe was designed primarily as an economy measure because nuclear weapons provided a cheaper deterrent than conventional forces.

Khrushchev's experience of foreign affairs before coming to power was extremely limited. He did not make his first trip abroad until 1954, when he was 60 years old. In that year he visited Poland and China. But despite his inexperience in foreign policy, Khrushchev was determined to make his mark and in May 1955 was a prominent member of the Soviet delegation that visited Belgrade to patch up the Yugoslav–Soviet rift. He also attended the 1955 GENEVA HEADS OF GOVERNMENT SUMMIT, where he made his first contact with President DWIGHT EISENHOWER. At Geneva, however, he maintained a low profile, and the Americans were uncertain of his importance in relation to Bulganin. Later that year, Bulganin and Khrushchev visited India and Burma, and in April 1956 they made a much-publicized visit to Britain.

Khrushchev will probably be best remembered for his "secret speech" before the 20th Party Congress in February 1956 in which he denounced Stalin. Until that time, the memory of Stalin had been preserved for fear that an attack on the man who had dominated communism for nearly 30 years would undermine the standing of communist parties everywhere. But the shadow of Stalin was also being used by party hard-liners to block essential political and economic reforms. Therefore, Khrushchev hit upon the idea of a "secret" speech addressed to party insiders but kept from the public. In it Khrushchev made a merciless attack on Stalin's cult of personality and on the dictator himself. He said that the personality cult had distorted political and economic development and enabled the dictator to murder many innocent people.

It proved impossible to keep such an attack on the architect of postwar Eastern Europe a secret, and when it leaked the speech had the effect feared by the party hardliners: The oppressed nations of Eastern Europe rebelled against the Stalinist rulers imposed on them by the former dictator. In June 1956 riots broke out in Poznan, Poland, and despite a personal intervention by Khrushchev and other members of the Soviet leadership, the Soviet Union was forced to accept the rehabilitation of the nationalist-oriented Polish communist, WLADYSLAW GOMULKA in order to keep Poland in the Soviet camp. (*See* POZNAN CRISIS.)

The discontent in Poland quickly spread to HUNGARY, where the people demanded the rehabilitation of IMRE NAGY, who had threatened to withdraw from the WARSAW PACT. This was a step too far, and Khrushchev ordered Soviet tanks into Hungary to suppress the rebellion.

The 20th Party Congress also saw the unveiling of some major changes in Soviet foreign policy. Khrushchev continued to accept the basic concept of an inevitable struggle between capitalism and communism, but he proposed that this struggle could be conducted within the framework of PEACEFUL COEXISTENCE, in the belief that the alternative was a suicidal nuclear war. Certainly, relations between the United States and the Soviet Union improved under Khrushchev. The 1955 Geneva Conference was seen as a diplomatic success even though its concrete achievements were limited. His determination to improve East–West relations was also largely responsible for the Austrian State Treaty. In 1959, Khrushchev became the first Soviet leader to visit the United States. His ebullient style delighted the American public, and U.S.–Soviet relations reached a postwar peak at a meeting at Camp David, Maryland, between President Eisenhower and the Soviet leader.

But Khrushchev was also determined to consolidate the wartime gains of the Soviet Union in Eastern Europe, and for him the foundation stone of the Soviet presence was East Germany and complete control of Berlin. The continued presence of British, American and French troops in West Berlin and the city's ties to West Germany provided a gateway to the West for dissatisfied East Germans and a capitalist enclave in the center of the most sensitive of the Soviet satellite states. In November 1958, Khrushchev announced that the Soviet Union was preparing "definite proposals" for the termination of the Allied administration in Berlin. He added, "We are not saying that we will go to war against the West" over the issue, but "if the aggressors attack the Soviet Union [or] the Socialist countries, they will be crushingly repulsed."

In the face of a strong response from the Western countries, Khrushchev was forced to back away slightly and proposed that Berlin become a demilitarized "free city" independent of either East or West Germany. When this was also rejected, he allowed the ultimatum attached to the proposal to lapse. But the rising tensions over Berlin continued and were exacerbated by the controversy surrounding the shooting down of a U.S. U-2 SPY PLANE over the Soviet Union on May 1, 1960. As a result of this incident, the U.S.–Soviet summit planned for Geneva in mid-May was cancelled.

The tensions over Berlin continued into the administration of JOHN F. KENNEDY, and the Soviet leader used his meeting with the new president in June 1961 to try to force him into an agreement on Berlin. Khrushchev appears to have been pressed as much by the communist authorities in East Germany as by the hardliners within his own Soviet Communist Party. The East Germans were becoming increasingly worried about the economic consequences of the flood of people fleeing from East Germany to the West through West Berlin. Between 1954 and 1961 an estimated 2,700,000 East Europeans (mainly Germans) fled across the Berlin border. In August 1961 the Berlin Wall was built and the flood stopped. The construction of the wall reduced the pressure on Khrushchev to force the West into a withdrawal from West Berlin but left behind a poignant symbol of the Soviet Bloc's failure to satisfy the aspirations of its own people.

The problems of Berlin may have contributed to Soviet involvement in CUBA and the Cuban Missile Crisis. Some analysts believe that Khrushchev's decision to deploy offensive nuclear missiles in Cuba was meant to force a Western withdrawal from Berlin. If so, the plan badly backfired, and after an American naval blockade Khrushchev was forced to withdraw the missiles in return for an American pledge not to invade Cuba.

Cuba was Khrushchev's greatest success at establishing a Soviet presence in the Third World. He was quick to realize the enormous attraction that communism held for anticolonial leaders governing newly independent countries. He won over many Third World leaders with a combination of military and financial aid, and he provided Soviet engineers and capital for several grandiose development projects. The most spectacular of these was the ASWAN HIGH DAM in Egypt (originally an American-sponsored project), which helped the Soviet Union to establish a political presence in the Middle East. Soviet engineers also helped with industrial project in GHANA, India, North Korea, Mongolia and AFGHANISTAN.

Military and political support was provided to PATRICE LUMUMBA in the CONGOLESE CIVIL WAR and to communists fighting in Vietnam, LAOS, Malaysia, the PHILIPPINES and elsewhere. In the Far East, a great deal of the aid was initially given in conjunction with Communist China (PEOPLE'S REPUBLIC OF CHINA). The Chinese, however, became increasingly worried about Khrushchev's de-Stalinization campaign and his policy of peaceful coexistence, both of which conflicted with the revolutionary ideology adhered to by the People's Republic. The Chinese were also concerned about the Soviet invasion of Hungary.

From 1957 onward, the previously warm relationship between Beijing and Moscow cooled. In 1958 the Chinese launched their Stalinist-style economic plan, the Great Leap Forward. The plan conflicted with Khrushchev's economic reforms, and he severely criticized it. At about the same time, Khrushchev agreed to help the Chinese to develop nuclear weapons, but in return he insisted that China officially subordinate its foreign and defense policies to that of the Soviet Union. The Chinese might have been able to accept this, but in 1959 Khrushchev withdrew the offer, allegedly as a result of American pressure. In 1960 Khrushchev withdrew some 1,300 Soviet technicians from China.

A split finally came at a meeting of the congress of the Soviet Communist Party in June 1960, when Khrushchev accused the Chinese of failing to understand "the character of the present era." The Chinese counterattacked by accusing Khrushchev of "revisionism." By the mid-1960s relations had deteriorated to such an extent that the two countries had heavily fortified their common border, and communist parties around the world had split into pro-Beijing and pro-Moscow camps.

In contrast to the deterioration in Sino-Soviet relations, relations between the United States and the Soviet Union rapidly improved following the 1962 Cuban Missile Crisis. The HOT LINE between the Kremlin and the White House was established in an attempt to avoid any future showdowns, and in 1963 the long-awaited NUCLEAR TEST BAN TREATY was signed.

But by the end of 1963, Khrushchev's domestic power base was beginning to crumble. His retreat from Cuba was interpreted as a major embarrassment for the Soviet Union, and his de-Stalinization campaign had led to the Sino-Soviet Split and a weakening of the Soviet hold on Eastern Europe. At home, his economic reforms were not producing the quantity or quality of consumer goods demanded, and his much-vaunted Virgin Lands scheme was encountering difficulties. By October 1964, Khrushchev's opponents were strong enough to bring him down, and on October 15, 1964, the Soviet news agency Tass reported that his resignation had been accepted for reasons of ill health.

Khrushchev went into a quiet and obscure retirement at his country *dacha* outside Moscow. He was occasionally photographed at election time, and whenever approached by a foreign correspondent for a comment on world affairs he always replied that he was "just a pensioner." His silence was broken in November 1970 with the publication in the West of Khrushchev's memoirs. *Khrushchev Remembers*, assembled by the journalist Edward Crankshaw, caused an uproar in ruling Soviet circles, and its authenticity was at first denied. But it later became clear that the memoirs had been dictated partly by Khrushchev himself and partly by members of his family. Khrushchev was bedridden at the time of publication and on September 11, 1971, died of a heart attack.

For Further Information:
Beschloss, Michael R. *The Crisis Years: Kennedy and Khrushchev, 1960–1963.* New York, 1991.
Crankshaw, Edward. *Khrushchev: A Career.* New York, 1966.
———. *Khrushchev Remembers.* New York, 1970.
Frankland, Mark. *Khrushchev.* London, 1966.
Khrushchev, Nikita Sergeevich, tr. and ed. Jerrold L. Schecter with Vyacheslav V. Luchkov. *Memoirs.* Boston, 1990.
Linden, Carl. *Khrushchev and the Soviet Leadership, 1957–1964.* Baltimore, 1966.
Owen, Richard. *Crisis in the Kremlin.* London, 1986.
Rush, Myork. *The Rise of Khrushchev.* New York, 1958.
Slusser, Robert M. *The Berlin Crisis of 1961; Soviet-American Relations and the Struggle for Power in the Kremlin, June–November 1961.* Baltimore, 1973.
Wolfe, Bertram. *Khrushchev and Stalin's Ghost.* New York, 1957.

Kiesinger, Kurt Georg   (April 6, 1904–March 9, 1988)

Kurt Kiesinger was leader of West Germany's Christian Democratic Union (CDU) and chancellor during the Grand Coalition with the Social Democrats from 1966 to 1969. He was a strong supporter of KONRAD ADENAUER's pro-Western foreign policy but as chancellor presided over a gradual relaxation in tensions with the Soviet Bloc.

After studying law at Berlin and Tübingen universities, Kiesinger entered private law practice. He joined the Nazi Party in 1933 but became disillusioned with Nazism, and in 1938 he refused to join the National Socialist Lawyers' Guild when it was formed. At that time he considered leaving the country, but he remained and during the war monitored radio broadcasts for the foreign ministry. After the war, his political opponents attempted to use Kiesinger's connections with the Nazi Party to discredit him. But it was revealed that Kiesinger had in fact used his position to obstruct the dissemination of anti-Semitic propaganda, and he was cleared by the Allies' de-Nazification program.

he was prepared to resign if an alternative government could be formed. The SPD under WILLY BRANDT called for interparty talks, and on November 26 it was announced that the two apparently implacable political foes, the SPD and the CDU, would form a grand coalition, with Kiesinger as chancellor and Brandt as his deputy and foreign minister.

Adenauer and Erhard had established West Germany's basic links with the West—membership in the NORTH ATLANTIC TREATY ORGANIZATION and the FRANCO–GERMAN TREATY OF FRIENDSHIP and membership in the EUROPEAN ECONOMIC COMMUNITY. It was left to Kiesinger and Brandt to make the first tentative moves toward the Soviet Bloc, which later found full expression in Brandt's OSTPOLITIK.

In January 1967 diplomatic relations were established with ROMANIA, in August 1967 a trade agreement was reached with CZECHOSLOVAKIA and in January 1968 diplomatic relations were established with YUGOSLAVIA. In May 1968, Kiesinger said in an interview with *Quick* magazine, "We have begun to build our bridges in the East. The opening of relations with Romania and Yugoslavia is a beginning. We are prepared to open such relations with all our neighbors in order to create a friendlier political climate in the whole of Europe."

But the WARSAW PACT's invasion of Czechoslovakia in August 1968 ended Kiesinger's attempts to initiate his own Ostpolitik. In a speech to the Bundestag, Kiesinger attacked the invasion as a "gross violation" of human rights and was particularly disgusted by the East German participation in the invasion.

Prior to the invasion of Czechoslovakia, Kiesinger had been attempting to establish some form of relations with East Germany. He supported Erhard's policy of increasing interzonal trade, and in April 1967 sent the East German Socialist Unity (Communist) Party 16 proposals for increased cooperation. These included youth exchanges, free traffic in newspapers and other literature, increased trade, technological cooperation, the easing of travel arrangements and more frequent visits across the Berlin Wall by relatives. All the proposals were designed to relieve the lives of East Germans while at the same time allowing Bonn to remain committed to its policy of eventual reunification. The East German government, however, was determined to settle for no less than full recognition of the East German state by Bonn and the establishment of diplomatic relations between the two German states. East German leader WALTER ULBRICHT also insisted that West Berlin be incorporated in the recognized East German state and that both German states join the United Nations.

This fruitless dialogue also abruptly ended with the invasion of Czechoslovakia, and Kiesinger did not have an opportunity to resume serious negotiations before he was voted out of office in September 1969 and replaced by an SPD–FDP coalition led by Brandt. Although Kiesinger had initiated the first steps toward Ostpolitik, he felt that Brandt's headlong rush into improved relations with the Soviet Bloc was too much too soon. He was especially opposed to Brandt's con-

Kurt Georg Kiesinger, chancellor of the Federal Republic of Germany from 1966 to 1969. Photo courtesy of the German Ministry of Foreign Affairs.

Kiesinger was one of the founding members of the conservative Christian Democratic Union (CDU) led by Konrad Adenauer and quickly established himself as an expert on foreign affairs, although Adenauer initially reserved the portfolio of foreign minister for himself. Kiesinger served as chairman of the Bundestag's foreign policy subcommittee. When Adenauer in 1957 signaled that he was prepared to relinquish control of foreign policy, Kiesinger expected to be offered the post. But Adenauer wanted to retain firm control over foreign policy and therefore appointed the more pliable Heinrich von Brentano. Kiesinger reacted by resigning from the Bundestag and returning to his native Baden-Württemberg, where he became minister-president (prime minister).

Adenauer resigned in October 1963 and was succeeded by LUDWIG ERHARD. In the September 1965 elections, the CDU, in a personal victory for Erhard, secured an unexpected 245 seats against 202 for the Social Democrats (SPD), but the centrist Free Democratic Party (FDP) held the balance of power, with 49 seats. The FDP joined Erhard's government, but a combination of fears of economic recession and the rise of neo-Nazism led the FDP to abandon the coalition in October 1966.

For a few weeks Erhard attempted to soldier on with a minority government, but on November 2 he announced that

cept of two states in one German nation, an idea that Kiesinger regarded as dangerous and confusing. Kiesinger resigned as leader of the CDU in October 1971. He died on March 9, 1988.

For Further Information:

Crawley, A.M. *The Rise of West Germany, 1945–1972.* New York, 1974.

Fritsch-Bournazel, Renata. *Confronting the German Question.* Oxford and New York, 1988.

Griffiths, William. *The Ostpolitik of the Federal Republic of Germany.* Cambridge, Mass., 1978.

Pfetsch, Frank. *West Germany, Internal Structures and External Relations: The Foreign Policy of the Federal Republic.* New York, 1988.

Prittie, Terence. *The Velvet Chancellors.* New York, 1979.

Kim Il-sung   (April 15, 1912–   )   Kim Il-sung has been the leader of the North Korean Workers' (Communist) Party and the dictator of North Korea since the end of World War II. His commitment to unite the Korean Peninsula under his Communist Party led to the KOREAN WAR and the maintenance of American troops in South Korea.

Kim was born Kim Song Ju. He joined the Korean Communist party in 1931 and throughout the 1930s led the armed resistance to the Japanese occupation of Korea. It was during this period that he adopted the name Kim Il-sung, the name of an earlier anti-Japanese guerrilla fighter.

Supported by the Soviet Union, Kim became the communist ruler of North Korea after World War II. His forces invaded South Korea in June 1950, launching the Korean War. U.S.-led United Nations forces succeeded in pushing the North Koreans back to near the Chinese border within a few months.

Kim's political career would probably have ended at this stage if the Chinese communists had not been concerned that the United States, emboldened by its success, was preparing to enlist the support of Chinese Nationalist leader CHIANG KAI-SHEK to topple the year-old communist government in Beijing. They offered their support to Kim, and on October 16, 1950, an estimated 300,000 Chinese troops crossed the Yalu River and joined with the North Koreans to push the UN forces back to Pusan in the southeast before themselves being pushed back to the 38th parallel. The two sides were effectively stalemated until the armistice was signed on July 27, 1953.

The Korean War formalized the division of the Korean Peninsula into a communist state and a capitalist state, each claiming the right to incorporate the other. The support by the United States of the South, and that of the Soviet Union and China of the North prevented an invasion of each by the other and at the same time restrained both from acting precipitously.

The two Koreas also became competing showcases for their respective sponsors, each trying to outdo the other in economic performance and international recognition. South Korea fared better on both counts, winning representation in the United Nations and establishing one of the most prosperous economies in Asia. However, its human rights record earned widespread criticism.

In North Korea, Kim Il-sung established a typically Stalinist state. Only one party was allowed, the Korean Workers' Party, and its leading role was written into the constitution. Agricultural land was gradually collectivized, so that by 1959 all private holdings had been abolished. Ninety percent of industry was taken over by the state and the remainder assigned to cooperatives.

Under Kim, North Korea became perhaps the most regimented society in the world. Kim established a secret police force known as the Protection and Security Bureau, controlled directly by himself. Resident security police were established in every city, town and village and given the task of controlling all movements of people. Every North Korean was required to carry an identification card and to secure a travel permit before being allowed to travel out of his or her designated residential and working area. The de-Stalinization process in Eastern Europe had no equivalent in North Korea.

Instead of de-Stalinizing, Kim simply replaced the cult of Stalin with the cult of Kim Il-sung. Statues of Kim sprung up around the country, along with posters with his likeness and quotations from his seven-volume collected works. He was idolized as a heroic, almost divine figure, and membership in the Communist Party became contingent on subservience to him. Kim also developed a national ideology known as *Juche,* loosely translated as "self-reliance" or "independence," which adapts Marxism-Leninism to the Korean context.

Juche has several strands of thought. One is the use of Korean history and culture to supplement Maxism, and the other is the stress laid on "the independent stand of rejecting dependence on others and of using one's own brains, believing in one's own strength and displaying the revolutionary spirit of self-reliance."

The self-reliance stressed by *Juche* was partly encouraged by the SINO-SOVIET SPLIT, which was formalized in the early 1960s. Until 1964 Kim had maintained a pro-Soviet policy, but he switched to the Chinese until the Red Guards singled him out for attack during the CULTURAL REVOLUTION. After 1966, Kim adopted an evenhanded policy toward China and the Soviet Union, and from the 1970s on the Soviet Union was North Korea's major arms supplier. But in 1978, Kim won plaudits from the Chinese when he refused to condemn Vietnam's invasion of Cambodia.

In the 1980s, Kim spent considerable time preparing the succession of his son Kim Jong Il, who at first appeared to take a harder line toward South Korea than his father. In recent years there have been signs that the elder Kim was preparing to step down in favor of his son, who was the subject of a deification campaign similar to the one launched for his father 30 years previously. Kim Il-sung, however, has remained in place.

For Further Information:
Berger, Carl. *The Korea Knot: A Military-Political History.* Philadelphia, 1964.
Brends, Williams J. *The Two Koreas in East Asian Affairs.* New York, 1976.
Kim, I.J. *Communist Policies in North Korea.* New York, 1975.

Kirkpatrick, Jeane   (November 19, 1926–   ) Jeane Kirkpatrick was U.S. ambassador to the United Nations from 1981 to 1985. She took a tough anti-communist line and became particularly involved in formulating the Reagan administration's policies toward Latin America.

Kirkpatrick attended Barnard College and Columbia University. She received her master's degree in political science from Columbia in 1950 and then returned to receive a doctorate in 1968. In the interim, Kirkpatrick studied political science at the Sorbonne, married and raised three children.

She and her husband, Evron Kirkpatrick, were both strong supporters of HUBERT HUMPHREY and the liberal wing of the Democratic Party. But by the late 1960s, both Kirkpatricks were becoming dissatisfied with the Democrats and began to shift further to the right, toward what they regarded as more traditional American political values.

In the early 1970s, Jeane Kirkpatrick joined other prominent right-wing Democrats to found the Coalition for a Democratic Majority, a major "neoconservative" group. But Kirkpatrick remained a member of the Democratic Party and loyally supported JIMMY CARTER in the 1976 election. After his election, however, she became increasingly critical of Carter's policies, especially those related to human rights and foreign affairs.

In 1979 she wrote an article for the conservative magazine *Commentary* in which she praised the deposed Nicaraguan dictator Anastasio Somoza and blamed Soviet expansionism for the problems of the Third World. She also maintained that America had a duty to intervene in the Third World to protect its interests from the threat of the Soviet Union. The article was passed on to presidential candidate RONALD REAGAN by his chief foreign policy adviser, RICHARD ALLEN (later national security adviser), who invited Kirkpatrick to join his foreign policy advisory council. After his election in November 1980, Reagan appointed Kirkpatrick ambassador to the United Nations.

Kirkpatrick quickly established her credentials as one of Reagan's most conservative foreign policy advisers and was effective in presenting the administration's foreign policy in the United Nations. She supported cutting American financial support for UN organizations whose policies ran contrary to perceived U.S. national interests. These included the UN Environmental Program, the UN Food and Agricultural Organization and UNESCO. She also criticized the proposed UN Universal Declaration of Human Rights for taking on "the character of a letter to Santa Claus."

Kirkpatrick's main interest lay in Latin America, and for this region she developed what became known as the "Kirkpatrick Doctrine" to justify American support for right-wing Latin American dictatorships. The Kirkpatrick Doctrine contended that it was in Washington's interest to support anti-communist governments unwaveringly, even if those governments were repressive. The doctrine was substantially modified in 1986 when some of the countries whose right-wing governments Kirkpatrick had supported, such as Argentina, Brazil and the Philippines, enthusiastically replaced those governments with more or less democratic ones.

Kirkpatrick played a major role in developing U.S. policy toward NICARAGUA, and inside and outside of the United Nations she defended American support for the anti-Sandinista Contra rebels. In March 1982, Kirkpatrick told the Senate Foreign Relations Subcommittee on Western Hemisphere Affairs that Nicaragua probably stood in "first place as a human rights violator" and asserted that the Sandinistas had become more repressive than the regime they had replaced.

(Kirkpatrick remained an active supporter of the Contras after her resignation in 1984. In October 1987 she visited Nicaragua and was enthusiastically received by the anti-Sandinista opposition. A prominent anti-Sandinista politician in Nicaragua hailed Kirkpatrick as "the U.S. politician who has most supported the cause of the Nicaraguan people." She was the only living American politician who had a Contra unit named after her.)

In the United Nations debate that followed the U.S. decision to invade Grenada in 1983, Kirkpatrick defended the invasion on the grounds that it was necessary as a defense against the "madmen" who had assumed power in Grenada. She also claimed that the heavy Cuban presence on the island meant that foreign intervention in Grenada had already taken place. Kirkpatrick, however, was unable to prevent a resolution "deeply" deploring the invasion and describing it as a "flagrant violation of international law and of the independence, sovereignty and territorial integrity" of Grenada.

Kirkpatrick had less interest or influence on policy outside the Western Hemisphere or on direct East–West relations. When she did become involved in East–West relations it was either to defend American actions or to launch an official attack on the Soviet Union. For instance, after the Soviet Union vetoed a resolution to send a UN peacekeeping force to Beirut, Kirkpatrick accused the Soviet Union of "sowing hate, watering it with lies and harvesting violence, refusing to cooperate and attacking others precisely for refusing cooperation."

Kirkpatrick also played an important role in the Reagan administration's attack on the Soviet Union following the shooting down of Korean Air Lines flight 007 in September 1983. Kirkpatrick played to the UN Security Council the American tapes of the conversation between the Soviet pilot and his ground control and declared that they established "that the Soviets decided to shoot down a civilian airliner, shot it down and lied about it." Kirkpatrick's forceful presentation helped to secure the strongly worded UN condemnation of the Soviet action and forced the Kremlin to use its veto.

Kirkpatrick hoped to be named national security adviser in October 1983 following William Clark's move from that post to the Department of the Interior, but the job went to Rear Admiral John Poindexter. She resigned her United Nations post at the end of 1984 to return to teaching, writing and lecturing. In February 1987 she was among a group of U.S. foreign policy experts who met for three hours with Soviet leader Mikhail Gorbachev.

Kirkpatrick also remained active in political circles and in April 1985 formally left the democrats for the Republican Party. Her tough stance at the United Nations had made Kirkpatrick a favorite with Republican right-wingers, who tried unsuccessfully first to convince her to run against GEORGE BUSH for the 1988 presidential nomination and then to persuade Bush to nominate Kirkpatrick as his vice presidential running mate.

Kissinger, Henry   (May 29, 1923–   )   Henry Kissinger has had a major impact on American foreign policy since 1954, when he became study director of the Council on Foreign Relations. He reached the peak of his influence during the Nixon administration, when he served first as the president's national security adviser and then as secretary of state (for a time holding the two offices simultaneously). In these posts he played a major role in prosecuting the VIETNAM WAR, reestablishing Sino-American relations, negotiating the first STRATEGIC ARMS LIMITATION TALKS agreement and establishing some of the basic tenets of détente.

Kissinger was born in Germany to an orthodox Jewish family. In 1938 the family fled the Nazis for New York, and Kissinger entered City College there to study accountancy. From 1943 to 1946 he served in the U.S. Army as an intelligence specialist and administrator in occupied Germany. When he left the army, Kissinger went to Harvard University to study government and international relations. He received his doctorate in 1954 with a dissertation on the 19th-century Austrian statesman Metternich. This was later published as a book and is still regarded highly by many.

The following year he was appointed study director for the Council on Foreign Relations and was placed in charge of a project examining policy alternatives for dealing with the Soviet military threat. The result was his book *Nuclear Weapons and Foreign Policy*, which accepted the Eisenhower administration's view of the Soviet Union as an expansionist power bent on world domination but criticized the administration for its heavy reliance on the policy of massive retaliation. He proposed that the United States develop and maintain a "spectrum of capabilities" to counter Soviet aggression at every stage. The concept, initially attacked by the administration's defense strategists, later became accepted as the policy of FLEXIBLE RESPONSE in the Kennedy administration.

Early in his career Kissinger developed a close relationship with NELSON ROCKEFELLER, and in 1956 Rockefeller appointed him to direct a gathering of prominent Americans to consider America's likely future foreign and domestic problems. He continued as an adviser to Rockefeller during the latter's unsuccessful campaigns for the Republican Party presidential nomination in 1960, 1964 and 1968. It was Rockefeller who later introduced Kissinger to RICHARD NIXON.

Kissinger returned to Harvard from 1957 to 1962, where he held several positions, including professor of government, associate director of the Harvard Center for International Affairs, and director of the Defense Studies Program. Kissinger used this time at Harvard to establish stronger ties with leading government officials and businessmen, and he was named an adviser to the National Security Council in 1961 and consultant to the ARMS CONTROL AND DISARMAMENT AGENCY in 1962. In 1965 he was appointed a consultant to the State Department.

The latter appointment was made at the request of HENRY CABOT LODGE, then U.S. ambassador to South Vietnam. Lodge wanted Kissinger to tour Vietnam and develop new ideas on the conduct of the war. As a result of Lodge's request, Kissinger visited Vietnam in October of 1965 and July–August of 1966. He came away convinced that the United States should remain in Vietnam to prevent communist expansion and maintain American credibility elsewhere in the world.

Although Kissinger was always convinced of the rightness of the American cause in Vietnam, growing public opposition to the war persuaded him to change his tactics, and he was responsible for the 1968 Rockefeller peace plan for Vietnam. The plan called for the gradual withdrawal of American troops and the Vietnamization of the war, internationally supervised free elections, the imposition of an international peacekeeping force and negotiations for a reunified Vietnam. The plan later became the basis of his and Nixon's negotiating strategy during the long-running PARIS PEACE TALKS with North Vietnamese negotiators Xuan Thuy and Le Duc Tho.

Following the election of Richard Nixon, Kissinger was persuaded to become the President's special assistant for national security affairs. He quickly became Nixon's chief foreign affairs adviser. The two men worked well together. They both distrusted the bureaucracy of Washington and had a penchant for personal and secret diplomacy. They were both basically conservative but recognized a need to develop a working relationship with the communist powers.

Kissinger's diplomatic role model was the subject of his doctoral thesis—Count Metternich. Like the 19th-century diplomat, Kissinger sought to create a balance of power that reduced the likelihood of conflict. This pragmatic, at times amoral, view of diplomacy produced a series of startling, if temporary, successes for Kissinger; this and his assiduous courting of the press led the press to dub him "Super K." But it also alienated him from both liberal Democrats and conservative Republicans, who both maintained that American foreign policy should be based on some consistent moral principle derived from American political traditions, rather than mere "realpolitik."

But the Kissinger approach fit well with the working assumptions of the Nixon administration, and Nixon was a strong enough political figure to ward off the right wing of the Republican Party. After Nixon was forced to resign, however, his successor, GERALD FORD, who had been appointed and not elected to office, felt he needed to be more responsive to grassroots party opinion. As a result, Kissinger's influence waned during the Ford administration, although he remained secretary of state throughout. During the CARTER and REAGAN years, Kissinger was kept out of office and vilified variously as either too conservative or too liberal.

Kissinger's first priority as national security adviser was ending the Vietnam War, which he saw as damaging to the American political fabric and as the single greatest obstacle to improved Soviet–American relations. But Kissinger opposed a sudden American withdrawal on the grounds that it would undermine U.S. "credibility" elsewhere in the world. As an alternative he supported Nixon's "peace with honor" campaign promise, which involved the gradual withdrawal of American troops and the "Vietnamization" of the war effort—and, indeed, a widening of the conflict to destroy Viet Cong and North Vietnamese bases in Cambodia and Laos before U.S. troops withdrew from Indochina.

Nixon quickly placed Kissinger in charge of the Paris peace talks with North Vietnam, and Kissinger expected an early success. He offered the North Vietnamese negotiators a "two-track" formula, which he hoped would break the deadlock of the talks. This formula projected a military settlement between the United States and North Vietnam and a political settlement between the South Vietnamese government and the South Vietnamese National Liberation Front (Viet Cong). As Kissinger's proposed military settlement involved the mutual withdrawal of American and North Vietnamese troops, the North Vietnamese rejected the formula because they maintained that they had a legitimate right to be in South Vietnam.

The rejection of the two-track formula led to a new stalemate. Nixon responded by increasing the military pressure on the North Vietnamese and instructed Kissinger to start secret negotiations with North Vietnamese negotiator Le Duc Tho. The stepped-up military pressure also included secret bombing raids on Viet Cong and North Vietnamese sanctuaries in Cambodia from 1969, the invasion of Cambodia in 1970 (leading to its subsequent engulfment in a bloody civil war) and then the invasion of Laos. Kissinger gave unqualified support to all these operations and found himself disowned by his former academic colleagues and several of his aides.

The secret negotiations between Kissinger and Le Duc Tho started in August 1969. They were broken off at various times, but in the summer of 1972, the president pressured Kissinger to produce an agreement in time for the November presidential election. On October 26, Kissinger announced that "peace is at hand" and unveiled the outline of a treaty to end American involvement in Vietnam. In late 1972—after Nixon's reelection—the United States carried out an intense bombing of North Vietnamese population centers. It had little effect on negotiations and is believed to have been meant as an assurance of continued support to the South Vietnamese government. The final agreement, essentially the same as the one negotiated before the bombing, was finally signed on January 27, 1973. Kissinger and Le Duc Tho were jointly awarded the Nobel Prize for peace for their part in negotiating the Paris agreement; Le Duc Tho refused to accept his share.

The treaty ended direct American military intervention in Indochina, but the cease-fire terms were largely ignored by the NLF and the North Vietnamese. Kissinger attempted to persuade Congress to continue bombing Cambodia in order to force North Vietnam to stick to the agreed cease-fire, but by this stage the American public was too relieved to be out of the war to worry about breaches of the treaty. The Viet Cong and North Vietnamese offensive continued, and South Vietnam fell in 1975.

Although the resolution of Vietnam was Kissinger's top priority, his ultimate aim was a working relationship with the Soviet Union. Kissinger rejected the early Cold War view of the Soviet Union as the directing force of an international communist monolith, although he did feel that Soviet or Chinese influence, rather than local politics and social grievances, were responsible for most of the unrest in the Third World. He felt that the policy of isolating the Soviet Union channeled Soviet foreign policy into capricious and anarchic actions. Kissinger therefore argued that the Soviet Union should be brought more into international discussions and encouraged to act as a responsible nation-state whose best interests would be served by constructing and maintaining a balance of power with the United States. This effectively became the policy of détente. Kissinger was not the originator of this policy—its earliest proponents were Europeans anxious to defuse tensions on their continent—but he played a leading role in securing American support for the idea.

At the core of détente lay the construction of a nuclear status quo through the Strategic Arms Limitation Talks (SALT). But Kissinger insisted on linking the SALT process to Soviet actions in other parts of the world, such as pressuring the North Vietnamese to make concessions in the Paris Peace Talks, or pressuring Soviet allies in the Arab world or in Eastern Europe to defuse tensions there. This policy of "LINKAGE" was best summed up by Nixon early in his administration when he responded to Soviet calls for SALT negotiations by saying that talks should be held "in a way and at a time that will promote, if possible, progress on outstanding political problems at the same time—for example, on the problem of the Middle East and other outstanding problems in which the U.S. and the U.S.S.R., acting together, can save the cause of peace."

The SALT negotiations started in Helsinki in November 1969 without any major progress on regional political problems. But Kissinger hoped that progress on SALT would lead to greater Soviet flexibility in other areas. The chief negotiator for the American delegation was GERARD SMITH, but the policies, statements and negotiating positions were directed from

Washington by Kissinger. The talks soon reached a deadlock over the Soviet insistence on separating defensive and offensive systems. The Soviets finally agreed to link the two in May 1971. In April 1972 Kissinger flew to Moscow to lay plans for the summit in May 1972 at which Nixon and Soviet leader LEONID BREZHNEV signed the SALT I Treaty and the ANTIBALLISTIC MISSILE TREATY. The Moscow summit also resulted in a number of cultural, educational, scientific and trade agreements between the United States and the Soviet Union.

The SALT process appeared to have had the desired effect of encouraging linkage when Soviet president NIKOLAI PODGORNY flew to Hanoi a few weeks after the Moscow Summit to pressure the North Vietnamese to make concessions in the Paris Peace Talks. In October 1972 the détente process continued with the signing of a three-year U.S.–SOVIET TRADE AGREEMENT. Détente reached its peak in 1975 during the Ford administration when the United States, Canada and the 35 nations of Europe signed the HELSINKI ACCORDS (although they were criticized by American conservatives as implicitly recognizing Soviet hegemony in Eastern Europe).

The greatest diplomatic triumph of the Nixon administration was the reestablishment of Sino-American relations. The ultimate credit for this diplomatic coup belongs to Nixon. Kissinger himself was at first skeptical of the advisability of rapprochement with communist China. He viewed China as an irresponsible power and at first feared that any improvement in Sino-American relations would damage the Soviet-American détente that lay at the heart of his foreign policy. But Kissinger quickly became convinced that the "China Card" was an effective lever in negotiations with the Soviet Union and in the Paris Peace Talks on Vietnam. In 1971 he secretly flew by way of Pakistan to Beijing to establish the initial opening and then accompanied President Nixon on his historic visit to China in February 1972.

It was at first thought that Kissinger's Jewish background ruled out a role for him in the Middle East. But he used it to great effect to achieve further diplomatic successes. As a victim of Nazi Germany, he was acceptable to Israel, and he could not so easily be accused of being anti-Semitic when he took a pro-Arab position. As a result he was able to negotiate a cease-fire to the 1973 Yom Kippur War, helping pro-Western Egyptian president ANWAR SADAT to avoid a longer conflict he could not win and keeping the United States from having to intervene militarily on the Israeli side. This kept both Egypt and Israel in the American camp and enabled the United States to apply pressure to both sides, eventually contributing to the Camp David Agreement under the Carter administration.

Kissinger's Middle East diplomacy, however, was not universally applauded. One of the results of the Yom Kippur War was the Arab oil embargo and the subsequent increase in oil prices. Western Europe and Japan, whose now prospering economies were heavily dependent on Arab oil, felt that Kissinger's policies in the region threatened their economic lifeline. Western Europe, as it fully recovered from World War II, also formed the cohesive political and economic unit of the European Community, leading it to pursue economic and foreign policies more independent of the United States.

President Nixon appointed Kissinger secretary of state in May 1973. The post guaranteed that Kissinger controlled foreign policy at a time when the president was absorbed by the scandal of Watergate. Kissinger managed to stay largely aloof from Watergate, although he was forced to admit that he had authorized the FBI to tap the telephone lines of officials and newsmen suspected of being involved in policy leaks. Kissinger managed to ride out this storm by claiming that the leaks had threatened national security. The Senate Foreign Relations Committee later declined to pursue perjury charges against Kissinger.

As Watergate progressed, the effectiveness of Kissinger's diplomacy waned as fewer and fewer world leaders wanted to make agreements with what had clearly become a lame-duck administration. Kissinger at first urged Nixon to cut all ties with fellow Watergate conspirators John Ehrlichman and H.R. Haldeman, provide copies of Watergate tapes to the special prosecutor and fully cooperate with the investigation, something Nixon was unable to do. As the crisis deepened and Nixon's impeachment became a virtual certainty, Kissinger, like many others, became convinced that the president must resign to prevent a complete breakdown in government and protect national security. Nixon did resign in August 1974.

Kissinger was retained as secretary of state by President Ford. His first task under Ford was to set up the VLADIVOSTOK Summit between Ford and Brezhnev. This summit laid the groundwork for SALT II by producing a tentative agreement on ceilings for strategic delivery vehicles and MIRV (MULTIPLE INDEPENDENTLY-TARGETED REENTRY VEHICLES) missiles. The two men also made a most-favored-nation trade agreement, which encountered fierce congressional opposition and was canceled by the Soviet Union after the JACKSON AMENDMENT tied most-favored-nation status to Soviet emigration policies.

During the Ford administration, conservatives in Congress became increasingly critical of Kissinger, who was regularly accused of "selling out" to the Soviets. It was claimed that his SALT and ABM agreements had given the Soviets a nuclear advantage and that the Vladivostok Accord had set too high a limit on the number of MIRVs.

Africa became increasingly important to American security during the Ford administration. The collapse of the Portuguese Empire in Angola and Mozambique led to the establishment of anti-Western governments with Soviet support in those countries and placed increasing pressure on the white supremacist regimes in Rhodesia and South Africa. Kissinger at first toyed with idea of direct support for the Rhodesian and South African governments but realized that this implied support for their racist policies and would damage American credibility throughout the Third World. Kissinger, working closely with the British, therefore tried a variation of his "shuttle diplomacy" in an attempt to negotiate the formation of a coalition government in Rhodesia that would include less militant black leaders. The interim government plans were eventually accepted by Rhodesian prime minister Ian Smith, but the interim government was roundly condemned by black Africa, and Kissinger sought to offset this damage by publicly attacking South Africa's apartheid policy and presence in Namibia. He also increased American aid to black Africa.

Out of office after the election of Jimmy Carter in 1976, Kissinger at first concentrated on writing his memoirs and acting the elder statesman. He supported the SALT II agreement, which was signed in 1979 but later rejected by Congress. He advised Ronald Reagan during his 1980 campaign, but Reagan's strong dependence on right-wing Republicans led Kissinger to keep a low profile, and later kept him out of the Reagan administration. In 1981 he was named international affairs adviser to Chase Manhattan Bank. He later formed his own Washington-based foreign policy consulting firm, Kissinger Associates, Inc., which offered its services to corporate clients. In 1983 Kissinger was named director of Reagan's Central American Policy Committee and toured Central America on behalf of the administration.

In January 1987 Kissinger was named to a defense strategy panel formed by Defense Secretary CASPAR WEINBERGER to develop long-term guidelines for defense technology. Later that year, he traveled to Moscow to meet with Soviet leader MIKHAIL GORBACHEV. In April 1987 he joined former president Nixon in criticizing Reagan for failing to link the agreement to remove medium-range missiles in Europe to an elimination of the Warsaw Pact advantage in conventional forces.

Kissinger was asked by GEORGE BUSH to act as cochairman of his National Security Task Force, which advised him on foreign policy issues during the 1988 presidential election. In 1989 the Bush administration came under heavy pressure to make a positive response to Gorbachev's repeated diplomatic initiatives. Kissinger proposed that the United States agree publicly to recognize Soviet interests in Eastern Europe but to link this recognition to improved human rights in the Soviet Union and Eastern Europe. The proposal was largely dismissed, but Kissinger's influence on the administration was regarded as having increased with the appointment of one of his aides, Lawrence Eagleburger, as deputy secretary of state. Eagleburger later became acting secretary of state in the last months of the Bush administration.

For Further Information:

Cleva, Gregory D. *Henry Kissinger and the American Approach to Foreign Policy.* Cranbury, N.J., 1989.

Hersh, Seymour M. *The Price of Power: Kissinger in the Nixon White House.* New York, 1983.

Isaacson, Walter. *Kissinger: A Biography.* New York, 1992.

Kalb, Marvin, and Bernard Kalb. *Kissinger.* Boston, 1974.

Kissinger, Henry. *The White House Years.* New York, 1979.

———. *Years of Upheaval.* New York, 1982.

Mazlish, Bruce. *Kissinger: The European Mind in American Policy.* New York, 1976.

Morris, Roger. *Uncertain Greatness: Henry Kissinger and American Foreign Policy.* New York, 1977.

Shawcross, William. *Sideshow: Kissinger, Nixon, and the Destruction of Cambodia.* London, 1986.

Sobel, Lester A., ed. *Kissinger & Detente.* New York, 1975.

Szulc, Tad. *The Illusion of Peace: Foreign Policy in the Nixon Years.* New York, 1978.

Thornton, Richard C. *The Nixon-Kissinger Years: Reshaping America's Foreign Policy.* New York, 1989.

Kitchen Debate   In July 1959 U.S. vice president RICHARD NIXON visited Moscow to open an exhibition of American goods. On July 24 Nixon and Soviet premier NIKITA KHRUSHCHEV engaged in a heated public debate over the respective merits of capitalism and communism. Part of the discussion took place in a model kitchen and thus became known as the "kitchen debate."

Khrushchev consistently laid a special emphasis on the ideological aspect of the Cold War conflict and usually enjoyed turning to it in any international meeting. He was determined to stress it during Nixon's visit, because the visit coincided with the American observance of "Captive Nations Week," drawing public attention to the status of Eastern Europe.

The Soviet leader, in a speech only 20 minutes before Nixon's arrival, attacked Captive Nations Week as a rude and unacceptable interference in Soviet internal affairs. He argued that the "only enslaved peoples are in capitalist countries" and challenged Nixon to meet and hear the ideas of "the real people here."

These remarks set the tone for the next day's meeting between the two men, part of which took place in Khrushchev's office and part at a preview of the American exhibition at Sokolniki Park. The latter part of the discussion was unusual because it was extemporaneous and occurred in front of American and Soviet television cameras. The debate ranged widely over the relative merits of communist and capitalist economies, the nature of the competition between the United States and the Soviet Union, and how the cause of peace might best be served. Comparisons were made between American color television sets and Soviet rockets. The discussion was inconclusive, although in the West Nixon is generally thought to have had the better of it. The widely publicized incident was a political asset for Nixon in his 1960 presidential campaign.

Kohl, Helmut   (April 3, 1930–   )   Helmut Kohl became chancellor of the Federal Republic of Germany in 1982. In this position he had the difficult task of steering a course between the security demands of NATO allies and the growing public demand for improved East–West relations. After the collapse of the Communist Party in East Germany in 1989, he led the successful diplomatic drive that culminated with the reunification of Germany in October 1990. Two months later he was reelected and became the first chancellor of a united Germany since World War II.

On December 2, 1990, Helmut Kohl, chancellor of the Federal Republic of Germany, became the first chancellor of the reunited Germany. Photo courtesy of the German Ministry of Foreign Affairs.

Kohl became an active member of the conservative Christian Democratic Union (CDU) in his teenage years. While at university in Frankfurt and Heidelberg, Kohl was elected to the ruling executive of his local CDU branch in Rhineland-Palatinate and was elected deputy chairman of the local young members' section.

Kohl received his law doctorate in 1958 and the following year was elected to the parliament of Rhineland-Palatinate. He built up a powerful base of support in the Palatinate which resulted in his being named to the CDU national executive in 1964; in 1969 he was elected prime minister of Rhineland-Palatinate.

In 1973 he was regarded as a possible future chancellor when he became chairman of the CDU national executive. In 1976 he was elected a member of the Bundestag (the West German lower house) and became parliamentary leader of the CDU. He became chancellor in October 1982, after the Free Democratic Party (FDP) left the Social Democratic Party–led coalition of HELMUT SCHMIDT to support Kohl and the CDU.

Kohl's first foreign trip as chancellor was to Paris to see French president FRANCOIS MITTERRAND. Both leaders regarded the 1963 FRANCO-GERMAN TREATY OF FRIENDSHIP as a cornerstone of their foreign policies, and Kohl immediately set out to increase Franco-German defense cooperation in order to offset West Germany's heavy dependence on the United States. This policy bore fruit on January 22, 1988, when Kohl and Mitterrand marked the 25th anniversary of the friendship treaty by establishing a joint defense council, which involved the stationing of a 4,000-strong joint defense brigade on West German soil.

Shortly after his trip to France, Kohl traveled to Washington for his first meeting with President RONALD REAGAN. In the latter stages of the Schmidt government, German-American relations were at times strained over the question of whether West Germany would allow the deployment of medium-range nuclear missiles on its soil if U.S.–Soviet arms talks failed to achieve an agreement. Kohl said that he wanted to "rescue the German-American relationship from the twilight and strengthen and stabilize this relationship." He strongly supported the NATO decision to deploy American medium-range nuclear missiles in Western Europe, arguing, "Only if the Soviet Union knows that it must definitely reckon with the stationing of American systems in Europe . . . can one count on their readiness to contribute to the negotiation results."

From the start of his chancellorship, Kohl had come under heavy attack for achieving power through parliamentary restructuring rather than through the ballot box. In January 1984 he succumbed to the increasing demands for a general election, and his coalition of the CDU, FDP and Christian Social Union (CSU) was returned to power. A major issue in the election was the deployment of medium-range missiles, and Kohl's victory was a fillip for American negotiators at the U.S.–Soviet INTERMEDIATE-RANGE NUCLEAR FORCES (INF) talks in Geneva.

Generally speaking, Kohl in the first five years of his government was supportive of President Reagan's hard-line anti-Soviet stand and tough negotiating position at nuclear arms talks. However, he opposed attempts by Reagan to breach the unratified SALT II accords. Kohl personally supported President Reagan's "Star Wars" initiative but faced opposition from his FDP coalition partners, who feared that SDI would lead to an escalation in the East-West arms race. The two parties eventually constructed a compromise in December 1985 that reiterated the government's political support for SDI but rejected formal German participation or public funding of research on a space-based antimissile system.

West Germany's position at the front line of the Western Alliance meant that security issues were a priority political issue after 1949. The West Germans were consistently concerned that the United States identify its security interests with theirs so that in case of a Soviet attack they would be guaranteed American support right up to the level of strategic nuclear weapons. At the same time, they balanced this desire for linkage to the frightening realization that Germany would be the main battleground of any East-West conflict. Therefore any diplomatic initiatives that reduced East-West tensions were favored, especially if they reduced the possibility of Germany's becoming a nuclear battlefield.

The positions of German politicians have varied widely, from total support for the nuclear deterrent and American weapons on German soil to total opposition. Kohl started off as a strong advocate for basing intermediate-range American missiles on German soil, so much so that after President Reagan and Soviet leader MIKHAIL GORBACHEV discussed the joint elimination of Soviet and American intermediate range missiles at the 1986 Reykjavik Summit, Kohl flew to Washington to urge Reagan to back away from what was called the "double-zero option." He only reluctantly accepted the policy when it was enshrined in the 1987 INF Treaty.

The public positions taken by Kohl were often at odds with the advice he gave to Western Alliance leaders in private, particularly after the January 1987 general election. He returned to office as chancellor, but the CDU saw its backing fall to the lowest level since the establishment of the Federal Republic in 1949. The drop in the size of the CDU vote was generally blamed on Kohl's own lackluster performance. His position within the government was further undermined by a 2.1% increase in the size of the vote for the FDP, his more liberal coalition partners. This strengthened the voice of the long-serving FDP foreign minister, HANS-DIETRICH GENSCHER, who approved in principle of nuclear weapons reductions and, in particular, felt that the West should be seen to be making concessions in nuclear negotiations in order to strengthen the *glasnost* policies of Gorbachev.

Kohl disagreed with many of Genscher's basic principles, but the two men were in agreement in their opposition to British and American demands to modernize the alliance's short-range nuclear weapons based in West Germany. British prime minister MARGARET THATCHER and presidents Reagan and GEORGE BUSH argued that such modernization was necessary after the withdrawal of intermediate-range forces. Kohl, however, countered that the emphasis on short-range nuclear weapons increased the likelihood of a war being fought on German soil and decreased the threat to the rest of Western Europe and therefore the likelihood of Germany's allies coming to its aid. Kohl argued even more forcefully in private that modernization of the weapons would erode the CDU's support at the polls.

Kohl, with some pressure from Genscher, therefore opposed the modernization program and demanded that the West start talks on the reduction of short-range nuclear systems. The issue, which threatened to split NATO on the eve of a heads-of-government summit to celebrate the alliance's 40th anniversary, was resolved at the last moment by a Bush compromise that linked negotiations on short-range nuclear systems to the progress of East–West negotiations to reduce conventional weapons. As part of the same package, Bush unilaterally reduced U.S. conventional forces in Europe.

Kohl's hard line on INF issues and his basic anti-Soviet positions made him an unpopular figure in Moscow, and he was never able to form the close relationship with Gorbachev that was enjoyed by other Western leaders. It took Gorbachev four years to arrange a visit to West Germany. German–Soviet relations were not helped by an interview Kohl gave *Newsweek* magazine in which he compared the public relations efforts of Gorbachev to those of Nazi propaganda chief Josef Goebbels. Kohl tried unsuccessfully to disown the comment.

Kohl's position also allowed for little real progress in relations between East and West Germany during his first seven years as chancellor. The SPD government in 1981 arranged for East German leader ERICH HONECKER to make a historic visit to West Germany in 1982. But after Kohl became chancellor, Honecker repeatedly put off the trip. He finally visited West Germany in September 1987 after Kohl accepted the principle of the double-zero option. But the talks produced only modest results, although the symbolism of the trip was widely regarded as setting the stage for a further improvement in inter-German relations.

Previous German governments had launched diplomatic initiatives either to strengthen the Western Alliance, as KONRAD ADENAUER had, or to extend peace feelers to Eastern Europe as had WILLY BRANDT and, to a lesser extent, Helmut Schmidt. Kohl avoided major initiatives. He was first and foremost an administrator who steered a difficult compromise course between West German commitments to the Western Alliance and a growing public desire to end the Cold War.

This situation abruptly changed with the collapse of the Socialist Unity (Communist) Party in East Germany at the end of 1989. The end of communist rule in East Germany led quickly to demands in both German states for reunification, and talks first for economic and then for political union started in 1990 after the Christian Democratic Union was elected to power in East Germany.

The last external obstacle was removed in July, when Kohl got Gorbachev to agree that a united, sovereign Germany could remain in NATO. The two-plus-four treaty was signed in Moscow in September, and "Unity Day" was celebrated on Oct. 3, 1990. Bolstered by his success, Kohl and the CDU won the December all-German elections, and threw the government into the work of integrating the country, a project that has proven more difficult and more costly than most Germans had anticipated. The Kohl government struggled to contain rising costs and growing unemployment, especially in the east, and concurrent social unrest from increasingly violent right-wing nationalist and neo-Nazi groups. Kohl himself has had to contend with accusations that he has been reluctant to enforce the law vigorously against extremists on the political right.

For Further Information

Pfetsch, Frank. *West Germany, Internal Structures and External Relations: The Foreign Policy of the Federal Republic.* New York, 1988.

KOR (Social Self-Defense Committee)   The KOR was the leading dissident organization in Poland before the creation of SOLIDARITY. It advised workers on the organization of the independent trade union, and its two leading members, Jacek Kuron and Adam Michnik, became prominent Solidarity activists.

The KOR was founded in September 1976 to help workers dismissed and imprisoned after the food riots and strikes in that year. Initially known as the Workers' Defense Committee, the group at first concentrated on providing legal advice and channeling funds to the workers' destitute families.

In September 1977, the name was changed to the KOR, or Social Self-Defense Committee, and the aims were redefined to embrace the collection and dissemination of information about the suppression of human rights in Poland. In a statement signed by 23 members, the group said it had changed its name because many of the original objectives had been reached.

The KOR launched an underground monthly newspaper titled *Glos* ("The Voice"), which became the main vehicle for the views of its two leading members, Michnik and Kuron. Writing in *Glos*, Michnik explained that KOR was not an opposition party in the traditional sense because it did not seek political power, but rather it acted as a pressure group to seek an improvement in human rights. In August 1978 KOR entered into a cooperative agreement with the Czechoslovak human rights group CHARTER 77.

In July 1980 Kuron started advising striking workers at the Lenin Shipyard in Gdansk on how to conduct wage negotiations and organize themselves. The strikers soon formed the independent trade union Solidarity, and Kuron became both a key adviser on legal matters and the chief liaison between Solidarity and the foreign press. He and 23 other members of KOR were arrested in August 1980 but were released shortly afterward.

The KOR continued to work closely with the Solidarity leadership and was responsible for the drafting of many of the union's political statements. On September 28, 1981, at the end of the second part of the first congress of Solidarity, KOR member Professor Edward Lipinski announced that the KOR considered its work completed and was disbanding itself, the struggle having been taken over by "the strong arm of Solidarity."

Kuron and Michnik continued to work closely with Solidarity and were regarded as Poland's most prominent dissidents. They were detained after the declaration of martial law in December 1981 and charged with treason. Kuron and Michnaik were released in August 1984 but were arrested again in February 1985 and in June were tried and convicted on charges of fomenting unrest and conducting illegal union activities. The month-long trial was closed to foreign journalists, and the conviction and three-year sentence raised an outcry from Solidarity activists and from supporters abroad. Solidarity leader LECH WALESA was the chief defense witness at the trial.

The men were freed in an amnesty the following year but continued to be harassed by the Polish secret police. It was not until 1989 that the authorities began to ease the pressure on them, and they were able to join the Solidarity team in roundtable negotiations with the government. Both men won parliamentary seats in elections in June 1989, and Kuron became the minister of labor in the new government.

For Further Information:

Ascherson, Neal. *The Polish August*. New York, 1982.

———. *The Struggles for Poland*. New York, 1988.

Brumberg, Abraham, ed. *Poland: Genesis of a Revolution*. New York, 1983.

Davies, Norman. *Heart of Europe: A Short History of Poland*. Oxford, 1984.

Persky, Stan. *At the Lenin Shipyard: Poland and the Rise of the Solidarity Trade Union*. Vancouver, 1981.

Sharman, T. *The Rise of Solidarity*. Vero Beach, Fla., 1987.

Korean Airlines (KAL 007) Incident   The shooting down of Korean Airlines flight 007 by the Soviet Union in September 1983 severely strained U.S.–Soviet relations.

KAL flight 007, a Boeing 747, was shot down on September 1, 1983, after overflying strategically sensitive Soviet territory. All 240 passengers and 29 crew were killed. The flight was enroute from New York to Seoul via Anchorage, Alaska.

It was the second time Soviet fighter planes had fired on commercial airliners that had strayed over Russian territory. In 1978 they had fired at another South Korean plane, and two passengers had been killed when it was forced to land on a frozen lake near Murmansk.

Flight 007 clearly strayed off its scheduled route and into Soviet airspace, and it was overflying sensitive Soviet military installations on the Kamchatka Peninsula when it was picked up by Soviet radar. The plane then headed straight toward Sakhalin Island, where other Soviet strategic bases were located. Two Soviet jet fighters were sent up to establish the identity of the plane and, if necessary, shoot it down.

At 3:12 A.M. the pilot of a SU-15 supersonic jet reported visual contact with the South Korean plane. In radio transmissions intercepted and taped by U.S. intelligence, he identified the plane only as "the target." The Soviet plane locked its radar on the target and performed a maneuver used by military aircraft to demand that a plane identify itself as "friend or foe." He received no response. At 3:26 A.M. the Soviet pilot fired his heat-seeking missiles and reported, "I have executed the launch. The target is destroyed." KAL 007 crashed into the Sea of Japan.

The Soviet Union on September 1 issued a statement claiming that a plane flying without navigational lights had violated Soviet airspace and resisted efforts by Soviet planes to guide it. The same day, U.S. secretary of state GEORGE SHULTZ accused the Soviet Union of knowingly shooting down an unarmed civilian airliner and revealed that the United States had recorded the conversation between the Soviet pilot and his ground command. President RONALD REAGAN condemned the jet's destruction as a "horrifying act of violence" and demanded an explanation from Soviet officials.

The president's rhetoric became more inflammatory as it became clear that the Soviet Union was not prepared to apologize for the incident. He referred to the downing of KAL 007 as the "Korean Airline Massacre" and said the issue had pitted "the Soviet Union against the world and the moral precepts which guide human relations among people everywhere."

It took the Soviet Union five days to acknowledge that it had shot down a commercial airliner. Officials insisted, however, that Soviet pilots had not known that the plane was a civilian aircraft and claimed that the Soviet pilot had fired tracer shells in warning "as envisaged by international rules." Shultz and Soviet foreign minister ANDREI GROMYKO met on September 7, at a previously scheduled international meeting in Madrid. Gromyko again defended Soviet actions, stating, "The borders of the Soviet Union are sacred."

At a Moscow press conference on September 9, Marshal Nikolai Ogarkov, chief of the Soviet General Staff, claimed that the "intrusion of the plane of the South Korean airlines into Soviet airspace was a deliberate, thoroughly planned intelligence operation . . . directed from centers in the territory of the United States and Japan."

A resolution condemning the Soviet action was brought before the United Nations Security Council on September 12; it was vetoed by the Soviet Union. President Reagan ordered Aeroflot, the Soviet airline, to close its offices in the United States, and a number of countries curtailed civil aviation links with the Soviet Union. Reagan also suspended negotiations on opening a U.S. consulate in Kiev and allowed negotiations for a new U.S.–Soviet transportation agreement and cultural and scientific exchanges to lapse.

There is strong evidence to suggest that the Soviet action was a case of mistaken identity, which politics would not allow the Soviet leadership to admit at the time. A number of U.S. defense intelligence analysts believe that Soviet radar and the Soviet pilot mistook the South Korean plane for an American RC-135 reconnaissance plane that had been flying an elliptical pattern near the Kamtchatka Peninsula at the same time.

The two planes flew very close to one another for about 10 minutes and may have appeared as one blip on Soviet radar screens. The RC-135 returned to base on a nearby Aleutian Island, and the KAL 007 continued on toward Sakhalin Island. Another indication that the incident was the result of a Soviet error was that a few weeks afterward there was a major shake-up in the Soviet Far Eastern Air Command, and the officers responsible for air defense were demoted. However, there has never been any good explanation for why the KAL flight was 150 miles off course, especially given the plane's advanced navigational instruments, other than that the instruments may have been damaged or set incorrectly when the plane was refueled in Anchorage.

For Further Information:

Dallin, Alexander. *Black Box. KAL 007 and the Super Powers.* Berkeley, Calif., 1985.
Johnson, R.W. *Shootdown: The Verdict on KAL 007.* New York, 1987.

Korean War   The Korean War was the first armed conflict of the Cold War. It was a victory for U.S. president HARRY TRUMAN's containment policy but left the United States with long-term military and political commitments in the Far East. The conduct of the war also started a major debate on the nature of communist expansion and the methods to be used in combating it.

Korea had for a long time been a political football among Czarist Russia, China and Japan. In 1910 the country was annexed by Japan and in the following years heavily exploited by the imperial government for its mineral and agricultural wealth. Korean culture was repressed and the Japanese police ruthlessly stamped out all political opposition. In the early 1930s, at the start of the Japanese invasion of China, the Japanese government conscripted Korean workers to work in Japanese factories in Manchuria and on the Japanese home islands. By the end of World War II, 4 million Koreans had been pressed into forced labor.

In these circumstances it was not surprising that anti-Japanese guerrilla activity developed even before the start of World War II. Much of this activity was organized by the Korean Communist Party or left-wing organizations sympathetic to its aims. This provided the communists with a well-established political base at the end of the war.

During the war, the Allied Powers, which included the Nationalist government of China, agreed to an "independent" postwar Korea and signed a pledge to that effect at the Cairo Conference in December 1943. The exact nature and political structure of the independent Korea was left unclear. Korea's future was further clouded by President FRANKLIN D. ROOSEVELT's desire to bring the Soviet Union into the war against Japan in order to open an Asian front to relieve the pressure on American troops island-hopping across the Pacific in preparation for an attack on the Japanese home islands.

At the YALTA CONFERENCE, Soviet leader JOSEF STALIN agreed to enter the war against Japan within three months of the end of the war in Europe. In return, Roosevelt agreed to Soviet control of the Kurile and Sakhalin islands, Dairen and Port Arthur on the Chinese coast, Chinese recognition of the Mongolian People's Republic and Soviet control of the Chinese Eastern and South Manchurian Railways. Roosevelt also proposed a four-power trusteeship of Korea that would involve China, the Soviet Union, Britain and the United States, but no agreement was reached at Yalta on this proposal.

At the POTSDAM CONFERENCE, American military leaders pressed the Soviet Union to enter the northern part of Korea, and it was informally agreed that the Soviets would occupy the country north of the 38th parallel and the Americans would be responsible for the territory south of the 38th parallel. At an agreed time, the Allied armies would withdraw and Korea would elect a government for the entire peninsula. On August 8, 1945, the Soviet Union declared war on Japan, and the following day Russian marines were landed at the Korean naval base of Rashin and the nearby port of Yuki. American troops did not land in Korea until September 8, 1945. The Soviets stuck to the agreement to remain north of the 38th parallel, but by the time of the American landing they had effectively sealed off their half of the country and were well on the way to installing a communist government under KIM IL-SUNG.

But communist influence was not restricted to the northern half of the peninsula. In the last year of the war, a Committee for the Preparation of Korean Independence (CPKI) was formed to oppose Japanese rule. Once again, the Communist Party dominated. In addition to the CPKI, hundreds of Red Peasant Unions sprang up all over the country. These organizations favored the redistribution of land and other socialist policies and in the confusion of victory started to implement the policies in South Korea as well as North Korea.

This did not fit in with the plans of General DOUGLAS MACARTHUR, at that time the commander of the Allied occupation forces in Japan and Korea, to incorporate Korea into the Western Bloc. He moved to disband the CPKI and left-wing trade unions and cancel their social and economic reform programs. To head the new government in South Korea, the Americans chose SYNGMAN RHEE, who had headed an American-based Korean government-in-exile before and during the war. Rhee had close contacts with extreme right-wing groups in China and employed similarly ruthless tactics to enforce similar policies.

But the left wing in South Korea was too well entrenched to be easily eliminated, and it now had the added advantage of a communist government in North Korea, which extended moral, political and military aid. The result was that by 1947 a guerrilla war had developed in South Korea. It was estimated that between the end of World War II and the start of the Korean War in June 1950, some 100,000 people died in fighting in South Korea.

In theory, the Soviet Union and the United States were both committed to a unified Korea. But each had fixed ideas of its political complexion, and neither side was prepared to make concessions. In negotiations in 1946 and 1947, the United States pressed for national elections on both sides of the 38th parallel and won the United Nations' support for the proposal. The Soviet Union refused to cooperate. Therefore, elections were held only in South Korea on May 10, 1948. The campaign and polling were marked by intimidation and violence. Syngman Rhee was confirmed in power and shortly afterward announced the formation of the Republic of Korea. On December 12, 1948, the UN General Assembly declared that the Republic of Korea was the only legitimate government of Korea; on October 12, the Soviet Union had recognized the People's Democratic Republic of Korea (North Korea) as the only lawful government of Korea. Both Syngman Rhee and Kim Il-sung were strong-willed nationalists who insisted on reunifying Korea on their own terms. Each government, therefore, represented a threat to the other.

The threat was reinforced by the actions of the United States and the Soviet Union, whose governments proceeded to provide military support to their respective client states. But neither country wanted to maintain expensive garrisons in Korea. During the course of reunification negotiations, both of the superpowers agreed to withdraw their forces. The Soviet Union was the first to start withdrawal, on October 19, 1948. Continuing unrest in South Korea delayed the withdrawal of American forces until June 29, 1949.

During the last two years of the American occupation of South Korea, relations between Washington and Seoul deteriorated as reports of Syngman Rhee's political repression multiplied. These reports played a major role in Congress' decision to refuse President Truman's request for a $150 million aid package for South Korea. It was also a factor, along with other limitations on defense resources, in Secretary of State DEAN ACHESON's decision to exclude South Korea from the American defense perimeter in the Far East. This policy was outlined in a speech to the National Press Club in Washington on January 12, 1950, when Acheson defined the defense perimeter as running "along the Aleutians to Japan and then to the Ryukus [and] from the Ryukus to the Philippine Islands." Acheson went on to add, "So far as the military security of other areas in the Pacific is concerned, it must be clear that no person can guarantee these areas against military attack. But it must also be clear that such a guarantee is hardly sensible or necessary within the realm of practical relationships."

Washington's ambivalent attitude toward South Korea and the growing domestic and international unpopularity of Syngman Rhee's government combined with the nationalist aspirations of Kim Il-sung and the international aspirations of Josef Stalin to spark the Soviet-supported invasion of South Korea by North Korean troops on June 25, 1950.

The United States moved quickly to secure United Nations condemnation of the North Korean attack. It was aided in this aim by the absence of the Soviet ambassador to the United Nations, Jakob Malik, who was boycotting UN proceedings in protest against the refusal to allow the new Chinese communist government to take China's seat. Before Malik could return from Moscow, the Security Council had voted 9 to 0 for an immediate cease-fire and the withdrawal of all forces to the 38th parallel.

At the same time, Truman ordered General MacArthur, the Supreme Allied Commander in the Pacific, to evacuate American citizens from South Korea and to provide naval and air support for South Korea, south of the 38th parallel. The president also dispatched the U.S. Seventh Fleet to the Taiwan Straits to act as a buffer between the communist government on the Chinese mainland and the Nationalist government of CHIANG KAI-SHEK on Taiwan.

In the meantime, South Korean troops were being routed by the North Korean attack spearheaded by Russian-made tanks and supported by Soviet aircraft. The United Nations, which had recognized the South Korean government as the only legitimate Korean government, faced its first test of credibility. On June 28, 1950, at American prodding, it responded by laying the foundations for the UN military command in Korea by recommending "that the members of the United Nations furnish such assistance to the Republic of Korea as may be necessary to repel the armed attack and to restore international peace and security in the area." On July 1 an American regiment arrived in South Korea, and on July 7, 1950, a British-sponsored resolution creating a UN command was passed by the General Assembly. It was agreed that the U.S. government would appoint the commander. President Truman immediately appointed General MacArthur.

The Soviet Union responded by accusing the United States of "direct acts of aggression" in Korea. Deputy Foreign Minister ANDREI GROMYKO said the United States had "violated the peace," presented the United Nations with its intervention as an accomplished fact and used "crude pressure" to turn the

Security Council into a branch of the U.S. State Department. He attacked the Security Council resolution on Korea as illegal, as both the Soviet Union and mainland China had been absent from the debate. He asked the council to demand the withdrawal of U.S. forces from Korea and said that the Soviet government would continue its policy of "nonintervention in the affairs of other states." Acheson responded to the Soviet statement by saying that "any contention that hostilities were started by [South Korea] is clearly in the category of the Nazi claims of 1939 that Poland started hostilities by attacking Germany."

The bulk of the UN forces in Korea were from the United States, and they bore the brunt of the initial fighting. But in the course of the war there also were ground units from Australia, Britain, the Philippines, Thailand, Turkey, Belgium, Colombia, Canada, Ethiopia, France, Greece, New Zealand, Norway and the Netherlands. Including monetary and supply contributions, 42 countries offered their aid to the UN forces.

One of the most controversial offers came from Chiang's government on Taiwan. Early in the conflict, he offered 33,000 "seasoned" troops for action in Korea. The offer was refused for several reasons: the troops were needed for the defense of Taiwan; they would have required the diversion of American naval and air services to transport them; and their use would have risked the possibility of widening the conflict by threatening retaliation by the Chinese communists.

The North Korean troops, in the meantime, continued to press forward. Their goal was the strategic South Korean port of Pusan, which was being used as the main debarkation point for foreign reinforcements and supplies. MacArthur's first action was to secure a defensive perimeter around the Pusan region in order to maintain a secure supply line. Truman, at the same time, asked for and received from Congress a $10 billion war program and proceeded to pour American troops into the Far East.

The capital of South Korea, Seoul, fell in the first week of fighting, and by the end of July, North Korean troops had overrun the southwestern corner of Korea and moved to within 50 miles of Pusan, in the southeast, before a defensive perimeter could be established. The North Koreans' rapid push south had left them with badly overextended and ex-

U.S. Marines moving forward against a North Korean position. By the end of 1950, the United Nations army fighting in Korea included troops from England, Turkey, Australia, the Philippines, the United States and South Korea.

posed supply lines. MacArthur devised a bold strategy to exploit this weakness by landing an attack force behind the North Korean lines, severing the supply lines and squeezing the enemy in a north–south pincer movement as the UN forces broke out of the Pusan perimeter.

On September 15, MacArthur made his move when an invasion fleet of 261 American and British vessels landed 40,000 American and South Korean troops at INCHON, 22 miles west of Seoul and 40 miles south of the 38th parallel. The North Koreans were caught by surprise. They had only 4,000 troops at Inchon, and they were able to put up only a light resistance. At the same time, North Koreans facing Pusan retreated before a strong counterattack. By September 26, Seoul had been liberated by the UN forces, and the North Koreans were fleeing back across the 38th parallel.

In the face of this success, the British government started to lobby the delegates for approval to invade North Korea in order to bring the whole Korean Peninsula under a government acceptable to the United Nations. The policy was adopted by the United States.

At the subsequent UN debate, Soviet foreign minister Andrei Vishynsky claimed the shelter of the 38th parallel for the North Korean forces. He also called for the withdrawal of all UN forces from Korea so that "all-Korean elections [could] be held to establish a unified, independent government." But the UN was flush with its victory at Inchon and distrustful of Soviet assurances. Vishynsky's proposal and a compromise resolution proposed by India were rejected. On October 4, the General Assembly's Political and Security Committee—in which the Soviets could not use their veto—passed a resolution "that all appropriate steps be taken to insure conditions of stability throughout Korea," so that a "unified, independent and democratic government" could eventually be established.

South Korean forces, which were not formally under the command of MacArthur, crossed the 38th parallel on October 1. Within five days, they had moved 50 miles. On October 7, MacArthur ordered American, British and Australian forces across the 38th parallel. The North Korean capital of Pyongyang was captured on October 19, 1950. South Korean forces reached the border with China on October 26, and North Koreans fled across the Yalu River into China.

MacArthur, at a meeting with Truman, assured the president that the fighting would cease by the end of November. He thought it unlikely that the Chinese would intervene, and he was confident that if they did, they could be easily defeated because they and the Soviets lacked proper air support.

The Chinese communists, however, had become convinced that their own political survival was at stake. They had come to power only a year before and still had to consolidate their political base. North Korea provided a buffer between American forces and the Chinese industrial heartland in Manchuria. They were also aware that a number of prominent American politicians advocated using Korea as a springboard into China and that MacArthur was in favor of using the Seventh Fleet to return Chiang's forces to the Chinese main-

land and open a second front against communist forces in Asia. The day after UN forces crossed the 38th parallel, Chinese foreign minister CHOU EN-LAI sent for the Indian ambassador to tell him that if the U.S. troops invaded North Korea, China would enter the war. On October 16, 1950, an estimated 300,000 Chinese troops started crossing the Yalu.

MacArthur, on November 6, ordered B-29 bombers to attack and destroy the bridges across the Yalu. Truman immediately ordered MacArthur to postpone the attack. The president was determined to limit the fighting to Korea and was concerned that an attack on the Yalu bridges would widen the conflict. He was also concerned that such an attack would be a violation of an agreement with Britain, America's principal ally in Korea, not to attack any targets on the Chinese side of the Yalu, and finally that it would divide the United Nations, upon which Truman was politically dependent for a mandate to remain in Korea.

The United Nations invited a Chinese communist delegation to UN headquarters, then at Lake Success, New York, to explain Chinese policy and to be persuaded that the United Nations did not intend an attack on China. Truman, at the same time, issued a statement in which he stressed, "We have never at any time entertained any intention to carry hostilities into China." The Chinese, however, accused the United States of intervening in the CHINESE CIVIL WAR, encircling China and preparing for World War III.

On November 24, MacArthur launched what he intended to be the final offensive in the Korean War. The first day, UN forces advanced 10 miles. On the second day, the Chinese counterattacked and broke through the UN lines. By the fourth day, the UN troops were in full retreat. Truman held a press conference at which he once again stressed that "neither the United Nations nor the United States has any aggressive intentions towards China." He went on to indicate that the United States would, if necessary, use the atomic bomb.

America's allies, particularly Britain, were now seriously worried about several possibilities:

1. Conservative pressures within the United States could lead to an American attack on China, either across the Yalu into Manchuria or through support for Chiang's troops across the Formosa Straits.
2. Such action would result in direct intervention by the Soviet Union, which had recently signed a Treaty of Mutual Assistance with China.
3. A widening and continuing conflict in Asia would require increasing defense resources that would result in leaving Western Europe dangerously exposed at a time of mounting East–West tensions.
4. Truman would use the atomic bomb and the Soviet Union would retaliate with a nuclear attack on Europe.

On December 4, 1950, British prime minister CLEMENT ATTLEE arrived in Washington for four days of talks with Truman. He had flown from Paris, where he and French prime minister René Pleven had held talks on the Korean War. Attlee set himself three goals for the Washington Summit: first, to convince Truman of Britain's reliability as an ally, second, to make sure that the president took account of world opinion in the conduct of the war; and finally, to do everything possible to prevent the use of nuclear weapons. As Truman was already personally committed to a policy of containment, the British leader had little difficulty; he provided the president with useful political ammunition to deal with those who wanted to widen the conflict.

The two allies, however, did have markedly different perceptions of the nature of communism and the Chinese communists, and these surfaced at the Washington meeting. The American delegation took the view that the Chinese communists were operating within the grand design of a Soviet-controlled strategy. The British, on the other hand, viewed China's action as the result of a misinterpretation of what the Chinese regarded as a threat to their national interests. Attlee foresaw the possibility of a SINO-SOVIET SPLIT at some point and urged the Truman administration to recognize communist China in order to be in a position to exploit the historical differences between Russia and China. This difference of understanding of the nature and threat of communism was to be a continuing factor in relations between the United States and its European allies.

While the British and American leaders conferred in Washington, the Chinese continued their push southward. By the end of the year they had driven the UN forces out of North Korea and were poised to cross the 38th parallel. On New Year's Eve they launched a major offensive across the dividing line and broke through the ranks of the South Korean troops facing them. On January 4, 1951, Seoul and the port of Inchon fell to the Chinese forces. The United Nations issued appeals for a Korean truce, but the Chinese refused any negotiations until UN troops were withdrawn from Korea and the U.S. Seventh Fleet from the Formosa Straits. Communist China also demanded that the Chinese have a seat at the United Nations and that peace negotiations be conducted in China. These demands were rejected by the United States.

The Chinese, like the North Koreans before them, had overextended their supply lines. On January 15, they had moved 50 miles south of Seoul when they stopped to consolidate their positions. Before reinforcements could be brought forward, the UN forces counterattacked. They made slow progress against strong Chinese opposition, but on March 14, Seoul was liberated a second time by UN forces. On March 31, 1951, the UN forces reached the 38th parallel for the second time.

By this time, Chinese intervention had created a major policy change among those countries that had supported the initial UN intervention and then authorized MacArthur to cross the 38th parallel. Frightened by prospect of a widening conflict, a majority of the UN members began to search for a negotiated solution to the Korean War. On January 13 Canadian foreign minister LESTER PEARSON proposed an immediate cease-fire in Korea and the creation of a UN committee, of which communist China would be a member, to negotiate a settlement of Far Eastern problems, including the Korean War and the future of Taiwan. Seven Communist Bloc countries voted against the resolution, but the American delegate joined 49 others to vote in favor of the proposal. However, the UN resolution came under heavy attack from Congress, and on January 15, Senator James Eastland introduced a resolution in the Senate to force the United States to withdraw from the United Nations if communist China were admitted. The resolution also directed Truman to defend Taiwan.

Both houses of Congress passed almost unanimous resolutions demanding that the United Nations brand China as an aggressor and apply sanctions if necessary. On January 20, Ambassador Warren Austin introduced a resolution to that effect. The result was a serious split between the United States and the other members of the United Nations. Even the British opposed the threat of sanctions. After two weeks of strained negotiations, a compromise was reached. China was branded the aggressor, but a Lebanese amendment was adopted that deferred the application of sanctions until further efforts had been made to reach a negotiated settlement. The divisions that surfaced during the negotiations underscored the difficulties the Truman administration faced in maintaining the continued support of the United Nations.

Throughout February 1951, the UN forces advanced against the Chinese and North Korean armies. But the progress was excruciatingly slow for MacArthur, who now began to actively press for American support of a Nationalist Chinese attack across the Formosa Straits. Public statements indicating MacArthur's desires and willingness to risk a full-scale war increased Truman's difficulties at the United Nations and strained the relationship between the president and his commander in Korea. The final break between MacArthur and Truman came after MacArthur, on March 20, 1951, wrote to Congressman Joseph Martin supporting Martin's suggestion that Chiang's forces be used to open "a second front in Asia." MacArthur concluded his letter with the comment, "It seems strangely difficult for some to realize that here in Asia is where the Communist conspirators have elected to make their play for global conquest, and that we have joined the issues thus raised on the battlefield; that here we fight Europe's war with arms, while the diplomats there fight it with words; that if we lose the war to Communism in Asia, the fall of Europe is inevitable; win it, and Europe would probably avoid war and yet preserve freedom."

The letter, which was read to Congress on April 5, was a direct attack on Truman's policies and a major threat to America's relations with the other members of the United Nations. The president summoned his top foreign and defense policy advisers, who unanimously agreed that the president should relieve MacArthur of his command. Truman did so. MacArthur, however, was hailed as a hero when he returned to America, and became the focal point for extreme conservatives opposed to Truman and the United Nations. He was replaced by General MATTHEW RIDGWAY, who had been commander of the 8th Army.

On June 1, after a UN counteroffensive had driven the Chinese north of the 38th parallel, UN secretary general TRYGVE LIE renewed efforts to open negotiations. The Chinese responded with threats to increase their commitment. UN forces pressed north across the 38th parallel to an area known as the "Iron Triangle," from which most of the south-bound offensives were launched. On June 12 this area fell to the UN forces, and the Chinese government shortly afterward extended peace feelers.

Concessions were also being made on the allied side. Lester Pearson and Acheson made statements indicating that the countries that contributed to the UN force would be prepared to accept a return to a divided Korea instead of the united democratic Korea envisaged in October 1950. On June 23, Malik said in a radio broadcast, "The Soviet peoples . . . believe that the . . . armed conflict in Korea could be settled. This would require the readiness of the parties to enter on the path of peaceful settlement of the Korean question. The Soviet peoples believe that, as a first step, discussions should be started between the belligerents for a cease-fire and an armistice providing for the mutual withdrawal of forces from the 38th Parallel." Two days later, Malik's proposal was endorsed by the Beijing *People's Daily*.

Truce negotiations began on July 10 at Kaesong, just south of the 38th parallel. The opening sessions were strained. The UN forces wanted a truce line just north of the 38th parallel; the Chinese continued to couple the truce to withdrawal of all foreign troops from the Korean Peninsula. On August 23 the Chinese communists claimed that a UN fighter aircraft had attacked Kaesong. They called off the truce negotiations and launched a fresh offensive on August 27–28. The UN forces successfully counterattacked and advanced until the Chinese and North Koreans agreed to resume truce negotiations at PANMUNJOM on October 25. This time the Chinese and North Koreans agreed to draw the truce line at the point of contact between the forces at the time of the signing of the truce.

Negotiations now faltered on the issue of the exchange of prisoners. The United States refused to return any Korean and Chinese prisoners who wanted to remain in the South or go elsewhere, of whom there were about 70,000, of the 132,000 prisoners held. This was a major problem for the Chinese, who faced considerable embarrassment over the issue. Prominent figures in the American military and Congress were prepared to return all Chinese and North Korean prisoners in order to end the war, but the issue became a matter of principle for Truman. The president prevailed, and the fighting continued throughout 1952 while talks were deadlocked over the prisoner exchange issue. Negotiations were further complicated when both sides claimed that the other was engaging in bacteriological warfare and when Syngman Rhee repeatedly pronounced that he would settle for nothing less than a united Korea.

The end of the war was undoubtedly brought closer by the almost simultaneous change of leadership in both the United States and the Soviet Union. President DWIGHT EISENHOWER, who took office in January 1953, was publicly committed to a speedy settlement. Then on March 5, 1953, Stalin died. On March 30, Chou En-lai returned from Stalin's funeral to declare that sick and wounded prisoners could be exchanged and those who refused should be handed over to a neutral state to ensure "a just solution to the question of their repatriation." Within a week truce negotiators had agreed to the first exchange of prisoners in more than three years.

For the next two months the negotiators argued over which neutral countries would deal with the prisoners and the guidelines for a "just solution" to their repatriation or otherwise. The two sides moved slowly toward an agreement. At the last moment, however, Syngman Rhee rejected the truce, saying "The present terms simply mean death to us." At the same time, on June 28 an estimated 25,000 Korean and Chinese prisoners were allowed by their South Korean jailers to escape. It was a clear attempt by the South Korean government to force a breakdown in the truce negotiations.

But Syngman Rhee's efforts to sabotage the truce failed. The communists lodged a formal protest but made it clear that they would continue with plans for an armistice. On July 27, 1953, the armistice was formally signed at Panmunjom. The UN forces had suffered more than 94,000 dead. About 55,000 Americans died in Korea and 113,000 were wounded. Approximately 1 million South Koreans and 2 million North Koreans died. The Chinese and North Korean military casualties were estimated at 1.5 million.

Neither side could legitimately claim victory. The United States had thwarted the establishment of a communist government on the entire Korean Peninsula, but it had failed in its revised objective of uniting the country under a pro-Western government. The Chinese had succeeded in maintaining a communist buffer in North Korea, but they had failed to force the withdrawal of American troops from the south, as some 35,000 remained to protect the government in Seoul. Perhaps more importantly, the Chinese intervention resulted in increased American support for the Nationalist government on Taiwan and ended the possibility of a speedy solution to the "two-China" problem.

For Further Information:

Berger, Carl. *The Korea Knot: A Military-Political History.* Philadelphia, 1964.

Blair Clay. *The Forgettable War: America in Korea, 1950–1953.* New York, 1987.

Caridi, Ronald J. *The Korean War and American Politics.* Philadelphia, 1969.

Collins, J. Lawton. *War in Peacetime: The History and Lessons of Korea.* Boston, 1969.

Donovan, Robert J. *Nemesis: Truman and Johnson in the Coils of War in Asia.* New York, 1984.

Goulden, Joseph C. *Korea, The Untold Story of the War.* New York, 1982.

Hastings, Max. *The Korean War*. New York, 1987.

MacArthur, Douglas. *Reminiscences*. New York, 1964.

Ridgway, Matthew B. *The Korean War: How We Met the Challenge*. Garden City, N.Y., 1967.

Stone, I.F. *The Hidden History of the Korean War*. New York, 1952.

Toland, John. *In Mortal Combat: Korea, 1950–1953*. New York, 1991.

Truman, Harry S. *Years of Trial and Hope*, Vol. 2 of *Memoirs*, Garden City, N.Y. 1956.

Whelan, Richard. *Drawing the Line: The Korean War, 1950–1953*. Boston, 1990.

Kosygin, Alexei   (February 20, 1904–December 18, 1980)

Alexei Kosygin was a key member of the Soviet triumvirate that succeeded NIKITA KHRUSHCHEV in 1964. As prime minister, he was mainly involved with the administration of government and the economy. However, he also played a major role in developing policy for the VIETNAM WAR and the SALT I negotiations.

Kosygin was born into a working-class family in St. Petersburg. At the age of 15 he enlisted in the Red Army, where he impressed his seniors with his devotion to the communist cause. When the civil war ended in 1921, Kosygin entered a training school to become an organizer for the cooperative movement, and following his graduation went to Siberia for five years to help integrate cooperative groups into the state-controlled economy.

It was not until 1927 that Kosygin formally joined the Communist Party. Two years later he returned to Leningrad, the renamed St. Petersburg, for an engineering course, and by 1934 he was director of a textile factory. He caught the attention of the party chief for Leningrad, Andrei Zhdanov, who in 1938 ushered Kosygin into the party machinery, first as the head of Leningrad's Industrial Transport Department and then, four months later, as mayor of Leningrad.

Kosygin was rapidly advancing up the political ladder. He was quickly elected to the Soviet parliament, the Supreme Soviet, and four months after becoming mayor was in the national cabinet as People's Commissar for the Textile Industry. In 1939, at the age of 35, he was elected to the Central Committee and the following year was made a deputy prime minister.

During World War II, Kosygin organized the evacuation of Leningrad in January 1942 and also organized wartime factory production. In 1943 he was appointed prime minister of the Russian Republic, the largest and most important of the Soviet republics. In 1946 his wartime work was recognized by JOSEF STALIN when he was made a candidate (non-voting) member of the ruling Politburo. He was made a full member and finance minister in February 1948.

Kosygin never claimed any driving political vision. His strength lay in his administrative skills; in a state shaped by ideological commitment this meant that he could never gain the control wielded by Stalin, Khrushchev or Brezhnev. However, his talents were such that he would always be able to make an invaluable contribution by introducing a pragmatic and moderating influence into policy debates.

In the late 1940s and early 1950s, Kosygin's lack of ideological identity probably saved him from Stalin's final purges. But after the dictator's death, it also kept him out of the newly formed, ruling Presidium that succeeded Stalin in 1953. Kosygin sought to regain influence by backing Khrushchev in his power struggle with GEORGI MALENKOV and in 1957 was named chief of economic planning.

By 1964, however, it became clear that Khrushchev had lost the support of the other members of the Politburo, and Kosygin was one of the key figures of the palace coup that overthrew Khrushchev in October 1964. Kosygin then became prime minister and part of the ruling triumvirate, which also included LEONID BREZHNEV as general secretary of the party and NIKOLAI PODGORNY as president. There was concern at first that the triumvirate would degenerate into a power struggle. But it appeared to work smoothly, with Podgorny assuming the ceremonial duties, Brezhnev the policy and party responsibilities and Kosygin the administrative role. Kosygin and Brezhnev were the two most important figures, and the two men worked together well. But it was clear from the start that whenever a disagreement occurred—which was rarely—it was Brezhnev who prevailed.

Kosygin's main responsibilities continued to lie in the administration of the economy, but he also took a keen interest in foreign policy and was often employed as a diplomatic troubleshooter. In September 1969 he visited Beijing for talks with Premier CHOU ENLAI. These talks resulted in a border agreement that temporarily halted the clashes between Chinese and Soviet troops and helped reduce tensions between the two countries.

Kosygin's main foreign policy interest, however, was the Vietnam War. Kosygin was infuriated by President LYNDON JOHNSON's decision to start bombing North Vietnam while Kosygin was visiting there, and for the next two years he refused to discuss the issue with the United States and encouraged the North Vietnamese not to enter any peace negotiations until the American bombings stopped. In 1968 Kosygin declared, "We cannot have normal relations with the United States as long as it continues the war. The Soviet people cannot approve of a policy of developing friendship with the United States while American troops kill absolutely innocent people, conduct an illegal war and seize foreign territories."

This hard line conflicted with the Johnson administration's assertion that the Vietnam War need not stand in the way of improved U.S.–Soviet relations, and President Johnson several times extended invitations to Kosygin to visit the United States. But Kosygin refused to visit as long as the bombings of North Vietnam continued. The Soviet leadership eventually decided that a meeting should take place, but the problem was in organizing the summit so that he did not appear to be backing down from the policy of no summit until the bombings were halted. The opportunity arose in 1967 when it was decided that Kosygin should attend the opening session of the UN General Assembly. Johnson, when he heard of this, invited Kosygin to extend his visit to meet with him at Glassboro, New Jersey.

The GLASSBORO SUMMIT, therefore, was not technically a U.S.–Soviet summit but rather a meeting in the midst of Kosygin's trip to the United Nations. The Glassboro Summit coincided with the 1967 Arab–Israeli War, and Kosygin tried to use the meeting to secure American concessions in the Middle East. Johnson had no intention of discussing the Middle East and went into the summit determined to start the first round of STRATEGIC ARMS LIMITATION TALKS. The two men talked at cross-purposes for two days and little was achieved, but Kosygin was able to report back to the Politburo the strong American commitment to strategic arms negotiations, and shortly thereafter the two countries agreed to start the SALT I negotiations.

The negotiations were due to start in October of 1968 but were postponed indefinitely by the WARSAW PACT invasion of CZECHOSLOVAKIA. Kosygin was a key member of the Soviet delegation that met with the Czech and Warsaw Pact leaderships in the months leading to the invasion and is believed to have counseled moderation. He is thought to have argued that the Czechoslovak leadership could have been more successfully brought back into line through a combination of negotiation, economic pressure and rewards. Other Warsaw Pact leaders, however, saw the Czech example as a major short-term threat to their regimes, and feared that by the time the Kosygin plan had borne fruit in Czechoslovakia their own governments would have fallen.

Brezhnev sided with the hawks, and military intervention came in August 1968. The invasion of Czechoslovakia was the watershed in the careers of Brezhnev and Kosygin in that it established Brezhnev's ascendancy over Kosygin on foreign policy issues and those issues related to the international role of the Communist Party. By 1970, it was clear that Brezhnev was completely in control. That was not to say that Kosygin did not still wield considerable power. He remained prime minister, and he became increasingly concerned with economic issues.

Kosygin was often critical of the Soviet Union's centralized economic planning and tried to decentralize it and improve production, especially in the agricultural sector. Shortly after coming to power in 1965, Kosygin pushed forward a bold economic plan to make profitability the primary index of economy efficiency. This plan reduced centralized controls and encouraged factory managers to take the initiative by rewarding them and their workers with bonuses. Kosygin's economics, however, consistently encountered opposition from the party ideologues, who considered his ideas too much of a retreat from Marxism-Leninism. In 1975 Kosygin warned the Communist Party Congress that a slowdown in the growth of the labor force meant that factories and farms must be encouraged to improve productivity. He encouraged the importation of Western technology and managerial techniques to stimulate the Soviet economy. But by this time, Kosygin was too seriously ill to push through his reforms against hard-line opposition, and the Soviet economy slid into a rapid decline. Kosygin died on December 18, 1980.

For Further Information:

Conquest, Robert. *Russia After Khrushchev*. London, 1965.

Dallin, Alexander, and Thomas B. Larson, eds. *Soviet Politics Since Khrushchev*. Englewood Cliffs, N.J., 1968.

Nogee, J.L. *Soviet Foreign Policy Since World War Two*. New York, 1988.

Owen, Richard. *Crisis in the Kremlin*. London, 1986.

L

Laird, Melvin (September 1, 1922–) Melvin Laird was secretary of defense during the first Nixon administration. He was also heavily involved in laying the groundwork for the post-Vietnam American defense policy and for policy positions in the SALT I talks.

Laird was born into a prosperous Wisconsin family. After graduation from Carleton College and wartime service in the U.S. Navy, he was elected to the Wisconsin State Senate. In 1952 he was elected to the U.S. House of Representatives, where he won a reputation as a conservative Republican and an expert on defense issues. Laird was an early and keen supporter of RICHARD NIXON in 1968.

As secretary of defense, Laird's most pressing task was the VIETNAM WAR. He agreed with Nixon's policy of Vietnamization. It was reported, however, that he differed with the president's plans to attack communist bases in Cambodia and Laos in order to improve the South Vietnamese military and political position prior to U.S. withdrawal. This difference resulted in the defense secretary's exclusion from a number of policy decisions related to the conduct of the war. Despite this, Laird publicly backed the administration's policy and in January 1971 justified the U.S. action in Cambodia on the grounds that it was crucial to U.S. troop withdrawals from South Vietnam.

Laird had a major impact in shaping American defense policy in other parts of the world. The Vietnam War had forced the United States to reexamine its assumption of the role of world policeman, and the Nixon administration decided that domestic political and financial problems precluded the United States from keeping the wide-ranging commitments outlined in the TRUMAN DOCTRINE. The emphasis instead shifted toward a greater reliance on regional military alliances, with the United States turning to regional allies to provide combat troops.

The new policy, which was known as the Nixon Doctrine, was described by Laird to Congress as a "prudent middle course between two policy extremes—world policeman or new isolationism." To put the policy into effect, Laird traveled widely, urging allies to increase their share of the defense burden. He succeeded, for instance, in persuading the Canadian government not to reduce its troop levels in Western Europe and persuaded West Germany and Britain to increase their defense spending.

Laird was deeply involved in the STRATEGIC ARMS LIMITATION TALKS (SALT I). He was a strong proponent of the Safeguard antiballistic missile system and of increased spending on strategic nuclear systems as a means of gaining negotiating leverage over the Soviets. He also argued that an effective ABM system was essential in case U.S. and Soviet negotiators failed to reach a SALT agreement.

Laird's record on defense spending was mixed. In March 1969 he announced a $2.5 billion cut in military outlays as part of the administration's anti-inflation policy. There was another cut in 1970, but in 1971 Laird reversed himself and asked for an $80 billion budget. In 1972 he asked Congress for a $6 billion increase. When the 1972 ANTIBALLISTIC MISSILE (ABM) TREATY came before Congress, Laird insisted that the legislators approve the treaty only if they also granted his requests for new weaponry.

At the end of 1972, Laird announced his resignation as defense secretary, effective at the end of Nixon's first term. But in May 1973 he returned to the White House as a domestic adviser and helped to select GERALD FORD as successor to Vice President Spiro Agnew, who had been forced to resign after plea-bargaining a criminal indictment. Laird managed to escape unscathed from the Watergate scandal, but he found it impossible to work in the atmosphere of distrust, fear and disillusionment that pervaded the final months of the Nixon White House and paralyzed the government machinery. He resigned in July 1974, calling for an "early impeachment vote" in order to resolve the government crisis quickly.

After leaving government, Laird became a director of several major companies while remaining active in Republican national politics.

For Further Information:
Kissinger, Henry. *The White House Years.* New York, 1979.
Litwak, R.S. *Detente and the Nixon Doctrine: American Foreign Policy and the Pursuit of Stability, 1969–1975.* New York, 1984.
Nixon, Richard. *RN: The Memoirs of Richard Nixon.* New York, 1978.
Small, M. *Johnson, Nixon and the Doves.* New Brunswick, N.J., 1988.

Lane, Arthur (June 16, 1894–August 12, 1956) Arthur Lane was United States ambassador to Poland in the immediate postwar period. He repeatedly clashed with Secretary of State JAMES E. BYRNES, whom he regarded as too soft on the Soviets.

Lane joined the diplomatic service after graduating from Yale University in 1916. He served in a number of posts in Europe and Latin America before being appointed ambassador to the Polish government-in-exile in London in September 1944. Lane, however, never presented his credentials to the London Poles because of Soviet insistence that the Western allies recognize the Lublin Committee government in Warsaw.

At the YALTA CONFERENCE in 1945, Britain and the United States agreed to accept the communist LUBLIN COMMITTEE government on the condition that its political base be broadened to include representatives from other Polish political parties in Poland and abroad and that the newly-created Government of National Unity would hold free elections as soon as possible.

However, neither the Lublin Committee nor the Soviet Union had any intention of admitting other political parties to the Government of National Unity. A delegation of 15 London-based Poles was promised safe conduct and flew to Warsaw for talks on the formation of the government. They were promptly arrested for anti-Soviet activities and imprisoned in Moscow. The Soviet Union's refusal to keep its Yalta promises on Poland led to a major argument between President HARRY TRUMAN and Soviet foreign minister V.M. MOLOTOV when they met for the first time in Washington, D.C., in April 1945.

But despite the growing differences over Poland, the Truman administration decided it was best to have a representative there, and Lane arrived in Warsaw in August 1945. From the outset, Lane regarded American policy toward Poland as a version of postwar appeasement. He demanded immediate free elections as promised at Yalta and the withdrawal of Soviet troops, advised against extending American aid to Poland, and attacked the political repression of the communist government.

Secretary of State Byrnes was at the time attempting to develop a postwar working relationship with the Soviet Union and was prepared to compromise on Poland in order to achieve this end. He was also more sympathetic to Soviet leader JOSEF STALIN's assertion that the Soviet Union needed a friendly government in Poland to protect itself from the possibility of another attack by Germany. In April 1946 Byrnes approved a $500 million loan to Poland in exchange for renewed Polish guarantees of free elections, compensation for nationalized American property and a favorable trade agreement.

Lane, however, continued to take a hard line and publicly attacked the government in speeches and statements in Warsaw. His positions made him increasingly unpopular with the communist government, and on September 8, 1946, a large crowd attacked his residence with shouts of "Down with the defenders of Germany!"

Elections were finally held on January 19, 1947, but they were blatantly rigged and marked by intimidation by the Red Army and fraudulent voting. The Truman administration accused the Polish government of failing "to carry out its solemn pledges" for free elections and accused it of "coercion and intimidation against democratic elements."

In protest against the election result, Lane boycotted the opening of the Polish parliament. But the Truman administration refused to break U.S.–Polish diplomatic relations, and in March 1947 Lane submitted his resignation so that he could discuss "openly . . . the present tragedy of Poland."

As a private citizen Lane wrote two books on Poland, *I Saw Poland Betrayed* and *How Russia Rules Poland*, in which he strongly attacked American policy in Eastern Europe. He advocated the armed liberation of Eastern Europe and became a strong supporter of Senator JOSEPH MCCARTHY. Lane died on August 12, 1956.

For Further Information:
Etheridge, Lynn. *The Cold War Begins*. Princeton, 1972.
Lane, Arthur. *How Russia Rules Poland*. New York, 1947.
———. *I Saw Poland Betrayed*. New York, 1948.

Lansdale, Edward   (February 6, 1908– February 23, 1987)   Major General Edward Lansdale was an American counterinsurgency specialist who believed that communism was best confronted by "democratic revolution". The theory was successful in the Philippines, but Lansdale failed to implement it in South Vietnam, where he became the inspiration for such famous novels as *The Quiet American* by Graham Greene and *The Ugly American* by Eugene Burdick and William Lederer.

During World War II, Lansdale served with the OFFICE OF STRATEGIC SERVICES, wartime predecessor to the CENTRAL INTELLIGENCE AGENCY, and with U.S. Army intelligence. After the war he was sent to the Philippines to organize resistance to the Communist HUKBALAHAP REBELLION. He did this with a combined program of military action and social reform.

Lansdale's success in the Philippines established him as the American military's foremost expert on counterinsurgency. In 1954 he was sent to Vietnam as head of the U.S. Military Mission. He was briefed by Secretary of State JOHN FOSTER DULLES to identify a local politician and direct efforts to see the politician installed in power. Lansdale chose NGO DINH DIEM and within weeks of Diem's taking power, Lansdale moved into the presidential palace as a close personal adviser. It was during this period that he became the model for the previously mentioned novels.

Following the division of Vietnam, Lansdale was appointed chief of the Saigon station of the CIA. He continued to advise Diem on a wide range of issues, including counterinsurgency programs, plans for the integration of North Vietnamese refugees, training for civil servants, intelligence operations and psychological warfare. Lansdale also advised Diem on his personal political problems and in November 1954 helped to thwart a coup against him. He also successfully opposed French attempts to remove Diem.

But by January 1956, Lansdale had become seriously worried about Diem's refusal to allow the creation of a recognized political opposition. He advised John Foster Dulles and CIA Director ALLEN DULLES to pressure Diem into accepting political reform. When they refused he asked to be transferred back to Washington.

In Washington, Lansdale became assistant to the secretary of defense for special operations. He did not return to Vietnam until January 1961. His subsequent report, while still critical of Diem's increasingly dictatorial methods, attacked American failure to give wholehearted support to Diem and proposed a wide-ranging American program of military, economic, political and social reform to demonstrate American commitment and to stabilize the country behind a pro-Western government. The report was read by President JOHN F. KENNEDY, who was reportedly so impressed that he considered appointing Lansdale ambassador to Vietnam. But Lansdale's opponents in the administration blocked the appointment.

Kennedy, however, appointed Lansdale to a special task force headed by Deputy Secretary of Defense ROSWELL GILPATRIC. The group had been established to discuss and suggest ways of preventing a communist takeover in Vietnam. The group's initial report repeated Lansdale's earlier suggestions and proposed that American policy in Vietnam be transferred to a permanent task force with Gilpatric in overall charge and Lansdale as chief of operations in Saigon. The report also proposed that Lansdale immediately go to Saigon for further study. However, the final draft, presented on May 6, was prepared by Undersecretary of State GEORGE BALL. The final version blocked Lansdale's appointment and the creation of the task force. Ball was backed by Defense Secretary ROBERT MCNAMARA.

Lansdale, however, was included in the October 1961 mission to South Vietnam headed by General MAXWELL TAYLOR and WALT ROSTOW. Lansdale clashed with Rostow and Taylor also but supported their proposals for a U.S. commitment of ground troops to Vietnam. During the mission, Diem repeatedly asked that Lansdale be assigned to Saigon. The request was repeated after the Taylor-Rostow Mission returned to the United States.

The main focus of Lansdale's attentions continued to be Southeast Asia, but in November 1961 he was asked by Attorney General ROBERT KENNEDY to prepare contingency plans for a scaled-down BAY OF PIGS type of operation to overthrow Cuban leader FIDEL CASTRO.

Lansdale did not return to Vietnam until 1965. By this time, his position within the Democratic administration had been substantially undermined. This, plus the overthrow of Diem in November 1963, meant that Lansdale had little further influence on American policy.

For Further Information:
Lansdale, Edward G. *In the Midst of Wars.* New York, 1972.
Wise, David, and Thomas B. Ross. *The Invisible Government.* New York, 1974.

Laos During the 1950s and early 1960s Laos became a major Cold War flashpoint when the United States tried to transform the country into a "bulwark against Communism." A 1962 agreement by the superpowers established the neutrality of Laos, but the agreement was effectively ignored and a "Secret War" was fought that was eventually won by the communist Pathet Lao forces in 1975.

The kingdom of Laos became a French protectorate and part of French Indochina in 1893. French rule was fairly relaxed, as the Laotian people were generally politically passive. But the Laotians also had strong links with the politically more dynamic Vietnamese, and in 1930 a small group of Vietnamese and Laotians established the Laotian Communist Party. This later became the Laos People's Revolutionary Party, whose military arm, the Pathet Lao, later spearheaded the communist attempt to overthrow first the French and then the American-supported or neutral governments in the capital at Vientiane.

There was, however, very little resistance to French rule until immediately after World War II. The Japanese occupied the country from 1940 to 1945, and at the end of the war, the Laotian political elite started an independence movement, but the French satisfied most of their aspirations in 1949 by giving Laos independence within the French Union.

The only major Laotian political group to reject the French solution was the Pathet Lao, headed by Prince Souphanouvong, whose half-brother, Prince Souvanna Phouma, became the most prominent pro-French Laotian and in 1951 formed his first government. The Pathet Lao established themselves in the northern provinces of Houa Phan and Phong Saly, close to the border with Vietnam, so that they could be supplied by the more powerful communist forces in North Vietnam. In 1953 Vietnamese communist troops crossed over into Laos and helped the Pathet Lao to establish a resistance government in the province of Houa Phan. The same year, France granted full independence to the government of Prince Souvanna Phouma.

The GENEVA CONFERENCE ON INDOCHINA AND KOREA in 1954 and the end of French rule in Southeast Asia further aggravated what had become a civil war in Laos. The conference agreement restricted the Pathet Lao forces to Houa Phan and Phong Saly and committed them to respect the "territorial and political integrity" of Laos and Cambodia, which would be demilitarized except for forces needed for self-defense. The French were allowed to continue training Laotian troops.

The Geneva agreement was largely ignored. The Pathet Lao found themselves in a substantially improved position with a communist government in North Vietnam, which became a conduit for Soviet weapons and the site of training facilities. The Eisenhower administration, for its part, refused to be bound by the Geneva Accords, and Secretary of State JOHN FOSTER DULLES set out to transform Laos into a "bulwark against Communism." In pursuit of this aim, the Eisenhower administration supplied Laos with $300 million in aid between 1955 and 1960, 85 percent of which was military-oriented.

The aid was more than the Laotian economy could absorb, and it encouraged the spread of corruption and increased the political power of the military.

The American aid also strengthened the position of the Pathet Lao, and Prince Souvanna Phouma was forced into negotiations with his brother. These resulted in November 1957 in the Vientiane Agreements, which established a neutral coalition government that included the Pathet Lao. The coalition government was strongly opposed by the Eisenhower administration, which ordered the CIA to undermine through covert operations both Prince Souvanna and the Pathet Lao. The CIA, against the wishes of the State Department, threw its support behind Phoumi Nosavan, who took power in July 1958. Prince Souvanna Phouma then joined forces with his brother Prince Souphanouvong, and the two men fled to the hills and to the Pathet Lao forces.

The new pro-Western government called for additional aid to fight the renewed civil war. At the same time, the Phoumi government went through coup and countercoup. North Vietnam and the Soviet Union increased their aid to the Pathet Lao. In 1961 the Royal Laotian Army suffered a major defeat on the Plain of Jars in February 1961.

President JOHN F. KENNEDY abandoned as unworkable Dulles's attempt to maintain Laos as a bulwark against communism. Instead he proposed that the neutrality of Laos be guaranteed by the great powers. The Laotian government's defeat on the Plain of Jars underscored the need for such an agreement. However, the Soviets and the North Vietnamese saw the routing of the pro-Western forces as an opportunity to establish a communist government, which would give them control of the upper reaches of the Mekong River and the Ho Chi Minh Trail to South Vietnam. They accordingly stepped up their support for the Pathet Lao forces, and the Soviets started a massive military airlift of weaponry. The result was the Laotian Crisis of 1961–62.

Kennedy believed that the only way to prevent a communist takeover and force his neutrality proposal on the Soviet Union was to threaten American intervention. At a White House press conference on March 23, 1961, he displayed a series of maps illustrating the advance of the Pathet Lao and claimed that the Soviet Union had flown more than 1,000 sorties into the battle area since December.

The president then stressed that there could be no peaceful solution to the problem of Laos without a "cessation of the present armed attacks by externally supported Communists." He added, "The security of all of Southeast Asia will be endangered if Laos loses its neutral independence. Its own safety runs with the safety of us all—in real neutrality observed by all . . . I know that every American will want his country to honor its obligations to the point that freedom and security of the free world and ourselves may be achieved."

Kennedy followed up his White House press conference by moving the Seventh Fleet to the area and placing American forces in the Far East on special alert. He also made approaches to all the members of the SOUTHEAST ASIA TREATY ORGANIZATION (SEATO). Laos was not a member of SEATO, but the alliance's security umbrella had been extended to include protection for South Vietnam, Cambodia and Laos. By March 27 troops had been pledged by Thailand, Pakistan and the Philippines, Britain had agreed to limited military intervention and Prime Minister HAROLD MACMILLAN, after a quick summit meeting with Kennedy in Bermuda, agreed to organize a multinational summit to negotiate a new neutrality agreement for Laos.

On April 24, 1961, Soviet leader NIKITA KHRUSHCHEV agreed to a cease-fire, and shortly afterward the British-organized summit was convened in Geneva. On July 23, 1962, agreements guaranteeing the freedom and neutrality of Laos were signed in Geneva by the diplomatic representatives of 14 Western, communist and neutral Asian nations, including the Soviet Union and the United States.

The agreement, however, merely moved the conflict underground and launched the "Secret War." The Soviet Union and North Vietnam continued to supply the Pathet Lao. The CIA was placed in full control of operations in Laos and effectively formed its own army using anti-communist guerrillas recruited from the Meo, the largest tribal group in Laos. By 1962, the guerrilla force numbered some 30,000 men. In addition to this army, there were another 17,000 American-financed mercenaries. The CIA also carried out air operations using planes from Air America and Continental Air Service for reconnaissance flights and occasional bombing runs.

Initially, the Secret War was waged to prevent a communist takeover in Laos, but after the U.S. intervention in Vietnam, operations became increasingly directed toward disrupting the Ho Chi Minh Trail and diverting communist resources away from the fighting in the south to disturbances in the Laotian foothills.

During the Secret War, the government in Vientiane underwent several changes from right to left and to locations in between. During most of the period, the government was controlled by Souvanna Phouma, who had split again with the Pathet Lao. In 1965, after an abortive coup, Phoumi Nosovan was forced into exile in Thailand. By 1974 the Pathet Lao forces were in control of three-quarters of the country.

The 1973 PARIS PEACE TALKS ON VIETNAM included provisions for a cease-fire in Laos. A new government was set up in April 1974 with participation by the royalist, neutral and Pathet Lao factions and with Prince Souvanna Phouma as prime minister and Prince Souphanouvong as chairman of a joint national political council. But the Pathet Lao forces already were in control of most of the country, and by November 1975 they were in complete control. Souvanna Phouma resigned as prime minister, and King Savang Vatthana abdicated his throne. By the start of 1976, a one-party communist government had been established in Laos with Prince Souphanouvong as president and Kaysone Phomvihan as prime minister.

The new Laotian government was firmly linked to the new communist government in Vietnam. In July 1977 a 25-year Treaty of Friendship was signed between the two countries.

The Laotian government sided with Vietnam and the Soviet Union during the attempted Chinese invasion of Vietnam in 1979 and supported the Vietnamese invasion of Cambodia and its imposition of the government of Heng Samrin in place of the murderous Khmer Rouge.

Throughout the 1980s, the communist government of Laos continued to face armed opposition from anti-communist guerrillas led by the exiled General Phoumi Nosavan, who formed the Royal Lao Democratic Government led by former Laotian military officers. Phoumi Nosavan's forces, however, made little headway against the government.

For Further Information:
Adams, Nina S., and Alfred W. McCoy. *Laos: War and Revolution.* New York, 1971.
Branfman, Fred. "The President's Secret Army: A Case Study—The CIA in Laos, 1962–72," in Robert Borosage and John Marks, *The CIA File.* New York, 1976.
Dommen, Arthur J. *Conflict in Laos; The Politics of Neutralization.* New York, 1971.
———. *Laos: Keystone of Indochina.* Boulder, Colo., 1985.
Fall, Bernard. *Anatomy of a Crisis: The Laotian Crisis of 1960–61.* New York, 1969.
Generous, Kevin M. *Vietnam: The Secret War.* New York, 1985.
Kirk, Donald. *Wider War: The Struggle for Cambodia, Thailand and Laos.* New York, 1972.
Stevenson, Charles A. *The End of Nowhere; American Policy Toward Laos Since 1954.* Boston, 1972.
Stuart-Fox, Martin. *Laos: Politics, Economics, and Society.* Boulder, Colo., 1986.
Zasloff, J.J. *The Pathet Lao.* Lexington, Mass., 1973.
Zasloff, Joseph J., and Leonard Unger, eds. *Laos: Beyond the Revolution.* New York, 1991.

Lattimore, Owen   (July 29, 1900–May 31, 1989)   Owen Lattimore was a prominent American scholar specializing in China whose advice to the government made him a target of the extreme right.

Lattimore spent his early years in China, where his father was an educational adviser to the Chinese government. In 1920 he joined a Shanghai newspaper. Shortly afterward he devoted himself to the study of Chinese history and culture, and by the end of the 1930s Lattimore was recognized as one of the leading American experts on China.

In 1937 he was appointed director of the Walter Hines Page School of International Relations at Johns Hopkins University and joined the Institute of Pacific Relations. At the institute he worked with a number of people who later became targets of Senator JOSEPH MCCARTHY.

During the war, Lattimore became a prominent adviser on relations with China. He successively served as Roosevelt's political adviser to CHIANG KAI-SHEK, deputy director responsible for Pacific operations at the Office of War Information and adviser to Vice President HENRY WALLACE during the latter's 1944 trip to China and Siberia. In 1945, Lattimore returned to Johns Hopkins University and published *Solution in Asia,* in which he urged Chiang Kai-shek to rid his government of corruption and introduce true democracy in China.

Lattimore's highly controversial book made him a principal target of the China Lobby. In 1950, Senator McCarthy started a formal inquiry into Lattimore's conduct and alleged that Lattimore was the "chief Soviet espionage agent in the United States." Two former communists, Louis Budenz and Fred Utley, testified that the Soviet Union had enlisted Lattimore to persuade the American public that the Chinese communists were merely agarian reformers.

Lattimore claimed that the testimony was a "plain, unvarnished lie." He went on the offensive against McCarthy, accusing the senator of damaging American civil liberties by abusing freedom of speech. Lattimore was strongly backed by President HARRY TRUMAN, who invoked the right of executive privilege to justify his refusal to release Lattimore's loyalty files. Lattimore was cleared by the bipartisan committee created to investigate the charges against him and career foreign service officer JOHN STEWART SERVICE.

But the continuing anti-communist furor led to another investigation in 1951 by the Senate Internal Security Subcommittee. This panel concluded that Lattimore had been "a conscious and articulate instrument of the Soviet conspiracy" and that he had perjured himself on five points before the subcommittee. A grand jury indicted him, but three years later a federal court threw out most of the key indictments for being too vague. The Justice Department dropped the remainder.

Lattimore remained a prominent target of the American right. In 1963 he left the United States to take up a teaching post at the University of Leeds in Britain. Lattimore retired to the United States in 1970. He died in Providence, Rhode Island on May 31, 1989.

For Further Information:
Koen, R.Y. *The China Lobby in American Politics.* New York, 1960.
Lattimore, Owen. *Ordeal by Slander.* Boston, 1950.

Leahy, Admiral William   (May 6, 1875–July 20, 1959)   Admiral William Leahy was a foreign and defense policy adviser to presidents FRANKLIN ROOSEVELT and HARRY TRUMAN and took a strong anti-Soviet line in the immediate postwar period.

Leahy was a career naval officer who graduated from the U.S. Naval Academy in 1897. He became a close friend of Franklin Roosevelt when the latter was assistant secretary of the navy. When Roosevelt became president he appointed Leahy chief of naval operations. In July 1942 he was appointed the president's chief of staff and became his closest military adviser. Truman retained Leahy as his senior military adviser, but Leahy's influence quickly waned. He was strongly opposed to the use of the atomic bomb against Japan; he regarded this act as morally repugnant.

Leahy was one of the first members of the American government to take a strong anti-Soviet position. He had accompanied Roosevelt to the Yalta Conference and expressed the opinion that the "Declaration of Liberated Europe," agreed upon at the conference, did not adequately protect Polish political rights. Leahy was a strong opponent of Secretary of State JAMES BYRNES, whom he regarded as an "appeaser," and voiced concern about pro-communist elements in the State Department.

Although Leahy was staunchly anti-Soviet, he was also opposed to the atomic bomb. He maintained that the United States, by being the first nation to use the bomb, had "adopted an ethical standard common to the barbarians of the dark ages."

Leahy retired in 1949 but continued to advise the government on defense organization until his death on July 20, 1959.

For Further Information:
Leahy, William D. *I Was There*. New York, 1950.

Lebanon Crisis   (1958)   The Lebanon Crisis of 1958 was the consequence of the 1957 EISENHOWER DOCTRINE and the first postwar intervention by American troops in the Middle East. The success of the American landings helped to postpone the Lebanese civil war, established the United States as a military power in the region and underscored the Soviet Union's difficulty in intervening in the Middle East.

The Lebanon Crisis of 1958 had its roots partly in the politically unstable Christian–Muslim constitutional division in Lebanon and partly in President DWIGHT EISENHOWER's fear that the Soviet Union would move to fill the vacuum left by the British following the SUEZ CRISIS.

The state of Lebanon was created by the French in 1920 in the aftermath of the collapse of the Ottoman Empire. The French also controlled Syria and sought to reestablish a political and economic union between the two countries. This was opposed by Lebanese Christians, mainly Maronite Catholics who identified with the West and were a slight majority of the total Lebanese population. In 1941, under the control of the Vichy French government, Lebanon gained its independence as a result of British and Free French intervention.

The Allied forces set out to resolve Lebanon's ethnic divisions by institutionalizing them in the National Pact of 1943. This recognized the Christians' numerical superiority but guaranteed political representation for other groups. The Maronites were thus guaranteed the presidency while, according to the pact, the premiership would always be held by a Sunni Muslim. The speaker of the parliament was to be a Shi'ite Muslim, the minister for defense a Druze and the deputy speaker a Greek Orthodox Christian.

The system prevented any one religious or ethnic group from dominating the government. But it also meant that the government failed to win the support of the entire population and, correspondingly, was unable to exert much control. The system worked as long as the rest of the Middle East remained politically stable, but when the region became unstable, outside forces exploited Lebanon's inherent divisions for their own ends.

From 1945 to 1956, British dominance in the region kept the Middle East relatively calm. But the Suez Crisis seriously damaged British influence, which in turn left a political vacuum. It also greatly enhanced Soviet prestige because the Soviets had supported Arab nationalist GAMAL ABDEL NASSER in his fight against the British, French and Israelis. Nasser's pan-Arabism, and, by association, the Soviet Union, moved to fill the political vacuum.

Lebanese president Camille Chamoun had championed the Eisenhower Doctrine and forged a close personal friendship with the U.S. president. He regarded the American policy as his best means of guaranteeing the peace in Lebanon and strengthening the pro-Western Christian forces in the country.

In April 1958 Chamoun pushed through a constitutional amendment that allowed him to run for an unprecedented second term. The result was a Muslim uprising in Beirut. Chamoun claimed that Egypt and Syria, which had formed a political union in January, were fomenting the uprising and on May 13, 1958, requested American and British help.

Eisenhower was at first wary of becoming involved in what was essentially a domestic dispute. His doubts were reinforced by UN secretary general DAG HAMMARSKJOLD, who reported to Eisenhower that Chamoun's claims of Syrian and Egyptian intervention were grossly exaggerated.

But then on July 14, 1958, the pro-Western Iraqi monarch King Faisal and his premier, General Nuri es-Said, were overthrown in a left-wing coup. Eisenhower later wrote, "Overnight our objective changed from quieting a troubled situation to facing up to a crisis of formidable proportions. Lebanon again came into our conscious concern because of the internal conflicts in that country and the pressures exerted by Syria."

Chamoun repeated his request for American and British military support. On July 15, 1958, some 10,000 U.S. Marines landed in Lebanon. British troops were held in reserve on Cyprus, and 2,200 British paratroopers were sent to Jordan to protect King Hussein, who was again believed to be in danger. A simultaneous State Department statement said that the landings were "in defense of Lebanese sovereignty and integrity" and stressed that troops had not been sent as "an act of war," but rather to "demonstrate the concern of the United States for the independence and integrity of Lebanon, which we deem vital to the national interest and world peace."

Eisenhower was determined that the American forces in Lebanon act only to prevent fighting rather than to participate in a civil war, and the troops became a temporary garrison force. The American landings were strongly condemned by the Soviet Union, Egypt, Syria and the new government in Iraq, and there were anti-American and anti-British demonstrations outside American embassies throughout the Arab world.

Nasser, who was visiting Yugoslavia just before the landings, immediately flew to Moscow to ask NIKITA KHRUSHCHEV for Soviet intervention if the West invaded or threatened to invade. Khrushchev refused to give such a pledge on the grounds that "it would raise the temperature, and at this point suddenly raising it could produce unforseeable consequences."

The Soviet reaction was therefore largely restricted to increasing the scale of scheduled Warsaw Pact maneuvers on the Bulgarian–Turkish border and to making diplomatic objections and resolutions in the United Nations. These actions, plus a Soviet call for an East–West summit on Lebanon, were all either ignored or dismissed by the Eisenhower administration. Khrushchev's inability to make any impact on the situation undermined his credibility with Nasser and the wider Arab world.

In the meantime, the American troops had had the desired effect of stabilizing the Middle East situation, and on July 31 General Chehab was elected Lebanese president in a special election. Chamoun remained in office until his term officially expired on September 23, and disturbances continued until his final departure from the presidential palace. The last American troops withdrew from Lebanon on October 25, 1958.

For Further Information:

Goria, Wade R. *Sovereignty and Leadership in Lebanon, 1943–1976.* London, 1985.

Heikal, Mohammed. *Sphinx and Commissar.* New York, 1978.

Korbani, Agnes G. *U.S. Intervention in Lebanon, 1958 and 1982: Presidential Decisionmaking.* New York, 1991.

Polk, William R. *The United States and the Arab World.* Cambridge, Mass., 1969.

Le Duc Tho *See* PARIS PEACE TALKS.

Lehman, John (September 14, 1942–   ) As United States secretary of the navy during the Reagan administration, John Lehman was responsible for a one-third increase in the size of the U.S. Navy.

Lehman came from a prominent Philadelphia family. Princess Grace of Monaco was his cousin. He studied at St. Joseph's College and Cambridge University, Johns Hopkins University, Yale and the University of Pennsylvania. He received his Ph.D. in international relations from the University of Pennsylvania. The main focus of his studies was strategic issues.

In January 1969, Lehman joined the Nixon administration as a staff assistant on the National Security Council. In September 1971 he was promoted to special counsel working directly for national security adviser HENRY KISSINGER, and in 1974 he joined the ARMS CONTROL AND DISARMAMENT AGENCY (ACDA) as a member of the U.S. delegation to the Mutual Balanced Force Reduction (MBFR) talks in Vienna. Six months later he was named deputy director of ACDA.

At ACDA, Lehman was placed in charge of the day-to-day administration of the agency. He developed a reputation as a conservative hard-liner and an opponent of the STRATEGIC ARMS LIMITATION TALKS (SALT I) then in progress. During the

Carter administration he became a vocal critic of the SALT II agreement and joined the neoconservative Committee on the Present Danger, which worked to defeat the treaty in Congress. He also criticized the Carter administration's cuts in conventional forces. Lehman became especially concerned about the effectiveness of the U.S. Navy and advocated an expansion of the nuclear-powered fleet. He played a key role in drafting the Republican Party's hard-line defense platform for the 1980 elections and was virtually assured of a major position in the Reagan administration after the Republican landslide victory. By this time, Lehman had become so committed to the cause of an expanded navy that he refused to accept any other post than that of secretary of the navy.

Shortly after taking office, Lehman told Congress that the number of ships in the navy would need to be increased by 33%, to 600 ships, to meet America's naval responsibilities. He said, "We are attempting to cover three oceans with a one-and-a-half-ocean navy." Lehman maintained that the growth of the Soviet Navy under Admiral SERGEI GORSHKOV had seriously undermined the naval superiority previously enjoyed by the United States and that American superiority should be reestablished as a matter of urgent priority.

As early as January 1981 Lehman was specific about the ships he wanted for his 600-ship navy. They included two Nimitz-class nuclear-powered aircraft carriers and three additional carrier battle groups. These ships would provide the core of an enlarged navy, which would simultaneously reestablish American superiority in the Pacific, protect the sea lanes between Europe and the Persian Gulf and effectively seal the GREENLAND–ICELAND–UK GAP sea route, which was the only route between the North Atlantic sea lanes and the Soviet naval base at Murmansk.

Lehman's proposed naval buildup won wide support but he faced criticism from some sections for his emphasis on large nuclear-powered vessels and attack vessels, which could be construed by the Soviet Union as a threat. One of his toughest critics was Admiral HYMAN RICKOVER, the "father" of the nuclear navy. He maintained that the proposed buildup was unnecessary. Lehman effectively silenced Rickover by forcing his retirement in 1982. Another critic was Senator William Proxmire, who claimed that Lehman's cost projections were unrealistically low. Lehman countered Proxmire by reducing cost estimates in negotiations with naval contractors and cutting the overall naval costs by recommissioning World War II battleships after relatively low-cost refits.

There were other critics, but Lehman successfully fought off all of them. By 1984 he had secured the appropriations he required for a 600-ship navy centered on 15 carrier groups. By the time Lehman left the navy for a business position in April 1987, the navy had reached 555 ships, an increase of 76 during his six years in office.

LeMay, General Curtis (November 15, 1906–October 1, 1990) General Curtis LeMay, a leading figure in the U.S. Air Force during World War II, went on to play a major role in commanding America's postwar strategic air forces. During the KENNEDY and JOHNSON administrations he became a major conservative voice within the Pentagon. He finished his career as running mate for Alabama governor George C. Wallace in the 1968 presidential election.

After obtaining an engineering degree from Ohio State University in 1928, LeMay joined the Army Air Corps. His greatest passion in life was flying, and he quickly rose through the ranks to become a major general by the age of 37. During World War II, he played a key role in planning bombing raids on West Germany and Japan, including the dropping of the atomic bombs on Hiroshima and Nagasaki.

Immediately after the war, LeMay was appointed Army Air Force deputy chief of staff for research and development and worked on some of the early plans for missiles, spacecraft and atomic weapons. He became an early and avid supporter of nuclear weapons and missile delivery systems.

In October 1947, LeMay became commander of the (now separate) U.S. Air Force in Europe. In this position, he was one of the main organizers of the 1948–49 Berlin Airlift. Code-named Operation Vittles, the airlift made a total of more than 200,000 flights and carried a million-and-a-half tons of supplies to 2.5 million people blockaded in West Berlin.

While the airlift was still in progress, LeMay was transferred back to Washington, D.C. to take charge of the Strategic Air Command (SAC). Under LeMay, SAC became the prime vehicle for America's strategic nuclear forces and the air force gained control of strategic nuclear policy. LeMay was an effective public speaker and lobbyist on behalf of the air force and in 1955 persuaded the Senate Armed Forces Committee to provide an additional $900 million for B-52 bombers. In 1956 he supported claims that a "bomber gap" existed between the United States and the Soviet Union, and after the launch of SPUTNIK by the Soviet Union LeMay took the argument one step further by claiming that the United States would be vulnerable to a Soviet attack by mid-1959 unless its strategic nuclear forces were quickly built up.

LeMay was appointed air force vice chief of staff in April 1957 but retained command of SAC. In June 1961 President John F. Kennedy promoted him to air force chief of staff. In this position he continued to press for increased production of air force bombers and more money for bomber research and development. On this issue, LeMay clashed with Defense Secretary ROBERT MCNAMARA, who wanted to increase expenditure on missiles at the expense of manned bombers. LeMay argued that the bombers were more flexible and took the issue to the Senate Armed Services Committee, which increased McNamara's proposed spending on bomber production.

McNamara, however, diverted $510 million of the $1.7 billion appropriated by Congress for the development of the B-70 bomber. This led to other fights between LeMay and the administration, and LeMay became increasingly critical of official Pentagon policy, opposing the development of the POLARIS missile and the Minuteman missile.

As the VIETNAM WAR escalated, LeMay took one of the most hawkish positions in the Pentagon, proposing that the United States launch massive air strikes against a wide range of North Vietnamese targets. His official position forced LeMay to moderate his public statements, and President Lyndon Johnson, who feared that LeMay could become a substantial conservative opponent out of office, repeatedly postponed the general's retirement in order to keep a tight rein on his political ambitions.

After LeMay finally retired in 1965, he launched a series of bitter attacks on the Johnson administration's conduct of the Vietnam War. In 1965 he wrote that he would end the war by bombing the North Vietnamese "back into the Stone Age" and criticized President Johnson for a "no-win" policy in Vietnam.

In 1968, the right-wing populist and segregationist governor George C. Wallace of Alabama formed the American Independence Party to sponsor his run for the presidency. Wallace chose LeMay as his running mate. During the campaign, LeMay attacked Johnson's decision to end the U.S. bombing of North Vietnam and advocated the use of nuclear weapons, if necessary, against the North Vietnamese. This hawkish statement was generally condemned and damaged Wallace's campaign.

For Further Information:
LeMay, Curtis. *Mission with LeMay: My Story.* New York, 1965.

Lend-Lease Act of 1941   The Lend-Lease Act of 1941 set up a program by which the United States supplied weapons and materiel to its Allies in World War II. The sudden decision to cancel Lend-Lease on August 21, 1945, strained relations between the United States and the Soviet Union and led to the ANGLO-AMERICAN FINANCE AND TRADE AGREEMENT of 1945.

The U.S. Congress passed the Lend-Lease Act to supply aid to Britain in March 1941. Later that year it was extended to the Soviet Union and China. The legislation, passed before American entry into World War II, empowered President FRANKLIN ROOSEVELT to provide aid to "any nation whose defense he believed vital to the U.S."—without, technically, violating U.S. neutrality. By the end of the war 38 nations had received $49.1 billion in aid in the form of military equipment, food, supplies and services. The president was authorized to accept repayment "in kind or property, or any other direct or indirect benefit which the President deems satisfactory."

On March 5, 1945, Leo T. Crowley, the U.S. foreign economic administrator, promised the House Foreign Affairs Committee that Lend-Lease would not be used "for the purposes of postwar rehabilitation and reconstruction." On August 21, 1945, President HARRY TRUMAN announced the sudden end of the aid program. The news came as a blow to Britain and the Soviet Union, who were both counting on a continuance of Lend-Lease until at least mid-1946 to help them reconstruct their economies. The British government immediately sent Lord Keynes to Washington, D.C., to negotiate the Anglo-American soft loan financial agreement to help cushion the blow.

The Soviet Union fared less well. Their Lend-Lease shipments were drastically cut when the war against Germany ended. Just before the Yalta Conference they had requested an American loan of $6 billion at 0.5% interest repayable over 25 years. By August 1945, when Lend-Lease was completely halted, the Soviets had reduced their request to $1 billion, but the Truman administration continued to delay and in February 1946 it demanded that the Soviets settle a number of outstanding issues before talks could begin on a loan. These included Soviet membership in the International Monetary Fund and the World Bank, future governments in Eastern Europe, and the settlement of Lend-Lease accounts and the claims of American citizens against the Soviet government. The Soviets charged that the United States was attempting to dictate Soviet economic policies, dropped their demand for a soft American loan and concentrated their efforts on obtaining reconstruction finance through war reparations from Germany.

For Further Information:
Pollard, Robert. *Economic Security and the Origins of the Cold War, 1945–1950.* New York, 1985.

Lie, Trygve **(July 16, 1896–December 30, 1968)** Trygve Lie was the first secretary general of the United Nations. His opposition to the North Korean invasion of South Korea led to his being boycotted by the Soviet Bloc countries and this in turn forced him to resign from the UN post in 1952.

Lie was born into a working-class family in Oslo and at the age of 16 joined the Norwegian Labor Party. In 1919 he graduated from Oslo University, where he had studied law, and was admitted to the Norwegian bar. At the same time he was appointed assistant to the secretary of the Labor Party.

From 1922 to 1935 Lie was legal adviser to the Trade Union Federation, and in 1926 he was elected to the national executive of the Labor Party. He was first elected to the Norwegian parliament in 1935 and in the same year entered the cabinet as minister of justice. One of his actions was to grant political asylum to Leon Trotsky; when Lie realized that Trotsky intended to use Norway as a base for his activities against Stalin, he had him deported, and Trotsky moved to Mexico.

In 1939 Lie moved from the Justice Ministry to the Ministry of Trade, Industry, Shipping and Fisheries, and in April 1940 he became foreign minister. Following the German invasion and occupation of Norway in 1940, Lie moved to London to become foreign minister of the Norwegian government-in-exile. In 1945 he represented Norway at the SAN FRANCISCO CONFERENCE at which the foundations of the United Nations were laid. During the conference he was chairman of the committee that drafted the section on the Security Council.

In December 1945 he was asked whether he would be prepared to be nominated for the position of president of the UN General Assembly. He agreed, but during the voting in London in January 1946 he was narrowly defeated by PAUL-HENRI SPAAK. In February the General Assembly met and elected Lie secretary general of the United Nations by a vote of 46 to three.

When Lie took office, the United Nations was still in its formative stage, and he had to build both the secretariat and a new headquarters. The offices were temporarily located in London, Paris, and Flushing Meadow and Lake Success, New York, before moving to their permanent headquarters in New York City. Lie developed the secretariat along American administrative lines. He also established many of the United Nations agencies such as the United Nations High Commissioner for Refugees, the International Court of Justice, the Food and Agricultural Organization, and the United Nations Educational, Scientific and Cultural Organization (UNESCO).

In the heady postwar days there were high hopes for the United Nations. The UN Charter, which set down its principles and operating statutes, was compared to the Magna Carta and the U.S. Constitution, and President HARRY TRUMAN described it as a declaration of "faith that war is not inevitable" and a "great instrument" for "security and progress." Some observers looked upon the United Nations as the nucleus of a world government that would use its security forces to stop aggressors and maintain world peace.

In this atmosphere, Lie's position as secretary general was a powerful one, and he was involved in most of the immediate postwar problems such as the proposed partition of Palestine and the subsequent founding of the state of Israel, United Nations trusteeships, the MARSHALL PLAN, the division of Korea, the problem of TRIESTE, the GREEK CIVIL WAR, the BERLIN BLOCKADE, the communist coup in CZECHOSLOVAKIA and the Soviet occupation of the AZERBAIJAN province of Iran.

In the first year of the United Nations, Lie generally enjoyed the backing of both the United States and the Soviet Union, although he did receive an inkling of things to come when the Soviet Union used its Security Council veto against France and Britain on the issue of troop withdrawals from Lebanon and Syria. By 1947 the Cold War had come to dominate international affairs. Lie tried to walk a tightrope between the two superpowers but found himself increasingly stepping over into the Western camp. This was mainly because Soviet leader JOSEF STALIN had become increasingly critical of both Lie and the United Nations. Stalin initially saw the United Nations as a means of preventing a resurgence of German and Japanese militarism and continuing the wartime alliance to the benefit of Moscow, but as the Cold War set in, the Soviet dictator increasingly viewed the United Nations as another tool of American foreign policy.

The lack of Soviet support quickly undermined the authority of Lie and the United Nations. In theory, the United Nations had substantial powers, but in practice it was hamstrung by the power of veto held by the five permanent members of the Security Council—Britain, France, the

United States, China and the Soviet Union. When any of these five powers found its interests jeopardized by a proposed UN action, it had only to use its veto to block the measure.

In the early Cold War years, the Soviet Union regularly employed its veto more than 45 times—between 1945 and 1950 and more than 100 times from 1950 to 1960. Soviet foreign minister Andrei Y. Vyshinsky said in 1948, "The veto is a powerful political tool. There are no such simpletons here as would let it drop. Perhaps we use it more, but that is because we are in the minority and the veto balances power. If we were in the majority, we could make such grandiloquent gestures as offering to waive the veto on this or that."

It was only because of a diplomatic blunder on the part of Moscow that the Soviet Union did not use its veto to block UN intervention in Korea. When the North Korean troops invaded South Korea on June 25, 1950, the Soviet ambassador to the United Nations, Jakob Malik, was in Moscow, boycotting the United Nations in protest against its refusal to allow the Chinese communist delegate to take China's seat at the organization. The United States asked Trygve Lie to call an emergency meeting of the Security Council on the following day, knowing that Malik could not return quickly enough to attend the meeting and use his veto.

In the absence of the Soviet delegate, the Security Council promptly passed a resolution calling for an immediate cessation of hostilities and a withdrawal of all forces to the 38th parallel. Lie himself took the initiative in having North Korea branded as the aggressor. The Security Council then passed a resolution recommending that the members of the United Nations furnish such assistance "as may be necessary to repel the armed attack and to restore international peace and security in the area." On July 7 the Security Council passed a British resolution setting up a unified UN command in Korea, the commander to be chosen by the United States.

The communist world now treated Trygve Lie as persona non grata. CHOU EN-LAI, the Chinese communist foreign minister and later premier, telegraphed a cable denouncing Lie and the Security Council's "illegal interference" in the internal affairs of Korea. In July 1950, the Soviet *Literary Gazette* called Lie a coward, a right-wing socialist, a stooge of Wall Street and an "abettor of American aggression" who only wanted to win reelection as secretary general. On October 12, Lie came up for reelection for a second five-year term. The Soviets used their veto for the 46th time to block the renewal of his term.

Lie was forced to turn toward the United States for help. America, which saw him as an essential part of its policy toward Korea, came to his aid by pressuring the General Assembly to extend his term for a further three years. But Vishynsky declared that the Soviet Union would not deal with him and called him "two-faced" and "unobjective."

At about the same time, Lie became embroiled in Senator JOSEPH MCCARTHY's hunt for communists in America. McCarthy accused Lie of giving jobs to disloyal U.S. citizens. Rather than challenge McCarthy, Lie dismissed several members of his staff who were named by McCarthy's investigators. The episode strongly damaged the morale and independence of the UN secretariat, and Lie has been severely criticized for his actions.

But Lie's main problem remained the Soviet Union, and on November 10, 1952, he announced his resignation because the Soviet Bloc's boycott of him prevented him from working effectively for a truce in the KOREAN WAR. In a letter read to the General Assembly, Lie said that a new secretary general "may be more help than I can be" in halting the Korean War. "I would not want . . . to hinder in the slightest degree any hope of reaching a new understanding that would prevent world disaster."

Lie's decision to resign before the expiration of his extended term threw the United Nations into a crisis, and it was several months before the Great Powers could agree on DAG HAMMARSKJOLD as the new secretary general. Lie finally left the UN post at the end of April 1953. After a lecture tour of the United States, he returned to Norway, where he wrote his memoirs and successfully reentered politics. Lie died in Norway on December 30, 1968.

For Further Information:
Lie, Trygve. *In the Cause of Peace.* New York, 1954.

Liebman, Marvin (July 21, 1923–   ) Marvin Liebman was an American ex-communist who shifted dramatically to the far right during the Cold War years. In 1953 he founded the powerful lobby organization, the COMMITTEE FOR ONE MILLION Against the Admission of Communist China to the United Nations.

Liebman was an active member of first the Young Communist League and then the American Communist Party during the 1930s and 1940s. But after the war he resigned in protest against JOSEF STALIN's purging of American Communist Party leader EARL BROWDER.

Almost overnight, Liebman moved to the far right of the political spectrum. He became involved with the Zionist right-wing terrorist organization Irgun Zvai Leumi and helped to smuggle political refugees out of Eastern Europe. At the same time, he built up a reputation as a public relations expert for right-wing causes.

In 1953 Liebman headed a group that went to the White House to present a petition signed by 210 prominent Americans calling for the Eisenhower administration to continue American opposition to communist China's admission to the United Nations. The signatories called themselves the Committee for One Million Against the Admission of Communist China to the United Nations, and the White House visit was the opening move in a campaign to secure one million American signatures on the petition and thus swing public opinion against the communist Chinese. Liebman was responsible for the campaign's fund-raising and publicity.

The one-millionth signature was secured on July 6, 1954, and Liebman set out to create a permanent lobbying organization, which became popularly known as the Committee of One Million. The committee was formally launched in 1955 with former UN ambassador WARREN AUSTIN as its honorary chairman and Liebman as the secretary and main driving force.

The committee had four goals: creation of a rightist bipartisan foreign policy; opposition to "appeasement" of communists; unqualified support for Nationalist China; and support for American resistance to "indirect" communist aggression in Asia. Liebman continued to act as the chief fund-raiser and publicist for the committee as well as keeping its members informed of the latest foreign policy positions of the United States and its European allies.

Liebman, through the committee, had a powerful impact on the China policy of the Eisenhower administration. His influence, however, waned during the KENNEDY and JOHNSON administrations. In 1969 Liebman closed his New York office and moved to London for a time to be a theatrical producer. The committee was disbanded in 1973 after President Richard NIXON's overtures to China. Liebman continued his political involvement as an occasional contributor to the conservative political journal *National Review*.

For Further Information:
Koen, R.Y. *The China Lobby in American Politics*. New York, 1960.

Lilienthal, David E.   (July 8, 1899–January 15, 1981)   As the first chairman of the U.S. ATOMIC ENERGY COMMISSION, David Lilienthal was instrumental in developing American nuclear policy and directing the development of the hydrogen bomb.

After graduating from Harvard Law School in 1923, Lilienthal practiced law in Chicago and became involved in progressive causes. His work in drafting a model regulation program for public utilities for the state of Illinois caught the attention of President FRANKLIN ROOSEVELT, who appointed Lilienthal a director of the Tennessee Valley Authority.

In January 1946 President HARRY TRUMAN asked Lilienthal to help prepare a report on international atomic energy control. The result, which became known as the Acheson-Lilienthal Report, was published on March 28, 1946, and proposed the establishment of an international authority with a world monopoly on uranium. The authority would forbid the production of explosive material but license the use of "denatured" plutonium for industrial and experimental work. The United States would stop the manufacture of nuclear weapons and effect a staged transfer of atomic information to the international authority. The report stressed, however, that the United States must not immediately release its atomic secrets.

The report became the basis for the Baruch Plan presented to the United Nations later that year. BERNARD BARUCH, however, insisted that Soviet compliance be ensured by adding a provision that prohibited Security Council members from using their veto when discussing atomic energy. Lilienthal,

along with DEAN ACHESON, opposed the addendum and warned that it would lead to Soviet rejection. Baruch's demands were met—and the Soviets rejected the plan.

On January 1, 1947, Truman created the Atomic Energy Commission (AEC) as a civilian successor to the military-controlled Manhattan Project. The AEC was charged with the development and production of all nuclear weapons and with directing and developing peaceful uses for nuclear technology. In February 1947 Lilienthal was nominated as the AEC's first chairman.

Lilienthal's nomination immediately encountered congressional opposition from conservative factions who opposed Lilienthal either because of his New Deal connections or because they felt that the Acheson-Lilienthal Report had committed him to nuclear disarmament. After personal intervention by Truman and moderate Republicans, Lilienthal was narrowly confirmed.

Lilienthal's problems with Congress did not stop with his confirmation. In May 1949 it was revealed that the AEC had granted fellowships to members of the Communist Party and that its Argonne National Laboratory in Chicago had lost some uranium compound. Senator Bourke Hickenlooper charged Lilienthal with "incredible mismanagement" and demanded his resignation. At the same time, the Senate forced Lilienthal to order all fellowship applicants and holders of current fellowships to sign loyalty oaths and affidavits swearing that they were not communists.

Lilienthal demanded a full congressional inquiry into his management of the AEC. The inquiry by the Joint Congressional Committee on Atomic Energy was concluded on October 13, 1949, and completely cleared Lilienthal of mismanagement. Shortly afterward, on November 21, 1949, Lilienthal announced his intention to resign. He told journalists that he had wanted to resign earlier but had waited for the results of the congressional inquiry so that he would not be perceived as leaving under a cloud.

Lilienthal finally left the AEC in February 1950 when he returned to practicing law. Shortly before leaving government, he warned that failure to control the production of atomic weapons would have "catastrophic consequences." Lilienthal remained active in Democratic Party politics until shortly before his death on January 15, 1981.

For Further Information:
Gilpin, Robert. *American Scientists and Nuclear Weapons Policy*. Princeton, 1962.
Jacobson, Harold D. *Diplomats, Scientists and Politicians*. Ann Arbor, Mich., 1966.
Lilienthal, David E. *The Journals of David E. Lilienthal: The Atomic Energy Years, 1945–60*. New York, 1964.
———. *This I Do Believe*. New York, 1949.

Lin Biao   (December 5, 1907–September 13, 1971)   Lin Biao was a major military and political figure in communist China. He was responsible for defeating CHIANG KAI-SHEK's Nationalist forces in Manchuria. In the 1960s his reorganization of the People's Liberation Army led to the CULTURAL REVOLUTION and Lin's promotion to second-in-command behind MAO ZEDONG. Lin was killed in an airplane crash in 1971 after an alleged attempt to overthrow Mao.

Lin was born into a peasant family in Hupeh province of central China. After completing his middle school (high school) education he joined the Socialist Youth League and enrolled in the Whampoa Military Academy in Canton. The Chinese communists at this time were allied with the Kuomintang Party of Chiang Kai-shek, who was head of the academy. Chiang quickly spotted Lin's talent as a military commander and, after only a year at Whampoa, gave Lin a batallion command on the 1926 military expedition against the northern warlords.

In 1927, however, Chiang started a bloody purge of the communists, and Lin joined Mao at his besieged base in Kiangsi in south China. Lin played a major part in defending the communist base against repeated attacks by Nationalist forces. During the legendary Long March to Shenshi province, Lin was placed in command of the First Army Corps, which acted as the march vanguard.

In 1937 Lin was badly wounded in a battle with the Japanese. The wound was to plague him for the rest of his life and kept him hospitalized in Moscow for large parts of World War II. In 1942, however, he returned to the communist headquarters at Yenan to take command of the party's Military and Political Academy. He was also elected to the party's Central Committee.

Lin had by this time perfected a military strategy based on guerrilla warfare, the support of the peasants and control of the countryside. These tactics were used to their greatest effect in Manchuria during the CHINESE CIVIL WAR between the Chinese communists and the Kuomintang. The capture of Manchuria was vital to the outcome of the conflict because of the region's heavy industry and its strategic position. Despite American aid in ferrying Kuomintang troops to the region, Lin's Fourth Field Army isolated the troops in the cities and eventually forced garrison after garrison to surrender. By 1948 the communists completely controlled Manchuria, and Lin's forces moved quickly south, capturing Beijing in January 1949, Wuhan in May and finally Canton in October 1949.

Lin later developed his Maoist military concepts to apply to revolutions in other countries. He argued that for a revolution to be successful it must rely primarily on internal support. The more dependent a revolution becomes upon foreign assistance, he argued in September 1965, the less likely its chance of success. Lin's military doctrine, developed in conjunction with Mao's political doctrine, became a model for Third World revolutionaries throughout the Cold War period.

As a reward for his military achievements, Lin was named head of the party for the central-south region of China. In 1954 he was named a vice premier and vice chairman of the National Defense Council and in 1955 became a member of the Politburo. In September 1959 he was appointed minister of defense.

Until this time, Lin's political exposure had been limited. But his control of the defense establishment provided him with a political base, and he started to build upon it. He began with a complete reorganization of the army to increase the soldiers' political consciousness and military efficiency. The idea was that the political debate and discipline of the army would become a model for the rest of the party and the country. Lin's reform of the People's Liberation ARMY (PLA) coincided with the Mao's loss of control of the party to DENG XIAOPING and LIU SHAOQI, who attempted to reintroduce market forces into the Chinese economy. The politicization of the army was done with the blessing and support of Mao, who intended to use Lin and the PLA to reassert his authority over the party. The ensuing struggle developed into the Cultural Revolution of 1965–1976 and the elevation of Lin to the position of heir-apparent to Mao.

During the Cultural Revolution the party and bureaucracy were so extensively purged that the administrative fabric of the country was in tatters. The only organized force left in China was Lin's People's Liberation Army, and the military thus effectively administered the country. Lin, as heir-apparent to Mao and minister of defense, became responsible for the day-to-day government of the country alongside Premier CHOU EN-LAI.

Mao came to fear that the military would take political control from the party. In 1971 he moved to purge Lin. According to a later account by Chou En-lai, when Lin heard of Mao's move he himself attempted to overthrow Mao. When the coup failed, Lin, his wife and son tried to escape to Moscow by plane. The plane crashed on September 13, 1971, in Mongolia. It has never been established if the plane was shot down or crashed accidentally.

For Further Information:
McFarquhar, Roderick. *The Origins of the Cultural Revolution.* London, 1974.
Meisner, Maurice. *Mao's China and After: A History of the People's Republic.* New York, 1986.
Robinson, Thomas W. *A Politico-Military Biography of Lin Piao.* New York, 1971.

Linkage Linkage was a U.S. foreign policy concept developed by HENRY KISSINGER in an attempt to encourage a more "responsible" Soviet foreign policy in return for American concessions on trade and technology and in negotiations on strategic arms limitation.

The policy of linkage was best summed up by President RICHARD NIXON in response to a Soviet request for early STRATEGIC ARMS LIMITATION (SALT) TALKS. He said that such talks would be feasible "in a way and at a time that will promote, if possible, progress on outstanding political problems at the same time—for example, on the problem of the Middle East and other outstanding problems in which the U.S. and the U.S.S.R., acting together, can save the cause of peace."

Linkage continued to be a major element of American foreign policy during the FORD, CARTER and REAGAN administrations. Although basically successful, the linkage policy did at times lead to disagreements between the Soviet Union and the United States and among policymakers within the United States and the Western Alliance over what issues should be linked.

For Further Information:
Kissinger, Henry. *The White House Years.* New York, 1979.
———. *Years of Upheaval.* New York, 1982.
Litwak, R.S. *Détente and the Nixon Doctrine: American Foreign Policy and the Pursuit of Stability, 1969–1975.* New York, 1984.
Nixon, Richard. *RN: The Memoirs of Richard Nixon.* New York, 1978.
Spanier, J.W. *American Foreign Policy Since World War Two.* Washington, D.C., 1988.

Li Peng   (October 1928–   )   Li Peng is a hard-line member of the Chinese Communist Party who was one of the key figures behind the decision to crush the student-led pro-democracy movement in May and June of 1989.

Li was born in Sichuan province into a communist family. His father, the writer Li Shouxun, was executed by Nationalist Chinese leader CHIANG KAI-SHEK in 1930 and the young Li was adopted by the future Chinese communist premier CHOU EN-LAI.

After studying engineering in China, Li went to Moscow in 1948 for a further degree. He remained in the Soviet Union for seven years and became president of the Association of Chinese Students in the U.S.S.R. His long stay in the Soviet Union later led critics to claim that he was pro-Soviet.

Between 1955 and 1965, Li worked on a series of engineering projects. At the start of the CULTURAL REVOLUTION he moved to Beijing, where he became acting party secretary for the Beijing Municipal Power Supply Bureau. In this position he was marked as a target of the Red Guards, but Chou's influence saved him.

After the death of MAO ZEDONG, Li was recruited by DENG XIAOPING to become deputy minister of power in 1979 and then minister of power two years later. In 1983 he became a deputy prime minister and in 1985 was elected to the Politburo and started to travel widely, including a trip to the Soviet Union to represent China at the funeral of KONSTANTIN CHERNENKO.

Within China, Li established a reputation as a cautious reformer. He supported Deng's efforts to relax economic controls, place more consumer goods on the shelves and open up China to international trade. But he opposed efforts to introduce accompanying political reforms. His position became increasingly similar to that of Deng and put him in opposition to the more reform-minded premier Hu Yaobang.

When pro-democracy student riots broke out at the end of 1985, Li claimed that they were the result of an excess of "bourgeois liberalism" and proposed that the state establish work programs so that students would learn "that capitalism is not feasible in China." When Hu Yaobang was forced to resign over the protests, Li supported Zhao Ziyang as premier and in November 1987 succeeded Zhao when the latter resigned the premiership to concentrate on his job as general secretary of the party.

But the two men quickly came into conflict. Zhao was committed to economic reform and was willing to accept the price of some dislocation of the economy to achieve this reform. Li, however, had come to realize that economic reform would eventually create popular pressures that would force the party to accept political reforms, which he steadfastly opposed. His approach to economic issues therefore became much more traditional and cautious.

In the weeks before the April 1988 Party Congress, at which Li was confirmed as prime minister, he let it be known that he thought Zhao was introducing the economic changes too quickly and that this would lead to political unrest. He quickly emerged as the leader of the hard-liners in opposition to the reformist movement headed by Zhao, and the Party Congress split between the two men. The aging Deng Xiaoping tried to mediate between the two factions but did not support either group until after riots broke out.

This split between hard-liners and moderates created an opportunity for the pro-democracy student movement to try to influence events in favor of political reform. In April 1989 they took to the streets to demonstrate in favor of Zhao and the late Hu Yaobang and to demand the resignation of Li. The demonstrations gathered momentum and by mid-May the students had control of Tiananmen Square at the center of Beijing and were able to disrupt the historic visit to China of Soviet leader MIKHAIL GORBACHEV. The growing power of the students threatened the very structure of the party, and martial law was declared. In June 1989, Li and Deng ordered troops into Tiananmen Square. They opened fire on the crowds, killing demonstrators and crushing the democracy movement.

In the prelude to and the immediate aftermath of the Tiananmen Square massacre the Communist Party leadership was wracked by a power struggle between the reformers led by Zhao and the hard-liners led by Li. Li for a time dropped from public view and it was rumored that he had been overthrown or even shot. But on June 9 Li appeared in public with Deng, thus receiving the "helmsman's" support. At the end of the month, Li was confirmed as the winner of the power struggle when the Central Committee voted Zhao out of office.

Lippmann, Walter   (September 21, 1889–December 14, 1974)   Walter Lippmann was a leading American liberal commentator of the early Cold War years and actually coined the term "Cold War." In his 60-year career he was one of the most respected and widely read journalists in the world.

Lippmann went into journalism after graduating from Harvard University in 1914. Three years later he became assistant secretary of war and helped to formulate President Woodrow Wilson's postwar internationalist policy. But Lippmann was dissatisfied with government work; shortly after the end of World War I he returned to journalism, and in 1931 he started his regular political column "Today and Tomorrow" for the *New York Herald-Tribune.* The column was eventually syndicated in 250 American newspapers and 25 newspapers overseas and won two Pulitzer prizes.

Lippmann argued that the United States should base its foreign policy on realpolitik considerations rather than on moral positions of abstract right and wrong. He felt that the United States should not attempt to challenge Soviet hegemony in Eastern Europe. He also criticized the TRUMAN administration's plans to rebuild postwar Germany as an unnecessary challenge to the Soviet Union.

Lippmann supported aid to Greece and Turkey because he believed it was in America's vital interests to protect the oil routes from the Middle East. But he opposed the TRUMAN DOCTRINE's offer of aid to any country fighting communism on the grounds that it went beyond protecting the national interest and was in effect a moral crusade. Lippmann also opposed GEORGE F. KENNAN's CONTAINMENT policy because he believed it would lead to "unending intervention" and enable the Soviets to maintain the initiative. Lippmann, in a series of articles on East–West relations, claimed that Kennan was waging a "cold war" and that the United States should instead pursue a "policy of settlement." The series of articles later became the basis of a book entitled *The Cold War,* published in November 1947.

During the EISENHOWER administration, Secretary of State JOHN FOSTER DULLES became a favorite target for Lippmann. He criticized Dulles for failing to define clearly the administration's "New Look" policy—the nuclear policy of "MASSIVE RETALIATION." During the QUEMOY AND MATSU crises Lippmann warned against a close alliance with Nationalist Chinese leader CHIANG KAI-SHEK. He also proposed that Germany be gradually neutralized and demilitarized in order to achieve unification. Lippmann argued that the best way to prevent the spread of communism was to encourage the growth of democratic institutions in neutral Third World countries.

In the 1960 presidential election campaign, Lippmann endorsed JOHN F. KENNEDY as the first candidate since Roosevelt who could stir and unite the American people. But the liberal journalist quickly became disillusioned with Kennedy's economic and foreign policies. He became a particularly vehement critic of the Kennedy and JOHNSON policies in Vietnam, and continued to attack U.S. involvement there until his retirement in 1968.

For Further Information:

Adams, Larry L. *Walter Lippmann.* Boston, 1977.
Blum, D. Steven. *Walter Lippmann, Cosmopolitanism in the Century of Total War.* Ithaca, N.Y., 1984.
Childs, Marquis, and James Reston, eds. *Walter Lippmann and His Times.* New York, 1959.
Dam, Hari N. *The Intellectual Odyssey of Walter Lippmann; A Study of His Protean Thought, 1910–1960.* New York, 1973.
Lippmann, Walter. *The Cold War.* New York, 1947.
———. *The Communist World and Ours.* New York, 1957.
———. *Public Opinion.* New York, 1956.
Steel, Ronald. *Walter Lippmann and the American Century.* Boston, 1980.

Lisbon Agreement (1952) The NORTH ATLANTIC TREATY ORGANIZATION's Lisbon Agreement of 1952 established many of the basic structures of NATO, laid foundation stones for the formation of a European army and the EUROPEAN DEFENSE COMMUNITY (EDC), which would include West Germany, and set ambitious goals for alliance defense forces.

The KOREAN WAR and successive crises in BERLIN had convinced the European members of NATO that there was a great danger that America's new worldwide commitments would leave it dangerously overstretched and leave Europe exposed to a military attack from the Soviet Union. The Europeans concluded therefore that they had to take on a greater share of the burden for their own defense and integrate their forces in a European army. At the same time, since Western Europe was still not fully recovered from World War II, it was necessary to strengthen America's defense and political ties to Western Europe through an expanded NATO organization.

These plans crystallized at a meeting of NATO foreign and defense ministers in Lisbon on February 20–25, 1952. The main points agreed upon by ministers at this meeting were:

1. Approval of plans for a European army to include West Germany.
2. A goal to have 50 NATO divisions active in Europe by the end of 1952 and produce 4,000 aircraft.
3. The inclusion of Greek and Turkish forces under the Supreme Allied Commander in Europe.
4. The reorganization of NATO's bureaucracy to create a secretary general, to increase the powers of the SUPREME ALLIED COMMANDER FOR EUROPE and establish a permanent council of ambassadors to NATO to take over from meetings of deputy ministers.
5. A declaration of aims that emphasized the defensive nature of the alliance.

The organizational changes went ahead and a NATO headquarters was installed later that year outside Paris. Lord Ismay, the British Commonwealth secretary, was named NATO's first secretary general. But a slight easing of tensions in Korea led the Europeans to reconsider their commitments to heavy defense expenditures. At his end-of-the-year report in December, Lord Ismay said that the alliance had fallen significantly short of its force goals. Plans for the European army under the EDC went ahead, and an agreement was signed in May 1952, but the pact collapsed after it was rejected by the French National Assembly in April 1953. This led to full West German membership in NATO and the WESTERN EUROPEAN UNION.

The main achievement of the Lisbon Agreement was that it demonstrated that if the threat were great enough, the

Europeans could find the political will and capacity to unite against it. The degree of unity demonstrated by the Lisbon Agreement caused a diplomatic panic in Moscow and prompted the Soviet Union on March 10 to ask Britain, France and the United States for early talks on German reunification. The Soviets also offered several concessions in a treaty draft, including allowing Germany sufficient land, air and sea forces for defense and an arms industry to equip them. The Soviets also proposed that the ODER-NEISSE LINE be made the permanent German–Polish boundary, that Germany refrain from joining NATO or the EDC, that basic civil rights be guaranteed all Germans, and full civil and political rights be restored to all ex-Nazis not convicted of war crimes.

The proposal was interpreted in the West as a Soviet attempt to seduce Germany away from an alliance with the United States or other European countries. The neutralization of Germany remained one of the centerpieces of Soviet foreign policy. Conversely, West German membership in the alliance was one of the foundation stones of American and Western foreign policy.

For Further Information:
Cook, Don. *Forging the Alliance*. London, 1989.
NATO Information Services. *NATO Facts and Figures*. Brussels, 1985.

Liu Shaoqi   **(1898–November 12, 1969)**   Liu Shaoqi was Chinese head of state in the early 1960s and the heir-designate to MAO ZEDONG for the chairmanship of the Chinese Communist Party. His moderate economic policies brought him into conflict with Mao, however, and this conflict was the major cause of the CULTURAL REVOLUTION, which led to Liu's being purged from the party.

Liu was born in Hunan province, the son of a wealthy peasant. He attended both middle (high) school and normal school and became involved in radical student politics at a young age. He joined the Socialist Youth League in 1920 and soon afterward went to Moscow, where he attended university and joined the newly formed Chinese Communist Party. In Moscow, Liu developed a strong attachment to the international communist movement, and he was never able to shed his internationalism.

In 1922 Liu returned to China and was appointed an aide to Mao Zedong in Hunan and given the task of organizing local trade unions. His work with the unions took Liu into urban areas, and when CHIANG KAI-SHEK's Nationalist Party turned on the Chinese Communist Party in April 1927, Liu's urban base was wiped out.

Chiang's attacks on Liu's cadres only served to strengthen Liu's position in the party. He moved into the Shanghai underground and in 1927 was elected a member of the Central Committee. Shortly afterward he was named director of the party's Workers' Department and in 1929 became secretary of the Manchurian Provincial Party Committee. In 1932 Liu joined Mao's forces in Kiangsi province and in 1934 was

elevated to the Chinese Communist Party's Politburo. When Mao left Kiangsi for his Long March to Yenan, Liu went to Beijing to foment antigovernment unrest. He was largely responsible for an outbreak of student violence in December 1935.

In 1939 Liu rejoined Mao in Yenan, where he assumed the role of party ideologue. In 1943 he was named secretary of the Central Secretariat and by the end of World War II was regarded as the chief spokesman for party affairs and the number-two man behind Mao. When the communist government was established on October 1, 1949, Liu was named vice chairman.

The early 1950s saw the laying of the basic political and economic foundation of communist China. Liu during this period adopted relatively moderate economic policies in opposition to the pro-Soviet Kao Kang and the radical Mao. In April 1955, the moderates and anti-Soviet figures were significantly strengthened when Liu's chief lieutenant, DENG XIAOPING, was promoted to the Politburo, Liu was promoted to the number-two position behind Mao, and Kao was purged.

The main thrust of Liu's influence at this stage was felt in the economic sphere, and he moved to reduce Soviet control of Chinese factories and the railway system. But the Soviet Union continued to exert a strong influence over the military and foreign policy, and the agricultural and intellectual fields were controlled by Mao.

Liu generally had control of the administrative machinery of government and had a large but not controlling influence on the party machinery. Mao preferred at this stage to concentrate more on doctrinal and policy issues. In 1955, however, he emerged from the shadows to reimpose his authority. This led to his "Hundred Flowers" campaign and the "Great Leap Forward." The first encouraged a diversity of intellectual thought in the hope that criticism would strengthen the party. Instead it led to dissidents' questioning the basic premises of communism. The Great Leap Forward was a bold effort to boost agricultural and industrial production, which also failed. The double failure undermined Mao's position in the party. In 1959 he was forced to retire as chairman of the People's Republic in favor of Liu, although he retained the position of chairman of the Chinese Communist Party.

Liu started to introduce a number of reforms to the Chinese economy designed to liberalize communist doctrine and increase the production of consumer goods. This was generally in line with the "New Look" policies then being introduced in the Soviet Union by NIKITA KHRUSHCHEV but was inconsistent with Maoist principles. Liu also took a more active interest in foreign affairs and was responsible for China's forging close relations with Ghana, North Vietnam, CAMBODIA, Pakistan, North Korea, CUBA and Indonesia under president Sukarno. It is difficult to determine his attitude toward the SINO-SOVIET SPLIT of the late 1950s and early 1960s. In the early 1950s he had been a proponent of close relations with Moscow and chairman of the Sino-Soviet Friendship Association, but his chief lieutenant, Deng, took a hard line in discussions with Moscow, and it appears unlikely that he would have been able to do so without the support of Liu.

Mao's weak position in the late 1950s prevented him from blocking Liu's foreign or domestic policies, and Mao appeared to slip further into the political wilderness. But in the early 1960s Mao formed a political alliance with Minister of Defense LIN BIAO, who agreed to restructure the People's Liberation Army along Maoist lines and introduce the teaching of Maoist ideological doctrine.

The first clear sign of Liu's fall from grace during the Cultural Revolution came after the extraordinary meeting of the Party Central Committee at the beginning of August 1966. At the first rally at which the Red Guards appeared, the notables presented were listed in a new order of importance, with Liu unaccountably dropped to seventh place. He still appeared in public for a further three months, but was increasingly vilified in a wall poster campaign. He was reported to have made a confession—deemed inadequate by the Red Guard—and later retracted it. By December 1966 Liu's public appearances stopped completely.

In October 1968 Liu was stripped of his party posts, and in April 1969 Lin Biao succeeded him as heir-designate of Mao. During this period, however, Liu continued to live in the special area near Beijing's Forbidden City reserved for the party elite. The exact date and cause of his death are clouded in mystery. Rumors of Liu's death started circulating among the foreign press corps in China toward the end of 1974, and on October 30 the communist newspaper in Hong Kong, *Wen Wei Po*, reported that he had died. No further details were given until May 1980, when the *Beijing Review* reported that Liu had died on November 12, 1969.

For Further Information:
Hsu, C.Y. *The Rise of Modern China*. New York, 1983.
Meisner, Maurice. *Mao's China and After: A History of the People's Republic*. New York, 1986.

Lodge, Henry Cabot   (July 5, 1902–February 27, 1985)
Henry Cabot Lodge was a prominent Republican figure in foreign affairs. As a U.S. senator during the Truman administration, he helped to swing liberal Republicans behind the Democratic president's foreign policy. Under President DWIGHT EISENHOWER he served as ambassador to the United Nations; he was the Republican Party's candidate for vice president in 1960 and later served as ambassador to Vietnam and headed the U.S. delegation to the PARIS PEACE TALKS.

Lodge came from an old and patrician New England family. He was raised by his grandfather, also named Henry Cabot Lodge, who was a prominent Republican senator from Massachusetts from 1893 to 1924. After graduating from Harvard in 1924, Lodge joined the staff of the *New York Herald-Tribune* as a reporter. In 1933 he was elected to the Massachusetts House of Representatives and in 1936 to the U.S. Senate. During World War II, Lodge served two tours of duty overseas. His experiences during the war convinced him that the United States must break away from the prewar isolationist policies championed by his grandfather, who had led the campaign to keep the United States out of the League of Nations.

After being reelected to the Senate in 1946, Lodge formed a close relationship with Senator ARTHUR VANDENBERG. Together they persuaded other prominent Republicans to support the MARSHALL PLAN, the TRUMAN DOCTRINE and the NORTH ATLANTIC TREATY ORGANIZATION.

Lodge urged General Dwight Eisenhower to seek the Republican nomination for president in 1952 and later helped to manage his campaign. In doing so, he neglected his own campaign and narrowly lost his Senate seat to JOHN F. KENNEDY. As a reward for his loyalty, Eisenhower appointed Lodge ambassador to the United Nations and a member of the National Security Council. At the United Nations, Lodge took a strong anti-communist stand and represented the United States at debates on the Hungarian Revolution, the SUEZ CRISIS and the QUEMOY AND MATSU ISLANDS crisis. His personal standing enabled him to develop an independence of action that no other American ambassador enjoyed.

Lodge resigned his UN post in 1960 to campaign as RICHARD NIXON's vice presidential running mate. Nixon hope that Lodge's extensive experience in foreign affairs and his East Coast establishment origins would complement Nixon's own West Coast following and his conservatism. The election was won, however, by the Democratic candidate, John F. Kennedy.

In November 1961 Lodge became director general of the recently created Atlantic Institute, which had been formed to work for an European–American–Canadian economic community. The project failed in the face of opposition from French president CHARLES DE GAULLE.

In June 1963 President Kennedy appointed Lodge, who was fluent in French, ambassador to South Vietnam. Lodge arrived in Saigon the day after troops of President NGO DINH DIEM had ruthlessly killed or arrested hundreds of Buddhist priests. The regime's attacks on the Buddhists quickly led Lodge to the conclusion that the Vietnamese war could not be won as long as Diem's corrupt and unpopular government remained in power. Within a few weeks, Lodge was being approached by high-ranking Vietnamese military officers and asked what the attitude of the United States would be to a military coup.

In cabling his reports back to Washington, Lodge advised both Secretary of State DEAN RUSK and President Kennedy to support a military coup. On August 24, Lodge received a State Department cable telling him to inform the generals that the United States would find it impossible to support Diem unless he instituted drastic political reforms. Unfortunately, the cable had not been cleared by Rusk or Kennedy, and Lodge was later instructed to back away from the earlier cable.

But the generals had already begun their plans for a coup. In early October, at the suggestion of Lodge, the Kennedy administration deferred approval of a portion of its foreign aid in an attempt to force Diem into reform. The military interpreted this as American approval for their coup and they moved on November 1, 1963.

Lodge remained in Saigon, and his political importance increased following the overthrow of Diem and the assassination of President Kennedy. In May 1964 he resigned his ambassadorship to return to the United States to challenge Senator Barry Goldwater for the Republican presidential nomination, but was unsuccessful.

In September 1964, Lodge was appointed President LYNDON JOHNSON's "consultant" on Vietnam and toured NATO countries explaining America's Vietnam policy. In July 1965 he was reappointed ambassador to Vietnam and began to press for a "pacification" program designed to provide protection to villagers and to carry out economic and social reforms aimed at raising rural living standards. The inevitable failure of the program, whose professed aims were in conflict with the interests of the South Vietnamese ruling elite, strengthened the position of those advising the president to press for a military solution in Vietnam. Lodge distanced himself from the military planning of the war, although he did recommend a resumption of bombing raids, after a pause from December 1965 to January 1966, in order to lure the North Vietnamese to the negotiating table.

In June 1966 Lodge became involved in secret negotiations with Hanoi and in November recommended a bombing pause in order to encourage a positive response from North Vietnam. In December 1966 Lodge was told by Polish intermediaries that the North Vietnamese were prepared to enter negotiations, but soon afterward the United States resumed bombing of civilian areas around Hanoi. Lodge tried to stop the air strikes but failed. The talks broke down and Lodge left Saigon on April 24, 1967.

In March 1968 Lodge became a member of the senior advisory group on Vietnam, which had been formed to consider the Pentagon's request for 200,000 additional troops following the TET OFFENSIVE. The group rejected the request and proposed a de-escalation policy, which Johnson accepted. From April 1968 until January 1969, Lodge served as the Johnson administration's ambassador to West Germany.

On January 5, 1969, President Richard Nixon appointed Lodge to replace AVERELL HARRIMAN as the chief of the U.S. delegation to the Paris peace conference on Vietnam. He forcefully presented the American proposals for a complete withdrawal of all outside forces within one year, a cease-fire under international supervision and free elections under international supervision. The North Vietnamese rejected these proposals—they did not regard themselves as an "outside" force—and demanded the immediate and total withdrawal of all American forces. Lodge resigned from his post on November 20. At the time he cited "personal matters at home," but his resignation letter also indicated that he was frustrated by the North Vietnamese negotiators' refusal to "reciprocate in any kind of meaningful way." Nixon's decision not to replace Lodge immediately was interpreted as a temporary downgrading of the peace talks.

On June 5, 1970, Nixon appointed Lodge special envoy to the Vatican. The position had special significance at the time because the Vatican had become a center for information about possible peace negotiations and American prisoners of war. At the same time, Lodge was named to a presidential commission to study American policy toward communist China. The commission's report, which was issued at the same time as a national U.S. Ping-Pong team arrived for a competition in China, recommended that the United States seek Chinese admission to the United Nations without the expulsion of Taiwan.

Shortly afterward, Lodge returned to his home in Massachusetts and concentrated on private business and the writing of his memoirs, which were published in 1973, and occasionally advised the government on foreign affairs issues.

For Further Information:
Hatch, Alden. *The Lodges of Massachusetts.* New York, 1973.
Lodge, Henry Cabot. *The Storm Has Many Eyes.* New York, 1973.
Miller, William J. *Henry Cabot Lodge.* New York, 1967.

London Foreign Ministers' Conference (1945)   The London Foreign Ministers' Conference of September 11–October 2, 1945, was the first postwar meeting of the Foreign Ministers' Council. Its failure helped to set the tone for postwar East–West relations.

On July 17, 1945, at the POTSDAM CONFERENCE, Soviet leader JOSEF STALIN, U.S. president HARRY TRUMAN and British prime minister WINSTON CHURCHILL agreed that a council of foreign ministers should be established to pave the way for a full peace conference and the signing of a formal peace treaty with Germany. The foreign ministers would come from Britain, France, the United States, China and the Soviet Union.

On September 11, 1945, GEORGES BIDAULT (France), Secretary of State JAMES BYRNES (United States), ERNEST BEVIN (Britain), V.M. MOLOTOV (Soviet Union) and Wang Shih-chich (China) met in London. On the first day, Molotov and Byrnes clashed over the meeting's agenda. Byrnes wanted the ministers to discuss the terms of the peace treaty. Molotov insisted that the council should discuss arrangements for the occupation of Japan.

The council remained deadlocked over the issue for the first two days, until Byrnes managed to move discussion onto the Italian peace treaty, using a draft submitted by Bevin. Byrnes and Bevin now clashed with Molotov over his demand that the Soviet Union be given control over a portion of the Italian colonies and that Trieste be handed over to Yugoslavia. This led to several more days of argument until the council moved on to the Romanian treaty, at which point Molotov, accurately, accused the Western ministers of being hostile to the Soviet-supported government of Premier Petru Groza.

The major disagreement, however, occurred over the French and Chinese presence at the council. On September 22, Molotov asked Byrnes and Bevin to meet him privately and told them that the Soviet government believed that it had been a mistake to include France and China in the Council of Foreign Ministers. He said China had no business discussing European affairs, and France should be excluded from discussions on all countries except Italy and Germany. When Molotov raised the issue again at the full council session, Bidault and Wang threatened to walk out. The meeting quickly deteriorated until it collapsed on October 2.

For Further Information:

Davis, Lynn Etheridge. *The Cold War Begins: Soviet American Conflict over Eastern Europe.* Princeton, 1974.

Donnelly, Desmond. *Struggle for the World.* New York, 1965.

Fleming, D.F. *The Cold War and Its Origins, 1917–1960.* Garden City, N.Y., 1961.

Fontaine, Andre. *History of the Cold War,* vols. 1 and 2. New York, 1965 and 1969.

Rose, Lisle A. *After Yalta: America and the Origins of the Cold War.* New York, 1973.

London Foreign Ministers' Conference (1947) The Soviet hard line at the London Foreign Ministers' Conference of November 25–December 15, 1947, helped to bring France firmly into the Western camp and helped to prepare the right psychological climate for the signing of the 1948 BRUSSELS TREATY.

The conference was called to continue discussions for a German and Austrian peace treaty, the organization of postwar Germany and Soviet demands for German war reparations. Those attending were U.S. secretary of state GEORGE C. MARSHALL, British foreign Secretary ERNEST BEVIN, Soviet foreign minister V.M. MOLOTOV and French foreign minister GEORGES BIDAULT.

The conference was heavily influenced by the introduction of the MARSHALL PLAN. On the first day of the London meeting, Molotov, in an obvious reference to the plan, accused the Western powers of seeking to impose "an imperialist peace," which held "the seeds of conflict and even war." Over the next three days the ministers split 3–1 on the issues of the eastern border of Germany, the future structure of a unified German government and the list of those to be invited to the German peace conference.

The first few days set the tone for the rest of the conference, which managed to agree only that France attend the German peace conference and that German steel production be raised from 5.8 million tons a year to 11.5 million tons. Even these minor agreements were nullified because they were conditional on an overall agreement on German unity. The meeting broke up on December 15, having failed even to set a date for another meeting.

In his closing speech, Marshall laid the failure of the meeting firmly on Soviet shoulders. He argued that the Soviets had refused to allow the German Saarland to be economically attached to France; had objected to a boundary commission for Germany; had refused to disclose how much it had already taken out of Germany in reparations payments; had refused to stop reparations from current production in their own zone; and had rejected a solution for Austria. He went on to say that the Soviet demand for reparations would "enslave the German people" and "seriously retard the recovery of Europe."

Molotov blamed Marshall, Bevin and Bidault for wrecking the conference. He said, "The three western delegations have united into a single front against the Soviet government's reparations claims." Bevin claimed that the Soviet Union had already taken $7 billion in reparations out of Germany. Bidault, who at previous meetings had attempted to conciliate between the East and West delegations, said that he was doubtful that this practice could continue.

For Further Information:

Davis, Lynn Etheridge. *The Cold War Begins: Soviet American Conflict over Eastern Europe.* Princeton, 1974.

Donnelly, Desmond. *Struggle for the World.* New York, 1965.

Fleming, D.F. *The Cold War and Its Origins, 1917–1960.* Garden City, N.Y., 1961.

Fontaine, Andre. *History of the Cold War,* vols. 1 and 2. New York, 1965 and 1969.

Rose, Lisle A. *After Yalta: America and the Origins of the Cold War.* New York, 1973.

London Protocol (1944) The London Protocol of September 12, 1944, established guidelines for the postwar geographic division of Germany and of Berlin. The agreement was negotiated by the Soviet, American and British members of the European Advisory Commission (EAC). A later zone was created for the French from the British and American zones. The main points of the protocol were:

1. Germany would, "for the purposes of occupation," be divided into three zones, one of which would be allotted to each of the three Allied Powers, and a special Berlin area which would be under joint occupation of the Three Powers.

2. The Eastern Zone of Germany was allocated to the Soviet Union, the Northwestern Zone to Britain and the Southwestern Zone to the United States. The United States was also given control of the ports of Bremen and Bremerhaven and transit rights through the British zone.

3. The Greater Berlin area, as defined by the law of April 27, 1920, would be jointly occupied by the armed forces of the United States, Britain and the Soviet Union, and the area would be divided into the northeastern part occupied by Soviet forces, the northwestern part occupied by British forces and the southern part occupied by American forces.

4. An Inter-Allied Governing Authority (Komendatura) consisting of the three national commandants would be established to jointly direct the administration of the Greater Berlin Area.

5. It was agreed that the protocol would come into force on the signature by Germany of the Instrument of Unconditional Surrender.

For Further Information:
Davis, Lynn Etheridge. *The Cold War Begins: Soviet American Conflict over Eastern Europe*. Princeton, 1974.
Donnelly, Desmond. *Struggle for the World*. New York, 1965.
Fleming, D. F., *The Cold War and Its Origins, 1917–1960*. Garden City, N.Y., 1961.
Fontaine, Andre. *History of the Cold War*, vols. 1 and 2. New York, 1965 and 1969.
Rose, Lisle A. *After Yalta: America and the Origins of the Cold War*. New York, 1973.

Lovett, Robert A.   (September 14, 1895–   )   Robert A. Lovett served as undersecretary of state and secretary of defense under President HARRY TRUMAN. In those positions he played an important role in administering the MARSHALL PLAN, the negotiations leading to the creation of the NORTH ATLANTIC TREATY ORGANIZATION and the U.S. involvement in Korea.

After serving as a pilot in World War I, Lovett graduated from Yale in 1919. He went on to Harvard Law School and the Harvard Graduate School of Business Administration and in 1921 joined the Wall Street investment banking firm Brown Brothers as a clerk. In 1926 he was made a partner, and in 1931 he organized the merger between Brown Brothers and W. A. Harriman & Co.

In April 1941 Lovett was named assistant secretary of war for air and given special responsibility for aircraft procurement and production. When the war ended he returned to investment banking, but two years later, in July 1947, he was asked by Secretary of State GEORGE MARSHALL to join him as undersecretary of state. The two men had become close friends during the war years. Lovett became known as Marshall's "troubleshooter" and frequently acted for the secretary when Marshall was abroad. During the summer of 1947 he oversaw the preparation of the Marshall Plan and pressed for the rehabilitation of Germany.

In 1948 Lovett concentrated his efforts on the creation of the North Atlantic Treaty Organization. He worked closely with Senator ARTHUR VANDENBERG to develop the VANDENBERG RESOLUTION, which cleared the way for American membership in NATO. Later he led the American delegation to secret talks in Europe, preparatory to the establishment of NATO, which established the principle that an armed attack upon one member country should be regarded as an armed attack upon all and that each "should take military or other action forthwith."

Lovett briefly returned to banking on Marshall's departure from the State Department early in 1949, but when Marshall became secretary of defense in 1950, Lovett went with him as his deputy with special responsibility for budget and procurement policies. Lovett also handled most of the day-to-day administration of the department. His main contribution while in this post was to develop arrangements with industry that would enable factories to move swiftly from civilian to military production in case of war.

Truman appointed Lovett secretary of defense upon Marshall's retirement in September 1951. As secretary, he ex-

panded research and development programs to include missiles and research into chemical and biological warfare. He also favored conscription and established the current procedure of an overall coordinated defense budget.

During the Eisenhower administration, Lovett returned to banking. When JOHN F. KENNEDY was elected president in 1960 he offered Lovett a choice of secretary of state, defense or treasury, but Lovett refused a cabinet post on grounds of ill health. He did work for Kennedy in an unofficial capacity, however, introducing him to prominent people from the Truman administration and appearing as an expert witness before the Senate Foreign Relations Committee. He was also a member of the inner circle that advised Kennedy during the CUBAN MISSILE CRISIS.

Lovett's influence declined during the Johnson administration, but in 1964 he contributed to a study of nuclear nonproliferation and another on general foreign policy issues. During the Nixon administration he supported the president's opposition to Senator MIKE MANSFIELD's attempts to reduce U.S. troop levels in Western Europe.

For Further Information:
Ferrell, Robert H. *George C. Marshall*. New York, 1966.

Loyalty Review Boards   The loyalty review boards were established by President HARRY TRUMAN in response to the growing influence of anti-communist conservatives in the United States, in and out of Congress, who perceived a threat from communist "subversives" in the federal government.

Truman was himself a consistent opponent of the "witch hunt" tactics of politicians such as Senator JOSEPH MCCARTHY. He called the investigations of the HOUSE UN-AMERICAN ACTIVITIES COMMITTEE a "red herring" and opposed both the MUNDT-NIXON BILL of 1948 and the INTERNAL SECURITY ACT of 1950.

But in the early postwar period he felt growing pressure from the right and sought to control it by making the first move. On November 25, 1946, Truman established a temporary commission on federal employment loyalty to:

1. Examine the standards and procedures for investigation of persons employed by the government or applicants for government jobs.
2. Devise means for the removal or disqualification of any disloyal or subversive persons.
3. Recommend improvements in existing legislative and administrative procedure in connection with loyalty investigations.
4. Establish administrative responsibility in loyalty cases and define standards of loyalty so as to protect the government against the employment of disloyal or subversive persons.
5. Establish standards of procedure to ensure fair hearings for persons accused of disloyal activities.

The commission's report, submitted on March 20, 1947, stressed that the whole topic of employee loyalty was subject to "hysteria, emotion and irresponsible thinking." It went on to recommend that each government department and agency establish its own loyalty procedures but that minimum standards be set by the White House. All prospective federal employees should be investigated for loyalty, in most instances by the Civil Service Commission. All current employees should be checked against the FBI files for evidence of disloyalty.

The commission recommended that the determination of loyalty cases be made by a loyalty board in each agency. A loyalty review board in the Civil Service Commission would coordinate agency policies, advise the president and the agencies and act as an appeal board. Any employee charged with disloyalty would be entitled to written notice of the charges and to an administrative hearing, including the right to be represented by counsel.

The report was accepted by Truman, who established the Loyalty Review Boards on March 22, 1947, with Executive Order 9835. The boards played a major role in the dismissals of prominent American diplomats such as JOHN STEWART SERVICE and JOHN PATON DAVIES.

For Further Information:
Feuerlich, Roberta. *Joe McCarthy and McCarthyism: The Hate That Haunts America.* New York, 1972.
Goldston, Robert. *The American Nightmare: Senator Joseph R. McCarthy and the Politics of Hate.* Indianapolis, 1973.

Lubbers, Ruud *See* NETHERLANDS.

Lublin Committee The Lublin Committee was the name given to the Polish provisional government supported by the Soviet Union in the closing years of World War II. The Lublin Committee formed the core of the postwar Polish government, and its creation and the Soviet Union's staunch support of it were a major cause of friction between the Soviet Union and the Polish government-in-exile in London and between the Soviet Union and the United States and Britain.

Following the fall of Poland in September 1939 a group of Polish statesmen led by Wladyslaw Sikorski, and later Stanislaw Mikolajczyk, established a government in exile in London. The government was recognized by the United States and Britain and later, after the Soviet Union was attacked by Germany, by the Soviets. But relations between the London Poles and Moscow were strained, partly because of the Soviet role in the 1939 dismemberment of Poland and partly because of the historical enmity and distrust between Poland and Russia.

One of the primary objectives of JOSEF STALIN's wartime strategy was to emerge from the war in control of Poland. Poor relations with the London Poles indicated that this could not be done if they returned to power in Warsaw. Therefore, Stalin in 1943 established a communist-dominated alternative known at first as the Union of Polish Patriots, an organization of Polish communists formed in Moscow. At first, the Soviet leader did not recognize the Polish communists as an alternative government. Then, in April 1943, the London Poles accused the Soviet Union of the murder of up to 15,000

Polish officers after its occupation of eastern Poland in September 1939.

Stalin used the accusation of the KATYN MASSACRE to break off diplomatic relations with the London Poles and bestow recognition on the Polish communists, who were led by Boleslaw Bierut and WLADYSLAW GOMULKA. Shortly afterward, on July 23, the Polish communists established headquarters in Lublin in Eastern Poland and issued a manifesto that declared themselves to be "the sole legal Polish executive power." There were now effectively two Polish governments. One was recognized by the Western Allies and the other by the Soviet Union.

As the Lublin Committee was already on Polish soil and allied with the invading Soviet Union, it was better placed to take power. The Lublin Committee suggested that the London Poles join a government of national unity in which the Lublin Committee would hold 18 cabinet posts and the London Poles only four. The immediate reaction of the London Poles was to reject the offer. Although they remained in London, they had strong support from the 300,000-strong Polish Home Army in Warsaw, led by General Tadeusz Komorowski. But this force was wiped out when the Red Army refused to come to its support during the WARSAW UPRISING from August 1 to October 2, 1944.

The defeat of the Home Army substantially weakened the position of Mikolajczyk in negotiations with the Lublin Poles in Moscow. The result was the formation of a national government in which the Lublin Poles emerged with 15 cabinet seats and the London Poles only six. Stalin had promised at YALTA and later at POTSDAM to hold free elections within a month. But no elections were held until January 19, 1947, by which time the dominant Lublin Poles had effectively repressed all political opposition.

For Further Information:
Davis, Lynn Etheridge. *The Cold War Begins: Soviet American Conflict Over Eastern Europe.* Princeton, 1974.
De Weydenthal, J.B. *The Communists of Poland.* New York, 1978.
Karski, Jan. *The Great Powers & Poland, 1919–1945: From Versailles to Yalta.* Lanham, Md., 1985.
Lukas, Richard C. *Bitter Legacy: Polish-American Relations in the Wake of World War II.* Lexington, Ky., 1982.
———. *The Strange Allies, the United States and Poland, 1941–1945.* Knoxville, 1978.
Polonsky, A. *The Little Dictators: The History of Eastern Europe Since 1918.* New York, 1975.
Polonsky, Antony, ed. *The Great Powers and the Polish Question, 1941–45: A Documentary Study in Cold War Origins.* London, 1976.
Toranska, Teresa. *"Them": Stalin's Polish Puppets.* New York, 1987.

Luce, Clare Boothe (April 10, 1903–October 9, 1987) Clare Boothe Luce was influential in the formation of U.S. foreign policy in the postwar years for three reasons. She was the wife and close adviser of Henry Luce, America's most influential news magazine publisher. She was elected to the U.S. Congress and subsequently was a U.S. ambassador.

Clare Boothe left home at 16 to become an actress in New York and four years later married millionaire clothing manufacturer George Brokaw. The marriage ended in divorce in 1929, and she took a number of journalist jobs before marrying HENRY LUCE, president of Time, Inc. in November 1935. She was also a successful playwright.

Shortly after the outbreak of war, Clare Luce toured China for *Life* magazine, and she and her husband developed a close friendship with Nationalist Chinese leader CHIANG KAI-SHEK and his wife Madame Chiang. This friendship was to be a major factor in the postwar politics of both Luces.

Upon her return from the Far East, Luce ran successfully as the Republican candidate for a seat in the U.S. House of Representatives from Connecticut. In the House she became a staunch critic first of President FRANKLIN ROOSEVELT's conduct of the war and later of Roosevelt and then of TRUMAN's postwar policies. Roosevelt, Luce maintained, had sold out the East Europeans at YALTA, and Truman had sold out Chiang Kai-shek to the Chinese communists.

Luce also pressed for U.S. economic aid for war-ravaged Europe and with Rep. Everett Dirksen of Illinois introduced aid legislation that became a forerunner to the MARSHALL PLAN. She left Congress in 1946 to return to writing, but remained active in Republican Party politics. She was a keen supporter of DWIGHT EISENHOWER for the 1952 Republican Party presidential nomination and was rewarded with the post of ambassador to Italy.

In Rome, Luce developed a reputation for meddling in Italian domestic politics. She publicly backed the Christian Democratic candidate ALCIDE DE GASPERI in the 1953 Italian general election and used her influence with her husband to put Gasperi on the cover of *Time* magazine just before the polling. She also persuaded the Eisenhower administration to cancel federal contracts with Italian companies where communist unions were in control.

Luce helped to resolve the long-standing Italian–Yugoslav dispute over TRIESTE by organizing a meeting in London between the two governments. When it was learned that Yugoslavian leader JOSIP BROZ TITO was taking a hard line in order to draw domestic attention away from the poor Yugoslav wheat crop, Luce arranged for a delivery of American wheat in return for concessions. The dispute was finally settled in October 1954.

Luce left Rome in 1956 because of ill health, but in 1959 Eisenhower nominated her ambassador to Brazil. The appointment was challenged by Senator Wayne Morse because of her record of interference in Italian domestic politics. The nomination was eventually confirmed by the Senate, but she resigned on the grounds that the dispute with Morse had made it impossible for her to do a proper job. Clare Boothe Luce returned to writing and remained active in Republican Party politics.

For Further Information:
Shadegg, Stephen. *Clare Boothe Luce.* New York, 1970.

Luce, Henry   **(April 3, 1898–February 28, 1967)**   As publisher and editor-in-chief of *Time* magazine and head of Time, Inc., Henry Luce was one of the most influential men in America from his founding of *Time* in 1923 until his death. He used this influence to further his conservative views, especially in regard to foreign policy.

Luce was the son of an American missionary in China, and he lived in that country until he was 14. His childhood experiences gave him a lifelong interest in the Far East. After graduating from Yale University in 1921 he entered journalism, and in 1923 Luce and his Yale classmate Britton Hadden launched *Time* magazine. The magazine was an instant success and the profits were used to found *Life* (1936) and *Fortune* (1930) magazines. In 1929, following the early death of Hadden, Luce took complete control of the company.

Luce never made any secret of his conservative views or his magazines' Republican and strongly anti-communist bias. President HARRY TRUMAN was regularly attacked in the news columns for being soft on communism, although Luce's publications did support the TRUMAN DOCTRINE and the MARSHALL PLAN.

Time magazine was particularly outspoken on American postwar policy in China. Luce and his wife, CLARE BOOTHE LUCE, had formed a close wartime friendship with Nationalist Chinese leader CHIANG KAI-SHEK and his wife Madame Chiang. This led him to become one of the most active and influential proponents of Chiang. Luce regularly rewrote the dispatches of his China correspondent Theodore White to portray Chiang in the best possible light and the Chinese communists in the worst (an editorial technique *Time* employed during the VIETNAM WAR as well). He also featured Chiang seven times on the cover of *Time*. He and his wife, who was a representative in the U.S. Congress from 1943 to 1947, personally lobbied for increased military and financial aid for the Nationalist government.

When Chiang's government fell in 1949, Luce singled out Secretary of State DEAN ACHESON and held him responsible for the "loss" of China. His support for Chiang was one of the reasons for Luce's backing of THOMAS E. DEWEY in the 1948 presidential election. He was led to believe that Dewey would support Chiang's attempts to win back control of the Chinese Mainland.

Luce and *Time* magazine backed DWIGHT EISENHOWER in the 1952 presidential campaign and strongly supported Secretary of State JOHN FOSTER DULLES's moral crusade against world communism. He tried to encourage American involvement in Vietnam following the French defeat at DIEN BIEN PHU in 1954 and supported it in the 1960s.

Luce's refusal to give an early endorsement to RICHARD NIXON, whose career he had helped to promote, is believed to have been a factor in JOHN F. KENNEDY's victory in the 1960 presidential campaign. Later Luce praised Kennedy's handling of the CUBAN MISSILE CRISIS. Luce's continuing support for Chiang Kai-shek is believed to have been a factor in Kennedy's continuing opposition to Chinese membership in the United Nations.

Luce retired as head of Time, Inc. in April 1964, but he remained editorial chairman and maintained a strong hold on editorial policy until his death on February 28, 1967.

For Further Information:

Baughman, James L. *Henry R. Luce and the Rise of the American News Media.* Boston, 1987.

Martin, Ralph G. *Henry and Clare: An Intimate Portrait of the Luces.* New York, 1991.

Neils, Patricia. *China Images in the Life and Times of Henry Luce.* Savage, Md., 1990.

Swanberg, W.A. *Luce and His Empire.* New York, 1972.

Lumumba, Patrice   (July 2, 1925–January 1961)

Patrice Lumumba was the first prime minister of the independent Congo and became a national hero. His anti-Western views led to an East–West clash in the Congo (later the Republic of Zaire) following independence from Belgium. His murder under mysterious circumstances at the age of 35 made him a martyr for African nationalists.

Lumumba was born in the small village of Onolua in the province of Kasai. He started his education in the American Methodist School at Wembo Nyama, but in his teens he was expelled for "immoral conduct" and finished his schooling at the Roman Catholic school.

After a course in teacher training, Lumumba entered the civil service and rose to become assistant postmaster of Stanleyville. But in 1956 he was found guilty of embezzlement, dismissed and given a short prison sentence. Shortly before this, he had become involved in African nationalist politics. After his release from prison in 1957, Lumumba founded the Congolese Nationalist Movement (MNC), dedicated to early independence and Congolese unity.

The mineral-rich Congo had been administered by the Belgian government since 1905. Among the European colonial powers in Africa, the Belgians had the worst record for treatment of the indigenous Africans and did little to prepare them for eventual self-rule. This and a policy of exploiting tribal differences in order to divide and rule, created a highly unstable situation when the Congo eventually achieved independence.

In 1958 Lumumba attended the Pan-African conference in Accra, Ghana where he formed a close relationship with the Ghanaian socialist leader Kwame Nkrumah. At the end of 1959 he was imprisoned by the Belgian authorities after being found guilty of inciting riots against Europeans. But by this time, Lumumba had become recognized as the only truly national figure capable of winning the support of all the Congolese people. The Belgian government, increasingly concerned about the attacks on Europeans, decided to pull out of the country and released Lumumba so that he could attend a round-table conference on independence in Brussels in January 1960.

The round-table conference negotiated a constitution based on a multiparty system with a president and prime minister. The pro-Western Joseph Kasavubu became president, but Lumumba's MNC was the overwhelming victor in a general election in May 1960. The socialist Lumumba officially became prime minister on July 1, 1960. Almost simultaneously, the army, which was led by the pro-Western Joseph-Désiré Mobutu (later Mobutu Sese Seko) mutinied, and the mineral-rich province of Katanga, led by Moise Tshombe, seceded with the support of Belgian mining interests. To protect the 90,000 Europeans still in the country, the Belgian government dispatched paratroopers.

Lumumba turned to the United Nations for help in ending the Katangan secessionist movement and to the Soviet Union for help in the expulsion of the Belgian troops. The United Nations sent peacekeeping forces, and Soviet premier NIKITA KHRUSHCHEV, who saw the request as an opportunity to establish a political toehold in the emerging African states, promised that the Soviet Union would not "shrink from resolute measures to curb the aggression." He quickly sent Soviet equipment and several hundred "technicians" to help Lumumba.

Lumumba's decision to turn to the Soviet Union alarmed Western countries. The EISENHOWER Administration was especially concerned, and the CENTRAL INTELLIGENCE AGENCY (CIA) developed several plots to assassinate Lumumba. None of these succeeded. Lumumba's actions also alarmed pro-Western elements in the Congolese government, and on September 5, 1960, President Kasavubu dismissed Lumumba from the premiership. Lumumba immediately challenged the legality of the dismissal, and for 10 days there were effectively two governments in the Congo. Then, on September 14, army leader Mobutu seized power and recognized the government of Kasavubu, which was in turn recognized by the United Nations. A number of African and Asian states, however, continued to recognize Lumumba as the head of government, as he had by then established himself as a popular Pan-African nationalist figure. The United Nations, while recognizing Kasavubu's government, provided protection for Lumumba in Leopoldville.

On November 27, Lumumba tried to travel from Leopoldville to Stanleyville. He was arrested by Kasavubu and Mobutu's forces before he reached his destination. In January 1961 he was handed over to Tshombe's secessionist government in Katanga. Shortly afterward he was murdered. The details of Lumumba's arrest, his delivery to his most bitter enemies and his subsequent murder have remained clouded in mystery, further feeding the myths surrounding the man.

The civil war continued for another year, eventually ending with the collapse of the Katangan secessionist government. After the civil war, the Congolese political factions that had opposed him united in declaring Lumumba a "national hero" and evoking his memory for their political cause. The Soviet Union also sought to exploit his name by naming a university after him. Throughout the rest of Africa, he became a model for the rising generation of African leaders.

For Further Information:

Albright, D.E. *Soviet Policy Toward Africa.* Washington, D.C., 1987.

Davidson, Basil. *Africa in Modern History: The Search for a New Society.* New York, 1978.

Jackson, Henry F. *From the Congo to Soweto: U.S. Foreign Policy Toward Africa Since 1960.* New York, 1982.

Magall, James. *Africa: The Cold War and After.* London, 1971.

Nielsen, Waldemar. *The Great Powers and Africa.* Washington, D.C., 1969.

Weissman, Stephen. *American Policy in the Congo, 1960–1964.* Ithaca, N.Y., 1974.

Luns, Joseph (August 28, 1911–   ) Joseph Luns was a Dutch politician and the longest-serving secretary general of the NORTH ATLANTIC TREATY ORGANIZATION, holding that position from 1971 to 1983.

After studying law at Leyden and Amsterdam universities, Luns attended the London School of Economics and Berlin University before entering the Dutch diplomatic service. During the war years he worked in Switzerland and Portugal in the embassies of the Dutch government-in-exile, and after the war he served at the United Nations from 1949 to 1952. He left the diplomatic service in 1952 to become minister of foreign affairs as a member of the Catholic People's Party. He remained minister of foreign affairs for an unprecedented 19 years.

As Dutch foreign secretary, Luns took a keen interest in military matters and NATO issues. He often attended Dutch and NATO naval maneuvers and published several studies and articles on naval matters and international affairs.

Luns was named secretary general of NATO on June 4, 1971. One of his greatest challenges came after it was learned that the Soviet Union was deploying intermediate-range SS-20 missiles. In November 1976 he announced that the alliance was considering steps to counter them. Eventually American cruise and PERSHING II missiles were deployed in Belgium, Italy and Britain, which in turn prompted the revival of the antinuclear movement throughout Europe.

In response to the widespread antinuclear and anti-NATO demonstrations, several European political parties, including Britain's Labour Party, adopted policies of unilateral nuclear disarmament and opposed the deployment of the cruise and Pershing missiles. Some governments, including that of Belgium, delayed the final decision on deployment until the last moment. Luns played a major part in pushing the deployment against this opposition. The Soviets eventually agreed to withdraw the SS-20s in return for the withdrawal of the American intermediate-range nuclear forces. The INTERMEDIATE RANGE NUCLEAR FORCES (INF) TREATY was signed in December 1987.

Luns retired as secretary general of NATO in June 1984. He was replaced by the former British foreign secretary, LORD CARRINGTON.

M

MacArthur, General Douglas (January 26, 1880–April 5, 1964) General Douglas MacArthur was the most controversial American military figure of the Cold War period. His support for CHIANG KAI-SHEK, his trenchant anti-communism and his public disagreements with President HARRY TRUMAN over the conduct of the KOREAN WAR led to his dismissal and to a major political battle over presidential power and Truman's foreign policy.

MacArthur is generally accepted to have been a brilliant soldier. He graduated in 1903 from the U.S. Military Academy at the top of his class. During World War I he was decorated 13 times and cited seven times for bravery. In 1930 he became America's youngest army chief of staff and a four-star general.

During the 1920s, MacArthur served a tour of duty in the Philippines, which left him with a strong interest in the Far East. In 1935 he retired and moved to Manila to serve as military adviser to the Philippine government. As war approached, President FRANKLIN ROOSEVELT asked MacArthur to return to active service in the U.S. Army, and in July 1941 MacArthur was appointed commander of United States Armed Forces in the Far East. In this post, he commanded first the unsuccessful defense of the Philippines and then the three-year island-hopping campaign against the Japanese in the Pacific.

At the end of the war, MacArthur took the surrender of the Japanese forces aboard the USS MISSOURI and was appointed supreme commander of the Allied Powers in the Pacific with responsibility for administering the occupation of Japan. At Moscow in December 1945, the British, American and Soviet foreign ministers agreed to establish a FAR EASTERN COMMISSION and Allied Council for Japan to "formulate policies, principles and standards" related to postwar Japan and to "exercise control" over the supreme commander (MacArthur).

From the start, MacArthur protested against the decision to include the Soviet Union in the Far Eastern Commission, and three months before its creation in 1945 he threatened to resign if the Soviet Union were allowed any further participation in occupation affairs. MacArthur was a war hero and his resignation at the time would have created unwanted problems for Truman before he had had time to settle into the presidency. Furthermore, Truman's experiences with the So-

viet Union had made him wary, and he too opposed giving the Soviets a major say in the administration of Japan. The United States therefore insisted on inserting a clause into the Moscow agreement that named the supreme commander as "the sole executive authority for the Allied Powers in Japan."

The final wording of the Moscow agreement gave MacArthur virtual dictatorial powers, and he used them vigorously and on the whole benignly. His main aim was the destruction of the ideology of Japanese militarism, followed by the creation of political and economic structures that would encourage democratic government and a sound economy. Military industries were dismantled and war crimes trials conducted. A constitution was written that enshrined basic democratic rights such as a free press and free speech. In the same document, Japan renounced forever the right to wage war.

As Supreme Allied Commander in the Pacific, MacArthur was also responsible for American forces in Korea. It had been agreed at the YALTA CONFERENCE that Korea would be occupied by Soviet and American troops. This agreement had been carried a step further at the POTSDAM CONFERENCE, where American negotiators had suggested dividing the country into two occupation zones, to the north and south of the 38th parallel. Korea, in effect, became the Germany of the Far East. But in contrast to Germany, the Soviets found a well-entrenched and genuinely popular Communist Party in Korea. The communists under KIM IL-SUNG had taken the lead in fighting the repressive Japanese rule, and the Soviets had little difficulty in establishing a communist government in their sector and withdrawing their troops in 1948.

MacArthur had a more difficult task in establishing a secure pro-Western government in the American occupation zone. His main criterion was that the government be anti-communist, and he selected the extreme right-winger SYNGMAN RHEE to head it. Rhee proceeded to eliminate his opponents on the left and in the center through intimidation, arrest and sometimes murder. Rhee's tactics made it difficult for politicians back in Washington to identify the United States closely with South Korea, but MacArthur remained close to Rhee, although his official connection ceased when the Republic of Korea was formed in 1948.

MacArthur also became a strong supporter of CHIANG KAI-SHEK, the Nationalist leader in China who was fighting a

General Douglas MacArthur, commander of UN forces in Korea, was removed from his position when he publicly challenged President Truman's war policies.

desperate civil war to prevent the Chinese communists from coming to power. MacArthur pressed Truman to provide military aid to Chiang's forces. When Chiang was forced to flee to the island of Taiwan, MacArthur predicted that the collapse of the Nationalist government marked the beginning of a general communist offensive in Asia.

His predictions appeared credible when North Korean troops invaded South Korea on June 25, 1950. On July 7, after securing a United Nations mandate, Truman appointed Mac-Arthur commander of UN forces in Korea with the task of repelling the North Korean attack. MacArthur decided to commit the U.S. Eighth Army in Japan and developed a brilliantly simple plan to defeat the North Koreans.

Kim Il-sung's forces had enjoyed an immediate and huge success with their first offensive. The South Korean forces had been routed, and North Korean troops swept into Seoul and beyond, so that South Korean, American and British troops were left to defend a small portion of the southeastern tip of the peninsula. MacArthur concluded that the North Korean success had left the enemy with an overextended supply line, which he cut by landing troops at INCHON on September 15. The North Koreans were forced to flee back across the 38th parallel, with UN forces in pursuit. It was a triumph for MacArthur.

But while planning this operation, MacArthur made a political error by flying to Taiwan for discussions with Chiang Kai-shek. The Nationalist Chinese leader saw the Korean War as an opportunity to launch an attack on mainland China and wrest control from the communists, who were genuinely popular but still consolidating their power. Mac-Arthur was sympathetic to Chiang's ambitions, but he found little support within the Truman Administration. At the start of the Korean War, Truman had ordered the Seventh Fleet into the Formosa Straits separating Taiwan from China. He announced that the ships were there to protect Taiwan from a Chinese communist attack, but it was understood that they were also there to prevent an attack by Chiang's forces on the mainland. Truman's policy, and the UN's, was to prevent the war from spreading beyond Korea.

The Chinese communists, however, looked upon the Seventh Fleet as a threat. MacArthur's discussions with Chiang seemed to confirm the communists' suspicions that they were in danger of a two-pronged attack—the first by UN forces in Korea across the Yalu River into Manchuria and the second by Chiang's troops ferried across the Formosa Straits by the U.S. Navy. The Chinese decided to act first and sent 300,000 troops across the Yalu to support North Korea. The scales tipped in favor of North Korea, and the UN forces were driven back beyond Seoul (they later launched a counteroffensive that took them back to the 38th parallel).

During this seesaw war there were intense diplomatic negotiations at the United Nations to reestablish the status quo of a divided Korean Peninsula. MacArthur, however, made repeated public statements supporting a policy of military victory over the Chinese communists and a unified pro-Western Korea. His attitude and public statements caused the administration increasing problems with Britain and the other countries that had contributed to the UN force, and relations between MacArthur and Truman deteriorated. MacArthur was finally relieved of his command by Truman on April 11, 1951.

From the time of his dismissal, MacArthur became a focal point for the conservative critics of Truman's foreign policy. He was a hero of three wars and many regarded him as America's outstanding soldier at a time when the military was at the height of its popularity. Upon his return to America he was accorded a triumphal salute in each city where he stopped—Honolulu, San Francisco, New York and finally Washington, D.C. In Washington he was given the singular honor of addressing a Joint Session of Congress, where he attacked the president's policies in Asia.

MacArthur's return was followed by hearings by the combined Senate committees on armed forces and foreign relations during which the chief witness was MacArthur. He was followed by Defense Secretary GEORGE C. MARSHALL and General OMAR BRADLEY, chairman of the Joint Chiefs of Staff, both of whom strongly defended Truman and his policies. The full committees voted against issuing a formal report, which might "renew a bitter discussion of methods for waging war" and would not help Korean cease-fire negotiations. But an eight-man Republican minority on the committees issued their own review, attacking MacArthur's recall as "ill-advised."

MacArthur was a candidate for the Republican Party's 1952 presidential nomination but was considered too controversial in comparison to the equally popular General DWIGHT EISENHOWER. He did, however, deliver the keynote address at the 1952 Republican National Convention. Shortly afterward he became chairman of the board of Remington Rand and thereafter kept out of politics. In 1962, Congress ordered a gold medal struck for him. MacArthur died two years later, on April 5, 1964.

For Further Information:

Feis, Herbert. *Conquest Over Japan*. New York, 1967.

Leckie, Robert. *The Korean War*. New York, 1963.

MacArthur, Douglas. *Reminiscences*. New York, 1964.

Manchester, William Raymond. *American Caesar: Douglas MacArthur, 1880–1964*. Boston, 1978.

Schaller, Michael. *Douglas MacArthur: The Far Eastern General*. New York, 1989.

Smith, Robert. *MacArthur in Korea: The Naked Emperor*. New York, 1982.

Spanier, John. *The Truman-MacArthur Controversy and the Korean War*. New York, 1959.

MacLean, Donald (1914–March 6, 1983)   Donald MacLean was one of a trio of British diplomats who spied for the Soviet Union during the Cold War years and handed over a number of important nuclear and political secrets.

MacLean was born into a prominent British political family and attended Cambridge University in the 1930s. While there he became a devoted communist and approached the Soviet Embassy in London in an attempt to obtain a visa to live in the Soviet Union. The Soviets refused him the visa and convinced him to remain in the West as a spy.

While at Cambridge, he became close friends with KIM PHILBY and GUY BURGESS, who were also recruited as Soviet agents. It is believed that Burgess and MacLean also had a homosexual affair and that this was later used to blackmail the bisexual MacLean.

At the urgings of his Soviet handler, MacLean joined the British Foreign Office. From 1944 to 1948 he served at the British Embassy in Washington, D.C. He was the British representative on the Combined Policy Committee for Joint Atomic Development among Britain, the United States and Canada, and twice a week delivered atomic secrets to the Soviet consulate in New York.

By 1949, MacLean came under suspicion after the FEDERAL BUREAU OF INVESTIGATION (FBI) discovered that he had misused his access pass to the U.S. Atomic Energy Commission to make unauthorized visits. The suspicions were strengthened by reports from double agents in the Soviet Union.

By this time Philby was working at the British Embassy in Washington. As liaison officer between American and British intelligence, Philby learned of the American suspicions and sent a warning to the KGB. But MacLean's Soviet handlers wanted to keep him in place. As the pressures grew on MacLean he started drinking heavily and suffered a nervous breakdown. The British Foreign Office, which initially dismissed the FBI suspicions, sent MacLean to Cairo for a short spell to recuperate and then brought him back to London, where he was appointed head of the American Desk at the Foreign Office. The post gave him access to British and American policies in the KOREAN WAR and allowed him to tell the Soviets of President HARRY S. TRUMAN's refusal to let General DOUGLAS MACARTHUR cross the YALU RIVER.

By 1951, however, British counterintelligence had also become suspicious of MacLean. Philby instructed Guy Burgess to warn MacLean that he was on the verge of arrest, and Burgess and MacLean escaped to Moscow. In the Soviet Union, MacLean became a Soviet citizen, was given the rank of colonel in the KGB, and worked as a foreign policy analyst under the name of Mark Petrovich Frazer. His American wife, Melinda, followed him to Moscow, but she later left MacLean for Philby. MacLean died of cancer on March 6, 1983.

Macmillan, (Maurice) Harold (February 10, 1894–December 29, 1986)   Harold Macmillan, later the Earl of Stockton, was British prime minister from after the SUEZ CRISIS until 1963. He restored the Anglo-American "special relationship," arranged the purchase of Britain's POLARIS submarine fleet and sought to mediate between the Soviet Union and United States.

Macmillan was born into the British upper middle class; his mother was American. His father was head of the Macmillan publishing company. Macmillan's education at Eton and Oxford was interrupted by World War I. He was badly wounded at the battle of the Somme in 1916 and limped for the rest of his life.

Macmillan entered politics as the Conservative candidate for Stockton-on-Tees in the general election of 1923. He narrowly lost to the Liberal candidate, but he won the seat in the 1924 general election. In the House of Commons, Macmillan gained a reputation as a liberal on economic issues and opposing appeasement of Germany. His tough stand against Germany kept Macmillan out of the government until WINSTON CHURCHILL became prime minister in 1940 and Macmillan was named junior minister for supply. Later he became British minister in Algiers, responsible for maintaining good relations among the Free French, British and American forces in North Africa. In this capacity he developed a close relationship with DWIGHT EISENHOWER and CHARLES DE GAULLE, which became useful in later years. As the Allies moved into Sicily and Italy, Macmillan's geographic responsibility increased, and Churchill relied increasingly on his judgment concerning Mediterranean issues. By the end of the war he was one of the most influential figures in that region of the world.

In 1951 Macmillan became minister of housing. Many considered it a demeaning post for a man of his talents, but the enthusiasm and efficiency with which he took on the unglamorous and thankless task of replacing the bombed-out homes of Britain substantially increased his popularity both inside and outside the Conservative Party.

In October 1954 Churchill appointed Macmillan secretary of defense. He inherited the ministry at the moment when the British defense forces were just coming to grips with their possession of the atomic bomb and at the same time were being forced by the poor state of the British economy and crippling war debts to cut back their defense commitments. Macmillan was not at the Ministry of Defense long enough to make any real impact. In April 1955 Churchill retired as prime minister. ANTHONY EDEN moved into the premiership, and Macmillan took Eden's job as foreign secretary. Eden, however, was not prepared to relinquish control of British foreign affairs, and after nine months Macmillan moved over to the treasury as chancellor of the exchequer.

Macmillan was at the treasury for only a short time when the Suez Crisis broke. It was his responsibility to tell the cabinet that Britain could not afford a war with Egypt after the United States threatened to withdraw dollar credits. After Eden resigned in January 1957, Macmillan was chosen as prime minister. He was initially regarded as a stopgap until the crisis passed.

His first foreign affairs priority was the restoration of Anglo-American relations in the aftermath of Suez. Toward this end he arranged a meeting with President Eisenhower at Bermuda in March 1957, which also helped to establish a precedent by arranging the sale of American missile systems to Britain.

Macmillan and Eisenhower had several more bilateral meetings: at Washington, D.C. in October 1957 to discuss pooling Anglo-American scientific resources in the wake of the Soviets' launching of SPUTNIK; at Washington in June 1958 when the two men discussed a nuclear test ban treaty; at Paris in December 1959 during a summit meeting among the British, French, German and American heads of government; and at Camp David, Maryland in March 1960 when the two men again discussed the proposed nuclear test ban treaty.

Like Churchill before him, Macmillan was staunchly anticommunist but sought a working relationship with the Soviet Union, and he felt that President Eisenhower and Secretary of State JOHN FOSTER DULLES were too blinkered in their approach to Moscow. He projected himself as a mediator between the Soviets and Americans, and in February 1959 became the first postwar British prime minister to visit the Soviet Union in an attempt to "break the ice . . . and get some feeling of the general situation." Macmillan's negotiations with Soviet leader NIKITA KHRUSHCHEV concentrated on Germany and the stalled nuclear test ban negotiations and the possibility of a four-power East-West summit. There were high hopes for the subsequently arranged meeting in Paris in May 1960, but they were scuttled by the Soviet downing of an American U-2 spy plane shortly before the four leaders met. The summit collapsed after only three hours.

Macmillan had high hopes for President JOHN F. KENNEDY after the latter's election in November 1960, and the two men formed possibly the closest postwar relationship between two heads of government. Arthur Schlesinger, participant in and historian of the Kennedy administration, said that Macmillan and Kennedy discovered a "considerable temperamental rapport. Kennedy, with his own fondness for the British political style, liked Macmillan's patrician approach to politics, his impatience with official ritual, his insouciance about professionals, his pose of nonchalance . . . Macmillan, for his part, responded to Kennedy's courage, his ability to see events unfolding against the vast canvas of history, his contempt for cliché, his unfailing sense of the ridiculous."

But despite the close relationship, there were differences. The first came over the CUBAN MISSILE CRISIS. Kennedy, for security reasons, did not tell Macmillan of his decision to impose a blockade on Cuba until 24 hours beforehand. This caused embarrassment at home for Macmillan, who had argued that his special relationship with Kennedy gave him added power in world councils. To protect Macmillan's prestige, the U.S. ambassador to Britain, DAVID BRUCE, was told to release the first public photographs of Soviet missile sites in Cuba through British sources.

America's unilateral decision to abandon the Skybolt missile project in 1962 was even more damaging. The move was a considerable embarrassment to Macmillan and the British Ministry of Defense, which had been counting on the system to replace their own failed Blue Streak. The problem was resolved at a meeting between Macmillan and Kennedy in December 1962 in Nassau, at which the United States agreed to sell Polaris submarines to Britain. The NASSAU AGREEMENT resulted in greater British dependence on American nuclear weapons technology. The arrangement greatly angered French president Charles de Gaulle, who was trying to limit American influence in Europe. He later used the agreement as one of his chief reasons for blocking British entry into the EUROPEAN ECONOMIC COMMUNITY. Macmillan, however, was a committed European and, although de Gaulle blocked British entry for many years, many of the negotiations that eventually resulted in British membership in the EEC were conducted by Macmillan.

Macmillan was prime minister at the time of the signing of the NUCLEAR TEST BAN TREATY. When negotiations first started during the Eisenhower administration, Macmillan was opposed to British involvement in the agreement because Britain's development of nuclear weapons was still in the early stages and scientists needed more time for testing. But when the tests were completed he became an avid proponent of the treaty, which was signed by Britain, the United States and the Soviet Union on July 25, 1963.

Britain was still a major colonial power at the start of Macmillan's government, and one of his principal achievements was to take Britain through the process of decolonization without the kind of major upheavals that had shaken France. By Macmillan's time it was clear that many of the former colonies and those fighting for independence were being attracted to the professed political philosophy of the Soviet Union. Macmillan made it clear in his famous February 1960 "winds of change" speech in Capetown, South Africa that in order not to "imperil the precarious balance of East and West" the Western world, and Britain in particular, must side with the progressive forces of African nationalism.

Macmillan was reelected in 1960 on the campaign slogan "You've never had it so good." But within a few years inflation and unemployment were beginning to eat into his credibility. The final straw was the Profumo affair, a lurid sex-and-spy scandal involving a member of Macmillan's cabinet. Macmillan resigned as prime minister in October 1963, ostensibly for health reasons. Upon his resignation from Parliament the following year, Macmillan was offered a peerage; he refused it, but later accepted the honor and became Earl of Stockton. He spent most of his long retirement writing his memoirs. Toward the end of his life he became a fierce critic of Prime Minister MARGARET THATCHER's economic policies.

For Further Information:
Evans, Harold. *Downing Street Diary: The Macmillan Years, 1957–1963*. London, 1981.
Fisher, Nigel. *Harold Macmillan: A Biography*. London, 1982.
Horne, Alistair. *Harold Macmillan*. New York, 1989–1991.
Macmillan, Harold. *Tides of Fortune, 1945–1955*. New York, 1969.
———. *Riding the Storm, 1956–1959*. New York, 1971.
———. *Pointing the Way, 1959–1961*. New York, 1972.
———. *At the End of the Day, 1961–1963*. New York, 1973.

Malay Emergency   The Malay Emergency from 1948 to 1960 was a state of emergency declared in the British colony of Malaysia to put down a communist insurrection. The long guerrilla war was eventually won by the British with a combination of military pressure and a village resettlement program.

From the beginning of the 19th century the Malay Peninsula was under British domination, although the colonial authorities worked closely with the Malay sultans, who retained a substantial, traditional authority in most areas. During the last half of the 19th century millions of Chinese and Indian immigrants arrived in Malaya to work in the booming rubber and tin industries. These workers were not allowed Malayan citizenship and in the 20th century became the subject of increasing ethnic tensions.

The Malayan Communist Party drew its membership almost exclusively from the Chinese community in Malaya and Singapore. This was both an asset and a liability for the party. It was an asset in that it gave the party strong ethnic as well as ideological roots in a country where the indigenous Malays were starting to discriminate against non-Malays. It was a liability in that the party was unable to move beyond this base.

The first Communist Party on the Malay Peninsula was founded in 1928 in Singapore as the South Seas Communist Party. The Malayan Communist Party was formed in 1930. Both parties had strong connections with the Soviet-controlled Comintern, and most of the top leadership of the Singapore and Malay parties came initially from Vietnam. Throughout the 1930s, the Communist Party agitated for an end to British rule on the Malay Peninsula, but in the generally prosperous climate of the day it found little support.

During World War II, the communists led the resistance to the Japanese occupation through the Anti-Japanese Army, and this considerably increased their influence. However, British and Commonwealth forces returned unopposed in September 1945.

Because of its record of fighting the Japanese the party was legalized for the first time in its history and admitted to the British governor's advisory council. In October 1945, the communists created a General Labor Union with the hope of using the infant trade union movement as a vehicle for their political aims. Postwar deprivation gave the Communist Party and its unions some early successes, but by 1947 the economic tide had turned with increased world demand for Malayan rubber and tin.

The British at this stage made a major political error in proposing a new constitution that gave the vote to the Chinese and Indian communities. The constitution alienated the indigenous Malays, and the British were forced to abandon the reform and return to a Malay-dominated federation, leaving the Chinese community without political power. To have it offered and then suddenly taken away was a major blow to the Chinese community and left the Chinese-dominated Communist Party convinced that it could take power only through military means.

The Communist Party had maintained its wartime command structure through an "Old Comrades Association" and after the war had hidden large caches of arms in the Malayan jungle. The actual revolt started in June 1948 with the murder of three European planters in Perak. This was quickly followed by a series of other attacks, murders and strikes. On June 16, 1948, the British authorities declared a state of emergency. The two most important parts of the emergency regulations were the compulsory registration and issuance of identity cards to all residents of Malaya and Singapore and the right of the authorities to arrest and detain without trial.

The communist guerrillas were under the command of Chin Peng, who in 1947 succeeded Lai Tek as secretary general of the Malayan Communist Party. Chin called his guerrilla force the Malayan Peoples' Anti-British Army; he based himself in the jungle and concentrated his attacks on British-managed rubber estates. He drew his support from Chinese squatter communities, which had been established by Chinese who had fled from the Japanese at the start of the war. Chin's plan was to establish a strong base of operations in the dense jungles and from it launch attacks on the tin mining fields and urban centers. By the end of 1948 more than 900 people had died.

The initial British reaction was to try to contain and defeat the communist forces with large-scale conventional maneuvers. These were invariably unsuccessful, as the guerrilla forces melted away into the jungles or villages before the British forces could face them. The result was that by 1951 the communist insurrection posed a serious threat to British and Malay rule.

In April 1950, the British appointed veteran jungle fighter

Sir Harold Briggs as director of operations. Working closely with High Commissioner Sir Henry Gurney, Briggs devised a strategy to cut the guerrillas off from the villages and win back the support of the people there. The first element of the Briggs Plan was the removal of 423,000 Chinese squatters from their jungle communities and resettlement in 400 newly built villages isolated from the communist guerrillas.

The resettlement program was completed in a year, and by mid-1951 the tide of the war started to turn in favor of the British. The communist guerrillas responded by launching increasingly reckless attacks, including the ambush and murder of Gurney in October 1951. The assassination marked the apex of the communist insurgency. The British had by that time developed an effective intelligence network and counterinsurgency strategy, and the guerrillas were starting to suffer heavy losses.

Gurney was succeeded by General Sir Gerald Templer, who was given virtual dictatorial powers to deal with the Emergency. By 1953 it was estimated that two-thirds of the communist guerrilla forces had been destroyed. In mid-1954 the British situation had improved to such an extent that Templer was able to hand over his post to his civilian deputy Sir Donald MacGillivray and the post of director of operations to Lieutenant General Sir Geoffrey Bourne.

Chin Peng made his first peace overtures in 1955, shortly before the first elections under a new constitution. Talks were held with the British authorities, who offered the guerrillas a full amnesty and help in reestablishing themselves in Malayan society if they would surrender their arms and renounce communism. Those who refused to renounce communism were given the option of repatriation to China. Chin offered to disband his army if the new chief minister of the Malay Federation, Tunku Abdul Rahman, would agree to legalize the Communist Party. Tunku refused this and the talks broke down.

But by this time the Malay communists' guerrilla army was a defeated force. Malaya became independent on August 31, 1957, but the British continued to help administer the country and direct the war against the remaining communist forces. The state of emergency remained in force but was gradually relaxed. Between 1957 and 1958 an estimated 1,500 guerrillas surrendered. This left Chin Peng with only 400 troops, who sought refuge in neighboring Thailand and who occasionally launched attacks across the Thai–Malay border. The emergency was officially ended on August 1, 1960.

For Further Information:
Clutterbuck, Richard. *The Long, Long War: The Emergency in Malaya, 1948–1960.* London, 1967.
Short, Anthony. *The Communist Insurrection in Malaya, 1948–1960.* London, 1975.

Malenkov, Georgi M.   (January 8, 1902–January 25, 1988)
Georgi M. Malenkov was briefly head of the Soviet Communist Party and premier of the Soviet Union following the death of JOSEF STALIN in 1953. He was purged from the party by NIKITA KHRUSHCHEV.

Unlike many of Stalin's close advisers, Malenkov was too young to have taken an active part in Communist Party activities before the Bolshevik Revolution in 1917. When the Winter Palace was stormed, Malenkov was only 15 years old. However, he almost immediately joined the Red Army; in 1920 he became a member of the Communist Party and was appointed political commissar for Turkestan, where he established his party reputation by suppressing rebellious Muslims.

Malenkov returned to Moscow in 1922 to study engineering at the Higher Technical School. After he graduated in 1925, he was appointed to an administrative post in the Central Committee. The job put him in close contact with Josef Stalin, whose protégé he became. In 1934 Malenkov was given the key job of party official responsible for personnel. This was during Stalin's Great Purge, and it fell to Malenkov to advise the Soviet leader who should be purged and who should be selected to replace the purge victims. The job enabled Malenkov to build a powerful political base within the party.

In 1939 Malenkov was elected a secretary of the Central Committee and in February 1941 a candidate (non-voting) member of the Politburo. He became a full member in March 1946. When Germany invaded the Soviet Union in June 1941, Malenkov was appointed to the State Defense Committee, the elite group that directed the Soviet war effort. Malenkov's primary responsibility on the committee was aircraft production, but after 1943 he also became responsible for the economic rehabilitation of liberated areas.

In the closing stages of the war and immediately after it, Malenkov was responsible for dismantling German industrial equipment and shipping it back to the Soviet Union. This strategy was a key part of the Soviet Union's reparations policy, and Malenkov's ruthlessness in carrying it out led to starvation conditions for thousands of Germans. It also contributed to the strained relations with the Western powers, which wanted to rehabilitate Germany in order to relieve the Western economies of the burden of supporting the German population.

In 1946, Malenkov was appointed a deputy premier and at this stage was regarded as second in command to Stalin. In October 1947, Malenkov, along with Andrei Zhdanov, represented the Soviet Union at the meeting in Poland that established the Communist Information Bureau (COMINFORM). Malenkov's position suffered a blow following an attack by Zhdanov on his handling of the dismantling of German industries, but by 1949 Malenkov had substantially recovered his influence. He gave the keynote address at the celebration of the Bolshevik Revolution on November 7, 1949, and declared that if the "imperialists" started another world war it would be "the grave . . . for the whole world of capitalism." In December 1949, he led the party celebrations for Stalin's 70th birthday.

When Stalin died in March 1953, Malenkov assumed the

post of general secretary of the party and premier and seemed set to assume Stalin's full mantle. But Malenkov was too much Stalin's man, and the other leading members of the Politburo were unwilling to concede ultimate authority to him. Only 11 days after Stalin's death, Malenkov was relieved of the post of general secretary and replaced by the relatively unknown Nikita Khrushchev. At the same time, a collective leadership emerged with Malenkov as premier.

Malenkov's premiership was marked by a somewhat more conciliatory attitude toward the West and by attempts to step up production of consumer goods and curb the role of the secret police. His economic policies, dubbed the "New Course," ran into heavy opposition from Khrushchev and NIKOLAI BULGANIN, who wanted to continue the Soviet economy's emphasis on investment in heavy industry. Malenkov lost the battle with Khrushchev and resigned from the premiership in February 1955. He remained a member of the Politburo and from that position tried to engineer Khrushchev's downfall. In 1957 he was named by Khrushchev as the leader of the "anti-party" group attempting to overthrow him and was expelled from both the Politburo and the Central Committee. He was expelled from the Communist Party in 1964.

Malenkov spent the remainder of his life in obscurity. To remove him from Moscow, Khrushchev placed Malenkov in charge of a power station in Kazakhstan in Soviet Asia. When he died in 1988, the authorities took 10 days to announce his passing.

For Further Information:
McCauley, M. *The Soviet Union since 1917.* London, 1981.
McNeal, Robert H. *Stalin: Man and Ruler.* New York, 1988.

Manhattan Project   The Manhattan Project was the United States' World War II program to develop the atomic bomb. It was named after the Manhattan Engineer District, in New York, where the first offices were located when the project was started by the War Department in June 1942.

Most of the major research work was done at facilities at Los Alamos, New Mexico, Oak Ridge, Tennessee, Hanford, Washington, the University of California at Berkeley and the University of Chicago.

The actual weapon was designed by Dr. J. ROBERT OPPEN-HEIMER, who headed the Project Y division at Los Alamos. The first experimental atomic bomb was detonated near Alamogordo, New Mexico on July 16, 1945.

Control of the atomic weapons program was taken away from the War Department and placed in civilian hands on January 1, 1947, when the ATOMIC ENERGY COMMISSION was created.

Mansfield, Mike (Michael J.)   (March 16, 1903–   )
Mike Mansfield played an influentil role in American foreign policy from the early years of the Cold War when he was elected to the U.S. House of Representatives and joined the Foreign Relations Committee. Later he was elected to the Senate and became a member of its Foreign Relations Committee and a prominent critic of the VIETNAM WAR. For 11 years Mansfield was U.S. ambassador to Japan.

Mansfield left school after the eighth grade. He held a number of manual jobs before completing his education, eventually receiving B.A. and M.A. degrees from Montana State University, where he went on to teach history.

In 1942 Mansfield, a Democrat, was elected to the House of Representatives from Montana and became a member of the Foreign Relations Committee. In 1944 President FRANKLIN ROOSEVELT sent Mansfield on a tour of China, and he began a lifelong interest in Asian affairs. In 1952 Mansfield was elected to the Senate and quickly joined the upper house's Foreign Relations Committee, where he gained a reputation as a critic of the EISENHOWER administration's foreign aid program.

Mansfield played a key role in formulating the congressional Democratic attitude to President Dwight Eisenhower's foreign policy. That this was generally supportive and bipartisan was reflected in Eisenhower's decision to appoint Mansfield as a delegate to the 1954 conference that established the SOUTHEAST ASIA TREATY ORGANIZATION.

In 1957 Mansfield became Senate majority whip and in 1961 succeeded LYNDON JOHNSON as Senate majority leader. During the KENNEDY administration Mansfield created a diplomatic furor when, in June 1961, he suggested that BERLIN be made a free, neutralized city under international guarantees and protection. This caused a panic among West Germans, who feared that the Kennedy administration, which often used Mansfield as its spokesman on foreign policy issues, was preparing to abandon Berlin. The State Department was forced to make it clear that Mansfield was speaking only for himself.

Mansfield started off a reluctant supporter of the Johnson administration's Vietnam policies. But in January 1966 he went on a fact-finding mission in Vietnam and returned convinced that a military victory was highly unlikely. From that time he became a prominent critic of the war and pressed for a negotiated end to American involvement. From the early 1970s he also played a leading role in the Senate's efforts to curb the president's powers in determining foreign policy.

Following President RICHARD NIXON's historic visit to communist China in February 1972, Mansfield made his own trip to Beijing with Senate minority leader Hugh Scott (R-Pennsylvania). Upon his return, Mansfield stated that the Chinese government was led by responsible men more concerned with China's internal development than the export of revolution. His statements about China did much to dispel the aura of suspicion that had surrounded the Chinese communists in the 1950s and 1960s.

In 1972 Mansfield again caused a diplomatic panic in Europe when he repeatedly tried to introduce legislation to reduce the number of American troops in Western Europe. The Mansfield Amendment was rejected by the Senate, but this did little to lessen the concern within Western Europe, where Mansfield was strongly disliked. Mansfield responded by attacking America's foreign policy as too Eurocentric and criticizing the increasingly wealthy West Europeans for not doing more to pay for their own defense.

Mansfield retired from the Senate following the 1976 elections, but in 1977 President JIMMY CARTER appointed him ambassador to Japan. Mansfield had a difficult time during the Carter administration when the president considered reducing the number of U.S. troops in South Korea. He had a better relationship with President RONALD REAGAN, whom Mansfield praised as the first U.S. president to show a "continuous interest" in Japan and the Pacific region. Mansfield played an important role in persuading the Japanese to liberalize their trade policies and increase defense spending. Mansfield finally retired in December 1988.

For Further Information:

Cyr, A.I. *U.S. Foreign Policy and European Security.* New York, 1988.

Spanier, J.W. *American Foreign Policy Since World War Two.* Washington, D.C., 1988.

Treverton, G.F. *Making the Alliance Work: The United States and Europe.* Ithaca, N.Y., 1985.

Mao Zedong   (December 26, 1893–September 9, 1976)
Mao Zedong was the leader of China from October 1949 to his death in 1976. His interpretation of Marxism for colonial and peasant-based economies became known as Maoism and was a model for many Third World political movements.

Mao was born in Hunan province, son of a wealthy peasant. He ran away from home to continue his education and at age 18 became involved in the revolution against the Manchu Dynasty. After the revolution, Mao resumed his education at the First Normal School of Changsha. While completing his studies he became involved in student politics and founded the New People's Study Society, many of whose early members later become prominent members of the Chinese Communist Party.

After Changsha, Mao went to Peking (Beijing) University shortly before the outbreak of the May 4 Movement in 1919, which may be said to have been the foundation of revolutionary China. Mao's experience during the Beijing riots helped him to formulate many of his political ideas and pushed him away from Western liberalism to Marxism. By 1920 Mao was a convinced Marxist, and in 1922 he helped to found the Chinese Communist Party. In 1925 he began to develop his theory of the revolutionary potential of the peasantry, rather than of the industrial workers of Marx and Lenin's revolutionary vanguard.

In 1923 the communists had formed an alliance with the Kuomintang led by Dr. Sun Yat-sen, the revolutionary founder of modern China. Mao left his teaching job to become a full-time party official. Sun died in 1925 and was succeeded by CHIANG KAI-SHEK, who was suspicious of the Chinese communists. In 1926 Chiang expelled the communists from most of the important posts within the Kuomintang, although Mao

was retained. In April 1927, however, Chiang carried out a bloody and extensive purge of the Chinese communists, which left only a handful of leaders alive.

Mao managed to escape the 1927 uprising, and with a group of Hunan peasants he established a base in the southern province of Kiangsi. Here he began to put into practice his theory of a peasant-based revolution, which Mao believed would "rise like a tornado or tempest—a force so extraordinarily swift and violent that no power, however great, will be able to suppress it."

Mao's closest associate in these early years in Kiangsi was CHU TEH, a military genius who worked with Mao to apply his political thinking to military doctrine. The result was the successful development of a guerrilla warfare strategy to be executed from bases in the countryside. By November 1931, the activities of Chu's guerrilla army had been successful enough for Mao to declare the founding of the Chinese Soviet Republic in Kiangsi. Mao was the first chairman. But Chiang gradually encircled the communist forces, and was on the verge of defeating them when they broke through and started their historic 6,000-mile Long March to the northwestern province of Shenshi.

In 1936 Mao, in association with a group of sympathetic northern warlords, kidnapped Chiang and forced him to form a Kuomintang–Chinese communist "United Front" against the invading Japanese. The common war against Japan enabled Mao's communists to expand both their base of operations and their army. Employing Chu Teh's guerrilla tactics and Mao's political tactics, the communists built an army of about 700,000 men controlling a population of nearly 85 million by the end of the war. The communist government was clearly popular. Mao instituted a widespread agrarian reform program in the areas he controlled, and American observers who visited the communist areas during the war contrasted his administration favorably with the corrupt and inefficient government in the areas controlled by Chiang Kai-shek.

With their solid northern base, the communists were in a good strategic position when the CHINESE CIVIL WAR broke out at the end of World War II. In the first year they suffered setbacks against Chiang's numerically stronger Nationalist forces, but they regrouped in the countryside while the Nationalist army stayed in the cities. By 1947, the communists were on the offensive, and the northern cities were beginning to fall under their control. The People's Republic of China was proclaimed by Mao on October 1, 1949.

Chiang fled to the offshore island of Taiwan and established a government that laid claim to all of China. In December 1949, seeking to protect his government from any American-supported attempt by Chiang to return, Mao went to Moscow and negotiated the SINO-SOVIET TREATY OF FRIENDSHIP, ALLIANCE AND MUTUAL ASSISTANCE, which pledged the two countries to come to each other's defense in case of attack. The treaty also included extensive Soviet financial and military aid. But Mao continued to worry about Chiang and the Americans, and this fear played a major part in his decision to attack UN forces during the KOREAN WAR.

After the signing of the Sino-Soviet treaty, Mao retired to a largely ceremonial role as chairman of the party and the People's Republic. The day-to-day administration of the country was left to party bureaucrats, who came increasingly under the influence of technical and military advisers from the Soviet Union. The political and economic structure of China was developed along the same lines as that of the Soviet Union, and many of Mao's theories on peasant-based revolution were pushed aside.

In 1955, however, Mao emerged from the shadows to start a battle to reimpose his authority and his doctrines. His failure undermined his position, and in 1959 he was forced to retire as chairman of the People's Republic in favor of LIU SHAOQI, although he retained the position of chairman of the Communist Party.

Mao's weak position at that time prevented him from blocking reforms of Liu and DENG XIAOPING. But in the early 1960s, Mao formed a political alliance with Minister of Defense LIN BIAO, who agreed to restructure the People's Liberation Army along Maoist lines. By 1964 Mao felt strong enough to start purging the army of Deng and Liu's supporters.

The following year Mao extended his purge to cultural and intellectual figures with the launching of what he called the Great Proletarian CULTURAL REVOLUTION. In February 1966, the supporters of Deng and Liu fought back within party circles. Mao turned to the students for additional support and struck a responsive chord among the Chinese youth.

The army was given responsibility for education and cultural affairs; the schools were effectively shut and the students organized into battalions of "Red Guards." The Red Guards were encouraged to hold mass meetings with Mao and were presented with copies of the *Quotations of Chairman Mao*, which became known as "the little red book." The students were then encouraged to go into the countryside and create local rebellions and overthrow the "capitalist roaders" who supported Deng and Liu. The party was purged to such an extent that the only effective power left in the country was the army, which took over the administration of the government.

By the summer of 1967, Mao's Cultural Revolution had brought China to the brink of civil war, and, after a series of disturbing armed clashes in the industrial city of Wuhan, Mao started to move against the excesses of the Cultural Revolution. By 1969 the first phase of the Cultural Revolution was over, and Mao and the People's Liberation Army were left in control of both the party and the country. Following the death of Lin Biao in 1971, Mao was in absolute control.

One of the results of the Cultural Revolution was the creation of the cult of Mao. His book of quotations was accorded scriptural authority and giant portraits of Mao sprung up all over the country alongside billboards displaying one of his many homilies. Mao later argued that the creation of the personality cult had been necessary to counter entrenched party interests.

The SINO-SOVIET SPLIT occurred during Mao's eclipse but was supported by him and owed much to Maoist thought. The Soviet leadership, in particular JOSEF STALIN, had long been opposed to Mao, whom they regarded as a nationalist agrarian reformer rather than a true communist because of his emphasis on peasant-based revolution rather than the proletariat-based strategy of Marx and Lenin. Stalin feared that the success of Mao could eventually lead to a doctrinal split within the communist camp and deprive the Soviet Union of its position as self-appointed leader of the communist camp. In the 1930s Stalin ordered Mao to abandon his rural base in Kiangsi and attack the cities in the hope of sparking a doctrinaire communist revolution by the factory workers. Mao refused.

After the Long March, Mao established his new base in the Northwest. It was assumed that he chose the area because the common border with the Soviet Union would enable him to be easily supplied from Moscow. But there is little evidence to suggest that the Soviets sent any more than basic materials. In 1942, at Stalin's insistence, the Chinese communists launched the "Rectification Campaign" to purge the party of any anti-Soviet figures. During the Chinese Civil War, Soviet troops did turn over the former Japanese-occupied areas to communist forces, but this was because Chiang's troops were based in the other half of the country. Stalin recognized

In October 1959, celebrations of the 19th anniversary of the People's Republic of China were led by Chinese Communist Party chairman Mao Zedong and visiting Soviet leader Nikita Khrushchev. Photo courtesy of Novosti Press Agency.

Chiang's Kuomintang as the government of China, and the Soviet ambassador was the only diplomat to accompany the retreating Nationalist forces to Canton after the fall of Nanking in April 1949. It was not until the signing of the Sino-Soviet mutual defense treaty in 1950 and the start of the Korean War that Stalin accepted Mao's commitment to international communism. But he remained concerned about the doctrinal differences.

The differences became more pronounced after Mao emerged victorious from the Cultural Revolution. The initial Sino-Soviet split was based primarily on political as distinct from ideological differences, and before the start of the Cultural Revolution there were signs that it might be resolved. But after the Cultural Revolution China's attacks on the Soviet Union increased in bitterness, and the dispute widened to encompass the basic differences between Maoism and Marxism-Leninism as well as more traditional conflicts over borders and trade.

The increasing bitterness of the Sino-Soviet dispute led Mao to look for allies against a possible Soviet attack. Guided by CHOU EN-LAI, he turned to the United States. In February 1972 Sino-American relations were reestablished after President Richard Nixon's historic visit to Beijing and discussions with Chairman Mao. But Mao by this time was plagued by illness, and the running of the country was left largely to Chou at first, and later to Mao's wife, Chiang Ch'ing (Jiang Qing). Her radical domestic policies ensured that many of the basis precepts of the Cultural Revolution continued in force until Mao's death on September 9, 1976.

For Further Information:
Ch'en, Jerome. *Mao and the Chinese Revolution.* New York, 1965.
Fitzgerald, C.P. *Mao Tse-tung and China.* New York, 1977.
Meisner, Maurice. *Mao's China and After: A History of the People's Republic.* New York, 1986.
Snow, Edgar. *Red Star Over China.* New York, 1937.
Wakeman, Frederic. *History and Will: Philosophical Perspectives of Mao Tse-tung's Thought.* New York, 1973.

Marshall, George C.   (December 31, 1880–October 16, 1959)   General George C. Marshall was the American Army chief of staff during World War II and under President HARRY TRUMAN served as secretary of state and secretary of defense and headed a U.S. mission to China to try to negotiate a peaceful end to the CHINESE CIVIL WAR. He also gave his name to the MARSHALL PLAN.

The son of a Pennsylvania coal merchant, Marshall joined the U.S. Army in 1902 after graduating from the Virginia Military Institute. He distinguished himself in World War I as chief of operations of the First Army and so impressed General John Pershing, leader of the American Expeditionary Forces, that Pershing made him his aide-de-camp. Marshall was appointed army chief of staff in 1938 and held that post throughout World War II. He emerged from the war a national hero and retired in November 1945, when he reached the mandatory age of 65.

A week after Marshall's retirement from the army, President Truman named him special emissary to China with the assignment of negotiating peace between the Chinese communists and the Nationalist government of CHIANG KAI-SHEK. At the time, Truman dubbed Marshall "the greatest living American."

Marshall managed with great difficulty to negotiate a shaky truce between the communists and the Nationalists, but it fell apart while he was in Washington, D.C., in March 1946 for consultations. Marshall tried to negotiate a fresh truce, but by then both the communists and Nationalists were committed to a military solution. Truman ended the mission in January 1947. In his report to the president, Marshall supported U.S. foreign service officers who blamed the rise of communism on corruption within the Nationalist government and warned that the only way to prevent a communist takeover in China was to commit the United States to a political and military situation from which it would "practically be impossible to withdraw." Because of this advice, Truman gradually wound down U.S. aid to Chiang's forces. After he became secretary of state, Marshall came under heavy pressure to boost American military aid to the beleaguered Chiang, but his experiences in China made him wary of any increased American commitment.

Marshall was still on his China mission when Truman offered him the post of secretary of state. His appointment was seen as apolitical and as a genuine attempt to remove foreign policy from the arena of party politics. Marshall himself stressed that his cabinet post was not political and he would not become involved in partisan issues.

The relationship between Truman and Marshall was close but not friendly. The president, a man whose early political career was tainted by association with a corrupt Kansas City political machine, was in awe of Marshall, who personified moral integrity and impartial wisdom to such a degree that the Senate unanimously approved his nomination without even a hearing.

From the start of his tenure as secretary of state, Marshall took a hard-line position against the Soviet Union. In this respect his appointment was seen to indicate an administration shift, as his predecessor, JAMES BYRNES, had been viewed as an appeaser.

One of Marshall's first actions as secretary of state was to reorganize the State Department. The new organization suited the rather aloof Marshall, who saw himself approving policy decisions worked out by undersecretaries, who were also responsible for the day-to-day workings of the diplomatic service. This gave a great deal of power to the undersecretaries. Marshall was fortunate in having a particularly close relationship with Undersecretary of State DEAN ACHESON, who pushed through U.S. aid to Greece and Turkey and formulated the TRUMAN DOCTRINE while Marshall prepared for the Moscow Conference of Foreign Ministers. Acheson also played a major role in developing the Marshall Plan.

The failure of the 1947 MOSCOW FOREIGN MINISTERS' CONFER-

ENCE convinced Marshall of the futility of attempting to reach agreements with the Soviet Union. It also led directly to the European Recovery Program, which became known as the Marshall Plan. Marshall believed that the Soviets' refusal to compromise over the issue of reparations was part of a plan to destroy Europe economically. He concluded that unilateral American action involving long-term financial aid was necessary to thwart this.

The Marshall Plan was proposed by the secretary of state in his commencement address at Harvard University on June 5, 1947, in which he said, "It is logical that the United States should do whatever it is able to do to assist in the return of normal economic health in the world, without which there can be no political stability and no assured peace. Our policy is directed not against any country or doctrine but against hunger, poverty, desperation and chaos. Its purpose should be the revival of a working economy in the world so as to permit the emergence of political and social conditions in which free institutions can exist."

The offer of American aid was extended to both Eastern and Western Europe. The governments of Western Europe responded enthusiastically and, after rapid negotiations, a four-year program of $17 billion in aid was agreed upon. The proposal was also welcomed by the governments of Czechoslovakia and Poland, but Soviet leader JOSEF STALIN denounced the Marshall Plan as "a repetition of the Truman Plan for political pressure with the help of dollars, a plan for interference in the domestic affairs of other countries."

Under strong pressure from Moscow, the Czech government withdrew from Marshall Plan negotiations. To counter the attractions of American aid, the Soviet Union offered its own aid package to Eastern Europe. At a conference of communist governments at Wiliza Gora, in Silesia, on September 22–23, 1947, the communist parties of Yugoslavia, Poland, Hungary, the Soviet Union, Czechoslovakia, Bulgaria, France and Italy established the Communist Information Bureau (COMINFORM) with the explicit purpose of fostering unrest in the West.

The Marshall Plan, therefore, saved Western Europe from ecomomic collapse but also reinforced the division of the continent into Western and Eastern blocs.

During the BERLIN Blockade Marshall convinced Truman to reject the advice of General LUCIUS CLAY, who wanted to respond to the Soviet blockade by sending armed American convoys through the Soviet zone to Berlin. Marshall instead urged him to airlift supplies to the city. He also had overall authority for the year-long East–West negotiations that eventually ended in the Soviet lifting of the blockade.

One of the few areas of conflict between Truman and Marshall was over U.S. policy toward the infant state of Israel. Marshall opposed immediate recognition because he thought Israel would lose the war against the Arab countries and because recognition would damage American relations with the Arabs, upon whom the United States was becoming increasingly dependent for oil imports. Truman, however, was told that he needed the Jewish vote in the 1948 presidential election and reluctantly came out in favor of immediate recognition of Israel.

Marshall was a supporter of GEORGE F. KENNAN's policy of containment and played a major role in the discussions that led to the formation of the NORTH ATLANTIC TREATY ORGANIZATION (NATO). He also initiated a series of alliances designed to prevent communist expansion in Latin America and persuaded the Latin American countries to sign the mutual defense treaty known as the RIO PACT. A year later, in 1949, he helped to establish the ORGANIZATION OF AMERICAN STATES.

While secretary of state, Marshall also supported Truman's plans to unify the services under a single secretary of defense and suggested the formation of an agency to coordinate foreign and military policy. This agency became the NATIONAL SECURITY COUNCIL, which was created in 1947. Marshall was initially a supporter of the BARUCH PLAN, which proposed United Nations control of atomic energy. But after the Soviet Union rejected the plan, Marshall changed course to advocate increased atomic weapons production and research and advised against unilateral disarmament.

Ill health forced Marshall to resign as secretary of state in January 1949. In July 1950 he returned to government service when Truman asked him to become secretary of defense to help deal with acute organizational problems created by the KOREAN WAR. Marshall reorganized the Pentagon and oversaw the buildup of American defense forces to 2.5 million men. He also secured a continuation of conscription.

Marshall backed Truman in his battle against General DOUGLAS MACARTHUR, who wanted to expand the Korean War from a limited police action to an attack on communist China. Marshall argued that MacArthur's plans would involve a massive influx of American and European troops into Asia and leave Western Europe dangerously unprotected.

Marshall approved of Truman's decision to relieve MacArthur of command in April 1951 and, in the following month, publicly supported Truman's decision at congressional hearings on the dismissal. Marshall was before the committee for two full-day sessions and five half-day sessions. Throughout his testimony, he maintained that MacArthur had been recalled for publicly disagreeing with the president's foreign and military policies. Marshall's testimony swung the tide for Truman and prevented the dismissal of MacArthur from developing into a foreign policy crisis.

Toward the end of his term as defense secretary, Marshall came under attack from Senator JOSEPH MCCARTHY, who alleged that he had allowed communists to continue working in the State Department and had played a major role in the "loss" of China. Marshall retired from government service in September 1951. In 1953 he won the Nobel Prize for peace for developing the European Recovery Plan and represented the United States at the coronation of Queen Elizabeth II. He died at Walter Reed Army Hospital in Washington, D.C., on October 16, 1959.

For Further Information:

Acheson, Dean. *Present at the Creation.* New York, 1969.

Ambrose, Stephen E. *Rise to Globalism.* New York, 1971.

Beal, John Robinson. *Marshall in China.* Garden City, N.Y., 1970.

Cray, Ed. *General of the Army: George C. Marshall, Soldier and Statesman.* New York, 1990.

Ferrell, Robert H. *George C. Marshall.* New York, 1969.

Mosley, Leonard. *Marshall, Hero for Our Times.* New York, 1982.

Pogue, Forrest C. *George C. Marshall.* New York, 1963–1987.

Stoler, Mark A. *George C. Marshall: Soldier-Statesman of the American Century.* Boston, 1989.

Marshall Plan (European Recovery Program)

The Marshall Plan was an American plan to aid the economic recovery of Western Europe after World War II. The plan played a major role in rebuilding European economies so that they could withstand political and military aggression from the Soviet Union. It also accelerated the political and economic split between East and West.

The basic tenets of the Marshall Plan were laid out by Undersecretary of State DEAN ACHESON in a memorandum to President HARRY TRUMAN on March 5, 1947, following a discussion on the progress of the TRUMAN DOCTRINE, which had extended American military and economic aid to Greece and Turkey. In this memorandum, Acheson said that Greece and Turkey were "only part of a much larger problem growing out of the change in Great Britain's strength and other circumstances . . . I believe it is important and urgent that study be given by our most competent officers to situations elsewhere in the world which may require analogous financial, technical and military aid on our part."

As a result of this memorandum an ad hoc committee was established to define the scope and nature of a program to provide widespread American financial assistance to Europe. On April 21, the committee reported that any U.S. aid program should "support economic stability and orderly political processes throughout the world and oppose the spread of chaos and extremism . . . prevent the growth or advance of national or international power which constitutes a substantial threat to U.S. security and well-being . . . [and] orient foreign nations toward the U.S."

The $16 billion Marshall Plan was first proposed publicly by Secretary of State George C. Marshall in a commencement address at Harvard University on June 5, 1947. From left to right: President Harry Truman, Secretary Marshall, Paul Hoffman and Averell Harriman.

The committee also urged that the United States restrict its aid to the economic sphere and ensure the cooperation of all participating countries; that the United States have full knowledge "of the manner in which the means provided [would be] distributed and used"; and that the recipient countries use the money for "the development and support of free and democratic institutions." The Soviet Union and Eastern Europe, suggested the committee, should be invited to participate, but heavy emphasis should also be placed on the revival of German industry.

The debate on the details of the plan continued within the State Department. The major participants in the planning process at this stage were Secretary of State GEORGE C. MARSHALL, Acheson, head of policy planning GEORGE F. KENNAN and WILLIAM CLAYTON, undersecretary of state for economic affairs. Marshall was at the MOSCOW FOREIGN MINISTERS' CONFERENCE of 1947 during most of the planning stages. While there he became more convinced of the Soviets' aggressive intent toward Western Europe and the need for American financial assistance to alleviate the poverty that might lead to unrest and revolution.

The first public airing of a massive American financial assistance program was made by Acheson in a speech in Cleveland, Mississippi, on May 7, 1947. He called on America to import more "in order that the financial gap between the world's needs and what it can pay for can be narrowed. There is no charity involved in this. It is simple common sense and good business."

Acheson then went on to propose that the United States "push ahead with the reconstruction of those two great workshops of Europe and Asia—Germany and Japan—upon which the ultimate recovery of the two continents so largely depends. It is wheat and coal and steel that are urgently required to stave off economic collapse, not just dollar credits." He concluded, "Not only do human beings and nations exist on narrow economic margins, but also human dignity, human freedom and democratic institutions. It is one of the principal aims of our foreign policy today to use our resources to widen these margins. It is necessary if we are to preserve our own freedoms and our own democratic institutions."

Acheson's speech received a warm welcome, clearing the way for Marshall's more important policy statement on June 4, at which the secretary of state outlined the plan that came to bear his name. In a commencement address at Harvard University, he outlined in graphic detail the poverty found throughout Europe and offered American help to alleviate "hunger, poverty, desperation and chaos." But he then added, "Before the U.S. government can proceed much farther in its effort to alleviate the situation and help start the European world on its way to recovery, there must be some agreement among the countries of Europe as to the requirements of the situation and the part those countries themselves will take in order to give proper effect to whatever might be undertaken by this government . . . The initiative, I think, must come from Europe . . . The program should be a joint one, agreed to by a number, if not all European nations."

The British press in Washington, D.C., had been briefed in advance that Marshall was making a major speech that required an immediate reaction from the British government. The result was a quick, positive response from British foreign secretary ERNEST BEVIN. There was also a positive response from French foreign minister GEORGES BIDAULT, who on June 7 cabled the French ambassador in Washington asking him to inform Marshall that the French government accepted his views. Nine days later, Bevin and Bidault met in Paris to further coordinate their reactions.

The Soviet Union was initially silent, although Foreign Minister V.M. MOLOTOV agreed to meet with Bidault and Bevin in Paris on June 27 for further discussions on how to coordinate a European-wide reaction to the proposed Marshall Plan. At this meeting, Bevin and Bidault proposed a survey of European needs followed by an overall European economic plan to be submitted to the United States. This was objected to by Molotov because it included Germany. He also wanted each European country to have complete control of the funds it received and wanted the United States to state in advance how much money it would make available.

The Soviets were in a difficult position; they did not want to become involved in the Marshall Plan because they regarded it as a form of financial imperialism, but the governments of two of the occupied East European countries, Poland and Czechoslovakia, had welcomed it. Molotov walked out of the three-power conference on July 2, and two days later Bevin and Bidault decided to go ahead with a Europe-wide conference on the Marshall Plan without the participation of the Soviet Union. Invitations were sent out to all European governments except that of Spain, which had not participated in the war, and where fascists still ruled. The Czechs initially accepted the invitation, but shortly afterward, under pressure from the Soviet Union, withdrew their acceptance. The official Soviet reaction to the Marshall Plan was made clear in an article in *Pravda* on July 16, which denounced it as "a repetition of the Truman Plan for political pressure with the help of dollars, a plan for interference in the domestic affairs of other countries."

The West European countries that attended the conference to discuss a wider response to the Marshall Plan quickly agreed upon a reply based on the initial proposal from Bevin and Bidault. The West Europeans' agreement did not mean automatic implementation of the plan by the Truman administration. Marshall still had to win acceptance for it from the U.S. Congress, and he encountered strong opposition from Republican conservatives, who were unwilling to give the Democratic Truman administration a major diplomatic triumph during an election year. But Marshall's substantial personal prestige, the support of senior Republican senator ARTHUR VANDENBERG, and the communist coup in Czechoslovakia ensured passage of the necessary legislation in March 1948. The funds were first made available that year and continued until 1952.

More than any other postwar political event, the Marshall

Plan became the watershed for almost every European country. The West European countries warmly welcomed it, and the East Europeans, under Soviet pressure, rejected it. Shortly after the West European nations' formal acceptance of the plan, foreign ministers from the nine communist European countries met in Wiliza Gora in Silesia on September 22–23 and formed the COMINFORM (Communist Information Bureau), which was meant to be a political counter to the Marshall Plan. The final Soviet Bloc rejection of the Marshall Plan came at the LONDON FOREIGN MINISTERS' CONFERENCE in December 1947. In 1949 the Soviet Union established the COUNCIL FOR MUTUAL AND ECONOMIC COOPERATION (COMECON), which proved to be ineffective as an economic counter to the Marshall Plan because it was able to provide regional economic planning only, without any major financial aid.

Some historians have argued that the Soviet Union had sound financial and political reasons for rejecting the Marshall Plan and that its implementation was a major cause of the Cold War. They argued that Marshall and Acheson had too little regard for the Soviet fear of a revived Germany and that the Marshall Plan's heavy emphasis on industrial redevelopment in the West would have forced the Soviet Union into the limited role of provider of agricultural products for a wealthier Western Europe.

Other critics also claim that the Marshall Plan aided American industry as much as it did that of Europe, as Congress stipulated that most of the $12.5 billion in aid be spent on American products. But the aid money distributed through the Economic Cooperation Administration, the administrative arm of the Marshall Plan, was the most important factor in boosting European industrial output to 35% above prewar levels and agricultural output to 10% above prewar levels by the end of the four years.

For Further Information:

Arkes, Hadley. *Bureaucracy, the Marshall Plan, and the National Interest.* Princeton, 1973.

Donovan, Robert J. *The Second Victory: The Marshall Plan and the Postwar Revival of Europe.* Lanham, Md., 1987.

Fossedal, Gregory A. *Our Finest Hour: Will Clayton, the Marshall Plan, and the Triumph of Democracy.* Stanford, Calif., 1993.

Gimbel, John. *The Origins of the Marshall Plan.* Stanford, Calif., 1976.

Hartmann, Susan M. *The Marshall Plan.* Columbus, Ohio, 1968.

Hogan, Michael J. *The Marshall Plan: America, Britain, and the Reconstruction of Western Europe, 1947–1952.* New York, 1987.

Maier, Charles S., ed., with Gunter Bischof. *The Marshall Plan and Germany: West German Development Within the Framework of the European Recovery Program.* New York, 1991.

Mee, Charles L. *The Marshall Plan: The Launching of the Pax Americana.* New York, 1984.

Pisani, Sallie. *The CIA and the Marshall Plan.* Lawrence, Kan., 1991.

Price, Harry. *The Marshall Plan and Its Meaning.* Ithaca, N.Y., 1955.

Masaryk, Jan   (September 14, 1886–March 10, 1948)

Jan Masaryk was foreign minister of Czechoslovakia in the immediate postwar period. A statesmanlike figure, he tried to act as a bridge builder between East and West while remaining committed to multiparty democracy in his own country. Masaryk's suspicious death in a fall shortly after the communist coup in Czechoslovakia persuaded many people in the West that it was a dangerous folly to try to work with the Soviet Union.

Masaryk was the son of the founder and first president of Czechoslovakia, Tomas Masaryk. In 1908 he emigrated to the United States, while his country was still part of the Austro-Hungarian Empire. Masaryk returned home shortly before the start of World War I and was drafted into the Austro-Hungarian Army. He became a lieutenant but was court-martialed for "political unreliability" after his father went into exile.

The end of World War I also saw the end of the Hapsburg empire and the creation of the republic of Czechoslovakia. Masaryk's father became president, and Jan Masaryk returned to his homeland to enter his newly created country's diplomatic service.

During the 1920s and 1930s, Masaryk served in Washington, D.C., and London. Following the German occupation of Czechoslovakia, Masaryk became one of his country's most respected figures overseas, and in July 1940 he was appointed the minister of foreign affairs in the Czechoslovak provisional government. In 1941 he was named prime minister as well. In 1945 Masaryk attended the SAN FRANCISCO CONFERENCE, which established the United Nations.

Masaryk was by nature a diplomat who sought always to build diplomatic "bridges" and find compromises. This often created immense political problems for him, for, as he once observed, "The problem with being a bridge is that people trample over you." Masaryk was convinced that postwar Czechoslovakia had to maintain friendly relations with the Soviet Union, although he was equally determined that his country would remain democratic, and Masaryk himself was always Western in his basic political orientation.

Masaryk played a major role in negotiating the wartime alliance between the Soviet Union and the provisional Czech government that was signed in December 1943 by President EDUARD BENEŠ. The treaty became the legal basis for the Soviet presence in Czechoslovakia in the immediate postwar period. It also enabled Beneš and Masaryk's government to return to its country in the postwar period—the only East European government-in-exile allowed by the Soviets to do so.

The communists were then in a politically powerful position within Czechoslovakia. They had gained credibility as the only major political organization to have stood up to the German occupation of the Sudetenland in 1938, and during the war they had organized the Czech resistance movement. In addition, the majority of Czechs had a genuine feeling of gratitude toward the liberating Red Army. In free multiparty elections held in 1946, the Communist Party, led by KLEMENT GOTTWALD, polled 40% of the vote.

Following the 1946 elections, most of the key positions in the coalition government were taken by the Communist Party. But Masaryk retained the powerful position of foreign minister and continued to use his reputation to try to improve Czechoslovakia's relations with the Soviet Union as well as relations between the Soviet Union and the West. In January 1947 he denied the existence of an IRON CURTAIN in Eastern Europe, saying, "I wouldn't live behind an Iron Curtain for two minutes."

Masaryk's political inclinations, however, clearly leaned toward the West, and when U.S. secretary of state GEORGE C. MARSHALL announced his MARSHALL PLAN for Europe, Masaryk eagerly embraced the concept and instructed Czech diplomats to work toward full Czech participation. Masaryk was opposed by Gottwald, who was under strict instructions from Stalin to block Czech participation. In July 1947, Masaryk and Gottwald flew to Moscow, where the Soviet dictator issued an ultimatum to pull out of the Marshall Plan or face Soviet retaliation. Masaryk reluctantly agreed and was presented with a face-saving five-year trade pact with the Soviet Union.

Masaryk loyally denied that Stalin had pressured him into taking Czechoslovakia out of the Marshall Plan. He said in August 1947 that Czechoslovakia had voluntarily stayed out to avoid being used as a tool in East–West rivalry.

The Czech withdrawal from the Marshall Plan and events elsewhere in Eastern Europe began to erode the popularity of the Czech communists, and the party moved to grab power by taking control of the police and security forces in preparation for a coup and the establishment of a Soviet-style one-party state. Masaryk had been prepared to accept Soviet domination, but he was not prepared to accept the end of the multiparty democratic system in Czechoslovakia.

For the communists, Masaryk represented a powerful asset. As the son of the founder of Czechoslovakia and a popular political figure in his own right, both at home and abroad, his support would provide any Czech government with credibility and legitimacy; for the same reasons withdrawal of his support would represent a threat to any Czech government.

In February 1948, the noncommunist cabinet members in the Czech government, including Masaryk, resigned in protest against the communist control of the police forces. Their hope was that this would force an early general election. But at the last moment the Social Democrats refused to join the rest of the noncommunist bloc, and in the ensuing political confusion the communist-controlled police arrested its opponents, suppressed nonparty newspapers, placed party members in other key positions and surrounded the capital with armed activists supported by the Soviet Red Army.

In the midst of this crisis, on March 10, 1948, Masaryk fell to his death from the window of his apartment in the Foreign Office. Gottwald claimed that Masaryk had committed suicide as a result of depression brought about by Western claims that he had sold out to Eastern Europe. But a number of Masaryk's friends and colleagues denied that he had been depressed. They said he had been on the verge of leaving the country and denouncing the communist government and that, to prevent this, communist activists had brutally beaten him and thrown him out the window. The latter account

seems to be more in keeping with the personality of Masaryk and the events of the day, and it is generally assumed that he was murdered. In death he continued to represent liberal Czech nationalism, and his memory was often invoked by Czech dissidents over the next 40 years.

Massive Retaliation   Massive retaliation, at the core of the Eisenhower administration's defense and foreign policies, threatened full-scale U.S. nuclear attack on the Soviet Union in response to "Communist aggression" in any part of the world.

The policy was outlined by Secretary of State JOHN FOSTER DULLES in a speech before the New York Council of Foreign Relations on January 12, 1954. He said that the United States would be prepared to meet aggression "with massive and instant retaliation by means and at places of our own choosing."

Dulles made it clear that a major purpose of the new policy was to reduce American military and foreign aid expenditure as a means of combating aggression. He said it was not sound military strategy to commit U.S. land forces to Asia to a degree that left no strategic reserves at home; it was not sound economics or good foreign policy to continue to support other nations and it was not sound to be committed to "military expenditures so vast that they lead to practical bankruptcy."

Neither Dulles nor President DWIGHT EISENHOWER explicitly linked massive retaliation to the threat to retaliate with nuclear weapons. But as the subsequent "NEW LOOK" DEFENSE POLICY decreased conventional forces to bolster strategic forces, the linkage became clear. This worried a number of defense planners, who felt that massive retaliation heightened the risk of nuclear war, while at the same time creating opportunities for communist-inspired guerrilla offensives at the lower end of the military spectrum. The result was the KENNEDY administration's decision to replace massive retaliation with FLEXIBLE RESPONSE, which called for the development of a wide range of American defense capabilities to allow the United States to counter a communist insurgency with an equivalent show of force. The policy, while reducing the nuclear threshold, also significantly increased American defense costs.

McCarran, Patrick   (August 8, 1876–September 28, 1954)
Senator Pat McCarran was a staunch anti-communist who led investigations into alleged subversion of the State Department, the United Nations and the American motion picture industry. He sympathized with and supported Senator JOSEPH MCCARTHY but employed a less showy approach in his search for communist subversion.

McCarran graduated from the University of Nevada in 1901 and became a full-time rancher and part-time law student. He was elected to the state legislature in 1903 and two years later passed his bar examination. He established a private legal practice in Reno, where he specialized in representing the area's growing silver mining industry. In 1912 he became a member of the State Supreme Court and in 1932 was elected to the U.S. Senate as a Democrat.

After World War II, McCarran became the leading Democratic senator convinced of the existence of a vast communist conspiracy attempting to overthrow the U.S. government. In 1947 he introduced an amendment to the State Department appropriations bill that allowed the department to dismiss any employee whose actions it considered harmful to the national interest. And in 1950 he sponsored the bill that became the INTERNAL SECURITY ACT—the anti-communist bill that criminalized sedition, tightened safeguards against espionage, stiffened penalties and allowed the State Department to bar or deport aliens who were members of the Communist Party. President HARRY TRUMAN vetoed the bill but Congress overrode his veto.

In 1951 McCarran became chairman of the newly created Internal Security Subcommittee and started a series of investigations into alleged communist influence and "subversion" in the motion picture industry, the trade unions, the State Department and the United Nations. One of McCarran's main victims was China scholar OWEN LATTIMORE, who had served as an adviser to the State Department and to Nationalist Chinese leader CHIANG KAI-SHEK during the war. In 1951 McCarran's subcommittee reported that "Lattimore was for some time, beginning in the middle of the 1930s, a conscious, articulate instrument of the Soviet conspiracy." Lattimore was indicted for perjury, but the indictment was later dismissed.

McCarran attributed much of the alleged subversion in the United States to immigration from communist-dominated parts of the world. In 1952 he helped to introduce a complete recodification of the U.S. immigration, naturalization and nationality laws. The McCarran-Walter Act established a quota system for each country, which effectively discriminated against immigrants from Asia, Southern Europe and Central Europe. McCarran said the bill was framed with the security of the United States in mind, because, "if this oasis of the world should be overrun, perverted, contaminated or destroyed, then the last flickering light of humanity will be extinguished." Truman again used his veto, describing the McCarran-Walter Act as "one of the most un-American acts I have ever witnessed in my public career." Congress again overrode the presidential veto.

Although McCarran opposed Truman on the issue of communist subversion, he supported the TRUMAN DOCTRINE, the MARSHALL PLAN, the KOREAN WAR and the president's response to the BERLIN BLOCKADE. He was, however, highly critical of the administration's China policy, accusing the State Department of abandoning Chiang Kai-shek to the communists. He successfully pressed for loans and U.S. military aid to Chiang's forces in 1949 and 1950.

McCarran was Senator McCarthy's strongest supporter in the Democratic Party and helped him to secure bipartisan support for many of his actions. In 1953, he joined McCarthy in an unsuccessful attempt to block the appointment of CHARLES BOHLEN as U.S. ambassador to the Soviet Union. After a special committee of the Senate recommended that McCarthy be censured, McCarran delivered a strong attack on the committee from the Senate floor. The following week, McCarran collapsed and died of a heart attack while addressing a political rally in Reno.

For Further Information:
Divine, Robert. *American Immigration Policy: 1924–1952*. New York, 1972.
Reeves, Thomas C., ed. *McCarthyism*. Hinsdale, Ill., 1973.

McCarthy, Eugene **(March 29, 1916–   )**   Senator Eugene J. McCarthy was an antiwar candidate for the Democratic Party's 1968 presidential nomination and became a focal point for the anti-VIETNAM WAR campaign. Although he failed to win the nomination, his ability to motivate and organize American youth in opposition to the war contributed to the end of American military involvement in Southeast Asia.

In the Senate, McCarthy had a reputation as a figure slightly out of place in the cut-and-thrust world of politics. This reputation was reinforced by his background. After graduating from St. John's University in Minnesota, he spent 13 years teaching sociology and economics at Catholic high schools and colleges. For nine months during World War II he was a novice Benedictine monk.

In the later stages of the war, McCarthy became involved in politics as a supporter of HUBERT HUMPHREY, and in 1948 he was elected to the U.S. House of Representatives from Minnesota, quickly establishing a liberal voting record and a record of leadership in domestic policy issues. In 1958 McCarthy was elected to the U.S. Senate, and in 1964 he was named to the Senate Foreign Relations Committee.

McCarthy's liberal leanings quickly came to the fore on the Foreign Relations Committee. He demanded greater congressional control of the CENTRAL INTELLLIGENCE AGENCY, called for an investigation of the CIA's role in various activities, and criticized American arms sales to Third World countries.

But it was in his opposition to the Vietnam War that McCarthy made his mark. This opposition, however, did not start until 1966. McCarthy voted in favor of the 1964 GULF OF TONKIN RESOLUTION and was a cautious supporter of the initial bombings. But in January 1966, McCarthy wrote to President LYNDON JOHNSON calling for the continued suspension of air strikes against North Vietnam. He said that bombing had not had a "beneficial political or diplomatic effect" and suggested that the war called for "a national debate . . . and a real searching of the mind and the soul of America."

McCarthy's opposition to the war gradually grew, and on February 25 he said that the war was "morally unjustifiable." He went on to attack the Johnson administration's broad interpretation of the Gulf of Tonkin Resolution and in October 1967 published *The Limits of Power*, a wide-ranging attack on American foreign policy. Shortly afterward McCarthy announced that he was a candidate for the Democratic presidential nomination. "I am concerned," he said "that the administration seems to have set no limit to the price which it is willing to pay for a military victory."

Political observers regarded McCarthy as a dark horse. His campaign was poorly organized. The candidate wrote his own speeches, and although they were generally pointed and witty, they were not rousing political oratory. And he was a one-issue candidate. But he won the backing of many of those who opposed the war, and thousands of idealistic young people volunteered to help his campaign. This led to a surprisingly strong showing in the New Hampshire primary election, where McCarthy won 42% of the vote compared to 49% for President Johnson.

The New Hampshire primary result led ROBERT KENNEDY, the Democratic Party's other major antiwar figure, to declare his candidacy. A few days later Johnson announced that he would not be a candidate for re-election, and Vice President Hubert Humphrey picked up the administration's banner. The fight for the antiwar vote was between Kennedy and McCarthy, with Kennedy gradually pulling ahead until his assassination in California on June 5.

The death of Kennedy left McCarthy the only antiwar candidate, but at the Democratic Convention in Chicago he failed to secure the backing of former Kennedy supporters, who rallied around Senator George McGovern. The antiwar demonstrations outside the convention hall also alienated many of the delegates, and Humphrey's adept handling of the political machinery secured him 1,760 delegate votes to McCarthy's 601. Humphrey, who had once called the Vietnam War "our finest hour," tried to win McCarthy's endorsement by taking an equivocal antiwar position, but McCarthy withheld his support until the last minute, seriously undermining Humphrey's campaign.

McCarthy resigned from the Senate Foreign Relations Committee after the 1968 campaign and left the Senate in 1971. He made two subsequent bids for the Democratic nomination, in 1972 and 1976, but they failed to generate the enthusiasm of his 1968 campaign.

For Further Information:
Dougan, C.A. *A Nation Divided.* Boston, 1984.
McCarthy, Eugene. *The Year of the People.* New York, 1969.
Small, M. *Johnson, Nixon and the Doves.* New Brunswick, N.J., 1988.
Smith, R.B. *An International History of the Vietnam War.* New York, 1986.

McCarthy, Joseph　(November 14, 1908–May 2, 1957)

Senator Joseph McCarthy was the leading American anti-communist figure of the late 1940s and early 1950s. His campaign against communist "subversion," based on half-truths and innuendo, ruined the careers of many and contributed substantially to the anti-communist hysteria that characterized American politics at that time. His campaign and tactics gave rise to the terms *McCarthyism* and *McCarthyite*.

McCarthy was raised in Wisconsin. He left school at age 14 to raise chickens on his father's farm. At age 20, he returned to complete his high school education in one year, and the following year he entered Marquette University. He received his law degree in 1935 and in 1939 was elected a

Wisconsin circuit court judge. In 1942 McCarthy volunteered for the Marine Corps and was sent to the South Pacific as an intelligence officer. In 1944, while still in the service, he made an unsuccessful bid for a U.S. Senate seat. In 1946, he was elected to the Senate.

McCarthy developed a reputation for bombast and anti-labor positions, but made little impact during his first four years in the Senate. He was not involved in the early, well-publicized anti-communist investigations, but he had exploited the issue profitably. He realized that such efforts offered substantial political benefits, especially if he could establish himself as the chief exposer of communist "subversives."

McCarthy made his move in February 1950 in Wheeling, West Virginia, when he waved a sheet of paper that he claimed contained the names of 205 Communist Party members currently employed in important positions at the State Department. A special subcommittee of the Democratic-controlled Senate Foreign Relations Committee was established to investigate McCarthy's sensational charges, and in July 1950 denounced them as false, attacking McCarthy for unethical tactics.

But the Republican minority called the report a whitewash and McCarthy continued his attacks. In the political climate of the time, they received a strong favorable response among the general public, and many political figures were afraid to attack McCarthy for fear of alienating voters.

McCarthy, emboldened by public support and the fear he engendered in both the administration and Congress, stepped

Senator Joseph McCarthy, whose name has become synonymous with the anti-communist hysteria that swept the U.S. in the late 1940s and 1950s. "Witch hunts" conducted by McCarthy and others ruined the careers of many.

up his attacks, making them more sensational and outrageous. In June 1951, he accused GEORGE C. MARSHALL, then secretary of defense, of near treason for his role in formulating America's China policy. Senator William Benton responded by proposing an investigation into McCarthy's behavior and was accused by McCarthy of being "a hero of every Communist and crook in and out of government." Benton was undeterred and became a leading figure in the anti-McCarthy camp.

After winning reelection in 1952, McCarthy secured the position of chairman of the Permanent Investigations Subcommittee of the Senate Government Operations Committee. His first major attack was on CHARLES E. BOHLEN, President DWIGHT EISENHOWER's nominee as ambassador to the Soviet Union. Eisenhower won the battle, but it left him wary of McCarthy and he avoided confronting him. It would be wrong, however, to say that Eisenhower supported McCarthy's campaign or tactics. He heartily disliked the man and reportedly said on several occasions that he would not "get in the gutter with him."

But the president's refusal to denounce McCarthy publicly only increased the senator's power. In April 1953, his committee started an investigation of American embassy libraries to determine whether they contained any subversive books. The subcommittee's chief counsel, ROY COHN, and chief consultant, G. David Schine, toured libraries in American embassies in Europe. The State Department panicked and ordered the removal of all material written by "Communists, fellow travelers, et cetera . . ." Many books were literally burned, and Eisenhower consequently issued his famous appeal to students not to join the "book burners," which was the closest he came to an attack on McCarthy.

In September 1953 McCarthy began an investigation of the army and the Department of Defense. Almost from the start he issued sensational revelations based on questionable or nonexistent evidence. The mere mention of a federal employee's name in the McCarthy hearings could lead to his dismissal or forced resignation. If the individual did not work for the government he still stood a good chance of losing his livelihood. McCarthy became so adept at whipping up public hysteria that his search for communist subversives spread throughout the government and into the private sector, and many congressmen and senators emulated his tactics. McCarthy's committee was not the only one investigating communist subversion. The HOUSE UN-AMERICAN ACTIVITIES COMMITTEE had begun its investigations long before McCarthy launched his first attack and continued long after his censure in 1954. But McCarthy's spotlight-grabbing tactics ensured that his name became synonymous with the anti-communist hunt, and his political fate became inextricably bound to this domestic aspect of the Cold War.

Each new investigation appeared to drive McCarthy to wilder excess. In November 1953, he appeared on television to launch an attack on President Eisenhower, claiming that the president had not acted to eliminate subversives from the federal government and that America had been "reduced to a state of whining and whimpering appeasement."

In December 1953, McCarthy started an investigation into the activities of an army dentist, Major Irving Peress, which eventually led to the senator's downfall. Peress, who was based at Camp Kilmer, New Jersey, was a member of the left-wing American Labor Party. In November 1953 he had been routinely promoted to the rank of major under the Doctor Draft Law, although he had invoked the Fifth Amendment in refusing to answer questions on loyalty certification forms. A few weeks later, however, the Pentagon discovered his background and ordered that he be discharged.

McCarthy called Peress before his subcommittee on January 30, 1954, shortly before his discharge. When asked by McCarthy about his political affiliations, Peress again took the Fifth Amendment. McCarthy demanded that Peress be court-martialed, but the army had already started to process his discharge, and immediately after his appearance before McCarthy he was honorably discharged.

Two weeks later, McCarthy called the commanding officer of Camp Kilmer, General RALPH ZWICKER, before the subcommittee and demanded that he reveal the names of all officers involved in granting Peress' discharge. Zwicker refused and McCarthy contemptuously attacked him as "not fit to wear that uniform" and as not having "the brains of a five-year-old." As a result of this attack, Secretary of the Army Robert Stevens refused to allow Zwicker to appear before McCarthy's subcommittee again. Stevens was forced to back down, but in doing so he convinced the political and military establishment that McCarthy had to be stopped.

McCarthy now came under fire from all sides. In March 1954, EDWARD R. MURROW used his respected and popular television program "See It Now" to launch an attack on McCarthy. The same day, Senator Ralph Flanders (R-Vt.) indicated that McCarthy was losing the support of his own party's conservatives; he also joined the attack on McCarthy when he ridiculed the discrepancy between his shrill statements and his limited "achievements." Soon afterward, the Republican Party's national chairman, Leonard Hall, who only weeks before had described McCarthy as an "asset" to the Republican Party, said that he could not "go along" with McCarthy when he attacked "persons who are fighting communism just as conscientiously as he is."

But perhaps the most damaging attack came from Vice President RICHARD NIXON. Speaking on behalf of the administration on March 13, 1954, he denounced the "reckless talk and questionable methods" of McCarthyites. Although Nixon did not mention McCarthy by name, his target was clear when he attacked "men who in the past" had done "effective work" in uncovering communism but who had made "themselves the issue rather than the cause they believe in so deeply." Such men had "diverted attention from the danger of Communism".

With the forces gathering against McCarthy, the army launched a counterattack when it alleged that McCarthy and Cohn were seeking preferential treatment for Schine, who had been drafted into the army in 1953. McCarthy claimed that the army was "trying to use Schine as a hostage to pressure us to stop our hearings on the Army." He added that John Adams, general counsel to the army, had suggested that McCarthy go after the navy and air force and offered to provide "plenty of dirt" to help his investigation. The allegations were denied by Adams and Stevens, and charges and countercharges flew between McCarthy and the army until eventually McCarthy's own subcommittee voted to investigate the claims of both sides.

The investigation was known as the Army–McCarthy hearings and began on April 22, 1954. During the hearings, McCarthy temporarily resigned his seat as chairman, which was taken by Karl Mundt (R-South Dakota). Cohn also temporarily resigned. The Democrats successfully insisted that the hearings be televised, and this turned out to be McCarthy's downfall. His bullying tactics and unsubstantiated allegations were witnessed by the entire nation and exposed him as irresponsible and dishonest.

By the time the hearings ended on June 17, 1954, McCarthy had lost the support of even the hard-core conservative Republicans. His own Wisconsin constituents circulated a recall petition, which attracted a staggering 400,000 signatures. Cohn, McCarthy's protégé, was forced to resign as counsel on July 19, and at the end of August the subcommittee issued its formal report, criticizing Cohn for having used his position to obtain preferential treatment for Schine. The Democrats also implicated McCarthy, but the Republicans on the panel said there was insufficient evidence to support this allegation.

By this time, however, the hearings and the report had been overshadowed by a Senate move to censure McCarthy officially. On July 30, Senator Flanders introduced a formal motion for censure. The proposed resolution was referred to a carefully chosen select committee of moderate conservatives. Hearings were carefully organized to deny McCarthy his usual theatrical props, and chairman Arthur Watkins (R-Utah) maintained a firm control over McCarthy's attempts to lower the tone of the proceedings.

The Watkins Report was issued on November 8 and recommended censure. The Senate debate started two days later with McCarthy claiming that the Select Committee was the Communist Party's "unwitting handmaiden" and "involuntary agent." He said the committee did the Communist Party's work, "cooperated in the achievement of Communist goals" and, "in writing its report, it imitated Communist methods."

McCarthy predicted that he would be censured and that this meant a temporary but major victory for the communists because it slowed the fight against communism. He called himself "the symbol of resistance to communist subversion" and claimed that the nation's fate was in some respect tied to his own. McCarthy insisted that he was being censured only because of his fight against communism.

On December 2, 1954, the Senate voted to censure McCarthy by a vote of 67 to 22. McCarthy responded with a bitter attack on President Eisenhower and his administration and apologized to the American people for having urged them to vote for the president. But the attack served only to further alienate the nation from McCarthy.

McCarthy spent another two-and-a-half years in the Senate, during which he continued to make his outrageous claims. In March 1955, for instance, he claimed that Secretary of State JOHN FOSTER DULLES had censored the records of the YALTA CONFERENCE. But McCarthy was increasingly shouting from a political wilderness. His health rapidly deteriorated as he turned increasingly to drink. McCarthy died on May 2, 1957, officially of acute hepatitis, but according to a number of sources, actually of cirrhosis of the liver.

For Further Information:
Buckley, William F., Jr., and L. Brent Bozell. *McCarthy and His Enemies: The Record and Its Meaning.* Chicago, 1954.

Feuerlich, Roberta. *Joe McCarthy and McCarthyism: The Hate That Haunts America.* New York, 1972.

Fried, Richard M. *Nightmare in Red: The McCarthy Era in Perspective.* New York, 1990.

Goldston, Robert. *The American Nightmare: Senator Joseph R. McCarthy and the Politics of Hate.* Indianapolis, 1973.

Griffith, Robert. *The Politics of Fear: Joseph R. McCarthy and the Senate.* Lexington, Ky., 1970.

Hellman, Lillian. *Scoundrel Time.* New York, 1976.

Hiss Alger. *In the Court of Public Opinion.* New York, 1957.

Hoffman, Nicholas von. *Citizen Cohn: The Life and Times of Roy Cohn.* New York, 1988.

Lattimore, Owen. *Ordeal by Slander.* Boston, 1950.

Matusow, Allen J., ed. *Joseph R. McCarthy.* Englewood Cliffs, N.J., 1970.

Oshinsky, David M. *A Conspiracy So Immense: The World of Joe McCarthy.* New York, 1983.

Reeves, Thomas C. *The Life and Times of Joe McCarthy: A Biography.* New York, 1982.

Rovere, Richard. *Senator Joe McCarthy.* New York, 1959.

Theoharis, Athan G. *Seeds of Repression; Harry S. Truman and the Origins of McCarthyism.* Chicago, 1971.

McCloy, John   (March 31, 1895–March 11, 1989)   John McCloy played an important role in the development of postwar Germany and the establishment of the international financial system in the early Cold War years. Later he became an expert on disarmament and defense issues and advised presidents EISENHOWER, KENNEDY and JOHNSON.

After graduating from Harvard Law School in 1921, McCloy entered a large New York law firm. His 1930–1939 investigation establishing responsibility for a 1916 sabotage case had made him an expert on German espionage, and in October 1940, Secretary of War Henry Stimson appointed him a special consultant. From April 1941 to November 1945 McCloy served as assistant secretary of war. At war's end, he became heavily involved in the debate over Allied plans for Germany. He opposed the Morgenthau Plan for the "pastoralization" of Germany and worked closely with General LUCIUS CLAY, the first military governor of the U.S. occupation zone, to revive the German economy.

While at the Pentagon, McCloy also participated in discussions for the division of Korea along the 38th parallel and worked on plans for defense pacts in the Western Hemisphere, Far East and Europe. He left government in November 1945 to return to private practice, but he remained in close contact with the Truman administration and served on the Acheson–Lilienthal committee whose work led to the BARUCH PLAN for control of nuclear technology. In February 1947 he returned to government as first president of the WORLD BANK.

McCloy saw his first task as reassuring the financial communities that the World Bank had not been established for the sole purpose of extending loans for political purposes, and he helped to establish the bank's policy of making loans conditional on the borrower's demonstrated ability to repay. As part of this policy, he opposed participation by the World Bank in relief programs for Europe. He felt this should be the responsibility of government agencies, and for this reason was a strong supporter of the MARSHALL PLAN.

McCloy was unable to avoid political pressure entirely in determining the bank's lending policies. He was obliged, for instance, to tell the Polish government that a $128.5 million loan to rebuild the Polish coal industry would be refused because of pressure from the American government. An application from Czechoslovakia suffered the same fate, and the treatment of the two countries contributed to their withdrawal from the World Bank and the INTERNATIONAL MONETARY FUND.

On May 18, 1949, President HARRY TRUMAN appointed McCloy military governor and U.S. high commissioner for Germany. His main task was to oversee the transition from military to civilian rule and strengthen the German economy. As part of the latter effort he modified the Allies' de-Nazification and de-cartelization (economic decentralization) programs and ended the dismantling of German factories in the American Zone. McCloy was also an active mediator in the Franco-German negotiations that led to the adoption of the Schuman Plan, one of the foundation stones of the EUROPEAN ECONOMIC COMMUNITY.

McCloy resigned from his post in Germany in August 1952 to return to private business as chairman of Chase National Bank. He also became a director of several other major corporations and was chairman of the Council of Foreign Relations and the Ford Foundation.

At the same time, he continued to perform diplomatic tasks. In 1956 he went to Egypt as UN secretary general DAG HAMMARSKJOLD's special financial adviser for the SUEZ CRISIS. He was a special adviser on disarmament issues to President Eisenhower, and in January 1961 President Kennedy appointed McCloy his principal disarmament adviser and negotiator. While at that post, McCloy drafted the legislation that established the ARMS CONTROL AND DISARMAMENT AGENCY (ACDA) and revived disarmament talks with the Soviet Union. After six months of futile negotiations, McCloy resigned in protest against Soviet intransigence. He was appointed to the general advisory committee of ACDA.

During the Johnson administration, McCloy served on the Warren Commission investigating the assassination of President Kennedy, and on various panels investigating nuclear nonproliferation. In April 1966 he was appointed special presidential consultant on the internal crises within NATO following French president CHARLES DE GAULLE's decision to withdraw from the alliance, British attempts to reduce their troop levels in Germany and the German desire to renegotiate their offset payments arrangements with the United States. President Lyndon Johnson proposed multilateral Anglo-German-American negotiations to resolve the problems and appointed McCloy as the American representative.

In March 1968, McCloy became a member of the Senior Advisory Group on Vietnam, which was formed to consider the Pentagon's request for 200,000 additional U.S. troops in the wake of the TET OFFENSIVE. The group rejected the request and recommended a de-escalation policy, which President Johnson accepted.

Throughout the 1960s, McCloy was also advising the U.S. government on how to deal with the Organization of Petroleum Exporting Countries (OPEC) and represented major American oil companies in their dealings with OPEC. He also made several unsuccessful attempts to persuade the antitrust division of the Justice Department to allow the oil companies to join forces in dealing with OPEC. During the 1970s, more and more of McCloy's time was taken up with oil diplomacy and the Middle East. He urged the NIXON, FORD and CARTER administrations to press for a Middle East peace settlement and to shift U.S. government support from Israel to the oil-producing states.

John J. McCloy—the "chairman of the establishment," as one journalist called him—died on March 11, 1989.

For Further Information:
Davis, Franklin M. *Come as a Conqueror: The United States Army's Occupation of Germany, 1945–1949*. New York, 1967.
Jonas, M. *The U.S. and West Germany*. New York, 1985.
Spanier, J.W. *American Foreign Policy Since World War Two*. Washington, D.C., 1988.

McCone, John   **(January 4, 1902–February 14, 1991)**
American politician John McCone had a reputation as a militant anti-communist and strong supporter of the doctrine of massive retaliation. During the early Cold War years he served in minor but influential government posts. His direction of the CENTRAL INTELLIGENCE AGENCY (CIA) during the KENNEDY and JOHNSON administrations coincided with some of the agency's most flagrant abuses of power, which in turn contributed to the crisis of confidence in the CIA and American foreign policy in the 1970s.

McCone was born into a prosperous California family, and after graduating with an engineering degree from the University of California at Berkeley in 1922, he took a job as a riveter and boilermaker for the Llewellyn Iron Works. By 1933 he was executive vice president, and in 1937 he left to found his own engineering company, Bechtel-McCone, which produced military aircraft during World War II.

In 1947 President TRUMAN appointed McCone to the Air Policy Commission, which examined the role of military aircraft in the overall American defense strategy. The following year he was appointed special deputy to Secretary of Defense JAMES FORRESTAL and helped to lay the foundation for the Central Intelligence Agency. In June 1950, at the outbreak of the KOREAN WAR, McCone was appointed undersecretary of the air force and given responsibility for increasing the production of military aircraft. By the time he resigned in October 1951, production had doubled.

McCone had formed a close relationship with General DWIGHT EISENHOWER while on the Air Policy Commission, and after Eisenhower's victory in the presidential election of 1952, he became a close adviser to the new president. He remained in private business, however, until June 1958, when Eisenhower asked him to become director of the U.S. ATOMIC ENERGY COMMISSION (AEC).

As director of the AEC, McCone attended talks with the Soviet Union on controlling nuclear testing and worked to expand international research on the peaceful uses of atomic energy. McCone resigned from the AEC when Eisenhower left office in January 1961, but in September 1961 President Kennedy asked McCone to return to government as director of the CIA. His appointment was designed to quiet Kennedy's conservative critics in the wake of the failed invasion of the BAY OF PIGS in Cuba.

Because of his strong right-wing bias, McCone was distrusted by more liberal elements within the Kennedy administration. He was the first to warn the president of the presence of Soviet missiles on Cuba but was initially ignored because of his right-wing views. However, McCone's undoubted administrative talents and contacts with key Republican figures led to his gradual increase in stature. He was one of the president's advisers during the CUBAN MISSILE CRISIS and recommended surgical air strikes to destroy the Soviet missiles.

After Cuba, Vietnam became a major preoccupation of McCone and the CIA. He was one of those who advised President John F. Kennedy against supporting a military coup against South Vietnamese president NGO DINH DIEM. During the Johnson administration, McCone took a hawkish line on the war.

During McCone's tenure at the CIA, the agency became involved in a number of covert activities for which it was later severely criticized. These included spending $3 million in the 1964 Chilean election to prevent communist-backed SALVADOR ALLENDE from winning; support for right-wing elements in Greece and Italy; a secret war in Laos; counterterrorist programs in Vietnam; illegal opening of foreign mail to U.S. citizens; and several unsuccessful attempts to assassinate foreign leaders, including FIDEL CASTRO and PATRICE LUMUMBA. McCone in 1974 and 1975 claimed in testimony for the Senate Select Committee on Intelligence Activities that he knew little or nothing about most of these activities because of the agency's ambiguous chain of command. The committee failed to find sufficient evidence to prove that McCone had broken the law.

McCone resigned from the CIA in April 1965 in protest against President Lyndon Johnson's refusal to support his efforts to centralize intelligence operations. In August 1965 he chaired an eight-person commission investigating the Watts riots in Los Angeles. Because of his Republican credentials, McCone expected to be offered a senior position in the Nixon administration, but he was disappointed and returned to private business.

For Further Information:
Allison, Graham. *Essence of Decision: Explaining the Cuban Missile Crisis.* Boston, 1971.
U.S. Senate Select Committee on Intelligence Activities. *Alleged Assassination Plots Involving Foreign Leaders.* Washington, D.C., 1975.
Wise, David, and Thomas B. Ross. *The Invisible Government.* New York, 1964.

McMahon, Brien   (October 6, 1903–July 28, 1952)
Senator Brien McMahon (D, Conn.) was the first chairman of the Congressional Joint Committee on Atomic Energy and framed the bill that created the U.S. ATOMIC ENERGY COMMISSION.

After attending Fordham University and Yale Law School, McMahon went into private law practice in 1927. From 1935 to 1939 he was in Washington, D.C., as assistant attorney general for the Justice Department's Criminal Division and enhanced his already considerable reputation as a trial lawyer. He was elected to the Senate from Connecticut as a Democrat on his first attempt, in 1944.

When the atomic research program became known, McMahon urged the Truman administration to establish an atomic energy policy, and proposed the creation of a congressional joint committee. When Congress established it in October 1945, McMahon was made chairman. His first objective was to wrest control of atomic energy from the military and place it under civilian control. The result was the Atomic Energy Act of 1946, which created the five-man civilian Atomic Energy Commission, declared it the sole owner of all the fissionable material in the U.S. and gave it full control over research.

McMahon was a keen advocate of both atomic development and controls. He urged the building of the hydrogen bomb and called for an increase in America's atomic energy program from an annual expenditure of $1 billion to $6 billion. At the same time he campaigned unsuccessfully for a $10 billion plan to force all members of the United Nations to submit to regular inspections in order to prevent nuclear proliferation.

McMahon's stalwart support of New Deal programs and of international initiatives such as the MARSHALL PLAN, the TRUMAN DOCTRINE, NATO and the POINT FOUR PROGRAM earned him the enmity of the Republican right wing. When he ran for re-election in 1950, Senator JOSEPH MCCARTHY personally campaigned against him, but McMahon was returned to the Senate with 53% of the vote. He continued as chairman of the Joint Committee on Atomic Energy until his death from cancer on July 28, 1952.

For Further Information:
Jacobson, Harold D. *Diplomats, Scientists and Politicians*. Ann Arbor, Mich., 1966.

McNamara, Robert S.   (June 9, 1916–   )   Robert S. McNamara was arguably one of the most influential American defense secretaries of the postwar period. He tightened civilian control of the Pentagon, introduced the policy of FLEXIBLE RESPONSE and built up America's arsenal of strategic nuclear missiles. McNamara was secretary of defense at the height of America's involvement in the VIETNAM WAR. In 1967 he became disillusioned with the war and resigned to become president of the WORLD BANK.

After attending the University of California and Harvard Business School, McNamara joined the teaching staff of the latter in 1940. Poor eyesight kept him out of combat during World War II, but McNamara found a role in planning support services for bomber operations in both Europe and the Far East.

At the end of the war, McNamara joined the financially troubled Ford Motor Company and helped to put the company back on its feet as general manager and vice president of the automotive division. In November 1960 he became the first person outside the Ford family to be named company president. McNamara held the position for only a month before President JOHN F. KENNEDY asked him to be secretary of defense.

McNamara set out to centralize control of the Pentagon in his office and to cut what he regarded as inefficient defense spending. This brought him into conflict with several of the service chiefs. The most notable clash was with the flamboyant air force chief of staff, General CURTIS LEMAY, who clashed with McNamara over the budget for the manned bomber program. When LeMay persuaded Congress to exceed McNamara's request and allocate $1.7 billion for the B-70 bomber, McNamara diverted $510 million of the money to other projects. LeMay also opposed McNamara's development of the POLARIS and Minuteman missiles and selection of General Dynamics for the TFX (Tactical Fighter Aircraft) contract.

The controversy over the TFX contract led to an investigation by the Senate Government Operations Subcommittee. LeMay and others maintained that the contract should have been awarded to Boeing. But McNamara, who wanted a swing-wing jet that could be used by both the navy and the air force, maintained that General Dynamics had presented the better proposal and that the cost of the Boeing design had been grossly underestimated. The subcommittee hearings came to an inconclusive end after nine months, during which differences within the Pentagon were embarrassingly aired in public.

The EISENHOWER administration's defense strategy had rested primarily on the doctrine of MASSIVE RETALIATION. This meant the development of strategic nuclear forces at the expense of counterinsurgency and conventional forces in the belief that the threat of massive nuclear retaliation against the Soviet Union would deter aggression and insurgency by communists everywhere. President John F. Kennedy, when he succeeded Eisenhower, was concerned that this policy made nuclear war more likely. He wanted to develop conventional forces so that the United States could fight at all levels without having to resort to nuclear weapons to protect vital interests. McNamara developed the theory of "flexible response" to fit Kennedy's strategy and expanded the size and mobility of America's conventional forces. These changes meant an increase in the defense budget from $45.9 billion in 1960 to $53.6 billion in 1964, with most of the money going to pay for 300,000 extra troops and additional air troop carriers.

Although McNamara was a registered Republican, he became a trusted and close adviser to President Kennedy, a Democrat. He was one of the inner circle who advised the president during the CUBAN MISSILE CRISIS and proposed the course of action—a naval quarantine—that Kennedy successfully employed. It was an essential part of the quarantine strategy that any unnecessary clashes with the Soviets be avoided in order not to give the Soviet Union an excuse to escalate the crisis or harden its position. McNamara was assigned to manage the deployment of the American ships and scrutinize their conduct to ensure that clashes were avoided. The operation was carried out with remarkable care, and only two ships were intercepted before the crisis was resolved.

Because of the close relationship between McNamara and Kennedy, the defense secretary, rather than Secretary of State DEAN RUSK, was given the primary policy-making role in Vietnam. During the Kennedy administration, McNamara was convinced that the American military advisers in South Vietnam (15,000 by the end of 1963) would complete the task of shoring up the South Vietnamese government and leave the country by 1965. But by 1964, he concluded that a much greater U.S. commitment was needed to defeat the North Vietnamese, and he pressed for a major escalation in U.S. troop levels. After a visit to Vietnam in March 1964, McNamara announced that U.S. forces in Vietnam had a "blank check" on defense funds. This led to a massive increase of $19.6 billion on defense spending for Vietnam between 1965 and 1967.

McNamara devoted almost all of his last three years at the Pentagon to the conduct of the Vietnam War. In August 1964, after the Gulf of Tonkin incident, he presented evidence of the alleged North Vietnamese attack on U.S. ships, which led to the GULF OF TONKIN RESOLUTION and to President LYNDON JOHNSON's decision to introduce U.S. ground troops in South Vietnam.

When General William Westmoreland, in October 1964, first proposed U.S. air attacks against North Vietnamese targets, he was opposed by McNamara, who argued that it would dangerously escalate the conflict and have little effect on North Vietnamese support for communist guerrillas in the South. Johnson, who had great respect for McNamara's views, accepted his advice. But in February 1965, after Viet Cong attacks on American bases in South Vietnam, McNamara reversed his position and agreed to retaliatory air strikes, which started the next month.

By this time, McNamara was completely committed to the Vietnam War. Yet neither the air strikes nor the introduction of 3,500 U.S. Marines had appeared to have any effect on the insurgency. McNamara therefore, in July 1965, approved a request by Westmoreland for 185,000 American troops. In November, Westmoreland asked for another 400,000 men, and again McNamara approved. In forwarding the requests for more troops to President Johnson, he also advised that the reserves be called up and taxes be raised to cover the greatly increased costs. Johnson agreed to the additional troops but rejected as politically too risky the rest of McNamara's advice.

By 1966, McNamara had begun to develop private doubts about the Vietnam War. He initially concentrated his skepticism on the morality and effectiveness of bombing raids on the North. In 1967 he began to press for a negotiated settlement. With Deputy Secretary of Defense PAUL NITZE he drew up the San Antonio Formula, which offered an end to the bombing in return for "productive discussions." The proposal was rejected by the North Vietnamese in October.

While McNamara's commitment to a military solution waned, President Johnson's remained firm. The defense secretary found himself increasingly in conflict with the president, who intensified the American bombing of the North. In testimony before the Senate Preparedness Subcommittee on August 25, 1967, McNamara said that the bombing of North Vietnam had not significantly affected North Vietnam's warmaking capacity. He added that there was no direct relationship between the level of bombing in the North and the U.S. forces required in the South.

In November 1967, McNamara wrote a memorandum to President Johnson in which he proposed that the administration end the bombing, freeze U.S. troop levels and turn over major responsibility for ground combat to the South Vietnamese Army. Johnson rejected his proposals, and shortly afterward McNamara announced his resignation to take up the post of president of the World Bank.

At the World Bank, McNamara set out to shift the emphasis of the bank's lending programs from major industrial projects to agricultural and educational development. In his first year, McNamara managed to increase lending by 87% and raised a total capital of $1.2 billion. In the 1970s the World Bank under McNamara became increasingly concerned about the world population problem and financed family planning activities; in 1971 a Population Projects Department was established. McNamara is generally regarded as the most successful of the World Bank's presidents. He was reelected in 1972 and 1977 and retired in 1982.

For Further Information:
Murdock, Clark A. *Defense Policy Formation; A Comparative Analysis of the McNamara Era.* Albany, 1974.
Roberty, James M. *Decisions of Robert S. McNamara: A Study of the Role of the Secretary of Defense.* Miami, 1970.
Shapley, Deborah. *Promise and Power: The Life and Times of Robert McNamara.* Boston, 1993.
Trewhitt, Henry L. *McNamara: His Ordeal in the Pentagon.* New York, 1970.
U.S. Department of Defense. *The Pentagon Papers*, Senator Gravel Edition. Boston, 1971.

McNaughton, John   (November 21, 1921–July 19, 1967)
John McNaughton was one of the leading U.S. experts on disarmament during the KENNEDY administration. During the JOHNSON administration he was heavily involved in U.S. planning for the VIETNAM WAR. He entered office as a hawk, but by 1967 he had become one of the key doves within the Pentagon.

McNaughton attended Harvard University and went on to Oxford University as a Rhodes Scholar. He returned to Harvard in 1956 as a professor of law. In July 1961 he joined the Pentagon as special assistant for disarmament affairs.

McNaughton believed that the United States could take unilateral steps to limit the arms race and enhance both its own security and the Soviet Union's. These steps, such as measures to prevent the accidental firing of nuclear weapons, would improve the political climate between the superpowers.

A key element in McNaughton's arms control theories was the maintenance of a defense structure capable of deterring an attack, especially a surprise attack. He argued that without this capability the United States or the Soviet Union would be tempted to launch a nuclear strike on the basis of ambiguous intelligence.

In July 1963, McNaughton joined Ambassador AVERELL HARRIMAN's mission to Moscow, which resulted in the Limited NUCLEAR TEST BAN TREATY. After its initialing in Moscow, McNaughton played a major role in lobbying for its passage through the U.S. Senate.

In July 1964, President Lyndon Johnson named McNaughton assistant secretary of defense for international security affairs, and he quickly established himself as the chief assistant to Defense Secretary ROBERT MCNAMARA in developing U.S. defense strategy in Vietnam. His early work included writing a report in September 1964 entitled "Plan for Action in South Vietnam," in which he proposed that the United States renew naval patrols off the coast of North Vietnam in the wake of the Gulf of Tonkin incident (see GULF OF TONKIN RESOLUTION). McNaughton also supported President Johnson's decision to start limited retaliatory air strikes against North Vietnamese targets.

McNaughton said at the time that he hoped that the U.S. attacks would force a counterattack from the North, which would provide the United States with a legitimate excuse to enter the war and start "a crescendo of military actions" aimed at forcing the North Vietnamese to the negotiating table. He argued that the United States had to be "willing to keep promises, be tough, take risks, get bloodied and hurt the enemy badly."

In March 1965, McNaughton took the lead in recommending that three U.S. and two Korean divisions be sent to Da Nang and Pleiku. At the same time he warned that it might require "massive deployment" of American troops to defeat the communists. He continued to take a hard line on the war throughout 1965, but by 1966 McNaughton, along with McNamara, had become increasingly pessimistic about the chances of winning the war and dubious about the effectiveness and morality of continued U.S. bombing of North Vietnam. By May 1967, McNaughton had completely reversed his earlier hawkish position and wrote to President Johnson warning him "of a feeling widely and strongly held that the Establishment is out of its mind. The feeling is that we are trying to impose some U.S. image on distant people we cannot understand." He strongly advised the president against sending more U.S. troops to Vietnam and urged him to place a stronger emphasis on a Vietnamization program.

McNaughton's reversal lost him a great deal of support within the military establishment and the White House. McNamara, however, called him "a voice of reason" within the Pentagon and later claimed that McNaughton's opposition to the bombing was a contributory factor in its eventual end in 1968.

In June 1967, McNaughton was appointed secretary of the navy. On July 19, just before he was due to take up the post, he, his wife and their youngest son were killed in an airplane crash in North Carolina.

For Further Information:
U.S. Department of Defense. *The Pentagon Papers*, Senator Gravel Edition, vols. 2 and 3. Boston, 1971.

Menzies, Stewart   (1890–May 30, 1968)   Sir Stewart Menzies was head of Britain's Secret Intelligence Service (MI6) throughout World War II and during the early postwar years, including the period when Soviet spies KIM PHILBY, DONALD MACLEAN and GUY BURGESS were most active. It is widely believed that Ian Fleming, author of the James Bond novels, modeled his character "M" on Menzies, who himself was generally referred to as "C."

Menzies was educated at the upper-class British public school Eton and the British military academy at Sandhurst, joining the elite Brigade of Guards on graduation. After a distinguished career in the military in which he reached the rank of major general, Menzies joined Britain's Secret Intelligence Service, also known as MI6 or the SIS, which is responsible for gathering overseas intelligence.

Shortly before the outbreak of war, in 1939, Menzies was named head of MI6. During the war, he was one of Prime Minister WINSTON CHURCHILL's closest advisers. He enjoyed great success in penetrating the German intelligence service, the Abwehr. Early in the war he personally headed a mission

to Poland to secure Polish help in breaking the Germans' Enigma Code, a vital contribution to the British war effort.

Menzies also advised the U.S. government in the establishment of the OFFICE OF STRATEGIC SERVICES (OSS), wartime predecessor of the CENTRAL INTELLIGENCE AGENCY. He formed a number of close contacts with men who would become major figures in the CIA, such as ALLEN DULLES and WILLIAM CASEY. After the war, Menzies agreed to assign a number of senior British intelligence officers to the TRUMAN administration to help in the establishment of the CIA. This early and vital contact led to a close relationship between the British and American intelligence services that lasted throughout the Cold War.

Menzies' experience in breaking the Enigma Code made him a keen exponent of electronic espionage, and he encouraged the development of Britain's General Communications Headquarters at Cheltenham and the American NATIONAL SECURITY AGENCY and the relationship between those two agencies.

In addition to enjoying a number of successes in espionage, Menzies was at the head of MI6 when it suffered its worst defeat of the Cold War years—the defection of Donald MacLean and Guy Burgess and the failure to detect the activities of Kim Philby. All three men had been recruited by Soviet intelligence while at Cambridge University and had during their student years publicly flirted with communism. This had been either ignored or completely missed when British security had cleared the men for their posts in either the Foreign Office or the intelligence service. It was said that at the time establishment credentials were more important than political affiliations.

During the war, Burgess, a notorious drunkard and homosexual, worked with MI6 and afterward at the Foreign Office. In 1950 he was posted to Washington, D.C., as British attaché responsible for Far Eastern affairs, a post that enabled him to pass on valuable information about British and American policy toward Korea. In 1951, he tipped off British diplomat Donald MacLean that MacLean was about to be arrested. MacLean, who had passed valuable atomic secrets at the British Embassy in Washington in the late 1940s, managed to escape with Burgess to Moscow.

Both men had been warned by their fellow Soviet agent Kim Philby that British and American intelligence were closing in on them. Philby had worked closely with Menzies during the war and at one time had been considered by the MI6 director as a possible successor. In 1944, Menzies had appointed Philby head of the anti-Soviet service, thus placing him in the perfect position to inform the KGB of British and American anti-Soviet operations.

After the defection of Burgess and MacLean, Philby also came under suspicion, but investigations at the time by Menzies and the British counterintelligence service MI5 failed to produce any evidence and Philby was cleared. He eventually escaped to Moscow in 1963, shortly before he was due to be arrested.

Sir Stewart retired as head of MI6 in 1953. He died on May 30, 1968.

Mery Plan   The Mery Plan of 1976 was a revision of France's anti-Soviet nuclear defense policy as outlined in the FOURQUET PLAN of 1969. Developed by Chief of Staff General Guy Mery, it steered a middle course between narrow national interests and wider Western alliance concerns.

This policy was encapsulated in the concept of "enlarged sanctuarization." The Mery Plan reaffirmed the Fourquet Plan's heavy emphasis on tactical nuclear weapons and graduated response and took France a step closer to alliance commitments by committing the French defense forces to a "forward first battle" in the event of a Soviet invasion of Western Europe.

(King) Michael of Romania   (October 25, 1921–   )
King Michael of Romania led the coup that overthrew the fascist, pro-Axis government of General Ion Antonescu and was king of Romania from August 1944 until Soviet-supported, local communists forced his abdication on December 30, 1947.

Michael's short first reign as monarch of Romania started in 1927 when he was only five years old. This followed the exclusion of his father, Carol II, from the royal succession as a result of his morganatic marriage. But Michael's three-man regency was dissolved and Michael was reduced to the rank of crown prince following the return of his father in June 1930 and the creation of a fascist "corporatist dictatorship."

After King Carol II was overthrown by the pro-German General Ion Antonescu in September 1940, Michael was effectively placed under house arrest. His position allowed him a limited amount of freedom, however, which he used to maintain contacts with opposition forces. In August 1944, as the Soviet Red Army was invading from the East, Michael led a coup against Antonescu, who was arrested on August 23. The Soviet Union hailed Michael as a hero and presented him with its rare diamond-studded Order of Victory.

King Michael was determined to encourage Western democratic principles and to this end he had himself declared a constitutional monarch and appointed the prominent pro-Western statesman General NICOLAE RADESCU as premier and minister of the interior. But Radescu was unacceptable to the Soviets. After fighting broke out in February 1945 between communist partisans and government forces, Soviet deputy foreign minister Andrei Vishynsky flew to Bucharest, met with King Michael and demanded the instant dismissal of Radescu.

Michael tried to delay making a decision, claiming that as a constitutional monarch he had to follow the constitutional practice of consulting party leaders. This assertion was rejected by Vishynsky, who repeated his demand for immediate action. Michael, whose country was occupied by the Red Army, had no choice but to accede to the demand and on March 3 Radescu was dismissed. At the same time the king announced that he was asking the anti-communist Prince Stirbey to form a government. The Romanian communists, who had been placed in key positions by the Red Army, refused to join a Stirbey government. Vishynsky then sent the king a note telling him that the Soviet Union wanted Romanian communist Petro Groza to be appointed premier. Once again, the king was forced to concede. On March 6 Groza announced the composition of his government: 13 members from the communist groups and only four from the pro-Western parties.

Groza immediately began to suppress political freedoms and arrest opponents, which brought him into opposition to the king. After a government-organized campaign of intimidation and repression, the communists managed to obtain four-fifths of the parliamentary seats in an election on November 19, 1946. Relations between the king and Groza continued to deteriorate, and in August 1947 Michael was actively seeking American and British support for the overthrow of Groza.

In November 1947 Michael became engaged to Denmark's Princess Anne of Bourbon-Parma, while attending the wedding of Princess Elizabeth in London. When he returned to Bucharest, Michael was told that the government had vetoed the expense of a state wedding. Groza used the excuse of the wedding to surround the royal palace on December 30, 1947, and present Michael with an abdication act for his signature. The government quickly voted to formally abolish the monarchy and create a "People's Republic."

On March 4, 1948, Michael repudiated his abdication, claiming that it had been imposed on him by force to clear the way for a communist government "utterly unrepresentative of the will of the Romanian people." Shortly afterward, Michael visited President HARRY S. TRUMAN at the White House.

Later that year, on May 22, Michael was deprived of his Romanian citizenship and property in that country. Throughout the Cold War he remained a focal point for many Romanian dissident groups.

After the revolution in Romania in December 1989, Michael offered himself as a constitutional monarch behind which the country could unite. The suggestion received a frosty reception from the country's ruling National Salvation Front, and when Michael attempted a brief return to Romania in April 1990 he was blocked by the authorities and quickly made to leave.

Middle East   The conflicting nationalist tensions within the Middle East combined with religious, economic and strategic considerations to encourage both the United States and the Soviet Union to exert their influence in the region. This inevitably resulted in the Middle East's becoming a major point of conflict between the superpowers and a primary Cold War tinderbox.

Following the end of World War II, the major cause of tension in the Middle East was the struggle between Arab nationalist forces and the colonial powers, mainly Britain, followed by the long-running Arab–Israeli conflict.

Britain had long had an interest in the region. The Middle East straddled the route to India, with the Suez Canal as the strategic link between India and Britain. Important British coaling stations were set up at Suez, Port Said and Aden. The areas around these stations were brought under British control either as colonies or as protectorates. The Arabian Peninsula and the areas of Palestine, Syria, Iraq and Lebanon were nominally part of the Ottoman Empire based at Constantinople (Istanbul), but in practice they were loosely governed by local leaders whose differences the British exploited in order to reduce the threat to their strategic interests.

During World War I, Turkey allied itself with Germany and Austria-Hungary. This increased the threat to British India, and Britain's policies changed from exploiting Arab differences to providing the Arabs inducement to unite to fight the Turks. The British encouraged the rise of Arab nationalism, leading to the Arab revolt against Turkey, which played a major role in driving the Turks out of the Arab world.

But at the end of the war, Britain (and France) attempted to ignore the nationalist feelings they had aroused and the promises they had made; instead of assisting Arab independence, they replaced Turkey as the colonial powers in the region. Under the terms of the Sykes-Picot Agreement between Britain and France, the Middle East was divided between the two allies with Britain gaining control of the Persian Gulf, Jordan and Palestine, and France in control of Lebanon and Syria. The only part of the region left more or less untouched was Saudi Arabia, which became loosely united under King Ibn Saud, the only Arab beneficiary of early Arab nationalism.

In the interwar period, two major events occurred. One was the application of the Balfour Declaration, which promised a "national home" for the Jews in Palestine. The other was the discovery of oil, which vastly increased the region's economic importance to Britain and the rest of Western Europe.

The Balfour Declaration was the result of pressure on the British government from the Zionist Movement, then based in London. The declaration did not, as is sometimes supposed, promise the creation of a Jewish state. It promised a Jewish "national home" in Palestine, whose form and legal status were not specified, which did not prejudice the "civil and religious" rights of the Arab population. This typical British compromise between contradictory assurances given during the war predictably failed to satisfy either the Zionist movement or the Arabs. European Jews, however, started to pour into Palestine, and the 1920s and 1930s were marked by intercommunal Arab–Jewish riots, with Britain, as the mandatory power, trying to negotiate a solution.

The intercommunal tension was exacerbated by Hitler's attempt to exterminate Europe's Jews. Before, during and after World War II, refugees from the Nazis and survivors of the Holocaust fled to Palestine as their only refuge (in part because Western nations like the United States and Britain would not allow them refuge within their own borders). The Holocaust also added an increased sense of moral obligation

to the pressure to transform the Jewish "home" into a Jewish state (which had been a Zionist goal for years before Hitler). Britain and the United Nations tried to negotiate a partition of Palestine, but they fell afoul of uncompromising sectarianism on both sides.

The Zionist movement, whose attitudes reflected its origins in 19th-century Europe, was insistent that only a Jewish state could provide Jews with freedom from persecution and that the state should be centered on the biblical Hebrews' homeland. The indigenous Arab residents of Palestine were equally determined, particularly after their anticolonial struggles, not to be displaced by a foreign people. Arabs in other countries did not wish to see an Arab country, located in the center of the Arab world, alienated through massive population transfers.

At this stage, the American Jewish community began to play a major role in the conflict. It was the largest and richest in the world and because of its size, organization and wealth, was able to play an increasingly significant role in domestic politics in the United States, which in 1945 was the most powerful nation in the world. The American Jewish community exercised considerable political pressure on the U.S. government to support the creation of a Jewish state. Britain, which was economically unable to maintain its military presence in Palestine and with few political options, decided to withdraw and leave the problem to the UN. The British formally gave up their mandate on May 14, 1948, and the Zionists immediately declared an independent Jewish state, Israel.

The proclamation of independence was immediately followed by the first Arab-Israeli War. The Arab fighters, largely enthusiastic volunteers from throughout the Arab world, were poorly organized, poorly led and poorly equipped. They were quickly defeated by the Israelis.

The state of Israel was immediately recognized by both the United States and the Soviet Union. The U.S. recognition was largely the result of pressure from the American Jewish lobby (in what was a presidential election year). The Arab lobby at that time largely consisted of American oil companies in Saudi Arabia.

The reasons for Soviet recognition, and the early close ties between Israel and the Soviet Union, were more complex. The first Israeli leaders were enthusiastic socialists. Many of them looked toward the Soviet Union for inspiration, and the successful and popular kibbutz system was modeled on socialist lines. The Israelis also represented a counterweight to the still dominant British imperial influence.

Czarist Russia and, after 1917, the Soviet Union had a long-established interest in the Middle East. It lay on the Soviet Union's southern borders and control of it could fulfill one of Russia's most cherished ambitions—a warm-water port. These strategic considerations were behind the Soviet attempt to gain control of the DARDANELLES in 1945 and 1946 and the occupation of the Iranian portion of the AZERBAIJAN region in the immediate postwar period. The Soviet Union also had two further interests in the region, oil and Islam.

The oil fields of the Caucasus had transformed the Soviet

Union into the world's largest oil producer in the 1930s. When oil production began in the Persian Gulf and, later, on the Arabian Peninsula, the Soviet Union took an interest in influencing both the economic and political policies of the governments of the area and hoped as well to increase the strategic importance of its own oil-producing region. The Soviet Union also had a very large Islamic population and, with the Communist Party's intolerance for religion and its necessary interest in suppressing nationalism within its borders, was concerned with the rise of Islamic political activism.

The rise of GAMAL ABDEL NASSER and the SUEZ CRISIS resulted in a major shift in the power politics of the Middle East. Nasser's ambitious brand of pan-Arab nationalism soon proved more damaging to British interests than previous varieties, and the Soviet Union successfully courted Nasser with economic and military aid. The British government of ANTHONY EDEN, attempting to exercise old-fashioned imperial power, then made the strategic error of allying itself with France and Israel in an attempt to topple Nasser and regain control of the Suez Canal. The resultant debacle seriously damaged British influence among the Arabs and increased the influence of both Nasser and the Soviet Union. Within a few years, rejuvenated Arab nationalism had led to the end of British control in South Yemen, Iraq and Libya; of French rule in Algeria and Tunisia; and of French influence in Syria and Lebanon.

The Soviet Union allied itself with the cause of Arab nationalism, whose main enemy after the colonial powers was the state of Israel. The United States, faced with the possibility of the Soviet Union's emerging as the dominant power in the Middle East, increased its support for Israel. In broad terms, the Arab nationalists thus became Middle East proxies for the Soviet Union and Israel became regional proxy for the United States. Britain still retained a strong influence in the Persian Gulf and in Jordan, and Saudi Arabia, although staunchly anti-Israel, remained pro-American both because of its strong ties to American oil companies and because its extreme social conservatism, as well as its role as protector of Islam's holy sites, ruled out close relations with communists.

By 1966, Soviet-supported Arab nationalists, still dominated by Nasser, had grown strong enough in Jordan, Syria and Egypt to pose a serious military threat to Israel. In November 1966, the Egyptian and Syrian governments signed a defense agreement. At the same time, attacks on Israel by Palestinian guerrillas based in the Egyptian Sinai, Jordan and Syria increased. Nasser moved Egyptian troops into the Sinai on May 14, 1967; on May 22 he ordered UN peacekeeping forces out of Egypt and closed the Straits of Tiran—Israel's link to the Red Sea—to Israeli shipping. All of these moves were either implicitly or explicitly encouraged by the Soviet Union. Nasser, in the belief tht he would be backed by the Soviet Union, prepared for a joint Syrian-Egyptian-Jordanian invasion of Israel.

The Israelis decided to preempt the Arab attack and launched their own surprise offensive on June 5, 1967. The Six-Day War was a major military victory for Israel. The Egyptian Air Force was destroyed on the first day, thus preventing the Egyptians from ever launching an effective attack. The Israelis took the Sinai, Syrian forces were driven off the Golan Heights, and the Jordanians were forced out of Jerusalem and the West Bank. The Soviets protested and threatened Israel, but they failed to give any practical assistance to the Arabs. This failure severely damaged Soviet influence over Arab countries.

American involvement in the Six-Day War was mostly limited to promises of economic and military aid and stationing the U.S. Sixth Fleet in the eastern Mediterranean to counter the limited Soviet naval presence there. It was not until after the war that U.S. military and economic aid substantially increased, partly in response to increased Soviet military aid for Syria and Egypt and partly as a result of pressure from the domestic Jewish lobby.

Nasser, for his part, had concluded that the only way that the Arabs could defeat Israel was to draw Soviet troops into battle on the Arab side. To this end he proposed a formal Soviet–Egyptian Defense Treaty. The Soviets shied away from this proposal because they feared that direct intervention in the Arab–Israeli conflict would bring them into direct conflict with the United States, which could quickly escalate into a nuclear war. The Soviets instead hoped that their rearming of Egypt and Syria would enable their two allies in the region to negotiate with Israel from a position of strength as well as tie the two countries closer to the Soviet Union.

The Arab-Israeli conflict was further complicated by the emergence of the Palestine Liberation Organization (PLO) as a force within the Arab world. The PLO was formed in 1964 to bring together the various Palestinian groups fighting to regain their territory from Israel. The organization at that time rejected any solution of the Arab–Israeli conflict other than the elimination of the Jewish state. Most of the Palestinian guerrillas based themselves in Jordan, where their activities soon created a virtual state within a state. Jordan's King Hussein was the most moderate of the Arab leaders and understood that the PLO's presence threatened his own position. In September 1970, Hussein moved to expel the PLO from Jordan. Syria, a strong PLO supporter, then attacked the Jordanian Army, and King Hussein secured promises of support from the United States, Israel and Britain. The United States also agreed to act against both the Soviet Union and Egypt if they assisted Syria. Hussein, however, was able both to expel the PLO and to stop the Syrian attack.

Nasser died of a sudden heart attack on September 28, 1970, and was succeeded by ANWAR SADAT, who had become disillusioned with the Soviet Union, partly because of Moscow's heavy-handed attempts to influence Egyptian policies and partly out of frustration at the Soviet Union's inability to pressure Israel to negotiate. Sadat concluded that the only country capable of forcing Israel into a negotiated settlement was the United States, and in July 1972 he ordered all Soviet advisers out of Egypt and revoked the Soviets' right to use military bases in the country.

But Sadat's break with Moscow failed to win any concessions from either the United States or Israel. He decided to improve his negotiating position by joining with Syria in attacking Israel on October 6, 1973, at the start of Yom Kippur. Syria had retained its close ties with the Soviet Union and, although Soviet advisers had been expelled from Egypt, the Soviet Union decided to back Sadat in his attack. The Egyptian forces made early and impressive gains across the Sinai. By October 12 Israeli prime minister Golda Meir was threatening to use "whatever means are required" to preserve the Jewish state. This was interpreted by the NIXON administration to mean that the Israelis would use a nuclear weapon, which many suspected they possessed. To prevent this the Americans sent more weapons to hold off the Arab attack.

By mid-October, the tide of war had turned and the Israelis had retaken the Sinai and crossed the Suez Canal, surrounding the Egyptian Third Army. This turn of events suited neither the United States nor the Soviet Union. Both countries wanted to see a negotiated settlement to the Arab–Israeli conflict, and the complete military defeat of either side would not have served that aim. HENRY KISSINGER, President Nixon's secretary of state, flew to Moscow where he and Soviet leader LEONID BREZHNEV worked out a Middle East cease-fire that provided for direct Egyptian-Israeli talks. Kissinger's next task was to stop the Israeli advance. The Israelis wanted to press their advantage and had to be threatened with a withdrawal of American aid if they continued to fight.

Sadat, anxious to further involve both superpowers in a negotiated settlement, proposed that both the United States and the Soviet Union send peacekeeping forces to the region to enforce the cease-fire. The Soviets agreed and threatened to act unilaterally if the Americans did not join them. The United States, concerned that a joint U.S.–Soviet intervention would damage its interests to the benefit of the Soviets, refused and placed American forces on a worldwide nuclear alert in response to what Kissinger claimed was a Soviet attempt to intervene militarily.

The Soviets backed down and Kissinger engaged in an exhausting round of shuttle diplomacy aimed at restraining the Israelis, winning the confidence of both Egypt and Syria, and enforcing the cease-fire resolution. His success confirmed America's role as mediator in the Middle East and friend of both Israel and Egypt.

An important side effect of the Yom Kippur War was the Arab oil embargo. Before attacking Israel, Sadat had arranged with Saudi Arabia and the other major Arab oil-producing countries that they would refuse to send oil supplies to any country that supported Israel. The oil embargo exposed the West's dependence on Arab-produced oil and encouraged the Organization of Petroleum Exporting Countries (OPEC) to quadruple oil prices and gain greater control of supplies and sales.

The emergence of oil as a weapon had an especially strong impact on Western Europe and Japan, which were more dependent upon imports for their oil supplies than was the United States. As a result, these countries adjusted their policies toward a more even-handed position, and in 1977 the European Economic Community passed a resolution favoring the creation of a Palestinian homeland.

The rise in oil prices also resulted in a major shift in the world's wealth. Billions of dollars poured into the Arab oil-producing countries. This money substantially improved the international position of the Arab world, and countries such as Saudi Arabia were able to increase their aid to the Palestinian cause. It also created sudden, simultaneous, inflation and recession in the Western world.

Finally, the oil embargo increased the political and economic power of the Soviet Union, still the world's largest oil producer. It enabled the Soviets to earn additional hard currency to subsidize their increasingly inefficient industries and made the East European satellites more dependent upon the Soviet Union for energy supplies, as Moscow was prepared to reduce oil prices to COMECON countries in return for political cooperation.

The eventual cease-fire agreed upon by Egypt and Israel ended with the Egyptians making a small net gain in the Sinai. Syria, which had suffered serious military defeats in the fighting, managed to regain 300 square miles of territory it had lost, but Israel retained the Golan Heights and an observation post on Mount Hermon. Angered by Sadat's willingness to negotiate, the Syrians moved closer to the Soviet Union.

Following the election of President JIMMY CARTER in 1976, the United States turned toward a comprehensive international conference as a means of resolving the Arab–Israeli conflict. This idea foundered on the Israeli government's refusal to allow PLO participation. Sadat, dismayed by American inability to pressure Israel, attempted to break the stalemate by making a historic visit to Israel in November 1977 to offer an Egyptian-Israeli peace. This eventually resulted in the Camp David Agreement of September 1978, which ended the conflict between Israel and Egypt and removed a major threat to the state of Israel.

Carter had hoped that Egypt would be quickly followed by Jordan. But widespread Arab condemnation of Sadat and his eventual assassination in 1981 kept Jordan out of the peace process. Syria, the PLO and other hard-line Arab states moved closer to the Soviet Union as chief protector of their interests. The PLO had by this time established itself in Lebanon, which it used both to house thousands of Palestinian refugees and as a base for attacks on Israel. This eventually led the Israelis to invade Lebanon in support of the Christian side in that country's intermittent civil war, and to a *cordon sanitaire* in the southern part of the country. The Syrians moved into the northern part of Lebanon in support of the Palestinians and the Lebanese Muslims. All of this led to an increasingly destructive civil war, the expulsion of the PLO from Lebanon and the effective destruction of that country as the various factions jockeyed for power.

The oil-rich nations of the Persian Gulf managed to remain largely aloof from the fighting in the eastern Mediterranean, although they provided military and financial aid to the Palestinians and the front-line Arab states. The lack of direct involvement in the Arab–Israeli conflict made it easier for most of these countries to remain pro-Western. This was particularly true of Iran and its leader, MOHAMMED RIZA SHAH PAHLEVI.

The Soviet Union's occupation of Iran's Azerbaijan region after World War II had made the shah intensely suspicious of Soviet motives. His animosity toward the Soviet Union was increased by the close relationship between the Soviet Union and Iraq, which was in a territorial dispute with Iran over the Shatt al-Arab Waterway. Iran became America's closest ally in the Persian Gulf. The United States supplied military equipment and advisers to the shah's government, and the shah allowed the United States to use Iranian territory for electronic surveillance of Soviet territory.

But the increasingly despotic shah became increasingly unpopular in his own country. Opposition to his rule coalesced around Islamic fundamentalists led by the exiled Ayatollah Khomeini. In January 1979 the shah was forced to flee the country, and on February 1 Khomeini arrived in Teheran to establish an Islamic state. Because of America's close association with the exiled shah and his government, Iran turned rabidly anti-American. On November 4, 1979, the depth of anti-American feeling was demonstrated by the seizure of the American Embassy and 60 American diplomats and staff members by students.

The crisis in the Persian Gulf was exacerbated by the Soviet invasion of AFGHANISTAN in December 1979. It appeared to many Western observers that the Soviet Union was taking advantage of the collapse of American influence in Iran and the turmoil in that country to begin a drive for a warm-water port on the Persian Gulf. This was one possible reason for the Soviet invasion, but primarily the Soviets were responding to internal problems within Afghanistan. The Soviet leadership felt it had to strengthen its position on its southern borders in order to prevent the spread of nationalist fundamentalism among the Islamic population of the Soviet Union.

Whatever the reasons for the Soviet invasion, it marked the end of the period of East-West détente and increased tensions in the Persian Gulf as both superpowers moved naval forces into the region to protect their positions.

Tensions increased further after the Iran–Iraq War broke out following the Iraqi invasion of Iran in the autumn of 1980. The seven-year war between the two traditional enemies threatened to spill over onto the southern shore of the Persian Gulf and to destabilize the conservative Arab monarchies, which were supporting Iraq. The war also provided an impetus to a transnational revolutionary Islamic fundamentalist movement, directed largely from Teheran. The fundamentalists were rabidly anti-Israel as well as opposed to the Arab monarchies, which they regarded as corrupt, having sold out to Western interests.

The rise of Islamic fundamentalism and the threat of Iran made the Arab countries aware that they faced threats other than the presence of Israel. This, and Egypt's separate peace with the Jewish state, pushed them toward an accommodation with Israel. In December 1988 the PLO, led by Yasir Arafat, publicly accepted the existence of the state of Israel. Arafat's statement led to the first official talks between PLO and American officials and renewed American pressure on Israel to negotiate a comprehensive Middle East settlement.

Formal negotiations among Israel, the Palestinians (though formally not the PLO) and the Arab states were organized by the BUSH administration and endorsed by the Soviet Union. The first round of negotiations was held in Madrid in late 1991; later the talks were moved to Washington, D.C.

In 1993 the Israeli government, in secret negotiations held in Norway, agreed to recognize the PLO as the body representing the Palestinian people, and came to an agreement with it promising Palestinian autonomy in parts of the occupied territories. Details were left for later discussion, but the accord was tacitly endorsed by several Arab governments and gave some hope that there would eventually be a peaceful resolution of the Arab-Israeli dispute.

For Further Information:
Adams, Michael, ed. *The Middle East*. New York, 1988.

Cooley, John K. *Payback: America's Long War in the Middle East*. Washington, 1991.

Drinan, Robert F. *Honor the Promise: America's Commitment to Israel*. Garden City, N.Y., 1977.

Efrat, Moshe, and Jacob Bercovitch, eds. *Superpowers and Client States in the Middle East: The Imbalance of Influence*. New York, 1991.

Freedman, Robert Owen. *Moscow and the Middle East: Soviet Policy Since the Invasion of Afghanistan*. New York, 1991.

Freiberger, Steven Z. *Dawn Over Suez: The Rise of American Power in the Middle East, 1953–1957*. Chicago, 1992.

Hakleh, Emile A. *Arab American Relations in the Persian Gulf*. Washington, D.C., 1975.

Lenczowski, George. *American Presidents and the Middle East*. Durham, N.C., 1990.

Mangold, Peter. *Superpower Intervention in the Middle East*. New York, 1978.

Quandt, William B. *Decade of Decisions: American Policy Toward the Arab-Israeli Conflict, 1967–1976*. Berkeley, Calif., 1977.

Safran, Nadav. *Israel, The Embattled Ally*. Cambridge, Mass., 1978.

Taylor, Alan R. *The Superpowers and the Middle East*. Syracuse, N.Y., 1991.

Yergin, Daniel. *The Prize: The Epic Quest for Oil, Money, and Power*. New York, 1991.

MI5 MI5 is Britain's counterintelligence organization. It is responsible for countering internal subversion and espionage in Britain and for directing counterintelligence operations against potential enemies.

MI5 was created in 1909 and was particularly effective in both world wars in undermining German espionage networks in Britain. There has always been a rivalry between MI5 and its sister organization MI6, which is responsible for gathering overseas intelligence. In the 1950s and 1960s, MI6 suffered a blow to its prestige and operations after one of its top agents, KIM PHILBY, was exposed as a Soviet spy and fled to Moscow.

This exposure increased the prestige of MI5, only to have it damaged by the revelation in 1981 that one of its agents, Anthony Blunt, had also been a Soviet spy and was suspected of having warned Philby of his imminent arrest. MI5's reputation was further tarnished by allegations that its long-time director, Sir Roger Hollis, was a Soviet mole, and revelations that it had carried out operations to undermine the Labour government of Prime Minister HAROLD WILSON.

Mikoyan, Anastas Ivanovich   (November 13, 1895–October 21, 1978)   Anastas Mikoyan was a chief foreign policy adviser to Soviet leader NIKITA KHRUSHCHEV. He was especially influential during the CUBAN MISSILE CRISIS, and after Khrushchev decided to withdraw the missiles, Mikoyan was given the task of trying to persuade FIDEL CASTRO to accept United Nations observers.

Mikoyan joined the Bolshevik Party in 1915 after initially training for the priesthood. He quickly rose through the party ranks to become a major revolutionary figure in the Caucasus region. After the revolution of 1917 he was arrested by British troops, who had intervened in support of the White Russian forces. He was released in 1920 and went to work as a party official. In 1923 he became a member of the Central Committee.

During the power struggle of the 1920s, Mikoyan supported JOSEF STALIN, and in 1926 he was rewarded with the post of commissar for external and internal trade. He was elected to the Politburo in 1935 and during the war was a member of the State Defense Committee, which administered the country.

From the late 1920s, Mikoyan specialized in economic and trade issues, especially foreign trade. During the war, he branched out slightly to supervise the procurement and transport of supplies, but in 1946 he returned to trade issues as deputy premier responsible for trade. In his later years, Stalin came to suspect Mikoyan of plotting to overthrow him, and there is strong evidence to suggest the dictator was planning Mikoyan's death when he himself died in 1953.

In the power struggle that followed the death of Stalin, Mikoyan at first supported GEORGI MALENKOV and his "New Course" economic policy, which aimed to introduce more consumer goods to Soviet shops. But when it became apparent that this policy would fail he switched his support to Nikita Khrushchev.

In 1955, Mikoyan was a key member of the Soviet delegation that visited Yugoslavia to apologize publicly for Stalin's actions and seek a rapprochement with JOSIP BROZ TITO. Mikoyan also paved the way for Khrushchev's denunciation of Stalin by being the first to criticize the dictator at the famous 20th Party Congress in February 1956. In his speech Mikoyan said that "for some twenty years [the Soviet Union] actually had no collective leadership" and instead "the cult of the individual had prevailed." A few days later Khrushchev delivered his "Secret Speech," attacking Stalin and exposing details of the Great Purges of the 1930s.

The denunciation of Stalin unleashed a wave of unrest in Eastern Europe, which led to rebellions in Poland and Hungary. Mikoyan was among the Soviet leaders who flew to Warsaw to warn the Poles of the repercussions of a complete break with Moscow. After the revolution in Hungary, Mikoyan appeared in Budapest on October 25 to conduct negotiations with Prime Minister IMRE NAGY for the withdrawal of Soviet troops from Hungary. On October 29 the Red Army began its withdrawal, and the following day Mikoyan flew back to Moscow. But Nagy then went too far for the Soviets. On October 31 he announced that Hungary was withdrawing from the Warsaw Pact and that the one-party system was being abolished. Soviet troops reentered Budapest on the night of November 3, and within a few days Mikoyan was back in Budapest to support the pro-Soviet government of Janos Kadar.

Mikoyan was by this stage Khrushchev's main supporter within the Politburo. In 1957 he helped him to defeat the "antiparty group" of Malenkov, V.M. MOLOTOV and Lazar Kaganovich. As a reward for this support, Mikoyan in 1957 became first deputy premier. Khrushchev used Mikoyan increasingly as his chief representative in contacts with foreign dignitaries. Between 1959 and 1961, Mikoyan made a number of official state visits, including trips to the United States, Japan and Mexico. He was also instrumental in negotiating the early Soviet-Cuban trade agreements that tied Castro economically to the Soviet Union. The first agreement, signed in February 1960, was a five-year treaty that pledged the Soviet Union to buy five million tons of sugar at world market prices and guaranteed a $100 million credit to Cuba to buy Soviet machinery and materials.

Mikoyan's early success in Cuba led to his being heavily involved in all Soviet decisions involving Cuba, including the decision to base Soviet missiles on Cuban soil. Mikoyan is believed to have initially supported the missile deployment that led to the Cuban Missile Crisis but later supported Khrushchev's withdrawal of the missiles. One of the conditions of the U.S.–Soviet agreement to end the missile crisis was that United Nations observers would oversee the withdrawal of the missiles. Castro refused to allow the observers on Cuban soil, and Mikoyan was sent to Havana to try to persuade the Cuban leader to change his mind. He remained in Havana for four weeks—during which time he missed his wife's funeral—but failed to sway Castro. In the end, President John F. Kennedy was forced to rely on American intelligence reports to verify Soviet compliance. In November 1963, Mikoyan represented the Soviet Union at Kennedy's funeral.

Mikoyan was too closely tied to Khrushchev to avoid being affected by the latter's fall from power in 1964. Mikoyan was moved to the largely ceremonial position of chairman of the Presidium of the Supreme Soviet and from 1964 onward had little impact on the Soviet decision-making process. In April 1966 Mikoyan was removed from the Politburo, but he remained a member of the Central Committee until his death on October 21, 1978.

For Further Information:

Crankshaw, Edward. *Khrushchev: A Career.* New York, 1966.

Nogee, J.L. *Soviet Foreign Policy Since World War Two.* New York, 1988.

Tatu, Michael. *Power in the Kremlin: From Khrushchev to Kosygin.* New York, 1969.

Ulam, Adam B. *Expansion and Coexistence: The History of Soviet Foreign Policy, 1917–1967.* New York, 1968.

Mindszenty, Jozsef   **(March 29, 1892–May 6, 1975)**   As head of the Roman Catholic Church in Hungary in the immediate postwar period, Jozsef Cardinal Mindszenty took a strong stand against the communist government. This led to his imprisonment, which transformed him into a martyr for Hungarian dissidents.

Mindszenty was politically active from the time of his ordination as a priest in 1915 and was consistently anti-communist. In 1919 this led to his first arrest, under the short-lived revolutionary soviet of Béla Kun. In the interwar years he supported the arrests of leading communists by the rightist dictatorship of Admiral Miklós Horthy, but during the war he opposed the Nazis and was jailed in 1944 when the Germans occupied Hungary.

Mindszenty was released in 1945 and in 1947 was made a cardinal and primate of Hungary. His prewar stand against communism made him an early target of attacks by the communist press. He was forced to wait eight days for an exit visa to fly to Rome to receive his cardinal's hat from Pope Pius XII.

Although the communists initially held only three cabinet positions in the postwar coalition government, they controlled the police and were backed by the occupying Soviet Army. From this position they quickly moved against Mindszenty and ordered the dissolution of Catholic associations. Cardinal Mindszenty responded by accusing the conservative Premier Ferenc Nagy of failing to "defend the honor of the Catholic Church." He also threatened to "impose with the spiritual power of the church, severe punishments upon those who decreed and implemented the dissolution of Catholic associations."

After seizing power in 1947, communist leader MATYAS RAKOSI effectively silenced opposition from traditional political parties through the use of intimidation, arrests and executions. Mindszenty's position as leader of the Catholic Church at first protected him, and for a time he was the only government critic at large in Hungary. Rakosi moved to silence all the churches by expropriating their property so that they were deprived of the income needed to run church schools. He then offered to finance the schools if priests and ministers took an oath that effectively removed them from politics. The Calvinist and Lutheran church leaders reluctantly agreed, but Mindszenty refused.

On May 23, 1948, Mindszenty issued a pastoral letter publicly opposing the nationalization of Hungarian schools and was supported in a broadcast by Pope Pius XII on May 30.

On June 6, Mindszenty issued another pastoral letter instructing Hungarian Catholics to boycott communist newspapers and radio broadcasts, which he denounced as filled with "falsehood, deceit and terror." He refused to hold any negotiations with the Rakosi government without an assurance that the church's schools, property, newspapers and associations would be unmolested.

This was too much for Rakosi, who, on November 27, issued a statement denouncing "spies, traitors, smugglers and Fascists dressed in the robes of a cardinal." A month later, on December 27, Mindszenty was arrested on charges of plotting against the government, spying, treason and blackmarket dealings in currency. His last pastoral letter before his arrest exhorted priests and church officials to make a stand against the Hungarian communists.

The arrest and subsequent trial of Mindszenty sparked demonstrations and government protests throughout the West. The Vatican excommunicated all Catholics who had a hand in the arrest and trial of Mindszenty, and U.S. secretary of state DEAN ACHESON described the Hungarian government's actions as a "conscienceless attack upon religious and personal freedom." None of this deterred the communist government, and Mindszenty was sentenced to life imprisonment on February 8, 1949.

In prison, Mindszenty became a living martyr of the communist government. When the first government of IMRE NAGY acted to improve personal freedoms, Mindszenty was moved out of prison but kept under house arrest at Felsoepeteny Castle. Nagy was preparing to release Mindszenty when he was expelled from the party in 1955.

When the Hungarian Revolution (see HUNGARY) began on October 29, 1956, the crowds demanded the reinstatement of Nagy and the release of Mindszenty. Nagy was returned to power on October 31, and the same day he released Mindszenty from Felsoepeteny Castle and restored him as Roman Catholic primate of Hungary. Upon his release, Mindszenty announced that he had been asked to lead a Christian People's Party, and on November 1 he stated that the party would join a government purged of those who had compromised themselves by working with the Soviet Union.

When 200,000 Soviet troops invaded Hungary on November 3–4, Mindszenty joined Nagy on Budapest Radio in denouncing the invasion and appealing to the West for political support and relief supplies for Hungarian refugees. He then fled to the U.S. legation in Budapest for sanctuary. Mindszenty lived in a small apartment on the top floor of the U.S. mission until 1971.

Effective leadership of the Hungarian Catholic Church returned to Archbishop Joseph Groesz, who was prepared to accept the dictates of the new Soviet-supported government. On May 23, 1957, he was attacked by Mindszenty for allowing the formation of a Catholic "Work of Peace" organization, which agreed to cooperate with the communist-organized peace and disarmament groups. Mindszenty's activities, however, were now severely limited by the American government, which was reluctant to become involved in a dispute with the Hungarians by allowing Mindszenty to use the legal sanctuary provided by the American mission for public attacks on the government.

At various times the cardinal was offered a safe conduct out of the country. But he refused, partly because his continued presence in the country represented a greater threat to the communist government and partly because he was concerned that he might suffer the same fate as Nagy, who had been offered a safe conduct out of the Yugoslav Embassy only be arrested, tried and executed. But as relations between Hungary and the West gradually improved, Mindszenty became an increasing diplomatic embarrassment. On September 15, 1964, the Vatican and the Hungarian government signed an agreement that restored the church's right to form a Roman Catholic hierarchy in Hungary. On September 28, 1971, Pope Paul VI asked Mindszenty to leave Hungary. On February 5, 1974, Pope Paul VI removed Mindszenty from his honorary position as Roman Catholic primate of Hungary in an attempt to improve Hungarian church-state relations. Mindszenty died in Vienna on May 6, 1975.

For Further Imformation:

Kovrig, Bennet. *Communism in Hungary from Kun to Kadar.* Stanford, Calif., 1979.

Mindszenty, Jozsef Cardinal. *Memoirs.* New York, 1974.

Minimum Daily Exchange Requirement   The Minimum Daily Exchange Requirement was the amount of money foreign visitors were required to take into East Germany for each day's visit. The purpose of the requirement was to discourage visits from West Germany and to increase East Germany's hard currency income.

The amount required was calculated in West German marks, and the money had to be exchanged into East German marks at an official exchange rate of one for one, although the bank rate in 1988 was four to one and the black market rate as high as 10 to one. The difference in the rates meant that visitors were forced to spend all of the money in East Germany.

From its introduction in 1972, the minimum daily exchange requirement fluctuated according to the East German economic situation and East-West political tensions. It started at 10 marks per person per day and a year later, on November 5, 1973, was increased to 15 marks as the East Germans sought to limit the political consequences of the flood of West German visitors to relatives in East Germany. On October 13, 1980, the exchange requirement was raised to 20 marks as East-West tensions rose in the wake of the Afghanistan and Poland crises. On August 1, 1984, the requirement was reduced again to 15 marks; in 1988 it was raised to 25 marks.

The minimum daily exchange requirement was abolished in December 1989 at the same time as the East-West German border was abolished and the Berlin Wall torn down.

Minimum Deterrence   A military strategy that relies on the minimum number of nuclear weapons needed to deter an attack. For such a strategy to be successful, the weapons must be invulnerable and carefully targeted to achieve the maximum political and military effect if used. France and Britain maintain a minimum deterrent. In the case of Britain, invulnerability is achieved by basing the nuclear weapons on submarines.

MI6   The British foreign intelligence gathering agency, MI6, is also known as the Secret Intelligence Service (SIS).

MI6 was formally founded in 1911 but can trace its roots back to Elizabethan England. In 1939 it was discovered that the organization had been infiltrated by German Nazis, and many of its wartime operations were taken over by the Special Operations Executive.

During the Cold War period, MI6 suffered another blow when it was discovered that one of its top agents, KIM PHILBY, was a Soviet agent. MI6 did, however, have a major Cold War success in the recruitment of KGB agent OLEG PENKOVSKY, who was executed by the Soviet Union in 1963 after passing valuable intelligence to MI6.

Officially neither MI6 nor its sister organization MI5, which is responsible for counterintelligence, exists. Their budgets and operations are a state secret. Attempts by the British Labour Party to make the intelligence services more accountable to the government and to the public have encountered strong opposition from the Conservative Party, the intelligence community and the British Foreign Office.

Missile Gap   The "missile gap" of the late 1950s and early 1960s was suggested by critics of the EISENHOWER administration's defense policies, who claimed that the Soviet Union was developing an unassailable lead in nuclear-armed missiles. The claims were later shown to be based on false data.

The claim of a three-to-one gap in favor of the Soviets was first made by President Dwight Eisenhower's second defense secretary, Neil McElroy. This was quickly seized upon by the Democrats, led by Senator STUART SYMINGTON, as evidence that the Republicans had allowed the American deterrent posture to deteriorate.

On January 19, 1960, THOMAS GATES, Eisenhower's third defense secretary, attempted to retrieve the position by using revised intelligence estimates to report to the House Defense Appropriations Committee that the initial estimate had been wrong and that there was "a clear balance in our favor."

The Democrats accused Gates and Eisenhower of juggling the statistics, and the "missile gap" became a major issue in the 1960 presidential election. However, after JOHN F. KENNEDY was elected president, his defense secretary, ROBERT MCNAMARA, dismissed the missile gap as illusory.

For Further Information:

Bottome, Edgar. *The Missile Gap: A Study of the Formation of Military and Political Policy.* Rutherford, N.J., 1971.

Gervasi, Tom. *The Myth of Soviet Military Supremacy*. New York, 1986.

McNamara, Robert S. *Blundering into Disaster: Surviving the First Century of the Nuclear Age*. New York, 1986.

Powaski, Ronald E. *March to Armageddon: The United States and the Nuclear Arms Race, 1939 to the Present*. New York, 1987.

Stein, Jonathan B. *From H-Bomb to Star Wars: The Politics of Stategic Decision Making*. Lexington, Mass., 1984.

Mitterrand, François **(October 26, 1916–   )** François Mitterrand was elected president of France in 1981 as the socialist candidate and was reelected in 1988. He has slowly moved French foreign policy closer to the United States while at the same time maintaining the independent stand of the Gaullists.

Mitterrand studied at the University of Paris, from which he received an advanced law degree. At the outbreak of war in 1939, he enlisted in the French Army and in June 1940 was wounded and captured by the Germans. He escaped in December 1941 and returned to France, where he joined the French Resistance while at the same time working in the civil service of the Vichy government.

After the liberation of France in 1944, Mitterrand was briefly secretary general for war prisoners and deportees. In November 1946 he was elected a deputy of the National Assembly as a member of the Democratic and Socialist Resistance Union. The following year he was named minister of war veterans and victims. Over the next 10 years he held a number of cabinet posts in the governments of the Fourth Republic, including minister for overseas territories, minister of state for justice and minister of the interior.

In 1958 he opposed the new constitution that established the Fifth Republic. This unpopular stand cost him his seat in the National Assembly in the parliamentary elections that year. He returned to the National Assembly in 1962 as the major opposition figure on the French left. Mitterrand was hamstrung, however, by the damaging divisions within the left and attempted to unite the various French socialist parties and the communists under his leadership. In 1965 he succeeded in winning the backing of a united left in his bid for the presidency and surprised political observers by forcing CHARLES DE GAULLE into an embarrassing second round. But in that runoff de Gaulle won comfortably, with 54.5% of the vote compared to 45.5% for Mitterrand.

Mitterrand, however, had created the Federation of the Democratic and Socialist Left (FGDS), which successfully projected itself as the only alternative to Gaullism. But in the wake of the student riots of May 1968 the FGDS collapsed in a series of intraparty feuds and political miscalculations that left Mitterrand without his political base. In June 1971 Mitterrand joined the small French Socialist Party and was immediately elected its secretary general. Once again, he entered into negotiations with the Communist Party to form a united left. This resulted in June 1972 in the Common Program, which pledged both parties to a common electoral

François Mitterrand, before the 1974 presidential elections in France. Photo courtesy of Popperfoto.

platform committed to improved social welfare, an extensive nationalization program, reduced presidential powers, continued membership in both the NORTH ATLANTIC TREATY ORGANIZATION (NATO) and the EUROPEAN ECONOMIC COMMUNITY (EEC), and higher wages and pensions.

The result of the Common Program was an immediate increase in the political fortunes of the Socialist Party in the parliamentary elections of March 1973. Then, in the presidential election of May 1973 Mitterrand was the leading candidate in the first round, but he narrowly lost in the runoff round to VALERY GISCARD-D'ESTAING, 50.7% to 49.3%. Despite a number of political problems, the Socialist Party continued to grow and Mitterrand managed to hold together the coalition of the French left. In May 1981 he won the presidency over Giscard, 50.8% to 49.2%.

The election of Mitterrand was a watershed in French postwar political history. It marked the end of 23 years of Gaullist government and the first left-wing government of the Fifth Republic. It was also a major personal achievement for Francois Mitterrand, who had developed a reputation as a perpetual also-ran. The election of Mitterrand also resulted in the admission of communists to the French cabinet for the first time since the immediate postwar period. The communists' role caused considerable concern among some members of the Western Alliance, but the communists were restricted to minor posts that had nothing to do with defense, security or foreign policy. Mitterrand himself took a decidedly pro-NATO stance and supported U.S. president RONALD REAGAN's defense buildup. Isolated within the government, the communists finally left the coalition in July 1984.

Mitterrand's more pro-American stance became apparent almost immediately. At an EEC heads-of-government summit in July 1981 he startled his fellow European leaders by denouncing "the dangers of galloping neutralism" in Western Europe and strongly supported the NATO plan to deploy U.S. PERSHING II and cruise missiles in Western Europe as a counter to the Soviet SS-20s. In October 1981 Reagan and Mitterrand met in Williamsburg, Virginia for celebrations to mark the bicentennial of the end of the American Revolution. The discussions revealed a broad range of agreement on strategic and defense issues, although they differed on relations toward the Third World and Central America. The Williamsburg Summit, however, marked the start of a close relationship between Mitterrand and Reagan, which was slightly marred later by differences over economic issues.

The differences over Central America were made plain by Mitterrand in an interview in October 1981 with *Time* magazine. While Reagan saw the first priority as the military defeat of the region's left-wing forces, Mitterrand made it clear that he believed that the U.S. policy of supporting right-wing dictatorships fighting left-wing guerrillas and right-wing guerrillas fighting leftist governments was only playing into the hands of the Soviet Union. He said, "The reality is that El Salvador lives under an unbearable, dictatorial oligarchy . . . We believe that the prolongation of those outdated systems in Latin America is a danger for the whole world. Do we speak of Communism? This is how it is introduced!" Mitterrand used a similar argument to develop close political and economic ties with the Sandinista government in NICARAGUA. He argued that it was important to keep open a channel of communication between Nicaragua and the Western Alliance. In May 1985 Nicaraguan president Daniel Ortega visited Mitterrand, who promised to expand commercial ties.

On strategic nuclear issues, Mitterrand broke with traditional Socialist Party policies to embrace wholeheartedly the maintenance and further development of the French nuclear deterrent. This was partly because an increased nuclear deterrent was a cheaper alternative to conventional forces and partly because Mitterrand accepted the basic Gaullist premise that while extended American nuclear deterrence was a fundamental contribution to the defense of Europe, it was primarily designed to protect the United States and only secondarily to protect Europe. Therefore, the credibility of the American nuclear umbrella was always shaky and needed to be supplemented by a European (preferably French) deterrent.

At the same time, however, the European deterrent could only be a backup for the American umbrella, and therefore it was important that the U.S. deterrent not be eroded or be allowed to uncouple itself from Western Europe's. Mitterrand

therefore placed a high priority on deploying Pershing II and cruise missiles, arguing that failure to do so would force West Germany into a damaging political accommodation with the Soviet Union. A basic element of France's security policy was that Germany should remain firmly anchored in the Western Alliance system.

Mitterrand thus continued the Gaullist policy of reassuring the West Germans of French support and of encouraging the Franco-German alliance, which had become one of the cornerstones of Europe's postwar political structure. At his first Franco-German summit in Bonn, Mitterrand agreed to consult West Germany on decisions relating to France's deterrent that could affect German security, and Mitterrand and West German chancellor HELMUT SCHMIDT agreed to establish a permanent commission for defense. On January 16, 1986, Mitterrand and Chancellor HELMUT KOHL met in Baden-Baden to agree to increased military cooperation. On February 28, at a Franco-German summit in Paris, Mitterrand announced that France would consult West Germany before using "prestrategic" weapons on its territory.

But the height of Franco-German cooperation came in January 1988 at celebrations to mark the 25th anniversary of the FRANCO-GERMAN FRIENDSHIP TREATY. In Paris, Mitterrand and Kohl signed agreements establishing a defense council to improve cooperation on military strategy, troop deployment and weapons procurement. They also established a 4,000-strong joint brigade to be based in West Germany. Finally, they established a joint economic council to strengthen monetary and financial ties and coordinate policy. It was not until the end of 1989 that Franco-German relations began to cool, over the issue of German reunification. Mitterrand, in common with many Frenchmen, wanted close relations with West Germany, but feared the economic, political and military consequences of a reunited Germany and was less enthusiastic about the prospect than Chancellor Kohl would have liked.

Mitterrand also enjoyed a good working relationship with British prime minister MARGARET THATCHER, although he often berated her for not being more supportive of the EEC. The British and French governments reached several agreements for joint research and production on conventional and nuclear weapons, and they shared the problem of resisting Soviet pressure to include their national deterrents in the U.S.–Soviet negotiations for an INTERMEDIATE-RANGE NUCLEAR FORCES (INF) TREATY. The Soviets repeatedly claimed that their intermediate-range nuclear weapons were meant as a counter to the British and French nuclear forces and that any reduction in the Soviet forces would have to be accompanied by a parallel reduction in the British and French nuclear arsenals. Thatcher and Mitterrand refused to accept this argument.

A major problem faced by Mitterrand was how to pursue the politically desirable goal of improving defense cooperation with France's European allies while remaining at arm's length from the United States and the U.S.-dominated NATO. There were some half-hearted attempts to include a military element in the EEC, but these were quickly blocked by Greece and Ireland. Mitterrand then hit upon the idea of reviving the moribund WESTERN EUROPEAN UNION (WEU). On October 27, 1984, the WEU was relaunched at a meeting in Rome of the foreign and defense ministers of Britain, France, Italy, West Germany, Belgium, Holland and Luxembourg. With the collapse of the communist governments in Eastern Europe and the reunification of Germany, however, Mitterrand again began reassessing the French relationship with NATO and European institutions.

On President Reagan's STRATEGIC DEFENSE INITIATIVE, Mitterrand reserved France's official position while at the same time not preventing French companies from taking part. This policy enabled some French companies to benefit both financially and in terms of access to American technology while at the same time limiting the political damage that too close a relationship with an American initiative would have on both the domestic and foreign fronts. Mitterrand also launched in July 1985 the joint European high technology research program known as the European Research Agency (Eureka) to increase coordination in the development of high technology. Mitterrand launched the opening Paris conference with a French contribution of $116 million.

In March 1986, Mitterrand suffered a major political setback when the right-wing RPR/UDF coalition won a majority of the seats in the National Assembly. The constitution of the Fifth Republic had been written for Charles de Gaulle, who demanded a strong executive presidency, which, he assumed, would control the legislative branch as well. This had been the case between 1958 and 1986, but the electoral success of the RPR/UDF coalition threatened a constitutional crisis. Mitterrand managed to avoid this by appointing RPR leader Jacques Chirac as prime minister. This led to a shaky *modus vivendi* dubbed "cohabitation," which had its ups and downs but for the most part worked because Mitterrand was determined that it should. Mitterrand's statesmanlike approach to cohabitation increased his standing with the French electorate; he was reelected to the French presidency in May 1988 while the socialists regained control of the National Assembly.

Chirac, however, did manage to introduce major changes in Mitterrand's economic policies. During his first month in office, Mitterrand had introduced a number of socialist policies, including a 10% increase in the minimum wage, a 25% increase in social security payments, a mandatory fifth week of vacation for all salaried employees and a reduction of the working week. Soon afterward he decentralized the government and nationalized a number of private banks and key companies in the chemical, electronics and defense industries. This he followed with a major increase in government spending. These economic changes boosted the French inflation rate, and even before March 1986 Mitterrand was forced to introduce austerity measures to bring the economy back into line. But most of the deflationary monetarist program was introduced after 1986. The cohabitation with Chirac enabled Mitterrand to blame the RPR/UDF for the unpopular social

effects of austerity economics while at the same time claiming credit for the general improvement in the economic climate.

While Franco-American relations improved during Mitterrand's presidency, Franco-Soviet relations initially deteriorated sharply. The conservative Gaullists had had far greater room to maneuver in their relations with Moscow as opposition to communism had always been among their basic political beliefs. Mitterrand, the socialist, was distrusted by conservative French business circles because of his occasional tactical alliance with the pro-Soviet, French Communist Party. It was important for Mitterrand quickly to establish his anticommunist credentials and win the confidence of the business community by taking a tough anti-Soviet stand. He thus strongly denounced the imposition of martial law in Poland, and after the Soviets shot down KOREAN AIRLINES Flight 007 he canceled a trip to Paris by Soviet foreign minister ANDREI GROMYKO.

But it was in his treatment of Soviet spies that Mitterrand took an especially hard line. The Gaullists had turned a blind eye to the activities of Soviet citizens in France in order to prevent any damage to their special relationship with Moscow. Mitterrand, in contrast, regularly expelled them. On February 3, 1986, France expelled four Soviet diplomats for spying and another three on April 2, 1987, after they had been discovered spying at the European Space Agency. The biggest expulsion order came on April 5, 1983, when Mitterrand personally ordered the expulsion of 47 Soviets for espionage activities. The French government issued a statement saying that French investigators had discovered that the Soviets were "engaged in a systematic search on French territory for technological and scientific information, particularly in the military area."

Mitterrand's anti-Soviet position did not extend to the economic sphere. The socialists were as eager to trade with Moscow as had been their Gaullist predecessors. On January 23, 1982, France became one of the first West European companies to agree to purchase Soviet gas when Mitterrand signed a major contract to buy 8 billion cubic meters of Soviet natural gas for 25 years, starting in 1984. President Reagan tried to block the sale of the gas to Western Europe by imposing a trade ban on companies involved in the Soviet gas pipeline. Mitterrand helped to push through the EEC statement condemning the ban as "an implied extraterritorial extension of United States jurisdiction . . . contrary to the principles of international law." Reagan's embargo was quietly lifted a year later. On February 3, 1984, France and the Soviet Union signed a five-year economic cooperation pact.

Mitterrand was among the first world leaders to recognize the importance of Soviet leader MIKHAIL GORBACHEV, and France was the first Western country Gorbachev visited after becoming secretary general of the Communist Party. In July 1989 Mitterrand invited Gorbachev back to France, and the two leaders used the occasion to sign 21 agreements on a wide range of issues including military exchanges, French training of Soviet managers, common standards for high-definition television and a joint declaration calling for an immediate cease-fire in Lebanon.

Mitterrand also played a major role in encouraging closer links between the West and Eastern Europe with a number of trips to the East European countries. In December 1985 he played host to the Polish president, General WOJCIECH JARUZELSKI. It was the first time that the Polish leader had been received in a Western capital since the imposition of martial law in Poland in 1981. In June 1989, Mitterrand made a three-day visit to Poland and announced that France would restructure its $1.15 billion Polish debt and provide Poland with a further $100 million in bank loans. He also played a major role in the creation of a European Recovery Bank.

For Further Information
Aldrich, Robert, and John Connell, eds. *France in World Politics.* New York, 1989.

Moby Dick Program   "Moby Dick" was the code name for a CIA/U.S. Air Force aerial reconnaissance program using balloons that flew over the Soviet Bloc countries in the early 1950s.

As a result of research by the RAND CORPORATION, the air force in 1951 started developing large polyethylene balloons capable of flying at altitudes of 50,000 to 100,000 feet. Each balloon carried a 600-pound gondola equipped with cameras and tracking instruments.

The first Moby Dick reconnaissance mission was launched in November 1955. The balloons were launched in Western Europe and carried eastward by the wind for three days across Eastern Europe and China. Once past China, an automatic ballasting system lowered the balloons to 28,000 feet, and the gondolas were released. Each gondola was equipped with a parachute that allowed it to float to the ground or be collected by an airplane in midair.

Some of the balloons landed prematurely in Soviet territory, and this resulted in a series of diplomatic incidents. But generally, the intelligence gathered by the Moby Dick program was judged to outweigh any political damage incurred. The program continued until 1956, when the balloons were replaced by U-2 reconnaissance airplanes.

For Further Information:
O'Toole, G.J.A. *The Encyclopedia of American Intelligence and Espionage.* New York, 1988.
Rostow, W.W. *Open Skies: Eisenhower's Proposal of July 21, 1955.* Austin, Tex., 1982.

Molotov, Vyacheslav Mikhaylovich   (March 9, 1890–November 8, 1986)   V.M. Molotov was a close confidant of JOSEF STALIN and was Soviet foreign minister in the early years of the Cold War. He represented the Soviet Union at almost all of the major East–West conferences between 1945 and 1949 and between 1953 and 1956, and he became known

Vyacheslav Molotov in 1947. As foreign minister, he represented the Soviet Union at almost all major East-West conferences between 1945 and 1949. Photo courtesy of Novosti Press Agency.

as the chief exponent of a Soviet hard line in dealings with the West.

Molotov was born into a middle-class family in the province of Byatka, later Sovietsk, in the Kirov region. His real name was Skriabin. When he joined the Bolshevik Party in 1905 he changed his name to "Molotov," which translates as "Man of the Hammer."

His parents planned for their son to join the Russian civil service, and Molotov was enrolled in the high school at Kazan and the polytechnic at St. Petersburg, two well-known routes to government service. But Molotov quickly became interested in revolutionary activities and participated in the unsuccessful 1905 uprising. In 1909 he was arrested by the Czarist police and sent into internal exile for two years. Upon his release he continued to work in the Bolshevik underground.

Molotov first met Stalin in 1912 when the two men worked together on the launching of the Bolshevik newspaper *Pravda.* They became firm friends. Molotov was arrested several times between 1912 and 1916 but managed eventually to escape and was one of the few Bolsheviks still at liberty and active in Russia at the time of the 1917 revolution.

After the revolution, Molotov was placed in charge of nationalization programs in the northwest. He took command of similar projects in the Volga and Ukraine regions. In 1920 he became secretary of the Ukraine Communist Party and in 1921 secretary of the Central Committee of the Russian Communist Party and a candidate member of the Politburo. He became a full Politburo member in 1926 and in 1930 was named prime minister.

In the 1930s, Molotov worked closely with Stalin to implement the great purges and took special responsibility for purging the party apparatus in Moscow. Molotov's loyalty to Stalin became almost legendary within Communist Party circles. Only once did he show any sign of rebelling against the dictator. That was in 1948, when he abstained in a Politburo vote to purge his own wife from the party and imprison her.

Molotov was named foreign secretary in May 1939 and shortly afterward signed the Molotov-Ribbentrop Pact, which led to the Soviet-German invasion of Poland and the start of World War II. After Germany invaded the Soviet Union in 1941, he arranged Soviet alliances with Britain and the United States. He attended the Allies' conferences at Teheran, YALTA and POTSDAM as well as the SAN FRANCISCO CONFERENCE, which created the United Nations. British prime minister WINSTON CHURCHILL described Molotov as "a man of outstanding ability and coldblooded ruthlessness."

Molotov was the first high-ranking Soviet official to meet HARRY S. TRUMAN after Truman succeeded FRANKLIN ROOSEVELT as president. At the meeting in April 1945, Truman took the opportunity to berate Molotov "in words of one syllable" on the Soviet Union's failure to live up to the Yalta accords. The early clash between the two men helped to set the tone for the Cold War.

Soviet foreign policy in the immediate postwar years was largely a joint operation between Stalin and Molotov. Stalin would usually set the broad guidelines in consultation with Molotov, who would represent them at international conferences. Usually Molotov would take a hard and uncompromising line in direct negotiations with the West and leave it to Stalin to make quiet concessions if they were necessary. The main guidelines of Soviet foreign policy in the late 1940s were the establishment of Soviet hegemony in Eastern Europe, the division of Western Europe, the withdrawal of U.S. troops from Europe and Asia, support for other communist parties through COMINFORM (the Communist Information Bureau), undermining of British influence in Europe, the dismantling of German industry and the imposition of crippling war reparations to finance the rebuilding of Soviet industry. Molotov became the chief architect of Soviet control of Eastern Europe and was so hated by the anti-Soviet population there that Hungarians during their 1956 uprising named their petrol bombs "Molotov cocktails" (although Molotov had resigned by that time).

In 1949 Stalin became convinced that he was the target of a coup and resolved to replace the Politburo Old Guard with younger men whom he could easily control. The so-called "Doctors' Plot" resulted in a demotion for Molotov, although there is no evidence to suggest that he was involved in any plan to overthrow his old friend.

After the death of Stalin in 1953, Molotov was reinstated as foreign minister. At the time, the Soviet Union under GEORGI MALENKOV and NIKOLAI BULGANIN was attempting to improve relations with the West, and Molotov was instructed to make concessions. Some of the results were the Treaty of TRIESTE, the Austrian State Treaty, and the agreements at the GENEVA CONFERENCE ON INDOCHINA AND KOREA in 1954. But whenever the issues of Eastern Europe, German reunification, German rearmament or West European defense or economic unification were raised, Molotov reverted to his Stalinist positions.

The rise of NIKITA KHRUSHCHEV meant the eventual downfall of Molotov. Khrushchev was a firm opponent of the old-style Stalinism, and Molotov despite his four years in the wilderness, refused to completely disown his old friend and mentor. Molotov resigned as foreign minister in June 1956. The following June he was officially associated with the leadership of the "antiparty group" and was expelled from the Politburo and the Central Committee and from all of his government posts. For the next five years, until his retirement in 1962, Molotov was relegated to insignificant diplomatic posts such as ambassador to Mongolia and permanent delegate to the International Atomic Energy Agency. Throughout this period, Molotov remained implacably opposed to Khrushchev and at every opportunity tried to organize opposition to him. Khrushchev finally expelled Molotov from the party in 1962.

Molotov was given a monthly pension of $400 and assigned a small apartment in Moscow. To anyone who would listen, he would maintain that Stalin's policies had been correct. Molotov remained in disgrace until he was rehabilitated by President KONSTANTIN CHERNENKO in July 1984, when he was given a large pension and a country dacha. In 1986, shortly before his death, Molotov gave an interview to *Moscow News* in which he praised the government of MIKHAIL GORBACHEV.

For Further Information:
Nogee, J.L. *Soviet Foreign Policy Since World War Two.* New York, 1988.
Shulman, Marshall D. *Stalin's Foreign Policy Reappraised.* New York, 1969.

Monnet, Jean (November 9, 1888–March 16, 1979)
Jean Monnet is widely regarded as the spiritual father of the EUROPEAN ECONOMIC COMMUNITY. He never held any elected national office.

Monnet started his career working abroad as a salesman in Canada for the family cognac business. In Canada he developed strong links with both the government and the business community, and during World War I he used these contacts to negotiate a major Canadian war loan for the French government.

The French government was so impressed with Monnet's abilities that it secured for him the post of deputy secretary general in the newly formed League of Nations after World War I. In this position he helped to reconstruct the Austrian economy. But Monnet disagreed fundamentally with both the league and the French government over the policy of punishing rather than rehabilitating Germany and left the league in 1923 to return to the family business. In 1925 he moved into international banking, and for the next 14 years he alternated between the private and public sectors of international finance, continuing to build on his reputation as a brilliant technocrat and solver of problems.

At the outbreak of World War II, Monnet was called upon to organize joint Anglo-French production and rearmament. But before his project could get underway, France fell. Monnet quickly realized that the future of France lay in British hands and offered his services to Prime Minister WINSTON CHURCHILL. Churchill personally endorsed his passport and sent Monnet to Washington, D.C. as a member of the British Supply Council. There he organized the diversion to Britain of supplies earmarked for France and conceived the idea of LEND-LEASE. Monnet also coined the term "Arsenal for Democracy," which was used to great effect by President FRANKLIN D. ROOSEVELT. In 1943, General CHARLES DE GAULLE named Monnet to the National Economic Council and charged him with planning the modernization of French industry.

Monnet's supranational banker's mind quickly led him to the conclusion that the best way to achieve French economic revival was through economic integration with the rest of Western Europe, and that the first step toward this integration was the pooling of coal and steel resources. He persuaded his close friend ROBERT SCHUMAN, then French foreign minister, to propose in November 1950 the creation of the EUROPEAN COAL AND STEEL COMMUNITY. The ECSC was enthusiastically welcomed by the Benelux countries of Belgium, the Netherlands and Luxembourg, which had already taken steps toward a customs union. The Schuman Plan, as it became known, was also welcomed by West Germany and Italy, which saw membership in such an organization as a step toward acceptance back into the European fold. Only Britain, with its empire and its traditional island mentality, remained aloof.

British coolness to his grand idea of a United States of Europe was a major blow to Monnet, who had based his career on a close relationship with the British establishment and a belief that Britain was an essential partner in his European federation. When Britain finally decided to join the Common Market in October 1971, the 82-year-old Monnet flew to London to watch the vote from the spectators' gallery of the House of Commons.

The ECSC went into operation in January 1952 and Monnet was elected the community's first president. He saw the creation of the ECSC not as an end in itself, but merely as the first step toward a fully united Europe. Even before he was ensconced in the ECSC headquarters in Luxembourg he began to work on the next step: integration of European defense systems. He persuaded another French politican, Rene Pleven, to launch his proposal for a EUROPEAN DEFENSE COMMUNITY (EDC) in what became known as the PLEVEN PLAN.

The EDC fell at the last hurdle, when the French National Assembly refused to ratify the necessary treaty in May 1954. Undeterred, Monnet left the ECSC and devoted himself to the creation of the European Economic Community. In this case he was rewarded with success when the Treaty of Rome was signed in 1957, and the Common Market of France, Belgium, the Netherlands, Luxembourg, West Germany and Italy was formed. Monnet said, "The people of Europe want this change. This new community is a revolution in Europe, perhaps the greatest Europe has known. We are embarked on the liberation of Europe from its past."

After the creation of the Common Market, Monnet formed and became president of the Action Committee for a United States of Europe, which concentrated on plans for European economic union. Monnet never held a national elected office because he felt that this might bring him into a conflict of interest with his pan-European ideals. He died at his country estate outside Paris on March 16, 1979, at the age of 90.

For Further Information:
Mayne, Richard. *The Recovery of Europe.* London, 1970.

Moorer, Thomas H.   **(February 9, 1912–   )**   Admiral Thomas Moorer was chairman of the Joint Chiefs of Staff during the NIXON administration. In this position he played a vital role in the closing stages of the VIETNAM WAR. Moorer also took a leading role in developing the U.S. military's hard-line attitude toward the STRATEGIC ARMS LIMITATION TALKS (SALT).

Moorer graduated from the U.S. Naval Academy at Annapolis in 1933. During World War II he saw action in both the Pacific and Atlantic. After the war, Moorer reached the rank of full admiral and was appointed commander of the Pacific Fleet in 1964. He was in that command when the USS *Maddox* either was or was not fired upon while patrolling the GULF OF TONKIN, leading to the Gulf of Tonkin Resolution, establishing the tenuous legal basis for direct American involvement in the Vietnam War.

In April 1965 Moorer assumed command of the Atlantic Fleet. While in this post he commanded the American invasion of the Dominican Republic. In April 1967 he was appointed chief of naval operations, and in July 1970 President Richard Nixon appointed him chairman of the Joint Chiefs.

Moorer was a consistent and unquestioning supporter of the administration's Vietnam policy. He supported and directed the American invasion of Cambodia in May 1970 and backed the administration's decision to provide tactical support for the South Vietnamese Army's invasion of Laos in February 1971. He also supported the resumption of bombing raids against North Vietnam and the mining of Hanoi and Haiphong harbors.

The only area in which Moorer differed with the administration was over strategic nuclear issues. He took the traditional military view that the only effective defense was a clear-cut superiority. In March 1971, Moorer told the House of Representatives Armed Services Committee that he was worried that the Soviet arms buildup could, within five years, lead the United States to find itself in a position of overall strategic inferiority.

Moorer publicly endorsed the ANTIBALLISTIC MISSILE TREATY and SALT I (Strategic Arms Limitation Talks) agreement in 1972. But his endorsement was conditional on a continuing strategic modernization program and an acceptable verification procedure to ensure Soviet compliance with the treaties.

Nixon reappointed Moorer for a second two-year term as chairman of the Joint Chiefs in July 1972, and Moorer was at the Pentagon when the Paris Peace Treaty ending American combat involvement in Vietnam was signed in January 1973. This presented him with the task of organizing the withdrawal of U.S. forces and at the same time continuing to provide material assistance to the South Vietnamese.

In 1973 Moorer became embroiled in a scandal involving the unauthorized transfer in 1971 of secret documents from the National Security Council to the Pentagon. The Senate Armed Services Committee investigated the incident and cleared Moorer after he admitted having received the documents and explained that he thought they had been sent to him through proper channels. Moorer retired from the navy in July 1974.

For Further Information:
Karnow, Stanley. *Vietnam: A History*. New York, 1983.

Morgenthau, Henry, Jr. **(May 11, 1891–February 6, 1967)** Henry Morgenthau was a key figure in the ROOSEVELT administration as treasury secretary and an active participant in international negotiations to establish postwar world financial structures. Later, outside the administration, he became a prominent critic of President HARRY TRUMAN's Cold War policies.

Born into a wealthy New York family with prominent connections to the Democratic Party, Morgenthau left Cornell University without graduating to become a farmer in upstate New York. One of his neighbors was Franklin D. Roosevelt, and the two became close friends. When Roosevelt was elected governor of New York in 1928, he appointed Morgenthau chairman of the agricultural advisory commission. The friendship continued to flourish, and when Roosevelt won the 1932 presidential election, Morgenthau moved with him to Washington, D.C. to become treasury secretary.

Prior to Morgenthau, U.S. Treasury secretaries generally let market forces take their course. But Roosevelt's New Deal policies demanded a different type of person, and Morgenthau quickly established a reputation as the most activist and interventionist treasury secretary in history.

Morgenthau's stature continued to grow during the war years as the demand for finance brought the Treasury Department increasingly into discussions of foreign and military policy. By 1944 he was directing plans for the postwar economic order, and at the Bretton Woods Conference in that year played a major role in planning for the creation of an INTERNATIONAL MONETARY FUND and WORLD BANK.

The treasury secretary suffered a major setback, however, with his demand for the "pastoralization" of Germany. Under this proposal, known as the Morgenthau Plan, German's heavy industry would be dismantled and the German economy focused on agriculture. Young children would be separated from their presumably Nazi parents and reeducated in special schools; the country would be divided into northern and southern halves, and eastern and western districts would go to Poland and France.

The Morgenthau Plan was strongly opposed by career officers in the U.S. State Department and by British prime minister WINSTON CHURCHILL. Roosevelt's position was unclear, but by the time of the YALTA CONFERENCE discussion was clearly leading away from Morgenthau's ideas. When Harry Truman succeeded Roosevelt as president he rejected the scheme.

Morgenthau tried to hang onto his office after the death of his close friend Roosevelt. But President Truman's attempts to isolate Morgenthau within the administration and his refusal to implement the plans for Germany made Morgenthau's position untenable. He resigned on July 5, 1945, and was replaced by Truman's close friend Fred Vinson.

In the following years, Morgenthau criticized Truman for failing to continue Roosevelt's policies of compromise with the Soviet Union. He was particularly adamant that Britain and America's plans for rebuilding Germany were damaging the prospect of constructive East–West relations. Various left-wing political groups courted the former treasury secretary, but he became disillusioned with politics and from 1947 until his death in February 1967 was involved mainly with Jewish philanthropies.

For Further Information:
Rose, Lisle A. *Dubious Victory*. Kent, Conn., 1973.

Mosaddeq, Mohammed **(1880–March 5, 1967)** Mohammed Mosaddeq was the strongly nationalist and populist premier of Iran from 1951 to 1953. His nationalization of British oil interests and alliance with local communists alienated him from the West and led to a CIA-organized coup that toppled him, restored MOHAMMED REZA PAHLEVI to power and left the United States the preeminent outside power in Iran.

Mosaddeq was born into the Iranian ruling elite. After graduating from the University of Lausanne, Switzerland, with a doctorate in law, he returned to Iran in 1914. Soon afterward he was appointed governor of Fars province. Mosaddeq continued to rise after Reza Khan came to power in 1921, serving as Reza Khan's minister of foreign affairs and minister of finance. But after Reza Khan named himself shah (Reza Shah Pahlevi) and created the Pahlevi dynasty, a disillusioned Mosaddeq retired from public life, only to return after Reza Khan was forced to abdicate in favor of his son Mohammed Riza in 1941.

From early in his career, Mosaddeq was an outspoken nationalist and opponent of British influence in Iran. Britain had been the preeminent power in Iran since the turn of the century and had maintained a stranglehold on the country's political and economic life through the monopoly of Iranian oil held by the Anglo-Iranian Oil Company (AIOC). In the postwar years, the nationalization of British oil interests in Iran became a popular rallying cry, and anti-British demonstrations were held regularly in Teheran. Mosaddeq took the lead in demanding the nationalization of the oil industry.

In 1948 talks opened between the Iranian government and the AIOC, with the British trying to negotiate a compromise solution. But these negotiations failed, and on April 28, 1951, the Iranian parliament (Majlis) passed the Oil Nationalization Act; Mosaddeq was appointed premier the following day. The nationalization resulted in a break with Britain, which at that time supplied the key personnel for the oil fields and markets for the oil. The Iranian economy suffered badly as a result.

This appeared to have little effect on Mosaddeq's popularity with the masses, although it did push him closer to the communist-controlled Tudeh Party and alienated him from the ruling elite and the West. He found himself increasingly in conflict with the young shah, who still retained considerable power through his control of the military. In July 1952, the shah managed to engineer the dismissal of Mosaddeq but was forced to reinstall him as premier after pro-Mosaddeq riots broke out. Mosaddeq returned with a greatly enhanced reputation and on August 11, 1952, managed to get a bill passed granting him emergency dictatorial powers.

During this time, the British Secret Intelligence Service (SIS) had approached the CENTRAL INTELLIGENCE AGENCY to request American help in coordinating a coup to overthrow Mosaddeq. ALLEN DULLES, director of the CIA, had become convinced that Mosaddeq was a crypto-communist and that if he stayed in power, the Soviet Union would gain direct access to the strategic Persian Gulf. He approved the British plan, and the CIA took the lead and approached the shah, who approved of the initial plan to dismiss Mosaddeq and replace him with General Fazlollah Zahedi. But Mosaddeq learned of the plot and launched a series of violent anti-shah demonstrations. The Shah fled the country.

The CIA, however, was still operating in Teheran. Under the direction of Kermit Roosevelt, grandson of Theodore Roosevelt, undercover CIA operatives organized huge pro-shah and anti-Mosaddeq demonstrations. They also kept communications open between the shah and the military, which had remained loyal to him. On August 19, only three days after the shah had left, the army, claiming the support of the CIA-organized crowds, moved against Mosaddeq and overthrew him.

The shah returned to Iran from Rome on August 22. Mosaddeq was sentenced to three years' imprisonment for treason. After he served his sentence, he was kept under house arrest until his death on March 5, 1967.

In 1954 a new oil agreement was negotiated. Iranian oil remained nationalized, but the government subcontracted the marketing to Western oil companies. The British lost their monopoly, although the AIOC (renamed British Petroleum) retained the largest share with 40% of the operations. In recognition of American involvement in restoring the shah to his throne, a consortium of five large American oil companies (Standard of New Jersey, Standard of California, Gulf, Texas Oil and Socony-Mobil) was given another 40% of the operations. The remaining 20% went to Dutch and French oil companies.

With Britain's monopoly of Iranian oil broken, the United States was free to becoming increasingly involved in Iranian affairs and developed closer and closer relations with the shah. Before long, the United States had replaced Britain as the preeminent foreign power in Iran and the main target of Iranian nationalists.

For Further Information:
Engler, Robert. *The Politics of Oil.* Chicago, 1961.
Keddie, Nikkie. *Roots of Revolution, an Interpretative History of Modern Iran.* New York, 1981.
Ramzani, R.K. *The U.S. and Iran: The Patterns of Influence.* New York, 1982.
Roosevelt, Kermit. *Countercoup.* New York, 1979.

Moscow Foreign Ministers' Conference (1945) The Moscow Foreign Ministers' Conference of December 16–27, 1945, was organized in an attempt to salvage postwar Allied cooperation after the failure of the London conference earlier in the year. The concessions made in Moscow by U.S. secretary of state JAMES BYRNES later led to his dismissal by President Harry Truman.

The London conference of foreign ministers from Britain, France, the Soviet Union, the United States and China had collapsed over the issues of Soviet involvement in the occupation of Japan and Soviet insistence that China and France be excluded from the bulk of the discussions.

Following the London conference, Byrnes tried to improve U.S.-Soviet relations by recognizing the provisional governments in Austria and Hungary and sending a well-known liberal, publisher Mark Ethridge, as his special representative to Moscow. Finally, under pressure from Britain and the Soviet Union, Byrnes agreed to include those two countries in the occupation of Japan. The final agreement, however, left control of Japan in American hands.

Byrnes then proposed another foreign ministers' meeting. As further concessions he proposed that the meeting be held in Moscow, that Soviet foreign minister V. M. MOLOTOV be the chairman and that France and China be excluded. The meeting reached agreement on the following issues:

1. A formal peace conference would be held in Paris no later than May 1, 1946.
2. Preliminary considerations of the peace treaty terms would be confined to the signatories of the armistices.
3. A FAR EASTERN COMMISSION would be formed and would meet in Washington, D.C.
4. An Allied Council for Japan would be formed and would meet in Tokyo.
5. The Romanian government would be broadened to include more anti-communists and would be recognized by Britain and the United States.
6. The Soviet Union would advise the Bulgarian government to broaden its political base and the government would be recognized by Britain and the United States.
7. Britain, the United States and the Soviet Union would recommend the creation of a United Nations Commission for the Control of Atomic Energy.
8. A "provisional Korean Democratic government" would be established with a joint U.S.–Soviet military commission to assist it.

The American press and Byrnes were pleased with the results of the conference, but they encountered a storm of congressional and presidential protests. Senator ARTHUR VANDENBERG called the Moscow agreement "one more typical American giveaway." Truman was angry because Byrnes had failed to achieve any discussion of the Soviet occupation of the Iranian province of AZERBAIJAN and had failed to keep him informed of the conference's progress. He accused Byrnes of "losing his nerve" at Moscow. The congressional and presidential reactions led Byrnes to take a tougher anti-Soviet line in subsequent negotiations.

Moscow Foreign Ministers' Conference (1947)   The Moscow Foreign Ministers' Conference of March 10 to April 24, 1947, further underscored what U.S. secretary of state GEORGE MARSHALL termed "the critical difficulties" of the postwar world. It was the first major East–West meeting after the announcement of the TRUMAN DOCTRINE.

The meeting was called primarily to discuss the differences in the administration of the four zones of occupied Germany and to settle the issue of German war reparations. Those attending were U.S. secretary of state Marshall, British foreign secretary ERNEST BEVIN, French foreign minister GEORGES BIDAULT and Soviet foreign minister V.M. MOLOTOV. Agreements were reached on the following:

1. The liquidation of Prussia as a German state.
2. The complete demilitarization and denazification of Germany.
3. An exchange of notes on China between Marshall and Molotov.
4. Revival of the Joint Commission on Korea.

The area of disagreements were, however, more widespread and more basic. They centered on the Soviet demand for German war reparations, four-power control of the industrial Ruhr area of Germany, the structure of a unified German government, a French plan for the economic incorporation of the German Saarland into France, the German–Polish border and German economic and political unity.

Molotov started the conference by repeating Soviet demands for $20 billion in German war reparations, half to go to the Soviet Union. He also demanded the annulment of the merger of the U.S. and British zones (BIZONAL AGREEMENT), four-power control of the Ruhr and a 45% increase in German industrial output to meet reparation payments. Marshall denied that the creation of Bizonia had been a breach of the POTSDAM Agreement, as claimed by Molotov, and argued that Germany must be made self-sufficient before reparations were skimmed from production. He went on to present an American plan for Germany, which included a unified economy and new currency.

Bevin suggested proposals for the new government of a unified Germany. He proposed immediate guarantees of basic rights, including freedom of movement and freedom from arbitrary arrest and imprisonment; a central government of limited powers, with the states (*Lander*) retaining all others; and a German president with a two-chamber legislature—one representing the federal structure and the other the states. Marshall went on to propose a three-step program toward the creation of a government. The first step was to be the creation of a provisional German government composed of heads of the *Lander*; the second, the drafting of a constitution; and the third, free elections.

Molotov proposed a strong central German government based on the pre-Hitler Weimar mode; a two-chamber parliament with the president elected by it; a national constitution drawn up by the parliament; guarantees of basic rights drawn up by the states; and constitutional guarantees on financial and other commitments to the Allies.

On April 9, Molotov claimed that the Potsdam Agreement had set Germany's Eastern border "irrevocably" on the ODER-NEISSE LINE. Marshall and Bevin said the Oder-Neisse line was provisional and that the "final delimitation" should await the final German Peace Treaty. Marshall went on to propose a "revision of the Polish frontier" with some of the Polish-occupied land being returned to Germany "in the interests of peace and the Central European economy." When Molotov rejected this, Bevin and Marshall proposed an international commission to investigate the issue. This was also rejected by Molotov.

Despite these basic disagreements, the foreign ministers agreed to meet again. Marshall blamed failure to reach agreement over Germany and Austria on Russian demands that would have "mortgaged" both countries to the Soviet Union. Bevin, in an assessment of the conference delivered to the British House of Commons, said, "I ask the British people to have patience. In framing the peace, we are not working for a day, but for generations to come."

For Further Information:
Davis, Lynn Etheridge. *The Cold War Begins: Soviet-American Conflict over Eastern Europe.* Princeton, 1974.
Donnelly, Desmond. *Struggle for the World.* New York, 1965.
Fleming, D.F. *The Cold War and Its Origins, 1917–1960.* Garden City, N.Y., 1961.
Gaddis, J.L. *The United States and the Origins of the Cold War, 1941–1947.* New York, 1972.
Rose, Lisle A. *After Yalta: America and the Origins of the Cold War.* New York, 1973.

Mozambique   The former Portuguese colony of Mozambique became a locus of the East-West power struggle during the late 1970s after the Marxist Frelimo party won independence from Portugal.

Mozambique became a Portuguese colony in the 15th century. Nationalist opposition groups began to form in the early 1960s, and in 1962 the Mozambique Liberation Front (Frelimo) was formed. It launched its military campaign against Portuguese rule in 1964. This continued until after the revolution in Portugal in April 1974 led to negotiations for Mozambican independence. Mozambique became fully independent on June 25, 1975, and the leader of Frelimo, Samora Machel, became Mozambique's first president.

At the time of independence, southern Africa was undergoing major political upheaval, with most of the attention focused on the neighboring, white-ruled British colony of Rhodesia (later Zimbabwe). Under Portuguese rule, the Mozambican authorities had been allied to the Rhodesian government of Ian Smith, which had unilaterally declared its independence from Britain to avoid black majority rule. The unilateral declaration of independence had led the British to secure an international embargo on trade with Rhodesia. This was honored by almost all of the international community except for South Africa and Mozambique.

After independence, the Frelimo government not only joined the embargo but gave sanctuary to the guerrilla forces of Robert Mugabe, which were fighting against the Smith regime. This led to a number of Rhodesian attacks on guerrilla bases in Mozambique and Rhodesian support for a right-wing anti-Frelimo guerrilla army known as the National Resistance Movement (Renamo).

The Frelimo government turned to the Soviet Bloc countries for military and economic aid. The new constitution described the communist countries as Mozambique's "natural allies," and in 1977 the Frelimo government signed a Treaty of Friendship and Cooperation with the Soviet Union. Moscow, for its part, was keen to become involved in Mozambique in order to influence better the black revolutionary movements both in Rhodesia and in the larger and strategically more important South Africa.

Both the South Africans and the Smith regime in Rhodesia were anxious to exploit the Soviet Bloc's presence in Mozambique (and in Angola on the western side of southern Africa) to stigmatize the black revolutionaries as communists and thus win American support. The argument was well received by American conservatives and right-wingers such as Jesse Helms, but the administration of JIMMY CARTER was more inclined to view the struggle in southern Africa as a battle for democratic and human rights rather than in East–West Cold War terms. Mozambique thus never became a major focal point of the Cold War. By the time Rhodesia gained its independence under majority rule in 1980, the Frelimo government had become disillusioned with the Soviets and turned increasingly toward Britain, the United States and Zimbabwe.

The problem of the Renamo guerrillas did not disappear with white-ruled Rhodesia. The South African government merely replaced it as Renamo's main supporter. The relationship between South Africa and Mozambique was complex and difficult. Each country despised the other's political system, but at the same time Mozambique's economy was almost entirely dependent on trade and communications with South Africa. South African goodwill was thus essential for the economic future of Mozambique and the government's political stability. The situation was further complicated by the fact that Renamo guerrillas directed most of their attacks on economic targets such as oil pipelines, power lines and road and rail links. And during the early 1980s South Africa crossed into Mozambique to attack ANC (African National Congress) bases in that country.

The Frelimo government thus desperately needed peace with South Africa, and in March 1984, South Africa and Mozambique signed a nonaggression pact known as the Nkomati Accord. Under this agreement, each government undertook to prevent opposition forces in its territory from launching attacks against the other. No specific forces were mentioned, but it was implied that South Africa would stop its support for Renamo and Mozambique would prevent the ANC from using its territory for attacks on South Africa.

Almost immediately after the signing of the Nkomati Accord, Mozambique police made a number of raids on the houses of ANC officers and forced ANC members into controlled refugee camps. South African support for Renamo, however, was increased, although the South African government publicly denied that it was extending aid to the right-wing guerrillas. By 1990, the security situation within Mozambique had deteriorated to such an extent that the Frelimo government was being forced to seek talks with the Renamo forces.

After two years of bloody skirmishes and occasional large-scale fighting, a truce was signed on August 7, 1992. A formal peace was made by treaty on October 4, 1992, requiring both the government and the Renamo forces to disband and surrender their arms to a United Nations peacekeeping force. In December, the UN Security Council voted unanimously to send such a force and eventually deployed 7,500 soldiers and civilian administrators.

For Further Information:
Serapiao, Luis B., and Mohamed El-Khawas. *Mozambique in the Twentieth Century.* Washington, D.C., 1979.

Multiple Independently-Targeted Reentry Vehicles (MIRVS)

A MIRV missile carries a number of warheads, which are released at the height of the missile's trajectory. Each warhead is programmed to hit a separate target.

MIRVing missiles substantially increases the destructive capability of a country's nuclear arsenal. It also increases the possibility of the nuclear warheads piercing the enemy's anti-ballistic missile (ABM) defenses by decreasing the response time available to the defenders and increasing the number of warheads to be stopped.

MIRVed missiles were major obstacles facing U.S. and Soviet disarmament negotiators because of the associated problem of verification. Any disarmament agreement is worthless unless each side can assure itself that the other is complying with the rules. Both the United States and the Soviet Union, especially the Soviet Union, opposed on-site verification because of fears of espionage. The other principal means of verification is by satellite or reconnaissance plane, but these can count only the number of launching pads or missiles. They cannot count how many warheads each missile carries, how many are dummies or how many are conventional or nuclear.

Multiple Reentry Vehicles (MRVs)

MRV missiles carry a number of warheads that are released at the height of the missile's trajectory. Each warhead then free-falls toward the target area. MRVs differ from MULTIPLE INDEPENDENTLY-TARGETED REENTRY VEHICLES (MIRVs) in that the latter are more advanced, with each warhead separately programmable to hit an individual target.

Arming missiles with MRVs or MIRVs substantially increases the destructive capability of a country's nuclear arsenal and increases the possibility of the nuclear warheads piercing the enemy's antiballistic missile (ABM) defenses.

Mundt–Nixon Bill

The Mundt–Nixon Bill was an early product of the anti-communist frenzy that shaped American politics in the late 1940s and 1950s. It also helped to establish the anti-communist credentials of its cosponsor, Representative RICHARD NIXON (R-Calif.).

The main force behind the bill, however, was conservative Republican Representative Karl Mundt (S.D.). In April 1947, Mundt was a prominent member of the HOUSE UN-AMERICAN ACTIVITIES COMMITTEE, where he called for compulsory registration of American communists and for the denial of federal labor law protection to communist-led trade unions. The following year he cosponsored the Mundt–Nixon Bill. The main provisions of the bill were:

1. The Communist Party would have been required to register the names of all its officers and members with the U.S. Justice Department.
2. Communist "front" organizations would have been required to register the names of all of their officers with the Justice Department and maintain a list of members for the department to inspect.
3. Members of the Communist Party would have been barred from federal employment.
4. Members of the Communist Party would have had their passports confiscated.

The bill passed the House of Representatives but was stopped in the Senate Judiciary Committee. However, most of the bill's provisions were later incorporated into the INTERNAL SECURITY ACT of 1950.

For Further Information:
Feuerlich, Roberta. *Joe McCarthy and McCarthyism: The Hate That Haunts America.* New York, 1972.
Goldston, Robert. *The American Nightmare: Senator Joseph R. McCarthy and the Politics of Hate.* Indianapolis, 1973.

Munich Conference (1947)

The Munich Conference of June 6–7, 1947, was the first and only meeting of political leaders from the Soviet- and Western-occupied sectors of Germany. Its failure was a major factor in preventing the early reunification of Germany.

The meeting was called by Hans Erhard, prime minister of Bavaria. He invited the heads of all the other German *Lander* (states) to a joint conference to discuss eventual economic and political reunification. The prime ministers of the five states in the Eastern Zone attended but refused to agree even on an agenda, and the meeting collapsed when the delegates from the Soviet zone walked out.

Murrow, Edward R.   (April 25, 1908–April 27, 1965)

Edward R. Murrow was a major broadcast journalist whose liberal views, combined with his unassailable credibility, served to undermine the far right during the TRUMAN and EISENHOWER administrations. In 1960 he was recruited by President JOHN F. KENNEDY to serve as director of the United States Information Agency.

Murrow graduated from Washington State College in 1930 and spent the next five years traveling in Europe. In 1935 he joined the Columbia Broadcasting System and at the start of World War II was assigned to Britain as London correspondent of CBS. His "This Is London" radio broadcasts during the Blitz were important in securing American sympathy for the British cause.

In 1951, Murrow went into television as anchorman for the weekly current affairs program "See It Now." In October 1953, the program came to the defense of Lieutenant Milo Radulovich, who was threatened with dismissal from the air force because his father and sister had been anonymously accused of left-wing sympathies. As a result of the program, Radulovich was fully reinstated and the communist witch hunt, which had reached a fever pitch in some U.S. circles, suffered a blow.

In March 1954, Murrow, after avoiding the subject for several years, took on Senator JOSEPH MCCARTHY, the most visible of the anti-communist crusaders, in a special program devoted to the senator and his tactics. Murrow concluded the program with the declaration, "This is no time for men who oppose Senator McCarthy's methods to be silent." McCarthy demanded and received equal air time to respond to Murrow. His vitriolic attack on the respected newsman backfired and contributed to his eventual downfall, although it did not help Murrow with his employers.

In 1958 a group of liberal democrats tried to persuade Murrow to run for the U.S. Senate from New York. He turned down the offer because he felt he was more effective as a newsman. But soon afterward Murrow became disenchanted with television as CBS and other networks started replacing news, documentary and commentary programs with soap operas, quiz shows and other light entertainment. He was thus in a receptive mood when President Kennedy offered him the directorship of the United States Information Agency (USIA) in January 1961.

Murrow agreed to take the job on the condition that he also be made a member of the National Security Council, be fully informed of foreign policy initiatives and be given a free hand in transforming the agency from a right-wing propaganda organization to an honest news information service.

But Murrow's own credibility was undermined one month later when he tried to stop the British Broadcasting Corporation from showing a CBS documentary that he had helped to produce. The program, "Harvest of Shame," exposed the sordid living and working conditions of American migratory farm workers. When information about Murrow's intercession was leaked by the BBC, he was attacked by the American Civil Liberties Union and backed down, admitting that he had been "foolish." Despite this setback, Murrow did manage to improve dramatically the credibility of the USIA and its broadcast arms, Voice of America and Radio Free Europe. He was particularly influential in raising awareness of American policy in Third World countries.

Murrow also proved himself adept at Washington infighting and quickly became a well-known figure in the White House and on Capitol Hill. In a battle with the National Aeronautics and Space Administration (NASA) he managed to secure astronaut John Glenn's space capsule for an around-the-world tour. In September 1961 he persuaded Kennedy and Secretary of State DEAN RUSK against the resumption of atmospheric nuclear tests on the grounds that it would "destroy the advantages of the greatest propaganda gift we have had in a long time."

Cancer severely hampered Murrow's work after the summer of 1962, when he had a lung removed. This kept him out of the consultations during the CUBAN MISSILE CRISIS, although earlier in the administration he had expressed strong opposition to the BAY OF PIGS operation. He resigned shortly after the assassination of Kennedy in 1963 and died of cancer on April 27, 1965.

For Further Information:
Kendrick, Alexander. *Prime Time: The Life of Edward R. Murrow.* Boston, 1969.

Sorensen, Thomas C. *The Word War: The Story of American Propaganda.* New York, 1968.

Mutual Assured Destruction (MAD)   The theory, or policy, of mutual assured destruction refers to an effective nuclear standoff whereby each side deters attack by having the capacity to inflict unacceptable retaliatory damage on the other.

The idea was favored by U.S. defense secretary ROBERT MCNAMARA and the KENNEDY and JOHNSON administrations. It was an essential element in the BALANCE OF TERROR.

For Further Information:
Bobbitt, Philip. *Democracy and Deterrence: The History and Future of Nuclear Strategy.* Hampshire, England, 1988.
Bottome, Edgar M. *The Balance of Terror: Nuclear Weapons and the Illusions of Security, 1945–1985.* Boston, 1986.
Bruce-Briggs, B. *The Shield of Faith: A Chronicle of Strategic Defense from Zeppelins to Star Wars.* New York, 1988.
Clemens, Walter C. *The Superpowers and Arms Control: From Cold War to Interdependence.* Lexington, Ky., 1973.
Holst, T.T., and Schneider, W., eds. *Why ABM? Policy Issues in U.S. Defense Policy.* Elmsford, N.Y., 1976.
Kissinger, Henry. *Nuclear Weapons and Foreign Policy.* New York, 1969.
Lebovic, James H. *Deadly Dilemmas: Deterrence in U.S. Nuclear Strategy.* New York, 1990.
Lowe, George E. *The Age of Deterrence.* Boston, 1964.
Mayers, T. *Understanding Nuclear Weapons and Arms Control.* London, 1986.
Molander, Roger C., and Robbie Nichols. *Who Will Stop the Bomb? A Primer on Nuclear Proliferation.* New York, 1985.
Moulton, Harland B. *From Superiority to Parity: The United States and the Strategic Arms Race, 1961–1971.* Westport, Conn., 1972.
Newhouse, John. *War and Peace in the Nuclear Age.* New York, 1989.
Porro, Jeffrey, ed., with Paul Doty, Carl Kaysen, and Jack Ruina. *The Nuclear Age Reader.* New York, 1989.
Powaski, Ronald E. *March to Armageddon: The United States and the Nuclear Arms Race, 1939 to the Present.* New York, 1987.
Rhodes, Edward Joseph. *Power and MADness: The Logic of Nuclear Coercion.* New York, 1989.

MX Missile System   The MX missile system is a controversial American INTERCONTINENTAL BALLISTIC MISSILE (ICBM) system the development and deployment of which encountered strong opposition from the U.S. Congress, environmentalists, religious leaders and disarmament advocates.

The main element of the system is the 4-stage ICBM, armed with 10 MULTIPLE INDEPENDENTLY-TARGETED RE-ENTRY VEHICLE (MIRV) warheads. Each warhead is specially equipped to improve resistance to nuclear antiballistic missile (ABM) systems and has a sophisticated computer guidance system, which enables it to destroy hardened targets. Each missile has a range of 5,000 miles and each warhead has an explosive yield of 500 kilotons.

Development of the MX (acronym for Mobile Experimental) started during the CARTER administration and continued under the Reagan administration. The Pentagon had become worried that America's land-based strategic nuclear deterrent was under increasing pressure from the Soviet Union's own land-based systems and feared that the weapons could be knocked out in a Soviet first strike, leaving America without any land-based weapons to engage in a retaliatory strike.

Planners therefore devised the MX system. As first envisioned, 40 MX installations were to be built. Each would consist of five oval-shaped "race tracks" for a total of 4,600 underground shelters and 10,000 miles of roadway. Each "race track" would have one missile and 23 shelters. Such a deployment system would allow the MX missiles to be shuttled quickly from one shelter to another in a "shell game" meant to confuse a possible Soviet first strike.

Critics of MX focused on cost. Projections in October 1977 for 300 missiles and trenches was $35–40 billion. In May 1980, defense officials discarded the controversial "race track" basing plan in favor of the "straight track" deployment, which would shuttle the missiles along a linear track and save $2 billion.

But the MX had also encountered strong opposition from the states of Nevada and Utah where the missile base was scheduled to be built. When Ronald Reagan was campaigning for the presidency in 1980 his close friend Paul Laxalt, a U.S. senator from Nevada, persuaded Reagan to oppose the MX and to review the entire proposal upon election.

In May 1981 the Mormon Church came out against the MX on moral, sociological and environmental grounds. Environmentalists filed a suit against the MX on June 8, claiming that it violated environmental regulations. The suit also charged that the environmental violations produced by the proposed basing method would be "of such magnitude as to impose an unconstitutional form of military rule heretofore unprecedented in our legal system."

A report issued in June 1981 by the House Interior and Insular Affairs Committee's subcommittee on public lands and national parks also attacked the MX basing as providing "only an illusion of survivability." The report cited the vulnerability of the system until completely assembled and the possibility that the whole project could be rendered useless if future technology enabled the Soviet Union to locate the missiles.

On October 2, 1981, Reagan dropped the original MX plan. But he did not immediately suggest an alternative basing system. Instead he recommended that 100 MX missiles be built, 36 of them to be deployed in existing, fixed Titan missile silos beginning in 1986. In the meantime research would continue into the best method of deployment for the 64 remaining missiles.

Among the basing possibilities discussed were placing them aboard airplanes in continuous flight, basing them in deep underground silos (the Citadel plan) or placing them in bases protected by an antimissile defense system of some kind.

Reagan himself preferred the "dense pack" basing mode,

and it was formally proposed to Congress on August 17, 1982. This system would group 100 missiles in hardened silos on a site of 10 to 15 square miles surrounded by interceptor missiles. The rationale for keeping them in a fairly tight formation was that the first Soviet warheads, in destroying some of the MX missiles, would set off a sympathetic detonation that would in turn destroy the warheads flying right behind them. Enough missiles would then be left, according to Pentagon planners, to use in a retaliatory attack.

The initial cost for construction of a base for the missiles was $25 billion. In the 1990s the silos could be fortified with ABM missiles, several new bases could be constructed so that they could be shuttled, and the missiles could be built into the side of the mountains.

By this time there was increasing concern that the MX system would constitute a breach of the 1972 ABM Treaty and the provisions of the unratified SALT II Treaty. Concern mounted as the strain in U.S.–Soviet relations appeared to make it increasingly unlikely that the two governments would be able to renegotiate the SALT II Treaty or a feasible substitute. Congress tied funding for the MX system to progress on arms talks and cut off all funds until an acceptable basing plan had been selected.

In an attempt to break the deadlock, Reagan in January 1983 appointed retired Air Force General Brent Scowcroft to chair the Presidential Commission on Strategic Forces to study MX basing options. The Scowcroft Commission report was published on April 11 and called for the MX missile to be based in existing Minuteman silos in Wyoming and Nebraska. It recommended building and deployment of 100 MX missiles to replace 100 Minuteman III missiles. The estimated cost was $14.6 billion.

The MX missiles would be supplemented by an undetermined number of new, smaller ICBMs that could be launched either from existing silos or from special trucks near the missile bases. The panel estimated that the new missiles could be operational by 1993 at a cost of $5.3 billion. The plan was endorsed by Reagan on April 19 and was released on April 21.

The Scowcroft Plan was largely put into effect and deployment of the MX missiles went ahead in 1987.

For Further Information:
Mayers, T. *Understanding Nuclear Weapons and Arms Control*. London, 1986.

My Lai Massacre   The massacre of innocent Vietnamese civilians in the village of My Lai by American troops in March 1968 was a turning point in American public opinion about the VIETNAM WAR. It also undermined Americans' confidence in their military and their role in the world.

From the start of U.S. involvement in South Vietnam, the American public and forces in Vietnam were told that they were in Southeast Asia to protect Vietnamese civilians from the communists. The problem was that it was often impossible to differentiate the Viet Cong guerrillas from the civilians. They often lived in the same villages and were sheltered and protected by the villagers, and quite often women and children were Viet Cong. The frustrating problem of telling friend from foe led many American soldiers simply to regard all Vietnamese as the enemy.

On March 15, 1968, an American infantry company under the command of Captain Ernest Medina swept through the district of Son My on a search-and-destroy mission. A platoon under the command of Lieutenant William Calley was given responsibility for the hamlet of My Lai. His force marched into My Lai and killed 102 innocent South Vietnamese civilians. At Calley's subsequent trial, witnesses charged that he and one of his platoon sergeants, Paul Meadlo, had fired on a group of "unarmed, unresisting men, women and children" who had been ordered to sit down on a trail. Some who "tried to run and didn't make it, were shot down in cold blood." A larger group of civilians, numbering more than 70, had been shoved into an irrigation ditch, and Calley had "ordered them executed and they were." A child observed running away from the ditch had been caught and picked up by Calley, who "threw it back into the irrigation ditch and shot and killed it."

The incident was reported by American helicopter pilots who witnessed the massacre from the air. Their report was investigated by Colonel Oran K. Henderson and General Samuel Koster, who took no action. This led to accusations of an army coverup.

News of the incident spread, and Calley and Staff Sergeant David Mitchell were charged with murder in November 1969. The North Vietnamese extracted the maximum favorable publicity out of the My Lai Incident. Immediately afterward, the Viet Cong's Provisional Revolutionary Government charged that My Lai was only one of "thousands and thousands of crimes perpetrated by the United States in Vietnam." This seemed to be confirmed by the scores of American soldiers who came forward after the initial My Lai charges to admit that they had participated in or witnessed other atroci-

ties by American forces in South Vietnam. Some of these atrocities were even worse than the incident at My Lai, but because of the publicity surrounding this episode it became synonymous with American war crimes in Vietnam.

At his court-martial, Calley claimed that he had been ordered by his commanding officer, Captain Medina, to kill every living being in My Lai because "they were all enemy." This was denied by Medina, who did, however, admit to covering up the atrocity. Medina was also court-martialed for mass murder but was found not guilty and given an honorable discharge.

Calley was found guilty of mass murder in March 1971 and was sentenced to life imprisonment, dismissal from the army and forfeiture of pay and allowances. The severity of the sentence raised a storm of protest from those members of the public who believed that Calley had become a scapegoat for higher-ranking officers and the collective American conscience. But the general feeling of the country was expressed by the prosecutor in the Calley trial, Captain Aubrey M. Daniel, who said Calley had "prostituted all the humanitarian principles for which this country stands. The accused failed in his duty to his troops, to his country, to mankind." Calley's sentence was later reduced to 10 years and Calley was paroled in 1974. No other participant was ever convicted of a crime.

For Further Information:
Bilton, Michael, and Kevin Sim. *Four Hours in My Lai.* New York, 1992.
Everett, Arthur, Kathryn Johnson, and Harry F. Rosenthal. *Calley.* New York, 1971.
Hersh, Seymour M. *Cover-up: The Army's Secret Investigation of the Massacre at My Lai 4.* New York, 1972.
———. *My Lai 4.* New York, 1970.
Peers, William R. *The My Lai Inquiry.* New York, 1979.
Sack, John. *Lieutenant Calley: His Own Story.* New York, 1971.
Smith, R.B. *An International History of the Vietnam War.* New York, 1986.
Stanton, S.L. *The Rise and Fall of an American Army.* Novato, Calif., 1988.

N

Nagy, Imre (June 7, 1896–June 16, 1958) Imre Nagy was a populist Hungarian communist who was thrust into the leadership of the 1956 Hungarian Revolution. His subsequent attempt to take HUNGARY out of the WARSAW PACT led to the Soviet invasion of Hungary and to Nagy's trial and execution.

Nagy was born into a Hungarian peasant family and was apprenticed to a locksmith before being drafted to fight with the Austrian Army in World War I. He was captured by the Czarist Russian Army and, while a prisoner, joined the Communist Party. After the Bolshevik Revolution he joined the Soviet Red Army. When the Hungarian communist Bela Kun came to power on March 21, 1919, Nagy was given a minor government post.

Kun's "Red Terror" was one of the most oppressive governments in modern European history. It lasted only five months before Kun and his supporters, including Nagy, fled to the Soviet Union. In Moscow, Nagy was given a post teaching economics at the Institute for Agrarian Sciences. During World War II he was placed in charge of broadcasting Soviet propaganda to Hungary.

Nagy returned to Hungary with the Red Army in 1944 and between 1944 and 1948 held the posts of minister of agriculture, minister of the interior, speaker of the parliament and deputy premier. At first Nagy was a member of the wing of the party that stressed its strong links with Moscow, but later he leaned toward the nationalist wing, which stressed Hungarian independence from the Soviet Union. He was also an advocate of increased agricultural production and support for small peasant farmers. These positions brought him into conflict with the Stalinist communist leader MATYAS RAKOSI, who was pushing through a rapid industrialization program, collectivizing the farms and strengthening links with the Soviet Union. In 1949 Nagy was expelled from the party.

After publicly recanting, Nagy was readmitted to party ranks. As a result of strong pressure from the farming community, he was appointed deputy premier on November 15, 1952. Following the death of Soviet leader JOSEF STALIN on March 5, 1953, the Hungarian communists turned against Rakosi, and on July 3, 1953, Nagy was named premier. Nagy immediately set about to de-Stalinize Hungary.

His reforms made Nagy immensely popular within Hungary and effectively lifted him to the status of national hero. But the Red Army's continued occupation of the country meant that the Soviet Union maintained the power of veto over Nagy's reforms. Between 1953 and 1955 it allowed Nagy to retain power while the Soviet premier GEORGI MALENKOV experimented with his own economic reforms. Malenkov, however, fell from power in February 1955, and the Soviet Union lurched back toward Stalinism. On April 14, 1955, Nagy was again expelled from the party and government because he "represented ideas that were detrimental to the interest of Hungary."

Rakosi was reinstated as premier, and Nagy went into the political wilderness until the Hungarian Revolution suddenly erupted on October 20, 1956, when students took to the streets to demand free elections, the withdrawal of Soviet troops from Hungary and the reinstatement of Nagy. That evening a huge crowd carrying torches gathered outside Nagy's home and escorted him to the parliament building, where they demanded his return to power. Eighty Soviet tanks entered Budapest, but they were beaten back by the Hungarians. The Communist Party had little choice but to reinstate Nagy in the Politburo and as premier on October 24, 1956. Soviet tanks started to withdraw on October 29, and on October 31 Nagy promptly abolished the one-party political system and promised to raise living standards.

Nagy later told a West German reporter that he believed the Soviet Union might have been prepared to accept these reforms, but Nagy made a mistake in announcing that Hungary was leaving the Warsaw Pact and demanded talks with the Soviet Union to organize the withdrawal of the Red Army from Hungary. The Soviets agreed to the negotiations, which started three days later. But their agreement had been a ruse, and they had moved 4,000 tanks and 200,000 troops into the northeast corner of Hungary for an attack on Budapest. When the Hungarian delegation arrived for negotiations they were arrested.

Nagy was at home when he heard that Soviet tanks were entering Budapest. He managed to reach the Budapest Radio Station, where he broadcast an emotional appeal for help. He then fled to sanctuary in the Yugoslav Embassy. His government collapsed, and the Soviets installed Janos Kadar in his place.

Nagy spent three months in the Yugoslav Embassy before Kadar agreed to allow him safe conduct to Yugoslavia. A bus was sent to collect him and some of his colleagues who had joined him in the embassy. As the bus pulled away, however, a group of Soviet KGB officers jumped aboard and ordered it driven to the Soviet military compound. From there Nagy and his colleagues were flown to Romania and imprisoned. Kadar at first claimed that Nagy had asked to go to Romania but later conceded that he had been "exiled." He denounced Nagy for having permitted the killing of "scores of Communists" during the "murderous counterrevolution."

Exactly what happened to Nagy next is not clear. It is known that he was charged with treason and placed on trial. The trial, however, was conducted in secret and its occurrence was not announced until after Nagy had been executed on June 16, 1958. His body was secretly buried in an unmarked grave in Budapest.

Official Hungarian history books denounced Nagy as a counterrevolutionary, but among the Hungarian people he was elevated to the status of martyr. Opponents of the regime used the memory of Nagy and his fate to keep alive opposition to the Communist Party. Kadar tried to win public support with political and economic reforms, but he refused to countenance the ultimate symbolic reform: the rehabilitation of Nagy.

However, as communist rule began to crumble in Eastern Europe in 1989, Kadar was forced to accept that Nagy's trial had been "judicially unlawful." On June 16, 1989, Nagy's body was exhumed from its unmarked grave and reburied with an accompanying memorial service organized by the opposition with the full support of the government. More than 250,000 people attended the nine-hour service. The following month, Kadar died and on the same day, Nagy was officially rehabilitated by the Communist Party.

For Further Information:

Brzezinski, Zbigniew K. *The Soviet Bloc: Unity and Conflict.* Cambridge, Mass., 1960.

Kovrig, Bennet. *Communism in Hungary from Kun to Kadar.* Stanford, Calif., 1979.

Vali, Ferenc. *A Rift and Revolt in Hungary; Nationalism vs. Communism.* Cambridge, Mass., 1961.

Zinner, Paul. *Revolution in Hungary.* New York, 1962.

Nassau Agreement   The Nassau Agreement of December 1962 between the United States and Britain resolved a crisis in the Anglo-American relationship over the American cancellation of the Skybolt missile project and provided Britain with American POLARIS MISSILES.

Between 1955 and 1960, Britain concentrated on the development of its own intercontinental ballistic missile, codenamed BLUE STREAK, but after spending $182 million on research, cancelled the program because of the $1.7 billion additional money needed to complete its development. Instead, the British government turned to the United States to provide it with the missile technology required for its nuclear deterrent. At a meeting at Camp David, Maryland in 1960 between President DWIGHT EISENHOWER and Prime Minister HAROLD MACMILLAN, the United States agreed to provide Brit-

ain with Skybolt missiles, then under development by the U.S. Air Force. Britain would provide the nuclear warheads for the missiles and would have to pay only for the missiles it actually acquired. All research and development costs would be borne by the United States. In addition, Britain agreed to provide facilities for American Polaris submarines at Holy Loch in Scotland.

Polaris missiles were suggested at that stage as an alternative to Skybolt, but Britain preferred Skybolt because it allowed them to extend the life of their Vulcan bombers, which then represented the mainstay of their nuclear deterrent. To use Polaris missiles, the Royal Navy would have had to switch its spending emphasis from aircraft carriers to submarines.

The American provision of Skybolt missiles became a major political issue in Britain and one in which the Conservative government of Macmillan invested considerable political capital. In November 1962 the Kennedy administration decided after a fifth test failure that the project was too expensive and unilaterally canceled it. In Britain, Conservative members of Parliament were furious with the United States and demanded that the government pursue the uneconomic course of developing its own system. The Labour Party demanded the closure of the Holy Loch base in retaliation for the cancellation of Skybolt.

The American axing of the Skybolt project and the resultant political furor in London threatened to undermine the "special relationship" at a time when it was already under a strain from Kennedy's failure to keep Macmillan fully informed during the CUBAN MISSILE CRISIS. Macmillan and Kennedy had arranged a meeting in Nassau, the Bahamas, for December 1962, and it quickly became apparent that the future of the British nuclear deterrent and its effect on Anglo-American relations would dominate the summit. The British entered the meeting angry and suspicious of the Kennedy administration, and British defense secretary Peter Thorneycroft was prepared, if necessary, to walk out.

The provision of Polaris was the obvious solution to the crisis, but this solution was complicated by the position of French president CHARLES DE GAULLE. The French leader was already wary of the Anglo-American relationship and feared that Britain would act as an American "trojan horse" should it be admitted to the EUROPEAN ECONOMIC COMMUNITY. Skybolt would have allowed Britain a greater degree of independence from the United States than Polaris, and de Gaulle was opposed to a British nuclear deterrent dependent on the United States for fear that this would increase American influence over British foreign policy.

At Nassau, Macmillan played down the fears surrounding the possible impact of Polaris on Britain's application to join the EEC. He argued that the main obstacle to British membership was differences over agricultural policy and that France and the rest of Europe would understand a British decision to buy Polaris.

Kennedy was committed to a proposed NATO-wide Polaris-based Multilateral Nuclear Force, and it was unclear how this would fit in with Britain's independent nuclear deterrent. This problem was resolved by a British commitment to merge its Polaris force with the proposed NATO force. British independence, however, was assured by a clause that allowed the British Polaris-equipped submarines to be transferred to exclusive British control when the British government decided national interests were at stake.

The basic terms of the Nassau Agreement were:

1. The United States would provide Britain with an unspecified number of Polaris missiles in place of Skybolt missiles.
2. The Polaris missiles would arm British-built nuclear submarines and would be equipped with British nuclear warheads.
3. The naval force would replace the Royal Air Force's Vulcan bombers as Britain's major nuclear deterrent.
4. The new British nuclear deterrent would become part of a NATO nuclear force subject to NATO command in all circumstances "except where Her Majesty's Government may decide that supreme national interests are at stake."
5. The British contribution to a new unified NATO nuclear force would be matched by "at least equal United States forces" to be similarly assigned to the unified force and made subject to NATO command and control.

As feared by the Europeanists, the agreement was used by de Gaulle as part of his reason for later blocking British entry into the Common Market. The Multilateral Nuclear Force pressed for by Kennedy never came into being because of British and French determination to keep their nuclear deterrents as independent as possible.

For Further Information:
Freedman, L. *Britain and Nuclear Weapons.* London, 1980.
Kissinger, Henry. *Nuclear Weapons and Foreign Policy.* New York, 1969.
Macmillan, Harold. *At the End of the Day, 1961–1963.* New York, 1973.

Nassar, Gamal Abdel (January 15, 1918–September 28, 1970)

Gamal Abdel Nasser was for nearly 20 years the personification of pan-Arab nationalism, and his close relationship with the Soviet Union provided the Soviets with a role in the strategic Middle East.

Nasser's father was a minor civil servant in British-ruled Egypt. From an early age, Nasser participated in anti-British demonstrations, and his antipathy for Britain was to be a major guiding force in his later life.

Nasser enrolled in the Egyptian Royal Military Academy in 1935 and upon graduation entered the Egyptian Army as a second lieutenant. Shortly afterward he and ANWAR SADAT formed a secret anti-British and antimonarchist revolutionary organization called the Free Officers. On July 23, 1952, the Free Officers overthrew King Farouk and established a Revolutionary Command Council under the titular leadership of General Mohammad Naguib, but in reality secretly controlled by Nasser. Two years later Nasser emerged from the shadows to oust Naguib and name himself prime minister.

The United States at first supported Nasser and together with Britain offered to provide finance for the building of the ASWAN HIGH DAM. But Nasser also wanted to purchase American arms to use against Israel. When Secretary of State JOHN FOSTER DULLES refused, Nasser started negotiations with the Soviet Union. Dulles viewed the arms deal as a dangerous drift to the left and in July 1956 cut off American aid for the Aswan project. The Soviet Union immediately offered to replace the American financing.

Nasser also used the cutoff of American and British aid as the occasion to end British control of the Suez Canal. Claiming that Egypt needed the revenues generated by use of the canal to pay for the dam, he nationalized the waterway. This resulted in the SUEZ CRISIS, which effectively ended British dominance in the Middle East and increased the regional authority of Nasser and, by association, the Soviet Union.

After the Suez War, Nasser projected himself as the leader of all Arabs. In his book *Philosophy of the Revolution* he wrote of his dream to lead the 55,000,000-strong Arab nation. To this end he supported anti-British nationalists throughout the Middle East and in 1958 formed the United Arab Republic with Syria, but the political merger fell apart three years later.

In the 1960s, opposition grew within Egypt to Nasser's rule, and he had to turn Egypt into a police state to hold onto power. The humiliating defeat in the 1967 Arab–Israeli Six-Day War further undermined his position within Egypt and in the wider Arab world.

In foreign affairs, Nasser became an active member of the nonaligned group of nations. To Western policy makers it appeared that his nonaligned status had a distinct pro-Soviet bent. Nasser was a regular visitor to Moscow; his defense forces were supplied by the Soviet Union; there were thousands of Soviet military advisers and technicians in Egypt; and the Soviet Union poured millions of dollars of aid into the country. But in reality, Nasser was first and foremost an Arab nationalist, and when the Soviet Union tried to pressure him into toeing Moscow's foreign policy line, he started to repair relations with the United States. He was on the verge of a major break with the Soviet Union when he died of a heart attack on September 28, 1970. It was left to his successor, Anwar Sadat, to expel the Soviets from Egypt and establish an alliance with the United States.

For Further Information:
DuBois, Shirley Graham. *Gamal Abdel Nasser, Son of the Nile; A Biography.* New York, 1972.
Eden, Anthony. *The Suez Crisis of 1956.* Boston, 1966.
Lacouture, Jean. *Nasser, A Biography.* New York, 1973.
Mikdadi, F.H. *Gamal Abdel Nasser.* New York, 1991.
Nutting, Anthony. *Nasser.* London, 1972.
Quandt, William B. *Decade of Decisions: American Policy Toward the Arab-Israeli Conflict, 1967–1976.* Berkeley, Calif., 1977.
Stephens, Robert. *Nasser: A Political Biography.* London, 1971.

National Foreign Intelligence Board (NFIB)   The National Foreign Intelligence Board (NFIB) advises the director of the CENTRAL INTELLIGENCE AGENCY (CIA) and coordinates the work of the different American intelligence services. Its membership consists of the directors of the DEFENSE INTELLIGENCE AGENCY (DIA), the State Department's Bureau of Intelligence and Research and the NATIONAL SECURITY AGENCY (NSA).

The board was created in 1946 as the Central Intelligence group. After the creation of the CIA in 1947, the board became the Intelligence Advisory Committee and was given the task of supervising the work of the newly created CIA and its director. Successive CIA directors, however, resented the committee's powers and succeeded in gradually whittling down its authority until it became little more than a mechanism for coordinating the functions of the U.S. intelligence agencies.

In 1958 the Intelligence Advisory Committee was merged with the United States Communications Intelligence Board to form the United States Intelligence Board, and in 1977 the USIB became known as the National Foreign Intelligence Board.

For Further Information:
Cline, Ray S. *The CIA, Reality vs. Myth.* Washington, D.C., 1982.
Karalekas, Anne. *History of the Central Intelligence Agency.* Laguna Hills, Calif., 1977.

National Intelligence Estimate (NIE)   The National Intelligence Estimate (NIE) is America's ultimate intelligence report designed for use by the upper echelons of government. Information for the report is gathered from all the U.S. intelligence agencies and compiled under the direction of the CENTRAL INTELLIGENCE AGENCY.

Most NIEs deal with the intelligence community's assessment of another country's future foreign policy or defense position or its reaction to an American course of action. The CIA, for instance, regularly produced annual and biannual NIEs on the Soviet Union's future defense and economic capabilities. Special reports have been produced on such subjects as the Soviet reaction to the CUBAN MISSILE CRISIS, U.S. support for the Contras in NICARAGUA and the likely Soviet reaction to the rise of Solidarity in POLAND.

NIEs were first introduced by CIA director WALTER BEDELL SMITH soon after he took office in 1950. They were originally compiled by a Board of National Estimates, whose members were drawn from the different intelligence agencies. In 1973 the board was abolished and replaced by a group of national intelligence officers with specialized knowledge in specific subjects. These officers had access to information from all the agencies but reported directly to the director of the CIA.

NIEs have occasionally come under critical attack. The best known example was in 1974 when General GEORGE KEEGAN, head of Air Force Intelligence, questioned an NIE report that détente with the Soviet Union was working and that the Soviets were not trying to use improved relations to gain a military advantage or make inroads in the Third World. Keegan ordered his expanded staff to write a rebuttal of the NIE. The Keegan report discredited the NIE and undermined the position of the CIA and the NIEs.

For Further Information:
Breckinridge, Scott D. *The CIA and the U.S. Intelligence System.* Boulder, Colo., 1986.
O'Toole, G.J.A. *The Encyclopedia of American Intelligence and Espionage.* New York, 1988.
Ransom, Harry Howe. *The Intelligence Establishment.* Cambridge, Mass., 1970.

National Security Act of 1947   The National Security Act of September 18, 1947, officially established the CENTRAL INTELLIGENCE AGENCY and NATIONAL SECURITY COUNCIL and unified the American defense establishment.

During World War II, the United States established the OFFICE OF STRATEGIC SERVICES to gather and assess intelligence. But in the euphoria of peacetime, the OSS was disbanded by President HARRY S. TRUMAN, who returned to the prewar intelligence arrangement of separate intelligence agencies in the army, navy and air force and the State Department's Bureau of Intelligence and Research. He quickly found that he was presented with many, often conflicting, intelligence reports, and in January 1946 he established the Central Intelligence Group to coordinate the work of the various intelligence services.

But the wartime OSS officers, such as ALLEN DULLES and General William Donovan, argued that in order for the CIG to be effective it had be separate from the departments of defense and state and equipped with its own intelligence officers and budget. The result was the National Security Act, which was signed by Truman on July 26, 1947, and took effect on September 8, 1947. The act not only created the CIA but laid down the rules under which it would operate.

For Further Information:
Karalekas, Anne. *History of the Central Intelligence Agency.* Laguna Hills, Calif., 1977.
Prados, John. *Keepers of the Keys: A History of the National Security Council from Truman to Bush.* New York, 1991.

National Security Agency (NSA)   The National Security Agency is the United States's electronic intelligence gathering operation. It is the largest such organization in the world and the main source of information for American intelligence operations.

The NSA had its origins in World War I with the establishment of a cryptography and electronic surveillance department known as MI8. Between 1917 and 1919 MI8, also known as the Black Chamber, broke the Japanese diplomatic and military code and established a working relationship with the American cable companies. In 1930, MI8 was superseded by the Signal Intelligence Service (SIS), which, during the war years, was replaced by Communications Intelligence (COMINT).

COMINT's early success in developing electronic surveillance equipment and in breaking the Japanese codes encouraged British signals intelligence to approach the United States in 1940 with an offer to exchange its information on German intelligence (garnered through the British success in breaking the German Enigma code) in return for access to American equipment and Japanese communications. The offer resulted in close Anglo-American wartime cooperation and the 1947 UNITED KINGDOM–UNITED STATES (UKUSA) AGREEMENT, which divided the world into electronic surveillance spheres of influence and established the postwar working relationship among the United States, Britain, Australia, New Zealand and Canada.

The National Security Agency officially came into being on November 4, 1952, under the direction of Major General Ralph Julian Canine. By 1957, NSA had established its headquarters on a site at Fort Meade, Maryland, halfway between Baltimore and Washington, D.C., and by the early 1980s it employed 70,000 people and had the capability to intercept every form of communication. The NSA is also responsible for breaking foreign codes, developing new American codes and developing electronic surveillance equipment for use in the field by CIA and other agents.

The NSA is comprised of four operational organizations, five staff and support operations and one training unit.

For Further Information:
Bamford, James. *The Puzzle Palace.* New York, 1982.

National Security Council (NSC)   The National Security Council is the most powerful U.S. government group dealing with intelligence matters. It is responsible for coordinating information from the main intelligence agencies and preparing intelligence assessments. The NSC reports directly to the president.

The National Security Council was established in 1947 by the NATIONAL SECURITY ACT, which also created the CENTRAL INTELLIGENCE AGENCY (CIA). In 1948 the council established the Office of Policy Coordination to counter Soviet covert activities inside and outside the United States. The NSC does not have direct control over American espionage agents.

The council is composed of senior members of the armed forces, the State Department and the directors of the various intelligence agencies.

For Further Information:
Etzold, Thomas H., and John Lewis Gaddis, eds. *Containment: Documents on American Policy and Strategy, 1945–1950.* New York, 1978.
Gaddis, John Lewis. *Strategies of Containment: A Critical Appraisal of Postwar American National Security Policy.* New York, 1982.
Lord, Carnes. *The Presidency and the Management of National Security.* New York, 1988.
May, Ernest R., ed. *American Cold War Strategy: Interpreting NSC 68.* New York, 1993.
Prados, John. *Keepers of the Keys: A History of the National Security Council from Truman to Bush.* New York, 1991.

National Security Council Report 68 (NSC-68)   The National Security Council Report 68 was the first postwar comprehensive review of American security policy and helped to establish PAUL NITZE as a leading foreign policy adviser.

In January 1950, Secretary of State DEAN ACHESON asked Nitze, then head of the State Department's policy planning staff, to chair an interdepartmental review of security policy. Nitze was a well-known hawk within the TRUMAN administration, and he started his review from the premise that the ultimate goal of Soviet foreign policy was world domination and that only the United States had the economic strength necessary for a defense buildup to deter the Soviets.

His report predicted that by 1954 the Soviet Union would be capable of a nuclear attack on the United States, and that this capability would deter the United States from protecting other non-communist countries. In order to counter this, Nitze advised that the United States institute a two- to four-fold expansion of American arms spending to increase both conventional arms and nuclear arsenals. This increase, argued Nitze, would enable the NORTH ATLANTIC TREATY ORGANIZATION (NATO) to deter a full-scale conventional attack on Western Europe and would allow the United States to take the lead in thwarting Soviet expansion elsewhere in the world.

Nitze's report was initially rejected by President HARRY TRUMAN, who blocked its publication but began to implement the recommendations at the start of the KOREAN WAR. Defense cuts during the Eisenhower administration, however, caused the abandonment of the dual conventional and nuclear capability in favor of a greater reliance on the policy of massive nuclear retaliation.

For Further Information:
Etzold, Thomas H., and John Lewis Gaddis, eds. *Containment: Documents on American Policy and Strategy, 1945–1950.* New York, 1978.
Gaddis, John Lewis. *Strategies of Containment: A Critical Appraisal of Postwar American National Security Policy.* New York, 1982.
May, Ernest R., ed. *American Cold War Strategy: Interpreting NSC 68.* New York, 1993.

NATO   See NORTH ATLANTIC TREATY ORGANIZATION.

NATO Heads of Government Summit (1957)   At the NATO Heads of Government Summit in Paris on December 16–19, 1957, the United States and Britain persuaded West Europeans to base American intermediate-range ballistic missiles on their territory.

The Paris summit was the first meeting of NATO heads of government since the organization's formation in 1949. The idea for the summit emerged from a meeting in Washington, D.C. in October 1957 between President DWIGHT EISENHOWER and British prime minister HAROLD MACMILLAN.

The two men were worried that as the direct military threat from the Soviet Union receded, the NATO alliance would start to fall apart and become more susceptible to subversion and political persuasion. They felt one way to combat this threat would be to tie the United States more closely to the defense of Europe by basing American intermediate-range nuclear weapons on European soil. The final agreement on this policy would be made at a NATO heads-of-government summit, which would reaffirm the political and defense commitments of all the signatories of the North Atlantic Treaty.

The alliance members were not unanimous in their desire for American nuclear weapons on their soil. The Scandinavian countries, Norway and Denmark, led the opposition to the proposal and tried to force a postponement of a decision on the issue. The West Germans accepted the need for American nuclear weapons in Europe, but Defense Minister FRANZ JOSEPH STRAUSS, who attended on behalf of the ill Chancellor KONRAD ADENAUER, said that it would be "militarily unwise" to base the missiles in West German defense areas open to massive Soviet attack.

To avoid a heads-of-government-level clash over the issue of basing, the final communiqué left open the question of the sites for the weapons. The SUPREME ALLIED COMMANDER FOR EUROPE was instructed to consult with European governments to find the best sites "in conformity with NATO defense plans and in agreement with the states directly concerned." General LAURIS NORSTAD, Supreme NATO commander, said that the 1,500-mile range of the weapons meant that they could be placed anywhere within the European alliance. In the end, the weapons were based in Britain, Turkey and Italy.

NATO Industrial Advisory Group (NIAG)

The NATO Industrial Advisory Group (NIAG) was formed in June 1968 by the NATO alliance's Conference of National Armaments Directors to encourage the exchange of information on weapons development and procurement.

The formation of NIAG was partly an American response to European fears that the U.S. defense industries were dominating weapons development at the expense of European businesses. A second reason for its formation was the need to standardize weapons procurement so that, for instance, German bullets could be fired by British rifles. The issue of standardization remained a major problem as national defense industries tried to increase their competitiveness by stressing the uniqueness of their product.

NIAG's stated purpose was to provide a forum for the free exchange of views on the various industrial aspects of NATO armaments questions; to foster a deeper feeling of international involvement in research, development and production; to seek closer cooperation among the industries of member countries; and to encourage the timely and efficient exchange of information between member governments and their defense industries.

NATO Military Committee

The NATO Military Committee is the highest military authority in the NORTH ATLANTIC TREATY ORGANIZATION. It is composed of the chiefs of staff of each member state except France and Spain. The committee meets at least twice a year. Each member of the committee also appoints a permanent military representative to a permanent military committee, which is based at NATO headquarters in Brussels.

The Military Committee is responsible for developing NATO military policies. All the NATO operational commands—SUPREME ALLIED COMMANDER EUROPE, SUPREME ALLIED COMMANDER ATLANTIC, Commander-in-Chief Channel and the CANADA–UNITED STATES REGIONAL PLANNING GROUP—report to the Military Committee.

The Military Committee is also responsible for the Military Agency for Standardization based in Brussels, the Advisory Group for Aerospace Research and Development in Paris and the NATO Defense College in Rome.

The Military Committee was created at the first meeting of NATO foreign ministers on September 17, 1949. Its first formal meeting was held on October 6, 1949, in Washington, D.C. In 1966 France withdrew from the integrated military structure of the alliance. Since then France has been represented on the Military Committee by a military mission rather than its chief of staff. Iceland, the only member without any military forces, is represented on the committee by a civilian.

Netherlands, The

The Netherlands is one of the founding members of the NORTH ATLANTIC TREATY ORGANIZATION, the WESTERN EUROPEAN UNION and the EUROPEAN ECONOMIC COMMUNITY. As a medium-size European country, it makes a valuable contribution to the Western Alliance. The Dutch port of Rotterdam, the largest port in Europe, would be vital to the supply of military forces to Europe if there were a conflict.

Before World War II, the foreign policy of the Netherlands was one of strict neutrality. During the war, the government-in-exile in London took some initial steps to establish greater cooperation among small and medium-size European countries as a bulwark against great-power aggression. In 1944 the Dutch government agreed with the governments of Belgium and Luxembourg to the formation of the Benelux Economic Union, which has become one of the most effective political and economic regional pacts of the postwar period and was a forerunner to the larger European Economic Community. The union became operational in 1948, but it was not until 1958 that the Treaty of the Benelux Economic Union was signed.

The war left the Netherlands' economic and social fabric in tatters. In the final years of the war, the country suffered severe food shortages and was on the verge of famine as millions were reduced to eating tulip bulbs during the harsh winter of 1945.

The country was in need of immediate economic aid, and this was extended by the U.S. government, which in 1946 gave more than $200 million in soft loans through the Export-Import Bank. The Dutch government gave an enthusiastic and early welcome to the MARSHALL PLAN.

On March 17, 1948, the Dutch government joined the governments of Britain, France, Luxembourg and Belgium in signing the BRUSSELS TREATY, which pledged the five countries to build a common defense system and established the Western European Union. The Brussels Treaty was a key forerunner to the North Atlantic Treaty of April 4, 1949, which established the North Atlantic Treaty Organization (NATO); again the Netherlands was a founding member. The Netherlands was also an enthusiastic supporter of the EUROPEAN DEFENSE COMMUNITY (EDC).

During the KOREAN WAR, some 1,000 Dutch soldiers fought with the United Nations forces. But the Netherlands was also one of the first countries to recognize the People's Republic of China and took a leading role in developing trade relations with the Soviet Union and East European countries.

In the aftermath of the collapse of the EDC, the Netherlands accepted the EDEN PLAN for the strengthening of British and American commitments to the defense of Western Europe and allowed a U.S. fighter-plan squadron to be based at the Soesterberg airbase. In 1989 2,800 American servicemen were based in Holland. The Dutch Army also helped with the forward defense of the alliance by deploying 5,700 troops in the British sector of West Germany. The Dutch Navy is deployed mainly in the North Sea and English Channel, although it also has commitments in the Caribbean. At the NATO HEADS OF GOVERNMENT SUMMIT in December 1957 it was agreed that the Netherlands would be a site for American INTERMEDIATE-RANGE BALLISTIC MISSILES.

In January 1961, the Soviet government said that the Netherlands "was the first government in the European continent to agree to the actual turning of its country into an American nuclear base." This decision, it said, was "fraught with grave consequences . . . for the existence of the Netherlands."

During the VIETNAM WAR, the Dutch government faced strong student opposition to support to American policy in Southeast Asia. The student opposition manifested itself most dramatically in October 1967 when about 13,000 people demonstrated outside the American consulate in Amsterdam. On January 15, 1973, the consulate was briefly occupied by Dutch antiwar demonstrators.

The Vietnam War was a turning point for Dutch–American relations. Running through Dutch politics is a strong puritanical and Christian flavor. Prior to the conflict in Southeast Asia, the Dutch public had seen the United States entirely in the role of benefactor, protector against Soviet aggression and upholder of sound Christian and Western values. The war caused Dutch public opinion to regard the United States instead as a nation that had been corrupted by its status as a superpower.

This shift had a major impact on Dutch-American relations and NATO after the alliance decision in December 1979 to base cruise and PERSHING II MISSILES in a number of West European countries, including 48 Pershing II missiles in the Netherlands. The center-right coalition government of Andries Van Agt at first agreed to the proposal, but he faced strong opposition from the antinuclear lobby, Christian parties and the left wing of the Dutch political spectrum.

Disagreements over the American missiles contributed to the eventual collapse of the Van Agt government. In November 1982 another center-right government was formed under Ruud Lubbers. By this time, public opposition to the missile deployment was so strong that Lubbers, who supported deployment, did not dare put the issue to a vote. Instead he delayed a final decision on the issue by suggesting a number of compromise proposals. These included accepting the missiles in installments to allow more time for U.S.–Soviet negotiations, exchanging the deployment of the Pershings for performing other NATO tasks, starting construction on the missile bunkers without accepting the missiles themselves and reducing the total number of missiles to be based on Dutch soil.

Growing opposition within the Netherlands began to have a ripple effect elsewhere in Western Europe where intermediate-range missiles were scheduled for deployment, and antinuclear movements in those countries increased in influence. The Netherlands became a test case for deployment throughout Europe. If the missiles could be successfully deployed in Holland, then the policy could be safely applied elsewhere on the Continent. If public opposition blocked deployment there, then the antinuclear campaigners would be immeasurably strengthened and encouraged.

In November 1985 Lubbers postponed a cabinet crisis over the issue by offering to stop the deployment if the Soviet Union would reduce the number of SS-20 missiles to 378. The offer was clearly designed to shift the focus of criticism away from the United States and NATO and to the Soviet Union. It succeeded. The offer was ignored by the Soviet Union, with the result that Lubbers was able to secure the parliamentary support he needed for a vote in favor of deployment. The official acceptance of the missiles came just before the Geneva summit meeting between President RONALD REAGAN and Soviet leader MIKHAIL GORBACHEV and is believed to have significantly strengthened the American negotiating position.

Neutron Bomb (Enhanced Radiation Weapon) The neutron bomb, or enhanced radiation weapon, is a small hydrogen bomb with only one-tenth of the blast, heat and fallout produced by a normal hydrogen bomb.

The bomb is designed to be detonated in the air. The radiation emitted by the blast kills the human occupants in the area, but leaves physical structures such as roads and buildings intact.

The effects of the radiation last only a few hours, enabling troops to move in and occupy the blast zone relatively quickly. President GERALD FORD secretly approved plans for the neutron bomb in 1976. Funds for the production of the weapon were included in the fiscal 1978 appropriations bill for public works and for the Energy Research and Development Administration.

When the existence of the project became public it was widely and vehemently debated. The Soviet Union and European antinuclear campaigners dubbed the enhanced radiation weapon the "capitalist's bomb" because it left property intact while killing people. Opponents of the bomb argued that the enhanced radiation weapon also significantly lowered the nuclear threshold over which a superpower had to cross before employing nuclear weapons.

Supporters of the neutron bomb argued that it provided a much more believable deterrent than other nuclear warheads since it could be unleashed more readily.

The bomb's opponents won the debate. President JIMMY CARTER shelved the project. Development and production were resumed by President RONALD REAGAN, but the end of the Cold War began before deployment.

"New Look" Defense Policy

The "New Look" Defense Policy was developed by President DWIGHT EISENHOWER in response to rising defense costs. It shifted the emphasis of American defense away from a high level of conventional forces to a credible, massive nuclear deterrent.

During the TRUMAN administration it was commonly believed that the powerful U.S. economy could afford any cost to defend national interests. As chief of staff and SUPREME ALLIED COMMANDER OF EUROPE, Eisenhower had become increasingly concerned about spiraling defense costs, and soon after he was inaugurated as president he instituted a study aimed at reorganizing the American defense structure.

In ordering this study, he was driven by the belief that the United States could "choke itself to death piling up military expenditures just as surely as it can defeat itself by not spending for protection." Another factor in Eisenhower's thinking was his belief that the United States would never initiate another war, therefore the focus of the armed forces should shift from the ability to wage war to the ability to deter aggression. These basic conditions made it inevitable that the president's "New Look" Defense Policy would result in a decrease in conventional forces and an increase in nuclear forces, where the military could achieve "more bang for the buck."

The change in military doctrine also involved changes in the budget allocations for each of the three main branches of the armed forces. The army and navy, where the conventional forces were concentrated, suffered a cutback in spending from $12.9 billion in 1954 for the army to $8.8 billion in 1955. The navy's budget was reduced from $11.2 billion in 1954 to $9.7 billion in 1955. The air force controlled the nuclear defense system and thus had its budget increased from $15.6 billion in 1954 to $16.4 billion in 1955. Not surprisingly, the army and navy objected to the changes and lobbied Congress to reject them. But they could do little against the military prestige of Eisenhower, and the "New Look" Defense Policy was fully implemented.

For Further Information:
Schilling, Warner, Paul Y. Hammond, and Glenn Snyder. *Strategy, Politics and Defense Budget.* New York, 1962.

Ngo Dinh Diem   (January 3, 1901–November 2, 1963)

Ngo Dinh Diem was first prime minister and then president of South Vietnam from 1954 until his overthrow and assassination in November 1963. Diem was adept at securing American support, but his narrow, corrupt and oppressive government failed to establish a popular base and prepared the ground for the ultimate victory of the more nationalist National Liberation Front (Viet Cong) and the North Vietnamese.

Diem was born into a prominent Roman Catholic family that had long been in imperial service. Diem's personal connections dated to the prewar period when he was in the French Indochina colonial administration, which he left in 1933. During World War II, the Vichy French were allowed to remain in Vietnam to administer it on behalf of the Japanese. Diem, a former collaborator with the French, refused to back the French collaborators with the Japanese, but neither did he join any of the Vietnamese nationalist groups fighting for independence from the French and the Japanese. Diem's failure to establish nationalist credentials at a critical juncture in his country's history was later used against him by his opponents.

Diem was, even at this stage, vehemently anti-communist, and when the Viet Minh took power at the end of World War II, Diem was captured and exiled to an obscure northern village. He was released in 1946 after an agreement between the Viet Minh and the newly returned Free French, but in the late 1940s was the target of several communist assassination attempts. In 1950 Diem left Vietnam for the United States.

In America, Diem concentrated on establishing contacts with political figures and prominent Catholics. Among those he saw were FRANCIS CARDINAL SPELLMAN and then-Congressman JOHN F. KENNEDY. On every possible occasion, Diem stressed both his nationalist and his anti-communist views, attacking both the French colonial rulers and the Viet Minh forces of HO CHI MINH. Diem foresaw that the United States would replace France as the dominant power in Indochina and that the Vietnamese politician who could claim American support could also lay claim to the leadership of his country.

In 1953 Diem moved to a monastery in Belgium and established contact with Vietnamese exile groups in Paris and his brother Ngo Dinh Nhu back in Vietnam. When it became clear that the French were going to relinquish power and accede to the temporary division of Vietnam, Diem offered himself to Emperor Bao Dai (who served as a kind of figurehead for the French) as the one Vietnamese politician whose contacts would ensure that the United States would supply the assistance necessary to keep South Vietnam in existence permanently. Bao Dai appointed Diem prime minister on June 18, 1954. The following year, Diem effectively overthrew Bao Dai in a fraudulent referendum and named himself president, assuming the roles of both head of state and head of government.

Diem's contacts in the United States did indeed result in

substantial financial assistance for South Vietnam. In 1955 U.S. secretary of state JOHN FOSTER DULLES pledged $300 million in aid. His brother, CIA director ALLEN DULLES, established a large CIA bureau in South Vietnam under Colonel EDWARD LANSDALE to direct covert operations against the North Vietnamese and dissidents inside South Vietnam.

Under the terms of the 1954 Geneva agreement that partitioned Vietnam, the two halves of the country were scheduled to hold elections for a government under which to unify the country in 1956. Diem, with the support of the United States, refused to hold the elections because he knew that Ho Chi Minh and the Viet Minh had more popular support than he did. Ho at this stage was in no position to challenge this breach as he was involved in a brutal collectivization program, and the Soviet Union was preoccupied with problems in Hungary and Poland. After 1956, however, Ho started providing assistance to South Vietnamese communists, who formed their own guerrilla army known as the Viet Cong.

The Viet Cong's main targets were local officials of the Saigon government. In 1961 alone, they killed 2,500. By this time, the Viet Cong army was estimated to be 100,000 strong. Diem responded by increasing CIA covert operations, cracking down on dissidents, increasing the size of his army and introducing a land reform program. Under initial American guidance, the land reform program started out with a redistribution of farming land, but as Viet Cong operations stepped up, it evolved into the forced removal of the peasants from their villages to heavily protected hamlets known as "agrovilles" where they were often required to work without pay. This policy only further alienated Diem from the people he ruled.

Faced with growing public opposition, Diem relied heavily on a few close friends and relatives, led by his brother Ngo Dinh Nhu and Nhu's wife, Madame Nhu. Nhu founded a secret political party and headed the secret police; Madame Nhu developed a reputation for personal evil. Many regarded them as the evil geniuses behind Diem. Another of Diem's brothers, Ngo Dinh Thuc, was the powerful Catholic bishop of Hue. As Diem concentrated more power in the hands of fewer political figures, from a narrow, wealthy and foreign-educated elite, corruption increased, as did popular dissatisfaction.

All this provided fertile ground for the Viet Cong, whose military operations were increasingly successful. At the same time, other dissident groups became more active. The largest such group was the Buddhist monks, whose opposition was both political and religious because of Diem's favoritism toward the Catholic Church—in Vietnam, the religion of a privileged minority. In May 1963 Buddhist monks in Hue rioted after being denied permission to fly the Buddhist flag. Diem dispatched troops to quell the riots, and nine people were killed. The Buddhists then launched a series of protests against Diem's government, culminating with self-immolation by monks (Madame Nhu publicly referred to this form of protest as "monk barbecues"). In August 1963 Diem retaliated by attacking Buddhist temples throughout the country, arresting thousands of monks and charging them with "subversion."

Diem's treatment of the Buddhists highlighted the repressive nature of his regime and American public opinion began to turn against him. At the same time, the Viet Cong appeared to be on the verge of a military victory over Diem's army. In August 1963 the recently arrived U.S. ambassador to South Vietnam, HENRY CABOT LODGE, cabled the State Department that the United States should start looking for a replacement for Diem. Lodge was instructed to press Diem to reform his government and remove his brother Nhu from power. At the same time, Lodge contacted the Vietnamese generals and informed them that the United States would countenance a coup.

On November 1, 1963, the generals moved against Diem. The following day Ngo Dinh Diem and his brother Nhu were shot to death.

For Further Information:

Barnet, Richard J. *Roots of War.* New York, 1972.

Bator, Victor. *Vietnam: A Diplomatic Tragedy: The Origins of the United States Involvement.* Dobbs Ferry, N.Y., 1965.

Fifield, Russell Hunt. *Americans in Southeast Asia: The Roots of Commitment.* New York, 1973.

Karnow, Stanley. *Vietnam: A History.* New York, 1983.

Lansdale, Edward G. *In the Midst of Wars: An American's Mission to Southeast Asia.* New York, 1972.

Nicaragua   Nicaragua was a Central American client state of the United States until 1979, when the right-wing dictatorship of Anastasio Somoza was overthrown in a popular revolt led by the leftist Sandinistas. For the next 10 years the United States tried to overthrow the Sandinista government, which it regarded as a Soviet beachhead on the American continent. In February 1990 elections the Sandinistas were unexpectedly defeated by a U.S.-backed coalition.

The United States had a long history of involvement in Nicaraguan affairs, starting with the discovery of gold in California in 1848. One of the quickest routes from the American East Coast to the goldfields was by ship, with an overland passage across Nicaragua. In 1852 the American millionaire Cornelius Vanderbilt opened a steamship and carriage company with the express purpose of moving the prospectors from the east to the west coast of Nicaragua. The strategic position of Nicaragua also attracted the ambitious American adventurer William Walker, who in 1855 organized an army that invaded Nicaragua and installed him as president. He was overthrown a year later.

Nicaragua was seriously considered as the site for the American-built canal across Central America, and the Nicaraguan government lobbied for the route to go through its territory. When the United States decided on Panama instead, the Nicaraguan government turned to European interests to provide the money for another canal. In 1909 U.S.

Marines invaded after two Americans were murdered for aiding a rebellion against the Nicaraguan government. The presence of the U.S. Marines put an end to Nicaraguan attempts to build a rival canal, and from that time onward the support of the American government was seen as a prerequisite for any Nicaraguan politician or general seeking the leadership of his country.

Political instability remained endemic in Nicaragua, and there were several attempts to overthrow the American-supported governments. One of the most prominent rebellions was led by Cesar Augusto Sandino from 1926 to 1933. In 1934 the American-supported General Anastasio Somoza Garcia positioned himself to assume power and began a political dynasty that ruled the country for the next 45 years. That same year, he lured Sandino into the capital, Managua, where he was murdered by the National Guard commanded by Somoza. The following year, Somoza formally assumed power. Anastasio Somoza was assassinated in September 1956 and was succeeded by his son Luis Somoza Debayle, who in turn was succeeded by his younger brother Anastasio Somoza Debayle in 1967. The Somozas did not always hold the office of president. Because of formal constitutional restrictions they had occasionally to relinquish the title, but they handpicked and controlled each of their successors, a policy known as continuismo.

The Somozas ruled Nicaragua as if it were their private property. The economy and the land were controlled by their family and a few close associates, who succeeded in blocking serious political or economic reform. There were various attempts to rebel against the Somoza dictatorship, and in 1962 the left-wing Frente Sandinista de Liberacion Nacional (Sandinista National Liberation Front) was founded. The Sandinistas named themselves after the 1930s rebel leader.

The Sandinistas and other dissident groups at first proved little more than a nuisance to the Somoza family. The American-trained National Guard's brutal repression of political dissidents kept them largely underground, and they did not initially attract a large popular base. This political situation was dramatically altered by the earthquake that shook Managua in December 1972. More than 6,000 people died and 300,000 were left homeless. Anastasio Somoza took personal control of the disaster relief program and proceeded to siphon off money for himself from international aid programs. Thousands died or suffered needlessly as the rubble remained uncleared and disease spread.

Somoza's reaction to the earthquake united the population against his regime, and the Sandinistas joined with other dissident groups and increased in power and influence. Somoza suffered another blow with the election of JIMMY CARTER as U.S. president in November 1976. Carter's relatively tough stand on human rights left the right-wing dictator without his traditional unconditional support in Washington and indicated that American forces would not be used to keep him in power. The final straw was the murder in January 1978 of Pedro Joaquin Chamorro, the editor and publisher of the newspaper *La Prensa* and founder of the opposition party, the Democratic Union of Liberation.

Chamorro's murder was followed by violent demonstrations and a general strike, and in August 1978 the Sandinistas occupied the national palace and held 1,500 hostages for two days, forcing the regime to release 59 political prisoners. Following increased repression by the National Guard, the moderate opposition was driven into the camp of the Sandinistas, who launched their final offensive against the discredited and now internationally isolated Somoza regime. The offensive quickly turned into a general uprising. On July 19, 1979, the Sandinistas marched into Managua and Somoza fled the country. He was assassinated in Paraguay in September 1980.

The Sandinistas, under the leadership of Daniel Ortega, quickly formed a leftist government with ties to Cuba and the Soviet Union. The Carter administration offered the new Nicaraguan government $75 million in economic aid in October 1980. But when RONALD REAGAN succeeded Carter in January 1981 he immediately froze the remaining $15 million balance in the aid account. In April he announced that aid to Nicaragua had been suspended indefinitely because, he said, the Sandinistas were supporting left-wing guerrillas attempting to overthrow the government of El Salvador. Reagan also imposed a boycott on trade with Nicaragua in May 1985.

At the same time, a 2,000-strong force of former members of Somoza's National Guard (known as Somocistas) established themselves in Honduras and launched guerrilla raids into Nicaragua. Almost simultaneously, the Sandinista government launched a campaign to integrate the English-speaking Miskito Indians more fully into Nicaraguan social structures. This drove the Miskitos into an alliance with the Somocistas. The two groups formed the nucleus of the counterrevolutionary forces or Contras.

It is not certain how actively involved the United States CENTRAL INTELLIGENCE AGENCY was in the original formation of the Somocistas and the Miskito rebel group MISURA, but it was certainly involved with the Contra rebels from an early stage. In 1981 Congress approved $10 million in support to the Contras. This figure was increased to $19 million the following year. The Reagan administration also established training camps in the United States. Further aid from private sources was channeled through the CIA to the Contras.

Within a few years, the Contra forces had grown to more than 15,000 men, most based in Honduras. In January 1983 the Contras launched a major offensive to coincide with joint U.S.–Honduran military exercises (code-named Big Pine) on the Honduran–Nicaraguan border. In April 1983 Eden Pastora Gomez, one of the heroes of the revolution that had overthrown Somoza, announced that he would be joining the Contra cause with raids from his base in Costa Rica.

Ortega declared a state of emergency in March 1982, and the country remained on a war footing from then until 1989. American spy planes regularly violated Nicaraguan airspace, and the United States at one point mined the country's principal harbor. These actions contributed to fears of an imminent invasion by American forces in support of the Contra rebels, and martial law was declared.

Under martial law the government imposed some restrictions on political and trade union activity. Censorship was reintroduced and political opponents were arrested. At the same time—due to the American trade boycott—the economy rapidly deteriorated. The Sandinistas had inherited from Somoza a country nearly bankrupt from years of neglect, corruption and civil war. It badly needed a respite and trade with the United States. Denied both, it turned necessarily toward the Soviet Bloc for military and financial aid. This allowed the Reagan administration to brand the Sandinistas as Soviet and Cuban puppets.

The Sandinistas held elections in November 1984. The results were an overwhelming victory for the Sandinistas over the political opponents who had agreed to participate in the campaign. The results were judged to be reasonably fair by international observers (including ex-President Carter), sent to monitor the campaign and polling, but they were denounced by the Reagan administration. The pro-American parties had refused to participate.

The election results followed the failure of a major Contra offensive, and this had the combined effect of swinging American congressional and public opinion away from the Contras. The Honduran government also became less enthusiastic, and the Costa Ricans eventually expelled all but a handful of the rebel forces. President Reagan, however, remained a strong supporter of the Contra cause and made financial and other support a key pillar of his foreign policy. In 1986, after a tough battle with the Congress, he managed to secure approval for $100 million in aid for military and "humanitarian" purposes for the period 1986–88.

Simultaneous with the Contra military offensive and the Iran–Contra arms scandal was a diplomatic offensive led by Costa Rican president Oscar Arias. In August 1987, Arias organized a summit meeting of five Central American presidents—of Costa Rica, Nicaragua, El Salvador, Guatemala and Honduras. At this and later meetings the Sandinista leader Daniel Ortega agreed to lift the state of emergency and participate in face-to-face talks with the Contra leadership.

The direct negotiations resulted in a move toward a ceasefire, an agreement to allow the Contras to participate in the domestic political dialogue and elections, a staged release of political prisoners and more detailed peace negotiations at a later stage. But full agreement evaded the negotiators' grasp, partly because of the Sandinistas' reluctance to hand over any control of the government and partly because of divisions among the Contra leadership.

The lack of a final agreement between the Contras and the Sandinista government led Arias to again take the diplomatic offensive. In February 1989 another summit of Central American presidents was held in El Salvador at which Nicaragua agreed to open and free elections in February 1990 in return for a draft plan to disarm and repatriate Contra rebels based in Honduras.

The U.S. Congress responded to the Arias diplomatic offensive by axing all military aid to the Contras, reducing humanitarian aid to $50 million and tying this aid to the February 1990 elections. The elections were held on February 25. The Sandinistas were expected to win, but were upset by the National Opposition Union led by Violeta Barrios de Chamorro, the widow of Pedro Joaquin Chamorro. Ortega duly handed over power to the new government and the Contra rebels were disarmed. The day after the elections U.S. president GEORGE BUSH lifted economic sanctions and pledged a " significant and meaningful aid package." U.S. aid, however, has been forthcoming only in token amounts.

For Further Information:
Ashby, T. *The Bear in the Backyard.* Lexington, Mass., 1987.
Burns, E.B. *At War in Nicaragua.* New York, 1987.
Dunkerley, James. *Power in the Isthmus.* London, 1988.
Feinberg, Richard E., ed. *Central America: International Dimensions of the Crisis.* New York, 1982.
Gettleman, Marvin, et al., eds. *El Salvador: Central America in the New Cold War.* New York, 1986.
Gutman, R. *Banana Diplomacy.* New York, 1988.
Lumar, Shiv. *U.S. Intervention in Latin America.* Chicago, 1987.
Miller, Nicola. *Soviet Relations with Latin America, 1959–1987.* New York, 1989.

Nitze, Paul (January 16, 1907–   )   Paul Nitze was one of the most influential American nuclear weapons strategists. His career as a defense adviser stretched from the TRUMAN to the REAGAN administrations, and he has played a role in almost every American strategic decision and negotiation with the Soviets.

Following graduation from Harvard University in 1928, Nitze joined the prestigious investment banking firm of Dillon, Read and Company. He remained in banking until he entered government service in 1941 as financial director of the Office of the Coordinator of Inter-American Affairs. From 1944 to 1946 he gained his first experience in strategic affairs as vice chairman of the U.S. Strategic Bombing Survey. But in 1946 he returned to economics, first as the director of the Office of International Trade Policy in the State Department and then as assistant secretary of state for economic affairs. In both positions he helped to prepare the MARSHALL PLAN.

In April 1949 Nitze joined GEORGE F. KENNAN's State Department policy planning staff, which was then developing America's long-term strategy toward the Soviet Union. His first major contribution to the East–West debate came after Secretary of State DEAN ACHESON asked Nitze to head an interdepartmental study group to review foreign and defense policy.

The result of this study was the NATIONAL SECURITY COUNCIL REPORT 68 (NSC-68), which laid the foundation for America's postwar security policy and established Nitze's reputation. Nitze started his review from the premise that the ultimate goal of Soviet foreign policy was world domination and that only the United States had the economic strength necessary to deter them.

Nitze advised the Truman administration to increase defense spending on conventional and nuclear weapons by 200–400%, to provide the weaponry to protect the members of the NORTH ATLANTIC TREATY ORGANIZATION (NATO) and to deter Soviet aggression elsewhere. Truman at first rejected this advice but reversed his decision at the start of the KOREAN WAR.

NSC-68, however, failed to find supporters within the EISENHOWER administration, whose key figures preferred a defense policy that relied on the less expensive threat of massive nuclear retaliation to any Soviet attack rather than on the mix of conventional and nuclear weapons advocated by Nitze. Senator JOSEPH MCCARTHY and Senator Robert Taft's opposition to NSC-68 blocked Nitze's appointment as assistant secretary of defense during the Eisenhower administration, although he was regularly called upon for his advice. In 1957 he worked with the Gaither Committee (see GAITHER REPORT), which was studying U.S. defense demands, and in 1959 he worked as an adviser to the Senate Foreign Relations Committee.

On December 24, 1960, President JOHN F. KENNEDY appointed Nitze assistant secretary of defense for international security affairs. In this position, he urged the United States and NATO to move away from the massive retaliation policy of the Eisenhower years toward a greater emphasis on conventional weapons as outlined in NSC-68. He also urged NATO to develop its own multilateral conventional and nuclear force.

During the BERLIN Crisis in 1961, Nitze chaired the task force created to develop strategy in case of a showdown. He helped to develop American policy toward the Soviet Union and Cuba during the CUBAN MISSILE CRISIS and later, along with special presidential assistant WALT ROSTOW, was given the task of analyzing the Kennedy administration's handling of the crisis.

In October 1963 Kennedy appointed Nitze secretary of the navy. He became enamored of high-tech weaponry, and his interest led him to favor development of the TFX swing-wing bomber project, criticized in the late 1960s and 1970s for cost overruns and technological problems.

In June 1967 President LYNDON JOHNSON appointed Nitze deputy secretary of defense. He and Defense Secretary ROBERT MCNAMARA coordinated their efforts to press for a de-escalation of the VIETNAM WAR. Of the senior advisory group on Vietnam formed by Johnson to study the Pentagon's request for 200,000 additional U.S. troops after the TET OFFENSIVE, Nitze was in the majority that opposed the request. The group's recommendation led to Johnson's decision on March 31, 1968, to de-escalate.

During his last year as deputy secretary of defense Nitze became more involved in strategic nuclear issues as an advocate of the Sentinel Antiballistic Missile (ABM) system as a defense against Chinese nuclear weapons. His expertise in the area made him a logical choice as the Pentagon's representative on the five-man American delegation to the STRATEGIC ARMS LIMITATION TALKS (SALT) in Helsinki in 1969. Nitze was among those members of the delegation who favored limiting the American ABM system to Washington, D.C. in order to make it symmetrical with Soviet ABM deployment around Moscow. During the SALT negotiations Nitze managed to develop cordial relations with the Soviet negotiators without compromising his own conservative views. These relations served him well in later discussions.

In March 1974 Defense Secretary JAMES SCHLESINGER proposed Nitze for assistant secretary of defense, but his appointment was blocked by Senator Barry Goldwater. On June 14, 1974, Nitze abruptly resigned from the SALT delegation in protest of President Richard Nixon's involvement in the Watergate affair. His resignation came just before the president was due to fly to Moscow and played a major role in undermining the visit.

Nitze became an early critic of President JIMMY CARTER. On February 28, 1977, he testified against Carter's appointment of Paul Warnke as director of the ARMS CONTROL AND DISARMAMENT AGENCY and chief negotiator at the SALT II negotiations. Nitze told the Senate Foreign Relations Committee that Warnke's ideas on arms control were "dangerous" and his knowledge of nuclear arms "inadequate." The committee's overwhelming endorsement of Warnke ensured that Nitze would remain out of office.

Nitze became one of the strongest critics of the direction of the SALT II negotiations. He claimed that SALT II would give the Soviet Union near-parity in heavy bombers and a 10-1 advantage in land-based ICBMs by 1985. Nitze's opposition to SALT II was a major factor in the Senate's decision not to ratify the 1979 treaty.

During the 1980 presidential election Nitze supported Ronald Reagan's opposition to the SALT II Treaty, and in 1981 Reagan appointed him to head the American delegation to the U.S.–Soviet talks in Geneva on intermediate-range and strategic-range nuclear forces. Nitze resigned as chief negotiator in 1983, but in December 1984 he was appointed adviser to Secretary of State GEORGE SHULTZ for a meeting with Soviet foreign minister ANDREI GROMYKO, called to discuss the stalled arms negotiations. He continued in that position after the meeting. In August 1986, Nitze led another American delegation to nuclear arms negotiations with the Soviets. The meeting was designed to prepare for another Gromyko–Shultz summit.

By 1987, however, there were signs that Nitze was becoming increasingly isolated within the Reagan administration because of his belief that the president's STRATEGIC DEFENSE INITIATIVE ("Star Wars") was a breach of the ANTIBALLISTIC MISSILE TREATY OF 1972, which he had helped negotiate. Nitze left government service May 1, 1989.

Nitze was critical of the arms control posture taken by President GEORGE BUSH and in the 1992 presidential election publicly endorsed first Ross Perot and then, after a serious policy difference with Perot's advisors, Bill Clinton.

For Further Information:

Callahan, David. *Dangerous Capabilities: Paul Nitze and the Cold War*. New York, 1990.

Clemens, Walter C. *The Superpowers and Arms Control: From Cold War to Interdependence*. Lexington, Mass., 1973.

Mayers, T. *Understanding Nuclear Weapons and Arms Control*. London, 1986.

Moulton, Harland B. *From Superiority to Parity: The United States and the Strategic Arms Race, 1961–1971*. Westport, Conn., 1972.

Newhouse, John. *Cold Dawn: The Story of SALT*. New York, 1973.

Nitze, Paul H. *Paul H. Nitze On Foreign Policy*. Lanham, Md., 1989.

Reardon, Steven L. *The Evolution of American Strategic Doctrine: Paul H. Nitze and the Soviet Challenge*. Boulder, Colo., 1984.

Talbott, Strobe. *Endgame: The Inside Story of SALT Two*. New York, 1979.

Nixon, Richard M. (January 9, 1913–   ) Richard Nixon's public career spanned most of the Cold War and owed a great deal to it. He came to national prominence with his involvement in the HOUSE UN-AMERICAN ACTIVITIES COMMITTEE investigation of ALGER HISS and his early attempts to legislate against the Communist Party. His popularity among conservatives led DWIGHT EISENHOWER to choose him as vice president. When he was president, Nixon's past exploitation of anti-communist hysteria helped him to win public acceptance for his reestablishment of relations with China and policy of détente with the Soviet Union. His foreign policy achievements, however, were ultimately undermined by the domestic Watergate scandal, and Nixon was forced to resign in disgrace.

Nixon was born into a lower middle-class Quaker family in Whittier, California. He was educated at Whittier College and Duke University Law School, where he graduated third in his class in 1937. After Duke, Nixon returned to Whittier to open his own law practice. During World War II he worked for a time in the Office of Price Administration before joining the U.S. Navy as a noncombatant officer. After his discharge in 1946 he returned to California and was elected to the U.S. House of Representatives in a campaign in which he accused the popular liberal incumbent, Jerry Voorhis, of communist associations.

His anti-communist campaign continued in Washington. Nixon joined the House Un-American Activities Committee and in 1948 joined Representative Karl Mundt in sponsoring a bill to require the federal registration of communists and communist-front organizations. The MUNDT-NIXON BILL, as it was known, also barred members of such political organizations from federal employment and called for the stiff punishment of convicted subversives. The bill passed the House but was killed in the Senate Judiciary Committee. Many of its basic features, however, were later incorporated into the INTERNAL SECURITY ACT of 1950.

At the end of 1947 Nixon was told that Alger Hiss, a former high-ranking State Department official then president of the Carnegie Foundation for Peace, had been a secret member of the Communist Party. On August 3, 1948, the accusation was made public by journalist WHITTAKER CHAMBERS. From then on Nixon took the leading role in the campaign against Hiss. He arranged a personal confrontation between Chambers and Hiss on August 17 and extracted from Hiss the confession that he had known Chambers in the 1930s. Later he subpoenaed the "Pumpkin Papers," microfilms of documents that allegedly had been stolen from the State Department by Hiss and hidden in a pumpkin on Chambers' Maryland farm. Hiss was eventually convicted of perjury in 1949.

Nixon's relentless pursuit of the former diplomat turned him into a national figure. In 1950 he decided to run for the U.S. Senate. His campaign was marked by attacks on the TRUMAN administration's handling of "domestic subversion" and on the alleged communist associations of his opponent, the liberal incumbent Helen Gahagan Douglas. The result was a landslide 680,000-vote majority for Nixon, which further increased his political standing with both the public and the Republican Party and led to his being chosen by Dwight D. Eisenhower as his running mate in the 1952 presidential election.

During the 1952 campaign, Nixon was accused of accepting money from wealthy businessmen for his personal use. The allegations led Eisenhower to comment that Nixon would have to prove himself "clean as a hound's tooth" to remain his running mate. Nixon went on television to deny the allegations and give what he claimed was an "unprecedented" and "complete" account of his finances, and to plead for the

Richard Nixon was president of the United States from 1969 until 1974, when he resigned in disgrace. Despite his involvement in the Watergate scandal and other illegal activities, Nixon's policy of détente with the Soviet Union and his reestablishment of diplomatic ties with China did help ease Cold War tensions.

public's sympathy. This apparently humiliating appearance, known as the "Checkers Speech" (after his children's dog, who was mentioned prominently), was a success, and Eisenhower declared Nixon "completely vindicated."

Nixon was an active vice president, especially in the field of foreign affairs. He chaired meetings of the NATIONAL SECURITY COUNCIL and traveled extensively. In May 1958 he proved his personal bravery by his calm reaction when a mob in Caracas, Venezuela stopped his car and nearly overturned it. In July 1959 Nixon became the highest-ranking American politician to visit the Soviet Union since NIKITA KHRUSHCHEV had come to power. During the visit the two men engaged in the famous KITCHEN DEBATE over the relative merits of capitalism and communism. The televised, impromptu discussion considerably enhanced Nixon's popularity with American voters.

Nixon's position on Senator JOSEPH MCCARTHY's anti-communist "witch hunt" demonstrated his willingness to adapt his political stance to changing circumstances. He started off as chief mediator between McCarthy and the Eisenhower administration. In 1953 he advised Eisenhower against a public break with McCarthy and arranged for Secretary of State JOHN FOSTER DULLES to praise McCarthy publicly for acting in the national interest, in return for a promise from McCarthy that he would coordinate his activities with the State Department. But after McCarthy's attacks on the army, Nixon abandoned him. Nixon's maneuver was a major contribution to the senator's downfall.

Throughout the Eisenhower administration, Nixon took a hard line on communist China and American policy in Asia. He backed the decision to defend the islands of QUEMOY AND MATSU and became a powerful figure in the pro-CHIANG KAI-SHEK China Lobby. In 1954 he also suggested sending American troops to Vietnam to support the French colonial authority over the Vietnamese.

In 1958 Nixon started organizing his campaign for the 1960 Republican presidential nomination, which he effectively secured after the withdrawal of his chief rival, New York Governor Nelson Rockefeller. His defeat in the election, the narrowest in American history, is generally credited to his opponent JOHN F. KENNEDY's success in televised debates. Nixon suffered a severe political setback in 1962 when he lost the election for the governorship of California.

Following that defeat, Nixon announced his withdrawal from active politics and joined a prominent New York law firm. But it soon became clear that Nixon had not abandoned his presidential ambitions. He spent the next five years rebuilding a national political base by touring the country in support of various Republican candidates. In 1964 he campaigned on behalf of Republican presidential candidate BARRY GOLDWATER. By 1967, Nixon had established a powerful political machine, which enabled him to win easily the 1968 Republican presidential nomination. He defeated Vice President HUBERT HUMPHREY and a badly divided Democratic Party in the election.

Foreign affairs was Nixon's area of special interest during his presidency, and the area in which he enjoyed his greatest success. He worked closely with HENRY KISSINGER, whom he appointed first as national security adviser and then, in September 1973, secretary of state. Nixon, from the start, was determined to set the basic guidelines of foreign policy himself rather than delegate the task to the departments of defense and state. Kissinger, with whom he shared basic political assumptions, became Nixon's tool for the implementation of those policies.

Nixon's greatest foreign policy triumph was his rapprochement with communist China. During the 1950s and 1960s recognition of communist China was a major domestic issue. Conservatives opposed recognition and liberals theoretically were in favor but were unable to act for fear of being attacked by conservative politicians exploiting anti-communist hysteria as being "soft on communism." The SINO-SOVIET SPLIT from 1960 on led Nixon privately to reverse his previous opposition on the grounds that American recognition of communist China would further alienate China from the Soviet Union and weaken Soviet influence in the Third World. Nixon also realized that his hard-line anti-communist career made him the first American president who could extend diplomatic recognition to communist China without being accused of being soft on communism.

Nixon began exploring the possibility of reestablishing Sino-American relations shortly after assuming office. But the first serious public step in his China initiative came in February 1970 when he said in a foreign policy report to Congress that "the Chinese are a great and vital people who should not remain isolated from the international community . . . It is certainly in our interest . . . that we take what steps we can toward improved practical relations with Peking [Beijing]."

As a result of that report, the Chinese secretly indicated that they would welcome a high-ranking American official to Beijing for talks, and the State Department eased travel and trade restrictions with communist China. Since 1958, there had been an accepted and partially public Sino-American diplomatic channel through the American and Chinese embassies in Poland. Nixon reinforced this channel with two more, through Romania and Pakistan. In March 1971, all travel restrictions were lifted, and the following month Beijing responded by inviting an American table tennis (Ping-Pong) team to China.

In April 1971 the government in Beijing reaffirmed "its willingness to receive publicly in Beijing a special envoy of the President," and at about the same time Life magazine published an interview with MAO ZEDONG in which the Chinese leader said he would welcome a visit by Nixon. Early in July, Kissinger secretly flew to Beijing for three days to arrange the visit, and on July 15 Nixon announced that he would be visiting China.

The actual visit took place on February 18–28, 1972. The 1,800-word Shanghai communiqué issued at the end of the visit emphasized that the United States and China remained in opposition across a whole range of foreign policy issues. But while recognizing the "essential differences," the communiqué also made it clear that "the two sides agreed on general rules of international relations" and that "normalization of relations" between them was "in the interests of all countries."

Nixon's conservative credentials also enabled him to make major strides toward improving U.S.–Soviet relations. His success in improving relations with China also pushed the Soviet Union toward concessions as it tried to adjust to the new balance of power represented by the Sino-American rapprochement. The Soviets' desire for détente was also heightened by the country's economic problems, which required a reduction in defense spending, an increase in Western technological expertise and importation of American grain.

Nixon was amenable to Soviet advances. By 1968 he had come to the conclusion that U.S. foreign policy had been "held hostage" for too long by the confining policies of the Cold War. He thus encouraged the STRATEGIC ARMS LIMITATION TALKS (SALT I), which had started during the JOHNSON administration. At the same time, however, he believed in negotiating from a position of strength and continued spending increases for new weapons, especially the Antiballistic Missile (ABM) system.

He also set out to link progress in nuclear weapons negotiations to Soviet concessions in other areas. This policy, which was carefully developed with Kissinger, became known as "LINKAGE." The Soviet leadership at first rejected linkage as a form of diplomatic blackmail. But the policy was eventually accepted, and after Nixon went to Moscow to sign the ABM and SALT I treaties in Moscow in May 1972, the Soviets put pressure on North Vietnam to make concessions in the PARIS PEACE TALKS. Nixon responded with the U.S.–SOVIET TRADE AGREEMENT and various cultural, scientific and educational agreements. An agreement to grant the Soviet Union most-favored-nation trading status was blocked by the JACKSON AMENDMENT, which tied the trade agreement to Soviet emigration policies.

Nixon's top foreign policy priority was the VIETNAM WAR. He accepted that remaining indefinitely in Vietnam had become politically impossible, but he argued that the other apparent alternative, withdrawal, was unacceptable because it would undermine other countries' confidence in American treaty commitments. Nixon's strategy therefore was to "Vietnamize" the conflict and withdraw American troops, but in such a way that the South Vietnamese forces would seem to be left with a significant political and military advantage. This policy included American and South Vietnamese moves into Cambodia and Laos to destroy Viet Cong and North Vietnamese bases there, and American bombing raids on North Vietnam to place pressure on its negotiators in Paris. Eventually an agreement was reached on the eve of the 1972 presidential elections. After a last and extraordinarily heavy bombing of North Vietnamese civilian areas at Christmas, a U.S.–North Vietnamese Peace Treaty was signed in January 1973.

But Nixon's policies and tactics were disapproved of by a growing proportion of the American public, especially the younger generation. Demonstrations, which had first taken place during the Johnson administration, increased in frequency and size. They reached a peak after Nixon ordered the invasion of Cambodia in 1970, which resulted in anarchy and a genocidal civil war in that country. Students, especially, were galvanized by an incident at Kent State University in which four student demonstrators were shot to death by Ohio National Guard troops.

Nixon and his White House aides responded to the public anger and mass demonstrations by developing a "siege" mentality. His assistants were directed to secretly gather information on antiwar protesters. This involved illegal wiretaps, breaking and entering and interfering with the mail. All of this illegal activity was justified on the grounds of national security.

It did not take long for Nixon and his key associates to equate national security and national interest with the president's interest in reelection. It was therefore a relatively easy decision to order that the same tactics used against antiwar demonstrators be employed against the Democratic opponents. On June 17, a group of men employed by the Nixon campaign's Committee to Reelect the President (CREEP) were caught breaking into the Democratic Party's national headquarters at the Watergate Hotel complex in Washington, D.C. The subsequent investigation by the press, led by the *Washington Post*, revealed not only widespread illegalities in other areas but also a massive coverup that extended all the way to the president.

The Watergate scandal dominated Nixon's last 18 months in the White House, and he was unable to give the attention he wanted to foreign policy, which was left increasingly in the hands of Henry Kissinger. At the same time, other countries, especially the Soviet Union, became increasingly reluctant to negotiate with what they regarded as a lame-duck administration. In July 1974 the Supreme Court ordered Nixon to release 64 secretly-made tapes of conversations in his office. These revealed that the president had known of and participated in the obstruction of the Justice Department's Watergate investigation. Within a few days the House Judiciary Committee passed three articles of impeachment. A straw poll showed that the House as a whole would vote in favor of impeachment, and rather than face the ordeal, on August 9, 1974, Nixon resigned from office.

Nixon was succeeded by Vice President GERALD FORD, who granted his predecessor an unprecedented blanket pardon for any crimes Nixon might have committed in office. Nixon himself has never admitted to criminal wrongdoing, although he has admitted to "grave errors" in his "handling" of the Watergate scandal. Out of office, Nixon returned to his law practice and began to write his memoirs. He has often written and spoken on foreign policy issues.

For Further Information:
Ambrose, Stephen E. *Nixon*, 3 vols. New York, 1987–1989.
Jones, Alan, ed. *U.S. Foreign Policy in a Changing World: The Nixon Administration, 1969–73.* New York, 1977.
Kissinger, Henry. *The White House Years.* New York, 1979.
———. *The Years of Upheaval.* New York, 1982.
Nixon, Richard M. *The Memoirs of Richard Nixon.* New York, 1978.
Parmet, Herbert S. *Richard Nixon and His America.* Boston, 1990.
Price, Raymond. *With Nixon.* New York, 1977.
Roberts, Chalmers. "Foreign Policy Under a Paralyzed Presidency," *Foreign Affairs* (July 1974).
Safire, William L. *Before the Fall: An Inside View of the Pre-Watergate White House.* Garden City, N.Y., 1975.
Schurmann, Franz. *The Foreign Politics of Richard Nixon: The Grand Design.* Berkeley, Calif., 1987.
Shawcross, William. *Sideshow: Kissinger, Nixon, and the Destruction of Cambodia.* London, 1986.
Sulzberger, C.L. *The World and Richard Nixon.* New York, 1987.
Szulc, Tad. *The Illusion of Peace: Foreign Policy in the Nixon Years.* New York, 1978.
Thornton, Richard C. *The Nixon-Kissinger Years: Reshaping America's Foreign Policy.* New York, 1989.

Nkrumah, Kwame   See GHANA.

Nonaligned Movement   The nonaligned movement was a group of mainly Third World countries that reacted against the division of the world into East–West power blocs by declaring their neutrality in the superpower struggle.

Throughout the 1950s, Third World countries came under increasing pressure from the Soviet Union and the United States to ally themselves with one or the other superpower. The EISENHOWER administration, for instance, was adamant that there could be no neutrals in the Cold War.

A number of countries, however, believed that the superpower conflict was about power, rather than political principle, and failed to offer them any useful help in addressing issues of importance to them, such as colonialism, racism and apartheid and various regional issues. They also feared that alliance with a superpower meant inevitable subordination of their own national identities and interests to those of the great world power.

The leading figures among those neutralist countries were Yugoslavia's JOSIP BROZ TITO, Egyptian president GAMAL ABDEL NASSER, Indonesian president Sukarno and Indian prime minister Jawaharlal Nehru. In September 1961 Tito invited these leaders and the leaders of 21 other neutral countries to a summit in Belgrade to form the nonaligned movement. On September 6, 1961, the conferees issued a 27-point declaration that included:

1. A denunciation of colonialism, Zionism and apartheid.
2. A declaration of "the absolute respect of the rights of ethnic or religious minorities to be protected in particular against . . . genocide or any other violation of their fundamental human rights."
3. A declaration that disarmament was "an imperative need and the most urgent task of mankind."
4. An agreement that "general and complete disarmament should include the elimination of armed forces, armaments, foreign bases, manufacture of arms . . . institutions and installations for military training . . . and the total prohibition . . . of nuclear and thermonuclear arms, bacteriological and chemical weapons . . ."
5. A denunciation of foreign military bases and "full support to countries who are endeavoring to secure the vacation of these bases."

Membership in the nonaligned movement grew to more than 100 nations by 1985. Its foreign ministers and leaders met regularly and in 1973 the movement established a headquarters in Belgrade. As well as encouraging political cooperation, the Belgrade-based secretariat also maintained special funds for agricultural development.

During the 1970s the nonaligned movement became an increasingly powerful force on the international stage, especially in the United Nations General Assembly, where its members often voted as a bloc on major international issues. In the United States, the organization was regarded by successive administrations as leaning too far to the left to warrant support. This view was reinforced by the membership of CUBA. The founders hoped that the movement would become a third power bloc to challenge the Soviet Union and the United States. This did not happen, but the nonaligned movement did succeed in drawing attention to issues of international relations beyond the Cold War.

The nonaligned movement currently has 108 members, and held its most recent summit in Jakarta, Indonesia in September 1992. The status of its Belgrade headquarters is questionable.

For Further Information:
Allison, Roy. *The Soviet Union and the Strategy of Non-Alignment in the Third World.* New York, 1988.
Brands, H.W. *The Specter of Neutralism: The United States and the Emergence of the Third World, 1947–1960.* New York, 1989.
David, Steven R. *Choosing Sides: Alignment and Realignment in the Third World.* Baltimore, 1991.
Zimmerman, William. *Open Borders, Nonalignment, and the Political Evolution of Yugoslavia.* Princeton, 1987.

Nordic Balance   The Nordic Balance is the Scandinavian structure of diplomatic and military alliances that has existed since the end of World War II and that many analysts believe has contributed to peace in that part of Europe.

The main elements of the Nordic Balance are the special relationship between Finland and the Soviet Union established by the FINNISH-SOVIET AGREEMENT of 1948; Swedish neutrality; Norwegian and Danish membership in the NORTH ATLANTIC TREATY ORGANIZATION; Denmark and Norway's refusal to allow either nuclear weapons or foreign troops to be based on their national territory during peacetime; and political and economic cooperation among all the Scandinavian countries through the Nordic Council and the European Free Trade Association (EFTA).

Norstad, Lauris   (March 24, 1907–September 12, 1988)

As NATO's SUPREME ALLIED COMMANDER FOR EUROPE, Lauris Norstad became an early advocate of an alliance-wide nuclear strike force. His championing of the European position on this issue led to his early resignation during the KENNEDY administration.

Norstad graduated from the U.S. Military Academy at West Point. He joined the Army Air Corps in 1939 and at the start of World War II became assistant chief of staff for intelligence of the Air Corps. In this capacity he helped direct Allied landings in North Africa and Sicily and the bombings in Japan, including the atomic bomb attacks on Hiroshima and Nagasaki.

After the war, Norstad was instrumental in establishing the air force as an independent service. In 1950 he was named to the command of the U.S. Air Force in Europe. In 1952 he became the youngest American to achieve the rank of full general. In 1953 Norstad was appointed NATO's air deputy to the Supreme Allied Commander Europe, and in November 1956 he became supreme commander of NATO forces in Europe.

General Lauris Norstad, former supreme commander of NATO. His stand on a nuclear strike force in Europe led to his resignation during the Kennedy administration. Photo courtesy of NATO.

Norstad's long experience in Europe had allowed him to develop close contacts with European allies, and he was often seen as their champion in policy disputes between them and Washington. At the same time, however, Norstad pressed for a greater nuclear and conventional weapons commitment from the Europeans, especially the British. On April 15, during a meeting of NATO defense ministers in Iceland, Norstad asked for an increase in conventional force strength to 32 divisions.

Norstad also supported the case for increasing the strength of the West German Army and basing nuclear weapons on German soil. He opposed the RAPACKI PLAN of 1958 put forward by the Polish foreign minister, which proposed a nuclear-free zone in Central Europe.

Norstad believed that the first deterrent should be conventional forces, but that an extra commitment to defense should be demonstrated by land-based ballistic missiles. During his tenure at Brussels, he increased the number of short-range missile battalions from 30 to 100. Norstad felt that the tactical weapons were an essential adjunct to the long-range strategic system. He at first accepted the American position that the United States should retain control of the nuclear weapons, but by 1959 he was advocating a nuclear force commanded and controlled on an alliance-wide basis.

Norstad also proposed the creation of a West German nuclear-armed force, which he described as "absolutely indispensable" for the effective defense of Western Europe. The proposal was seen as too provocative to Europeans in both East and West, but as a result of Norstad's efforts, the Bonn government was given permission to develop air-to-air and surface-to-air missiles. In 1959 West Germany was equipped with nuclear-capable missiles, but they remained under Norstad's direct command.

During the 1961 BERLIN Crisis, Norstad urged President John F. Kennedy to reassure the European allies that he would use nuclear weapons to protect West Berlin. Kennedy's refusal to do so led to increased determination by Britain and Germany to build up European nuclear forces. In response to this pressure, Kennedy agreed to commit Polaris submarines to a multilateral NATO force. The Kennedy proposal, which was unveiled at Nassau in December 1961, gave each alliance member a veto over the use of the nuclear missiles.

Norstad felt that the veto clause was too clumsy and during an attack would hamper command and control procedures and possibly prove fatal. He proposed that the decision to launch the missiles be made by a majority vote among the alliance's three nuclear powers, Britain, France and the United States. He also wanted land-based nuclear systems rather than Polaris.

Norstad's differences with Kennedy led to his early resignation in January 1963. He became president of the international division of Owens-Corning in 1963 but continued to speak out on defense issues. In April 1964 he urged the Republican Party to press for an independent NATO nuclear force, and he repeated his support for such a force in May 1966 before the Senate Subcommittee on National Security and International Operations.

Norstad was part of a group of elder statesmen called to the White House on May 13, 1971, for consultation on the Mansfield Amendment, which would have reduced U.S. troop levels in Europe. The group's unanimous opposition to troop reductions played a major role in the Senate's defeat of the amendment.

North Atlantic Council

The North Atlantic Council is the principal decision-making body of the NORTH ATLANTIC TREATY ORGANIZATION. The chairman of the council is the secretary general of NATO.

The council meets at various levels. Heads of government meet as occasion demands; the foreign ministers generally meet twice a year, once in Brussels and once in the capital of a member nation. Their meetings usually take place in December and June.

When the council meets at the level of permanent representatives (who act as the member governments' ambassadors) it is known as the council in permanent session. In theory, the permanent representatives meet once a week on Wednesdays. In practice, they often meet four or five times a week. In fact, the permanent representatives are on constant standby 24 hours a day, and a council meeting can be arranged at two hours' notice.

Nineteen committees report to the council. They are: Nuclear Defense Affairs Committee; Economics Committee; Defense Review Committee; Conference of National Armaments Directors; Senior NATO Logistics Conference; Security Committee; Senior Civil Emergency Planning Committee; NATO Joint Communications Electronics Committee; Infrastructure Committee; Science Committee; Committee on the Challenges of Modern Society; Committee on Information and Cultural Relations; NATO Air Defense Committee; Committee for European Airspace Coordination; Council Operations and Exercises Committee; Civil and Military Budget Committees; Command, Control and Information Systems; and Automatic Data Processing Committee.

The structure and duties of the council have changed several times since the creation of NATO in 1949. At first it was decided that the council would be comprised of foreign ministers who would meet once a year. At the same time a council of defense ministers was established. Shortly afterward, in November 1949, the alliance also established a defense and economic committee comprised of finance ministers.

This system was too cumbersome to deal with ongoing problems. Therefore, in 1950, it was decided to establish the Council of Deputies, which became the forerunner of the permanent representatives. The main structures of the existing North Atlantic Council were established at the Lisbon foreign ministers' meeting in 1952.

At first, the council was based at NATO headquarters in Paris. But it moved to Brussels with the rest of the NATO offices after France left the military structure in 1966.

North Atlantic Treaty Organization (NATO)

The North Atlantic Treaty Organization is a defense and political alliance of Western nations founded in 1949 to protect Western Europe from attack by the Soviet Union. The alliance quickly became the primary institutional framework linking the United States and Canada to the protection of Europe.

In the aftermath of World War II it was hoped that the peacekeeping force of the United Nations would maintain international security. But the Soviet Union's excessive use of its Security Council veto blocked any effective use of the UN's military potential. As early as 1946 it became apparent that a regional defense alliance would be needed to protect Western Europe from the Soviet Union. In that year Canadian external affairs minister LOUIS ST. LAURENT proposed an "Association of Democratic Peace-Loving States" under the umbrella of the United Nations.

It was obvious to all concerned that the only country powerful enough to give any real meaning to such an alliance was the United States. In 1947 the TRUMAN administration demonstrated its unwillingness to return to prewar isolation with the TRUMAN DOCTRINE and the MARSHALL PLAN. Further proof of American commitment was given by the Berlin Airlift, which started in 1948.

But to overcome isolationist opponents, the Truman administration required signs of a European commitment to Europe's own defense. This was provided by the 50-year ANGLO-FRENCH TREATY OF ALLIANCE AND MUTUAL ASSISTANCE of 1947 and then the BRUSSELS TREATY of 1948, which committed the governments of Belgium, France, Luxembourg, the Netherlands and Britain to build a common defense system.

Shortly after the Brussels Treaty was signed, the Soviets imposed the BERLIN BLOCKADE, which acted as a further impetus to West European defense cooperation and cooperation between Europe and the United States and Canada. In April 1948, St. Laurent proposed the creation of a single mutual defense system to supersede the Brussels Treaty. This was welcomed by the Europeans led by British foreign secretary ERNEST BEVIN and French foreign minister GEORGES BIDAULT.

In Washington, the ground for American membership in a Western Alliance was cleared by a former isolationist, Senator ARTHUR VANDENBERG, whose VANDENBERG RESOLUTION recommended "the association of the United States, by constitutional process, with such regional and other collective arrangements as are based on continuous and effective self-help and mutual aid" and its "contribution to the maintenance of peace by making clear its determination to exercise the right of individual or collective self-defense . . . should any armed attack occur affecting its national security."

The passage of this resolution cleared the way for the State Department to start negotiations for American membership in the alliance. The North Atlantic Treaty, which established NATO, was signed on April 4, 1949, in Washington, D.C.

The initial signatories were Canada, the United States, Britain, Belgium, the Netherlands, France, Luxembourg, Denmark, Iceland, Italy, Norway and Portugal. Greece and Turkey joined in 1952. West Germany became a member in 1955 and Spain joined in 1982. France withdrew from the integrated military structure in 1966 but remained a member of the political structure. Greece withdrew from the military structure following the Turkish invasion of Cyprus in 1974 but rejoined it in October 1980. Under the treaty the signatories agree:

1. "That an armed attack against one or more of them in Europe or North America shall be considered an attack against them all; and consequently they agree that, if such an armed attack occurs, each of them, in exercise of the right of individual or collective self defense . . . will assist the party or parties so attacked by taking forthwith, individually and in concert with the other parties, such action as it deems necessary, including the use of armed force, to restore and maintain the security of the North Atlantic area . . ."
2. To strengthen "free institutions."
3. To "seek to eliminate conflict in their international economic policies" and "encourage economic collaboration between any and all of them."
4. That through "continuous and effective self-help and mutual aid" they will "maintain and develop their individual and collective capacity to resist armed attack."
5. To "consult whenever, in the opinion of any of them, the territorial integrity, political independence, or security of any of the parties is threatened."
6. That the geographic area covered by the treaty includes the territory of any of the parties in Europe or North America, as well as French Algeria; occupation forces of any party in Europe; islands under the jurisdiction of any party in the North Atlantic area north of the Tropic of Cancer; or the vessels or aircraft in this area of any of the parties. The treaty was later amended to exclude Algeria.
7. Not to sign conflicting defense treaties.
8. To establish a North Atlantic Council to implement the treaty and oversee its operation.

NATO's first six years were absorbed by organizational matters. At the September 1949 meeting of the North Atlantic Council it was agreed that foreign ministers and defense ministers would meet annually. A military committee consisting of the chiefs of staff of the member countries was also established. In November 1949, the council established the Defense Financial and Economic Committee, composed of the national finance ministers, to coordinate finance guidance for defense programs. The military Production and Supply Board was also established to promote standardized armaments production (a problem that was never adequately resolved).

In December 1949, the defense ministers agreed on a strategic concept for the integrated defense of the treaty area

and an integrated military production plan. In May 1950, the NATO foreign ministers established a Council of Deputies that would meet in permanent session in London (later moved to Brussels). The deputies became known as the permanent representatives or ambassadors of their countries to NATO.

After the outbreak of the KOREAN WAR in June 1950, each of the alliance members was urged to provide support to the South Korean government. The focus of the alliance then shifted to the development of a "Forward Strategy," which allowed the NATO countries to be defended as far to the east as possible. This inevitably led to the conclusion that a formula must be found for West German involvement in the Western Alliance.

In December 1950, the alliance members took the momentous military step of approving the Defense Committee's plans for an integrated European defense force and the appointment of a SUPREME ALLIED COMMANDER FOR EUROPE (SACEUR) for those forces. General DWIGHT D. EISENHOWER was the first SACEUR. Since then, SACEUR has always been an American officer. The political head of the organization, the secretary general, has always come from a European country.

In 1952, the NATO foreign ministers' meeting in Lisbon set ambitious goals for NATO conventional force levels and endorsed the plans for a EUROPEAN DEFENSE COMMUNITY (EDC), which would bring West Germany into the Western Alliance and strengthen West European defenses. The Lisbon goals were later found to be financially unrealistic, especially in the light of the collapse of the EDC, and the alliance's failure to meet these goals led to Western Europe's long-term dependence on the United States. In the same year new military commands were established: SUPREME ALLIED COMMANDER ATLANTIC (SACLANT), based at Norfolk, Virginia and responsible for NATO naval forces in the Atlantic; Allied Commander-in-Chief Channel (CINCHAN), based at Northwood, England and responsible for NATO naval forces in the English Channel; and the CANADA-U.S. REGIONAL PLANNING GROUP, based in Washington, D.C. and responsible for coordinating the defense of North America. Other commands were established later and included the Commander-in-Chief of Allied Forces in Northern Europe, based in Norway; the Commander-in-Chief of Allied Forces in Central Europe, based in the Netherlands; and the Commander-in-Chief of Allied Forces Southern Europe, based in Naples. A Nato Defense College was also established in Rome.

The French National Assembly's rejection of the EDC Treaty in 1954 threw the alliance into temporary disarray. The crisis was resolved by the EDEN PLAN FOR GERMAN REUNIFICATION, which committed Britain and the United States to maintaining their troops in West Germany, and West Germany was recognized as a sovereign state and invited to join NATO. The Soviet Union responded to West German membership in NATO by forming the WARSAW PACT.

The Eden Plan finally resolved the political and military foundations of the NATO alliance, which for the next 10 years concentrated on consolidating the military situation. The continuing economic difficulties of the European countries, and the increasing costs to the United States of maintaining large numbers of conventional forces in Europe, meant that the emphasis of the defense shifted from conventional forces to nuclear forces. Tactical, battlefield and intermediate-range American nuclear weapons were based in West Germany, Britain and Turkey in order to deter the large Soviet conventional forces in East Germany, Czechoslovakia, Hungary and Poland.

The heavy emphasis on nuclear defense worried the nonnuclear members of the alliance. They were concerned that this dependence on nuclear weapons over which they had no military control meant that the weapons could be used on their territory without their approval. To assuage these concerns, President JOHN F. KENNEDY proposed the creation of a NATO Multilateral Nuclear Force (MLF), which involved the commitment of some of the American nuclear forces and all of the French and British forces to an alliance-wide command structure. This proposal eventually collapsed because of British and French refusal to relinquish full control of their nuclear deterrent. Eventually, the nonnuclear countries were provided with a say in nuclear planning issues through the creation of a NATO Nuclear Planning Group (NPG), which established the alliance's nuclear policies.

The next NATO crisis came in 1966 with the withdrawal of France from the military structure. French president CHARLES DE GAULLE was concerned that the predominance of the United States within NATO might circumscribe independent French political and military action. In March 1966 he officially announced that French personnel would be withdrawn from the NATO integrated military headquarters, and that French forces would end their assignment to international headquarters, allied units and installations or bases not falling under the control of the French authorities. He also expelled American forces from France and the French military headquarters, which was then based outside Paris. The crisis was resolved by moving the military headquarters to Brussels and maintaining political consultations with France. There was never any suggestion that France had turned against its former alliance partners. It remained committed to the defense of Western Europe, and this was demonstrated by the FRANCO–GERMAN FRIENDSHIP TREATY of 1963. It has been generally assumed that, in the event of an outbreak of war, France would quickly reintegrate its forces with those under NATO command.

The withdrawal of France coincided with the start of the détente period. NATO's response to détente found its expression in the HARMEL REPORT of 1967, which defined the main political task of the alliance as "to pursue the search for progress towards a more stable relationship in which the underlying political issues can be solved." The ultimate political purpose of the alliance was described as the achievement of "a just and lasting peaceful order in Europe accompanied by appropriate security guarantees."

The report presented several specific proposals in pursuit of these goals. They included alliance-wide discussions on German reunification issues; an ongoing examination and review of suitable policies designed to achieve a just and stable order in Europe, to overcome the division of Germany and to foster European security; the start of East–West negotiations on the reduction of conventional forces in Europe; greater consultation on military conflicts outside the North Atlantic Treaty area; and an increase in NATO's Mediterranean forces to counterbalance increased Soviet activity in the MIDDLE EAST.

The following 10 years were absorbed with implementation of the Harmel Report as the détente period bore fruit with the Salt I and Salt II agreements (the second of which was unratified), the start of the Mutual Balance Force Reduction (MBFR) Talks (which were eventually replaced by the Conventional Forces in Europe talks), OSTPOLITIK, the QUADRIPARTITE AGREEMENT OF 1971 and the CONFERENCE ON SECURITY AND COOPERATION IN EUROPE (CSCE).

NATO policies shifted dramatically in 1979 with the Soviet invasion of AFGHANISTAN and the decision in December of that year to deploy American cruise and PERSHING II intermediate-range nuclear missiles in Western Europe in response to the Soviet deployment of its highly mobile intermediate-range SS-20 missiles. The NATO decision to protect Western Europe with American missiles sparked off a series of vociferous protests from many Europeans. Groups such as the British-based CAMPAIGN FOR NUCLEAR DISARMAMENT were revived and organized antinuclear demonstrations across Europe. The protesters were worried that the increase in intermediate-range systems was adding another twist to the nuclear arms spiral, lowering the nuclear threshold and making it more, rather than less, likely that a war between the superpowers would result in a nuclear exchange confined to the European theater.

As the protests grew, so did the pressure on the governments of the European members of NATO to force the United States either to reach a quick agreement with the Soviet Union or to retreat from the December 1979 decision. This pressure was increased by a series of "peace initiatives" by the Soviet leadership, which, until 1985, were generally short on substance and long on rhetoric and clearly designed to drive a wedge between the American and European members of NATO.

The situation was further complicated by what many Europeans regarded as President RONALD REAGAN's hostile anti-Soviet rhetoric and the American negotiators' initial plans to link the intermediate nuclear force (INF) weapons negotiations to talks aimed at reducing the strategic nuclear arsenals of the superpowers. These STRATEGIC ARMS REDUCTION TREATY talks (START) became increasingly bogged down by President Ronald Reagan's STRATEGIC DEFENSE INITIATIVE (SDI, or Star Wars), which the Soviets regarded as a breach of the 1972 ANTIBALLISTIC MISSILE TREATY.

The alliance crisis over the INF negotiations was resolved

with the signing of the INTERMEDIATE-RANGE NUCLEAR FORCES TREATY in December 1987. But in the interim a number of factors had come into play that would affect the long-term future of the alliance. These included the increased political cooperation among West European states through the EURO-PEAN ECONOMIC COMMUNITY, sometimes in opposition to the United States; growing concern within the United States about the cost of maintaining a large military presence in Western Europe; and, finally, the accession to power of Soviet leader MIKHAIL GORBACHEV, the subsequent collapse of Soviet power in Eastern Europe, reunification of GERMANY, and finally the dissolution of the Soviet Union.

These last changes negated the military need for the alliance. By June 1990, NATO foreign ministers concluded that the Western Alliance no longer faced a military threat from Eastern Europe and the Soviet Union. This statement had been preceded by a decision not to modernize the alliance's tactical nuclear weapons in West Germany and by President GEORGE BUSH's announcement that he was reducing American forces in Europe and elsewhere in the world in response to a lessening of East–West tensions. At the start of the 1990s alliance members generally agreed that for the alliance to remain a viable force, it should shift the emphasis of its activities from the military to the political sphere.

For Further Information:
Cook, Don. *Forging the Alliance.* London, 1989.
Cyr, A.I. *U.S. Foreign Policy and European Security.* New York, 1988.
Grosser, Alfred. *The Western Alliance: European-American Relations Since 1945.* New York, 1980.
Kennan, George F. *The Fateful Alliance.* New York, 1984.
NATO Information Services. *NATO Facts and Figures.* Brussels, 1985.
Treverton, G.F. *Making the Alliance Work: The United States and Europe.* Ithaca, N.Y., 1985.

Northern Flank   The Northern Flank is the narrow border between Norway and the former Soviet Union or between Norway and Finland. Control of the Northern Flank was vital to Soviet naval operations in the North Atlantic.

The only way that the Soviet Union could move its Western fleet out of Murmansk on the Arctic Ocean to a position where it could threaten the North Atlantic sea lanes was through the narrow GREENLAND-ICELAND-UK GAP, which is well protected by the American and British air forces and the British Royal Navy. To dislodge NATO forces from the GIUK Gap, the Soviet Union would have to invade and occupy Norway. This would have given the Soviet Union a land base on the eastern edge of the GIUK Gap from which it could launch air and naval operations in support of the Soviet Navy.

To combat the threat, NATO established the Northern European Command to coordinate British, American, Norwegian, Dutch and Canadian forces assigned to the defense of Norway and the Baltic Sea approaches. Because the Norwegian government does not allow foreign troops to be permanently based on its soil in peacetime, stocks were prepositioned and member countries' troops were flown to Norway for annual defense exercises.

Northern Territories   The Northern Territories are a group of islands at the northern end of the Japanese archipelago that have been occupied by the Soviet Union since the end of World War II. The Soviet refusal to return the islands is the major source of friction between Japan and the Soviet Union and has prevented the two countries from signing a formal peace treaty.

The islands of Habomai, Shikotan, Kunashiri and Etorofu stretch in a northeasterly direction off the northeastern tip of the Japanese island of Hokkaido. The Soviets claim that they are part of the Kurile Islands, which are directly north of the Northern Territories, but the Japanese claim that they are a separate group. Before the Soviet Army occupied the islands in September 1945, more than 16,000 Japanese lived on them.

The Russo-Japanese conflict over the islands stretches back to the 19th century, when Russia tried to colonize the islands. In 1855 the two countries signed a treaty establishing a line between Etorofu and Uruppu islands as the boundary between Japan and Russia. Sakhalin Island was to have no national boundary but to remain a mixed settlement for both nations. In 1875, Japan abandoned all of Sakhalin Island in exchange for the Kurile Islands. The Japanese claim to the islands is based on these treaties.

At the YALTA CONFERENCE, the allied leaders agreed that southern Sakhalin, its adjacent islands and the Kurile Islands should be handed over to the Soviet Union in return for Soviet entry into the war against Japan. The Soviets declared war on Japan on August 9, 1945, and by early September had occupied all of Sakhalin, the Kuriles and adjacent islands. The Soviet Union's claim to the islands is based on the Yalta Agreement. The Yalta Agreement was later reinforced by the POTSDAM CONFERENCE and the 1951 San Francisco Peace Treaty, both of which give either implicit or explicit control of Sakhalin and the Kurile Islands to the Soviet Union.

But the Japanese claim that the Northern Territories are not part of the Kurile Islands. They point out that neither the Potsdam nor Yalta agreement had the effect of a binding treaty and neither specifically stated which islands were part of the Kurile group. They also point out that Japan's position on the Northern Territories was made clear during the San Francisco Peace Conference. In September 1956, Japan won the formal support of the United States when the EISENHOWER administration issued a statement saying that Kunashiri, Etorofu, Habomai and Shikotan have always been part of Japanese territory and should "in justice" be acknowledged to be under Japanese sovereignty. This position was restated in a note sent to the Soviet Union in May 1957 after the shooting down of a U.S. aircraft over Hokkaido.

The Soviet Union refused to sign the 1951 peace treaty, claiming that it would pave the way for a new war in the Far East. Japan thus decided to conclude a separate treaty with the Soviet Union, and negotiations started in June 1955. But no agreement could be reached on the territorial question except as regarded Habomai and Shikotan, so the two countries agreed to shelve the peace treaty negotiations, although they did reestablish diplomatic relations in October 1956. The Soviet Union used the reestablishment of relations to claim that the two countries had effectively settled the territorial issue.

The issue remained more or less unresolved and undiscussed until January 1972, when Soviet foreign minister AN-DREI GROMYKO agreed to reopen negotiations for a peace treaty. In October 1973, Japanese prime minister Kakuei Tanaka visited the Soviet Union to try to settle the issue of the Northern Territories. But Tanaka and Soviet leader LEONID BREZHNEV could agree only that the territorial issue could be resolved only within the terms of a final peace treaty and that further talks were needed.

Further negotiations were held in January 1975 in Moscow between Gromyko and Japanese foreign minister Kiichi Miyazawa. During this round the Soviet government said that the Japanese view concerning the territorial question could not serve as the basis for a peace treaty and asked that Japan take a "realistic attitude." In January 1976, Gromyko visited Japan and again the issue of the Northern Territories blocked the conclusion of a peace treaty. Later that year, the Soviet Union, ignoring long-established practice, demanded that those Japanese wishing to visit family graves in the Northern Territories must acquire passports with Soviet visas, on the grounds that the islands were Soviet territory. Because this would result in an implicit Japanese recognition of Soviet sovereignty, the annual visit to Japanese graves was canceled.

In March 1977 the Soviet Union extended its territorial fishing zone, including waters around the disputed islands, to 200 miles. The Japanese made a formal protest, and the Soviet Union issued a statement claiming that there was no "territorial issue" outstanding between Japan and the Soviet Union and that it had never agreed to discuss the Northern Territorial issue, which "the Japanese artificially created." Japan and the Soviet Union did, however, sign a fishing agreement in May 1977, which explicitly stated that it did not in any way prejudice Japan's claim to the Northern Territories.

In 1978 the Soviet Union started constructing military facilities on Kunashiri and Etorofu. This resulted in a fresh round of Japanese protests and a demand that the Soviet Union immediately remove its military forces and installations from the Northern Territories. The protest was ignored by the Soviet Union and all negotiations were suspended. In January 1986 Soviet foreign minister EDUARD SHEVARDNADZE visited Japan, and peace treaty negotiations were resumed. There have been talks and summit meetings since between Japan and the Soviet Union, and later Russia, but the issue has remained unresolved.

Norway Norway is the key country on the NORTHERN FLANK of the NORTH ATLANTIC TREATY ORGANIZATION (NATO). It was one of only two NATO countries to have a common border with the Soviet Union, and at the same time is located at the eastern end of the GREENLAND-ICELAND-UK (GIUK) GAP and the Baltic Sea approaches through which the Soviet Union's European fleet would have had to pass to reach the North Atlantic.

Until 1905, Norway was linked to the Swedish Crown. In 1905 the union with Sweden was peacefully dissolved, and the Norwegians elected their own monarch. At the same time, they opted for the traditional Scandinavian foreign policy of neutrality. This kept them out of World War I, but not World War II.

Norway's strategic position on the northeastern edge of the Atlantic presented the Germans with an opportunity to dominate this approach to the ocean and the route from Britain to Russia through the Norwegian Sea and the Arctic. German troops invaded Norway in April 1940 and by June had conquered it and established a puppet government under Vidkun Quisling, the leader of the small Norwegian Nazi Party. The king and the government fled to London, where they established a government-in-exile.

After the Germans invaded the Soviet Union in 1941, the Norwegian government in London became increasingly concerned that Soviet troops would attempt to take Norway. The Norwegians were concerned that this would lead to communist domination and pressured the Americans and the British to demand that the liberation of Norway be the sole responsibility of the Western Allies. The Americans and British reluctantly agreed, but nevertheless Soviet troops moved into the northernmost section of Norway (Finnmark) in October 1944. But after 65 miles, the Soviet offensive stopped. It is believed that Soviet leader JOSEF STALIN did not want to tie his forces down fighting the large German contingent in Norway when he had an opportunity to secure control of the more strategic Central European countries. The Soviets, however, occupied an estimated 1,000 square miles of Norwegian territory. At the same time, the Soviet foreign minister, V.M. MOLOTOV, requested that Norway formally cede its Arctic Ocean territories—the Svalbard Archipelago—so that the Soviet Navy could protect the shipping lanes from Murmansk and Arkhangel'sk to the Atlantic.

The Norwegians revealed the Soviet demand to British foreign secretary Sir ANTHONY EDEN, knowing that Eden would attempt to block the Soviet action as it had been long-standing British policy to prevent the establishment of a Russian base on the Atlantic. Eden reacted as expected. At the time of the German surrender, the Soviets claimed an occupation zone of 14,000 square miles in the northernmost part of Norway. The central part of Norway was controlled by Norwegian forces and the southern part was occupied by British and American forces. But the foreign troops were there mainly to organize the surrender of 350,000 German troops. Within eight months the British, American and Soviet troops had withdrawn from the country.

In the immediate postwar period, the Norwegian Labor Party formed an electoral pact with the Norwegian Communist Party, which had grown in stature because of its role in wartime resistance. But in elections in the autumn of 1945 Labor won a decisive majority, which enabled it to form a government without the help of the communists. Labor remained in power at the head of a series of coalitions until 1965.

Norway's wartime experience demonstrated both the inability of the small Norwegian population to defend itself from attack by a great power and the inadvisability of a continuance of Norway's prewar policy of neutrality. The issue, then, was not whether to seek an alliance, but the exact nature of that alliance. The Norwegians were greatly attracted to the concept of the United Nations and their foreign minister, TRYGVE LIE, became the first UN secretary general. Within the United Nations, Norway saw itself as a bridge between the Anglo-American-dominated Western powers and the Soviet-dominated East. Defense could be guaranteed by the United Nations.

The Norwegians drew a number of similarities between themselves and the immediate postwar government of CZECH-OSLOVAKIA. Thus when the communist coup took place in Czechoslovakia in March 1948 the bridge-building policy and search for UN protection was quickly abandoned in favor of a pell-mell race for a regional alliance to protect Norway from a Soviet attack. By the end of March the Swedish, Danish and Norwegian governments were involved in negotiations for a Nordic Defense Alliance, and by the end of the year a joint defense scheme was ready for political approval. But the plan fell apart because Sweden insisted that Norway and Denmark substantially increase their defense spending and because the Norwegians refused to enter into any Nordic Alliance that was not guaranteed by either Britain or the United States.

In February 1949, the Norwegian defense minister, Oscar Torp, and foreign minister, Halvard Lange, flew to Washington to explore the possibility of joining the proposed North Atlantic Treaty Organization. The Soviets responded by demanding an assurance from the Norwegians that they would not join an Atlantic alliance. In response, the Norwegians undertook to "make no agreement with other states which lays obligations upon Norway to open bases on Norwegian territory to the armed forced of foreign powers, so long as Norway is not attacked or exposed to threats of attack." In this statement lies the Norwegians' steadfast refusal to allow Canadian, American or British troops to be based on Norwegian soil or to allow any nuclear weapons on Norwegian territory.

The issue of membership in NATO was discussed by the Norwegian Storting (parliament) in a secret debate in March 1949, and Norway was among the founding members of the alliance in April.

As the guardian of the long and sparsely populated Northern Flank, it was clear that Norway could not protect all of its territory on its own. But at the same time, its pledge to the Soviet Union meant that other NATO forces could not be based in Norway. A compromise was reached to retain the delicate NORDIC BALANCE. The headquarters for NATO's Northern Flank, the Northern European Command, was based in Oslo under a British general. No Allied troops were permanently based in Norway, but Dutch, Canadian (until 1988), American and British troops were regularly flown to Norway for exercises, especially during the winter months. It was also made clear that in time of emergency these troops would be flown to Norway and based there, along with nuclear weapons. In 1980 it was decided to stockpile American non-nuclear military equipment in central Norway for use in case of war.

The Soviet Union tacitly accepted this compromise but at the same time based a large naval, air force and army establishment at Murmansk on the Kola Peninsula, only a few miles from the Norwegian border.

Relations with the Soviet Union in the 1950s and 1960s settled into an armed truce. But in the 1970s the problem of the Svalbard Archipelago again cropped up. The Norwegians had rejected Molotov's demand in 1944 that the archipelago be handed over to the Soviets but had allowed them to share in the islands' rich coal deposits. But by the 1970s, it became clear that the surrounding waters were also rich with oil deposits and fishing.

In 1977 Norway declared a 200-mile exclusive economic zone from its coastline. But a counterclaim by the Soviet Union left an overlap of 155,000 square miles. In 1978 a "gray zone," in which both countries could exercise control of fisheries, was established as a temporary measure. But at the end of 1983 the Soviet Union began drilling for oil on the eastern edge of the gray zone.

Norwegian–Soviet relations were further damaged in January 1984 when diplomat and Labor deputy minister Arne Treholt was arrested and charged with being a Soviet spy. Treholt had played a prominent role in negotiations with the Soviet Union about territorial and fishing rights and about the division of the Barents Sea continental shelf. He also had provided the Soviets with details of NATO's defense of the Northern Flank. A month later, five Soviet diplomats were expelled from Norway for activities "incompatible with their diplomatic status." Treholt was found guilty in June 1985 and sentenced to 20 years' imprisonment.

Norwegian foreign policy was never completely in the Western camp. It retained strong links with Sweden and Finland through membership in the Nordic Council, and a significant portion of the Norwegian population was drawn toward closer Scandinavian ties and the traditional Scandiavian policy of neutrality. This was a major contributing factor in the Norwegian voters' decision to leave the EUROPEAN ECONOMIC COMMUNITY less than a year after joining it. It also almost led to the defeat in 1983 of the conservative government of Kare Willoch over the issue of the basing of American cruise and PERSHING II missiles in Europe, even though none of the missiles would have been based in Norway.

The traditional Scandinavian abhorrence of nuclear weapons encouraged the Soviet Union in 1983 to propose a nuclear-free zone for the Baltic Sea. This was rejected, but in November 1986, in an apparent attempt to revive the proposal, the Soviet Union announced that it had withdrawn medium-range nuclear missiles from the Kola Peninsula and was prepared to withdraw ballistic missile submarines from the Baltic. In October 1989 Soviet leader Mikhail Gorbachev made another unilateral gesture by withdrawing the last four Soviet Golf-class nuclear-armed submarines in the Baltic. Although the left wing of the Norwegian Labor Party was attracted to the idea of a nuclear-free zone, the mainstream politicians realized that it would be a one-sided agreement, as no Nordic countries have any nuclear weapons, and that the Soviet Union could easily have hit any NATO bases in Norway with missiles or planes based elsewhere in the Soviet Union. On the other hand, Norwegian agreement to such a pact would only have damaged relations with the United States and Britain.

The Norwegians maintain an active defense force of 36,500 troops. Their main contribution to the protection of the Northern Flank was air cover and reconnaissance by eight fighter aircraft squadrons.

For Further Information:
Derry, Thomas. *A History of Modern Norway.* Oxford, 1973.
Udgaard, Nils Morten. *Great Power Politics and Norwegian Foreign Policy: A Study of Norway's Foreign Relations, November 1940–February 1948.* Oslo, 1973.

Nosenko, Yuri   *See* ANGLETON, JAMES JESUS.

Novotny, Antonin   (December 10, 1904–January 28, 1975) Antonin Novotny was a hard-line communist who became general secretary of the Czechoslovak Communist Party in 1953. In that capacity he restrained reformist tendencies of President ANTONIN ZAPOTOCKY and in 1957 succeeded him in the presidency. In January 1968 Novotny was forced to resign in favor of ALEXANDER DUBCEK, but he was rehabilitated in 1971.

From 1948 to 1953, President KLEMENT GOTTWALD was one of the most slavish disciples of JOSEF STALIN and Soviet policy, and Novotny was recognized as his closest disciple in Prague. When Gottwald died suddenly in March 1953 he was succeeded by Antonin Zapotocky, who wanted to end the repression of the Gottwald years and started by attempting to introduce a limited economic and monetary reform. But on June 1, 1953, workers in PILSEN rioted, destroying factory machinery, pillaging the town hall and trampling on the Soviet flag. Troops opened fire and six demonstrators were killed.

The riots strengthened the Stalinist wing of the party led by Novotny. Zapotocky's moves toward reform were quashed, and in September 1953 Novotny was named party secretary general. Zapotocky, however, made another attempt at reform toward the end of 1953, which led Novotny's hard-line faction to appeal formally to Moscow in 1954 to stop Zapotocky's initiatives. The Czechoslovak leadership was invited to Moscow, and Zapotocky was told to adhere to the principle of "collective leadership." This further strengthened Novotny's position, and he was able to thwart Zapotocky's reforms thereafter. Zapotocky, however, continued as president until his death on November 14, 1957, when he was succeeded by Novotny.

Novotny was a die-hard Stalinist, and this was reflected in his public statements and actions. In July 1960 he introduced a new constitution, which he described as "the basis for the advent of pure Communism." The constitution, which renamed CZECHOSLOVAKIA the Czechoslovak Socialist Republic, laid down that "education and all cultural policy [would be] carried out in the spirit of scientific Marxism-Leninism" and limited personal property to "consumer goods" and "savings acquired through work."

Novotny's Stalinist economics failed to raise living standards, and by 1963 it had become clear that the country needed a serious economic reform. The issue eventually led to Novotny's replacement by reformist Slovak leader Alexander Dubcek. Novotny invited Soviet leader LEONID BREZHNEV to Prague to intervene personally, but Brezhnev refused to become involved. Dubcek secured the support of a majority of the Central Committee members, and on January 5, 1968, he succeeded Novotny as general secretary of the Communist Party. Novotny for a short time managed to retain the now largely ceremonial position of president. But Novotny was thoroughly discredited and never regained his former position within the party.

Nuclear-free Zones   Nuclear-free zones are geographic areas in which nuclear weapons are banned. The best-known example of a nuclear-free zone is the one established throughout Latin America by the 1967 TREATY OF TLATELOLCO. There have been attempts to establish nuclear-free zones in other regions. Some states are de facto nuclear-free zones; Sweden and Finland are two examples.

It is almost impossible for a country to declare itself a nuclear-free zone and remain in alliance with a nuclear power. When New Zealand declared itself a nuclear-free zone it led to the break up of the Australia, New Zealand, United States Treaty Organization (ANZUS). Some local government authorities have declared themselves nuclear-free zones. This usually amounts to little more than a political gesture, but it can create difficulties if the central government needs local cooperation in moving nuclear materials.

Nuclear Parity   Nuclear parity is the concept that hostile states can best deter attack by maintaining nuclear forces of roughly equal destructive capability.

Nuclear parity was considered essential to the maintenance of the BALANCE OF TERROR that characterized East–West defense relations throughout most of the Cold War.

There has not always been nuclear parity, and defense planners are divided about its benefits. Throughout the 1940s and 1950s, the United States enjoyed nuclear superiority vis à vis the Soviet Union. At the end of the 1950s, the launching of the Soviet satellite SPUTNIK led many American defense planners to believe that the Soviets had achieved nuclear parity and were fast moving toward superiority. The CUBAN MISSILE CRISIS resulted in a reassessment in favor of the United States.

But by the mid-1960s, the Soviet Union had reached a rough nuclear parity, and the administration of President LYNDON JOHNSON decided that it was better to enshrine this parity in a strategic arms agreement than to engage in an increasingly expensive arms race. This policy was later accepted by the NIXON, FORD and CARTER administrations. But the REAGAN administration returned to the policy of attempting to achieve superiority, although it continued strategic nuclear weapons negotiations with the Soviet Union.

Nuclear Planning Group (NPG)

The Nuclear Planning Group of the NORTH ATLANTIC TREATY ORGANIZATION (NATO) is responsible for planning and advising member governments on all nuclear-related matters. This includes nuclear strategies, disarmament, negotiations and weapons procurement and deployment. Membership in the NPG is restricted to seven allied countries. These include the nuclear powers and a rotating membership among the other alliance members.

The NPG was formed on December 14, 1966, and held its first meeting on April 6–7, 1967, in Washington, D.C. The NPG was formed to give the nonnuclear members a forum for airing their views on nuclear issues and to give the U.S. secretary of defense a forum for briefing nonnuclear allies on U.S. nuclear strategy.

NPG meetings are held at defense minister level and usually take place twice a year at the same time as regular NATO defense ministers' meetings. At other times, most of the work of the NPG is done by the Nuclear Defense Affairs Committee, which is based in Brussels and reports to the Permanent Representatives Council of NATO.

Nuclear Test Ban Treaty   (1963)

The Nuclear Test Ban Treaty of 1963 prohibited the signatories from testing nuclear weapons in the atmosphere, in space or under water. Although the treaty did not limit or reduce any nuclear weapons systems, it is generally regarded to have paved the way for serious arms limitation negotiations.

The treaty was described by U.S. secretary of state DEAN RUSK at the time as "a first step" in reducing international tension.

The Nuclear Test Ban Treaty was initially signed by the British, American and Soviet governments. The French and Chinese governments refused to sign and continued to conduct atmospheric tests. The signing ceremony was held on August 5, 1963, in Catherine Hall in the Kremlin's Great Palace. Rusk signed on behalf of the United States, Foreign Minister ANDREI GROMYKO on behalf of the Soviet Union and Foreign Secretary Lord HOME on behalf of Britain.

The test ban treaty emerged from the GENEVA SUMMIT in July 1955 as a proposal that was both desirable and achievable. By the start of 1956 the Soviet, British and American governments had agreed that a ban on atmospheric testing would be to the advantage of all three governments. They disagreed, however, on the means of verifying compliance with such a ban and on whether a test ban treaty should be negotiated as part of a wider disarmament agreement or to pave the way for wider disarmament talks.

The two Western governments favored on-site inspections and wider disarmament negotiations. The Soviet Union was opposed to both positions but in June 1957 agreed to the principle of on-site inspection "of the area of any unidentified explosion." Formal negotiations among the Soviets, the United States and Britain started in Geneva on October 31, 1958. The three negotiators were Semyon K. Tsarapkin (Soviet Union), James J. Wadsworth (United States) and David Ormsby-Gore (Britain).

The negotiations stumbled on year after year with the main sticking point being the issue of verification. To try to give the talks an added impetus, British prime minister HAROLD MACMILLAN visited Moscow in February 1959, and the following month the British and American governments dropped their requirement that the test ban treaty be negotiated as part of a wider disarmament agreement.

The negotiations were seriously jeopardized when a U.S. U-2 spy plane was shot down over the Soviet Union on May 1, 1960. In November 1961 the Soviet Union withdrew its acceptance of the principle of on-site inspection and accused the United States and Britain of demanding on-site inspections for the purpose of conducting espionage. On January 29, 1962, after 353 sessions, the three-power Geneva talks collapsed when the Soviet delegation walked out.

The negotiations were kept alive within the 17-nation disarmament conference, which continued to meet in Geneva. But experts believe that the treaty would have been delayed a great deal longer if the CUBAN MISSILE CRISIS had not pointed to the danger of increasing East–West tensions. In February 1963 the United States agreed to reduce its demands for on-site verification inspections, and in June of that year the three powers agreed to resume negotiations, which started in Geneva between Soviet foreign secretary Andrei Gromyko, Lord Hailsham for Britain and AVERELL HARRIMAN for the United States.

The preamble of the Nuclear Test Ban Treaty proclaimed that the principal aim of the three signatories was the "achievement of an agreement on general and complete disarmament under strict international control. . . which would put an end to the armaments race and eliminate the incentive to the producing and testing of all kinds of weapons, including nuclear weapons."

Article I of the treaty prohibits the signatories from carrying out or encouraging any nuclear weapon test explosion, or any other nuclear explosion, in the atmosphere, outer space or under water.

Article II allows amendements to the treaty if the majority of the signatories agree.

Article III opens the treaty to any and all states.

Article IV states that the treaty is of unlimited duration but allows any signatory to withdraw at three months' notice "if it decides that extraordinary events . . . have jeopardized the supreme interests of its country."

For Further Information:

Blacker, Coit, and Gloria Duffy. *International Arms Control: Issues and Agreements.* Stanford, Calif., 1984.

Clemens, Walter C. *The Superpowers and Arms Control: From Cold War to Interdependence.* Lexington, 1973.

Dean, Arthur. *Test Ban and Disarmament: The Path of Negotiation.* New York, 1966.

Kissinger, Henry. *Nuclear Weapons and Foreign Policy.* New York, 1969.

Moulton, Harland, B. *From Superiority to Parity: The United States and the Strategic Arms Race, 1961–1971.* Westport, Conn., 1972.

Nunn Amendment   The 1984 Nunn Amendment proposed the withdrawal of up to a third of American troops in Western Europe unless European members of the NORTH ATLANTIC TREATY ORGANIZATION increased their support of conventional forces. The proposal was narrowly defeated but led to some increases in European defense budgets.

Successive American administrations had argued that the United States bore a disproportionate share of the cost of maintaining conventional forces in Western Europe. This had been acceptable immediately after World War II when Western Europe had been incapable of defending itself and the United States had enjoyed a large surplus of trade with the rest of the world. But by the mid-1970s the American budget and trade deficits were growing, and Western Europe had recovered to the extent that the combined gross national product of the European NATO members was roughly equivalent to that of the United States. In the early 1970s, Senate Democratic leader MIKE MANSFIELD was calling for a reduction in American troop levels in Europe, but at that stage little support was found for the proposal.

In 1984, however, America's defense budget was approximately 7.5% of its gross national product, compared to an average of under 3% for the West European countries. This led to a growing political demand for renewed pressure on the European allies to increase their defense budgets. When the defense budget for 1985 was presented, Senator Sam Nunn (D, Georgia) moved an amendment to the budget calling for the withdrawal of 100,000 American troops by 1990 unless European NATO members increased their conventional forces.

Nunn argued that the United States was bearing a disproportionate share of conventional defense costs, which he said must be maintained in order to avoid the possibility of a rapid escalation from conventional to nuclear war in any East–West conflict. Opponents of the amendment, who included President RONALD REAGAN, feared that the amendment would damage relations between the United States and its NATO allies. The amendment was defeated on June 20, 1984, by 55 votes to 41.

The proposal, however, shook the European allies, and in the following year they responded favorably to the U.S. Conventional Defense Initiative, which proposed the partial funding of some U.S. defense procurement costs by Western Europe.

For Further Information:

Treverton, G.F. *Making the Alliance Work: The United States and Europe.* Ithaca, N.Y., 1985.

O

Oder-Neisse Line The Oder-Neisse Line is the post–World War II boundary between Poland and Germany and resulted in the loss of 40,000 square miles of German territory to Poland. Hundreds of thousands of ethnic German families were forced either to flee to West Germany or to become Polish citizens.

The Oder-Neisse Line follows the course of the western Neisse River and the Oder River, as it runs out to the Baltic Sea west of Swinemünde. It gives Poland control of the great Baltic port of Stettin and of Pomerania, East Prussia and Lower Silesia. At the end of World War I, Germany lost control of West Prussia and Upper Silesia to Poland.

The Oder-Neisse Line was proposed by Soviet leader JOSEF STALIN at the YALTA and POTSDAM conferences. He insisted on the German sacrifice for two reasons: to compensate the Poles for the land they lost to the Soviet Union east of the CURZON LINE and to contribute to his policy to destroy the political and economic strength of the German nation.

The British and Americans opposed the Oder-Neisse Line because they felt it overcompensated the Poles, and it was their policy to encourage an economically viable Germany in order to effect a successful reconstruction of Europe. The issue remained unresolved at the Yalta and Potsdam conferences, and subsequent meetings of foreign ministers failed to find a solution. In July 1946 U.S. secretary of state JAMES BYRNES proposed that the Oder-Neisse Line be accepted as the provisional border, but that the border be formally set when a final peace treaty with Germany was signed.

The West German government implicitly accepted the boundary as part of the OSTPOLITIK policy of Social Democratic chancellor WILLY BRANDT. This de facto acceptance found opposition within the conservative Christian Democratic Union, but the issue lay dormant throughout the 1970s and most of the 1980s. It was not until the communist government collapsed in East Germany in 1989 that the Oder-Neisse Line again became an issue. The government of Chancellor HELMUT KOHL formally accepted it as the German-Polish border in 1990 in return for Polish and Soviet recognition of German reunification.

For Further Information:
Terry, Sarah Meiklejohn. *Poland's Place in Europe: General Sikorski and the Origin of the Oder-Neisse Line, 1939–1943.* Princeton, 1983.

Office of Strategic Services (OSS) The Office of Strategic Services (OSS) was the World War II predecessor of the U.S. CENTRAL INTELLIGENCE AGENCY. It was the first major American civilian intelligence service, and many of its members went on to play key roles in the development and administration of the CIA.

The driving force behind the creation of the OSS was General William Donovan, who in 1940 was persuaded by British Intelligence that the United States should develop a centralized intelligence agency reporting directly to the White House in preparation for entry into World War II. Donovan was a close associate of President FRANKLIN D. ROOSEVELT and persuaded the president to create a civilian-run intelligence agency. In July 1941 the Office of Coordinator of Information (COI) was established by presidential order under the direction of Donovan. After America's entry into the war the COI became known as the Office of Strategic Services.

In the early days of the war the British Secret Intelligence Service (SIS) played a major role in the supply of intelligence information and administrative advice in establishing the OSS. This close relationship between the two national intelligence services continued throughout the war and formed the basis for the close links between the CIA and SIS during the Cold War. During the war, the British clearly played the role of big brother to the American service, but by the mid-1950s the roles had reversed.

The OSS had a number of special operations branches, including a maritime unit that infiltrated agents behind enemy lines by sea, conducted maritime sabotage and helped to supply resistance groups. The special projects office worked on the development of secret weapons, and the OSS operational groups trained paramilitary groups to fight with resistance units. The activities of OSS agents proved their worth time and time again, tying up regular German and Japanese troops, sabotaging military and economic targets and providing valuable intelligence.

The American political establishment, however, viewed the OSS as primarily a wartime instrument, and at the war's end, in September 1945, President HARRY TRUMAN disbanded it and divided its responsibilities among the State Department and the branches of the armed forces. The president, however, quickly discovered that a central body was needed to assimilate and coordinate the sometimes contradictory reports reaching the White House from four different sources. In 1946 he created the Central Intelligence Group. It soon became apparent that any central intelligence body needed its own agents and statutory powers. Thus, on July 26, 1947, Truman signed the NATIONAL SECURITY ACT, which created the CIA.

For Further Information:
Karalekas, Anne. *History of the Central Intelligence Agency.* Laguna Hills, Calif., 1977.
Roosevelt, Kermit. *War Report of the OSS.* New York, 1976.
Smith, R. Harris. *OSS: The Secret History of America's First Central Intelligence Agency.* Berkeley, Calif., 1972.

Open Skies President DWIGHT D. EISENHOWER's Open Skies proposal at the GENEVA SUMMIT in July 1955 was an early American attempt to create a climate of mutual confidence through acceptable and mutual verification of Soviet and American defense capabilities. The Soviet rejection of the plan led to the deployment of the U-2 spy plane and more sophisticated high-tech reconnaissance devices.

Eisenhower formally presented his Open Skies proposal on the last day of the meeting of the heads of government of Britain, France, the United States and the Soviet Union. The major points of Eisenhower's proposal were:

1. The Soviet Union and United States would exchange military blueprints and charts that would fully describe and accurately locate every military installation within the two countries' national territory or overseas.
2. Both countries would station reconnaissance units at a fixed number of isolated airfields in the other's territory for the purpose of inspecting the other country's military installations. The size and type of reconnaissance units would be mutually agreed upon.
3. One of the crew members from each reconnaissance plane would come from the country being inspected.

British prime minister Sir ANTHONY EDEN and French premier Edgar Faure supported Eisenhower's proposals and offered to open their national skies to aerial inspection. NIKOLAI BULGANIN, who was heading the Soviet delegation, also seemed interested, but he was overruled by NIKITA KHRUSH-CHEV, who, according to Eisenhower's memoirs, denounced the plan as "a bald espionage plot against the U.S.S.R."

The Open Skies proposal was revived in 1989, and a number of international conferences were held before the dissolution of the Soviet Union.

For Further Information:
Eisenhower, Dwight D. *The White House Years, Mandate for Change, 1953–56.* Garden City, N.Y., 1963.

Operation Valuable Operation Valuable was the code name given to a covert Anglo-American operation to overthrow the communist government in ALBANIA. The plan was undermined by the activities of the British traitor KIM PHILBY, and hundreds of agents died as a result.

In 1948 the British and American governments agreed to overthrow an East European government in the hope that this would create a chain reaction throughout the region. Albania was chosen as the target because it was regarded as the weakest in political and economic terms and because there was a well-established émigré group prepared to fight the regime of ENVER HOXHA.

A joint CIA and MI6 (or SIS) committee was established in Washington, D.C. The British representative on the committee was Philby, who at the time was also the MI6 liaison officer in Washington. The British made available facilities in Malta for the training of hundreds of Albanian émigrés, and the United States provided air backup from its base in Libya as well as financial support.

At the end of 1948, a forward base was established on the Greek island of Corfu, only three miles off the Albanian coast. In December 1949 the first small group of Albanians was ferried to the mainland by patrol boat. But Philby had notified Soviet Intelligence of the operation, and they in turn had warned the Albanians, who were waiting for the émigré forces. As soon as the first landed, they were captured and their radio equipment was confiscated.

Albanian and Soviet intelligence officers used the captured radio equipment and cypher equipment to signal back to the Anglo-American base that the first guerrillas had successfully landed and made contact with opposition forces. This was the signal for other Albanian émigrés to make their way to the mainland, either by patrol boat or by parachute from American planes. All of them found communist troops waiting for them and all were shot. Some 300 men were killed in the operation before one of them managed to escape to Greece and warn British and American intelligence that they had been betrayed.

British and American intelligence launched similar operations in the Ukraine, Poland, Latvia, Lithuania and Estonia. Philby was involved in the betrayal of most of the schemes, but defense and intelligence analysts believe that they stood little chance of success anyway, and were largely the result of ill-considered political pressure to "roll back" the IRON CURTAIN.

For Further Information
Knightley, Phillip. *Philby: KGB Masterspy.* New York, 1988.

Oppenheimer, J. Robert (April 22, 1904–February 18, 1967) Dr. J. Robert Oppenheimer was heralded by President HARRY TRUMAN as "father of the atomic bomb." He played a leading role in the development of both the weapon and nuclear weapons policies in the early Cold War years. Earlier left-wing associations, however, led to his falling out of favor during the MCCARTHY period.

Oppenheimer started teaching physics at the University of California at Berkeley in 1929 after receiving degrees from

J. Robert Oppenheimer, heralded by President Truman as "the father of the atomic bomb," was later accused of being a communist sympathizer.

Harvard, Cambridge University and the University of Göttingen. At Berkeley, Oppenheimer quickly developed a worldwide reputation. In common with many other intellectuals of the day, Oppenheimer also developed left-wing sympathies, although he never joined the Communist Party. In 1940 he married Katherine Puening, a former communist, and began to disengage himself from politics.

From 1939 onward, Oppenheimer worked on the development of the atomic bomb. At first his work was done on his own initiative, but he was later asked to join the Manhattan District Project. Because of his earlier left-wing connections, security officials were reluctant to clear Oppenheimer for the top-secret work, but they did so when they were told that he was vital to the project. In March 1943, Oppenheimer was appointed director of the scientific group working on the atom bomb at the laboratory at Los Alamos, New Mexico.

Later that year Oppenheimer voluntarily told U.S. Army counterintelligence officers that the Soviets had sought to gain atomic secrets from him through his Berkeley colleague Haakon Chevalier and British engineer George Eltenton. The fact that he had been approached and then had delayed nine months reporting it further aroused the suspicions of counterintelligence officers.

After the bomb was successfully developed, Oppenheimer advised President Truman to use it against a dual military and civilian target, without prior warning. He and other advisers argued that this was the best way to bring a speedy end to the war and to save American lives. When the war ended Truman awarded Oppenheimer the Medal of Merit.

In September 1945, Oppenheimer resigned from Los Alamos to help write the Acheson-Lilienthal Report, which later led to the BARUCH PLAN, the first proposal for international control of atomic weapons. In 1947 he returned to teaching as director of the Institute for Advanced Study at Princeton, but he continued to advise the government and later in the year was appointed chairman of the General Advisory Committee (GAC) of the ATOMIC ENERGY COMMISSION (AEC).

By this time, Oppenheimer had become increasingly concerned about the destructive power of the atomic bomb, and in 1949 he led the GAC recommendation against development of the hydrogen bomb on the grounds that it was both morally and economically unjustifiable. In 1951, the committee reversed its previous position when new technology cut the production costs. But Oppenheimer and the other scientists on the GAC continued to press for negotiations to limit the nuclear arms race while at the same time maintaining a strong defense posture.

During the KOREAN WAR, Oppenheimer worked on the development of tactical nuclear weapons, and in 1952 Truman appointed him chairman of the special State Department Advisory Committee on Disarmament. The committee's report advised the EISENHOWER administration to educate the public about the dangers of nuclear warfare and to share weapons secrets with its allies. Eisenhower rejected the advice.

In November 1953, at the height of the anti-communist hysteria, William Borden, former executive director of the Joint Committee on Atomic Energy, accused Oppenheimer of disloyalty. He exposed the scientist's former left-wing connections, claimed that he had brought communist scientists to work on the MANHATTAN PROJECT and had intentionally retarded development of the hydrogen bomb, and asserted that "more probably than not he [had] since been functioning as an espionage agent."

Eisenhower ordered Oppenheimer's security clearance suspended pending a review by the AEC. At the subsequent hearing a number of prominent scientists spoke in Oppenheimer's defense. The only one who spoke against him was Edward Teller, who supported Borden's claim that he had delayed work on the hydrogen bomb. The panel also went over Oppenheimer's FBI files and unearthed the Chevalier affair. In May 1953 the panel unanimously declared Oppenheimer a "loyal citizen," but two of its members voted to maintain the suspension of his security clearance on the grounds that his "continuing conduct and associations . . . reflected a serious disregard for the requirements of the security system."

Oppenheimer continued his work at Princeton University

and became a living martyr of the McCarthy era. An AEC review of the case in January 1958 characterized the proceedings against him as "a primitive abuse of the judicial system" but took no action. President JOHN F. KENNEDY, under attack from Republican conservatives, also refused to reopen the case, although he showed his sympathies in the case by inviting Oppenheimer to a White House dinner and awarding him with the AEC's Enrico Fermi Award. The presentation was made in December 1963 by President JOHNSON. Oppenheimer died of throat cancer on February 18, 1967.

For Further Information:

Gilpin, Robert G., Jr. *American Scientists and Nuclear Weapons Policy.* Princeton, 1962.

Jacobson, Harold D. *Diplomats, Scientists and Politicians.* Ann Arbor, Mich., 1966.

Major, John. *The Oppenheimer Hearing.* New York, 1971.

Rhodes, Richard. *The Making of the Atomic Bomb.* New York, 1982.

York, Herbert F. *The Advisers: Oppenheimer, Teller and the Superbomb.* San Francisco, 1976.

Organization for Economic Cooperation and Development (OECD)   The Organization for Economic Cooperation and Development was established in 1961 as the successor to the MARSHALL PLAN'S ORGANIZATION FOR EUROPEAN ECONOMIC COOPERATION (OEEC). Its purpose is to coordinate the economic policies of the industrialized democracies.

The idea behind the OEEC and the OECD is the belief that economic well-being is the best way to prevent communism. The major postwar threat from communism was to Western Europe, but by the end of the 1950s Western Europe had recovered and Western planners perceived a need to widen the base of the OEEC in order to prevent communist political dominance elsewhere in the world.

Most of the negotiations for the new organization were handled by a four-man committee comprised of delegates from Britain, the United States, Greece and France and debated more fully within the full council of the OEEC. The only major difference was over whether OECD decisions should be binding, as proposed by the European members. This was opposed by the United States and eventually dropped.

The OECD charter was signed in Paris on December 14, 1960. President JOHN F. KENNEDY signed the convention providing for U.S. membership in the OECD on March 23, 1961, and the OECD came into formal existence at its first meeting in Paris on September 30, 1961.

Organization for European Economic Cooperation (OEEC)   The OEEC was established on April 16, 1948, initially to coordinate MARSHALL PLAN aid to European countries. When the aid program ended, the OEEC continued to work for economic cooperation between European countries. The OEEC is regarded by some as an American-inspired forerunner of the EUROPEAN COAL AND STEEL COMMUNITY and the later EUROPEAN ECONOMIC COMMUNITY. It was expanded in 1961 to include the United States and Canada. At that time it was renamed the Organization for Economic Cooperation and Development (OECD). In 1988 the OECD had 25 members.

Organization of American States (OAS)   The Organization of American States was formed in 1948 to strengthen the RIO PACT of 1947 and increase U.S. dominance of the Western Hemisphere. It has become the major vehicle for multilateral cooperation within the Western Hemisphere and has been used by the United States to isolate the communist government in CUBA.

The Bogota Pact, which established the OAS, was a series of treaties signed in Bogota, Colombia on April 30, 1948. The treaties established that the governing board of the Pan American Union in Washington, D.C. would become the permanent consultative council, secretariat and central economic, social, juridical and cultural agency. The pact also specified that the chief political organ of the OAS would be the Inter-American Council of Foreign Ministers, under which would function a military Inter-American Defense Council.

The conference had a strong anti-communist undertone, which was exaggerated by riots inspired by the left wing in Colombia. Encouraged by the United States and Colombia, the 21 nations attending the conference unanimously agreed that "agents in the service of international Communism" must be thwarted in the Western Hemisphere by "constitutional methods in each country."

This clause was later strengthened in 1954 by the Declaration of Solidarity for the Preservation of the Political Integrity of the American States Against the Intervention of International Communism. These two agreements were later used by the U.S. government to organize OAS opposition to the communist government in Cuba. In 1961 Cuba was suspended from the OAS after a meeting of foreign ministers. The following year, OAS approval was a key part of President JOHN F. KENNEDY's plan to remove Soviet missiles from Cuba.

The OAS also served as a vehicle for the creation of the Inter-American Development Bank, the Inter-American Telecommunications Network and the Economic Commission for Latin America. It also provided the framework for discussions that led to the TREATY OF TLATELOLCO, in 1967, which established a Latin American NUCLEAR-FREE ZONE. The OAS became a forum at which members on 16 occasions would invoke the Rio Pact, which stipulated that an attack against any nation in the Western Hemisphere would be considered an attack against all.

In 1970 a General Assembly of the OAS was created to replace the Inter-American Conferences and the three councils as the main political organs of the organization. With the establishment of the General Assembly, the United States lost some of its control over the OAS, which became more outspoken about lack of financial aid from the United States and the dominance of American multinationals.

For Further Information:

Berle, Adolf A., Jr. *Latin America: Diplomacy and Reality.* New York, 1962.

Burr, Robert N. *Our Troubled Hemisphere: Perspectives on United States–Latin American Relations.* Washington, D.C., 1967.

Lumar, Shiv. *U.S. Intervention in Latin America.* Chicago, 1987.

Walton, Richard J. *The United States and Latin America.* New York, 1972.

Ostpolitik   Ostpolitik was the name given to West German chancellor WILLY BRANDT's policy of improving relations with the Soviet Bloc countries.

Ostpolitik ("Eastern Policy") was very much the creation of Brandt. Its purpose was to improve the conditions of Germans living in East Germany and elsewhere in Eastern Europe by relaxing East–West tensions, making it easier for them to emigrate to West Germany, offering West German loans and trade and permitting increased contact with families and friends in the West.

Under previous governments, the policy had been to reject the division of Germany and to work toward eventual reunification as a Western-oriented democratic state. Crucial to the success of this policy was Western, and in particular American, political and military support for the West German state and its foreign policy aims.

Through the 1940s and 1950s this support was forthcoming. Then came the traumatic watershed of the Berlin Wall. The wall had the dramatic and immediate consequence of cutting off millions of Germans in the East from reaching their families, friends and political sanctuary in the West. It also graphically demonstrated the West's inability, or unwillingness, to prevent the permanent division of Germany. But under West Germany's BASIC LAW the West German state had a legal responsibility to protect the rights of the Germans in the East. If it were unable to secure those rights through eventual reunification, then another course had to be found.

Few people were more shaken by the erection of the Berlin Wall and its consequences than Brandt, who at the time was mayor of BERLIN. He pressed both President JOHN F. KENNEDY and ADENAUER for action and when it was not forthcoming began to turn his mind to a reconstruction of West Germany's foreign policy. He quickly reached the conclusion that the only alternative practical possibility was a policy of peaceful coexistence and détente. Over the next five years Brandt's thoughts were further refined as he rose through the ranks of the Social Democratic Party (SPD) to emerge as its leader.

In November 1966, following the collapse of the Erhard government, Brandt's SPD formed a grand coalition with the Christian Democratic Union under KURT GEORG KIESINGER. Brandt became deputy chancellor and foreign minister and Kiesinger became chancellor. Brandt was now able to start putting a limited form of his Ostpolitik into practice. In January 1967, diplomatic relations were established with ROMANIA, in August 1967 a trade agreement was reached with CZECHOSLOVAKIA and in January 1968 diplomatic relations were established with YUGOSLAVIA. In May 1968, Kiesinger said in an interview with *Quick* magazine, "We are prepared to open such relations with all our neighbors in order to create a friendlier political climate in the whole of Europe."

Kiesinger had also been attempting to establish some form of relations with East Germany. He supported Erhard's policy of increasing interzonal trade and in April 1967 sent the East German Socialist Unity (Communist) Party 16 proposals for increased cooperation. These included youth exchanges, free traffic in newspapers and other literature, increased trade, technological cooperation, the easing of travel arrangements and more frequent visits across the Berlin Wall by relatives. All the proposals were designed to improve the lives of East Germans while at the same time allowing Bonn to remain committed to its policy of eventual reunification. The East German government, however, was determined to settle for no less than full recognition of the East German state by Bonn and the establishment of diplomatic relations between the two German states. East German leader WALTER ULBRICHT also insisted that West Berlin be incorporated into East Germany and that both German states join the United Nations.

This fruitless dialogue abruptly ended with the invasion of Czechoslovakia in August 1968, and Kiesinger did not have an opportunity to resume serious negotiations before his government was voted out of office in September 1969 and replaced by a Social Democratic/Free Democratic coalition led by Brandt.

Brandt's first major Ostpolitik initiative as chancellor was a meeting in March 1970 with East German Premier Willi Stoph at Erfurt, East Germany. The talks were initially inconclusive. Stoph continued to insist on international legal recognition of the East German state and indemnification of 100 billion marks for losses incurred by East Germany's economy through emigration to West Germany before the building of the Berlin Wall in 1961. At a second meeting, at Kassel in West Germany, Brandt presented a list of 20 "principles and elements" designed to lead to a treaty normalizing relations between the two German states. These included the establishment of diplomatic missions in each other's capitals. Stoph did not press his earlier demand for indemnification but repeated his demand for legal recognition of the East German government and branded as "absolutely unacceptable" Brandt's use of phrases such as "inter German" or "intra-German" to describe relations between two states with "contradictory social orders" and "utterly different basic interests." Brandt managed to circumvent the problem of West Germany's constitutional commitment to a reunified Germany by calling for the acceptance of two German states within one German nation. This was denounced by the opposition as confusing, but it struck a popular chord in both East and West Germany.

Despite the cool response from the East German government, Brandt pushed forward, and his effort finally bore fruit in August 1970 when, after extended negotiations, he and Soviet premier ALEXEI KOSYGIN signed a West German–Soviet nonaggression pact. The pact included a pledge to renounce territorial claims against each other and to refrain from the use of force in the settlement of disputes, and the recognition of all boundaries, including the borders between East and West Germany and between Poland and East Germany.

Brandt's recognition of the ODER-NEISSE LINE as Poland's western border cleared the way for a treaty between West Germany and Poland. This treaty was signed in Warsaw in December 1970 by Brandt and Polish premier Jozef Cyrankiewicz.

The United States, Britain and France, the three Western powers responsible for West Berlin, had mixed feelings about Brandt's Ostpolitik policy. France was generally in favor, and its government had formed a close relationship with Brandt's. The British were won over by Brandt's enthusiastic support of their application to join the EUROPEAN ECONOMIC COMMUNITY.

The United States, however, was more suspicious. HENRY KISSINGER, then national security adviser, was concerned that Ostpolitik could lead to a resurgence of German nationalism. At the same time, he recognized that West Germany's HALLSTEIN DOCTRINE was an increasingly dangerous political anachronism that had lost support in West Germany. In order to retain some control of events, he offered his support for Brandt's policy. In August 1971, Britain, France, the United States and the Soviet Union made their contribution to Ostpolitik when they signed the QUADRIPARTITE AGREEMENT, which established the right of unhindered traffic between West Germany and West Berlin, allowed West Berliners to travel to the East and formally determined the city's status in relation to West Germany.

In recognition of his work in defusing East–West relations, Brandt was awarded the Nobel Prize for peace in October 1971. The East Germans were now forced to take a more serious view of Brandt's Ostpolitik, and in November 1972 East and West Germany signed a treaty normalizing relations between them. The treaty also allowed the reunification of families and the release of prisoners. This treaty was signed only a few days before a West German general election and helped Brandt's SPD-FDP coalition to increase its majority to 48 seats.

In his second term, Brandt concluded economic agreements with the Soviet Union and Romania. In December 1973 West Germany and Czechoslovakia signed a treaty recognizing each other's postwar boundaries.

Brandt appeared to be politically impregnable when in April 1974 his close aide GUNTER GUILLAUME was arrested and charged with being a spy for East Germany. The subsequent scandal forced Brandt to resign the chancellorship the following month.

For Further Information:

Brandt, Willy. *People and Politics.* New York, 1978.
Crawley, A.M. *The Rise of West Germany, 1945–1972.* New York, 1974.
Fritsch-Bournazel, Renata. *Confronting the German Question.* Oxford, 1988.
Griffiths, William. *The Ostpolitik of the Federal Republic of Germany.* Cambridge, Mass., 1978.
Pfetsch, Frank. *West Germany, Internal Structures and External Relations: The Foreign Policy of the Federal Republic.* New York, 1988.
Prittie, Terence. *The Velvet Chancellors.* New York, 1979.

P

Pahlevi, Mohammed Reza (October 26, 1919–July 27, 1980) Mohammad Reza Pahlevi was the ruler of Iran from 1941 until his overthrow in 1979. Throughout that period he was the West's staunchest ally in the Persian Gulf region, and in 1955 he took Iran into the BAGHDAD PACT.

Pahlevi was the son of Iranian Army Col. Reza Khan. In 1921 Reza Khan seized power in a coup d'état and four years later, when Mohammad Reza was six years old, declared himself shah (king) and his son crown prince, establishing the Pahlevi dynasty. The prince was educated at a Swiss boarding school and the Teheran Military College, from which he graduated in 1939.

Reza Shah Pahlevi sympathized with the Germans during World War II and refused to let British war supplies be shipped through his country to the Soviet Union. As a result, British and Soviet troops occupied Iran and forced him to abdicate in favor of his son, who acceded to the throne in September 1941.

The new shah signed an agreement with Britain and the Soviet Union to allow their troops to occupy Iran until six months after the end of the war. The United States was later added to this agreement. But when the war ended, the Soviets, who had been refused an Iranian oil concession, instead of withdrawing their forces from Iranian AZERBAIJAN, added to their numbers and in December 1945 announced the formation of an Azerbaijani revolutionary government, which demanded "autonomy." The Soviets intended to play on Azerbaijani nationalist aspirations to pressure Teheran, clearly implying a future combination of Soviet and Iranian Azerbaijan into one Soviet-controlled province.

In January 1946, the shah's government formally charged the Soviet Union before the UN Security Council with interference in Iranian internal affairs. The British and American governments promised to support Iran and sent strong protests to Moscow. In May 1946 the Soviets withdrew on the promise of future oil concessions, to be authorized by the parliament. Late that year the Soviet-installed government collapsed, and in 1947, U.S. secretary of state GEORGE MARSHALL promised the shah's government $30 million in military equipment. In October 1947 the United States and the shah signed an agreement for an American Army mission to Iran to assist in "enhancing the efficiency of the Iranian Army." The oil concessions to the Soviets were rejected.

The Azerbaijan incident was the start of a close military and political link between the shah and the United States which resulted in Iran's becoming a major purchaser of American military equipment. The shah also allowed the Americans to build a series of electronic listening posts along the Iranian-Soviet border, maintained close links with American intelligence agencies, and took Iran into the Baghdad Pact (later the Central Treaty Organization).

Iran quickly became America's closest and most important client in the Persian Gulf. This link was not based on broad relations with a friendly country sharing similar political values, but on a strategic relationship between the U.S. government and the person of the shah, who rules as an absolute monarch. The situation was further complicated by the British role in Iran. Britain, before the war, had been the premier Western influence in Iran and continued to have a strong impact through the Anglo-Iranian Oil Company, which dominated Iran's oil industry. In the immediate postwar years, Britain derived more revenue from taxing the company's profits than Iran did through its royalties on the oil involved. The shah accepted this state of affairs because he realized that his position depended largely on the good will of the Americans and British. But the increasingly powerful Iranian parliament (the Majlis) was resentful of British control of Iranian oil and in March 1951 voted to nationalize the oil industry, at the same time demanding that the shah name as prime minister MOHAMMED MOSADDEQ. This was done, and Mosaddeq moved quickly to implement the nationalization order.

But Anglo-Iranian Oil refused to accept the measure and persuaded other oil concerns to impose an embargo on supplies and expertise. Iran lacked the trained personnel to operate the fields and pumping stations, and the oil industry virtually ceased operations. At about the same time, the British Secret Intelligence Service (SIS) approached the CENTRAL INTELLIGENCE AGENCY (CIA) to request American help in coordinating a coup to overthrow Mosaddeq. The approach was approved by ALLEN DULLES, who regarded Mosaddeq as a crypto-communist who would bring the Soviet Union back into Iran if he stayed in power. The CIA approached the shah, who approved of the initial plan to dismiss Mosaddeq and replace him with General Fazlollah Zahedi. But at the last moment, Mosaddeq learned of the plot and organized a series of violent public demonstrations against the shah, who was forced to flee the country for Rome.

The CIA, however, was still operating in Teheran. Under the direction of KERMIT ROOSEVELT (grandson of Theodore Roosevelt) undercover CIA operatives organized huge pro-shah and anti-Mosaddeq demonstrations. They also kept open communications between the shah and the military, which had remained loyal to the monarch. On August 19, only three days after the shah had left for Rome, the Iranian Army, claiming the support of the CIA-organized crowds, moved against Mosaddeq and overthrew him. The shah returned on August 22, even more dependent than before on the United States. Consequently, the United States became even more closely identified with the monarchy.

After the Mosaddeq incident, the shah set about consolidating his power by appointing close associates to key positions in the military and circumscribing the power of the Majlis. Finally in 1961, he dissolved the Majlis. The dissolution signaled the start of the "White Revolution," through which the shah attempted to broaden his personal base of support through a directly ordered land reform program. He also substantially improved educational facilities and literacy rates. In foreign affairs, the shah improved relations with the Soviet Union (while maintaining his close relations with the United States) and developed close relations with Israel, which bought the bulk of its oil from Iran.

The White Revolution was followed in 1973 by the quadrupling of world oil prices, which resulted in a major jump in government spending and improved living conditions for Iran's population of 30 million. Between 1960 and 1977, the country's per capita income increased from $176 in 1960 to $2,160 in 1977.

But this improvement in Iranian living standards was made at great sacrifice in personal and political liberty and at the expense of the powerful Islamic clergy who, before 1961, had been the country's largest landowners and had controlled the education system.

By the mid-1970s there had been several Islamic-organized riots and anti-shah demonstrations. The country's leading cleric, Ayatollah Ruhollah Khomeini, had been forced into exile in 1962, whence he regularly issued calls for the overthrow of the shah. A growing number of anti-shah activists found themselves in and out of prisons run by the shah's dreaded, American-trained SAVAK secret police. The shah, for his part, became increasingly isolated from political reality by his circle of advisers.

In 1977, the shah made the fatal step of accusing Khomeini of conspiring against him with Iranian communists. This led to an anti-shah demonstration in the holy city of Qum. The shah's police opened fire on the crowd and 20 people were killed. Instead of quelling the disturbances, the shooting only fueled more unrest in Qum and other cities. After a year of bloody riots, the shah was forced to appoint long-time opposition figure Shahpour Bakhtiar as prime minister, and in January 1979, Riza Shah Pahlevi left the country for an exile that took him to Egypt, Panama, Mexico, Morocco and the Bahamas.

The departure of the shah resulted in the abrupt end of American influence in Iran. American businessmen, diplomats and military had become inextricably linked in the Iranian public mind with the hated figure of the shah. This connection became more pronounced after Ayatollah Khomeini returned to Iran on February 1, 1979, and shortly afterward declared Iran an Islamic state opposed to both the "Great Satan" of the United States and the officially atheistic Soviet Union. The shah was sentenced to death in absentia, and Khomeini made it clear that any country that provided the shah sanctuary was committing an unfriendly act. On October 4, 1979, the shah, suffering with cancer, with the permission of President JIMMY CARTER flew to New York for a major medical operation. The Iranian government protested and on November 4, 1979, Islamic militants stormed the U.S. Embassy in Teheran and took hostage the American diplomatic staff. The diplomats were held for over 14 months, causing major political unrest in the United States.

For Further Information:

Amuzegar, Jahangir. *The Dynamics of the Iranian Revolution: The Pahlavis' Triumph and Tragedy.* Albany, N.Y., 1991.

Bill, J.A. *The Eagle and the Lion.* New Haven, Conn., 1988.

Chubin, Shahram, and Sephr Zabih. *The Foreign Relations of Iran.* Los Angeles, 1974.

Gitisetan, Dariush. *Iran, Politics and Government Under the Pahlavis, An Annotated Bibliography.* Metuchen, N.J., 1985.

Milani, Mohsen M. *The Making of Iran's Islamic Revolution: From Monarchy to Islamic Republic.* Boulder, Colo., 1988.

Ramzani, R.K. *The U.S. and Iran: The Patterns of Influence.* New York, 1982.

Roosevelt, Kermit. *Countercoup.* New York, 1979.

Shawcross, William. *The Shah's Last Ride: The Fate of an Ally.* New York, 1988.

Zonis, Marvin. *Majestic Failure, The Fall of the Shah.* Chicago, 1991.

Panmunjom   Panmunjom is a small Korean village on the 38th parallel that became the venue for the final cease-fire and armistice negotiations of the KOREAN WAR and later was the scene for the exchange of prisoners. Since the end of the war, the deserted village has become the accepted venue for Red Cross–supervised negotiations between the two Korean governments. It is as much a symbol of a divided Korea as the BERLIN WALL was a symbol of a divided Germany.

The initial truce negotiations were held just south of the 38th parallel in Kaesong, which was occupied by North Korean and Chinese troops. That city was declared a neutral zone during the course of negotiations, but the communist negotiators regularly accused the UN forces of violating the zone's neutrality, and after one such allegation they broke off negotiations on August 23, 1951.

On September 20, 1951, the communists offered to resume negotiations in Kaesong. But General MATTHEW RIDGWAY, commander of the UN forces, had decided against Kaesong on the grounds that it was too difficult to have a neutral zone occupied by one of the belligerent armies. He proposed that a site be chosen as close as possible to the 38th parallel in the no-man's-land that separated the two armies. His first proposed site, Songhyen, a village eight miles east of Kaesong, was rejected by the communist commanders, General KIM IL-SUNG and General Pleng Teh-huai. They proposed instead that the talks be held in Panmunjom, which would be at the center of a jointly policed neutral zone including Panmunjom, Kaesong and Munsan. Ridgway accepted Panmunjom but rejected the proposed enlarged neutral zone. Formal truce negotiations started at Panmunjom on October 25, 1951.

The negotiations and the fighting dragged on for nearly two more years as President HARRY TRUMAN refused to return forcibly the many Chinese and North Korean prisoners who wished to remain in the West. The two sides eventually compromised by agreeing that a committee of neutral nations would decide which prisoners should be returned and which should remain. The armistice agreement was signed at Panmunjom on July 27, 1953.

For Further Information:
Leckie, Robert. *The Korean War*. New York, 1963.
Lewis, D.S. *Korea: Enduring Division*. Chicago, 1980.

Paris Peace Talks on Vietnam   The Paris Peace Talks on Vietnam lasted from May 1968 until January 1973. Their eventual outcome ended American involvement in Vietnam and paved the way for a communist victory.

President LYNDON JOHNSON offered the North Vietnamese negotiations from the early stages of American involvement in the VIETNAM WAR. But the North Vietnamese refused to negotiate while the United States continued its bombing of North Vietnam. After the communist TET OFFENSIVE of January–February 1968, Johnson announced an end to the bombing and a renewed willingness to negotiate.

In his statement on March 31, 1968, Johnson designated veteran diplomat AVERELL HARRIMAN as his personal representative "to any forum, at any time, to discuss the means of bringing this ugly war to an end." In addition, the United States ambassador to the Soviet Union, LLEWELLYN THOMPSON, was placed on standby to join Harriman "at Geneva or any other suitable place just as soon as Hanoi agrees to a conference."

Johnson refused to establish any preconditions other than that the eventual settlement be based on "political conditions that permit the South Vietnamese—all the South Vietnamese—to chart their course free of any outside domination or interferences, from us or from anyone else."

Three days later, on April 3, the North Vietnamese agreed to establish direct contact in order to arrange the cessation of American bombings and start formal peace negotiations. After a 34-day dispute over the site for the negotiations, Paris was chosen, and the talks began on May 10. The American delegation was led by Harriman and included CYRUS VANCE, Lieutenant General Andrew Goodpaster and Philip Habib.

The North Vietnamese delegation was led by Minister of State Xuan Thuy, a secretary of the Central Committee of the Indochina Communist Party. Substantive negotiations started on May 13 and within a week reached an impasse. The deadlock centered on North Vietnamese insistence on an unconditional halt to the American bombing of North Vietnam and the American demand for a North Vietnamese pledge of some military reciprocation in exchange. The talks continued with each side exchanging accusations until October 23, when they were adjourned. The only major achievement of this period was that the North Vietnamese agreed to allow the South Vietnamese government to participate in the talks in exchange for a complete ban on American bombings of North Vietnam.

Talks resumed on December 2 and continued intermittently for four years. Very few concessions were made by either side. The American negotiating position was weak because the United States government had clearly lost its people's support for the war, and was seeking a way to extricate itself even though the fighting was not over. In addition, the South Vietnamese and National Liberation Front (NLF) delegations refused to deal with each other directly.

President RICHARD NIXON's national security adviser (later secretary of state) HENRY KISSINGER took over direct responsibility for the negotiations in 1969. He started by offering the North Vietnamese a "two-track" formula that projected a military settlement between the United States and North Vietnam and a political settlement between the South Vietnamese government and the NLF. Kissinger's proposed settlement involved the mutual withdrawal of American and North Vietnamese troops, and the North Vietnamese rejected it. To have accepted would have been to concede that they were a "foreign" or "outside" force, as the Americans contended.

Nixon and Kissinger quickly came to the conclusion that for any talks to be effective they had to be held in secret and that the South Vietnamese and NLF delegations would have to be excluded. In August 1969, Kissinger started a series of secret meetings with North Vietnamese Politburo member Le Duc Tho. The official talks continued but served only as a cover for the more substantive secret negotiations. In September 1972 Kissinger made a major concession in agreeing that North Vietnamese troops could remain in South Vietnam after a cease-fire, and Le Duc Tho agreed that South Vietnamese President Nguyen Van Thieu could remain in office after the signing of a treaty. On October 26, 1972, on the eve of the U.S. presidential elections, Kissinger announced that peace was at hand and that the main points of a peace treaty had been agreed. These points were:

1.   A cease-fire that left North Vietnamese troops in place.
2.   The withdrawal of U.S. troops and the dismantling of American bases within 60 days of the signing of the treaty.
3.   An exchange of prisoners of war.

4. Foreign troops to be withdrawn from Cambodia and Laos and troop and supply movements through those countries to be banned.

5. A demilitarized zone to be provisionally set between the border of North and South Vietnam until such time as peaceful reunification was achieved.

6. An international commission to deal with the release and exchange of prisoners of war and the holding of eventual countrywide elections.

7. President Thieu's continuation in office pending elections.

The terms encountered strong opposition from Thieu, who insisted that they be amended to include a guarantee of continued American support for his government. When the North Vietnamese refused, Nixon ordered the renewed bombing of Hanoi in December 1972. On January 8, 1973, the talks resumed. The final treaty was signed on January 27, 1973. The terms were not significantly different from those announced in October.

For Further Information:
Karnow, Stanley. *Vietnam: A History.* New York, 1983.
Kissinger, Henry. *The White House Years.* New York, 1979.
Smith, R.B. *An International History of the Vietnam War.* New York, 1986.

Parsons, J. Graham (October 28, 1907–October 20, 1991) Graham Parsons was assistant secretary of state for Far Eastern affairs at a time when the United States was heavily involved in trying to prevent communists from controlling the Laotian government. He was later deputy chairman of the U.S. delegation to the STRATEGIC ARMS LIMITATION TALKS.

Parsons entered the diplomatic service after graduating from Yale University in 1929 and served in a number of posts in Asia, including Tokyo, China, New Delhi and Nepal. In 1956 he was named ambassador to Laos.

After he had been ambassador for 16 months, Parsons was promoted to deputy assistant secretary of state for Far Eastern affairs, and he was named assistant secretary of state in 1959. As a result of holding these three consecutive positions, Parsons was able to wield a strong influence on American policy in LAOS.

After the 1954 division of Vietnam and the creation of the SOUTHEAST ASIA TREATY ORGANIZATION, the maintenance of a pro-Western government in Laos became a priority of American foreign policy. Between 1954 and 1960, the United States flooded the small country with $300 million in aid, mainly to support the army. This led to corruption and an inordinate amount of power in the hands of the military.

At the same time, the communist-supported Pathet Lao had managed to gain control of the northeastern corner of the country and, with supplies from the Soviet Union and North Vietnam, constituted a major threat to the government. The prime minister, Prince Souvanna Phouma, favored taking a neutral course in the East–West conflict in order to reach a negotiated settlement with the Pathet Lao. The EISENHOWER administration, however, equated neutrality with anti-Americanism.

Parsons' main task as ambassador was to prevent Prince Souvanna from forming a coalition with the Pathet Lao. As Prince Souvanna moved closer to the Pathet Lao, the CIA gave its support to the pro-American army officer, General Phoumi Nosavan, who grabbed power in 1959 only to be overthrown in August 1960 by Air Force Captain Kong Le. Le returned Prince Souvanna to the prime minister's office.

By this time Parsons, now assistant secretary of state, supported Ambassador WINTHROP BROWN, who advocated a neutralist government, but without any representation of the Pathet Lao. Parsons, however, was opposed to Prince Souvanna, whom he regarded as naive about the threat of communism. In taking this position, Parsons was running contrary to policy directives from the White House, which was demanding full support for Phoumi. Parsons tried to keep American options open while Brown attempted to negotiate a new coalition.

On October 12, 1960, Parsons led a mission to Laos to set down the conditions under which the American government would support Prince Souvanna. He demanded that the prince end his coalition talks with the Pathet Lao and offer Phoumi a major position in a new government. He also insisted that Kong Le, who was funneling American military supplies to the Pathet Lao, be restrained and that the capital be moved to Luang Prabang in the center of the Western-controled sector. Prince Souvanna, who later described Parsons as "the most nefarious and reprehensible of men," refused all of the American demands and shortly afterward turned to the Soviet Union for military aid to help fight Phoumi.

After Prince Souvanna turned to the Soviets, Parsons dropped his support for a Souvanna-led coalition and joined his superiors in pressing for Souvanna's overthrow and replacement by Phoumi. In November 1960, Phoumi overthrew Prince Souvanna, who fled into exile.

President JOHN F. KENNEDY quickly switched American foreign policy to support a neutralist Laos. Parsons, who was too closely identified with the Eisenhower administration, was in February 1961 appointed U.S. ambassador to Sweden. He became senior foreign service inspector in 1967 and in 1969 was appointed deputy chairman of the U.S. delegation to the Strategic Arms Limitation Talks, but he had little influence over the negotiations.

For Further Information:
Adams, Nina S., and Alfred W. McCoy. *Laos: War and Revolution.* New York, 1971.
Barnet, Richard J. *Roots of War.* New York, 1972.
Fall, Bernard. *Anatomy of a Crisis: The Laotian Crisis of 1960–61.* New York, 1969.
Goldstein, Martin. *American Policy Toward Laos.* Rutherford, N.J., 1973.

Pauling, Linus **(February 28, 1901–   )** Linus Pauling is a prominent American chemist who after World War II became a leading antinuclear campaigner and peace activist. He won the Nobel Prize for chemistry in 1954 and in 1963 was awarded the Nobel Prize for peace. Pauling was only the second person to receive two Nobel prizes; the other was Marie Curie.

Pauling graduated from Oregon State College in 1922 and three years later received his doctorate in physical chemistry from the California Institute of Technology (Cal Tech). During the 1930s he did research at Cal Tech, which later led to the development of various drugs, plastics and synthetic fibers. Pauling also successively applied his research into molecular structures to the study of proteins and hemoglobins.

During World War II, Pauling served in the explosives division of the National Defense Research Commission and on the consultative committee on medical research of the Office of Scientific Research and Development. After the war, Pauling became the leader of a small group of scientists who opposed nuclear testing and supported multinational disarmament. Because of his views, he was accused of being a communist by Senator JOSEPH MCCARTHY. The charge was vehemently denied by Pauling, but the State Department still refused to issue him a passport in 1952 and 1954, although he was given one after he won the 1954 Nobel Prize for chemistry for his study of the molecular structures of proteins.

After he was awarded the Nobel Prize, Pauling's views were taken more seriously. In 1955 he was a leading participant at the first PUGWASH CONFERENCE, which was composed of scientists who supported disarmament. In 1957 he presented the United Nations with a petition signed by more than 9,000 scientists and calling for an immediate halt to nuclear tests.

In 1958 Pauling's book *No More War* was published. The book ascribed the arms race to political misunderstanding and ignorance and warned that both the Soviet Union and the United States had enough nuclear weapons to completely destroy each other. He went on to warn about the dangers of radioactive fallout from continued nuclear tests, including the increased risk of cancer, leukemia and birth defects.

On the day that the NUCLEAR TEST BAN TREATY was signed in October 1963, it was announced that Pauling had won the Nobel Prize for peace. In his acceptance speech at Oslo, Pauling proposed that the United Nations supervise nuclear weapons stockpiles. He also urged United Nations membership for the PEOPLE'S REPUBLIC OF CHINA (Communist China) and the end of research on, development of and use of biological and chemical weapons.

In 1963 Pauling took a leave of absence from Cal Tech to join the Center for the Study of Democratic Institutions, where he continued to work for general disarmament. After 1966, Pauling became increasingly involved in the protests against the VIETNAM WAR. In 1967 he joined Dr. Benjamin Spock and 318 other prominent citizens in signing the "Call to Resist Illegitimate Authority." The statement asserted that the Vietnam War outraged the "deepest moral and religious sense" of Americans and called on the nation's youth to resist the draft.

Pauling returned to his research at Cal Tech in 1967. He resigned from Cal Tech, a state-run university, in 1969 and moved to the private Stanford Univeristy in protest against the State of California's educational policies under Governor RONALD REAGAN. In September 1975 he was awarded the National Medal of Science.

For Further Information:
Gilpin, Robert. *American Scientists and Nuclear Weapons Policy.* Princeton, 1962.

Peaceful Coexistence   Peaceful Coexistence is a term coined by Soviet leader NIKITA KHRUSHCHEV to characterize a state of affairs in which the superpowers would continue their political and economic competition without resorting to war. As Khrushchev said in 1963, "Your representatives of the Western countries do not like our social system, and we disapprove of the systems that exist in your countries . . . But we, the Soviet people, firmly stand for the social and class questions, the questions of international social and political systems, to be settled not through war between states but by the people of every country without any interference from outside. I . . . would like to repeat that in present conditions the choice is between peaceful coexistence and world thermonuclear war. The Soviet Union firmly adheres to the Leninist position of peaceful coexistence of states with different social systems."

Pearson, Lester B. **(April 23, 1897–December 27, 1972)** Lester Pearson was Canadian secretary of state for external affairs from 1948 to 1957. During that period he also served as president of the UN General Assembly and chairman of the NATO Council and won the Nobel Prize for peace for helping to negotiate a solution to the SUEZ CRISIS. He was prime minister from 1963 until his retirement in 1968.

After serving in World War I as a pilot, Pearson won a scholarship to Britain's Oxford University and then returned to Toronto University to teach history. In 1928 he entered the Canadian diplomatic service. During World War II he served in London and Washington, D.C.; he became Canadian ambassador to Washington in 1945.

Pearson was attracted to the ideals of the United Nations, and in the closing stages of the war he was senior adviser to the Canadian delegation at the SAN FRANCISCO CONFERENCE. Pearson was nominated for the post of secretary general of the United Nations in 1945 and 1953, but on both occasions his appointment was blocked by the Soviet Union. Pearson, however, was chairman of the Political and Security Committee of the General Assembly and in this post helped to achieve the Palestine partition resolution.

In 1948 Canadian prime minister LOUIS ST. LAURENT persuaded Pearson to leave the diplomatic service for Liberal Party politics and the post of secretary of state for external affairs. He took up the post at a time when Canada was coming out from under the wing of Britain to become a strong middle power on the world stage. It was also the start of the Cold War, and Pearson fought against the traditional Canadian isolationism to bring Canada's newfound political weight firmly into the Western camp in support of Western European unity, the NORTH ATLANTIC TREATY ORGANIZATION and the KOREAN WAR.

In 1952, the same year Pearson was elected president of the United Nations General Assembly, he presided over the NATO Lisbon Conference, at which new and substantially increased force levels were set for the member countries. In 1952 and 1953 he played a leading role in negotiating the truce that ended the Korean War.

Pearson's active involvement in the United Nations was a reflection of Canada's own keen interest in the organization. Pearson also laid other major foundations of Canadian postwar foreign policy, such as support for the Commonwealth, close relations with the Third World, an extensive foreign aid program and a willingness to criticize American foreign policy.

Canada sent forces to the Korean War, but Pearson made it clear that the Canadian government regarded the war not as an attempt to "contain" or "roll back" communism but as a UN action to uphold the peace settlement that had divided Korea at the 38th parallel. Pearson was also critical of American refusal to recognize communist China, although he did give in to American pressure and also withheld recognition.

Pearson remained external affairs minister until the Liberals' defeat in the Canadian general election of June 1957. The following year St. Laurent retired from politics, and Pearson replaced him as leader of the Liberal Party and the opposition. In 1963 he became prime minister at the head of a minority government, and he held the post until his retirement in 1968.

As prime minister, much of Pearson's time was absorbed with the problem of keeping his minority government in power and dealing with the separatist movement in French-speaking Quebec. Pearson did oppose the VIETNAM WAR, and Canada became a refuge for thousands of young Americans fleeing the military draft. Pearson also became involved in implementing the decision of the previous Conservative government to deploy nuclear warheads with the Canadian forces in West Germany. The move provoked an outcry from the Liberal Party's left wing, led by Pierre Trudeau, and after Trudeau assumed the premiership in 1968 the Canadian forces were denuclearized.

After his retirement from politics in 1968, Pearson became chancellor of Carleton University in Ottawa. He also became heavily involved in projects for Third World countries.

For Further Information:
Balawyder, Aloysius. *Canada-Soviet Relations, 1936–1980*. Winnipeg, Manitoba, 1982.
Bothwell, R. *Pearson*. New York, 1978.
Hurs, Donald, and John Miller. *The Challenge of Power: Canada and the World*. New York, 1979.
Pearson, Lester. *Mike: The Memoirs of the Rt. Hon. Lester Pearson*, 3 vols. Buffalo, N.Y., 1975.
Stursberg, Peter. *Lester Pearson and the American Dilemma*. Garden City, N.Y., 1980.

Penkovsky, Oleg   (April 23, 1919–May 1963)   Oleg Pen-kovsky was one of the most prominent Soviet double agents during the Cold War. He provided valuable information to American and British intelligence before and during the CUBAN MISSILE CRISIS. Before he could be spirited out of the Soviet Union, Penkovsky was arrested, tried and executed.

Penkovsky had a distinguished career in the Soviet military. He attended the prestigious Frunze Military Academy and during World War II was a much-decorated artillery officer. By the age of 40, Penkovsky was a full colonel.

At this stage he was chosen for the military intelligence service, the GRU (Glavnoye Razvedyvatelnoye Upravleniye), and was posted to Turkey as assistant military attaché. Penkovsky later wrote that, about this time, he had become convinced that the foreign policy of Soviet leader NIKITA KHRUSHCHEV would eventually cause the world to blunder into a nuclear war and felt he had a moral obligation to subvert that policy. He made his first contact with the West in late 1960 through British businessman Greville M. Wynne, who had extensive contacts with the British Intelligence community.

In April 1961 Penkovsky led a Soviet delegation to London, where he met British and American intelligence officers and arranged to hand over information. He returned to Moscow and was given the code name "Alex" by his British and American handlers. Between April 1961 and August 1962, Penkovsky passed more than 5,000 copies of top secret political, military and economic documents to Western intelligence.

Wynne, whose business activities took him on regular business trips into Eastern Europe, acted as the main conduit between Penkovsky and MI6 and the CENTRAL INTELLIGENCE AGENCY (CIA). Penkovsky's assessments of Soviet foreign policy and nuclear defense capabilities played a major part in formulating American foreign policy at the time of the Cuban Missile Crisis.

In the months before the crisis, British Intelligence became aware that the Soviets were increasingly suspicious of Penkovsky's activities. They started planning for his escape to the West, but Penkovsky, increasingly worried about the threat of nuclear war, refused to be withdrawn while the missile crisis was at its height.

In October, Wynne crossed into Hungary with a small convoy of trucks, one of which was designed to be used to smuggle out Penkovsky. Almost as soon as he entered Hungary, Wynne was arrested on espionage charges (he was imprisoned in the Soviet Union and released in 1964 in a prisoner exchange). The same day, October 22, 1962, Penkovsky was arrested in Moscow. After a trial, he was found guilty of high treason, sentenced to death and shot. His journal, *The Penkovsky Papers*, was published in 1965.

For Further Information:
Penkovsky, Oleg. *The Penkovsky Papers*. New York, 1965.

Perle, Richard N. (September 16, 1941–   ) Richard Perle was assistant secretary of defense for international security during the REAGAN administration. He was one of the leading hardliners in the administration.

The son of a California businessman, Perle studied at the University of Southern California, the London School of Economics and Princeton University. After graduate work in international relations, Perle went to Washington, D.C. to work with DEAN ACHESON and PAUL NITZE to help promote the ANTIBALLISTIC MISSILE (ABM) TREATY. In 1969 Senator HENRY M. JACKSON hired Perle as an aide on foreign affairs and arms control issues. In this position, Perle advised Jackson in regard to the SALT I (STRATEGIC ARMS LIMITATION TALKS) negotiations that any treaty on offensive nuclear arms should be based on "the principle of equality."

Perle and Jackson, who supported the 1972 ABM Treaty in principle, were angry when the NIXON administration agreed to reduce the number of American ABM sites from four to two. Jackson had too much political prestige invested in the ABM Treaty to withdraw his support, but with Perle's help he launched an attack on the corollary SALT I agreement and organized a purge of the officials at the ARMS CONTROL AND DISARMAMENT AGENCY (ACDA) who had conducted the negotiations.

Perle now became an unabashed opponent of arms control agreements with the Soviet Union, and his statements took on a more strident anti-Soviet tone. In 1973, at Jackson's behest, Perle was appointed a professional staff member of the Permanent Subcommittee of the Senate Investigations Committee on Government Affairs. In this position he became part of the Senate forces opposed to the SALT II Treaty. The treaty was signed by president JIMMY CARTER and Soviet president LEONID BREZHNEV in 1979 but failed to secure ratification in the U.S. Senate, not so much because of the efforts of Jackson and Perle but because of the Soviet invasion of Afghanistan and the taking of American diplomatic hostages in Iran.

In 1981 Perle reached the pinnacle of his power when he was appointed assistant secretary of defense for international security. The position is a relatively minor one in the Pentagon, but Perle's well-established contacts and the closeness of his views to those of President Ronald Reagan invested the job with new importance, and for at least six years Perle was possibly the greatest intellectual influence on American arms control policy. His major contribution was to shift the debate over arms control to the question of Soviet trustworthiness and the need for verification.

Perle did not restrict his work to arms control issues. He was an avid supporter of Israel on the grounds that the Jewish state was America's most reliable ally. He was also one of the principal figures behind moves to tighten control of exports to the Soviet Union from third countries.

In Perle's view, the prospect of a successful arms control agreement with the Soviet Union was very low because the "terrible failure" of the Soviet system had left that country dependent on "sheer brute force." He went on to maintain that agreements that merely controlled the development of nuclear weapons were worthless and that the only type of agreement worth negotiating was one that reduced nuclear forces to an equitable, balanced and verifiable level.

Perle's hard line made him especially unpopular with America's European allies. DENIS HEALEY, the British Labour Party spokesman on defense, labeled him "The Prince of Darkness." Perle struck back at the West Europeans. At the annual Wehrkunde Conference on Western security at Munich in Feburary 1987, Perle accused West European leaders of being "mealy-mouthed" in expressing their views on East–West issues and said that they too often resorted to "misty blandishments" rather than directly criticize the Soviets on arms control issues. He went on to say "it is as though the words *violation* and *cheating* cannot be said in well-mannered company. How hard our allies find it to distinguish between the unspeakable and the unspoken." Perle's comments caused an uproar among Europeans. Michael Alexander, British ambassador to NATO, called them "gratuitously offensive." Various European leaders complained to President Reagan and Defense Secretary CASPAR WEINBERGER, and in March 1987 Perle announced that he was resigning.

Pershing II Missiles The Pershing II missiles were nuclear-armed intermediate-range missiles deployed in West Germany in the 1980s as a response to the Soviet Union's SS-20 program. The missiles were withdrawn as a condition of the INTERMEDIATE-RANGE NUCLEAR FORCES (INF) TREATY in 1987.

The Pershing II missile was the successor to the Pershing 1A missile deployed in West Germany in the 1970s. The first-generation Pershing had a range of 100 miles and was armed with a 400-kiloton nuclear warhead. The missile's limited range and massive explosive power made it unsuitable for battlefield use in Germany, where the public was becoming increasingly concerned about their country being destroyed in a battlefield nuclear exchange regardless of the final outcome.

The introduction of the Pershing II owed as much to public opposition to the Pershing 1A as it did to the introduction of the highly mobile Soviet SS-20 missiles in the late 1970s. The new Pershing II had a range of up to 460 miles and an explosive yield of 5 to 50 kilotons. It also had a more sophisticated guidance system that enabled the U.S. Army to use it as a ground-to-ground missile against hardened military targets in Eastern Europe.

Under an agreement reached at a NATO foreign ministers' meeting in December 1979, a total of 572 American Pershing II and cruise missiles were to be deployed in Western Europe.

Of these, a total of 120 Pershing II missiles were based in West Germany. Under the terms of the INF Treaty of 1987, the Pershing II missiles, along with other American and Soviet INF weapons in Europe, were not only withdrawn but also destroyed.

Philby, H.A.R. (Kim) (January 1, 1912–May 11, 1988)

Kim Philby was the most notorious of a group of British double agents who operated for the Soviet Union during the Cold War. At one time, he was head of the anti-Soviet section of Britain's MI6 and liaison officer between the CENTRAL INTELLIGENCE AGENCY (CIA) and MI6. He helped to organize the escape of two other double agents, GUY BURGESS and DONALD MACLEAN; undermined an Anglo-American operation to overthrow the communist government in ALBANIA; and is believed to have done more damage to British and American intelligence operations than any other Soviet spy.

Philby was born into a British colonial family. His father, St. John Philby, was a renowned expert on the Middle East and adviser to Saudi Arabia's King Abdul Aziz. While studying at Cambridge University during the 1930s, Kim Philby was attracted to communism, and was recruited as a Soviet spy in 1933. Philby always gave the impression of being a committed member of the British establishment and after university joined the staff of the London *Times*. He was sent to Spain to cover the civil war there and was awarded a medal by General FRANCISCO FRANCO. But he also provided valuable intelligence to the Soviet Union, which promoted him to the rank of general in the KGB.

With the start of World War II, Philby joined MI6, the British Intelligence agency responsible for overseas intelligence. By the end of the war, his capacity for hard work and his personal charm had led to his being marked as a possible future director of the agency. In 1944 Philby was appointed head of MI6's anti-Soviet service, thus placing him in the perfect position to inform the KGB of British and American anti-Soviet operations. In the late 1940s, MI6 and the CIA organized an attempt to overthrow the communist government in Albania. Philby kept the KGB fully informed. When hundreds of paratroopers were dropped into Albania they were machine-gunned to death before they reached the ground.

In 1949 Philby was assigned to Washington, D.C. as the chief liaison officer between the CIA and MI6. At the time, the CIA was still in its formative stages and relied heavily on the more experienced MI6 for guidance and help. This provided Philby with invaluable information on CIA intelligence activities, which he passed on to Moscow. American agents began to suspect Philby in 1950. Their suspicions appeared to be confirmed after the double agents Burgess and MacLean fled to Moscow shortly before they were to have been arrested. The CIA was convinced that they had been tipped off by Philby and demanded that he be arrested. But after an investigation by Britain's counterintelligence organization, MI5, Philby was cleared.

H.A.R. (Kim) Philby (standing) denies that he is a Soviet spy at a press conference on August 11, 1955. Photo courtesy of Popperfoto.

The Burgess and MacLean case had seriously impaired relations between American and British intelligence organizations, and the CIA made it clear that it still did not trust Philby, who was sent into an intelligence wilderness for four years. In 1955 he emerged in Beirut working for MI6 under the cover of journalist for the *Observer* and the *Economist*. MI5 had continued its investigations and was on the verge of arresting Philby when he escaped to Moscow in January 1963. Shortly before he disappeared, Philby admitted to being a Soviet double agent.

In Moscow, Philby joined the British section of the KGB and was treated as a Soviet hero with a comfortable Moscow apartment and full access to foreign journals and books. He was married to a Russian woman, and until his dying day he maintained a firm belief in communism and the Soviet system. Kim Philby was buried with full military honors when he died on May 11, 1988. British Labour Member of Parliament Ted Leadbitter said Philby's death "brings to an end . . . the unhappiest period of betrayal of this century." British journalist Phillip Knightley, who had conducted extensive interviews with Philby shortly before his death, said, "Philby was the most remarkable spy in the history of espionage. He stuck to his beliefs through thick and thin with a doggedness of purpose and total commitment."

For Further Information:
Boyle, Andrew. *The Climate of Treason.* London, 1979.
Knightley, Phillip. *Philby: KGB Masterspy.* London, 1988.
Philby, Kim. *My Silent War.* New York, 1968.

Philippines

During the Cold War the Philippines was a vital American base of operations in the Asia–Pacific region.

The history of the relationship between the Philippines and the United States has been marked by changes in character from ostensible friendship to colonialism to alliance to neo-colonialism. It started at the end of the 19th century, when, in the guise of aiding the Filipino nationalist struggle against Spanish colonial rule, American forces occupied the islands. After the bloody suppression of a two-year revolt against

American rule (1899–1901), the Philippines became part of an American empire.

During the next 40 years, the U.S. colonial administration successfully contained violent opposition, and achieved substantial improvements in social, political and economic conditions. In 1934, a self-governing "commonwealth" was established, and in 1946, after World War II, the Philippines became independent. But the war and the Japanese occupation destroyed the country's infrastructure and left the economy in ruins.

The government of President Manuel Roxas turned to the United States for aid. The TRUMAN administration extended generous help (see HUKBALAHAP REBELLION) but in return demanded that U.S. citizens be given equal rights with Filipinos in the exploitation of natural resources (a move that ensured American economic dominance) and that the United States be given a 99-year lease on a number of military and naval bases. The Philippines thus remained America's base of operations in the region.

During the KOREAN WAR, Filipino troops fought alongside American forces; in 1952 the Philippines signed its own Mutual Defense Treaty with the United States, and it was a founding member of the SOUTHEAST ASIA TREATY ORGANIZATION (SEATO) in 1954. During the VIETNAM WAR, noncombatant Filipino engineers augmented American forces, and the American bases in the Philippines were crucial to U.S. military operations.

As of 1989, there were six American bases in the Philippines. The most important were the Subic Bay Naval Base and Clark Air Force Base (the others were subsidiary to these).

Subic Bay was regarded by defense experts as the U.S. Navy's most important installation outside the United States. Equipped with a large and well-protected harbor, the base was the headquarters for the U.S. Navy's Seventh Fleet operating in the Indian Ocean and the Pacific. Clark Air Force Base was the headquarters of the U.S. 13th Air Force, responsible for American air operations in the West Pacific.

Filipino opposition to the bases, however, was widespread. The nonmutuality of the base treaties and their perpetuation of an old-style colonial relationship were major issues in Philippine politics for years. In 1965 the size and number of U.S. bases were reduced, and in 1966 the base leases were shortened to 25 years. In 1979 the United States yielded to demands from President Ferdinand Marcos that the base areas be further limited; formal jurisdiction was passed to the Philippine government, U.S. compensation was increased, the lease period was reduced to five years, and the United States had to give an explicit commitment to defend Filipino interests outside the Philippines.

In June 1983, the agreement was extended for another five years until October 1989, and American compensation was increased from $500 million to $900 million. After the overthrow of President Marcos in February 1986, opposition to the bases only grew, since the United States was identified with the authoritarian role of Marcos. The new government of President Corazon Aquino took a tough line in negotiations to renew the leases, and on October 17, 1988, an interim accord was signed extending them to the end of 1991. This arrangement was also attacked by Filipino opposition groups, as were its financial terms.

Negotiations for a new lease continued, but the end of the Cold War, followed by the considerable physical damage caused by the eruption of the Mount Pinatubo volcano, substantially lowered the value of the bases to the United States. In September 1991, the Philippine senate failed to ratify a new agreement, and the U.S. decided to allow the leases to end. The subsequent American withdrawal was completed in 1992.

Pilsen Riots   (1953)   The riots in Pilsen (Plzen), Czechoslovakia in 1953 were in response to President ANTONIN ZAPOTOCKY's attempts to introduce economic and monetary reforms. They resulted in an improved position for the hardline Stalinists within the Czechoslovak Communist Party.

Communist leader KLEMENT GOTTWALD had imposed a dogmatic Stalinist government on Czechoslovakia. There were extensive political purges in addition to widespread nationalization of industry and agriculture. The combined effect of these actions was political and economic stagnation by the time of Gottwald's death in March 1953.

His successor, Zapotocky, set out to loosen the political and economic repression of his predecessor. To provide a firm financial foundation for the changes, Zapotocky on May 30, 1953, revalued the Czechoslovak currency on a plan under which old "crowns" were worth $\frac{1}{5}$ to $\frac{1}{50}$ the value of the new. All state loans and securities issued since 1945 were canceled. The effect of the revaluation was to deprive farmers and better-off workers of their savings.

On June 1, 1953, employers of the Lenin Works, a weapons manufacturing complex in Pilsen, started a protest march. The march quickly spread to other factories in Pilsen, and within a few hours the protest had turned into a riot as workers destroyed factory machinery, pillaged the town hall, trampled a Soviet flag and pictures of communist leaders, and waved American and British flags.

Troops were called in to restore order and they fired on the rioters, killing six people. Other demonstrations took place in Moravia, Ostrava, the Vaclav Sofie mines, the Bohumin Iron Works and the Stalingrad Iron Works in Liskovec. Sporadic firing was reported as late as June 4. The Czech government at first denied the riots, but they were finally confirmed on June 15 by President Zapotocky when he said that demonstrations against currency reform had been subdued.

Pleven Plan   The Pleven Plan formed the basis for discussions on the formation of a EUROPEAN DEFENSE COMMUNITY and a common European army and on German rearmament. The EDC Treaty was rejected by the French National Assembly, but the basic concepts led to West German membership in the NORTH ATLANTIC TREATY ORGANIZATION (NATO) and the WESTERN EUROPEAN UNION.

The start of the KOREAN WAR in June 1950 convinced some Europeans that they were in danger from the Soviet Union. With American troops committed in Korea, it was therefore necessary that they unite against the common foe. The United States was convinced that a common European defense program would need to include a rearmed West Germany. But this encountered strong opposition from a public unable to forget German atrocities committed only five years before.

French prime minister René Pleven attempted to break the deadlock by proposing a European army, the creation of which would be contingent upon serious restrictions on the size and nature of a German defense force. The main points of the Pleven Plan were as follows:

1. A European defense minister would be appointed and would be responsible to a European assembly, which would either be elected or appointed by the governments of its members.
2. A European defense council comprised of West European defense ministers would be created.
3. The European defense council would have a single defense budget.
4. Each member of the European defense council would contribute troops from its own national forces.
5. West Germany would contribute to the European army and be represented on the council, but would not have its own separate national army or defense minister.

The strong anti-German tone of the Pleven Plan annoyed the West Germans, who wanted to be admitted as full partners to the Western Alliance. The final EDC Treaty eliminated most of the anti-German sentiments, and for this reason the French National Assembly rejected it.

Podgorny, Nikolai   (February 18, 1903–January 12, 1983)

Nikolai Podgorny was a close associate of NIKITA KHRUSHCHEV but helped to overthrow his mentor in 1964. He became president of the Soviet Union in 1965 and traveled widely, especially among Third World countries, until abruptly removed from office in 1977.

Podgorny was born into a working-class Ukrainian family and started factory work at the age of 15. At almost the same time, he joined the Young Communist League (Komsomol) and started attending evening classes in engineering. He eventually won a place at an engineering college in Kiev and graduated with his degree in 1931. He became a full member of the Communist Party in 1930.

Podgorny's first engineering jobs were in a series of sugarbeet factories, which gave him a good grounding in the country's agro-industries. In 1939, after a series of bloody purges, he was named deputy people's commissar for the Ukrainian food industry. In 1940 he moved to Moscow to do the same job at the national level and throughout the war helped to organize Soviet food production.

Podgorny was named to the Council of Ministers in 1946, and in 1950 he began his climb up the party ladder when he was named first secretary of the Kharkov province in the Ukraine. Three years later he was second secretary of the entire Ukrainian party and in 1957 became its leader. In 1956, Podgorny became a member of the Central Committee. He was elevated to the Politburo as a candidate (non-voting) member in 1958 and became a full member in 1960.

Podgorny's rapid climb through party ranks in the 1950s owed much to his close friendship to Communist Party leader and fellow Ukrainian Nikita Khrushchev. Khrushchev considered Podgorny such a close ally that he openly talked of him as his most likely successor. But by 1963, Podgorny realized that Khrushchev was on the way out, and he sided with LEONID BREZHNEV and ALEXEI KOSYGIN in engineering the overthrow of Khrushchev in October 1964. Podgorny's reward was the post of chairman of the Presidium of the Supreme Soviet (president or head of state). Kosygin and Brezhnev held the other key posts.

The Soviet presidency was largely a ceremonial role, although Podgorny retained considerable influence as a member of the Politburo and the person responsible for local party units and officials. This led some political observers to report that he would come to dominate the triumvirate. It soon became apparent, however, that Brezhnev's position as leader of the party made him the dominant member.

Podgorny's main task appeared to be to travel to Third World countries, where his protocol position of head of state gave the host country an exaggerated sense of importance and enhanced Soviet prestige. After one especially well-publicized tour of Africa in 1977 Podgorny was abruptly pushed out of the presidency so that Brezhnev could take over the post of head of state, with its protocol advantages in dealing with foreign leaders. It was speculated at the time of Podgorny's resignation that it was the result of policy differences over Africa. His removal could also have been linked to the draft of a new Soviet constitution, completion of which was announced on the same day that Podgorny was removed from the Politburo. Podgorny slipped into a quiet and uneventful retirement.

For Further Information:

Conquest, Robert. *Russia After Khrushchev*. London, 1965.
Dallin, Alexander, and Thomas B. Larson, eds. *Soviet Politics Since Khrushchev*. Englewood Cliffs, N.J., 1968.
Owen, Richard, *Crisis in the Kremlin*. London, 1986.

Point Four Program (International Development Act)   The

Point Four Program was effectively the start of America's postwar foreign aid program to the underdeveloped world. It was based on the premise that communism thrived on poverty, and therefore the best way to combat it was to raise the world's standard of living.

The program was the fourth point of a foreign policy plan

outlined by President HARRY TRUMAN in his inaugural address of January 20, 1949. The first three points were continued support for the United Nations and its related agencies, continuation of the program for world economic recovery and strengthening of "freedom-loving nations" against the dangers of aggression. Truman's fourth, and most controversial, proposal was to make American investment capital and scientific and technical expertise available to underdeveloped countries in order to raise the worldwide standard of living.

Truman saw the Point Four Program as the logical extension of the MARSHALL PLAN and the special aid extended to Greece and Turkey under the TRUMAN DOCTRINE.

On June 24, 1949, Truman requested $45 million to inaugurate the program. On June 5, 1950, the program became law when the president signed the International Development Act. A great deal of the money went to UN agencies, but specialized American agencies were also established. Distribution of the aid was the responsibility of the State Department, which established an International Development Advisory Board under the chairmanship of NELSON ROCKEFELLER. By March 1951, a total of 350 technicians were at work on more than a hundred technical cooperation projects in 27 countries. By 1953 Congress had increased the budget to $155,600,000.

For Further Information:
Clark, Paul F. *American Aid for Development.* New York, 1972.
Eberstadt, Nicholas. *Foreign Aid and American Purpose.* Washington, D.C., 1988.

Poland   The treatment of Poland at the end of World War II was one of the chief causes of the Cold War. JOSEF STALIN's refusal to allow Poland to hold the free elections that had been promised at the YALTA CONFERENCE severely strained relations among the wartime allies, and the Soviets' continuing occupation of Poland and repression of Polish nationalism was viewed in the West as evidence of the Soviet Union's hegemonic designs. Later, the rise of Solidarity in the 1980s prefigured many of the protests that led to the fall of communism throughout Eastern Europe at the end of the decade.

The Polish issue has its roots in medieval history and in Poland's unfortunate geographic situation, with no natural barriers, between Europe's two great land powers, Russia and Germany. Because of its position the country was in recent centuries either divided among its more powerful neighbors or used as a corridor for attacks aimed at either Moscow or Berlin.

During the second half of the 18th century, Poland was divided among Russia, Austria and Prussia. The partition of 1795 effectively erased the Polish state until after World War I. During the intervening 124 years, Polish language, culture and nationalism were brutally repressed by the great European powers. The Roman Catholic Church was one of the few Polish institutions allowed to remain intact, and it became the repository of Polish nationalism, thus giving the church sub-

stantial political power. The end of World War I saw the collapse of the Prussian, Austrian and Russian empires, and the Polish state was revived.

The victorious allies agreed that Poland's border with the Soviet Union should be set roughly along the Bug River and the former frontier between the old Austrian and Russian empires. However, the new Polish government took advantage of Russia's ongoing civil war to lay claim to and occupy not only the former Russian zone of Poland but also the western Ukraine region. The Red Army retaliated in May 1920 and advanced to within a few miles of Warsaw. At this stage the Poles appealed for Allied intervention, and British foreign secretary Lord Curzon offered a mediated solution, which again formally offered the Bug River as the border. This proposed border became known as the CURZON LINE.

Unexpectedly, the Poles decisively defeated the Red Army and pushed it back beyond the western Ukraine. Their victories led them to ignore the proferred Curzon Line. The new border, set in March 1921 by the Treaty of Riga, gave Poland an additional 52,000 square miles east of the Curzon Line. It also left the Soviet government determined to recover the lands that it had lost.

The Soviets' opportunity to reverse the Treaty of Riga came when Hitler offered Stalin a secret alliance to attack and divide Poland. The Molotov–Ribbentrop Pact (named for the foreign ministers of Germany and the Soviet Union) set a seal on the start of World War II. With an alliance with the Soviet Union, Hitler's eastern flank was secure, and he was free to throw the full might of his defense forces against Britain and France. On September 1, 1939, Hitler's army invaded Poland. On September 3, Britain and France, who had guaranteed Polish independence, declared war on Germany. On September 17, Soviet troops attacked Poland, and on September 27, Warsaw fell.

A Polish government-in-exile was established under Wladyslaw Sikorski in Paris. After the fall of France it moved to London and was recognized as the official Polish government by Britain and, after the German attack on the Soviet Union and the Japanese attack on Pearl Harbor, by the Soviet Union and the United States as well. But relations between the Soviets and the London Poles were marked by distrust.

Polish suspicions appeared to be confirmed when the Germans announced that they had discovered in the Katyn Forest in the U.S.S.R. a mass grave of thousands of Polish officers. Signs indicated that the Poles had been massacred by the Red Army during its early wartime occupation of Poland. The KATYN MASSACRE led to a series of charges and countercharges between Stalin and STANISLAW MIKOLAJCZYK (who succeeded Sikorski after the latter died in a plane crash). Stalin used the dispute to break off diplomatic relations with the London-based Poles and form an alternative, Soviet-supported government led by Polish communist BOLESLAW BIERUT.

On July 21, 1944, the Red Army crossed the Curzon Line, and Bierut's Polish National Liberation Committee was installed at Lublin. It became known as the LUBLIN COMMITTEE. Bierut's presence on Polish soil placed him in a strong position to form the postwar Polish government, but the deciding factor was his absolute obedience to Stalin and Stalin's determination to crush the London Poles and create a pro-Soviet communist government in Poland.

Stalin's opportunity came during the WARSAW UPRISING of 1944. Shortly after the Red Army crossed the Curzon Line, Radio Moscow called on the Poles in Warsaw to stage a general uprising against the Germans, promising to come to their aid. On August 1, 1944, the commander of the Home Army in Poland, General Tadeusz Bor-Komorowski (also known as General Bor), ordered his forces to arms. The Red Army, however, instead of coming to the aid of the Poles, was ordered by Stalin to halt its advance. The result was that for 63 days the poorly equipped Poles fought the German Army in Warsaw. An estimated 200,000 Poles were killed and the Home Army (the military arm of the London Poles) was effectively destroyed, leaving the Soviet Red Army as the only Allied military power in Poland.

Mikolajczyk reluctantly accepted Bierut's demand for 14 seats in the Provisional Polish Government of National Unity. When the government was finally formed on June 21, 1945, Bierut was named president of the National Council. Mikolajczyk was reduced to a second deputy prime minister and minister of agriculture.

Stalin's heavy-handed tactics in Poland had made the British and American governments suspicious of Bierut and Stalin's plans. The Polish question dominated the Yalta Conference in February 1945, and Stalin had to promise free elections within a month in order to secure American and British recognition of the Bierut government. But neither Stalin nor Bierut had any intention of holding any elections in Poland until Bierut had had ample opportunity to eliminate political opposition through the traditional Stalinist methods of political intimidation, arrests and executions.

It was two years before elections took place. The delay was one of the major causes of early postwar strains in East–West relations, but Stalin clearly felt that it was worth it to consolidate his control. The elections held on January 19, 1947, resulted in Bierut's Polish Workers' Party securing 383 out of the 444 seats in the Polish Sejm (parliament). Mikolajczyk described the result as a "classic in the annals of electoral fraud." Bierut formally assumed the title of president of the Polish Republic.

(Mikolajczyk was accused of being an ally of foreign imperialists, and in October 1947 he fled first to Britain and then to the United States, saying he wanted to avoid "being shot and killed like a sheep." In the United States he sought to rally anticommunist forces among the large Polish-American community and lobbied the U.S. administration for action against Stalin and the Bierut government. In November 1948 his account of the Soviet occupation of his country, *Rape of Poland*, was published. Mikolajczyk died in Chevy Chase, Maryland on December 13, 1966.)

Meanwhile, Poland's boundaries were again changed. The eastern border was established along the Curzon Line, thus reestablishing Soviet control in the Ukraine. To compensate the Poles for the loss of their eastern territories, the Soviets proposed that 40,000 square miles of German territory be granted to Poland and that the German–Polish border be drawn along the ODER-NEISSE LINE. This was provisionally accepted by the United States and Britain as a temporary arrangement. It was accepted by the West German government in 1970 with the signing of the GERMAN-POLISH TREATY, and reconfirmed in 1991 as part of the German reunification process.

After the 1947 elections, Bierut moved to Stalinize Poland. He introduced forcible collectivization of farms, suppressed the Roman Catholic Church and nationalized all businesses with more than 50 employees. He also strengthened Polish ties with the Soviet Union by appointing a Russian, Marshal Konstantin K. Rokossovsky, as Polish defense minister. On July 22, 1952, the Sejm approved a Soviet-style constitution.

Bierut, however, faced opposition from a nationalist wing within the Communist Party led by WLADYSLAW GOMULKA. Bierut won the resultant power struggle and in July 1951 Gomulka was arrested and imprisoned.

Bierut replaced Gomulka as first secretary of the Communist Party and reorganized the party and governmental structures so that the party leader became the de facto ruler of the country. In 1952 he resigned from the largely ceremonial position of president and became premier, an administrative post that he in turn quit in 1954, leaving himself with only the all-important position of party first secretary.

Throughout this period Bierut continued to consolidate his power base through the ruthless use of the secret police and army. He emerged virtually unscathed from the turmoil following the death of Stalin in 1953 and appeared to be unaffected by the Yugoslav-Soviet rapprochement, which undermined other East European Stalinists. But in 1956 he went to Moscow for the 20th Party Congress, where on February 26 NIKITA KHRUSHCHEV delivered his famous "secret speech" denouncing the crimes of Bierut's mentor Stalin. Bierut was so badly shaken that he suffered a heart attack and died in Moscow on March 12.

Bierut's death, along with the anti-Stalinist campaign of Nikita Khrushchev and the political rehabilitation of Yugoslavia, freed the pent-up forces of Polish nationalism.

On April 6, 1956, Gomulka was released from prison and "rehabilitated," and the government announced its intention to free 30,000 political prisoners. These events significantly raised the political temperature in Poland, and workers started agitating for increased political freedoms and higher wages. Events boiled over in Poznan on June 28, 1956, when workers rioted for bread, political liberty, free elections and the withdrawal of Soviet troops.

The subsequent POZNAN CRISIS contributed to the Hungarian Uprising, to the rise of power of Gomulka, and to an agreement between Gomulka and Khrushchev that Poland would be allowed greater control of its internal affairs in return for a firm pledge to remain within the WARSAW PACT.

At this stage, Gomulka was regarded as a great Polish hero. An estimated 250,000 Poles swept into the Warsaw city center to cheer him. He had a clear mandate for a sweeping reform of the political and economic system. But Gomulka was a communist as well as a nationalist and his reforms fell short of public aspirations. There were some significant changes. The forced agricultural collectivization program was abandoned, the Catholic Church was allowed greater freedom and the activities of the secret police were curbed. But the economy remained centrally controlled, the press was censored and the Communist Party continued to dominate all aspects of life.

It was widely believed inside and outside Poland that the limited scope of Gomulka's reforms was the result of pressure from Moscow and that this demonstrated the continuing stranglehold of the Soviet Union on Poland. There is an element of truth in this, but it is also fair to state that Gomulka limited his reforms out of conviction. He demonstrated this in 1961 when Khrushchev launched a second de-Stalinization campaign. Elsewhere in Eastern Europe, especially in Hungary, this campaign led to economic reforms that substantially improved living conditions, but Gomulka refused to exploit the situation.

From this point, Gomulka's power base began to crumble. In 1968, opposition to Gomulka culminated in student riots in Warsaw, Lublin, Poznan and Lodz, in protest against the Warsaw Pact invasion of Czechoslovakia. Gomulka responded by closing down the universities and forcing the students to apply for readmission. Student leaders were denied permission to reenter, and an estimated 1,300 students were drafted into the army.

At the party conference in November 1968, Gomulka managed to hold onto his post of secretary general, but the party itself split between those seeking to identify more closely with Eurocommunism in Western Europe and those who looked toward Moscow for leadership. Gomulka sided with the Moscow faction. From this point on, his political decline quickened, although in 1969 and 1970 his work in helping to establish the foundations of West German chancellor WILLY BRANDT's OSTPOLITIK policy slightly revived his political fortunes.

The main issue became the state of the national economy, which had stagnated under Gomulka's strict central control. In May 1970, Gomulka tried to revive the economy with an incentive program for individual workers. This was followed by a massive increase in basic food prices. Two days later, on December 15, 1970, riots broke out among workers in the port city of Gdansk and quickly spread to other major cities. In one day 300 people were killed. On December 20, Gomulka resigned and was replaced by Edward Gierek.

Gierek won popular support by rescinding most of the price increases and set out to correct some of the basic imbalances in the Polish economy by attempting to improve Polish productivity and exports to the West. To do this he imported Western machinery and borrowed from Western banks to pay for the modernization program. But the world recession that followed the quadrupling of oil prices in 1973–74 badly affected Gierek's export drive, and Poland was left with heavy debts to Western banks.

Gierek placed his own supporters, such as Stanislaw Kania, in the Politburo. But Gierek still faced opposition from such men as Stefan Olszowski and Tadeusz Grabski, who opposed his policy of increased centralization of the economy and his relatively soft line on opposition outside the party.

In June 1976 the government was again forced to introduce large increases in basic prices. The result was another round of strikes and riots. This time the government used political repression to suppress the workers and sent hundreds of them to prison. Gierek's heavy hand temporarily eased the political situation, but economic circumstances continued to deteriorate. These were complicated by the election in October 1978 of Karol Cardinal Wojtyla, the archbishop of Krakow, as Pope JOHN PAUL II. Because of the special historical and political position of the Roman Catholic Church in Poland, the election of a Polish pope further stoked the nationalist fires, and in June 1979 more fuel was added with the pope's triumphant visit to his homeland.

The election of a Polish pope, continuing economic problems for Polish workers, continuing Soviet domination, the Polish debt and Polish nationalism led, in August 1980, to fresh strikes at the Baltic port of Gdansk. The strikes, led by an electrician named LECH WALESA, quickly spread to other cities, and a committee was formed to coordinate strike activities. This committee became the nucleus of SOLIDARITY, Poland's first postwar independent trade union.

Solidarity issued a list of demands, including the right to organize independent trade unions, a rollback of meat price rises, family allowances and pensions, higher wages, an end to censorship, the right to strike and the release of political prisoners.

Gierek offered negotiations and pay increases, but he flatly refused political reform and ordered the workers to return to their jobs. When they refused, the government arrested a number of dissidents, broke off negotiations and cut telephone links to the Gdansk shipyard. Gierek's actions only inflamed the workers, and by August 24 the strike had spread to include 300,000 men.

Gierek was forced into concessions. He restored telephone links to the shipyards, reopened negotiations, and, in the first sign of an acceptance of a link between political and economic demands, dismissed Premier Edward Babiuch and three other hard-line members of the Politburo. He also promised free elections for a new leadership of the officially recognized trade unions. On August 30 the government acceded to most of the demands of the strikers, including the right to form independent trade unions and the right to strike. The government also promised increased food supplies, an end to press censorship, improved church access to the media and increased pay.

In return, the strike leaders promised that "the new unions [would] fulfill all constitutional principles and recognize the leading role of the party, the state and all of Poland's alliances and international obligations."

The government concessions represented a major defeat for Gierek, who was forced to resign as party leader on September 6, 1980. He was replaced by Stanislaw Kania, who immediately went to Gdansk to meet with Walesa to pledge his commitment to the agreement. On September 17, 1980, representatives from workers' groups throughout the country met in Gdansk and agreed to form a single national trade union. Solidarity was officially registered on September 24, 1980. It started with a membership of 3 million workers in 3,500 factories. This was roughly equal to the size of the Polish Communist Party.

The size of Solidarity and the circumstances that led to its creation meant that it could not be only a trade union concerned with pay and working conditions. It quickly became the only legal alternative to the Communist Party and therefore a threat to the party's existence. At the same time, because of the speed with which Solidarity sprang into being, Walesa had no time to consolidate his authority throughout the organization and was powerless to control the many wildcat strikes by workers anxious to exercise their newfound freedom.

The government, for its part, faced even more severe difficulties. It had agreed to the creation of Solidarity because it needed economic peace to introduce economic reforms. Solidarity's inability to control its members delayed the introduction of reforms, which in turn poisoned relations with the trade union and led to further strikes. At the same time, Polish communists were coming under increasing attack from other East European communists who saw the creation of Solidarity and the government's subsequent concessions as a threat to their own political futures. The Polish Communist Party had to find ways to curb Solidarity's political power in order to maintain its own dominance and prevent intervention by the Warsaw Pact.

The concern of other Soviet Bloc countries reached its peak when the Soviet Union called a summit meeting of East European leaders in Moscow on December 5 to discuss the Polish crisis. Kania's main purpose at the meeting was to prevent an invasion of Poland, which he believed would end in a bloodbath. He pledged Poland's continued "loyalty to the Socialist Commonwealth." The response from other Warsaw Pact leaders was an ambivalent communiqué, which expressed their confidence in Poland's ability to "overcome its present difficulties" and renounced "the use or the threat of the use of force." The communist leaders vowed, however, that Poland "was, is, and will be a socialist state" that could "firmly count on the fraternal solidarity and support" of the Warsaw Pact.

The last part of the statement was interpreted in the West as political shorthand for a threatened invasion of Poland unless moves were taken to curb Solidarity. To reinforce this interpretation, Soviet and East German troops gathered on their borders with Poland. Western aerial reconnaissance of the area was increased, and a meeting of NATO foreign ministers warned that intervention in Poland would wreck East–West détente. STEFAN Cardinal WYSZYNSKI, the Catholic primate of Poland, warned Polish dissidents that their action "could raise the danger of a threat to the freedom and statehood of the fatherland."

However, neither Wyszynski's appeal for moderation nor the threat of invasion appeared to have any effect on Polish workers. On January 10, 1981, Solidarity unilaterally declared a five-day working week and ordered its members to take Saturday off. At the same time, the nation's farmers announced their intention to form a Rural Solidarity. On January 22 wildcat strikes were staged in 10 Polish cities over the issue of Saturday work. The government responded by warning that it would "take the necessary steps" to halt the labor unrest. Walesa appealed for an end to the wildcat action but threatened a general strike on February 1 unless the government agreed to the five-day week, allowed Solidarity to publish a weekly newspaper and accepted the formation of Rural Solidarity.

The government, at a meeting with Solidarity on January 26–31, reluctantly accepted all of the demands except the formation of Rural Solidarity. The government negotiators were led by Premier Josef Pinkowski, who was made the scapegoat for another government failure in its dealings with Solidarity. On February 9, at a plenary session of the Polish Communist Party's Central Committee, Pinkowski was replaced by the country's defense minister, General WOJCIECH JARUZELSKI, who retained the defense portfolio.

Jaruzelski appealed for a halt to industrial actions to allow the government to deal with Poland's urgent economic problems. For a few weeks there was relative quiet, but it was against a background of a continuing deterioration in relations between Solidarity and the government. On March 19, riot police forcibly broke up a demonstration of farmers in Bydgoszcz town hall. Several farmers were injured in the first use of police force since the start of the labor unrest. Solidarity members demanded a national strike. Walesa appealed for moderation and nearly quit the leadership of Solidarity over the issue. At the same time, Warsaw Pact exercises in East Germany were extended, and U.S. president RONALD REAGAN warned that any measures "aimed at suppressing the Polish people" would have a "grave effect on the whole course of East–West relations."

The immediate crisis passed when Walesa regained control of the Solidarity leadership and suspended the national strike called for March 31. In return, the government agreed to give official recognition to Rural Solidarity.

The government's tactics now shifted from trying to contain Solidarity to reaching a working arrangement with it. The political and economic crisis created by the industrial unrest had, by June 1981, reduced the national income to 75% of the 1978 level. There had been a substantial drop in exports, and

Poland was unable to purchase essential food imports, let alone service the large debt that had helped to create the economic crisis.

At the same time, Solidarity's political power had increased. It was estimated that a third of the membership of the Communist Party also belonged to Solidarity. This had created a groundswell of opinion within the party in favor of political reform. At the party congress in July 1981, secret ballots were used for the first time in the election of party officials. This led to widespread changes within the Central Committee, although Kania, for the time being, remained first secretary.

Walesa was prepared to discuss greater cooperation with the government but demanded that the government in turn allow them a say in the management of the economy. On September 22 a compromise agreement was reached that gave Polish workers a greater role in running the nation's factories. But Walesa was by now a moderate within an increasingly radical Solidarity. At the union's first congress in September 1981, he was only narrowly elected leader and was censured for the compromise with the government.

The same congress also made a direct challenge to the Communist Party's monopoly of power by calling for free parliamentary elections, although, at Walesa's insistence, it tempered this action by voting against a resolution to change the union's constitution so that it no longer acknowledged the "leading role" of the party.

The increasingly radical position of many Solidarity members and Walesa's own difficulties in controlling them made the union and Walesa less attractive to the government as a partner in the fight against Poland's economic problems, and Communist Party hard-liners began to gain power. On October 18 Stanislaw Kania was dismissed as first secretary and replaced by Jaruzelski, who retained the premiership, the defense portfolio and the post of commander of the armed forces. He was the first military officer to head the Polish Communist Party, and his appointment signaled the start of a crackdown on Solidarity as Polish Army units were deployed throughout the country.

Under the auspices of Archbishop Jozef Glemp, the Roman Catholic primate, Jaruzelski and Walesa met in November 1981. Glemp proposed the establishment of a "Front of National Agreement," which was described as "a permanent platform for dialogue and consultation of political and social forces on the basis of the constitution." Jaruzelski, however, insisted that Solidarity be limited to one seat on the front's council and rejected Walesa's demands for a larger role in economic policy, access to the media and greater democracy.

Throughout this period, industrial action had continued to snowball. Hundreds of businesses were idled because of industrial action, students were on strike at more than 100 universities, and Rural Solidarity was proposing to swell the membership of Solidarity by merging the two unions. On December 2, 1981, soldiers attacked the Warsaw firemen's training school where 300 cadets had been on strike and had occupied the premises for several weeks.

On December 7, Warsaw Radio accused the Solidarity leaders of advocating the overthrow of the government. Walesa urged a moderate response, but he was overruled by the hard-liners, who responded with a call for a general strike on December 17 and a demand for a national referendum on the future of the Communist Party, the issue of free elections and membership in the Warsaw Pact. This was the last straw for Jaruzelski; on December 12, 1981, he declared a state of emergency and issued a decree of martial law curtailing civil rights and suspending the operations of Solidarity. A new leadership composed of Poland's highest-ranking military officers moved swiftly to consolidate its power. There was a midnight raid on Solidarity headquarters; Walesa and other union activists throughout the country were arrested, as were many former government officials; a communications blackout was imposed; and tanks and troops were deployed.

On December 23, 1981, President Reagan ordered economic sanctions against Poland. The move was soon echoed by the Western allies. The American sanctions included: (1) the suspension of Poland's civil aviation privileges in the United States; (2) withdrawal of Poland's right to fish in American waters; (3) an end to Export-Import Bank credit insurance to Poland; and (4) suspension of U.S.-sponsored shipments of agriculture and dairy products to Poland.

A week later, on December 29, Reagan, who blamed the Soviets for the imposition of martial law in Poland, announced sanctions against the Soviet Union. These included: (1) suspension of all U.S.-bound flights by the Soviet airline Aeroflot; (2) nonrenewal of U.S.–Soviet scientific exchange agreements; (3) closure of the New York-based Soviet Purchasing Commission; (4) expansion of the list of oil and natural gas equipment for which U.S. exporters to the Soviet Union needed government licenses and the suspension of the issuance of such licenses; (5) suspension of the issuance or renewal of U.S. export licenses for electronic equipment, computers and other high technology; (6) suspension of talks on a new maritime accord and restricted access to American ports by Soviet ships; and (7) postponement of negotiations on a new long-term grain agreement to replace the one expiring in September 1982.

In Poland itself the imposition of martial law was followed by widespread rioting and strikes. But the arrest of thousands of dissidents left the protests uncoordinated, and they collapsed in the face of a well-organized military repression. Solidarity was forced underground, and several key figures, not including Walesa, fled overseas. With the military firmly in control, Jaruzelski was able to implement the necessary economic changes. It was not until July 21, 1983, that martial law was lifted, although Solidarity remained banned.

Jaruzelski, however, failed to solve the economic crisis that had created the conditions for the rise of Solidarity. In the following years he discovered that a solution remained beyond his grasp as long as he was without the cooperation and support of Solidarity. However, he was effectively blocked from speaking to the union leadership by the Soviet Politburo. The accession to power in Moscow of MIKHAIL GORBACHEV in March 1985 dramatically changed the situation. Gorbachev was committed to his own political and economic reform program and could not be seen to be blocking a similar program in Poland.

In 1989, following a visit by Gorbachev and a series of fresh Solidarity strikes, Jaruzelski and Walesa met in Warsaw and agreed to roundtable negotiations. As a precondition for the talks, Walesa successfully demanded the legalization of Solidarity.

Both sides effectively accepted each other's demands by agreeing to a major reorganization of the Polish political structure that would allow multiparty elections to a more powerful Sejm. The new parliament would in turn elect an executive president. The distribution of the 460 seats, however, was agreed upon beforehand, with 157 seats (34.1%) going to the United Workers' (Communist) Party and 107 seats (23.3%) reserved for the communists' political allies. The independents and opposition (Solidarity) would be allowed a maximum of 161 seats (35%).

The subsequent elections in June 1989 were a resounding victory for Solidarity. The trade union, which formed a political wing for the elections, won every seat that it contested. The predetermined division of seats kept Solidarity from securing a parliamentary majority. The voting results, however, demonstrated the depth of popular support for Solidarity.

The political situation was further complicated by the desertion of the communists' allies who saw greater political opportunity in supporting Solidarity. The result was that on August 17, 1989, Walesa forced the Communist Party into a coalition government led by a leading Solidarity member, Tadeusz Mazowiecki. In December Jaruzelski was elected president by only one vote, and only because Walesa had decided that it was important to retain Jaruzelski in the short term.

The main political development in Poland in 1990 was the split within Solidarity between its leftist blue-collar base, headed by Walesa, and its free-market intellectual wing, led by Mazowiecki. The split was accentuated when Walesa decided to run for president, charging the government with neglecting the working class. His direct entry into politics was opposed by other Solidarity leaders, who viewed him as a blundering egoist and potential demagogue. But Walesa won the initial vote in November, triumphed in the runoff election in December and replaced Jaruzelski as president. Mazowiecki resigned and was followed by a succession of three different premiers over the next year and a half, during which Polish politics were dominated by parliamentary paralysis and calls by Walesa for greater presidential powers to overcome the impasse.

With the end of the Cold War, Poland acquiesced to the reunification of GERMANY in 1990 in exchange for a German pledge that it would not seek to change its current border with Poland. The Soviet Union, for its part, began withdrawing its troops from Poland in April 1991.

For Further Information:
Garton Ash, Timothy. *The Polish Revolution: Solidarity 1980–1982.* London, 1983.
Kaminski, Bartolomiej. *The Collapse of State Socialism: The Case of Poland.* Princeton, 1991.
Karski, Jan. *The Great Powers & Poland, 1919–1945: From Versailles to Yalta.* Lanham, Md., 1985.
Kaufman, Michael T. *Mad Dreams, Saving Graces: Poland, A Nation in Conspiracy.* New York, 1989.
Lukas, Richard C. *Bitter Legacy: Polish-American Relations in the Wake of World War II.* Lexington, Ky., 1982.
———. *The Strange Allies, The United States and Poland, 1941–1945.* Knoxville, Tenn., 1978.
Sanford, George. *Polish Communism in Crisis.* New York, 1983.
Wandycz, Piotr Stefan. *The United States and Poland.* Cambridge, Mass., 1980.
Wedel, Janine R., ed. *The Unplanned Society: Poland During and After Communism.* New York, 1992.

Polaris Missiles　Polaris missiles were the first submarine-launched ballistic missiles (SLBMs). Developed by the United States, they added a new dimension to the U.S. nuclear deterrent through the creation of a highly mobile and virtually invulnerable nuclear strike force. The U.S. Polaris force was quickly replaced by the next generation of SLBMs, the Poseidon, but became the mainstay of the British nuclear deterrent.

On July 20, 1960, the first underwater firing of a Polaris missile was successfully conducted from the USS *George Washington* off Cape Canaveral, Florida. Eventually, the most advanced version had a range of 2,500 nautical miles and carried either a single-megaton warhead or a MIRVed warhead with three 200-kiloton bombs.

In December 1962, President JOHN F. KENNEDY agreed to sell American Polaris missiles to Britain as a replacement for the cancelled Skybolt project. When the development of the Soviet antiballistic missile system was deemed to have made the Polaris obsolete, the United States replaced it with the more advanced POSEIDON. Poseidon was also offered to Britain, but the British government rejected it for a combination of political and technical reasons. Instead they developed a complex system of upgrading and modernization that extended the life of the Polaris until the mid-1990s. It had been due to be replaced at that time by the American-built Trident system, but the fate of that program has been in contention since the end of the Cold War. The British have maintained four nuclear-powered submarines, each carrying 16 Polaris missiles. Each missile is MIRVed with three warheads.

Poseidon C-3　The Poseidon C-3 is a two-stage nuclear-armed American missile designed for launch from submerged submarines. The Poseidon missile was the successor to the Polaris A-2 and A-3 systems.

Each Poseidon missile has a range of 2,900 miles and is equipped with 10 MULTIPLE INDEPENDENTLY-TARGETED REENTRY VEHICLES (MIRVs) capable of carrying a nuclear warhead with the explosive yield of 100 kilotons.

The first Poseidon missiles were tested in August 1968 and became operational in March 1971. The exact number of Poseidon warheads has never been disclosed. Virtually all of the Poseidon submarines are deployed in the North Atlantic and committed to NATO defense.

In 1984 the REAGAN administration started replacing Poseidon missiles with the new TRIDENT I and TRIDENT II systems. It was estimated at the time that the Poseidon missiles and submarines would be completely phased out by the year 2000, but with the end of the Cold War the eventual fate of the Trident program has not been determined.

Potsdam Conference   (1945)   The Potsdam Conference was the first major diplomatic forum at which it became apparent that the wartime alliance might not survive the postwar peace; East–West differences came to the fore, especially over the issue of Poland.

The Potsdam Conference took place in July 1945, five months after the YALTA CONFERENCE, which had been attended by U.S. president FRANKLIN D. ROOSEVELT, Soviet leader JOSEF STALIN and British prime minister WINSTON CHURCHILL. In the intervening period the world had changed dramatically. Germany had surrendered and the Soviet Union was preparing to enter the war against Japan. Roosevelt had died and there had been a general election in Britain, although Labour leader CLEMENT ATTLEE was not declared Churchill's successor until halfway through the conference. The Soviet Union had tightened its hold on Eastern Europe and failed to hold the elections it had promised in Poland; and the day before the conference started the United States had successfully tested the world's first atomic bomb (the world was ignorant of this last change).

The conference opened on July 17 in the Berlin suburb of Potsdam. Attending the meeting were Stalin, President HARRY TRUMAN, Churchill and Attlee. Churchill and Attlee returned to Britain halfway through the meeting for the counting of the

Stalin (second left), Truman (center) and Churchill (right) with their interpreters during the first session of the Allied three-power talks at Potsdam, Germany, July 17, 1945.

votes in the general election, and the victorious Attlee, with the new foreign secretary ERNEST BEVIN, returned.

The meeting opened auspiciously when all the leaders accepted Truman's suggestion that a council of foreign ministers comprised of the five members of the newly established United Nations Security Council be established to prepare for a peace conference. This was the only easy decision of the conference, which lasted until August 1 and included 13 plenary sessions and 11 formal foreign ministers' meetings as well as a number of bilateral meetings and informal sessions.

It soon became apparent that East–West differences over Poland would dominate Potsdam as it had Yalta. Stalin on the first day sought to consolidate the power of the communist government in Warsaw by demanding the transfer of assets from the London-based Poles to those in Warsaw. This was strongly opposed by Churchill, who made it clear that support for the London Poles "involves the honor of His Majesty's Government."

Stalin next tried to fix the Polish–German boundary along the ODER-NEISSE LINE with the Baltic port of Stettin going to Poland. He was opposed by both Churchill and Truman, who argued that the land involved was the traditional breadbasket of Germany and that its loss would make it difficult for Germans to feed themselves.

The conference remained deadlocked over the issue, and Truman proposed that members of the provisional Polish government attend the conference to give their views. The provisional government was dominated by the communists but included some members of the former London government-in-exile, primarily STANISLAW MIKOLAJCZYK. Both Mikolajczyk and the communist leader BOLESLAW BIERUT supported the proposed boundary changes, but Mikolajczyk used the conference to warn Britain and America that neither Stalin nor Bierut intended to honor his pledge of free elections in Poland.

The results of the successful test of the atomic bomb were cabled to Truman at Potsdam. He immediately informed Churchill, and the two men were in complete agreement to use the bomb against Japan. Truman informed Stalin of the existence of the atom bomb after a plenary session on July 24.

On July 29 the conference returned to the Polish problem, with Bierut present. Under ruthless questioning from Ernest Bevin, Bierut was forced to give an assurance that elections would be held in Poland not later than the first half of 1946. He also agreed to allow foreign correspondents into Poland. Neither of these agreements was honored.

The next major problem was the administration of postwar Germany and German reparations. It had been agreed at Yalta that Germany would be divided into four zones of occupation, with Britain, France, the United States and the Soviet Union each occupying a zone. Berlin was to be similarly divided. Britain and the United States, however, believed that this did not preclude the administration of Germany as one unit, although no central German government was to be established for the time being. It became clear that the Soviets

regarded each occupation zone as a separate administrative unit and the leaders failed to reach a compromise on the issue.

On reparations, the Soviet delegation repeated its demand for $10 billion and made it clear that the former German territory Stalin wanted to have handed over to Poland would not be subject to reparations payments. American secretary of state JAMES BYRNES proposed that the Soviet Union extract its reparations payments from the Soviet-occupied zone. Soviet foreign minister V.M. MOLOTOV, however, demanded that a further $3 billion in reparations come from the British-occupied Ruhr, a major industrial region in western Germany.

Byrnes, in a clear attempt to placate the Soviets, went on to propose that Britain and the United States accept Stalin's reparations demands and proposed German–Polish border pending a final German peace treaty. In return, the Soviets would accept an American demand that Italy be admitted to the United Nations. This was agreed to after Stalin secured the right to remove 15% of Germany's capital equipment from the Western zones in return for food and coal from the Soviet Zone. In addition, he was to receive further reparations, amounting to 10% of the nonessential capital equipment for which he would not have to deliver supplies.

For Further Information:

Davis, Lynn Etheridge. *The Cold War Begins: Soviet American Conflict over Eastern Europe*. Princeton, 1974.

Donnelly, Desmond. *Struggle for the World*. New York, 1965.

Fontaine, Andre. *History of the Cold War*, vols. 1 and 2. New York, 1965 and 1969.

Gaddis, J.L. *The United States and the Origins of the Cold War, 1941–1947*. New York, 1972.

Rose, Lisle A. *After Yalta: America and the Origins of the Cold War*. New York, 1973.

Thomas, Hugh. *Armed Truce: The Beginnings of the Cold War, 1945–1946*. New York, 1986.

Powers, Lieutenant Francis Gary (August 17, 1929– August 2, 1977) Lieutenant Francis Gary Powers was the pilot of an American U-2 spy plane whose capture by the Soviets and subsequent confession led to the breakdown of the 1960 Geneva Summit, the cancellation of a visit to the Soviet Union by President DWIGHT D. EISENHOWER and a setback in U.S.–Soviet relations, which had started to improve after a trip to the United States by Soviet leader NIKITA KHRUSHCHEV in September 1959.

Powers joined the CENTRAL INTELLIGENCE AGENCY in January 1956 and trained to fly U-2 spy planes over the Soviet Union. In November 1956 he was assigned to Incirclik Air Force Base in Turkey and started spy flights over Soviet territory. The Eisenhower administration claimed that the U-2 squadron was conducting weather observation flights. The Soviets were aware of the true nature of the squadron but were unable to do anything about it because the U-2 was capable of conducting accurate aerial reconnaissance at 80,000 feet, out of range of Soviet attack aircraft. But by 1960 the Soviet Union had developed ground-to-air missiles capable of hitting U-2 aircraft, and on May 1, 1960, Powers was shot down while on a reconnaissance flight from Peshawar, Pakistan to Bodo, Norway.

The plane had been equipped with a self-destruct mechanism, and Powers had been given a suicide pill. But instead of using them, Powers bailed out over the Soviet city of Sverdlovsk and was taken prisoner. His capture came two weeks before President Eisenhower and Soviet leader Nikita Khrushchev were due to meet in Geneva. Khrushchev, in announcing the downing of the spy plane, denounced the American reconnaissance flights as "aggressive provocation," but he cleverly kept secret Powers' capture and confession and the acquisition of reconnaissance film until after the State Department issued a statement claiming that the U-2 was a weather plane flying off course.

The timing of the Soviet disclosures seriously embarrassed the Eisenhower administration, which was forced to admit the true nature of Powers' flight. This enabled Khrushchev to demand a public apology from Eisenhower as a precondition for attending the Geneva Summit. The summit started on May 16 but broke down after only three hours because of Khrushchev's insistence on an apology.

Powers went on public trial in Moscow on August 17, 1960. He pleaded guilty to charges of espionage and was sentenced to prison for 10 years. In his final plea to the court, Powers said that he had "committed a grave crime" but stressed that he was no "enemy" of the Soviet people and was "deeply repentant."

A U.S. Senate investigating committee later cleared Powers of any misconduct, but he was criticized by American conservatives for his failure to destroy the plane and commit suicide as well as for his confession and conduct at the trial. Martin McKneally, national commander of the American Legion, attacked Powers as a "weak American" who had "served his country badly."

On February 10, 1962, Powers was exchanged for Soviet spy RUDOLF ABEL and shortly afterward joined the Lockheed Aircraft Corporation as a test pilot. At home he continued to receive criticism from American conservatives. During the 1970s Powers became a Los Angeles helicopter traffic reporter. He was killed in a helicopter crash on August 2, 1977.

For Further Information:

Beschloss, Michael R. *Mayday: Eisenhower, Khrushchev and the U-2 Affair.* New York, 1986.
O'Toole, G.J.A. *The Encyclopedia of American Intelligence and Espionage.* New York, 1988.
Powers, Francis Gary, with Curt Gentry. *Operation Over-flight: The U-2 Spy Pilot Tells His Story for the First Time.* New York, 1970.

Poznan Crisis   (1956)   The Poznan Crisis was the first major uprising in POLAND after World War II. It provided the spark for the Hungarian Revolution and helped to establish the Polish Communist Party as one of the most independent in Eastern Europe.

Soviet control of Poland was the main aim of Stalin's postwar policy in Eastern Europe. Poland was the historic invasion route to Russia, and three times in 150 years Western armies had marched across the Polish plains to the gates of Moscow. Stalin was determined to seal the route by installing an obedient government in Warsaw and ruthlessly suppressing the Polish nationalism that had for centuries been a thorn in Russia's side.

Stalin began to create the conditions for Soviet control during the war. He installed a loyal communist movement in Poland, led by BOLESLAW BIERUT and WLADYSLAW GOMULKA, and saw to it that it was firmly entrenched after the war.

In 1956, the almost simultaneous political rehabilitation of Yugoslavia, denouncement of Stalin and death of Bierut combined to release the suppressed nationalist forces within the Polish Communist Party and the country as a whole. On April 6, 1956, Gomulka, who had been Bierut's most effective opponent within the party, was released from prison and "rehabilitated," and the government announced its intention to release 30,000 political prisoners. Workers started agitating for increased political freedoms and higher wages.

Events boiled over in Poznan on June 28. A deputation of workers from the city's major engineering factory had been sent to Warsaw to demand better working conditions. They returned empty-handed on June 27. On the following day a 50,000-strong crowd gathered in the main square outside a hotel where foreign visitors were staying during the city's international trade fair. They demanded bread, political liberty, free elections and the withdrawal of Soviet troops.

The city's police authorities seem to have been taken by surprise. Under strict orders not to allow any signs of dissent to reach foreign ears, they opened fire on the crowd and 70 people were killed. The result was a riot. Some sympathetic Polish police left their ranks and joined the rioters. They stormed the local prison, freed the prisoners and then turned on police headquarters.

Party officials in Warsaw at first appeared to take the traditional Stalinist line of blaming the riots on "Western agents" and "provocateurs." Then on June 29 Polish premier Jozsef Cyrankiewicz made a major departure from Soviet-dictated policy when he said that the provocateurs had taken advantage of "the undoubtedly existing dissatisfaction in a number of industrial enterprises" caused by "mistakes" that "must and will be immediately corrected." Cyrankiewicz went on to promise that the riots would not stop "the process of democratization of Poland's political life."

These and subsequent statements set warning bells ringing in Moscow. On July 21, NIKOLAI BULGANIN arrived in Warsaw and told the Polish party that it must cease talking about socialist mistakes as the cause of the riots. But Polish nationalism had been revived within the communist ranks. In September and October 1956 the leading Stalinists within the party were forced to resign from their posts, and it was announced that Gomulka was being asked to resume the post of party first secretary at the party plenum.

Just as Gomulka was preparing to deliver his speech at the

plenum it was announced that a Soviet plane carrying Khrushchev and other leading members of the Soviet Politburo was landing at Warsaw airport. The Polish Politburo, at that stage still led by Edward Ochab, and Gomulka immediately drove to the airport, where Khrushchev informed them that Soviet tanks were moving toward the capital and demanded that the old Polish Politburo be retained and the democratization program stopped.

Ochab was undeterred. He told Khrushchev that the Polish Communist Party was determined to go ahead with the election of Gomulka and that Polish workers were ready to fight Soviet tanks. The Polish Communist Party leadership then returned to the conference to elect Gomulka, while the Soviet leaders retired to the Soviet embassy. That night there was a second meeting between Gomulka and Khrushchev at which Gomulka reiterated the demands that the Poles be allowed to choose their own leaders. Gomulka mollified Khrushchev by promising him that Poland would not withdraw from the WARSAW PACT.

It was a delicate balancing act on the part of Gomulka. In order to maintain order within Poland he had to be seen to be leading a Polish government whose prime loyalties were to Poland rather than to the Soviet Union. But he knew that the Soviet tanks could easily crush Poland. Khrushchev did not want to invade Poland; his main concern was that Poland remain firmly in the Soviet camp. Gomulka's pledge made it possible for the Soviet leader to accept the new Politburo gracefully on October 20. The next day Marshal Rokossovsky was removed from the Politburo and returned to the Soviet Union. An estimated 250,000 Poles gathered in the Warsaw city center to cheer Gomulka.

For Further Information:
Brzezinski, Z.K. *The Soviet Bloc: Unity and Conflict.* Cambridge, Mass., 1960.
De Weydenthal, J.B. *The Communists of Poland.* New York, 1978.
Stehle, Hansjakov. *The Independent Satellite.* New York, 1965.

Prague Spring   *See* CZECHOSLOVAKIA.

Prevention of Surprise Attacks, Geneva Conference on (1958)   The Geneva Conference on the Prevention of Surprise Attacks was one of the early efforts at disarmament negotiations. The positions of the U.S. and Soviet negotiators proved to be irreconcilable, and the negotiations broke down after only a month, but they enabled American diplomats to develop their first concrete proposals for arms limitation.

The conference was proposed by President DWIGHT D. EISENHOWER in the diplomatic note to Soviet leader NIKITA KHRUSHCHEV on April 28, 1958, in which Eisenhower also proposed a nuclear test ban treaty. The talks, attended by the United States, Britain, France, Canada, Italy, Poland, Czechoslovakia, Romania, Albania and the Soviet Union, opened in Geneva on November 10, 1958. The American delegation was headed by WILLIAM FOSTER and the Soviet delegation by Vasily Kuznetsov.

From the outset, the conference was deadlocked over the issues, scope and purpose of the negotiations. The Western position was presented by Foster, who argued that the major threat to surprise attacks lay in either side's ability to deliver nuclear weapons. He therefore proposed that they negotiate limitations on existing delivery systems and outlined a proposal for the development of a comprehensive inspection system to deal with existing weapons.

Kuznetsov, for the Soviet side, argued that the issue of control was "inseparable" from the wider problem of disarmament and therefore the talks should focus on general disarmament. He maintained that reliable measures to prevent surprise attack would be feasible "only on the condition" that nuclear weapons be banned, foreign military bases liquidated and conventional armaments reduced.

The conference ended on December 18 after failing to reach an agreement on an agenda. But the work done by the American delegation provided valuable data for future negotiations. It also marked the first time the United States had developed concrete proposals rather than vague principles for weapons control.

It was, moreover, a major turning point in U.S. thought on the issue of disarmament and arms control. Instead of focusing on control of nuclear weapons materials, the United States stressed the elimination of nuclear warfare through the control of delivery systems. The conference also helped to establish the credentials of William Foster, who, in September 1961, became the first director of the ARMS CONTROL AND DISARMAMENT AGENCY.

Pueblo Incident   The Pueblo Incident involved the capture of the American intelligence ship USS *Pueblo* by North Korean naval forces on January 23, 1968. One member of the crew was killed, and the remainder were taken prisoner and held in North Korea for 11 months.

According to American sources the lightly armed *Pueblo* was cruising 15 miles off the east coast of North Korea (three miles beyond the 12-mile territorial limits claimed by North Korea) when it was challenged by two North Korean submarine chasers and four North Korean torpedo boats. The North Koreans claimed that the *Pueblo* was only seven miles off the coast.

North Korean naval forces were quickly joined by jet fighter planes, which buzzed the ship and fired warning shots. The *Pueblo* tried to outrun the Korean ships, but it was not built for speed and was quickly surrounded and boarded. During the chase and boarding operation four men aboard the *Pueblo* were wounded, one fatally. Six officers, 75 enlisted men and two civilians were taken prisoner, and the ship was towed into Wonsan Harbor.

American public reaction loudly condemned the capture, and there were repeated calls for military retaliation against the North Koreans. This was echoed by prominent politicians on Capitol Hill. Senator Richard Russell called the capture of the ship "a breach of international law amounting to an act

On January 23, 1968, the U.S.S. Pueblo was seized as a spy ship by North Korean naval forces. Photo courtesy of the U.S. Navy.

of war." Congressman Robert Wilson said that the United States must retake the ship, even "if this means sending in military and naval forces . . . It must be done—and done at once."

President LYNDON JOHNSON increased the size of the American air forces in South Korea and called to active duty selected units of the Air National Guard and Air Force Reserve. He also considered mining Wonsan Harbor, mining other North Korean harbors, interdicting coastal shipping, seizing a North Korean ship or striking selected North Korean targets by air and naval gunfire. But he later wrote in his memoirs that "in each case we decided that the risk was too great and the possible accomplishment too small."

Johnson also became convinced later that the North Koreans' seizure of the *Pueblo* was not an isolated incident but part of a coordinated plan worked out in conjunction with the Soviet Union and North Vietnam to distract American and South Korean attention and troops away from South Vietnam on the eve of the TET OFFENSIVE, which was launched in South Vietnam eight days later, and from a North Korean plot to assassinate South Korea's president, Chung Hee Park.

Johnson therefore quickly switched the emphasis of his response from the military to the diplomatic initiative. This took the form of pressure on the Soviet Union to reason with the North Koreans and action in the United Nations to condemn the seizure of the ship. Direct U.S.–North Korean talks were held at the Korean truce village of PANMUNJOM.

The North Koreans, for their part, extracted confessions from several members of the crew to the effect that the *Pueblo* had been in North Korean territorial waters at the time of its capture. In March 1968 the North Koreans delivered an open letter from the crew of the *Pueblo* to Johnson asking him to publicly admit that the ship had violated North Korean territorial waters, apologize for the action and "give assurances that they will not be repeated." In July the captain of the *Pueblo*, Commander Lloyd M. Bucher, appeared on Japanese television reading what was described as "a joint letter of apology."

The United States finally decided on what Secretary of State DEAN RUSK called a "strange procedure" in agreeing to admit publicly that the *Pueblo* had violated North Korean waters while denying the admission before it was signed. The admission was signed on December 21 at Panmunjom by Major General Gilbert H. Woodward, but before signing it Woodward read into the record a statement disavowing the confession.

The ship was kept by the North Koreans, but the crew was released the following day. The State Department that day emphasized the U.S. disclaimer. It said that the *Pueblo* crewmen had been "illegally seized and have been illegally held as hostages by the North Koreans." At a press conference in Seoul, Bucher said that he had been kept in solitary confinement for the entire 11 months and that he and other members of his crew had been regularly beaten with fists, boards and clubs. He described North Korea as a country "completely devoid of humanity, completely devoted to enslavement of men's minds." Bucher said he had signed a false confession when the North Koreans had threatened to shoot one member of the crew daily until he complied.

For Further Information:

Brandt, Edward. *The Last Voyage of the U.S.S.* Pueblo. *New York, 1969.*

Bucher, Lloyd M. *My Story.* Garden City, N.Y., 1970.

Pugwash Conferences   The Pugwash Conferences were a series of informal conferences organized by the American industrialist CYRUS EATON.

In the early 1950s Eaton became a crusader for U.S.–Soviet rapprochement. He regularly invited leading nuclear scientists and intellectuals from East and West to his home in Pugwash, Nova Scotia to exchange views. The first such meeting was held in April 1954. On April 11, 1958, the gathering issued a statement urging a ban on atmospheric nuclear tests. Later meetings were held in Austria, West Germany and Moscow.

The Soviet Union used the December 1960 Pugwash Conference in Moscow to signal its desire to reopen arms negotiations with the KENNEDY administration.

Q

Quadripartite Agreement (1971) The Quadripartite Agreement on Berlin regularized West Berlin's postwar status and removed the constant Soviet threat, which had been hanging over the Western sector of the city since the end of World War II.

The agreement among the United States, the Soviet Union, Britain and France was an expression of superpower approval of West German chancellor WILLY BRANDT's OSTPOLITIK ("Eastern Policy"). Legally, under the terms of the London Agreement of September 1944, Berlin was the property and responsibility of the United States, Britain, France and the Soviet Union, and no major change could be made without the agreement of those governments.

The discussions were complex and bureaucratic as they involved four different countries and excluded West Germany, the country with the biggest stake in the talks. The United States was in a particularly difficult position. U.S. negotiators knew that the Soviet Union wanted to encourage Ostpolitik and regularize the Berlin situation. The NIXON administration was prepared to play for time in order to win concessions on other strategic issues such as the STRATEGIC ARMS LIMITATION TALKS. The Germans, however, were impatient for an agreement.

A combination of pressure from West Germany and concessions from the Soviet Union on the links between West Berlin and West Germany helped to get the negotiations moving after a meeting between U.S. national security adviser HENRY KISSINGER and Soviet ambassador ANATOLY DOBRYNIN on January 9, 1971. The United States was committed to negotiations after a meeting between Kissinger and Egon Bahr, the foreign policy adviser to Chancellor Brandt, on January 30.

Formal negotiations started in Berlin on February 5, and the formal agreement was signed on September 3, 1971. The Quadripartite Agreement was composed of three parts, four annexes, one note and two "agreed minutes." The first part pledged the signatory powers to strive to eliminate tension in the area. It also obliged the signers to relinquish the use or threat of force in solving problems relating to Berlin and to see to it that the document was not "changed unilaterally."

The text also affirmed that although West Berlin would "continue not to be a constituent part of the Federal Republic of Germany," its ties with West Germany would be maintained and developed. The Soviet Union also promised to improve communications between the two halves of Berlin and to allow visits for compassionate, family, religious, cultural or commercial reasons, or for tourists.

The four governments agreed that they would "mutually respect their individual and joint rights and responsibilities, which remain unchanged." The Soviets pledged not to block traffic through East Germany to West Berlin. West Germany was also allowed to perform consular services for West Berlin and to represent the Western sector at international meetings.

For Further Information:
Bell, Coral. *The Diplomacy of Detente: The Kissinger Era.* New York, 1977.

Brandt, Willy. *People and Politics.* New York, 1978.

Griffiths, William. *The Ostpolitik of the Federal Republic of Germany.* Cambridge, Mass., 1978.

Jonas, M. *The U.S. and West Germany.* New York, 1985.

Pfetsch, Frank. *West Germany, Internal Structures and External Relations: The Foreign Policy of the Federal Republic.* New York, 1988.

Prittie, Terence. *Willy Brandt.* London, 1974.

Quemoy and Matsu Islands The Chinese communist shelling of the Nationalist-held Quemoy and Matsu Islands in 1954–55 and a second threat to the islands in 1958 brought the United States to the brink of war with China and caused a major split between the United States and its Western allies over America's China policy.

The Quemoy and Matsu Islands are two groups of small islands occupied by the Nationalist Chinese forces just off the coast of mainland China. In 1949 CHIANG KAI-SHEK's forces fled to Taiwan, a large island 100 miles from China, but they maintained a military presence on Matsu and Quemoy in anticipation of a future invasion of the mainland. In the interim, the islands were used as bases for guerrilla attacks.

The official American regional defense perimeter stopped at the Pescadores Islands halfway between Taiwan and the mainland, but President DWIGHT EISENHOWER supported Chiang's presence on Quemoy and Matsu. He considered the belief in a future Kuomintang invasion vital to morale on Taiwan and to the securing of the island as a bulwark against the spread of Chinese communist influence. Eisenhower's views, however, conflicted with those of Britain, New Zealand, Australia and other allies, which opposed an invasion of mainland China and saw the Nationalist presence on Quemoy and Matsu as an unnecessary provocation. They repeatedly urged Eisenhower to force Chiang to withdraw his forces to Taiwan.

In 1954 tensions between Taiwan and mainland China increased as Chiang promised an attack "in the not too distant future" and later called for a "holy war" against communism. On July 28, 1954, South Korean president SYNGMAN RHEE, speaking before a joint session of the United States Congress, proposed that America provide naval and air support for a Nationalist Chinese and South Korean invasion of the Chinese mainland.

Two weeks later, on August 11, 1954, Chinese premier CHOU EN-LAI urged the "liberation" of Taiwan as an "exercise of China's sovereignty" and warned the United States that if it tried to prevent a Chinese attack on Taiwan it would face "grave consequences." President Eisenhower responded by warning that any attack on Taiwan would have to go through the American Seventh Fleet, which had been protecting Taiwan since the early days of the KOREAN WAR.

On August 26 a group of communist guerrillas landed on Quemoy and killed 10 Nationalist soldiers before returning to the mainland. Then on September 3, 1954, the communist forces started shelling the islands of Quemoy and Matsu. The Nationalists responded with air and naval attacks on mainland positions facing Quemoy.

The American position was now vital. U.S. support was essential if the Nationalist forces were to remain on Quemoy. On the other hand, providing that support meant that the United States risked an armed conflict with China and the Soviet Union, which had promised to help defend China if the mainland were attacked by American forces. At the same time, none of America's main allies supported Chiang's presence on Quemoy and Matsu.

Within the United States, however, there was strong support for Chiang Kai-shek. Senate Majority Leader William Knowland, for instance, demanded that the United States impose a naval blockade on the Chinese mainland. This was opposed by Eisenhower, but on December 2, 1954, Secretary of State JOHN FOSTER DULLES and Dr. George K.C. Yeh, the Nationalist Chinese foreign minister, signed a mutual defense treaty that committed the two countries to come to the other's aid if either was attacked. The pact did not mention the Quemoy and Matsu Islands, but it specifically mentioned the Pescadores and included "other territories under the jurisdiction of the parties." At the same time, the Eisenhower administration sought to restrain Chiang Kai-shek by negotiating a second, secret agreement in which the Nationalist government pledged not to invade the mainland without the permission of the U.S. government.

Chiang, however, did not feel restrained in his 1955 New Year's message in which he again forecast war "at any time." The Chinese communists responded with another attack, this time on the Nationalist-held Tachen Islands north of Quemoy and about 200 miles from Taiwan. On January 18,

Chinese communist troops successfully defeated the 1,000-strong Nationalist garrison on the island of Ichiang, just seven miles north of the Tachens.

Eisenhower decided to evacuate the Tachens but extend the December defense treaty to include Quemoy and Matsu explicitly. On January 24, 1955, he asked Congress for wide-ranging discretionary military powers "to act in whatever fashion might be necessary." Congress overwhelmingly approved his request.

Chou En-lai declared the congressional approval tantamount to a message of war, and the Chinese communists increased their artillery and air attacks on Quemoy and Matsu. After a visit to the Far East in March 1955, Secretary of State Dulles reported to the president, "Before this problem is solved I believe there is at least an even chance that the United States will have to go to war." At a press conference on March 16, Eisenhower sought to deter a Chinese attack by threatening to use tactical nuclear weapons "against a strictly military target" in defense of Taiwan.

At this stage, the Chinese communist government started a diplomatic retreat. On April 23, at the Asia–Africa BANDUNG CONFERENCE, Chou said, "The Chinese people are friendly to the American people. The Chinese people do not want to have war with the U.S.A. The Chinese government is willing to sit down and enter into negotiations with the U.S. government to discuss the question of relaxing tension in the Far East and especially the question of relaxing tension in the Taiwan area." The United States refused to enter negotiations unless the Nationalist government was included. This was unacceptable to the Chinese communists, but on May 17, Chou said that China was "willing to strive for the liberation of Taiwan by peaceful means so far as it is possible." By May 22 there was an informal cease-fire in the Taiwan Straits.

Between 1955 and 1958 the Quemoy and Matsu Islands and the Taiwan Straits were relatively quiet. But in 1957–58 Chiang Kai-shek started building up his forces on the islands so that by the summer of 1958 there were some 100,000 Nationalist troops there. They had been deployed against the advice of the Eisenhower administration, which viewed the move as unnecessarily provocative and militarily unsound, as it was almost impossible to protect them if the communists decided to launch a major invasion of the islands. Eisenhower, however, remained fully committed to supporting Chiang's occupation of the islands and drew up plans for attacks on Chinese shipping and airfields and for the possible use of nuclear weapons.

On August 22, 1958, the Chinese communists launched a major artillery bombardment of the offshore islands. In the first day, 20,000 rounds fell on Quemoy and Matsu. The initial attack was followed by a bombardment of about 8,000 rounds a day, air attacks and a naval blockade that effectively sealed the islands off from Taiwan for two weeks.

Eisenhower responded by ordering the Seventh Fleet into a position from which it could quickly intervene to defend Taiwan, increasing the number of destroyers in the Taiwan

Straits and doubling the fleet's aircraft carrier force to four. American forces in the Far East were put on a war footing and told to be ready to escort Nationalist Chinese supply vessels from Taiwan to Matsu and Quemoy.

On September 4, 1958, Secretary of State Dulles released a statement restating the U.S. commitment to the defense of Taiwan and making it clear that the Eisenhower administration regarded the attack on Quemoy and Matsu Islands as the first stage of an attack on Taiwan. But the same statement offered negotiations based on the "mutual and reciprocal renunciation of force, except in self-defense . . . without prejudice to the pursuit of policies of peaceful means."

On September 6, Chou En-lai said his government was prepared to start negotiations in Poland between the Chinese and American ambassadors there. Eisenhower accepted this proposal but stressed that his acceptance in no way lessened his determination to provide military support to Chiang's forces.

In the interim, the Nationalist Chinese Navy, with U.S. naval support, had succeeded in breaking the blockade of Quemoy. On September 17, the Nationalist Chinese landed 7,500 tons of supplies on the island. On October 5, the Chinese communists announced that the artillery bombardment of Quemoy would stop for a week if American destroyers ceased their escort duty. The American vessels returned to regular duties, and in one day of the unilateral cease-fire the Nationalist Chinese succeeded in landing 20 days' worth of supplies.

The Chinese communists unilaterally extended their cease-fire, and Dulles flew to Taiwan on October 16 for three days of talks with Chiang. The purpose of the visit was to persuade the Nationalist leader to reduce his forces on Quemoy and Matsu to the minimum necessary and to renounce the use of force to achieve his return to the mainland. Dulles made it clear that the United States would not provide military or logistic support for a Nationalist invasion of the mainland but would continue to defend Taiwan and its outposts on the outlying islands. Faced with the threat of a withdrawal of American support, Chiang had no choice but to renounce the use of force and to reduce his presence on Quemoy and Matsu.

The Nationalist Chinese presence on the two islands continued to drop in the 1960s, 1970s and 1980s. By 1990 the only bombardment between the islands and the mainland was from loudspeakers blasting propaganda speeches across the water at each other.

For Further Information:
Bachrack, Stanley D. *The Committee of One Million: China Lobby Politics, 1953–1971.* New York, 1976.
Clubb, Oliver E. "Formosa and the Offshore Islands in American Policy 1950–1955," *Political Science Quarterly* (December 1959).
Eisenhower, Dwight D. *The White House Years, Mandate for Change, 1953–1956.* Garden City, N.Y., 1965.
———. *The White House Years, Waging Peace, 1956–1961.* Garden City, N.Y., 1965.
Rankin, Karl Lott. *China Assignment.* Seattle, Wash., 1964.

Radescu, General Nicolae (March 30, 1874–May 16, 1953)   General Nicolae Radescu was the only anticommunist prime minister of postwar Romania. His overthrow, only two weeks after the end of the YALTA CONFERENCE, was the first Soviet-inspired coup in Eastern Europe.

Radescu followed family tradition and entered the Romanian Army. During World War I he fought with distinction and was rewarded with the post of military attaché in London. While in London, Radescu developed a strong attraction for the British parliamentary form of government. At the time, Romania's own fledgling democracy was under threat and then was eliminated when the fascist King Carol II ascended to the throne on June 8, 1930, and announced a "corporatist dictatorship." Shortly afterward, Radescu resigned from the army in protest.

After the pro-German General Ion Antonescu forced the abdication of King Carol on September 6, 1940, Radescu was interned at the Targu-Jiu concentration camp, where he remained until August 1944 when Antonescu was overthrown by the invading Red Army and an anti-fascist coup led by King Michael (see MICHAEL OF ROMANIA). The new king appointed Radescu chief of the Romanian general staff. On December 2, 1944, he was named premier and minister of the interior.

By February 1945, fighting had broken out between the government forces and the Soviet-supported communist partisans. Radescu appealed for American and British assistance, and the U.S. and British members of the Control Commission for Romania immediately asked for a meeting to deal with the crisis. The request was turned down by the Soviet member.

In the meantime, Soviet deputy foreign minister Andrei Vishynsky flew to Bucharest to protest the shooting of communists and to demand the immediate dismissal of Radescu. King Michael, who was in no position to argue with the Red Army occupying his country, capitulated, and Radescu was dismissed on March 3, 1945. He was replaced by the Soviet-supported Romanian communist, Petro Groza. Radescu fled the country for Cyprus and then eventually New York, where he died on May 16, 1953.

Rakosi, Matyas (March 14, 1892–February 5, 1971)   Matyas Rakosi was the first postwar communist leader in HUNGARY. His hard-line Stalinist policies and repressive political system did much to create the climate for the 1956 Hungarian Revolution.

Rakosi joined the Hungarian Social Democratic Party while still in school. When World War I broke out he was drafted into the Austrian Army and sent to fight against Russia. He was taken captive and while a prisoner of war joined the Russian Communist Party. He returned to Hungary in 1918 and served as commissar for socialist production during Bela Kun's "Red Terror" of 1919. The repressive Kun regime lasted only five months before it was overthrown by a successful counterrevolution.

Rakosi, along with other prominent Hungarian communists, fled to the Soviet Union and became a Soviet citizen. In 1924 Lenin sent him back to Hungary to organize an underground Hungarian Communist Party, the old party having by this time been banned. In 1925 Rakosi was arrested by the authorities and sentenced to eight years in prison. As soon as he was released in 1934, he was rearrested and sentenced to death, but his sentence was commuted to life imprisonment.

With the outbreak of war in 1939, Hungary sought to mollify its communist neighbor the Soviet Union and in 1940 extradited a number of communist political prisoners to Russia, Rakosi among them. He joined the Red Army and rose to the rank of brigadier general. In 1943 he was one of the signatories of the order that dissolved the Comintern. In 1944 Rakosi returned to Hungary with the Red Army and became the leading communist in the coalition government installed by the Soviet Union. After elections on November 5, 1945, produced a majority for the Smallholders Party, the Soviet Union allowed Smallholders leader Ferenc Nagy to take over the premiership, but the Soviets insisted on a continuation of the coalition government and demanded that Rakosi be given responsibility for the police along with fellow communist JANOS KADAR. With the Red Army occupying Hungary, the Smallholders Party had no choice but to acquiesce to the demands.

Rakosi and Kadar, with Soviet support, spent the next two years using their control of the police to intimidate and arrest political opponents and establish a power structure based on political repression. Just before the elections in August 1947, Rakosi made his move for power. While Ferenc Nagy was on vacation in Switzerland, Rakosi charged him with "conspiracy against Hungarian democracy," arrested the Smallholders in the government and demanded that Nagy return and face trial. He then enacted a law that disenfranchised 500,000 conservative voters, whom he termed "enemies of democracy." The communists, however, still failed to win an outright majority despite widespread electoral fraud. But Rakosi's police state tactics ensured that the other political parties accepted communist dominance, and he pushed through a constitution modeled on that of the Soviet Union. Rakosi later boasted that "before the U.S. could rub its eyes everything was perfectly put over" by the "iron-fisted Communist Party."

Opposition to Rakosi now came from only two sources—from within his own party and from Catholic religious leaders. The Hungarian Communist Party was divided between the Nationalist and Muscovite wings. The Nationalist Wing, led by Laszlo Rajk, favored greater independence from the Soviet Union and populist left-wing policies such as support for farmers, more consumer goods and government support to maintain wages and keep down prices. Rakosi led the Muscovite Wing, which based its entire policy on close links with Moscow and the implementation of Stalinist policies such as the rapid development of heavy industry and the forced collectivization of farms. In 1949 Rakosi moved against the Nationalist Wing, arrested its members and ordered the execution of Rajk.

The clergy presented a more difficult problem, and after the elimination of the political opposition, the clergy became the major source of criticism. Rakosi's doctrinaire communism dictated that religion be stamped out. But the Lutheran, Calvinist and Roman Catholic churches had a hold on the people through their control of the educational system, and were also major landowners. In 1949 Rakosi expropriated the church lands, depriving the churches of the income needed to maintain their schools. Rakosi offered to pay for running the schools in return for the churches' silence on political issues. The Calvinist and Lutheran churches agreed, but the Roman Catholic Church refused. Rakosi arrested the Roman Catholic primate for Hungary, Cardinal JOZSEF MINDSZENTY, and the church reluctantly agreed to Rakosi's demands.

As the leader of the party's Muscovite wing, Rakosi was a slavish follower of Stalin's foreign policy directives. In 1948 Stalin ejected Yugoslavia from the COMINFORM because of JOZIP BROZ TITO's nationalist tendencies. Rakosi denounced Tito and demanded his overthrow. His strong stand on the issue severely strained Yugoslav–Hungarian relations and later contributed to his downfall.

Between 1949 and 1953 Rakosi was effectively the Stalinist dictator of Hungary. He owed his position, however, to the dominance in the Soviet Union of Stalin. When Stalin died on March 5, 1953, Rakosi's power base crumbled, and on July 4, 1953, he was replaced by the populist communist, IMRE NAGY. Rakosi, however, remained in the party leadership, and when the Stalinists made a short-lived comeback in Moscow in 1955, Rakosi was reinstated as premier. At this stage, his

too strident denouncement of Tito, made in 1948, came back to haunt him. In 1956 NIKITA KHRUSHCHEV decided to heal the Soviet–Yugoslav breach. As part of his price for cooperation, Tito demanded the removal of Rakosi, who was replaced by ERNO GERO on July 18, 1956. Shortly afterward, the Hungarian Revolution broke out, Gero was overthrown and crowds marched through the streets demanding that Rakosi be put on trial.

After the invasion by 200,000 Soviet troops put down the revolution, the Soviets installed Janos Kadar as the new Hungarian leader. Rakosi had fled to the Soviet Union at the start of the revolution. His unpopularity within Hungary and with other East European governments kept him in exile in the Soviet Union until his death on February 5, 1971.

For Further Information:
Kovrig, Bennet. *Communism in Hungary from Kun to Kadar.* Stanford, Calif., 1979.

Rand Corporation   The Rand Corporation is the United States' premier defense "think tank." Its research and reports have played a crucial part in the development of American strategic thinking during the Cold War.

The Rand Research and Development Corporation was started by the United States Air Force in 1948 as the first of the Cold War think tanks. Its initial purpose was to develop strategic policies of benefit to the air force, and its early successes in this field contributed to the air force's dominance of nuclear strategy.

The Rand Corporation, for instance, helped to develop the plans for the establishment of the Strategic Air Command, and almost all of the major government defense planners have at one time worked in the think tank's offices in Santa Monica, California.

The Rand Corporation is technically independent of the government but receives most of its funding from air force contracts, although it does accept nongovernmental work.

Rapacki Plan   The Rapacki Plan, proposed by Polish foreign minister Adam Rapacki on February 14, 1958, called for a nuclear-free zone that would encompass East Germany, West Germany, Poland and Czechoslovakia. The plan also proposed a phased reduction of conventional forces in the same area.

The plan was rejected by the EISENHOWER administration because:

1. It was "too limited in scope to reduce the danger of nuclear war or provide a dependable basis for the security of Europe."
2. It failed to deal "with the essential question" of nuclear weapons production or "the fact that present scientific techniques are not adequate to detect existing nuclear weapons."
3. It did not affect "the central sources of power [the United

States, Britain and the Soviet Union] capable of launching a nuclear attack."

4. It would "perpetuate the basic cause of tension in Europe by accepting the continuation of the division of Germany."

Reagan, Ronald Wilson   (February 6, 1911–   )   Ronald Reagan was president of the United States from 1981–1989. He reversed many of the détente policies of the 1970s and substantially increased American military spending. At the same time, his administration successfully negotiated the first reduction in U.S. and Soviet nuclear weapons and, in its second term, witnessed a dramatic decline in direct Soviet influence in Eastern Europe, Afghanistan, Africa and Southeast Asia.

Reagan often related his basic conservative values to his personal experiences of the past. He was the son of a sometime shoe salesman who suffered recurring bouts of alcoholism. Despite the lack of money, Reagan managed to attend Eureka College and graduated in 1932. His first job was as a radio sportscaster. In 1937 he moved into motion pictures with a five-year film contract with Warner Brothers.

Reagan subsequently appeared in more than 50 films, usually playing the all-American "good guy," a role he continued with great effect while in the White House. During the 1940s, Reagan became involved in liberal Democratic politics and

Ronald Reagan, president of the United States from 1981 to 1989. His administration favored high military budgets and aid to anti-communist governments.

was elected president of the Screen Actors Guild. But by the late 1940s his views had shifted significantly to the right, and in 1949 he cooperated with the movie industry's purge of actors with alleged communist associations. Reagan completed his shift to the conservative cause in 1962 when he became a registered Republican.

Reagan proved his Republican credentials in 1964 when he was the major force in Senator Barry Goldwater's presidential election campaign in California. His support for Goldwater convinced many wealthy California Republicans that Reagan's extremely likable personality made him a substantial political asset, and they recruited him to run for governor. He was subsequently elected in November 1966.

As governor of California, Reagan was able to put many of his conservative beliefs into practice, and he successfully turned the state's $200 million budget deficit into a surplus that allowed credits of 20% to 35% on state income taxes—while seriously weakening state programs in areas such as education, mental health and social welfare. On foreign policy issues Reagan deepened his hard-line anti-Soviet views, favored an escalation of the VIETNAM WAR and advocated criminal punishment for opponents of the war.

Reagan quickly established himself as the standard-bearer of the Republican Party's far-right wing and made a last-minute bid for the Republican Party presidential nomination in 1968. But when it was clear that his campaign was too little too late, Reagan threw his support behind RICHARD NIXON, and in 1970 was reelected governor.

Reagan was a firm supporter of Nixon's Vietnam War policies and in 1971 toured Asia on behalf of the president. When disgraced Vice President Spiro T. Agnew was forced to resign, Reagan was one of those considered to replace him. By 1972, however, Reagan had become increasingly critical of the détente policies of the Nixon administration. In June 1975 he declared that all Americans should oppose the accords signed by President GERALD FORD in Helsinki as part of the CONFERENCE ON SECURITY AND COOPERATION IN EUROPE.

In 1976, Reagan decided to challenge Ford for the Republican presidential nomination and singled out détente and Secretary of State HENRY KISSINGER for attack. During the New Hampshire primary he declared that détente had become "a one-way street" to the advantage of the Soviet Union. He also called on the Ford administration to demand that Soviet and Cuban troops leave Angola or face American intervention.

In March 1976 Reagan charged that the United States had fallen behind the Soviet Union in military might during the Ford administration and claimed that Kissinger was the man most responsible for the relative decline in American military power. Although Reagan failed to win the 1976 nomination, the popular success of his attacks on Kissinger, détente and the ongoing Panama Canal negotiations forced Ford to move the foreign policy plank of his platform further to the right.

Reagan was even more critical of President JIMMY CARTER's foreign and defense policies. He attacked Carter's level of defense spending, the failure to deploy the MX missile and the neutron bomb, and the Panama Canal Zone treaty. He called on the Senate to reject the SALT II treaty and advocated a new one that "finally, genuinely reduces the number of strategic nuclear weapons."

A significant popular swing to the right led to Reagan's election as president in 1980. He won 51% of the vote compared to Carter's 41% (8% went to third-party candidate John Anderson) and 489 of the electoral college votes compared to 49 for Carter. Reagan underscored his intention to act on his strong anti-Soviet position in his first press conference following his inauguration. In reply to a question about the future of détente, he repeated earlier assertions that détente was a one-way street and added that the Soviet Union had always aspired to "world revolution and a one-world socialist or communist state . . . The only morality they recognize," he continued, "is what will further their cause, meaning they reserve to themselves the right to commit any crime, to lie, to cheat, in order to attain" that goal.

The statement was seen by many as the opening shot in a war of rhetoric between Reagan and the Soviet leadership. The Soviet Union responded to Reagan's opening statements by saying that his term's beginning had been marked by "an appetite for confrontation." Reagan later characterized the Soviet Union as "the Evil Empire" and in turn was condemned by the Soviet Union for trying "to plunge international relations back into the times of the Cold War."

Reagan did not plan to reestablish the Nixon-Kissinger détente policy and form a political structure in which the American and Soviet systems could peacefully compete and sometimes cooperate. He viewed communism as not merely wrong but inherently predatory and American world power as inherently good. The thrust of his foreign policy was that the United States should be overwhelmingly more powerful than the Soviet Union. By the end of the Reagan administration it was clear that the United States was indeed again in a dominant position.

But it is difficult to assess whether the general contraction of Soviet influence that occurred in the second half of the 1980s would have happened without Reagan's tough anti-Soviet foreign policy. Soviet leader MIKHAIL GORBACHEV inherited a fundamentally unsound economy incapable of maintaining the Soviet Union's elaborate and overextended global web of military and financial commitments. Faced with the unpalatable choice of economic collapse or a major reconsolidation process, Gorbachev chose the latter course. The result was that in the second half of the Reagan administration the Soviets withdrew from Afghanistan; the Soviet-supported Vietnamese announced their withdrawal from Cambodia; liberalizing reform was encouraged in Poland, Hungary and even the Soviet Union; Soviet aid to Cuba was reduced (causing Cuban withdrawal from Angola); and aid to Ethiopia and other left-wing governments and groups was severely curtailed.

AFGHANISTAN was one of the most pressing problems inherited by Reagan. The Soviet Union had invaded the country in December 1979. The invasion coincided with the fall of the shah of the Iran, and there were fears that the Soviet Union had moved into Afghanistan to use that country as a springboard into Iran and the oil-rich Persian Gulf. President Carter had responded by substantially increasing the U.S. naval presence in the Indian Ocean and Persian Gulf and by suspending U.S. grain shipments to the Soviet Union. Despite his anti-Soviet rhetoric, Reagan soon restored grain shipments, arguing that the embargo was hurting American farmers more than it was the Soviet economy.

At the same time, however, Reagan substantially increased American aid to Pakistan, which bolstered defenses along its border with Afghanistan and channeled money to the Afghan Mujahideen guerrillas based in Pakistan but fighting Soviet and Afghan government troops. (It has also been alleged that Pakistan used American assistance to develop a covert nuclear arms program whose eventual target was India.) Reagan also increased direct U.S. covert aid to the Afghan guerrillas; some observers estimated that the guerrillas received $300 million in American military assistance and training in 1985 alone. The guerrillas succeeded in tying down the Soviet troops in a long, expensive and unwinnable guerrilla war, and in May 1988 the Soviets started to withdraw. The administration assumed that the Soviet-supported government of President Najibullah would quickly collapse, but it proved more resilient than expected.

A strong military was at the heart of Reagan's foreign policy. He believed that it was essential that the United States negotiate from a position of strength. This was underscored by an increase in the military budget from $126.3 billion in 1979 to $312 billion in 1988. These increases are all the more significant when contrasted with reductions in taxes and spending in social and welfare programs. The fiscal result was enormous budget deficits and an increase in the national debt greater than that accumulated from 1776 to 1980. New money was spent mainly on improving the efficiency of the army, increasing the size of the navy, strengthening the global reach of American forces, weapons accumulation and development of new weapons systems. A great deal was also spent on Reagan's STRATEGIC DEFENSE INITIATIVE (SDI) or "Star Wars" nuclear defense program.

The SDI program was one of the most controversial of the Reagan administration. Reagan launched the program in March 1983 when he called on Western scientists to develop a space-based, antimissile system to shoot down attacking missiles with laser beams. The program was criticized by most scientists as being technically impossible as well as prohibitively expensive. It was also attacked by the Soviet Union as a breach of the 1972 ANTIBALLISTIC MISSILE TREATY, and Soviet negotiators repeatedly threatened to pull out of various nuclear weapons negotiations unless Reagan abandoned SDI research. Reagan responded, somwhat illogically, by offering the Soviet Union "Star Wars" protection against U.S. missiles and continuing the research program. SDI was a major issue dividing the United States and the Soviet Union in arms negotiations. It was the main stumbling point in the failure of the 1986 Reykjavik Summit.

The second Strategic Arms Limitation Treaty (SALT II) had been signed by Carter and Soviet leader LEONID BREZHNEV in 1979, but because of American dissatisfaction both with the agreement and Soviet actions in Afghanistan and elsewhere, the treaty was never submitted to the Senate for ratification. Reagan continued to comply with the SALT II accords while at the same time accusing the Soviet Union of breaching the treaty. But the thrust of his arms control policy was directed not toward SALT II, but toward a new agreement that would achieve genuine reductions in strategic nuclear weaapons. The different aim of these negotiations was reflected in the name given to them by the Reagan administration: "Strategic Arms Reduction Talks" (START, see STRATEGIC ARMS REDUCTION TREATIES).

The START talks became inextricably tied up with U.S.–Soviet talks on intermediate-range nuclear forces (INF) in Europe. These involved U.S. and Soviet nuclear-armed missiles, and in December 1987 Reagan and Gorbachev signed the INF Treaty, which for the first time pledged the United States and Soviet Union to the complete elimination of a category of nuclear weapons. The negotiations on strategic weapons, however, were less successful. Both sides proposed 50% reductions in their strategic arsenals, but the Soviets also insisted that any agreement include a ban on Star Wars development.

Ronald Reagan transformed the climate of arms control negotiations. Some of the credit is owed to Gorbachev, but the two men had an entirely different approach to nuclear policy. Gorbachev was a pragmatist. Reagan was an idealist, who, in the words of Henry Kissinger, "genuinely hoped to write the end" to the age of nuclear weapons.

A major component of his success in the INF negotiations was his twin-track technique of deploying American intermediate-range nuclear forces and at the same time negotiating to eliminate them. But Reagan's idealistic commitment to the abolition of nuclear weapons thoroughly alarmed European governments when he proposed the move to Gorbachev during their failed Reykjavik Summit in September 1986. The proposal, made without any prior consultation with the European allies, undercut a basic strategic premise—that the American nuclear deterrent was necessary to deter a conventional attack on Western Europe by the vastly superior Soviet conventional forces.

America's European allies admired Reagan's political tenacity, feared his simplistic good-guy-versus-bad-guy view of the world and were at times angered by his attempts to force his views on them. One of the early clashes was over policy toward the construction of a Soviet gas pipeline from Siberia to Western Europe. Reagan opposed the purchase of the gas and the sale of construction equipment for the pipeline. In December 1981 he used the crackdown in Poland to ban the sale of oil and natural gas equipment to the Soviet Union by American companies. In June 1982 the ban was widened to include foreign subsidiaries and licensees of American companies. The decision provoked an immediate reaction in the European Economic Community, which said that the ban on foreign subsidiaries "implies an extraterritorial extension of United States jurisdiction . . . contrary to the principles of international law." The embargo was quietly lifted a year later.

There were no successful Middle East initiatives during the Reagan administration, although there were several military interventions. The first was in Lebanon, where in September 1983 U.S. Marines led a multinational force of 2,000 French, 2,000 Italians, 1,600 Americans and 100 British troops in an attempt to separate the warring Lebanese factions. When it became clear that the force was becoming a party to the fighting (on the side backed by Israel) it was attacked and finally withdrawn.

There were several clashes between American forces and those of Libyan leader Colonel Muammer el-Qaddafi, whom Reagan charged with being a "Soviet stooge" and a major source of state-sponsored terrorism. The most serious clash occurred on April 14, 1986, when Reagan ordered a bombing attack on Tripoli in retaliation for the bombing of a West Berlin discotheque. The attack on Libya met with widespread approval in the United States Congress and among the American public but was criticized by most West European governments.

Reagan also intervened in the Persian Gulf conflict in 1987. The war between Iran and Iraq had become increasingly dangerous to the shipping of other countries. Kuwait was especially affected because of its support of Iraq, and the Soviet Union offered the Kuwaiti ships escort protection by Soviet naval ships. Reagan was concerned that Kuwaiti acceptance of the offer would provide the Soviets with a foothold in the Persian Gulf and countered with a similar American offer, which was accepted by Kuwait. The U.S. Navy patrols led to several clashes with Iranian forces. The most serious occurred on July 3, 1988, when the USS *Vincennes* mistook an Iran Air passenger plane for an attacking jet fighter and shot it down, causing the death of 290 passengers.

Reagan provided covert support for UNITA rebels fighting the Cuban- and Soviet-supported MPLA government in Angola (see ANGOLA AND NAMIBIA CONFLICTS). His efforts were hampered by the need to distance the United States from the apartheid regime in South Africa, which was supporting UNITA, especially after Congress, against the administration's wishes, imposed full economic sanctions against South Africa in response to that country's declaration of martial law. But the Reagan administration continued to apply pressure on Angola, Cuba and the Soviet Union, and in August 1988 the administration was rewarded with an agreement to withdraw Cuban and Soviet forces from Angola and South African forces from Angola and Namibia.

One of the main focuses of Reagan's foreign policy was in the Caribbean and Central America, where he prevented the establishment of a far-left government in GRENADA and worked to topple the leftist Sandinista government in NICARA-

GUA. The Reagan administration had for some time been concerned about growing links between Grenada and Cuba, and the CIA had reported that an airport being built on the island was destined for use as a major staging post for Soviet maneuvers in the Caribbean. American intervention in Grenada came on October 25, 1983, after a coup in which far-left elements murdered Prime Minister Maurice Bishop and seized power. A total of 1,999 U.S. military personnel invaded the island, restored order and organized fresh elections.

Of greater concern to Reagan was the presence of the Sandinista government in Nicaragua. The Sandinistas had seized power in July 1979 in a popular revolt against the right-wing, American-supported dictator General Anastasio Somoza. The Sandinistas, led by Daniel Ortega, were interested in establishing a democratic government, but by late 1981 it had become clear that it was to have a socialist cast. Reagan believed that Ortega had allowed Nicaragua to become a base for Soviet operations, and froze all aid to Nicaragua. Through the CIA, he helped to create, and provided covert aid to the Contra rebel force based in Honduras and fighting the Sandinista regime. In 1981 he provided $10 million and in 1982 $19 million. Substantial American military aid was also provided to the right-wing governments of Honduras, El Salvador and Guatemala.

Eventually Reagan's requests for increased aid to the Contras encountered opposition from a Congress skeptical both of the effectiveness of the aid and of Reagan's assertions about the Sandinistas' Soviet links. This led Reagan's national security staff to breach an embargo on arms sales to Iran in order to secure money for the purchase of weapons for the Contras. The illegal transactions were uncovered and led to investigations by the administration-appointed Tower Commission and by a congressional committee, both of which cleared Reagan of any direct involvement. Evidence that has come to light since suggests that this was not the case.

Many observers believed that the Iran–Contra Arms Scandal would cripple the final year of the Reagan administration and possibly even result in the impeachment or resignation of the president. But Reagan's immense personal popularity made it possible for him to recover from this setback with relative ease, though he never again enjoyed the trust of such a large part of the public. Although he left office in January 1989 as one of the most well-liked presidents in American history, his popularity out of office declined rather rapidly.

For Further Information:
The Aspen Strategy Group. *The Strategic Defense Initiative and American Security.* Lanham, Md., 1987.

Blumenthal, Sidney. *Our Long National Daydream: A Political Pageant of the Reagan Era.* New York, 1988.

Boaz, David, ed. *Assessing the Reagan Years.* Washington, D.C., 1988.

Brzezinski, Zbigniew. *In Quest of National Security.* Boulder, Colo., 1988.

Cannon, Lou. *President Reagan: The Role of a Lifetime.* New York, 1991.

Churba, Joseph. *The American Retreat: The Reagan Foreign and Defense Policy.* Chicago, 1984.

Haig, Alexander Meigs. *Caveat: Realism, Reagan, and Foreign Policy.* New York, 1984.

Hyland, William G., ed. *The Reagan Foreign Policy.* New York, 1987.

Johnson, Haynes Bonner. *Sleepwalking Through History: America in the Reagan Years.* New York, 1991.

Mandelbaum, Michael. *Reagan and Gorbachev.* New York, 1987.

Morley, Morris H., ed. *Crisis and Confrontation: Ronald Reagan's Foreign Policy.* Totowa, N.J., 1988.

New American Library. *The Reagan Foreign Policy.* New York, 1987.

Oye, Kenneth, Robert Lieber, and Donald Rothchild, eds. *Eagle Resurgent?: The Reagan Era in American Foreign Policy.* Boston, 1987.

Rogin, Michael. *Ronald Reagan, the Movie, and other episodes in Political Demonology.* Berkeley, Calif., 1987.

Schaller, Michael. *Reckoning with Reagan: America and Its President in the 1980s.* New York, 1992.

Shimko, Keith L. *Images and Arms Control: Perceptions of the Soviet Union in the Reagan Administration.* Ann Arbor, Mich., 1991.

Sick, Gary. *October Surprise: America's Hostages in Iran and the Election of Ronald Reagan.* New York, 1991.

Spanier, J.W. *American Foreign Policy Since World War Two.* Washington, D.C., 1988.

Talbott, Strobe. *The Russians and Reagan.* New York, 1984.

Wills, Garry. *Reagan's America: Innocents at Home.* New York, 1987.

Refugees   Throughout the Cold War years, refugees fled from Eastern to Western Europe and from other Socialist Bloc countries such as Vietnam, Cuba and North Korea.

The biggest movement of refugees was from Eastern to Western Europe in the immediate postwar years, especially from East to West Germany. From 1951 until the Berlin Wall was built in 1961, an estimated 3.5 million people fled from East to West Germany via BERLIN.

There were also hundreds of thousands of refugees from other East European countries, especially POLAND, CZECHOSLOVAKIA and HUNGARY. After the 1956 Hungarian Revolution some 200,000 Hungarians fled to the West.

By the early 1960s, the Soviets had consolidated their hold on Eastern Europe, and the flood of refugees to the West was reduced to a trickle. The next major changes did not come until 1989, after Hungary opened its borders with the West and tens of thousands of East Germans took advantage of the standing offer of West German citizenship to escape to the West, first through Hungary and then through Poland and Czechoslovakia.

Throughout the Cold War years, the prosperous and growing economies of Western Europe were able to absorb the refugees into their economic and social structures. The refugees spent only a limited time in special camps and did not pose a significant external threat to the security of Eastern Europe, although they represented a popular dissatisfaction with the Socialist Bloc's political, economic and social structures.

The problem was different in other parts of the world. In Korea, the problem was exacerbated by the KOREAN WAR, with populations moving to avoid the fighting as well as "voting with their feet," and a large number of Koreans fled both the right-wing regime of SYNGMAN RHEE and the communist government of KIM IL-SUNG. The problem was further complicated by discussions over prisoners of war in the final negotiations between the North Koreans and Chinese and the United Nations forces. Some 50,000 of the 117,000 Chinese and North Korean prisoners of war requested asylum in South Korea. The Chinese and North Koreans, fearing a major loss of face, demanded the return of all prisoners. President Syngman Rhee, in an attempt to sabotage the negotiations, arranged a mass escape by the prisoners.

Refugees from Cuba established themselves mainly in southern Florida, where they became a potent political force applying pressure on successive American administrations to either overthrow or maintain the severe isolation of FIDEL CASTRO's Cuba. Men from this group of refugees formed the invasion force that attempted the abortive BAY OF PIGS invasion in 1961.

In Southeast Asia, the refugees were mainly from Vietnam (see VIETNAM WAR), LAOS and CAMBODIA. They fled across the border into refugee camps in Thailand or by boat to Malaysia, Singapore, Indonesia and Hong Kong. In the late 1970s and early 1980s, the flood of refugees from Southeast Asia averaged 9,000 per month. The refugee camps in Thailand also became protected areas for Western-supported guerrillas fighting the Soviet-supported regime in Cambodia.

Many of the Vietnamese refugees found homes in Australia, Western Europe, Canada and the United States. Other Southeast Asian countries were unable or unwilling to accept the refugees. Many of the "boat people" were turned back and some died at sea because passing freighters refused to pick them up. In Hong Kong, over 50,000 Vietnamese refugees were locked into crowded and unsanitary camps by the British authorities, and in 1989 the British government reached an agreement with Vietnam for the forcible repatriation of these refugees.

Some of the largest movements of refugees followed the Soviet invasion of AFGHANISTAN in December 1979. Eventually some 3.5 million Afghans were provided with refuge in Pakistan and another 2 million in Iran. These refugee camps also became military bases for Mujahideen guerrillas to plan their attacks, train troops, liaise with Western and Pakistan intelligence officers, and buy and store equipment. Pakistan's decision to allow these activities severely strained Pakistan's relations with the Soviet Union.

Many refugee camps are administered by the United Nations High Commissioner for Refugees, which was established in 1951. The UNHCR's stated function is to extend international protection to refugees, protect them against their forcible return, and ensure that they receive asylum and internationally recognized standards of treatment.

Rhee, Syngman (April 26, 1875–July 19, 1965) Syngman Rhee was the first president of the Republic of Korea and held the post before, during and after the KOREAN WAR. He was heavily committed to the reunification of Korea under his authority; the brutal methods he used to achieve this goal, and his dictatorial rule, were often embarrassments to the United States.

Rhee was educated in a nominally independent but Japanese-controlled Korea. In 1896 he started his long battle for Korean independence from Japan when he helped to form the Independence Club. Two years later, he was imprisoned for his political activities. After his release in 1904, Rhee went to the United States, where he attended Princeton University. He returned to Korea in 1910 but soon afterward Japan formally annexed the country, and Rhee fled again to the United States, where he found a job as a high school principal.

Rhee quickly became the focal point for exiled Koreans, many of whom had fled to the United States, and in 1919 he was elected president of the Korean Provisional Government-in-exile. During World War II, he established an office in Washington, D.C. and conducted an energetic and successful lobbying campaign for American assurances of postwar Korean independence.

The question of postwar Korea was raised at the Cairo, YALTA and POTSDAM conferences. It was agreed by the Allied powers that Korea would have its independence and that in the immediate aftermath of the war the United States would occupy the half of the peninsula south of the 38th parallel and the Soviet Union the northern portion of the country.

Rhee's wartime work in Washington had made him well known in the political establishment, and he persuaded his contacts to allow him to return to the American-occupied zone ahead of rival American-based Korean figures. In the political vacuum, he was able to establish a powerful right-wing political network, the Korean Democratic Party (KDP), supported by security police who liquidated his more moderate political opponents. In July 1948 he was formally elected president of the Republic of South Korea.

Almost from the moment of his return, Rhee campaigned for a policy of immediate independence from military administration and unification of the country under his rule. In the northern half of the country, however, the Soviet Union had established a government based on the Soviet model and led by former Red Army Major KIM IL-SUNG, who also demanded that the entire country be unified, but under his rule. U.S.–Soviet negotiations aimed at establishing a unified and independent Korea were as unsuccessful as similar negotiations over the future of Germany.

Rhee faced an additional problem within South Korea from communist-controlled People's Committees, which had been formed during the war to organize resistance against the Japanese. During the war, the committees had seized land from Japanese landlords and wealthy Koreans and redistributed it to the peasants. Rhee quickly moved to disband the committees and reverse their land-reform program. The result was a guerrilla war in the southern half of the country. It has been estimated that 100,000 people were killed during the guerrilla warfare before the start of the Korean War in June 1950.

Both Rhee and Kim Il-sung made it clear that they were prepared to go to war in order to secure control of the entire country. They also cultivated relations with the United States and the Soviet Union, respectively, in order to secure military supplies. In October 1949 Congress voted Rhee's government $10.2 million in military aid and $110 million in economic aid for fiscal year 1950. A further $11 million in military aid was approved in March 1950. Officials in Washington disapproved of Rhee's totalitarian methods, but by 1947 they were in the midst of the Cold War and were unprepared to allow any communist victory. Rhee's position was further strengthened by the close relationship that he managed to foster with General DOUGLAS MACARTHUR, the commander of U.S. forces in the Far East and Pacific.

Kim Il-sung was the first of the two Korean leaders to move. On June 25, 1950, North Korean troops stormed across the 38th parallel and swept the South Korean forces toward the southern tip of the country. The United States managed to win United Nations backing for a UN force to intervene in support of Rhee, and in the fighting that followed the South Koreans, supported by American-led UN forces, managed to push the North Korean forces back to within a few miles of the Chinese border. Rhee believed that he was on the verge of gaining control of the entire country when communist China entered the war and drove his supporters back to the southern tip. Over the following two years, the UN forces fought their way back to the 38th parallel and long armistice negotiations with the Chinese and North Koreans.

Throughout the war Rhee opposed any negotiated settlement that would leave the country divided. He saw the war as his best opportunity to gain control as long as he had the support of American forces, and he was prepared to continue fighting until his ultimate goal was achieved. But by the end of 1952, the United States was tired of the inconclusive war and was prepared to make concessions at the armistice negotiations at PANMUNJOM. In June 1953 there was a breakthrough in negotiations, and the two sides moved quickly toward an agreement. Rhee protested to U.S. President DWIGHT EISENHOWER, and when that failed to halt the march toward peace he ordered South Korean guards to permit a mass escape of 25,000 prisoners in the hope that this would sabotage the talks.

The communists protested to the American negotiators, asking them pointedly whether the United States was able to live up to any agreement to which Rhee might be a party. Eisenhower, in turn, sent a strong letter to Rhee in which he expressed his "grave concern" over the release of the prisoners and warned him that any future such actions would "make impractical for the UN Command to continue to operate jointly" with him.

By this stage, Rhee was planning to continue the war without the support of the United States, and Eisenhower had to send Assistant Secretary of State Walter Robertson to Seoul to persuade Rhee that such a course would be both futile and dangerous. Rhee only reluctantly agreed to stop fighting after the Eisenhower administration promised to maintain American forces in South Korea and sign a mutual defense treaty with his government. Fortunately, the Chinese were as anxious to end the war as the Americans were, and the release of the prisoners and Rhee's obstinance delayed the signing of an armistice agreement by only a few weeks.

After the war, Rhee continued his authoritarian rule of South Korea. Popular discontent against his government continued to grow. In 1956, despite massive electoral fraud, an opposition candidate was elected vice president. This led to even greater electoral fraud in the May 1960 elections, and when Rhee announced that he had secured 90% of the popular vote, student-led riots erupted throughout the country. The National Assembly supported the popular demands for Rhee's resignation, and he was forced to resign and leave South Korea for exile in Hawaii. He died there on July 19, 1965.

For Further Information:
Berger, Carl. *The Korea Knot: A Military-Political History.* Philadelphia, 1964.
Collins, J. Lawton. *War in Peacetime: The History and Lessons of Korea.* Boston, 1969.
Cummings, B. *The Origins of the Korean War.* Princeton, 1981.
Rees, David. *Korea: The Limited War.* New York, 1964.
Stone, I.F. *The Hidden History of the Korean War.* New York, 1952.

Rickover, Admiral Hyman   (January 27, 1900–July 8, 1986)   Admiral Hyman Rickover is regarded as the father of the United States' nuclear-powered navy. His long naval career extended from 1922 to 1982 and included the building of the first nuclear-powered submarine. He served for more than 20 years as head of the Naval Reactors Branch of the Atomic Energy Commission.

Rickover was born in Russia and immigrated to America at the age of six. He was raised in Chicago and attended the U.S. Naval Academy at Annapolis, from which he graduated in 1922.

Rickover was appointed director of the electrical section of the Bureau of the Ships in 1939 and remained in that position throughout World War II. In 1945 he was assigned to the Manhattan Project and began a long love affair with nuclear power, especially as it pertained to submarines.

Rickover encountered strong opposition from the tradition-bound U.S. Navy for a research project to investigate the feasibility of developing a nuclear submarine. He overcame the opposition, however, by building powerful political contacts, which later helped in his promotion from captain to rear admiral.

The navy reluctantly started construction of the nuclear-powered submarine *Nautilus* in June 1952. It was launched on January 21, 1954. Its nuclear-powered engines made it capable of cruising around the world without refueling and of crossing the Atlantic submerged at a full speed of 20 knots.

During the KENNEDY administration, Rickover clashed with Defense Secretary ROBERT MCNAMARA over construction of a second nuclear-powered aircraft carrier. McNamara maintained that the project was too expensive, but in April 1962 Rickover told the Joint Congressional Committee on Atomic Energy that multiple production of nuclear-powered submarines had reduced their costs and that there was no reason why the same cost factors would not apply to surface ships. Rickover was supported by the U.S. Navy's surface fleet officers, but McNamara's influence on Capitol Hill led to the defeat of the project.

In 1963 President John F. Kennedy asked Rickover to investigate the possibility of using nuclear-powered submarines for the proposed Multilateral Force for NATO. Rickover advised the president that allocating nuclear-powered submarines to the international naval task force would present insuperable security problems.

Rickover was a stern critic of the American educational system, which he said undermined national security. This criticism won him recognition on the wider public stage. Rickover was also critical of the workmanship of American defense contractors and the cozy relationship between the military and the defense industry, which he said encouraged the military's acceptance of inferior work and materials. Rickover blamed inferior materials for the sinking of the American nuclear submarine *Thresher* in 1963.

Rickover was due to retire in 1964, but his firm grasp of the navy's nuclear program prompted President LYNDON JOHNSON to ask him to remain at his post as chief of the Naval Reactors Branch of the Atomic Energy Commission. The request was extended by presidents NIXON, FORD and CARTER. Rickover continued his battle against defense contractors. In April 1971 he gave the Congressional Joint Economic Committee the names of 17 firms he alleged had failed to comply with a federal law that required them to supply the government with cost and pricing information. In April 1975 Rickover told the committee that the Renegotiation Board, the federal agency responsible for recovering excess profits from defense contractors, was probably "the biggest sieve" in government.

In the 1970s, Rickover also became increasingly worried about the lack of government spending on the navy and the threat of the Soviet Navy being developed by Admiral SERGEI GORSHKOV. In May 1971 he told the House Appropriations Committee that America's naval might was declining and that this could cause the United States to become "a second-rate world power." In May 1976 Rickover testified before the Armed Services Committee that the Soviet Union outnumbered the United States in total number of missile-launching submarines and that the Soviets had the only submarines that could launch missiles against surface ships. He maintained that the United States had lost the chance to match the numerical strength of the Soviet fleet and should opt for building a lesser number of multipurpose nuclear ships.

Rickover had a particularly close relationship with President Jimmy Carter, who had been his staff aide during the early development of the nuclear submarine program. Carter wrote of Rickover in his autobiography, "Admiral Rickover had a profound effect on my life—perhaps more than anyone except my own parents." In June 1977 Rickover accompanied Carter on a nine-hour voyage on the nuclear submarine USS *Los Angeles* as part of the president's investigation of American defense capabilities.

President RONALD REAGAN finally retired Rickover in January 1982. In a characteristically sharp-tongued and irreverent farewell address, Rickover excoriated defense contractors for their irresponsibility, censured the Defense Department for its inefficiency, and attacked large corporations, which he said had become "another branch of government . . . without assuming any of the responsibilities." He attacked the nuclear arms race relaunched by Reagan as "nonsense." Rickover said he was not proud of his own role in building a nuclear navy, which he called a "necessary evil," and he called for the outlawing of both nuclear weapons and nuclear power.

During his retirement, Rickover's tough stand on defense contractors was undermined when it was revealed that he had received $67,628 in gifts from General Dynamics between 1961 and 1977. As a result of the revelation he was sent an official letter of censure by the navy.

Ridgway, General Matthew (March 3, 1895–July 26, 1993) General Matthew Ridgway was General DOUGLAS MACARTHUR's successor as commander of the United Nations forces in Korea. Later he served as supreme commander of NATO forces in Europe and as army chief of staff. He advised President LYNDON JOHNSON to limit the U.S. commitment to Vietnam.

Ridgway graduated from the U.S. Military Academy at West Point in 1917 and spent the first two decades of his army career serving on bases in Central America and the Far East. In September 1939 he was assigned to the War Department General Staff. He remained in Washington, D.C. until January 1942, when he secured an active command in Europe, first as assistant division commander and then as commander of the 82nd Infantry Division. He led the division in fighting in Sicily, Italy and Normandy.

In November 1945 Ridgway was appointed to the Military Staff Commission of the United Nations, which prepared a report calling for an armed force controlled by the Security Council. Ridgway sympathized with the thinking behind the report but warned Americans not to think that they could confide their military security to the United Nations.

In August 1948 Ridgway was appointed commander of the Caribbean Defense Command and the Panama Canal Department. He remained there until the outbreak of the KOREAN WAR in June 1950, when he was appointed field commander of the 8th Army under General MacArthur. When MacArthur was relieved of his command on April 11, 1951, President HARRY TRUMAN appointed Ridgway commander of the UN forces in Korea and supreme commander for the Allied Powers in the Far East. Ridgway succeeded in pushing

General Matthew Ridgway succeeded General Douglas MacArthur as commander of the UN forces in Korea in 1951.

the Chinese and North Korean forces back across the 38th parallel and kept them there through two years of protracted truce negotiations.

On April 28, 1952, Truman appointed Ridgway to succeed General Dwight Eisenhower as supreme commander of the Allied Forces in Europe. In July 1952 his command was widened to include the naval and air forces of the Eastern Atlantic, Europe and the Mediterranean. Shortly after his arrival, Ridgway faced a budget battle with the cost-conscious NATO council, which wanted to reduce by $224 million the construction budget for building air bases, jet fuel pipelines, and communications and headquarters installations in Western Europe. The money was cut in December 1952, but after intensive lobbying Ridgway persuaded the council to restore the funds in February 1953.

On May 12, 1953, Eisenhower, by then president, named Ridgway army chief of staff, in which position he became an opponent of the administration's "NEW LOOK" DEFENSE POLICY, which emphasized strategic nuclear weapons over troops on the ground. He maintained that the United States should concentrate on building up NATO strength, including manpower, not on substituting "new and untried weapons" for soldiers.

Ridgway was known as the voice of moderation on the Joint Chiefs of Staff during the Eisenhower administration. He

opposed supporting French action in Vietnam and was the lone dissenter when the Joint Chiefs of Staff argued that CHIANG KAI-SHEK should be allowed to shell the Chinese mainland following the Chinese communist shelling of QUEMOY AND MATSU ISLANDS in the autumn of 1954.

Ridgway retired as army chief of staff in June 1955 and became a director of Colt Industries. He continued to express his opinion on defense and foreign policy issues. In articles and speeches, Ridgway stressed the need for a greater emphasis on manpower so that the United States could respond to threats ranging from a small guerrilla war to a nuclear attack. His proposals were eventually incorporated into the KENNEDY administrations's FLEXIBLE RESPONSE policy.

Ridgway was one of the military men who opposed American military involvement in Vietnam. His opposition was based mainly on fear of Chinese intervention. Ridgway supported a negotiated settlement, a permanent halt to air strikes against the north, and a limit on American troop activity to coastal areas in the south. President LYNDON JOHNSON appointed Ridgway in March 1968 to the senior advisory group on Vietnam. It was this group's advice that led to Johnson's announcement on March 31, 1968, that he was suspending air and naval bombings of North Vietnam, de-escalating American involvement and seeking peace talks.

For Further Information:

Berger, Carl. *The Korea Knot: A Military-Political History.* Philadelphia, 1964.
Rees, David. *Korea: The Limited War.* New York, 1964.
Ridgway, Matthew. *The Korean War: How We Met the Challenge.* Garden City, N.Y., 1967.
———. *Soldier: The Memoirs of Matthew B. Ridgway.* New York, 1956.
Stone, I.F. *The Hidden History of the Korean War.* New York, 1952.

Rio Pact (Inter-American Treaty of Reciprocal Assistance, 1947)   The Rio Pact was an American-inspired defense treaty designed to thwart communism in the Western Hemisphere. It is generally accepted as an extension of the 19th-century Monroe Doctrine.

The treaty was the first postwar regional defense alliance and affirmed the dominant role of the United States in the Western Hemisphere. It stipulated that an attack against any nation would be considered an attack against all, but it added that signatories would not be required to use their armed forces without their consent. The defense pact was reaffirmed the following year when the ORGANIZATION OF AMERICAN STATES was formed by the Pact of Bogota. The OAS became the main administrative arm of the Rio Pact.

The Rio Pact was signed on September 2, 1947, at the end of the Inter-American Defense Conference in Rio de Janeiro. A total of 103 delegates from 19 nations attended the meeting. President HARRY TRUMAN, who attended the conference, stated just before the signing that the pact "made it clear to any possible aggressor that the American republics are determined to support one another against attacks . . ."

The defense zone extended from the North Pole to the South Pole and included all of North and South America, the Aleutian Islands, Greenland and a quarter of Antarctica but excluded the Hawaiian Islands. Articles 1–6 of the treaty condemned war and the "threat or use of force in any manner inconsistent with" the United Nations Charter; pledged efforts to settle all disputes between signatory nations peacefully, before they were referred to the United Nations; agreed on joint defense of any American nation attacked within its own territory; and allowed for joint action against aggressions that had not reached the shooting stage.

Article 7 prescribed that if fighting broke out between American states, they could be called upon to suspend hostilities and "restore the status quo ante bellum" pending peaceful adjustment. "Rejection of the pacifying action [would] be considered in the determination of an aggressor." Article 8 specified actions that could be taken against an aggressor (diplomatic or economic sanctions or armed force).

Article 9 further defined aggressions as unprovoked armed attack against "the territory, the people or the land, sea or air forces of another state" or armed invasion that violated legal boundaries or a region "under the effective jurisdiction of another state."

For Further Information:
Berle, Adolf A., Jr. *Latin America: Diplomacy and Reality.* New York, 1962.

Rockefeller, Nelson Aldrich   (July 8, 1908–January 26, 1979) Nelson Rockefeller was an early advocate of Pan-American unity as a safeguard against Soviet influence. Later he played a major role in formulating Republican Party foreign policy positions and in furthering the career of HENRY KISSINGER. From 1974 to 1977 he was vice president of the United States.

Rockefeller was born into one of the wealthiest families in America. He graduated from Dartmouth College in 1930 and joined the family oil business. President FRANKLIN D. ROOSEVELT appointed Rockefeller first coordinator of Inter-American Affairs and then, in 1944, assistant secretary of state for Latin American affairs.

After World War II, Rockefeller became heavily involved in lobbying for a Pan-American alliance to prevent Soviet encroachments in the Western Hemisphere. This meant the forgiving of formerly pro-fascist governments such as that of Argentina, which the United States had promised the Soviet Union it would bar from the United Nations. Rockefeller's aggressive lobbying on behalf of Argentina and his proposed Pan-American alliance came in 1945 when the United States and Soviet Union still enjoyed reasonably good relations. It alienated a number of senior Democrats, including Secretary of State JAMES BYRNES and Undersecretary of State DEAN ACHESON, and Rockefeller was dismissed in August 1945. Many of Rockefeller's proposals, however, were later adopted by the Truman administration.

Rockefeller maintained his influence in Latin American affairs by using some of the family money to found the American International Association for Economic and Social Development (AIA) and the International Basic Economy Corporation (IBEC). The AIA distributed money directly to Latin Americans in the form of agrarian aid, and the IBEC provided funds for industrial capital investment. From 1950 to 1951 Rockefeller was an adviser on the POINT FOUR PROGRAM but had little influence over policy.

A liberal Republican, Rockefeller supported General DWIGHT D. EISENHOWER in the 1952 presidential election. He hoped in return to win a cabinet post, or at least a senior position in the State Department. He was disappointed when he was nominated undersecretary for the newly-created Department of Health, Education and Welfare. In 1954 he left HEW to become a special assistant to the president on foreign policy and was given special responsibility for developing long-range economic and military aid programs. One of Rockefeller's suggestions was the OPEN SKIES proposal. But again Rockefeller faced opposition from within the administration, and resigned at the end of 1955.

In 1956 Rockefeller started the Special Studies Project of the Rockefeller Brothers Fund. The purpose of the project was to bring together the best minds in America to make policy recommendations in economics, education and defense. Among the participants in the project was Henry Kissinger, who established his reputation with a report for the project entitled "International Security: The Military Aspect." Through the project, Kissinger became a key adviser to Rockefeller. Kissinger later wrote that Rockefeller "would have made a great president" but was politically hamstrung by his enormous wealth.

In 1958 Rockefeller defeated AVERELL HARRIMAN for the governorship of New York. As governor he reinforced his liberal credentials by introducing extensive social welfare programs, expanding education facilities, and establishing a State Housing Finance Authority. He viewed the governorship, however, as a stepping stone to the White House, and as soon as he entered the governor's mansion he established a campaign organization for the 1960 presidential election.

Rockefeller failed to defeat Vice President RICHARD NIXON for the Republican nomination. In the aftermath of the convention, though, he forced Nixon to accept many of his foreign and defense policy positions by threatening to withhold his endorsement, a move that would have split the Republican Party into liberal and conservative camps. Rockefeller also tried and failed to win the Republican nomination in 1964 and 1968.

In July 1968, Rockefeller presented the details of a peace plan for Vietnam. It proposed the gradual withdrawal of troops by the United States and North Vietnamese, free elections, and direct negotiations between North and South Vietnam that would include the National Liberation Front (Viet Cong), on the condition that it renounce force. The proposal helped to establish Rockefeller's foreign policy credentials and, by association, those of Kissinger, whom Nixon appointed national security adviser.

Kissinger's presence in Washington provided Rockefeller with entry back into foreign affairs. In 1969 Nixon asked him to formulate policy recommendations on Latin America. After a series of tours, Rockefeller compiled a report that indicated a "climate of growing instability, extremism and anti-U.S. nationalism." The report recommended increases in military aid, renegotiated foreign debts and major trade concessions.

In December 1973 Rockefeller resigned the governorship of New York, and in August 1974 he was nominated for the vice presidency by President GERALD FORD, who had succeeded Richard Nixon in mid-term. After a lengthy Congressional confirmation process, Rockefeller was approved. In December 1974 Ford gave him the task of investigating allegations that the CENTRAL INTELLIGENCE AGENCY had conducted illegal domestic espionage. The subsequent report of the Rockefeller Commission was the mildest of the indictments of CIA activities in 1975. It concluded that "the great majority" of CIA activities were within the law, but it did concede that the CIA had engaged in activities that were "plainly unlawful and constituted improper invasions upon the rights of Americans."

In June 1975, Ford chose Rockefeller as his running mate in the 1976 presidential election. But the choice encountered strong opposition from the right wing of the Republican Party. In November 1975, in an attempt to head off a conservative challenge to Ford from RONALD REAGAN, Rockefeller withdrew his name from consideration. Rockefeller retired in January 1977 and died of a heart attack on January 26, 1979.

For Further Information;

Collier, Peter, and David Horowitz. *The Rockefellers*. New York, 1976.

Moscow, Alvin. *The Rockefeller Inheritance*. New York, 1977.

Rogers, William P.   (June 23, 1913–   )   William Rogers was U.S. secretary of state throughout most of the NIXON administration. He was essentially a State Department administrator, as most foreign policy was determined by President RICHARD NIXON and National Security Adviser HENRY KISSINGER.

Rogers graduated from Colgate University in 1934 and went on to Cornell Law School, graduating fifth in his class in 1937. In 1938 Rogers joined the office of Manhattan (New York) District Attorney THOMAS E. DEWEY and started his association with politics.

During the war Rogers served in the U.S. Navy, and afterward he moved to Washington, D.C. to become counsel to the Senate Special Committee to Investigate the National Defense Program. In Washington, Rogers met and became a close friend of Congressman Richard Nixon, and over the following 20 years he was involved in most of Nixon's major political decisions. These involved pressing the young con-

gressman to pursue ALGER HISS on charges of espionage, advising Nixon to make his famous "Checkers Speech," and encouraging him, as vice president, to adopt a statesmanlike role following President Dwight Eisenhower's heart attack in 1955.

The close bond with Nixon ensured Rogers a role in the Eisenhower administration, first as deputy attorney general from 1953 to 1957 and then as attorney general from 1957 to January 1961. He had little to do with foreign policy, although he did accompany Nixon to Austria in 1956 to visit refugees of the Hungarian Revolution.

After Nixon's defeat in the presidential election in 1960, Rogers returned to his private law practice in New York and Washington. He became a member of the U.S. delegation to the UN General Assembly and a delegate to the UN Committee on Southwest Africa. But his interest in foreign affairs remained peripheral.

Rogers was expected to be appointed to the cabinet after Nixon's election to the presidency in 1968, but his lack of foreign affairs experience meant that he was a surprise choice as secretary of state. Nixon later made it clear that he had chosen Rogers partly because he wanted to maintain complete control of foreign policy and he needed a close friend to manage "the recalcitrant bureaucracy of the State Department." Rogers also took on the role of managing foreign policy public relations both with the Congresss and foreign countries.

Foreign policy itself was not determined or even managed by Rogers but by Nixon in consultation with National Security Adviser Henry Kissinger. Rogers was excluded from many important meetings and negotiations. For example, he did not attend the first meeting between Nixon and Soviet ambassador ANATOLY DOBRYNIN in February 1969.

Nixon kept his private exchange in 1969 with North Vietnamese president HO CHI MINH a secret from Rogers until 48 hours before he revealed it on television. Neither did Rogers know of the secret negotiations in 1971 between Kissinger and Dobrynin that led to the breakthrough in the SALT I negotiations. And he was not told of Kissinger's trip to China in July 1971 until the latter was on the plane.

The respective talents of Kissinger and Rogers could have been successfully used to complement each other. But Kissinger and Nixon's penchant for secrecy alienated Rogers and led to a conflict between the secretary of state and the national security adviser. Kissinger, instead of using Rogers, "tended to view him as an insensitive neophyte who threatened the careful design of our foreign policy," as he later wrote in his memoirs.

The antipathy between the two men led Kissinger to develop his own mini-State Department within the White House through which he established his own relations with foreign governments. This further undermined the influence of Rogers, demoralized U.S. diplomats working for him, and confused foreign governments, who were often presented with conflicting American policies.

The only area in which Rogers was able to make an impact was the Middle East. In October 1969 he proposed his Rogers Plan, calling for Israel to withdraw from the Occupied Territories in return for a binding Arab commitment to peace. The plan was rejected by Arabs and Israelis, but Rogers in 1970 managed to secure agreement from Egypt, Jordan and Israel to a cease-fire and new negotiations.

The conflict between Kissinger and Rogers led to the resignation of Rogers in January 1973. Kissinger assumed the title of secretary of state, and Rogers returned to his law practice. He supported RONALD REAGAN during the 1980 presidential election, and during the Reagan administration he participated in a mock nuclear war drill to hone emergency drill procedures and advised the administration on policy toward Central America.

For Further Information:
Kissinger, Henry. *The White House Years.* New York, 1979.
Nixon, Richard. *The Memoirs of Richard Nixon.* New York, 1978.

Romania Romania managed in the latter part of the Cold War to combine a repressive Stalinist form of government while at the same time pursuing a foreign policy relatively independent of the Soviet Union.

Romania has strong historical reasons for being wary of the Soviet Union. Russia has invaded Romania on 13 separate occasions. After the Bolshevik Revolution in 1917, Romania became one of the chief targets of communist subversion. The Romanian Communist Party was banned, and in 1940 the country allied itself with Germany under the fascist dictatorship of General Ion Antonescu.

In August 1944 King Michael (see MICHAEL OF ROMANIA) led a coup against Antonescu as the Red Army invaded Romania from the east. Michael was determined to encourage Western democratic principles, and to this end he had himself declared a constitutional monarch and appointed the prominent pro-Western statesman General NICOLAE RADESCU as premier and minister of the interior. But Radescu was unacceptable to the Soviets and fighting broke out between government forces and communist partisans. In February 1945, Soviet deputy foreign minister Andrei Vishynsky flew to Bucharest and demanded that King Michael dismiss Radescu. Michael, whose country was occupied by the Red Army, had no choice but to accede to the demand, and the Romanian communist Petro Groza was named prime minister.

Groza immediately began to suppress political freedom and arrest opponents. After a government-organized campaign of intimidation and repression, the communists managed to obtain four-fifths of the parliamentary seats in an election on November 19, 1946. On December 30, 1947, Groza forced King Michael to abdicate. In the same year, Romania ceded Bessarabia and northern Bukovina to the Soviet Union and southern Dobrudja to Bulgaria. It was allowed to retain Transylvania, which was historically dominated by ethnic Hungarians.

In the following year the Communist Party and the Social Democrats merged to form the Romanian Workers' Party, with GHEORGHE GHEORGHIU-DEJ as its new leader. Gheorghiu-Dej quickly emerged as the strongman of Romanian politics and in 1952 succeeded Groza as prime minister. Gheorghiu-Dej instituted a number of vicious purges to consolidate his power and in 1952, following a purge of the Romanian Workers' Party, forced the adoption of a Soviet-style constitution.

In the 1950s, Gheorghiu-Dej slavishly followed Soviet directives on both foreign and domestic policies. The first tangible sign of Soviet–Romanian differences surfaced at a meeting of the Council for Mutual and Economic Cooperation (COMECON) in June 1962. The meeting had been organized by Soviet leader NIKITA KHRUSHCHEV to endorse his proposal that the Soviet-controlled COMECON secretariat allocate specific economic duties in order to avoid duplication of effort. The proposal was vehemently blocked by Gheorghiu-Dej.

The Romanian leader's opposition stemmed from Romanian national interest. Romania is a country rich in natural resources, especially oil and grain, but relatively underdeveloped in industrial terms. Gheorghiu-Dej feared that closer economic integration within the Soviet Bloc would prejudice his country's chances of industrial advancement. Romanian opposition to Khrushchev's plan meant that COMECON was forced to accept Romania's right to reject economic proposals that its government deemed incompatible with Romania's national interest.

Gheorghiu-Dej died in March 1965 and there was a brief struggle for the leadership of the party between NICOLAE CEAUSESCU and the head of the secret police, Alexandru Draghici. After Ceausescu emerged victorious, he purged the secret police and placed it firmly under his control. In 1967 Ceausescu was declared head of state and in March 1974 he created and occupied the post of president. Ceausescu perpetuated the Stalinist-type personality cult employed by Gheorghiu-Dej and retained all the trappings of a repressive police state.

Ceausescu also continued Gheorghiu-Dej's independent economic line, which had by 1964 extended to foreign affairs as well. Alone among East Europeans, the Romanian leader maintained close relations with Beijing following the Sino–Soviet Split. In 1979 he refused to endorse a WARSAW PACT declaration condemning Chinese policy in Southeast Asia. He also opposed the occupation of Cambodia by Soviet-backed Vietnam. Romania was a member of the Warsaw Pact but after 1967 did not participate in military exercises nor allow Pact troops on its soil. In 1968, after the Soviet invasion of CZECHOSLOVAKIA, Ceausescu hinted at mobilization to fend off a possible similar invasion of Romania.

In 1979 Ceausescu criticized the Soviet invasion of AFGHANISTAN. In 1977 he opposed Warsaw Pact plans to increase defense spending and reduced the Romanian defense budget, diverting the money to social projects. He also spoke out in favor of multilateral nuclear disarmament in Europe, and

Romania was the only East European country to attend the 1984 Los Angeles Olympics.

Ceausescu's independent foreign policy line meant that successive United States administrations and West European governments were prepared to turn a blind eye to his repressive internal policies in order to encourage division within the Warsaw Pact. Romania was awarded most-favored-nation status by the United States and gained massive credits and favorable tariff treatment for its exports from other Western countries. In 1971 Romania became the first COMECON country to join the General Agreement on Tariffs and Trade (GATT) and in 1972 it joined the International Monetary Fund. It was also the first Socialist Bloc country to sign a trade agreement with the EUROPEAN ECONOMIC COMMUNITY in 1979.

Throughout the 1970s and early 1980s, Ceausescu's independent foreign policy made him the West's favorite East European leader. But following the accession to power in Moscow of MIKHAIL GORBACHEV, the Soviet Union and Eastern Europe started to democratize political and economic structures and to develop a more accommodating foreign policy. Ceausescu became less valuable to the West as a foreign policy tool and was an embarrassment because the West's earlier economic support had bolstered his Stalinist internal order.

Ceausescu was especially damaged by his decision in 1988 to bulldoze thousands of villages in Transylvania. Thousands of ethnic Hungarians fled into Hungary, and the Hungarian government, whose liberal economic and political policies had won it Western support, delivered a strong protest that was echoed in both the Western and Eastern camps. Ceausescu found himself isolated from both major power blocs and in 1988 and 1989 traveled extensively through the Third World offering generous aid in an effort to gain support from that sector of the international community.

At the same time, by 1989, he was facing serious economic and political difficulties at home, which were being exacerbated by ethnic problems.

The regime's end came with stunning rapidity, although, unlike the relatively peaceful fall of other Eastern European communist governments, it took a virtual civil war (albeit a brief one) to achieve. On December 15, 1989, a mass protest in the Transylvanian city of Timisoara was crushed by the Securitate—the feared and hated force that served as both national security police and Ceausescu's palace guard—with an unknown but apparently large loss of life. The massacre led to huge demonstrations in Bucharest December 21, with a large crowd jeering a speech by Ceausescu, which turned out to be his last. The next day, the army—poorly paid and equipped, and long resentful of the elite Securitate—joined the revolt, handing out weapons to civilians and joining in heavy fighting around the central Palace Square. Hundreds died in street combat in the capital and in other cities around the country over the next week, until the last of the Securitate were killed, surrendered or fled.

Meanwhile, Ceausescu and his wife Elena were captured December 22 trying to flee the country. The couple was convicted by a secret "extraordinary military tribunal" December 25 and immediately executed by firing squad. A videotape was broadcast of the dictator's bloody corpse.

The National Salvation Front (NSF) took control with the aid of the army, and Ion Iliescu, a former Communist Party official who had been expelled from the Central Committee in the early 1980s, was named interim president. Although many ministers in the new cabinet had been CP members as well, the party was declared "dead" and the NSF promised broad democratic reforms. (The CP was officially outlawed in January 1990, then revived as the Socialist Labor Party the following November.)

In May 1990, Iliescu and the NSF won Romania's first free presidential and parliamentary elections in more than half a century. But the campaign was plagued by violence, which continued afterward and reached a peak in June, with bloody riots between student-led antigovernment protesters, upset over food shortages and the presence of communist holdovers in the new regime, and progovernment coal miners. The miners themselves ultimately became angry with the regime's liberal economic reforms and staged riots in Bucharest in September 1991 that prompted the cabinet to resign and be replaced by a coalition government. Iliescu split off from the NSF and was reelected in the fall of 1992. A new government, opposed to radical reform and favoring a slower transition to a market economy, took over in November.

For Further Information:

Behr, Edward. *Kiss the Hand You Cannot Bite: The Rise and Fall of the Ceausecus.* New York, 1991.

Fischer-Galati, Stephen A. *Twentieth Century Rumania.* New York, 1991.

Floyd, David. *Romania, Russia's Dissident Ally.* London, 1965.

Govender, Robert. *Nicolae Ceausescu.* London, 1988.

Hale, Julian. *Ceausescu's Romania, A Political Documentary.* Toronto, 1971.

Ratesh, Nestor. *Romania: The Entangled Revolution.* New York, 1991.

Saiu, Liliana. *The Great Powers and Rumania, 1944–1946: A Study of the Early Cold War Era.* New York, 1992.

Shafir, Michael. *Romania, Politics, Economics and Society: Political Stagnation and Simulated Change.* London, 1985.

Rome Treaty   *See* EUROPEAN ECONOMIC COMMUNITY.

Roosevelt, Anna Eleanor   (October 11, 1884–November 7, 1962)   Eleanor Roosevelt, the wife of U.S. President FRANKLIN D. ROOSEVELT, established an independent reputation as a humanitarian liberal and internationalist.

Mrs. Roosevelt married her distant cousin Franklin in 1905 and became an active partner in his political career. When polio forced him to retire temporarily in the 1920s she stood in for him at Democratic Party functions and developed her own independent political power base. Throughout the New Deal period, Mrs. Roosevelt traveled extensively in the United States and was known to be one of the more liberal figures with an influence on the president. She was a highly public figure.

After her husband's death on April 12, 1945, friends urged Mrs. Roosevelt to remain politically active, and in December 1945 President HARRY TRUMAN asked her to join the U.S. delegation to the United Nations conference in London. Mrs. Roosevelt developed a special interest in humanitarian affairs and became chairman of the Commission on Human Rights, which drafted the universal statement on human rights. The two-year debate on the document became a focus of a major ideological debate between the Western and Soviet Bloc countries, and Mrs. Roosevelt had the difficult task of attempting to mediate between the two sides. The final document leaned heavily toward the Western camp but still included most of the economic rights demanded by the Soviets such as the right to shelter, food and education.

Mrs. Roosevelt at first supported the liberal former vice president, HENRY WALLACE, in his attacks on Truman's anticommunist foreign policies, but she gradually came to support the president's policy of containment, although she believed that the policy would best be carried out by economic rather than military means.

By the end of 1947 Mrs. Roosevelt had become completely disenchanted with Wallace because of the latter's growing links with the Communist Party and his refusal to denounce Soviet repression in Eastern Europe. In January 1948 she helped found and became the first honorary chairman of the liberal Americans for Democratic Action (ADA), an anticommunist alternative to Wallace's Progressive Citizens of America. The organization supported Truman in the 1948 election.

Following DWIGHT EISENHOWER's election to the presidency in 1952, she returned to private life, although she continued to be active within the United Nations and the ADA and campaigned for Adlai Stevenson in the 1956 presidential election. Mrs. Roosevelt had mixed feelings toward JOHN F. KENNEDY as president, partly because of her dislike of his father, Joseph, and partly because she felt he lacked maturity. This, along with her failing health, prevented her from taking a more active role in the Kennedy administration, but she did attend the UN General Assembly in March 1961 as an American delegate and served on various commissions, mainly in a ceremonial role. Mrs. Roosevelt died on November 7, 1962. Her funeral was attended by President Kennedy and former presidents Eisenhower and Truman.

For Further Information:
Lash, Joseph P. *Eleanor: The Years Alone.* New York, 1972.

Roosevelt, Franklin Delano   (January 30, 1882–April 12, 1945)   Franklin D. Roosevelt was president of the United States from 1933 until his death in 1945. Roosevelt's policies in the last days of World War II, especially at the YALTA CONFERENCE in February 1945, helped to lay the foundations for the Cold War.

Born into a privileged New York family, Roosevelt attended the exclusive Groton School and Harvard University. He was a distant cousin of President Theodore Roosevelt, whose political success is believed to have had a major impact on the young Franklin. Another influence was Theodore Roosevelt's niece, ELEANOR ROOSEVELT, who introduced the future president to the problems of the underprivileged. They were married on March 17, 1905.

Franklin Roosevelt established a powerful political base in New York State as a reformer opposed to the political stranglehold of Tammany Hall. In 1910 he was elected to the state senate; he supported Woodrow Wilson's presidential campaign in 1912 and was rewarded the next year with the post of assistant secretary of the navy.

In 1920 Roosevelt was the nominee for vice president on the unsuccessful Democratic ticket, but in August 1921 his political career appeared to have come to an abrupt end when he was struck down and partially paralyzed by polio. However, he continued in an elder statesman role while his wife, Eleanor, represented him at political meetings. In 1928 he had recovered sufficiently to contest and win the governorship of New York. And in 1932, at the bottom of the Depression, he was elected president after promising a "New Deal."

Roosevelt's New Deal was a mixture of wealth redistribution, government regulation and job creation schemes. It proved immensely popular with a broad range of voters, who returned him to office in 1936, 1940 and 1944. When war broke out in Europe in 1939 Roosevelt offered Britain "all aid short of war." This abruptly changed when Japan bombed Pearl Harbor on December 7, 1941, and the United States entered the war on the side of the Allies against the Axis Powers.

During the war, Roosevelt maintained good relations with both the British prime minister WINSTON CHURCHILL and the Soviet leader JOSEF STALIN. But like many liberals of his generation, he distrusted the imperial power of Britain and worked hard in the cause of anticolonialism. At the same time he was in a small way attracted to the revolutionary experiments of Stalin.

Roosevelt hoped to establish a postwar peace based on the strength of the four major allied powers—the United States, Britain, the Soviet Union and China. Each would be responsible for maintaining the peace in its regional sphere of responsibility and all would sit as permanent members of the Security Council in an organization of united nations. The plan was flawed from the outset by the parlous economic state of Britain, the total collapse of CHIANG KAI-SHEK in China and Stalin's ruthless oppression in Eastern Europe. However, none of this was clear during the war years.

Roosevelt's first meeting with Stalin was at TEHERAN from November 28 to December 1, 1943. The meeting was also attended by Churchill, who tried to persuade Roosevelt and Stalin to push the second European front in the Mediterranean, possibly through Turkey and Greece into Eastern Europe. This was opposed by Stalin, who wanted to establish the Red Army's hegemony in that area. Roosevelt supported him, and it was agreed that the Allies would open the second front on the French coast. Roosevelt's main aim at the conference was to bring the Soviet Union into the war against Japan. Stalin agreed to enter the war after the defeat of Germany, provided that the Soviet Union was granted strategic concessions.

Roosevelt was strongly opposed to increased British involvement in the Far Eastern war because he feared that this would lead to demands from Churchill for additional colonial possessions from the dismembered Japanese Empire. Roosevelt, however, realized that he did need additional military help. The atomic bomb had not been tested at that stage; Roosevelt's military advisers had told him that China's internal conflicts made it useless as an ally and that an American-only landing on the Japanese islands would involve the loss of at least 1 million American lives. The Soviet Union, therefore, seemed the only alternative.

It was at Teheran that Roosevelt, Churchill and Stalin agreed to the regional division of GERMANY. The Polish issue was also informally raised at the Teheran Conference for the first time. The question of postwar POLAND and Germany was destined to become a major stumbling block at future meetings and a major cause of East–West friction.

Poland was to play a bigger role at the YALTA CONFERENCE, February 5–12, 1945. In the intervening period the Soviets had engineered the destruction of the Polish Home Army and effectively installed a puppet communist government (the LUBLIN COMMITTEE) in Warsaw while the government-in-exile, recognized by Britain and the United States, watched in frustration from London.

At Yalta, Roosevelt was clearly a dying man and, in fact, had only two months to live. A number of historians claim that this affected the president's judgment and that Stalin seized the opportunity of Roosevelt's illness to take the diplomatic offensive.

At Yalta, Churchill attacked Stalin's recognition of the Lublin Committee and demanded a broad-based administration in Poland. Roosevelt, while basically supporting Churchill, attempted to mediate between the two. Stalin refused to withdraw his recognition of the puppet regime but promised elections in about a month. Roosevelt and Churchill accepted Stalin's word, realizing that they had no alternative, as the Red Army by that stage occupied all of Eastern Europe.

Also at Yalta, Stalin and Roosevelt reached a secret agreement on the Soviet Union's entry into the war against Japan. Before Yalta, it was agreed that, in return for the help of the Red Army, the Soviet Union would be given control of Port Arthur and Dairen on the Chinese coast, the Kurile Islands and southern Sakhalin Island north of Japan and the Eastern and South Manchurian Railways, and that China would recognize the Mongolian People's Republic. The introduction into Asia of the Red Army altered the regional balance of power and put the Soviet Union in a position later to support the government of North KOREA and the PEOPLE'S REPUBLIC OF CHINA.

Roosevelt's health declined quickly after the Yalta Conference. His post-summit address to Congress had to be delivered sitting down, and doctors ordered him to his estate in Warm Springs, Georgia, for a rest. He died there of a cerebral hemorrhage on April 12, 1945.

For Further Information:
Burns, J.M. *Roosevelt.* New York, 1970.
Davis, Lynn Etheridge. *The Cold War Begins: Soviet American Conflict over Eastern Europe.* Princeton, 1974.
Donnelly, Desmond. *Struggle for the World.* New York, 1965.
Fleming, D.F. *The Cold War and Its Origins, 1917–1960.* Garden City, N.Y., 1961.
Gaddis, J.L. *The United States and the Origins of the Cold War, 1941–1947.* New York, 1972.
Rosenman, S.I., ed. *The Public Papers and Addresses of Franklin D. Roosevelt.* New York, 1969.

Roosevelt, Kermit (February 16, 1916–   ) Kermit Roosevelt was the CIA agent who organized the overthrow of Iran's Premier MOHAMMED MOSSADEQ. He was also deeply involved in the SUEZ CRISIS.

Roosevelt was the grandson of Theodore Roosevelt. He graduated from Harvard University in 1938 and during World War II worked for the wartime predecessor of the CIA, the OFFICE OF STRATEGIC SERVICES. During the war he became an expert in Middle Eastern affairs.

In 1953 the EISENHOWER administration became concerned about the rise to power of Premier Mossadeq. After Mossadeq nationalized the Anglo-Iranian Oil Company (later, British Petroleum) and established contacts with the Iranian Communist Party, President Dwight Eisenhower and CIA Director ALLEN DULLES began to suspect that Mossadeq was a communist, or at least a communist sympathizer.

After an initial approach from the British Secret Intelligence Services (SIS), Dulles dispatched Roosevelt to Iran to coordinate the downfall of Mossadeq. Roosevelt approached the ruler of Iran, Shah MOHAMMED REZA PAHLEVI, who agreed to dismiss Mossadeq and replace him with a pro-Western premier. But at the last minute Mossadeq discovered the plot, organized anti-shah demonstrations and forced the shah to flee the country.

Roosevelt remained in the country and contacted pro-shah elements in the army. He also organized and paid professional agitators to organize pro-shah and anti-Mossadeq demonstrations. As the demonstrators marched through the streets the army moved against Mossadeq. The premier was overthrown on August 19, 1953, and imprisoned, and the shah returned to power.

During the Suez Crisis of 1956, Roosevelt was sent to Egypt to try to persuade President Gamal Abdel Nasser not to accept Soviet military aid. He was followed by Undersecretary of State George Allan, and conflicting messages from the two men are reported to have contributed to Nasser's ultimate decision to accept the Soviet aid as well as his later anger over the American decision to cut off financial support for the ASWAN DAM.

Roosevelt resigned from the CIA in 1958, but he maintained close contacts with the agency. In 1961 he and Dulles approached Postmaster General J. Edward Day to discuss the CIA's plans for an illegal mail surveillance operation, which was later put into effect.

In 1960 Roosevelt became a director of the Gulf Oil Corporation and in 1960 was made a vice president of the company. In 1964 he established his own consulting firm. In June 1975 the Senate Foreign Relations subcommittee on multinational corporations reported that Roosevelt had used his contacts in the CIA to secure nearly $1 billion worth of business for the Northrop Corporation.

For Further Information:
Ramzani, R.K. *The U.S. and Iran: The Patterns of Influence.* New York, 1982.
Roosevelt, Kermit. *Countercoup.* New York, 1979.
Upton, J.M. *The History of Modern Iran.* Cambridge, Mass., 1960.
Wise, David, and Thomas B. Ross. *The Invisible Government.* New York, 1964.

Rosenberg, Julius and Ethel (Ethel: September 28, 1915– June 19, 1953) (Julius: May 12, 1918–June 19, 1953) Julius and Ethel Rosenberg were convicted by the United States in 1951 of selling atomic weapons secrets to the Soviet Union. They were executed for treason.

Julius Rosenberg was raised in a poor but devout Jewish family in New York. In his late teens he became involved in radical politics. This involvement was reinforced when he met his future wife, Ethel Greenglass, a fellow activist, at a union meeting. After he obtained an engineering degree from the City College of New York, Julius and Ethel were married.

In 1943, Julius secured a civilian job as an engineer with the Army Signal Corps. He lost the position in 1945 for alleged communist activities. He and Ethel were arrested in 1950. During their trial they were accused of transmitting atomic bomb secrets to the Soviet Union in 1944 and 1945.

American government lawyers accused them of being at the center of an espionage ring that included Klaus Fuchs, Harry Gold, MORTON SOBELL, a Russian diplomat, and Ethel's brother David Greenglass. The prosecution claimed that while Greenglass was working as a machinist on the atomic bomb project at Los Alamos, New Mexico, the Rosenbergs had persuaded him to pass them secret sketches and drawings via Harry Gold. They in turn had passed the information to a Russian diplomat in New York.

Gold and Greenglass pleaded guilty, but the Rosenbergs and Sobell claimed that they were innocent. The Rosenbergs were convicted largely on the evidence of Ethel's brother, who testified that he had delivered to the Rosenbergs diagrams and sketches of the detonating mechanism of the atomic bomb. Sobell was sentenced to 30 years in jail, and, on April 5, 1951, the Rosenbergs were sentenced to die in the electric chair.

After numerous appeals and pleas for clemency and stays of execution, the Rosenbergs were executed on June 19, 1953, at Sing Sing Prison.

The Rosenbergs' case provoked strong and conflicting responses from around the world. Liberals portrayed Ethel and Julius as victims of anti-Semitism and the anti-communist witch hunt of the early Cold War period (the judge at the trial had accused them of virtual responsibility for the KOREAN WAR). Among those who joined pleas for clemency were ALBERT EINSTEIN and French president Vincent Auriol. But the anti-communist lobby was even more vociferous in its demand for the death penalty. Both presidents TRUMAN and EISENHOWER believed that the evidence pointed clearly to their guilt. In his memoirs, Eisenhower maintained that commuting the sentences to life imprisonment would have encouraged future spies.

For Further Information:
Schneir, Walter and Miriam. *Invitation to an Inquest: A New Look at the Rosenberg-Sobell Case.* Baltimore, 1973.

Rostow, Eugene D. (August 25, 1913–) Eugene Rostow was undersecretary of state for political affairs during the JOHNSON administration, when he maintained a hawkish posture on the VIETNAM WAR. During the early part of the REAGAN administration, Rostow was director of the Arms Control and Disarmament Agency.

Rostow, elder brother of WALT ROSTOW, attended Yale University, graduating in 1937. During the World War II he served as an adviser to the State Department and afterward he returned to Yale Law School to teach. In 1955 he was appointed dean of the Law School, but he retained close contact with government officers. Rostow remained at Yale until 1965, when President LYNDON JOHNSON brought him into government as undersecretary of state for political affairs. In October 1966 Rostow was named an alternate governor of the International Monetary Fund and the World Bank.

In May 1968 Rostow represented the United States in important negotiations over the financing of American troops in West Germany. It was a time when American public opinion was becoming increasingly concerned about the cost of maintaining 300,000 troops in an economically prosperous West Germany. As a result of Rostow's efforts, the West German government agreed to reimburse the United States for a large part of the cost of maintaining the troops.

Rostow was a consistent supporter of the Johnson administration's policy in Vietnam, maintaining that the peace lobby was stimulating a dangerous new isolationist spirit in the United States.

In January 1969 Rostow left public service to return to Yale as Sterling Professor of Law and Public Affairs. But he continued to write and lecture on foreign policy and in 1972 published a defense of American postwar diplomacy, *Peace in the Balance: The Future of U.S. Foreign Policy.* In this book Rostow argued for continued attention to the international balance of power as "the key to any system of law . . . that seeks to assure liberty in peace."

Rostow's support for the Vietnam War and balance-of-power politics earned him a reputation as one of the leading neoconservatives in the Democratic Party. This reputation was enhanced by Rostow's decision to help found the Committee on the Present Danger, a neo-conservative lobby formed to oppose the 1979 Strategic Arms Limitation Treaty (SALT II).

Rostow's activities drew the attention of RONALD REAGAN, who after his election to the presidency in 1980 sought a figure from the Democractic Party to appoint to a senior arms-control position in an attempt to head off criticisms of being too tough on the Soviet Union. Reagan referred to Rostow as "a man of unquestionable liberal credentials."

Rostow was made director of the ARMS CONTROL AND DISARMAMENT AGENCY in early 1981 and spent much of that year establishing a new U.S. position in strategic arms negotiations. In August he headed the American delegation to preliminary U.S.–Soviet talks in Washington, D.C. In testimony before the Senate Foreign Relations Committee, Rostow expressed doubt about the Soviets' willingness to comply with arms control agreements and supported deployment of additional Trident submarines, a fleet of B-1 bombers, MX missiles, production of the neutron bomb, additional cruise and tactical ballistic missiles and expanded civil defense planning.

In June 1982, Rostow appeared on the television program "Meet the Press" and supported the NATO policy of FLEXIBLE RESPONSE, which left open the option of the first use of nuclear weapons in response to a WARSAW PACT conventional attack. Rostow said, "The question of uncertainty about that response has been the main element of deterrence now for a generation."

But Rostow came into increasing conflict with more conservative elements in the Reagan administration. After the president's Zero Option proposal, Rostow instructed PAUL NITZE to expand negotiations with the Soviet negotiating team in Geneva. These negotiations, in the eyes of many administration hard-liners, indicated an American willingness to compromise on basic issues, and on January 12, 1983, Reagan dismissed Rostow as director of ACDA and appointed the even more conservative Kenneth Adelman in his place.

For Further Information:
Brownstein, Ronald, and Nina Easton. *Reagan's Ruling Class.* Washington, D.C., 1982.
Rostow, Eugene. *Peace in the Balance: The Future of U.S. Foreign Policy.* New York, 1972.

Rostow, Walt W.   (October 7, 1916–   ) Walt Rostow was one of the leading American strategists during the VIETNAM WAR. Throughout the conflict he maintained a prowar position. He began his government service in 1961 as deputy special assistant to the president for national security affairs and ended in January 1969, when he retired from the post of special assistant to the president for national security affairs.

Rostow studied at Yale University and attended Oxford University as a Rhodes Scholar. During World War II he served with the OFFICE OF STRATEGIC SERVICES, the wartime forerunner of the CENTRAL INTELLIGENCE AGENCY (CIA). After the war he spent five years with the U.S. diplomatic service before joining the economics faculty of the Massachusetts Institute of Technology (MIT).

At MIT, Rostow established an impressive reputation as a political economist. His book *The Stages of Economic Growth: A Non-Communist Manifesto,* which challenged the Marxist theory of dialectic materialism, was considered a major contribution to political economic thought.

In 1958 Rostow started providing foreign policy advice to Senator JOHN F. KENNEDY, and during the presidential campaign of 1960 he served on Kennedy's advisory council. This placed Rostow in a good position to secure a key job in the new administration, and he was subsequently named deputy to MCGEORGE BUNDY, special assistant to the president for national security affairs.

Rostow almost immediately became involved in planning American policy in Vietnam—a country that was to dominate his life in government. In January 1961 he passed on to the president a report by EDWARD LANSDALE urging a major increase in the U.S. commitment to South Vietnam. As early as May 1962, Rostow proposed the bombing of North Vietnam.

In April 1961 Rostow pressed the president to deepen America's commitment to South Vietnam by appointing a special task force to coordinate policy and by dispatching additional U.S. forces to the war zone. Rostow's pressure led Kennedy to send ROSWELL GILPATRIC, deputy secretary of defense, to South Vietnam to conduct a full-scale reevaluation of American policy.

In October 1961, the president sent Rostow and General MAXWELL TAYLOR to South Vietnam to conduct another review of America's Vietnam policy. The subsequent report of the Taylor-Rostow mission proposed that the United States encourage a series of political and economic reforms within South Vietnam, increase military aid, send additional advisers, and change the American role in Vietnam from advisory to "limited partnership." Most of the recommendations were put into effect, laying the foundations for wider U.S. involvement. An additional proposal by General Taylor for the introduction of 8,000 combat troops was shelved by Kennedy.

Rostow was shifted away from the Vietnam issue in November 1961 when President Kennedy appointed him chairman of the State Department policy planning council, responsible for long-range analysis. This involved him more deeply with the problems of Berlin and Cuba. In April 1963, Rostow also visited India and Pakistan in an attempt to mediate in the two countries' dispute over Kashmir. Rostow was also named U.S. representative to the Inter-American Committee on the Alliance for Progress in May 1964.

Rostow, however, maintained a strong interest in Vietnam

and in December 1963 prepared a paper that became known as the "Rostow Thesis." In it, he argued that an externally supported guerrilla war could be won only by taking military action against the source of the external support—in this case, North Vietnam. Therefore, said Rostow, the United States should institute a series of escalating military actions against North Vietnam.

The "Rostow thesis" was not widely circulated within the Johnson administration until August 1964. Despite some initial opposition from Defense Secretary ROBERT MCNAMARA, the document became the theoretical basis for America's escalation of the Vietnam War after August–September 1964. Rostow's attentions shifted back to Southeast Asia.

In March 1966, President LYNDON JOHNSON, who had a close relationship with Rostow, appointed him special assistant to the president for national security affairs to succeed McGeorge Bundy. In this position, Rostow became Johnson's closest foreign policy adviser for the next two years.

By 1966 the administration was divided over the issue of continued bombing of North Vietnam. McNamara and the key figures in his department, such as JOHN MCNAUGHTON, opposed the bombing on ethical and political grounds. Rostow, however, remained firmly committed to "systematic and sustained" bombing raids and a military resolution of the war. In May 1966 he successfully proposed that the Air Force launch attacks on oil refineries and storage facilities in the Hanoi–Haiphong area. The proposal, which represented a major escalation in the bombings, was accepted by Johnson, and the raids were carried out that summer.

Rostow, however, was not completely dismissive of the concerns of McNamara and McNaughton. In November 1967 he supported McNamara's proposal to freeze U.S. troop levels in South Vietnam and to shift the burden of combat from U.S. ground forces to the South Vietnamese Army. He remained committed, however, to a continuation of the bombing raids, and his influence with the president on this issue led to the resignation of McNamara in November.

The hard-line position of Rostow suffered a major blow with the TET OFFENSIVE of January–February 1968, in which the North Vietnamese gained the upper hand—politically, if not militarily. In its aftermath, Johnson ordered another policy review under the new defense secretary, CLARK CLIFFORD. Rostow, who participated in the review, continued to support the bombing raids. Clifford, however, became increasingly pessimistic about the U.S. position in Vietnam and persuaded Johnson on March 31 to order a total halt to bombing and a de-escalation of the war.

Although Vietnam dominated Rostow's time and efforts, he also advised Johnson on the entire spectrum of foreign policy issues. He accompanied the president on all his foreign travels and sat in on all meetings with visiting heads of state and government. In June 1967 Rostow accompanied the president to the GLASSBORO SUMMIT with Soviet premier ALEXI KOSYGIN, and he played a major role in developing U.S. policies in the Middle East following the 1967 Arab–Israeli War.

Rostow's strong association with the Vietnam hawks left him estranged from the American academic community, most of which was vehemently opposed to the war. In 1968 he tried to return to his teaching position at MIT but was rebuffed. President Johnson eventually secured a position for him as professor of economics and history at the University of Texas, where a Lyndon B. Johnson School of Public Affairs was planned. He continued to defend American involvement in Vietnam and in 1972 published *The Diffusion of Power, 1957–72.*

For Further Information:
Halberstam, David. *The Best and the Brightest.* New York, 1972.
Rostow, W.W. *The Diffusion of Power, 1957–72.* New York, 1972.
U.S. Department of Defense. *The Pentagon Papers.* Senator Gravel Edition, vols. 3 and 4. Boston, 1971.

Rusk, Dean (February 9, 1909–   ) Dean Rusk's high-level diplomatic career spanned the height of the Cold War years and took him from director of the Office of Special Political Affairs in 1947 to secretary of state under presidents Kennedy and Johnson. He was probably best known for his hard-line stand in support of the VIETNAM WAR.

After graduating from Davidson College in 1931, Rusk attended Oxford University as a Rhodes Scholar. When he returned to the United States in 1934 he took a job teaching government at Mills College in California. During the war he served as deputy chief of staff to General Joseph Stilwell, commander of the Allied Forces in China.

In 1947 Rusk joined the State Department as director of the Office of Special Political Affairs and was given responsibility for helping to formulate America's early policy toward Israel. In March 1950 he was appointed assistant secretary of state for Far Eastern affairs and played a key role in formulating American policy toward China, Taiwan and Korea. After the North Korean attack in June 1950, it was Rusk who advised President HARRY TRUMAN to secure international backing for American military action by coordinating all moves through the United Nations. Rusk also argued for firm action in Korea, although he opposed extending the war to Chinese soil.

Rusk was a keen supporter of Nationalist Chinese leader CHIANG KAI-SHEK and consistently supported the policy of nonrecognition of communist China, which he regarded as a Soviet puppet. In a speech to the United Nations on May 18, 1951, Rusk stated that the U.S. government regarded the Chinese communist government as "not Chinese." He went on to say that the Chinese people were assured of "added strength" if they tried to throw off the communist "tyranny." Rusk's speech was followed by a quick and embarrassing denial that he was offering active American support for an anti-communist coup.

On December 6, 1951, Rusk left the State Department to become president of the Rockefeller Foundation, where he stayed until 1961. At the foundation, Rusk distributed more than $250 million in aid to Third World countries. Much of this money helped to finance the "green revolution," which significantly improved agricultural production in the under-developed world. Other projects included research into the hazards of nuclear fallout and programs to encourage the peaceful use of nuclear energy.

In 1954 the Rockefeller Foundation was accused by right-wing Republican congressmen on the House Special Committee to Investigate Tax-Exempt Foundations of having "directly supported subversion" by financing reports by left-wing writers. Rusk attacked the accusations as "flimsy allegations . . . without the support of trustworthy evidence." Rusk denied that the foundation had been infiltrated by communists and said that the investigation would in no way influence the foundation on the type of research it funded.

Rusk had a professorial air and a reputation for being more a consultant than an active decision maker. These attributes, plus the Establishment contacts Rusk developed at the Rockefeller Foundation, made him attractive to President JOHN F. KENNEDY. Kennedy believed that foreign policy should be controlled by the president and that the secretary of state's role was to implement that policy and occasionally consult with the president.

Rusk was named secretary of state soon after Kennedy's election in 1960. He confined himself mainly to improving the administration of the State Department and improving the department's relations with the Pentagon, CENTRAL INTELLIGENCE AGENCY (CIA) and Congress. Rusk himself was not a member of the Kennedy inner circle and was only rarely consulted on major foreign policy issues. He was involved in the meetings related to events such as the BERLIN Crisis, the BAY OF PIGS and the CUBAN MISSILE CRISIS, but he usually followed Kennedy's directives rather than offering his own advice. This was partly because of Kennedy's dominance and partly because Rusk was more conservative in his attitudes toward communist China and Third World countries.

After LYNDON JOHNSON became president, however, Rusk's influence and input into the foreign policy-making process substantially increased, especially on issues related to the Vietnam War. Rusk was a strong proponent of increased American involvement in Vietnam, which he saw as another Korea. He maintained that defeat in Vietnam would result in "a drastic loss of confidence in the will and capacity of the free world to oppose aggression."

In 1964 and 1965 Rusk opposed attempts to negotiate a settlement with the North Vietnamese on the grounds that North Vietnamese successes meant that the United States would be negotiating from a position of weakness. For the same reason, he opposed the bombing halt at the end of 1965.

Rusk soon became the chief defender of Johnson's Vietnam War policy. At a Washington news conference on October 12, 1967, he justified the presence of American troops in Vietnam on the grounds that they were opposing Chinese communist policy. "Within the next decade or two," he said, "there will be a billion Chinese on the mainland armed with nuclear weapons . . . The free nations of Asia will make up at least a billion people. They don't want China to overrun them on the basis of a doctrine of the world revolution."

On January 31, 1968, the North Vietnamese and the Viet Cong launched the TET OFFENSIVE. They attacked the streets of Saigon and even entered the compound of the U.S. Embassy. The Pentagon responded by asking President Johnson for a further 200,000 American troops. Rusk was adamant that he supply the men. Johnson, however, established a special bipartisan panel to consider the request, and it advised him to de-escalate American involvement. From the moment Johnson accepted their advice, Rusk's influence began to wane. By the time the PARIS PEACE TALKS started in May 1968, Rusk was playing only a minor role. The American delegation was headed by AVERELL HARRIMAN.

After RICHARD NIXON's election victory in 1968, Rusk left government service to return to academic life, first as a fellow of the Rockefeller Foundation and then as a professor of international law at the University of Georgia.

For Further Information:
Halberstam, David. *The Best and the Brightest.* New York, 1972.
Hoopes, Townsend. *The Limits of Intervention.* New York, 1969.
Johnson, Richard A. *The Administration of United States Foreign Policy.* Austin, Tex., 1971.

S

Sadat, Anwar **(December 25, 1918–October 6, 1981)**
Anwar Sadat was president of Egypt from 1970 until his assassination in 1981. He was responsible for severing Egypt's formerly close relations with the Soviet Union and establishing relations with archenemy Israel. The two moves did much to increase American influence in the Middle East.

After studying at the Egyptian Royal Military Academy, Sadat entered the army in 1938 as a second lieutenant and was posted to the Sudan. There he met fellow lieutenant GAMAL ABDEL NASSER, and the two men formed the secret anti-British and antimonarchy revolutionary organization, the Free Officers. During the war Sadat was imprisoned by the British for treason but escaped. In 1952 he participated in the Free Officers' coup that overthrew King Farouk and established a Revolutionary Command Council. When Nasser emerged from the shadows in 1954 to name himself prime minister, Sadat was alongside him.

Sadat held a number of high positions under Nasser and in 1964 was named vice president. He became president when Nasser died of a sudden heart attack on September 28, 1970. Nasser's anti-British policies had led him to establish close relations with the Soviet Union, which gave Moscow a major foothold in the Middle East. But shortly before his death Nasser had become increasingly disenchanted with the Soviets and started making the initial moves toward reestablishing relations with the United States.

Nasser, and later Sadat's, disenchantment with the Soviet Union was a result of the beginnings of Soviet–U.S. détente and of the efforts of U.S. secretary of state HENRY KISSINGER to link progress in the Middle East to improved U.S.–Soviet relations and to the STRATEGIC ARMS LIMITATION (SALT) TALKS. As a result of these policies, the Soviets backed away from providing Egypt with the military equipment needed for a successful attack on Israel. At the same time, the Soviets demanded that the Egyptians continue their pro-Soviet foreign policy in return for the aid they did receive.

On July 18, 1972, Sadat ordered the immediate withdrawal from Egypt of Soviet military advisers and experts, a total of 5,000 men. They were followed by a further 15,000 Soviet combat personnel who flew MiG-23 jets and operated Egyptian air defense systems. The Soviet–Egyptian breach was partially repaired in October 1972, and Soviet arms shipments were resumed.

On October 6, 1973, Egypt and Syria attacked Israel at the start of the Yom Kippur holiday. At first the Egyptian forces advanced, and the Soviets increased their arms shipments. The United States increased its shipments to Israel, and tensions rose accordingly. As the tide turned against Egypt, both the United States and the Soviet Union worried that a humiliating defeat for Sadat would destroy the balance of power in the Middle East. Secretary of State Henry Kissinger flew to the region and negotiated a truce that left Egyptian forces on the Eastern bank of the Suez Canal. The truce was a political victory for Sadat, who concluded that the United States was the only country capable of extracting concessions from Israel and that he could achieve more by dealing directly with the Americans. In March 1976 he put Egypt completely into the U.S. camp by abrogating the 1971 Soviet–Egyptian Treaty of Friendship.

Sadat knew that Israel's superior military position and strong links with the United States meant that Egypt was unlikely ever to defeat Israel. The Yom Kippur War was mainly designed to improve Egypt's negotiating position following its humiliating defeat in 1967. Having achieved this, Sadat now set out to negotiate a peace with Israel. In 1977, in order to overcome Israeli suspicions, Sadat made his historic trip to Jerusalem and addressed the Israeli Knesset (parliament). This breakthrough visit led to a series of talks with Israeli prime minister Menachem Begin, hosted by President JIMMY CARTER. The talks resulted in the Israeli–Egyptian Peace Treaty, signed at Camp David, Maryland in September 1978.

The Camp David Accords, however, were universally rejected by the rest of the Arab world, and Sadat was vilified as a traitor to the Arab cause. Egypt, which had been the standard-bearer of Arab nationalism, was expelled from the Arab League, and various Arab leaders called for Sadat's assassination. On October 6, 1981, Sadat was assassinated by Muslim fundamentalists while reviewing a military parade commemorating the Yom Kippur War.

For Further Information:
Ayoob, Mohammed, ed. *The Middle East in World Politics.* London, 1981.
Freedman, Robert. *The Middle East Since Camp David.* Boulder, N.Y., 1984.

Golan, Matti. *The Secret Conversations of Henry Kissinger: Step-By-Step Diplomacy in the Middle East.* New York, 1976.

Hirst, David. *Sadat.* London, 1981.

Israeli, Raphael. *Man of Defiance: A Political Biography of Anwar Sadat.* London, 1985.

Lippman, Thomas W. *Egypt After Nasser: Sadat, Peace, and the Mirage of Prosperity.* New York, 1989.

Perlmutter, Amos. *The Life and Times of Menachem Begin.* Garden City, N.Y., 1987.

Quandt, William B. *Decade of Decisions: American Policy Toward the Arab-Israeli Conflict, 1967–1976.* Berkeley, Calif., 1977.

Sadat, Anwar. *In Search of Identity: An Autobiography.* New York, 1978.

St. Laurent, Louis   (February 1, 1882–July 25, 1973)

Louis St. Laurent was Canadian external affairs minister from 1945 to 1948 and prime minister from 1948 to 1957. He played a crucial role in the formation of the NORTH ATLANTIC TREATY ORGANIZATION (NATO) and the laying of the foundations of Canadian postwar foreign policy.

After graduating with his law degree from Laval University in Quebec, St. Laurent opened his own law practice and quickly became one of the wealthiest and most prominent lawyers in French-speaking Canada.

After Canada entered World War II in 1939, Liberal prime minister Mackenzie King was faced with the major problem of overcoming opposition to conscription among French Canadians. He turned to St. Laurent for help, as a respected French Canadian who could win the support of his community. In December 1941, St. Laurent entered the government. He was 60 years old at the time and had never before held or sought any public office.

St. Laurent's first cabinet post was as minister of justice, where he performed the task of maintaining French Canadian loyalty despite the overwhelming unpopularity of conscription in Quebec province. At the end of the war, St. Laurent was moved to the ministry of external affairs. In this position he was deputy chairman of the Canadian delegation to the SAN FRANCISCO CONFERENCE, which established the United Nations.

Canada emerged from World War II a major middle power in the world. Europe lay in ruins. Britain, in whose shadow Canada had stood for more than a century, was absorbed with its own reconstruction and heavily in debt to both the United States and Canada. St. Laurent thus found Canada in a position of international influence unknown to it before the war, and he was able to exercise it effectively.

St. Laurent was attracted to the ideals of the United Nations, and support for the United Nations quickly became a Canadian national passion. St. Laurent hoped that the United Nations would be able to ensure world peace through its peacekeeping forces, but quickly realized that it would fall short and that regional alliances would be needed to buttress it. He was especially keen to form an alliance between the western European states, the United States and Canada that would tie the United States to the defense of Western Europe and prevent a Soviet attack. In pursuit of this goal he allied himself with British foreign secretary ERNEST BEVIN and U.S. undersecretary of state DEAN ACHESON.

Canadian membership in a transatlantic alliance was important to its American supporters, who did not want the United States to be seen as the only North American country committed to the defense of Western Europe. Thus on April 28, 1948, in the Canadian House of Commons St. Laurent was the first to propose formally a single mutual defense system, superseding the BRUSSELS TREATY, which already linked Britain, France and the Benelux countries. It was warmly welcomed a week later by Bevin, and on June 11, 1948, the U.S. Senate passed the VANDENBERG RESOLUTION supporting American involvement in regional alliances for "collective self-defense."

By this time, St. Laurent had replaced Mackenzie King as prime minister and leader of the Liberal Party and recruited LESTER PEARSON as secretary of state for external affairs. Pearson and St. Laurent worked closely and together devised what became known as the "Canadian Clause" of the NATO Treaty, which tried to widen the scope of the alliance to encompass political and economic affairs as well as defense. This was incorporated as Article 2 of the North Atlantic Treaty, but it has never been actively pursued.

Pearson was also a strong proponent of the United Nations and was twice nominated for the post of secretary general. He and St. Laurent were instrumental in ensuring that the KOREAN WAR remained a UN action, albeit led by the United States. Canada sent forces to Korea, but it was made clear that the Canadian government regarded the war not as an attempt to contain or roll back communism but as a UN action to uphold the peace settlement, which had divided Korea at the 38th parallel.

St. Laurent was as determined as Pearson to see that Canada maintained a foreign policy independent of the United States, but he was more accommodating to Washington than Pearson was. This was especially apparent in the two men's attitude toward recognition of communist China. In March 1954 Pearson said that Canada was considering recognition of the Beijing government if Beijing adopted a conciliatory attitude at the 1954 GENEVA CONFERENCE ON INDOCHINA AND KOREA, ceased aggression in Korea and took an "honest line" in world affairs. Within hours, Pearson was being contradicted by St. Laurent, who told the Canadian House of Commons that he knew of no prospects at that time for recognition of communist China.

After his defeat by John Diefenbaker's Conservatives in the 1957 general election, St. Laurent retired to his Quebec law practice at the age of 75.

For Further Information:

Hurst, Donald, and John Miller. *The Challenge of Power: Canada and the World.* New York, 1979.

Pearson, Lester. *Mike: The Memoirs of the Rt. Hon. Lester B. Pearson,* 3 vols. Buffalo, N.Y., 1975.

Thompson, D.C. *Louis St. Laurent.* Toronto, 1967.

Sakharov, Andrei   (May 21, 1921–December 14, 1989)

Andrei Sakharov was the "father" of the Soviet Union's hydrogen bomb and later became his country's most famous dissident. His political rehabilitation by Soviet leader MIKHAIL GORBACHEV was seen in the West as a sign of the genuineness of Gorbachev's commitment to policies of democratization.

Sakharov graduated with honors in physics from Moscow State University in 1942. His extraordinary scientific abilities led to his exemption from military service during World War II in order to continue his studies. In 1945 Sakharov joined the famous P.N. Lebedev Physics Institute of the Soviet Academy of Sciences.

In 1948 Sakharov published a series of articles outlining his theories on the magnetic thermal isolation of ionized gas. The articles significantly altered Soviet research into controlled thermonuclear reaction, and as a result Sakharov was assigned exclusively to the development of atomic and hydrogen bombs. In 1950, with Igor Tamm, Sakharov formulated the theoretical basis for the hydrogen bomb. In 1953 he was elected the youngest-ever member of the Soviet Academy of Sciences.

Sakharov's first tentative steps into the political arena were made in 1958 when he published an article in *Pravda* in which he criticized NIKITA KHRUSHCHEV's educational program. His criticisms, designed to improve training for scientifically minded youth, were eventually incorporated into the Soviet educational system.

In the 1960s Sakharov became embroiled in a debate over the work of Soviet agronomist Trofim D. Lysenko, whose pseudoscientific theories dominated official Soviet science during the Stalin regime. Lysenko had become so closely associated with Stalin that an attack on him became an oblique attack on Stalin and his policies. Sakharov thus emerged as the leading anti-Stalinist figure within the Soviet scientific community.

While Khrushchev was in power this worked to Sakharov's advantage, but after his fall in 1964, the new leadership cracked down on the Soviet intellectual community and Sakharov became a prime target. In 1966 Sakharov put his name to a letter to LEONID BREZHNEV warning the new Soviet leader that the Soviet people would not accept a resurgence of Stalinism. Later that year he attacked a decree banning public demonstrations.

In 1965 Sakharov refused to cooperate with any further research into nuclear weapons development and shifted his research to the physical structure of the universe. That same year he published a ground-breaking article dealing with the theory of an expanding universe.

But by this time, Sakharov was more involved in dissident politics than scientific issues, and he formally launched himself into this arena on July 22, 1968, when his 10,000-word article "Progress, Coexistence and Intellectual Freedom" was published in the *New York Times*. In this article Sakharov warned that "the division of mankind threatens it with destruction" and maintained that "intellectual freedom is essential to human society." In many ways, the article was as critical of the United States as it was of the Soviet Union. American forces in Vietnam, for instance, were accused of "violating all legal and moral norms" and of "carrying out flagrant crimes against humanity."

But Sakharov's criticisms of the Soviet Union were more damaging because they struck directly at the foundations of the Soviet system, as "a threat to the independence and worth of the human personality, a threat to the meaning of human life."

The purpose of Sakharov's article, however, was not to attack the superpowers, but to demonstrate that neither of them could claim a monopoly on political morality and that the leaders of both countries should seek a measured rapprochement in order to deal with the threats of thermonuclear war, famine, environmental pollution, overpopulation and police-state dictatorships. To this end, he proposed a four-point timetable for U.S.–Soviet rapprochement by the year 2000, leading to social democracy and economic justice worldwide.

After the Soviet invasion of CZECHOSLOVAKIA in August 1968, Sakharov became increasingly critical of the Soviet system and of Brezhnev. In March 1970 Sakharov joined physicist Valery F. Turchin and historian Roy Medvedev in issuing a manifesto attacking the threat that thought control posed to scientific and technological progress. Shortly afterward, Sakharov wrote to Brezhnev appealing for the release of Medvedev's brother, dissident scientist Zhores Medvedev, who had been forcibly detained in a psychiatric hospital.

In November 1970 Sakharov helped to found the Committee for Human Rights. In January 1972 he protested against the trial of dissident Vladimir Bukovsky and asked UN secretary general KURT WALDHEIM to intervene on Bukovsky's behalf. In August 1973 Sakharov warned the West against détente, saying that it could be "very dangerous" if it were not accompanied by the democratization of Soviet society and reduced Soviet isolation from the rest of the world.

Sakharov's attacks on Brezhnev and the Soviet system were matched by mounting attacks on Sakharov in the Soviet press. In July 1973 he was denounced by the Soviet news agency Tass for "supplying the reactionary press with anti-Soviet slander." In August 1973 Sakharov was attacked by fellow members of the Academy of Soviet Sciences. President Mstislav Keldysh charged that Sakharov had joined "the most reactionary imperialist circles which actively oppose the course of peaceful coexistence."

The following month, Sakharov was offered a teaching position at Princeton University and applied for an exit visa. He was denied permission to leave the Soviet Union because of his extensive knowledge of Soviet nuclear secrets. In June 1973 he staged a six-day hunger strike to protest "the illegal and brutal repression" of political prisoners.

In October 1975 Sakharov received his greatest honor, the Nobel Prize for peace. In citing Sakharov, the committee said, "Uncompromisingly and forcefully, Sakharov has fought not only against the abuse of power and violations of human dignity in all their forms, but he has with equal vigor fought for the ideal of a state founded on the principle of justice for all."

The award of the Nobel Prize confirmed Sakharov as the Soviet Union's leading dissident. In some respects, this protected him because it focused the attention of the world's press on him. But it also ensured that his comments were given prominence in the Western press, and this led to a battle between Sakharov and his Western supporters and the Soviet leadership on the issue of Moscow's right to control the statements and actions of its citizens.

In January 1980 Brezhnev decided that he could no longer allow Sakharov unfettered access to Western news media. On January 22 he was stripped of all of his awards and sent into internal exile in the closed city of Gorky. Announcing the move, Tass said Sakharov "has been conducting subversive activities against the Soviet state for a number of years." The internal exile met with a storm of protest from the international community. President JIMMY CARTER called the Soviet action "a scar on their system that the Soviet leaders cannot erase by hurling abuse." Protests were also issued by the EUROPEAN ECONOMIC COMMUNITY and Western European communist parties. Sakharov, in a statement smuggled out of Gorky, described his banishment as "a gross violation of my basic right to receive and disseminate information" and called for a public trial.

For years before his internal exile, Sakharov had been carefully watched by the Soviet KGB. His telephone had been tapped, his apartment ransacked and visitors, friends and relatives regularly interrogated and photographed. This harassment and the constant attacks in the press took their toll. In exile, he placed an additional burden on his health by staging a hunger strike in order to obtain an emigration visa for the wife of his stepson. In December 1981, Sakharov was admitted to the hospital with heart problems, which plagued him for the next five years.

Following the accession to power of Mikhail Gorbachev there was increased speculation that Sakharov would be allowed to return to Moscow. In December 1986, Gorbachev personally telephoned Sakharov to tell him that he had been pardoned and would be allowed to return to the capital. Two months later, he was the surprise speaker at a Soviet-organized peace forum, where he appealed for a "more open and democratic Soviet Union."

In January 1988 Sakharov met with Gorbachev. During the meeting, Sakharov handed the Soviet leader a list of 200 dissidents still held in prisons, labor camps and psychiatric hospitals. After the meeting, Sakharov praised Gorbachev as the "kind of leader . . . needed in a great country at such a decisive moment in history." The free Sakharov now became a symbol of Gorbachev's *glasnost* and *perestroika* policies. He was encouraged to speak and to travel. In May 1988 he was a guest at the Moscow state dinner for visiting U.S. president RONALD REAGAN, and in December he attended a meeting in Paris to mark the 40th anniversary of the United Nations Declaration of Human Rights. He went from Paris to Washington, D.C., where he had a private discussion with Reagan. Sakharov's political rehabilitation was completed in April 1989 when he was elected to the reorganized Soviet parliament.

In parliament, Sakharov quickly established himself as a leading opponent of the Communist Party and of Soviet involvement in AFGHANISTAN. In July 1989 he joined forces with communist maverick BORIS YELTSIN to form a group of opposition legislators known as the Inter-Regional Group of People's Deputies. At the opening of the December session of the Congress of People's Deputies Sakharov took a leading role in trying to organize a motion to debate the constitutional clause entrenching the Communist Party's monopoly on political power.

In the middle of this campaign, Sakharov died suddenly of a heart attack, on December 14. More than 80,000 mourners attended the funeral service, and 100,000 filed past his body while it lay in state at the Moscow Palace of Youth. Among those who paid their respects at the grave were Gorbachev and several members of the Politburo.

For Further Information:
Sakharov, Andrei. *My Country and the World.* New York, 1975.
———. *Memoirs.* New York, 1990.

San Francisco Conference (1945)   The San Francisco Conference, which started on April 26, 1945, established the framework of the United Nations and ended with the signing of the UN Charter on June 26.

The conference was marred by a number of East–West disagreements, starting on the first day when Soviet foreign minister V.M. MOLOTOV rejected a motion that U.S. secretary of state EDWARD STETTINIUS be named permanent chairman of the conference. He counterproposed that the foreign ministers of the Big Four Powers (the United States, the Soviet Union, Britain and China) be cochairmen with equal powers. A compromise proposal from British foreign secretary ANTHONY EDEN saved the conference from becoming bogged down in procedural questions on the first day. The compromise left Stettinius as chairman of all "steering committee" meetings while the chairmanship of plenary sessions was rotated among the delegates of the Big Four.

POLAND was also a major East-West issue at the conference. At the time, Britain and the United States were pressing the Soviets to honor their pledge to hold free elections in Poland. The Soviet Union, for its part, was working toward international recognition for the communist government it had installed there. It tried to secure a seat at the San Francisco Conference for the LUBLIN COMMITTEE, as it was known, but the American and British delegations blocked the move.

Britain and the United States had already reluctantly accepted that Belorussia and Ukraine be given seats in the new United Nations, even though they were not separate nations but part of the Soviet Union. The Soviets insisted on this because some countries that were part of the British Empire were being seated at the United Nations. Molotov also wanted Belorussia and the Ukraine to participate in the work of the steering committees meeting in San Francisco, as this would give him two extra votes. At first the British and Americans objected, but they eventually conceded.

The major problem of the conference concerned the veto in the Security Council. It had been agreed at the Dumbarton Oaks Conference in 1944 and at the YALTA CONFERENCE in February 1945, when the structure of the United Nations was first being discussed, that each of the Big Four Powers would be given a permanent seat and a veto on a special committee to be called the Security Council. At San Francisco the United States maintained that the veto could be used only to stop *action* by the Security Council. The Soviet Union argued that the Big Four members should be allowed to veto Security Council *discussion* of an issue.

Stettinius threatened to advise the American government against signing the UN Charter if the Soviet proposal were passed. The conference became deadlocked over the issue, and on May 9 Molotov walked out, leaving ANDREI GROMYKO to head the Soviet delegation. The conference was saved by U.S. presidential adviser HARRY HOPKINS, who secured Stalin's approval of the American proposal during a trip to Moscow on May 25–28, 1945.

For Further Information:
Fleming, D.F. *The Cold War and Its Origins, 1917–1960.* Garden City, N.Y., 1961.
Fontaine, Andre. *History of the Cold War*, vols. 1 and 2. New York, 1965 and 1969.

Satellite Reconnaissance   Satellite reconnaissance is the gathering of intelligence by satellites orbiting the Earth above target areas. The intelligence gathered can be either electronic, in the form of monitored telecommunications traffic, or photographic.

Both the Soviet Union (and now Russia) and the United States have conducted satellite reconnaissance since the 1970s, although it is generally recognized that American technology in this field is far superior.

The first U.S. reconnaissance satellite was developed in the mid-1950s, and the first launching was in August 1960. This was the *Discoverer* satellite, which carried still-photograph cameras. When the satellite had completed its orbit the capsule gondola was released; it fell back toward Earth and was recovered in midair by American planes. This was succeeded in 1961 by the *Samos I* satellite, which carried a television camera capable of transmitting signals back to Earth.

In the 1970s the United States started to launch the KH or Keyhole satellites, which have since been the mainstay of American satellite reconnaissance. The KH-9, or "Big Bird," travels on a north–south orbit at an altitude of up to 167 miles and transmits television-like pictures back to a ground receiv-

ing station. The KH-11 is the largest reconnaissance satellite, standing 75 feet tall and weighing over 15 tons. It gathers SIGNAL or electronic INTELLIGENCE and takes photographs by radio command from the ground. The KH-12 was first launched in 1986 and, like the KH-8, has the ability to detect objects on the ground that are less than six inches across.

The United States also operates the Rhyolite reconnaissance satellite, the geosynchronous orbit of which allows it to remain in a fixed position relative to one place on the Earth's surface. From there it monitors telecommunications and telemetry and relays the intercepts back to a ground station.

Other American reconnaissance satellites include the *Vela*, which is deployed to watch for nuclear explosions and verify Soviet/Russian compliance with nuclear test bans, and the *Midas* early-warning satellite, which is designed to provide an early warning of the launching of missiles toward the United States.

The improvements in satellite technology have made virtually redundant reconnaissance aircraft such as the U-2 and SR-71 spy planes. Newer technology has also made it easier for each side to verify the other's compliance with weapons treaties.

For Further Information:
Klass, Philip J. *Secret Sentries in Space.* New York, 1971.
O'Toole, G.J.A. *The Encyclopedia of American Intelligence and Espionage.* New York, 1988.
Taylor, John, and David Mondey. *Spies in the Sky.* New York, 1972.

Schlesinger, James   (February 15, 1929–   ) James Schlesinger served during the NIXON and FORD administrations first as director of the CENTRAL INTELLIGENCE AGENCY and then as secretary of defense. He established a reputation as a hard-liner on the VIETNAM WAR and U.S.–Soviet détente.

After completing his Ph.D. in economics at Harvard in 1956, Schlesinger taught at the University of Virginia and the Naval War College. In 1963 he joined the air force-funded think tank the RAND CORPORATION as director of strategic studies. In 1968 he joined the Nixon administration as deputy director of the Office of Management and Budget.

In July 1971 Schlesinger was appointed chairman of the Atomic Energy Commission, and in December 1972 he was appointed to succeed RICHARD HELMS as director of the Central Intelligence Agency. At the CIA Schlesinger started some of the first investigations into illegal agency activities and cut the number of agents by 1,000 in his first year. Nixon was so impressed by his work that he appointed Schlesinger chairman of the Intelligence Resources Advisory Commission, giving him responsibility for the activities of the NATIONAL SECURITY AGENCY and the DEFENSE INTELLIGENCE AGENCY. As director of the CIA, Schlesinger attended NATIONAL SECURITY COUNCIL meetings, where he established a reputation as a hawk on the Vietnam War and relations with the Soviet Union. At the height of the Watergate crisis, Schlesinger was moved from the CIA to the Pentagon to become secretary of defense.

A major issue during Schlesinger's tenure at the Pentagon was the second set of STRATEGIC ARMS LIMITATION TALKS (SALT II). The interim SALT I agreement had been signed in May 1972 with a commitment to fresh negotiations and a permanent treaty on offensive weapons within five years. Schlesinger was a major participant in these negotiations.

In the closing days of the Watergate scandal, the SALT II negotiations became deadlocked over the issue of mutual ceilings on MIRVed (MULTIPLE INDEPENDENTLY-TARGETED REENTRY VEHICLES) missiles. Secretary of State HENRY KISSINGER wanted to continue the negotiations, but Schlesinger began openly to block the talks. He took the view that the Soviet Union's growing nuclear capacity had given it an effective second-strike capability and that the SALT process was "seeking to forestall the development of an asymetrical situation which would be beneficial to the Soviet Union." His proposed response to this situation was an increased emphasis on limited nuclear warfare and the retargeting of American missiles from Soviet population centers to missile bases.

Schlesinger's views on limited nuclear warfare were especially controversial. As explained in a Pentagon paper released in May 1975, adopting a policy of limited nuclear warfare would allow the United States to use limited nuclear weapons in any general war in Western Europe as a means of underscoring U.S. determination to prevent Soviet aggression and of forcing the Soviets to negotiate without resorting to all-out nuclear warfare. Opponents argued that such a policy only made nuclear war more likely. America's European allies were especially worried that the policy made it more likely that their countries would become a nuclear battlefield.

Relations between the United States and its allies in the NORTH ATLANTIC TREATY ORGANIZATION (NATO) were also strained by Schlesinger's attacks on their lack of support for American policies. This was brought into the open during the 1973 Yom Kippur War, when the Europeans refused to support Israel openly for fear of alienating the oil-producing Arab states. In October 1973 Schlesinger said that the lack of support would cause the United States to "reflect" on its concepts of military strategy. In December 1974 he warned NATO defense ministers not to undertake defense cuts in the mistaken belief that the United States would bail them out militarily.

Schlesinger's aggressive policies made him a number of enemies within the administration, in the Soviet Union and among NATO allies. He was finally dismissed by President Gerald Ford in November 1975. His dismissal was welcomed in almost all quarters except China, where his tough anti-Soviet stand had made him a popular figure.

Schlesinger returned to government as President JIMMY CARTER's secretary of energy but was dismissed from that post in July 1979. He continued to speak out on defense issues and during the Reagan administration expressed doubts about the president's STRATEGIC DEFENSE INITIATIVE, pointing out to the House Armed Services Committee in February 1985 that a space-based missile defense system would still be vulnerable to low-flying Soviet cruise missiles launched from submarines or bombers. In April 1987 Schlesinger was put in charge of an investigation of security at U.S. embassies after it was learned that the new U.S. Embassy in Moscow was riddled with Soviet listening devices.

For Further Information:
Zumwalt, Elmo. *On Watch*. New York, 1976.

Schmidt, Helmut   (December 23, 1918–   )   Helmut Schmidt succeeded WILLY BRANDT as the chancellor of West Germany. In his early days in the Social Democratic Party (SPD) he was known as a left-winger, but as chancellor he adopted a relatively moderate course. He played a leading role in the decision in 1979 to deploy American cruise and PERSHING II missiles in Western Europe.

Schmidt joined the Hitler Youth as a boy, and during World War II he served as a lieutenant commanding an antiaircraft artillery battery. Some of his political opponents tried in later years to turn his peripheral connections with the Nazi regime against him. But Schmidt was never a convinced Nazi and made it clear that he had fought for his country and not for Hitler.

During the battle of the Bulge Schmidt was taken prisoner by the British, and he was converted to the cause of the Social Democratic Party by his fellow prisoners. In 1945 he enrolled at the university in his native Hamburg, where he studied politics and economics, and the following year joined the SPD. In 1947 he was elected the national chairman of the Socialist Student League.

Schmidt secured a job in the Hamburg city government in 1948 and worked there until he was elected to the Bundestag (the lower house of the West German legislature) in 1953. Schmidt began his political career on the left wing of the party and was at first opposed to basing American nuclear weapons

Helmut Schmidt (right), former Social Democratic chancellor of West Germany, with Franz-Joseph Strauss, long-time leader of the Bavaria-based Christian Social Union. Photo courtesy of the German Ministry of Foreign Affairs.

on German soil. In 1958 he asserted that putting nuclear weapons in Germany was as bad as the Enabling Act, which had given Hitler dictatorial powers. He also enthusiastically supported the RAPACKI PLAN, which called for a nuclear-free zone in Central Europe. Later he felt that he had been "jointly guilty" of preaching a mistaken policy.

The SPD in the 1950s was controlled largely by a prewar old guard, and the ambitious and impatient Schmidt felt blocked from further advancement. In 1961 he resigned his Bundestag seat and returned to Hamburg, where he was appointed the city's minister for internal affairs. The post made his political career. In February 1962 Hamburg was struck by sudden and drastic floods that breached the city's sea defenses. The mayor was on holiday, and Schmidt took command of the relief operations. His actions saved several thousand lives and transformed him overnight into a national hero.

In 1964 Schmidt re-entered the Bundestag and was made SPD shadow minister of defense. He was elected deputy chairman of the SPD in 1966, and when the Grand Coalition was formed in 1967 he became minister of defense under Chancellor Willy Brandt. Schmidt was now accepted as the heir-apparent to Brandt.

By the time of Schmidt's appointment as minister of defense, his political thinking had moved him from the left to the right wing of the SPD. His initial anti-Americanism had been replaced by a desire for full military cooperation with the United States, and he abandoned his earlier calls for a nuclear-free zone. In 1967 Schmidt wrote the book *The Balance of Power*, in which he declared himself in full favor of détente, but added, "It would be foolish to strive for détente while neglecting to provide for the military protection of one's own existence."

From 1972 to 1974 Brandt was first minister of economics and finance and then minister of finance alone. These posts were considered to be part of the process of grooming Schmidt for the chancellorship. Brandt's resignation came sooner than expected in May 1974, when it was discovered that one of his key assistants, GUNTER GUILLAUME, was an East German agent. Brandt assumed responsibility for the security breach and resigned. Schmidt quickly and quietly assumed the chancellorship.

By that time West Germany had shed most of its baggage of guilt from the war and had established itself as the economic powerhouse of Western Europe. But the fact that other European powers continued to fear and distrust West Germany limited Schmidt's scope for political, economic or security initiatives. On issues affecting the EUROPEAN ECONOMIC COMMUNITY (EEC) he continued to let France take the lead, but he developed an extraordinarily close relationship with French President VALERY GISCARD-D'ESTAING, which served to increase West German influence. On security and alliance issues, Schmidt offered no challenge to American leadership.

Schmidt quickly moved to establish good relations with the U.S. administration. In December 1974 he visited Washington, D.C. for talks with President GERALD FORD and Secretary of State HENRY KISSINGER, whom he had first met 20 years earlier when Kissinger had visited Germany. German–American relations under Ford and Schmidt were generally cordial. The VIETNAM WAR, the major potential sore point, was coming to its inglorious end. There was a general consensus that a balance of power was being struck in Europe and that the focus of attention should shift to preventing the spread of Soviet influence in Africa. Schmidt's only serious difference with the Ford administration was over American concern that the German supply of nuclear reactors to Brazil could provide that country with a nuclear weapons capability.

Schmidt did not get on so well with President JIMMY CARTER. He was angered and upset by Carter's decision to halt the deployment of the NEUTRON BOMB because, in his view, it showed an unacceptable weakness by the leader of the Western Alliance. He was also concerned that Carter's tough stand on human rights would lead to a hardening of the Soviet Bloc position rather than to an improvement in the human rights situation.

West Germany felt its attitude toward human rights policy deserved special attention. This was not only because of the 17 million Germans in East Germany but also because of the 300,000 ethnic Germans in Poland and elsewhere in the Soviet Bloc. Brandt's OSTPOLITIK had been specifically designed to ease the plight of those Germans. In Poland 284,000 ethnic Germans had applied for the right to immigrate to West Germany, and in October 1975 Schmidt's government provided 2.3 billion marks in soft loans and partial restitution for Nazi war atrocities to encourage the Polish government to allow them to leave the country. By 1977 this policy was beginning to bear fruit; a total of 55,000 ethnic Germans were allowed to leave East European countries, compared to a total of 63,000 in the previous two years combined.

Relations with East Germany also gradually improved under Schmidt. At the 35-nation CONFERENCE ON SECURITY AND COOPERATION IN EUROPE in 1975, Schmidt and East German leader ERICH HONECKER became the first East German and West German leaders to meet. They met again when Schmidt visited East Germany in December 1981. Schmidt used West Germany's growing financial power to buy additional concessions from the East Germans. In November 1978 new transit agreements were reached that provided for West Germany to build a $700 million autobahn from West Berlin to Hamburg and a $50 million canal around South Berlin. Schmidt's government also agreed to pay an estimated $100 million to the East German government to offset the cost to the East German economy of the emigration of East German pensioners. Schmidt continued the policy of paying the East German government for East German workers who wanted to immigrate to West Germany. In 1978 the East German government released an estimated 1,000 East Germans at an estimated cost to the West German treasury of $50 million.

On the issue of German reunification, Schmidt had started off his political career an ardent advocate and had been prepared to accept neutralization as a necessary price to be paid. But by the early 1970s he was urging his fellow SPD members to instead work to consolidate the good and sound political structures that they had already established in the Federal Republic. By the time Schmidt became chancellor, West German diplomats were being briefed to inform allies that the Schmidt government was in fact wary of reunification because the two Germanies had grown too far apart in political, social and economic terms. Officially, however, Schmidt remained committed to the principle of German reunification.

Relations between Schmidt and Soviet leader LEONID BREZHNEV appeared to get off to a good start when Schmidt visited Brezhnev in Moscow in October 1974. At this meeting Schmidt proposed that West Germany build a nuclear power station for the Soviet Union at Kaliningrad in return for a supply of nuclear power from the station to West Berlin. Schmidt also offered to supply West German pipe for a gas pipeline in return for Soviet natural gas. The nuclear power project was shelved, but the gas pipeline went ahead and later caused a rift between the Reagan administration and America's European allies.

In May 1978 Brezhnev visited Bonn and Schmidt again visited Moscow. In his state-of-the-nation address that year, Schmidt stressed that German–Soviet relations still fell short of the desired goal. At the same time, he stressed that German–Soviet trade was expanding rapidly. In 1978 it was worth nearly $20 billion.

Brezhnev carefully cultivated his relationship with Schmidt and upgraded the Soviet Union's diplomatic staff in Bonn. He believed that the new German leader was preparing a bid for the leadership of Western Europe, and he wanted to be in a position to ensure that this did not involve renewed demands for German reunification. German–Soviet relations suffered a severe setback with the Soviet invasion of AFGHANISTAN and the crackdown on the SOLIDARITY trade union in POLAND. In June 1980 Schmidt visited Moscow and told Brezhnev that the Soviet invasion of Afghanistan "threw a long shadow over East–West relations in Europe."

On strategic issues, Schmidt was a firm supporter of the American position. He enthusiastically endorsed the SALT II Treaty and urged the U.S. Senate to ratify the 1979 agreement quickly. Toward the end of 1978, Schmidt became increasingly concerned about the Soviet deployment of intermediate-range SS-20 nuclear missiles. The presence of the SS-20 missiles on their own threatened to give the Soviet Union the capability to conduct a nuclear war in Europe at the intermediate-range level. The only American nuclear response at that stage was at the tactical nuclear level (which was designed to deter a conventional Soviet attack) or with the U.S.-based long-range strategic weapons. Schmidt, whose strategic thinking had been heavily influenced by Giscard of France, feared that in those circumstances the United States would refuse to counter a Soviet nuclear attack on Western Europe with its strategic arsenal, arguing that the strategic

missiles were needed to deter or counter an attack on the United States. Schmidt's fears appeared to be further justified by increased pressure from the U.S. Congress to reduce U.S. conventional forces in West Germany.

Schmidt and his foreign minister, HANS-DIETRICH GENSCHER, feared that this combination of factors would leave West Germany—and Western Europe—exposed and vulnerable to political and military pressures from the Soviet Union. To counter this threatened "decoupling" process Schmidt proposed that the United States demonstrate its commitment to the defense of Western Europe by deploying American intermediate-range nuclear weapons in Europe as a counter to the SS-20s. This policy was accepted at the NATO foreign ministers' meeting in December 1979, and in 1983 the United States began deployment of cruise and PERSHING II missiles in Western Europe. At the same time, the NATO foreign ministers made it clear that the missiles were being deployed to force the Soviets to negotiate the reduction or withdrawal of their SS-20s.

The deployment of the missiles, however, also sparked a divisive debate in Germany and in the rest of Western Europe. The Germans wanted protection, but they also wanted peace. Many Germans feared that deployment of the missiles was another twist in the arms spiral that brought the world closer to a nuclear disaster that would leave both East and West Germany a pile of irradiated ashes. Their fears were reinforced by the hard-line rhetoric of U.S. president RONALD REAGAN, and the SPD gradually turned against the policy of deployment.

From 1980 to 1982, Schmidt had to fight a constant battle against his own party to secure continued support for the alliance-wide policy that he had initiated. In May 1981 Schmidt had to threaten to resign to secure his party's support for a Bundestag resolution favoring deployment of American intermediate-range missiles on German soil. Even so, several members of the SPD voted against the motion and it passed only narrowly. In March 1982, a group of SPD parliamentarians formed a new left-wing party, the Democratic Socialists, in protest against Schmidt's support for the deployment of the U.S. missiles and his increasingly conservative economic policies.

In October 1982 Schmidt was ousted from power after his coalition partners in the Federal Democratic Party (FDP) deserted him and joined a new coalition with the Christian Democratic Union (CDU), led by HELMUT KOHL. At the SPD conference in Cologne in November 1983 the party voted by a margin of 383 to 14 to oppose deployment of the American missiles. Schmidt was among the 14. The same year, the Social Democrats and Schmidt were soundly beaten in federal elections. In reaction, the party moved further to the left and away from Schmidt's policies. Schmidt announced his resignation from active politics in September 1986, effective January 1987. But he continued to write and speak on security issues after his formal retirement. He is now a principal editor of a weekly political journal published in Hamburg, Die Zeit.

For Further Information:

Bark, Dennis L., and David R. Gress. *A History of West Germany.* Cambridge, Mass., 1989.

Carr, J. *Helmut Schmidt.* New York, 1985.

Fritsch-Bournazel, Renata. *Confronting the German Question.* Oxford and New York, 1988.

Hanrieder, Wolfram F., ed. *Helmut Schmidt, Perspectives on Politics.* Boulder, Colo., 1978.

Jonas, M. *The U.S. and West Germany.* New York, 1985.

Pachter, Henry Maximilian. *A History of Modern Germany: From Wilhelm II to Helmut Schmidt.* Boulder, Colo., 1978.

Pfetsch, Frank. *West Germany, Internal Structures and External Relations: The Foreign Policy of the Federal Republic.* New York, 1988.

Prittie, Terence. *The Velvet Chancellors.* New York, 1979.

Schmidt, Helmut. *The Balance of Power.* London, 1971.

———. *Men and Powers: A Political Retrospective.* New York, 1989.

———. *People and Power.* New York, 1987.

Robert Schuman (left) on November 26, 1947, shaking hands with Paul Ramadier, whom he succeeded as premier of France. Photo courtesy of Popperfoto.

Schuman, Robert   (June 29, 1886–September 4, 1963)

Robert Schuman was one of the key figures of the campaign to unite Europe. As foreign minister of France he was the author of the Schuman Plan, which proposed the formation of the EUROPEAN COAL AND STEEL COMMUNITY, and also played a role in the negotiations that led to the proposal for a EUROPEAN DEFENSE COMMUNITY.

Schuman was born in Luxembourg to prosperous parents and was raised in Metz, in Lorraine, which was then under German rule. He studied law at the universities of Munich, Bonn and Berlin. After the war, Alsace-Lorraine was returned to France, and in 1919 Schuman entered French politics as a deputy for the Popular Democratic Party (PDP) representing Moselle.

At the start of World War II, Schuman was named undersecretary of state responsible for refugees from eastern France. In September 1940 he was arrested by the Germans. He escaped the following year and made his way to Lyon, where he helped to organize Resistance activities.

A devout Roman Catholic, Schuman became a leading figure in the postwar Catholic Left party, the Mouvement Republicain Populaire (MRP), which gained the support of nearly three-quarters of the National Assembly in 1945. Schuman became finance minister in 1946, and he was prime minister from November 1947 until September 1948. It was a frustrating period for him, as most of his time was spent grappling with party divisions that blocked his attempts at economic reform. His government finally fell over Allied plans for West Germany.

Schuman immediately moved to the foreign ministry, where he remained for four years and made his real impact on the structure of postwar Europe. Along with other European statesmen such as JEAN MONNET, he believed that the best way to prevent another European war was to increase the economic interdependence of West European countries. This would, be believed, also lead to political integration, strengthening the European states and enabling them to withstand Soviet pressures without overreliance on the United States.

In May 1950, after discussions with Monnet, Schuman made the first step toward a United States of Europe when he proposed that the coal and steel resources of France and Germany be pooled under a common authority. This would be open to all European countries, and Schuman expressed the hope that it would lead to eventual "European federation." This proposal became known as the Schuman Plan.

The concept was enthusiastically welcomed by the smaller European countries such as Belgium, Holland and Luxembourg, which had already agreed to the Benelux Customs Union. West Germany and Italy were eager to be rehabilitated politically and economically, and France saw itself as able to dominate the new structure. The only unenthusiastic country was Britain, which maintained its traditional policy of interest in, but detachment from, European affairs.

The subsequent treaty establishing the European Coal and Steel Community (ECSC) took effect in June 1952. Under the presidency of Monnet, the ECSC was a political and economic success and encouraged the negotiations that led to the establishment of the EUROPEAN ECONOMIC COMMUNITY.

Schuman's second step toward European integration was the proposal to form a common European army, to be known as the European Defense Community (EDC), which he proposed with Defense Minister René Pleven in November 1950. The EDC was also intended to enable a rearmed Germany to participate in the defense of Western Europe while at the same time checking a possible resurgence of German militarism. But French suspicion of Germany overwhelmed both fear of the Soviet Union and desire for European integration, and the EDC treaty was rejected by the National Assembly in 1954.

Schuman had moved from the Foreign Ministry to the Ministry of Justice before the treaty came before the National Assembly and thus did not play an essential role in its ratifi cation campaign. But he remained strongly committed to the principle of European unity, and when the European Parliamentary Assembly first met in Strasbourg in March 1958 he was elected president by popular acclaim. Schuman held that post until March 1960 and was honorary president until February 1963. He died on September 4, 1963.

For Further Information:

Lodge, J. *Institutions and Policies of the European Community*. London, 1982.

Mason, Henry. *The European Coal and Steel Community*. The Hague, 1955.

Mayne, Richard. *The Recovery of Europe*. New York, 1970.

Mayne, Richard, ed. *Handbooks to the Modern World: Western Europe*. New York, 1986.

Schuman, Robert. *Pour L'Europe*. Paris, 1963.

Scowcroft, Brent (March 19, 1925–   ) Lieutenant General Brent Scowcroft was national security adviser to President GERALD FORD and President GEORGE BUSH. During the REAGAN administration he was chairman of the Scowcroft Commission, which investigated the best means of deploying the MX MISSILE system.

Scowcroft graduated from the U.S. Military Academy at West Point in 1947. He concentrated on the academic side of military life, becoming an instructor in Russian history at West Point in the 1950s and teaching political science at the U.S. Air Force Academy in the 1960s. In 1967 he received his Ph.D. in international relations from Columbia University. He speaks fluent Russian and Serbian.

From 1964 to 1967, Scowcroft was involved in long-range planning at the Pentagon. In 1968 he was on the staff of the assistant secretary of defense for international security affairs, and from 1969 to 1971 he was assistant to the director of the staff of the Joint Chiefs of Staff. He joined the White House staff in November 1971 as military aide to President RICHARD NIXON. In January 1973 he retired from the army and succeeded General ALEXANDER HAIG as deputy to national security adviser HENRY KISSINGER.

Scowcroft became a loyal member of the Kissinger staff, prepared to stay in the shadows while his boss took the limelight. The two men developed a close working relationship, and Kissinger came to rely heavily on Scowcroft's administrative and diplomatic skills. In November 1975 President Gerald Ford reshuffled his cabinet, and Kissinger gave up the dual posts of national security adviser and secretary of state to concentrate on his State Department duties. Scowcroft replaced him at the NATIONAL SECURITY COUNCIL (NSC).

Scowcroft stayed at the NSC until the end of the Ford administration. He continued to remain in the shadow of Kissinger and was criticized by some as "Kissinger's errand boy." By the end of the Ford administration Scowcroft was, in the eyes of many Republican conservatives, tarred by association with Kissinger. This kept him out of formal office when the right-wing RONALD REAGAN assumed office in 1981.

Scowcroft, however, had become an acknowledged expert in arms control and foreign policy issues. In 1983 Reagan named him to head a bipartisan commission on strategic forces. The commission was given a mandate to examine all land-based strategic policy options, but with a special emphasis on the controversial MX Missile system. In its report in April 1983 the commission recommended that the MX system be based in existing Minuteman silos in Wyoming and Nebraska and that a smaller, single-warhead intercontinental ballistic missile be developed for mobile land-based deployment in the 1990s. The recommendations were not fully endorsed by the Reagan administration, and the problem of how best to modernize the U.S. land-based strategic deterrent remained unresolved throughout the Reagan years.

In 1987 Scowcroft joined former Senator John Tower's investigation into the Iran–Contra arms-for-hostages scandal, which plagued the final year of the Reagan administration. He played a major part in composing its less- than-scathing report on the White House national security machinery.

Scowcroft himself has restricted his role to coordinating advice from the bureaucracy and helping the president to devise and implement foreign policy, following the original intent of the 1947 law that established the national security apparatus. He was named national security adviser by president-elect George Bush on November 23, 1988. The two men had come to know each other when Bush served as director of the CENTRAL INTELLIGENCE AGENCY from 1975 to 1976. Bush referred to Scowcroft as "a trusted friend who understands how the White House, the Congress and the intelligence community work."

Seabed Treaty (1971) The 63-nation Seabed Treaty of 1971 prohibited the installation of nuclear weapons on the ocean floor. The treaty was seen as part of the U.S.–Soviet SALT I process, which at the time of the Seabeds Treaty had reached deadlock. (See STRATEGIC ARMS LIMITATION TALKS.)

The treaty was signed on February 11, 1971, at ceremonies in Washington, D.C., Moscow and London. It barred from the seabed beyond the signatories' 12-mile coastal zones "any nuclear weapons and launching installations or any other facilities specifically designed for storing, testing or using such weapons."

Both U.S. president RICHARD NIXON and Soviet premier ALEXEI KOSYGIN welcomed the treaty as part of wider disarmament talks.

Second-Strike Capability   Second-strike capability is a country's ability to survive a nuclear attack and counterattack with its own nuclear weapons.

The maintenance of second-strike capability by both superpowers was at the core of the concept of BALANCE OF TERROR and is believed to have been a successful deterrent; presumably, if one side lost its second-strike capability then the other would be tempted to launch a preemptive strike, which could not then be responded to.

Second-strike capability is maintained in a number of ways. The first is to deploy an increasing number of nuclear missiles so that the enemy cannot possibly eliminate them all in a first strike. Another is to protect land-based intercontinental ballistic missiles by placing them in hardened silos, mounting them on movable launching pads or surrounding them with an effective antiballistic missile system. Finally, nuclear missiles are placed on difficult-to-detect submarines or aircraft such as the TRIDENT submarine or Stealth bomber.

For Further Information:
Kissinger, Henry. *Nuclear Weapons and Foreign Policy.* New York, 1969.
Mayers, T. *Understanding Nuclear Weapons and Arms Control.* London, 1986.

Service, John Stewart   (August 3, 1909–   ) John S. Service was a leading American career diplomat in China whose doubts about the viability of CHIANG KAI-SHEK's Nationalist government made him a target of the extreme political right in the United States.

Born to American missionaries in China, Service returned to China as a Foreign Service officer after graduating from Oberlin College. During the war he was assigned as a political adviser to General Joseph Stilwell and in 1944 was chosen to accompany a military mission to the Chinese communist forces based at Yenan.

His experiences working with both the Nationalist government in Chungking and the communists in Yenan convinced Service that the communists would eventually come to power. Therefore, he advised the U.S. administration to increase its aid to the communist forces to maintain American influence over them. These views conflicted with those of Ambassador PATRICK HURLEY, who accused Service of being pro-communist and campaigned for his removal from the diplomatic service.

Service's cause was further damaged by his involvement in the *Amerasia* affair. Service had supplied Philip Jaffe, the editor of *Amerasia* magazine, with background material, not knowing that Jaffe was suspected of possessing secret government documents. After a raid on the *Amerasia* offices, the FBI charged Service with passing the documents to Jaffe. Service was subsequently cleared by a grand jury, a House Judiciary subcommittee and the State Department Loyalty Review Board.

In 1950, however, Senator JOSEPH MCCARTHY took up the case against Service and charged him with being "a known associate and collaborator with Communists." McCarthy's campaign forced another investigation by the State Department Loyalty Review Board. This time it ruled that there was a "reasonable doubt" about the diplomat's loyalty. He was dismissed by the State Department on December 13, 1951.

Service was reinstated in January 1957 after successfully testing the constitutionality of his dismissal before the Supreme Court. He was reinstated in the State Department with all back pay, but his diplomatic career had been ruined. In 1962 Service left government service to become a resident China scholar at the University of California at Berkeley.

For Further Information:
Kahn, E.J. *The China Hands.* New York, 1973.

Shevardnadze, Eduard   (January 25, 1928–   ) Eduard Shevardnadze was MIKHAIL GORBACHEV's foreign minister during the key years of the 1980s that saw a major lessening of East-West tensions and the beginning of the end of the Cold War. The prime architect of Gorbachev's "new thinking" on foreign policy, he developed a close working relationship with his counterparts in the Reagan and Bush administrations, with whom he helped negotiate U.S.–Soviet arms control pacts and other cooperative measures.

Shevardnadze was born in the Soviet republic of Georgia, where his father was a teacher and local politician. Shevardnadze joined Komsomol, the youth wing of the Communist Party, in 1946, and two years later the party itself. His higher education was confined to a correspondence degree in history from the Kutaisi State Pedgagogical Institute. From 1946 on he concentrated on climbing the ladder of the Georgian Communist Party. In 1965 he was placed in charge of Georgia's police as minister of internal affairs.

As head of the police, Shevardnadze launched a ruthless and successful campaign against corruption, which brought him to the attention of the party leaders in Moscow. In September 1972 he was named secretary general of the Georgian Communist Party and stepped up his fight against apparently endemic corruption. He had hundreds of party officials arrested and imprisoned, and some senior figures in the party hierarchy were forced to surrender illegal posessions.

Shevardnadze was named to the Central Committe of the national Communist Party in 1976 and in 1978 became a candidate (non-voting) member of the Politburo. On July 1, 1985, he was made a full member of the Politburo and on July 2 was named foreign minister in succession to veteran diplomat ANDREI GROMYKO.

Shevardnadze was a surprise appointment as he was relatively young and had no experience in foreign affairs. Western observers were caught unaware and watched carefully Shevardnadze's first major public appearance in July 1985, at the conference in Helsinki on the 10th anniversary of the HELSINKI ACCORDS. Shevardnadze used the conference to sound some of the themes of the new Soviet government's conduct of foreign policy. To start with, his private discussions with other ministers and diplomats were informal and friendly, in marked contrast to the stiff and formal approach usually employed by the Soviet. His speech before the conference was devoid of the usual party rhetoric, and he surprised all those present with a public relations coup in the form of an unprecedented Western-style press conference complete with unrehearsed questions and answers.

The Helsinki Conference also offered an opportunity for Shevardnadze and U.S. secretary of state GEORGE SHULTZ to hold a three-hour bilateral meeting. Afterward, Shultz said, "From all indications we should have an easy ability to talk to each other in a direct and useful way." The major substantive issue discussed by the two men was the agenda for the forthcoming Geneva summit between U.S. President RONALD REAGAN and Soviet leader Mikhail Gorbachev.

The next meeting between Shultz and Shevardnadze took place during the 1985 session of the UN General Assembly, when Shevardnadze stressed that the Soviet Union wanted to "build normal, stable relations with the United States" and added that the Cold War between the United States and the Soviet Union was not the result of "a fated clash of national interests." Much of Shevardnadze's speech, however, was devoted to an attack on President Ronald Reagan's proposed STRATEGIC DEFENSE INITIATIVE (SDI). After his UN speech and meeting with Shultz, Shevardnadze traveled to the White House, where he presented Reagan with a letter from Gorbachev proposing a reduction of up to 50% in the strategic nuclear arsenals of the United States and the Soviet Union.

Shevardnadze continued to play an active role in formulating Soviet arms policy and directing negotiations. He accompanied Gorbachev to all major summit meetings with President Reagan, including the Geneva Summit in 1986, the Reykjavik Summit, the signing of the INTERMEDIATE-RANGE NUCLEAR FORCES (INF) TREATY in 1987 and the follow-up summit meeting in Moscow in 1988. He was consistently opposed to SDI on the grounds that it would effectively breach the 1972 ANTIBALLISTIC MISSILE (ABM) TREATY. He also supported all of Gorbachev's unilateral reductions in defense forces and his proposals to reduce nuclear arsenals.

After making his initial statements on arms negotiations, Shevardnadze concentrated on improving Soviet relations with previously hostile countries in different parts of the world. He carefully coordinated his travels and statements with Gorbachev. Shevardnadze was dispatched on extensive travels, generally to solicit information for a new diplomatic initiative by Gorbachev, to prepare the way for a visit by the Soviet leader or to explain how he was applying *glasnost* principles to Soviet foreign policy. Shevardnadze gave especially high priority to the Asian and Pacific countries, particularly Japan and China.

Soviet–Japanese relations had been strained since the end of World War II, when the Soviet Union occupied four islands at the northern end of the Japanese archipelago. The Japanese had refused to sign a peace treaty or normalize relations with the Soviet Union until the issue was resolved. In January 1986 Shevardnadze became the first Soviet foreign minister to visit Japan in more than a decade. Cultural, trade and technological agreements were signed, but the NORTHERN TERRITORIES issue remained unresolved.

China was a more difficult problem. Gorbachev and Shevardnadze repeatedly stated their desire for an end to the long-running SINO–SOVIET SPLIT, but the Chinese refused to normalize relations until the Soviet Union withdrew from AFGHANISTAN, substantially reduced troop levels on the Chinese–Soviet border and in Mongolia, and persuaded the Vietnamese to withdraw their troops from Cambodia. These demands were gradually met over a four-year period. Shevardnadze visited Beijing in February 1989 to discuss the details for Gorbachev's visit at the end of May 1989.

Afghanistan was the most difficult problem inherited by Shevardnadze. The Afghan war had become the Soviet Union's Vietnam, and its presence in the country seemed only to unite the fundamentalist Islamic guerrillas against the Soviet-supported government. The continued Soviet presence in Afghanistan was also blocking improved relations with other countries and was draining the overstretched Soviet economy. Shevardnadze spent two years trying to negotiate a solution to the Afghan War that involved Pakistan and the Afghan government. Talks finally collapsed because of Pakistan's unwillingness or inability to control the Afghan guerrillas based in its territory. By the start of 1988 Shevardnadze and Gorbachev decided to cut Soviet losses, and the unilateral nine-month withdrawal of Soviet troops began on May 15, 1988. During the withdrawal, Shevardnadze continued to try for a negotiated solution and regularly visited Pakistan to try to persuade the government to end its support of the guerrillas. There was also a failed last-minute attempt to negotiate a coalition government. The Soviets, however, continued to supply the government of President Najibullah after their withdrawal.

Shevardnadze appeared more than willing to link progress on regional issues to progress on arms negotiations and general East–West relations. This flexibility on regional issues is largely explained by Soviet economic problems and the high cost of supporting communist governments in the Third World. On trips to Ethiopia, Angola, CUBA and Vietnam, Shevardnadze made it clear that the Soviet Union could no longer afford to subsidize their economies or their military adventures. This led to the withdrawal of Cuban troops from Angola, the withdrawal of Vietnamese forces from Cambodia, and peace talks between the Ethiopian government and Eritrean rebels. Soviet pressure on the Palestine Liberation Organization (PLO) and its efforts to reestablish diplomatic relations with Israel increased the acceptability of the Soviet Union as a participant in future Middle East negotiations.

In Western Europe, Soviet foreign policy concentrated on gaining access to technical information, establishing trade contacts and winning support for Gorbachev's many arms control initiatives. Shevardnadze focused his attentions on West Germany and secured the support of Chancellor HELMUT KOHL and Foreign Minister HANS-DIETRICH GENSCHER for negotiations to eliminate, or at least reduce, short-range nuclear forces in Europe. British and American opposition to the talks led to a split within the ranks of the NORTH ATLANTIC TREATY ORGANIZATION (NATO) on the eve of a heads-of-government summit to celebrate the 40th anniversary of the founding of the NATO alliance. A major crisis was avoided at the last minute by a compromise solution offered by U.S. president GEORGE BUSH.

In Eastern Europe, Shevardnadze and Gorbachev relaxed the Soviet Union's vise-like control of satellite countries' internal affairs. Shevardnadze represented the Soviet Union at the two-plus-four talks on German reunification that culminated in the signing of the historic unity treaty in September 1990. He was also the primary agent of Gorbachev's policy of noninterference in Eastern Europe as the communist regimes there crumbled under the weight of popular discontent. In October 1989, on the eve of the collapse of the Berlin Wall, he hailed the "historic" changes taking place in the Eastern Bloc nations, vowed a gradual pullout of Soviet troops, and said Moscow was prepared to work toward the dissolution of both the WARSAW PACT and the North Atlantic Treaty Organization—although ultimately it was only the former that would disband.

Perhaps the signature aspect of Shevardnadze's years of service was the constructive and cordial relationship he established with both Shultz and his successor JAMES BAKER, of the Bush administration. He met with both men numerous times, negotiating the INF treaty with Shultz and the 1990 Conventional Forces in Europe pact with Baker, setting the stage for the START accord of 1991, and laying the groundwork for the frequent and successful U.S.–Soviet summits of the Gorbachev era.

He established a particularly close relationship with Baker, with the two men even spending vacations together. It was a far cry from the formal, frosty encounters between senior American and Soviet officials in the earlier years of the Cold War. A high point in the new cooperative relationship came in August 1990, when Shevardnadze joined Baker in issuing a strong denunciation of Iraq for its invasion of Kuwait. The joint statement set the tone for subsequent events, as the Soviet Union worked closely with the United States in the UN Security Council to back military measures against Iraq, a former Soviet ally.

Shevardnadze's close ties with Washington, his role in cutting Eastern Europe loose, his opposition to high levels of defense spending and his strong support for Gorbachev's domestic reforms all combined to make him a suspect figure in the eyes of conservatives in the Communist Party and the Soviet military establishment. Chafing under the increasing attacks on his stewardship, and disheartened by Gorbachev's own shift to the right, Shevardnadze stunned Moscow by announcing his resignation on December 20, 1990.

In an address to the Congress of People's Deputies he said he had grown especially tired of having to defend his policies on German reunification and the Persian Gulf crisis from incessant criticism. He warned that Soviet democratic reformers were retreating before a wave of conservatism that was pushing the U.S.S.R. toward a military dictatorship. Gorbachev was caught unawares by his old friend's abrupt resignation, which he called "unforgivable." He said there was "no evidence" that the country was "on the brink of a coup by the military." Shevardnadze, of course, turned out to be correct, as the August 1991 coup attempt against Gorbachev demonstrated.

Shevardnadze was succeeded by Alexander Bessmertnykh, who was then fired for keeping a low profile during the coup and replaced by Boris Pankin. Meanwhile, Shevardnadze in July 1991 founded the moderate opposition Democratic Reform Movement and quit the Communist Party. He briefly became foreign minister for a second time in November, once again lending his prestige to Gorbachev as he struggled to keep the Soviet Union from breaking apart, which it did the following month.

In March 1992, the ruling military council of the now-independent republic of Georgia chose Shevardnadze to become chairman of a newly created state council. But as the year progressed, Shevardnadze found that even his diplomatic skills were inadequate to the task of ending the bitter civil war that had erupted in Georgia in 1991.

For Further Information:
Bukowski, Charles, and J. Richard Walsh, eds. *Glasnost, Perestroika, and the Socialist Community*. New York, 1990.
Eisen, Jonathan, ed. *The Glasnost Reader*. New York, 1990.
Ledeen, Michael Arthur. *Superpower Dilemmas: The U.S. and the U.S.S.R. at Century's End*. New Brunswick, N.J., 1992.
Oberdorfer, Don. *The Turn: From the Cold War to a New Era: The United States and the Soviet Union, 1983–1990*. New York, 1991.
Shevardnadze, Eduard Amvrosievich. *The Future Belongs to Freedom*. London, 1991.
Staar, Richard Felix. *Foreign Policies of the Soviet Union*. Stanford, Calif., 1991.

Shevchenko, Arkady (October 11, 1930–   ) Arkady Shevchenko was one of the Soviet Union's highest-ranking defectors to the West. His debriefings by the CENTRAL INTELLIGENCE AGENCY exposed a number of Soviet spies, revealed details of Soviet positions on disarmament negotiations and confirmed the KGB's penetration of United Nations agencies.

Shevchenko was born in the Ukraine and in 1949 entered the prestigious Moscow State Institute of International Relations. He specialized in nuclear weapons, strategic issues and international law. He received his doctorate in 1963, with a thesis on Soviet disarmament policy.

While still writing his thesis, Shevchenko joined the Ministry of Foreign Affairs and was assigned to the United Nations desk. In 1958 he joined the Communist Party. From 1960 onward he was an adviser to the Soviet government on nuclear disarmament issues. From 1963 to 1970 he was counselor at the Soviet mission to the United Nations, and from 1970 to 1973 he served with the rank of ambassador as personal political adviser to Foreign Minister ANDREI GROMYKO.

In April 1973, Gromyko nominated Shevchenko to the post of undersecretary general for political and Security Council affairs in the secretariat of the United Nations. The post involved Shevchenko in outer space and disarmament issues, and he was the chief UN official responsible for preparing analyses on those issues for Secretary General KURT WALDHEIM.

Shevchenko, in his book *Breaking Out*, claimed that his observation of the American way of life while in New York made him realize the hypocrisy of the Soviet ruling classes. He said he considered resigning from his UN post and returning to the Soviet Union to join the "dissidents who fight the regime," but realized that this would lead to his spending the rest of his life "in jail or in a mental institution."

Shevchenko claims that he discussed his problems with an American diplomat friend who put him in touch with the CIA. As a result, he says, for two and a half years he was a reluctant spy for American intelligence. At the end of March 1978, Shevchenko received a cable summoning him back to the Soviet Union for consultations. He was convinced that his espionage activities had been discovered and that he was about to be arrested. On April 6, 1978, he formally defected to the United States and was given sanctuary by the CIA. His wife publicly denounced him and returned to the Soviet Union. (According to Soviet authorities, she committed suicide with an overdose of sleeping tablets in May 1978.)

After several months of extensive debriefings, the CIA offered Shevchenko a new identity to protect him from KGB agents. But although Shevchenko had been sentenced to death in absentia for treason, he chose to live a relatively open life and to make his living from writing, broadcasting and giving public lectures.

For Further Information:
Shevchenko, Arkady. *Breaking Out*. New York, 1985.

Shultz, George (December 13, 1920–   ) George Shultz was U.S. secretary of state from June 1982 to January 1989. Working closely with President RONALD REAGAN, he helped to reverse many of the détente policies of the 1970s. At the same time he oversaw successful negotiations for the first reduction in U.S. and Soviet nuclear weapons, at a time of dramatic decline in Soviet world influence.

Shultz was born into a wealthy New York family and was educated at a private school in Connecticut and at Princeton University. He graduated cum laude from Princeton in 1942 and immediately joined the U.S. Marine Corps. During World War II he saw action in the Pacific and rose to the rank of captain.

After the war, Shultz studied for his doctorate in industrial economics at Massachusetts Institute of Technology. After completing his degree he joined the M.I.T. teaching staff as an assistant professor of industrial relations. In 1955 Shultz took a leave of absence from M.I.T. to accept a position as senior staff economist on President DWIGHT EISENHOWER's council of economic advisers. In 1957 he moved to the University of Chicago, where he became dean of the Graduate School of Business.

During the KENNEDY and JOHNSON administrations, Shultz served as a consultant on labor-management relations. President RICHARD NIXON nominated him as secretary of labor in December 1969 and then in June 1970 moved him to the newly created Office of Management and Budget. In May 1972 Shultz was moved again, this time to take over as secretary of the treasury. This brought him into the foreign policy field, and Shultz represented the United States at meetings of the International Monetary Fund and the General Agreement on Tariffs and Trade and signed a series of trade agreements with the Soviet Union in June 1972. Following the resignation of Nixon, Shultz stayed briefly with the FORD administration, but left in March 1975 without having been tarnished by the Watergate scandal.

After leaving Washington, Shultz joined the Bechtel Corporation as executive vice president and soon was made president. Following the election of Ronald Reagan as president in November 1980, Shultz was the front-runner for the post of secretary of state. But Reagan also wanted to nominate Bechtel executive Caspar Weinberger as secretary of defense and decided he could not appoint two Bechtel executives to two key positions in his administration. Therefore, he appointed General ALEXANDER HAIG as his first secretary of state. Haig's style clashed with the other members of Reagan's foreign policy team, and when he resigned in June 1982, the president asked Shultz to take over at the State Department.

Shultz was well suited to the role of secretary of state in the Reagan administration. He was a negotiator and mediator by training and inclination, complementing Reagan's more confrontational style. Shultz's instinct for the negotiated solution did at times bring him into conflict with the president and some of his more right-wing advisers, especially with the succession of national security advisers and occasionally with Weinberger. It also led many conservative Republicans to brand the secretary of state as a "closet liberal." Shultz, however, was as innately conservative as Reagan, and the two men appeared to think along similar, if not identical, lines on most of the major foreign policy issues.

One of Shultz's first tasks was to resolve the dispute between the Reagan administration and its European allies over the sale of Soviet natural gas to Western Europe and over the help provided by Western Europe in building the pipeline to carry the gas from Siberia. Reagan opposed both the purchase of the gas and the sale of construction equipment for the pipeline, arguing that these actions made West European economies unacceptably dependent of the Soviet Union.

Shultz quietly defused the crisis at an informal meeting of NATO foreign ministers in Montreal at which he agreed to end U.S. opposition to the pipeline in return for a general NATO economic policy toward the Soviet Union.

While the CENTRAL INTELLIGENCE AGENCY (CIA) under Reagan used Pakistan to supply arms to Muslim rebels fighting Soviet troops in AFGHANISTAN, Shultz pursued the diplomatic track. In April 1988 he signed an agreement to guarantee that Pakistan would abide by a simultaneous agreement not to interfere or intervene in the affairs of Afghanistan, thus setting the stage for the withdrawal of Soviet troops.

Shultz understood that the Soviet economy and those of other Soviet Bloc countries were in serious trouble and that this was forcing them to make economic reforms that would likely bring political reforms in their wake. He promised U.S. support for individuals and groups in communist countries who "seek peaceful change."

Shultz was a strong supporter of Reagan's tough defense policy, but he became embroiled in the controversy over the STRATEGIC DEFENSE INITIATIVE and whether it violated the 1972 ANTIBALLISTIC MISSILE (ABM) TREATY. Key foreign and defense policy figures soon split over the stand to take on SDI. The dividing point was the ABM Treaty. Those wholly in favor of SDI regardless of Soviet sensibilities favored a new, "broad interpretation" of the ABM Treaty, which would allow deployment of space-based defense systems. The "narrow" interpretation, subscribed to by previous administrations, forbade such deployment. Defense Secretary Caspar Weinberger supported the broad interpretation and Reagan leaned toward this view. Shultz, however, supported the narrow interpretation and managed to win the president over to a grudging acceptance of this position during debates of the issue in the NATIONAL SECURITY COUNCIL or at cabinet meetings.

Shultz's main concern about SDI was that it would scuttle the INTERMEDIATE-RANGE NUCLEAR FORCES (INF) and STRATEGIC ARMS REDUCTION (START) TREATY talks being held in Geneva. The START talks, which succeeded the unratified SALT II Treaty, involved U.S. and Soviet strategic nuclear weapons systems, while the INF talks involved intermediate-range systems based in Europe.

In May 1988 Shultz went with Reagan to Moscow for the fourth Reagan–Gorbachev summit. While there he signed two new U.S.–Soviet arms agreements. One required either superpower to notify the other 24 hours before the test launching of a land- or sea-based ballistic missile, and the other codified a 1987 agreement in principle on monitoring the yields of underground nuclear tests. Shultz and Shevardnadze also launched East–West talks on reducing conventional forces in Europe (known as "CFE"), which replaced the moribund Mutual Balance Force Reduction (MBFR) talks.

Shultz developed a good working relationship with Soviet foreign minister EDUARD SHEVARDNADZE and a possibly even closer relationship with MIKHAIL GORBACHEV. He met the Soviet president for the first time at the funeral of KONSTANTIN CHERNENKO in March 1985 and discovered that the two men had a common interest in economics. At the end of Shultz's tenure at the State Department, Gorbachev paid him the rare compliment of singling him out as the leading figure in the Reagan administration who had worked for improved Soviet–American relations and added that Shultz was somebody who "defends the American position very well" and who is "solid and reliable."

Shultz also had to deal with a deterioration in America's strategic position in the Pacific. The first blow was the election of the New Zealand Labor Party, whose government, under Prime Minister David Lange, banned visits to New Zealand ports by ships carrying nuclear weapons. This effectively ended defense cooperation between New Zealand and the United States and led to the breakup of the ANZUS alliance of Australia, New Zealand and the United States. In an attempt to replace ANZUS, Shultz forged closer bilateral political and security links with Australia. Australia in turn increased its bilateral cooperation with New Zealand.

The PHILIPPINES presented another set of problems. The overthrow of Philippine dictator Ferdinand Marcos in 1986 was welcomed by Shultz. But the new government of Corazon Aquino came under strong pressure from its left-wing supporters to close the American military bases on the islands. The bases were regarded as essential to American policy in the Far East and Pacific, and Shultz opened negotiations with Foreign Minister Raul Manglapus. These talks resulted in a new U.S.–Philippines Treaty, signed in October 1988, which kept the bases open but increased the cost to the U.S. Treasury by two-and-a-half times, to $481 million in military and economic assistance.

Central America, and in particular the leftist Sandinista government of NICARAGUA, which had taken power after a popular revolt against an American-supported dictator, was a dominant factor in the Reagan administration's foreign policy. In June 1984 Shultz visited Nicaragua for talks with President Daniel Ortega. Shultz's trip was billed not as an attempt at "bilateral negotiation" but as part of a diplomatic process initiated by the "Contadora Group" of Central American heads of state in an attempt to find an adequate political resolution to the American-sponsored Contra insurgency.

The conditions laid down by Shultz, however, were impossible for Ortega to agree to, and by February 1985, Shultz threw his weight behind President Reagan's hard-line policy of military and financial support for the Contra rebels. He told the U.S. Senate Foreign Relations Committee that month that the Contras deserved help because they were "fighting for freedom." He later argued before the U.S. House Foreign Affairs Committee that Nicaragua under the Sandinistas was a "Communist tyranny" and that those who opposed aid to the Contras were, in effect, consigning Nicaragua to "endless darkness." This led Democratic Representatives Ted Weiss and Peter Kostmayer to accuse Shultz of "red-baiting."

The logic of Shultz's support for the Contras also led him toward increased support for covert actions and right-wing subversion or guerrilla warfare against left-wing governments everywhere. This policy, which became known as the Reagan Doctrine, was outlined by Shultz in an article in the Spring 1985 edition of the journal *Foreign Affairs* entitled "Shaping American Foreign Policy: New Realities and New Ways of Thinking." Shultz wrote that if the United States did not support anti-leftist rebels "we would be conceding the Soviet notion that Communist revolutions are irreversible while everything else is up for grabs." He added, "So long as Communist dictatorships feel free to aid and abet insurgencies in the name of 'socialist internationalism,' why must the democracies, the target of this threat, be inhibited from defending their own interests and the cause of democracy itself?"

But Shultz's support for covert action did not extend to involvement in the Iran–Contra arms scandal. He told the congressional committee investigating the affair that he had been kept in the dark about the operation and claimed that when he had discovered the details in November 1986 he had told Reagan, "Back off—all the way." The subsequent Tower Commission report claimed that Shultz and Weinberger had "simply distanced themselves from the plan." National security adviser John Poindexter, later convicted on charges related to the scandal, said that he hadn't withheld anything from them that they hadn't wanted withheld.

After leaving the government at the end of the Reagan administration in January 1989, Shultz moved back to California to teach part-time at Stanford University and work as a consultant to the Bechtel Corporation.

Signal Intelligence   Signal intelligence (Sigint) is intelligence gathered from the interception of messages such as telephone conversations, telegrams, telexes, radio, radar and electronic impulses.

With the increased reliance on electronic communications since World War II, Sigint has taken on an increasingly important role and provides a significant portion of the raw data gathered by intelligence communities.

In the Soviet Union, Sigint was handled by the KGB and the GRU. In the United States it is operated by the NATIONAL SECURITY AGENCY (NSA), which works closely with Britain's GOVERNMENT COMMUNICATIONS HEADQUARTERS (GCHQ) at Cheltenham. Since the 1950s the British and Americans have maintained a string of land-based radar listening posts encircling the Soviet Union and China. They also operate listening posts from air- and sea-based platforms. A large proportion of the Soviet listening platforms were based on ships. In recent years, both the United States and the U.S.S.R. (and now Russia) have come to rely increasingly on SATELLITE RECONNAISSANCE for their signal intelligence.

By the early 1970s, American equipment was so sophisticated that the National Security Agency was able to intercept radio-telephone conversations of senior Soviet officials traveling around Moscow in their limousines.

For Further Information:
Bamford, James. *The Puzzle Palace.* Boston, 1982.

Sino–Soviet Split   The Sino–Soviet Split (the break in relations between the PEOPLE'S REPUBLIC OF CHINA and the Soviet Union from 1960 to 1989) divided the communist world into two major camps and substantially weakened it as an international force. It also provided a diplomatic opportunity, which was exploited by the United States.

In February 1950 China and the Soviet Union signed the SINO-SOVIET TREATY OF FRIENDSHIP, ALLIANCE AND MUTUAL ASSIS-

TANCE and created what CHOU EN-LAI called a force of 700 million people "which it is impossible to defeat."

For the first six years of the 30-year treaty, the two countries seemed inextricably tied together, with the Soviet Union cast in the role of senior partner and China approaching the status of satellite. The Chinese Army was modeled along Soviet lines, and Soviet technical advisers played an increasing role in Chinese industry. In 1956, however, two events shook Chinese confidence in the Soviet leadership. The first was NIKITA KHRUSHCHEV's denunciation of Stalin and the second was the Soviet invasion of Hungary.

After the attack on Stalin, Chinese leader MAO ZEDONG called a special meeting of the Chinese Communist Party Politburo to discuss how to deal with the change in Moscow. The consensus was that the Chinese should do everything possible to limit the attack to Stalin's personality and not let it become an attack on his economic and political policies, which were the models for China's policies.

In repressing the Hungarian Revolution the Soviet Union was seen to be forcing its policies on another socialist country. The Chinese were particularly sensitive on this issue because of their own historical experience with colonialism. They supported sending Soviet troops into HUNGARY but argued that the invasion would have been unnecessary if the Soviet Union had not pursued hegemonic policies in Eastern Europe. Mao seemed to climb down from this position the following year when he declared, "The socialist camp must have a head and this head is the Soviet Union." But the two issues—nationalist-inspired communism versus Soviet-controlled communism and Stalinism versus the more liberal policies of Khrushchev—eventually produced a distinct Maoist variety of communism, which brought the Chinese into increasing conflict with the new leadership in Moscow.

In 1958 China launched its "Great Leap Forward" campaign, promoting massive collectivization and state-sponsored industrialization reminiscent of the Stalinist program for Soviet industry and agriculture in the 1930s. This was developed and launched without the approval of Khrushchev who, when he learned of its details, criticized it severely.

At about the same time, the Soviet Union agreed to help the Chinese to develop nuclear weapons. But they tied their assistance to an insistence that China officially subordinate its foreign and defense policies to those of the Soviet Union. Mao might have been able to accept this, but in 1959 Khrushchev withdrew the offer, allegedly under pressure from the United States.

Khrushchev and Mao also became increasingly divided over what policies to adopt toward the United States. Khrushchev was trying to improve relations through his policy of PEACEFUL COEXISTENCE. Mao, who was fearful of an American-supported attack by CHIANG KAI-SHEK, opposed any rapprochement with the United States.

By the summer of 1960, the two communist giants had approached an open split. This came at a meeting of the congress of the Soviet Communist Party in June 1960 when

Khrushchev circulated a letter to the other delegations accusing the Chinese of failing to understand "the character of the present era." The letter went on to attack Chinese behavior and pointed out the folly of China's internal policies. The Chinese counterattacked by accusing Khrushchev of "revisionism." With the split in the open, Khrushchev withdrew all Soviet technicians from China, creating an economic crisis in that country. Attempts were made to restore relations at a conference of communist parties in Moscow in November 1960 and again in October 1961. But these conferences served only to underscore the differences and to enlarge the split.

By the mid-1960s, relations had deteriorated to such a level that the two countries had heavily fortified their common border. Because of historical differences over the exact line of the boundary, there were sporadic military clashes, which threatened to erupt into war until a temporary border agreement was negotiated by Chou En-lai and ALEXEI KOSYGIN.

In the meantime, the international communist camp had split into two factions—those supporting China and those supporting the Soviet Union. Most communist governments, with the exception of Albania's, supported the Soviet Union because of their heavy reliance on Soviet aid. Some such as North Korea and North Vietnam steered an uneasy course between the two. In countries where communists were still struggling for power, the Maoist faction invariably took the more radical course, and the traditional Communist Party followed Moscow. The bitterness of the dispute meant that even in the most obscure corners of the world, the two factions spent more time fighting each other than the capitalist social system they both aspired to replace.

The growing overt hostility of the Soviet Union forced China to look toward the West for protection. The U.S. government, because of its basic mistrust of communist China and because of the powerful pro-Taiwan lobby in the United States, was slow to react. It was not until 1971–72 that President RICHARD NIXON played the "China Card" and reestablished diplomatic contact with Beijing.

Soviet president LEONID BREZHNEV made several halfhearted attempts to heal relations, but always on Soviet terms. These were repeatedly rebuffed by China, and the Soviet Union set out to increase its military advantage by further reinforcing the Sino-Soviet border and providing extensive military aid to China's traditional enemy, Vietnam. The Chinese also claimed that the Soviet invasion of AFGHANISTAN was part of a Soviet policy of encirclement.

It was not until MIKHAIL GORBACHEV came to power in Moscow that the Soviet Union made a major attempt at reconciliation. He was at first rebuffed by the Chinese leadership, which insisted that relations could not be improved until the Soviet-backed Vietnamese withdrew their forces from Cambodia, Soviet forces in Afghanistan were withdrawn and the Soviets agreed to withdraw their forces from Mongolia and the Sino–Soviet border. Gorbachev, who could not afford to maintain the heavy defense expenditures of the Brezhnev era, agreed, and the split was formally ended when he visited Beijing in May 1989. However, Soviet relations with the rest of the Communist Bloc countries had changed so dramatically that there was no suggestion that the Sino–Soviet relationship would return to the same level it had reached in 1950–56.

For Further Information:

Camilleri, J. *Chinese Foreign Policy: The Maoist Era and Its Aftermath.* Seattle, 1980.
Clubb, Oliver Edmund. *China and Russia: The "Great Game."* New York, 1971.
Ginsburgs, G., and C.F. Pinkele. *The Sino-Soviet Territorial Dispute, 1949–1964.* New York, 1978.
Griffiths, William E. *The Sino-Soviet Rift.* New York, 1964.
Low, A.D. *The Sino-Soviet Dispute.* Rutherford, N.J., 1976.
Segal, G. *The Soviet Union in East Asia.* Boulder, Colo., 1983.
Zagorian, Donald. *The Sino-Soviet Conflict, 1956–1961.* Princeton, 1962.

Sino–Soviet Treaty of Friendship, Alliance and Mutual Assistance (1950) The Sino–Soviet Treaty of Friendship, Alliance and Mutual Assistance, signed in February 1950, marked the high point of relations between communist China and the Soviet Union. For many years it was used by the pro-Taiwan "China Lobby" in the United States as proof that communist China was a Soviet satellite and therefore should be denied diplomatic recognition.

The agreement was signed in Moscow on February 14, 1950, after nine weeks of negotiation. Two other agreements—one promising the return of Soviet-held properties in Manchuria and the other giving China a five-year, $300 million loan for Soviet industrial equipment—were signed at the same time. The main points of the agreement were:

1. The treaty was to last for 30 years and replace the Soviet Union's friendship treaty with the Nationalist government of China.
2. The two countries promised that if either country were attacked by Japan or "any other state that directly or indirectly would unite with Japan in acts of aggression" the other country would "immediately render military or other aid with all means at its disposal."
3. China and the Soviet Union pledged to respect each other's "sovereign and territorial integrity," practice "non-intervention in the internal affairs of the other country" and "render each other every possible economic aid."

After the signing of the pact, Chinese foreign minister CHOU EN-LAI said that the Soviet Union and China were welded into a single force of 700 million people, "which it is impossible to defeat." U.S. secretary of state DEAN ACHESON said that the pact meant trouble for China, as the Soviet Union would use it to make China a Soviet satellite.

During the first few years of the agreement, the Soviets did in fact use the agreement to play an increasing role in Chinese affairs. The Soviets even agreed to supply the Chinese with nuclear weapons, only in exchange for Soviet control of Chinese foreign and defense policy. At this point, the Chinese began to back away from Moscow. The differences were heightened by NIKITA KHRUSHCHEV's denunciation of Stalin in 1956, and the countries drifted further apart until the formal SINO–SOVIET SPLIT in 1960 and the subsequent renunciation of the 1950 treaty.

For Further Information:
Clubb, Oliver Edmund. *China and Russia: The "Great Game."* New York, 1971.
Ginsburgs, G., and C.F. Pinkele. *The Sino-Soviet Territorial Dispute, 1949–1964.* New York, 1978.
Griffiths, William E. *The Sino-Soviet Rift.* New York, 1964.
Low, A.D. *The Sino-Soviet Dispute.* Rutherford, N.J., 1976.

Smith, Gerard   (May 4, 1914–   )   Gerard Smith was director of the ARMS CONTROL AND DISARMAMENT AGENCY (ACDA) and chief U.S. negotiator at the STRATEGIC ARMS LIMITATION TALKS (SALT I). The negotiations resulted in the SALT I and ANTIBALLISTIC MISSILE (ABM) treaties of 1972, the first negotiated limitations on strategic nuclear weapons.

Smith graduated from Yale Law School in 1938 and served with the U.S. Navy during World War II. After the war he worked in private law practice before joining the Atomic Energy Commission in 1950. During the KENNEDY and JOHNSON administrations he served as counsel to the Washington Center for Foreign Policy Research. In 1969 President RICHARD NIXON appointed Smith director of ACDA and chief delegate to the SALT I negotiations.

Preparations for the negotiations had been made in the closing stages of the Johnson administration, but the talks had been indefinitely postponed after the Warsaw Pact invasion of CZECHOSLOVAKIA in August 1968. They did not start until November 1969. In the intervening period the Nixon administration committed itself to the deployment of an antiballistic missile system to counter the Soviet Galosh ABM system already in place.

The commitment had been made with considerable debate, with the opponents of ABM deployment arguing that a pro-ABM decision would only fuel the spiraling arms race and send the wrong signals to Moscow. Smith favored ABM deployment, testifying before the U.S. Congress in November 1969 that the system would be a valuable "bargaining chip" in SALT talks and would reduce the Soviet capability for a surprise attack.

Before the ABM system won congressional approval, the Soviet emphasis had been on limiting offensive weapons where the United States enjoyed a three-to-one superiority. But the victory of the pro-ABM faction led the Soviets to shift the focus of their concern from offensive to defensive systems. They realized that the United States had the technological edge and that if it came to an ABM race the Americans would win. Therefore, it would benefit the Soviet Union to reach an agreement on defensive systems while it still had an advantage.

Formal negotiations began in Helsinki on November 17, 1969. Smith led the American negotiators, and the Soviets were led by Deputy Foreign Minister Vladimir Semyonov. Although Smith conducted the talks, most of the policy for the American team was established and directed by national security adviser HENRY KISSINGER, working with a small team in Washington known as the verification panel. The negotiations themselves alternated between Helsinki and Vienna.

Running in tandem with the SALT negotiations were talks on Seabed Arms Control and a Nuclear Accident Agreement. Smith also conducted these negotiations, which were concluded in 1971 (see SEABED TREATY [1971]). The first prohibited the installation of nuclear weapons on the seabed outside the 12-mile limit of any nation, and the second established cooperative procedures in the event of a nuclear accident. Both countries also agreed to ban biological warfare.

Despite this progress, it became clear by the end of 1970 that SALT was deadlocked over several issues, including the Soviet desire for an ABM-only treaty, Soviet insistence that American forward-based systems (FBS) be included in negotiations, and American efforts to tighten limits on land-based ICBMs (INTERCONTINENTAL BALLISTIC MISSILES) and relax limits on SLBMs (submarine-launched ballistic missiles) where America's easier access to open waters gave the United States the advantage.

With the negotiations between Smith and Semyonov deadlocked, Kissinger turned to the "back channel" and initiated secret negotiations between himself and ANATOLY DOBRYNIN, the Soviet ambassador in Washington. Smith knew little or nothing about these negotiations and carried on talking with Semyonov, sometimes making suggestions completely at variance with Kissinger's.

The secret negotiations, however, did achieve a breakthrough when the two sides agreed to separate negotiations on offensive and defensive weapons and to aim for two treaties. Because there were fewer areas of difference on ABM systems, Smith and his negotiators concentrated on that side of the strategic equation with the result that the negotiations for the offensive systems were not completed until hours before the treaty was signed on May 23, 1972, in Moscow by President Richard Nixon and Soviet leader LEONID BREZHNEV.

After the signing of the treaties, Smith lobbied for their passage through Congress. He resigned as head of ACDA in January 1973. In 1977 Smith joined the CARTER administration as an ambassador-at-large involved with the problem of nuclear proliferation. During the REAGAN administration he became an opponent of the president's STRATEGIC DEFENSE INITIATIVE and "broad interpretation" of the ABM Treaty.

For Further Information:
Newhouse, John. *Cold Dawn: The Story of SALT.* New York, 1973.
Smith, Gerard. *Doubletalk.* Garden City, N.Y., 1980.

Smith, Walter Bedell   (October 5, 1895–August 9, 1961)   General Walter Bedell Smith held three key positions from

1946 to 1954: U.S. ambassador to the Soviet Union, director of the CENTRAL INTELLIGENCE AGENCY and undersecretary of state. He is generally regarded as a leading Cold War hawk. After his official retirement, he continued to advise the EISENHOWER administration on disarmament issues.

Smith started his career in the army with the Indiana National Guard. During World War I he served in France and then remained in the peacetime army. By 1942 he was a brigadier general. He was assigned to General Dwight Eisenhower's staff, where he developed a close relationship with the future president, planning the invasions of Italy, North Africa and Normandy.

In February 1946, President HARRY S. TRUMAN appointed Smith ambassador to the Soviet Union. He remained at the post until March 1949. He was also the American representative at U.S.–Soviet negotiations during the BERLIN Blockade.

Upon his return to Washington, Smith wrote *My Three Years in Moscow*, in which he argued that the Soviets would not seek peaceful coexistence with the West because of an ideological determination to destroy capitalism. He believed that the Soviet Union was unlikely to attack Western Europe as long as the West maintained strong defenses.

Smith left the diplomatic service to return to the military as commander of the First Army, but in October 1950 Truman asked him to take over from ROSCOE HILLENKOETTER as director of the CIA. Hillenkoeter had seemed unable to cope with the Washington bureaucracy, adversely affecting the agency's intelligence activities in Korea, where it failed to predict the North Korean invasion. Smith set about to reorganize the CIA. Among the changes he made were: creation of the Office of National Estimates to evaluate intelligence; tighter control of covert operations; establishment of a directorate for administration to oversee the budget, personnel, and logistical support for overseas operations; creation of the Directorate for Intelligence to conduct political and scientific studies; and the establishment of the Directorate of Plans. The structure Smith created remained intact for the next 20 years.

On January 10, 1954, Eisenhower named Smith undersecretary of state. Smith hoped that the combination of the number-two position in the State Department and his past relationship with Eisenhower would give him a major say in foreign policy, but Secretary of State JOHN FOSTER DULLES organized the department so that he himself dominated policy. Smith's main role was as an administrator.

He did, however, play an important role in American policy in Indochina as head of the National Security Council's Special Committee on the United States and Indochina. The committee was formed to develop an American response to the deteriorating French situation in Vietnam. The committee, at Smith's urging, proposed that the administration and its main allies establish a mutual defense treaty to protect the area from further communist insurgency. This led to the establishment of the SOUTHEAST ASIA TREATY ORGANIZATION.

Smith also advocated direct American involvement in Indochina in support of the French, preferably in tandem with Britain. When British foreign secretary ANTHONY EDEN refused British support, Smith proposed that the United States enter the war with Australia or New Zealand. The fall of DIEN BIEN PHU on May 7, 1954, prevented this. Smith was sent to Geneva to represent the United States at the talks that led to the partition of Vietnam.

Smith went into official retirement in October 1954, but he continued to act as an unofficial adviser on disarmament issues. He died on August 9, 1961.

For Further Information:

Cline, Ray S. *The CIA: Reality vs. Myth.* Washington, D.C., 1982.
O'Toole, G.J.A. *The Encyclopedia of American Intelligence and Espionage.* New York, 1988.
Ranelagh, John. *The Agency: The Rise and Decline of the CIA.* New York, 1986.
Smith, Walter Bedell. *My Three Years in Moscow.* New York, 1949.

Sobell, Morton (April 11, 1917–) Morton Sobell was convicted as a Soviet spy, along with JULIUS AND ETHEL ROSENBERG, on charges of selling American atomic secrets, but he has consistently maintained that he is an innocent victim of the 1950s communist witch hunt.

After graduating from the City College of New York in 1938, Sobell took a job in Washington, D.C. with the Navy Bureau of Ordnance. During World War II he worked in General Electric's aircraft and marine engineering divisions. Later he moved to New York City, where he worked for the Rees Instrument Corporation, which manufactured top-secret radar equipment for the government.

Sobell was arrested on August 18, 1950, in Laredo, Texas after being deported from Mexico. He was a former classmate and close friend of Julius Rosenberg and was charged with belonging to the same spy ring that gave atomic secrets to the Soviet Union. Sobell maintained his innocence from the moment he was arrested.

Sobell was convicted mainly on the evidence of Max Elitcher, who testified that Sobell and Julius Rosenberg had tried to recruit him as a Soviet spy. Sobell's case was further damaged by his trip to Mexico and the fact that he had written from there using several aliases. Sobell maintained that he was in Mexico on holiday with his family and that he had been kidnapped by the FBI. The prosecution maintained that Sobell had fled to Mexico on his way to Eastern Europe. On the advice of his lawyers, Sobell declined to testify on his own behalf.

Sobell was found guilty by a federal jury on March 29, 1951, and sentenced to 30 years in prison. The conviction marked the start of a long campaign by Sobell, his wife and others to clear his name and, by association, the names of Julius and Ethel Rosenberg, who had been found guilty and executed. During the 1950s the campaign was led by Sobell's wife Helen, who formed the Committee to Free Morton Sobell.

Between 1953 and 1958 there were eight attempts to

persuade the U.S. Supreme Court to review the Sobell case. All were refused. In 1953 Sobell reversed his earlier decision not to testify and submitted a detailed affidavit explaining his activities prior to leaving for Mexico and while in Mexico, in hopes that this would secure him a retrial. This also failed as did a 1962 petition for clemency signed by such leading liberal figures as Martin Luther King, Senator Lee Metcalf and Reinhold Niebuhr.

Sobell was released in 1969 after serving 17 years and nine months in prison. In 1971 his parole board refused Sobell permission to attend anti-VIETNAM WAR demonstrations. He successfully sued the parole board for violation of his constitutional rights. In 1974 he wrote *On Doing Time*, which gave his version of the case and related his experiences while in prison. He and his wife continued to campaign to clear his and the Rosenbergs' name.

On June 15, 1979, in an article in the *New Republic*, Sol Stern and Ronald Radosh concluded that Sobell and the Rosenbergs had indeed been Soviet spies. They based the conclusion on more than 200,000 pages of files released by the FBI under the Freedom of Information Act and on interviews with people involved in the case.

For Further Information:

Buranelli, Vincent, and Nan Buranelli. *Spy/Counterspy: An Encyclopedia of Espionage*. New York, 1982.
Radosh, Ronald, and Joyce Milton. *The Rosenberg File: A Search for the Truth*. New York, 1983.
Schneir, Walter, and Miriam Schneir. *Invitation to an Inquest*. Baltimore, 1973.

Solidarity *See* POLAND.

Solzhenitsyn, Alexander (December 11, 1918–   )
Alexander Solzhenitsyn is the most prominent Soviet dissident author. His works such as *One Day in the Life of Ivan Denisovich* graphically portray the horrors of the Stalinist labor camps and won him the Nobel Prize for literature. Solzhenitsyn was denounced by the Brezhnev regime and in 1974 became the first person since Trotsky to be stripped of his Soviet citizenship and expelled from the country.

Solzhenitsyn was raised in the south Russian port city of Rostov-on-Don. He attended the University of Rostov, from which he graduated in 1941 with a degree in physics and mathematics. During World War II he commanded an artillery battery and distinguished himself during the battle of Leningrad.

Toward the end of the war, Solzhenitsyn wrote a letter to a friend in which he criticized JOSEF STALIN. The letter fell into the hands of the KGB, and in February 1945 Solzhenitsyn was arrested and sentenced to eight years' imprisonment. He spent some of his imprisonment as a laborer in Moscow, some in a research institute and most of it at a labor camp in Kazakhstan. During his confinement, Solzhenitsyn contracted cancer, which was successfully arrested.

Solzhenitsyn was released in 1956 and took a teaching job in the industrial city of Ryazan. In 1962 he submitted his short novel *One Day in the Life of Ivan Denisovich* to the Soviet literary journal *Novy Mir*. The book, based on Solzhenitsyn's own experiences, described a routine day in the life of a Russian sentenced to a labor camp on trumped-up espionage charges. The editor of *Novy Mir* was so impressed by the novel that he sent the manuscript to the Communist Party Central Committee. Soviet leader NIKITA KHRUSHCHEV saw it and decided to allow the novel's publication as part of his anti-Stalinist campaign. The story of Ivan Denisovich was an overnight bestseller, established Solzhenitsyn in the first rank of Soviet authors and gained him admission to the prestigious Union of Soviet Writers.

Solzhenitsyn continued to write short anti-Stalinist novels, which were published in *Novy Mir* and republished in the West, where they also won high praise. But a number of Politburo members questioned Khrushchev's decision to allow publication of Solzhenitsyn's works. The first indication that the writer was falling out of favor came in 1964 when he failed to win the Lenin Prize for literature because, it was said, his work failed to distinguish between "honorable and good people" on the one hand and "criminals and traitors" on the other.

Official disapproval of Solzhenitsyn grew after the overthrow of Khrushchev in October 1964. His novel *Cancer Ward* was denied publication, and the manuscript of his novel *First Circle* was confiscated, along with a number of short stories and plays. Solzhenitsyn fought back in May 1967 when he launched a scathing attack on the Soviet leadership for its censorship of Soviet literature. In a letter distributed at the Fourth National Congress of Soviet Writers, he called on the congress to "demand . . . the abolition of all censorship, overt or hidden, of all fictional writing," and called on the Union of Soviet Writers to establish "guarantees for the defense of . . . members who are subjected to slander and injustice."

Solzhenitsyn was not allowed to address the congress in person, but his letter was widely circulated and was published in the *New York Times*. The Soviet leadership, however, continued to denounce him and bar the publication of his works.

In 1968 a copy of the *Cancer Ward* manuscript was smuggled out of the Soviet Union and published in London in both Russian and English. The book was based on Solzhenitsyn's own experiences in Soviet hospitals and uses human cancer as a metaphor for the cancerous growth of totalitarianism in the Soviet Union. At one point, Solzhenitsyn asks, "A man sprouts a tumor and dies—how then can a country live that has sprouted camps and exile?"

Later that same year, a New York publisher announced that it would publish Solzhenitsyn's novel *First Circle*. In November 1969 Solzhenitsyn was expelled from the Soviet Writers' Union and effectively became a nonperson in the Soviet Union. The expulsion only increased Solzhenitsyn's status in the West. In October 1970 he was awarded the Nobel Prize for literature. The Swedish Academy said the award was being presented to Solzhenitsyn "for the ethical force with which he has pursued the indispensable tradition of Russian literature."

Solzhenitsyn declared his willingness to travel to Stockholm to receive the prize but was blocked from doing so by the Soviet authorities. The official Novosti Press Agency used the occasion of the award to launch a stinging attack on the author.

Solzhenitsyn had by this time joined other prominent Soviet dissidents, such as nuclear physicist ANDREI SAKHAROV, in the Human Rights Committee. In December 1973, Solzhenitsyn's *Gulag Archipelago* was published in the West. The nonfiction work provided a detailed firsthand account of Stalin's secret police system and his extensive network of labor camps. The book was attacked by the Soviet news agency Tass as an "unfounded slander against the Soviet people" and "a New Year present to the enemies of his motherland."

On February 12, 1974, Solzhenitsyn was arrested, stripped of his Soviet citizenship and deported to West Germany, becoming the first Soviet citizen since Leon Trotsky to be expelled from his country. Solzhenitsyn at first went to live in Switzerland, and in 1975 he moved to the United States. Shortly after his arrival, he said that the West had already lost World War III by allowing the Soviet Union "to devastate and enslave 20 countries."

Solzhenitsyn settled into a largely reclusive life in Vermont. In 1985 he applied for and was granted American citizenship. The reforms of President MIKHAIL GORBACHEV created a new climate in the Soviet Union, and in July 1989 Solzhenitsyn was reinstated in the Soviet Writers' Union and his *Gulag Archipelago* was serialized in *Novy Mir*. The government hoped that Solzhenitsyn would return and extend his legitimacy to the new regime, but the writer refused to accept a restoration of his Soviet citizenship.

Solzhenitsyn's pronouncements since, on the state of the West and the future of Russia, have revealed a strain of political thinking deeply at odds with the assumptions of Western liberalism, as well as Russian ethnocentric and anti-Semitic attitudes that have tarnished his reputation.

Sonnenfeldt, Helmut   (September 13, 1926–   )   Helmut Sonnenfeldt is an American expert on Soviet affairs who worked closely with HENRY KISSINGER during the NIXON and FORD administrations.

Sonnenfeldt was educated in England and at Johns Hopkins University in Baltimore after his Jewish parents fled Nazi Germany. While with the U.S. Army in Germany he met and became close friends with Henry Kissinger, another child refugee from the Nazis.

In 1952 Sonnenfeldt joined the State Department, where he won a reputation as an expert political analyst and hardline anti-communist. Despite his strong anti-Soviet views, Sonnenfeldt in 1960 came under suspicion for passing classified information to the press and foreign governments. He was cleared after a lengthy investigation but remained under heavy surveillance, which included bugging of his telephone. Sonnenfeldt became director of the International Political Activities Division of the State Department in 1966 and the following year was appointed head of the Soviet and East European Research Section of the Office of Research and Analysis.

When Kissinger was appointed President Richard Nixon's national security adviser, he moved Sonnenfeldt over to the NATIONAL SECURITY COUNCIL as his top aide. The two men had not only remained close friends, but also enjoyed near identical views on almost every major foreign policy issue. Sonnenfeldt's almost symbiotic relationship with Kissinger guaranteed his close involvement in all of Kissinger's activities, including the STRATEGIC ARMS LIMITATION TALKS, the rapprochement with China, the VIETNAM WAR and the PARIS PEACE TALKS.

In April 1973 Sonnenfeldt was nominated to the post of undersecretary of the treasury, where he was expected to oversee the growing U.S.–Soviet trade. In May 1973 he visited Moscow for four days of talks with Soviet leader LEONID BREZHNEV on the granting of most-favored-nation trading status to the Soviet Union. But because of the 1960 investigation, his nomination was held up in the Senate for eight months and eventually was withdrawn. In the interim, Kissinger had moved from the National Security Council to the State Department and asked Sonnenfeldt to rejoin him.

In March 1974 Sonnenfeldt represented the United States at a special consultation forum of members of the NORTH ATLANTIC TREATY ORGANIZATION (NATO) to discuss U.S.–European policy differences. The meeting had been called after European complaints that the United States had not consulted adequately with its NATO allies during the 1973 Yom Kippur War. Sonnenfeldt, however, used the meeting to criticize the Europeans for what he labeled their own inadequate consideration of U.S. policy interests. He also expressed concern that the EUROPEAN ECONOMIC COMMUNITY's efforts to improve trade with Arab nations would undermine Kissinger's diplomatic initiative in the Middle East.

Sonnenfeldt became the center of a politically damaging controversy in March 1976, during the Ford administration. Syndicated columnists Rowland Evans and Robert Novak wrote that at a meeting of American ambassadors in Europe Sonnenfeldt had proposed that a permanent union between the Soviet Union and Eastern Europe was necessary to avoid World War III. The article was picked up by President Gerald Ford's rival for the Republican presidential nomination that year, RONALD REAGAN, and turned into an election issue. The text of the off-the-record speech, which was later released, showed that Sonnenfeldt's remarks had been misconstrued. He had in fact argued that the Soviet Union's strength called for a more "realistic interpretation" of the situation in Eastern Europe.

Sonnenfeldt said that the United States should concentrate on attempting to influence the development of Soviet policies by drawing the U.S.S.R. into a series of relationships in which the West was the senior partner. He also argued that it was more important to prevent the rise of communist parties in Western Europe than to encourage anti-Soviet elements in Eastern Europe.

Reagan's attack, however, forced Ford onto the defensive and then into a reappraisal of détente, in the middle of the Republican primaries. In the end, Ford had to accept major foreign policy changes in order to secure the support of the skeptical right wing of his party and win the nomination.

Sonnenfeldt retired from the State Department at the end of the Ford administration. He took a teaching job at Johns Hopkins University and joined the RAND CORPORATION. He continued to speak out on international affairs and became a familiar figure on the international lecture circuit. But his controversial views and close association with Kissinger kept him out of public office.

For Further Information:
Kissinger, Henry. *The White House Years.* New York, 1979.
———. *Years of Upheaval.* New York, 1982.
Litwak, R.S. *Détente and the Nixon Doctrine: American Foreign Policy and the Pursuit of Stability, 1969–1975.* New York, 1984.
Spanier, J.W. *American Foreign Policy Since World War Two.* Washington, D.C., 1988.
Szulc, Tad. *The Illusion of Peace: Foreign Policy in the Nixon Years.* New York, 1978.

Sorensen, Theodore   (May 8, 1928–   )   Theodore Sorensen, a close aide to JOHN F. KENNEDY throughout his political career, was special counsel to Kennedy during his presidency and had a major liberalizing influence on his foreign policy.

Sorensen's father was a liberal political reformer, and while at the University of Nebraska Sorensen himself campaigned for racial integration. He registered with the military draft as a conscientious objector.

Sorensen graduated from the University of Nebraska Law School in 1951 and joined the Federal Security Agency as an attorney. In 1953 he started his long and close relationship with Kennedy when he joined the newly elected senator's staff as a researcher. Sorensen later stated that for the next 11 years Kennedy "was the only human being who mattered to me."

Sorensen took over the role of Kennedy's chief speech writer and adviser and became the primary liberalizing influence on the young senator, drawing him away from the more conservative positions held by Kennedy's father. As chief speechwriter, Sorensen is credited with writing Kennedy's most notable speeches, including his inaugural address. (He is also said to have been the real author of *Profiles in Courage,* the book that won Kennedy a Pulitzer Prize in 1956.)

Appointed the president's special counsel, Sorensen in the first few months of the Kennedy administration was involved mainly in education policy. But after the abortive BAY OF PIGS invasion in April 1961, he became increasingly involved in foreign affairs. He advised Kennedy during the 1961 BERLIN Crisis and during the civil war in LAOS, each time counseling the president to avoid the use of military force and confrontation.

Sorensen was a key adviser during the 1962 CUBAN MISSILE CRISIS and was a member of Excom, the special group gathered to counsel the president after the discovery of Soviet missiles in October 1962. Sorensen was among those who successfully advised the imposition of a naval blockade rather than an air strike.

Sorensen left the White House shortly after the assassination of Kennedy and in 1965 published his book *Kennedy.* In 1966 he joined the leading New York law firm of Paul Weiss, Rifkind, Wharton and Garrison, and in 1970 he made an unsuccessful attempt for the Democratic nomination to the U.S. Senate from New York. In 1973 he became involved in the defense of DANIEL ELLSBERG and Anthony Russo in connection with their trial for the unauthorized disclosure of the "Pentagon Papers" dealing with the U.S. involvement in Vietnam.

In December 1976, president-elect JIMMY CARTER nominated Sorensen as director of the CENTRAL INTELLIGENCE AGENCY. But the Sorensen nomination encountered strong opposition from CIA officials and Senate conservatives who thought that the former Kennedy aide would not be tough enough. Several members of the Senate Select Committee on Intelligence expressed concern over what they called Sorensen's "pacifist" approach to military service in 1945. On January 17, 1977, Carter asked Sorensen to withdraw his nomination, saying that "a substantial portion of the U.S. Senate and the intelligence community is not yet ready to accept as director of central intelligence an outsider who believes as I believe."

For Further Information:
Anderson, Patrick. *The President's Men.* New York, 1968.
Schlesinger, Arthur M. *A Thousand Days.* New York, 1965.
Sorensen, Theodore. *Kennedy.* New York, 1965.

Southeast Asia Treaty Organizaton (SEATO)   The Southeast Asia Treaty Organization was one of the string of American-inspired postwar military alliances designed to contain communist expansion. But lack of support from Britain and France proved the alliance ineffectual during the VIETNAM WAR, and it was disbanded shortly after the fall of Saigon.

The concept of a defensive alliance for Southeast Asia was first voiced by U.S. secretary of state DEAN ACHESON during the KOREAN WAR. The idea went no further at that time because of the French military commitment to the region. The proposal was revived by Secretary of State JOHN FOSTER DULLES in 1954 when it became clear that France was unable to defeat the communist-led Vietnamese nationalist movement on its own.

Dulles wanted an Anglo–French–American military force to rescue the French Army in Vietnam. He faced opposition, however, from both Britain and France—Britain because of doubts about the winability of the war in Vietnam and France because it was tired after eight years of fighting and was ready to allow Vietnamese independence.

The issue came to a head during the 1954 GENEVA CONFERENCE ON INDOCHINA AND KOREA, where increasing American pressure threatened a rift among the Western allies. To avoid this rift, British foreign secretary ANTHONY EDEN proposed in June 1954 that two treaties be negotiated. The first would be a nonaggression treaty among China, the Soviet Union and the Western powers, which would guarantee the neutrality and independence of Laos, Cambodia and Vietnam. The second would be a non-communist Southeast Asian defensive alliance.

The proposal was accepted. On July 7, the Geneva Agreement on Indochina was signed by China, the Soviet Union and Britain. The United States withheld its signature but accepted the provisions. Accompanying the Geneva Agreement was a further agreement between France and the Vietnamese communists that divided Vietnam temporarily along the 17th parallel. Shortly afterward talks began in Washington, D.C., among representatives from Britain, France, the United States, Thailand, Australia, New Zealand and Pakistan. The treaty forming SEATO was signed in Manila on September 8, 1954.

The treaty fell far short of Dulles's plans for the region. He wanted a military alliance similar to the NORTH ATLANTIC TREATY ORGANIZATON with specific commitments of troops and a command structure. British Prime Minister WINSTON CHURCHILL dashed his hopes by specifically opposing the use of either British or American troops in Indochina except as a "rescue" operation. Eden and Churchill saw British membership more as a means of restraining what they regarded as America's tendency to irrational action in Asia than as a firm defense commitment. This view was shared by France, whose unfortunate experience in Vietnam made the French government even less likely to recommit troops to the region.

The pact was also hampered by British and French commitment to the maintenance of the neutrality of Indochina. This meant that neither Cambodia, Laos nor South Vietnam could join SEATO, and the problem had to be circumvented by a special protocol that extended the protective arm of SEATO to those countries without making them formal members.

Another problem was that the Asian members of the alliance—Thailand, Pakistan and the Philippines—felt as threatened by other regional powers as by the Soviet Union and communist China and hoped that the treaty would protect them from those powers as well as the communist giants. When this policy failed—most notably during the Indo-Pakistan War—it led to the withdrawal of Pakistan from the alliance.

The first major test for SEATO came during the Laotian Crisis of 1960 and 1961 when first the EISENHOWER and then the KENNEDY administration tried to use the alliance for a united intervention. At a SEATO council meeting in Bangkok in March 1961, the alliance agreed to take joint action in Laos if the civil war required it, but they rejected immediate intervention. Because of British and French fears that it would endanger chances for a diplomatic settlement of the crisis, the communiqué issued from the meeting represented a position far short of the warning of military intervention sought by Secretary of State DEAN RUSK.

In May 1962 U.S. troops and the U.S. Seventh Fleet were sent to Thailand to counter the perceived threat to that country from communist forces in Laos. These were joined a month later by a British air squadron and a small force of New Zealand and Australian air and ground units. But the Americans regarded their allies' response as tepid, and a report prepared in 1962 by the House Foreign Affairs Committee asserted that SEATO "offer[ed] no security" to the nations of Southeast Asia and might even have had a harmful effect by hampering the creation of effective defense arrangements. The committee traced the pact's ineffectiveness to its requirement of unanimity and "the lack of support of Britain and France." The study concluded that "either the rule of unanimity should be abolished or the treaty itself should be terminated."

The next test came in 1965 when the United States called for SEATO intervention in the Vietnam War. France boycotted a crucial SEATO meeting called to pledge increased aid to South Vietnam. Pakistan attended the meeting but refused to sign the communiqué, which criticized the North Vietnamese, because of "concern over the consequences of the continuance of armed conflict in Vietnam."

SEATO thus played virtually no role in the Vietnam War, although four of its members—the United States, Australia, New Zealand and Thailand—sent forces, as did a non-SEATO member, South Korea. In November 1972, New Zealand prime minister Norman Kirk indicated a decline in New Zealand's interest in the alliance when he said that his government would "be most interested in an arrangement to supersede SEATO—but not a defensive arrangement." French opposition to America's Vietnam policy led to its withdrawal of financial support for the alliance.

In March 1972, U.S. senator Frank Church called the SEATO pact "a corpse" that had been abandoned by at least three U.S. allies, and said it deserved a "decent burial." After the Philippines' recognition of communist China in June 1975, the Marcos government announced that it would be reviewing its membership in the alliance. And in July Thailand and the Philippines called for a gradual dismantling of the organization "to make it accord with the new realities of the region," an allusion to the collapse of South Vietnam. SEATO was formally disbanded on February 20, 1976, at a ceremony in Manila.

The main points of the 1954 SEATO treaty were:

1. The signatories agreed to "maintain and develop their individual and collective capacity to resist armed attack and to prevent and counter subversive activities directed from without against their territorial integrity and political stability."

2. The signatories agreed to "strengthen their free institutions" and cooperate to promote "economic progress and social well-being."

3. Each signatory recognized "that aggression by means of armed attack in the treaty area against any of the parties or against any state or territory which the parties by unanimous agreement may . . . designate, would endanger its own peace and safety," and agreed to meet the common danger in accordance with its constitutional processes.

4. If any of the signatories or other agreed countries were threatened by subversion then the signatories would "consult immediately in order to agree on the measures which should be taken for the common defense."

5. The treaty area was defined as "the general area of Southeast Asia, including also the entire territories of the Asian parties and the general area of the Southwest Pacific not including the Pacific area north of 21 degrees 30 minutes north latitude."

For Further Information:
Barnet, Richard J. *Roots of War*. New York, 1972.
Karnow, Stanley. *Vietnam: A History*. New York, 1983.
Sobel, Lester, ed. *South Vietnam: U.S.-Communist Confrontation in Southeast Asia*, 4 vols. New York, 1966–1974.

Southern Flank   The Southern Flank is the term used to describe the member countries of the NORTH ATLANTIC TREATY ORGANIZATION (NATO) bordering the Mediterranean—Spain, France, Italy, Greece and Turkey.

The area is in practice subdivided into three further groups: Spain and Portugal; Italy, where NATO's Mediterranean naval command is headquartered; and Greece and Turkey.

The most strategic part of the Southern Flank is the Greek–Turkish sector because of Turkey's long border with the Soviet Union and its control of the DARDANELLES. It was the strategic importance of this region, and Soviet pressure on it, that inspired the 1947 TRUMAN DOCTRINE.

Greece and Turkey also represent the weakest political and military link in the Southern Flank. Differences between the two countries over the island of Cyprus brought the two NATO allies to the brink of war in the 1970s and 1980s. There is no military cooperation between them, and U.S. military and economic aid to Turkey has strained U.S.–Greek relations.

Spaak, Paul-Henri   **(January 25, 1899–July 21, 1972)**
Paul-Henri Spaak was one of the leading forces for European unity and played a major role in the formation of the EUROPEAN COAL AND STEEL COMMUNITY, the EUROPEAN ECONOMIC COMMUNITY, the NORTH ATLANTIC TREATY ORGANIZATION and the COUNCIL OF EUROPE. He was also chairman of the North Atlantic Council and secretary of NATO from 1957 to 1961.

Spaak came from a well-known Belgian family. His mother was a member of the Belgian senate; his uncle, Paul Emile Janson, was prime minister; and his father was a well-known

Paul-Henri Spaak, the Belgian statesman who served as second secretary-general of NATO. Photo courtesy of NATO.

writer. In 1916, during World War I, Spaak tried to cross the Dutch frontier to rejoin the Belgian Army but was captured and interned by the Germans. After the war, Spaak studied law at Brussels University and upon graduation plunged straight into Socialist Party politics.

In 1932 Spaak was elected deputy for Brussels and was appointed minister of transport. He quickly rose through Socialist Party ranks and from 1936 to 1938 was foreign minister; he then served as prime minister from 1938 until the collapse of Belgium in 1939. Spaak, along with most of the other leading Belgian politicians, managed to escape to Britain, where he joined the government-in-exile of Hubert Pierlot as foreign minister.

While in London, Spaak became convinced that his country's interests, and the wider interests of Europe, would best be served by the creation of a supranational European authority, which would bind the nations of Europe together in such a way that war between them would become unthinkable. His initial emphasis was on economic union, as this would undermine national industries and financial structures that provided the essential props to national war machines. Spaak found initial support for his ideas from Holland and Luxembourg. Along with Belgium they were the natural invasion route between Germany and France and lacked the economic or military means to protect themselves. By 1944 the three countries had agreed on the details of the Benelux Customs Union, which took effect in 1948. The customs union became the progenitor of the European Economic Community.

Spaak's efforts in London earned him a reputation as a man determined to achieve political union as an alternative to war. On the strength of this reputation he was appointed the first president of the UN General Assembly from 1946 to 1947. In 1947 he returned to Brussels as prime minister and foreign minister. In 1948 he played a key role in the signing of the BRUSSELS TREATY, which established a regional defense alliance among Britain, the Benelux countries and France. The Brussels Treaty was the first West European defensive alliance to recognize, implicitly, that the major postwar threat to peace in Europe was not Germany but the Soviet Union. In 1948 Spaak told the UN General Assembly, "There is but one great power that emerged from the war having conquered other territories and that power is the USSR." Spaak went on to play a major role in the negotiations that led to the formation of NATO in April 1949.

In August 1949 Spaak was appointed president of the first assembly of the Council of Europe. At the end of that first session he declared, "I came to Strasbourg convinced of the need for a United States of Europe. I leave with the certainty that union is possible." Spaak, however, became frustrated and disillusioned with the progress of talks at the council and two years later resigned in disgust. In his memoirs he wrote of the Council of Europe, "Of all the international bodies I have known, I have never found any more timorous or more impotent."

When it came to the issue of European unity, Spaak was a man who wanted to deal in practical realities rather than the theories discussed at the Council of Europe. He was thus much more at home as president from 1952 to 1953 of the Common Assembly of the European Coal and Steel Community, which laid down the administrative structure for West European cooperation in these two key industries and established the foundations of the wider European Economic Community (EEC). Spaak went on to play a major role in the negotiations that led to the signing in March 1957 of the Treaty of Rome, which established the EEC and the European Atomic Energy Community (Euratom). He also continued during this period to play a role in Belgian politics as foreign minister from 1954 to 1957.

As foreign minister, Spaak was involved in the events leading up to and immediately following the French National Assembly's rejection of the EUROPEAN DEFENSE COMMUNITY Treaty in 1954. Spaak was a keen supporter of the EDC and German rearmament and wholeheartedly opposed the attempts of the French to amend the treaty. Spaak made it clear that if the French National Assembly rejected the treaty, the Benelux countries would support the NATO alternative proposed by British foreign secretary ANTHONY EDEN. Spaak's support for the Eden plan was essential to its later implementation.

Spaak's support for NATO after the failure of the EDC led to his appointment as secretary-general of NATO, the Western Alliance's top political post, on May 15, 1957. He was immediately embroiled in the alliance's debate, which has never ended, over the correct mix of conventional and nuclear forces in Europe. Other major issues during Spaak's tenure at NATO were the Soviet launching of SPUTNIK and the subsequent debate over the MISSILE GAP, the EISENHOWER DOCTRINE, and the BERLIN Crisis. During the EDC debate, his relations with French leaders had deteriorated. This continued while he was at NATO and encouraged the independent foreign policy of President CHARLES DE GAULLE.

Spaak left NATO in 1961 to join the Belgian coalition government of Theo Lefevre as deputy prime minister and foreign minister from 1961 to 1965. He retired from politics in 1966 to go into private business. He died July 21, 1972, of kidney failure.

For Further Information:
Grosser, Alfred. *The Western Alliance: European-American Relations Since 1945.* New York, 1980.
Mayne, Richard. *Postwar: The Dawn of Today's Europe.* New York, 1983.
———. *The Recovery of Europe.* London, 1981.
Spaak, Paul-Henri. *Why Nato.* New York, 1959.

Spellman, Francis J.   (May 4, 1889–December 2, 1967)
Francis Cardinal Spellman was a leading American conservative clergyman and anti-communist campaigner. Toward the end of his career, his hawkishness brought him into conflict with the Vatican and liberal American Catholics.

Spellman was ordained a Roman Catholic priest in 1916. He was ordained archbishop of New York in 1939 and cardinal in 1946. During World War II Spellman forged close links with the military establishment as Catholic vicar-general of the U.S. armed forces. He was one of the first public figures to attack the Soviet Union, comparing communism to "a wild beast in the forest."

In the early years of the Cold War, Spellman became heavily involved in the cause of imprisoned Catholic clergymen in Eastern Europe. He was particularly active in the campaign to free his personal friend Cardinal JOZSEF MINDSZENTY of HUNGARY. Spellman was also a strong supporter of South Korean president SYNGMAN RHEE.

During the EISENHOWER administration Spellman further enhanced his Cold Warrior image by supporting the anti-communist campaign of Senator JOSEPH MCCARTHY even after the senator had been censured by the U.S. Senate. He also supported calls for American intervention in Vietnam in 1954 and condemned the 1954 Geneva agreement that partitioned the country. In September 1959, a week before Soviet leader NIKITA KHRUSHCHEV visited the United States, Spellman summoned the archdiocese to participate in an hour of prayer for America.

Spellman's anti-communist extremism brought him into conflict with the more liberal Vatican policies of Pope John

XXIII. His unconditional support for the VIETNAM WAR isolated him from many American Catholics, and in December 1965 Catholic college students picketed his office. By 1966 Spellman was in direct conflict with the peace initiatives of Pope Paul VI, and the Vatican issued a statement on December 27 of that year saying that the cardinal "did not speak for the Pope or the church" on the issue of Vietnam. Spellman offered to resign as archbishop but was refused by the Vatican. Catholic antiwar demonstrations against Spellman continued until he died from a stroke on December 2, 1967.

For Further Information:

Cooney, John. *The American Pope: The Life and Times of Francis Cardinal Spellman.* New York, 1984.

Gannon, Robert. *The Cardinal Spellman Story.* Garden City, N.Y., 1962.

Steibel, Warren. *Cardinal Spellman, The Man.* New York, 1966.

Sputnik *Sputnik* was the first man-made satellite to orbit the Earth. Its launching by the Soviet Union in October 1957 undermined American claims to world leadership in science. It also led to fears that the Soviet Union had a massive lead in guided-missile technology and that outer space could become an invulnerable Soviet military base from which the U.S.S.R. could control the world. This is turn led to America's creation of the National Aeronautics and Space Administration (NASA) and propelled the U.S.–Soviet space race.

The initial Soviet lead in the space race has been attributed to the Soviet defense establishment's decision to invest heavily in guided-missile and rocket technology immediately after World War II. The United States, in contrast, did not initially foresee that rockets would replace manned bombers as the primary delivery vehicle for bombs.

It was not until 1952 that the United States began to invest large sums in missile research. By then the Soviets were well ahead. In April 1955 they named a scientific commission to work toward the launching of a space satellite. In June 1957, Soviet scientists at an International Geophysical Year meeting reminded the world of their intention, and in September they repeated their reminder, this time announcing estimates of the satellite's approximate weight.

On October 5, 1957, *Sputnik I* was launched. By current standards it was a primitive affair. Equipped with little more than a radio beacon, the satellite weighed 184 pounds. Its spheroid shape was only 22.8 inches in diameter and it reached a maximum altitude of 560 miles as it orbited the Earth on a north–south route, circling the globe once every 96.2 minutes. The satellite had been carried into space by a three-stage rocket. The first stage reached a speed of 4,650 miles per hour, the second 12,400 miles per hour and the third 18,000 miles per hour.

News of the launching of *Sputnik* prompted a major national debate. Several U.S. senators demanded an investigation into the U.S. program of missile development. Senator HENRY M. JACKSON called the launching of *Sputnik* a "devastating blow to the prestige of the United States." Senator STYLES BRIDGES declared that it was time for Americans to be "prepared to shed blood, sweat and tears if this country and the free world are to survive."

In response to the national uproar, the EISENHOWER administration increased spending on scientific education and in July 1958 created the National Aeronautics and Space Administration. President Eisenhower also secretly commissioned H. Rowan Gaither, former president of the Ford Foundation, to investigate Soviet offensive capabilities. The subsequent GAITHER REPORT estimated that the Soviet Union would achieve missile superiority over the United States in 1959. When the report was leaked to the press, it led to a fresh controversy over the "MISSILE GAP."

Stalin, Josef **(December 21, 1879–March 5, 1953)** Josef Stalin was arguably the most powerful political figure of the Cold War—even after his death in 1953. Consolidator of the Revolution, creator of the Soviet economy, destroyer of political opposition, Stalin was the brutal absolute ruler of the Soviet state and guiding light of communist parties everywhere from 1929 until he died. Stalin governed ruthlessly, practicing a mixture of revolutionary Marxism, Russian chauvinism, czarist-style authoritarianism, national pride and personal paranoia. After World War II, he installed and dominated the governments of Eastern Europe in the interests of the Soviet Union. Partly because of his role as putative world leader of the prewar opposition to fascism—a role that was solely his due to the default of the leaders of the Western democracies in the 1930s—and partly from his role as undisputed master of the mighty force that defeated Hitler, he was a larger-than-life figure for an entire generation. He was greatly feared in the West.

Stalin was born Iosif Vissarionovich Dzhugashvili in Georgia. He adopted the name Stalin, which means "Man of Steel," after becoming active in revolutionary politics. Stalin's mother wanted her son to enter the priesthood and sent him to seminary. But Stalin had by this time already become attracted to the teachings of Karl Marx and decided on a career as a communist revolutionary. He joined the political underground as a union agitator in 1900 and in 1903 met and became a disciple of Vladimir Ilyich Lenin. Between 1902 and 1913 Stalin was arrested 12 times for his revolutionary activities.

In 1912 Stalin became a member of the Bolshevik Party's first Central Committee and for a brief period edited the party newspaper *Pravda* before being arrested again and sent into exile in Siberia. He remained there until March 1917 when the czarist government collapsed and was replaced by a patchwork provisional government. Stalin returned to Moscow and rejoined the Central Committee and the Politburo. He at first advocated that the Bolsheviks cooperate with the Mensheviks in forming a coalition government, but he later joined Lenin and Leon Trotsky in the November 7 revolution.

During the civil war that followed, Stalin was sent as a political commissar to various frontline posts to organize supplies and resistance to the Western-supported White Russian forces. He developed a reputation for cutting through red tape and for a hatred of the Western powers—Britain, France, Japan and the United States—that were sending troops and supplies in support of the White Russians. Stalin was later to contend that this period, and the interwar years of diplomatic hostility, proved that the Western powers were the implacable enemies of the Soviet Union and that this unalterable hostility should be a determining factor in Soviet foreign policy.

It was also during the civil war, which lasted until 1921, that Stalin first demonstrated his willingness to resort to brutal killings and torture as tools for the implementation of policy. He was an eager supporter of Lenin's Red Terror campaign, which swept the country.

While acting as a roving political commissar, Stalin also held two key ministerial posts, as commissar for nationalities and for state control. In 1922 he was appointed general secretary of the party's Central Committee. At the time the post was considered to be an unglamorous administrative job, but Stalin within a short time turned it into a powerful political base, which later enabled him to grab control of the party and the country from his rival Leon Trotsky. He held the post of general secretary until his death, and every successive Soviet leader found it necessary to control this position.

From 1921 onward Stalin came into increasing conflict with Lenin. He opposed his mentor's New Economic Policy as a retreat into capitalism and criticized Lenin's plans to establish a system of largely autonomous Soviet republics, rather than a centrally controlled system. When Lenin died in 1924 his final political testament, which Stalin suppressed, called for the removal of Stalin, but by then Stalin was too well entrenched. In the subsequent power struggle all of Stalin's opponents were either killed or exiled. In 1929 he succeeded in expelling Trotsky and assumed dictatorial powers. Trotsky fled to Mexico, where he was assassinated in 1940.

In 1928 Stalin discarded Lenin's New Economic Policy for a state-organized drive toward industrialization and collectivization of Soviet agriculture. Some 25 million farmers were forced onto state farms. Those who refused were shot. The result was widespread terror and, because of the dislocation, famine. An estimated 10 million people died as a result of this policy. But the agricultural system was reconstructed on communist lines, and the Soviet Union became an industrial power, rising from 15th in industrial output to second, behind only the United States, by 1937.

In 1934 Stalin launched his great purge of the Communist Party as he sought to eliminate all opposition and establish his stranglehold on the party apparatus through the implementation of terror. There was an endless round of show trials, fabricated confessions and executions extending from the top of the party down to the local party committees and then into the academic, art, medical and literary worlds. Another 3 million people are believed to have died during the great purge.

Domestic upheavals in the Soviet Union during the interwar years gave Stalin little time for foreign policy. He gave a high priority to foreign affairs but felt that aiding foreign revolutions had to wait until he had consolidated "Socialism in one country." His own belief in the inevitability of conflict between the Soviet Union and the West was made clear from the earliest days of the Soviet government. In 1920 he declared that the world was "definitely and irrevocably split into two camps: the camp of imperialism and the camp of socialism . . . the earth is too small for both . . . one of them must perish if peace is to be established."

Stalin, however, realized that the Soviet Union needed a period of peace to establish a secure economic and political base that would be strong enough to sustain such prolonged conflict. For this reason he established trade and diplomatic relations with Britain in the 1920s and supported the policy of "peaceful struggle" that lasted through the 1930s. At the same time, he encouraged the formation of communist movements in the colonial world, in the accurate belief that these countries would eventually fight for independence from their colonial masters.

Britain was the major enemy during the interwar years, but Stalin was one of the few statesman to recognize the importance of the United States. He went out of his way to encourage business contacts with America and personally saw many visiting American businessmen. He professed to be a great admirer of President FRANKLIN D. ROOSEVELT, but when others claimed that Roosevelt's New Deal economic program would lead to a convergence of the socialist and capitalist systems Stalin replied that Roosevelt remained a "captain of the modern bourgeois world" and had no intention of undermining the foundations of American capitalism.

Most of all, Stalin was a practical politician. Although he believed in the inevitable triumph of Soviet-style socialism, he employed traditional great-power diplomacy toward that end. This meant trade and diplomatic relations with the West and the attempt to make an alliance with Britain and France in the 1930s against Nazi Germany. When those countries refused such an alliance, preferring not to confront Hitler, he agreed to the 1939 Molotov-Ribbentrop Pact with Hitler that led to the division of Poland and the start of World War II. Stalin's purpose was not primarily territorial gain; it was to buy additional time to strengthen the Soviet economy and secure his domestic power base.

When Hitler—to Stalin's apparent surprise—turned against the Soviet Union on June 22, 1941, British prime minister WINSTON CHURCHILL immediately offered an alliance. Despite the obvious benefits to both countries, it was another year before a formal treaty was signed. Even at that early stage Stalin's view of the postwar world differed markedly from that of Churchill and Roosevelt, who had just signed the Atlantic Charter.

This became clear when British foreign secretary ANTHONY EDEN flew to Moscow in December 1941, and Stalin demanded a secret protocol on postwar frontiers. These included the redrawing of the Soviet–Polish border along the CURZON LINE and a realignment of the Soviet–Romanian border. POLAND and ROMANIA would be compensated with land taken from GERMANY and HUNGARY, respectively. Poland and Romania would also be recognized by Britain and America as within the Soviet sphere of influence, and the Soviet Union would have the right to establish military bases in Romania. The three Baltic states of Lithuania, Estonia and Latvia, which had been absorbed by Stalin in 1940, would remain part of the Soviet Union. The Soviet–Finnish border would be restored as of June 1941, and the Soviet Union would have the right to base troops in Finland. In return for these territorial concessions, Stalin offered Britain military bases in Denmark, Norway and France. He also raised the issue of postwar German reparations and suggested an armed council of the victorious powers to maintain the peace following Germany's defeat.

Eden realized that Britain, and especially the United States, could not formally accept such a proposal. It ran directly counter to the Atlantic Charter supporting the right of national self-determination and appeared to cast the Allied Powers in the same land-grabbing political mold as Hitler (and Stalin). At the same time, beleaguered Britain could not afford not to make an alliance. The result was a vague 20-year Treaty of Mutual Assistance eventually signed on May 26, 1942. The treaty did not reject Stalin's territorial ambitions, and he felt free to pursue them unilaterally and intermittently seek tacit Anglo–American approval.

For the two years after the signing of the treaty, the Grand Alliance was strained by the fact that the Soviet Union bore the brunt of the German offensive. Stalin harbored a secret fear that the United States and Britain intended to sit on the sidelines while Germany and the Soviet Union fought to a common death. At every opportunity he pressed Roosevelt and Churchill for the launching of a second front in France and warned that its postponement created diplomatic problems. Stalin later claimed that the Soviet Union's unequal sacrifices entitled it to a larger share of the war spoils. Churchill retorted by pointing out that it was German–Soviet connivance that had led to the start of the war and that for two years Britain had stood alone while the Soviet Union had adopted a neutral stance.

Within the Soviet Union, the war became a vehicle for Stalin to turn himself into a popular hero. He had already

Josef Stalin (second left) with President Truman (second right) in Potsdam.

launched the "cult of personality" in the 1930s. At the outset of the war he declared himself "supreme commander in chief." When the Germans threatened Moscow in the winter of 1941, he won widespread respect by staying in the capital and organizing a successful counteroffensive. He also personally commanded the successful battles of Stalingrad and Kursk.

The turning point for Stalin's postwar plans was the Teheran Conference in 1943. It was the first meeting among Stalin, Roosevelt and Churchill and the first time they discussed postwar Europe. Stalin had expected strong American opposition to his Eastern Europe policy, especially as it related to Poland. The ailing President Roosevelt did raise some objections but couched them in the context of the effect Soviet ambitions would have on the ethnic vote during the 1944 U.S. presidential elections. According to many Sovietologists, this led Stalin to believe that Roosevelt's opposition would evaporate after November 1944.

In the 1930s Stalin had provided sanctuary to East and Central European communists who had been forced to flee their own countries, all of which were under fascist influence or control. They had been carefully cultivated in Moscow and during the war had planned, with the support of the Soviet Union, to take power in their countries when the fighting finished. One of the most important of these figures was the Polish communist BOLESLAW BIERUT, who helped to ensure the satellite status of Poland. In 1943 Stalin severed relations with the London-based Polish government-in-exile of Stanislaw Mikolajczyk over the KATYN MASSACRE of Polish officers. He then recognized the Moscow-based government of Bierut in its stead, connived to destroy the Polish Home Army in Warsaw and, after the Red Army had occupied Poland, established Bierut in power.

Similar formulas were used in Romania, Hungary, Czechoslovakia, Albania, Bulgaria, East Germany and North Korea. Poland, however, became for the West a test case of Soviet intentions and the focal point of East–West differences. From the British point of view, the invasion of Poland had been the cause for the start of the war, and therefore the restoration of Polish national sovereignty was the main reason for the fighting. But from Stalin's point of view, Poland represented the traditional corridor of attack from Western Europe into the Russian heartland; one of the main reasons he had made his pact with Hitler in 1939 was to gain control of that corridor.

Poland thus became the major issue at the YALTA CONFERENCE and the POTSDAM CONFERENCE in 1945, as well as at a number of foreign ministers' meetings. At Yalta Stalin avoided an East–West confrontation over Poland by promising to hold free elections within a month. The elections never took place, and this led to a serious argument at the subsequent Potsdam Conference. But with the Red Army occupying all of Eastern Europe and half of Germany, Britain and the United States had no leverage over Stalin.

At Yalta, Roosevelt and Stalin also negotiated the terms for the Soviet Union's entry into the war against Japan. Roosevelt agreed that Stalin would occupy the northern half of Korea and be given sovereignty over islands in the northern part of the Japanese archipelago. Thus, at the end of the war, Stalin achieved all of his prewar territorial ambitions and more. He was the leader of the dominant land power in Europe and Asia. The Soviet Union and the United States had emerged from World War II as the world's two superpowers.

The emphasis of Stalin's foreign policy thus shifted to the consolidation of Soviet gains and the postwar destruction of Germany as an economic and political unit. Germany was, in Stalin's view, still the major threat to Soviet security. It had risen from the ashes of defeat after World War I to invade the Russian heartland again and kill an estimated 20 to 25 million Soviet citizens. Unless it was destroyed as an economic and political unit, argued Stalin, it would eventually do it again. There was another element of national self-interest in Stalin's German policy. That was the massive reparations he demanded either in cash or in industrial equipment, both of which were needed by the Soviet Union to rebuild its industrial base and construct a defense industry able to maintain the Red Army in Eastern Europe.

Britain and the United States, however, quickly came to the conclusion that an economically revived Germany was essential to their national self-interests. They could not, as Stalin did, allow the German people in their sectors to starve, and the cost of feeding the German people and maintaining the basic infrastructure was proving to be a massive drain on their national treasuries. The only alternative was to create a viable political and economic unit that would not only support the German people but, it was hoped, would also return to its traditional role as the industrial engine of Europe. These basic differences led eventually to the establishment of the American- and British-supported Federal Republic of Germany and the Soviet-supported German Democratic Republic.

From January 1946 it had become apparent to policy makers in both East and West that the wartime alliance would not survive the peace. It seems that Stalin had hoped it would, but on his own terms. For the next 18 months Stalin switched his policy toward the West from an entente back to the prewar policy of peaceful struggle. But either way it was to be on Stalin's terms, which meant continued Soviet control of Eastern Europe and concessions in Iran, Turkey and Greece. This was unacceptable to Britain, but Britain was too weakened to thwart Stalin on its own. In 1947 Britain requested American aid to prevent a communist takeover in Greece. President HARRY TRUMAN responded with the TRUMAN DOCTRINE, and Stalin found himself locked into a Cold War with the United States.

It is not clear whether Stalin expected the American opposition, and his subsequent actions were the result of a plan, or whether he did not expect the opposition, and reacted defensively to the unexpected Truman Doctrine and the subsequent MARSHALL PLAN and formation of the NORTH ATLANTIC TREATY ORGANIZATION (NATO). The evidence suggests the latter, but Stalin had complete control of Soviet domestic and foreign policy during this period, and his increasing paranoia led him to conceal his intentions from the rest of the Soviet hierarchy. His true motives will probably never be known.

Stalin, however, believed in the inevitable triumph of communism over capitalism and was committed to the Soviet Union's political dominance of a worldwide communist movement. In September 1947 he launched COMINFORM (the Communist Information Bureau), the publicly stated aim of which was to direct the activities of communist parties elsewhere in the world. And certainly the whole of Western Europe, and many of the emerging Third World countries, appeared to be politically unstable and ready for revolution.

But Stalin knew that he was in no position to challenge the dominant Western power—the nuclear-armed United States—and would be unlikely to do so for years. His foreign adventures, with the exception of his imposition of the BERLIN Blockade, were mainly directed at points of Western weakness. Whenever he encountered strong resistance, Stalin quickly retreated. At the same time, he pushed the development of a Soviet nuclear weapons program.

The successful testing of a Soviet atomic bomb in September 1949 came only a few months after the end of the Berlin Blockade and a week before a communist government came to power in China. This plus the start of the KOREAN WAR in June 1950 led to panic among West Europeans, who feared that Stalin was trying to divert American troops away from the protection of an impoverished Western Europe so that he could use his new atomic weapon and vastly superior conventional forces to impose his political system on the rest of the European continent.

The West Europeans countered this threat with an unprecedented show of unity. Stalin in the meantime appears to have drifted into paranoia. Not only was he fearful of an American attack on the Soviet Union, he also became increasingly convinced that he was the target of a coup. According to NIKITA KHRUSHCHEV and Stalin's daughter Svetlana, from 1949 onward Stalin progressively lost his grasp on reality. In January 1953 he ordered the arrest of a number of Kremlin doctors, whom he accused of having medically murdered certain leading communists. It was clear that Stalin was preparing to use the "Doctor's Plot" as a pretext for another great purge of the party when he died suddenly on March 5, 1953.

Stalin left behind an international climate of mistrust and a Communist Party in charge of an elaborate bureaucracy of ministries, trade unions, the military, secret and political police, and rubber-stamp legislative bodies. This system continued to rule Soviet society for decades after his death.

For Further Information:
Bullock, Alan. *Hitler and Stalin: Parallel Lives.* London, 1991.
Conquest, Robert. *The Great Terror: A Reassessment.* New York 1990.
———. *Power, Policy and the U.S.S.R.* New York, 1961.
———. *Stalin: Breaker of Nations.* New York, 1991.
———. *Stalin and the Kirov Murder.* New York, 1989.
Deutscher, Isaac. *Stalin; A Political Biography.* New York, 1949.
Feis, Herbert. *Churchill, Roosevelt, Stalin.* New York, 1957.
Laqueur, Walter. *Stalin: The Glasnost Revelations.* New York, 1990.
Medvedev, Roy Aleksandrovich. *Let History Judge: The Origins and Consequences of Stalinism.* New York, 1989.
Payne, Robert. *Rise and Fall of Stalin.* New York, 1965.
Rapoport, Louis. *Stalin's War Against the Jews: The Doctor's Plot and the Soviet Solution.* New York, 1990.
Taubman, William. *Stalin's American Policy: From Entente to Détente to Cold War.* New York, 1982.
Tucker, Robert C. *Stalin in Power: The Revolution From Above, 1929–1941.* New York, 1990.
Ulam, Adam. *Stalin.* New York, 1973.

Standing Consultative Commission (SCC)   The Standing Consultative Commission (SCC) is a permanent United States–Soviet (now Russian) commission established in 1972 in accordance with the ANTIBALLISTIC MISSILE (ABM) TREATY to review treaty compliance.

The SCC is responsible for considering questions of compliance, amendments, reviews and "further measures aimed at limiting strategic arms." In the 1980s, a great deal of the SCC's time was taken up by allegations from both the Soviet Union and the United States that the other side was breaching the ABM treaty or the unratified SALT II accords.

Star Wars   *See* STRATEGIC DEFENSE INITIATIVE.

Stassen, Harold   (April 13, 1907–   )   Harold Stassen was a regular candidate for the Republican presidential nomination, who during the EISENHOWER administration was, first, director of foreign operations administration and later special assistant to the president for disarmament.

Stassen, who came from an impoverished background in Minnesota, worked his way through the University of Minnesota and the University of Minnesota Law School. He went straight into state politics after graduating from law school in 1929 and in 1938, at the remarkably young age of 31, was elected governor. In 1943, after being twice reelected, he resigned to go on active duty in the U.S. Naval Reserve.

In 1945 he was one of the two Republican members of the American delegation to the first organizational meeting of the United Nations in San Francisco. After the conference, Stassen concentrated on winning the Republican nomination for the U.S. presidency. He made his first bid in 1948 as a progressive Republican favoring international cooperation. Stassen at first opposed the get-tough policy with the Soviet Union, and in 1947 he visited Moscow and met JOSEF STALIN. But the following year he supported American aid to Greece and Turkey.

Stassen was a leading contender at the start of the Republican primaries in 1948 but lost support after a radio debate in which he supported the outlawing of the Communist Party. After the convention, Stassen became president of the University of Pennsylvania, but he continued to speak out on foreign policy issues. His status within Republican circles was enhanced by the defeat in 1948 of Dewey.

Stassen's foreign policy pronouncements at this time were contradictory as he vacillated between favoring negotiations with the Soviet Union and threats of a military attack. In February 1950, he proposed "a major mid-century conference" to forestall a third world war, but in a national radio broadcast on August 15, 1950, he suggested that the United States warn the Soviet Union that if there were a communist attack anywhere in the world it "[would] mean that war [would] come to Moscow, to the Urals and to the Ukraine." In April 1950 Stassen asked Stalin for a meeting to discuss ways of establishing "a just world peace," only to follow that up in December 1950 with a proposal to use atomic weapons against China.

Stassen's bid for the 1952 Republican presidential nomination failed after Dwight Eisenhower entered the race and undercut his base of support. But Stassen remained in the race until the convention, where his 19 Minnesota delegates were crucial to Eisenhower's narrow victory over Robert Taft. Eisenhower rewarded Stassen's support at the convention by naming him director of the Foreign Operations Administration in August 1953.

As director of the FOA, Stassen was responsible for the government's foreign aid program. In March 1955 Eisenhower appointed Stassen special assistant to the president for disarmament, with a seat at the cabinet table. Stassen's role was to develop and negotiate a disarmament program with the Soviet Union, and in particular to promote Eisenhower's "OPEN SKIES" policy, which was unveiled at the Geneva summit conference in July 1955.

Stassen had a difficult time persuading Secretary of State JOHN FOSTER DULLES and other administration hawks to accept the principle of disarmament. Dulles believed that any disarmament negotiations would undercut the American deterrent policy of "massive retaliation," upon which American security policy was based. Stassen, on the other hand, argued that as the two superpowers reached nuclear parity, disarmament negotiations were vital to avoid a dangerous and financially debilitating arms race. A nuclear weapons ban was one of Stassen's major objectives. He was especially anxious to have a ban in force while the United States had a technological edge over the Soviets.

Stassen found his way blocked by the Soviets' unwillingness to submit to verifiable inspections and their insistence on conducting aerial inspections of Western Europe. During negotiations in London in 1957, Stassen committed a diplomatic blunder by submitting a proposal to the Soviets that would have blocked the development of the hydrogen bomb by Britain. The proposal, which had not been discussed first with the British, resulted in a protest from Prime Minister HAROLD MACMILLAN. Eisenhower was forced to "reprimand" Stassen publicly. He resigned in February 1958.

Stassen remained active in Republican Party politics but was never again a major force, although he continued to run for the Republican nomination in every presidential election through 1984.

For Further Information:

Clark, Paul F. *American Aid for Development.* New York, 1972.
Clemens, Walter C. *The Superpowers and Arms Control: From Cold War to Interdependence.* Lexington, 1973.
Eberstadt, Nicholas. *Foreign Aid and American Purpose.* Washington, D.C., 1988.
United States Arms Control and Disarmament Agency. *Arms Control and Disarmament Agreements: Texts and Histories of Negotiations.* Washington, D.C., 1980.

Stettinius, Edward R.   (October 22, 1900–October 31, 1949)   Edward R. Stettinius was U.S. secretary of state during the YALTA CONFERENCE and the first American ambassador to the United Nations.

Stettinius was born into a prominent New York banking family. He failed to graduate from the University of Virginia and for a time toyed with the idea of becoming a clergyman before family connections secured him a job with General Motors. He climbed through the business world eventually to become chairman of U.S. Steel in 1938.

In 1939 President FRANKLIN D. ROOSEVELT appointed Stettinius chairman of the War Resources Board, and in 1941 he was appointed director of priorities for the Office of Production Management. Roosevelt moved Stettinius to the State Department as undersecretary of state in 1943. He was appointed secretary of state in 1944 following the resignation of Cordell Hull.

Stettinius was never a dynamic or innovative secretary of state. He owed his position entirely to his friendship with Roosevelt, who wished to exploit the administrative skills he had developed in the business world. His failure to establish a wider political base undermined his effectiveness even during the Roosevelt administration, and led to his political downfall under President HARRY TRUMAN. During Stettinius' short tenure at the State Department, from December 1944 to June 1945, almost all foreign policy making was directed by President Roosevelt or his close confidant HARRY HOPKINS, and after Roosevelt's death by President Truman.

Stettinius was present as secretary of state at the decisive Yalta Conference, and it fell to him to propose formally the "Declaration of Liberated Europe." This declared that the Soviet Union, Britain and the United States were committed to emergency relief measures and free elections throughout Europe. Stettinius participated in discussions related to the formation of the United Nations, and opposed Treasury Secretary HENRY MORGENTHAU's plan for the "pastoralization" of postwar Germany. He also opposed the Soviet demand for German war reparations. Roosevelt excluded him from the portion of the Yalta talks that dealt with the Soviet Union's entry into the war against Japan.

As soon as Truman took office, Stettinius handed in his resignation as secretary of state. The new president did not have confidence in Stettinius and had already earmarked

JAMES BYRNES for the job. However, Truman decided to post-pone acceptance of the resignation until after the United Nations organizational conference in San Francisco, where Stettinius made two major contributions. The first was on August 27, 1945, when he opposed a Czechoslovak motion to admit the Lublin government of Poland to the United Nations. The second was a strongly worded threat to take the United States out of the United Nations over a Soviet demand that the permanent members of the Security Council have the power to veto even the discussion of a dispute.

In June 1945, Truman appointed Stettinius as the first U.S. ambassador to the new United Nations, and Stettinius attended the first UN General Assembly in London in 1946. But his lack of a political base placed him at an increasing disadvantage in conflicts with influential men such as senators ARTHUR VANDENBERG and Tom Connally as well as JOHN FOSTER DULLES and Secretary of State Byrnes. Stettinius resigned in June 1946 after a disagreement with Byrnes. A heart condition curtailed his public activities from the time of resignation to his death on October 31, 1949.

For Further Information:
Finger, A. *American Ambassadors at the United Nations.* New York, 1988.

Stevenson, Adlai   (February 5, 1900–July 14, 1965)   Adlai Stevenson personified the Democratic Party's liberal tradition in the 1950s and early 1960s. He was twice the party's presidential candidate and took a strong stand against Senator JOSEPH MCCARTHY and the foreign policy of President DWIGHT EISENHOWER and Secretary of State JOHN FOSTER DULLES. President JOHN F. KENNEDY appointed him ambassador to the United Nations.

Stevenson was born into a patrician political family. His grandfather was Grover Cleveland's vice president and another forebear was a Supreme Court associate justice. Stevenson was educated at the exclusive Choate School and then Princeton University, from which he graduated in 1922. He received his law degree from Northwestern University in 1926.

After a law career in both private and state practice, Stevenson in 1941 entered politics in Washington, D.C., as special assistant to the secretary of the navy. In 1945 he was named special assistant to Secretary of State EDWARD STETTINIUS and in 1946 was senior adviser to the American delegation to the first UN General Assembly in London.

In 1948 Stevenson was elected governor of Illinois, where he firmly established his liberal credentials by establishing a fair employment practices commission, increasing pensions and unemployment benefits and vetoing an antisubversive activities bill. He also appeared as a character witness for ALGER HISS during the latter's perjury trial in 1949.

Stevenson won the 1952 Democratic presidential nomination on the third ballot. During the campaign he denounced McCarthyism but as a liberal Cold Warrior supported President HARRY TRUMAN's major domestic and foreign policies, including the conduct of the unpopular KOREAN WAR. Stevenson's campaign was characterized by his thoughtful and eloquent speeches, which were impressive but enabled the opposition to ridicule him as an intellectual "egghead" out of touch with ordinary people. Republican candidate Dwight Eisenhower won in a landslide.

After the election Stevenson made a six-month world tour, and upon his return he wrote a series of articles for *Look* magazine in which he advocated the promotion of economic development in backward countries as opposed to anti-communist "preaching," which he said "wins few hearts."

Stevenson quickly established himself as the Democratic Party's leading critic of the Eisenhower administration. He attacked Dulles' policy of MASSIVE RETALIATION as leading to World War III. He also continued his attacks on McCarthyism, stating, "It is wicked and it is subversive for public officials to try deliberately to replace reason with passion; to substitute hatred for honest difference . . ."

In 1955, Stevenson opposed the Formosa Resolution, which committed the United States to the protection of Taiwan. He also warned that the United States might lose allies if it went to war over the islands of QUEMOY AND MATSU. When the dispute over the islands flared up again in 1958, Stevenson was scathing in his attack on the Eisenhower administration. He said that the United States had had nearly "four years of grace" to extricate itself since the last crisis over the islands but that instead had "allowed CHIANG KAI-SHEK to bring us closer to war" over small islands "useless to the Formosa government."

Stevenson easily won the Democratic Party's presidential nomination for the 1956 election and in his second campaign employed more traditional campaign tactics. But he suffered another landslide defeat by Eisenhower. During the campaign he proposed the end of the draft and a unilateral halt to the testing of hydrogen bombs.

In 1958 Stevenson visited the Soviet Union and met Soviet leader NIKITA KHRUSHCHEV. He came away convinced that the Soviet leadership had become more pragmatic in its approach to international relations. Before going to Moscow, he proposed the establishment of regular twice-a-year summits between the Soviet and American leaders. At a Democratic-Farmer-Labor Party rally in November 1958, Stevenson claimed that the United States had lost ground in foreign affairs under the Eisenhower administration. He said, "We should be willing to talk with the Russians at every level . . . Russia is here to stay, and so is China—and we may as well face it."

Stevenson reluctantly supported John F. Kennedy in the 1960 presidential election, and this helped Kennedy to secure the support of the liberal wing of the Democratic Party. Stevenson expected to be rewarded with the post of secretary of state. Instead, he was disappointed with the job of ambassador to the United Nations.

Stevenson had a poor relationship with Kennedy. It

started with the president's failure to inform his ambassador to the United Nations about the April 1961 BAY OF PIGS invasion, which led Stevenson unknowingly to misinform the Security Council, telling it that the United States had committed no aggression against Cuba. Kennedy did not repeat this mistake during the 1962 CUBAN MISSILE CRISIS. The ambassador was a member of Excom, the inner circle that met daily to discuss the crisis and develop policies to deal with it. Stevenson proposed that the United States press for a UN-guaranteed demilitarization of Cuba and opposed a surgical air strike against the Soviet missile bases on the island.

Stevenson remained at the United Nations following Kennedy's assassination and vigorously defended President LYNDON JOHNSON's decision to invade the DOMINICAN REPUBLIC and to commit troops to Vietnam. But by April 1965 he was urging a "subtle shift" in American policy on Vietnam toward a greater reliance on mediation through international organizations. His friends claim that Stevenson was on the verge of resigning his UN post and joining the antiwar movement when he died of a heart attack while visiting London on July 14, 1965.

For Further Information:

Brown, Stuart Gerry. *Conscience in Politics: Adlai E. Stevenson in the 1950s.* Syracuse, N.Y., 1961.

Davis, Kenneth S. *The Politics of Honor.* New York, 1967.

Stikker, Dirk Uipko **(February 5, 1897–December 24, 1979)** Dirk Stikker was a prominent Dutch politician and diplomat and served as secretary general of the NORTH ATLANTIC TREATY ORGANIZATION (NATO) from 1961 to 1964.

After studying law at the University of Gröningen, Stikker entered the banking industry and became director of a number of Dutch banks and industrial companies. In 1946 he founded the centrist Party for Freedom and Democracy and became its first chairman. The same year he was elected to the First Chamber of the States General (Senate), and from 1948 to 1952 he served as the Netherlands' minister of foreign affairs.

In 1952 Stikker began a career as a diplomat when he was appointed ambassador to London, a post he held until 1958. At the same time he was ambassador to Iceland and chairman of the Dutch delegation to the Economic and Social Council of the United Nations. In 1958 he was appointed permanent representative to NATO and to the Organization for European Economic Cooperation, a body he had helped to found earlier in the decade. He was named secretary general of NATO on April 21, 1961, in succession to PAUL-HENRI SPAAK.

During Stikker's tenure at NATO, he dealt with a number of issues, including the debate over the proposed Multinational Nuclear Force (MLF), the BERLIN Crisis and the Berlin Wall, the BAY OF PIGS invasion and the CUBAN MISSILE CRISIS, the NUCLEAR TEST BAN TREATY, the Anglo-American POLARIS deal

and the Greek–Turkish dispute over Cyprus. Stikker left NATO in August 1964 to return to business life as a director of Shell Oil Company.

Stimson, Henry L. **(September 21, 1867–October 20, 1950)** As secretary of war from 1940 to 1945, Henry L. Stimson played a major role in the closing days of World War II and the first days of the Cold War. He was also head of the committee that advised the president to use the atomic bomb against Japan.

Stimson was the son of a New York banker. After graduating from Yale he attended Harvard Law School for two years and was admitted to the New York bar in 1891. In 1910 he ran unsuccessfully for the governorship of New York.

As a prominent Republican he held a number of important positions before FRANKLIN ROOSEVELT's election to the presidency in 1932, including secretary of war, secretary of state, special envoy to Nicaragua and governor-general of the Philippines. Although Roosevelt and Stimson occupied opposing political positions, they were close friends, and when Roosevelt sought to widen his political base to prepare for war, Stimson was a logical choice for high office.

Stimson participated in all the major military and foreign policy decisions of World War II and, from May 1, 1943, was Roosevelt's top adviser on the military use of atomic energy.

Stimson's attitude toward the Soviet Union in the closing days of the war was ambivalent. He sympathized with Stalin's desire to surround the Soviet Union with friendly states and advised President HARRY TRUMAN that friendly relations with the Soviet Union were more important than democracy in Eastern Europe. At the same time, he was shocked at the repressive measures taken by the Soviet government and the occupying Red Army in Eastern Europe.

As head of the interim committee charged with advising Truman on the use of the atomic bomb, Stimson was responsible for making the final decision as to whether to recommend dropping it on Hiroshima. Stimson was reluctant to use the bomb and flew uninvited to the POTSDAM CONFERENCE to try to convince Truman that the Japanese could be persuaded to surrender without the use of the bomb. He later defended the use of the bomb, maintaining that no responsible leader "could have failed to use it and afterward looked his countrymen in the face."

In September 1945, shortly before his retirement, Stimson wrote to Truman questioning the wisdom of continuing the American nuclear monopoly. He correctly predicted that future relations with the Soviet Union would be dominated by possession of nuclear weapons and that failure to control their spread would lead to a major arms race. He proposed that the United States halt production of atomic weapons, impound existing stockpiles and formulate an international agreement to outlaw nuclear weapons. After the Soviet Union rejected the BARUCH Plan for nuclear weapons control, Stimson reversed his position and advocated the production of "as many atomic missiles as possible."

Stimson retired on September 21, 1945. He died of a heart attack on October 20, 1950.

For Further Information:
Donnelly, Desmond. *Struggle for the World.* New York, 1965.
Gaddis, J.L. *The United States and the Origins of the Cold War, 1941–1947.* New York, 1972.
Thomas, Hugh. *Armed Truce: The Beginnings of the Cold War, 1945–1946.* New York, 1986.

Stockholm International Peace Research Institute (SIPRI)

The Stockholm International Peace Research Institute (SIPRI) is the world's leading independent center for peace research.

It publishes data on stockpiles of nuclear and conventional weapons and an annual survey of arms control agreements and negotiations and analysis of their implementation. It also monitors arms sales on a worldwide basis.

SIPRI is funded primarily by the Swedish government. Although the focus of its work is meant to encourage pacifism and neutralism, the institute is well known for its objective reports.

Strategic Arms Limitation Talks, 1972 (SALT I Treaty)

The SALT I Treaty of 1972 was the first agreement by the Soviet Union and the United States to limit their offensive nuclear weapons and was one of the high points of the détente era.

Perhaps more importantly, SALT I enshrined the principle of mutual deterrence, that is, the understanding by the Soviet Union and the United States that the maintenance of nuclear deterrents by both made nuclear war less likely. Both sides also implicitly accepted that an element of control by each side over the size and nature of the other's strategic nuclear system was a legitimate component of an adequate deterrent.

American assessments of Soviet strategic capabilities during the 1950s and 1960s were often based on ideological assumptions or domestic political considerations, which resulted in overestimates or underestimates. The Soviet detonation of a nuclear device in 1948 followed by the first BERLIN Crisis and the KOREAN WAR led the United States to embark on the successful development of the hydrogen bomb and massive nuclear superiority. Then the launching of SPUTNIK in 1957 led to a further exaggeration of Soviet capabilities. From 1961 to 1965, the pendulum swung in the other direction, prompted by the exposure of the supposed "MISSILE GAP" as nonexistent and Soviet leader NIKITA KHRUSHCHEV's acquiescence during the CUBAN MISSILE CRISIS. From 1965 to 1969, the United States overreacted to the Chinese missile program and failed to notice the qualitative improvement in Soviet strategic systems.

The first substantive moves toward limiting strategic arms were begun by President LYNDON JOHNSON. In January 1964 Johnson wrote to Khrushchev and suggested scrapping an equal number of obsolescent American B-47 and Soviet TU-16 strategic bombers. The proposal was not taken seriously because the United States had already stated publicly its intention to dispose of the B-47s unilaterally.

In August 1964 the Johnson administration suggested freezing the "number and characteristics" of strategic offensive and defensive weapons delivery vehicles. This proposal quickly foundered on the problem of on-site verification, an issue that was to bedevil the entire SALT process.

To circumvent the problem of on-site verification, American arms control experts proposed that arms limitation proposals focus on verifying numbers of missiles and launchers rather than production facilities. This could be achieved with spy satellites.

This approach was accepted as potentially the most profitable but encountered problems in the development of the Soviet Galosh antiballistic missile system (ABM) and in the development of MIRVed (MULTIPLE INDEPENDENTLY-TARGETED REENTRY VEHICLES) and MRVed (MULTIPLE REENTRY VEHICLES) systems. The latter two developments allowed either superpower to pack an unknown number of nuclear warheads in each missile, thus making it impossible to calculate the number of warheads by counting missiles or launching pads.

In 1965 and 1966 the Soviet Union's rapid development of its ABM system and land-based intercontinental ballistic missiles (ICBMs) equipped with MIRVed and MRVed warheads seemed to indicate that Moscow was aiming to develop first- and second-strike capability. Therefore a secure and effective agreement would have to address both defensive and offensive systems.

The development of the Soviet ABM system emphasized the need for a strategic arms limitation agreement. The United States in the mid-1960s enjoyed an estimated three-to-one superiority in nuclear warheads, but if these warheads were likely to be shot down before reaching their targets then this superiority was ineffectual. The Johnson administration therefore countered by announcing plans to develop an American ABM system, to equip its Minuteman arsenal with MIRVs and to seek to negotiations with the Soviet Union to limit both offensive and defensive nuclear systems.

At this stage, the emphasis of the American plans was on limiting defensive ABM systems where the Soviets enjoyed a clear if momentary lead. The Soviets, when sounded out on the possibility of talks by Ambassador LLEWELLYN THOMPSON, were lukewarm and were more concerned about limiting offensive systems, in which the Americans had superiority.

As a concession to the Soviet Union, Thompson was instructed to tell Soviet prime minister ALEXEI KOSYGIN that the United States was willing to discuss limiting offensive weapons as well as defensive systems. On March 2, 1967, Johnson announced that Kosygin had agreed to U.S.–Soviet negotiations on "limiting the arms race in offensive and defensive nuclear missiles" and went on to suggest that the talks should aim to set upper limits on offensive systems.

Johnson pressed for talks when he met Kosygin for a summit meeting in Glassboro, New Jersey in June 1967. But Kosygin refused to set a date for the start of negotiations and was especially opposed to any attempt to limit ABM systems. Some observers believe, though, that the intensity with which Johnson put the case for holding talks convinced Kosygin to investigate the possibility further.

On June 27, 1968, Soviet foreign minister ANDREI GROMYKO told the Supreme Soviet that the Soviet government was ready to discuss the "mutual limitation and subsequent reduction of strategic means of delivery of nuclear weapons, both offensive and defensive, including antiballistic missiles." Formal U.S.–Soviet negotiations were set to start on September 30 with a meeting in Leningrad between Johnson and Kosygin. But on August 20, 1968, Warsaw Pact forces invaded Czechoslovakia and the talks were indefinitely postponed.

In the months prior to the decision to start negotiations, the Johnson administration had engaged in a vigorous internal debate over negotiating tactics and strategies. These centered largely on the development and deployment of the American antiballistic missile system Safeguard. At the start of the process, the U.S. defensive systems were inferior to those of the Soviet Union, and there was a strong argument for developing an ABM system to counter the Soviet system—partly for military reasons and partly because some arms experts believed that the deployment of an American ABM system would improve the leverage of American negotiators at any subsequent SALT talks. Others, however, argued that the development of an American ABM system was unnecessarily provocative to the Soviets, was potentially destabilizing and would lead to a new and dangerous twist in the arms race spiral. The same logic was applied by both factions to plans for MIRV programs.

RICHARD NIXON was among those arguing for stronger defenses, and in the 1968 presidential campaign he ran on a promise "to restore our objective of clear-cut military superiority." Nixon's support for the pro-ABM faction led the U.S. Congress to approve deployment of the Safeguard System to protect Minuteman ICBM sites. The Soviet Union had 64 ABM launchers in place around Moscow.

The victory of the pro-ABM faction in the United States led the Soviets to shift the focus of their concern from offensive to defensive systems. They realized that the United States had the technological edge and that if it came to an ABM and MIRV race, the Americans would win. Therefore, it would benefit the Soviet Union to reach an agreement on defensive systems while it still had an advantage.

Talks began in Helsinki on November 17, 1969. By the end of 1970 it had become clear that the talks were deadlocked.

The Nixon administration, through national security advisor HENRY KISSINGER, turned to secret negotiations with Anatoly Dobrynin, Soviet ambassador to Washington. These negotiations produced an agreement to negotiate two separate treaties, one to deal with ABM systems, the other to deal with offensive weapons.

The Nixon administration, however, refused to sign an ABM Treaty without an accompanying agreement on offensive weapons. As Nixon made clear on February 25, 1971, "To limit only one side of the offense–defense equation could rechannel arms competition rather than curtail it."

But American negotiators, following the course of least resistance, concentrated on the ABM negotiations, partly because they were easier and partly because they hoped that success in this area would encourage Soviet concessions on offensive weapons. A further impetus to talks was given by an agreement to hold a U.S.–Soviet summit meeting in Moscow in May 1972, thus providing the negotiators with a deadline.

Pressure to reach agreement was also applied to the American negotiating team by the forthcoming 1972 presidential elections. Soviet leader LEONID BREZHNEV, for his part, was facing pressure from within the Politburo to produce tangible results from his détente policy. He was also concerned by the prospect of a Sino–American rapprochement, which threatened a new anti-Soviet alignment on the Soviet Union's eastern border.

The ABM Treaty was ready for signing when Nixon arrived in Moscow in May 22, 1972. But the SALT I Treaty still needed a great deal of work on the issues of submarine-launched ballistic missiles, mobile land-based missiles and the size of missiles. The problem of forward-based systems had been temporarily resolved by agreeing to ignore it for the time being.

The United States wanted to ban mobile missiles and obtain more precise language on missile size than had been agreed in the preceding negotiations. The Soviets refused to discuss mobile ICBMs, and this issue, like the FBS, was shelved. The issue of missile size—which dealt with silo modifications and sublimits on large missiles—was dealt with by the Soviets, who agreed that increases in land-based missile silos be restricted to 10–15%. But the issue of sublimits was also left for later negotiations.

The last hurdle involved SLBMs. The Soviets wanted to increase the size of their nuclear submarine fleet, but the United States successfully insisted that each additional SLBM must be matched by the retirement of an old missile.

American and Soviet negotiators worked around the clock to complete the SALT I Treaty before Nixon was due to leave Moscow. The final details were actually worked out on the final day of Nixon's visit, May 26, and the treaty was signed, along with the ABM Treaty, at St. Vladimir Hall in the Kremlin. The main points of the SALT I Treaty were:

1. Neither the Soviet Union nor the United States would "start construction of additional fixed land-based ICBM launchers after July 1, 1972."
2. Submarine-launched ballistic missile launchers and "modern ballistic missile submarines" were to be limited "to the numbers operational and under construction on the date of signature" of the interim agreement.
3. Modernization and replacement of existing missiles and launchers could be undertaken.
4. The agreement was to last five years.

5. Both parties agreed "to continue active negotiations for limitations on strategic offensive weapons."

The protocol attached to the interim agreement limited the United States to no more than 710 SLBMs and no more than 44 missile-launching submarines. The Soviet Union was limited to 950 SLBMs and 62 modern submarines. Some replacements were to be permitted for "launchers of older types deployed prior to 1964."

For Further Information:
Newhouse, John. *Cold Dawn: The Story of SALT.* New York, 1973.
Smith, Gerard. *Doubletalk.* Garden City, N.Y., 1980.

Strategic Arms Reduction Treaties (START)   After the signing of SALT II (which remained unratified by the United States but which both countries continued to abide by), Washington and Moscow in 1982 began the Strategic Arms Reduction Talks, which ultimately became the first Strategic Arms Reduction Treaty, known as START. Aside from a break during a period of East–West tension, from 1983 to 1985, the bilateral negotiations were continuous until START I was finally signed in July 1991. It was the first treaty to reduce, rather than merely limit, the number of long-range nuclear weapons. It was followed in relatively short order by START II, signed in January 1993.

Soviet president MIKHAIL GORBACHEV and U.S. president RONALD REAGAN initially sought to have the treaty cut both sides' strategic arsenals by 50%. But as it was ultimately crafted, START I amounted to an average reduction of 30%: The Soviets would slash their arsenal by about 35%, from 11,000 warheads to 7,000, and the United States would cut its by some 25%, from 12,000 to 9,000. Although the pact allowed both countries to deploy an additional 1,000 warheads each over the next decade, budget restraints made such increases unlikely.

(In theory, START was to limit both sides to no more than 6,000 warheads and 1,600 strategic delivery systems each. However, under a complex formula, nuclear weapons carried by long-range strategic bombers—bombs, short-range missiles, and cruise missiles—in some cases counted as less than one warhead. Therefore, both sides actually ended up being permitted to deploy considerably more than 6,000 weapons each.)

With the reductions, the United States still would maintain its edge in submarine-launched intercontinental ballistic missiles (ICBMs), while the Soviet Union would keep its numerical advantage in land-based ICBMs.

President GEORGE BUSH, traveling to Moscow for the first post-Cold War superpower summit, joined with Gorbachev in signing START I on July 31, 1991. Once ratified, the treaty was to be in effect for 15 years, renewable after that point for successive five-year periods until replaced by a new treaty. However, the situation became more complicated with the breakup of the Soviet Union and the resignation of Gorbachev in December 1991. In a follow-up action, the United States and the four nuclear-armed members of the new Commonwealth of Independent States—Russia, Ukraine, Belarus and Kazakhstan—signed protocols in May 1992 vowing compliance with START. The treaty was ratified by the U.S. Senate on October 1, by a vote of 93 to 6. Kazakhstan and Russia also ratified the pact in 1992, leaving only Belarus and Ukraine as holdouts.

Meanwhile, Russian president BORIS YELTSIN traveled to Washington in June 1992 for a summit with Bush. There, in an unexpected breakthrough, both sides agreed on a sweeping new package of arms reductions that went significantly beyond START I. In essence, it called for the American arsenal to be cut to 3,500 warheads and Russia's to 3,000 by the year 2003. The accord was made possible when Yeltsin agreed to abandon the concept of strategic parity, or a roughly equal balance of arms—a principle that had been at the center of all previous Cold War arms-control talks.

Whereas previous arms-control treaties had taken up to a decade each to negotiate, START II took only six months, a reflection both of the new post-Cold War world and of Bush's wish to have the treaty finished before he left office. The accord was signed by Bush and Yeltsin on January 3, 1993, in Moscow.

START II called for both sides to slash their arsenals by about one-third of current levels within a decade. It would entirely eliminate MIRVs (MULTIPLE INDEPENDENTLY TARGETED REENTRY VEHICLES), or multiple warheads, on all land-based ICBMs, including the Soviet SS-18 and the U.S. MX missile, each of which carried 10 warheads.

Many analysts saw the agreement as being particularly advantageous to the United States. They noted that while it would scrap MIRVs on land—which had long been the strength of the Soviet and now Russian arsenal—it did not forbid submarine-launched MIRVed missiles, where the United States had a considerable lead. (The pact would, however, cut the number of American sub-launched warheads in half, to 1,728.)

Since the June 1992 summit, conservatives in the Russian parliament and military establishment had been criticizing Yeltsin for supposedly bargaining away Moscow's strength and capitulating to Washington. To bolster Yeltsin's position and assist him in getting the treaty ratified, the United States made a number of concessions in the final draft. They included: allowing the Russians to keep 90 of their SS-18 fixed silos, as long they were rendered unfit for SS-18 basing; permitting Moscow to convert 105 of its SS-19 six-warhead missiles into single-warhead missiles (the United States could do the same with its three-warhead Minuteman III missiles); counting each nuclear weapon carried by a bomber as equal to a missile warhead; allowing each side to verify the actual number of weapons carried by each kind of bomber; and allowing Moscow a one-time controlled inspection of the new U.S. B-2 Stealth bomber.

Both Russia and the U.S. agreed that START II would not be implemented until all parties to START I had honored the provisions of that pact. START II was intended to supplement, not replace, START I.

Strategic Coupling   Strategic coupling describes a political and/or military link between two regions or countries that ensures that one region comes to the aid of the other in case of attack. The term *decoupling* is used to describe the breaking of this strategic link.

The best example of strategic coupling and decoupling is the relationship between the United States and Western Europe. The military support of the United States is vital to the protection of Western Europe, and the two regions are strategically coupled by the presence of American troops and nuclear weapons in Western Europe as well as by NATO treaty obligations. During the Cold War these factors taken together ensured that a Soviet attack on Western Europe would result in an American attack on the Soviet Union.

Strategic Defense Initiative (SDI: "Star Wars")   The Strategic Defense Initiative, or "Star Wars," is a land- and/or space-based defensive shield proposed by President RONALD REAGAN. It has been attacked by critics as being technologically unfeasible and for allegedly breaching the 1972 ANTIBALLISTIC MISSILE (ABM) TREATY, threatening a new arms race and undermining strategic arms negotiations with the Soviet Union and its successor states. SDI's supporters claim that the "prefect" defense envisaged would make nuclear war unwinable and thus pointless.

Reagan's SDI program was very much a personal initiative. It was launched on March 23, 1983, in a nationally televised address in which he called for the long-term development of antiballistic missile technology that would render nuclear missiles "impotent and obsolete" and hold out "the promise of changing the course of human history."

The system, as envisaged by Reagan and his advisers, was to be based on land and in space and would employ advanced technology, including lasers, microwave devices, particle beams and projectile beams deployed in several defensive layers to destroy attacking nuclear missiles far above the Earth's surface.

Until the launching of Reagan's Strategic Defense Initiative, the guiding defense principle of the nuclear weapons states had been MASSIVE RETALIATION. According to the principle, no one country would dare to launch a nuclear attack on any of the others for fear that it would itself be subject to a massive nuclear retaliatory attack.

It was further argued that a foolproof defensive system increased the likelihood that the owner of that system would be tempted to launch a FIRST-STRIKE attack, secure in the knowledge that it was protected from retaliation. This thinking lay behind the 1972 Antiballistic Missile (ABM) Treaty, which limited the antinuclear defensive systems of the two superpowers.

SDI was attacked by Reagan's critics within the United States and the Western Alliance and by the Soviet Union as a breach of the ABM Treaty. The Soviet Union also insisted on tying progress on Strategic Arms Reduction Talks (see STRATEGIC ARMS REDUCTION TREATIES) to an American commitment to halt its SDI program. Critics also questioned the technical and financial feasibility of the program and warned that further advances would force the Soviet Union into a dangerous new arms race.

Reagan, however, regarded his SDI as a "moral imperative" and said that deployment of such a system would "pave the way for arms control measures to eliminate the [nuclear] weapons themselves."

The debate over SDI became a major factor in U.S.–Soviet relations and U.S.–European relations during the Reagan administration, and between major figures within the U.S. government. America's allies were concerned primarily with the effect that the SDI program was having on strategic arms negotiations and general East–West tensions. But this was offset somewhat by a U.S. offer to West European companies to share in the SDI research program.

Within the U.S. administration, the key figures broke down into those who supported a "narrow interpretation" of the 1972 ABM Treaty, which would effectively block or limit SDI, and those who supported the "broad interpretation," which would allow SDI to go ahead. The narrow camp was led by Secretary of State GEORGE SHULTZ and stemmed from his concern over the effect that the program was having on arms negotiations. The broad camp was led by Defense Secretary Caspar Weinberger, who wanted to take advantage of America's technological lead and was concerned about Soviet violations of the ABM Treaty and increases in the Soviet Union's land-based intercontinental ballistic missile systems.

President GEORGE BUSH affirmed his support for SDI when he entered the White House in 1989, but the program's close identification with Reagan personally meant that it lost some of its impetus during the changeover of administrations. This plus the changes in Soviet policies initiated by MIKHAIL GORBACHEV led at the end of 1989 to cuts in SDI budget of more than 25%, from $4.1 billion to $3.57 billion. This was the first real cutback in SDI funding since the program's inception.

Research and testing continued, however. The initially proposed laser-type defense systems were largely abandoned to concentrate on the less expensive and allegedly more feasible kinetic systems known as autonomous space-based interceptors, nicknamed "Brilliant Pebbles."

The program continues to be funded at minimal levels, more for political than strategic reasons in a weak post-Cold War economy, but its future is in doubt.

For Further Information:
Aspen Strategy Group. *The Strategic Defense Initiative and American Security.* Lanham, Md., 1987.
Payne, Keith B. *Strategic Defense: Star Wars in Perspective.* Lanham, Md., 1986.

Strauss, Franz Josef   (September 6, 1915–October 3, 1988)
Franz Josef Strauss was the longtime leader of the Bavarian-

based Christian Social Union (CSU) and played a major role in rebuilding West Germany's international voice and stature.

Strauss graduated from the University of Munich with a top degree in classics. During World War II he served in an antiaircraft unit and was captured by U.S. forces. Shortly after his release, he set about to establish the CSU. The party is based entirely in Bavaria, but Strauss from the start was determined that it should have a national voice.

Strauss was elected to the Bundestag in the first West German elections in 1949. He served there until 1978, when he became state premier of Bavaria. Strauss knew that as a regional party, the CSU could not on its own win a majority in the Bundestag. He therefore formed an alliance with the Christian Democratic Union (CDU) led by KONRAD ADENAUER. Under this arrangement the CDU restricted its activities to the northern part of the country and the CSU remained in Bavaria, but both parties respected each other's separate identities.

As a result of the alliance, Strauss was in 1953 called into Adenauer's second government as minister without portfolio. In 1955 he became minister for atomic affairs and the following year minister of defense. Strauss was defense minister at a crucial period in his country's history. West Germany had just been given back its sovereignty and been admitted to the NORTH ATLANTIC TREATY ORGANIZATION (NATO). At the same time, the Soviet Union was offering inducements, including guaranteed German neutrality, both to West Germany and Western Europe to reverse their decision to admit West Germany as a member of the Western Alliance.

Strauss had to convince Germany's new West European partners that a rearmed West Germany posed no threat to them, would be a firm ally against Soviet expansionism and would not succumb to the appeal of neutralism. He also had to structure a West German defensive system that protected West German national territory in conjunction with NATO forces, while not posing an offensive threat to Soviet forces based in East Germany. Strauss managed to pull off this delicate balancing act and in doing so established himself as a major force in East–West relations.

Strauss's initial success as West German minister of defense probably would have landed him the chancellorship if not for his clumsy handling in 1962 of the *Der Spiegel Affair.* The West German news magazine, *Der Spiegel* had published an article on NATO that allegedly contained state secrets. Strauss ordered the police to raid the magazine and arrest its publisher. In a subsequent statement to the Bundestag he misled the parliament, and he was forced to resign.

However, Strauss remained the dominant force within the CSU and Bavarian politics, and it was inevitable that whenever the CSU held the balance of power, he would be in a position to return to office. The opportunity came in 1966 with the "Grand Coalition" of the CDU, CSU and Social Democratic Party (SPD), and Strauss was appointed finance minister. After the defeat of the conservative CDU/CSU

alliance in the 1969 election, Strauss went into a 13-year period of opposition.

In opposition, Strauss became an implacable foe of the OSTPOLITIK ("Eastern Policy") of Chancellor WILLY BRANDT. He described the German–Soviet Treaty of August 1970 as "the advance can opener of a Pandora's box of mischief."

Strauss was clearly the major conservative force in West German politics, but many found him to be too volatile personally and too extreme in his anti-Soviet views. He might have been able to overcome this reputation if, in October 1971, the Federal Audit Board had not severely criticized him for his procurement of the accident-prone U.S. Lockheed Starfighter F-104 jet when he was defense minister. The report said that Strauss had purchased the planes without waiting for the normal trial period in the plane's development and accused him of inadequately informing, and sometimes misleading, parliamentary defense and budget committees about the Starfighter's capabilities. The release of the report followed the 140th crash of a Starfigher (not all the planes were German).

The Starfighter scandal destroyed Strauss's dreams of becoming chancellor. He made a vain attempt in 1980 but was decisively defeated, and his defeat paved the way for HELMUT KOHL to take over as the undisputed conservative leader. Before the January 1987 campaign, Strauss had hopes of increasing the CSU share of the vote and unseating HANS-DIETRICH GENSCHER, the leader of the Free Democratic Party (FDP), as foreign minister. But the FDP increased its share of the vote and Genscher retained the foreign minister's portfolio.

In the last two years of his life, Strauss appeared to move toward a rapprochement with the Soviet Union and East Germany. He developed a friendly relationship with East German leader ERICH HONECKER and helped to negotiate a key $500 million West German credit for East Berlin. In December 1987 he visited the Soviet Union for the first time and met with MIKHAIL GORBACHEV. During this visit he called for improved ties in East–West trade and technology. Strauss's moves in this direction made it easier for Kohl and Genscher in 1988 and 1989 to call on Britain and the United States to reduce the number of short-range nuclear missiles in West Germany as part of an effort to improve East–West relations. Strauss died on October 3, 1988, of a sudden heart attack while delivering a campaign speech in his Bavarian homeland.

For Further Information:
Crawley, A.M. *The Rise of West Germany, 1945–1972.* New York, 1974.
Pfetsch, Frank. *West Germany, Internal Structures and External Relations: The Foreign Policy of the Federal Republic.* New York, 1988.
Strauss, Franz Joseph. *The Grand Design.* New York, 1965.

Streibert, Theodore   (August 29, 1899–January 18, 1987)
Theodore Streibert was the first director of the United States Information Agency (USIA) and helped to establish its reputation as a disseminator of anti-communist propaganda.

After graduating from Wesleyan University in 1921,

Streibert went on to Harvard Business School. In 1935 he started a career in radio, which culminated 18 years later in his being named chairman of the board of the Mutual Broadcasting System.

In April 1953 President DWIGHT EISENHOWER proposed to strip the State Department of its overseas information functions and pass those duties to a newly created United States Information Agency, under the aegis of the NATIONAL SECURITY COUNCIL. The USIA would be responsible for running the Voice of America, the International Press Service and the International Educational Exchange Service. The proposal was approved by Congress in the following month, and Streibert was confirmed as the USIA's first director in August 1953.

In a press conference on October 28, 1953, Eisenhower said that the purpose of the USIA was "to submit evidence to peoples of other nations . . . that [U.S.] objectives and policies . . . are in harmony with and will advance their legitimate aspirations for freedom, progress and peace." He then released a letter from Streibert in which the new director said that the USIA would avoid "a propagandistic tone."

But despite this early pledge, the USIA under Streibert developed a reputation as the main propaganda arm of America's Cold Warriors. The agency regularly depicted the dark side of Soviet totalitarianism and stocked USIA libraries with such books as *The Death of Science in Russia* and *Forced Labor in Soviet Russia*.

The agency also praised the American-sponsored overthrow of the popularly-elected left-wing Arbenz government in Guatemala, calling it a victory of free men over "red colonialism." It tried to persuade nonaligned countries that they were pawns of Soviet foreign policy.

In spite of the agency's strident anti-communist campaign, it became a target of Senator JOSEPH MCCARTHY, who claimed that USIA had been infiltrated by communist "subversives." In November 1953, Streibert was forced to order his office of security to carry out a search for communists. In January 1954, Streibert told the Senate Foreign Relations Committee that only 20 out of 7,800 employees had been dismissed as security risks.

Streibert was appointed to the National Security Council in 1955, and from January 1956 he attended cabinet meetings. He resigned his post in November 1956 to join the business staff of Nelson and Laurence Rockefeller. He became a vice president of Time-Life Corporation in 1960 and in 1962 was named president of the Radio Free Europe Fund. He retired in 1965.

Suez Crisis The Suez Crisis ended Britain's immediate postwar role as a superpower, destroyed its lingering imperial pretensions, undermined British influence in the Middle East, distracted world attention from the simultaneous Hungarian Revolution, created a dangerous strain in Anglo–American relations and underscored Britain's weakness as an independent foreign policy maker.

The Suez Canal was regarded by British policy makers as the vital link between Europe and its interests in the oil fields of the Persian Gulf, India and the Far East. The company that controlled the canal was Anglo–French, and, under a 1936 Anglo–Egyptian 30-year treaty imposed by the British, the Canal Zone was occupied by British troops.

In the immediate postwar years, the Egyptian government came under strong pressure from nationalist and Islamic fundamentalist forces to renegotiate the 1936 treaty. A number of anti-British riots took place. The ensuing political instability was fertile ground for the coup that eventually toppled the monarchy in July 1952. The coup was led by Colonel GAMAL ABDEL NASSER, who did not take absolute power until April 1954.

Nasser was vehemently anti-British, anti-Israeli and a strong advocate of pan-Arabism in order to combat what he regarded as two outside colonial powers entrenched in the Arab world. A primary goal for Nasser became the ownership of the Suez Canal and the withdrawal of British troops from Egyptian territory. In 1954 he succeeded in renegotiating the 1936 treaty to force the gradual withdrawal of British troops. Nasser continued his diplomatic attacks on Britain after the 1954 treaty and gradually started to shift his foreign policy toward a closer relationship with the Soviet Union. Nasser's growing popularity throughout the Arab world appeared to undermine traditional British influence in the Middle East. ANTHONY EDEN, who became British prime minister in 1955, became convinced that Nasser had to be overthrown in order to protect vital British and Western interests. For Eden, the final straw came when Nasser, in response to Britain and America's decision to withdraw from the Aswan Dam project, nationalized the Suez Canal Company on July 26, 1956.

Two days after the nationalization of the canal, the British Treasury froze all Egyptian assets in Britain. France and the United States quickly followed suit. Eden also ordered the mobilization of 20,000 army reservists and dispatched military reinforcements to the eastern Mediterranean. France also threatened military force. U.S. president DWIGHT EISENHOWER responded by organizing a canal users' conference to try to force a settlement on Nasser. Nasser refused to attend.

Britain and France lost American support shortly afterward when Secretary of State JOHN FOSTER DULLES became convinced that the two European powers wanted to push Egypt into a war. On October 1, 1956, Dulles called a press conference to dissociate the Eisenhower administration from British and French actions in the Middle East and announced that the United States intended to play "a somewhat independent role." Some historians believe that the Dulles press conference undermined the moderates in the British government and finally convinced Eden that war was the only option.

Britain and France continued to go through the motions of trying to reach a negotiated settlement, although the vehicle for these negotiations shifted from the canal users' conference to the United Nations. Egypt, under heavy political pressure from all sides, agreed effectively to share management of the canal with the Suez Canal Users' Association, but the Egyptian concessions were rejected by the British and French, who would accept nothing less than the proposals agreed to earlier by the Canal Users' Conference.

While the negotiations were in progress, French prime minister Guy Mollet had been holding secret negotiations with Israel to involve that country in an attack on Egypt. Under the terms of the 1954 Anglo–Egyptian treaty, the British could reoccupy the canal zone if either Egypt or the canal came under attack from a third country. Mollet therefore proposed that Israel attack Egypt and thus provide Britain and France with a legal excuse to intervene. Each of the three countries had its own reason for attacking Nasser. Britain wanted to regain control of the Suez Canal. France wanted to eliminate a government that was supporting rebel forces in Algeria, and Israel wanted to gain access to the Suez Canal. The French and Israelis needed the support of British bombers based in Cyprus in order to stage a successful attack.

On October 13 Mollet sent Acting Foreign Minister Albert Gazier and General Maurice Challe, deputy chief of staff for the French Air Force, to meet with Eden and formally propose British involvement in the plot. The plan encountered strong opposition from Arabists in the British Foreign Office, but it was approved by Eden, who, along with Foreign Secretary Selwyn Lloyd, went to Paris on October 16 to confer directly with Mollet and Israeli prime minister David Ben-Gurion.

The Israelis were at first skeptical about British and French support for their action, but on October 25 they finally agreed to attack Egypt across the Sinai. The Eisenhower administration was kept completely in the dark, and on October 29, 1956, Israel attacked Egypt. On October 30 the British and French governments issued an ultimatum to both sides to withdraw their forces to 10 miles from either side of the Suez Canal. The ultimatum gave Egypt and Israel 12 hours to reply. If no reply was received within the allotted time, then British and French troops would intervene to seize and protect the canal.

The Israelis, of course, accepted the ultimatum. The Egyptians rejected it. Up to this point, Eden's strong anti-Nasser stand had been supported by the Labour opposition. But when he reported to the House of Commons on October 31 he faced heavy criticism from the Labour party, which already suspected Anglo–French–Israeli collusion. The absence of bipartisan support throughout the Suez Crisis was one of the reasons for British withdrawal.

British aircraft bombed four Egyptian airfields on the night of October 31–November 1 and a further nine the next day, effectively wiping out the Egyptian bomber force and preventing an Egyptian reprisal attack on Israeli citizens. British and French paratroopers were dropped at the northern end of the Suez Canal on November 5.

In the intervening five days, Britain and France came under heavy political pressure to withdraw. Within the Commonwealth; British action was either condemned or "regretted." The Soviet Union warned that Britain and France must bear the "dangerous consequences" of taking "the road of aggression." But the most damaging opposition came from the United States, where President Eisenhower on October 31 described the attack as an action "taken in error," promised that there would be no U.S. involvement in the hostilities and warned Britain and France against using American weapons. On Novembver 2, the UN General Assembly approved an American-sponsored resolution that all parties involved in hostilities in the area agree to an immediate cease-fire and halt the movement of military forces and arms. On November 4, Israel and Egypt agreed to a cease-fire, thus negating the need for Anglo–French forces in the area.

One of the most damaging pressures on Britain and France was economic. The Syrians destroyed a pipeline from Iraq, and Saudi Arabia halted all of its oil shipments to Britain and France. This meant that the two European countries had to purchase their oil in dollars on the open market rather than in sterling from British-controlled sources. But Britain's dollar reserves had been seriously depleted by a run on sterling, and the Eisenhower administration refused to extend Eden's government any credit while British troops remained in the canal zone.

The result was that even before the Anglo–French paratroopers landed, Eden had decided to climb down and accept a Canadian proposal that a UN emergency force replace British and French troops in the canal zone. Despite Eden's reversal, the British and French governments went ahead with their attack on Port Said on November 5, and fighting broke out between Egypt and the Anglo–French forces. A final cease-fire, which included the British and French, was agreed to on November 6.

Eden hoped to keep the Anglo–French force in the canal zone as part of a UN force, but the Eisenhower administration refused to extend essential financial credits unless the British and French forces were, at the very least, seen to be withdrawing. Eden and Mollet were reluctant to agree to these terms, and gasoline rationing was introduced in both countries. Eden, who was seriously ill, went on a three-week holiday from November 21, leaving Deputy Prime Minister R.A. Butler in charge of the government. At the end of November Lloyd and French foreign minister Christian Pineau agreed to withdraw by December 22 and to the replacement of the Anglo–French force by a 4,000-strong UN force drawn from the Scandinavian countries, India, Brazil, Indonesia and Colombia. On December 1, Eisenhower announced that he had authorized American oil companies to start supplying oil to Britain and France on favorable credit terms. Shortly afterward Eden resigned, citing ill health.

For Further Information:
Carlton, David. *Britain and the Suez Crisis.* New York, 1989.
Cooper, Chester L. *The Lion's Last Roar: Suez, 1956.* New York, 1978.
Eden, Anthony. *The Suez Crisis of 1956.* Boston, 1966.
Freiberger, Steven Z. *Dawn Over Suez: The Rise of American Power in the Middle East, 1953–1957.* Chicago, 1992.

Louis, William Roger, and Roger Owen. *Suez 1956: The Crisis and its Consequences*. New York, 1989.

Lucas, W. Scott. *Divided We Stand: Britain, the US and the Suez Crisis*. London, 1991.

Nutting, Anthony. *No End of a Lesson*. London, 1967.

Stephens, Robert. *Nasser: A Political Biography*. London, 1971.

Supreme Allied Commander Atlantic (SACLANT) The Supreme Allied Commander Atlantic is the officer responsible for all NORTH ATLANTIC TREATY ORGANIZATION (NATO) naval commands in the Atlantic Ocean. His area of responsibility extends from the coastal waters of North America to those of Europe and Africa. It does not include the British Isles and the English Channel, which come under the command of Allied Commander-in-Chief Channel (CINCHAN). SACLANT's command is based at Norfolk, Virginia and is always headed by an American naval officer.

In peacetime, SACLANT is responsible for preparing defense plans, conducting joint and combined training exercises, laying down training standards and determining the establishment strength of naval units.

In wartime, SACLANT would be responsible for ensuring the security of the entire Atlantic by guarding the sea lanes. SACLANT is also responsible for islands in this area such as the Faeroes and the Azores and, in wartime, would be responsible for conventional and nuclear attacks against enemy naval bases and airfields.

Supreme Allied Commander Europe (SACEUR) SACEUR is the most powerful military commander in the NORTH ATLANTIC TREATY ORGANIZATION (NATO) alliance. In time of war, he would be responsible for all land, sea and air operations in Europe, the most likely scene of an East–West conflict.

SACEUR is traditionally a senior American officer. He has direct access to NATO's Military Committee, the individual chiefs of staff of each NATO country, the defense ministers of each NATO country and the heads of government of each NATO country. Previous SACEURS have included DWIGHT EISENHOWER and ALEXANDER HAIG.

In peacetime, SACEUR is responsible for training, assigning and equipping all NATO forces under his command, including all U.S. troops committed to European defense. SACEUR is also responsible for preparing defense plans for submission to the Military Committee.

Suslov, Mikhail (November 21, 1902–January 26, 1982) Mikhail Suslov was for many years the Soviet Communist Party's ideological arbiter. His hard-line views are believed to have played a major role in the decision to invade CZECHOSLO-VAKIA in 1968 and AFGHANISTAN in 1979.

Suslov was born into a Russian peasant family in the Volga River valley. At the age of 15 he became involved in the Bolshevik Revolution as a member of the Youth Communist League. When he turned 19 he joined the Communist Party

and was sent to Moscow for an accelerated high school education at a special workers' school.

In 1924 Suslov entered the Plekhanov Institute of the National Economy, the training ground for the Soviet Union's first generation of economic planners and political economists. In 1928 he moved on to graduate studies at the Moscow Communist Party school, the Economics Institute of Red Professors. He also taught economics at Moscow University and at the Industrial Academy at the same time.

While studying and teaching, Suslov continued his work for the Communist Party and was recognized for his loyalty to the party leadership. In 1931 he was appointed to help supervise the Stalinist purges in the Urals and in the Chernigov region of the Ukraine. He climbed through the party ranks during the period of the purges, and in 1939 was appointed first secretary of the local party in the Stavropol territory of the Caucasus. He was elected to the Central Committee in 1941.

During World War II, Suslov remained in the Caucasus and helped to organize the resistance in the areas occupied by the Germans in 1942. In 1944 he helped to supervise the deportation of ethnic minorities accused of collaboration with the Germans. Shortly afterward, Suslov was moved to Lithuania to supervise the political integration of that formerly independent country. He was responsible for the arrest and deportation to Siberia of thousands of Lithuanians who opposed Soviet rule.

In March 1946 JOSEF STALIN summoned Suslov to Moscow, where he was put in charge of the Central Committee department responsible for domestic ideological controls. But Suslov quickly moved over into the foreign affairs field, where he earned a reputation as a "young political philosopher." In 1947 Suslov was instrumental in establishing the multinational COMINFORM (Communist Information Bureau) and took responsibility for relations with other national communist parties. In 1949 he went back to domestic matters as editor of *Pravda*, but in 1952 was promoted to the Politburo, then known as the Presidium. He moved into foreign affairs and, despite his age, was quickly recognized as the leading interpreter of Marxist-Leninist doctrine on the ruling Presidium.

Suslov continued in this role of, in effect, chief ideologue until his death in 1982. In a government purporting to be organized and run according to a universally applicable "scientific" doctrine, the person who held the position of doctrinal arbiter wielded immense power. If there was any major difference of opinion over policy within the Politburo, it was often Suslov who would break the deadlock by deciding which course of action was doctrinally correct in Marxist-Leninist terms. He also had to approve the ideological credentials of all potential senior appointments within the party apparatus, was responsible for relations with other national communist parties and approved foreign trips by senior Soviet officials.

Suslov never sought the top position within the Soviet Communist Party, but his support became an essential prerequisite for anyone else seeking the general secretaryship of the party. For this reason, Suslov became known as "the kingmaker." In 1957, he voted for NIKITA KHRUSHCHEV in his bid for power, but Suslov was never pro-Khrushchev. The two disagreed over Khrushchev's economic program of shifting emphasis from heavy industry and armaments to the production of consumer items. Suslov also opposed Khrushchev's cultural liberalization and felt that the Soviet leader had gone too far in denouncing Stalin and in dealing with YUGOSLAVIA and POLAND. Suslov's support for LEONID BREZHNEV is believed to have been crucial to the latter's decision to oust Khrushchev in October 1964 and his eventual emergence as the leading figure in the triumvirate of Brezhnev-Podgorny-Kosygin that succeeded Khrushchev.

Suslov was generally viewed as a conservative on both foreign and domestic issues. On domestic issues, he was the guardian of communist purity who was on constant watch for any signs of Western subversion through literature, the arts, television or education. He was a powerful advocate of suppressing dissident voices.

Abroad, he fought against the development of Eurocommunism and efforts by East European communist parties to take a more independent line from Moscow. He was in HUNGARY shortly before the Hungarian Revolution of 1956 and sought to keep Stalinist leader MATYAS RAKOSI in power. In 1968 he was a strong advocate of WARSAW PACT intervention in Czechoslovakia, and he is believed to have pressed for Soviet intervention in Poland in 1980 to suppress Solidarity. In 1979 he supported the Soviet invasion of Afghanistan.

As the Politburo member responsible for interparty relations, Suslov often traveled abroad as the head of Soviet delegations to the congresses of other communist parties. He rarely met any Western political figures. He visited France in 1972, Cuba in 1975, Vietnam and East Germany in 1976 and Poland in 1980. He was awarded four Orders of Lenin as well as the title of Hero of Socialist Labor.

Suslov died on January 26, 1982, at a time when the Communist Party was considering a successor to the ailing Brezhnev. His death, shortly before Brezhnev's, left a major vacuum within the Politburo that helped Brezhnev's successors to shift to a more pragmatic approach to policy-making.

For Further Information:
Conquest, Robert. *Russia After Khrushchev*. London, 1965.
Dallin, Alexander, and Thomas B. Larson, eds. *Soviet Politics Since Khrushchev*. Englewood Cliffs, N.J., 1968.
Owen, Richard. *Crisis in the Kremlin*. London, 1986.

Svoboda, Ludvik   (November 25, 1895–September 20, 1979)   General Ludvik Svoboda was a Czech military hero who lent his prestige to the reforms of the Prague Spring of 1968 when he accepted the largely ceremonial post of president. After the Soviet invasion, Svoboda was retained as president by the hard-liners in order to lend legitimacy to their government.

Svoboda was born into a farming family when Czechoslovakia was still part of the Austro-Hungarian Empire. During World War I he was drafted into the Austro-Hungarian Army and fought on the Russian front. He was captured and joined the Czechoslovak Legion, which was fighting for his country's independence.

After the war, Svoboda returned home to join the newly independent Czechoslovakia's army. He became a career officer and an instructor at the national military academy. At the time of the Munich Crisis in 1938, when Germany annexed the Czech Sudetenland, he took command of an infantry battalion.

When the Germans seized the rest of Czechoslovakia in March 1939, Svoboda fled to Poland. There he organized a military unit of fellow Czech refugees, and after the German invasion of Poland he moved the unit, which had by this time grown to a brigade, to the Soviet Union. Svoboda, now a general, commanded the brigade throughout World War II as it fought alongside the Red Army, moving toward Czechoslovakia. At the end of the war, Svoboda was a war hero and had been given 50 medals, including the Soviet Union's Order of Lenin and Hero of the Soviet Union and the American Legion of Merit.

After the war, Svoboda was named defense minister and charged with rebuilding the Czech Army. He was generally believed to be apolitical, but refused to intervene when the communists seized power in 1948. Svoboda was allowed to remain in the government, first as defense minister and then as deputy prime minister. In 1951 he was himself purged; after an initial imprisonment, he was moved to a bookkeeping job on a collective farm.

In 1955 Soviet leader NIKITA KHRUSHCHEV visited Czechoslovakia and asked about Svoboda, with whom he had fought during the war. Khrushchev's inquiries resulted in Svoboda's rehabilitation, and he was appointed head of the Klement Gottwald Military Academy. He remained there until his retirement from the army in 1959.

Czechoslovakia's Stalinist leadership under ANTONIN NOVOTNY managed to survive the upheavals that shook the rest of Eastern Europe in 1956, but by 1967 a combination of dissatisfaction with the economy and the nationalist aspirations of the Slovaks was undermining the power base of Novotny, who held the posts of president and first secretary of the Communist Party. In January 1968 it was decided to separate those positions, and ALEXANDER DUBCEK replaced Novotny as first secretary. Novotny retained the ceremonial post of president until March 30, 1968, when Svoboda was voted into the position by a secret ballot of the members of the Czechoslovak parliament.

Svoboda was seen as a man who embodied the Czechoslovak national spirit, including the sense of betrayal that followed the Stalinist purges of the early 1950s. It was felt that as president, he would act as a unifying force while Dubcek implemented his program of political and economic reforms. Svoboda also had a high standing in the Soviet Union, where he was as much a war hero as he was in Czechoslovakia.

As Dubcek's democratic reforms moved Czechoslovakia further out of the Soviet orbit, the Soviet Union and other WARSAW PACT countries became increasingly concerned about the implications of the reforms of the Prague Spring. Soviet troops were massed on the Czechoslovak border, and the Dubcek government asked for a meeting with the Soviet Politburo to explain its program. Three days of talks were held in the small town of Cierna on the Slovak–Soviet border starting on July 29. On the first day of talks the Czech government met with a frosty Soviet response. But on the second day, Svoboda made an impassioned defense of his country's right to carry out the liberalization program. The Soviets were apparently so struck by Svoboda's address that they recommended to a summit of Warsaw Pact leaders that the Prague Spring be allowed to continue.

The Bratislava agreement led to wild rejoicing in the streets of Prague. But the celebrations were short-lived because on August 20, 1968, the Warsaw Pact countries, claiming that the Dubcek regime had broken pledges made at Cierna, invaded Czechoslovakia and arrested the entire leadership, including Svoboda. However, he was allowed to retain the post of president because his presence lent political credibility to the new hard-line regime and to the Soviet presence. Svoboda agreed to stay in office, at first to try and rescue the reform program, later to prevent bloodshed.

In the immediate aftermath of the Warsaw Pact invasion, Svoboda took over the reins of government and launched a radio appeal for public support. He urged the Czechoslovak people "to avoid any action or contacts that would exacerbate the atmosphere in our country and our relations with the representatives of the foreign armies." On August 23, he flew to Moscow for talks with Soviet leaders, who demanded that Svoboda appoint a pro-Moscow government. Svoboda refused and threatened to walk out of the talks unless Dubcek was also brought to the negotiations. Dubcek was quickly brought in. Svoboda's stand delayed the resignation of Dubcek, and he believed that he had negotiated the gradual withdrawal of the Soviet troops.

But it quickly became apparent that the Soviet troops were not going to leave, and on October 16 Svoboda, under duress, signed a new Soviet–Czech Treaty authorizing the "temporary stay" of Soviet troops in Czechoslovakia and legalizing the presence of the Warsaw Pact forces. The treaty was signed in Prague and Svoboda refused to greet or see off the Soviet delegation at the airport, as was demanded by diplomatic protocol.

Svoboda became a member of the new Central Committee and Politburo and continued to support Dubcek as he headed for the status of "nonperson" in 1969. He was in the minority when the Czech Politburo voted seven to four in 1970 to deprive Dubcek of his party membership. Svoboda's unimpeachable reputation and character, however, protected him from the ruthless purges of liberals that started in 1972. But he became increasingly isolated and was virtually powerless when he died on September 20, 1979.

For Further Information:
Mlnar, Z. *Nightfrost in Prague.* New York, 1980.
Tokes, Rudolf, ed. *Opposition in Eastern Europe.* Baltimore, 1979.
Valenta, J. *Soviet Intervention in Czechoslovakia 1968: Anatomy of a Decision.* Baltimore, 1979.

Symington, Stuart   (June 26, 1901–December 14, 1988)
Senator Stuart Symington was an early supporter of the U.S. Air Force and a strong nuclear bomber fleet, first as secretary of the Air Force under President HARRY TRUMAN and later as a senator from Missouri from 1953 to 1977. Throughout the 1950s and early 1960s, Symington was regarded as a defense hawk, but by 1967 he had come to oppose the VIETNAM WAR and in the 1970s supported moves to curb the president's foreign policy-making powers.

Symington enlisted in the army while still a teenager in order to fight in World War I. After the war he attended Yale University, but because of a poor mathematics record he did not receive his degree until 1943. After leaving Yale in 1923, Symington went into business, and in 1938 he became president of Emerson Electric Manufacturing Company in St. Louis, Missouri. He developed a reputation for good labor relations, and his successes were brought to the attention of President Truman who, in July 1945, appointed Symington chairman of the Surplus Properties Board with the responsibility for disposing of the country's war surplus. On January 18, 1946, Truman appointed Symington assistant secretary of war for air.

Symington quickly became a proponent of a centralized military structure under a single secretary of defense. He also supported defense budget increases and a strong air force as the cornerstone of a powerful nuclear-based defense force. As part of this campaign he pressed for the establishment of an independent presidential commission to investigate postwar air power. The subsequent report, published in January 1948, called for an immediate large increase in air force spending in order to maintain American superiority in delivery systems for atomic warfare. After the Soviet Union exploded its first atomic bomb in September 1949, Symington called for an increase in the air force from a 48-wing group to a 70-wing group.

But Truman and Defense Secretary Louis Johnson were determined to reduce the defense budget, and in March 1950 Symington resigned in protest against cuts in the air force budget. In April 1950, Symington was appointed director of the National Security Resources Board, which was responsible for mobilization for the KOREAN WAR. A year later he moved to the Reconstruction Finance Corporation as administrator. He was elected to the U.S. Senate as a Democrat in November 1952.

Shortly after taking his seat, Symington returned to the subject of defense spending to attack the new EISENHOWER administration for lagging behind the Soviet Union in the development of bombers and missiles. He went on to accuse Defense Secretary CHARLES WILSON of having done a "wrecking job" on the air force. Symington was not mollified by Eisenhower's "NEW LOOK" DEFENSE POLICY, which increased the air force budget at the expense of the army and navy. In April 1956 he chaired a special subcommittee of the Senate Armed Forces Committee that conducted hearings into the state of American air power. The subcommittee report issued on January 29 charged that American defenses had been weakened because of "a tendency to either ignore or underestimate Soviet military progress" and that U.S. vulnerability to sudden attack "had increased greatly."

In 1959 Symington became one of the leading figures warning about a "bomber gap" and "MISSILE GAP" between the United States and Soviet Union. The issue became a major topic during the 1960 presidential election. Symington predicted that because of greater research and development and more investment in production facilities, the Soviet Union would within a few years have a three-to-one advantage over the United States in intercontinental ballistic missiles and that this would enable the Soviets to "wipe out our entire manned and unmanned retaliatory force" with a single nuclear strike.

Although Symington was regarded as a single-issue politician, he also became involved in opposing the anti-communist campaign of Senator JOSEPH MCCARTHY. He defended Pentagon clerk Annie Lee Moss, accused of being a communist, and played a major role in the Army–McCarthy hearings, which eventually led to McCarthy's fall from power.

In 1960 Symington entered the Democratic presidential primaries, using his campaign to launch a series of attacks on the Eisenhower administration's defense cuts. Symington eventually threw his support behind LYNDON JOHNSON.

During the KENNEDY administration, Symington participated in an investigation of military education programs that were "soft on Communism" and a second investigation into charges that the Eisenhower administration had built up excessive defense stockpiles in order to aid specific companies.

In 1961 Symington joined the Senate Foreign Relations Committee. He thus became a greater force in foreign affairs as the only senator to sit on both the Foreign Relations and Armed Services committees. He later said that his experience on the Foreign Relations Committee caused him to shift from the position of "Cold Warrior" to a more realistic foreign policy approach that took into account all of America's global commitments. By 1967, Symington had joined Senators J. WILLIAM FULBRIGHT and MIKE MANSFIELD in opposing the Vietnam War. He also started opposing foreign aid bills and specific defense projects—including an expanded antiballistic missile system—on the grounds that the United States was already overcommitted.

During the 1970s, Symington spearheaded congressional attempts to make the president more accountable to Congress in foreign policy-making. His stand on this issue was partly the result of a 1969 subcommittee investigation that discovered that, as a result of a series of secret agreements, the United States had 429 major military bases around the world, many of which involved important commitments that had not been approved by Congress, as the Constitution required.

Symington's increasingly liberal stands alienated him from his Midwestern constituents, and he was narrowly reelected in 1970. He did not run again and retired from the Senate, after completing his last six-year term. He died of a heart attack on December 14, 1988.

For Further Information:
Lewis, Flora. "The Education of a Senator," *Atlantic Monthly* (December 1971).

Taiwan   *See* CHINA, REPUBLIC OF.

Taylor, Maxwell D.   (August 26, 1901–April 19, 1987)

General Maxwell Taylor served in several key American military and diplomatic positions, including commander of the Eighth Army during the final stages of the KOREAN WAR, army chief of staff under President DWIGHT EISENHOWER, chairman of the Joint Chiefs of Staff under President JOHN F. KENNEDY and ambassador to Vietnam during the JOHNSON administration. His military theories and emphasis on building up conventional forces shaped America's early responses to the VIETNAM WAR.

Taylor graduated fourth in his class from the U.S. Military Academy at West Point in 1922. During World War II he served as artillery commander of the 101st Airborne Division, and after the war rose to the rank of general and became superintendent of West Point. In 1949 he was appointed the first commander of the American military government in Berlin. During the final stages of the Korean War, Taylor commanded the Eighth Army, and in 1955 he was briefly the commander of UN forces in the Far East.

In June 1955 President Eisenhower appointed Taylor army chief of staff. Eisenhower thought that Taylor would be sympathetic to his cost-cutting "NEW LOOK" DEFENSE POLICY, which diverted money from conventional forces to nuclear forces. Publicly Taylor at first went along with the policy, but privately he had doubts about its effectiveness. The doubts did not solidify into a coherent military doctrine until Eisenhower's second term.

The New Look Policy depended heavily on the idea of MASSIVE RETALIATION, that is, the belief that the Soviet Union would not launch either a conventional or nuclear attack out of fear of a massive nuclear retaliatory strike by the United States. The U.S. government's GAITHER REPORT, released in 1951, undermined the policy by warning that the Soviet Union was on the verge of nuclear parity with the United States. Taylor and others concluded that this would result in a nuclear standoff, which would enable the Soviet Union to utilize its superior conventional forces. The United States, Taylor argued, should therefore rebuild its conventional forces in order to have the ability to fight limited as well as nuclear wars.

This brought Taylor into direct conflict with Eisenhower.

As a result, he was eased out of the Pentagon and into retirement on June 30, 1959. In retirement his attacks on the administration's defense policies became more strident. In December 1959 he published his book *The Uncertain Trumpet*, in which he outlined his policy of "FLEXIBLE RESPONSE" to enable the United States to deal with "anything from general war to infiltration, aggression" or subversion. He maintained that such a policy could be executed only by building up and maintaining both conventional and nuclear forces.

Taylor's book impressed John F. Kennedy, who used the general's arguments to attack Eisenhower's defense policies during the 1960 presidential campaign. After Kennedy's victory, Taylor became one of his chief advisers. One of his first tasks was to compile a report on the CIA role in the failed BAY OF PIGS invasion and the U.S. capability for conducting paramilitary operations. Taylor concluded that the paramilitary operations should be left to the Defense Department rather than the CIA.

On June 26, 1960, Kennedy appointed Taylor to the newly created post of military representative to the president. It was generally acknowledged that it was an interim appointment until Taylor could be appointed chairman of the Joint Chiefs of Staff. As Kennedy's military adviser, Taylor in October 1961 led a mission with WALT ROSTOW to South Vietnam to assess the American response to a series of communist victories. He recommended that the United States send 8,000 combat troops to South Vietnam to reassure President NGO DINH DIEM of America's commitment to the region. Taylor's report was backed by Secretary of Defense ROBERT MCNAMARA but was opposed by the State Department. Kennedy approved a compromise plan that involved an increase in military aid, the dispatch of American helicopter pilots and an increase in the number of military advisers.

On July 20, 1962, Taylor was appointed chairman of the Joint Chiefs of Staff. He was a key figure during the CUBAN MISSILE CRISIS and supported measures to eliminate Soviet missiles from the island quickly. He also played a major role in winning military and congressional backing for the NUCLEAR TEST BAN TREATY.

In September 1963, Taylor and McNamara were sent to Vietnam following demonstrations against the regime by Buddhists. Taylor continued to express confidence in President Ngo Dinh Diem and reported that the war was going well.

McNamara, however, was less optimistic on both counts, and this led to tacit American approval of the military coup that overthrew Diem November 1963.

Taylor remained at the Joint Chiefs of Staff until President Lyndon Johnson appointed him ambassador to South Vietnam in June 1964. Taylor became increasingly concerned that the repressive nature of the South Vietnamese government was hampering the war effort, and he unsuccessfully pressed for political reform. His attitude toward American military involvement was at this stage ambivalent. He supported the sustained American bombing of North Vietnam that began in March 1965, but when it failed to have any military effect he resisted U.S. military pressure to commit more combat troops. He argued that the arrival of large numbers of American forces would lead to anti-Americanism, result in an ever-increasing spiral of American military involvement and encourage the South Vietnamese Army to slacken its efforts.

Taylor's views were at first accepted, but in April 1965 rejected, when it was decided to commit an additional 40,000 American troops. In June, General WILLIAM WESTMORELAND, U.S. commander in South Vietnam, reported that the situation had deteriorated further and requested additional troops. He was supported by Taylor, who from this point fully committed himself to increased American military involvement in Vietnam.

In July 1965 Taylor left South Vietnam, and later in the year he was named a special presidential consultant. But his influence on administration policy declined following his recall from Vietnam. He was, however, a member of the senior advisory group on Vietnam, which in March 1968 unsuccessfully supported Westmoreland's request for an additional 200,000 troops. From 1968 to 1970 he was chairman of the Foreign Intelligence Board. In 1972 he published his memoirs, *Swords and Plowshares*. Taylor died on April 19, 1987.

For Further Information:
Halberstam, David. *The Best and the Brightest*. New York, 1972.
Taylor, General Maxwell. *Swords and Plowshares*. New York, 1972.
————. *The Uncertain Trumpet*. New York, 1959.

Tet Offensive   The Tet Offensive, carried out by the North Vietnamese and Viet Cong in January and February 1968, is generally regarded as the turning point in the VIETNAM WAR. It resulted in the first serious questioning by the Johnson administration of the optimistic military reports from American field commanders, President LYNDON JOHNSON's decision to halt the American bombing of North Vietnam and the start of the PARIS PEACE TALKS.

American ground combat forces had operated in Vietnam from shortly after the GULF OF TONKIN RESOLUTION in August 1964. By 1968 they totaled nearly 500,000, fighting an inconclusive war against the Viet Cong guerrilla army of approximately 200,000 and the North Vietnamese force of about 500,000. In October 1967 the North Vietnamese Army (NVA) started operations in the Central Highlands and along the borders of Cambodia and Laos. The Americans and South Vietnamese responded with a massive show of strength that resulted in the deaths of an estimated 10,000 Vietnamese, compared with 500 American lives.

The Central Highlands operation, however, was a feint designed to draw the American and South Vietnamese forces away from the cities. As the Americans consolidated their position in the highlands, the Viet Cong/NVA forces struck at the unprotected urban areas.

They chose the start of the lunar New Year, Tet, to launch their offensive, breaking a truce to do so. On January 30, 1968, the offensive started in the central provinces. The following day the assault was extended to 36 of South Vietnam's 44 provincial capitals. They hit five of the six largest cities and a quarter of the 242 district capitals. In Saigon, a Viet Cong suicide squad in civilian clothes blasted a hole in the wall surrounding the U.S. Embassy compound and entered the grounds. They were killed by U.S. Marine guards.

The Communists' greatest success of the offensive was in the imperial capital of Hue, which they managed to capture and hold for 26 days. To protect the cities, American and South Vietnamese forces quickly retreated from the rural positions they had just captured, leaving the Viet Cong once again in control of those areas.

The Tet Offensive reinforced an increasingly popular view that the United States was fighting an unwinable war and sparked a fresh round of antiwar protests in the United States and among America's allies. But the American commander in Vietnam, General WILLIAM WESTMORELAND, maintained that the Viet Cong and North Vietnamese forces had in the end "suffered a military defeat" despite "some temporary psychological advantage." He added that he did not believe North Vietnam could "hold up under a long war." At the same time, Westmoreland asked President Johnson for an additional 200,000 troops.

Meeting such a request involved the politically unpopular decision to call up Army Reserve forces. Johnson was reluctant to do this without further advice. He therefore formed a senior advisory group on Vietnam, which advised him against meeting Westmoreland's request, to stop the bombing of North Vietnam and to de-escalate American involvement in Vietnam. Johnson accepted the advice and announced it on March 31, 1968. In May 1968 peace talks started in Paris between North Vietnamese and American negotiators.

For Further Information:
Braestrup, Peter. *Big Story: How the American Press and Television Reported and Interpreted the Crisis of Tet 1968 in Vietnam and Washington*. New Haven, 1983.
Karnow, Stanley. *Vietnam: A History*. New York, 1983.
Oberdorfer, Don. *Tet!* Garden City, N.Y., 1971.
Shulimson, Jack. *Tet-1968*. New York, 1988.
Smith, R.B. *An International History of the Vietnam War*. New York, 1986.
Wirtz, James J. *The Tet Offensive: Intelligence Failure in War*. Ithaca, N.Y., 1991.

Thant, U (January 22, 1909–November 26, 1974) U Thant was secretary-general of the United Nations from 1961 until December 1971. His tenure at the United Nations coincided with the end of the CONGOLESE CIVIL WAR, the 1967 Arab–Israeli War, the VIETNAM WAR, the CUBAN MISSILE CRISIS and the Indo–Pakistan War.

Thant was born in Burma. He attended high school in his home town of Pantanaw and went on to the University College at Rangoon. Before he graduated, Thant's father died, and he was forced to return home to help support his family. He took a job teaching at his old school and eventually rose to headmaster.

During the war, the British colony of Burma was occupied by the Japanese, and Thant was appointed secretary to the educational reorganization committee of the Japanese occupation government. After the war, his old university friend U Nu became prime minister of Burma, and Nu recruited Thant into government service as government press director in 1947. Thant became director of broadcasting in 1948 and in 1949 secretary in the Ministry of Education. In 1953 he was appointed secretary for projects in the Office of the Prime Minister, and in 1955 executive secretary of Burma's Economic and Social Board.

Thant first became involved with the United Nations in 1952 as a member of Burma's delegation to the United Nations. In 1957 he was appointed permanent representative to the United Nations and in 1959 was elected vice president of the General Assembly. In October 1961, Secretary-General DAG HAMMARSKJOLD was killed in an airplane crash over the Congo. The Soviet Union, which had over the years faced increasing pressure from the United Nations, demanded that Hammarskjold be replaced by a three-man executive. This was opposed by the United States, which wanted to maintain a powerful secretary-general. The two superpowers eventually agreed to the appointment of Thant as acting secretary-general to fill Hammarskjold's unexpired term until April 1963. As a concession to the Soviets, the United States also agreed to the creation of five assistant secretaries-general, to include one from the Soviet Union and one from the United States. Thant, however, was given full authority to make executive decisions.

Thant was the ultimate compromise choice at a time when the very structure of the United Nations was in danger from the Cold War. He was clearly from neither of the two power blocs and at his appointment made it clear that his experience as a Burmese diplomat would be carried over into his job at the United Nations. "My country," he said, "has steadfastly pursued over the years a policy of nonalignment and friendship for all other nations whatever their ideologies. In my new role I shall continue to maintain this attitude of objectivity." He later added, "My belief is countries can be neutral but it will be very difficult for an individual to be neutral on the burning issues of the day."

Thant's first problem as secretary-general was the unresolved civil war in the Congo. New fighting broke out in December 1961 and then again in December 1962. On the second occasion, UN forces established the right of complete freedom of movement throughout the troubled province of Katanga. This effectively halted the secessionist movement of Moishe Tshombe, and by June 1964 the UN forces in the Congo were able to withdraw.

In October 1962, Thant became involved in the Cuban Missile Crisis. As tensions over the crisis reached their peak, Thant appealed to both President JOHN F. KENNEDY and Soviet leader NIKITA KHRUSHCHEV to suspend both the American naval blockade of Cuba and the shipments of Soviet arms for two to three weeks so that negotiations could take place. He also appealed to Cuban leader FIDEL CASTRO to halt work on the missile installations. Thant received conciliatory messages from all three parties, and this helped to start negotiations that enabled Khrushchev to back away from a direct confrontation with the United States.

Thant was deeply troubled by the Vietnam War, which he described as "barbarous," but any diplomatic initiatives he launched to resolve the crisis could be only personal ones since neither North Vietnam nor communist China belonged to the United Nations. Thant forcefully expressed his frustration at the UN position when he said that the international body's image was "somewhat tarnished by its seeming impotence in this, the greatest crisis of present times." Thant did, however, make two personal initiatives. In 1968 he visited Britain and the Soviet Union—cochairmen of the 1954 GENEVA CONFERENCE ON INDOCHINA AND KOREA—to try to persuade them to launch a diplomatic initiative. He also spoke to North Vietnamese representatives in Paris and supported their call for a halt to American bombing before any cease-fire negotiations could be started.

In September 1965, the Indo–Pakistan War created another international crisis. Thant was instructed by the UN Security Council to visit the Asian subcontinent to "exert every possible effort to secure an end to hostilities." By September 22, a UN-observed cease-fire was in force along the Indo–Pakistan border. This continued until March 1968, when the two governments negotiated a withdrawal to previous positions.

In 1967, the simmering MIDDLE EAST crisis flared up when the United Arab Republic demanded the immediate withdrawal of the 10-year-old UN emergency force from the armistice lines and frontier between Israel and Egypt. Thant had no legal option but to comply with the demand as Egypt had the unilateral right to abrogate the agreement that had put the forces in place. As soon as the forces were withdrawn, the Israelis launched a preemptive strike against Egypt, Syria and Jordan. Thant played an important role in the subsequent cease-fire negotiations and in securing a role for UN peacekeeping forces.

Thant retired from the United Nations and active public affairs on December 31, 1971. He died of cancer in a New York hospital on November 26, 1974. Thant had fallen out of favor with the Burmese government since his friend U Nu had been overthrown by Ne Win. The new government arranged for Thant's body to be buried in a public cemetery. This infuriated pro-Nu students, who stole the body upon its arrival in Rangoon and placed it in a mausoleum on the grounds of Rangoon University. Government troops had to storm the university to recover the body. Fighting and rioting quickly spread throughout the city. Hundreds of students were arrested and several killed.

For Further Information:

Bingham, June. *U Thant: The Search for Peace.* New York, 1966.

Thatcher, Margaret (Hilda)   (October 13, 1925–   )

Margaret Thatcher was Conservative prime minister of Britain from May 1979 to November 1990. She was noted for a tough anti-communist stand, rigidly right-wing domestic policies and a strong pro-American foreign policy.

Thatcher studied chemistry at Britain's Oxford University and was elected president of the Oxford University Conservative Association. After graduating in 1947, she took a job as a research chemist for three years and in 1951 qualified as a barrister, specializing in taxation and patent law. In October 1951 she also made an unsuccessful attempt to win a seat in the House of Commons and married British businessman

Margaret Thatcher, prime minister of Britain from May 1979 until November 1990, was known for her inflexible position toward the Soviet Union, as well as her domestic opponents. Photo courtesy of the British Conservative Central Office.

Denis Thatcher. Mrs. Thatcher succeeded in her second attempt to win election to Parliament in October 1959.

Thatcher's first government post came in 1961 when she was appointed joint parliamentary secretary to the Ministry of Pensions and National Insurance. When the Labour Party returned to power in 1964, Thatcher joined the Conservative front benches, responsible alternatively for housing, land, transport and energy. When the Conservatives returned to power in June 1970 under EDWARD HEATH, Thatcher was appointed secretary of state for education. She quickly developed a reputation as a doctrinaire conservative rigidly opposed to the mixed socialist-capitalist economy, against the trade union movement, in favor of high defense spending and opposed to détente with the Soviet Union.

The British Conservative Party at the time was going through a crisis of identity in which it tried to respond to the postwar growth in the Labour Party by adopting its support for the principles of the welfare state. This was largely the position of Heath, but in 1974 the Conservatives lost two general elections in quick succession, and the Heath wing of the party came under attack from the right. In December 1975 Thatcher, with the support of the Conservative right, announced that she was challenging Heath for the Conservative leadership, and in February 1975 she won an unexpected and resounding victory over the former prime minister.

In January 1976, Thatcher made her first foray into foreign affairs when she attacked the Soviet Union for its failure to pursue "genuine détente." She said that Soviet intervention in Angola clearly indicated that Moscow was "bent on world domination" and urged that there be no weakening of the NORTH ATLANTIC TREATY ORGANIZATION's defense structures. Thatcher's statements drew an official protest from Nikolai Lunkov, the Soviet ambassador in London, who accused the Conservative leader of "extreme hostility and even open hostility." *Krasnaya Zvezda,* the official newspaper of the Soviet Ministry of Defense, soon afterward published an article in which it dubbed Thatcher the "Iron Lady." The intended sarcasm backfired. Thatcher adopted the epithet happily as a compliment to her strength of purpose, a Soviet confirmation that she was not a leader who would back down in the face of adversity.

By May 1979, the British electorate was looking for an Iron Person to deal with the country's acute economic problems. In the elections that month, the Conservatives won a comfortable majority in the House of Commons, and Thatcher succeeded JAMES CALLAGHAN as prime minister.

Thatcher's first foreign policy problem was the long-standing Rhodesia crisis. Her conservatism steered her away from the left-wing Patriotic Front led by Joshua Nkomo and Robert Mugabe toward recognition of the internal government, which was led by Bishop Abel Muzorewa and kept in place by the rebel white leader Ian Smith. Thatcher allowed herself to be led by her more experienced foreign secretary, Lord PETER CARRINGTON, who advised that recognition of the Muzorewa government would never win international acceptance and would only create increased opportunities for the Soviet Union in southern Africa.

Thatcher's rejection of Muzorewa and Smith at the Commonwealth Summit in Lusaka in August 1979 paved the way for the Rhodesia constitutional conference. After four months of difficult negotiations under Carrington's chairmanship, the conference ended in success and Rhodesia was brought to legal independence as the state of Zimbabwe.

Carrington's success in resolving the Rhodesia crisis increased his stature on both the international and national stages, and for the next four years Thatcher left the conduct of foreign affairs largely in his hands while she concentrated on economic issues. This changed radically with the 1982 Falklands War. The Foreign Office's failure to predict the Argentine invasion of the British islands in the South Atlantic led to Carrington's hasty departure from government. Thatcher took over the conduct of the war, quickly dispatched a British fleet to the South Atlantic and by June had recovered the islands with a minimum loss of life and a maximum gain of national prestige.

The "Falklands Factor" and Thatcher's Iron Lady image in standing up to opponents at home and abroad were a major factor in her reelection victory in June 1983. Other issues that contributed to Thatcher's success were splits within the Labour Party and public concern over Labour's swing to the left and its advocacy of unilateral nuclear disarmament.

Thatcher was a consistent supporter of the 1979 NATO decision to deploy United States cruise and PERSHING II intermediate-range nuclear missiles in Western Europe. A total of 166 cruise missiles were earmarked for deployment in Britain, and Thatcher took a tough line against demonstrators who tried to stop their delivery to Greenham Common, where most of the missiles were based. Thatcher also repeatedly rebuffed Soviet attempts to include the British and French nuclear deterrents in U.S.–Soviet negotiations for an INTERMEDIATE-RANGE NUCLEAR FORCES (INF) TREATY, the Soviets postulating that their intermediate-range systems were a necessary counter to the British and French nuclear arsenals. Thatcher maintained that the British system was strategic rather than intermediate-range and that the cuts proposed by successive Soviet leaders would have a disproportionate effect on the relatively tiny British nuclear arsenal.

At the same time, Thatcher pressed ahead with a plan to modernize the British nuclear deterrent by replacing the Royal Navy's POLARIS fleet with TRIDENT II submarines and missiles. The policy encountered strong opposition from the Labour Party, which maintained a policy of unilateral nuclear disarmament until 1989, and from the revived CAMPAIGN FOR NUCLEAR DISARMAMENT. But it also served to further enhance Thatcher's Iron Lady image, which had proved popular with the British electorate.

British voters gave a mixed reception to Thatcher's exceptionally close relationship with U.S. president RONALD REAGAN. The two leaders found that they shared a common perception of the Soviet Union and of economic matters. Reagan also deeply admired Thatcher's strong principles and her refusal to compromise. The result was that Thatcher enjoyed an access to the White House that no British prime minister had achieved since the days of President JOHN F. KENNEDY and Prime Minister HAROLD MACMILLAN. But she paid the additional price of unswerving support for virtually every American foreign policy initiative and action; even when other European countries expressed their reservations or criticism of American policy in countries such as NICARAGUA, Libya and Chile, Thatcher provided unstinting support. On one occasion, after American forces were allowed to use bases in Britain to attack Libya, the opposition, employing a historic British political insult, derided Thatcher as "Mr. Reagan's poodle."

There were two occasions, however, when British and American policy diverged. The first was the U.S. invasion of GRENADA in 1983. The U.S. intervention in a Commonwealth country, which recognized the queen as its head of state, was an embarrassment to the Thatcher government and drew a muted protest. The second was over sanctions against South Africa. Reagan himself was opposed to sanctions, but their imposition by the U.S. Congress led to some friction with Thatcher, who refused to impose more than token sanctions in the face of criticism from Britain's partners in the Commonwealth and the European Community (EC) and from the U.S. Congress.

Anglo-American relations dipped during the BUSH administration partly as a reaction to Reagan's overzealous admiration for Thatcher and partly because President George Bush saw Thatcher's policies toward the Commonwealth and the European Community as alienating Britain from its partners in those organizations and reducing British influence. Thatcher had never had a close relationship with the Commonwealth, which she saw primarily as a brake on British foreign policy in the Third World. When the Commonwealth voted to impose sanctions against South Africa, relations between Thatcher's government and the former British colonies edged toward the breaking point. Relations with the EC were also stormy. Thatcher spent the first few years of her government renegotiating Britain's contributions to the EC budget and then from 1988 onward trying to slow the pace of economic and political integration for fear that it would infringe British sovereignty.

Thatcher's relations with Soviet leader LEONID BREZHNEV were distant. Brezhnev regarded Thatcher as little more than an American stooge and an impediment to his efforts to drive a wedge between Europe and the United States. Brezhnev tried to deal with the problem of Thatcher by ignoring the British leader as much as possible. This was not the case with MIKHAIL GORBACHEV. He and Thatcher first met in December 1983, shortly before Gorbachev succeeded KONSTANTIN CHERNENKO as general secretary of the Soviet Communist Party. Thatcher had been briefed beforehand that Gorbachev could soon emerge as the new Soviet leader and that he was inclined toward reform. After their meeting, she declared, "I like Mr. Gorbachev. We can do business together." For Gorbachev, Thatcher became an acceptable conduit to the United States at a time when Washington was skeptical about his commitment to political and economic reform.

But while praising Gorbachev and his reforms, Thatcher also urged that the Western Alliance take a cautious approach toward defense negotiations and security arrangements. She argued that Gorbachev's policies entailed a strong element of risk for the Soviet leader and that if he failed he could be replaced by a more hard-line communist figure who would take a tougher position on East-West relations.

Britain's relations with China were dominated by the negotiations for the return of the British colony of Hong Kong to China in 1997. In 1984 Thatcher agreed that the colony would be returned, and formal negotiations on the details started soon afterward. The Chinese refused to accept anything less than full sovereignty over the territory after 1997, while the British tried to negotiate the establishment of structures that would ensure the continuation of the status quo in post-1997 Hong Kong. The British colony's existence had depended on the goodwill of China since 1949, and it quickly became apparent that Thatcher had virtually no room to maneuver in negotiations with Beijing. This led to a crisis of confidence in Hong Kong, which threatened the economic viability of the colony. The crisis worsened after the Tiananmen Square Massacre in June 1989 demonstrated the Chinese leadership's attitude toward demands for democratic reform. In order to prevent a mass exodus from Hong Kong Thatcher offered Britain as a final refuge for 250,000 prominent and wealthy Hong Kong citizens in the hope that this would encourage them to stay and work with the post-1997 administration.

Thatcher's primary focus, however, was on domestic social and economic issues. She is credited with having curbed runaway inflation and the power of the British trade union movement, and having substantially reduced public spending. Her uncompromising right-wing policies, however, are also blamed for producing massive structural economic dislocation, high levels of unemployment and increased class hostility. She won the 1987 general election, but as the true economic situation became clearer, she and her aggressive approach became increasingly unpopular. In 1990 she was deposed from the leadership of her party, and thus from office. She has since been elevated to a peerage and continues to speak out on public issues.

For Further Information:

Louis, William Roger, and Hedley Bull. *The "Special Relationship": Anglo-American Relations since 1945.* Oxford, 1986.

Ogden, Chris. *Maggie: An Intimate Portrait of a Woman in Power.* New York, 1990.

Smith, Geoffrey. *Reagan and Thatcher.* London, 1990.

Wapshott, Nicholas, and George Brock. *Thatcher.* London, 1983.

Young, Hugo. *The Iron Lady: A Biography of Margaret Thatcher.* New York, 1989.

———. *One of Us: A Biography of Margaret Thatcher.* London, 1991.

Thompson, Llewellyn (August 24, 1904–February 2, 1972) Llewellyn Thompson was an American career diplomat who served in several key posts, including high commissioner to AUSTRIA, ambassador to Austria and twice as American ambassador to the Soviet Union and special adviser on Soviet affairs.

After graduating from the University of Colorado in 1928, Thompson entered the American diplomatic service. He served in Ceylon and Switzerland until November 1940, when he was posted as second secretary to the U.S. Embassy in Moscow. Here he became an expert on Russian language and culture, and began his long involvement in Soviet and East European affairs. After the war Thompson served in a variety of positions relating to Eastern Europe, including chief of the division of Eastern European affairs, deputy director for European affairs and deputy assistant secretary of state for European affairs.

In July 1952, Thompson was appointed high commissioner and ambassador to Austria. In Vienna, his two main responsibilities were the negotiations for the Austrian Peace Treaty, which was eventually signed in 1955, and the TRIESTE Settlement, which was signed in 1954 and resulted in the division of the Trieste area between Italy and Yugoslavia.

In 1957, U.S. president DWIGHT EISENHOWER appointed Thompson ambassador to the Soviet Union. He had little influence over U.S. policy toward the Soviet Union at this stage, when it was handled almost entirely by Secretary of State JOHN FOSTER DULLES. He remained in Moscow for the first two years of the KENNEDY administration, during which time he became more involved in forming policy. Thompson first met President John F. Kennedy in February 1961, when he proposed a summit meeting with Khrushchev to try to remedy the failure of the 1960 Paris Summit. The result was the VIENNA SUMMIT, held on June 3–4, 1961, which many diplomatic observers now believe to have been a mistake. During the 1961 BERLIN Crisis, Thompson opposed direct military action in favor of a combined policy of military buildup and diplomatic action. This advice was adopted by Kennedy, and eventually Khrushchev dropped his "free city" proposal, which had sparked the crisis.

Thompson also advised Kennedy on disarmament issues, especially during the negotiations leading to the NUCLEAR TEST BAN TREATY of 1963, and was instrumental in persuading the administration to drop its demand for a total ban on nuclear testing and instead negotiate a limited ban.

In September 1962, Thompson returned to Washington as special adviser to the State Department on Soviet affairs. He was a member of the inner circle that advised Kennedy during the CUBAN MISSILE CRISIS. He argued that the Soviet Union would not risk military action to protect the missiles, but would probably use them as a bargaining chip to win concessions elsewhere in the world. When Khrushchev later offered to withdraw the missiles from Cuba in return for a withdrawal of American missiles from Turkey, Thompson advised the president against this tradeoff on the grounds that the Soviets would regard it as a sign of weakness.

Thompson attended all high-level U.S.–Soviet talks during the Kennedy and JOHNSON administrations and regularly briefed Congress on Soviet developments. His standing with the Soviet leaders was so high that, after an American RB-66 aircraft was shot down over East Germany in March 1964, President Lyndon Johnson asked him to reassure the Soviets personally that the plane had not been, as they claimed, on a spy mission. Johnson correctly assumed that the Soviets knew that Thompson's prestige was too high to be risked by being caught in a lie.

In January 1967, Thompson returned as ambassador to Moscow in an attempt to improve relations strained by the VIETNAM WAR. To this end, he arranged the June 1967 GLASSBORO SUMMIT between President Johnson and Soviet premier ALEXEI KOSYGIN. Thompson resigned in January 1969 and worked as a foreign affairs consultant until his death on February 2, 1972.

Titan II For many years, until the program was deactivated at the end of 1987, the Titan II missile carried America's largest nuclear warheads with an explosive yield of nine megatons.

These INTERCONTINENTAL BALLISTIC MISSILES (ICBM) were an improved version of the Titan missile and entered service with the Strategic Air Command in 1963.

The Titan II missiles were powered by a two-stage rocket and had a range of 7,500 miles. They were deployed in hardened missile silos in Nebraska and Wyoming and had a launch reaction time of 60 seconds from the time of pressing the launch button to leaving the silo. The missile was dismantled in 1987 to comply with provisions of the first Strategic Arms Limitation Treaty (SALT I, see STRATEGIC ARMS LIMITATION TALKS).

Tito, Josip Broz (May 7, 1892–May 4, 1980) Josip Broz, Marshal Tito was the communist leader of Yugoslavia for 35 years. His refusal to accept Soviet dominance in Yugoslav affairs led to the first split among the communist Bloc countries and undermined the monolithic nature of JOSEF STALIN's regime in Eastern Europe. Later Tito played a leading role in the formation of the NONALIGNED MOVEMENT, which sought a middle course between the two superpowers.

Tito was born in Croatia as Josip Broz; he adopted the name Tito as a party pseudonym in 1934. His parents were poor peasants, and at the age of 13 Tito was apprenticed to a locksmith. During his World War I service in the Austrian Army, he was seriously wounded, captured and taken to Russia, where he eventually escaped, became a communist and participated in the civil war. Tito returned from Russia in 1920 and threw himself into political activity with the Yugoslav Communist Party, which was illegal. He was arrested three times between 1923 and 1928, the last time to be imprisoned for six years. When he was released in 1934, Tito

Communist President Josip Broz Tito of Yugoslavia (center) with East German leader Walter Ulbricht (left) and Horst Sindermann at a German-Yugoslav friendship rally in Halle, German Democratic Republic, on November 6, 1965. Photo courtesy of Popperfoto.

was named to the party's Central Committee and to the Politburo. In 1937 he became general secretary.

In 1935 Tito left Yugoslavia for Moscow to work in the Balkan section of the Comintern. His animosity toward Josef Stalin probably dates from 1937, when the Soviet dictator extended his purge to Yugoslav communists living in exile in Moscow. More than 800 were killed. Tito was on the list to be liquidated also, but intervention by Georgi Dimitrov, the Bulgarian communist leader in exile in Moscow, saved the remaining Yugoslavs.

Following Nazi Germany's attack on Yugoslavia in April 1941, Tito issued a proclamation for a general uprising and returned to Yugoslavia to lead it. He was the only East European communist who returned to his country to fight the Germans, and he defied Stalin to do it. The result was the most successful guerrilla operation of the war. Within a year, Tito's partisan groups were in control of half of Yugoslavia and were tying up hundreds of thousands of German troops. Tito was an active commander and was wounded several times during the fighting, which established his charismatic leadership abilities and personal bravery.

At the Teheran Conference in 1943 the Allied powers granted Tito's partisans the official status of ally, and the Soviet Union and Britain agreed to send military missions and aid. Later Stalin and WINSTON CHURCHILL agreed that Yugoslavia should be a shared Anglo–Soviet postwar sphere of influence. Churchill's purpose in the deal was to create a coalition government between the Soviet-supported and popular partisan leader Tito and the Western-supported émigré government in London. Tito rejected the arrangement and emerged from the war in total control of the country and in a close alliance with the Soviet Union.

Relations between the West and Tito quickly deteriorated, starting with Tito's rejection of émigré politicians and his decision to establish a socialist state. In 1946 relations were severely strained after Yugoslavia shot down an American transport plane and detained its crew. Tito's support for communist guerrillas in the GREEK CIVIL WAR appeared to confirm initial American and British fears that Tito was acting as Stalin's tool in the Balkans.

But the major point of friction between Yugoslavia and the West was the port city of TRIESTE and its hinterland, which was claimed by both Italy and Yugoslavia and occupied by British, American and Yugoslav forces. Trieste remained a major problem until it was resolved in October 1954.

From 1945 to 1947, Tito had a close relationship with the Soviet Union. But by 1947, he and Stalin were starting to part company. Tito's support for the Greek communists, for instance, appears to have largely been against Stalin's advice. But the serious difficulties began when Stalin tried to dictate senior appointments within the Yugoslav Communist Party. In March 1948, the Soviet Communist Party wrote to the Central Committee of the Yugoslav Party making serious charges against Tito's policies and demanding that he mend his ways. Tito responded by liquidating a number of Yugoslav Stalinists and purging the army. On June 28, 1948, the Soviet-controlled COMINFORM (Communist Information Bureau) denounced Tito and called on the Yugoslav Communist Party to overthrow him or face expulsion from the Cominform. Yugoslavia was duly expelled, and the following year Stalin canceled the Yugoslav–Soviet defense treaty.

The Yugoslav–Soviet split continued for seven years, with Tito and the Soviet leadership exchanging insults and accusing each other of deviating from the true course of Marxism-Leninism. Tito, who was also isolated from the West, was clearly at a disadvantage, and Stalin tried to use this to his advantage by threatening invasion, instituting an economic blockade and inciting various border incidents. His hope was that the pressure would result in an internal coup that would overthrow Tito. But Stalin's tactics had the opposite effect. Yugoslavia united behind Tito, who was seen increasingly as a heroic figure.

After Stalin's death in 1953, the new Soviet leadership began mending relations with Yugoslavia. But Tito rejected the initial advances, holding out for Soviet recognition of the right of communist states to pursue national policies independent of the Soviet Union. He was finally rewarded with a visit on June 2, 1955, by Soviet leader NIKITA KHRUSHCHEV during which the two leaders agreed to a relationship based on mutual respect for each other's sovereignty and independence and mutual noninterference in each other's internal affairs.

The agreement was a major diplomatic triumph for Tito. It also raised the hopes of other East European communists, particularly in POLAND and HUNGARY, and contributed to the crises in those countries. Despite the 1955 statement, Soviet–Yugoslav relations never again reached the high point of the immediate postwar period and were again strained at times afterward. In 1957, the Yugoslav delegation to an interna-tional communist conference in Moscow refused to sign the final communiqué because it referred to "the necessity of resolutely overcoming revisionism . . ." In 1958, the Chinese Communist Party said that Stalin's decision to expel Yugoslavia from "the Socialist camp" had been "basically correct," and in May 1958 the Soviet government suspended credits and other financial assistance to Yugoslavia.

Yugoslav–Soviet relations hit another low after the Soviet invasion of CZECHOSLOVAKIA in 1968. The invasion was denounced by Tito as a violation of sovereignty and a blow to progressive forces everywhere. Fearful that the invasion might be the precursor to a similar move against Yugoslavia, Tito ordered the creation of partisan units to strengthen the regular army forces.

Anything that divided the communist camp was clearly to the benefit of the Western alliance, and the United States exploited the divisions by supplying generous financial aid to Tito's government. Tito, however, steered clear of a close association with America. He remained a committed communist. His differences with the Soviet Union centered on national rather than ideological issues and made him a more avid supporter of Third World revolutionaries because their independent existence helped his own nationalist course.

In 1961 Tito sought to reinforce this independence by helping to found the Non-Aligned Movement. After 1961, support for nonalignment became the primary aim of Tito's foreign policy, and he traveled extensively thoughout the Third World to urge the emerging nations to eschew alliances with either major power bloc and instead join the Non-Aligned Movement. His success turned the movement into a major international force as its members coordinated policies for presentation at the United Nations General Assembly.

In later years, Tito's interest shifted from foreign affairs to domestic concerns. Yugoslavia was not a unitary state but a collection of small, mutually hostile national republics and ethnic enclaves. Tito was able to suppress these differences by the force and prestige of his powerful personality, but he realized the danger of ethnic and national hostilities resurfacing after his death. In 1974 he established a collective presidency to succeed him. Tito died on May 4, 1980.

The collective presidency failed to control the national and ethnic passions that Tito had feared, with open warfare breaking out in 1990.

For Further Information:
Auty, Phyllis. *Tito.* New York, 1970.

MacLean, Fitzroy. *Disputed Barricade: The Life and Times of Josip Broz Tito.* New York, 1957.

———. *Tito, a Pictorial Biography.* New York, 1980.

Neal, F.W. *Titoism in Action: The Reforms in Yugoslavia after 1948.* New York, 1958.

Togliatti, Palmiro   (March 26, 1893–August 21, 1964)
Palmiro Togliatti was leader of the Italian Communist Party (PCI) from 1926 to 1964. He turned the PCI into the largest

communist party in Western Europe while at the same time maintaining close links with the Soviet Union.

Togliatti was born into a lower-middle-class family in Genoa and won a scholarship to Turin University, where he studied law. During World War I, Togliatti served in the medical corps for the first two years of the fighting before receiving a medical discharge.

Like many Europeans of his day, Togliatti was deeply influenced by the Russian Revolution. While at university he had formed a close friendship with Antonio Gramsci and together they founded a left-wing journal in May 1919. In January 1919, the Italian Communist Party was founded, and Gramsci became its first leader. Togliatti, although not instrumental in the founding of the party, was an original member.

The rise of Benito Mussolini in 1922 led to a crackdown on Communist Party leaders. Gramsci fled to Moscow and others were arrested. Togliatti remained at liberty because he was not at that time regarded as being in the first rank.

In Moscow, Gramsci persuaded the Russians to appoint him acting party secretary with responsibility for organizing a semi-clandestine organization. Back in Italy in 1926, Gramsci was arrested and kept imprisoned until he died in 1937. Togliatti took over as general secretary of the PCI and held the position until his death.

Forced into exile himself, Togliatti fled to Moscow, where he became the Italian representative on the Soviet-dominated Comintern. In the years before his return to Italy he divided his time between Moscow, France (where the bulk of the PCI's exiled membership resided) and Spain, where he was responsible for the political morale of the communist units in the International Brigade. During World War II, Togliatti based himself in Moscow, from where he broadcast resistance messages to Italy.

His broadcasts made Togliatti a household name in Italy, and when he returned in 1944 he was appointed to the cabinet of Marshal Pietro Badoglio as minister without portfolio. His decision to accept the cabinet post (leaders of the anti-fascist resistance refused to work with Badoglio, who had loyally served Mussolini) was in keeping with Stalin's immediate postwar policy of capitalizing on the wartime prestige of the communist parties to try to win power through constitutional means. In 1945, Togliatti was named vice premier under ALCIDE DE GASPERI. In the government, Togliatti tried to shift Italian foreign policy to favor the Soviet Union. De Gasperi, however, was determined on a westward-leaning policy. In January 1947 he flew to Washington, D.C. to organize a $100 million American "soft" loan and emergency food supplies. The American ties infuriated Togliatti as did de Gasperi's introduction of tough anti-communist measures upon his return to Rome. Togliatti protested; de Gasperi resigned and formed a new government without the PCI.

Out of office, the PCI, with encouragement from the COMINFORM, organized a series of damaging anti-government strikes, and in September 1947 Togliatti warned that he could call on "30,000 well-armed partisans." Togliatti also denounced the U.S. "world dictatorship" for trying to "spread another war." The strength of the PCI, which then stood at 2 million members, and Togliatti's statements terrified the U.S. government, which feared that Italy was on the verge of a communist takeover, through either revolution or elections. The TRUMAN administration directed the newly created CENTRAL INTELLIGENCE AGENCY to give a high priority to Italy, and an estimated $10 million in covert CIA aid flowed into the Christian Democrats' April 1948 campaign. The Soviet Union, in turn, is believed to have substantially contributed to Togliatti's 1948 campaign.

As a result of Togliatti's talk of armed partisans, de Gasperi mobilized 100,000 police and soldiers on the eve of the crucial April 1948 elections in case the PCI made an attempt to grab power if the results went against them. But despite his implicit threat of violence, Togliatti promised to accept the election results, and the elections passed relatively peacefully. The results were a victory for de Gasperi's Christian Democrats, who won a 53.7% majority in the new Chamber of Deputies. The PCI, however, emerged as the largest opposition party, with 31% of the vote and 135 deputies in parliament. This alignment of the Christian Democrats in government and the communists leading the opposition was to dominate Italian postwar politics and continually frustrate Togliatti and his successors.

Togliatti's pledge of no violence was dealt a major blow three months after the election when a gunman shot the PCI leader twice in the chest and once in the head. The party leadership blamed the assassination attempt on de Gaspari's anti-communist campaign and an angry membership launched four days of riots and strikes, which forced the government to mobilize 300,000 policemen and troops to maintain essential services and quell the disturbances. Togliatti quickly recovered from the shooting, however, and brought his membership under control.

Togliatti stuck to what he termed his "Italian Road to Socialism" despite continued pressure from Stalin to resort to subversive tactics. Several times in the 1950s, Togliatti's tactics appeared to be on the verge of parliamentary success, and the United States, fearful of a communist election victory, continued to supply covert CIA aid to the Christian Democrats.

Despite American fears, the only occasion on which Togliatti resorted to violence was in July 1960, when Premier Fernando Tambroni turned to the neo-fascist Italian Social Movement to keep his shaky coalition in power. Communist-led riots and strikes broke out throughout the country, and on July 12 Togliatti threatened fresh riots unless Tambroni renounced his neo-fascist links and resigned the premiership. Tambroni's government collapsed and in August was replaced by a cabinet led by Amintore Fanfani and supported by a coalition of Christian Democrats, Liberals, Democratic Socialists and Republicans. The riots had resulted in the deaths of more than 11 people and over 1,000 injuries and were a graphic demonstration of Togliatti's potential power.

In the early 1960s a great deal of Togliatti's efforts were directed toward trying to negotiate a solution to the SINO-SO-VIET SPLIT. Although Togliatti spoke of the Italian Road to Socialism and in 1956 was criticized by Moscow for coining the word *polycentrism,* there was never any doubt of his acceptance of the Soviet Union as the leader of the international communist movement. This was most aptly demonstrated by Togliatti's slavish adherence to the Soviet opposition to any moves toward West European integration. As the mainstream of European politics moved closer to these ideals and policies, the PCI under Togliatti found itself moving further away from the aspirations of the electorate. By the time Togliatti died on August 21, 1964, the PCI was starting to reexamine its relationship with the Soviet Union and moving toward what became known as EUROCOMMUNISM.

For Further Information:

Blackmer, Donald, and Sidney Farrow. *Communism in Italy and France.* Princeton, 1975.

Campbell, John, ed. *Successful Negotiation: Trieste 1954.* Princeton, 1976.

Hughes, H. Stuart. *The United States and Italy.* Cambridge, Mass., 1965.

Kogan, Norman. *A Political History of Postwar Italy: From the Old to the New Center Left.* New York, 1981.

Nicholas, Peter. *Italia, Italia.* New York, 1974.

Sassoon, Donald. *The Strategy of the Italian Communist Party: From the Resistance to the Historic Compromise.* London, 1981.

Urban, Joan. *Moscow and the Italian Communist Party: From Togliatti to Berlinguer.* Ithaca, N.Y., 1986.

Treaty of Tlatelolco   (1967)   The Treaty of Tlatelolco bans nuclear weapons from Central America, South America and the Caribbean and thereby established the first nuclear-free zone in an inhabited area of the world. Signatories include all nations in Latin America except Cuba and Guyana.

The treaty was signed on February 14, 1967. Its official title was the "Treaty for the Prohibition of Nuclear Weapons in Latin America." In the area covered it outlawed the "testing, use, manufacture, production or acquisition by any means whatsoever of any nuclear weapons." It also prohibited the "receipt, storage, installation, deployment and any form of possession of any nuclear weapon," and the "engaging in, encouraging or authorizing . . . or in any way participating in the testing, use, manufacture, production, possession or control of any nuclear weapons."

The treaty did not prohibit the use of nuclear energy for peaceful purposes, particularly for "economic development and social progress."

Triad   Also known as Nuclear Triad, Triad is a term used to encompass the three different basing systems used for the United States' strategic nuclear arsenal. The systems are land-based intercontinental ballistic missiles (ICBMs), strategic bombers and nuclear-equipped submarines.

The theory behind the maintenance of the three systems is that it would be almost impossible for the enemy to destroy all three in a first-strike attack. Therefore, the United States maintains a strong second-strike capability and continues to deter a nuclear attack.

Trident I   Also known as Trident C-4, Trident I is a U.S. submarine-launched ballistic missile (SLBM) developed as a successor to the POSEIDON System. Each Trident I missile is armed (MIRVed) with eight MULTIPLE INDEPENDENTLY-TARGETED REENTRY VEHICLES with an explosive yield of 100 kilotons each. The Trident I is also equipped with a computer guidance system that allows it to correct its flight path based on star sightings.

The Trident I can be launched from submerged or surfaced submarines. The missile itself is ejected by the pressure of expanding gas within launch tubes. Once it gains a sufficient height, the first-stage motor is ignited. It is a three-stage rocket. By 1988 an estimated 384 Trident I missiles were deployed.

Trident II   Also known as Trident D-5, Trident II is a U.S. submarine-launched ballistic missile (SLBM) that was first deployed in 1989. It was planned that there would be 312 Trident II missiles deployed by 1998, but the program is in doubt with the end of the Cold War.

Each missile was to be MIRVed (equipped with 10 to 15 MULTIPLE INDEPENDENTLY-TARGETED REENTRY VEHICLES each capable of carrying a nuclear warhead with an explosive yield of 300–475 kilotons). The missiles have a range of 4,100 miles. The first test of Trident II was successfully conducted in January 1987.

Trieste   Trieste is a major Adriatic port city. It became a major source of Italian–Yugoslav and, by extension, East–West conflict in the early Cold War years. The issue was finally resolved in 1954.

Prior to World War I, Trieste was the major port city of the Austro-Hungarian Empire. After the war the city and the surrounding province of Venezia Giulia were ceded to Italy. At the end of World War II, American and British troops occupied Trieste, while the Yugoslav Army occupied the province around it and claimed both the province and the city.

Under an agreement signed on June 9, 1945, the British and American troops continued to occupy their section of the province, which was renamed Zone A, and the Yugoslavs occupied their section, which was renamed Zone B. The Italian Peace Treaty of February 10, 1947, awarded most of Venezia Giulia to Yugoslavia but also created the Free Territory of Trieste, the independence of which was guaranteed by the United Nations Security Council. The Free Territory, like the wider province, was divided into an Anglo-American Zone A, and a Yugoslav Zone B. The treaty, which was guaranteed by the British, Americans and Soviets, also stipulated that the UN Security Council would appoint a governor of Trieste, who in turn would establish a legislature and police force. This never happened because of East-West differences, and the three-power military occupation and government continued.

Both the Italians and Yugoslavs objected to the division of Trieste. Both also claimed the whole of the city for their own state. The Soviets supported the Yugoslav claim even after the expulsion of JOZIP BROZ TITO from the COMINFORM in 1948 and the abrogation of the Soviet–Yugoslav Treaty in September 1949.

In February 1952, Tito proposed the integration of Zones A and B, with the united zone to be administered by a governor who would be alternately appointed by Italy and Yugoslavia for a three-year term. This was rejected by Italian prime minister ALCIDE DE GASPERI, who feared it would result in a communist government in Trieste. In May 1952, the British and Americans agreed to share responsibility for their zone with the Italian authorities. The Soviet Union and Yugoslavia objected, and Yugoslavia formally extended its laws into Zone B.

The United States and Britain found themselves in a difficult diplomatic dilemma. They wanted to be seen as supporting their NATO ally, Italy, but at the same time, they did not want to do anything that would bring Yugoslavia and the Soviet Union back together. The Italians, under de Gasperi and his successor Giuseppe Pella, warned that anything less than full Anglo–American support could jeopardize Italian membership in NATO, American bases in Italy and Italian ratification of the EUROPEAN DEFENSE COMMUNITY (EDC), treaty.

The British and French concluded that the answer lay in some form of permanent partition. To facilitate this aim, the U.S. State Department and British Foreign Office simultaneously announced on October 8, 1953, that they were planning to turn over Zone A to Italian administration and withdraw their troops at the earliest possible date. Tito responded by threatening to send troops into Zone A, and a fleet of American warships was dispatched to the Upper Adriatic. Tito then proposed an Anglo-Italian-American-Yugoslav conference before any transfer of Zone A to Italy. The Italian government, however, refused to attend unless Yugoslavia left Zone B. This was rejected by Tito.

The situation became further complicated by the growth of the Italian Communist Party. CLARE BOOTHE LUCE, U.S. ambassador to Italy, warned U.S. president DWIGHT EISENHOWER that failure to hand over the administration of Zone A to the Pella government would undermine the ruling Christian Democrats and lead to the inclusion of the communists in the Italian government.

The path to a negotiated settlement, however, was blocked by Italian and Yugoslav refusal to meet without major advance concessions from each other. The British and American negotiations circumvented this problem by starting separate, secret negotiations with both governments in London in February 1954. The first negotiations were among Britain, the United States and Yugoslavia and ended on May 31 with a number of concessions by Yugoslavia. Negotiations with Italy started in June 1954 against the backdrop of the French refusal to ratify the EDC treaty, and the Italians tied their participation in NATO and American bases on Italian soil firmly to the Trieste issue. After several more months of negotiation, the final treaty was eventually signed October 5, 1954. Its main points were:

1. Italy was to take responsibility for the administration of Zone A (the northern half of the territory, which included the city of Trieste).
2. The 6,000 American and British troops in Zone A were to withdraw.
3. A six-square-mile strip of territory on the southern edge of Zone A, including the town of Crevatini, was to be transferred to the Yugoslav sector.
4. Yugoslavia was to have free use of the port of Trieste.
5. Yugoslavia was to substitute civil administration for the military government in Zone B (southern half of the Trieste territory).
6. The agreement noted that it had been impossible to put into effect the provisions of the Italian Peace Treaty to establish a Free Territory of Trieste through the United Nations. The United States, Britain and Yugoslavia therefore acted to terminate military occupation, which "it was never intended . . . should be other than temporary."

The Italian-speaking community in Trieste staged parades through the city on October 5 in celebration of the agreement. The Yugoslav Tanjug News Agency said the settlement represented "heavy sacrifice" of "justified national demands" for all of the Trieste territory. But Acting Foreign Secretary Ales Bebler called the agreement a "reasonable compromise."

For Further Information:
Campbell, John, ed. *Successful Negotiation: Trieste 1954.* Princeton, 1976.
Carrillo, Elisa. *Alcide de Gasperi.* Notre Dame, Ind., 1965.
Novak, Bogdan, *Trieste, 1941–1954.* Chicago, 1970.

Trizonal Agreement   *See* BIZONAL AGREEMENT.

Truman, Harry S.   **(May 8, 1884–December 26, 1972)**
Harry S. Truman was president of the United States in the early years of the Cold War and laid the foundations of America's Cold War policies. Some of the key foreign affairs events of his administration were the first use of the atomic bomb, development of the hydrogen bomb, formulation of the TRUMAN DOCTRINE and MARSHALL PLAN, the formation of the NORTH ATLANTIC TREATY ORGANIZATION, the communist victory in China, formulation of the U.S. policy of containment, and U.S. participation in the BERLIN airlift and the KOREAN WAR.

Truman was born in rural Missouri. Because of his father's financial reverses, he was unable to go to college, but during World War I he served with distinction as an army artillery captain in France. After the war he started several businesses, but none was a success.

Truman's family had longtime connections with the state's Democratic Party, and Truman himself established a link with the powerful Pendergast machine in Kansas City. In 1922 he was elected judge of the Jackson County Court. The Pendergast machine was later found to be hopelessly corrupt and fell from power. Truman was able to dissociate himself from the scandals, but not before he secured the backing of Tom Pendergast to win a U.S. Senate seat in 1934.

His first 10 years in Washington, D.C., were unspectacular, but he became genuinely popular with fellow senators and congressmen and gained a reputation as a hard-working pragmatist. In 1944 the Democratic Party was torn between HENRY A. WALLACE and JAMES BYRNES as the choice for President FRANKLIN D. ROOSEVELT's running mate. Truman was chosen as the compromise figure who would offend the fewest people.

In 1944 no one expected Truman to become president. He was regarded as a stopgap vice president who would serve one term and then step down when the party chose a replacement for Roosevelt in 1948. Roosevelt certainly did not treat him as a potential successor. He was excluded from all major discussions, especially those related to foreign policy. But only 83 days after the start of his fourth term, Roosevelt died of a massive cerebral hemorrhage, and Truman became president.

Truman was in office for only three months when he met with British prime minister WINSTON CHURCHILL, Churchill's successor CLEMENT ATTLEE, and Soviet leader JOSEF STALIN at the POTSDAM CONFERENCE from July 17 to August 1, 1945. The new president was initially well disposed toward the Soviet Union and wanted to continue Roosevelt's policy of compromise and

Harry S. Truman (hand on bible) is sworn in as president of the United States by Chief Justice Harlan F. Stone, April 12, 1945.

alliance with Moscow. But at Potsdam Truman first encountered Soviet intransigence, and his conversion to an anti-Soviet stand began. The shift, however, was not immediate and for a time he vacillated between compromise and a hard-line foreign policy.

Just before the Potsdam Conference officially started, on July 16, 1945, the United States successfully tested the first atomic bomb. The British, who knew well in advance about the test, had already given formal sanction to Truman to use the bomb at his discretion. It was at Potsdam that Truman made the final decision to use the weapon, and on July 24 he informed Stalin of its existence.

Before the atomic bomb test, the military had been planning a massive invasion of the Japanese islands. It was estimated that such an invasion might have cost a million American lives. After the test Truman postponed the invasion and then accepted the recommendation of an advisory committee to make a surprise drop of the new weapon on a combined military and civilian target. He rejected advice from scientists and Secretary of State James Byrnes that the Japanese be shown the power of the new bomb with a demonstration explosion and then be given the chance to surrender.

An atomic bomb was dropped on Hiroshima on August 6, 1945. Three days later a second bomb was dropped on Nagasaki. On August 14 Japan surrendered after Truman agreed to let the Japanese retain the monarchy.

Truman did not go into the peace determined to become the world's policeman and arms supplier. One of his first acts after the Japanese surrender was to end the LEND-LEASE program of aid to European countries. He also made it clear that he would maintain only as many American troops in Germany and Japan as were necessary for administrative purposes. The emphasis was on an attempt to return to prewar normality, albeit without the isolationism of the past.

Government advisers such as GEORGE KENNAN, AVERELL HARRIMAN and Senator ARTHUR VANDENBERG, however, strongly advised Truman that the United States had to take the lead in containing Soviet power and influence. By the start of 1946, Truman had accepted their premises. During 1946 he took a hard line in demanding that the Soviet Union withdraw its troops from Iran, sent American warships to Greece and Turkey to deter Soviet intervention in local politics, supported the merger of the American and British occupation zones in Germany to ensure the economic rehabilitation of that country and supported the Baruch Plan for future control of nuclear weapons.

In 1947 Truman continued an interventionist U.S. foreign policy, replacing Britain in Greece and Turkey in order to prevent communist governments from coming to power. This policy, which became known as the Truman Doctrine, effectively committed the United States to preventing the spread of communism throughout Europe. The Truman Doctrine was followed by the Marshall Plan, which provided Western Europe with the economic means to rebuild its economies and thus resist communism's appeal. The Truman Doctrine was enunciated in a speech to the U.S. Congress on March 12, 1947. This speech marked the public abandonment of prewar isolationism and Roosevelt's hopes of preserving world peace by cooperating with the United States' wartime allies through the United Nations.

Truman was reluctant to engage the Soviets directly with American arms. He preferred instead to use economic muscle. The aid extended to Greece and Turkey was almost entirely financial, about $400 million worth. The Marshall Plan was also a financial package. Truman refused to introduce U.S. troops to prevent the communist takeover in Czechoslovakia in 1948, and when the Soviet Union blockaded Berlin in June 1948 he ignored repeated appeals from the military to send in American troops to reopen the roads. Instead he defied the blockade by supplying the city by air (see BERLIN).

Truman's tough stand against the Soviet Union in Europe led him into conflict with Roosevelt administration officials such as Secretary of State James Byrnes, Commerce Secretary Henry A. Wallace and former Treasury secretary, HENRY MORGENTHAU. But his policy toward events in Asia, especially China, led to charges from right-wing Republicans that he was "soft" on communism.

In the final stages of the war and immediately afterward, America's career foreign service officers were predicting that the corrupt and unpopular regime of CHIANG KAI-SHEK would eventually collapse before the Chinese communists. Their views were supported by General GEORGE MARSHALL, who was sent by Truman to China in an attempt to bring the communists and Nationalists together. Truman accepted this advice and gave only halfhearted support to Chiang Kai-shek. This infuriated the powerful right-wing China Lobby, and Truman was forced to increase American support in the final days of Chiang's tenure on the mainland. But it was not enough to prevent the inevitable and served only to increase accusations that Truman had "lost" China, with the result that the president was forced into recognition of Chiang's government on Taiwan.

The "loss" of China, the Soviet Union's development of an atomic bomb and cynical allegations that there were communists at high levels of the U.S. government contributed to an anti-communist hysteria that had begun in 1946 and reached its peak in the early 1950s. Truman was strongly opposed to the "investigations" of Senator JOSEPH MCCARTHY; he backed State Department officials whose careers were ruined by McCarthy and vetoed the INTERNAL SECURITY ACT, which would have required the registration of communists. But, at the same time, he did make his own contribution to the mood of the times by describing his foreign policy as a "crusade" against communism.

Some of Truman's anti-communist rhetoric can be described as a response to the Republicans' assertions that he was "soft on Communism" and to their 1946 campaign pledge to "clean the Communists and fellow travelers out of the government." Truman was also concerned about the Republican reaction to the discovery of a communist spy ring in Canada and FBI reports of communist infiltration in Washington. In 1947 he ordered an investigation of communist activities and a stringent "loyalty" check of all federal employees.

The Cold War reached an early peak on June 25, 1950, when the Soviet-equipped armies of North Korea attacked South Korea. Truman's quick and firm reaction did more than anything else to counter Republican claims that he was soft on communism. But the president's subsequent disagreements with and recall of the popular though insubordinate General DOUGLAS MACARTHUR, who commanded the United Nations forces in Korea, damaged Truman's position.

President Truman and Secretary of State DEAN ACHESON were firmly of the opinion that the Korean War was part of a grand Soviet-controlled strategy. They believed that the Soviets planned to embroil the Western powers in the Far East in order to give themselves a free hand in Europe.

The war rapidly ended the shortlived, post-World War II demobilization and hardened American suspicion of the Eastern bloc. It also widened the gulf between communist China and the United States. Early in the conflict Truman dispatched the Seventh Fleet to the Taiwan Straits, between Taiwan and the mainland. The fleet had the dual task of preventing Chiang from widening the conflict by attacking the Chinese mainland—something the American right wing often called for—and deterring the Chinese communists from using Korea as a diversion to attack and eliminate the nationalists on Taiwan. The communists viewed the introduction of the Seventh Fleet, and the American-led prosecution of the Korean War as aggression against them.

Their suspicions appeared to be justified by General MacArthur's attempts to persuade Truman to allow Chiang to attack China. Truman's repeated assurances to the Chinese that neither the United States nor the UN forces had any "aggressive intentions" toward China failed to assuage their fears, and Chinese troops intervened in the Korean War just as the UN forces were on the verge of victory.

The Korean War confirmed Sino-American enmity, established the United States' role as policeman in the Pacific and Asia and brought the European powers firmly behind the Truman administration's policy of "containing" the Soviet Union by encircling it with a group of American-sponsored defensive alliances. The most effective of these, the North Atlantic Treaty Organization (NATO), quickly evolved into an effective military and political alliance to unite Western Europe against a Soviet attack, which Western policy planners expected to come at any time during the Korean War. Other alliances were the Australia–New Zealand–United States (ANZUS) Alliance formed in 1951, the SOUTHEAST ASIA TREATY ORGANIZATION (SEATO) formed in 1954, and the Central Treaty Organization (CENTO) or BAGHDAD PACT, formed in 1955.

Deteriorating East–West relations also forced Truman to reorganize American defense and intelligence agencies. The NATIONAL SECURITY ACT OF 1947 brought the armed services into a single Department of Defense headed by a secretary of defense. It also created the NATIONAL SECURITY COUNCIL, the NATIONAL SECURITY AGENCY and the CENTRAL INTELLIGENCE AGENCY.

After the successful testing of the Soviet atomic bomb on September 23, 1949, Truman ordered a complete reappraisal of U.S. defense and nuclear policy. This led to a crash program to develop the hydrogen bomb and the issuing of NATIONAL SECURITY COUNCIL REPORT 68, which recommended that the United States assume responsibility for leading the defense of the noncommunist world and called for a buildup of American forces.

At the start of Truman's second term, rumors began to spread of financial scandals involving senior White House officials. Truman himself was never implicated, but his support for friends damaged his public standing. In addition to this, the 1950 congressional elections weakened his position on Capitol Hill and effectively killed his Fair Deal, a comprehensive New Deal-style program that included a national health insurance program as well as proposed civil rights measures. These factors and discontent over Truman's handling of the Korean War led the president to announce in March 1952 that he would not run for reelection that year.

Assessments of Truman's foreign policy vary. Left-wing critics claim that he overreacted to Stalin's legitimate security concerns in Eastern Europe and misinterpreted a nationalist war in Korea as part of a communist plot. They claim that his failure to recognize the communist Chinese government led to a dangerous isolation of that country. Some insist that Truman's decision to respond to the Soviet explosion of an atomic bomb with the development of the hydrogen bomb started the nuclear arms race.

Right-wing critics claim that if Truman had given full military and political backing in the immediate postwar years to Chiang Kai-shek, then the Chinese communists would never have come to power and the Korean War would have been prevented.

In his final State of the Union message on January 7, 1953, Truman confirmed that the United States had developed a hydrogen bomb and publicly warned Stalin that war would mean "ruin" for the Soviet Union. He urged that the United States continue to lead the way in establishing a strong collective Western defense as a deterrent to Soviet expansionism.

During the Eisenhower administration, Truman became a vociferous critic of his successor's foreign and defense policies. He was a consistent supporter of American policy in Vietnam. Truman died on December 26, 1972, in Independence, Missouri.

For Further Information:
Caute, David. *The Great Fear: The Anti-Communist Purge Under Truman and Eisenhower.* New York, 1978.
Cochran, Bert. *Harry Truman and the Crisis Presidency.* New York, 1973.
Donovan, Robert J. *Conflict and Crisis: The Presidency of Harry S. Truman, 1945–1948.* New York, 1977.
———. *Nemesis: Truman and Johnson in the Coils of War in Asia.* New York, 1984.
———. *Tumultuous Years: The Presidency of Harry S. Truman, 1949–1953.* New York, 1982.
Gaddis, John Lewis. *The United States and the Origins of the Cold War.* New York, 1972.
Goldman, Eric F. *The Crucial Decade and After: America, 1945–60.* New York, 1960.
McCoy, Donald R. *The Presidency of Harry S. Truman.* Lawrence, Kan., 1984.
McCullough, David G. *Truman.* New York, 1992.
Messer, Robert L. *The End of an Alliance: James F. Byrnes, Roosevelt, Truman, and the Origins of the Cold War.* Chapel Hill, N.C., 1982.
Pemberton, William E. *Harry S. Truman: Fair Dealer and Cold War.* Boston, 1989.
Theoharis, Athan G. *The Truman Presidency: The Origins of the Imperial Presidency and the National Security State.* New York, 1979.
Truman, Harry S. *Memoirs.* 2 vols. New York, 1955–56.

Truman Doctrine   The Truman Doctrine was the policy by which the United States undertook to prevent communists from coming to power in Greece and Turkey, and by extension anywhere it felt its interests threatened. It prevented the United States from returning to its prewar isolation and was the first postwar military commitment to protect Western Europe from the Soviet Union.

In the closing days of World War II and in the war's aftermath, Greece became embroiled in a civil war between British-backed conservative forces and communist guerrillas. At the same time, the Soviet Union applied diplomatic and military pressure against Turkey in order to gain unfettered access to the DARDANELLES. Britain had taken on the responsibility for defending the Aegean, but by the end of 1946 it became apparent that the perilous state of the British economy made Britain's withdrawal inevitable.

On February 21, 1947, British foreign secretary ERNEST BEVIN was told by the treasury that from March 31 Britain could not contribute any more aid to Greece. Bevin immediately warned U.S. undersecretary of state DEAN ACHESON of the forthcoming British withdrawal. He suggested that the burden of defending the region be shouldered by the United States. Acheson felt that "Great Britain had within the hour handed the job of world leadership, with all its burdens and all its glory, to the United States."

President HARRY S. TRUMAN and Secretary of State GEORGE MARSHALL ordered an immediate assessment of the British cable and discovered complete unanimity within the administration in support of Bevin's proposal. To secure congressional support, Truman called a meeting with ARTHUR VANDENBERG, Republican chairman of the Senate Foreign Relations Committee, and other congressional leaders. The administration's case was put by Acheson, who warned of the grave international dangers resulting from the decline of British power and concluded, "Only two great powers remain in the world: the United States and the Soviet Union."

The congressional leaders were persuaded of the need to provide assistance to Greece and Turkey, and on March 12, 1947, Truman announced the Truman Doctrine before a joint session of Congress. Nowhere in his speech did Truman mention the Soviet Union by name, but it was clear that the policy was directed against Moscow.

The president summarized the situation in terms of fundamental ideological opposition and "alternative ways of life" rather than great-power politics; an opposition between "free institutions, representative government, free elections . . . individual liberty, freedom of speech and religion and . . . [freedom] from political oppression" on one side and "terror and oppression" on the other. When the latter are imposed on "free peoples, by direct or indirect aggression," international peace is undermined and the security of the United States is threatened. The United States, Truman implied, had the right and the duty to intervene in such situations, to assure that a "free people" could work out its destiny in its own way. Truman in this address essentially set the tone for the U.S. effort for the entire Cold War.

Specifically, Truman requested $400 million for aid to Greece and Turkey through June 30, 1948, and authority to detail American civilian and military personnel to Greece and Turkey to supervise the use of funds and material assistance and to instruct and train Greek and Turkish personnel.

The president's request did not receive overwhelming praise. Many congressmen wanted a withdrawal to prewar isolation and argued that intervention in Greece and Turkey would lead to World War III. But the support of the former isolationist Vandenberg proved a key factor, and Truman's request was approved.

For Further Information:
Donnelly, Desmond. *Struggle for the World.* New York, 1965.
Fontaine, Andre. *History of the Cold War, vols. 1 and 2.* New York, 1965 and 1969.
Lukacs, John. *A New History of the Cold War.* Garden City, N.Y., 1966.

Turkey   Turkey is one of the only two members of the NORTH ATLANTIC TREATY ORGANIZATION to border on the (former) Soviet Union. It is the guardian of the straits linking the Black Sea and the Mediterranean. Soviet claims on this waterway contributed to the formulation of the TRUMAN DOCTRINE and to Turkish membership in the Western Alliance. In the 1970s and 1980s, the Turkish invasion of Cyprus seriously endangered the SOUTHERN FLANK of NATO.

Turkey's position in the history of the Cold War is intermeshed with its own emergence as a national state following the collapse of the Ottoman Empire in 1918 and with the centuries-old rivalry between the Turks and the Russians for control of the Turkish Straits.

The Turkish Straits, comprised of the DARDANELLES at its Aegean entrance, the Bosporous at the entrance to the Black Sea—and the Sea of Marmara linking the two narrow waterways, provides the only sea link between the Soviet Union or Russia and the Mediterranean. Control of the Turkish Straits has been a long-standing aim of Russian foreign policy, as it would immediately transform the country from a land-based Central European power to a Central European and Mediterranean power.

Between 1475 and 1775, the Ottoman Empire controlled not only the Straits but also the entire Black Sea and would allow only Turkish vessels on it. In 1775, Russia under Catherine the Great gained access to the Black Sea and the right to sail through the Straits, but the Turks retained the right to close the Straits to any foreign warships. For the next 150 years one of the major aims of Russian foreign policy was to destroy the Ottoman Empire and gain total control of the Straits.

Russia might have achieved this ambition at the end of World War I if it had stayed in the war on the side of the Allies. Britain and France in 1915 agreed that the Straits, the city of Constantinople (Istanbul) and the province of Thrace would all be incorporated into the Russian Empire at the end of the war. But because the new Bolshevik government took Russia out of the war, the Straits were placed under the administration of the Great Powers at the end of World War I, backed up by the British- and French-supported Greek Army. In 1922 the Greek Army was defeated by the Turkish nationalist general Mustafa Kemal Pasha (Ataturk), and modern-day Turkey emerged from the ashes of the Ottoman Empire.

The rules governing passage through the Straits were first established at Lausanne in 1923 and were substantially revised at Montreux in 1936. The Montreux Convention allowed complete freedom of transit in time of peace to any merchant ship. In time of war, the same provisions apply if Turkey is not a belligerent. If Turkey is a belligerent, then merchant vessels that do not belong to a country at war with Turkey continue to enjoy full freedom of transit provided "they do not in any way assist the enemy." In time of peace, warships of non–Black Sea powers are allowed through the Straits only when their maximum aggregate tonnage does not exceed 10,000 tons, their number does not exceed nine vessels, and they do not carry guns with a caliber exceeding eight inches. The same restriction applies to Black Sea powers' warships, except that they are allowed to exceed the 10,000-ton limit on the condition that they pass singly and are escorted by no more than two destroyers. Black Sea states are also allowed to send submarines through the Straits. The same rules on warships apply during war, if Turkey is not a belligerent and the ships do not belong to a belligerent power. The warships of belligerent powers are not allowed to pass through the Straits. When Turkey is at war, the entry and passage of warships of other nations is left to the discretion of the Turkish government.

The Soviet Union, which was a party to the Montreux Convention, had won a concession in blocking access to the

Black Sea by Western navies, but at the cost of blocking its own navy into the inland sea. At the time of the Montreux Convention, the Soviets were more concerned about protecting the young Bolshevik state than they were about expanding Soviet influence and power. This situation dramatically altered during the course of World War II.

At the YALTA CONFERENCE in February 1945 Soviet leader JOSEF STALIN asserted that the Montreux Convention was outdated and demanded a revision, as it was impossible for the Soviet Union to accept a situation in which Turkey had "a hand on Russia's throat." Both British prime minister WINSTON CHURCHILL and U.S. president FRANKLIN D. ROOSEVELT agreed that the Montreux Convention was due for a revision and that it should be discussed by the foreign ministers of the Allied powers. Yalta was quickly followed by Soviet pressure on Turkey to effectively hand control of the Straits over to Moscow. In March, Soviet foreign minister V.M. MOLOTOV refused to extend the 1925 Turkish–Soviet Treaty of Neutrality, and in June he demanded two Turkish provinces that had previously formed part of the Russian Empire, a revision of the Montreux Convention, and the establishment of Soviet bases on Turkish territory in order to "help to defend" the Straits.

The demands were rejected outright by Turkey. Britain and the United States, however, at first continued to support Soviet demands for a revision of the Montreux Convention, although they opposed Molotov's demand for Soviet bases along the Straits. In November 1945 the Truman administration proposed a revision to give unlimited access to the Straits by Black Sea powers while maintaining restrictions on non–Black Sea states. This proposal was backed by the British.

The Turkish government immediately launched a diplomatic offensive in both Washington and London against the American proposal. But at the same time, the Soviet government deployed troops along its border with Turkey. It also established a puppet communist government in the Iranian province of AZERBAIJAN, which borders Turkey, and in Greece communist rebels appeared on the verge of seizing power. These factors, plus the general worsening of East–West relations, led Britain and the United States to reconsider their position on the Montreux Convention. In February 1946, British foreign secretary ERNEST BEVIN reminded the House of Commons that Britain had a treaty of alliance with Turkey, and in June 1946 the American battleship *Missouri* was sent to Istanbul accompanied by two destroyers.

In August 1946 the Soviet Union formally demanded that it be allowed to share in the organization of the "joint means of defense" for the Straits. This was rejected by Turkey, Britain and the United States, although they all agreed to call a conference to revise the Montreux Convention. Stalin, however, appeared unwilling to discuss anything short of a Soviet military presence in the Straits and continued to apply political pressure on Turkey.

Protection of Turkey and Greece was generally considered to be Britain's responsibility, but by March 1947 it was clear that the weakened British economy could no longer bear the cost of the GREEK CIVIL WAR and the supply of military aid to Turkey. President HARRY S. TRUMAN decided to fill the gap, announcing what became known as the TRUMAN DOCTRINE and asking Congress for $400 million in immediate aid for Greece and Turkey to help them withstand Soviet pressures.

Turkey was now firmly in the Western camp, and the protection of the Turkish state and the Turkish Straits became a vital element of American foreign policy. In terms of Turkish foreign policy, the United States replaced Britain as Turkey's chief protector, and until the early 1960s the Turkish government did everything possible to please Washington.

Turkey, however, was not one of the founding members of the North Atlantic Treaty Organization. Several of the original members objected to Turkish membership on the grounds that Turkey was not really a European power and did not share the common cultural, social and political heritage of the other NATO members. But the massive size of the Turkish Army and Turkey's status as guardian of the Dardanelles outweighed the factors against Turkish membership, and Turkey was admitted to NATO in 1951. In the KOREAN WAR, Turkey sent the second largest contingent after that of the United States.

The Soviet Union responded to Turkish membership in NATO by warning the Turkish government that it considered such a move to be an unfriendly act toward Moscow. The result was that Turkish-Soviet relations plunged to new depths, and the Turkish-Soviet border became one of the most heavily fortified in the world.

There was a brief improvement in relations between Turkey and the Soviet Union following the death of Stalin in March 1953. In May 1953, the Soviet government renounced its territorial claims against Turkey and dropped its demand for the joint defense of the Straits. But the Turkish government remained wary of Soviet intentions and insisted that the provisions of the Montreux Convention remain in force. In April 1955 Turkey was a founding member of the BAGHDAD PACT, which formed the Middle Eastern link in the Western chain encircling the Soviet Union. The Baghdad Pact evolved into the Central Treaty Organization, and the Turkish capital, Ankara, became the headquarters of CENTO. Turkey also provided bases for American nuclear missiles, bases for American U-2 spy planes and facilities for electronic listening posts.

The Soviet Union, for its part, tried to persuade the Turkish government to forsake the Western Alliance for neutrality. Following the Turkish military coup in May 1960, Soviet leader NIKITA KHRUSHCHEV wrote to Prime Minister General Cemal Gursel offering "close" Soviet-Turkish "cooperation" if Turkey opted for neutrality and stopped "squandering" its resources on defense expenditures. Gursel replied that Turkish-Soviet relations could improve with Turkey remaining in NATO and stressed that without a system of international disarmament Turkey had to remain loyal to a collective security system.

The U.S.–Turkish relationship received its first jolt with the CUBAN MISSILE CRISIS of 1962. Turkey had accepted American Jupiter missiles on its soil, and part of the negotiated solution to the Cuban Missile Crisis was the withdrawal of those outdated missiles in return for the withdrawal of the Soviet missiles from Cuba. The deal was struck without any consultations with Ankara and left the Turkish government reconsidering its dependence on the United States.

This dependence was made even more apparent during the Cyprus Crisis of 1964. The administration of President LYNDON JOHNSON learned that Turkey was considering intervening on the island of Cyprus in behalf of Turkish Cypriots. In June 1964, Johnson wrote to Premier Ismet Inonu that the United States could not "agree to the use of any United States–supplied military equipment for a Turkish intervention in Cyprus." He said that a Turkish intervention would almost certainly result in a Greek-Turkish clash and warned that if such Turkish action was followed by a Soviet attack then American assistance might not be forthcoming.

Johnson's threat succeeded in forcing the Turkish government to back down, but at the cost of losing the blind obedience of Turkey. Successive governments moved their foreign policy toward a more independent course. Relations with the Soviet Union were improved, as were relations with European, Middle Eastern and African countries. In 1965 the Turkish government launched negotiations aimed at gaining greater control over American activities on Turkish soil.

U.S.–Turkish relations plummeted in 1974 after the Turkish invasion of Cyprus and the partition of the island. In reaction, the U.S. Congress in February 1975 imposed a complete embargo on all arms deliveries to Turkey. The ban was partially lifted in September, but in the interim Turkey had closed all American installations and abrogated the 1969 U.S.–Turkish Defense Agreement. At the same time, Turkey's relationship with Greece continued to deteriorate, and the two guardians of NATO's Southern Flank moved to the brink of war.

The Ford and Carter administrations tried to improve relations with Turkey in an effort to ease the threat to the Alliance, but each time they were blocked by Congress, demanding the withdrawal of Turkish forces from Cyprus. It was not until September 1978 that the embargo was lifted and American forces were allowed to return to their bases. In March 1980 a new U.S.–Turkish Cooperation on Defense and Economy Agreement was signed that formalized the resumption of the U.S.–Turkish alliance.

However, in September 1980, a new crisis arose in Turkey when the military overthrew the government of Premier Bulent Ecevit. Relations between Ankara and Washington remained on a steady course, but relations between the Turkish military government and the European members of NATO deteriorated rapidly. Turkey responded by strengthening its ties with the United States and by forging new links with the Middle East countries, especially the new Islamic fundamentalist government in Iran. After the return of civilian rule under Turgut Ozal in 1983, relations with Europe gradually improved. In 1987 Turkey applied for membership in the European Community, but the EC has not made any official response.

For Further Information:
Alvarez, David J. *Bureaucracy and Cold War Diplomacy: The United States and Turkey, 1943–1946.* Thessaloniki, 1980.
Bolukbasi, Suha. *The Superpowers and the Third World: Turkish-American Relations and Cyprus.* Lanham, Md., 1988.
Finkel, Andrew, and Nukhet Sirman, eds. *Turkish State, Turkish Society.* New York, 1990.
Harris, George Sellers. *Troubled Alliance: Turkish-American Problems in Historical Perspective, 1945–1971.* Washington, 1972.
———. *Turkey: Coping with Crisis.* Boulder, Colo., 1985.
McGhee, George Crews. *The U.S.-Turkish-NATO Middle East Connection: How the Truman Doctrine and Turkey's NATO Entry Contained the Soviets.* New York, 1990.
Rozakis, Christos, and Petros N. Stagos. *The Turkish Straits.* Boston, 1987.
Rustow, Dankwart A. *Turkey, America's Forgotten Ally.* New York, 1989.
Schick, Irvin C., and Ertugrul Ahmet Tonak, eds. *Turkey in Transition: New Perspectives.* New York, 1987.
Shaw, Stanford J. *History of the Ottoman Empire and Modern Turkey.* New York, 1976.
Vali, Ferenc A. *The Turkish Straits and NATO.* Stanford, Calif., 1972.

Twining, Nathan　(October 11, 1897–March 29, 1982)
General Nathan Twining played a key role in the development of America's nuclear air weapons and missile systems while serving first as air force chief of staff from 1953 to 1957 and then as chairman of the Joint Chiefs of Staff from 1957 to 1960.

Twining graduated from the U.S. Military Academy at West Point in 1918. During the 1920s he served as an Army Air Force flight instructor. When World War II broke out, Twining was a major, but by the end of 1942 he was a general commanding the Thirteenth Air Force in the Solomon Islands. In 1943 Twining was transferred to the Mediterranean. After the defeat of Germany, he returned to the Pacific to direct bombing raids against Japan, including the dropping of the atomic bombs on Hiroshima and Nagasaki.

After the war, Twining returned to the Pentagon, where he climbed the bureaucratic ladder to reach the post of air force chief of staff in June 1953. Twining took a consistently hard anti-communist line and was a strong advocate of the development and maintenance of a large nuclear arsenal to be delivered by a powerful air force.

Twining's emphasis on nuclear as distinct from conventional forces was in keeping with President DWIGHT EISENHOWER's views, but he opposed the president on spending cuts in the "NEW LOOK" DEFENSE POLICY. During his Senate confirmation hearings, Twining testified that the proposed cuts would "delay" the creation of the 143 wings (air force units comparable in organizational status to an army regiment or brigade) he thought necessary for American security.

Twining supported the projection of U.S. military power, including nuclear weapons, to prevent communists from coming to power. In 1954, he proposed the use of atomic weapons to relieve the French forces at DIEN BIEN PHU. He successfully argued for American intervention in LEBANON in 1958. During the Chinese communist sieges of QUEMOY AND MATSU ISLANDS, Twining and Admiral Arthur Radford, then chairman of the Joint Chiefs of Staff, proposed that the Nationalist Chinese be allowed to bomb the mainland and that American forces support them if the Chinese communists retaliated.

Twining was one of the first military figures to issue public warnings about the so-called "bomber gap." In 1953 he warned that the Soviet Union had 1,000 bombers capable of delivering atomic weapons and about a third of them would be able to breach American defenses. In 1956, Twining told the Senate Appropriations Committee's subcommittee on defense that the U.S. Air Force could repel a Soviet air attack that year, but, because of proposed defense cuts, he was not sure how long he could guarantee that this would be the case. As a result of his testimony, the air force budget for 1957 was increased by $1 billion.

When he was appointed chairman of the Joint Chiefs of Staff in April 1957, Twining was forced to take a broader look at spending priorities and generally took a more supportive view of the administration's defense budgets. For instance, he supported plans for cutbacks in missile development, development of the B-70 bomber and production of B-52 bombers.

Twining retired in 1960 to become chairman of the board of publisher Holt, Rinehart and Winston. In August 1963 he appeared before the preparedness subcommittee of the Senate Foreign Relations Committee to testify against the NUCLEAR TEST BAN TREATY. He also supported American involvement in Vietnam. In 1964 he advised Republican presidential candidate BARRY GOLDWATER on defense issues and was a member of Goldwater's "Peace Through Preparedness" task force, which proposed that the NATO commander be given authority to use tactical nuclear weapons.

In 1966, Twining was an unsuccessful Republican candidate for a U.S. Senate seat from New Hampshire. During the campaign he took a strong stand in support of the VIETNAM WAR. In 1969 he compiled a report for the American Security Council, which described the antiballistic missile (ABM) system as "the soundest insurance for peace and against war that the United States can buy in 1969 for use in the 1970s." General Twining died of a heart attack on March 29, 1982, at Lackland Air Force Base in San Antonio, Texas.

U

Ulbricht, Walter   (June 30, 1893–August 1, 1973)   Walter Ulbricht was the leader of the East German Communist Party after World War II. He added the post of head of state in 1960 and was largely responsible for the building of the BERLIN Wall. He was ousted from power because of his poor response to WILLY BRANDT's OSTPOLITIK ("Eastern Policy").

Ulbricht was the son of a Leipzig tailor who was heavily involved in the German socialist movement. As a boy, Ulbricht distributed tracts and joined the socialist youth movement at the age of nine. He joined the Socialist Party in 1912 at the age of 19 and quickly established a reputation as one of the most active members in the Leipzig area.

After World War I, Ulbricht became disillusioned with the Socialist Party and switched his allegiance to the German Communist Party. In 1921 he went to the Soviet Union, where he developed a close relationship with JOSEF STALIN and undertook a long period of training. He returned to GERMANY in 1928 and was elected to the Reichstag.

When Adolf Hitler crushed the German Communist Party in 1933, Ulbricht was one of the few not arrested and imprisoned. He escaped to Paris, where the German communists established a party-in-exile with Ulbricht as its secretary.

From 1936 to 1938 Ulbricht, on Stalin's orders, was attached to the Republican Army Headquarters in Spain, where he was responsible for the liquidation of party members whose loyalties were suspect. During World War II, Ulbricht was based mainly in Moscow, and he did not return to Germany again until a week before the surrender in May 1945. In the chaos that followed the collapse of government, Ulbricht was able to establish the essential elements of a communist administration in the Soviet-occupied part of Germany. From the start, he was known for his slavish adherence to policies dictated by Moscow.

Following instructions from Stalin, Ulbricht moved quickly to establish a communist system in the Soviet-occupied sector of Germany. In July 1945 all private banks were closed, farms larger than 250 acres were nationalized without compensation, and all individuals and businesses were ordered to surrender all their currency, title deeds and other valuables. Four main antifascist parties were legalized: the Communist Party of Germany (KPD), the Christian Democratic Union (CDU), the Social Democratic Party (SPD) and the Liberal Democratic Party (LDPD). It was clear from the start, however, that the Communist Party under Ulbricht, Wilhelm Pieck and OTTO GROTEWOHL dominated the scene, and communists were moved into key administrative positions by the Soviet authorities. In April 1946, the Communist Party and the SPD merged to form the communist-dominated Socialist Unity Party (SED), which won an overwhelming victory in local elections that year. At the same time, Ulbricht carried out a ruthless purge of the Communist Party ranks to eliminate the old guard and ensure an elite personally dependent on himself.

In 1949, the Soviet Union established the German Democratic Republic following the Berlin Blockade and in response to the West's creation of the Federal Republic of Germany. Ulbricht was officially named deputy chancellor and secretary-general of the SED. Otto Grotewohl was named president and Wilhelm Pieck chancellor, but as in most one-party states, the real political power was concentrated in the hands of the secretary-general of the party. Ulbricht achieved complete power in name as well as in fact in 1960 when, following the death of Pieck, he was named chairman of the newly created Council of State and head of the armed forces, thus combining leadership of both the government and party.

Between 1949 and 1953, Ulbricht concentrated his efforts on trying to achieve the reunification of Germany on terms that would leave the Communist Party dominant and the reunited country dependent on the Soviet Union. In 1950, Ulbricht proposed on ALL-GERMAN COUNCIL to establish a provisional all-German government, which, he proposed, would draw up a constitution and then hold elections on the basis of that constitution. East German and West German governments would be represented equally on the council and in the provisional governments. The West Germans and the Western Allies rejected this proposal on the grounds that the East German government had not been freely elected and therefore should not have equal representation in a provisional government charged with negotiating a constitution.

From about 1950 onward, Ulbricht, working closely with the Soviet Union, began gradually to shift his efforts from trying to reunite Germany under his terms to consolidating his and his party's position. This effort was intensified after the EAST GERMAN UPRISING of June 1953, when workers rioted following an attempt to raise prices. To help the East German economy, the Soviets annulled the remaining $3.2 billion in reparations payments, and a soft loan of $125 million was extended to the East German government. On March 25, 1954, it was announced that the German Democratic Republic had become a sovereign state. In the same year, East Germany became a full member of COMECON (the COUNCIL FOR MUTUAL AND ECONOMIC COOPERATION), and it was a founding member of the WARSAW PACT in May 1955.

With the division formally completed, the two Germanies became the showcases of their respective socioeconomic systems; every success was a reflection on either capitalism or communism. The East German economy, however, was damaged by the flight of thousands of refugees to the West, many of them university graduates or skilled workers. To deal with this problem, Ulbricht favored the closure of the East–West border.

Construction of the Berlin Wall in 1961 made Ulbricht feel secure enough to relax some of his more doctrinaire policies. At the SED Party Congress in 1963 he took the lead among East European leaders in pressing for economic reform, although he forcefully opposed the introduction of a market mechanism. At the same time he showed a greater disposition to seek better relations with West Germany, and he made a number of overtures to the West German Social Democratic Party (SPD).

Ulbricht, however, was not prepared to accept the reformist Prague Spring movement in CZECHOSLOVAKIA. He urged the Warsaw Pact to invade Czechoslovakia in 1968 and overthrow the government of Alexander Dubcek. Ulbricht reasoned that the withdrawal of Czechoslovakia from the Soviet sphere would lead to similar pressures in East Germany, which the SED would be unable to withstand. Therefore it was better to prop up the Czechoslovak "domino" before it fell on him.

But the invasion of Czechoslovakia ironically led to the downfall of Ulbricht. Before 1968, Ulbricht had been able effectively to veto any contacts between the Soviet Bloc countries and West Germany, and by doing so increased his own influence within Eastern Europe. But after 1968, Soviet leader LEONID BREZHNEV decided to take a more direct involvement in East European affairs and in relations with West Germany. This coincided with the Ostpolitik of West German chancellor Willy Brandt, which the Soviet Union saw as an opportunity to establish a direct link with Bonn and gain recognition of its dominance over Eastern Europe.

Ulbricht found himself being pushed by the Soviet Union into an unwelcome rapprochement with West Germany, and relations between him and Brezhnev became strained. In 1970 Brandt met with East German premier Willi Stoph to discuss normalizing relations between the two Germanies. In December 1972 the two men signed the BASIC TREATY, which laid the legal foundation for relations between the two German states. The treaty included a form of joint diplomatic recognition. But it was politically impossible for any West German government to abandon totally the principle of a single German nation and the goal of eventual reunification.

Therefore the two Germanies, at the insistence of Brandt, recognized each other as states within a single German nation. Ulbricht was reluctant to accept this concept because he feared it undermined the legitimacy of the East German state. But Moscow saw the joint recognition as a vital element in its own plan to win Western recognition of postwar borders and forced the resignation of the reluctant Ulbricht, who was replaced with the more amenable ERICH HONECKER. Ulbricht went into a quiet retirement.

For Further Information:

Brant, Stefan. *The East German Rising*. London, 1954.
Fritsch-Bournazel, Renata. *Confronting the German Question*. Oxford, 1988.
Goeckel, Robert F. *The Lutheran Church and the East German State: Political Conflict and Change Under Ulbricht and Honecker*. Ithaca, 1990.
Griffiths, William. *The Ostpolitik of the Federal Republic of Germany*. Amherst, Mass., 1978.
Mander, J. *Berlin: The Eagle and the Bear*. New York, 1962.
McCauley, Martin. *The German Democratic Republic Since 1945*. London, 1983.
McElvoy, Anne. *The Saddled Cow: East Germany's Life and Legacy*. Boston, 1992.
Mezerik, A.F., ed. *Berlin and Germany: Berlin Crisis, Wall, Free State, Separate Treaty, Cold War, Chronology*. New York, 1962.
Sanford, Gregory W. *From Hitler to Ulbricht: The Communist Reconstruction of East Germany, 1945–46*. Princeton, 1983.
Strauss, Franz Joseph. *The Grand Design*. New York, 1965.
Turner, Henry Ashby. *The Two Germanies Since 1945*. New Haven, Conn., 1987.
Whetten, Lawrence. *Germany East and West*. New York, 1980.

Union of Soviet Socialist Republics (Soviet Union, U.S.S.R.) *See* Index for specific subjects.

United Kingdom (Britain, Great Britain, U.K.) *See* Index for specific subjects.

United Kingdom–United States (UKUSA) Agreement (1947) The UKUSA agreement of 1947 established a close partnership among the electronic intelligence organizations of Britain, the United States, Canada, Australia and New Zealand.

The agreement had its origins in Britain's success in breaking Germany's Enigma code in World War II. British prime minister WINSTON CHURCHILL in April 1940 offered the intelligence gathered from Enigma in return for access to American equipment. An agreement to this effect was signed in November 1940. A second wartime agreement, the British–United States Agreement (BRUSA), was signed in May 1943 and provided for full wartime cooperation, including the exchange of information between British and American electronic intelligence organizations. The successful implementation of the BRUSA agreement led to the postwar UKUSA agreement.

In the immediate postwar years, Britain had effective control of the intelligence organizations of Canada, Australia and New Zealand, and the foreign policies of those countries were closely tied to that of Britain. The UKUSA agreement expanded the wartime BRUSA agreement to include the three Commonwealth countries. It also provided for the exchange of personnel among them and the regular exchange of intelligence and equipment, and divided the world into areas of responsibility.

For Further Information:
Bamford, James. *The Puzzle Palace*. New York, 1982.

United States (U.S., USA)   *See* Index for specific subjects.

U.S.–Soviet Trade Agreement (1972)   The U.S.–Soviet Trade Agreement of October 1972 was one of the high points of the détente era. The agreement granted most-favored-nation trading status to the Soviet Union. The agreement was canceled, however, after the U.S. Congress tied most-favored-nation status to a relaxation of Soviet emigration regulations.

The agreement followed hard on the heels of the 1972 STRATEGIC ARMS LIMITATION and ANTI-BALLISTIC MISSILE treaties and was seen as an essential element in the NIXON administration's policy of linking concessions in U.S.–Soviet trade to progress in the political and defense issues. The actual three-year agreement was signed by U.S. secretary of state WILLIAM ROGERS and Soviet foreign trade minister Nikolai Patolichev on October 18, 1972. The main points of the agreement were:

1. The Soviet Union would settle its $722 million LEND-LEASE debt from World War II.
2. The United States government would secure congressional authorization for a reduction of duties on Soviet imports "generally applicable to like products of most other countries" (thereby conferring (most-favored-nation status).
3. The U.S. Export-Import Bank would extend credits and guarantees for sales to the Soviet Union.

It was believed that the agreement would likely triple the rate of trade between the two countries in the previous three years. The agreement, however, fell afoul of the JACKSON AMENDMENT, which tied most-favored-nation status for the Soviet Union to a relaxation of Soviet emigration restrictions. When Congress refused to repeal the amendment, the Soviet Union abrogated the treaty on the grounds that it was an unwarranted interference in Soviet domestic affairs.

Ustinov, Dimitri   (October 30, 1908–December 20, 1984) Marshal Dimitri Ustinov was a major figure in Soviet military affairs, first as minister of armaments under STALIN, later as minister of defense industry under KHRUSHCHEV and finally as minister of defense under BREZHNEV and CHERNENKO.

Ustinov was born into a working-class family in the Russian town of Kuibyshev. In 1927 he joined the Communist Party, and during the two next two years he worked at various factory jobs. In 1929 he entered Bauman Higher Technical School, from which he graduated at the top of his class in 1934. He entered the Soviet armaments industry as an engineer and worked at the Naval Artillery Research Institute in Leningrad and then at the Bolshevik Arms Factory in Leningrad as deputy chief designer and manager.

In the latter job he came to the attention of the party hierarchy, and when Germany attacked the Soviet Union in June 1941 Ustinov was appointed people's commissar (as ministers were then known) of armaments. In this post, Ustinov played the key role in organizing the evacuation of the Soviet arms industry to the area beyond the Urals, thus preventing it from falling into the hands of the advancing Germans.

Ustinov continued as commissar and then minister of armaments in the postwar and early Cold War years, helping to direct the growth in the Soviet armaments industry so that the Soviet Union eventually rivaled the United States in military strength. In 1948, military expenditure in the Soviet Union was $13.1 billion, $3 billion greater than in the United States. By 1969 this figure had grown to $89.8 billion, a great proportion of which went to the armaments industry, which developed the atomic bomb, the hydrogen bomb and a series of missiles capable of delivering nuclear weapons. Ustinov's contribution to Soviet defense was recognized in 1952 when he became a member of the Central Committee. In the following year he was named minister of defense industry, a post he held until 1957, when he was made a deputy chairman of the Council of Ministers while still retaining overall responsibility for the armaments industry.

Ustinov, however, did not have a good relationship with Soviet leader Nikita Khrushchev, and this kept him out of the Politburo until he was made candidate (non-voting) member in 1965, a year after Khrushchev's overthrow. In the same year, Ustinov became a secretary of the Central Committee responsible for the military, the defense industry and the KGB. In the latter position, he developed a close working relationship with KGB chief YURI ANDROPOV, who later became general secretary.

In 1967 the post of minister of defense fell vacant. Ustinov was one of the front-runners for the post, but traditionally the job had gone to a career military officer. Although almost his entire career had been connected with the military, Ustinov had been in the Red Army for only one year in the early 1920s. The Defense Ministry therefore went to Marshal Andrei Grechko, who had an added advantage in that he had served with Brezhnev during the war.

In 1976 Grechko died suddenly, and Ustinov was quickly moved into the Ministry of Defense and simultaneously made a marshal of the Soviet Union and a full member of the Politburo. He quickly established a reputation as one of the Politburo members who was prepared to take a stand independent from that of Brezhnev, especially on domestic issues and arms control negotiations.

Throughout the 1970s, Ustinov played a major role in the U.S.–Soviet SALT I (STRATEGIC ARMS LIMITATION TALKS) and

SALT II negotiations. He played an especially prominent role in 1979 at the Vienna summit meeting between President JIMMY CARTER and Soviet leader Leonid Brezhnev. U.S. national security adviser ZBIGNIEW BRZEZINSKI was struck by the warm relations among Ustinov, Brezhnev and Soviet foreign secretary ANDREI GROMYKO and by Ustinov's "quick and shrewd mind."

By the time Brezhnev died in 1982, Ustinov was being talked about as a possible successor. He was a pallbearer at Brezhnev's funeral and was the second speaker after Yuri Andropov. But Ustinov was by this time too old and too ill to make a serious play for power. Instead he teamed up with Gromyko to play the role of kingmaker and to ensure that the reform-minded Andropov was named to the top party position. Both Gromyko and Ustinov had come to the conclusion that the Soviet Union was badly in need of radical reform, and both men carried considerable weight within the Politburo as they owed their positions not to party patronage but to proven managerial and diplomatic skills.

It was a bitter blow to Ustinov and Gromyko when Andropov died on February 9, 1984. Neither man was well enough to fill the top post, and the other serious candidate, MIKHAIL GORBACHEV, was not well enough placed politically to present a serious challenge. Ustinov reluctantly agreed that Brezhnev's chief protégé, Konstantin Chernenko, would succeed Andropov, but he and Gromyko insisted on guarantees that Chernenko would not return to the Brezhnev policies. At the same time, he helped to push Gorbachev into the political limelight so that by the time Chernenko died on March 10, 1985, Gorbachev was well placed to succeed him. Ustinov, however, had died by then, on December 20, 1984.

For Further Information:
Scott, Harriet, and William F. Scott. *The Armed Forces of the USSR.* Boulder, Colo., 1981.

U-2 Spy Plane   The U-2 spy plane was one of the most important American intelligence-gathering devices of the 1950s and 1960s. Aerial reconnaissance by U-2 planes played an important role during the 1962 CUBAN MISSILE CRISIS. The Soviet downing of a U-2 on May 1, 1960, led to the breakdown of a scheduled summit meeting that month.

The development of the U-2 was the result of the Soviets' rejection of President DWIGHT EISENHOWER's "OPEN SKIES" plan.

Eisenhower had unveiled his proposal on July 21, 1955, at that year's GENEVA HEADS OF GOVERNMENT SUMMIT. The plan called on the Soviet Union and the United States to exchange military blueprints and allow mutual air reconnaissance over their military installations.

After the Soviet rejection, RICHARD BISSELL, assistant director of the CENTRAL INTELLIGENCE AGENCY, persuaded CIA Director ALLEN DULLES and President Eisenhower to develop a high-altitude spy plane that could collect the information the Open Skies plan would have made available, while operating outside the attack range of Soviet aircraft.

Research on such an aircraft was already being conducted by the Lockheed Aircraft Company, and by September 1956 U-2 squadrons operated by the CIA were being deployed in Turkey, Western Europe and Japan for reconnaissance flights over Eastern Europe, the Soviet Union and China.

The plane was capable of four-hour flights at altitudes of 80,000 feet. The true nature of the U-2 squadrons was kept top secret. The planes were fitted with self-destruct mechanisms, and pilots were given suicide pills.

The Soviets, however, were aware of the true nature of the planes and by 1958 were trying to shoot them down with ground-to-air missiles. On May 1, 1960, they succeeded in downing a U-2 plane piloted by Lieutenant FRANCIS GARY POWERS, whose subsequent confession seriously embarrassed the Eisenhower administration and led to the breakdown of the May 1960 Geneva summit.

The U-2, however, continued to be a mainstay of the CIA's high-tech intelligence gathering program. The planes were used during the abortive BAY OF PIGS invasion of Cuba, and they were responsible for photographing the installation of Soviet missiles in Cuba. The pilot who first spotted the installations, Major Rudolph Anderson, was shot down over Cuba in the later stages of the Cuban Missile Crisis. Although some planes remained operational into the 1970s, they became obsolete with the increased use of SATELLITE RECONNAISSANCE.

For Further Information:
Ambrose, Stephen E. *Ike's Spies: Eisenhower and the Espionage Establishment.* Garden City, N.Y., 1981.
Beschloss, Michael R. *Mayday: Eisenhower, Khrushchev and the U-2 Affair.* New York, 1986.
O'Toole, G.J.A. *The Encyclopedia of American Intelligence and Espionage.* New York, 1988.

V

Vance, Cyrus (March 27, 1917–   ) Cyrus Vance served as secretary of the army under President JOHN F. KENNEDY and as deputy secretary of defense and diplomatic trouble-shooter under President LYNDON JOHNSON. He became secretary of state in 1977 in the CARTER administration, and helped to negotiate the SALT II treaty, the normalization of Sino–American relations, the Anglo–American agreement on Rhodesia, the Camp David Accords and other issues.

Vance attended Yale University, where he received his law degree in 1942. After serving in the U.S. Navy during World War II, he entered private practice in New York City. In 1957 he became special counsel to the U.S. Senate committees investigating the satellite and missile programs and worked closely with Senator Lyndon Johnson.

When Johnson became vice president in 1960, he recommended Vance to President John F. Kennedy, who appointed him secretary of the army under Defense Secretary ROBERT MCNAMARA. Vance developed a good working relationship with McNamara and in January 1964 was appointed deputy secretary of defense.

After Johnson became president he also used Vance as a diplomatic troubleshooter. In January 1964 Vance was sent to Panama to try to negotiate the restoration of diplomatic relations after U.S. troops fired on rioters protesting the American presence in the Canal Zone. The following year, Vance went to the DOMINICAN REPUBLIC to try to establish a coalition government to end the civil war there. In 1967 he was assigned by Johnson to try to negotiate a truce in the Cyprus civil war, and following the seizure of the USS *Pueblo* Vance was sent to South Korea to assure the government of continuing American support.

Vance was known as a hawk on the VIETNAM WAR who, according to the Pentagon Papers, was "overwhelmingly in favor of prosecuting the war vigorously," of intensified bombing of North Vietnam and of increased efforts to "create a viable government in the South."

Vance left the Defense Department at the end of 1967 because of ill health. But he continued to advise the president on Vietnam and was a member of the senior advisory group created by Johnson to consider the military's request for an additional 200,000 troops to fight the war. By this time Vance had revised his attitudes toward the war and joined the other members of the advisory group in recommending de-escalation.

In May 1968, at the start of the PARIS PEACE TALKS ON VIETNAM, Vance was appointed a deputy delegate to the negotiations. His main responsibility was handling organizational details such as seating arrangements and the sizes of the delegations. Vance resigned this post in 1969 to resume his New York law practice, but he remained active in Democratic Party politics.

Jimmy Carter and Vance first met in 1971 at a meeting of the Trilateral Commission, but they remained no more than acquaintances until 1976, when Carter asked Vance to join his campaign staff as a foreign policy adviser. In December 1976, after a visit to Plains, Georgia, Vance was nominated as secretary of state by the president-elect.

Carter stressed that he wanted a collegiate approach to his administration. Vance accepted this with the reservation that he wanted "only the president and his secretary of state . . . to have responsibility for defining the administration's foreign policy publicly." This position conflicted with the ambitions of national security adviser ZBIGNIEW BRZEZINSKI, and according to Vance, Brzezinski's "actions became a serious impediment to the conduct of our foreign policy." Vance's position was further complicated by Carter's penchant for becoming closely involved with every aspect of government and at times making foreign policy decisions without consulting the State Department.

Vance was convinced that the bipolar world of 1945 to the late 1960s had given way to a more complicated set of relationships that did not fit neatly into a simple East–West Cold War context. He further believed that the Nixon and Ford administrations had failed to recognize this diffusion of power and that their thinking had been too firmly rooted in the concept of a U.S.–Soviet "geopolitical" struggle. Vance's view of the world wrongly led many to label him as a "dove" on U.S.–Soviet relations. He tried to steer the Carter administration away from the Kissinger–Nixon policy of linkage between strategic negotiations and Soviet actions elsewhere in the world, although he favored a linkage between political issues and economic concessions. However, he ran into opposition from Brzezinski and some key figures on Capitol Hill. The result was that Carter tended to vacillate between Brzezinski's hard line and Vance's more complex one.

This shifting position confused the Soviet Union and delayed the STRATEGIC ARMS LIMITATION negotiations (SALT II).

The agreement was not signed until June 1979, when Carter and Soviet leader LEONID BREZHNEV met in Vienna. Vance strongly supported the treaty, which he described as "a balanced, carefully wrought set of agreements that left us with virtually full freedom of action to modernize our strategic forces . . . while requiring a significant reduction in Soviet strategic forces." The treaty's opponents, however, accused Carter and Vance of "appeasement." The treaty faced a difficult ratification fight, but because of the Soviet invasion of AFGHANISTAN, was never submitted for approval.

The Afghanistan matter was, along with the Iranian revolution and its consequences, one of the two major foreign policy crises during Vance's tenure at the State Department. The invasion came at a time when the United States was preoccupied with the collapse of the shah of Iran and the taking of the U.S. diplomatic hostages in Teheran. Many took the view that the Soviet Union was exploiting American weakness in the region to place itself in a position to dominate events in Pakistan and post-shah Iran. Vance took the view that the invasion was partly the result of Soviet fears of a fundamentalist regime taking power in Afghanistan and partly a result of a general deterioration in U.S.–Soviet relations. In late January 1980, he urged Carter to talk with Brezhnev. The president refused. He also refused to allow Vance to meet personally with Soviet foreign minister ANDREI GROMYKO to stress the threat that Afghanistan posed to U.S.–Soviet relations.

Vance did not place a high priority on relations with Western Europe. He saw the major Western European governments as hamstrung, either by economic problems or narrow political majorities. Vance opposed Carter's making an early European tour and suggested that most meetings with West European heads of government should take place in Washington, D.C. He did emphasize the need to encourage European integration and involve the West Europeans in maintaining the floundering North–South dialogue (between developed and developing nations) and improving NATO's strength. Less important items on Vance's European agenda were EUROCOMMUNISM and the Mutual Balance Force Reduction Talks in Vienna.

Vance was more concerned with African affairs. He was especially alarmed by southern Africa, where a number of observers believed that the Soviet Union, with the help of the Cubans, was successfully exploiting the black nationalist movements in Rhodesia, Namibia and South Africa to gain influence in the strategically important and mineral-rich region.

Working closely with British foreign secretary David Owen, Vance pressured the South Africans to stop or at least reduce their aid to Rhodesian prime minister Ian Smith in order to force him to the negotiating table and into real concessions. In September 1977, Owen announced the Anglo–American plan for a Rhodesian settlement, which included universal suffrage, a bill of rights, an internationally supervised cease-fire, free elections, the establishment of a

new army based on the guerrilla force and constitutional protection for the white minority.

On the MIDDLE EAST, Vance initially argued in favor of a continuation of the step-by-step approach employed by HENRY KISSINGER. The ultimate aim involved the Arabs' agreeing to normalization of relations with Israel in exchange for return of most of the territories occupied by Israel in 1967. Vance, in a memorandum to Carter in 1976, also proposed asking for Soviet help, "at the appropriate time," in reaching such an agreement.

In February 1977, Vance made a Middle East tour, during which he shuttled for eight days among Israel, Egypt, Jordan, Saudi Arabia and Syria. He returned convinced that the United States should abandon step-by-step shuttle diplomacy in favor of an all-parties, Geneva-type conference on the Middle East. The proposed negotiations faced increasing opposition from Israel. The impasse was finally resolved by Egyptian president ANWAR SADAT with his historic visit to Israel in November 1977. Sadat's initiative pushed Vance back into the step-by-step approach that eventually culminated in the Camp David Accords, which were largely negotiated by Carter himself.

When Vance moved into the State Department, China's government (see PEOPLE'S REPUBLIC OF CHINA) was undergoing its change from radical Maoists to the more pragmatic supporters of DENG XIAOPING. In a 1976 memorandum, Vance argued forcefully that the Carter administration should support a policy of "normalization of diplomatic relations" between the United States and China but saw "no reason to alter the current arms sales policy to TAIWAN."

The decision to normalize relations and exchange ambassadors with China was announced in December 1978. Vance had hoped that he would be assigned the task of flying to Beijing to formalize the arrangements, because he felt it was important that the State Department maintain control of Sino–American relations. In the end, however, Carter sent Brzezinski to Beijing and Vance to Moscow for further SALT II negotiations. In January 1979, Chinese leader Deng Xiaoping visited the United States.

Early on, Vance proposed that Carter send a presidential envoy to Hanoi to discuss the issue of American soldiers still listed as missing in action (MIAs) in the Vietnam War. During the visit, the special emissary would probe Vietnam's intentions and would be authorized to say that the Carter administration would be prepared to put to Congress a program of humanitarian assistance once there was a full accounting for the MIAs. Vance saw this as the first step on the road to normalization of relations and proposed AVERELL HARRIMAN as the special emissary. Improved U.S.–Vietnamese relations were blocked by the plight of the Vietnamese boat people, the Vietnamese invasion of CAMBODIA and Vietnam's decision to sign a treaty of friendship with the Soviet Union in November 1978.

During his confirmation hearings, Vance signaled his intention to improve relations with CUBA. He and Carter both believed that U.S. interests would best be served by maintaining diplomatic relations with countries with whom the United States had political differences. In his memoirs, Vance wrote: "Our objective was to see whether it might be possible slowly to change Castro's perspective on relations with the U.S. from one of fear and hostility to one in which he might see benefits in restraining his revolutionary adventurism and in lessening his dependence on the Soviet Union."

FIDEL CASTRO initially responded favorably. But improved relations foundered on the hostility engendered on Capitol Hill by Cuban activities in Angola and the Horn of Africa. A further complication was the discovery that the Soviet Union was supplying to Cuba MiG-23 aircraft, which some defense experts believed were capable of carrying nuclear weapons in breach of the 1962 U.S.–Soviet agreement on Cuba. The Soviet Union delivered a public assurance that the aircraft were nonnuclear, but the publicity further damaged U.S.–Cuban relations and delayed passage of the SALT II Treaty.

The collapse of the shah of Iran was the other major foreign policy crisis of the Carter years and eventually led to Vance's resignation. United States strategy in the Persian Gulf had become increasingly reliant on the American relationship with the despotic MOHAMMED REZA PAHLEVI of Iran. But the shah's relationship with the United States and the tactics of his feared American-trained secret police, Savak, were opposed by his increasingly angry subjects. In January 1979, the shah was forced to flee after massive demonstrations organized by the Islamic clergy, who had become the focus of the anti-shah movement. Shortly afterward, the exiled Islamic leader Aytollah Ruhollah Khomeini returned to Teheran and established an Islamic state. Vance tried to form a relationship with the Khomeini regime, but the United States was firmly denounced by the ruling clergy as the "Great Satan."

The depth of anti-American feeling in Iran was underscored when Iranian students seized control of the American Embassy on November 4, 1979, and took hostage the American diplomats there. Vance believed that "the hostages would be released safely once they had served their political purpose in Iran," and as time passed he became increasingly convinced that the "chances of physical harm to the hostages diminished." While Vance was away on a weekend holiday with his wife, a meeting of the NATIONAL SECURITY COUNCIL was called, and it was agreed to use military force to free the hostages. Vance later said that he had been "stunned and angry that such a momentous decision had been made in my absence" and he demanded and got a special meeting of the National Security Council to present his objections to the use of the military. But no one at the second meeting supported his plan for continued diplomatic pressure, and the plans went ahead for the rescue attempt. In protest against the mission, Vance resigned on April 20, but he agreed not to make his decision public until after the attempt, which failed with tragic consequences for the would-be rescuers.

Vance returned to his private law practice in New York. He maintained close contact with Carter and in 1983 was named a foreign policy adviser to the Carter Center in Atlanta, Georgia. He remained a consistent supporter of the SALT II Treaty he had negotiated and a firm opponent of President RONALD REAGAN's foreign and defense policies. In February 1985 he appeared before the Senate Foreign Relations Committee to argue against deployment of the MX MISSILE on the grounds that it would push the Soviets to "develop new missile technology." He also advised against pursuing the STRATEGIC DEFENSE INITIATIVE beyond the research stage.

Cyrus Vance has not chosen to enjoy a peaceful retirement. Since 1991 he has worked as a United Nations special envoy to Yugoslavia and South Africa.

For Further Information:
Brzezinski, Zbigniew. *In Quest of National Security*. Boulder, Colo., 1988.

Carter, Jimmy. *Keeping Faith*. New York, 1982.

Spanier, J.W. *American Foreign Policy Since World War Two*. Washington, D.C., 1988.

Talbott, Strobe. *Endgame: The Inside Story of SALT Two*. New York, 1979.

Vance, Cyrus. *Hard Choices*. New York, 1983.

Vandenberg, Arthur (March 22, 1884–April 18, 1951)

Senator Arthur Vandenberg played a major role in forging a bipartisan postwar foreign policy and bringing the Republican Party out of its prewar isolationism. His support for the TRUMAN DOCTRINE and the MARSHALL PLAN ensured their passage through Congress, and in 1948 he was author of the resolution that provided the constitutional basis for American entry into the NORTH ATLANTIC TREATY ORGANIZATION.

Vandenberg started his career in 1902 as a journalist on the *Grand Rapids Herald*. Within five years he was the newspaper's publisher and editor. In 1928, the Republican Vandenberg was appointed to fill a vacant seat in the U.S. Senate. In the prewar years he was an isolationist and in 1939 led the Republicans in opposing modifications to the Neutrality Act. Vandenberg moved away from isolationism after the bombing of Pearl Harbor. He fully supported President FRANKLIN ROOSEVELT's war measures, served on a bipartisan committee to forge a bipartisan postwar policy and in April 1944 publicly renounced isolationism.

Roosevelt appointed Vandenberg as the leading Republican on the American delegation to the negotiations to form the United Nations. At the SAN FRANCISCO CONFERENCE in 1945, Vandenberg successfully fought for approval of Article 51 of the UN Charter, which permitted member states to enter into regional security pacts for the maintenance of international peace and security. This article later provided the legal basis for the VANDENBERG RESOLUTION.

Vandenberg had a large Polish-American constituency and took a special interest in the Soviet occupation of Poland and Eastern Europe. In the immediate aftermath of the war Vandenberg was a member of American delegations to Big Three talks to implement the YALTA and POTSDAM agreements. After the Paris Conference from April to June 1946, he returned to the United States to report that a "Cold War" now existed between the United States and Soviet Union and that Washington should adopt a "talking tough" policy in dealing with the Soviets.

In 1946 Vandenberg became chairman of the Senate Foreign Relations Committee. His senior position within the Republican Party and the Senate as well as his oratorical gifts made Vandenberg a key figure in the TRUMAN administration's efforts to deal with the Soviet Union. He was a regular visitor to the White House, where he conferred with President Harry Truman and his advisers on how best to steer foreign policy initiatives through Congress. It was on Vandenberg's advice that Truman decided to couch his request for military and economic aid to Greece in the terms of a moral crusade against communism. In a speech supporting the Truman Doctrine aid program Vandenberg warned that defeat of the program would "give the green light" to aggression everywhere.

Vandenberg also helped to frame the legislation for the Marshall Plan, which he described as a program that would "help stop World War III before it starts." In an emotional speech to the Senate in December 1947 he said that if the plan failed, "we have done our final best. If it succeeds our children and our children's children will call us blessed."

Perhaps Vandenberg's greatest contribution to the history of the Cold War period was the Vandenberg Resolution, which provided the political and legal basis for American entry into NATO and the signing of the RIO PACT. The need for a Western Alliance involving the United States had first been formulated by British foreign secretary ERNEST BEVIN, who paved the way for American involvement by negotiating a series of security agreements between Britain and West European governments.

On April 11, 1948, Secretary of State MARSHALL opened talks with Vandenberg and Senator Tom Connally on the problem of security in the North Atlantic region. It was agreed that, following a commitment from Canada and Britain, Vandenberg would propose that the Congress act under Article 51 of the UN Charter. On April 28, 1948, Canadian prime minister LOUIS ST. LAURENT proposed a single mutual defense system to supersede the agreements already negotiated by Bevin. The Canadian premier's proposal was warmly welcomed by Bevin a week later. On June 11, 1948, the Vandenberg Resolution was adopted by the Senate, and the way was clear for the United States to sign the North Atlantic Treaty on April 4, 1949.

In his last few years Vandenberg suffered terrible physical pain as a result of cancer. He was able to steer the North Atlantic Treaty through the Senate, however, and continued to support a bipartisan foreign policy until his death on April 18, 1951.

For Further Information:
Gazell, James A. "Arthur Vandenberg, Internationalism and the United Nations," *Political Science Quarterly*, 88 (1973): 375–94.

Vandenberg, Hoyt   (January 24, 1899–April 2, 1954)
General Hoyt Vandenberg was air force chief of staff from 1948 to 1953 and led the argument for a strengthened air force during the early 1950s.

Vandenberg, nephew of the influential Senator ARTHUR VANDENBERG, entered the Army Air Corps after graduating from the U.S. Military Academy at West Point. By 1938, he was America's chief instructor in fighter plane tactics.

During the early war years, Vandenberg helped plan the Allied invasion of North Africa, and in 1944 he was given command of the Ninth Air Force. He also attended wartime diplomatic conferences at Cairo, Teheran and Quebec. After the war, Vandenberg served briefly as head of American Intelligence, but in 1947 he returned to the Army Air Corps as its chief of staff.

After the establishment in 1947 of the air force as an independent branch of the armed forces, President HARRY TRUMAN appointed Vandenberg air force chief of staff. Vandenberg immediately launched himself into a campaign for a stronger air force to counter increased Soviet production of bombers and jet fighters. In January 1950, Vandenberg wrote that the United States' "greatest deterrent to military aggression is the existence of a strategic force capable of inflicting damage sufficient to make aggression extremely unprofitable."

Vandenberg was also a leading figure in the drive for a unified Armed Services and supported Truman's dismissal of General DOUGLAS MACARTHUR from his command in Korea.

After DWIGHT EISENHOWER became president in 1953, Vandenberg became a leading critic of the "NEW LOOK" DEFENSE POLICY, which significantly reduced the defense budget. Cuts included a $5 billion reduction in appropriations for the air force and precluded the service's anticipated addition of 143 wings (regiment- or brigade-size units). In June 1953, Vandenberg testified before the Senate Appropriations Committee that the 143-wing increase was the absolute minimum needed for American air defense and that anything short of that "would increase the risk to national security beyond the dictates of national prudence."

Vandenberg claimed that the air force was being crippled by five types of restriction: new base construction, personnel, appropriations, force levels, and expenditures on research. He said that he had heard no sound military reason for the cuts "at a time when we face an enemy who has more modern jet fighters than we have and enough long-range bombers to attack this country in a sudden all-out atomic effort." Vandenberg added that the proposed reductions would reduce the U.S. Air Force to a "one-shot" service without the reserves to counterattack the Soviets.

Vandenberg, however, was suffering from terminal cancer. He retired in July 1953 and the cuts took effect immediately afterward. He died on April 2, 1954.

Vandenberg Resolution   The Vandenberg Resolution, sponsored by U.S. Senator ARTHUR VANDENBERG (R, Mich.), was a congressional repudiation of America's prewar isolationism and provided the constitutional basis for American entry into the NORTH ATLANTIC TREATY ORGANIZATION. It passed the Senate on June 11, 1948.

The resolution was introduced by Senator Vandenberg after Canadian prime minister LOUIS ST. LAURENT and British foreign secretary ERNEST BEVIN proposed a mutual security pact to supersede the postwar defense agreements negotiated between Britain and the Benelux countries and France. The resolution, which was not legally binding, declared it to be the sense of the Senate that the United States should enter into collective international defense arrangements as provided for by Article 51 of the UN Charter, and pursue other strategies to achieve peace through the UN.

Vienna Summit Conference (1961)

The Vienna Summit in June 1961 between U.S. president JOHN F. KENNEDY and Soviet leader NIKITA KHRUSHCHEV was the first meeting of the two men. It resolved none of the differences between the superpowers, and Kennedy's reportedly poor performance is believed to have encouraged Khrushchev to precipitate the Berlin crisis of August 1961 and to base Soviet missiles in CUBA.

The first day of the conference (June 3) was spent in an abstract ideological debate during which each leader attempted to persuade the other of the rightness of his own political philosophy. The second day of the conference concentrated on LAOS, a test ban treaty and Berlin.

Khrushchev used the meeting to press for Western withdrawal from Berlin. He warned that the Soviet Union would soon sign a treaty with the German Democratic Republic (East Germany) and that once this was done the Western Powers, in his opinion, would have no juridical right to remain in West Berlin. Kennedy maintained that American abandonment of West Berlin would signal an intention to abandon Western Europe.

Negotiations on a NUCLEAR TEST BAN TREATY had begun after the GENEVA HEADS OF GOVERNMENT SUMMIT in July 1955, and had been seriously jeopardized when a U-2 spy plane flown by Lieutenant FRANCIS GARY POWERS was shot down on May 1, 1960. Kennedy had hoped to revive negotiations in Vienna, but he encountered opposition from Khrushchev, who opposed any more than three on-site inspections a year and wanted to tie a test ban agreement to a wider Soviet disarmament proposal.

The only real progress was made on the issue of Laos. Both Kennedy and Khrushchev wanted to disengage from an increasingly difficult situation in that country. The two leaders' agreement on the need for a resolution to the Laotian crisis led to a cease-fire and the start of negotiations, which established formal Laotian neutrality. Unfortunately, the agreement fell apart by 1963, and Laos again collapsed into civil war.

For Further Information:
Crankshaw, Edward. *Khrushchev: A Career.* New York, 1966.
Fontaine, Andre. *History of the Cold War, vols. 1 and 2.* New York, 1965 and 1969.
Schlesinger, Arthur. *A Thousand Days: John F. Kennedy in the White House.* New York, 1965.
Walton, Richard. *Cold War and Counterrevolution: The Foreign Policy of John F. Kennedy.* New York, 1972.

Vietnam War

The Vietnam War was America's biggest setback of the Cold War. It destroyed the myth of American military invulnerability and undermined the cherished American belief in the moral superiority of the United States. The American experience in Vietnam has acted as a brake on subsequent U.S. military adventures in other parts of the world.

American involvement in Vietnam dated back to the early 1950s, when the TRUMAN administration first supported the French in their colonial war, against the Viet Minh, the communist-led coalition fighting for national independence. President DWIGHT EISENHOWER and Secretary of State JOHN FOSTER DULLES also saw the maintenance of a pro-Western government in Vietnam and neighboring LAOS as an essential bulwark against communist influence spreading from China and the Soviet Union.

The Eisenhower administration supplied substantial military aid to the French government, and American air strikes to relieve the besieged French garrison at DIEN BIEN PHU were discussed in 1954. But the French were not prepared to continue the war and agreed to withdraw at the GENEVA CONFERENCE ON INDOCHINA AND KOREA in 1954. The Eisenhower administration did not like the Geneva Accords, which temporarily divided Vietnam along the 17th parallel pending elections for a unified government in 1956 and effectively forbade the introduction of foreign troops. The chief American negotiator, Undersecretary of State WALTER BEDELL SMITH, refused to sign the accords, instead issuing a unilateral declaration stating that the United States would "refrain from the threat or the use of force to disturb" the armistice agreements. The statement added that the United States "would view any renewal of the aggression in violation of the aforesaid agreements with grave concern and as seriously threatening international peace and security."

The U.S. stand on the Geneva Accords left the United States in the position of chief supporter of any anti-communist leader who came to power in South Vietnam. This proved to be NGO DINH DIEM, who in 1955 was asked by Emperor Bao Dai (a figurehead maintained by the French) to become prime minister. The following year, Diem overthrew Bao Dai and declared himself president of the Republic of Vietnam. Diem managed to secure massive American financial assistance from the Eisenhower administration, which also supplied covert CENTRAL INTELLIGENCE AGENCY (CIA) support directed by Colonel EDWARD LANSDALE.

The 1956 elections never took place because the Eisenhower administration and Diem were convinced that the Viet Minh led by communist nationalist leader HO CHI MINH would win. Neither the Soviets nor the Chinese pressed for elections. The Soviet Union was preoccupied with problems in HUNGARY and POLAND, and the PEOPLE'S REPUBLIC OF CHINA was concerned about an Indochinese repeat of the KOREAN WAR. Ho was also pursuing a brutal policy of forced collectivization and, as he had withdrawn most of his troops to the north following the 1954 agreement, he had little military leverage in the south. The de facto partition of Vietnam therefore continued, with South Vietnam and the United States committed to the division's permanence. North Vietnam, however, remained committed to the concept of a unified Vietnam.

Diem continued in power in South Vietnam, but his government lacked any popular base and became increasingly dependent on the support of corrupt officials for its existence. The focal point for dissidence became the continuing public protests of Buddhist monks. The Roman Catholic Diem arrested thousands of monks, accusing them of sympathizing with the communists. Diem's treatment of the Buddhists alienated American public opinion, and U.S. ambassador HENRY CABOT LODGE argued that Diem had to be replaced. The result was a military coup, in November 1963, which ended with the murder of Diem and his brother Ngo Dinh Nhu.

Between 1956 and the overthrow of Diem, antigovernment guerrilla operations in South Vietnam had substantially increased (as had American military assistance to the government). Most such operations were conducted by a communist-directed South Vietnamese guerrilla force known as the Viet Cong. By 1963 there were an estimated 150,000 active Viet Cong guerrillas. They were supplied by the local population (not always voluntarily) and by North Vietnam along what became known as the Ho Chi Minh Trail. They were also given sanctuary in North Vietnam and, to a lesser extent, in CAMBODIA and Laos. It was not until 1964 that North Vietnamese regulars entered the war. In 1961, President JOHN F. KENNEDY began to raise the number of American military personnel in South Vietnam, and by the time of Kennedy's death in November 1963, there were 16,200.

Kennedy shelved proposals from the Pentagon to introduce up to 200,000 American combat troops into the war. But he did allow American bombers, helicopters and fighter aircraft to provide air support to Vietnamese troops. Diem's death also contributed to increased American involvement. His murder was followed by a political vacuum, which the United States was forced to fill in order to counter increasing communist gains. Eventually a stable government emerged in 1965 under Air Vice-Marshal Nguyen Cao Ky. In 1967 he was replaced by General Nguyen Van Thieu following rigged elections. It was always clear that these governments depended on the United States for their existence and that the United States had become the effective political as well as military power in the country.

The final decisions to commit a large force of American combat troops to Vietnam were taken by President LYNDON B. JOHNSON after the American destroyer USS *Maddox* was involved in what became known as the Gulf of Tonkin Incident. Whether an attack was actually made by the North Vietnamese, or it was fabricated or provoked to provide Johnson with an excuse to enter the war, has never been clear. It is clear that before the incident, the administration had drafted a congressional resolution giving the president the power to commit American forces in Southeast Asia. After the alleged incident, the GULF OF TONKIN RESOLUTION was approved unanimously in the House of Representatives, and with only two dissenting votes in the Senate. At this stage, public opinion polls showed the American public 85% in favor of the war.

In February 1965, the Viet Cong raided an American encampment near Pleiku, South Vietnam, killing eight Americans. In retaliation, Johnson ordered the bombing of North Vietnam. The bombing continued with only a few breaks until the end of March 1968 and became one of the major factors in the war, with the United States offering to halt the bombing in return for substantive peace negotiations and the North Vietnamese refusing to negotiate until the bombing stopped. The bombings also helped to turn international public opinion against the United States.

At the height of the war, there were over 500,000 American troops in Vietnam, and President Johnson was fully committed to the war. He was convinced that American troops were needed to prevent a Soviet- and Chinese-inspired communist takeover that would threaten Western interests throughout the Pacific and Indian Ocean regions. He was also convinced that the South Vietnamese could and would, with American support, win the war. The NLF and the North Vietnamese, however, fought primarily as nationalists rather than communists, and assured themselves the support of the peasants in the South Vietnamese countryside.

The belief of the NLF and North Vietnamese leaders in their ultimate victory was given further support by the growing antiwar movement in the United States. Intellectuals and a growing number of others could not understand why the United States was fighting to support a government that was clearly corrupt, despotic and unpopular. The antiwar movement was especially strong among students, who faced the prospect of being drafted to fight in the war.

At the start of 1968, President Johnson was seriously considering a major new troop commitment—until the huge TET OFFENSIVE of January–February 1968. This took North Vietnamese and Viet Cong forces into the heart of the towns and cities of South Vietnam. The old imperial capital of Hue was held for 25 days, and the Viet Cong even managed to break into the U.S. Embassy compound in Saigon.

U.S. commanders argued that the Tet Offensive was a last desperate effort by the Viet Cong and North Vietnamese and that their offensive was, in purely military terms, a failure. They also requested an additional 200,000 troops, which would have involved calling up the reserves. Johnson, faced with growing public disenchantment and no longer taking the military's optimistic projections at face value, created a senior advisory group to consider the request, and ultimately rejected it. On March 31, 1968, he announced that he would stop the bombing and de-escalate American involvement in Vietnam. He also announced that he would not seek reelection that year.

American policy thus became the eventual withdrawal of American ground forces, to be replaced by a more effective South Vietnamese Army supported by American air power. This was known as "Vietnamization." At the same time, the United States hoped to negotiate a complete end to the fighting. Negotiations started in Paris in May 1968 and continued off and on until January 1973 when an agreement was reached.

Johnson was succeeded by a Republican president, RICHARD M. NIXON, who campaigned on the slogan of "peace with honor." Early in his presidency, Nixon came to the conclusion that he could not successfully "Vietnamize" the war without destroying the communist bases and supply lines. U.S. forces thus attacked North Vietnamese and Viet Cong bases in Cambodia and Laos as well as in North Vietnam—a strategy that substantially widened the geographic scope of the war (and sparked a whole new round of antiwar protests).

In Cambodia, this resulted in a right-wing coup by pro-American military officers. Then, in April 1970, Nixon ordered a full-scale ground and air invasion of Cambodia with the purpose of finding and destroying the presumed field headquarters of the communist war effort. The invasion completely destabilized Cambodia and eventually led to the establishment of the ruthless Khmer Rouge government under Pol Pot. The invasion also sparked a new series of antiwar demonstrations in the United States. More than 100,000 protesters surrounded the White House and 420 colleges were shut by strikes. At Kent State University in Ohio, four students were shot to death on May 4, 1970, by National Guardsman called out in response to the demonstrations.

In May 1972 there was a fresh offensive by North Vietnamese and Viet Cong forces. This was countered by renewed American bombing of North Vietnam and the mining of Haiphong harbor. This offensive produced inconclusive results which, along with pressure from the Soviet Union and China, led the North Vietnamese to consider making concessions at the PARIS PEACE TALKS.

Secretary of State HENRY KISSINGER and chief North Vietnamese negotiator Le Duc Tho began secret negotiations in the summer of 1972. A breakthrough was made when Le Duc Tho dropped his former insistence that the South Vietnamese regime be replaced by a coalition government that included the Viet Cong and Kissinger dropped America's objection to the presence of North Vietnamese troops in South Vietnam. The deal, which was informally agreed upon in October, also arranged a cease-fire between the United States and North Vietnam, complete American withdrawal, the repatriation of American prisoners of war and an agreement that the future of Vietnam would be determined entirely by the Vietnamese.

The deal was strenuously objected to by South Vietnamese President Nguyen Van Thieu, who maintained that it constituted an American sellout. When the arrangements were made public, he insisted that the United States continue to guarantee the existence of the Republic of South Vietnam. The North Vietnamese refused to agree to this, and Nixon ordered saturation bombing of North Vietnam in December 1972. The final peace treaty, signed on January 17, 1973, made no concessions to Thieu and was essentially the same as the October agreement.

The Paris Peace Treaty allowed the United States to resupply the South Vietnamese Army and to provide air support. At the time of the treaty, the South Vietnamese Army totaled 1 million troops, and the air force was the fourth largest in the world. But the South Vietnamese government had never succeeded in establishing its legitimacy, and without unrestricted American support could not protect itself. For the first 18 months after the signing of the Paris Peace Treaty, the North Vietnamese and Viet Cong consolidated their positions. In January 1975 there was a major offensive by North Vietnamese forces, which was a total success unexpected even by the North. On April 17, 1975, Saigon fell to the communist forces and was renamed Ho Chi Minh City. Shortly before, communist governments had taken power in Laos and Cambodia.

More than eight-and-a-half-million Americans fought in Vietnam. Approximately 58,000 died or were listed as missing in action. More than 300,000 were wounded. An estimated 800,000 Viet Cong and North Vietnamese forces and 220,000 South Vietnamese were killed, and hundreds of thousands of civilians on both sides. Australian and New Zealand casualties totalled 469, Thai 351 and South Korean 4,406. An estimated 750,000 Cambodian civilians died and about 150,000 Laotians. The financial cost of the war for the United States has been estimated at $155 billion (in early 1970s dollars), and the heavy expenditure with its deficit financing was one cause of the worldwide inflation of the 1970s.

For Further Information:

Fifield, Russell Hunt. *Americans in Southeast Asia: The Roots of Commitment.* New York, 1973.

FitzGerald, Frances. *Fire in the Lake: The Vietnamese and the Americans in Vietnam.* New York, 1973.

Gelb, Leslie H., and Richard K. Betts. *The Irony of Vietnam: The System Worked.* Washington, D.C., 1979.

Halberstam, David. *The Best and the Brightest.* New York, 1972.

Herring, George C. *America's Longest War: The United States and Vietnam, 1950–1975.* Philadelphia, 1986.

Kahin, George McTurnan. *Intervention: How America Became Involved in Vietnam.* New York, 1986.

Karnow, Stanley. *Vietnam, A History.* New York, 1984, 1991.

Lewy, Guenter. *America in Vietnam.* New York, 1978.

Shawcross, William. *Sideshow: Kissinger, Nixon and the Destruction of Cambodia.* New York, 1979.

Sheehan, Neil. *A Bright Shining Lie: John Paul Vann and America in Vietnam.* New York, 1988.

Summers, Harry G. *Vietnam War Almanac.* New York, 1985.

Young, Marilyn. *The Vietnam Wars, 1945–1990.* New York, 1991.

Vinson, Carl (November 18, 1883–June 1, 1981)   U.S. congressman Carl Vinson (D, Ga.) was an advocate for a strong navy and substantial ground forces. As chairman of the House Naval Affairs Committee and later the House Armed Services Committee he had a powerful platform for his views.

Vinson worked his way through Georgia state politics after receiving his law degree from Mercer University in 1902. In 1914 he was elected to the U.S. House of Representatives and almost immediately directed his attention to military affairs, especially issues related to the navy. In 1931 he was named chairman of the House Naval Affairs Committee.

Before World War II Vinson pressed for a strong navy as a deterrent against attack. In 1934 he cosponsored the Vinson–Trammell Act, which laid the foundation for a permanently enlarged navy with separate fleets in the Atlantic and the Pacific. During the war he advocated legislation to increase military production, and when the rest of Congress favored demobilization in the immediate postwar period, Vinson proposed the maintenance of wartime levels.

At the urging of Navy Secretary JAMES FORRESTAL, Vinson opposed consolidating the separate armed services into a single Department of Defense. But the merger went ahead, and to reflect the changed executive structure, the House and the Senate each merged their separate military committees into one Armed Services Committee in the House and one in the Senate. In 1949 Vinson was named chairman of the House committee. He held the post until 1953 and then again from 1955 to 1965, when he retired.

As chairman of House Armed Services Committee, Vinson continued to oppose defense cuts and support increased naval spending. In 1949 he claimed that the TRUMAN administration was "letting the Navy air force die on the line."

Vinson was an old-style Democratic politician whose long tenure in the House of Representatives had enabled him to establish a complex and successful system of political patronage. He dominated the Armed Services Committee, arranged defense contracts in the districts of congressmen who supported him and determined which congressmen were selected for "inspection tours." Vinson's adroit handling of patronage meant that almost all legislation related to the military in the lower house had to be personally approved by him, and almost all legislation adopted by his committee was approved by the House of Representatives. He was also a jealous guardian of Congress' constitutional rights in the military field.

Vinson was an opponent of President DWIGHT EISENHOWER's "NEW LOOK" DEFENSE POLICY, which shifted the emphasis from conventional forces to the nuclear deterrent. He believed that even in the nuclear age the United States would require a large conventional force to fight limited wars in different parts of the world. Vinson reluctantly accepted Eisenhower's cut in the army from 1.1 million troops to 900,000, but when the administration tried to cut troop levels further to 870,000 in 1958, he led a successful congressional campaign to restore them to 900,000.

Vinson also opposed President JOHN F. KENNEDY's decision to switch the emphasis in nuclear delivery systems from manned bombers to guided missiles and unmanned bombers. In 1961 he was instrumental in Congress' appropriation of $800 million more than the Kennedy administration requested for manned bombers. Secretary of Defense ROBERT MCNAMARA refused to spend the money, and this led to a constitutional clash, with Vinson claiming that Congress had the legal right to raise and support armies. McNamara accepted Congress' constitutional powers but still did not spend the money.

Vinson retired from Congress in 1965 after serving 51 years in the House of Representatives. He was the longest-serving member of Congress at the time of his decision not to seek reelection. Vinson died on June 1, 1981.

Vladivostok Accords (1974)   The Vladivostok Accords of 1974, signed by U.S. president GERALD FORD and Soviet leader LEONID BREZHNEV, laid the foundation for further Strategic Arms Limitation (SALT II) negotiations by resolving major differences on the numbers of MULTIPLE INDEPENDENTLY-TARGETED REENTRY VEHICLES (MIRVs).

The accords were published after a meeting on November 23–24 in the Siberian port city of Vladivostok. It was the first meeting between Ford and Brezhnev, and the result was hailed by Secretary of State HENRY KISSINGER as a "breakthrough" that would "mean that a cap has been put on the arms race for a period of ten years."

The SALT II process formally began in November 1972 with the objective of replacing the five-year interim SALT I agreement (see STRATEGIC ARMS LIMITATION TALKS, 1972) with a more comprehensive treaty of indefinite duration. But negotiations quickly encountered difficulties because of the complexity of balancing the quantity of weapons against their quality or destructive capability.

The development of missiles fitted with multiple independently target (MIRV) nuclear warheads further complicated negotiations. The destructive power of each missile was multiplied several times, and warning time for the targeted nation was substantially reduced.

In the early 1970s, the Soviet Union enjoyed an advantage in MIRVed missiles. Kissinger in 1973 and 1974 tried various means of limiting Soviet MIRVs but without success. The U.S. Congress, in the meantime, was pressing for acceptance of the principle of equal aggregates. This was reluctantly accepted by Brezhnev and became the basis for the Vladivostok Accords.

The key feature of the accords was a ceiling of 2,400 for total offensive strategic missiles and a further subceiling of 1,320 launchers for MIRVed warheads. The Soviets also dropped their insistence that the SALT II agreement restrict U.S. nuclear weapons based in Europe. The United States dropped its insistence on a cutback in Soviet heavy missiles and agreed that the 2,400 ceiling on strategic launchers would include heavy bombers—an area in which the United States enjoyed an overwhelming superiority.

Ford and Kissinger hoped that the Vladivostok Accords would lead to an early SALT II agreement. But a continuing Soviet buildup, regional tensions and definition problems delayed the final agreement until the CARTER administration. This treaty was ultimately not ratified by the Senate.

For Further Information:

Smith, Gerard. *Doubletalk*. Garden City, N.Y., 1980.
Talbott, Strobe. *Endgame, The Inside Story of SALT Two*. New York, 1979.

Von Braun, Werner   (March 23, 1912–June 16, 1977)

Werner Von Braun laid the technological foundations of America's guided-missile program. He also helped to build the Apollo rockets for the National Aeronautics and Space Administration (NASA), which carried men to the moon.

Von Braun was born into an aristocratic Prussian family and began studying rockets in 1932 as an engineering student in Berlin. He was put in charge of technical research for the German rocket program, and was responsible for the development of the V-1 and V-2 rockets that devastated London during World War II. He joined the Nazi Party in 1940. In 1945 Von Braun surrendered to the Americans and soon signed a contract with the U.S. Army to develop missiles.

At first, Von Braun's work was restricted to teaching American personnel how to build and handle wartime V-2 rockets, but by 1950 he was working on guided missiles capable of delivering atomic warheads. During the KOREAN WAR, Von Braun's budget was considerably expanded, and he moved his Army Ordinance Guided Missile Center to Redstone Arsenal in Huntsville, Alabama.

Von Braun's first major task was the development of a surface-to-surface ballistic missile with a range of 500 miles. The rocket, called the Redstone, was successfully tested in August 1953. Two years later, Von Braun's team developed their research further to build the Jupiter intermediate-range ballistic missile (IRBM).

In February 1956, the Army Ballistic Missile Agency was established, and Von Braun became its first director. By this time it had become accepted military doctrine that if another war took place it would be dominated by nuclear weapons. This had led to a fierce rivalry among the armed services for control of the delivery systems for nuclear warheads. The air force emerged as the dominant service in the nuclear field with control of intercontinental ballistic missiles and nuclear-capable bombers. The navy developed the Polaris system. The army and Von Braun were restricted to the development of IRBMs.

Von Braun's career was dramatically altered by the Soviet launching on October 5, 1957, of SPUTNIK. The successful orbiting of a Soviet satellite provoked a storm of concern in the United States that the Soviets would gain control of outer space and be able to use it as an invulnerable military platform.

Von Braun, who had long been an advocate of the development of space travel, had proposed in 1951 that the United States build a space station. The following year he wrote *Mars Project*, proposing the eventual construction of an interplanetary space fleet. These suggestions were at first dismissed as flights of fancy, but not after *Sputnik*.

In December 1957 Von Braun appeared before the Senate Preparedness Subcommittee to propose the establishment of a national space agency with a $1.5 billion budget and the aim of placing a man in orbit within five years and on a space station in 10. In July 1958 the National Aeronautics and Space Administration (NASA) was formed, and Von Braun became director of the George C. Marshall Flight Center in Huntsville.

Von Braun supervised the development of the Saturn rocket used by Project Apollo and was a major decision maker in the Apollo missions. He also acted as a spokesman for NASA on numerous occasions. Von Braun was director of the Marshall Center until 1970 and a NASA director for two more years. In 1972 he joined Fairchild Industries as a vice president. He died five years later, on June 16, 1977.

For Further Information:

Young, Hugo, Bryan Silcock, and Peter Dunn. *Journey to Tranquility: The Long Competitive Struggle to Reach the Moon*. Garden City, N.Y., 1970.

W

Waldheim, Kurt (December 21, 1918–   )   Kurt Waldheim was secretary-general of the United Nations from 1972 to 1981. In 1986 he was elected president of Austria despite his alleged participation in Nazi war crimes.

Waldheim was born in a lower-middle-class Viennese family. His father was briefly jailed after the German Anschluss in 1938 because of his anti-Nazi views. At the time, Kurt Waldheim was studying Austrian and international law at the University of Vienna. Shortly afterward he joined the Nazi Party, and later joined the party's militia, the SA (storm troopers), known as the Brownshirts.

When war broke out, Waldheim became a lieutenant in the German Army. According to his autobiography, he left the army after being wounded in 1941. But German records showed that he became an intelligence officer for the German Army Group E, which was responsible for a number of war crimes against Jews and Yugoslav partisans. Waldheim later admitted his army role after 1941 but denied any knowledge of or participation in war crimes.

Waldheim entered the Austrian diplomatic service at the end of the war and by 1955 held ambassadorial rank. In 1956 he was appointed ambassador to Canada, and he returned to Austria in 1960 to head the western political department until 1962. He headed the political affairs department from 1962 to 1964, when he was posted to New York as Austria's permanent representative to the United Nations. In 1968 Waldheim was named foreign minister, and he had the difficult task of maintaining Austria's strict neutrality during the Soviet invasion of Czechoslovakia.

In 1970 Waldheim returned to the United Nations as Austria's representative. In 1971, when U THANT decided against running for a third term, Waldheim declared himself a candidate for the UN secretary-generalship. He was elected and took office in January 1972 despite opposition from the newly admitted communist China.

Waldheim became secretary-general at a time when shifts in the international political structure wrought by decolonization were becoming apparent. This, and the maintenance of détente in East–West relations, shifted the focus of the secretary-general's duties. After years of acting as East–West referee, the holder of that office now had to concern himself with extinguishing regional brushfires and negotiating an international consensus among the East and West and the Third World.

During his first term as secretary-general, Waldheim's major efforts were directed toward keeping alive peacekeeping initiatives in Vietnam, Cyprus and the Middle East. He set modest and achievable step-by-step goals rather than pursuing grand solutions. The greatest achievement of Waldheim's first term came during the 1973 Yom Kippur War when he was instrumental in persuading the Egyptians and Israelis to begin negotiations.

In his second term, Waldheim's major problems were the war in AFGHANISTAN; the Gulf War between Iran and Iraq; the Israeli occupation of southern Lebanon; CAMBODIA; Namibia and Angola (see ANGOLA AND NAMIBIA CONFLICTS); and the Iranian hostage crisis. The Soviet invasion of Afghanistan in December 1979 put an end to détente, and during his last two years at the United Nations Waldheim concentrated on preventing regional conflicts from becoming East–West confrontations. He formed a close working relationship with President JIMMY CARTER, who used Waldheim as an envoy during the Iran hostage crisis. But he failed to establish a rapport with the more conservative President RONALD REAGAN, and relations between the United Nations and the United States deteriorated as the Reagan administration became increasingly critical of what it regarded as the international forum's left-wing bias.

Waldheim tried but failed to secure a third term as secretary-general and was succeeded in 1982 by Peruvian diplomat Javier Pérez de Cuéllar. From 1982 to 1984 Waldheim was a visiting professor of diplomacy at Georgetown University, and then in 1986 he was the conservative People's Party candidate for the Austrian presidency.

In the middle of the campaign, the World Jewish Congress produced documentary evidence of Waldheim's previously unknown war record and turned an international spotlight on Waldheim, on Austria, and on the normally dull Austrian presidential elections. Waldheim was condemned internationally, but on July 8, 1986, he was elected to a six-year term with 53.9% of the vote. During his single term in office Waldheim was shunned by most of the international community. The Israeli government withdrew its ambassador to Austria, and many Western countries made it clear that the new president would not be welcome to visit them. The United States barred Waldheim as a suspected war criminal. Waldheim's foreign travels were restricted to an audience with Pope John Paul II and trips to Arab countries.

Walesa, Lech   (September 29, 1943–   )   Lech Walesa founded Poland's trade union movement Solidarity and played an important role in ending communist rule in POLAND.

Walesa received a basic education and then attended a vocational school in Lipno, near Popow. After graduation he moved to the ancient Baltic port city of Gdansk, where he found a job as an electrician at the Lenin Shipyard. In December 1970, the Gdansk shipyard was the center of violent demonstrations following the Polish government's decision to raise food prices (see GDANSK RIOTS). Walesa was among the protesters who forced the resignation of WLADYSLAW GOMULKA and the withdrawal of the price increases.

Within six years, the government of Edward Gierek was forced into a fresh round of increases. Walesa again protested and was fired. For both financial assistance and political advice he turned to the KOR (Workers' Defense Committee), founded in September 1976 to provide legal advice and funds for families of the men fired from their shipyard jobs. Through the KOR, Walesa became increasingly active in dissident activities and was several times arrested between 1976 and 1980.

On July 1, 1980, the mounting debts of the Polish government forced another round of increases in food prices. Unofficial strikes broke out all over Poland as workers demanded pay raises to compensate for the price increases. By mid-August, 100,000 workers were on strike. Soon the focus of the industrial action centered on what had become the traditional seat of labor unrest—the Lenin Shipyard. On August 14, shipyard workers seized the yard and successfully demanded the reinstatement of Walesa, who had scaled the wall to join the workers inside. Walesa was quickly elected the workers' leader.

Walesa realized that the best hope of securing the workers' demands was to coordinate strike activities among workers at different Polish factories. On August 17, the workers in Gdansk announced the formation of an interfactory strike committee, chaired by Walesa. The committee established links with workers at 20 other striking factories in Gdansk, Gdynia and Sopot. The committee was soon coordinating and organizing all over Poland and became known as Solidarity.

The failures of 1970 and 1976 had taught Walesa and the other strike leaders that the solution to workers' problems lay not with cosmetic economic changes but with fundamental alterations to the political system. Therefore, they expanded their demands beyond calls for more money into the political sphere, calling for the right to strike, the release of political prisoners, abolition of government censorship and free access for all religious groups to the mass media. The Gierek government eventually gave in, in return for Solidarity's recognition of the Communist Party's supremacy.

Lech Walesa's role in forcing unprecedented concessions from a communist government catapulted him into the national and international spotlight. On September 7, 1980, the new Polish leader, Stanislaw Kania, went to Gdansk to meet with him and personally pledged his commitment to the Gdansk accords. On September 17, workers' groups throughout the country met in Gdansk and officially formed the national trade union Solidarity, which was registered on September 24. It started with a membership of 3 million workers in 3,500 factories and quickly became Poland's de facto political opposition.

Walesa then found himself caught between the increasing demands of his membership and the threat of Soviet military action that was brought home to him repeatedly in regular discussions with government ministers. His first priority, however, was to retain the loyalty of his members. Therefore within the Solidarity councils he argued for moderation, but with government ministers he took the agreed-upon hard line.

In January 1981, Defense Minister General WOJCIECH JARUZELSKI was appointed prime minister in a sign of hardening government attitudes. After a year of increasing industrial, social and political unrest, and threats of Soviet intervention, Jaruzelski declared martial law in December 1981, driving Solidarity underground. Walesa was arrested and spent the next few years either in prison, under arrest or being questioned. The systematic harassment to which Walesa was subjected at one point began seriously to affect his health, and doctors expressed fears that he would suffer a heart attack.

Outside Poland, Solidarity and Walesa remained symbols of opposition to communist rule, and in December 1983 Walesa was awarded the Nobel Prize for peace. Crowds at Warsaw's central railroad station burst into applause when the award was announced on the evening television news. Walesa later donated the $195,000 prize money to the National Gift Fund, an emergency fund established to provide help in health care, education and social welfare. The prize

Lech Walesa (right), a founder and leader of Poland's independent labor union Solidarity, with Prime Minister Tadeusz Mazowiecki in 1989. Photo courtesy of the Polish Ministry of Foreign Affairs.

was collected in Oslo by Walesa's wife, Danuta, because the Solidarity leader feared that if he left the country the Polish government would bar his return.

Finally, in an effort to solve the country's continuing economic crisis, and after the effective internal collapse of the Soviet Union Jaruzelski in 1989 began talks with the opposition and met several times with Walesa. At Walesa's insistence, Solidarity was legalized. Political reforms were enacted that increased the power of the Sejm (parliament), and Solidarity candidates gained a key share of power when they won the seats they were allowed to contest. The result was that Walesa was able to force the Communist Party into a coalition government with Solidarity. Walesa could have taken the premiership himself but remained the leader of Solidarity and possibly Poland's most powerful political figure, although he held no official government post.

After the creation of the first non-communist government in postwar Poland, Walesa became his country's leading ambassador. He traveled to the United States and Western Europe, meeting with world leaders and urging them to contribute money to support the Polish economy and the embryonic democratic government.

In 1990, Walesa announced his interest in running in national elections to replace Jaruzelski as president. He criticized the current government as elitist and out of touch with the working class. He was opposed by Mazowiecki, leader of Solidarity's free-market intellectual wing, which viewed Walesa as something of a demagogue motivated by personal ambition. Despite the strong opposition from within Solidarity, Walesa went on to win the initial vote in November 1990 in a campaign with undertones of anti-Semitism, and won the run-off election the following month, defeating Jaruzelski. Over the next year and a half he sparred with a series of premiers and unsuccessfully called on parliament to grant him emergency powers to break Poland's continuing political stalemate.

For Further Information:
Ascherson, Neal. *The Polish August.* New York, 1982.
————. *The Struggles for Poland.* New York, 1988.
Persky, Stan. *At the Lenin Shipyard: Poland and the Rise of the Solidarity Trade Union.* Vancouver, 1981.
Sharman, T. *The Rise of Solidarity.* Vero Beach, Fla., 1987.
Walesa, Lech. *A Way of Hope.* New York, 1987.

Wallace, Henry A.   **(October 7, 1888–November 18, 1965)**   Henry A. Wallace was a noted American liberal in the immediate postwar years. A former vice president, he argued for postwar Soviet–American cooperation and split with the TRUMAN administration on the issue. He joined the left-wing Progressive Citizens of America and was their candidate in the 1948 presidential election.

Wallace was born into a prominent Iowa family. After graduating from Iowa State Agricultural College in 1910, he followed his father's footsteps, first into teaching and writing about agriculture and then into politics.

The refusal of successive Republican administrations to provide farming subsidies drove Wallace out of the Republican Party and into the liberal wing of the Democratic Party. In 1933 President FRANKLIN D. ROOSEVELT rewarded Wallace for his support among Midwestern farmers by naming him secretary of agriculture, and in 1940 Roosevelt chose him as his running mate in that year's presidential elections.

As vice president, Wallace's interest shifted from agriculture to international affairs and civil rights issues. In common with many liberal Democrats of the day, he distrusted Britain and believed that its empire had left it morally bankrupt. He also admired the economic and social achievements of the Soviet Union and thought that the future for America lay in the socialization of the capitalist system while retaining its basic free-market principles.

The vice president's outspoken beliefs found little support among the Democratic Party machinery. A staunch civil rights campaigner, he was especially unpopular among the Southern Democrats. By 1944 Roosevelt became convinced that he would have to drop Wallace from his ticket in order to avoid a damaging split at the nominating convention. To get Wallace out of the way in the months leading up to the convention, Roosevelt sent him to China and the Soviet Union. This was Wallace's first major exposure to the Soviet Union, and he came away convinced that JOSEF STALIN wanted postwar cooperation with the United States, was not really an international revolutionary and had no designs on China.

After the 1944 election, Roosevelt named Wallace secretary of commerce, and he continued in that post under President HARRY TRUMAN. But Wallace's real interest remained foreign policy, and he neglected his duties at the Commerce Department to speak out on what he regarded as the sad deterioration of Soviet–American relations, which he blamed on the machinations of the British government and Eastern Establishment figures.

He opposed Truman's decision in 1945 to sever economic aid to the Soviet Union, Truman's refusal to share atomic secrets with the Soviets, the MARSHALL PLAN, and the supply of American military and economic aid to Greece and Turkey. On March 19, 1946, at a dinner for Russian relief, Wallace defended Soviet domination of Eastern Europe on the grounds that "the Soviets . . . are out to make every boundary secure. They fear capitalist encirclement. They . . . feel that time is short to prepare for a possible capitalist-provoked war."

On July 23, 1946, Wallace sent Truman a memo in which he argued that the United States should recognize Soviet interests in Eastern Europe, make concessions on atomic weapons and extend economic aid to the Soviet Union and Eastern Europe. The memo was ignored by Truman, and a frustrated Wallace decided to make his objections more public. In a speech in Madison Square Garden on September 12, 1946, he attacked the "get tough with Russia" policy, saying that "the tougher we get, the tougher the Russians will get."

Wallace criticized the Truman administration's close relations with Britain as "the height of folly" and added that "the real peace treaty we now need is between the U.S. and Russia . . . . The Russians have no more business in stirring up native Communists to political activity in Western Europe, Latin America and the U.S. than we have in interfering in the politics of Eastern Europe and Russia."

The Madison Square Garden speech came at the same time as Secretary of State JAMES BYRNES was taking a hard line in negotiations with the Soviet Union at the Paris Conference. He and other senior foreign policy makers were incensed at the commerce secretary's attempts to undermine the administration's position at the talks, and Truman was forced to ask Wallace to resign on September 19.

Wallace became editor of the *New Republic* and used that magazine as a forum to continue his attacks on Truman's foreign policies. He quickly became the focal point for liberals opposed to Truman's anti-Soviet foreign policy, and in 1947 the Progressive Citizens of America (PCA) asked Wallace to be their presidential candidate in the 1948 elections. The PCA was a coalition of liberals and American communists, and Wallace came under increasing attack for allowing members of the Communist Party to work on his campaign. He replied, "If the Communists are working for peace with Russia, God bless 'em. If they are working for the overthrow of the government by force, they know I'm against them."

At one time during the campaign it was thought that Wallace would be appealing enough to the liberal wing of the Democratic Party to split the Democrats and allow Republican candidate THOMAS E. DEWEY to defeat President Truman. But Wallace's refusal to repudiate the communists severely damaged his prospects. In the end Wallace received only 1.2 million votes compared to 24 million for Truman and 22 million for Dewey.

Wallace retired to his farm in South Salem, New York, and remained active in the PCA until right-wing pressure forced its disbandment in 1950. After the collapse of the PCA, Wallace's foreign policy outlook shifted toward the right. He supported Truman's decision to intervene in Korea, and in the presidential elections of 1956 and 1960 he endorsed the Republican Party's nominee. He died on November 18, 1965.

For Further Information:
Walton, Richard H. *Henry Wallace, Harry Truman and the Cold War.* New York, 1976.

Walters, Vernon (January 3, 1917–   )   General Vernon Walters' career as a soldier, intelligence officer and diplomat has spanned nearly 50 years and made him a participant in many of the key events of the Cold War. He has served in a number of positions, including ambassador-at-large and ambassador to the United Nations during the Reagan administration and ambassador to West Germany during the Bush administration.

Walters was born in New York, the son of a British insurance executive. In 1923 his family returned to Europe, and Walters was educated in France and Britain, where he developed an aptitude for languages. He eventually became fluent in seven languages and could converse in many others. This linguistic ability played a major role in the development of Walters' career.

Walters' family returned to New York in 1929 and after finishing his education in Britain, he joined his father's insurance business in 1934. He enlisted in the U.S. Army in May 1941, but his language skills led to a quick promotion to lieutenant and assignment to the Intelligence Corps operating in Morocco. His skills in this field brought him to the attention of General MARK CLARK, who appointed him his aide-de-camp.

Walters accompanied Secretary of State GEORGE C. MARSHALL to Europe as an interpreter during the MARSHALL PLAN negotiations. He performed so well that he became one of President HARRY TRUMAN's top interpreters, sitting in on many of the major meetings of the early Cold War years. During the 1950s, Walters became an assistant to veteran diplomat AVERELL HARRIMAN and accompanied him on missions to Korea, Iran and Yugoslavia. From 1956 to 1960 he was a staff assistant to President DWIGHT EISENHOWER.

Walters twice served as U.S. military attaché in Brazil, once immediately after World War II and then again in 1964, when he accurately predicted a military coup. In 1967 he was appointed military attaché at the U.S. Embassy in Paris and helped smuggle White House national security advisor HENRY KISSINGER in and out of Paris during his secret negotiations with Le Duc Tho to end the VIETNAM WAR.

In 1972 President RICHARD NIXON appointed Walters deputy director of the CENTRAL INTELLIGENCE AGENCY. In this position he was responsible mainly for coordinating liaisons with foreign intelligence services. He became briefly involved in the Watergate scandal when he threatened to resign if the White House repeated its early attempts to involve the CIA in the Watergate cover-up. The CIA eventually awarded Walters a medal for resisting external pressure on the agency.

Walters left the CIA and retired from the army in 1978 with the rank of lieutenant general, even though he had never commanded any troops. He became a consultant for an American arms company and an international oil cartel. In 1980 President RONALD REAGAN asked Walters to join the State Department as ambassador-at-large.

In this role, Walters became Reagan's chief diplomatic troubleshooter, traveling around the world to visit various hot spots, sometimes secretly. It was estimated that in four years he flew 1.5 million miles and visited 108 countries. In February 1985 he was named to succeed Jeane Kirkpatrick as U.S. ambassador to the United Nations. Less than a year later, the United States created a financial crisis at the United Nations when Congress voted to withhold half of its assessed dues until certain reforms were introduced. Walters was left with the difficult task of persuading the United Nations to move toward meeting the demands and then to argue for Congress to fulfill its financial obligations to the international organization.

While at the United Nations, Walters also became involved with the problem of international terrorism. In September 1985 he visited Syria to negotiate the release of the Rev. Benjamin Weir, who was being held hostage in Lebanon. He also visited the Soviet Union and Syria as part of the negotiations for a cease-fire in the Iran-Iraq War.

After the election of GEORGE BUSH as president in 1988, Walters was appointed to the sensitive post of U.S. ambassador to West Germany. He was faced with the task of persuading the West German government not to succumb to the tempting diplomatic initiatives of Soviet leader MIKHAIL GOR-BACHEV. But West German foreign minister HANS-DIETRICH GENSCHER remained convinced that the West must make a positive response to the Gorbachev initiatives and strongly advocated negotiations on reducing short-range nuclear missiles. The West German position was strongly opposed by the British and American governments, which had difficulty accepting the honesty of Gorbachev's motives, and at one point it seemed that the cohesiveness of the NORTH ATLANTIC TREATY ORGANIZATION was threatened by the issue. Walters helped hammer out the compromise solution agreed to at the NATO heads of government summit in Brussels in May 1989.

For Further Information:
Walters, Vernon. *Silent Missions.* New York, 1978.

Warsaw Pact   The Warsaw Treaty of Friendship, Cooperation and Mutual Assistance (known as the Warsaw Pact) was created in May 1955 as a counter to the NORTH ATLANTIC TREATY ORGANIZATION, Western moves toward the EUROPEAN DEFENSE COMMUNITY and the rearming of West Germany. The Warsaw Pact disbanded in July 1991, following the end of the Cold War.

After the formation of NATO there was no immediate need for the Soviet Union to create an alliance of East European countries because it had effective political and military control of the region, embodied in a series of bilateral defense treaties and a network of military bases. By 1954, however, the Soviets were becoming increasingly worried about moves toward greater West European integration through the proposed European Defense Community (EDC) Treaty and proposals for economic union. These they regarded as a greater long-term threat, partly because they involved the rearming of West Germany and partly because they represented a viable alternative within Europe rather than the more distant appeal of the United States.

The 20-year Warsaw Pact was duly signed on May 14, 1955, by the foreign ministers of the Soviet Union, Albania, Bulgaria, Czechoslovakia, East Germany, Hungary, Poland and Romania. Marshall Ivan S. Knoiev, defense minister of the Soviet Union, was named its first supreme commander. Communist China's defense minister, Peng Teh-huai, was present as an observer.

The text of the treaty stated that the ratification of Western agreements authorizing a remilitarized West Germany increased "the danger of a new war" and created "a threat to the national security of peace-loving states."

In subsequent negotiations, the Soviets indicated that they were prepared to disband the Warsaw Pact in return for a reversal of the Western Alliance's decision to allow the arming of West Germany and a substantial reduction in the size of NATO forces. This was rejected by the West because it regarded the Warsaw Pact as little more than the formalization of a military arrangement that had existed since 1945.

The Political Consultative Committee, comprised of heads of government of Warsaw Pact members, was originally intended to meet twice a year, but after 1972, meetings usually took place every other year. The Committee of Defense Ministers was established in 1969; it usually met annually. Also established in 1969 was a Military Council of national chiefs of staff or deputy ministers of defense, which normally met twice a year. According to the International Institute for Strategic Studies, the combined forces of the Warsaw Pact countries in 1988 totaled 5,155,000 troops. This excluded approximately 1,140,000 border guards, internal security forces and construction troops.

The alliance regularly held combined defense maneuvers, but the system proved more useful to Moscow as a means of containing internal dissension within Eastern Europe. The only time the Warsaw Pact armies ever conducted a joint military action was in 1968 when they intervened in Czechoslovakia.

For Further Information:
Faringdon, Hugh. *Strategic Geography: NATO, the Warsaw Pact, and the Superpowers.* New York, 1989.
Fodor, Neil. *The Warsaw Treaty Organization: A Political and Organizational Analysis.* Hampshire, England, 1990.
Gati, Charles. *The Bloc That Failed: Soviet-East European Relations in Transition.* Bloomington, Ind., 1990.
Holden, Gerard. *The Warsaw Pact: Soviet Security and Bloc Politics.* New York, 1989.
Moreton, N. Edwina. *East Germany and the Warsaw Alliance: The Politics of Detente.* Boulder, Colo., 1978.
Nelson, Daniel N. *Alliance Behavior in the Warsaw Pact.* Boulder, Colo., 1986.

Warsaw Uprising   The Warsaw Uprising of 1944 destroyed the Polish Home Army of the anti-Soviet, London-based Polish government-in-exile and ensured that the Soviet-supported Lublin Poles and the Soviet Red Army would take control of postwar POLAND.

Control of Poland has been a major element of Russian policy for centuries. Soviet leader JOSEF STALIN was determined to continue this policy, and his resolve was strengthened by the anti-Soviet nature of the independent Polish government during the interwar years.

The historical enmity between Poland and Russia continued during World War II with a strained relationship between Stalin and the Polish government-in-exile in London. In April 1943 diplomatic relations between them were severed after the London Poles, led by STANISLAW MIKOLAJCZYK, accused the Red Army of the massacre of thousands of Polish officers in the KATYN Forest near Smolensk after the Soviets occupied eastern Poland in 1939.

Stalin established an alternative Polish government-in-exile under the Polish communist BOLESLAW BIERUT. But the London Poles were still recognized by the British and American governments and, more importantly, had the support of the Polish people and the Polish Home Army, a guerrilla force commanded after July 1943 by General Tadeusz Komorowski (also known as "Bor").

Bor maintained a large and secret army in Warsaw, which he planned to hold in reserve until the Red Army approached the city. The plan was for the army to rise and take control of the city so that the capital would be controlled by the London Poles when the Soviets reached Warsaw. To succeed the Warsaw Uprising required the support of the Soviet Union, first in continuing its advance toward Warsaw so that German troops would be drawn away from any fighting in the city, and second in either sending supplies or allowing British and American planes to send supplies to the forces in Warsaw. Without this support, Bor reckoned he could last no longer than 10 days.

According to Polish sources, Stalin promised to go along with the plan and to signal the Polish Home Army when to start the uprising. The Red Army crossed the Polish frontier on January 5, 1944. By July 25, 1944, Russian forces had reached the suburbs of Warsaw, and on July 29 Moscow Radio broadcast that liberation was at hand and the Poles in Warsaw should attack. On July 31, Soviet tanks broke through German defenses on the eastern edge of the city.

The following day, at exactly 5:00 P.M., the Warsaw Uprising began. On Bor's orders, a 14,000-strong army launched a surprise attack on Germans throughout the city. At the same time, the Soviet advance halted.

News of the uprising reached the London Poles the following day. They immediately appealed to the British and American governments for an airdrop of supplies to Warsaw. British prime minister WINSTON CHURCHILL immediately cabled Stalin telling him that the Royal Air Force planned to drop 60 tons of ammunition and equipment to the Polish Home Army. Stalin cabled back that reports of the uprising were "greatly exaggerated."

Despite the cool response, Polish volunteers serving with the Royal Air Force tried to get through to Warsaw. But they found themselves being shot at by Soviet as well as German antiaircraft weapons, and they were forced to turn back after suffering heavy casualties. On August 14, Moscow Radio broadcast a statement from Tass, the official news agency, denying any responsibility for the uprising or its consequences. The statement said, "Information from Polish sources on the rising in Warsaw in August by order of the Polish émigrés in London has recently appeared in various newspapers abroad. The Polish press and radio of the émigré government in London have asserted that the Warsaw insurrectionists were

in contact with the Soviet High Command and that this Command has sent them no help. The announcement is either a misunderstanding or a libel against the Soviet High Command.

"Tass is in possession of the information which shows that the Polish circles in London responsible for the Warsaw rising made no attempt to coordinate this action with the Soviet High Command. In these circumstances, the only people responsible for the results of the events in Warsaw are the Polish émigré circles in London."

The statement caused an uproar in London and Washington, D.C. The American ambassador in Moscow, AVERELL HARRIMAN, asked the Soviet government for permission for American aircraft participating in an airlift to Warsaw to refuel in Soviet-held territory. The Soviet government refused on the grounds that "the Soviet Government did not wish to associate themselves directly or indirectly with the adventure in Warsaw."

On August 20, a joint statement from Churchill and U.S. president FRANKLIN D. ROOSEVELT was sent to Stalin asking for either a Soviet airdrop or for permission for British and American aircraft to undertake the mission. On August 22, Stalin replied that "sooner or later the truth about the group of criminals who have embarked upon the Warsaw adventure in order to seize power will become known to everybody."

In Berlin, Adolf Hitler responded to the uprising by ordering the German High Command to destroy Warsaw. Entire districts were razed and the inhabitants were shot. Much of the fighting was done in the city sewers in hand-to-hand fighting. The uprising, which was meant to take only 10 days, went on for 63 days before Bor was forced to surrender to the German Army. Out of Bor's command of 40,000 troops, 15,000 were killed. Nearly 200,000 inhabitants of Warsaw died. The Germans lost 17,000 men. The Red Army did not cross the Vistula River into Warsaw until January 1945, giving the German commander three more months to fulfill Hitler's order to destroy the city.

The Polish Home Army was completely destroyed as a military force. At the height of the uprising Mikolajczyk was in Moscow trying to heal the diplomatic rift with Stalin and persuade the Soviet leader to come to the aid of the Warsaw Poles. His failure to do so completely destroyed Mikolajczyk's political credibility, and the London Poles were forced to accept a junior position in a postwar national government headed by Bierut.

Wedemeyer, Albert (July 9, 1897–December 17, 1989) U.S. General Albert Wedemeyer was a major figure in America's immediate postwar relations with China and Korea, as chief of staff to Nationalist Chinese leader CHIANG KAI-SHEK and later as the head of a mission to assess the prospects of a rapprochement between the communist and Nationalist forces in China.

Wedemeyer graduated from the U.S. Military Academy at West Point in 1918, and in 1936 he became the first American to study at the German General Staff School. At the outbreak of World War II, Wedemeyer was assigned to the Plans Group of the War Department under DWIGHT EISENHOWER. Three years later, he replaced General Joseph Stilwell as Chiang Kai-shek's chief of staff.

Wedemeyer's first task was to restore the equilibrium of Sino–American relations after a stormy period brought on by the corruption of the Kuomintang government and Stilwell's frustration with it. The major problem faced by Stilwell was persuading Chiang to use his American-equipped forces against the Japanese. Chiang maintained a greater distrust for the communist forces of MAO ZEDONG than for the Japanese, and he sent his best troops to blockade the communists (who were fighting the invaders), in the northwest corner of the country.

An essential element in President FRANKLIN ROOSEVELT's postwar foreign policy was a strong and unified China as the dominant Asian power. As the war drew to a close, the emphasis in Wedemeyer's task shifted from fighting the Japanese to encouraging the conditions for a unified China, and he worked closely with the president's special representative, PATRICK J. HURLEY.

The pro-Chiang Hurley believed that he could negotiate an agreement between the two sides, but Wedemeyer was more skeptical and was convinced that little progress could be made in Kuomintang–communist negotiations until Chiang's government was thoroughly purged of corruption. On November 23, 1946, after war had broken out between the two sides, Wedemeyer briefed Eisenhower, then army chief of staff, that if unification of China under Chiang was to be American policy, then "involvement in fratricidal warfare and the possibility of war with the Soviet Union must be accepted," and that such a war would require more American forces than were presently in China. Wedemeyer's report was a factor in President Harry Truman's decision to restrict American military support to Chiang.

In 1947 Truman sent Wedemeyer back to the Far East to assess the situation in China and Korea. He repeated his criticisms of corruption within the Kuomintang and said that military force alone could not eliminate communism in China. Wedemeyer, however, had also become even more anti-communist and proposed that Chiang's government be sent $1.5 billion in American aid and that U.S. military advisers be dispatched to Chiang's staff. These recommendations were not accepted.

As a result of his visit to Korea in 1947, Wedemeyer predicted the invasion of South Korea and maintained that the Soviets would leave behind a North Korean army "sufficiently well established to carry out Communist objectives without the presence of Soviet troops." He recommended that the United States continue American military and economic support "to cope with the threat from the North." During the 1952 presidential campaign Eisenhower charged that Truman had "disregarded and suppressed" Wedemeyer's report on Korea. This was supported by Wedemeyer but denied by Secretary of State DEAN ACHESON.

Wedemeyer retired from the army in July 1951 and went into business. In 1958 he published his memoirs, *Wedemeyer Reports!*, in which he claimed that withdrawal of U.S. aid to Chiang had given rise to communism in China.

For Further Information:
Wedemeyer, Albert. *Wedemeyer Reports!* New York, 1958.

Western European Union (WEU) The Western European Union was formed in 1955 after the collapse of the EUROPEAN DEFENSE COMMUNITY. For most of its history the WEU has been overshadowed by the NORTH ATLANTIC TREATY ORGANIZATION, but in the 1980s there were significant attempts to revive the organization.

The WEU has its roots in the BRUSSELS TREATY signed in 1948 by Belgium, France, Luxembourg, the Netherlands and Britain, which provided for collective self-defense, mutual military assistance and collaboration in economic, social and cultural affairs. It was an important forerunner of the North Atlantic Treaty Organization.

The Brussels Treaty was also meant to help prepare for the formation of a European army controlled by a European defense community, which would end Western Europe's heavy reliance on British and American troops. The French rejection of the EDC Treaty in 1954 threw the plans into disarray, and a conference was hastily convened in London by British foreign secretary ANTHONY EDEN in an attempt to rescue the cause of common European defense and the reintegration of West Germany into the political and military structure of the Western alliance.

On October 3, 1954, the "Final Act of the London Conference" was drawn up. It stated that the occupation government of West Germany would end, that West Germany would join NATO, and that the Brussels Treaty would be strengthened and extended, making it a more effective instrument for European integration; West Germany and Italy would also be invited to accede to it.

Thus the military commitments embodied in the original Brussels Treaty would be extended to seven European countries (and later to Spain, Portugal, Greece and Turkey). In addition, Britain guaranteed to base on the continent four divisions and its second Tactical Air Force and not to withdraw these forces against the wishes of the majority of the WEU powers except in the case of acute overseas emergency.

Over the next few weeks the nine-power conference completed discussions for a renegotiated Brussels Treaty, which formally took effect on May 6, 1955. The principal features of the modified Brussels Treaty were:

1. The WEU would encourage the progressive integration of Europe.
2. A Council of Western European Union would be established. This council would cooperate closely with the North Atlantic Treaty Organization.
3. The council would present an annual report to an assem-

bly composed of representatives of the WEU powers to the Council of Europe Assembly.

4. The system of cooperation in social and cultural matters would be extended to cover West Germany and Italy.
5. West Germany's army and air force would be restricted in size and placed under the command of NATO's SU-PREME ALLIED COMMANDER, EUROPE.
6. An agency would be established to control the level of stocks of armaments held by each member of the WEU and to prevent the manufacture of certain types of armaments.

The WEU Assembly and meetings of foreign and defense ministers provided a useful forum for discussion of European security issues, but because the assembly had no political control of defense forces it was overshadowed by NATO, and Western Europe continued to be heavily dependent on American security guarantees.

In the early 1980s, however, West Europeans, led by France, became increasingly concerned about the viability of the American commitment to Europe. This led them to investigate the possibility of reviving the moribund WEU as a vehicle for increased European defense cooperation. A meeting of WEU foreign and defense ministers in Rome in October 1984 decided to make better use of the organization by holding semiannual meetings to harmonize views on European security issues in the areas of arms control and disarmament, East–West relations, ways of bolstering the European contribution to the NATO alliance and European cooperation in weapons development and manufacture.

Wheeler, Earle   (January 13, 1908–December 18, 1975)
General Earle Wheeler was chairman of the U.S. Joint Chiefs of Staff at the height of the VIETNAM WAR. He was a well-known hawk but remained at his post and implemented President LYNDON JOHNSON's decision to de-escalate the war.

Wheeler rose to prominence in the U.S. Army during the 1950s when his skills as an administrator and liaison between politicians and the military were noted. In 1960 he was assigned to the office of the Joint Chiefs of Staff as staff director and formed a good relationship with President JOHN F. KENNEDY, who appointed him army chief of staff in October 1962. President Johnson appointed Wheeler chairman of the Joint Chiefs in July 1964.

From the early 1960s, Wheeler advocated an extensive American troop commitment in Vietnam. In April 1965, he told Johnson that 850,000 U.S. soldiers would be needed over a seven-year period to secure the defeat of the North Vietnamese. In addition to supporting the ground commanders' requests for more troops, Wheeler also urged the president to begin and continue massive bombing raids against North Vietnamese targets.

After the resignation of Defense Secretary ROBERT MCNAMARA in 1968, Wheeler assumed responsibility for channeling communications between the military commanders in Vietnam and the White House. This substantially increased his power and strengthened those who advocated an escalation in the U.S. commitment. On February 26, 1968, after the TET OFFENSIVE, he supported General WILLIAM WESTMORELAND's request for 200,000 additional ground troops. The offensive and subsequent request led to a complete reappraisal of the U.S. commitment, which resulted in Johnson's speech on March 31 in which he announced that he was de-escalating the war.

The president's decision placed Wheeler, as one of the leading hawks, in a difficult position. He was urged to resign in protest but decided to stay at his post to prevent a rash of high-level resignations that would do long-term damage to the national defense structure. Wheeler's success in carrying out the presidential instructions was evidenced by his persuading Westmoreland that he could achieve his military goals with only 15,000 of the 200,000 men that he had requested.

After the election of President RICHARD NIXON, Wheeler remained at the Joint Chiefs of Staff and tried unsuccessfully to persuade Nixon to reverse the withdrawal policy. He supported Nixon's decision in 1970 to invade Cambodia on the grounds that it bought much-needed time.

Wheeler retired from the army in July 1970 and became a director of the Monsanto Corporation. In July 1973 he was called before the Senate Armed Services Committee to answer allegations that senior officials had falsified reports to conceal secret U.S. air strikes against Cambodian targets in 1969 and 1970. Wheeler said the air strikes had been personally ordered by Nixon and denied that documents had been falsified, although a system of dual reports had been used for "security reasons." Wheeler died two years later, on December 18, 1975.

White, Harry Dexter   (October 9, 1892–August 16, 1948)
Harry Dexter White was a high-ranking official in the U.S. Treasury Department and the first American executive director of the INTERNATIONAL MONETARY FUND. Around the time of his death in 1948 he won notoriety when he was accused of being a communist agent.

White was the son of Lithuanian immigrants. After serving in World War I, he studied economics at Stanford and Harvard universities. He wrote an award-winning thesis on *The International Payments of France, 1880–1913*, then took up a teaching post at Lawrence College in Wisconsin. Shortly afterward, he started consulting for the United States government.

In 1936 White moved to Washington, D.C., to work in the Treasury Department in the international monetary division. He became increasingly involved in foreign affairs and international finance. In the months before the bombing of Pearl Harbor, he strenuously proposed a series of major financial concessions to Japan in order to avoid a U.S.–Japanese confrontation.

After American entry into the war, White was promoted

to assistant secretary and placed in charge of the Treasury Department's international relations. His major responsibility was to plan the postwar international financial structure, and he was a key figure in the negotiations that led to the Bretton Woods Conference in 1944 and the creation of the International Monetary Fund (IMF) and the WORLD BANK. White also helped to draw up the MORGENTHAU PLAN, which advocated the "pastoralization" of Germany through the destruction of its industrial base and pressed for a postwar $10 billion U.S. loan to the Soviet Union. Both of the latter proposals were rejected by President HARRY TRUMAN.

In January 1946 White was appointed the first American executive director of the IMF, and he stayed in that post until he left it for the private sector in May 1947. On July 31, 1948, confessed former communist spy ELIZABETH BENTLEY told the House Un-American Activities Committee that White was part of an espionage network in the American government. Her testimony was backed up by WHITTAKER CHAMBERS in testimony before the committee on August 3, 1948.

On August 13, 1948, White appeared before the committee to deny ever having seen or met Bentley or Chambers and to proclaim, "I am not now and never have been a Communist, nor even close to becoming one . . . My creed is the American creed."

White did, however, admit that he was a good friend of Nathan Silversmith, who had been named by Chambers and Bentley as a leading Soviet agent, but he continued to emphatically deny that he had any communist links.

Three days later White died of a heart attack. But the accusations against him continued. In his autobiography published in 1952, Chambers claimed that White had regularly given him information to pass to the Soviet Union. Chambers claimed in further testimony in 1951 that White had placed communists in high-ranking positions in the Treasury and had developed pro-Soviet policies such as the Morgenthau Plan.

On November 6, 1953, Attorney General Herbert Brownell declared, "Harry Dexter White was a Communist spy," and maintained that Truman had been informed of this in an FBI report and had known of White's activities before he appointed him to the IMF post. The allegations were denied by Truman, but in testimony before the Senate Internal Security Subcommittee FBI director J. EDGAR HOOVER admitted telling Truman's attorney general, Tom Clark, that the White appointment to the IMF was "unwise." The subcommittee took no action, and the issue of White's political allegiances remained unresolved.

For Further Information:
Rees, David. *Harry Dexter White: A Study in Paradox.* New York, 1973.

White Paper on China   *See* CHINA, WHITE PAPER ON.

Wilson, Charles E.   **(July 16, 1890–September 26, 1961)**
Charles E. Wilson was U.S. secretary of defense at a crucial period during the EISENHOWER administration when the United States was switching its defense emphasis from conventional to strategic weapons.

Wilson graduated in 1909 from the Carnegie Institute of Technology with an electrical engineering degree. By 1929 he was a vice president of the General Motors Corporation. He became the company's president in 1941. During the war years he conferred regularly with Dwight Eisenhower on armaments production. The two men became close friends, and in November 1952 president-elect Eisenhower offered Wilson the post of secretary of defense.

Wilson's Senate confirmation encountered difficulties when he at first refused to sell his shares in General Motors. When asked if his General Motors shareholdings constituted a conflict of interest that would make it difficult for him to make a decision unfavorable to General Motors, Wilson gave the famous reply, "For years, I thought what was good for the country was good for General Motors and vice versa." On January 22, 1953, however, he bowed to Senate pressure and sold his shares in order to secure the nomination, but his somewhat arrogant approach to the hearings soured his relationship with Congress and it never improved.

Eisenhower's military experience made it inevitable that he would dominate defense policy. Wilson was brought in because of his management expertise. His main task was to cut Defense Department spending. In this area he as a success. In his first four months in office, Wilson reduced the number of civilian employees in the Department of Defense by 40,000.

Wilson's biggest cost-cutting exercise involved Eisenhower's "NEW LOOK" DEFENSE POLICY, which shifted priorities from conventional to strategic nuclear forces. It also involved a cutback in army and navy budgets and an increase in the budget of the U.S. Air Force, which would have primary responsibility for the American nuclear deterrent. Between December 1953 and June 1955, the army budget was cut from nearly $13 billion to $7 billion, and the number of troops was reduced by 500,000, to 1 million. Naval and marine manpower was cut from 1 million to 870,000, while the air force increased from 950,000 to 970,000 and the air force budget rose from $16.4 billion in 1955 to $18 billion in 1957. Wilson defended the Eisenhower policy as a "sound, long-range" program that assured the country of a "retaliatory" force with "tremendous power to perform essential tasks in the initial phases of a general war."

The New Look Defense Policy inevitably led to dissatisfaction among senior army and navy officers, and many of them blamed Wilson for failing to fight Eisenhower over the cuts. Frustrated by their inability to win over Wilson, senior officers started leaking classified information in an attempt to take their case directly to the public. This led to further arguments between the officers and Wilson, and in August 1957 a dissatisfied Wilson resigned from the Pentagon. He returned to business as a director of General Motors and the National Bank of Detroit and as chairman of the Michigan Advisory Committee to the U.S. Commission on Civil Rights.

Wilson, Harold (March 11, 1916–   ) Harold Wilson was the son of an industrial chemist and was educated at Oxford University, where he distinguished himself in economics. After graduation he accepted a post lecturing in economics at the university's New College, and the following year was made a Fellow of University College. While at Oxford, Wilson collaborated with Sir William Beveridge on the report that set down the foundations for Britain's postwar welfare state.

During World War II, Wilson was drafted into the civil service as the director of economics and statistics at the Ministry of Fuel and Power. While there he wrote a book on the coal industry, which became the basis of the Labour Party's postwar nationalization of the industry.

In 1945 Wilson was elected to Parliament in the Labour's postwar, landslide victory. In 1947 he became the youngest British cabinet minister since William Pitt when he was named president of the Board of Trade, but he resigned in April 1951 in protest against the introduction of national health service charges to finance British involvement in the KOREAN WAR.

After Britain acquired a nuclear bomb in 1953, the Labour Party split over whether to keep the weapon or to opt for unilateral nuclear disarmament. From 1956 onward, the unilateralists increased in power, buoyed by the activities of the increasingly vociferous CAMPAIGN FOR NUCLEAR DISARMAMENT (CND). Finally, in 1960 the unilateralists managed to overturn a national executive policy decision and won a party conference vote in favor of unilateral nuclear disarmament. The following year, moderate Labour leader Hugh Gaitskell successfully overturned the conference decision, but the Labour Party remained badly split on the issue. Wilson by this time had become de facto leader of the Labour left and moved some way toward adopting the unilateralist stand.

In January 1963, at the height of his power and influence,

Harold Wilson (left), Britain's prime minister from 1964 to 1970, with Patrick Gordon Walker (right) and Nikita Khrushchev. Photo courtesy of the Labour Party.

Gaitskell suddenly died, and the leadership of the Labour Party and its future defense position, were open to question. Wilson, with the party's unilateralist left wing behind him, was narrowly elected party leader over deputy leader George Brown. The party now appeared unalterably committed to unilateral nuclear disarmament, and this seemed to be confirmed by Wilson when he flew to Washington, D.C., in April to tell President JOHN F. KENNEDY that if Labour came to power it would "denegotiate" the Nassau Pact under which America provided Britain with POLARIS missiles. Wilson added that he did not oppose Britain's demotion to the status of a second-class power "if being a first-rate military power means being a nuclear power."

But after he became prime minister in October 1964, Wilson backed away from this position. At a summit meeting of the NORTH ATLANTIC TREATY ORGANIZATION in Washington in December 1964, he said he would retain Britain's Polaris fleet and its nuclear-armed Vulcan bombers but proposed that they be incorporated into an ATLANTIC NUCLEAR FORCE that would give all NATO allies a greater say over nuclear weapons policy and deployment. The proposal never went much further than the discussion stage, and the Polaris missiles were quietly put into operation while discussions continued. The unilateralist wing of the Labour Party and the CND campaign suffered a major setback and did not recover its former political influence until the 1980s, when the debate arose over the deployment of American intermediate-range cruise and PERSHING II missiles.

Wilson's switch on unilateralism discredited him with the left wing of his party, and for the rest of his tenure as leader he had to struggle to maintain party unity. This had an effect across a wide range of government policy and meant that the prime minister was too often forced into short-term, politically expedient measures rather than long-term programs. Thus a number of issues were not addressed and resolved because the measures required would be unpalatable to either the left or right wing of the party, both of which distrusted Wilson's leadership.

Wilson's wavering stand on nuclear arms soured his relationship with the incoming administration of U.S. president LYNDON B. JOHNSON. He tried to improve relations by offering to mediate in the VIETNAM WAR, in conjunction with the Soviet Union. This effort had little effect on the outcome of the war, although Wilson claimed in February 1967 that the Anglo–Soviet efforts had brought peace within grasp. But British diplomacy did have the effect of allowing Washington to seem to take a more reasonable position through Britain while portraying the North Vietnamese as more obdurate.

Wilson and Foreign Secretary Michael Stewart were initially consistent in their support of American action in Southeast Asia, and at one time there was talk of limited British military support. The Labour Party as a whole, however, turned increasingly against the war. In 1965 a resolution demanding the end of American bombing of North Vietnam was narrowly defeated at the annual Labour Party conference.

But in 1967 the party conference successfully passed a motion calling on the government to dissociate itself completely from American policy in Vietnam. Wilson's problems with the party over Vietnam continued to sour relations with Johnson, who believed that he was too dependent on Labour's left wing to be an effective partner. Wilson had a much closer relationship later with the more conservative RICHARD NIXON, who was a sincere believer in the Anglo–American special relationship and furthermore believed that Wilson also gave top priority to the transatlantic link.

Johnson also had differences with Wilson over general British defense and foreign policy, especially over the 1967 decision to withdraw from east of Suez, which was forced on Britain by economic factors. The Kennedy administration had placed a high value on the presence of British forces in Asia, and in February 1962 Defense Secretary ROBERT MCNAMARA told the London *Times* that "British withdrawals in Asia would constitute a virtual invitation to the Sino–Soviet bloc to move into a power vacuum." Johnson also held this view and objected to the withdrawal. His objections were slightly assuaged by the Wilson government's decision to allow the establishment of an American military base on the strategically located British-held island of Diego Garcia in the Indian Ocean.

Wilson placed a high premium on developing a "special relationship" with the Soviet Union. He visited Moscow several times, the first time in February 1966. Soviet chairman ALEXEI KOSYGIN visited London in February 1967. Wilson's visit had a three-fold purpose: to further his attempts to mediate the Vietnam War, to encourage Anglo–Soviet trade and to encourage the movement toward East–West détente. Wilson believed that the threat of an imminent Soviet attack on Western Europe had long passed and that the time was right to start laying the foundations for a relaxation of East–West tensions. A major tool in this policy was increased trade. Anglo–Soviet trade jumped from $328.8 million in 1964 to $628.8 million in 1968. During Kosygin's visit to London in February 1967, he and Wilson agreed that preparations should start for the conclusion of a long-term trade agreement, and in August 1968 the Soviet Union held its largest-ever overseas trade exhibition in London.

Anglo–Soviet relations, however, were set back by the Soviet invasion of CZECHOSLOVAKIA in August 1968. Wilson denounced the WARSAW PACT invasion of Czechoslovakia as a "flagrant violation of the United Nations Charter and of all accepted standards of international behavior." He said that it had dealt a "serious blow" to East–West relations but urged the West not to be deterred from its search for détente with the Soviet Bloc and rejected any return to "the frozen immobilism of the Cold War."

In 1970, Wilson and Labour were defeated by the Conservatives led by EDWARD HEATH, who remained in office until February 1974, when Labour returned to power with a narrow majority. In February 1975 Wilson traveled to Moscow for a five-day visit, during which he signed a series of political and economic agreements. These included the British provision of $2.4 billion worth of low-interest credits for Soviet purchases of British equipment and machinery over the following five years. Wilson described his talks with Soviet leader LEONID BREZHNEV as opening "a new phase in Anglo–Soviet relations." The Soviets, however, took up only half of the offered credits and dealt a major blow to Labour's claim of a special relationship with Moscow.

Wilson's attitudes toward Western Europe and the EUROPEAN ECONOMIC COMMUNITY (EEC) were to a large degree directed by Britain's economic troubles. Under the EDEN PLAN FOR GERMAN REUNIFICATION initiated in 1955, Britain was committed to maintaining a significant military presence in West Germany until the year 2005. The cost of this presence, however, was proving to be a drain on the weakened British economy. In 1966 and 1967, Wilson secured new offset payments covering most of the foreign exchange costs of the British forces in West Germany, some £72 million out of the total cost of £82 million. The United States as well as the Federal Republic of Germany contributed. But even with this new agreement, Wilson had to withdraw one brigade group of the BRITISH ARMY OF THE RHINE and one squadron of the Royal Air Force from Germany.

Economic circumstances were also the major factor in determining Wilson's attitude toward the EEC. In common with a large proportion of the Labour Party, Wilson started off opposed to British membership in the Common Market, which he regarded as a supranational capitalist-oriented organization that would place an unacceptable brake on the party's socialist goals. At the same time, there was a fear within both the Labour and Conservative parties that membership in the EEC would damage Britain's relationship with its former colonies in the Commonwealth. In June 1962, as Labour foreign affairs spokesman, Wilson warned that "if a choice has to be made between Europe and the Commonwealth, there can be no doubt where our duty and loyalty lie."

But by 1965 Wilson had moved toward the center of the Labour Party and looked toward the EEC as a natural haven for the battered British economy. In February 1965 Wilson told the House of Commons that "the position of the British government is and remains that if a favorable opportunity were to arise for negotiating entry we would be prepared to negotiate if, and only if, the necessary conditions relating to essential British and Commonwealth interests could be fulfilled." In the spring of 1967, Wilson launched a new round of negotiations for British entry, but in November 1967 French president CHARLES DE GAULLE again vetoed British membership.

The subject of British membership in the Common Market largely languished until the pro-European Edward Heath became prime minister after the 1970 general election. Heath made major concessions on the agricultural agreements and budgetary contributions, and Britain entered the EEC in January 1972. The terms were denounced by Wilson, who promised a referendum on the issue of British membership if

Labour returned to power. But when the referendum was finally held in June 1975, Wilson campaigned in favor of British membership while a number of his Labour colleagues campaigned against. Wilson's support was considered to have played a vital role in securing the 67.2% vote in favor of continued membership.

A great proportion of Wilson's diplomatic efforts were absorbed by the problems of southern Africa, particularly the British colony of Rhodesia (later Zimbabwe). In the late 1950s and early 1960s, the white settlers in Rhodesia came under pressure from black nationalists and the British government to accept an independent multiracial government. This was rejected by the whites, who in 1963 formed the white supremacist Rhodesia Front Party under Ian Smith. The Rhodesia Front was elected in 1964, and in November 1965, after a series of abortive talks between Wilson and Smith, the Rhodesian government unilaterally declared itself independent of Britain.

Wilson's critics maintain that a long-running crisis over Southern Africa could have been averted if he had immediately sent British troops into Rhodesia to put down what he described as a "treasonable" rebellion. Wilson did not regard this as a practical option and instead sought and won an international embargo on trade with Rhodesia. The embargo, however, was ignored by the Portuguese colony of Mozambique and the white-ruled government in South Africa. This allowed the Smith regime to stay afloat financially and fight a long civil war against black nationalist guerrillas, who turned increasingly toward the Soviet Bloc for assistance.

Between 1965 and 1970, Wilson made several more attempts to resolve the Rhodesia Crisis and bring the rebellious colony to legal independence. The most important of these meetings was in December 1966 aboard the Royal Navy cruiser HMS *Tiger* off Gibraltar, at which Wilson offered to accept an interim government headed by Smith that would be committed to eventual black majority rule. This proposal was rejected by the Rhodesian cabinet.

The Conservative government of 1970–1974 also failed to resolve the Rhodesia Crisis, and by the time Wilson once again became prime minister in 1974 it was recognized that Rhodesia was a political quagmire, and Wilson left the problem to his foreign secretary, JAMES CALLAGHAN. The problem was eventually resolved by Conservative foreign secretary Lord PETER CARRINGTON in December 1979.

Wilson unexpectedly resigned as prime minister in March 1976. He first retired to the back benches and concentrated on writing his memoirs. In 1983 he was elevated to the House of Lords and assumed the title Baron Rievaulx.

For Further Information:

Callaghan, James. *Time and Chance*. New York, 1984.

Donoghue, Bernard. *Prime Minister: The Conduct of Policy under Harold Wilson and James Callaghan*. London, 1987.

Dorril, Stephen and Robin Ramsay. *Smear! Wilson and the Secret State*. London, 1991.

Falkender, Marcia. *Downing Street in Perspective*. London, 1983.

Frankel, Joseph. *British Foreign Policy, 1945–1973*. New York, 1975.

Healey, Denis. *The Time of My Life*. London, 1989.

Leigh, David. *The Wilson Plot: The Intelligence Services and the Discrediting of a Prime Minister*. London, 1988.

MacLean, Donald. *British Foreign Policy Since Suez, 1956–1968*. London, 1970.

Morgan, Austen. *Harold Wilson*. London, 1992.

Wilson, Harold. *Memoirs, The Making of a Prime Minister, 1916–1964*. London, 1986.

———. *Memoirs, The Labour Government, 1964–1970*. London, 1971.

———. *Memoirs, The Governance of Britain*. London, 1976.

———. *Memoirs, Final Term: The Labour Government, 1974–1976*. London, 1979.

Window of Vulnerability   The "window of vulnerability" was a concept current among conservatives in the United States in the late 1970s and early 1980s that a gap had appeared in the American nuclear defenses that could allow the Soviet Union to launch a relatively safe first-strike nuclear attack.

The window of vulnerability theory was used to great effect during the 1980 presidential election by RONALD REAGAN in much the same way as JOHN KENNEDY had used the MISSILE GAP debate of the late 1950s to his political benefit. In office, Reagan used the window of vulnerability to increase defense spending substantially during his administration.

The theory was based on an analysis of the Soviet Union's large force of land-based intercontinental ballistic missiles (ICBMs) equipped with MIRVed (MULTIPLE INDEPENDENTLY-TARGETED REENTRY VEHICLE) warheads. The U.S. Department of Defense reported that the Soviet ICBM force was capable of destroying up to 90% of America's land-based and air-based nuclear forces and would have sufficient ICBM reserves to hold American cities hostage in order to prevent an American retaliatory strike by U.S. submarine-based nuclear missiles. In retrospect, the "window" appears to have been just as much a mirage as the "missile gap" had been in the late 1950s.

Wisner, Frank   (June 23, 1909–October 29, 1965)   Frank Wisner was a leading intelligence agent who established America's postwar anti-communist covert operations. He remained the leading figure in the CENTRAL INTELLIGENCE AGENCY's covert operations until a mental breakdown forced his resignation in 1958.

After graduating from the University of Virginia Law School in 1934, Wisner joined a New York law practice. During World War II he joined the OFFICE OF STRATEGIC SERVICES (the wartime forerunner of the CIA) and served as station chief in Bucharest. In the immediate postwar period, Wisner served under ALLEN DULLES, the OSS station chief in Berlin, and he persuaded Dulles that American intelligence should shift its emphasis from hunting ex-Nazis to watching Soviet activities.

When the OSS was disbanded in September 1945, Wisner returned to his New York law firm, but he maintained close contacts with the intelligence community. In June 1948 he was appointed director of the Office of Policy Coordination (OPC), which was responsible for the CIA's covert operations. The OPC's work included psychological, economic, political and paramilitary activities.

Technically, the OPC was part of the CIA. But Wisner had organized the command structure so that he worked directly with the White House, the State Department and the Pentagon rather than with CIA director ROSCOE HILLENKOETTER. The operation quickly expanded. In 1949 the OPC had 302 agents in five stations financed by a budget of $5 million. Three years later the budget was $84 million, the staff nearly 6,000, and there were 47 stations. Among the OPC's early activities were a failed attempt to overthrow the Albanian government in 1950, strikebreaking in France, influencing elections in Italy and raising private armies for a possible invasion of Eastern Europe.

In 1950 the OPC was brought under the direct control of the CIA, and in 1952 it was merged with the Office of Special Operations (OSO) to form the Directorate for Plans; Wisner was named deputy director.

From 1951 onward, Wisner worked closely with Allen Dulles, who joined the agency in that year as deputy director and in 1953 was named director. Dulles gave Wisner special responsibility for covert operations in Eastern Europe, and in 1956 Wisner argued strongly for direct American intervention in support of the Hungarian Uprising (see HUNGARY). The EISENHOWER administration's failure to support the Hungarians left Wisner disillusioned with American policy, and Dulles shifted his operations to Asia, where Wisner was responsible for the failed attempt to overthrow Indonesia's President Sukarno.

In 1958 Wisner suffered a nervous breakdown and resigned as deputy director for plans. After a rest period, he was appointed London station chief. Wisner committed suicide on October 29, 1965.

For Further Information:
Dulles, Allen W. *The Craft of Intelligence.* New York, 1974.

World Bank (International Bank for Reconstruction and Development)   The World Bank was established on December 27, 1945, following the Bretton Woods Conference of July 1944. Its initial purpose was to supply seed capital for the reconstruction of postwar Europe, but its membership has expanded to include 148 states. Because it is dominated by the United States, the Soviet Union referred to the bank as an expression of American imperialism.

The bank was started with an initial capital of $9.1 billion and initially had 44 members. By 1988 the bank's capital exceeded $58 billion. Most of the bank's lendable funds come from its borrowing in world capital markets, from retained earnings and from the flow of repayments on its loans.

The stated purpose of the bank is to make loans or guarantee private bank loans to the governments of member countries whose current credit rating might not be sound but whose future prospects look promising. The loans are meant to "assist in the reconstruction and development" of member countries and to promote "private foreign investment" and the "long-range balanced growth of international trade." In practice this means that the bank has a good deal of leverage over a borrowing government's economic and fiscal policies, and it has often exercised it in ways detrimental to a country's social well-being (as distinct from its government's fiscal soundness). This in turn has led to political unrest. The bank works closely with the INTERNATIONAL MONETARY FUND, which was established at the same time. Both organizations are based in Washington, D.C.

Wyszynski, Stefan   **(August 3, 1901–May 28, 1981)**
Stefan Cardinal Wyszynski was the postwar Roman Catholic primate of Poland for 32 years. In this position he took the leading role in first opposing and then reaching a gradual accommodation with the communist authorities.

Wyszynski was educated at the University of Lublin and was ordained a priest at the age of 23. Between the wars, he taught at Catholic universities and seminaries, and soon after the war ended, in 1946, Wyszynski was named bishop of Lublin.

The Roman Catholic Church has had a unique position in Polish history. It always kept itself separate from the government, enabling it to act as the custodian of Polish culture, language and national identity during the many years when Poland was divided among the German, Russian and Austro-Hungarian empires. The church continued this traditional role when it became clear that Poland was being absorbed into a new Soviet empire.

The Communist Party was quick to recognize the power of the Polish church and in September 1945 moved to curb it by repudiating the 1925 Concordat with Rome, which had given the church full freedom to conduct its own affairs within Poland. The Vatican retaliated by refusing to recognize the new Polish government, continuing to recognize Polish bishops in the eastern territories ceded to the Soviet Union and refusing to appoint bishops for the German territories now administered by Poland.

Wyszynski took a major role in establishing these early policies, and in November 1948 he became the church's major spokesman in the fight against the party when he was named archbishop of Geniezno and Warsaw and primate of Poland. In a determined effort to stop Wyszynski before he had time to establish a power base, the government nationalized church hospitals, confiscated church lands and took over direct supervision of the church's welfare organization, Caritas.

Wyszynski decided it was best to seek an accommodation with the Communist Party, and on April 14, 1950, he signed an agreement that acknowledged the supremacy of the government in all secular matters in return for freedom of worship. The agreement also allowed the Roman Catholic Church to run its own newspaper, teach religion in public schools and operate the Catholic University at Lublin.

The agreement did not last. The new constitution, adopted

on July 22, 1952, made all church appointments subject to government approval. The Vatican rejected this and asserted the church's independence by naming Wyszynski a cardinal on November 29, 1952. At the investiture ceremony at the Vatican on January 12, 1953, Wyszynski was conspicuous by his absence. He had been told that he would be granted an exit visa, but that it was unlikely that he would be allowed to reenter Poland.

The government was determined to silence Wyszynski. In March 1953, the Catholic weekly *Tygodnik Powszechny* was shut down. Finally, on September 28, the government announced it was using its constitutional veto over church appointments to suspend Wyszynski as primate and to imprison him in a Polish monastery. The arrest of Wyszynski sparked a series of international protests, and Pope Pius XII excommunicated all Roman Catholics who had any part in the affair.

With Wyszynski in prison, the government was able to force its policies on the church. The teaching of catechism was banned in Polish churches, and on December 17, 1953, Polish bishops took an oath of loyalty to the government. The Vatican claimed that the oath was forced on the bishops by "long, moral, administrative and physical violence" and would not be recognized by the church.

Wyszynski became one of the leading symbols of Stalinist repression in Poland, and it was natural that his release led the demands of Polish anti-Stalinists such as WLADYSLAW GOMULKA, who became first secretary of the Polish Communist Party after the POZNAN CRISIS of 1956. Wyszyinski was therefore released on October 30, 1956, and returned to the primacy of Poland.

Gomulka and Wyszynski negotiated a new church–state agreement in which Wyszynski expressed support for all government policies aimed at the extension of Polish democracy. In return, the government promised to lift all barriers to full religious freedom in Poland.

Wyszynski had his own difficulties in dealing with the communist government. He did not like it but he depended on its acquiescence in order to maintain the church's role in Polish life. The Communist Party, in turn, saw the Catholic Church and Wyszynski as major obstacles to control of the Polish people. But it also realized that a frontal assault on the authority of the church would only alienate the intensely religious Poles. Therefore the party's best chance lay in gradually chipping away at the structure of the church.

The result was an attack by the government followed by a counterattack by Wyszynski and then a new agreement, which lasted for a limited time until a new series of attacks and counterattacks. As government restrictions gradually increased throughout the 1960s, Wyszynski moved closer to the secular opposition to strengthen the church's position. After student riots in 1968, he demanded the release of arrested students and warned that "a truncheon is never an argument in a free society."

Two years later, Gomulka fell from power and was succeeded by EDWARD GIEREK after nationwide riots sparked by Gomulka's decision to increase food and fuel prices dramatically. His downfall was coupled with the signing of a treaty between Poland and West Germany, which implicitly recognized the ODER-NEISSE LINE as the German–Polish border. This cleared the way for the Vatican to recognize Polish sovereignty over the region, which in turn resulted in a major improvement in church–state relations. In June 1971, the church was granted title to 7,000 former church buildings in the Oder–Neisse territories plus 2,000 acres of land.

But Gierek's concessions to the church were too little too late as far as Wyszynski was concerned. His experiences with Gomulka and the WARSAW PACT invasion of CZECHOSLOVAKIA in 1968 had left him convinced that the Communist Party was institutionally incapable of political reform. He moved closer to the secular opposition, forging unofficial but close links with opposition groups such as the KOR (Workers' Self-Defense Committee) and the ROPCiO (Movement for the Defense of Human and Civil Rights).

On January 25, 1976, Wyszynski publicly attacked proposed amendments to the Polish constitution. These amendments established the "leading role of the party," made legal rights conditional on "the honest fulfillment of duties" and set in legal concrete Poland's "unshakeable bond" with the Soviet Union. An amendment to prosecute those seeking "to use religion for political ends" was dropped because of opposition from Wyszynski.

Later that year, after food riots, Wyszynski accused the authorities of police brutality, and on December 12 he urged workers to fight for their rights and demand more pay if they believed their salaries were inadequate.

The elevation of Karol Cardinal Wojtyla, the archbishop of Krakow, to the papacy on October 16, 1978, dramatically altered Polish church–state relations and the position of Cardinal Wyszynski. Pope JOHN PAUL II's election led to a resurgence of church-based Polish nationalism, which the government was forced to recognize. This increased Wyszynski's leverage in negotiations with the Communist Party, and it again became advantageous for him to seek a working relationship.

This relationship was upset by the Gdansk riots and strike and the creation of Solidarity in 1980. Although Wyszynski felt a strong sympathy with the cause of Solidarity, and a number of Catholic priests publicly backed it, Wyszynski himself took an ambivalent position.

Throughout 1981 Wyszynski urged moderation upon both the government and Solidarity. He met with both party leader General WOJCIECH JARUZELSKI and Solidarity leader LECH WALESA in an attempt to mediate a settlement between the two. But before he could effect an agreement, Wyszynski died of stomach cancer on May 28, 1981.

For Further Information:

Dunn, Dennis. *Détente and Papal-Communist Relations, 1962–1978.* Boulder, Colo., 1979.

Pomian-Szrednicki, Machiej. *Religious Change in Contemporary Poland: Secularization and Politics.* London, 1982.

Yalta Conference The Yalta Conference was held in the Crimean resort town of Yalta on February 4–11, 1945, and was attended by U.S. president FRANKLIN D. ROOSEVELT, British prime minister WINSTON CHURCHILL and Soviet leader JOSEF STALIN. The conference set the terms for Soviet entry into the war against Japan, agreed to the four-power occupation of Germany and, in the opinion of many historians, implicitly accepted Soviet postwar occupation of Eastern Europe.

The conference was held in the Livadia Palace. The first item was the postwar dismemberment of Germany. The three powers had accepted the principle at previous meetings and in correspondence, but had not worked out the details. Roosevelt wanted to divide Germany into five constituent parts. Churchill favored a division into Prussia and Austria–Bavaria, with the German industrial heartland of the Ruhr and Westphalia under international control. Churchill also pressed for a zone of occupation for France. This was initially opposed by Stalin but later was accepted. It was agreed to leave the exact boundaries of the occupation zones to later discussions.

The second item on the agenda was the formation of the United Nations. Roosevelt proposed that the United Nations have a security council; that the four permanent members of this council be Britain, the United States, China and the Soviet Union; and that they each have a veto. This was accepted by Churchill and Stalin. The Soviets also dropped a previous demand that all 16 Soviet republics be given a seat at the United Nations. Instead, Stalin asked that two of the republics (the Ukraine and Belorussia) be allowed representation. Churchill and Roosevelt accepted this demand as an obvious improvement on the previous position.

The third item on the agenda was German war reparations. The Soviet Union wanted Germany to pay the Allies $20 billion in reparations, with half of that money going to the Soviet Union. Churchill opposed any reparations and stressed that the crippling reparations levied on Germany at the end of World War I had helped to create the political climate that had led to the rise of Hitler and the start of World War II. Differences on this issue were left unresolved, with the three leaders agreeing only to refer the issue to a reparations commission.

U.S. secretary of state EDWARD STETTINIUS then proposed a "Declaration on Liberated Europe." This declared that the three powers promised to "(a) establish conditions of internal peace; (b) carry out emergency measures for the relief of distressed peoples; (c) form interim governmental authorities broadly representative of all democratic elements in the population and pledged to the earliest possible establishment through free elections of governments responsive to the will of the people; and (d) facilitate where necessary the holding of such elections." The declaration was accepted almost without debate, and Britain and the United States later used it to claim that the Soviet Union had broken the agreement by virtue of its actions in Eastern Europe.

Discussions related to the Soviet entry into the Far Eastern war were conducted almost exclusively between Stalin and Roosevelt. Roosevelt was strongly opposed to an increased British involvement in the Far Eastern war because he feared that this would lead to demands from Churchill for additional colonial possessions from the dismembered Japanese Empire. Roosevelt, however, realized that he needed additional help as the atomic bomb had not been tested at that stage; also, his military advisers had told him that China was destined for a disastrous civil war and an American-only landing on the Japanese islands would involve the loss of a million American lives. The Soviet Union, therefore, seemed the only alternative.

At Yalta, Stalin agreed to enter the war against Japan within three months of the end of the war in Europe. In return, Roosevelt agreed to certain strategic concessions in favor of the Soviet Union. There were control of the Kurile and Sakhalin islands north of Japan and of Dairen and Port Arthur on the Chinese coast, Chinese recognition of the Mongolian People's Republic and control of the Chinese Eastern and

Josef Stalin (left) with President Franklin D. Roosevelt at Yalta in February 1945.

South Manchurian Railways. In the end, Stalin entered the Asian war exactly three months after the war in Europe ended. The Soviet entry also came two days after the atomic bomb was dropped. The strategic concessions agreed to by Roosevelt, and the presence of the Red Army in Asia, left Stalin in a position later to support North Korea and the PEOPLE'S REPUBLIC OF CHINA.

The final and most difficult subject on the Yalta agenda was POLAND. In the year before Yalta, relations between Stalin and the Polish government-in-exile in London had become severely strained. The Red Army now occupied Poland and most of the rest of Eastern Europe and had recognized as the Polish government a group of communists they had installed in Warsaw (the LUBLIN COMMITTEE). It was generally recognized that Poland was a test case for all of Eastern Europe.

The two Western leaders were quickly put on the defensive when Stalin compared Soviet hegemony in Eastern Europe with Anglo–American dominance in Italy. Stalin had vainly sought a role in the wartime administration of Italy and had been repeatedly rebuffed. At Yalta he claimed that this established a precedent along the lines of spheres of responsibility based upon the presence of the Allied Powers' respective armies.

The American and British leaders had to accept the logic of this argument but continued to argue vehemently against the communist government in Poland. Churchill took the strongest line against the Lublin Committee, maintaining that it commanded the support of less than a third of the Polish people. He pointed out that Britain had gone to war against Germany over the issue of Polish sovereignty and that Britain "could never be content with any solution that did not leave Poland a free and independent state."

Stalin responded by pointing out that Poland was the historical corridor of attack against Russia and that it was therefore essential that the Soviet Union be able to shut that corridor. On the basis of this statement Churchill and Roosevelt concluded that Stalin could not be moved on the issue of the Lublin Committee. The conference looked as if it might be deadlocked until Stalin promised that free elections would be held within a month. The Soviet leader effectively ignored his promise of free elections, however, and this played a major role in the rapid deterioration in postwar relations with the United States and Britain.

For Further Information:
Davis, Lynn Etheridge. *The Cold War Begins: Soviet American Conflict over Eastern Europe.* Princeton, 1974.
Donnelly, Desmond. *Struggle for the World.* New York, 1965.
Fleming, D.F. *The Cold War and Its Origins, 1917–1960.* Garden City, N.Y., 1961.
Gaddis, J.L. *The United States and the Origins of the Cold War, 1941–1947.* New York, 1972.
Graebner, Norman. *Cold War Diplomacy: American Foreign Policy, 1945–1960.* Princeton, 1962.

Yalu River The Yalu River forms the border between North Korea and Manchuria in the PEOPLE'S REPUBLIC OF CHINA. During the early stages of the KOREAN WAR it took on major political significance as a debate raged on the issue of whether to attack targets on the Chinese side of the Yalu.

Those in favor of attacking argued that the North Koreans found sanctuary in China from which they could return to the offensive. The only way to deny them that sanctuary was to control the Yalu and possibly the northern bank. Those opposed argued that crossing the Yalu made it likely that the Soviet Union would send troops to protect China and North Korea, thus increasing the possibility of a U.S.–Soviet war.

The major advocate in favor of attack was General DOUGLAS MACARTHUR, commander of the UN forces in Korea. After his successful INCHON landings on September 15, 1950, his UN forces routed the North Koreans, who fled back across the 38th parallel. Flushed with MacArthur's success, the United Nations changed his mandate and instructed him to occupy all of the Korean Peninsula in order to unify the country under a single democratic government.

MacArthur pressed forward and had actually reached the Yalu at Hyesanjin when 300,000 Chinese communist troops started to cross the river. MacArthur announced on November 6, "A new and fresh army faces us, backed up by a possibility of large alien reserves and adequate supplies within easy reach of the enemy but beyond the limits of our present sphere of military action."

The same day he ordered 90 B-29 bombers to attack the bridges across the Yalu in order to prevent more Chinese from crossing into North Korea and so trap those already on the southern bank. President HARRY TRUMAN heard about the order less than three hours before the planes were due to take off. He immediately ordered a postponement on the grounds that such an attack would inevitably mean dropping bombs on the Chinese side of the river and that the United States had a firm commitment to Britain, its chief ally in Korea and main diplomatic support at the United Nations, not to attack any targets on the Chinese side of the Yalu without prior consultation.

Truman's decision to countermand his general's orders led to the first major disagreement between the two men. MacArthur replied to the president that he was suspending the air strike "under the gravest protest that I can make." Shortly afterward the Chinese launched their offensive, and the UN forces were pushed back to the southern end of the Korean Peninsula.

For Further Information:
Caridi, Ronald, J. *The Korean War and American Politics.* Philadelphia, 1969.
Collins, J. Lawton. *War in Peacetime: The History and Lessons of Korea.* Boston, 1969.
Higgins, Trumbull. *Korea and the Fall of MacArthur: A Précis in Limited War.* New York, 1960.
MacArthur, Douglas. *Reminiscences.* New York, 1964.
Stone, I.F. *The Hidden History of the Korean War.* New York, 1952.

Yeltsin, Boris (February 1, 1931–   )   Boris Niko-layevich Yeltsin became recognized as one of the leading Soviet reformers while head of the Communist Party in Moscow. His forced removal from that post was seen as a victory for conservative hardliners, but he later staged a comeback by being elected to the Soviet parliament and became the focal point for the reformist movement in opposition to Soviet president MIKHAIL GORBACHEV. Ultimately, he became Russian president, outlasting Gorbachev and even the U.S.S.R. itself.

Yeltsin trained as an engineer at the Kirov Polytechnic and after graduation in 1955 worked on a number of construction projects until entering politics full-time in 1968. It was not until he was 30 years old that Yeltsin joined the Communist Party, and he quickly developed a reputation as an avid reformer. In 1976 he was appointed first secretary of the Sverdlovsk District Central Committee.

Yeltsin's breakthrough came when Gorbachev became general secretary of the party in 1985. Gorbachev needed supporters for his reformist policies to counter the entrenched positions of the Brezhnev old guard. In July 1985 he moved Yeltsin to Moscow to be secretary of the Central Committee for Construction, and within six months Yeltsin was first secretary of the party apparatus in Moscow, one of the most powerful positions in the Soviet Union. The following year, Yeltsin was elevated to the Politburo as a candidate (non-voting) member.

Yeltsin was given the immediate task of clearing the city bureaucracy of corruption. In April 1986 he announced the arrest of hundreds of corrupt officials and publicly named several corrupt bureaucrats. He also advocated the abolition of special privileges for senior party officials, such as special stores and chauffeur-driven cars. In February 1986, he shocked party officials at the 27th Party Congress when he criticized himself for "inaction and hypocrisy" during the Brezhnev years. Later, he stressed that self-sacrifice rather than self-aggrandizement should become the standard for all Communist Party workers.

Yeltsin's attacks on party officials made him increasingly unpopular within the party apparatus, so he set out to construct a popular base outside the party structure. He established a distribution network to ensure that fresh vegetables would reach the capital. He encouraged street cafés and the contruction of colorful markets with private market stalls. An urban planning council was established to preserve historic buildings and beautify the city. All of these moves made Yeltsin a popular figure with the residents of Moscow.

Both the improvements within Moscow and the attacks on party abuses throughout the Soviet Union brought Yeltsin into increasing conflict with the entrenched party interests led by Yegor Ligachev. And for his part, Yeltsin became increasingly frustrated that Gorbachev's perestroika and glasnost were not moving fast enough. On October 21, 1987, Yeltsin took the unprecedented move of resigning from both the Politburo and his post as Moscow party secretary because of his dissatisfaction with the speed of the perestroika program.

The astonishing resignation led to a public split between Gorbachev and Yeltsin. The Soviet leader clearly believed that his former supporter was insensitive to the problems he faced in the reform program and wanted to move too quickly too soon. He joined the old guard in criticizing Yeltsin and accused him of "political adventurism." Yeltsin responded by calling for more and faster reforms and accusing Gorbachev of cultivating a "cult of personality." Yeltsin was eventually forced to apologize, and his fall from power was seen as a major setback for perestroika.

But Yeltsin's popular base in Moscow meant that the party leadership could not afford to ignore him without a damaging political crackdown in the capital. Yeltsin stayed largely in the political background until the 1989 elections to the Congress of Deputies. In these first relatively democratic elections, Yeltsin was overwhelmingly elected a deputy from Moscow to the congress, which was to elect from its ranks the members of the Supreme Soviet (parliament). But the number of seats reserved in the congress for the Communist Party effectively blocked Yeltsin from being elected to the Supreme Soviet, even though he had won more popular votes than any other deputy. Muscovites threatened political riots unless their representative was elected, and the situation was resolved only at the last minute when a candidate from Siberia resigned his seat in favor of Yeltsin, who was carried through the streets of Moscow in a torchlight procession.

The whole episode established Yeltsin as the focal point for reformers in the Soviet Union and leader of the legal political opposition.

He consolidated his political base in Russia in 1990, capturing a seat in the republic's Supreme Soviet and then winning a parliamentary contest to become Russia's president in May. In June 1991, he cemented his position and national stature when he won 60% of the vote in a popular election for Russia's newly-created executive office of president.

Throughout 1990 and 1991, Yeltsin engaged in an increasingly bitter power struggle with Gorbachev over the slow pace of reforms. His moment of glory came during the August 1991 hard-line coup attempt against Gorbachev, when he and his followers stood up to the tanks of the "putschists" in the Kremlin and rallied national and international opinion against the coup.

After this, Yeltsin's star rose dramatically while Gorbachev's sank. Although Gorbachev was still Soviet president, in actuality the two men functioned as co-leaders, with more and more authority flowing to Yeltsin. In November, the Russian government granted him emergency powers to rule by decree, and he became the republic's premier as well. He was the leading personality in negotiating and signing the Commonwealth of Independent States accord that led to the dissolution of the U.S.S.R. in December, and managed to convince his long-time rival Gorbachev to accept the inevitable and resign peacefully.

But the rose of independence lost its bloom in 1992, as the populace objected to Yeltsin's introduction of harsh austerity measures to shock the Russian economy into a free-market system. There were near-constant political crises as his reforms were opposed in parliament by an opposition bloc of hard-line nationalists, military industrialists and conservative former communists. Nevertheless, both sides continued to compromise at the last minute, and the long-predicted "second coup" against Yeltsin and his team of pro-Western market-oriented reformists did not occur. (Ultimately, Yeltsin brought the situation to a head in the autumn of 1993.)

Meanwhile, Yeltsin finally won the international acclaim that had long been denied him, when he had labored in Gorbachev's shadow. He visited Washington in June 1992 and agreed to steep cuts in land-based nuclear missiles that went far beyond anything negotiated by Gorbachev. The details were finalized when President Bush traveled to Moscow in January 1993 and joined Yeltsin in the historic signing of START II (see STRATEGIC ARMS REDUCTION TREATIES).

For Further Information:

Felshman, Neil. *Gorbachev, Yeltsin, and the Last Days of the Soviet Empire.* New York, 1992.

Morrison, John. *Boris Yeltsin: From Bolshevik to Democrat.* New York, 1991.

Solovev, Vladimir. *Boris Yeltsin: A Political Biography.* New York, 1992.

Yucca Flats   Yucca Flats was the United States' premier nuclear weapons testing ground in the 1950s.

As America's nuclear weapons program expanded, scientists and defense analysts found it increasingly difficult to perform the necessary tests at remote sites such as BIKINI ISLAND. In July 1951 Gordon Dean, chairman of the ATOMIC ENERGY COMMISSION, suggested to President HARRY TRUMAN that a test site be set up in the continental United States and proposed Yucca Flats, approximately 70 miles north of Las Vegas.

Truman gave his approval and in September the first tests were carried out. These involved 5,000 American servicemen who were used to determine how soon after a nuclear explosion troops can be sent into the damaged zone. These and other tests led to a number of cases of radiation contamination and later cost the Defense Department a considerable amount of money in lawsuits.

Yugoslavia   Yugoslavia was the first communist-controlled country to break away successfully from Soviet domination. The country went on to become a major player in the NON-ALIGNED MOVEMENT. But beginning in 1990, it dissolved into civil war.

Yugoslavia was not a nation-state, but rather a federated collection of small Balkan national states, the main ones being Serbia, Croatia, Slovenia and Bosnia-Herzegovina. It was not until the collapse of the Austro-Hungarian Empire in 1918 that the state of Yugoslavia came into being as the Kingdom of Serbs, Croats and Slovenes. In October 1929, King Alexander formally changed the name to Yugoslavia.

In the early years of World War II, Yugoslavia followed a pro-German foreign policy, but in March 1941 the regent, Prince Paul, was overthrown in a military coup; 17-year-old King Peter II was placed on the throne, and Yugoslavia formally allied itself with the Allies. Italy and Germany responded by invading and occupying Yugoslavia in April 1941.

The Germans faced two major centers of resistance. The first one was led by the pro-monarchist faction, under General Draza Mihailovic, which operated in Serbia. The other group was dominated by the communist leader JOSIP BROZ TITO and operated mainly in Bosnia, Croatia, Montenegro and Slovenia. In the early war years, the two partisan armies spent as much time fighting each other as they did the Germans; but by 1943 the communists had emerged as the more powerful force, and the Allied governments shifted their support to Tito. On November 29, 1943, Tito's National Liberation Army proclaimed its own government in liberated areas, and the following year King Peter was formally deposed. Mihailovic was summarily tried and executed in 1946.

Unlike other East European communist parties, Yugoslavia's communists came to power without any help from the Soviet Union, and Tito was in control of the country before the Red Army was in a position to occupy the Balkans. This provided Tito with a popular base within Yugoslavia, which in turn allowed him to operate independently of Moscow.

Tito's strong position also allowed him to pursue his dream of a communist Balkan federation extending from TRIESTE to Greece, and in the aftermath of the war he set out to achieve this aim. Yugoslavia occupied the Italian-claimed port city of Trieste, formed a monetary and customs union with Albania and supported communists in the GREEK CIVIL WAR. The pursuit of this dream brought Yugoslavia into conflict not only with the Western Powers but also with JOSEF STALIN. The Soviet leader tried to restrain Tito's enthusiasm, partly because he did not want the Soviet Union, by association, to be committed to unwinable conflicts and partly because he wanted to dictate policies to the Yugoslav government.

An outright Yugoslav-Soviet split occurred in 1948–49 and continued into the mid-1950s, when there was a brief warming of ties after the death of Stalin and the rise of NIKITA KHRUSHCHEV. But the rapprochement lasted only until 1956, foundering on Chinese opposition to improved relations with "deviationist" Tito and the nationalist aspirations that Yugoslavia inspired in other East European countries. In 1961, Tito sought to bolster his independent course by helping to found the Nonaligned Movement. Support for nonalignment soon became the primary aim of Yugoslav foreign policy, and the country's key position within the group of nonaligned countries gave Yugoslavia international political influence out of all proportion to its military or economic power.

In 1962 relations between Yugoslavia and the Soviet Union reached another peak when Tito visited Moscow. But relations worsened again after the fall of Khrushchev, and when

Yugoslavia condemned in turn the WARSAW PACT invasion of CZECHOSLOVAKIA in 1968, Soviet support for the Vietnamese occupation of CAMBODIA, and the 1979 Soviet invasion of AFGHANISTAN.

Another factor that contributed to a worsening in Yugoslav–Soviet relations was Yugoslavia's decision to move away from a strict socialist economy to a more mixed market-oriented system. In 1966 MILOVAN DJILAS was released from prison. Once a high-level aide to Tito, he had been the country's strongest critic of a centralized economy and had advocated a two-party political system for Yugoslavia.

Tito also moved to decentralize political power. He had been able to suppress the strong Balkan national rivalries by the force of his personality and his unique historical position, but as he grew older, the Yugoslav leader realized the danger of ethnic and national differences resurfacing after his death. In 1971 he established the principle of a collective presidency, and a new constitution was promulgated that devolved substantial power from the federation to the republics and provinces.

The collective presidency took power upon Tito's death on May 4, 1980, and rotated regularly on the basis of ethnic parity. The rotating presidency substantially increased the powers of the provincial governments, where the leadership was chosen in a more traditional fashion. The strong provincial governments left Yugoslavia without a firm political or economic direction, and the historic and divisive national differences reemerged with savage virulence, leading to the breakup of the Yugoslav state and the open warfare and horrendous cruelties of an ethnic civil war.

The worst tensions surfaced in Croatia, Slovenia and Bosnia-Herzegovina, all of which found themselves facing militant Serb minorities backed by the Yugoslav federal army and pursuing the old dream of a "Greater Serbia," articulated for the 1990s by Serbian communist leader Slobodan Milosevic. After months of clashes, open civil war broke out when Croatia and Slovenia declared independence in June 1991. Thousands died (most of them Croats slain by Serb guerrillas and federal troops), and many European Community-brokered cease-fires failed before the EC and United Nations helped negotiate an end to the conflict in January 1992. The UN deployed peace-keeping troops, and the EC formally recognized the independence of Croatia and Slovenia, signaling an end to the 75-year-old Yugoslav federation.

Then, in late February 1992, the international spotlight moved to independence-minded Bosnia, where the conflict pitted Serbs (who made up about 31% of the republic) against an alliance of Muslim Slavs (who constituted a plurality of 43%) and Croats (about 17%). The Muslims and Croats wanted a unitary, multi-ethnic state, while the Bosnian Serbs wanted their own independent republic.

As the year wore on, the conflict became progressively more gruesome as Serbian irregulars (well-armed by the departed federal troops) besieged the capital of Sarajevo and engaged in the apparently genocidal process of "ethnic cleansing"—using such techniques as concentration camps, mass rapes, and slaughter of civilians to drive Muslims out of areas the minority Serbs deemed to be rightfully "theirs." More than 100,000 people were believed to have died, and many more were forced to become refugees. The international community continued to wring its hands, but did little aside from engaging in ineffectual negotiations and dispatching UN troops to guard humanitarian aid shipments to Sarajevo and a few outlying areas.

For Further Information:

Banac, Ivo. *With Stalin Against Tito: Cominformist Splits in Yugoslav Communism.* Ithaca, N.Y., 1988.

Beloff, Nora. *Tito's Flawed Legacy: Yugoslavia & the West Since 1939.* Boulder, Colo., 1985.

Clissold, Stephen. *Djilas, The Progress of a Revolutionary.* Middlesex, England, 1983.

Glenny, Misha. *The Fall of Yugoslavia.* London and New York, 1992.

Phillips, John. *Yugoslav Story, 1943–1983.* Belgrade, 1980.

Singleton, Frederick Bernard. *A Short History of the Yugoslav Peoples.* New York, 1985.

Wilson, Duncan. *Tito's Yugoslavia.* New York, 1979.

Zukin, Sharon. *Beyond Marx and Tito: Theory and Practice in Yugoslav Socialism.* New York, 1975.

Z

Zapotocky, Antonin **(December 19, 1884–November 13, 1957)** Antonin Zapotocky was a key figure in the Czechoslovak Communist Party. As leader of the trade unions, he played a major role in the communist coup of 1948. Under the leadership of KLEMENT GOTTWALD he implemented widespread socialization and purges, and from 1953 to 1957 he was president of CZECHOSLOVAKIA.

Zapotocky was drafted into the Austro-Hungarian Army in 1914 and fought in Italy and the Balkans. After World War I, he returned to his home town and entered radical socialist politics. In 1920 he was arrested for his involvement in a series of industrial disturbances and was sentenced to two-and-a-half-years' imprisonment. After his release, Zapotocky joined the newly formed Communist Party and was quickly named to the powerful and important position of secretary of the Prague branch.

Zapotocky was elected to the Czechoslovak parliament in 1925 and retained his seat until the Germans marched into Czechoslovakia in 1939. Zapotocky was also secretary-general of the Communist Trade Union from 1929 to 1939. He remained in Czechoslovakia after the German invasion. He was captured and sent to a concentration camp, where he remained until released by the Soviet Red Army. He immediately returned to Prague where he served as chairman of the Czechoslovak Revolutionary Trade Union, which was composed of all of Czechoslovakia's organized trade unions but through Zapotocky's leadership quickly came under the control of the Communist Party.

Czechoslovakia in the immediate postwar period was the only Eastern Bloc country with a free government and was seen by many in the West as a test case for Soviet intentions in Eastern Europe. But after President EDVARD BENES resigned in June 1948, he was immediately succeeded by Klement Gottwald, who appointed Zapotocky premier and promoted him to the party politburo.

Gottwald, as leader of the party and president, was the leading figure in Czechoslovakia, but Zapotocky was given the key task of seeing that Gottwald's orders were implemented. These included Stalinist-type purges of all noncommunists and party deviationists, which involved thousands of arrests, show trials, imprisonments and executions. He also enforced collectivization of the agricultural system and a shift from the production of consumer items to heavy industry.

Gottwald died in March 1953. He was succeeded as president by Zapotocky and as party leader by ANTONIN NOVOTNY, who together continued Gottwald's Stalinist policies. Within a few months, they were faced with antigovernment riots in Pilsen and other industrial cities. The new president responded with a purge of Czech trade unions on the grounds that they hid "former entrepreneurs and bourgeois who inspired panic, unrest and hostile acts."

Zapotocky and Novotny kept Czechoslovakia's foreign policy closely allied with that of the Soviet Union and in 1955 made Czechoslovakia a founding member of the WARSAW PACT. Under Zapotocky, Czechoslovakia also played a role in the Middle East by helping to supply arms to the government of Egyptian leader GAMAL ABDEL NASSER.

Zapotocky's greatest achievement, however, was maintaining a firm control on the domestic situation while neighboring POLAND and HUNGARY were torn apart by riots and revolution in 1956. But by 1957, fresh cracks were also appearing within the Czechoslovak Communist Party. In July 1957, Soviet Communist Party leader NIKITA KHRUSHCHEV and Soviet premier NIKOLAI BULGANIN visited Prague to warn Zapotocky and Novotny to maintain order in their own party. The communiqué at the end of the meeting called on all communists to exercise their "sacred duty" in "unflagging struggle" against "all expression of factionalism" within their parties. Zapotocky was preparing for a fresh purge of the party ranks when he died on November 13, 1957. He was succeeded by Novotny, who continued the Stalinist policies of his predecessors.

For Further Information:
Silnitsky, Frantisek, et al., *Communism and Eastern Europe*. New York, 1979.
Tokes, Rudolf, ed. *Opposition in Eastern Europe*. Baltimore, 1979.
Valenta, J. *Soviet Intervention in Czechoslovakia, 1968: Anatomy of a Decision*. Baltimore, 1979.

Zhivkov, Todor **(September 7, 1911–)** Todor Zhivkov was the leader of the Bulgarian Communist Party from 1954 to 1989, making him the longest-serving East European leader. He established one of the most pro-Soviet and repressive governments in Eastern Europe before being forced to resign by reformers in 1989.

Zhivkov's formal education stopped after he attended the

High School of Drawing and Engraving in Sofia, where he trained as a print worker. The Bulgarian print unions were at that stage almost completely controlled by the Bulgarian Communist Party, and Zhivkov joined their ranks in 1932.

Bulgaria sided with the Axis powers during World War II. After the German attack on the Soviet Union, he joined the communist underground organizing armed resistance to the government and German forces in the country. In September 1944, the right-wing Bulgarian government was overthrown and replaced with a government led by the communist-dominated Fatherland Front. The communists secured the key government posts, which enabled them to liquidate several thousand opponents in 1945 and placed them in a position to win the elections held in 1946.

At the height of the purges, Zhivkov became a candidate member of the Central Committee. He became a full member in 1948 when he was also named general secretary of the party in the capital of Sofia. By 1950, Zhivkov had attracted the attention of Bulgaria's Stalinist leader Vulko Chervenkov, who promoted Zhivkov to the secretariat of the Central Committee and the following year made him a member of the Politburo.

After the death of Stalin in March 1953, Chervenkov came under strong pressure to relinquish either the premiership or the leadership of the Bulgarian Communist Party. Believing that Zhivkov was a loyal lieutenant, he appointed him leader of the party while retaining the premiership. But Chervenkov had lost Moscow's support. Zhivkov, after carefully cultivating NIKITA KHRUSHCHEV, managed in 1962 to secure Khrushchev's support for a successful challenge to Chervenkov and assumed the additional title of premier.

In April 1965 reform-minded members of the Communist Party attempted to overthrow Zhivkov and develop a policy more independent of the Soviet Union. The plot was discovered at the last minute and crushed. Zhivkov said a week afterward, "There is no force that can separate Bulgaria from the Soviet Union."

Zhivkov went on to earn a reputation as the leader of the Soviet Union's most loyal satellite. He denounced the Chinese Communist Party; Bulgarian troops participated in the 1968 WARSAW PACT invasion of CZECHOSLOVAKIA, which crushed the Prague Spring reform movement; and Bulgaria was the first East European country to join the Soviet Union in the boycott of the 1984 Los Angeles Olympics. In return for this loyalty, Zhivkov was in 1977 awarded the title of Hero of the Soviet Union.

In the 1970s Zhivkov oversaw a general improvement in relations between Bulgaria and the West alongside the improvement in U.S.–Soviet relations. But relations between Bulgaria and the West, and in particular between Bulgaria and Italy, became strained in November 1982 after Mehmet Ali Agca, a Turkish citizen, claimed Bulgarian involvement in his attempt to assassinate Pope JOHN PAUL II in 1981. Another cause of conflict between Bulgaria and the West was Zhivkov's policy of forced "Bulgarization" of the ethnic Turk-

ish minority; its repressive excess caused thousands of ethnic Turks to flee across the border into Turkey. In 1989 Soviet leader MIKHAIL GORBACHEV pointed out to Zhivkov that the policy was damaging Bulgaria's international reputation. There were also disputes with Greece over Bulgaria's diversion of the Nestos River and with Yugoslavia over Macedonia.

Zhivkov ruled Bulgaria as an old-style Stalinist leader. Signs of a Stalinist-type personality cult were evident throughout Bulgaria. Zhivkov's portrait was omnipresent, as were his words. He regularly broadcast long and didactic speeches on television. Other political figures were denied any opportunity to present a challenge to Zhivkov through his policy of regularly rotating those serving in party and government posts in order to prevent anyone from developing a political base.

In the 1970s Zhivkov also displayed dynastic ambitions by promoting his daughter, Lyudmila Zhivkova, to the Politburo. She was also made chairman of the State Committee on Culture. Her sudden death in 1981 was a major setback for Zhivkov's plans.

Zhivkov at first appeared to be in total control of Bulgaria in the latter part of the 1980s while the rest of Eastern Europe went through the turmoil of political and economic reform. His only major problem, it seemed, was opposition to his policy of the Bulgarization of the ethnic Turkish minority. But the introduction of Mikhail Gorbachev's *glasnost* and *perestroika* policies forced Zhivkov to take the same road, as he had based his government on slavish adherence to the policies of whoever was in power in Moscow.

But it quickly became apparent to Zhivkov and the party leadership that a man who had become intimately identified with Stalinist methods could not successfully introduce *perestroika* in Bulgaria. He was forced to resign on November 10, 1989, and was replaced by Petur Mladenov.

The following month, Zhivkov was expelled from the party and placed under house arrest while the Bulgarian parliament launched an investigation into charges of corruption. On September 4, 1992, Zhivkov was convicted of embezzlement and sentenced to seven years in prison. He became the first of Eastern Europe's ousted communist rulers to be convicted in a court of law.

For Further Information:
Brown, James F. *Bulgaria Under Communist Rule*. London, 1970.
Fischer-Galati, G.S., ed. *Eastern Europe in the 1980s*. London, 1980.
Linden, Ronald, ed. *The Foreign Relations of Eastern Europe*. New York, 1980.
Silnitsky, Frantisek, et al., eds. *Communism and Eastern Europe*. New York, 1979.

Zhukov, Georgi Konstantinovich (1896–June 18, 1974)
Marshal Georgi Konstantinovich Zhukov was the commander of the Red Army that defeated Hitler and occupied Eastern Europe. His immense popularity led Stalin to relegate him to minor posts, but Zhukov regained some of his influence

Marshal Georgi Zhukov, commander of the Soviet Army that defeated Hitler and occupied Eastern Europe, in 1971. Photo courtesy of Novosti Press Agency.

following the dictator's death and from 1955 to 1957 was Soviet minister of defense.

Zhukov served as a conscript in the Russian Imperial Army during World War I and as a cavalry commander with the Red Army during the civil war that followed the 1917 Bolshevik Revolution. Because of his early achievements he was given a place at the Frunze Military Academy and later was sent to study military tactics in Germany.

In ᴊ9, Zhukov established a reputation as an expert in the deployment of armor during Soviet clashes with the Japanese along the Mongolian–Manchurian border near Nomonhan. Zhukov's success against the Japanese led the Japanese Imperial General Staff to construct a policy of avoiding war with the Soviet Union. This enabled the Soviet Union to concentrate its forces on its western front after the German invasion in June 1941.

At the start of World War II, Zhukov was chief of staff of the Soviet army. He was transferred to command the Kiev military district and in January 1941 was appointed chief of the General Staff. After the German invasion of the Soviet Union, he commanded the defense of both Leningrad and Moscow, and the counteroffensive against the German forces, which started in December 1941. In January 1943, Zhukov was made a marshal of the Soviet Union and became JOSEF

STALIN's chief military planner, first as deputy supreme commander under Stalin and than as commander in chief of the Red Army. In April 1945, Zhukov personally commanded the final assault on Berlin.

In the immediate postwar period, Zhukov was in command of the Red Army that occupied all of Eastern Europe, and the structures he established played an important role in ensuring continued Soviet dominance in the region. He was also the Soviet representative on the Allied Control Commission for Germany and was personally responsible for the administration of the Soviet occupation zone in Germany.

Zhukov's adroit handling of the Western military commanders resulted in a number of major diplomatic achievements and ensured Soviet control of eastern Germany. The most significant of these achievements occurred in June 1945 when the British and American representatives met with Zhukov at his Berlin headquarters to point out that their forces had no formal access routes to their sectors of Berlin. Zhukov maintained that such access was a privilege to be granted by the Soviet occupation authorities rather than a right to be assumed by the Western powers. The Western representatives' reluctant acceptance of this point was later used by Soviet authorities to justify their closure of the access routes between West Germany and Berlin.

Zhukov returned to Moscow in 1946 as a popular hero. But his very popularity caused his fall from power. Stalin, in 1946, was on the verge of one of his paranoid purges. Zhukov's popularity was viewed by the dictator as a threat to his own position, and he removed Zhukov from command of the Red Army and relegated him to a series of provincial posts.

Zhukov, however, remained a popular figure with the army, and after Stalin's death in March 1953 the new leaders brought him back to Moscow as the deputy minister of defense in order to ensure the support of the military. In the subsequent power struggle within the Politburo, Zhukov supported NIKITA KHRUSHCHEV against GEORGI MALENKOV because of the latter's proposals to reduce defense spending. In February 1955 Khrushchev forced the resignation of Malenkov and moved NIKOLAI BULGANIN from the defense ministry to the premiership. As his reward, Zhukov was promoted to the post of minister of defense and elected a candidate member of the Politburo.

As minister of defense, Zhukov was part of the five-man Soviet delegation at the four-power GENEVA HEADS OF GOVERNMENT SUMMIT in July 1955. His wartime experiences had allowed him to form a closer relationship with President DWIGHT EISENHOWER than the other members of the Soviet delegation—Bulganin, Khrushchev, MOLOTOV and GROMYKO. In the middle of the summit, on July 22, Eisenhower invited Zhukov to his villa for a private meeting in an unsuccessful attempt to reach a diplomatic breakthrough.

Zhukov remained primarily a soldier. He organized the Soviet invasion of Hungary in 1956 and executed a major overhaul of the armed forces. This involved extensive retraining, replacing artillery with missiles and increasing the mobility of the army in order to improve its offensive capability. But Zhukov's reorganization also emphasized traditional military structures rather than the political indoctrination programs insisted upon by the party. This put Zhukov into conflict with Khrushchev, and for a time the CIA had reports that Zhukov was planning a coup.

Khrushchev was at this time indeed facing growing opposition, from a faction known as the antiparty group, which included Malenkov and Molotov. In June 1957 they moved against Khrushchev during a crucial meeting of the Communist Party Central Committee. Zhukov threw his support behind Khrushchev and played a vital role in shifting the balance of power by providing airplanes to fly absent Central Committee members back to Moscow for a vital vote. As a reward for this service, Zhukov was promoted to full membership in the Politburo.

In his enhanced position, Zhukov attempted to push through his proposed reorganization. Khrushchev, however, remained adamantly opposed to the changes and on October 26, 1957, dismissed the man he had promoted only a few months before. Zhukov went back into the political wilderness until Khrushchev's fall from power in October 1964, when he was again rehabilitated. He was awarded the Order of Lenin in 1966, but he never again played a major role in Soviet policy making.

For Further Information:
Zhukov, Georgi. *The Memoirs of Marshal Zhukov*. New York, 1971.

Zumwalt, Elmo   (November 29, 1920–   )   Admiral Elmo Zumwalt was U.S. chief of naval operations during the NIXON administration. He successfully campaigned for the TRIDENT missile system and, after leaving office, became a vociferous critic of détente and the SALT process.

Zumwalt graduated from the U.S. Naval Academy at Annapolis in 1942 and saw service on a number of destroyers during and after World War II. In 1948 he was appointed an assistant professor of naval science at the Naval War College in Washington, D.C. While there he delivered a lecture on "The Problems of Succession in the Kremlin," which attracted the attention of PAUL NITZE.

When Nitze became secretary of the navy in 1963, he made Zumwalt his executive assistant. In 1965 Zumwalt was promoted to admiral and given command of a cruiser–destroyer flotilla. The following year he started a two-year tour of duty in Vietnam as commander of U.S. naval forces and chief of the naval advisory group.

In July 1970, Zumwalt returned to Washington as chief of naval operations and introduced a number of controversial reforms. These included the relaxation of regulations regarding dress, conduct and shore leave. He also started a program to recruit more black naval officers and open all navy jobs to women, including general sea duty. The reforms encountered strong opposition from naval traditionalists, and after being forced to discharge 3,000 enlisted men deemed a "burden to

command" in 1973, recruitment standards were revised to emphasize educational and "character" qualifications.

As chief of naval operations, Zumwalt became increasingly concerned about the buildup of the Soviet navy under Admiral SERGEI GORSHKOV. Faced with budget restraints, he tried to offset the overall reduction in the size of the U.S. fleet with increases in specific areas. These included support for the F-14 navy fighter jet to boost air attack capability; more small, high-speed ships; and the controversial Trident missile program.

In April 1971, Zumwalt told the House Armed Services Committee that updating America's fleet was necessary to maintain nuclear parity with the Soviet Union, to enable the navy to provide greater logistical support to other nations, to balance an increasingly powerful Soviet navy and to compensate for the small number of new ships built during the VIETNAM WAR. Shortly before his retirement in July 1974 Zumwalt claimed that the U.S. Navy would be unable to maintain control of the seas in the event of war with the Soviet Union. The claim was disputed by his successor, Admiral James L. Holloway.

In retirement, Zumwalt became a stern critic of Secretary of State HENRY KISSINGER and his détente policy. In December 1975 he appeared before the House Select Committee on Intelligence to charge that Kissinger had withheld information from President GERALD FORD about "gross violations" by the Soviet Union of the 1972 ANTIBALLISTIC MISSILE (ABM) TREATY and the interim Strategic Arms Limitation Treaty (SALT I, see STRATEGIC ARMS LIMITATION TALKS). Zumwalt suggested that Kissinger's lack of candor was the result of a personal and political commitment to U.S.–Soviet détente that made him "reluctant to report the actual facts."

Zumwalt launched another bitter attack on Kissinger in his book *On Watch*, published in 1976. He claimed in the book that in a conversaton he had had with Kissinger, the secretary of state had compared the United States to Athens and the Soviet Union to an up-and-coming Sparta. He quoted Kissinger as saying, "The day of the U.S. is past and today is the day of the Soviet Union. My job as Secretary of State is to negotiate the most acceptable second-best position available." Both attacks were dismissed by Kissinger, who claimed that Zumwalt "got carried away by his political ambitions."

Zumwalt's political ambitions at the time were a seat in the U.S. Senate, and in 1976 he ran as the Democratic candidate in Virginia but failed to defeat the incumbent independent senator, Harry F. Byrd. He continued to speak out on foreign and defense issues, however, and joined the right-wing Committee on the Present Danger, which called for large increases in defense spending.

For Further Information:
Zumwalt, Elmo. *On Watch*. New York, 1976.

Zwicker, Ralph W.   (April 17, 1903–   )   General Ralph W. Zwicker was an unwitting but key figure in the political downfall of Senator JOSEPH MCCARTHY.

Zwicker was a graduate of the U.S. Military Academy at West Point and a hero of the D-Day landings at Normandy. In 1953 he was in command of Camp Kilmer, New Jersey where an army dentist, Major Irving Peress, was promoted while his loyalty was being probed by Senator McCarthy's investigators. Three days later Peress was honorably discharged.

McCarthy insisted that Peress was a communist and that he be courtmartialed. On February 18, 1954, he hauled Zwicker before his Government Operations Committee's Permanent Investigations Subcommittee and insisted that he name the officers responsible for Peress's discharge.

McCarthy was the only subcommittee member present at the hearing, which was held behind closed doors in New York. When Zwicker refused to disclose the identities of the superior officers who had ordered the discharge, McCarthy launched a vicious attack on the general's character and intelligence. He said that Zwicker was "not fit to wear that uniform," should "be removed from any command" and did not have "the brains of a five-year-old." Later, McCarthy accused the army of "coddling Communists." Zwicker later said the McCarthy's account of the closed hearings was "so colored and slanted" that it was "not truthful."

The attack on the army and Zwicker convinced Army Secretary Robert Stevens that McCarthy was unbalanced and must be opposed. He refused to allow Zwicker to appear before McCarthy again because, he said, "I cannot permit loyal officers of our Armed Forces to be subjected to such unwarranted treatment." Stevens was forced to back down, but it

was a Pyrrhic victory for McCarthy. At the time, the U.S. Army was one of America's most respected institutions. McCarthy's bullying of Zwicker and Stevens united conservatives and liberals in a counterattack against the senator.

On March 11 the army responded to McCarthy by charging the senator and his legal aide Roy Cohn with seeking preferential treatment for an army draftee, David Schine. McCarthy responded by accusing the army of holding his former aide as a hostage to blackmail him into ending his investigation of communism in the Armed Forces. The result was the televised Army–McCarthy hearings, which opened on April 22, 1954. Throughout the hearings, McCarthy came across as an ill-informed and abusive bully, while military officers projected themselves as intelligent and honorable. A few months after the hearings ended, McCarthy was censured by the Senate.

Soon after his confrontation with McCarthy, Zwicker was transferred to Japan, where he was assistant chief of staff for American military personnel in the Far East. In 1957 he was promoted to major general. During hearings conducted by the Senate Armed Services Committee into his nomination, Zwicker admitted that he may have been uncooperative toward McCarthy. But he said this was to avoid accidentally revealing classified information. McCarthy used this statement to try to retrieve his reputation by having Zwicker charged with perjury. He failed, and Zwicker's promotion was approved with only McCarthy and Senator George Malone dissenting.

BIBLIOGRAPHY

LATIN AMERICA AND THE CARIBBEAN

Adams, Jan S. *A Foreign Policy in Transition: Moscow's Retreat From Central America & the Caribbean.* Durham, N.C., 1992.

Ashby, T. *The Bear in the Backyard.* Lexington, Mass., 1987.

Berle, Adolf A., Jr. *Latin America: Diplomacy and Reality.* New York, 1962.

Berman, Karl. *Under the Big Stick: Nicaragua and the United States Since 1848.* Boston, 1986.

Bonachea, Roland, and Nelson P. Valdes, eds. *Che: Selected Works of Che Guevara.* Cambridge, Mass., 1969.

Bonsal, Philip W. *Cuba, Castro and the United States.* Pittsburgh, 1971.

Burns, E.B. *At War in Nicaragua.* New York, 1987.

Burrowes, R.A. *Revolution and Rescue in Grenada.* Westport, Conn., 1988.

Dunkerley, James. *The Long War: Dictatorship and Revolution in El Salvador.* London, 1982.

———. *Power in the Isthmus.* London, 1988.

Feinberg, Richard E., ed. *Central America: International Dimensions of the Crisis.* New York, 1982.

Gettleman, Marvin, et al., eds. *El Salvador: Central America in the New Cold War.* New York, 1986.

Gutman, R. *Banana Diplomacy.* New York, 1988.

Harris, Richard L. *Marxism, Socialism & Democracy in Latin America.* Boulder, Colo., 1992.

James, Daniel. *Che Guevara.* New York, 1970.

Lumar, Shiv. *U.S. Intervention in Latin America.* Chicago, 1987.

Martin, John Barlow. *Overtaken by Events: The Dominican Crisis from the Fall of Trujillo to the Civil War.* New York, 1966.

Miller, Nicola. *Soviet Relations with Latin America, 1959–1987.* New York, 1989.

Petras, James F. *The United States and Chile: Imperialism and the Overthrow of the Allende Government.* New York, 1975.

Shearman, P. *The Soviet Union and Cuba.* New York, 1987.

Sklas, Holly. *Washington's War on Nicaragua.* Boston, 1988.

Slater, Jerome. *Intervention and Negotiation: The United States and the Dominican Intervention.* New York, 1970.

Szulc, Tad. *Fidel: A Critical Portrait.* New York, 1986.

Tulchin, Joseph S. and Hernandez, Rafael, eds. *Cuba & the United States: Will the Cold War in the Caribbean End?* Boulder, Colo., 1991.

Uribe Arce, Armando. *The Black Book of American Intervention in Chile.* Boston, 1975.

WESTERN EUROPE

Adenauer, Konrad. *Memoirs,* 4 vols. New York, 1966–1967, 1968.

Alison, Roy. *Finland's Relations with the Soviet Union, 1944–1984.* New York, 1985.

Aldrich, Robert, and John Connell, eds. *France in World Politics.* New York, 1989.

Archer, Clive. *Nordic Nuclear Free Zone.* Oslo, 1984.

Augstein, Rudolf. *Konrad Adenauer.* London, 1964.

Ausland, John. *Nordic Security and the Great Powers.* Boulder, Colo., 1986.

Bader, William. *Austria Between East and West, 1945–1955.* Stanford, Calif., 1966.

Beyme, Klaus von, and Hartmut Zimmerman, eds. *Policy Making in the German Democratic Republic.* Aldershot, Hants., England, 1984.

Blackmer, Donald, and Sidney Farrow. *Communism in Italy and France.* Princeton, 1975.

Brandt, Willy. *People and Politics.* New York, 1978.

———. *The Ordeal of Coexistence.* Cambridge, Mass., 1963.

Brant, Stefan. *The East German Rising.* London, 1954.

Campbell, John, ed. *Successful Negotiation: Trieste 1954.* Princeton, 1976.

Carr, J. *Helmut Schmidt.* New York, 1985.

Carrillo, Elisa. *Alcide de Gasperi.* Notre Dame, Ind., 1965.

Childs, David. *The GDR: Moscow's German Ally.* New York, 1983.

Crawley, A.M. *The Rise of West Germany, 1945–1972.* New York, 1974.

Cromwell, William C. *The United States & the European Pillar: The Strained Alliance.* New York, 1992.

Cronin, Austrey Kurth. *Great Power Politics and the Struggle Over Austria, 1945–1955.* Ithaca, N.Y., 1986.

Crozier, Brian. *Franco: A Biographical History.* London, 1967.

Danish Information and Welfare Service. *Brief Introduction to Danish Foreign Policy and Defense.* Copenhagen, 1989.

Davis, Franklin M. *Come as a Conqueror; the United States Army's Occupation of Germany, 1945–1949.* New York, 1967.

Davison, Walter Phillips. *The Berlin Blockade: A Study in Cold War Politics*. Princeton, 1958.

Derry, Thomas. *A History of Modern Norway*. Oxford, 1973.

Donoughue, Bernard. *Prime Minister: The Conduct of Policy under Harold Wilson and James Callaghan*. London, 1987.

Ellul, J. *The Political Illusion*. New York, 1973.

Fisher, Nigel. *Harold Macmillan*. London, 1982.

Frankel, Joseph. *British Foreign Policy 1945–1973*. New York, 1975.

Fritsch-Bournazel, Renata. *Confronting the German Question*. Oxford, 1988.

Gilbert, Martin. *Winston S. Churchill, 1945–1965*. London, 1988.

Griffiths, William. *The Ostpolitik of the Federal Republic of Germany*. Cambridge, Mass., 1978.

Grosser, Alfred. *The Western Alliance: European–American Relations Since 1945*. New York, 1980.

Grove, Eric, ed. *NATO's Defense of the North*. London, 1989.

Harris, George S. *Turkey: Coping with Crisis*. Boulder, Colo., 1985.

Harris, Kenneth. *Attlee*. London, 1982.

Hartley, Anthony. *Gaullism: The Rise and Fall of a Political Movement*. New York, 1972.

Haskel, Barbara G. *The Scandinavian Option: Opportunities and Opportunity Costs in Postwar Scandinavian Foreign Policies*. Oslo, 1976.

Healey, Denis. *The Time of My Life*. London, 1989.

———. *Labour and a World Society*. London, 1985.

———. *Labour, Britain and the World*. London, 1963.

Heath, Edward. *Europe*. London, 1990.

———. *A British Approach to European Foreign Policy*. Leeds, England, 1986.

Hoffman, Stanley. *Decline or Renewal?: France since the 1930s*. New York, 1974.

Home, Lord. *The Way the Wind Blows*. London, 1976.

Horne, Alistair. *Macmillan, 1957–1986*. London, 1989.

Howley, F. *Berlin Command*. New York, 1950.

Hughes, H. Stuart. *The United States and Italy*. Cambridge, Mass., 1965.

James, Robert Rhodes. *Anthony Eden*. London, 1986.

Jonas, M. *The U.S. and West Germany*. New York, 1985.

Johnsson, Albert. *Iceland, NATO and the Keflavik Base*. Reykjavik, 1989.

Kennan, George F. *The Fateful Alliance*. New York, 1984.

Kirby, D.G. *Finland in the Twentieth Century*. Minneapolis, 1980.

Kogan, Norman. *A Political History of Postwar Italy: From the Old to the New Center Left*. New York, 1981.

Koivisto, Mauno. *Landmarks, Finland in the World*. Helsinki, 1985.

Korhonen, Kujo, ed. *Urho Kekkonen: A Statesman for Peace*. Helsinki, 1975.

Kuklick, Bruce. *American Policy and the Division of Germany: The Clash with Russia over Reparations*. Ithaca, N.Y., 1972.

Laqueur, Walter. *Europe in Our Time: A History*. New York, 1992.

Ledeen, M. *West European Communism and American Foreign Policy*. New York, 1987.

Lippmann, Heinz. *Honecker*. Cologne, 1971.

Lodge, J. *Institutions and Policies of the European Community*. London, 1983.

Louis, William Roger, and Hedley Bull. *The "Special Relationship:" Anglo-American Relations since 1945*. Oxford, 1986.

Lundestad, Geir. *America, Scandinavia and the Cold War*. New York, 1980.

Mander, J. *Berlin: The Eagle and the Bear*. New York, 1962.

Maude, George. *The Finnish Dilemma: Neutrality in the Shadow of Power*. New York, 1976.

McCauley, Martin. *The German Democratic Republic since 1945*. New York, 1983.

———. *Marxism-Leninism in the GDR: The Socialist Unity Party (SED)*. New York, 1979.

MacKay, D. *The United States and France*. Westport, Conn., 1983.

Maclean, Donald. *British Foreign Policy Since Suez*. New York, 1970.

McNeill, William H. *Greece: American Aid in Action, 1947–1956*. New York, 1956.

Matthews, Kenneth. *Memories of a Mountain War: Greece, 1945–1949*. London, 1972.

Mayne, Richard. *Handbooks to the Modern World: Western Europe*. New York, 1986.

———. *Postwar: The Dawn of Today's Europe*. New York, 1983.

———. *The Recovery of Europe*. London, 1981.

Meisel, James. *The Fall of the Republic*. Ann Arbor, 1962.

Mezerik, A.F., ed. *Berlin and Germany: Berlin Crisis, Wall, Free State, Separate Treaty, Cold War, Chronology*. New York, 1962.

Ministry of Defense. *Defense White Paper 1966–67*. London, 1967.

Monnet, Jean. *Memoirs*. Garden City, N.Y., 1978.

NATO Facts and Figures. Brussels, 1985.

Newhouse, John. *De Gaulle and the Anglo-Saxons*. New York, 1970.

Nicholas, Peter. *Italia, Italia*. New York, 1974.

Novak, Bogdan. *Trieste, 1941–1954*. Chicago, 1970.

O'Ballance, Edgar. *The Greek Civil War, 1944–1949*.

Nunnerly, David. *President Kennedy and Britain*. New York, 1972.

Petersen, Nikolaj. *Denmark and Nato, 1949 to 1987*. Copenhagen, 1987.

Pfetsch, Frank. *West Germany, Internal Structures and External Relations: The Foreign Policy of the Federal Republic*. New York, 1988.

Pittman, Avril. *From Ostpolitic to Reunification: West German-Soviet Political Relations Since 1974*. New York, 1992.

Porck, Douglas. *The Portuguese Armed Forces and the Revolution*. Stanford, Calif., 1977.

Prittie, Terence. *Willy Brandt*. London, 1974.

———. *Konrad Adenauer*. London, 1972.

———. *The Velvet Chancellors*. New York, 1979.

Puntila, L.A. *The Political History of Finland*. Helsinki, 1975.

Riess, Curt. *Berlin Story*. Toronto, 1952.

Robinson, Richard. *Contemporary Portugal: A History*. Boston, 1979.

Rozakis, Christos, and Petros N. Stagos. *The Turkish Straits*. Boston, 1987.

Ryan, H.B. *The Vision of Anglo-America*. Cambridge, 1987.

Sassoon, Donald. *The Strategy of the Italian Communist Party: From the Resistance to the Historic Compromise*. London, 1981.

Schulz, Eberhard, ed. *GDR Foreign Policy*. New York, 1982.

Stern, Carola. *Ulbricht: A Political Biography*. New York, 1965.

Strauss, Franz Joseph. *The Grand Design*. New York, 1965.

Taylor, William, Jr., and Paul Cole, eds. *Nordic Defense Comparative Decision Making*. Lexington, Mass., 1985.

Tokes, R.L. *Euro-Communism and Detente*. New York, 1978.

Treverton, G.F. *Making the Alliance Work: The United States and Europe*. Ithaca, N.Y., 1985.

Treverton, Gregory F. *America, Germany & the Future of Europe*. Princeton, 1992.

Trythall, J.W.D. *Franco*. London, 1970.

Turner, Arthur Campbell. *The Unique Partnership: Britain and the United States*. New York, 1971.

Tusa, Ann, and John Tusa. *The Berlin Blockade*. New York, 1989.

Udgaard, Nils Morten. *Great Power Politics and Norwegian Foreign Policy: A Study of Norway's Foreign Relations, November 1940–February 1948*. Oslo, 1973.

University of Leicester. *The Foreign Policy of the British Labour Governments, 1945–1951*. Leicester, England, 1984.

United States Department of State. *Documents on Germany, 1944–1985*. Washington, D.C., 1986.

Urban, Joan. *Moscow and the Italian Communist Party: From Togliatti to Berlinguer*. Ithaca, N.Y., 1986.

Vali, Ferenc A. *The Turkish Straits and NATO*. Stanford, Calif., 1972.

Viola, T. *Willy Brandt*. London, 1989.

Wapshott, Nicholas, and George Brock. *Thatcher*. London, 1983.

Wegs, J. Robert. *Europe Since 1945: A Concise History*. London, 1984.

Whetten, Lawrence. *Germany East and West*. New York, 1980.

Williams, Philip. *Crisis and Compromise: Politics in the Fourth Republic*. London, 1964.

Wilson, Harold. *Memoirs, The Making of a Prime Minister, 1916–1964*. London, 1986.

———. *Memoirs, Final Term: The Labour Government, 1974–1976*. London, 1979.

———. *Memoirs, The Governance of Britain*. London, 1976.

———. *Memoirs, The Labour Government, 1964–1970*. London, 1971.

Wiskemann, Elizabeth. *Italy Since 1945*. New York, 1971.

Young, John W. *Cold War Europe, 1945–89*. New York, 1991.

ESPIONAGE

Agee, Philip. *Inside the Company: CIA Diary*. New York, 1975.

Ambrose, Stephen E. *Ike's Spies: Eisenhower and the Espionage Establishment*. Garden City, N.Y., 1981.

Andrew, C. *Secret Service*. London, 1985.

Bamford, James. *The Puzzle Palace*. Boston, 1982.

Barron, John. *KGB: The Secret Work of Soviet Secret Agents*. New York, 1974.

Beck, Melvin. *Secret Contenders: The Myth of Cold War Counterintelligence*. New York, 1984.

Berman, Jerry J., and Morton H. Halperin, eds. *The Abuses of the Intelligence Agencies*. Washington, D.C., 1975.

Beschloss, Michael R. *Mayday: Eisenhower, Khrushchev and the U-2 Affair*. New York, 1986.

Bialoguski, Michael. *The Case of Colonel Petrov*. New York, 1955.

Bittman, Ladislav. *The Deception Game: Czechoslovak Intelligence in Soviet Political Warfare*. Syracuse, N.Y., 1972.

Boyle, Andrew. *The Climate of Treason*. London, 1979.

Breckinridge, Scott. *The CIA and the U.S. Intelligence System*. Boulder, Colo., 1986.

Bulloch, John, and Henry Miller. *Spy Ring*. London, 1961.

Buranelli, Vincent, and Nan Buranelli. *Spy/Counterspy: An Encyclopedia of Espionage*. New York, 1982.

Cline, Ray S. *The CIA: Reality vs. Myth*. Washington, D.C., 1982.

Colby, William, and Peter Forbath. *Honorable Men: My Life in the CIA*. New York, 1978.

Cookridge, E.F. *Gehlen: Spy of the Century*. London, 1971.

Copeland, Miles. *Without Cloak or Dagger*. New York, 1975.

Dallin, David J. *Soviet Espionage*. New Haven, Conn., 1963.

Dulles, Allen W. *The Craft of Intelligence*. New York, 1963.

Earley, Pete. *Family of Spies: Inside the Walker Spy Ring*. New York, 1989.

Gehlen, Reinhold. *The Gehlen Memoirs*. London, 1972.

Hagen, Louis. *The Secret War for Europe*. New York, 1969.

Kessler, Ronald. *Escape From the CIA: How the CIA Won & Lost the Most Important KGB Spy Ever to Defect to the US*. New York, 1991.

Knightley, Phillip. *The Second Oldest Profession*. London, 1986.

———. *Philby: KGB Masterspy*. London, 1988.

Marchenko, Anatoly. *My Testimony*. New York, 1969.

Marchetti, Victor, and John D. Marks. *The CIA and the Cult of Intelligence*. New York, 1974.

O'Toole, G.J.A. *The Encyclopedia of American Intelligence and Espionage*. New York, 1988.

Penkovsky, Oleg. *The Penkovsky Papers*. New York, 1965.

Philby, Kim. *My Silent War*. New York, 1968.

Powers, Francis Gary, and Curt Gentry. *Operation Overflight*. New York, 1970.

Ranelagh, John. *The Agency: The Rise and Decline of the CIA*. New York, 1986.

Richelson, Jeffrey T. *The U.S. Intelligence Community*. Cambridge, Mass., 1985.

Romanov, A.I. *Nights Are Longest There: Smersh from the Inside*. London, 1972.

Schecter, Jerrold, and Peter Deriabin. *The Spy Who Saved the World: How a Soviet Colonel Changed the Course of the Cold War*. New York, 1992.

U.S. Commission on CIA Activities within the United States. *Report to the President by the Commission on CIA Activities within the United States*. Washington, D.C., 1975.

U.S. Senate, Select Committee on Intelligence Activities. *Alleged Assassination Plots Involving Foreign Leaders*. Washington, D.C., 1975.

———. *Intelligence Activities and the Rights of Americans*. Washington, D.C., 1976.

Wise, David, and Thomas B. Ross. *The Invisible Government*. New York, 1964.

Wright, Peter, *Spycatcher: The Candid Autobiography of a Senior Intelligence Officer*. New York, 1987.

EASTERN EUROPE

Ascherson, Neal. *The Struggle for Poland*. New York, 1988.

———. *The Polish August*. New York, 1982.

Auty, Phyllis. *Tito*. New York, 1970.

Bermeo, Nancy, ed. *Liberalization & Democratization: Change in the Soviet Union & Eastern Europe*. Baltimore, 1992.

Bethell, Nicholas. *Gomulka: His Poland and His Communism*. London, 1969.

Boll, Michael. *Cold War in the Balkans: American Foreign Policy and the Emergence of Communist Bulgaria, 1943–1947*. Lexington, Ky., 1984.

Brock, Peter. *The Slovak National Awakening*. Toronto, 1976.

Bromke, Adam, and John Strong. *Gierek's Poland*. New York, 1973.

Brumberg, Abraham, ed. *Poland: Genesis of a Revolution*. New York, 1983.

Brown, James F. *Bulgaria Under Communist Rule*. London, 1970.

Brzezinski, Zbigniew. *The Soviet Bloc: Unity and Conflict*. Cambridge, Mass., 1960.

Cynkin, T.M. *Soviet and American Signalling in the Polish Crisis*. New York, 1988.

Davies, Norman. *Heart of Europe: A Short History of Poland*. Oxford, 1984.

Dunn, Dennis. *Detente and Papal-Communist Relations, 1962–1978*. Boulder, Colo., 1979.

Fischer-Galati, G.S., ed. *Eastern Europe in the 1980s*. London, 1980.

Floyd, David. *Romania, Russia's Dissident Ally.* London, 1965.

Frankland, Mark. *The Patriot's Revolution: How Eastern Europe Toppled Communism & Won Its Freedom.* Salem, Ore., 1992.

Govender, Robert. *Nicolae Ceausescu.* London, 1988.

Hale, Julian. *Ceausescu's Romania, A Political Documentary.* Toronto, 1971.

Halliday, Jon, ed. *The Artful Albanian: Memoirs of Enver Hoxha.* London, 1986.

Havel, Vaclav. *Open Letters: Selected Writings, 1965–90.* New York, 1992.

Keithly, David. *The Collapse of East German Communism: The Year the Wall Came Down.* Westport, Conn., 1992.

Keren, Michael, and Gur Ofer, eds. *Birth Pangs of Market Economies: East-Central Europe in Transition.* Boulder, Colo., 1992.

Kovrig, Bennet. *Communism in Hungary from Kun to Kadar.* Stanford, Calif., 1979.

Lavigne, Marie, ed. *The Soviet Union & Eastern Europe in the Global Economy.* New York, 1992.

Linden, Ronald, ed. *The Foreign Relations of Eastern Europe.* New York, 1980.

MacLean, Fitzroy. *Disputed Barricades: The Life and Times of Josip Broz Tito.* New York, 1957.

———. *Tito: A Pictorial Biography.* New York, 1980.

Menar, Z. *Nightfrost in Prague.* New York, 1980.

Michta, Andrew. *East Central Europe After the Warsaw Pact: Security Dilemmas in the 1990s.* Westport, Conn., 1992.

Mindszenty, Jozsef Cardinal. *Memoirs.* New York, 1974.

Neal, F.W. *Titoism in Action: The Reforms in Yugoslavia after 1948.* New York, 1958.

Persky, Stan. *At the Lenin Shipyard: Poland and the Rise of the Solidarity Trade Union.* Vancouver, 1981.

Pollo, S. *The History of Albania.* New York, 1981.

Pomian-Srzednicki, Maciej. *Religious Change in Contemporary Poland: Secularization and Politics.* London, 1982.

Radu, Michael, ed. *Eastern Europe and the Third World.* New York, 1981.

Schnytzer, A. *Stalinist Economic Strategy in Practice.* Oxford, 1983.

Shafir, Michael. *Romania, Politics, Economics and Society: Political Stagnation and Stimulated Change.* London, 1985.

Sharman, T. *The Rise of Solidarity.* Vero Beach, Fla., 1987.

Silnitsky, Frantisek, et al., eds. *Communism and Eastern Europe.* New York, 1979.

Starr, Richard. F. *East-Central Europe & The USSR.* New York, 1991.

Stehle, Hansjakov. *The Independent Satellite: Society and Politics in Poland since 1945.* London, 1965.

Szakolczai, Arpad, and Agnes Horvath. *The Dissolution of Communist Power: The Case of Hungary.* New York, 1992.

Tokes, Rudolf, ed. *Opposition in Eastern Europe.* Baltimore, 1979.

Valenta, J. *Soviet Intervention in Czechoslovakia, 1968: Anatomy of a Decision.* Baltimore, 1979.

Vali, Ferenc. *A Rift and Revolt in Hungary: Nationalism vs. Communism.* Cambridge, Mass., 1961.

Walesa, Lech. *A Way of Hope.* New York, 1987.

Zinner, Paul. *Revolution in Hungary.* New York, 1962.

UNITED STATES AND CANADA

Acheson, Dean. *Power and Diplomacy.* Cambridge, Mass., 1958.

———. *Sketches from Life.* New York, 1961.

———. *Present at the Creation: My Years in the State Department.* New York, 1969.

Allison, Graham. *The Essence of Decision: Explaining the Cuban Missile Crisis.* Boston, 1971.

Ambrose, Stephen E. *Rise to Globalism: American Foreign Policy, 1938–1976.* Baltimore, 1976.

Balawyder, Aloysius. *Canada-Soviet Relations, 1936–1980.* Winnipeg, Manitoba, 1982.

Barson, Michael. *Better Dead Than Red! A Nostalgic Look at the Golden Years of Russophobia, Red-baiting & Other Commie Madness.* Westport, Conn., 1992.

Berding, Andrew. *Dulles on Diplomacy.* Princeton, 1965.

Berman, W.C. *William Fulbright and the Vietnam War.* Kent, Ohio, 1988.

Bogart, Leo. *Premises for Propaganda: The United States Information Agency's Operation Assumptions in the Cold War.* New York, 1976.

Bothwell, R. *Pearson.* New York, 1978.

Bowles, Chester. *Promises to Keep.* New York, 1971.

Brands, H.W. *Cold Warriors.* New York, 1988.

Brzezinski, Zbigniew. *Power and Principle: Memoirs of the National Security Adviser, 1977–1981.* New York, 1985.

———. *In Quest of National Security.* Boulder, Colo., 1988.

Buckley, William F., Jr., and L. Brent Bozell. *McCarthy and His Enemies: The Record and Its Meaning.* Chicago, 1954.

Buhle, Mari J., et al., eds. *Encyclopedia of the American Left.* Champaign, Ill., 1992.

Carter, Jimmy. *Keeping Faith.* New York, 1982.

Chabot-Smith, John. *Alger Hiss: The True Story.* New York, 1976.

Chace, James. *The Consequences of Peace: The New Internationalism & American Foreign Policy.* New York, 1992.

Chambers, Whittaker. *Witness.* New York, 1952.

Chomsky, Noam. *Deterring Democracy.* New York, 1992.

Clark, Paul F. *American Aid for Development.* New York, 1972.

Cyr, A.I. *U.S. Foreign Policy and European Security.* New York, 1988.

Donovan, John C. *The Cold Warriors: A Policy-Making Elite.* Lexington, Mass., 1974.

Druks, Herbert. *Harry S. Truman and the Russians, 1944–1953.* New York, 1966.

Drummond, Roscoe, and Gaston Coblentz. *Duel at the Brink: John Foster Dulles' Command of American Power.* Garden City, N.Y., 1960.

Eberstadt, Nicholas. *Foreign Aid and American Purpose.* Washington, D.C., 1988.

Feuerlich, Roberta. *Joe McCarthy and McCarthyism: The Hate That Haunts America.* New York, 1972.

Finger, A. *American Ambassadors at the United Nations.* New York, 1988.

Ford, Gerald. *A Time to Heal.* New York, 1979.

Forsythe, D.P. *Human Rights and U.S. Foreign Policy.* Tampa, Fla., 1988.

Fulbright, J. William. *The Arrogance of Power.* New York, 1967.

Galbraith, John Kenneth. *A Life In Our Times: Memoirs.* Boston, 1981.

Goldman, Eric. *The Tragedy of Lyndon Johnson.* New York, 1969.

Goldston, Robert. *The American Nightmare: Senator Joseph R. McCarthy and the Politics of Hate.* Indianapolis, 1973.

Goodman, Walter. *The Committee: The Extraordinary Career of the House Committee on Un-American Activities.* New York, 1968.

Griffith, Robert. *The Politics of Fear: Joseph R. McCarthy and the Senate.* Lexington, Ky., 1970.

Gujiral, M.L. *U.S. Global Involvement: A Study of American Expansionism.* New Delhi, 1975.

Gukin, Michael. *John Foster Dulles: A Statesman and His Times.* New York, 1972.

Hellman, Lillian. *Scoundrel Time.* New York, 1976.

Henderson, John W. *The United States Information Agency.* New York, 1969.

Hilsman, Roger. *To Move a Nation: The Politics of Foreign Policy in the Administration of John F. Kennedy.* Garden City, N.Y., 1967.

Hiss, Alger. *In the Court of Public Opinion.* New York, 1957.

Hoffman, Nicholas von. *Citizen Cohn: The Life and Times of Roy Cohn.* New York, 1988.

Hogan, M.J. *The Marshall Plan.* New York, 1987.

Hoopes, Townsend. *The Limits of Intervention.* New York, 1969.

Hurs, Donald, and John Miller. *The Challenge of Power: Canada and the World.* New York, 1979.

Immerman, Richard H., ed. *John Foster Dulles & the Diplomacy of the Cold War.* Princeton, 1992.

Johns Hopkins University. *The Strategic Defense Initiative and U.S. Foreign Policy.* Baltimore, 1987.

Johnson, Lyndon B. *Vantage Point.* New York, 1971.

Jordan, Amos, et al. *American National Security: Policy and Process.* Baltimore, 1989.

Jordan, Hamilton. *Crisis: The Last Year of the Carter Presidency.* New York, 1982.

Kennan, George F. *Memoirs, 1950–1963.*

———. *Memoirs, 1925–1950.* Boston, 1968.

———. Boston, 1972. *Russia and the West Under Lenin and Stalin.* New York, 1951.

Kennedy, Robert F. *Thirteen Days: A Memoir of the Cuban Missile Crisis.* New York, 1969.

Kepley, David R. *The Collapse of the Middle Way.* New York, 1988.

Kissinger, Henry. *The White House Years.* New York, 1979.

———. *Years of Upheaval.* New York, 1982.

Koen, R.Y. *The China Lobby in American Politics.* New York, 1960.

Lattimore, Owen. *Ordeal By Slander.* Boston, 1950.

Litwak, R.S. *Détente and the Nixon Doctrine: American Foreign Policy and the Pursuit of Stability, 1969–1975.* New York, 1984.

MacArthur, Douglas. *Reminiscences.* New York, 1964.

Major, John. *The Oppenheimer Hearing.* New York, 1971.

Morgenthau, Hans. *Truth and Power.* London, 1970.

New American Library. *The Reagan Foreign Policy.* New York, 1987.

Nixon, Richard. *RN: The Memoirs of Richard Nixon.* New York, 1978.

Pearson, Lester. *Mike: The Memoirs of the Rt. Hon. Lester Pearson,* 3 vols. Buffalo, N.Y., 1975.

Schoenbaum, Eleanora, ed. *Political Profiles* (series).
The Truman Years. New York, 1978
The Eisenhower Years. New York, 1978.
The Kennedy Years. New York, 1976.
The Johnson Years. New York, 1976.
The Nixon-Ford Years. New York, 1979.

Pollard, Robert. *Economic Security and the Origins of the Cold War, 1945–1950.* New York, 1985.

Rabe, S.G. *Eisenhower and Latin America.* Durham, N.C., 1988.

Rovere, Richard. *Senator Joe McCarthy.* New York, 1959.

Ryan, H.B. *The Vision of Ango-America.* Cambridge, 1987.

Schlesinger, Arthur. *A Thousand Days: John F. Kennedy in the White House.* New York, 1965.

Small, M. *Johnson, Nixon and the Doves.* New Brunswick, N.J., 1988.

Sorensen, Thomas. *The World War: The Story of American Propaganda.* New York, 1968.

Spanier, J.W. *American Foreign Policy Since World War Two.* Washington, D.C., 1988.

Spanier, J.W., and Eric M. Uslaner. *How American Foreign Policy Is Made.* New York, 1974.

Stern, Laurence. *The Wrong Horse: The Politics of Intervention and the Failure of American Diplomacy.* New York, 1977.

Stoessinger, John. *Henry Kissinger: The Anguish of Power.* New York, 1976.

Stursberg, Peter. *Lester Pearson and the American Dilemma.* Garden City, N.Y., 1980.

Szulc, Tad. *The Illusion of Peace: Foreign Policy in the Nixon Years.* New York, 1978.

Thompson, D.C. *Louis St. Laurent.* Toronto, 1967.

Walton, Richard. *Cold War and Counterrevolution: The Foreign Policy of John F. Kennedy.* New York, 1972.

Weiley, Lawrence, and Anne Patricia Simmons. *The United States and the United Nations.* New York, 1967.

Weinstein, Allen. *Perjury: The Hiss-Chambers Case.* New York, 1978.

Wood, R.E. *From Marshall Plan to Debt Crisis.* Berkeley, Ca., 1986.

NUCLEAR ISSUES

The Aspen Strategy Group. *The Strategic Defense Initiative and American Security.* Lanham, Md., 1987.

Baylis, John, and John Garnett. *Makers of Nuclear Strategy.* New York, 1991.

Beckman, Peter R., et al. *The Nuclear Predicament: Nuclear Weapons in the Cold War & Beyond.* New York, 1991.

Blacker, Coit, and Gloria Duffy. *International Arms Control: Issues and Agreements.* Stanford, Calif., 1984.

Bottome, Edgar. *The Missile Gap: A Study of the Formation of Military and Political Policy.* Rutherford, N.J., 1971.

Brennan, Donald G., ed. *Arms Control, Disarmament and National Security.* New York, 1961.

Bull, Hedley. *The Control of the Arms Race.* New York, 1961.

Burns, Edson L.M. *A Seat at the Table.* Toronto, 1972.

Clemens, Walter C. *The Superpowers and Arms Control: From Cold War to Interdependence.* Lexington, Ky., 1973.

Dean, Arthur. *Test Ban and Disarmament: The Path of Negotiation.* New York, 1966.

Freedman, L. *Britain and Nuclear Weapons.* London, 1980.

Gilpin, Robert. *American Scientists and Nuclear Weapons Policy.* Princeton, 1962.

Holst, T.T., and W. Schneider, eds. *Why ABM? Policy Issues in U.S. Defense Policy.* Elmsford, N.Y., 1976.

Jacobson, Harold D. *Diplomats, Scientists and Politicians.* Ann Arbor, Mich., 1966.

Johns Hopkins University. *The Strategic Defense Initiative and U.S. Foreign Policy.* Baltimore, 1987.

Kahn, H. *On Thermonuclear War.* Princeton, 1960.

Kissinger, Henry. *Nuclear Weapons and Foreign Policy.* New York, 1969.

Labrie, Roger P., ed. *SALT Handbook: Key Documents and Issues, 1972–1979.* Washington, D.C., 1979.

Lowe, George E. *The Age of Deterrence.* Boston, 1964.

Mayers, T. *Understanding Nuclear Weapons and Arms Control.* London, 1986.

Moulton, Harland B. *From Superiority to Parity: The United States and the Strategic Arms Race, 1961–1971.* Westport, Conn., 1972.

Newhouse, John. *Cold Dawn: The Story of SALT.* New York, 1973.

Owen, David. *The Politics of Defense.* New York, 1972.

Payne, Keith B. *Strategic Defense: Star Wars in Perspective.* Lanham, Md., 1986.

Reiss, Edward. *The Strategic Defense Initiative.* New York, 1992.

Roberts, Chalmers M. *The Nuclear Years: The Arms Race and Arms Control, 1945–1970.* New York, 1970.

Schilling, Warner R. "The H-Bomb Decision," *Political Science Quarterly,* 81 (1961): 24–46.

Simon, Jeffrey. *NATO Warsaw Pact Force Mobilization.* Washington, D.C., 1988.

Smith, Gerard. *Doubletalk: The Story of the First Strategic Arms Limitation Talks.* New York, 1980.

Spanier, John W., and Joseph L. Nogee. *The Politics of Disarmament: A Study in Soviet–American Gamesmanship.* New York, 1962.

Talbott, Strobe. *Endgame: The Inside Story of SALT Two.* New York, 1979.

Ungar, Sheldon. *The Rise & Fall of Nuclearism: Fear & Faith as Determinants of the Arms Race.* University Park, Pa., 1992.

United Nations Department for Disarmament Affairs. *The United Nations Disarmament Yearbook.* New York, 1988.

United States Arms Control and Disarmament Agency. *Arms Control and Disarmament Agreements: Texts and Histories of Negotiations.* Washington, D.C., 1980.

York, Herbert F. *The Advisers: Oppenheimer, Teller and the Superbomb.* San Francisco, 1976.

Zuckerman, Edward. *The Day after World War III: The U.S. Government's Plan for Surviving a Nuclear War.* New York, 1984.

———. *Nuclear Illusion and Reality.* London, 1982.

CHINA AND KOREA

Beal, John Robinson. *Marshall in China.* Garden City, N.Y., 1970.

Berger, Carl. *The Korea Knot: A Military–Political History.* Philadelphia, 1964.

Camilleri, J. *Chinese Foreign Policy: The Maoist Era and Its Aftermath.* Seattle, 1980.

Caridi, Ronald, J. *The Korean War and American Politics.* Philadelphia, 1969.

Ch'en, Jerome. *Mao and the Chinese Revolution.* New York, 1965.

Chiang Ching-kuo. *Calm in the Eye of a Storm.* Taipei, 1978.

Chiang, H.T. *The United States and China.* Chicago, 1988.

Clubb, Oliver Edmund. *China and Russia: The "Great Game."* New York, 1971.

Collins, J. Lawton. *War in Peacetime: The History and Lessons of Korea.* Boston, 1969.

Cummings, B. *Child of Conflict: The Korean–American Relationship, 1943–1953.* Seattle, 1983.

———. *The Origins of the Korean War.* Princeton, 1981.

Dallin, Alexander. *Black Box: KAL 007 and the Super Powers.* Berkeley, Calif., 1985.

DesForges, Roger V., et al., eds. *Chinese Democracy & the Crisis of 1989.* Buffalo, N.Y., 1993.

Dittmer, Lowell. *Liu Shao-chi and the Cultural Revolution.* Berkeley, Calif., 1974.

Dulles, Foster Rhea. *American Policy toward Communist China, 1949–1969.* New York, 1972.

Fairbank, John King. *The United States and China.* Cambridge, Mass., 1971.

Feis, Herbert. *The China Tangle.* New York, 1953.

Fitzgerald, C.P. *Mao Tse-tung and China.* New York, 1977.

Frends, William, J. *The Two Koreas in East Asian Affairs.* New York, 1976.

Furuya, Keiji. *Chiang Kai-shek: His Life and Times.* New York, 1981.

Ginsburg, G., and C.F. Pinkele. *The Sino–Soviet Territorial Dispute, 1949–1964.* New York, 1978.

Griffiths, William E. *The Sino–Soviet Rift.* New York, 1964.

Han Lih-wu. *Taiwan Today.* Taipei, 1980.

Harding, Harry. *A Fragile Relationship: The United States & China Since 1972.* Washington, D.C., 1992.

Higgins, Trumbull. *Korea and the Fall of MacArthur: A Précis in Limited War.* New York, 1960.

Hinton, Harold C. *An Introduction to Chinese Politics.* New York, 1978.

Hsu, C.Y. *The Rise of Modern China.* New York, 1983.

Johnson, *Shootdown: The Verdict on KAL 007.* New York, 1987.

Kai-yu Hsu. *Chou En-lai: China's Gray Eminence.* Garden City, N.Y., 1968.

Kim, I.J. *Communist Policies in North Korea.* New York, 1975.

Koen, R.Y. *China Lobby in American Politics.* New York, 1960.

Koh, Byung Chul. *The Foreign Policy Systems of North and South Korea.* Berkeley, Calif., 1984.

Kwoh-ting Li. *Economic Transformation of Taiwan.* London, 1988.

Lasater, M.L. *Taiwan.* New York, 1987.

———. *The Taiwan Issue in Sino–American Strategic Relations.* Boulder, Colo., 1984.

Leckie, Robert. *The Korean War.* New York, 1963.

Lewis, D.S. *Korea: Enduring Division.* Chicago, Ill., 1980.

Li Tien-min. *Chou En-lai.* New York, 1978.

Low, A.D. *The Sino–Soviet Dispute.* Rutherford, N.J., 1976.

MacArthur, Douglas. *Reminiscences.* New York, 1964.

McFarquhar, Roderick. *The Origins of the Cultural Revolution.* London, 1974.

Meisner, Maurice. *Mao's China and After: A History of the People's Republic.* New York, 1986.

Robinson, Thomas W. *A Politico-Military Biography of Lin Piao.* New York, 1971.

Rees, David. *Korea: The Limited War.* New York, 1964.

Ridgway, Matthew B. *The Korean War: How We Met the Challenge.* Garden City, N.Y., 1967.

Rose, Lisle A. *Roots of Tragedy: The United States and the Struggle for Asia 1945–1953.* Westport, Conn., 1976.

Segal, G. *The Soviet Union in East Asia.* Boulder, Colo., 1983.

Segal, G., ed. *The China Factor: Peking and the Superpowers.* London, 1982.

Snow, Edgar. *Red Star Over China.* New York, 1937.

Solomon, R.H. *Mao's Revolution and the Chinese Political Culture.* New York, 1971.

Solomon, R.H., ed. *The China Factor: Sino–American Relations and the Global Scene.* Englewood Cliffs, N.J., 1981.

Stone, I.F. *The Hidden History of the Korean War.* New York, 1952.

Sutter, Robert. *China Watch: Toward Sino–American Reconciliation.* Baltimore, 1978.

Tuchman, Barbara. *Stilwell and the American Experience in China.* New York, 1971.

Wakeman, Frederic. *History and Will: Philosophical Perspectives of Mao Tse-tung's Thought.* New York, 1973.

Weinstein, Franklin, and Fuji Kamiya, eds. *The Security of Korean: U.S. and Japanese Perspectives on the 1980s.* Boulder, Colo., 1980.

Wilson, Dick. *Chou En-lai: The Story of Zhou Enlai, 1898–1976.* London, 1984.

Wilson, Dick. *Mao: The People's Emperor.* New York, 1979.

Wren, Christopher. *The End of the Line: The Failure of Communism in the Soviet Union & China.* New York, 1990.

Zagorian, Donald. *The Sino–Soviet Conflict, 1956–1961.* Princeton, 1962.

SOUTH ASIA, SOUTHEAST ASIA AND THE PACIFIC REGION

Adams, Nina S., and Alfred W. McCoy. *Laos: War and Revolution.* New York, 1971.

Barnet, Richard J. *Roots of War.* New York, 1972.

Bator, Victor. *Vietnam: A Diplomatic Tragedy: The Origins of the United States Involvement.* Dobbs Ferry, N.Y., 1965.

Branfman, Fred. "The President's Secret Army: A Case Study—the CIA in Laos, 1962–72." In Robert Borosage and John Marks, *The CIA File.* New York, 1976.

Clutterbuck, Richard. *The Long, Long War: The Emergency in Malaya, 1948–1960.* London, 1967.

Crouch, Harold. *The Army and Politics in Indonesia.* Ithaca, N.Y., 1978.

Dahm, Bernhard. *Sukarno.* Ithaca, N.Y., 1969.

Dougan, C.A. *A Nation Divided.* Boston, 1984.

Fall, Bernard. *Anatomy of a Crisis: The Laotian Crisis of 1960–61.* New York, 1969.

Fryer, D.W., and James C. Jackson. *Indonesia.* Boulder, Colo., 1976.

Galloway, John. *The Gulf of Tonkin Resolution.* Rutherford, N.J., 1970.

Generous, Kevin M. *Vietnam: The Secret War.* New York, 1985.

Goldstein, Martin. *American Policy Toward Laos.* Rutherford, N.J., 1973.

Griffiths, J.C. *The Conflict in Afghanistan.* Hove, England, 1987.

Halberstam, David. *The Best and the Brightest.* New York, 1972.

Ho Chi Minh. *On Revolution.* London, 1967.

Hudson, W.J. *Australia in World Affairs.* Boston, 1980.

Jones, Howard P. *Indonesia: The Possible Dream.* New York, 1971.

Karnow, Stanley. *Vietnam: A History.* New York, 1983.

Kerkvliet, Benedict H. *The Huk Rebellion: A Study of Peasant Revolt in the Philippines.* Berkeley, Calif., 1977.

Kim Sung Yong. *United States–Philippine Relations, 1945–1956.* Washington, D.C., 1968.

King, Peter. *Australia's Vietnam.* Boston, 1983.

Kirk, Donald. *Wider War: The Struggle for Cambodia, Thailand and Laos.* New York, 1972.

Krepinovich, A.F. *The Army and Vietnam.* Baltimore, 1986.

Lahica, Eduard. *The Huks: Philippine Agrarian Society in Revolt.* New York, 1971.

Lansdale, Edward G. *In the Midst of Wars: An American's Mission to Southeast Asia.* New York, 1972.

———. "Lessons Learned: The Philippines, 1946–1956." *Alert,* 6A (December 11, 1962).

Legge, J.D. *Sukarno: A Political Biography.* London, 1972.

McMichael, Scott. *Stumbling Bear: Soviet Military Performance in Afghanistan.* New York, 1991.

Maprayil, C. *The Soviets and Afghanistan.* New Delhi, 1986.

May, Brian. *The Indonesian Tragedy.* Boston, 1978.

Milburn, Price, ed. *New Zealand in World Affairs.* Wellington, 1977.

Pugh, Michael. *The ANZUS Crisis.* Cambridge, 1989.

Reese, Trevor. *Australia, New Zealand and the United States, 1941–1968.* New York, 1969.

Shalom, Stephen R. *The United States and the Philippines: A Study of Neocolonialism.* Philadelphia, 1981.

Shawcross, William. *Sideshow: Kissinger, Nixon and the Destruction of Cambodia.* New York, 1979.

Sihanouk, Varman, Norodom. *My War With the CIA: The Memoirs of Prince Norodom Sihanouk.* New York, 1973.

Short, Anthony. *The Communist Insurrection in Malaya, 1948–1960.* London, 1975.

Smith, R.B. *An International History of the Vietnam War.* New York, 1986.

Sobel, Lester, ed. *South Vietnam: U.S.–Communist Confrontation in Southeast Asia,* Vols. 1–4. New York, 1966–74.

Special Operations Research Office. *U.S. Army Area Handbook for Indonesia.* Washington, D.C., 1964.

Stanton, S.L. *The Rise and Fall of an American Army.* Navato, Calif., 1985.

Sukarno (as told to Cindy Adams). *Sukarno: An Autobiography.* New York, 1965.

Sullivan, Marianna P. *France's Vietnam Policy: A Study in French–American Relations.* Westport, Conn., 1978.

Thakur, I.C. *In Defense of New Zealand.* New York, 1986.

Thakur, Ramesh, and Carlyle A. Thayer. *Soviet Relations with India and Vietnam.* New York, 1992.

U.S. House of Representatives Committee on Foreign Affairs. *Regional Security Developments in the South Pacific.* Washington, D.C., 1989.

Zasloff, J.J. *The Pathet Lao.* Lexington, Mass., 1973.

SOVIET UNION (GENERAL)

Arbatov, Georgi. *The System: A Life in Soviet Politics.* New York, 1992.

Berliner, Joseph. *Soviet Economic Aid.* New York, 1958.

Bermeo, Nancy, ed. *Liberalization & Democratization: Change in the Soviet Union & Eastern Europe.* Baltimore, 1992.

Bronke, A., and D. Novak, eds. *The Communist States in the Era of Détente, 1971–1977.* Oakville, Ont., 1979.

Conquest, Robert. *Russia After Khrushchev.* London, 1965.

Crankshaw, Edward. *Khrushchev: A Career.* New York, 1966.

Currie, Kenneth M. *The Soviet Military: An Introduction.* New York, 1991.

Dallin, Alexander, and Thomas B. Larson, eds. *Soviet Politics Since Khrushchev.* Englewood Cliffs, N.J., 1968.

Deutscher, I. *Stalin: A Political Biography.* New York, 1967.

Dibb, P. *The Soviet Union: The Incomplete Superpower.* London, 1985.

Djilas, Milovan. *Conversations With Stalin.* New York, 1962.

Donaldson, Robert, ed. *The Soviet Union in the Third World: Successes and Failures.* Boulder, Colo., 1981.

Duncan, Raymond. *Soviet Policy in the Third World.* New York, 1980.

Felshman, Neil. *Gorbachev, Yeltsin & the Last Days of the Soviet Empire.* New York, 1992.

Feuchtwanger, E.J., and Peter Nailor, eds. *The Soviet Union and the Third World.* New York, 1981.

Ginsburg, G., and A.Z. Rubinstein, eds. *Soviet Foreign Policy Toward Western Europe.* New York, 1978.

Goldman, Marshall. *Soviet Foreign Aid.* New York, 1967.

Gorbachev, Mikhail. *Towards a Better World.* New York, 1987.

———. *Reykjavik.* New York, 1987.

———. *A Time for Peace.* New York, 1985.

Gromyko, Andrei. *Memories.* New York, 1989.

Hammond, T.T. *Red Flag Over Afghanistan.* Boulder, Colo., 1984.

Holman, P., et al. *The Soviet Union After "Perestroika."* New York, 1991.

Hosmer, Stephen, and Thomas Wolfe. *Soviet Policy and Practice Towards the Third World Conflicts.* Lexington, Mass., 1983.

Hyland, William, and Richard Wallace Shryock. *The Fall of Khrushchev*. New York, 1970.

Jukes, G. *The Soviet Union in Asia*. Berkeley, Calif., 1973.

Kanet, Roger, ed. *The Soviet Union and the Developing Nations*. Baltimore, 1974.

Kanet, Roger E., et al., eds. *Soviet Foreign Policy in Transition*. New York, 1992.

Lavigne, Marie, ed. *The Soviet Union & Eastern Europe in the Gobal Economy*. New York, 1992.

Malia, Martin E. *The Soviet Tragedy: A History of Socialism in Russia*. New York, 1992.

McCauley, M. *The Soviet Union Since 1917*. London, 1981.

McNeal, Robert H. *Stalin: Man and Ruler*. New York, 1988.

Medvedev, Zhores. *Gorbachev*. New York, 1986.

————. *Andropov: His Life and Death*. New York, 1984.

Mellor, R.E.M. *The Soviet Union and Its Geographical Problems*. London, 1982.

Menon, Rajan. *Soviet Power and the Third World*. New Haven, Conn., 1986.

Moreton, E., and G. Segal, eds. *Soviet Strategy Toward Western Europe*. London, 1984.

Nogee, J.L. *Soviet Foreign Policy Since World War Two*. New York, 1988.

Nove, A. *An Economic History of the USSR*. London, 1969.

Owen, Richard. *Crisis in the Kremlin*. London, 1986.

Reamington, W.A. *Warsaw Pact*. Cambridge, Mass., 1971.

Sakharov, Andrei. *Memoirs*. New York, 1990.

————. *My Country and the World*. New York, 1975.

Schmid, Alex P. *Soviet Military Interventions Since 1945*. New Brunswick, N.J., 1985.

Schmidt-Hauer, Christian. *Gorbachev: The Path to Power*. London, 1986.

Schopflin, George, ed. *The Soviet Union and Eastern Europe*. New York, 1986.

Schwartz, Harry. *The Red Phoenix: Russia Since World War II*. New York, 1961.

Scott, Harriet Fast, and William F. Scott. *Soviet Military Doctrine, Continuity, Formulation and Dissemination*. Boulder, Colo., 1988.

Shearman, P. *The Soviet Union and Cuba*. New York, 1987.

Shub, Anatole. *An Empire Loses Hope: The Return of Stalin's Ghost*. New York, 1970.

Shulman, M.D. *Stalin's Foreign Policy Reappraised*. New York, 1969.

Shultz, Richard H. *The Soviet Union and Revolutionary Warfare*. Stanford, Calif., 1988.

Sokolovski, V.D., ed. *Soviet Military Strategy*. Englewood Cliffs, N.J., 1963.

Starr, Richard F. *East-Central Europe & the USSR*. New York, 1991.

————. *USSR Foreign Policies After Détente*. Stanford, Calif., 1987.

Tatu, Michael. *Power in the Kremlin: From Khrushchev to Kosygin*. New York, 1969.

Ulam, Adam B. *Expansion and Coexistence: The History of Soviet Foreign Policy, 1917–1967*. New York, 1968.

Veen, Hans-Joachim. *From Brezhnev to Gorbachev: Domestic Affairs and Soviet Foreign Policy*. Boulder, Colo., 1986.

Watson, Bruce, and Susan Watson, eds. *The Soviet Navy*. Boulder, Colo., 1987.

Wolfe, Bertram. *An Ideology in Power: Reflections on the Russian Revolution*. New York, 1969.

Wolfe, Thomas. *Soviet Power and Europe, 1945–1970*. Baltimore, 1970.

Wren, Christopher S. *The End of the Line: The Failure of Communism in the Soviet Union & China*. New York, 1990.

MIDDLE EAST AND AFRICA

Albright, D.E. *Soviet Policy Toward Africa*. Washington, D.C., 1987.

Allen, Robert L. *Middle Eastern Economic Relations with the Soviet Union, Eastern Europe & Mainland China*. Westport, Conn., 1985.

Aluko, Olajide. *Africa and the Great Powers in the 1980s*. Lanham, Md., 1988.

Ayoob, Mohammed, ed. *The Middle East in World Politics*. London, 1981.

Bar-Siman-Tov, Y. *Israel, the Superpowers and the War in the Middle East*. New York, 1987.

Bill, J.A. *The Eagle and the Lion*. New Haven, Conn., 1988.

Carpenter, Ted G., ed. *America Entangled: The Persian Gulf Crisis & Its Aftermath*. Washington, D.C., 1991.

Chubin, Shahram, and Sephr Zabih. *The Foreign Relations of Iran*. Los Angeles, 1974.

Davidson, Basil. *Africa in Modern History: The Search for a New Society*. New York, 1978.

Dawisha, Adeed, and Karen Dawisha. *The Soviet Union in the Middle East: Politics and Perspectives*. London, 1982.

Drinan, Robert F. *Honor the Promise: America's Commitment to Israel*. Garden City, N.Y., 1977.

Eden, Anthony. *The Suez Crisis of 1956*. Boston, 1966.

Efrat, Moshe, and Jacob Bercovitch, eds. *Superpowers & Client States in the Middle East: The Imbalance of Influence*. New York, 1991.

Freedman, Robert. *The Middle East Since Camp David*. Boulder, Colo., 1984.

Glassman, John D. *Arms for the Arabs: The Soviet Union & War in the Middle East*. Baltimore, 1976.

Golan, Galia. *Soviet Policies in the Middle East: From World War II to Gorbachev*. New York, 1990.

Golan, Matti. *The Secret Conversations of Henry Kissinger: Step-by-Step Diplomacy in the Middle East*. New York, 1976.

Hakleh, Emile A. *Arab American Relations in the Persian Gulf*. Washington, D.C., 1975.

Hammond, Paul Y., and Sidney S. Alexander. *Political Dynamics in the Middle East*. New York, 1972.

Harris, M.F. *Breakfast in Hell*. New York, 1987.

Hersh, Seymour. *The Samson Option*. New York, 1991.

Hodges, Tony. *Angola to the 1990s: The Potential for Recovery*. London, 1987.

Hoveyda, Feredour. *The Fall of the Shah*. London, 1980.

Ismael, Tareq, et al. *The Middle East in World Politics: A Study in Contemporary International Relations*. Syracuse, N.Y., 1974.

Jackson, Henry F. *From the Congo to Soweto: U.S. Foreign Policy Toward Africa Since 1960*. New York, 1982.

Kempton, Daniel R. *Soviet Strategy Toward African National Liberation Movements*. Westport, Conn., 1989.

Laidi, Zaki. *The Superpowers in Africa: The Constraints of a Rivalry*. Chicago, 1990.

Lenczowski, George. *The Middle East in World Affairs*. Ithaca, N.Y., 1980.

Magall, James. *Africa: The Cold War and After*. London, 1971.

Mangold, Peter. *Superpower Intervention in the Middle East*. New York, 1978.

Nielson, Waldemar. *The Great Powers and Africa*. Washington, D.C., 1969.

Nutting, Anthony. *No End of a Lesson*. London, 1967.

————. *Nasser*. London, 1972

Ojo, Olatunde, D.K. Orwa, and C.M.B. Utete. *African International Relations*. London, 1980.

Pahlavi, Mohammed Reza. *Answer to History*. New York, 1980.

Perlmutter, Amos. *The Life and Times of Menachem Begin*. Garden City, N.Y., 1987.

Polk, William R. *The United States and the Arab World*. Cambridge, Mass., 1969.

Quandt, William B. *Decade of Decisions: American Policy Toward the Arab–Israeli Conflict, 1967–1976*. Berkeley, Calif., 1977.

Ramzani, R.K. *The U.S. and Iran: The Patterns of Influence*. New York, 1982.

Reich, Bernard. *Quest for Peace: United States–Israeli Relations and the Arab–Israeli Conflict*. New Brunswick, N.J., 1977.

Roosevelt, Kermit. *Countercoup*. New York, 1979.

Safran, Nadav. *Israel, The Embattled Ally*. Cambridge, Mass., 1978.

Samuels, Michael, ed. *Africa and the West*. Boulder, Colo., 1980.

Shaw, Timothy, and Sola Ojo, eds. *Africa and the International Political System*. New York, 1982.

Shawcross, William. *The Shah's Last Ride: The Story of the Exile, Misadventures and Death of the Emperor*. London, 1989.

Smertin, Y. *Kwame Nkrumah*. New York, 1987.

Spencer, J.H. *Ethiopia at Bay*. Algonac, Mich., 1987.

Stephens, Robert. *Nasser: A Political Biography*. London, 1971.

Thiam, Doudou. *The Foreign Policy of African States*. London, 1965.

Trefan, Barbara. *Angola: Politics, Economics and Society*. Boulder, Colo., 1986.

Upton, J.M. *The History of Modern Iran*. Cambridge, Mass., 1960.

Weissman, Stephen. *American Policy in the Congo, 1960–1964*. Ithaca, N.Y., 1974.

Whitaker, Jennifer Seymour. *Africa and the United States: Vital Interests*. New York, 1978.

Wubnesh, M. *Ethiopia*. Boulder, Colo., 1988.

COLD WAR (GENERAL)

Bialer, Seweryn, and Michael Mandelbaum. *The Global Rivals: The Soviet–American Contest for Supremacy*. New York, 1989.

Clawson, Robert, ed. *East–West Rivalry in the Third World*. Wilmington, Del., 1986.

Crockett, Richard, ed. *The Cold War Past and Present*. Boston, 1987.

Crozier, Brian, Drew Middleton, and Jeremy Murray-Brown. *This War Called Peace*. London, 1984.

Davis, Lynn Ethcridge. *The Cold War Begins: Soviet-American Conflict over Eastern Europe*. Princeton, 1974.

Donnelly, Desmond. *Struggle for the World*. New York, 1965.

Dukes, Paul. *The Last Great Game: U.S.A. Versus U.S.S.R.; Events, Conjectures, Structures*. London, 1985.

Dulles, Eleanor Lansing, and Robert Dickson Crane. *Détente: Cold War Strategies in Transition*. New York, 1965.

Facts On File Yearbook. New York. Annually, 1941 through 1992.

Feis, Herbert. *Between War and Peace: The Potsdam Conference*. Princeton, 1960.

Fleming, D.F. *The Cold War and Its Origins, 1917–1960*. Garden City, N.Y., 1961.

Fontaine, Andre. *History of the Cold War*, Vols. 1 and 2. New York, 1965 and 1969.

Gaddis, John L. *The United States & the End of the Cold War*. New York, 1992.

————. *The Strategies of Containment*. New York, 1982.

————. *The United States and the Origins of the Cold War, 1941–1947*. New York, 1972.

Garten, Jeffrey E. *A Cold Peace: The Struggle for Supremacy in the Post-Cold War World*. New York, 1992.

Glynn, Patrick. *Closing Pandora's Box: Arms Races, Arms Control, & the History of the Cold War*. New York, 1992.

Graebner, Norman. *Cold War Diplomacy: American Foreign Policy, 1945–1960*. Princeton, 1962.

Graebner, Norman, ed. *The Cold War: A Conflict of Ideology and Power*. New York, 1976.

Halle, Louis J. *Cold War as History*. New York, 1991.

Halliday, Fred. *The Making of the Second Cold War*. New York, 1986.

Herring, George C. *Aid to Russia: Strategy, Diplomacy, and the Origins of the Cold War*. New York, 1973.

Hogan, Michael J., ed. *The End of the Cold War: Its Meanings & Implications*. New York, 1992.

Hough, Jerry H. *The Struggle for the Thrid World*. Washington, D.C., 1986.

La Feber, Walter. *America, Russia and the Cold War*. New York, 1976.

Lukacs, John. *A New History of the Cold War*. Garden City, N.Y., 1966.

McNeill, William. *America, Britain and Russia: Their Cooperation and Their Conflict*. New York, 1970.

Millar, T.B., ed. *Current International Treaties*. London, 1984.

Rose, Lisle A. *After Yalta: America and the Origins of the Cold War*. New York, 1973.

Shulman, Marshall D., ed. *East–West Tensions in the Third World*. New York, 1986.

Solberg, Carl. *Riding High: America in the Cold War*. New York, 1973.

Stevenson, Richard W. *The Rise and Fall of Détente*. London, 1985.

Thomas, Hugh. *Armed Truce: The Beginnings of the Cold War, 1945–1946*. New York, 1986.

Ulam, Adam. *The Rivals: America and Russia Since World War II*. New York, 1971.

Vadney, T.E. *The World Since 1945: A Complete History of Global Change from 1945 to the Present*. New York, 1987.

INDEX

Boldface locators indicate major treatment of a subject

603